Handbook of Research on Acquiring 21st Century Literacy Skills Through Game-Based Learning

Carol-Ann Lane
University of Toronto, Canada

Volume I

A volume in the Advances in Game-Based Learning (AGBL) Book Series

Published in the United States of America by
IGI Global
Information Science Reference (an imprint of IGI Global)
701 E. Chocolate Avenue
Hershey PA, USA 17033
Tel: 717-533-8845
Fax: 717-533-8661
E-mail: cust@igi-global.com
Web site: http://www.igi-global.com

Copyright © 2022 by IGI Global. All rights reserved. No part of this publication may be reproduced, stored or distributed in any form or by any means, electronic or mechanical, including photocopying, without written permission from the publisher. Product or company names used in this set are for identification purposes only. Inclusion of the names of the products or companies does not indicate a claim of ownership by IGI Global of the trademark or registered trademark.
 Library of Congress Cataloging-in-Publication Data

Names: Lane, Carol-Ann, 1966- editor.
Title: Handbook of research on acquiring 21st century literacy skills
  through game-based learning / Carol-Ann Lane, editor.
Other titles: Handbook of research on acquiring twenty-first century
  literacy skills through game-based learning
Description: Hershey, PA : Information Science Reference, 2022. | Includes
  bibliographical references and index. | Summary: "This book offers
  findings in digital technology and multimodal ways of acquiring literacy
  skills in the 21st century, highlighting research in discovering new
  pedagogical boundaries by focusing on ways that youth learn from digital
  sources such as video games"-- Provided by publisher.
Identifiers: LCCN 2021044535 (print) | LCCN 2021044536 (ebook) | ISBN
  9781799872719 (hardcover) | ISBN 9781799872733 (ebook)
Subjects: LCSH: Reading--Computer-assisted instruction. | Video games in
  education.
Classification: LCC LB1050.37 .A38 2022 (print) | LCC LB1050.37 (ebook) |
  DDC 372.4028/4--dc23
LC record available at https://lccn.loc.gov/2021044535
LC ebook record available at https://lccn.loc.gov/2021044536

This book is published in the IGI Global book series Advances in Game-Based Learning (AGBL) (ISSN: 2327-1825; eISSN: 2327-1833)

British Cataloguing in Publication Data
A Cataloguing in Publication record for this book is available from the British Library.

All work contributed to this book is new, previously-unpublished material. The views expressed in this book are those of the authors, but not necessarily of the publisher.

For electronic access to this publication, please contact: eresources@igi-global.com.

Advances in Game-Based Learning (AGBL) Book Series

Robert D. Tennyson
University of Minnesota, USA

ISSN:2327-1825
EISSN:2327-1833

Mission

The **Advances in Game-Based Learning (AGBL) Book Series** aims to cover all aspects of serious games applied to any area of education. The definition and concept of education has begun to morph significantly in the past decades and game-based learning has become a popular way to encourage more active learning in a creative and alternative manner for students in K-12 classrooms, higher education, and adult education. **AGBL** presents titles that address many applications, theories, and principles surrounding this growing area of educational theory and practice.

Coverage

- Curriculum Development Using Educational Games
- Digital Game-Based Learning
- Edutainment
- Electronic Educational Games
- Game Design and Development of Educational Games
- MMOs in Education
- Pedagogical Theory of Game-Based Learning
- Psychological Study of Students Involved in Game-Based Learning
- Role of instructors
- Virtual worlds and game-based learning

IGI Global is currently accepting manuscripts for publication within this series. To submit a proposal for a volume in this series, please contact our Acquisition Editors at Acquisitions@igi-global.com or visit: http://www.igi-global.com/publish/.

The Advances in Game-Based Learning (AGBL) Book Series (ISSN 2327-1825) is published by IGI Global, 701 E. Chocolate Avenue, Hershey, PA 17033-1240, USA, www.igi-global.com. This series is composed of titles available for purchase individually; each title is edited to be contextually exclusive from any other title within the series. For pricing and ordering information please visit http://www.igi-global.com/book-series/advances-game-based-learning/73680. Postmaster: Send all address changes to above address. Copyright © 2022 IGI Global. All rights, including translation in other languages reserved by the publisher. No part of this series may be reproduced or used in any form or by any means – graphics, electronic, or mechanical, including photocopying, recording, taping, or information and retrieval systems – without written permission from the publisher, except for non commercial, educational use, including classroom teaching purposes. The views expressed in this series are those of the authors, but not necessarily of IGI Global.

Titles in this Series

For a list of additional titles in this series, please visit: www.igi-global.com/book-series

Esports Research and Its Integration in Education
Miles M. Harvey (University of New Mexico, USA) and Rick Marlatt (New Mexico State University USA)
Information Science Reference • © 2021 • 313pp • H/C (ISBN: 9781799870692) • US $195.00

Exploring the Cognitive, Social, Cultural, and Psychological Aspects of Gaming and Simulations
Brock R. Dubbels (McMaster University, Cnada)
Information Science Reference • © 2019 • 333pp • H/C (ISBN: 9781522574613) • US $190.00

Design, Motivation, and Frameworks in Game-Based Learning
Wee Hoe Tan (Sultan Idris Education University, Malaysia)
Information Science Reference • © 2019 • 306pp • H/C (ISBN: 9781522560265) • US $175.00

Handbook of Research on Collaborative Teaching Practice in Virtual Learning Environments
Gianni Panconesi (Esplica, Italy) and Maria Guida (National Institute for Documentation, Innovation, and Educational Research, Italy)
Information Science Reference • © 2017 • 637pp • H/C (ISBN: 9781522524267) • US $240.00

Gamification-Based E-Learning Strategies for Computer Programming Education
Ricardo Alexandre Peixoto de Queirós (uniMAD, Escola Superior de Media Artes e Design, Portugal) and Mário Teixeira Pinto (Polytechnic Institute of Porto, Portugal)
Information Science Reference • © 2017 • 350pp • H/C (ISBN: 9781522510345) • US $200.00

Handbook of Research on Serious Games for Educational Applications
Robert Z. Zheng (University of Utah, USA) and Michael K. Gardner (The University of Utah, USA)
Information Science Reference • © 2017 • 496pp • H/C (ISBN: 9781522505136) • US $285.00

Handbook of Research on 3-D Virtual Environments and Hypermedia for Ubiquitous Learning
Francisco Milton Mendes Neto (Federal Rural University of the Semiarid Region, Brazil) Rafael de Souza (Federal Rural University of the Semiarid Region, Brazil) and Alex Sandro Gomes (Federal University of Pernambuco, Brazil)
Information Science Reference • © 2016 • 673pp • H/C (ISBN: 9781522501251) • US $235.00

Handbook of Research on Gaming Trends in P-12 Education
Donna Russell (Walden University, USA) and James M. Laffey (University of Missouri at Columbia, USA)
Information Science Reference • © 2016 • 663pp • H/C (ISBN: 9781466696297) • US $325.00

701 East Chocolate Avenue, Hershey, PA 17033, USA
Tel: 717-533-8845 x100 • Fax: 717-533-8661
E-Mail: cust@igi-global.com • www.igi-global.com

Editorial Advisory Board

Daisy Alexander, *School of Law, Christ University, India*
Smitha Baboo, *Christ University, India*
Cathlyn Niranjana Bennett, *Christ University, India*
Robert Costello, *Middlesbrough College, UK*
Jonathan deHaan, *University of Shizuoka, Japan*
Marta Ferreira Dias, *University of Aveiro, Portugal*
Hacer Dolanbay, *Muş Alparslan University, Turkey*
Nilofer Hussaini, *Christ University, India*
Fritz Ngale Ilongo, *University of Eswatini, Eswatini*
Sunitha Abhay Jain, *School of Law, Christ University, India*
Sunil John, *School of Law, Christ University, India*
Yogesh Kanna, *Christ University, India*
Janna Jackson Kellinger, *University of Massachusetts, Boston, USA*
Hulisani Mulaudzi, *University of Venda, South Africa*
Brian Angus McKenzie, *Maynooth University, Ireland*
Ana Nobre, *Universidade Aberta, Portugal*
Bidisha Sarkar, *Business and Management, Christ University, India*
Sam von Gillern, *University of Missouri, USA*

List of Contributors

Abrose, Yogendran / *Universiti Sains Malaysia, Malaysia* 750
Água, Pedro B. / *Naval Aacdemy, Portugal* 946
Ahmad, Nur Jahan / *Universiti Sains Malaysia, Malaysia* 750
Alam, Atm S. / *Queen Mary University of London, UK* 455
Alam, Md Jahangir / *University of Dhaka, Bangladesh* 716
Alexander, Daisy / *CHRIST University (Deemed), India* 138
Amirnuddin, Puteri Sofia / *Taylor's Law School, Taylor's University, Malaysia* 472
Amorim, Marlene / *GOVCOPP, DEGEIT, University of Aveiro, Portugal* 533
Andreini, Daniela / *University of Bergamo, Italy* 488
Ashrafuzzaman, Md. / *Bangabandhu Sheikh Mujibur Rahman Digital University, Bangladesh* 78
Azim, Farhan / *University of Melbourne, Australia* 78
Baboo, Smitha / *CHRIST University (Deemed), India* 58
Bampasidis, Georgios Eleftherios / *National and Kapodistrian University of Athens, Greece* 646
Baturay, Meltem Huri / *Atilim University, Turkey* 510
Bengsch, Geraldine / *Kings College London, UK* 905
Bennett, Cathlyn Niranjana / *CHRIST University (Deemed), India* 58
Biswas, Annesha / *CHRIST University (Deemed), India* 832
Brin, Pavlo / *National Technical University "Kharkiv Polytechnic Institute", Ukraine* 927
Buttrey, Kristina M. / *Murray State University, USA* 289
Chelawat, Anshita / *Vivekanand Education Society's Institute of Management Studies and Research, India* 810
Chellaswamy, Karthigai Prakasam / *CHRIST University (Deemed), India* 122
Çinar, Cafer Ahmet / *Çanakkale Onsekiz Mart University, Turkey* 510
Correia, Anacleto / *Naval Academy, Portugal* 946
Costello, Robert / *Middlesbrough College, UK* 788
Culatta, Barbara Ellen / *Brigham Young University, USA* 671
Dam, Tinanjali / *CHRIST University (Deemed), India* 832
Dhamija, Ankit / *Amity University, Haryana, India* 31
Dhamija, Deepika / *Amity University, Haryana, India* 31
Dias Soeiro, Joaquim / *School of Hospitality, Tourism, and Events, Taylor's University, Malaysia* 472
Dolanbay, Hacer / *Muş Alparslan University, Turkey* 363
Donald, Cecil / *CHRIST University (Deemed), India* 1
Durmaz, Burcu / *Süleyman Demirel University, Turkey* 13
February, Pamela Jennifer / *University of Namibia, Namibia* 431

Ferreira Dias, Marta / *GOVCOPP, DEGEIT, University of Aveiro, Portugal* 533
Galani, Apostolia / *National and Kapodistrian University of Athens, Greece* 646
García-Molina, María / *University of Córdoba, Spain* 554
Goosen, Leila / *University of South Africa, South Africa* 580
Gouveia, Patrícia / *LARSyS, Interactive Technologies Institute (ITI), Faculdade de Belas-Artes, Universidade de Lisboa (FBAUL), Portugal* 180
Guetzoian, Emily / *Anderson School of Management, UCLA, USA* 164
Gururaj Rao, Nagarjuna / *CHRIST University (Deemed), India* 122
Hall-Kenyon, Kendra M. / *Brigham Young University, USA* 671
Huertas-Abril, Cristina A. / *University of Córdoba, Spain* 554
Hussaini, Nilofer / *CHRIST University (Deemed), India* 138
Ilongo, Fritz Ngale / *University of Eswatini, Eswatini* 606
Islam, Sheikh Rashid Bin / *Bangladesh Consulting Services, Bangladesh* 716
Jain, Sunitha Abhay / *CHRIST University (Deemed), India* 138
John, Sunil / *CHRIST University (Deemed), India* 138
Kaithathara, Seena Thomas / *CHRIST University (Deemed), India* 107
Kanna, Yogesh / *CHRIST University (Deemed), India* 58
Kellinger, Janna Jackson / *University of Massachusetts, Boston, USA* 888
Kok Ming, Goh / *SJKC Chi Sheng 2, Malaysia* 750
Küçükaydın, Menşure Alkış / *Eregli Faculty of Education, Necmettin Erbakan University, Turkey* 13
Kureethara, Joseph Varghese / *CHRIST University (Deemed), India* 832
Kurien, Georgy P. / *CHRIST University (Deemed), India* 122
Lambert, Richard G. / *University of North Carolina at Charlotte, USA* 731
Lane, Carol-Ann / *University of Western Ontario, Canada* 269
Le Rossignol, Karen / *Deakin University, Australia* 302
Li, Yixun / *The Education University of Hong Kong, Hong Kong* 381
Lim, Ji Soo / *Dokkyo University, Japan* 846
Lima, Luciana / *LARSyS, Interactive Technologies Institute (ITI), Faculdade de Belas-Artes, Universidade de Lisboa (FBAUL), Portugal* 180
Lombardi, Gaia / *Istituto Comprensivo Statale Via dei Salici, Legnano, Italy* 697
Luce, Hannah E. / *The University of North Carolina at Charlotte, USA* 731
M. Y., Manjula / *CHRIST University (Deemed), India* 1
M., Darshan S. / *CHRIST University (Deemed), India* 107
Madaleno, Mara / *GOVCOPP, DEGEIT, University of Aveiro, Portugal* 533
Mahoney, Jamie / *Murray State University, USA* 289
Makhanikhe, Tshimangadzo J. / *University of Venda, South Africa* 418
Manivannan, Anand Shankar Raja / *CHRIST University (Deemed), India* 122
Marlatt, Rick / *New Mexico State University, USA* 320
Marshall, Marinda / *Lectorsa, South Africa* 249
Marshall, Minda / *Lectorsa, South Africa* 249
McKenzie, Brian Angus / *Maynooth University, Ireland* 220
Mulaudzi, Hulisani / *University of Venda, South Africa* 418
Munroe-Lynds, Cora-Lynn / *Dalhousie University, Canada* 194
Muzambi, Absolom / *University of South Africa, South Africa* 580
N., Shabarisha / *CHRIST University (Deemed), India* 107

Nadolny, Larysa / *Iowa State University, USA* ... 320
Naomee, Iffat / *University of Dhaka, Bangladesh* ... 78
Nobre, Ana / *Universidade Aberta, Portugal* ... 630
Nobre, Vasco / *Universidade Aberta, Portugal* ... 630
Ogawa, Keiichi / *Kobe University, Japan* ... 716
P., Swarnalatha / *CHRIST University (Deemed), India* ... 1
Patil, Anand / *CHRIST University (Deemed), India* ... 1
Peck, Sharon / *State University of New York College at Geneseo, USA* ... 344
Pedeliento, Giuseppe / *University of Bergamo, Italy* ... 488
Qiao, Jianshu / *Queen Mary University of London, UK* ... 455
R., Gowri Shankar / *CHRIST University (Deemed), India* ... 107
Raj, Reena / *CHRIST University (Deemed), India* ... 1
Raman, Sreedhara / *CHRIST University (Deemed), India* ... 122
Ramatswi, Talifhani Trevor / *University of Venda, South Africa* ... 397
Reuter, Jessica / *GOVCOPP, DEGEIT, University of Aveiro, Portugal* ... 533
Salunkhe, Vikas / *CHRIST University (Deemed), India* ... 107
Samsudin, Mohd Ali / *Universiti Sains Malaysia, Malaysia* ... 750
Sant, Seema / *Vivekanand Education Society's Institute of Management Studies and Research, India* ... 810
Santos, Elvira Lázaro / *Instituto Superior de Lisboa e Vale do Tejo, Portugal* ... 772
Santos, Leonor / *Instituto de Educação, Universidade de Lisboa, Portugal* ... 772
Sarkar, Bidisha / *CHRIST University (Deemed), India* ... 138
Sendurur, Emine / *Ondokuz Mayis University, Turkey* ... 868
Şendurur, Polat / *Ondokuz Mayıs University, Turkey* ... 868
Setzer, Lee Ann / *Brigham Young University, USA* ... 671
Shohel, M. Mahruf C. / *University of Surrey, UK* ... 78
Shypilova, Mariia / *Great Wall School, China* ... 927
Siala, Haytham / *Business School, Newcastle University, UK* ... 488
Skordoulis, Constantine / *National and Kapodistrian University of Athens, Greece* ... 646
Stufft, Carolyn / *Berry College, USA* ... 320
Sundararajan, Binod / *Dalhousie University, Canada* ... 194
Tanni, Sanjida Akter / *Jagannath University, Bangladesh* ... 78
Taylor, Samantha / *Dalhousie University, Canada* ... 194
Tshifhumulo, Rendani / *University of Venda, South Africa* ... 397, 418
Tshikukuvhe, Livhuwani Daphney / *University of Venda, South Africa* ... 397
Unterholzner, Anna / *LARSyS, Interactive Technologies Institute (ITI), Faculdade de Belas-Artes, Universidade de Lisboa (FBAUL), Portugal* ... 180
Varghese, Sharon / *CHRIST University (Deemed), India* ... 122
Varma, Sankar / *CHRIST University (Deemed), India* ... 832
Veloso, Cláudia / *GOVCOPP, DEGEIT, University of Aveiro, Portugal* ... 533
von Gillern, Sam / *University of Missouri, USA* ... 320
Woodward, John R. / *Queen Mary Univeristy of London, UK* ... 455
Yangin Ekşi, Gonca / *Gazi University, Turkey* ... 510
Yastibaş, Ahmet Erdost / *Gazi University, Turkey* ... 510
Zou, Lin / *Primary School Affiliated to South China Normal University, China* ... 381

Table of Contents

Preface xxxv

Acknowledgment li

Volume I

Section 1
Gamification in Higher Education

Chapter 1
The Game of Game-Based Learning 1
  Reena Raj, CHRIST University (Deemed), India
  Cecil Donald, CHRIST University (Deemed), India
  Anand Patil, CHRIST University (Deemed), India
  Manjula M. Y., CHRIST University (Deemed), India
  Swarnalatha P., CHRIST University (Deemed), India

Chapter 2
Games in Education: Bibliometric Analysis 13
  Menşure Alkış Küçükaydın, Eregli Faculty of Education, Necmettin Erbakan University, Turkey
  Burcu Durmaz, Süleyman Demirel University, Turkey

Chapter 3
Amalgamation of Game-Based Learning With Interactive Instructional Strategies for Active
Learner Engagement 31
  Ankit Dhamija, Amity University, Haryana, India
  Deepika Dhamija, Amity University, Haryana, India

Chapter 4
A Systematic Review on the Neuro-Cognitive Correlates of Game-Based Learning in Higher
Education Learning Environments 58
  Smitha Baboo, CHRIST University (Deemed), India
  Yogesh Kanna, CHRIST University (Deemed), India
  Cathlyn Niranjana Bennett, CHRIST University (Deemed), India

Chapter 5
Game-Based Teaching and Learning in Higher Education: Challenges and Prospects 78
    M. Mahruf C. Shohel, University of Surrey, UK
    Md. Ashrafuzzaman, Bangabandhu Sheikh Mujibur Rahman Digital University, Bangladesh
    Iffat Naomee, University of Dhaka, Bangladesh
    Sanjida Akter Tanni, Jagannath University, Bangladesh
    Farhan Azim, University of Melbourne, Australia

Chapter 6
A Paradigm Shift in Higher Education: Evidence-Based Cross-Sectional Study Conducted in South India 107
    Vikas Salunkhe, CHRIST University (Deemed), India
    Seena Thomas Kaithathara, CHRIST University (Deemed), India
    Darshan S. M., CHRIST University (Deemed), India
    Gowri Shankar R., CHRIST University (Deemed), India
    Shabarisha N., CHRIST University (Deemed), India

Chapter 7
Effectiveness of Game-Based Learning as a Pedagogy Among the MBA Students 122
    Karthigai Prakasam Chellaswamy, CHRIST University (Deemed), India
    Nagarjuna Gururaj Rao, CHRIST University (Deemed), India
    Sharon Varghese, CHRIST University (Deemed), India
    Georgy P. Kurien, CHRIST University (Deemed), India
    Sreedhara Raman, CHRIST University (Deemed), India
    Anand Shankar Raja Manivannan, CHRIST University (Deemed), India

Chapter 8
Game-Based Learning in Higher Education: An Effective Pedagogical Tool for Enhanced Competency Building 138
    Sunitha Abhay Jain, CHRIST University (Deemed), India
    Nilofer Hussaini, CHRIST University (Deemed), India
    Sunil John, CHRIST University (Deemed), India
    Daisy Alexander, CHRIST University (Deemed), India
    Bidisha Sarkar, CHRIST University (Deemed), India

Chapter 9
Gamification Strategies for Higher Education Student Worker Training 164
    Emily Guetzoian, Anderson School of Management, UCLA, USA

Chapter 10
Interactive Multimedia Experiences in Higher Education: Gaming, Augment and Virtual Reality, and Research 180
    Patrícia Gouveia, LARSyS, Interactive Technologies Institute (ITI), Faculdade de Belas-
        Artes, Universidade de Lisboa (FBAUL), Portugal
    Luciana Lima, LARSyS, Interactive Technologies Institute (ITI), Faculdade de Belas-Artes,
        Universidade de Lisboa (FBAUL), Portugal
    Anna Unterholzner, LARSyS, Interactive Technologies Institute (ITI), Faculdade de Belas-
        Artes, Universidade de Lisboa (FBAUL), Portugal

Chapter 11
Live Long and Educate: Adult Learners and Situated Cognition in Game-Based Learning 194
    Samantha Taylor, Dalhousie University, Canada
    Binod Sundararajan, Dalhousie University, Canada
    Cora-Lynn Munroe-Lynds, Dalhousie University, Canada

Chapter 12
Worldbuilding, Gaming, and Multiliteracies in an Online First-Year Seminar 220
    Brian Angus McKenzie, Maynooth University, Ireland

Section 2
Exploring Literacy in Game-Based Learning

Chapter 13
Using Game-Based Learning to Improve Boys' Literacy 249
    Minda Marshall, Lectorsa, South Africa
    Marinda Marshall, Lectorsa, South Africa

Chapter 14
Game-Based Pedagogy: Educate, Collaborate, and Engage 269
    Carol-Ann Lane, University of Western Ontario, Canada

Chapter 15
Using Gamification to Improve Literacy Skills 289
    Jamie Mahoney, Murray State University, USA
    Kristina M. Buttrey, Murray State University, USA

Chapter 16
Digital Storyworlds: Transformative Ways to Play 302
    Karen Le Rossignol, Deakin University, Australia

Chapter 17
Minecraft and Elementary Literacy Learning: The Perspectives and Ideas of Preservice Teachers .. 320
    Sam von Gillern, University of Missouri, USA
    Carolyn Stufft, Berry College, USA
    Rick Marlatt, New Mexico State University, USA
    Larysa Nadolny, Iowa State University, USA

Chapter 18
Play Is the Game: Literacy Learning Through Game-Based Instruction 344
    Sharon Peck, State University of New York College at Geneseo, USA

Chapter 19
The Transformation of Literacy and Media Literacy 363
    Hacer Dolanbay, Muş Alparslan University, Turkey

Chapter 20
The Application of AI Teachers in Facilitating Game-Based Literacy Learning: An Introduction to Theories and Evidence-Based Tools 381
    Yixun Li, The Education University of Hong Kong, Hong Kong
    Lin Zou, Primary School Affiliated to South China Normal University, China

Section 3
Culturally-Based Game-Based Pedagogy

Chapter 21
Enhancing Literacy Skills Using Indigenous Games 397
    Rendani Tshifhumulo, University of Venda, South Africa
    Livhuwani Daphney Tshikukuvhe, University of Venda, South Africa
    Talifhani Trevor Ramatswi, University of Venda, South Africa

Chapter 22
Exploring the Use of African Indigenous Games in Teaching Critical Thinking Skills 418
    Hulisani Mulaudzi, University of Venda, South Africa
    Rendani Tshifhumulo, University of Venda, South Africa
    Tshimangadzo J. Makhanikhe, University of Venda, South Africa

Chapter 23
GraphoGame: A Computer-Assisted Reading Acquisition Tool – An Enabling Support to Reading in the African Classroom 431
    Pamela Jennifer February, University of Namibia, Namibia

Chapter 24
Educational Video Games for Learning English Vocabulary: Methodology of Empirical Research 455
    Jianshu Qiao, Queen Mary University of London, UK
    John R. Woodward, Queen Mary Univeristy of London, UK
    Atm S. Alam, Queen Mary University of London, UK

Volume II

Chapter 25
Gamification, Learning, and the Acquisition of 21st Century Skills Amongst Malaysian Law Students 472
    Joaquim Dias Soeiro, School of Hospitality, Tourism, and Events, Taylor's University, Malaysia
    Puteri Sofia Amirnuddin, Taylor's Law School, Taylor's University, Malaysia

Chapter 26
The Effect of Religiosity on Learning Ethics in Serious Gaming Environments: Religious Influences in Serious Educational Games 488
    Haytham Siala, Business School, Newcastle University, UK
    Giuseppe Pedeliento, University of Bergamo, Italy
    Daniela Andreini, University of Bergamo, Italy

Chapter 27
A Game-Based Content and Language-Integrated Learning Practice for Environmental Awareness
(ENVglish): User Perceptions 510
    Meltem Huri Baturay, Atilim University, Turkey
    Ahmet Erdost Yastibaş, Gazi University, Turkey
    Gonca Yangin Ekşi, Gazi University, Turkey
    Cafer Ahmet Çinar, Çanakkale Onsekiz Mart University, Turkey

Section 4
Teacher Perceptions of Game-Based Learning

Chapter 28
Educators as Facilitators of Game-Based Learning: Their Knowledge, Attitudes, and Skills 533
    Jessica Reuter, GOVCOPP, DEGEIT, University of Aveiro, Portugal
    Marta Ferreira Dias, GOVCOPP, DEGEIT, University of Aveiro, Portugal
    Marlene Amorim, GOVCOPP, DEGEIT, University of Aveiro, Portugal
    Mara Madaleno, GOVCOPP, DEGEIT, University of Aveiro, Portugal
    Claúdia Veloso, GOVCOPP, DEGEIT, University of Aveiro, Portugal

Chapter 29
Spanish Teacher Attitudes Towards Digital Game-Based Learning: An Exploratory Study Based
on the TPACK Model 554
    Cristina A. Huertas-Abril, University of Córdoba, Spain
    María García-Molina, University of Córdoba, Spain

Section 5
Gamification, Mobile Learning, and Education Policy

Chapter 30
Factors Affecting the Successful Implementation of an E-Education Policy and Community
Engagement: Acquiring 21st Century Skills Through E-Learning 580
    Absolom Muzambi, University of South Africa, South Africa
    Leila Goosen, University of South Africa, South Africa

Chapter 31
Game-Based Pedagogy and Learner Identity Development: Mechanical vs. Autotelic Identities 606
    Fritz Ngale Ilongo, University of Eswatini, Eswatini

Chapter 32
Gamification and Mobile Learning: New Pedagogical Strategies 630
    Ana Nobre, Universidade Aberta, Portugal
    Vasco Nobre, Universidade Aberta, Portugal

Chapter 33
Astronomy and Space-Themed Mobile Games: Tools to Support Science Education or Learning Barriers Due to the Misconceptions They Generate?..646
    Georgios Eleftherios Bampasidis, National and Kapodistrian University of Athens, Greece
    Apostolia Galani, National and Kapodistrian University of Athens, Greece
    Constantine Skordoulis, National and Kapodistrian University of Athens, Greece

Section 6
Game-Based Pedagogy for Primary-Elementary Educators

Chapter 34
Incorporating Digital Literacy Materials in Early Childhood Programs: Understanding Children's Engagement and Interactions 671
    Barbara Ellen Culatta, Brigham Young University, USA
    Lee Ann Setzer, Brigham Young University, USA
    Kendra M. Hall-Kenyon, Brigham Young University, USA

Chapter 35
Acquiring Problem-Solving Skills Through Coding Games in Primary School 697
    Gaia Lombardi, Istituto Comprensivo Statale Via dei Salici, Legnano, Italy

Chapter 36
Discrete Primary Education Curriculum in Bangladesh: Implications of Gamification for Quality Education 716
    Md Jahangir Alam, University of Dhaka, Bangladesh
    Sheikh Rashid Bin Islam, Bangladesh Consulting Services, Bangladesh
    Keiichi Ogawa, Kobe University, Japan

Chapter 37
Providing Validity Evidence for Ignite by Hatch: A Digital Game-Based Learning Experience for Preschool Children 731
    Hannah E. Luce, The University of North Carolina at Charlotte, USA
    Richard G. Lambert, University of North Carolina at Charlotte, USA

Chapter 38
Levelling Up Primary School Students' 21st Century Skills Through Minecraft-Game-Based Learning 750
    Mohd Ali Samsudin, Universiti Sains Malaysia, Malaysia
    Goh Kok Ming, SJKC Chi Sheng 2, Malaysia
    Nur Jahan Ahmad, Universiti Sains Malaysia, Malaysia
    Yogendran Abrose, Universiti Sains Malaysia, Malaysia

Section 7
Learner Assessment, Motivation, and Behaviors in Game-Based Learning

Chapter 39
How Gaming and Formative Assessment Contribute to Learning Supplementary and Complementary Angles 772

Elvira Lázaro Santos, Instituto Superior de Lisboa e Vale do Tejo, Portugal
Leonor Santos, Instituto de Educação, Universidade de Lisboa, Portugal

Chapter 40
Gamification Design Principles and Mechanics to Improve Retention 788

Robert Costello, Middlesbrough College, UK

Chapter 41
Learner Motivation Through Gamification in E-Learning: A Study on Game-Based Formative Assessment in E-Learning 810

Anshita Chelawat, Vivekanand Education Society's Institute of Management Studies and Research, India
Seema Sant, Vivekanand Education Society's Institute of Management Studies and Research, India

Chapter 42
Political Economy Inside the Strategy of Line Game 832

Annesha Biswas, CHRIST University (Deemed), India
Tinanjali Dam, CHRIST University (Deemed), India
Joseph Varghese Kureethara, CHRIST University (Deemed), India
Sankar Varma, CHRIST University (Deemed), India

Chapter 43
The Process of Prosocial Behavior Between Players/Characters in Digital Games: A Multidimensional Approach to the Situational Context and Gameplay 846

Ji Soo Lim, Dokkyo University, Japan

Section 8
Game-Based Learning: Code and Play

Chapter 44
Students as Gamers: Design, Code, and Play 868

Polat Şendurur, Ondokuz Mayıs University, Turkey
Emine Sendurur, Ondokuz Mayis University, Turkey

Chapter 45
Learning Coding Through Gaming 888

Janna Jackson Kellinger, University of Massachusetts, Boston, USA

Chapter 46
Using Custom-Built, Small-Scale Educational Solutions to Teach Qualitative Research Literacy:
No Code, Code, and Complex Applications 905
    Geraldine Bengsch, Kings College London, UK

Section 9
Virtual Teaching and Project-Oriented Game-Based Learning

Chapter 47
Project-Oriented Game-Based Learning: Managers From Fairytales 927
    Pavlo Brin, National Technical University "Kharkiv Polytechnic Institute", Ukraine
    Mariia Shypilova, Great Wall School, China

Chapter 48
Virtual Training for Scuba Divers 946
    Anacleto Correia, Naval Academy, Portugal
    Pedro B. Água, Naval Aacdemy, Portugal

Compilation of References lii

About the Contributors cxciii

Index ccxiv

Detailed Table of Contents

Preface xxxv

Acknowledgment li

Volume I

Section 1
Gamification in Higher Education

Chapter 1
The Game of Game-Based Learning 1
Reena Raj, CHRIST University (Deemed), India
Cecil Donald, CHRIST University (Deemed), India
Anand Patil, CHRIST University (Deemed), India
Manjula M. Y., CHRIST University (Deemed), India
Swarnalatha P., CHRIST University (Deemed), India

Games have been an inevitable part of education since the beginning. They have indescribably transformed the educational landscape with a higher emphasis on the learner-centric pedagogy. The educational games can be considered to be a contemporary manifestation of these centuries' old philosophies and practices aimed at imparting strategic and tactical thinking, language, logic, and mathematical skills amongst the learners. This chapter explores the meaning, significance, and scope of game-based learning as an instructional tool. It provides an interesting account of several games that are popularly used to facilitate effective learning in various settings. This chapter also examines the relevance and implications of games in education.

Chapter 2
Games in Education: Bibliometric Analysis 13
Menşure Alkış Küçükaydın, Eregli Faculty of Education, Necmettin Erbakan University, Turkey
Burcu Durmaz, Süleyman Demirel University, Turkey

In this study, a study was made on the Web of Science index by using the words "game-based learning," "video games," "game-based pedagogy," "digital games," "gamification," and "game." The study was carried out with data obtained from the SCI-E, SSCI, and A&HCI indices covering the years 1975-2021. A total of 1,376 articles were reached in accordance with the inclusion criteria. Retrieved articles were subjected to bibliometric analysis. In line with the relevant analysis, the most influential authors, journals, institutions, and articles were revealed under the title "games in education." In addition, based on the articles examined within the scope of this research, a co-word network structure was visualized in terms of cooperation among institutions and authors. As a result of the research, the trends in topics related to games were revealed, and the changes in this area are subsequently discussed.

Chapter 3
Amalgamation of Game-Based Learning With Interactive Instructional Strategies for Active Learner Engagement 31
    Ankit Dhamija, Amity University, Haryana, India
    Deepika Dhamija, Amity University, Haryana, India

In recent years, the teaching-learning process in higher education has undergone unprecedented change. Learners from across the world can enroll in any university using online platforms. This learning freedom is fantastic for all stakeholders, but it raises some serious concerns, such as how to ensure effective learner engagement and make the learning experience meaningful for the learners. While technology has aided learning, it has also become a significant source of distraction for students, as they spend too much time on gadgets solely for entertainment. This necessitates innovative and engaging teaching styles from educators. Designing course content as a game makes learning more engaging as learners get a sense of motivation and accomplishment. However, aligning games with lesson plans, designing assessment criteria, and learning outcomes takes a significant amount of time and effort. Hence, this chapter proposes learner-centered interactive instructional strategies that employ GBL to pique learners' curiosity and recommends popular GBL platforms for creating educational games.

Chapter 4
A Systematic Review on the Neuro-Cognitive Correlates of Game-Based Learning in Higher Education Learning Environments 58
    Smitha Baboo, CHRIST University (Deemed), India
    Yogesh Kanna, CHRIST University (Deemed), India
    Cathlyn Niranjana Bennett, CHRIST University (Deemed), India

Game-based learning is one of the sustainable education methods for future professionals from the higher education learning environment. To attain these innovative and sustainable teaching pedagogies, the components of games and simulations need to be incorporated into the teaching-learning content. The integration of neuroscience and cognitive concepts has become an essential feature in understanding various phenomena in game-based learning with regard to higher education learning environments. Several neural and cognitive processes are involved while engaging in such activities. These activities have played a pivotal role in the pedagogy and teachers had to think on their feet while engaging students in higher education as well. Game-based learning has proven to be a very effective method of engaging higher education students.

Chapter 5
Game-Based Teaching and Learning in Higher Education: Challenges and Prospects 78
    M. Mahruf C. Shohel, University of Surrey, UK
    Md. Ashrafuzzaman, Bangabandhu Sheikh Mujibur Rahman Digital University, Bangladesh
    Iffat Naomee, University of Dhaka, Bangladesh
    Sanjida Akter Tanni, Jagannath University, Bangladesh
    Farhan Azim, University of Melbourne, Australia

Game-based pedagogies use games for achieving learning outcomes by guiding the learners through specific tasks, which can be digital and/or non-digital and can promote deep meaningful learning. Therefore, the design of game-based learning helps learners to engage in the meaning-making process and ensure better participation. As the boundaries of classroom learning become blurred through blended or hybrid learning approaches, game-based learning enhances digital literacies for digital natives to prepare them for building a knowledge economy. By exploring existing literature, this chapter highlights how technology can support teachers and learners to go beyond their existing pedagogical boundaries by focusing on ways games may serve as digital sources of learning. It also explores the role game-based pedagogies and digital learning design frameworks play in enhancing learner engagement, collaboration, and cultural understanding.

Chapter 6
A Paradigm Shift in Higher Education: Evidence-Based Cross-Sectional Study Conducted in South India 107
    Vikas Salunkhe, CHRIST University (Deemed), India
    Seena Thomas Kaithathara, CHRIST University (Deemed), India
    Darshan S. M., CHRIST University (Deemed), India
    Gowri Shankar R., CHRIST University (Deemed), India
    Shabarisha N., CHRIST University (Deemed), India

Game-based learning is widely followed at the school level in India, but the higher education system has been longer in adopting it. The pandemic situation has transformed teaching and learning processes from the traditional to the technical method, which requires a more versatile approach. Because of the rapid change from the offline mode to the online mode in higher education, there is little evidence available on the inefficiency of implementing the traditional system of teacher-centered education on online platforms. There comes a lot of the significance in of adapting technology-based games in order to engage and motivate students throughout their course of study. The aim of this chapter is to provide an overview of the effectiveness of game-based learning strategies over traditional learning methods. Moreover, the results of a cross-sectional study conducted by the authors in South Indian universities at the higher education level is included.

Chapter 7
Effectiveness of Game-Based Learning as a Pedagogy Among the MBA Students 122
    Karthigai Prakasam Chellaswamy, CHRIST University (Deemed), India
    Nagarjuna Gururaj Rao, CHRIST University (Deemed), India
    Sharon Varghese, CHRIST University (Deemed), India
    Georgy P. Kurien, CHRIST University (Deemed), India
    Sreedhara Raman, CHRIST University (Deemed), India
    Anand Shankar Raja Manivannan, CHRIST University (Deemed), India

Game-based learning is an exciting and interactive tool used by many teachers across the globe. This research aims to check whether any significant change is found in the learning of the student before and after introducing game-based learning in classroom teaching. MBA students were identified as the target group for this research. The production dice game was used for this experiment. The teacher engaged the first session traditionally and later with the production dice game. Student learning was captured through a Google form before and after the game. The Google form had questions ranging from understanding to analyzing to application-level to capture exactly the effectiveness of game-based learning, Paired sample t-test was applied to check the before and after test results, and it was found that there was a significant change in the learning among the identified target group. Through this study, the authors conclude that game-based learning provides better results in student learning as compared to regular classroom teaching.

Chapter 8
Game-Based Learning in Higher Education: An Effective Pedagogical Tool for Enhanced Competency Building 138
    Sunitha Abhay Jain, CHRIST University (Deemed), India
    Nilofer Hussaini, CHRIST University (Deemed), India
    Sunil John, CHRIST University (Deemed), India
    Daisy Alexander, CHRIST University (Deemed), India
    Bidisha Sarkar, CHRIST University (Deemed), India

The technological developments and innovations have thrown open many challenges in the field of higher education. We are growing up in a society of digital natives who are exposed to the digital environment from their birth. Of late, the focus has shifted from traditional teaching methods to finding innovative ways and means to engage the students. Competence building instead of rote learning is the need of the hour. In order to prepare the students to face the challenges of the real world and make them future ready, it is important for higher educational institutions to focus on imparting to learners 21st century skill sets such as creativity, problem solving, and critical thinking, amongst others. Game-based learning is gaining momentum and is becoming a popular pedagogical tool as it is learner-centric and fosters creativity.

Chapter 9
Gamification Strategies for Higher Education Student Worker Training 164
    Emily Guetzoian, Anderson School of Management, UCLA, USA

This chapter discusses gamification strategies in the context of higher education student worker training. Specifically, it builds on the concepts of gamification in corporate training contexts and gamification in the academic classroom environment. It also considers various options to support gamified training content and methods to support student worker engagement and knowledge retention. It explains how these strategies relate to the concept of information literacy for an adult, higher education population. This chapter is ideal for higher education staff, faculty, or administrators who design training curricula for student workers.

Chapter 10
Interactive Multimedia Experiences in Higher Education: Gaming, Augment and Virtual Reality, and Research 180
    Patrícia Gouveia, LARSyS, Interactive Technologies Institute (ITI), Faculdade de Belas-
        Artes, Universidade de Lisboa (FBAUL), Portugal
    Luciana Lima, LARSyS, Interactive Technologies Institute (ITI), Faculdade de Belas-Artes,
        Universidade de Lisboa (FBAUL), Portugal
    Anna Unterholzner, LARSyS, Interactive Technologies Institute (ITI), Faculdade de Belas-
        Artes, Universidade de Lisboa (FBAUL), Portugal

This chapter presents experiences in using gaming and interactive media in higher education environments since 2017 culminating in the 2020/21 years when the COVID-19 pandemic forced teachers and students to adopt different work methodologies. Participatory design strategies merged with a tradition of critical and interdisciplinary studies in humanities mediated by online technologies helped shape these strategies enhanced by the cooperation from three different faculties from Lisbon University in Portugal (Universidade de Lisboa, UL), namely FBAUL, IST, and IGOT. The aim of these experiments was to augment the potential for innovation and research taking advantage of gaming research methodologies to involve teachers and students in a common context. This chapter also shows research done in interactive media, augmented and virtual reality, game art, and gender equity. The year 2020 showed how institutional collaboration can open learning spaces to a more focused approach on the interests of young people and to promote a more sustainable and dynamic future.

Chapter 11
Live Long and Educate: Adult Learners and Situated Cognition in Game-Based Learning 194
    Samantha Taylor, Dalhousie University, Canada
    Binod Sundararajan, Dalhousie University, Canada
    Cora-Lynn Munroe-Lynds, Dalhousie University, Canada

Using the lenses of Vygotskian constructivism, situated cognition, the antecedents of flow, and a pedagogy interwoven with the multiliteracy framework, the authors present a COVID-19 simulation game. The game has multiple levels, challenges, disrupters, and allows for student player groups to work together (i.e., collaborate within and across player groups) to achieve the strategic objectives of the game. The player groups have an overall goal to minimize loss of life, while other parameters need to be optimized, depending on the stakeholder group that the player group is role-playing. While the game can be digitized, it is presented in a manner that allows instructors to implement the game simulation right away in their classrooms. Assessment rubrics, decision matrix templates, and debriefing notes are provided to allow for student learners to reflect on their decisions (based on course concepts) both individually and as a player group.

Chapter 12
Worldbuilding, Gaming, and Multiliteracies in an Online First-Year Seminar 220
    Brian Angus McKenzie, Maynooth University, Ireland

This chapter provides a case study of the use of worldbuilding for role-playing games as the foundation for a first year multiliteracies seminar. The author provides an overview of teaching and learning during the pandemic in the Irish context. The chapter provides practical advice on using a MediaWiki installation as the infrastructure for worldbuilding projects. The author shows how this imparts important digital literacies and allows for a critical apprehension of Wikipedia itself. The author argues that online learning and professional development benefit from a multiliteracies approach and, furthermore, that worldbuilding is a useful strategy for overcoming the limitations of online learning while at the same time achieving rigorous learning outcomes.

Section 2
Exploring Literacy in Game-Based Learning

Chapter 13
Using Game-Based Learning to Improve Boys' Literacy 249
    Minda Marshall, Lectorsa, South Africa
    Marinda Marshall, Lectorsa, South Africa

This chapter foregrounds an online gamified visual intelligence innovation (eyebraingym) developed to enhance visual processing skills, improve memory and vocabulary, and increase reading fluency. The explicit aim of the innovation is to improve comprehension towards visual intelligence. Ninety-eight Grade 8 learners at a South African Boy's School completed their online development during the 2021 academic year. These learners were part of a group of students participating in a whole school reading and literacy intervention program. The innovation is an integral part of this ongoing project. Their interaction with the innovation consists of 15 sessions completed once or twice a week for 20 – 40 minutes over five months. The results of the project are positive. It shows that most participating students improved their perceptual development and reading speed (VPF) and cognitive development and comprehension skills (CDF). In addition, these outcomes transferred to improved relative efficiency when working with information (AIUF).

Chapter 14
Game-Based Pedagogy: Educate, Collaborate, and Engage 269
    Carol-Ann Lane, University of Western Ontario, Canada

Interpretations of the cultural meanings made by each of the boys in the study, based on their individual unique experiences engaging with video games, can provide readers with insights into how to approach adolescent aged boys' literacy development through game-based pedagogy. In this chapter the author describes how these four boys developed their multimodal ways of learning by engaging with visual perspectives of video games. The methodological approach documented what boys are saying, as much as possible, which is currently understudied in the literature surrounding boys and their video gaming practices. This chapter addresses some boys' out-of-school video gaming practices for meaning-making and gaining cultural knowledge. Studying the ways in which boys make meanings through multimodal ways of learning can offer insights into strategies for cyber culture that can potentially reinvent traditional literacy pedagogical boundaries and establish new ways and practices for building knowledge.

Chapter 15
Using Gamification to Improve Literacy Skills 289
    Jamie Mahoney, Murray State University, USA
    Kristina M. Buttrey, Murray State University, USA

Students in the 21st century are learning by doing and playing. Teachers need to incorporate technology into everyday tasks. Games assist students in the learning process. Once students have learned a task through the playing process, they will remember this much easier and longer than simply doing a worksheet. Research shows students enjoy interactive and engaging activities and will choose these types of activities over pencil and paper types of activities. Teachers must prepare students for the future which involves more critical thinking and technological types of skills. Traditional teaching methods and styles have underused technology tools and pedagogical methods. The 2020 Covid pandemic and remote learning delivery style assisted teachers in developing new tools and methods to reach and teach all students with various and diverse needs.

Chapter 16
Digital Storyworlds: Transformative Ways to Play... 302
    Karen Le Rossignol, Deakin University, Australia

The digital storyworld model is conceptualised in this chapter as an innovative digital storytelling that incorporates both transmedia and meaning-making narrative approaches. Working with Aristotelian story elements in a non-linear digital series of mini-worlds, the higher education narrator-as-learner enters real-world situations mirrored in a fictional and fragmented environment. The model encourages a playful engagement in the experiential learning process through a range of points of view, encouraging empathy for differing perspectives that are transferable to real-life environments.

Chapter 17
Minecraft and Elementary Literacy Learning: The Perspectives and Ideas of Preservice
Teachers 320
    Sam von Gillern, University of Missouri, USA
    Carolyn Stufft, Berry College, USA
    Rick Marlatt, New Mexico State University, USA
    Larysa Nadolny, Iowa State University, USA

This research examines the perceptions and instructional ideas of preservice teachers as relates to using Minecraft, a popular video game, to facilitate game-based learning opportunities in their future elementary classrooms. The participants were 21 preservice teachers who played Minecraft as part of a teacher preparation program course and then completed essays on their experiences with the game and its potential to support student learning in the elementary English language arts classroom. These essays were coded and analyzed for themes. Three primary results were found in data analysis. First, three groups emerged from the data with each group indicating either no interest, some interest, or high interest in using Minecraft in their future teaching. Second, the preservice teachers illustrated various potential instructional strategies for integrating the game into the classroom, and third, participants identified a variety of ways that Minecraft integration can support English language arts instruction and learning.

Chapter 18
Play Is the Game: Literacy Learning Through Game-Based Instruction 344
    Sharon Peck, State University of New York College at Geneseo, USA

Drawing on a multimodal framework, this chapter looks at the ways engagement and embodiment of learning are mediated through play as sixth graders learn to skin or repurpose board games to represent the story of The Lightning Thief. Studying game design for the purpose of skinning, that is, applying a new theme or skin to a game, provides a literacy learning process that can foster collaborative, creative, and authentic learning. Outcomes demonstrated gains in social skills and interactions, critical thinking, reading comprehension, visual representation, graphic design, and writing for specific purposes. Analysis revealed that students were immersed in the learning process to the extent that they felt comfortable acting informally, responding in the moment, and being playful. This chapter shows a way to foster academic growth, engagement in learning, and collaboration is to engage students in skinning games based on literature and integrated a playful learning environment.

Chapter 19
The Transformation of Literacy and Media Literacy.. 363
    Hacer Dolanbay, Muş Alparslan University, Turkey

Whether we call it the age of information, the age of digitalization, or the informatics, this century is an era in which rapid technological developments are taking place and will continue without stopping. The importance of using the media consciously and appropriately is increasing by reducing the effects of the media on individuals with many positive and negative characteristics. Having media literacy skills, which is one of the basic skills of the new century, is important in learning how tool live with the media. Becoming a conscious media consumer and producer, the way to realize the reality in the media is to have media literacy skills which is one of the basic skills of the new century. This chapter is mainly aimed at studying the dynamics that makeup media literacy and media literacy skills. How the century has transformed to meet the needs of its students will be highlighted within the context of media literacy. Then, the chapter will be completed by explaining how media literacy is reflected in pedagogy with examples suitable for different courses and levels.

Chapter 20
The Application of AI Teachers in Facilitating Game-Based Literacy Learning: An Introduction to Theories and Evidence-Based Tools 381
    Yixun Li, The Education University of Hong Kong, Hong Kong
    Lin Zou, Primary School Affiliated to South China Normal University, China

This chapter discusses the theoretical frameworks for artificial intelligence (AI) teachers and how AI teachers have been applied to facilitate game-based literacy learning in existing empirical studies. While the application of artificial intelligence (AI) in education is a relatively emerging research area, it has received increasing attention in the scientific community. In the future, AI teachers are likely to be able to serve as powerful supplementary tools in classroom teaching in support of human teachers. The main goal here is to provide the readers with new insights on promoting game-based literacy learning from the perspectives of AI teachers. To this end, the authors introduce the readers to the key concepts of AI teachers, the merits and demerits of AI teachers in education, scientific research on AI teachers in literacy learning, and some highlighted examples of AI teachers in literacy classrooms for practical concerns.

Section 3
Culturally-Based Game-Based Pedagogy

Chapter 21
Enhancing Literacy Skills Using Indigenous Games 397
    Rendani Tshifhumulo, University of Venda, South Africa
    Livhuwani Daphney Tshikukuvhe, University of Venda, South Africa
    Talifhani Trevor Ramatswi, University of Venda, South Africa

This chapter explores the possibility of enhancing literacy skills using indigenous games played by Vhavenda children at foundation phase. It critically analyses different types of Vhavenda games played by children which are ndode, mufuvha, muravharavha, and tsetsetse or trere-tsere to solicit the possibility to enhance literacy skills. Methodologically, this study aligns with the use of qualitative approach where researchers collected data using interviews and observations. The focus is on Vhavenda indigenous games that can be adopted by other cultures to enhance learning inside and outside the classroom environment. The results found that indigenous games develop several literacy skills inclusive of school, arithmetic, communication, cultural, emotional, and physical literacies which are very important for total development of children. Games are enjoyable and interesting and as such make learning fun.

Chapter 22
Exploring the Use of African Indigenous Games in Teaching Critical Thinking Skills 418
    Hulisani Mulaudzi, University of Venda, South Africa
    Rendani Tshifhumulo, University of Venda, South Africa
    Tshimangadzo J. Makhanikhe, University of Venda, South Africa

Critical thinking skills are fundamental for both undergraduate and postgraduate students in the academic environment. These skills allow students to question and reflect on the knowledge and information presented to them. These skills can be learned differently through various instruments. This chapter explores how this game can contribute towards teaching critical thinking skills. There are various indigenous games played in Vhavenda culture. The researchers focus on an indigenous game, Duvheke. The chapter employs game-based pedagogy as a theory that underpins this study. Methodologically, the chapter assumes a qualitative complexion because it seeks to collect in-depth information about Duvheke and how it can be used in teaching critical thinking skills first entering students in a rural university. The data collection method used is interviews which were collected from first entering students. Preliminary findings suggest that critical thinking is needed to play Duvheke. The chapter suggests that Duvheke can be a valuable tool in teaching critical thinking skills.

Chapter 23
GraphoGame: A Computer-Assisted Reading Acquisition Tool – An Enabling Support to Reading in the African Classroom 431
    Pamela Jennifer February, University of Namibia, Namibia

This chapter investigates the effectiveness of a digital reading tool, called GraphoGame, that could be employed as one of the solutions to the poor reading results of learners that have been revealed in both national and international assessments in Namibia, specifically, and Sub-Saharan Africa in general. Following a research study, this chapter sets out to demonstrate that, through pre-and post-tests, GraphoGame Afrikaans improved the initial reading skills of Grade 1 learners. The results have implications for the utilization of computer-assisted tools to support reading acquisition in the lower grades. As GraphoGame employs a scaffolded approach by presenting learners with letters and words, it can be utilized to support learners individually in classes with large numbers, as is typical in Africa.

Chapter 24
Educational Video Games for Learning English Vocabulary: Methodology of Empirical Research 455
    Jianshu Qiao, Queen Mary University of London, UK
    John R. Woodward, Queen Mary Univeristy of London, UK
    Atm S. Alam, Queen Mary University of London, UK

Researchers have been exploring the potential of educational video games for learning English vocabulary. The primary focus is on two questions: (1) Can educational video games motivate students to learn English vocabulary (which explores students' attitudes)? and (2) Are educational video games effective in acquiring English vocabulary (which explores learning outcomes)? Good quality empirical research on this is rare because of the shortage of games specific to educational purposes. In addition, although some researchers have contributed to answering these two questions, their methodology is not convincing. Therefore, this chapter aims to provide an overview of their methodologies by introducing participant groups, popular educational video games, pre-test, post-test, and data analysis. Finally, this chapter will inspire researchers to conduct more reliable empirical research, thereby making better-found contributions to the field.

Volume II

Chapter 25
Gamification, Learning, and the Acquisition of 21st Century Skills Amongst Malaysian Law Students 472
> *Joaquim Dias Soeiro, School of Hospitality, Tourism, and Events, Taylor's University, Malaysia*
> *Puteri Sofia Amirnuddin, Taylor's Law School, Taylor's University, Malaysia*

The diversification of pedagogic tools remains essential for a fruitful learning experience among the Gen Z students by embedding technology such as gamification in learning. Recent literature has discussed the acquisition of 21st century skills and the educational challenges generally faced by Asian students due to their cultural traits. Against this background, the findings of this study open reflections relating to the benefit of gamification in acquiring 21st century skills. The objective of this chapter is to identify whether gamification is a suitable pedagogic tool among Malaysian law students in order to support the acquisition of 21st century skills. The respondents are from Year 1 and Year 2 of a three-year Bachelor of Laws degree with the majority being Malaysian students. The data collected showed that gamification helps in the acquisition of 21st century skills. Evidently, it showed that gamification can be a suitable alternative pedagogic tool to support the students to learn skills such as critical thinking, creativity, innovation, leadership, or communication.

Chapter 26
The Effect of Religiosity on Learning Ethics in Serious Gaming Environments: Religious Influences in Serious Educational Games 488
> *Haytham Siala, Business School, Newcastle University, UK*
> *Giuseppe Pedeliento, University of Bergamo, Italy*
> *Daniela Andreini, University of Bergamo, Italy*

The multi-disciplinary literature on ethics asserts that the relationship between religiosity and ethical perceptions and judgements is an under-researched topic. Despite its importance, few studies have examined the relationship between religiosity and the learning of business ethics. This research investigates whether religiosity is conducive to the learning of business ethics in a digital learning environment: a serious 3D ethics game. A cross-sectional survey was conducted on 302 final-year students from two different academic institutions based in the UK. The results of a structural equation modelling analysis suggest that religiosity does not inform the ethical perceptions and decisions of religious individuals in digital learning environments. Religious individuals perceive the utilitarian aspects of a serious game such as ease of use to be more important for learning ethics than religion. In contrast, less religious individuals perceive the hedonic aspects of a serious game to be a key catalyst for enhancing the learning of ethics.

Chapter 27
A Game-Based Content and Language-Integrated Learning Practice for Environmental Awareness (ENVglish): User Perceptions 510
> *Meltem Huri Baturay, Atilim University, Turkey*
> *Ahmet Erdost Yastibaş, Gazi University, Turkey*
> *Gonca Yangin Ekşi, Gazi University, Turkey*
> *Cafer Ahmet Çinar, Çanakkale Onsekiz Mart University, Turkey*

Increasing human activities in the environment have created severe effects; therefore, handling such effects by raising environmental awareness through several ways has become significant to sustain the environment, which can enhance 21st century skills including critical thinking and information literacy. Digital games can be used for this because they create an environment for learning with higher engagement, motivation, and excitement besides fostering cognitive attainment and retention. Accordingly, a mobile game-based content and language-integrated learning practice (an educational digital game called ENVglish) was developed to raise EFL students' environmental awareness in this qualitative study. During the design and development phases of the game, students' and teachers' perceptions regarding it were collected with semi-structured interviews. The data were content analyzed. The findings indicated that both students and teachers had positive perceptions about the game and that students could improve their English and have environmental awareness with the game.

Section 4
Teacher Perceptions of Game-Based Learning

Chapter 28
Educators as Facilitators of Game-Based Learning: Their Knowledge, Attitudes, and Skills 533
    Jessica Reuter, GOVCOPP, DEGEIT, University of Aveiro, Portugal
    Marta Ferreira Dias, GOVCOPP, DEGEIT, University of Aveiro, Portugal
    Marlene Amorim, GOVCOPP, DEGEIT, University of Aveiro, Portugal
    Mara Madaleno, GOVCOPP, DEGEIT, University of Aveiro, Portugal
    Claúdia Veloso, GOVCOPP, DEGEIT, University of Aveiro, Portugal

Innovative educational methods such as gamification are gaining ground in more formal environments and have great potential to improve learning in education. However, the implementation of this strategy in the classroom is assumed to be a complex practice for beginners and requires the development of new competencies by educators. This chapter aims to contribute to the advancement of knowledge about the main competencies needed for educators to perform as facilitators of educational games. The study was developed through critical literature review, interviews, and questionnaires. The outcome is the development of a framework of competencies of an educator willing to use game-based learning. The study highlights the importance of institutional support to boost the development of pedagogical, technological, and social skills among educators. The conclusions of the chapter are valuable for educators aiming to adopt game-based learning and to higher education decision makers committed to expanding innovative learning contexts on their institutions.

Chapter 29
Spanish Teacher Attitudes Towards Digital Game-Based Learning: An Exploratory Study Based on the TPACK Model 554
    Cristina A. Huertas-Abril, University of Córdoba, Spain
    María García-Molina, University of Córdoba, Spain

The consideration that the only goal of games is the achievement of entertainment is still commonly accepted, although there is now an outgrowing perspective that believes in the use of games to promote learning. This exploratory quantitative research examines both in-service and pre-service Spanish teacher perceptions (n = 112) about using digital games in their lessons, paying a special attention to the TPACK model, and comparing the results regarding age, gender, and professional situation. Responses show a positive attitude towards the potential use of video games in their lessons, although there are differences considering the results of the items concerning technological, pedagogical, or content knowledge. The data presented in this study is relevant to guide the design of curriculum and training programs, as well as to develop strategies to support and scaffold pre-service and in-service teachers' knowledge and practical implementation of digital game-based learning (DGBL).

Section 5
Gamification, Mobile Learning, and Education Policy

Chapter 30
Factors Affecting the Successful Implementation of an E-Education Policy and Community Engagement: Acquiring 21st Century Skills Through E-Learning 580
    Absolom Muzambi, University of South Africa, South Africa
    Leila Goosen, University of South Africa, South Africa

In order to provide readers with an overview and summarize the content, the purpose of this chapter is stated as reporting on an investigation around acquiring 21st century skills through e-learning. This study takes place against the background of the factors affecting the successful implementation of an e-education policy and community engagement. In terms of research methodology, a case study is used of a specific high (secondary) school in the Metro North district of the Western Cape province, South Africa.

Chapter 31
Game-Based Pedagogy and Learner Identity Development: Mechanical vs. Autotelic Identities 606
    Fritz Ngale Ilongo, University of Eswatini, Eswatini

This chapter explores the potentially negative and positive impacts of game-based pedagogy on personality development. The methodology of this chapter is qualitative basic research, while the theoretical framework is critical theoretical analyses, articulated around psychodynamic theory, analytic psychology, and positive psychology. The negative view of game-based personality development presupposes 'learners for technology' or the pessimistic view, while the positive view of game-based personality development considers 'technology for learners' as being a perspective which facilitates media literacy, higher order thinking, higher emotional intelligence, and pro-social behaviors. The conclusion is that the positive view of game-based personality development would facilitate learners' effective and efficient acquisition of 21st century literacy skills, that is, information literacy, media literacy, and technology literacy.

Chapter 32
Gamification and Mobile Learning: New Pedagogical Strategies 630
    Ana Nobre, Universidade Aberta, Portugal
    Vasco Nobre, Universidade Aberta, Portugal

Gamification has been a very frequent research topic in the area of education in recent years, with some positive results, such as increasing student engagement and motivation. However, studies on gamification as an instructional strategy are recent and need more data to help teachers in its use in the classroom. Thus, this work describes a gamification experience of a social game with graduate students, teachers in primary and secondary education, and discusses how the elements present in games can provide engagement and favor learning. Furthermore, the authors present the Kahoot app as a possibility to stimulate and engage students in the teaching-learning process, analyzing some implications of learning with a mobile device. The results had a positive impact on increasing student engagement in both Game Social and Kahoot. Therefore, gamification and mobile learning can be good alternatives to increase the quality of teaching, generating meaningful experiences in the classroom.

Chapter 33
Astronomy and Space-Themed Mobile Games: Tools to Support Science Education or Learning
Barriers Due to the Misconceptions They Generate? 646
 Georgios Eleftherios Bampasidis, National and Kapodistrian University of Athens, Greece
 Apostolia Galani, National and Kapodistrian University of Athens, Greece
 Constantine Skordoulis, National and Kapodistrian University of Athens, Greece

This chapter aims to contribute to the discussion of incorporating mobile games with astronomy and space themes in order to support science learning. One concern is when these games include erroneous science content. In this case, they may build or enhance misconceptions or misunderstandings, which eventually create learning barriers. The authors try to determine the learning strategies or pedagogies which can be used to incorporate such games in science education. Research on which characteristics these games should have is also presented. Game-based learning is in alignment with acquiring and developing 21st century literacy skills. One of these skills, information literacy, is related to domain knowledge learning.

Section 6
Game-Based Pedagogy for Primary-Elementary Educators

Chapter 34
Incorporating Digital Literacy Materials in Early Childhood Programs: Understanding Children's
Engagement and Interactions 671
 Barbara Ellen Culatta, Brigham Young University, USA
 Lee Ann Setzer, Brigham Young University, USA
 Kendra M. Hall-Kenyon, Brigham Young University, USA

Use of digital media in early childhood literacy programs offers significant opportunities for interaction, engagement, and meaningful practice of phonic skills—and also a few pitfalls. The purpose of this chapter is to review 1) considerations for use of digital media in early childhood settings, 2) selection of appropriate media to facilitate early literacy learning, and 3) inclusion of digital media as an integral component of early literacy instruction, rather than an add-on. With an emphasis on practical ideas and solutions for instructors, the authors draw on studies in which interactive, personalized ebooks and an early literacy learning app were used in conjunction with face-to-face, hands-on activities drawn from Project SEEL (Systematic and Engaging Early Literacy).

Chapter 35
Acquiring Problem-Solving Skills Through Coding Games in Primary School 697
 Gaia Lombardi, Istituto Comprensivo Statale Via dei Salici, Legnano, Italy

Play is a spontaneous and free activity of the child and its role in learning processes has been recognized by pedagogical studies from Piaget onwards. Game-based learning places the pupil at the center of the teaching-learning process, creating a motivating and challenging environment in which the pupil can learn freely, proceeding by trial and error, learning to evaluate their choices and those of other players and monitor a number of variables. Game-based learning therefore stands as an individualized and inclusive learning environment, which allows all students to achieve maximum educational success. In more recent years, the spread of online games, the use of coding as a teaching tool, and distance learning experiences have contributed to spreading game-based didactics. In this chapter, the author proposes a path of coding games for the development of problem solving in primary school with interdisciplinary links and to the mathematics curriculum.

Chapter 36
Discrete Primary Education Curriculum in Bangladesh: Implications of Gamification for Quality Education 716

    Md Jahangir Alam, University of Dhaka, Bangladesh
    Sheikh Rashid Bin Islam, Bangladesh Consulting Services, Bangladesh
    Keiichi Ogawa, Kobe University, Japan

The curriculum is an essential and integral part of the education system for lifelong learning and better children's outcomes. The sum of experience throughout their schooling journey can be defined as an educational curriculum expressed in a much broader sense. The school's type of school, study materials used, teaching methods, available school facilities, and the qualifications of schoolteachers provided at the end of primary schooling often diverge with different educational curricula due to the government policy dilemma. There is no unified primary education curriculum in Bangladesh's case. More than three mainstream educational curricula can be founded, each with its own unique set of traits, benefits, and shortcomings. This chapter explores what factors affect a school's choice, which is linked with the educational curriculum being offered, and how it affects the student's quality of education. This chapter also explores gamification theory's implementation to ensure quality primary education in Bangladesh.

Chapter 37
Providing Validity Evidence for Ignite by Hatch: A Digital Game-Based Learning Experience for Preschool Children 731

    Hannah E. Luce, The University of North Carolina at Charlotte, USA
    Richard G. Lambert, University of North Carolina at Charlotte, USA

The authors of this study seek to provide practitioners with evidence to support the instructional value of Ignite by Hatch, a digital learning game designed for preschool children. Analyses were conducted using the entire population of three- and four-year-old children who used Ignite during the 2020-2021 academic year (n = 29,417) and included the use of descriptive statistics to explore patterns of growth and the Rasch measurement model to explore item difficulty. This chapter also features a preliminary crosswalk establishing the alignment between the domains, subdomains, and games presented within the Ignite game environment and the learning goals provided by the North Carolina Foundations for Early Learning and Development framework. Results suggest strong preliminary evidence in support of the instructional value of Ignite by Hatch. Further research is recommended to understand how knowledge and skill acquisition within the game environment translate to developmental growth outside of the gaming environment.

Chapter 38
Levelling Up Primary School Students' 21st Century Skills Through Minecraft-Game-Based Learning 750

    Mohd Ali Samsudin, Universiti Sains Malaysia, Malaysia
    Goh Kok Ming, SJKC Chi Sheng 2, Malaysia
    Nur Jahan Ahmad, Universiti Sains Malaysia, Malaysia
    Yogendran Abrose, Universiti Sains Malaysia, Malaysia

The aim of this study was to investigate the effectiveness of Minecraft-game-based learning towards on 21st century skills among primary school students. This study employed quasi-experimental methodology. The dependent variable of this study was the 21st century skills. During Minecraft-game-based learning session, students were given the opportunity to build and recreate a world based on certain themes inside Minecraft world based on their creativity and imagination. The session involved a learning process of different skills and knowledge relevant to school and real world which was imitate inside the Minecraft world. The result shows that the intervention of Minecraft-game-based learning is effective in enhancing and retaining the 21st century skills among students. The implication of the study suggests that the functionality of Minecraft as a digital learning tool should be promoted as it involves students to work in a team to solve problems and have fun while acquiring and sharpening the students' 21st century skills.

Section 7
Learner Assessment, Motivation, and Behaviors in Game-Based Learning

Chapter 39
How Gaming and Formative Assessment Contribute to Learning Supplementary and Complementary Angles 772
Elvira Lázaro Santos, Instituto Superior de Lisboa e Vale do Tejo, Portugal
Leonor Santos, Instituto de Educação, Universidade de Lisboa, Portugal

This chapter presents an empirical research where the authors developed tasks based on a digital game supported by assessment strategies. The study is interpretative in nature, in a case study design. The authors designed tasks with technology and assessment strategies in a collaborative work context implemented in a mathematics classroom with 5th grade students (students 10 years old). The results evidence that the use of a digital game and formative assessment have contributed to the learning of complementary and supplementary angle pairs, giving meaning to their utilization as an effective strategy.

Chapter 40
Gamification Design Principles and Mechanics to Improve Retention 788
Robert Costello, Middlesbrough College, UK

The design and guidelines for gamification offer designers a range of solutions to provide empowerment and engagement to assist with retention within education. This chapter addresses a knowledge gap around the effective use while improving retention. With gaming mechanics as a driving point, specific design considerations were explored: badges, leader boards, points and levels, and challenges. The educator must think from the learner's perspective and find new ways of creating challenges and motivation techniques to provide value. Gamification, when applied to different disciplines, has the potential to facilitate the individual within learner-centricity. Current research indicates that gaming mechanics can encourage and motivate the learner while enriching their experience when applied to education.

Chapter 41
Learner Motivation Through Gamification in E-Learning: A Study on Game-Based Formative Assessment in E-Learning 810
Anshita Chelawat, Vivekanand Education Society's Institute of Management Studies and Research, India
Seema Sant, Vivekanand Education Society's Institute of Management Studies and Research, India

It is a proven fact that learning with the element of fun and games makes the learning process interesting and also helps in student retention. Especially, in the context of e-learning environment, where learner motivation and engagement level are not easy to monitor, it is required to implement some mechanism which can improve their intrinsic motivation and make them self-motivated. Gamification in education and using game-based formative assessment tools will be of great help to not only motivate learners to opt for e-learning courses, but to complete till the end. The current study, thus, focuses on use of game-based formative assessment to improve learners' motivation in the e-learning environment so that their drop-out rates can be controlled, and their engagement level can be improved. Also, it intends to assess the past literature and identify the essential gaming mechanics which can possibly impact the learner motivation. It will also highlight the theoretical perspective used in previous studies on gamification, engagement, and motivation.

Chapter 42
Political Economy Inside the Strategy of Line Game.. 832
    Annesha Biswas, CHRIST University (Deemed), India
    Tinanjali Dam, CHRIST University (Deemed), India
    Joseph Varghese Kureethara, CHRIST University (Deemed), India
    Sankar Varma, CHRIST University (Deemed), India

In today's world, the concept of the game and game theory is turned into new methods of knowing and understanding some of the human behaviours followed by society. In the 21st century, behavioural economics plays a major role in understanding the concept of the `line' game and hence the strategies followed by it. It is a country game played in many parts of India. It is a two-person game with very simple rules and moves. It can be played indoors. Students play the game during the break-outs. The game keenly and minutely determines the objectivity of the game and the behaviour of the players involved inside the game and the way one starts moving helps the other players to understand what one is trying to portray through the game whether it is winning or losing. The strategies involved can be put forth and looked upon from different perspectives. Referring to one such perspective, it can be looked at from a concept of Pareto efficiency, a microeconomic concept. It helps develop logical skills and learn winning strategies.

Chapter 43
The Process of Prosocial Behavior Between Players/Characters in Digital Games: A
Multidimensional Approach to the Situational Context and Gameplay 846
    Ji Soo Lim, Dokkyo University, Japan

To understand the influence of video games on the player, several important questions must be answered. First, what accounts for the higher level of engagement in digital games relative to other entertainment media? Furthermore, what kind of experience does the player have during gameplay? Specifically, what does the player think when he or she interacts with other characters in the game? This study examines digital games with a focus on the interaction between the game itself and the person playing it. Among the various social behaviors elicited by digital games, much attention has been given to players' prosocial behavior within the context of a game's virtual world. A multidimensional view of behavior is used to analyze the game's situational contexts and players' interpretation of behavior.

Section 8
Game-Based Learning: Code and Play

Chapter 44
Students as Gamers: Design, Code, and Play 868
    Polat Şendurur, Ondokuz Mayıs University, Turkey
    Emine Sendurur, Ondokuz Mayis University, Turkey

Games have been considered as an important part of child development and can roughly be defined as fictional structures with certain rules to be followed to achieve certain goals. Modern games (ex. Minecraft) sometimes require quite sophisticated skills to move on, and these skills mostly match up with 21st century skills. From this perspective, this chapter tries to explain the relationship between 21st century skills and game playing skills, the design thinking approach where students are game designers, coders, and players.

Chapter 45
Learning Coding Through Gaming... 888
    Janna Jackson Kellinger, University of Massachusetts, Boston, USA

This chapter begins by arguing that computational thinking and coding should be included as two more C's in the Partnership for 21st Century Learning's list of essential skills. It does so by examining how coding and computational thinking can be used to manipulate people. It argues that gaming uses all the C's, including the two new ones proposed. It then explores connections between playing video games and computer programming. It claims that game-based learning would be an optimal way to leverage these connections to teach coding and describes ways in which to do so, including specific challenges that could be included in game-based learning and a sequence of introducing them so students can "level up." It briefly examines different coding games and describes ways in which educators can create their own coding games. It concludes by arguing that educators can make the connections between gamer thinking and computational thinking visible, use games designed to teach coding, or create their own coding games to take advantage of near transfer.

Chapter 46
Using Custom-Built, Small-Scale Educational Solutions to Teach Qualitative Research Literacy:
No Code, Code, and Complex Applications 905
    Geraldine Bengsch, Kings College London, UK

This chapter considers ways in which educators can create their own educational applications to integrate into their teaching. It is argued that interactive uses of technology can aid student engagement and encourage uptake of skills presented to them. Today, tools available allow everyone to create not only static websites, but also functional applications. It is possible to get started without knowing how to code, empowering anyone with an interest in technology to become a creator. While these no and low code solutions may come with some restrictions, they may encourage users to explore more traditional ways to engage with code and its possibilities for teaching. The chapter aims to encourage readers to look at technology as a creative practice to include into their teaching. It suggests strategies to help readers select the most appropriate tool for their projects.

Section 9
Virtual Teaching and Project-Oriented Game-Based Learning

Chapter 47
Project-Oriented Game-Based Learning: Managers From Fairytales 927
    Pavlo Brin, National Technical University "Kharkiv Polytechnic Institute", Ukraine
    Mariia Shypilova, Great Wall School, China

In this chapter, the authors investigate the potential of project-oriented game-based learning in making students of educational institutes more engaged and gain a deep understanding of the curriculum content. The literature review presents the main definitions and benefits of project-oriented game-based learning, followed by its contribution to improving the performance of students' training. The results of the research are based on testing the main statements of project-oriented game-based learning empirically – if it really can provide additional value for learners in higher education. The empirical data have been collected based on Ukrainian case study and allow the authors to prove the influence of project-oriented game-based learning on increasing students' engagement, satisfaction, performance, and improving learning outcomes. The main idea of the teaching project was to take as an object of the research a character from a fairytale and analyze its managerial activities. The chapter also analyzes the e-learning instruments which can be used in remote teaching.

Chapter 48
Virtual Training for Scuba Divers.. 946
    Anacleto Correia, Naval Academy, Portugal
    Pedro B. Água, Naval Aacdemy, Portugal

Virtual reality (VR) is a technology that is becoming more common for applications in the field of education and training. VR can be used to create simulated two- and three-dimensional scenarios, promoting interactions between the user and the environment, which allows experiencing virtual training situations very close to real actions. The aim of this text is to describe the development of a teaching and training tool using VR technology for scuba divers' operations within the aquatic context for enhancing critical thinking. To this end, a survey of requirements based on real procedures was carried out in order to transpose them into a synthetic environment. After the construction of the artefact, it was tested and evaluated by qualified users, and the results are promising.

Compilation of References lii

About the Contributors cxciii

Index ccxiv

Preface

Over the past few decades, pedagogical trends have mainly focused on e-learning, digitizing learning, multiliteracies, and multi-modal learning. These trends have been synonymous with planning goals for twenty-first century learning. Global scholars and many educators embraced these trends with optimism and total conversion, while others preferred hybrid learning models and maybe even relying on or reverting to traditional learning models. However, the global pressures of policy makers and covid-19 worldwide lockdowns required an immediate dramatic shift in ways learners could consume information. Solutions were necessary to fulfil learners' needs whether in educational, management, retail or healthcare. Digital learning was here to stay, and traditional literacies was becoming a thing of the past. The race was real to embrace technology from k-12 to higher education institutions, workplace training, government, and health care providers. The needs were high to ensure synchronous and asynchronous learning was successful. Technological demands for virtual, digital, multimodal, gamification, e-learning, zoom sessions, have steadily intensified to meet learners' needs, especially for k-12 and higher ed. Let's be clear, gamification and/or game-based learning (GBL) can be digital or non-digital and is based on applying game-based principles to real settings or scenarios to enable learner or user engagement, motivation, and learning. GBL is not a theory which integrates games for students to play as a reward for finishing their homework, or having good behavior, but it is used to increase learner engagement by designing learning activities that can incrementally introduce concepts, and guide users towards an end goal (Pho & Dinscore, 2015).

Scholars and educators have acknowledged the need to address the gaps currently facing today's learners. Recent trends indicate many educators and policy makers have responded by revising pedagogical models by including technological/digital designs and framework that support multimodal, multiliteracies and gamification elements. Scholars have acknowledged the potential contribution of video gaming to complex forms of learning, identifying links between gaming and engagement, experiential learning spaces, problem-solving, strategies, transliteracy reflectivity, critical literacy, and metacognitive thinking. Despite this movement toward the inclusion of video gaming in literacy teaching, concerns about certain risks raised by scholars have slowed the adoption of using video games to foster learning. The adoption of video games as an alternative classroom multiliteracies resource is acknowledged in technology and multiliteracies discourses as a strategy for meaning-making and developing cultural knowledge (Cope & Kalantzis, 2009; The New London Group, 2000). These concerns (largely associated with negative identity construction, violent content, distraction, and time commitment for integration), have slowed the adoption of video games for their potential contribution as spaces/media that encourage complex forms of learning (Gee, 2003, 2007; Squire, 2006; Steinkuehler, 2007, 2011).

Emerging technologies such as multiliteracies, learning by design frameworks and gamification are becoming more prevalent in global classrooms. Traditional literacy pedagogies are shifting toward game-based pedagogy which supports the call to addressing 21st century learners (C21 Canada, 2017). Therefore, within this context there remains a need to study ways to engage learners in meaning-making perhaps with some element of visual design. Multimodal ways of learning can offer insights for reinventing traditional literacy pedagogical boundaries and establish new ways and practices for building knowledge. Educators today need to be positioned with a broad perspective of technology enabling a critical understanding of assessing ways in which technology is universally integrated in our knowledge culture.

Today's educators need to be well versed in technological platforms to meet the needs of 21st century learners. To be successful, in k-12 and higher education levels, educators require foundational knowledge and skills in instructional design. When it comes to the topic of positive learning outcomes, educators will readily agree that tools and strategies that create student-centered learning spaces and engage students' interest are beneficial. Principles of instructional design are grounded in cognitive and constructive learning philosophies. Research in pedagogical online delivery included the community of inquiry model, developed by Garrison et al. in 2000, interconnecting elements of teacher presence, cognitive presence, and social presence to initiate successful learning experiences (Lane, 2011). Since that time new models have emerged which aim to facilitate transformational learning by fostering an environment of collaboration, community, and knowledge development. One of the central models was TPACK developed by Punya Mishra and Matthew Koehler in 2006 and updated in 2016. It is used in many higher education settings and is based on technological pedagogical content knowledge which is intricately linked. Lee and Kim in 2014 implemented the model in a multidisciplinary technology course by integrating the 3 core domains (technology tools, pedagogy, and content). They argue preservice teachers were well versed in the content they are teaching but experienced challenges with pedagogical knowledge when it comes to effective use of technology to address learners' needs (such as group and peer discussions, think/pair/share). They found pre-service teachers had a lack of understanding of pedagogy (being a facilitator, student-centered community, active and engaged learning) which hindered learning of integrated knowledge (applying their knowledge such as adaptability across different contexts, persistence, and collaborative problem solving needed, but also being a reflective practitioner). Swan (2005) suggests creating virtual spaces that foster and support active learning for knowledge acquisition.

Knowledge is transformative in nature and socially constructed. Vygotsky (1978) argues cognitive functions are activated when children socially collaborate. When children exchange words and language with their peers, they are collaborating and socially interacting with each other, which, Vygotsky argued, contributes to the ways they actively learn, and gain knowledge from each other. Therefore, constructivism theory underpins the need for both face-to-face and online learning environments to be learner-centered, knowledge-centered, assessment centered, and community-centered (Swan, 2005). One of the challenges for educators is how to link learner needs, pedagogy and technology to construct more engaging and student-centered environments.

Research indicates the potential of digital technology as a learning process can foster collaborative, creative and authentic learning (Cope & Kalantzis, 2009). Lane (2018) focuses on using the Learning by Design framework, which offers multiple modalities of meanings and a range of knowledge processes and allows practitioners to create pedagogical scaffolds, which do not assume every learner is at the same level (Cope & Kalantzis, 2016). For example, the idea of youth learning from video games is echoed by emerging research recognizing benefits and challenges of integrating video games in classrooms as a pedagogical strategy to gain literacy skills (Beavis, Muspratt, & Thompson, 2015; DeCoito & Richardson,

Preface

2016; Duret & Pons, 2016). Hommel (2010) also highlighted that many researchers argue meaningful learning, including critical thinking, decision-making in video games may model engaging and effective instructional techniques. Sider and Maich (2014) also suggest effective literacy teaching strategies for some learners include software programs that provide a multimodal experience. Technology supports the universal design learning (UDL) framework because it can increase access meaningful engagement in learning and reduce barriers (Israel, Marino, Delisio, & Serianni, 2014, p. 16). Recently, important research emerged for use of multimodal and multiliteracy models, adaptive technology, and artificial intelligence (AI) for core curriculum to address learners who have exceptionalities. Integrating technology for core curriculum is a positive approach in the right direction to acknowledge the efficacy of GBL. Yet, focusing solely on using gamification for learning exceptionalities may further compartmentalize these approaches and limit the promotion of scholarly focus to broaden integration within k-12 and higher education settings.

Global need for innovation and adoption in multimodal approaches, gamification, GBL, AI, has been the priority at an alarming pace for many institutions since the announcement of covid-19. This growing need for technological adoption and accessibility has surpassed traditional literacy and instructional approaches. Institutions unwilling to adopt technological innovations and adapt to multimodal, GBL approaches to meet the growing needs of 21st century learners, due to lack of funding or unwillingness to change traditional practices, will find themselves further limiting marketability of their institutions as open, barrier-free opportunities for learning. Mindsets need to change for educators and policy makers to become main players in educational innovation. According to Cope and Kalantzis (2009), learners play multiple roles based on their experiences. Todays' learners have grown up with technology and secondary sources of learning such as video games have increasingly shifted to primary sources of learning especially during the global pandemic. Cope and Kalantzis (2009) also recognize the pedagogical weaving between school learning with practical out-of-school experiences that are based on individual interests (Kalantzis & Cope, 2012).

Educators sometimes consider video gaming as students' rich cultural out-of-school practices; however, more research is surfacing about transitioning these practices into in-school literacy experiences (Beavis, 2014; Cope & Kalantzis, 2009; Kalantzis & Cope, 2012). Video games involve complex forms of text, literacy, and action where stories reveal a variety of genres (Beavis, 2014; Gee, 2003, 2007). Beavis (2014) urges educators to recognize the privileged place that students give to video games as a form of popular culture. She also sees video games as emergent cultural forms because they include stories that fuse words and images and other elements to reposition players as readers, writers, interpreters, and creators who play an active role in the stories. Video games have become increasingly rich in multimodal elements. Games are multilayered, intertextual, and exemplify literacy with the combination of words, pictures, sounds, colours, symbols, music, light effects, and movement (Ajayi, 2011; Beavis, 2014). These interrelations of text and visual images within video games form part of a multiple semiotic system, how we use signs. Semiotic systems are relied upon by meaning-makers in their knowledge designing processes (Cope & Kalantzis, 2009; Kalantzis & Cope, 2012). Steinkuehler (2007) views interrelations of text in video games as gateways for meaning makers to rely on for "textually produced verbal interaction and, therefore, on story-telling" (p. 195).

Some of the themes addressed by Freeman, Adams Becker, Cummins, Davis, and Hall Giesinger (2017) in the NMC/CoSN Horizon Report K-12 Edition (Horizon Report) indicate a future focus over the next five years to position pedagogical strategies—including learning and visualization technologies—to foster creative inquiry. Video games are not specifically named in the report which leads me to believe there remains a certain reluctance by educators to adopt these, perhaps due to scholars' reservations about stereotypical themes (such as themes of power, violence, and misogyny) that may be embedded in video game plots and characters. However, scholarly systemic reviews bridging designs for game-based learning or gamification in learning correlated with learner performance have been lacking in literature. Digital learning as a significant tool for learning both in k-12 and higher education has always existed but full adoption in these settings has been slow due to overreaching research about what games and how games are perceived both in terms of media and/or resistance due to technological knowledge gaps for instructors. This adoption hesitancy for game-based pedagogical models has lingered from 2012 and was acknowledged in the 2019 Horizon report (Alexander, et al., 2019) as fading interest and budget funding pressures for institutions who did not foresee the need for experimenting with these models. In addition, Alexander, et al. (2019) emphasized slow adoption of game-based learning was primarily due to a growing concern of privacy issues surrounding game developers tracking user behavior. In addition, concerns were raised about the suitability of commercially based games for classroom experiences and educational based games may too be limited on the market for widespread use (Alexander, et al., 2019). (p. 39). The Horizon Report in education for 2021 by Pelletier et al., tracked some higher education institutions that implemented full open digital courses, including game-based learning to support learner goals and degree requirements. Moreover, Brull and Finlayson (2016) suggest that gamification has been recognized as a powerful instructional method in k-12 education, as well as top colleges and universities. They also explain how some industries remain in the early adoption stages such as health care, which may relate to gaps in knowledge or technological competency.

Yet, Bohyn Kim (2013) provided several examples of how educational institutions, government, and workplaces that successfully integrated game-based learning to increase engagement, motivation, and knowledge acquisition for learners. For example, gamification was used in training and recruitment in America's army, lead generation marketing, public relations, continuous professional development, health professions and development of health skills. Kim (2013) also suggests gamification can increase motivation and engagement in many higher education settings. A professor at Michigan University converted his undergrad class to game-based learning to empower students to achieve learning goals, having them participate in guilds and giving them rapid responses maintained by his teaching assistances. Kim (2013) argued this gamified approach gave students increased autonomy to become more invested in what and how they learn. Similarly, Purdue University developed a digital passport system whereby students could earn and display badges to demonstrate their competencies and achievements (Pho & Dinscore, 2015). Kim (2015) explains digital badges are used in many higher education settings and organizations including MIT, NASA, US Department of Veteran Affairs and Education, and public broadcasting, to name a few. Pho and Dinscore (2015) emphasize digital badges are identified as significant gamification element. However, they caution instructors to consider their students' proficiency with technology so that the technology itself doesn't become a barrier to learning.

It is important to note that game-based trends in educational settings need empirical research that helps to provide a framework for learner engagement but also support mechanisms for design effectiveness. In a comprehensive review Abdul Jabbar and Felicia (2015) aimed to address the lack of empirical evidence of the impact of game design on learning outcomes, identify how the design of game-based activities may affect learning and engagement, and develop a set of general recommendations for GBL instructional design. Their findings illustrate the impact of key gaming features in GBL at both cognitive and emotional levels. Abdul Jabbar and Felicia (2015) also identified gaming trends and several key

Preface

drivers of engagement created by the gaming features embedded within GBL, as well as external factors that may have influences on engagement and learning.

The findings imply that students need multiple support measures for motivation and learning in gameplay. A lack of support and rewards for improvement decreases students' engagement (Ke & Abras, 2013) because they expect more rewards as recognition of their efforts and achievements (Tzeng & Chen, 2012). From their review, three recommendations were provided by Abdul Jabbar and Felicia (2015) as follows:

1. Promoting gameplay and learning: Game design must be accompanied with multiple learning tools and interesting tasks and materials that facilitate and help students to explore and complete gaming and learning activities in accordance with their needs and abilities. Many of the papers (Admiraal et al., 2011; Barab et al., 2012; Hou, 2012; Hsu, Wu, & Huang, 2008; Huizenga, Admiraal, Akkerman, & ten Dam, 2009; G.-J. Hwang, Wu, & Chen, 2012; Liao et al., 2011; Meluso et al., 2012; Miller et al., 2011; Sadler et al., 2013; Sanchez & Olivares, 2011; Suh et al., 2010) illustrate that multirole-play or collaborative role-play works effectively when coupled with learning tools and interactive elements and materials (Lennon & Coombs, 2007; Liu & Chu, 2010) to motivate and help learning. When presented with such tools, students are encouraged to work collaboratively to understand the learning tools provided (Hung et al., 2012; Sung & Hwang, 2013; Virvou & Katsionis, 2008) and to meet their individual and collective goals within the game.
2. Motivating gameplay and learning: The elements in GBL must be fully incorporated into the learning activities to provide a sense of enjoyment and motivation that is rewarding for students.

Gaming activities must match students' gender, game type preferences, and preferred mode of gameplay, as well as their abilities and the games' learning tasks (Clark et al., 2011). Challenges and conflicts must match students' abilities and knowledge (Bottino et al., 2007); they must provide equal opportunities for self-efficacy (Cheng et al., 2009; Tzeng & Chen, 2012), avoid causing frustration (Ke & Abras, 2013), and keep pupils focused (Rosas et al., 2003).

3. Supporting gameplay and learning: Gameplay must be supported with appropriate feedback and scaffolding; these can be provided in various forms depending on students' learning requirements (Ke, 2013; Sadler et al., 2013; Sun et al., 2011; Wang, 2008) so that the students can complete tasks and solve problems.

Adoption of Game-based learning for core curriculum classes is becoming more widespread in higher education settings. According to the 2021 Horizon Report on education (Pelletier et al., 2021), an American university in Texas is offering a series of short on-line, game-based academic courses to enable students to complete their degree requirements. Similarly, a North-Carolina state university created a gamified design framework for flipped and self-regulated learning, based on cognitive, metacognitive, and motivational theories. Pelletier, et al. (2021) reported that the North Carolina university implemented this gamified framework since the Fall of 2019 and was applied in redesigning four large undergraduate courses in the fields of business, biochemistry, computer science, and math.

This research handbook attempts to address these needs through a comprehensive compilation of game-based pedagogical models in broad-based settings, from education, including k-12 and higher education institutions, to workplace including healthcare, retail, and some government settings. It also includes perspectives from educators, management, and learners. These perspectives emphasize global integration of games to development of artificial intelligence pedagogical models and include culturally rich technological and non-technological approaches that have been successfully implemented. Game-based learning is not always full technological immersion but surprisingly both can have astonishing learner performance outcomes.

Technological innovation has continued to evolve and offers a much wider spectrum of capabilities even reducing the need for human interaction. Artificial intelligence can be developed to drive learner goals, instructional aims, be responsive to learner needs and address overall methods such as assessment and performance. According to Pellas, Fotaris, Kazanidis, and Wells (2019), a significant body of research relating to augmented reality (AR) already exists; however, they contend not with game-based learning (ARGBL) and how it may be applicable to global k-12 settings. Therefore, integrating instructional strategies with ARGBL may offer the potential to impact students' motivation and learning performance. Pellas et al. (2019) argue ARGBL can potentially influence students' attendance, knowledge acquisition, digital experience, and positive behaviors towards learning. In a similar vein, Bakan and Bakan (2018) conducted a meta-analysis, based on a 12-year review, of scientific databases (such as Web of Science (WoS) database in SCI, SSCI and AHCI) of game-based applications in learning and teaching environments. Emphasizing cognitive retention, Bakan and Bakan (2018) found that game studies, as well as cognitive understanding and application-level knowledge of the field are more effective in learning and in student achievements.

Many scholars have focused on the collaborative aspects of video games (Alexander, 2009; Apperley & Beavis, 2011; Huizenga et. al., 2009; Sanford & Madill, 2006), similarities were found from Vogel et al.'s (2006) analysis revealing significant results for cognitive gains from playing the video game. What the study by Vogel et al. (2006) also revealed was that "females showed significant cognitive gains favoring the interactive simulation and game method" (p. 234). Since these studies focused on elementary students and mathematics, there is still a need to explore the use of computer games, specifically focusing on boys, at the high school level. Recent research is also emerging supporting integration of science, technology, engineering, and mathematics (STEM) concepts in digital games (Decoito & Richardson, 2016). A study by Decoito and Richardson (2016) focused on introducing digital games as a pedagogical tool for K-12 science teacher candidates at a Canadian university. The participants explored the use of video games (for example, an online game, History of Biology) for teaching STEM concepts, and Decoito and Richardson (2016) found that teacher candidates expressed an "overwhelming agreement for including digital online games in science teaching" (p. 10). The participants also expressed the importance of using digital online games for science teaching for "engagement, relevance, reinforcement of content areas, and promoting 21st century skills" (p. 10). Decoito and Richardson (2016) also recognized some concerns surrounding learners' lack of expertise in the game, as well as technical challenges which posed frustration when completing the game. Lopez-Morteo and Lopez's (2007) study also focused on improving learning through an "electronic collaborative learning environment based on interactive instructors of recreational mathematics (IIRM), thus establishing an alternative approach for motivating students towards mathematics" (p. 618). They used an online collaborative environment combined with support elements to bridge content and context for the learning experience. The study had positive results as students were more motivated and excited to learn math when using computer games; however, some negative results included issues with computer failures. Researchers indicated that online collaborative games promoted greater interaction among students, even though students preferred to play games that did not support online interaction. Additionally, results showed students found usefulness of math in

Preface

daily life, which increased their level of confidence and attitudes towards learning math. Research has continued to indicate how video games can be used as an alternative approach to improve learning experiences. According to an investigation by Byun and Joung (2018), digital games can improve students' motivation and performance in mathematics education.

Research is beginning to emerge documenting how video games, a multimodal form, can represent an alternative pathway to learning, both inside and outside of school. Scholars have identified links between gaming and factors that affect the depth of learning: engagement, experiential learning spaces, problem-solving, strategic transliteracy reflectivity, critical literacy, and metacognitive thinking (see for example, Alexander, 2009; Apperley & Beavis, 2011; Cope & Kalantzis, 2009; Sanford & Madill, 2007; Squire, 2013; The New London Group, 1996, 2000; Van Sledright, 2002). These scholars explained the complex forms of interactive visuals—intertextual and multimodal—that are part of video games, and key to inviting players to understand a variety of texts in a variety of circumstances. They also found that these multimodal aspects help to create a rich environment that invites gamers to interact with a variety of significant learning and literacy experiences. Practitioners remain skeptical of GBL as a direct primary method of knowledge acquisition, preferring to perceive GBL as a secondary, leisure activity with little to no educational value (De Freitas, 2006). Yet the reality is digital fluency remains high among 21st century learners, combined with positive levels of motivation, acceptance, and expectation of acquiring knowledge in an innovative way, which in turn, influences the ways in which they self-regulate their learning. To improve adoption and effectiveness in practice, GBL has been widely examined and used not only as an alternative educational resource but in practice for knowledge acquisition in a variety of settings. It is equally important to note that full of adoption of GBL in the educational stream can benefit learners in not only what they learn but how they learn. According to a study conducted by De Freitas (2006), perceptions are changing about GBL as game design and theory courses are being offered widely in higher education settings. Game-based learning is often experienced-based or exploratory, and therefore relies upon experiential, problem-based or exploratory learning approaches. De Freitas (2006) emphasizes that GBL enables learners to role play, to identify with others, to use games for therapy, to rehearse skills, to explore in open-ended spaces, to learn in groups and to develop higher cognitive skills. Learning environments can include game-spaces which are highly immersive and can be collaborative (De Freitas, 2006). According to Duncum (2004), multiliteracies education is concerned with the relationship between written words and images, which is complex and needs to be recognized. Duncum (2004) further explains that images are not just a mirror to the meaning found in the text, but also offer subtle nuances of interpretation and a range of other cognitive functions, including emotional quality of an image, which all contribute to the uniqueness of modality of multiliteracies forms. As such, Squire (2013) argued that many video games are experiential with the aim to engage and immerse players in interactive gameplay. Jenkins (2002) also argued that video game spaces allow players to co-construct, deconstruct, and reconstruct the plot. Jenkins (2002) also explained that game designers over the years have become narrative architects by developing games with narrative potential, enabling the story-constructing activity of players. These game-based immersive approaches help to create "an emotionally compelling context for the player" (Squire, 2013, p. 110). Further to this point, Squire (2013) argued that good games emotionally connect players and invite them into a world of learning. Jenkins (2005) similarly argued that games can imitate different art forms by offering players "new aesthetic experiences and transform the computer screen into a realm of experimentation and innovation that is broadly accessible" (p. 3). Educators sometimes consider video gaming as students' rich cultural out-of-school practices; however, more research is surfacing about transitioning these practices into in-school literacy experiences (Beavis, 2014; Cope & Kalantzis, 2009; Kalantzis & Cope, 2012). Squire (2013) explained that games are now recognized as experiential learning spaces where learners engage in rich collaborative interactions, and where they can utilize a variety of complex tools to develop complex problem-solving skills (see for example, Alexander, 2009; Gros, 2007).

ORGANIZATION OF THE RESEARCH HANDBOOK

This research handbook is organized into 48 chapters. The handbook is organized into nine sections. These sections include gamification in higher education, exploring literacy in game-based learning, culturally based game-based pedagogy, teachers' perceptions of game-based learning, gamification, mobile learning and education policy, game-based pedagogy for primary-elementary educators, learner assessment, motivation and behaviors in game-based learning, game-based learning: code and play, and virtual teaching and project-oriented game-based learning.

A brief description of each of the chapters follows:

Chapter 1 explores the meaning, significance, and scope of game-based learning as an instructional tool. It provides an interesting account of several games that are popularly used to facilitate effective learning in various settings. This chapter also examines the relevance and implications of games in education.

Chapter 2 identifies a trend in digital learning by examining several articles in the Web of Science index by using the words "game-based learning", "video games", "game-based pedagogy", "digital games", "gamification", and "game". As a result of the research, the trends in topics related to games were revealed, and the changes in this area are subsequently.

Chapter 3 emphasizes how designing course content as a game makes learning more engaging as learners get a sense of motivation and accomplishment. It proposes learner-centered interactive instructional strategies that employ GBL to pique learners' curiosity and recommends popular GBL platforms for creating educational games.

Chapter 4 describes how game-based learning reflects sustainable education for future professionals from the higher education environment. To attain these innovative and sustainable teaching pedagogies the components of games and simulations need to be incorporated into the teaching-learning content. The chapter examines neural and cognitive processes of game-based learning.

Chapter 5 highlights how technology can support teachers and learners to go beyond their existing pedagogical boundaries by focusing on ways games may serve as digital sources of learning. It also explores the role game-based pedagogies and digital learning design frameworks play in enhancing learner engagement, collaboration, and cultural understanding.

Chapter 6 provides an overview of the effectiveness of game-based learning strategies over traditional learning methods. Moreover, the results of a cross- sectional study conducted by the authors in south Indian Universities at the higher education level is included.

Chapter 7 explores the efficacy of game-based learning in classroom teaching for MBA students in higher education. Student's learning was captured through a google form before and after a dice game.

Chapter 8 explores technological developments and innovations in the field of higher education. To prepare the students to face real world challenges, it is important for higher educational institutions to focus on imparting to learners creative, problem solving and critical thinking skills.

Preface

Chapter 9 discusses gamification strategies in the context of higher education student worker training. Specifically, it builds on the concepts of gamification in corporate training contexts and gamification in the academic classroom environment. It also considers various options to support gamified training content and methods to support student worker engagement and knowledge retention.

Chapter 10 shows research done in interactive media, augmented and virtual reality, game art, and gender equity. The year 2020 showed how institutional collaboration can open learning spaces to a more focused approach on the interests of young people, and to promote a more sustainable and dynamic future.

Chapter 11 uses the lenses of Vygotskian constructivism, situated cognition, the antecedents of flow, and a pedagogy interwoven with the multiliteracy framework, the authors present a COVID19 Simulation game. The game has multiple levels, challenges, disrupters, and allows for student player groups to work together (i.e., collaborate within and across player groups) to achieve the strategic objectives of the game.

Chapter 12 provides a case study of the use of worldbuilding for role-playing games as the foundation for a first year multiliteracies seminar. The author provides an overview of teaching and learning during the pandemic in the Irish context. The chapter provides practical advice on using a MediaWiki installation as the infrastructure for worldbuilding projects. The author shows how this imparts important digital literacies and allows for a critical apprehension of Wikipedia itself.

Chapter 13 foregrounds an online gamified visual intelligence innovation (eyebraingym) developed to enhance visual processing skills, improve memory and vocabulary, and increase reading fluency. The explicit aim of the innovation is to improve comprehension towards visual intelligence.

Chapter 14 addresses some of boys' out-of-school video gaming practices for meaning-making and gaining cultural knowledge. Studying the ways in which boys make meanings through multimodal ways of learning can offer insights into strategies for cyber culture that can potentially reinvent traditional literacy pedagogical boundaries and establish new ways and practices for building knowledge.

Chapter 15 focus on games that assist students in the learning process. Once students have learned a task through the playing process, they will remember this much easier and longer than simply doing a worksheet. Research shows students enjoy interactive and engaging activities and will choose these types of activities over pencil and paper types of activities.

Chapter 16 conceptualizes an innovative digital storytelling that incorporates both transmedia and meaning-making narrative approaches. Working with Aristotelian story elements in a non-linear digital series of mini-worlds, the higher education narrator-as-learner enters real-world situations mirrored in a fictional and fragmented environment. The model encourages a playful engagement in the experiential learning process through a range of points of view, encouraging empathy for differing perspectives that are transferable to real-life environments.

Chapter 17 examines the perceptions and instructional ideas of preservice teachers as relates to using Minecraft, a popular video game, to facilitate game-based learning opportunities in their future elementary classrooms. The participants were 21 preservice teachers who played Minecraft as part of a teacher preparation program course and then completed essays on their experiences with the game and its potential to support student learning in the elementary English language arts classroom.

Chapter 18 shows a way to foster academic growth, engagement in learning, and collaboration is to engage students in skinning games based on literature and integrated a playful learning environment. Analysis revealed that students were immersed in the learning process to the extent that they felt comfortable acting informally, responding in the moment, and being playful.

Chapter 19 studies the dynamics that makeup media literacy and media literacy skills. How the century has transformed to meet the needs of its students will be highlighted within the context of media literacy. It also explains how media literacy is reflected in pedagogy with examples suitable for different courses and levels.

Chapter 20 discusses the theoretical frameworks for Artificial Intelligence (AI) teacher and how AI teacher has been applied to facilitate game-based literacy learning in existing empirical studies. It also introduces key concepts of AI teacher, research on AI teacher in literacy learning, and some highlighted examples of AI teacher in literacy classrooms for practical concerns.

Chapter 21 explores the possibility of enhancing literacy skills using indigenous games played by Vhavenda children at foundation phase. It critically analyses different types of Vhavenda games played by children which are ndode, mufuvha, muravharavha and tsetsetse or trere-tsere to solicit the possibility to enhance literacy skills.

Chapter 22 focuses on an indigenous game duvheke. The chapter employs game-based pedagogy as a theory that underpins this study. Methodologically, the chapter assumes a qualitative complexion because it seeks to collect in-depth information about Duvheke and how it can be used in teaching critical thinking skills first entering students in a rural based university. The chapter suggests that duvheke can be a valuable tool in teaching critical thinking skills

Chapter 23 investigates the effectiveness of a digital reading tool, called GraphoGame. It sets out to demonstrate that, through pre-and post-tests, GraphoGame Afrikaans improved the initial reading skills of Grade 1 learners. As GraphoGame employs a scaffolded approach by presenting learners with letters and words, it can be utilized to support learners individually in classes with large numbers, as is typical in Africa.

Chapter 24 examines whether the intrinsically motivational factors of digital games could motivate students to learn English vocabulary and achieve better learning outcomes. English vocabulary is always a huge hurdle for students in non-speaking English countries because (a) they lack an English environment to practice vocabulary; (b) traditional memory is quite boring, and (c) they unavoidably forget remembered words. Therefore, this chapter aims to provide an overview of how to comprehensively conduct experimental research, which will expedite further research.

Chapter 25 identifies whether gamification is a suitable pedagogic tool among Malaysian law students to support the acquisition of 21st century skills. The respondents are from Year 1 and Year 2 of a 3-year Bachelor of Laws degree with the majority being Malaysian students. The data collected showed that gamification can be a suitable alternative pedagogic tool to support the students to learn skills such as critical thinking, creativity, innovation, leadership, or communication.

Chapter 26 examines the relationship between religiosity and the learning of business ethics. This research investigates whether religiosity is conducive to the learning of business ethics in a digital learning environment: a serious 3D ethics game. A cross-sectional survey was conducted on 302 final-year students from two different academic institutions based in the UK. The results of a structural equation modelling analysis suggest that religiosity does not inform the ethical perceptions and decisions of religious individuals in digital learning environments.

Chapter 27 introduces a mobile game-based content and language integrated learning practice (an educational digital game called ENVglish) to raise EFL students' environmental awareness. During the design and development phases of the game, students', and teachers' perceptions regarding it were collected with semi-structured interviews. The findings indicated that both students and teachers had posi-

Preface

tive perceptions about the game and that students could improve their English and have environmental awareness with the game.

Chapter 28 aims to contribute to the advancement of knowledge about the main competencies needed for educators to perform as facilitators of educational games. The outcome is the development of a framework of competencies of an educator willing to use game-based learning. The study highlights the importance of institutional support to boost the development of pedagogical, technological, and social skills among educators.

Chapter 29 examines both in-service and pre-service Spanish teachers' perceptions (n = 112) about using digital games in their lessons, paying a special attention to the TPACK model, and comparing the results regarding age, gender, and professional situation. Responses show a positive attitude towards the potential use of video games in their lessons, although there are differences considering the results of the items concerning technological, pedagogical, or content knowledge.

Chapter 30 explores the factors affecting the successful implementation of an e-education policy and community engagement. In terms of research methodology, a case study is used of a specific high (secondary) school in the Metro North district of the Western Cape province, South Africa.

Chapter 31 explores the potentially negative and positive impacts of game-based pedagogy on personality development. The methodology of this paper is qualitative basic research, while the theoretical framework is critical theoretical analyses, articulated around psychodynamic theory, analytic psychology, and positive psychology. The negative view of game-based personality development presupposes 'learners for technology' or the pessimistic view, while the positive view of game-based personality development considers 'technology for learners' as being a perspective which facilitates, media literacy, higher order thinking, higher emotional intelligence, and pro-social behaviors.

Chapter 32 describes a gamification experience of a Social Game with graduate students, teachers in primary and secondary education and discusses how the elements present in games can provide engagement and favor learning. Furthermore, it presents the Kahoot app as a possibility to stimulate and engage students in the teaching-learning process, analyzing some implications of learning with a mobile device. The results had a positive impact on increasing student engagement in both Game Social and Kahoot. Therefore, gamification and mobile learning can be good alternatives to increase the quality of teaching, generating meaningful experiences in the classroom.

Chapter 33 aims to contribute to the discussion of incorporating mobile games, with astronomy and space themes to support science learning. The authors try to determine the learning strategies or pedagogies which can be used to incorporate such games in science education. Research on which characteristics these games should have been also presented.

Chapter 34 reviews, a) considerations for use of digital media use in early childhood settings, b) selection of appropriate media to facilitate early literacy learning, and c) inclusion of digital media as an integral component of early literacy instruction, rather than an add-on. With an emphasis on practical ideas and solutions for instructors, the authors draw on studies in which interactive, personalized ebooks and an early literacy learning app were used in conjunction with face-to-face, hands-on activities drawn from Project SEEL (Systematic and Engaging Early Literacy).

Chapter 35 proposes a path of coding games for the development of problem solving in primary school, with interdisciplinary links and to the mathematics curriculum. Game-based learning places the pupil at the center of the teaching-learning process, creating a motivating and challenging environment in which the pupil can learn freely, proceeding by trial and error, learning to evaluate their choices and those of other players and monitor several variables. Game-based learning therefore stands as an individualized and inclusive learning environment, which allows all students to achieve maximum educational success.

Chapter 36 explores what factors affect a school's choice, which is linked with the educational curriculum being offered, and how it affects the student's quality of education. There is no unified primary education curriculum in Bangladesh's case. More than three mainstream educational curricula can be founded, each with its own unique set of traits, benefits, and shortcomings. This chapter also explores Gamification theory's implementation to ensure quality primary education in Bangladesh.

Chapter 37 provides practitioners with evidence to support the instructional value of Ignite by Hatch, a digital learning game designed for preschool children. This chapter also features a preliminary crosswalk establishing the alignment between the domains, subdomains, and games presented within the Ignite game environment and the learning goals provided by the North Carolina Foundations for Early Learning and Development framework.

Chapter 38 investigates the effectiveness of Minecraft-Game Based Learning towards on 21st Century Skills among primary school students. During Minecraft Game-Based Learning session, students were given the opportunity to build and recreate a world based on certain themes inside Minecraft world based on their creativity and imagination. The result shows that the intervention of Minecraft Game Based Learning is effective in enhancing and retaining the 21st Century Skills among students.

Chapter 39 presents empirical research where we developed tasks based on a digital game supported by assessment strategies. The study is interpretative in nature, in a case study design. The authors designed tasks with technology and assessment strategies in a collaborative work context implemented in a Mathematics classroom with 5th grade students (students with 10 years old). The results evidence that the use of a digital game and formative assessment have contributed to the learning of complementary and supplementary angle pairs, giving meaning to their utilization as an effective strategy.

Chapter 40 addresses a knowledge gap around the effective use of while improving retention. With gaming mechanics as a driving point, specific design considerations were explored: badges, leader boards, points and levels, and challenges. The educator must think from the learner's perspective and find new ways of creating challenges and motivation techniques to provide value. Gamification, when applied to different disciplines, has the potential to facilitate the individual within learner-centricity.

Chapter 41 focuses on use of game-based formative assessment to improve learners' motivation in the e-learning environment so that their drop-our rates can be controlled, and their engagement level can be improved. It highlights the theoretical perspective used in previous research on gamification, engagement, and motivation.

Chapter 42 suggests behavioral economics plays a major role in understanding the concept of the `line' game played in many parts of India. The game keenly and minutely determines the objectivity of the game and the behavior of the players involved inside the game and the way one starts moving, helps the other players to understand what one is trying to portray through the game whether it is winning or losing. The strategies involved can be put forth and looked upon from different genres of perspectives. Referring to one of such perspectives, it can be looked at from a concept of Pareto efficiency, a microeconomic concept. It helps develop logical skills and learn winning strategies.

Chapter 43 examines digital games with a focus on the interaction between the game itself and the person playing it. Among the various social behaviors elicited by digital games, much attention has been given to players' prosocial behavior within the context of a game's virtual world. A multidimensional view of behavior is used to analyze the game's situational contexts and players' interpretation of behavior.

Preface

Chapter 44 explains the relationship between 21st century skills, and game playing skills, the design thinking approach where students are game designers, coders, and players. Games have been considered as an important part of child development and can roughly be defined as fictional structures with certain rules to be followed to achieve certain goals.

Chapter 45 examines how coding and computational thinking can be used to manipulate people. It then explores connections between playing video games and computer programming. It briefly examines different coding games and describes ways in which educators can create their own coding games. It concludes by arguing that educators can make the connections between gamer thinking and computational thinking visible, use games designed to teach coding, or create their own coding games to take advantage of near transfer.

Chapter 46 considers ways in which educators can create their own educational applications to integrate into their teaching. Today, tools available allow everyone to create not only static website, but also functional applications. It is possible to get started without knowing how to code, empowering anyone with an interest in technology to become a creator. The chapter aims to encourage readers to look at technology as a creative practice to include into their teaching. It suggests strategies to help readers select the most appropriate tool for their projects.

Chapter 47 investigates the potential of project-oriented game-based learning in making students at educational institutes more engaged and gain a deep understanding of the curriculum content. The empirical data have been collected based on Ukrainian case study and allow the authors to prove the influence of Project Oriented Game Based Learning on increasing students' engagement, satisfaction, performance and improving learning outcomes. The main idea of the teaching project was to take as an object of the research a character from a fairy tale and analyze its managerial activities.

Chapter 48 explores how virtual reality (VR) is a technology that is becoming more common for applications in the field of education and training. VR can be used to create simulated two and three-dimensional scenarios, promoting interactions between the user and the environment, which allows experiencing virtual training situations very close to real actions. The aim of this text is to describe the development of a teaching and training tool using VR technology for scuba divers' operations within the aquatic context for enhancing critical thinking. To this end, a survey of requirements based on real procedures was carried out to transpose them into a synthetic environment. After the construction of the artefact, it was tested and evaluated by qualified users and the results are promising.

REFERENCES

C21 Canada. (2017). *Canadians for 21st Century Learning and Innovation.* Retrieved from: http://c21canada.org/mission/

Abdul Jabbar, A. I., & Felicia, P. (2015). Gameplay engagement and learning in game-based learning: A systematic review. *Review of Educational Research, 85*(4), 740–779. doi:10.3102/0034654315577210

Ajayi, L. (2011). A multiliteracies pedagogy: Exploring semiotic possibilities of a Disney video in a third grade diverse classroom. *The Urban Review, 43*(3), 396–413. doi:10.100711256-010-0151-0

Alexander, B., Ashford-Rowe, K., Barajas-Murphy, N., Dobbin, G., Knott, J., McCormack, M., Pomerantz, J., Seilhamer, R., & Weber, N. (Eds.). (2019). *EDUCAUSE Horizon Report: 2019 Higher Education Edition*. EDUCAUSE.

Alexander, J. (2009). Gaming, student literacies, and the composition classroom: Some possibilities for transformation. *College Composition and Communication, 61*(1), 35–63.

Apperley, T., & Beavis, C. (2011). Literacy into action: Digital games as action and text in the English and literacy classroom. *Pedagogies, 6*(2), 130–143. doi:10.1080/1554480X.2011.554620

Bakan, U., & Bakan, U. (2018). Game-based learning studies in education journals: A systematic review of recent trends. *Actualidades Pedagógicas, 72*(72), 119–145. doi:10.19052/ap.5245

Beavis, C. (2014). Games as text, games as action. *Journal of Adolescent & Adult Literacy, 57*(6), 433–439. doi:10.1002/jaal.275

Beavis, C., Muspratt, S., & Thompson, R. (2015). Computer games can get your brain working': Student experience and perceptions of digital games in the classroom. *Learning, Media and Technology, 40*(1), 21–42. doi:10.1080/17439884.2014.904339

Brull, S., & Finlayson, S. (2016). Importance of gamification in increasing learning. *Journal of Continuing Education in Nursing, 47*(8), 372–375. doi:10.3928/00220124-20160715-09 PMID:27467313

Byun, J., & Joung, E. (2018). Digital game-based learning for K–12 mathematics education: A meta analysis. *School Science and Mathematics, 118*(3-4), 113–126. doi:10.1111sm.12271

Cope, B., & Kalantzis, M. (2009). "Multiliteracies": New literacies, new learning. *Pedagogies, 4*(3), 164–195. doi:10.1080/15544800903076044

Cope, B., & Kalantzis, M. (2016). *A pedagogy of multiliteracies: Learning by design*. Palgrave Macmillan UK. Retrieved from https://books.google.ca/books?id=N6GkCgAAQBAJ

De Freitas, S. (2006). *Learning in immersive worlds: A review of game-based learning*. Academic Press.

DeCoito, I., & Richardson, T. (2016). Focusing on integrated STEM concepts in a digital game. In M. Urban & D. Falvo (Eds.), *Improving K-12 STEM Education* (pp. 1–23). IGI Global.

Duncum, P. (2004). Visual culture isn't just visual: Multiliteracies, multimodality and meaning. *Studies in Art Education, 46*(1), 252–264. doi:10.1080/00393541.2004.11651771

Duret, C., & Pons, C.-M. (2016). *Contemporary research on intertextuality in video games*. IGI Global. doi:10.4018/978-1-5225-0477-1

Freeman, A., Adams Becker, S., Cummins, M., Davis, A., & Hall Giesinger, C. (2017). *NMC/CoSN Horizon Report: 2017 K–* (12th ed.). The New Media Consortium. Retrieved from https://cdn.nmc.org/media/2017-nmc-cosn-horizon-report-k12-EN.pdf

Gee, J. P. (2003). *What video games have to teach us about learning and literacy* (1st ed.). Palgrave Macmillan. doi:10.1145/950566.950595

Preface

Gee, J. P. (2007). *Good video games and good learning: Collected essays on video games, learning, and literacy*. P. Lang. doi:10.3726/978-1-4539-1162-4

Gros, B. (2007). Digital games in education: The design of games-based learning environments. *Journal of Research on Technology in Education*, *40*(1), 23–38. doi:10.1080/15391523.2007.10782494

Herring, M. C., Koehler, M. J., & Mishra, P. (Eds.). (2016). *Handbook of technological pedagogical content knowledge (TPACK) for educators*. Routledge. doi:10.4324/9781315771328

Hommel, M. (2010). Video games and learning. *School Library Monthly*, *26*(10), 37–40.

Huizenga, J., Admiraal, W., Akkerman, S., & Dam, G. (2009). Mobile game-based learning in secondary education: Engagement, motivation and learning in a mobile city game. *Journal of Computer Assisted Learning*, *25*(4), 332–344. doi:10.1111/j.1365-2729.2009.00316.x

Israel, M., Marino, M., Delisio, L., & Serianni, B. (2014). *Supporting content learning through technology for K-12 students with disabilities*. CEDAR Document IC-10.

Jenkins, H. (2002). Game design as narrative architecture. In P. Harrington & N. Frup-Waldrop (Eds.), *First Person*. MIT Press.

Jenkins, H. (2005). Art form for the digital age. In J. Goldstein (Ed.), *Handbook for Video Game Studies*. MIT Press.

Kalantzis, M., & Cope, B. (2012). *Literacies*. Cambridge University Press. doi:10.1017/CBO9781139196581

Kim, B. (2013). *Gamification. Keeping Up With...*. ACRL. https://www.ala.org/acrl/publications/keeping_up_with/gamification

Kim, B. (2015). *Understanding gamification*. ALA TechSource.

Lane, C. A. (2011). *Social presence impacting cognitive learning of adults in distanced education*.

Lane, C. A. (2018). *Multiliteracies meaning-making: How four boys' video gaming experiences influence their cultural knowledge—Two ethnographic cases*. Academic Press.

Lee, C. J., & Kim, C. (2014). An implementation study of a TPACK-based instructional design model in a technology integration course. *Educational Technology Research and Development*, *62*(4), 437–460. doi:10.100711423-014-9335-8

Lopez-Morteo, G., & Lopez, G. (2007). Computer support for learning mathematics: A learning environment based on recreational learning objects. *Computers & Education*, *48*(4), 618–641. doi:10.1016/j.compedu.2005.04.014

Mishra, P., & Koehler, M. J. (2006). Technological pedagogical content knowledge: A framework for teacher knowledge. *Teachers College Record*, *108*(6), 1017–1054. doi:10.1111/j.1467-9620.2006.00684.x

Pellas, N., Fotaris, P., Kazanidis, I., & Wells, D. (2019). Augmenting the learning experience in primary and secondary school education: A systematic review of recent trends in augmented reality game-based learning. *Virtual Reality (Waltham Cross)*, *23*(4), 329–346. doi:10.100710055-018-0347-2

Pelletier, K., Brown, M., Brooks, D. C., McCormack, M., Reeves, J., Arbino, N., Bozkurt, A., Crawford, S., Czerniewicz, L., Gibson, R., Linder, K., Mason, J., & Mondelli, V. (2021). *2021 EDUCAUSE Horizon Report Teaching and Learning Edition.* Boulder, CO: EDU. Retrieved November 9, 2021 from https://www.learntechlib.org/p/219489/

Pho, A., & Dinscore, A. (2015). *Game-based learning. Tips and trends.* Academic Press.

Sanford, K., & Madill, L. (2006). Resistance through video game play: It's a boy thing. *Canadian Journal of Education, 29*(1), 287–306, 344–345. doi:10.2307/20054157

Sanford, K., & Madill, L. (2007). Understanding the power of new literacies through video game play and design. *Canadian Journal of Education, 30*(2), 432–455. doi:10.2307/20466645

Sider, S., & Maich, K. (2014). *Assistive technology tools: Supporting literacy.* Ministry of Education Learners in the Inclusive Classroom.

Squire, K. (2006). From content to context: Videogames as designed experience. *Educational Researcher, 35*(8), 19–29. doi:10.3102/0013189X035008019

Squire, K. D. (2013). Video game-based learning: An emerging paradigm for instruction. *Performance Improvement Quarterly, 26*(1), 101–130. doi:10.1002/piq.21139

Steinkuehler, C. (2007). Massively multiplayer online gaming as a constellation of literacy practices. *E-Learning and Digital Media, 4*(3), 297–318. doi:10.2304/elea.2007.4.3.297

Steinkuehler, C. (2011). *The mismeasure of boys: Reading and online videogames.* Wisconsin Center for Education Research, University of Wisconsin.

The New London Group. (1996). A pedagogy of multiliteracies: Designing social futures. *Harvard Educational Review, 66*(1), 60–93. doi:10.17763/haer.66.1.17370n67v22j160u

The New London Group. (2000). A pedagogy of multiliteracies: Designing social futures. In B. Cope & M. Kalantzis (Eds.), *Multiliteracies: Literacy learning and the design of social futures.* Routledge.

VanSledright, B. A. (2002). Fifth graders investigating history in the classroom: Results from a researcher-practitioner design experiment. *The Elementary School Journal, 103*(2), 131–160. doi:10.1086/499720

Vogel, J. J., Vogel, D. S., Cannon-Bowers, J., Bowers, C. A., Muse, K., & Wright, M. (2006). Computer gaming and interactive simulations for learning: A meta-analysis. *Journal of Educational Computing Research, 34*(3), 229–243. doi:10.2190/FLHV-K4WA-WPVQ-H0YM

Vygotsky, L. S. (1978). Readings on the development of children. *Mind & Society,* 79–91.

Acknowledgment

The editor would like to acknowledge the help of all the people involved in this project and, more specifically, to the authors and reviewers that took part in the review process. Without their support, this book would not have become a reality.

First, the editor would like to thank each one of the authors for their contributions. My sincere gratitude goes to the chapter's authors who contributed their time and expertise to this handbook.

Second, the editor wishes to acknowledge the valuable contributions of the reviewers regarding the improvement of quality, coherence, and content presentation of chapters. Most of the authors also served as referees; I highly appreciate their double task.

Carol-Ann Lane
University of Toronto, Canada

Section 1
Gamification in Higher Education

Chapter 1
The Game of Game-Based Learning

Reena Raj
CHRIST University (Deemed), India

Anand Patil
CHRIST University (Deemed), India

Cecil Donald
CHRIST University (Deemed), India

Manjula M. Y.
CHRIST University (Deemed), India

Swarnalatha P.
CHRIST University (Deemed), India

ABSTRACT

Games have been an inevitable part of education since the beginning. They have indescribably transformed the educational landscape with a higher emphasis on the learner-centric pedagogy. The educational games can be considered to be a contemporary manifestation of these centuries' old philosophies and practices aimed at imparting strategic and tactical thinking, language, logic, and mathematical skills amongst the learners. This chapter explores the meaning, significance, and scope of game-based learning as an instructional tool. It provides an interesting account of several games that are popularly used to facilitate effective learning in various settings. This chapter also examines the relevance and implications of games in education.

INTRODUCTION

Games have been an inevitable part of education from ancient times. It has indescribably transformed the educational landscape with a higher emphasis on the learner-centric pedagogy. Games are forms of experiential learning which unwrap new aesthetic experiences facilitating innovative problem-solving through experimentation. The history of Game-based learning (GBL) dates back to the era of board games such as Chess, Mancala and Kalaha pointing their origin to Asian and African roots. Ancient

DOI: 10.4018/978-1-7998-7271-9.ch001

Greeks were also known for using a combination of play-based learning with physical activities for educational purposes (Hellerstedt & Mozelius, 2019). Thus, the educational games can be considered to be a contemporary manifestation of these centuries' old philosophies and practices aimed at imparting strategic and tactical thinking, language, logic and mathematical skills amongst the learners.

According to Salen & Zimmerman (2004), a game is "a system in which players engage in an artificial conflict, defined by rules, that results in a quantifiable outcome". In the 1970s, Clark C Abt introduced the term 'serious games', which signifies games with explicit educational purposes but not necessarily entertaining (Wilkinson, 2015). The definitions of game-based learning also mostly emphasize that it is a form of game-play, which could be digital or non-digital, with well-defined learning outcomes (Shafer, Halverson, Squire & Gee, 2005). A good games-based learning should be designed based on six important elements: flow, clear goals, feedback loops, scaled challenges, self-determination, and fun. "Flow is a mental state where individuals are completely absorbed and engrossed in the activity" (Kiili, 2005). Great games fully engross their players and clearly link them in the environment created. Good game-based learning design also incorporates clear goals for players to achieve while providing feedback loops for individuals to determine if their actions are helping them achieve those goals. However, activity alone doesn't make a great Game Based Learning application. If the game isn't engaging and fun for players – then it won't matter how educational it is.

The advantages of GBL are numerous. The researchers suggest that the games contribute to cognitive development of the learners by allowing them to draw representations that allow the learners to transcend their immediate reality (Plass, Homer & Kinzer, 2015) and enhance symbolic thinking. It is also argued that games that cannot cognitively engage the participants, are not likely to facilitate the achievement of their learning goals. Furthermore, GBL promotes risk-taking and exploration behaviour (Hoffman & Nadelson, 2010) and facilitates the learning and execution of goal-setting strategies and monitoring the achievement of the intended goals (Barab, Warren, & Ingram-Goble, 2009; Kim, Park, & Baek, 2009). It also fosters team collaboration, communication, creativity, systems thinking, and socio-emotional skills of the players (Denning, Flores, & Flores, 2011), which make it one of the most preferred approaches in the teaching-learning process.

Game based learning also has applications in the digital realm through the use of simulations and pervasive ambient games. These advanced applications can be played anytime and anywhere allowing players to engage with content via mobile devices in environments that blur the boundary between the virtual and real world. Overall, game based experiential education is an emerging and powerful field. Its applications for both students and educators are now being realized. The main objective of Game Based Learning is to make learning permanent. This experiential learning makes learning fun which can create a lot of interest in learners.

However, there are several determinants of the efficacy of GBL as an instructional tool. The educational games should provide a challenge, facilitate response and offer feedback to the participants. It can choose a behaviourist approach, which provides a challenge where the players respond to a limited set of choices available and receive the corrective feedback. On the other hand, the games can also have a constructivist approach, which allows the learners to set their own challenges, to construct a response with available tools and receive peer feedback. The design and mechanics of games used for educational purposes must offer unique and playful experiences through advanced levels of learning engagement. The instructional designers must ensure an alignment of the games chosen with the learning ecosystem, specific goals and learner characteristics so as to create a balance between the cognitive, affective,

The Game of Game-Based Learning

behavioural and socio-cultural engagement. Customizable, personalized and adaptive games can make learning interesting and effortless for learners while fostering application-based learning.

This paper explores the meaning, significance and scope of Game based learning as an instructional tool based on various studies conducted by researchers. It presents an interesting account of several games that are popularly used to facilitate effective learning in various settings. It also examines some of the challenges, implications and the future of gamified education.

BACKGROUND STUDY

The changing dimensions of modern education has raised concern among the practitioners and educational researchers about the effectiveness of teaching and learning. There is a gradual shift in education from teaching methodology to learning methodology to make education more effective and interesting because ultimately the learning community is the largest stakeholder of the education industry. Therefore, there is a need to focus on the effectiveness of learning. The effectiveness of learning depends on the strategies and pedagogies. Traditionally many techniques like almanac (Yearbook), cases, cartons, collections, cross matrix, cross puzzles, dances, debate, family trees, group discussions, hobbies, lectures, mock conventions, newspapers and oral history are used to ensure the successful achievement of learning outcomes. Due to the technological innovations and changing needs of learners the question arises as to whether these tools will be effective?

The innovations in the teaching pedagogies and innovations in the field of technology have given birth to several new developments in the field of education. The shift in education from teaching centric approach to learning centric approach indicates the need for efforts towards making the learning process simple, interesting, and entertaining. The digitalization in education with the help of games made many educationalists to think about a learning pedagogy which will ensure achieving learning outcomes effectively with simple efforts, funds and motivation. The educationalists realized that this is possible by a pedagogy called Game Based Learning (GBL). The term digitalization in education and Game based learning is used interchangeably. However, there is a difference: Game Based Learning (GBL) is a 5000-year-old tool in the field of education whereas digitalization in education is an emerging phenomenon. In the 20th century Game Based Learning (GBL) was introduced as a pedagogical approach. In the present century the pedagogical approach is becoming an integral part of learning. (Hellerstedt & Mozelius, 2019)

Thomas (2018) designs and researches the creation of games for higher education. The education in the kindergarten is very interesting because most of the concepts are taught through different games. The learning process is facilitated by doing. The process of learning by doing is gaining much importance nowadays, this indicates the need for the Game Based Learning (GBL). If the class room is only limited to listening to the lectures, watching the videos and writing exams that will not contribute to effective learning. The learner needs to be facilitated with the task of doing things to ensure that the learning outcomes are achieved. For example, the pot maker learns pot making by doing it, driver learns to drive by driving and cooking is learnt by practical cooking. The very purpose of highlighting the above examples does not mean that classroom learning is not good, it means the learning needs to be facilitated with the art of doing things (i.e., the art of application-based learning) and that is the concept of Game Based Learning.

The evaluation process of education declares the learners as successful with a grade and percentage. There will be failures in the examinations even though nobody wants to fail. Post result the failed candidates need a motivation to re prepare and write. If they are asked to read the same material and in the same way they previously prepared for the test it's not going to motivate those learners. But if game-based learning is adopted it will not declare the learner as a winner unless and until the learner successfully finishes the game. Even the learner cannot go to the next level unless he finishes the earlier level. The losers keep on playing the game again and again till they win. If the learner fails or loses in a game he can rewind and redo again and again to complete which really helps to learn effectively This shows the motivation created by games for the learners (Thomas, 2018). That is how Game Based Learning makes the learning process fun and immersive. The Game Based Learning (GBL) provides a different way of learning repetitive attempts to overcome the difficulties and challenges, a safe and entertaining environment with motivation.

CONCEPT OF GAME BASED LEARNING

The concept of game-based learning helps the learners to achieve the learning outcomes through different games incorporated in the curriculum. In the process of Game Based Learning the learner(player) starts the learning slowly and completes the game successfully ensuring the victory. During the play the learner comes across many difficulties which will be considered as doubts and sorted with the help option.

Meaning of Game Based Learning:

The term Game Based Learning (GBL) refers to the application of gaming principles to the real life setting to engage the learner to achieve the desired learning outcomes (Trybus, 2015). "Game-based learning (GBL) is a type of game play that has defined learning outcomes. Generally, game-based learning is designed to balance subject matter with game play and the ability of the player to retain, and apply said subject matter to the real world" (Garrido et al., 2011).

Game Based Learning (GBL) allows the learners to engage with educational material in a play full and dynamic way. Game Based Learning (GBL) is not just creating the games for the students to play. It is designing learning activities that can incrementally introduce the concepts and guide the users towards an end goal (Pho & Dinscore, 2015).

Scope of Game Based Learning:

1. There are various terms used to explain game-based learning. The wider scope of GBL includes the terms like edutainment, digital games, simulations, gamifications. These terms are discussed in the following paragraphs (Tang, Hanneghan & Rhalibi, 2007)
2. Edutain Games: Educating games are developed using software. These games are developed keeping in mind the needs of the students who are having lower expectations of interaction. The different components used in these games are storytelling and game playing.
3. Digital Game Based Learning: In digital game-based learning the curriculum is digitalized to teach the learners. For example, the games project to teach the projects.

4. Simulations: In the simulation case different situations related to a specific problem requiring a decision are integrated in the software. The learner is provided with the inputs to solve the problem with the help of simulations which are usually executed through an algorithm.
5. Serious Games: The term serious games are the extended version of digital games. In the serious games the entertainment element will be absent. These games are used in the field of health and public policy.
6. Gamification: The term gamification refers to the process of adding game elements to make the learner experience an increased engagement or enjoyment.

TYPES OF GAMES FOR LEARNING

Game based learning is a vast and emerging area in the field of academics. Even though the concept of games is not new, the application of the game concepts to the learning process is a current phenomenon. Different types of games are used in different areas. Tables 1 and Table 2 show a list of popular games used in the selected areas.

The above are a few of the games in the selected areas. There are a number of games in all the areas, in the case of medical science there is a game called the Fold it game for protein identification for scientists and games for cancer patients. In the field of science, there are several lab-based games. All these games are very useful in the process of acquiring learning skills in the respective areas.

REVIEW OF LITERATURE

In virtual worlds, students can experience the concrete realities that words and symbols describe. Through such experiences, across multiple contexts, students can understand complex concepts without losing the connection between abstract ideas and the authentic problems that can be used to solve.

Nonoo (2019) has shown that our brains are "wired for pleasure" and that games are an effective way to learn because they simulate adventure and keep our brains engaged and happy. In an era consumed with teaching 21st-century soft skills, games are good at building collaboration skills or critical thinking.

In a study of 40 undergraduates, Smiderle et al. (2020) noticed that gamified environment systems affect users based on their characteristics. Specifically, it contributed to the comprehension of how gamification affects the engagement and learning behaviour of university students based on their personality traits. Jackson and McNamara (2013) found that adding game elements improved student engagement and enjoyment in an intelligent tutoring system. Sitzmann and Ely (2009) reported that students learned more from computer games supplemented by other instruction than from games alone. Their analysis of 55 studies found that learners using computer-based simulation games outscored control groups on self-efficacy, declarative and procedural knowledge, and retention.

Table 1. List of games for acquiring learning skills

Name of the Game	Resources	How to Play	Purpose
Charades Game	i. Physical or virtual classroom ii. Board or Digital Board iii. Marker or chalk iv. Laptop with net connection in case of virtual class	In this game, one student will be selected from the class, and he will be asked to act out a word. The rest of the class needs to guess the word, or the concepts acted upon.	This is a game to motivate the learners for active participation in the class.
Hangman Game	i. Physical or virtual classroom ii. Board or Digital Board iii. Marker or chalk Physical iv. Division of class into groups or breakout rooms v. Laptop with net connection in case of virtual class	In this game, the class will be divided into teams or breakout rooms. One of the selected learners from a group will be asked to think about a word related to the subject under discussion. After that, he will put spaces on the board and the other learners from the other group will be asked to fill the space. The correct guess will be rewarded.	This game helps the learners to improve their subject knowledge
Scatter-gories Game	i. Physical or virtual classroom ii. Board or Digital Board iii. Marker or chalk in case of Physical class iv. Division of class into groups or breakout rooms v. Laptop with net connection in case of virtual class	In this game, the game facilitator divides the class into small groups or breakout rooms and allots a few minutes time to think about a topic with a clue of alphabets or words. After the allotted time the groups will be asked to present.	This game enhances the subject knowledge
Puzzles Game	i. Physical or virtual classroom ii. Board or Digital Board iii. Marker or chalk in case of Physical class iv. Division of class into groups or breakout rooms v. Laptop in case of virtual class	The groups will be provided with puzzles to solve together.	It's a traditional game particularly good for team or group work.
Draw Foils Game	i. Physical or virtual classroom ii. Board or Digital Board iii. Marker or chalk in case of Physical class iv. Division of class into groups or breakout rooms v. Laptop in case of virtual class vi. Printed materials in case of physical class	In this game, the class will be divided into groups. Each group needs to nominate one learner. The nominated learner will be provided with a resource either hardcopy or softcopy or online to search and find a given concept or a word.	This game is to enhance the thinking capacity of the learner
Pictionary Game	i. Physical or virtual classroom ii. Board or Digital Board iii. Marker or chalk in case of Physical class iv. Division of class into groups or breakout rooms v. Laptop in case of virtual class	In this game, some drawings are drawn by a selected learner about the earlier topics discussed in the class. The other members will be asked to recall and find the topic and explain.	This game is for refreshing the memories of the students who forget the things they have studied earlier.
Quiz	i. Physical or virtual classroom ii. Board or Digital Board iii. Marker or chalk in case of Physical class iv. Division of class into groups or breakout rooms v. Laptop in case of virtual class	In this game, the trainer or the facilitator constructs the quiz consisting of different types of questions using pictures, tables, and other materials and runs the quiz either manually or through using different applications or websites.	This game is to assess the learnings of the students.

The Game of Game-Based Learning

Table 2. List of games in business management studies for acquiring learning skills

Name of the Game	Resources	How to Play	Purpose
Business Strategy Game	i. Physical or virtual classroom ii. Board or Digital Board iii. Marker or chalk in case of Physical class iv. Data and the strategies	In this game, the learners will be placed with data in a team and informed to come up with the strategy needed with different decisions. For example, an issue related to merger of a bank.	This game helps to learn and improve the decision-making process.
Supply Chain Management Game	i. Laptop with net connect	The students will be divided into teams to compete against each other with the provided assignments. The teams will be provided with different demand patterns and different regions. the teams are informed to set different parameters in the area of supply chain	This game helps the learners to manage a virtual supply chain To step up the process of invert turnover
Capsim Game	i. Management students from different areas ii. Problem iii. Opportunity extraction situation	In this game the management learners from different areas are involved in interaction to find a solution to a business problem or find a business opportunity.	To create a healthy competition among the students
Forio	i. Virtual simulation ii. Complex business problem	In this game simulations are used to explain the solution to complex business problems	To find solution to a business problem
Ball Toss	i. Ball ii. Questions iii. Even Spinner option during virtual class	In this game, questions are written on a ball and thrown among the learners. The learner who catches the ball needs to answer the questions.	Ice breaking
Two Truths and a Lie Game	i. Prior information about the topic to the participants ii. Reading materials	In this game, the learner needs to write 3 sentences out of which two facts, and one is a lie about a situation or a company or a concept. Once he reads the others in the group need to identify the lie.	This a game for improving observation skills, which is very important for a manager

RELEVANCE OF GAMES IN EDUCATION

Games now are replacing rote memorization and lecture-based learning methods. The entire education scenario is transforming iconoclastically as games are occupying the classrooms and the implementation is bringing in success through amusement in many countries.

The foremost advantage of games in a classroom is that there is hundred percent involvement of the class with no discrimination. Games teach them that small losses and failures are a part of life as everyone does not win every time. Another specific feature is the movement within the classroom, the noise made during discussions and the laughter that makes it lively which can even make students move out of the closed shells, they have been living in due to timidity and shyness for many reasons. Moreover, the curiosity of what next is kindled within the learners.

A curiosity as to what next? Am I going to win or what should I do to win? What made me lose? Will be kindled in the minds of the learners. A healthy play way competency is developed, where an automatic self-analysis is made by the learners. These are the general features that games can inculcate in the student body making them self-researchers. The teacher need not be the only resource person in the class. The whole class becomes a repertoire of resources. Games develop not just minds but also the physique like exposure to sunlight that strengthens the bone naturally, relieves stress, sharpens the mind, develops motor skills eye- hand coordination, body and mind coordination et cetera.

A few developmental disorders might vanish in course of time with the implementation of games in the learning process. Games can also help learners in identifying their skills when they play certain games. Triggering creative thought processes on the go along with the inception of concepts and their implementation for every idea that playfully springs in the minds can manifest as a colossal entity.

CHALLENGES IN GAME BASED LEARNING

Any new pedagogy has its own challenges and also resistance from some sections of the society. Apart from the proficiency and knowledge required to develop a game, some other challenges in Game Based Learning are (Ecke, 2006).

- Whether the game is aligned with the curriculum and learning outcomes.
- Is the competitiveness in the game different from the competitive games played?
- How to increase the appeal of the game among all the stakeholders, especially parents?
- Cost associated with the development and implementation of the game in the classroom set-up.
- Whether the game is in accordance with the cultural ethos of the society.
- Whether the game can be played by learners with different learning abilities.

Oblinger (2006) lists some challenges in implementation that Game Based Learning faces like

- Are computer laboratories available where students can play games?
- Are they appropriately configured?
- Are they available for the extended hours that game play involves?
- Is the right equipment available, such as headphones, speakers, and special consoles?
- Is support available for the game, both technically and in terms of game play?
- Is gaming integrated into the curriculum or just added on?

IMPLICATIONS OF GAME BASED LEARNING

Games encourage the individual to think out of the box, thus the creative propensities of the individual get kindled. They provide a safe space for learning. Here the individual can explore, create, analyse and synthesize. There is no humiliation if they fail to do some activity and, in the melee, they learn to face failure, which is a very important learning especially for the teenagers. In a game-based approach learning can be fun, less stressful and more enjoyable. Different types of games can be designed to teach/learn different concepts and the learning is likely to get strengthened because the variety of activities reduce the boredom that is seen in a traditional teaching/learning environment. Game based learning with its immediate reinforcers encourages the students to involve themselves fully in the learning process, and thus contributing to greater learning. Learners experienced a heightened level of reported goal clarity and autonomy with non-competitive games when game-based learning was administered individually, rather than in a group format (Chan, Van & King, 2021). If the teacher is creative and can effectively incorporate Game Based Learning along with traditional learning strategies, it will benefit the students.

The Game of Game-Based Learning

Some of the Controversies Related to Game Based Learning

Because of the immediate reinforcement that the participant gets, the shift may focus from learning to winning.

Unless collaborative games are included, chances are that the students may become more competitive, which may create a hostile environment in the learning process.

While introducing Game Based Learning it is important to keep in mind that Technology is important but it is not the whole and sole in the learning process. We should not miss the woods for the trees.

THE ROAD AHEAD

Information and communication technologies have taken education to newer heights. It continues to offer numerous opportunities to academia as well as industry specially in revolutionizing the learning arena with an increased focus on experiential learning. With the increasing innovations in technological offerings including Artificial intelligence, Augmented Reality, Virtual Reality and Mixed Reality, learning is becoming more comprehensive, realistic and enjoyable. It is expected that simulations, virtual games and exercises, scenario-based learning etc. will continue enabling the instructors, trainers and learners to explore, experiment and evolve in the areas of education and research like never before. The accessibility beyond the physical boundaries through the computers and mobile devices, the freedom and flexibility offered for individuals and teams, the applicability of both individual and collective learning, all make it the most desirable choice of learning and training. Educational institutions are redesigning the curricula in order to integrate specifically designed games with clear learning and assessment goals in the respective domain keeping learner empowerment as a focus. The trainer and trainee can also co-create highly creative and engaging games specific to situations both as a training technique as well as solution to the problem on hand. Needless to say, this will be a mutually rewarding experience.

Serious games have become a serious business for corporates too. Organizations across the globe continue to invest heavily in learning technologies such as extended reality in order to tap the opportunity. "The three countries with the highest revenues from gamification in 2018 are China, the US, and India, respectively," reports Adkins. By 2023, the US (with a compound annual rate of five-year global growth of 47.6%) will again be the leading country, followed by China. India will retain the third position through the forecast period." (Ibanez, 2018). As a result, constructive collaborations between academia and industry will be instrumental in transforming the teaching, learning and training terrains. Businesses are likely to develop more realistic, situation-based games aimed at specific job roles and support academia. The industry experts also are expected to join hands with academic experts in creating innovative games for teaching and training.

The very understanding of the increased scope of Gamified education has stimulated the need for constant research in the design, development and administration of innovative and more challenging games as both a classroom instructional tool and a training methodology. The experiments do not confine to the evolution of various types of games but also extend to crafting games with newness, excitement and engagement. The scholars are also trying to understand the applications of games in various disciplines ranging from engineering to psychology to medical research. The migration of computer to mobile games is another area of constant exploration. How virtual reality, augmented reality and 3D technology are influencing the learning experience is another interesting terrain to discover. Lots of research have been conducted in these areas, but there is a lot more to be unravelled. Nevertheless, its guaranteed that these disruptive research studies would bring out a huge transformation in the topography of higher education across the globe.

CONCLUSION

It has been proved that game-based methods facilitate powerful learning which ensures higher engagement for learners making knowledge acquisition a pleasant and memorable experience. Educators across the world, therefore, have been seriously involved in designing and delivering games in their disciplines from ancient times. However, designing games that appropriately align the learning ecosystem with the specific learning requirements still remains a challenge. The instructional designers, thus need to place greater emphasis on devising adaptive, personalized and more engaging games with an emphasis of application-based learning.

REFERENCES

Barab, S., Ingram-Goble, A., & Warren, S. (2009). Conceptual play spaces. In R. E. Ferdig (Ed.), *Hand-book of Research on Effective Electronic Gaming in Education* (pp. 989–1009). IGI Global. doi:10.4018/978-1-59904-808-6.ch057

Chan, K. H. W., Wan, K., & King, V. (2021). *Performance over enjoyment? Effect of game-based learning on learning outcome and flow experience.* doi:10.3389/feduc.2021.660376

Denning, P. J., Flores, F., & Flores, G. (2011). Pluralistic coordination. In M. M. Cruz-Cunha, V. H. Varvalho, & P. Tavares (Eds.), *Business, technological, and social dimensions of computer games: Multidisciplinary developments* (pp. 416–431). Information Science Reference. doi:10.4018/978-1-60960-567-4.ch025

Eck, R. V. (2006). Digital Game-Based Learning: It's Not Just the Digital Natives Who Are Restless. *EDUCAUSE Review, 41*(2), 16–30.

Garrido, P. C., Miraz, G. M., Ruiz, I. L., & Gomez-Nieto, M. (2011). *Use of NFC- based pervasive games for encouraging learning and student motivation.* doi:10.1109/NFC.2011.13

Hellerstedt, A., & Mozelius, P. (2019). *Game-based learning - a long history.* https://www.researchgate.net/publication/336460471_Game-based_learning_-_a_long_history

Hoffman, B., & Nadelson, L. (2010). Motivational engagement and video gaming: A mixed methods study. *Educational Technology Research and Development, 58*(3), 245–270. doi:10.100711423-009-9134-9

IbanezF. C. (2018). https://elearningindustry.com/elearning-authors/felipe-casajus-ibanez

Jackson, G.T., & McNemara, D. (2013). *Motivation and Performance in a Game-Based Intelligent Tutoring System.* Academic Press.

Kiili, K. (2005). Digital game- based learning: Towards an experiential gaming model. *The Internet and Higher Education*, *8*(1), 13–24. doi:10.1016/j.iheduc.2004.12.001

Nonoo, S. (2019). *Playing Games Can Build 21st-Century Skills*. Research Explains How.

Oblinger, D. G. (2006). Games and Learning. Digital games have the potential to bring play back to the learning experience. *EDUCAUSE Quarterly*, 29.

Pho A & Dinscore A. (2015). *Game Based Learning*. Tips and Trends Instructional Technologies.

Plass, J. L., Homer, B. D., & Kinzer, C. K. (2015). Foundations of Game-Based Learning. *Educational Psychologist*, *50*(4), 258–283. doi:10.1080/00461520.2015.1122533

Salen, K., & Zimmerman, E. (2004). *Rules of Play - Game Design Fundamentals*. The MIT Press. https://gamifique.files.wordpress.com/2011/11/1-rules-of-play-game-design-fundamentals.pdf

Shaffer, D. W., Squire, K. R., Halverson, R., & Gee, J. P. (2005). Video games and the future of learning. *Phi Delta Kappan*, *87*(2), 105–111. doi:10.1177/003172170508700205

Sitzmann, T., & Ely, K. (2009). A meta-analytic examination of the effectiveness of computer-based simulation games. Advanced Distributed Learning Technical Report.

Smiderle, R., Rigo, S.J., Marques, L.B., Coelho, J.A.P.D.M., & Jaques, P.A. (2020). *The impact of gamification on students' learning, engagement and behaviour based on their personality traits*. doi:10.1186/s40561-019-0098-x

Tang, S., Hanneghan, M., & El Rhalibi, A. (2007). *Describing games for learning: terms, scope and learning approaches*. https://www.academia.edu/25962572/Describing_Games_for_Learning_Terms_Scope_and_Learning_Approaches

Thomas, A. (2018). *TEDx Talk on The Effective Use of Game-Based Learning in Education*. https://www.youtube.com/watch?v=-X1m7tf9cRQ

Trybus, J. (2015). *Game-Based Learning: What it is, Why it Works, and Where it's Going*. New Media Institute. http://www.newmedia.org /game-based-learning--what-it-is-why-it -works-and-where-its-going.html

Wilkinson, P. (2015). *A Brief History of Serious Games*. https://core.ac.uk/download/pdf/157768453.pdf

ADDITIONAL READING

Babu, S. K., McLain, M. L., Bijlani, K., Jayakrishnan, R., & Bhavani, R. R. (2016). Collaborative Game Based Learning of Post-Disaster Management: Serious Game on Incident Management Frameworks for Post Disaster Management. *2016 IEEE Eighth International Conference on Technology for Education (T4E)*, 80-87, 10.1109/T4E.2016.024

Carron, T., Marty, J. C., & Heraud, J. M. (2007). Teaching with game-based learning management systems: Exploring a pedagogical dungeon. *Simulation & Gaming*, *39*(3), 353–378. doi:10.1177/1046878108319580

Ding, D., Guan, C., & Yu, Y. (2017). Game-Based Learning in Tertiary Education: A New Learning Experience for the Generation Z. *International Journal of Information and Education Technology (IJIET)*, *7*(2), 148–152. doi:10.18178/ijiet.2017.7.2.857

Ebner, M., & Holzinger, A. (2007). Successful implementation of user-centered game-based learning in higher education: An example from civil engineering. *Computers & Education*, *49*(3), 873–890. doi:10.1016/j.compedu.2005.11.026

Freina, L., & Canessa, A. (2015). *Immersive vs Desktop Virtual Reality in Game Based Learning. 9th European Conference on Games Based Learning (ECGBL)*, Steinkjer, Norway.

Leoste, J., Jõgi, L., Un, Õ., Pastor, T., San Martín, L., López, J., & Grauberg, I. (2021). Perceptions about the Future of Integrating Emerging Technologies into Higher Education—The Case of Robotics with Artificial Intelligence. *Computers*, *10*(9), 110. doi:10.3390/computers10090110

Oyelere, S. S., Bouali, N., Kaliisa, R., Obaido, G., Yunusa, A. A., & Jimoh, E. R. (2020). Exploring the trends of educational virtual reality games: A systematic review of empirical studies. *Smart Learn. Environ.*, *7*(1), 31. doi:10.118640561-020-00142-7

Shabalina, O., Malliarakis, C., Tomos, F., & Mozelius, P. (2017). *Game-Based Learning for Learning to Program: From Learning Through Play to Learning Through Game Development. European Conference on Games Based Learning*, Graz, Austria.

Squire, K. D. (2013). Video Game-Based Learning: An Emerging Paradigm for Instruction. *Performance Improvement Quarterly*, *26*(1), 101–130. doi:10.1002/piq.21139

Zielke, M. A. (2017). Developing Virtual Patients with VR/AR for a natural user interface in medical teaching. In *IEEE 5th international conference on Serious Games and Applications for Health (SeGAH)* (pp. 1–8). 10.1109/SeGAH.2017.7939285

Chapter 2
Games in Education:
Bibliometric Analysis

Menşure Alkış Küçükaydın
Eregli Faculty of Education, Necmettin Erbakan University, Turkey

Burcu Durmaz
Süleyman Demirel University, Turkey

ABSTRACT

In this study, a study was made on the Web of Science index by using the words "game-based learning," "video games," "game-based pedagogy," "digital games," "gamification," and "game." The study was carried out with data obtained from the SCI-E, SSCI, and A&HCI indices covering the years 1975-2021. A total of 1,376 articles were reached in accordance with the inclusion criteria. Retrieved articles were subjected to bibliometric analysis. In line with the relevant analysis, the most influential authors, journals, institutions, and articles were revealed under the title "games in education." In addition, based on the articles examined within the scope of this research, a co-word network structure was visualized in terms of cooperation among institutions and authors. As a result of the research, the trends in topics related to games were revealed, and the changes in this area are subsequently discussed.

INTRODUCTION

A game is generally defined as an activity that serves to achieve various gains without limitations such as the number of players or rules and that comes to life in various ways (Lai et al., 2018). Salen and Zimmerman (2004) defined the game as *"an artificial conflict system with a rule-defined and measurable outcome"* (p. 83) Although there is no one-size-fits-all definition of what a game is in the literature, the basic features of one should generally be the same. Accordingly, for an activity to be considered a game, the game must have a rule-based system, variable and measurable results, different values / points given for different results during the game, and outputs that change with the effort of the player; at the same time, all players must feel emotionally connected to the outputs obtained during the game, and play must

DOI: 10.4018/978-1-7998-7271-9.ch002

emerge because of a debatable activity (Juul, 2005). As with the definition of what a game is, there are also different approaches for game types. For example, games can be classified in various ways according to whether they are digital or not, the platform / environment they are played in, the tools used during the game, the participation status of the players, and game flow (Cojocariu & Boghian, 2014; Lai et al., 2018). However, it can be inferred that games can be grouped under the following categories: serious games and digital games, which are commonly and increasingly used today.

Serious games, which are frequently used in education, primarily serve the purpose of teaching professional skills and life skills (Clapper, 2018). Serious games can act as a supportive strategy to increase student participation and satisfaction, as well as being effective learning tools for knowledge and skill acquisition (Sipiyaruk et al., 2018). Research on serious games has shown that this type of game facilitates students' understanding of concepts holistically; enables them to acquire cognitive abilities; supports teaching; has positive effects on students' attitudes; provides them with flexible learning opportunities, improves learning outcomes; increases their motivation; attracts their attention; changes their behavior; facilitates socio-cultural learning; supports cognitive development; allows for multiple assessment; provides equal opportunities in terms of participation in the lesson, makes learning more enjoyable; opens opportunities for constructive feedback; and enables peer interaction (Allery, 2014; Clapper, 2018; De Freitas, 2018; Lai et al., 2018; Zhonggen, 2019).

Another type of game that has been increasingly used in education in recent years is the digital game. Many types of digital games have been used as auxiliary tools in teaching for a long period to support elements such as student participation and learning outcomes (Bado, 2019; Ke, 2016). Studies have shown that using digital games in the educational process can meet a wide range of needs. For example, Shah et al. (2018) pointed out that interventions presented in the digital game format can play a positive role in the prevention and elimination of mental disorders. In addition, compared to traditional teaching, digital games seem to be more effective in terms of variables such as attitude, motivation, skill acquisition, and student participation (Jackson et al., 2018). Therefore, different types of games used in education, whether it takes place in or out of school, provide important contributions to both students and teachers. Their potential has been explained in different ways by many theorists. To reveal these forms of expression, first, the theoretical foundations of the game will be mentioned in this study; then, the basic dynamics of the study will be outlined.

Game Theories

Theories with various discourses have tried to draw on the framework they have attributed to games, in line with their definitions and acceptance of what a game constitutes. From this perspective, the game, according to the theory of surplus energy, is an action in which a person spends this energy through purposeless activities: activities that gather energy according to the theory of relaxation and recreation and instinctive preparation for skills that must be acquired in preparation for life according to the pre-practice theory. According to the recapitulation theory, the game as an action represents activities that enable people to repeat developmental processes. When the viewpoint of what makes up a game is examined by theorists working on children's cognitive, social, and affective skills, Freud, as a leading psychoanalytic theorist, considered play as a serious action, and therefore emphasized that play is an important need in children (Lenormand, 2019). While Erikson, another psychoanalytic theorist, saw play as a tool that balances internal and external needs (Chien-Pen et al., 2014), Vygotsky, a cognitive theorist, believed that games play a key role in cognitive gains. Focusing on social learning, Bruner draws attention to the fact that the game provides not only cognitive but also social development (Frost et al., 2012). Huizinga, one of the theorists who evaluated the game in terms of cultural transfer, considered the game as a source of culture, while Bateson and Garvey emphasized the communicative and linguistic processes in games (Frost et al., 2012; Garvey, 1990; Singer, 2013). From these perspectives, all theories that directly or indirectly explain what a game is relate the meanings they attribute to the game to its functions and benefits to the individual / society.

Games in Education

It can be said that game-based learning, which responds to different skills, student levels, and disciplines—from health to law, pre-school to higher education, climate change to research skills—can play a key role in educational processes by feeding the learner's intrinsic motivation if used correctly and appropriately (Yuratich, 2020; Silva et al., 2021). Studies have supported this position. For example, it may be possible to achieve positive outcomes by successfully integrating game-based learning or gamification into teaching to increase the learning motivation, participation, and performance of higher education students (Subhash & Cudney, 2018). In addition, Connolly et al. (2012) researched experimental studies on computer games and serious games and found that games were associated with many outputs related to perceptual, cognitive, affective, behavioral, and motivational areas. The authors also found a field of application in many different disciplines. However, the fact that game-related research has been carried out based on very different contexts and disciplines may cause researchers to look at the concept of the game from a narrow perspective (De Freitas, 2018). As a result, it is important to examine the research on games from a holistic point of view because of the mixed findings on the effects of games in the literature and especially because digital games have started to find more of a place in the classroom compared to previous or normal conditions due to the global pandemic (Connoly et al., 2012; Gorbanev et al., 2018; Silva et al., 2021). For this reason, it can be said that the findings obtained from the research need to be gathered and examined under a general framework. Thus, it is anticipated that this study will reveal the main contributions of the game, render the literature coherent and holistic, harmonize the perspectives of different disciplines, and help to overcome some methodological difficulties / challenges (De Freitas, 2018). With this research, the latest trends in game studies will be examined by determining the general trends in the gaming environment and reveal the pioneers in the field; also, the productivity status of the researchers who have studied this subject will be clarified. In line with this, the study's aim is to examine academic publications related to games in terms of bibliometric indicators. With this aim in mind, answers to the following questions were pursued:

1. What is the distribution of the most influential authors, journals, institutions, articles, countries, and developments in game studies in education?
2. Regarding the game in educational terms, what kind of a structure emerges in the context of co-authors among countries and authors with a co-word network?

Previous Research

This book chapter is very valuable in terms of examining bibliometric analysis of studies on games in education because a very specific evaluation is included in this review. However, previous bibliometric studies have a certain context. For example, Irmade and Anisa (2021) discussed the latest trends in serious game studies and included proceedings, books, and notes that were included in the Scopus database between 1984 and 2019 without limitations by discipline. According to the findings of this study, serious game studies have increased in recent years.

Trinidad et al. (2021) focused on gamification studies. In that study, all indexes within the scope of Web of Science (WoS) were examined, and the studies published between 1900 and 2019 were included in the research. In the study, which also revealed themes related to gamification, other types of publications other than the article were included in the analysis, and current developments related to gamification were mentioned.

Martí-Parreño et al. (2016) conducted a bibliometric review in the context of gamification. In their study, they covered trends in studies published between 2010 and 2014 based on the keywords "games" and "gamification". A bibliometric review of gamification published between 2010 and 2013 in search of titles was conducted via Google Scholar by Harman et al. (2014). In their study, the authors did not perform a disciplinary-specific screening.

Liu et al. (2020) searched ScienceDirect, Web of Science, PsychInfo, ERIC, and IEEE Xplore databases using the keywords "learning game", "educational game", and "game-based learning". Bibliometric analysis, qualitative thematic analysis, and meta-analysis of the publications reached in accordance with the inclusion criteria were then made. Based on the results obtained, recommendations were submitted for policymakers and grant foundation administrators.

Finally, Schöbel et al. (2021) conducted a bibliometric analysis of games used in digital learning environments via WoS. They examined a total of 10,000 studies by including all publications in their surveys covering 2000-2019. At the end of the study, they clarified the basic concepts of digital learning. Bibliometric examination of research related to the game was carried out, and a broad perspective prevails in these studies can be observed. However, it is known that studies on the concept of games have shifted to focusing on gamification or video games in recent years. Based on this reality, it is thought that the studies carried out in the field of education and accepted by certain indexes will better contribute to the bibliometric literature for game research. Therefore, in this study, an attempt was made to determine the publication trends about games in education, the handling of the game in different parts of the world, influential articles on games, and how the leading researchers guided game literature. For this purpose, bibliometric analysis and data sets of game articles carried out in the field of education were used here.

METHOD

Bibliometric analysis was used in this study to examine the research carried out on games in education. Bibliometric analysis is accepted as an interdisciplinary basis allowing examination of the level of development of scientific research (Samiee & Chabowski, 2012). With bibliometric analysis, identifying and evaluating countries, universities, research institutions, journals, special research topics, and the characteristics of various disciplines is quite effective (Huang et al., 2006). In this analysis, the connection between any publication, author, or cited author with other publications and authors is revealed through visual maps (Zupic & Čater, 2015). Thus, it is possible to learn what the general trends are in any field, what kind of publication cooperation the authors in the field have, and the general situation of cited publications. Bibliometric analysis and general trends of the publications are revealed with data analysis programs that offer different visual maps. Therefore, in this study, bibliometric analysis and studies on games in the field of education are discussed.

Data Collection

The data were obtained by using WoS, one of the primary international citation indexes. The keywords "game-based learning", "video games", "game-based pedagogy", "digital games", "gamification", and "game" are used in the title of the relevant article. An online search was conducted in the WoS database covering the dates 1975 to 31 August 2021. In the data collection phase of the study, the Preferred Reporting Items for Systematic Review and Meta-Analysis (PRISMA) (Moher et al., 2009; Pham et al., 2021) model was used (Fig. 1). At this point, first, the WoS database was searched using relevant keywords. In this way, a total of 41,674 studies were accessed. The search started in July 2021, and the last search was carried out on 31 August 2021. All years (1975-2021) in the SSCI, SCI-Expanded, and A&HCI indices were included in this search. In these related studies, the "education/educational research" filter was used as the study area, and 1,686 studies were accessed in this way. Subsequently, among these, studies with the terms "book reviews" (n = 100), "early access" (n = 77), "editorial material" (n = 59), "review articles" (n = 36), "notes" (n = 14), "software reviews" (n = 11), "corrections" (n = 9), "letters" (n = 7), "meeting abstracts" (n = 2), and "new items" (n = 1) were extracted, and a total of 1,376 studies were reached. The code for how the WoS content was searched is as follows:

TS = "game-based learning" (Title) or "video games" (Title) or "game-based pedagogy" (Title) or "digital games" (Title) or "gamification" (Title) or "game" Refined by: WEB OF SCIENCE CATEGORIES: (EDUCATION EDUCATIONAL RESEARCH)] DOCUMENT TYPES: (ARTİCLES) Timespan: All years. Indexes: SCI-EXPANDED, SSCI, A&HCI.

Figure 1. PRISMA diagram for game in wos database

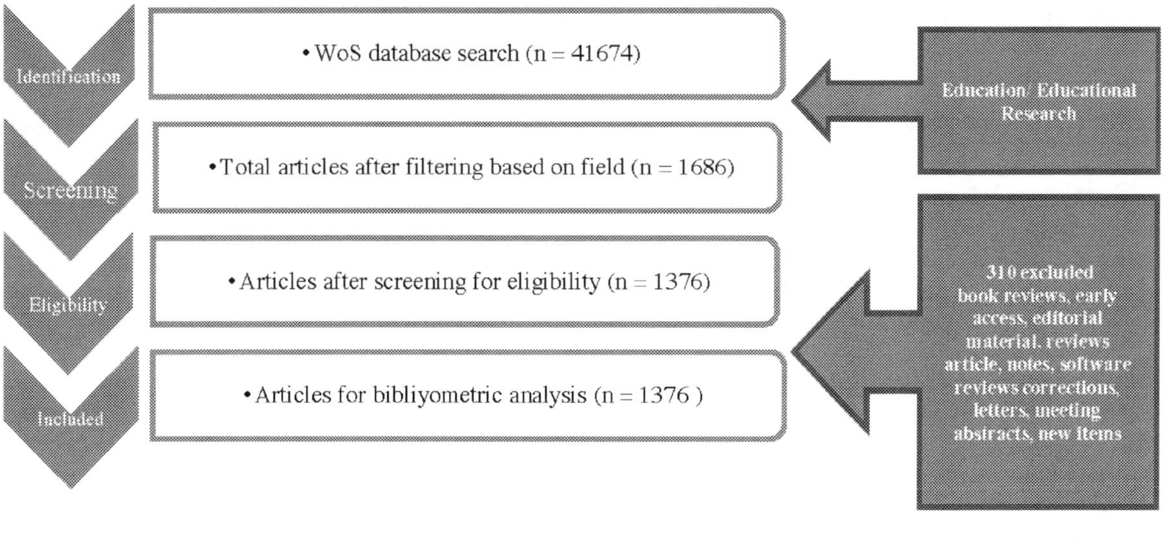

- Identification: WoS database search (n = 41674) ← Education/ Educational Research
- Screening: Total articles after filtering based on field (n = 1686)
- Eligibility: Articles after screening for eligibility (n = 1376) ← 310 excluded book reviews, early access, editorial material, reviews article, notes, software reviews corrections, letters, meeting abstracts, new items
- Included: Articles for bibliyometric analysis (n = 1376)

Data Analysis

Bibliometric analysis and descriptive statistics were used in the analysis of the 1,376 studies obtained from the PRISMA diagram. In this context, the distribution of game studies in the field of education by years, the top 10 most cited articles, the authors who contributed to the field and their number of publications, the top journals about games, the countries active in game studies, institutions, and the funds supporting game studies were analysed using bibliometric analysis techniques. Collaboration network analysis was used to determine co-word analysis and author co-citation network analysis in the articles examined in the research. The VOSviewer (Version 1.6.9) (Van Eck & Waltman, 2010) package program was preferred as an analytical tool in collaboration network studies. Data obtained from WoS have been converted into a text format suitable for the VOSviewer package program. Data obtained in this way were visualised with maps. In addition, the data obtained using WoS's own system was transferred to an Excel package program, and the achieved values were summarised in this way.

RESULTS

The findings of the studies obtained with the PRISMA diagram, in line with the previously mentioned research questions, are presented below, respectively:

The distribution of 1,376 articles, which emerged as a result of the surveying made on WoS, according to years, was examined and is presented in Fig. 2. Accordingly, can be seen that articles on games in education began appearing in 1975. After 2005, game studies as a topic started to regularly increase, and most publications (n = 145) were found to have appeared in 2020. This situation has a share of 10,538%, compared to all years. As of August of 2021, 57 articles on the game as a topic were reached.

A total of 1,376 articles about games in education were written by a total of 3,022 researchers. The list of researchers who have the most publications about games and that are in the top 10 is presented in Fig. 3. Among the researchers, the largest percentage belongs to Hwang, G.J. (17%, n = 21). The second largest percentage (15%, n = 18) is attributed to Hong, J.C. These two ratios were followed by 16 articles written by Hwang, M.Y. and 11 by Cheng, M.T.

It was observed that there are 207 journals that include research on games in education. Among these journals, the top journals that give the most importance to game research are listed in Fig.4. Accordingly, it is seen that most publications belong to the journal *Computers & Education* (n = 195). In second place, with a shared total number of articles on gaming, is the following group of journals: *British Journal of Educational Technology, Educational Technology & Society,* and *Simulation & Gaming* (n = 72). The impact factor of the first ranked journal is 8,538 (WoS).

Figure 2. Record of item research about games between 1985 and August 2021.

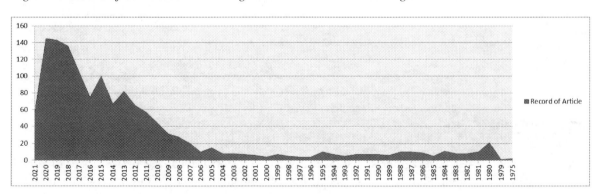

Figure 3. Top researchers in game-related research.

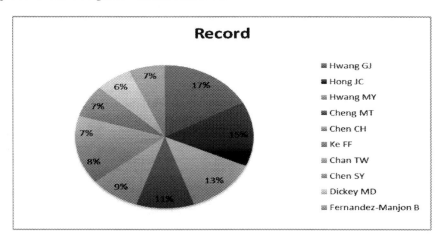

Figure 4. List of top journals.

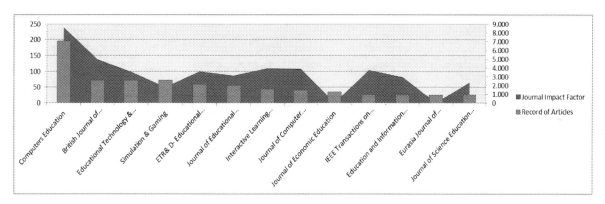

In the study, co-citation analysis of the journals that included research on games was also performed (Fig. 5). Accordingly, the journals that included research on games were gathered in 13 clusters. There are 3 journals that intersect with each other in these clusters. These journals are *Computer & Education*, *Educational Technology & Society*, and the *British Journal of Educational Technology*. These journals are also the ones that contain the most articles on games. When co-citation analysis of the journals is evaluated according to years, it can be seen that the co-citations made to the journals *Computer & Education* and *Educational Technology & Society* increased after 2014.

The distribution of the research carried out on games in education in institutions, the language of the article, countries, and regions is presented in Table 1. When the articles prepared by 1,151 institutions in total were examined, it was seen that the National Taiwan Normal University made the greatest contribution with 52 articles. The second institution with the most articles is the State University System of Florida (n = 39). While 74 different countries are working on research related to games in total, most articles are from the USA (n = 510). This rate was followed by Taiwan (232 articles) and England (84 articles). When the publication language of the articles was examined, it was seen that there were articles in 7 different languages. While 1,345 of these are in English, 13 of them are in Portuguese, 8 in Spanish, and 4 in German and Turkish. One article was written in Dutch and one in French.

Figure 5. Co-citation in the journals.

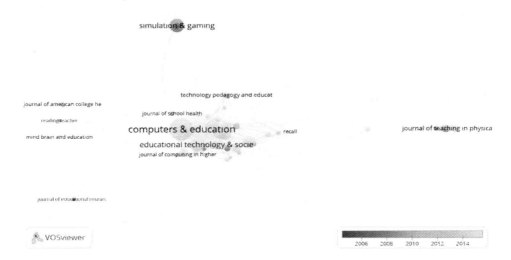

Table 1. Top affiliates, countries/regions, and article language.

Rank	Affiliates	Total Articles	Rank	Countries/ Regions	Total Articles	Rank	Languages	Total Articles
1	National Taiwan Normal University	52	1	USA	510	1	English	1,345
2	State University System of Florida	39	2	Taiwan	232	2	Portuguese	13
3	National Taiwan University of Science Technology	38	3	England	84	3	Spanish	8
4	National Central University	27	4	Australia	73	4	German	4
5	University of North Carolina	26	5	China	58	5	Turkish	4
6	National Yang Ming Chiao Tung University	21	6	Netherlands	52	6	Dutch	1
7	National Changhua University of Education	20	7	Canada	43	7	French	1
8	North Carolina State University	20	8	Turkey	39			
9	University of Wisconsin System	20	9	Finland	37			
10	The Pennsylvania State System of Higher Education	19	10	Germany	27			

The funds that support the related articles were also examined in this study. In this context, we can see that a total of 414 instances of funding supported articles on games in education. The top 10 funds that offered the most support among these funding agencies are presented in Fig. 6. Accordingly, we see that the most support is provided by the Ministry of Science and Technology of Taiwan (n = 98), the National Science Foundation (n = 51), and the European Commission (n = 34).

Figure 6. Funding agencies

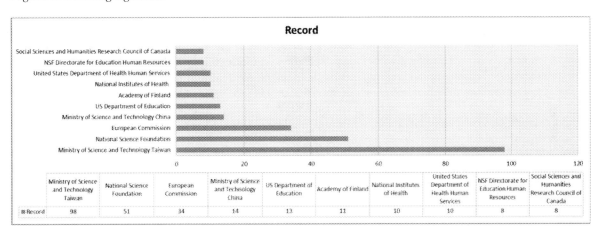

The list of the most cited articles among those concerning games in the field of education is presented in Table 2. Accordingly, the most cited article belongs to the *Computers & Education* journal with the title "Digital game-based learning in high school computer science education: Impact on educational effectiveness and student motivation." This article was published by Papastergiou, M. in 2009. A total of 717 citations were made from the relevant article. An article published in the same journal in 2015, written by Hanus, M.D. and Fox, J., with a total of 5,313 citations, is "Assessing the effects of gamification in the classroom: A longitudinal study on intrinsic motivation, social comparison, satisfaction, effort, and academic performance". When the top 10 most cited articles are examined, we can see that all of them deal with the game in a digital context.

In the second stage of the study, co-authorship between countries and authors was discussed. First of all, the co-authorship network in the countries where articles on games in education are carried out was taken into account (Fig. 7). The image below shows 30 countries and a total of 87 connections between these countries. Thirty countries are gathered in 8 clusters. The countries with the highest number of links among the countries in the image are the USA (22 links), England (18 links), Australia (11 links), the Netherland (9 links), China (9 links), and Taiwan (8 links). This shows that the number of USA and England-related articles is high. Therefore, the co-authorship social networks of these countries seem to be stronger.

In Fig. 8, the results of the co-authorship analysis network among authors are given. In the analysis, it is seen that there are a total of 12 connections and 4 clusters. We can also see that Hwang, G.J., who is in the first cluster, was connected with 6 authors and that Tsai, C.C. is linked with 4 authors. Other authors, on the other hand, seem to have established bilateral connections or conducted their studies alone.

Table 2. Articles with the most citations

Article	Author(s)	Publication Date	Journal	Times Cited
1. Digital game-based learning in high school computer science education: Impact on educational effectiveness and student motivation	Papastergiou, M.	2009	Computers & Education	717
2. Assessing the effects of gamification in the classroom: A longitudinal study on intrinsic motivation, social comparison, satisfaction, effort, and academic performance	Hanus, M.D. & Fox, J.	2015	Computers & Education	531
3. Gamification in education: A systematic mapping study	Dicheva, D., Dichev, C., Agre, G. & Angelova, G.	2015	Journal of Educational Technology & Society	459
4. Making learning fun: Quest Atlantis, a game without guns	Barab, S., Thomas, M., Dodge, T., Carteaux, R. & Tuzun, H.	2005	Educational Technology Research and Development	453
5. Successful implementation of user-centered game based learning in higher education: An example from civil engineering	Ebner, M. & Holzinger, A.	2007	Computers & Education	331
6. Beyond Nintendo: Design and assessment of educational video games for first and second grade students	Ebner, M. & Holzinger, A.	2007	Computers & Education	325
7. Investigating the impact of video games on high school students' engagement and learning about genetics	Annetta, L.A., Minogue, J., Holmes, S.Y. & Cheng, M.T.	2009	Computers & Education	311
8. Video games and the future of learning	Shaffer, D.W., Squire, K.R., Halverson, R. & Gee, J. P.	2005	Phi Delta Kappan	304
9. Exploring the potential of computer and video games for health and physical education: A literature review	Papastergiou, M.	2009	Computers & Education	280
10. Engaging by design: How engagement strategies in popular computer and video games can inform instructional design	Dickey, M.D.	2005	Educational Technology Research and Development	274

The co-citation authors' network analysis of those working on topics related to games is presented in Fig.9. When the cut-off point for at least 100 citations was determined among 27,576 authors working on the concepts related to "play", the number of authors decreased to 23. When the co-citation network of 23 authors was examined, it was revealed that there were 3 clusters. The number of connections in each of the 3 clusters is 22. In the first set (in blue), we find the following authors: Gee, J.P., Shaffer, D.W., Squire, K., Vygotsky, L.S., and Barab, S. With the exception of Vygotsky's work, all of the researchers in this cluster have worked on video games. Therefore, it is possible to say that the researchers in this cluster are mostly cited in terms of video games research. Researchers in the second cluster (in red) are Ryan, R.M., Cohen, J., Clark, D.B., Mayer, R.E., Wouters, P., Bandura, A., Killi, K., and Csikszentmihalyi, M. The researchers in this cluster mainly work in the fields of statistics, methods, measurement and evaluation, and educational psychology. Therefore, it is possible to say that researchers in this cluster are mostly referred to in terms of analysis and explanation of general theorems. Researchers in the third cluster (in green) are Garris, R., Connolly, T.M., Ke, F.F., Malone, T.W., Hwang, G.J., Papastergiou, M., Prensky, M., van Eck, R., and Dickey, M.D. The fields of work of these researchers are games, games and motivation, serious games, and computers games. In general, a very dense citation network is not seen between these 3 clusters but, rather, an inter-cluster citation network structure emerges. When the co-citation network between the authors is considered as a whole, it can be seen that game studies are mostly carried out in the digital field, and researchers from different disciplines are cited.

Figure 7. Co-authorship network among countries.

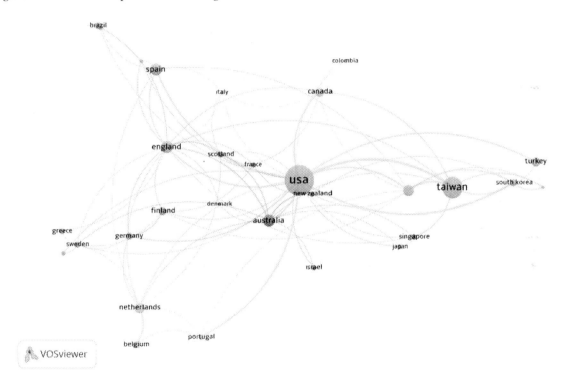

Figure 8. Co-authorship network among authors.

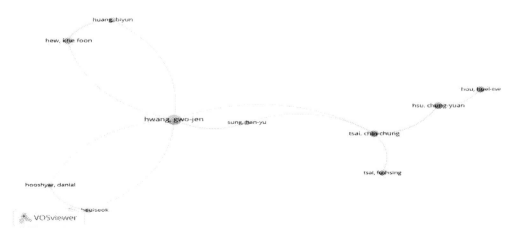

Figure 9. Co-citation authors' network.

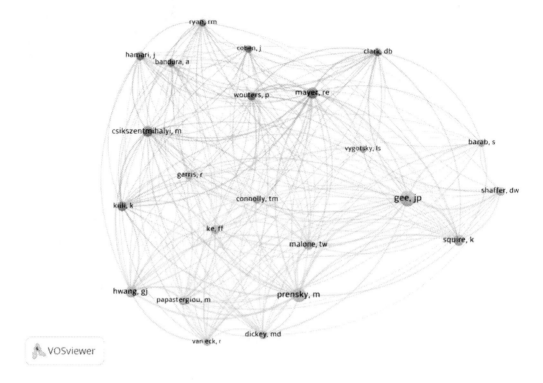

Finally, a relevant co-word analysis was performed. In the co-word analysis, the frequency of the keywords used in the articles and the relationship networks between them were explored and revealed in line with the survey made on WoS (Fig. 10). In the co-word analysis, it is seen that there are basically 2 main clusters. These clusters are shaped around "game-based learning" and "interactive learning environment". In addition, there have been some changes in the relevant keywords over the years. It is seen that the words "game", "board game", and "game theory" are generally used between 2012 and 2014. The words "game-based learning", "games", "educational games", "gaming", and "elementary education" were used between 2014 and 2016. The words "gamification", "computational thinking", "digital game", "higher education", "mobile learning", and "learning analytics" are observable on the same map between 2016 and 2018.

SOLUTIONS AND RECOMMENDATIONS

In this study, in which bibliometric analyses of articles on games in education were carried out, a search was initiated on the WoS database covering the dates 1975 to 31 August 2021. A total of 1,376 studies were accessed according to the relevant inclusion criteria. First, a descriptive analysis of the accessed articles was made. According to the analysis, the number of studies has steadily increased after 2005; the first study on games was carried out in 1975. Most articles on games were published in 2020. The increase in interest in the subject of games and gaming after 2005 can be associated with the change in the understanding of education in many countries. This is because, during this period, a constructivist understanding of education was dominant, and this situation can be explained due to student's personal access to information these days. In this respect, the idea of learning by having fun and mastering knowledge in this way may have guided the increasing trend in game studies in education. Similarly, Hwang and Wu (2012) stated that there was a marked increase during the 2005-2010 period in the research in which they analysed the trends in the studies related to games. According to these two authors, this increase was evident especially in higher education studies.

Figure 10. Co-word analysis

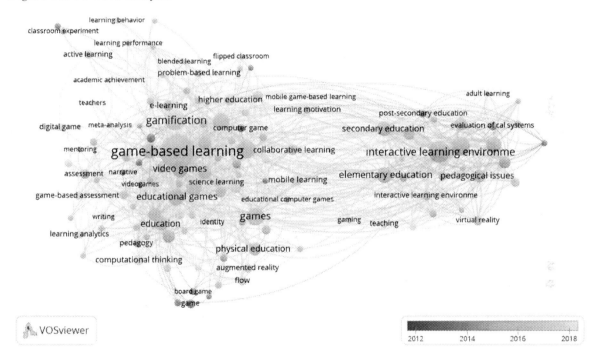

The researchers with the most articles on gaming are Hwang, G.J., Hong, J.C., Hwang, M.Y., and Cheng, M.T. According to WoS records on Hwang, G.J., the number of citations is also quite high; the author is currently working in the field of educational technologies. Hwang, G.J also appears to have strong links in the co-authorship analysis results. This reveals the effect of cooperation in scientific studies on the number of publications. When other researchers and journals that contain the highest number of game studies papers are evaluated together, this shows that game studies researchers publish in journals with predominantly technology-related content. This shows that games and gaming are integrated with technology and with studies in the field of educational technologies that tend to focus on computer games. In fact, in the co-citation analysis of journals that included game-related topics, 3 journals intersect with all of the clusters that had emerged. These journals are Computer & Education, Educational Technology & Society, and the British Journal of Educational Technology, which all include the most game-related articles. These journals frequently include related studies. Therefore, there are citation associations even if they are not directly related.

Considering the distribution of the articles carried out on games in education in terms of the institution, the language of the article, the country, and the region, it can be seen that National Taiwan Normal University has the highest number of articles. When evaluated in terms of countries, most publications originate in the US. America is also the country with the most connections in research. In terms of language, it is observed that the number of publications in English is high. This shows that the country with the highest number of articles and the language of publication overlap. Therefore, both the language used and the high number of collaborative social connections lead to an increase in the number of publications. However, the funds available to researchers should also be taken into account. When examined in terms of funding, it is clear that the institution that provides the most support to researchers is the Ministry of Science and Technology in Taiwan. This indicates that funding is an important source of motivation in terms of support for research, regardless of the number of researchers and language used. In many bibliometric studies, the contribution of funds to research has been emphasized (Huang et al., 2006; Sánchez et al., 2017).

As a result of this descriptive analysis, it was seen that the most cited article is "Digital game-based learning in high school computer science education: Impact on educational effectiveness and student motivation" by Papastergiou,M. Another article by the same author titled "Exploring the potential of computer and video games for health and physical education: A literature review" was published in 2009 and is the 9th most cited publication. Both articles were published in Computers & Education with an h-index of 8,538 (WoS). The high citation rate of the first mentioned article may be due to both the publication of the article in a highly visible journal and the fact that it was a game study about higher education, a publication trend that increased after 2005. Indeed, these findings confirm each other in terms of both the publication year trends and the education medium in which the publication was made.

In this study, current research topics in the field were also revealed by co-word analysis. The use of the terms "gamification", "computational thinking", "digital game", "higher education", "mobile learning", and "learning analytics", especially between 2016-2018, matches the findings above. In other words, game studies in education are carried out in digital environments and are shifting from primary school to higher education levels. This can be associated with the presentation of more design-oriented game education platforms to pre-service teachers.

There are some limitations in this study. First of all, the data of this bibliometric review was pulled from the WoS database, and only the SCI-E, SSCI, and A& HCI indexes were searched in WoS. There is a valid reason for this; since a transparent and rigorous review structure, the most accepted and recognized everywhere, was adopted, these 3 indexes were searched only. However, this situation naturally resulted in a limitation for many studies on games. Both surveying these indexes only and including only accepted articles in the review narrowed the data set. In future studies, these limitations can be overcome and a larger dataset can be examined.

The second limitation of the study is related to search strategies. Within the scope of this research, the keywords "game-based learning", "video games", "game-based pedagogy", "digital games", "gamification", and "game" were surveyed only in the title tab. In other words, the relevant keywords were evaluated in terms of their being included only in the article title, not in the subject content or author keywords. Thus, even if these keywords are included in the content of the subject, it prevented articles that are not very relevant from being included in the bibliometric analysis. This can be perceived as both a limitation and evidence of strong reliability. Therefore, in future studies about games, related keywords could be searched under all headings, but it will be very difficult to separate studies that are not related to games from those that are in the analysis.

Finally, the deadline for the data received over WoS in the related study is 31 August 2021. WoS is constantly updated. Therefore, very different results may be obtained in a search performed on a different date. This shows that the content of the datasets is related to WoS. This may not be seen as a limitation, but if the code specified at the beginning of the study is written in WoS, it may be possible to obtain different results. We believe that the reader should be informed about this issue. This study is very specific in terms of both the restriction in the indexes and the search strategies and inclusion criteria. Therefore, the results achieved are quite unique. A broader perspective can be obtained by expanding the inclusion criteria for searches in different databases.

We hope that this chapter will contribute to the knowledge of general readers, researchers, and game studies as a whole. Another important addition concerns the results of the bibliometric examination and the importance of the funds provided for these types of research. This study is also important for politicians and funding agencies in their support for research as it shows that games have recently been significantly integrated with technology and that combining.

REFERENCES

Allery, L. (2014). Make use of educational games. *Education for Primary Care*, 25(1), 65–66. doi:10.1080/14739879.2014.11494245 PMID:24423808

Bado, N. (2019). Game-based learning pedagogy: A review of the literature. *Interactive Learning Environments*, 1–13. doi:10.1080/10494820.2019.1683587

Chien-Pen, C., Neien-Tzu, H., & Yi-Jeng, H. (2004). *Life education based on game learning strategy for vocational education students in Taiwan.* http://163.21.114.214/ezfiles/0/1000/img/4/20130527-d17.pdf

Clapper, T. C. (2018). Serious games are not all serious. *Simulation & Gaming*, 49(4), 375–377. doi:10.1177/1046878118789763

Cojocariu, V. M., & Boghian, I. (2014). Teaching the relevance of game-based learning to preschool and primary teachers. *Procedia: Social and Behavioral Sciences*, 142, 640–646. doi:10.1016/j.sbspro.2014.07.679

Connolly, T. M., Boyle, E. A., Macarthur, E., Hainey, T., & Boyle, J. M. (2012). A systematic literature review of empirical evidence on computer games and serious games. *Computers & Education*, 59(2), 661–686. doi:10.1016/j.compedu.2012.03.004

De Freitas, S. (2018). Are games effective learning tools? A review of educational games. *Journal of Educational Technology & Society*, 21(2), 74–84.

Frost, J. L., Wortham, S. C., & Reifel, S. (2012). *Play and child development* (4th ed.). Pearson Education Inc.

Garvey, C. (1990). *Play*. Harvard University Press.

Gorbanev, I., Agudelo-Londoño, S., González, R. A., Cortes, A., Pomares, A., Delgadillo, V., Yepes, F. J., & Muñoz, Ó. (2018). A systematic review of serious games in medical education: Quality of evidence and pedagogical strategy. *Medical Education Online*, *23*(1), 1438718. doi:10.1080/10872981.2018.1438718 PMID:29457760

Harman, K., Koohang, A., & Paliszkiewicz, J. (2014). Scholarly interest in gamification: A citation network analysis. *Industrial Management & Data Systems*, *114*(9), 1438–1452. doi:10.1108/IMDS-07-2014-0208

Huang, Y. L., Ho, Y. S., & Chuang, K. Y. (2006). Bibliometric analysis of nursing research in Taiwan 1991-2004. *The Journal of Nursing Research*, *14*(1), 75–81. doi:10.1097/01.JNR.0000387564.57188.b4 PMID:16547908

Hwang, G. J., & Wu, P. H. (2012). Advancements and trends in digital game-based learning research: A review of publications in selected journals from 2001 to 2010. *British Journal of Educational Technology*, *43*(1), E6–E10. doi:10.1111/j.1467-8535.2011.01242.x

Irmade, O., & Anisa, N. (2021, March). Research trends of serious games: Bibliometric analysis. [). IOP Publishing.]. *Journal of Physics: Conference Series*, *1842*(1), 012036. doi:10.1088/1742-6596/1842/1/012036

Jackson, L. C., O'Mara, J., Moss, J., & Jackson, A. C. (2018). A critical review of the effectiveness of narrative-driven digital educational games. *International Journal of Game-Based Learning*, *8*(4), 32–49. doi:10.4018/IJGBL.2018100103

Juul, J. (2005). *Half-real: Video games between real rules and fictional worlds*. MIT Press.

Ke, F. (2016). Designing and integrating purposeful learning in gameplay: A systematic review. *Educational Technology Research and Development*, *64*(2), 219–244. doi:10.100711423-015-9418-1

Lai, N. K., Ang, T. F., Por, L. Y., & Liew, C. S. (2018). The impact of play on child development - a literature review. *European Early Childhood Education Research Journal*, *26*(5), 625–643. doi:10.1080/1350293X.2018.1522479

Lenormand, M. (2019). The importance of not being Ernest: An archaeology of child's play in Freud's writings (and some implications for psychoanalytic theory and practice). *The International Journal of Psycho-Analysis*, *100*(1), 52–76. doi:10.1080/00207578.2018.1489708 PMID:33945712

Liu, Z., Moon, J., Kim, B., & Dai, C. P. (2020). Integrating additivity in educational games: A combined bibliometric analysis and meta-analysis review. *Educational Technology Research and Development*, *68*(4), 1931–1959. doi:10.100711423-020-09791-4

Martí-Parreño, J., Méndez-Ibáñez, E., & Alonso-Arroyo, A. (2016). The use of gamification in education: A bibliometric and text mining analysis. *Journal of Computer Assisted Learning*, *32*(6), 663–676. doi:10.1111/jcal.12161

Moher, D., Liberati, A., Tetzlaff, J., & Altman, D. G. (2009). Preferred reporting items for systematic reviews and meta-analyses: The PRISMA statement. *International Journal of Surgery*, *8*(5), 336–341. doi:10.1016/j.ijsu.2010.02.007 PMID:20171303

Pham, H. H., Vuong, Q. H., Luong, D. H., Nguyen, T. T., Dinh, V. H., & Ho, M. T. (2021). A bibliometric review of research on international student mobility's in Asia with Scopus dataset between 1984 and 2019. *Scientometrics*, *126*(6), 5201–5224. doi:10.100711192-021-03965-4

Salen, K., & Zimmerman, E. (2004). *Rules of play: Game design fundamentals*. MIT Press.

Samiee, S., & Chabowski, B. R. (2012). Knowledge structure in international marketing: A multi-method bibliometric analysis. *Journal of the Academy of Marketing Science*, *40*(2), 364–386. doi:10.100711747-011-0296-8

Sánchez, A. D., Del Río, M. D. L. C., & García, J. Á. (2017). Bibliometric analysis of publications on wine tourism in the databases Scopus and WoS. *European Research on Management and Business Economics*, *23*(1), 8–15. doi:10.1016/j.iedeen.2016.02.001

Schöbel, S., Saqr, M., & Janson, A. (2021). Two decades of game concepts in digital learning environments–A bibliometric study and research agenda. *Computers & Education*, *173*, 104296. doi:10.1016/j.compedu.2021.104296

Shah, A., Kraemer, K. R., Won, C. R., Black, S., & Hasenbein, W. (2018). Developing digital intervention games for mental disorders: A review. *Games for Health Journal*, *7*(4), 213–224. doi:10.1089/g4h.2017.0150 PMID:30106642

Silva, R. D. O. S., Pereira, A. M., Araújo, D. C. S. A. D., Rocha, K. S. S., Serafini, M. R., & De Lyra, D. P. Jr. (2021). Effect of digital serious games related to patient care in pharmacy education: A systematic review. *Simulation & Gaming*, *52*(5), 104687812098889. doi:10.1177/1046878120988895

Singer, E. (2013). Play and playfulness, basic features of early childhood education. *European Early Childhood Education Research Journal*, *21*(2), 172–184. doi:10.1080/1350293X.2013.789198

Sipiyaruk, K., Gallagher, J. E., Hatzipanagos, S., & Reynolds, P. A. (2018). A rapid review of serious games: From healthcare education to dental education. *European Journal of Dental Education*, *22*(4), 243–257. doi:10.1111/eje.12338 PMID:29573165

Subhash, S., & Cudney, E. A. (2018). Gamified learning in higher education: A systematic review of the literature. *Computers in Human Behavior*, *87*, 192–206. doi:10.1016/j.chb.2018.05.028

Trinidad, M., Ruiz, M., & Calderón, A. (2021). A bibliometric analysis of gamification research. *IEEE Access: Practical Innovations, Open Solutions*, *9*, 46505–46544. doi:10.1109/ACCESS.2021.3063986

Van Eck, N. J., & Waltman, L. (2010). Software survey: VOSviewer, a computer program for bibliometric mapping. *Scientometrics*, *84*(2), 523–538. doi:10.100711192-009-0146-3 PMID:20585380

Yuratich, D. (2020). Ratio! A game of judgment: Using game-based learning to teach legal reasoning. *The Law Teacher*, 1–14.

Zhonggen, Y. (2019). A meta-analysis of use of serious games in education over a decade. *International Journal of Computer Games Technology*, *17*, 1–8. doi:10.1155/2019/4797032

Zupic, I., & Čater, T. (2015). Bibliometric methods in management and organization. *Organizational Research Methods*, *18*(3), 429–472. doi:10.1177/1094428114562629

ADDITIONAL READING

Gülmez, D., Özteke, İ., & Gümüş, S. (2021). Overview of educational research from Turkey published in international journals: A bibliometric analysis. *Education in Science*, *46*(206), 1–27.

Hallinger, P., & Kovačević, J. (2019). A bibliometric review of research on educational administration: Science mapping the literature, 1960 to 2018. *Review of Educational Research*, *89*(3), 335–369. doi:10.3102/0034654319830380

Klock, A. C. T., Gasparini, I., Pimenta, M. S., & Hamari, J. (2020). Tailored gamification: A review of literature. *International Journal of Human-Computer Studies*, *144*, 102495. doi:10.1016/j.ijhcs.2020.102495

Sánchez, A. D., Del Río, M. D. L. C., & García, J. Á. (2017). Bibliometric analysis of publications on wine tourism in the databases Scopus and WoS. *European Research on Management and Business Economics*, *23*(1), 8–15. doi:10.1016/j.iedeen.2016.02.001

Song, P., & Wang, X. (2020). A bibliometric analysis of worldwide educational artificial intelligence research development in recent twenty years. *Asia Pacific Education Review*, *21*(3), 473–486. doi:10.100712564-020-09640-2

KEY TERMS AND DEFINITIONS

Bibliometric Analysis: The numerical analysis of publications produced by individuals or institutions in a certain area, during a certain period, and in a certain region, along with the relations or connection points between these publications.

Educational Game: A teaching technique that ensures the reinforcement of learned information and its repetition in a more comfortable environment.

Gamification: This consists of the reward systems and competitive elements used in games using digital game design techniques in non-game elements, especially in the education world in an interactive and attractive way.

Chapter 3
Amalgamation of Game-Based Learning With Interactive Instructional Strategies for Active Learner Engagement

Ankit Dhamija
https://orcid.org/0000-0003-4456-9680
Amity University, Haryana, India

Deepika Dhamija
Amity University, Haryana, India

ABSTRACT

In recent years, the teaching-learning process in higher education has undergone unprecedented change. Learners from across the world can enroll in any university using online platforms. This learning freedom is fantastic for all stakeholders, but it raises some serious concerns, such as how to ensure effective learner engagement and make the learning experience meaningful for the learners. While technology has aided learning, it has also become a significant source of distraction for students, as they spend too much time on gadgets solely for entertainment. This necessitates innovative and engaging teaching styles from educators. Designing course content as a game makes learning more engaging as learners get a sense of motivation and accomplishment. However, aligning games with lesson plans, designing assessment criteria, and learning outcomes takes a significant amount of time and effort. Hence, this chapter proposes learner-centered interactive instructional strategies that employ GBL to pique learners' curiosity and recommends popular GBL platforms for creating educational games.

DOI: 10.4018/978-1-7998-7271-9.ch003

INTRODUCTION

Every person enjoys playing games of some kind because they want to have fun, and games have the characteristics to provide that enjoyment. It's a never-ending phenomenon, and people will continue to play computer games for years to come (Sailer, Hense, Mayr, & Mandl, 2017). This is due to the fact that games keep people engaged in achieving some goal, keeps them focused on a specific goal, and when that goal is achieved, the game player feels a sense of accomplishment (Dias, 2017). People who play games experience a significant increase in efficiency and morale, and they simply feel inspired and happy. (Gee, 2007; Ryan, Rigby, & Przybylski, 2006) after playing games. Individuals' positive characteristics can be effectively used in the teaching learning process through game-based learning or gamification. Since 2011, this term has caught the interest of the academic community (Deterding, Dixon, Khaled, & Nacke, 2011). Several definitions of game-based learning have been proposed in the literature, with researchers proposing definitions of game-based learning in various contexts. (Pho & Dinscore, 2015; Al Fatta, Maksom, & Zakaria, 2019) defined it as an instruction-based system that relies on quantifiable procedures and outcomes. (Brown et al., 2018; Lengyel, 2020; Talib et al., 2019) proposed the concept of connecting games with technology and software and then using it for education, which they termed as "digital game based learning." To put it simply, game-based learning is a creative instructional style or pedagogy used by educators in which highly engaging games are designed for learners using digital technology and software. This statement encapsulates the entire goal of incorporating games into education. According to a report by (Forbes, 2019), games are very popular among young learners, and they spend an average of seven hours per week playing them. Some of the reasons for this are the affordability of smart devices, low-cost internet plans, and the highly captivating nature of games and entertainment as a sole purpose. There's nothing wrong with playing games, but it's common knowledge that gaining access to anything can be dangerous. The same is true here, where students who spend more time playing video games may find it difficult to concentrate on their studies. Learners can often be seen engrossed in their gadgets for hours, even while in classrooms, because the minds will always seek some sort of excitement and challenge. Classrooms were thought to be the ideal place for teacher-learner interaction where both can share ideas (Wade, 1994), but with access to all of these devices, the learners are distracted, have such a feeling of boredom during lectures since they believe that all resources pertaining to the course are easily available on the internet, and they consider themselves to be digital learners who have access to just about everything (Wade, 1994). (Andone, Dron, Boyne, and Pemberton, 2005) asserted that digital learners can be trained in their own way, i.e. through technology. As a result, in order to maximise learner participation and keep them from becoming passive, teachers have turned to innovative instructional strategies for active learner engagement. It encompasses a variety of techniques and pedagogies, some of which utilise technology and others that do not; however, each of these is student-centric and, when used effectively, can be beneficial in generating student interest in a particular course under consideration. (Dhamija, 2020) proposed thirteen such strategies, only a few of which used technology and the rest did not. Gamification, also known as game-based learning, is a technology-based innovative instructional strategy that can be used for active learner engagement in both a classroom setting and a diverse online environment.

Hence, the purpose of this chapter is to bring to fore, the recent advancements in game based learning and interactive instructional strategies where efforts have been made to explain both these concepts in great detail with an objective to enhance students' learning experience and their active engagement. Since GBL requires the use of IT tools, the chapter also presents a discussion on some most relevant platforms for GBL. The chapter will assist teachers, students as well as academic administrators & educators in understanding the concepts of GBL and interactive instructional strategies. The authors firmly believe that after reading this chapter, the teachers will be more equipped with relevant knowledge, techniques, and approaches about GBL and innovative instructional strategies and how these can be used together for effective classroom teaching. For students, the chapter will bring in new perspective in the way they learn and for academic administrators and educators, the chapter is going to bring a realization that the teaching-learning process requires modern methods and innovative pedagogies to remain relevant. In this way, the chapter is quite relevant to all the stakeholders.

This chapter begins with a detailed background and analysis of recent advancements in game-based learning and innovative instructional strategies where emphasis has been made to explain the need of game based learning in modern day teaching-learning. Following that, various game based interactive instructional strategies are presented. Further, the chapter also discusses the various issues and challenges associated with implementation of game based learning. Furthermore, the chapter discusses the scenarios in which these innovative instructional strategies can be used. Finally, the chapter ends with key recommendations and a conclusion.

BACKGROUND AND LITERATURE REVIEW

This section throws light on the factors that led to the development of game based learning and interactive instructional strategies, how these are related to each other. The advancements that have taken place in GBL to the present state are presented through an exhaustive literature review of recent studies which highlights the recent advancements in game-based learning in various educational domains. Also presented are recent studies emphasizing the use of innovative teaching pedagogies for active learner engagement.

It is critical to understand the most important element in the teaching-learning process, which is the student, in order to give a background of game-based learning and innovative instructional methodologies. Because today's students have access to digital devices and high-speed internet, they spend the majority of their time utilizing these devices for amusement, such as video watching, information seeking, and game playing, to mention a few. When playing video games, the player remains concentrated and engaged in the game, which is a favorable attribute when viewed through the eyes of a teacher. This is because the academic community around the world is concerned about the continued decline in student participation. When students sit silently in classrooms with nil or minimal class engagement, expressing indifference in the topic being taught and being unresponsive to teacher's enquiries, they are described as "passive" (Mohd Yusof, et al 2011; Hussein, 2010; Bas, 2010). The key reasons for this passive behaviour are classroom size (Shaheen, Cheng, Audrey, & Lim, 2010), classmate perception (Maziha, Suryani, and Melor, 2010), and instructor behaviour, skill set, and pedagogy chosen (Kamarudin et al., 2009). As a result, the teaching community has shifted its focus to employing novel teaching pedagogies to excite students and increase their participation in class. Moving ahead from using regular IT tools like power-point slides and videos, teachers are now designing and delivering course content as a game with elements of challenge, pleasure, and learning, leveraging the positive attribute of game playing. Since 2011, GBL research has accelerated, and it is now being used successfully in a variety of fields. Furthermore, traditional instructional approaches must be replaced with new teaching methods, which are referred to as 'innovative instructional strategies', in order to deliver course information as a game and stimulate curiosity about the game. These are learner-centered teaching pedagogies that have been deliberately created with the goal of encouraging learners to engage in active learning. These include blended learning (Cummings et al., 2015), flipped classroom (Gilboy, Heinerichs and Pazzaglia, 2015; Clark, 2015), brain storming & discussion, reciprocal teaching, fieldtrips, writing, roleplaying, storytelling and visualization (Tate, 2013) and many others. Student interaction is a common feature of all of these new innovative educational strategies. Learners will be able to think in higher order with the help of these methods. As a result, delivering course content using an innovative instructional technique combined with game-based learning can be quite effective in engaging students. Hence, this chapter proposes a combinatorial approach of games with innovative instructional methodologies.

The section further presents a systematic review of the trends in digital game-based learning where efforts have been made to include studies which apply GBL in various domains and which used an innovative pedagogy. The review has been categorized according to various platforms and disciplines

Studies Utilizing Gaming Platforms

Few authors utilized various gaming platforms for game creation where (Esteves et al., 2018) used mobile technologies such as EDPuzzle, Kahoot, and Socrative to assess the impact of a game-based learning approach in an engineering classroom. The EDPuzzle allowed for video editing and question inserting, Kahoot encourages learner collaboration in a variety of subject areas, and Socrative allows for the creation and implementation of various activities, including quizzes, with the class. The Kahoot platform was used as a GBL tool with over 300 participants, and three assessment methods were used. The results showed that learners had a higher percentage of correct answers. Similarly, the effects of combining game-based learning with Kinect technology on students' attitudes toward the English language were studied by (Yükseltürk, Altiok, and Baser, 2018) through two experimental questionnaire-based approaches. A survey was conducted on 62 students where and a significantly positive change in participants' attitude and self-efficacy scores was recorded as Kinect technology detected motions, gestures, and voice commands using a camera, microphone, and sensors., In the same year, (Li et al., 2018) identified a lack of information literacy skills as a barrier to achieving the Web Intelligence course's learning outcomes. To overcome this barrier, game-based learning was used in conjunction with the online role-playing platform MEGA World. The research was conducted using questionnaires and surveys. The outcomes showed that the technique used effectively facilitated the development of information literacy.

Studies from Engineering Discipline

(Jin et al., 2018) investigated the effectiveness of game-based learning in raising cybersecurity awareness among high school students by creating four game-based cybersecurity course modules that included hands-on activities. The findings revealed that the proposed approach was successful in raising awareness through innovative teaching methods and an expanded curriculum. Similarly, (Mavromihales, Holmes, and Racasan, 2019) used an experimental approach to teach a course on Computer Aided Design by using game-based learning in the mechanical engineering discipline where a Resin Puzzle game was created in which color-coded polymer pieces were used by learners who were divided into two groups: experiment and control. The experiment group consisted of students who played the game while the control group participants did not. The learning experiences of both groups were compared across a variety of parameters, and the results revealed that the majority of students applied skills and knowledge, found it enjoyable and competitive, and that the activity encouraged collaboration among learners.

Studies from Management and Social Science Discipline

(Vasquez et al., 2017) used a game-based learning approach to help students improve their social and management skills. The approach was implemented as two games: Recursion and Simulation, the first based on a programming course and the second on improving the learners' marketing management skills. The outcomes had a positive impact on the students, and teamwork and collaborative skills were learned. In another study, the utility of game-based learning as an instructional strategy for tertiary education was investigated by (Ding et al., 2017) through a survey-based approach for finance students. They created an online stock trading game, and compared the results to traditional learning methods. The results demonstrated that the game-based method was more effective for the students. (Silva, Rodrigues, and Leal, 2019) used flow theory to assess the impact of game-based learning in Portuguese undergraduate accounting and management students. The impact of game characteristics on students' learning flow was assessed using structured equation modelling. The findings indicated that students were more interested and motivated. (Cipto, Yogi, and Dudung, 2020) used 100 samples from accounting, economics, and management student groups and used the gain scores method for analysis, where the learning outcomes of the experimental group with learning game treatment and the control group learning outcomes were examined and analysed to determine their effectiveness. Analyses revealed that using game-based learning to improve learning outcomes is extremely effective. GBL has seen applications in in psychology domain also where (Stansbury and Earnest, 2017) used gamification to design and quantitatively evaluate an industrial organisational psychology course that included elements of roleplay, narration, and social interaction. The experiment was carried out by dividing students into experimental and control groups, with the experimental group experiencing higher levels of motivation, engagement, and enjoyment.

Language Based Studies

(Lin and Hwang, 2018) used a two-way approach to teach business writing in an English as a Foreign Language (EFL) course by integrating game-based learning with flipped classroom. They asserted that context-based GBL can be an effective method of engaging students. The experimental approach demonstrated that the flipped contextual game-based learning approach not only improves the time involvement of the students' learning but also improves the English writing performance of the EFL students. Tan, Ganapathy, and Kaur (2018) sought to assess the motivation and engagement levels of undergraduate English language students in the media. Kahoot!, a game based learning platform was used to conduct the study and the results show that using it fosters and reinforces learning in participants.

General Survey Based Studies

A recent study by (Chang and Hwang, 2019) looked into the major countries that use game-based learning, the major types of games and learning styles used, and so on. The game types were classified into nine categories, with the results revealing that role playing, simulation, and gamification are the most commonly used game types. Furthermore, smartphones are the most commonly used device for imparting game-based learning, and the subjects where mobile-enabled game-based learning was used ranged from engineering to social science, arts, languages, mathematics, and business management, among others. This breadth demonstrates that game-based learning can be used effectively in almost any field. They concluded that more effective pedagogical approaches can be used by taking personalised feedback on students' reflections and psychological support into account, and that highly engaging gamification models are required to engage students. (Hosseini, Hartt, and Mostafapour, 2019) investigated the effectiveness of games in higher education without the use of technology, as well as students' perceptions of learning and engagement in computer science courses. The findings revealed a pressing need for formal assessment methods for game-based learning, as well as increased student engagement and teamwork. (Gündüz and Akkoyunlu, 2020) worked to highlight the efficacy of gamification in flipped learning. The study was conducted using a mixed-methods sequential explanatory design, which entails collecting and analysing quantitative and then qualitative data, and students were divided into experimental and control groups. The results showed that the experimental group outperformed the control group in terms of interaction data, participation, and achievement.

Table 1 provides an overview of the key findings from papers on gamified learning frameworks.

Table 1. Summary of recent work about game based learning in higher education

Author(s)	Year	Study Focus	Key Findings
Chang and Hwang	2019	Review of trends in GBL. Various fields like Engineering, Management, Arts, Mathematics etc	• Categorized games into nine types. • Simulation and gamification being most popular game types. • Smartphones being the mostly utilized device for GBL.
Vasquez et al.	2017	• Aimed towards improving the social and management skills of the students. • Based on Programming and Management course	• Implemented as Recursion and Simulation game. • Positive impact on teamwork and collaborative skills observed in students.
Ding et al.	2017	• Tertiary education • Used for Finance students.	• Game implemented for online stock trading and results compared with traditional learning methods. • Game based method to be more effective for the students.
Esteves et al.	2018	• To assess the impact of GBL using various technologies like Kahoot, Socrative etc. • Used in Engineering discipline	Upon usage of three assessment methods, the GBL approach resulted in higher percentage of correct answers from learners.
Li et al.	2018	• Usage of GBL to improve information literacy skills of learners. • Used in Web Intelligence course • Utilization of online Role Playing platform MEGA World	Adopted GBL technique effectively facilitated the development of information literacy.
Lin and Hwang	2018	• Combined approach of connecting GBL with Flipped classroom. • Used for English as Foreign Language course	• Enhanced time involvement of the students' learning was observed. • Improved English writing performance observed.
Jin et al.	2018	• To evaluate the GBL effectiveness • Used for Cyber Security course. • Development of four game based course modules.	• Awareness created through innovative teaching methods and enriched curriculum.
Yükseltürk, Altiok and Baser	2018	• Merging of GBL with Kinect technology. • Used in English Language course	• Recorded significantly positive change in attitude and self-efficacy scores of participants.

continues on following page

Table 1. Continued

Author(s)	Year	Study Focus	Key Findings
Mavromihales, Holmes and Racasan	2019	• Application of GBL in mechanical engineering discipline. • Design of Resin Puzzle game.	• Students applied skills and knowledge, found it enjoyable and competitive. • Activity promoted collaboration among learners.
Tan, Ganapathy and Kaur	2018	• Evaluation of motivation and engagement levels of undergraduate students. • Used in English language for the media	• Fostered and reinforced learning in participants using Kahoot!.
Stansbury and Earnest	2017	• evaluating an industrial organizational psychology course when taught using GBL	High motivation levels, engagement and enjoyment experienced by students.
Silva, Rodrigues and Leal	2019	• To determine the impact of GBL in Portuguese undergraduate students. • Used in Accounting and Management education	Higher interest and motivation levels among students was observed.
Hosseini, Hartt, and Mostafapour	2019	• To assess the effectiveness of games without the use of technology in higher education. • Used for Computer Science course.	• Formal assessment methods are required to leverage full benefits of GBL. • Increased student engagement and teamwork was observed.
Cipto, Yogi and Dudung	2020	• To measure the effectiveness of game based learning. • Used for Accounts, Economics and Management students	GBL based pedagogic approach prove to be highly effective in improving learning outcomes
Gündüz and Akkoyunlu	2020	To evaluate the effectiveness of gamification in flipped learning.	High scores achieved by experiment group students in terms of interaction data, participation, and achievement.

A close examination of the above table reveals that in recent years, game-based learning has grown in popularity and is being adopted as the preferred pedagogical tool in higher education by teachers. Figure 1 depicts this with various Domain areas.

ISSUES AND CHALLENGES IN GAME BASED LEARNING

Although more universities, teachers, and students recognise the value of Game Based Learning, there are still many issues and challenges that must be addressed before this type of learning can be adopted by masses.

1. Aligning games with course curriculum and objectives

In order to be instructive and valuable in the classroom, Game Based Learning approaches must achieve certain learning outcomes. To adapt the games to these diverse results, a variety of difficulty levels, challenges, and a number of steps or levels to "win" the game are required. Also, teachers should consider which sections of the course curriculum may be conveniently taught as a game.

Figure 1. Recent areas leveraging game based learning

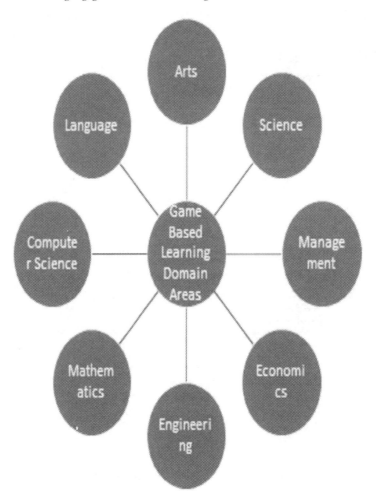

2. Providing appropriate gaming environment

Although the majority of today's students have grown up with access to the internet, smart portable devices, and computers, this does not apply to all learners. As a result, teachers must ensure that each learner is comfortable using these devices, and that the games are developed with a basic graphical user interface (GUI) and clear instructions on how to play the game are present.

3. Breaking through cultural boundaries

Dealing with learners and parents from various cultural backgrounds is another problem that teachers confront when implementing GBL. Parents continue to believe that games are a waste of time and that learning cannot occur through game play. As a result, altering this mindset and persuading them of the benefits of GBL is a difficult process.

4. Cost and Effort Factor

Teachers and institutions must put in sufficient effort in terms of time, money, and knowledge to ensure that the GBL is effectively contributing to improving students' learning experiences. Due to the high expense of game development, not every institution will have this kind of resource available.

5. Aligning Games with Assessment Criteria

Aligning games with evaluation criteria is another difficult challenge in GBL deployment. How will the learners' game performance be assessed? How important will game play be in the final evaluation? How many times can the students try during the game? Before GBL can be used in classrooms, these and other comparable questions must be answered.

GAME BASED INTERACTIVE INSTRUCTIONAL STRATEGIES AS SOLUTION

To address the concerns raised in the preceding section, games must be strategically integrated into the curriculum, with teachers considering which modules/topics from the curriculum could be given as a game. Furthermore, creating a game is not enough; its implementation is equally crucial. The students must be given trust, fully briefed on the purpose, and help at various stages must be provided. All of these tasks can be easily completed with the help of a well-chosen interactive instructional strategy. In the recent past, teachers have been turning to innovative instructional strategies in order to ensure active engagement and participation from learners. (Tate, 2013) presented several instructional strategies for effectively engaging the learners' brains, including brainstorming and discussion, reciprocal teaching, drawing and artwork, writing, field work, problem-based learning, humour and games, and story-telling. Then, for online and blended learning environments, various learner-centered active learning strategies were proposed by (Cummings, Shelton, Mason, & Baur, 2015). They advocated for the use of simulations (creating a replica of the original system with which learners can interact), role playing (imagining oneself as a character in a story), problem-based and project-based learning (giving learners real-world problems to solve using required skill set), case-based learning, wikis and blogs, peer collaboration, peer assessment and peer instruction, and feedback. According to them, such instructional strategies improve higher order thinking and must be carefully incorporated by instructors in their course content delivery.

Using these as a starting point, (Dhamija & Dhamija, 2020) classified various innovative teaching pedagogies into thirteen categories, as shown in Figure 2. They emphasised that all of these innovative strategies can be used with or without technological support, and that it is entirely dependent on the individual teacher's imagination, creativity, and efforts.

(Munoz, Duart, & Sancho-Vinuesa, 2014) argued that by combining technology and human interaction, instructional strategies can become interactive, and knowledge can emerge as a result of such interaction. Further, (Dhamija, Sharma and Dhamija, 2020) analysed the present state of EdTech organization penetration in South Asia where they assessed several EdTech companies operating in this region on various parameters. The result revealed that Byju's is the most popular EdTech platform which is incorporating game based learning for content delivery.

Figure 2. Innovative teaching pedagogies

The authors also propose using game-based learning in conjunction with technology to deliver content through interactive instructional strategies. Although game-based learning can be implemented without the use of technology, it can also be done through quizzes, fun games in the classroom, interactive sessions, flipped classrooms, roleplays, and many other methods. However, with today's information and communication technologies, game-based learning can be implemented more sophisticatedly and its benefits reaped more effectively. As a result, the author discusses two major important interactive instructional strategies implemented through game-based learning in the following section.

1. E-Meta Plan through Game Based Learning

Meta plan is an interactive learning method developed by Meta plan, a German company (Habershon,1993). The method's goal is to collect and organise information, ideas, and points of view based on some common characteristics. This strategy is used by instructors to organise their students' learning and problem-solving activities in groups. It can also be regarded as a method of group facilitation. It is also a group facilitation method and a communication model in which opinions are formed, a common

Amalgamation of Game-Based Learning With Interactive Instructional Strategies for Learner Engagement

understanding is formed, and objectives, recommendations, and action plans are developed to focus on a problem and its potential solutions. This method is also employed when moderating group discussions. This technique is distinctive in that it can be used in the classroom without the use of technology. The only requirement for using Meta plan is the availability of some stationery material such as various coloured chart papers, rectangular and oval shaped cards, multiple colour markers, cello tape, glue or bonding agent, scissor, board pins, pin boards, and some A4 size white sheets. This is a traditional method of implementing Meta Plan in the classroom that allows students to be engaged effectively. Figure 3 depicts the required material, students participating in a Meta plan session, and a meta plan cluster created by students and a teacher to explain the concept via a Meta plan cluster.

Figure 3. Meta plan implementation in classroom

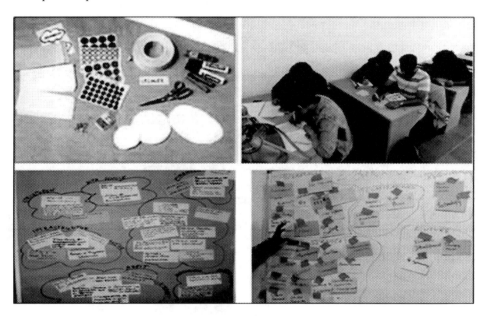

The modern implementation of Meta Plan includes a game element and inclusion of technology and is suitable for an online environment. This means that physical presence of learners and teacher in classroom is not necessarily required and students can participate in the activity through their laptop with stable internet connection and that too from the comfort of their home. This type of Meta Plan implementation is being referred by authors as E-Meta Plan. The stepwise process of implementing E-Meta Plan is listed below:

a. In an online classroom setting, the teacher initiates a topic by giving a brief introduction.
b. Instead of using stationery items, the teacher creates a Powerpoint presentation with Briefing of the topic as first slide and Rules to be followed on second slide. The third slide will have 8-10 square shapes of different colors.
c. The students may be divided in teams of 2-3 and the presentation can be shared online and each student is added as a collaborator on the presentation with editing permissions.

d. According to the rules stated on the slide, the student groups must work on their designated slide by taking appropriate shapes, adding appropriate keyword/text to the shape, and placing it in the most appropriate place on the slide, resulting in several clusters formed by each student group.
e. By switching the slides, the teacher can monitor the progress of all groups and clear any student doubts.
f. The teacher must develop an ideal Meta Plan cluster and assessment criteria, which can be shared with students either before or after they complete the task.
g. Once each group has completed their respective Meta Plan, the students are asked to share their thought process and explain their Meta Plan cluster, and also the teacher should share the ideal assessment criteria and evaluate each group's Meta Plan cluster and complete the assessment.

Figure 4 depicts the various stages of E-Meta Plan implementation. The teacher first creates a presentation on a topic and announces the team description, instructions for creating Meta Plan, and assessment criteria, and then provides the various coloured shapes that students use to create their e-meta plan.

Figure 4. E-meta plan implementation through technology

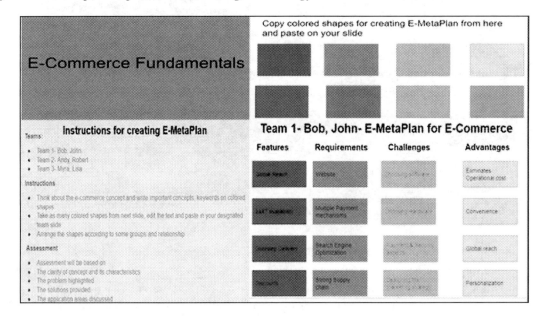

This is an effective method of engaging students in an online setting; students will find it interesting, engaging, thought provoking, and knowledge application will occur. However, there are a few requirements that must be met for this type of environment to function, such as the use of laptop computers, a stable internet connection, and knowledge of presentation and word processing software.

2. Game Based Role Play

Role-playing is a method that is being used in a variety of settings and subject areas (Rao & Stupans, 2012). In essence, it is the technique of having students act out certain roles - usually unfamiliar to them - in a case-based scenario in order to absorb course content or comprehend "difficult or ambiguous concepts" (Sogunro, 2004). Role-playing has been hailed as a more effective technique than more traditional teaching approaches for meeting the demands of today's college student (see Rosa, 2012, and Bobbit et. al., 2001). By putting themselves in the shoes of another person, students practise empathy and perspective taking. This can result in increased self-awareness and contemplation on the student's part (Westrup and Planander, 2013; Sogunro, 2004) Students form a stronger cognitive link with the subject when they put what they've learned in theory into practise, making it easier for them to learn (Johnson & Johnson, 1997). Finally, using role-playing as a training method allows students to modify their behaviours and apply best practises in real-world situations (Beard et al., 1995) Figure 5 depicts a group of people engaged in roleplaying.

Figure 5. Role play in a traditional setting

Combining Role Play with technology and game-based learning necessitated extensive thought on the part of teachers. It must be ensured that role play is both a fun activity and a source of enhancing participants' existing knowledge. Furthermore, the assessment criteria must be thoroughly designed and clearly communicated to students so that they are aware of the parameters against which they will be evaluated. A sample Game Based Role Play sequence for a programming or software engineering course in a Computer Science class is described in the steps below:

a. As a first step, the students are divided into teams of 8-10 students in each group.
b. The game instructions are explained to the students. For example, for this scenario, each group is supposed to follow the stages of Software Development Life Cycle (SDLC) and take various roles for each of the participants.

c. Next, the groups are asked to choose roles for each participant like the Client, Requirement Analyst, Designers, Developers, Testers, Maintenance personnel etc.
d. Based on each participant's skill set, the group members assign roles to each participant.
e. Then, the details of a small sample software project with very few lines of code is assigned to each group.
f. The Client need to explain his requirement to Requirement Analyst as an informal written document.
g. The Requirement Analyst is required to convert this informal requirement document into a formal Software Requirement Specification (SRS) document with all the necessary details.
h. Then taking input from the SRS, the designer needs to apply their knowledge and create designs of the software various techniques.
i. The designs serve as input for the development/coding team who do all the programming for the software application.
j. The testing team apply various testing techniques on the developed application and record the results, find the errors and communicate those to development team.
k. The errors, if any, are removed by the developers and application is again tested by testing team members and approve it as OK.
l. The maintenance team creates the manuals for usage of the application and prepare the schedule for its maintenance.
m. Finally, the software is delivered to the client.

This is a complete description of the software development process that each group must complete by applying the knowledge gained in the Software Engineering and Programming course. If necessary, the teacher can create assessment criteria for each stage of the game, which may include various rubrics. The clarity of the SRS document, how correct the designs have been made, is the code error free, what and how many errors are found by the testing team, and so on may all be factors in the assessment. Following the completion of the allotted time, each group is asked to give a presentation on the tasks completed by them, and the teachers can evaluate their work based on the assessment criteria decided upon beforehand.

Figure 6. Game based role play illustration

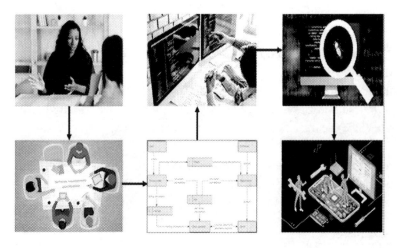

Amalgamation of Game-Based Learning With Interactive Instructional Strategies for Learner Engagement

This new Role Play variant can be used in both a physical setting, such as a computer lab, and an online setting, where all participants must stay connected remotely and work collaboratively. This method ensures a high level of student engagement, and the various stages present a variety of challenges that keep students engaged in the game. Furthermore, it fosters traits such as teamwork and leadership among participants. Figure 6 displays the sequence of game based roleplay approach.

3. Learning through Video Embedded Questions

Learners enjoy watching videos, as long as they are engaging and interesting. As a result, video-based learning has enormous potential. Teachers can innovate in video-based learning by embedding questions at regular intervals in the video and teaching the entire course as a game in which students can watch videos at their own pace, answer the questions that keep popping up in the video, and then continue with the video. The correct answers and scores obtained upon completion of a video may be displayed. Upon completion of the entire course, a cumulative score can be displayed, as well as the students' rank.

As a result, Badges serve as a motivator for learners, and they feel a sense of accomplishment when they reach a certain level. The teacher can decide when the student should earn a badge, such as a bronze badge at 25% completion of the course, a silver badge at 50% completion, a gold badge at 75% completion, a diamond badge at 90% completion, and a platinum badge at course completion! Figure 13 depicts a sample badge earned by a learner after completing a module and putting in 10 hours of reading time. Figure 7 displays a sample badge design.

Figure 7. An example of badges

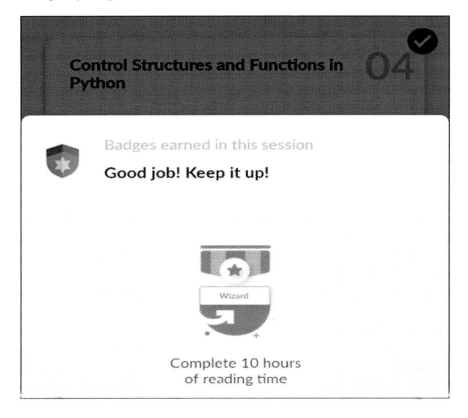

Another concept that can be introduced is a leader board, which publishes the names of the course's top performers. As displayed in Figure 8, leaderboard boosts participants' motivation and encourages them to work harder to complete the course. The use of animated graphics, emojis, and other forms of reward are also becoming more popular, and when combined, all of these elements make the video platform more interactive and generate interest among students.

Figure 8. Leader board showing top performers

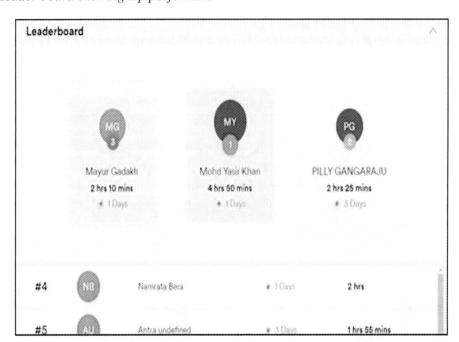

PROMINENT GAME BASED LEARNING PLATFORMS

Furthermore, due to the popularity of game-based learning, there are a plethora of popular platforms available where games can be created for educational purposes and students can actively participate in playing these games and applying their learnings in the game. Some of the most important gaming technologies and platforms are listed below:

1. Kahoot!

Kahoot! is a global learning platform organisation that helps students and teachers realise their full potential by providing highly engaging games that encourage students to learn and apply concepts in a fun way. In higher education, classes can be made more engaging by including assessment provisions, and better learning outcomes can be achieved.

Figure 9 provides a screenshot of the Kahoot platform, which allows games to be filtered by subject area, grade level, and preferred language. Kahoot! provides a variety of features. Polls, puzzles, brainstorming questions, student-paced challenges, and the ability to create Kahoot! Collections, an image reveal feature, an interactive slides layout, the ability to ask open-ended questions, up to 100-200 players per game, formative assessment, and a slew of other customised features Existing research has revealed that Kahoot! When compared to traditional pedagogical approaches in higher education, it has a positive effect on learning. Kahoot! can be used in a variety of domains such as information technology, media and communication, programming, educational technology, bioengineering, physics, chemistry, vocational training, and so on.

Figure 9. Snapshot of Kahoot! web platform

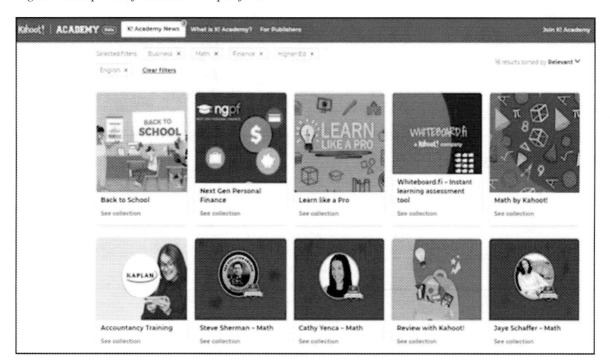

2. EdPuzzle

EdPuzzle is yet another popular platform for game-based learning in which students can be engaged through videos and games. It was founded in 2013 and now has over eight million video lessons and thirty-five million students, with 70 percent of them residing in the United States. It is very simple to use EdPuzzle; simply select a relevant video, add questions to the video, and assign the video to the class.

Another noteworthy feature of EdPuzzle is that it can be seamlessly integrated with a variety of other platforms such as Google Classroom, CANVAS, Moodle, BlackBoard, and others. EdPuzzle's assessment feature distinguishes it as a unique platform because teachers can track individual students' progress, allowing them to differentiate their instruction mechanism for different students. The features available include, but are not limited to, the creation of interactive videos and access to existing videos, the addition of questions, access to detailed analytics, and many others.

Figure 10. Home page of EdPuzzle website

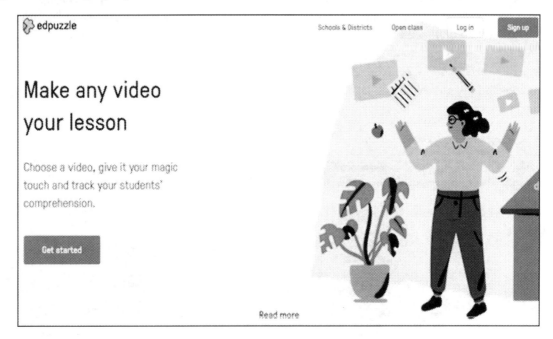

3. Socrative

Socrative is another excellent tool for actively engaging students. It is also available as a mobile application, which allows teachers to conduct quizzes, receive immediate feedback on a specific question, and provides an efficient way to monitor and evaluate learning, saving time for educators while providing fun and engaging interactions for learners.

Figure 11. A Socrative PRO for higher education snapshot

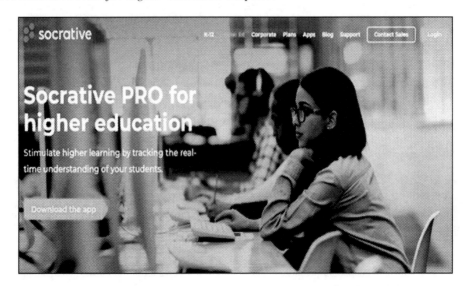

Amalgamation of Game-Based Learning With Interactive Instructional Strategies for Learner Engagement

Key features include provisions for customised assessment design, the ability to quickly review each learner's performance and share results, the ability to encourage friendly competition through a unique fun element in the quiz, visualisation and analysis of results, instant feedback, and personalised activities. Up to 20 activities, such as quizzes, surveys, and mini-competitions, can be launched at the same time. Socrative's most amazing feature is that it is completely free for all students and is available on all devices. Socrative, which has nearly 3 million users worldwide and is available in 14 languages, has also been a fantastic tool for conducting formative assessment.

4. Mega World

Mega World is a fantastic educational role-playing game that can be played by multiple players. It's a browser-based cross-platform game available in two versions: one for testing (version 1.0) and one for everyone (version 2.0). The game promotes educational games by allowing players to navigate difficult environments and interact with animated characters. Furthermore, the game provides participants with quests that test their knowledge of the subject, and students can learn the concepts while playing the game.

Figure 12. Various aspects of mega game

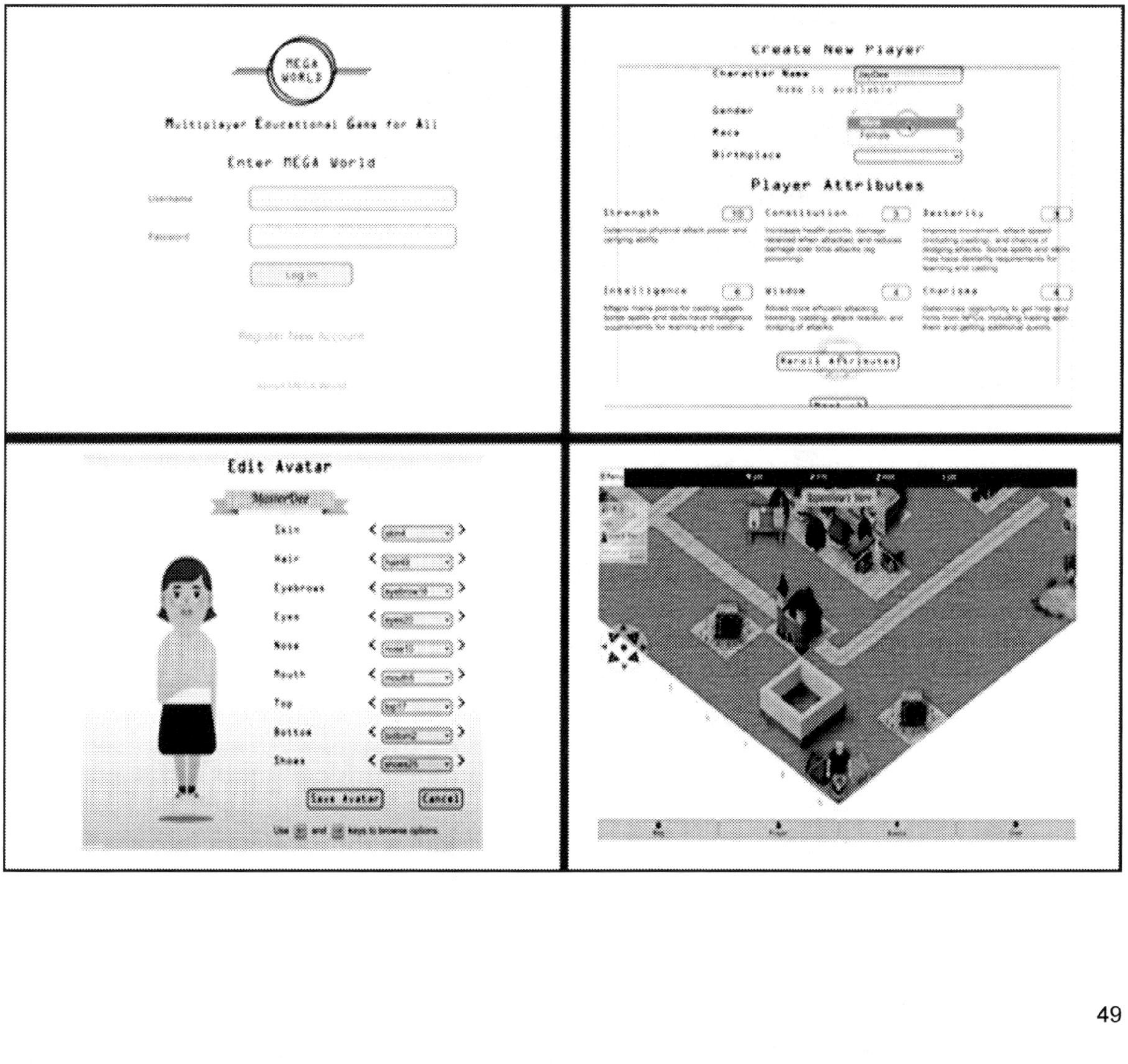

In addition, players can customise their avatars' attributes such as strength, wisdom level, intelligence, and so on. The game is available as a happy farm in which participants must make decisions and complete tasks. Social awareness, curiosity, and control, understanding the dark side of humans, collaboration and competition, taking on challenges, and so on are some of the benefits that can be gained by playing such role playing games.

5. Microsoft Kinect

Kinect Math, for example, is a Kinesthetic Learning Experience that enables teachers to make abstract mathematical concepts more interactive by utilising the Kinect. Students can play with graphs, variables, and other elements. Kinect, on the other hand, can be used in a variety of educational domains. Kinect has the potential to improve classroom interactions and expand student participation opportunities. Figure 13 provides of Kinect components.

Figure 13. Kinect components and installation in a classroom

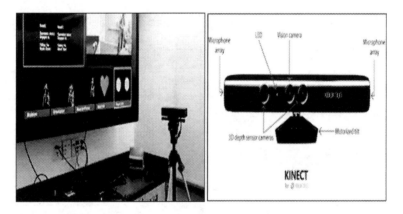

Miller (2012) stated that combining brain-based physical learning and gestures with content learning, Individual users can be identified using the Kinect system's facial and speech recognition feature.

Further, (Chang et al, 2015) created a Kinect game for students to learn about orbital physics and tested it at an Athabasca University science outreach summer camp. They wanted to see if the students' attitudes toward computer/video games influenced their perceptions of the developed Kinect game, and if their performance in the game was influenced by a lack of prior knowledge of the law of orbits. The findings revealed that students' attitudes toward computer/video games had no effect on their perceptions of the developed Kinect game's usability.

Figure 14 depicts a female student playing the game, another depicts the player about to throw the ball with her hands, and the third depicts the game's gesture recognition subsystem.

Figure 14. Kinect Game for Orbital Physics Learning

SELECTING THE BEST APPROACH

Following the discussion of the four types of game based interactive instructional strategies, you may be wondering which one is the best, can ensure maximum student involvement in the classroom, and can be implemented quickly. The answer to these questions is that no single method works well in every situation. It is determined by factors such as technology availability, class size, and desired learning outcomes. As a result, Table 2 defines all three techniques and identifies the factors that influence the teacher's decision to use them.

RECOMMENDATIONS

Although the chapter has already presented sufficient literature on game-based learning, popular platforms for game creation, and innovative instructional strategies leveraging technology and game play, this section is focused on providing relevant tips and recommendations about the best ways to integrate games and learning without requiring a significant shift in one's teaching style. In fact, current classroom teaching pedagogies can be slightly tweaked and a game element thoughtfully incorporated to make it more interesting. To begin with, games should be enjoyable to play. As a result, elements such as a point system, leaderboard, badges, digital rewards, and so on must be present in games. Incorporating these small elements will boost morale and generate curiosity among students and interest in the game. Second, game-based learning tools can be utilised. The appropriate platform for game creation should be selected based on the nature of the course. Third, it is not necessary to create full-fledged games using complex tools; the games can be created using regular IT tools such as powerpoint, MCQ questionnaires, interactive videos, and so on; however, a fun element should be present. Fourth, commercial games can be viewed as a medium in which little effort is required on the part of teachers because the game is already present and the teacher can focus on its integration into the curriculum and its assessment aspects. Fifth, some aspects should be taken seriously, such as a course outcome being associated with a game, game aspects of learning being meaningful and applicable to the concept taught, and the purpose of GBL being learning rather than just playing. Finally, the game's rules should be clearly explained, learners should be given feedback, a story-telling method should be used, and some rewards should be offered during game play. The authors are confident that if teachers' pay close attention to these recommendations, they will be able to implement the GBL approach with ease.

Table 2. Scenario for using games with interactive instructional strategies

Approach	Class Size	Benefits	Limitations
E-MetaPlan through Game Based Learning	Small to medium	• Interesting • Engaging • Thought provoking • Promotes Teamwork and collaboration • Imbibes Leadership skills	Requirement of: • Laptops • Online platforms like Zoom, Google Meet, WebX, Microsoft Teams • Stable internet connection • knowledge of Presentation & Word processing software is required
Game Based Role Play	Medium to large	• Applicable in both- offline & online classroom setting • Active student engagement • Interesting • Fun based learning • Teamwork and collaboration • Leadership skills • Clarity of the concepts	• Difficult to explain the concept to students. • Effort required from teacher in designing and executing the activity. Requirement of: • Laptops • Online platforms like Zoom, Google Meet, WebX, Microsoft Teams • Stable internet connection • knowledge of Presentation & Word processing software is required
Learning through Video embedded Questions	Any	• Flexibe learning • Self paced • Ensures students' active participation • Raises students' motivation through rewards like badges, leader board etc. • Thought Provoking and challenging • Concept clarity	• One time effort from teacher in designing the course. • Student may feel imposed participation. Requirement of: • Laptops • Stable internet connection

CONCLUSION

The goal of this chapter was to propose innovative instructional strategies that are implemented as a game using information technology tools that teachers can use to embrace learner-centered instruction in the physical classroom or in an online classroom environment. According to the extensive literature review conducted during the course of this chapter, game-based learning has a positive impact on learners, and as a result, many education domains are leveraging the benefits of game-based learning.

The focus of this chapter, however, was to propose active instructional strategies that can be used in conjunction with game-based learning using information technology tools. As interactive instructional strategies, three such innovative strategies have been discussed: E-Meta Plan, Game Based Role Play, and Learning through Video Embedded Questions. The detailed procedure for implementing these strategies has been presented in detail. Furthermore, the scenarios in which these strategies may be appropriated, the benefits they provide, and the limitations of their use are emphasised.

Given the nature of all interactive educational methodologies, one factor will almost always have an impact. It's due to the fact that the students are changing. Their ability to retain interest in subject knowledge, as well as their behaviour both inside and outside of the classroom, is changing. There will be learners who respond positively to such teaching approaches and find them useful and engaging; however, there will also be learners who oppose and avoid attending class because these methods necessitate active participation from students.

Furthermore, a proper combination of all interactive instructional strategies is required for digital learners, with the instructor ensuring that the learners are comfortable with the use of technology devices, that they have the necessary IT tools to study at home, and that the content created and delivered with technology is engaging and interesting.

Trust is the most important aspect of teacher-student communication. When working on a project, both teachers and students require certainty. Learners have the right to a welcoming environment in which they can express themselves freely in front of their teachers. Teachers must act as facilitators, providing opportunities for students to speak up, and must thus practise active listening skills in addition to using the best teaching pedagogy. Furthermore, when selecting an instructional technique, extreme caution must be exercised. The technique chosen must be consistent with the course's learning objectives and student learning outcomes, must focus on developing learners' professional skill set in some way, and the teacher must be comfortable implementing it in the classroom.

There is still a lot of room for research in this area because researchers can try out new teaching strategies in the classroom and see how they affect learner classroom participation. Additionally, innovative solutions to various constraints that limit the implementation of active learning methodologies in classrooms may be presented.

REFERENCES

Al Fatta, H., Maksom, Z., & Zakaria, M. H. (2019). Game-based learning and gamification: Searching for definitions. *International Journal of Simulation: Systems, Science & Technology*, *19*, 10–5013.

Andone, D., Dron, J., Boyne, C., & Pemberton, L. (2005). Digital Students and Their Use Of Elearning Enviroments. *IADIS International Conference on WWW/Internet*.

Bas, G. (2010). effects of multiple intelligences instruction strategy on students achievement levels and attitudes towards English lesson. *Cypriot Journal of Educational Sciences*, *5*(3).

Beard, R. L., Salas, E., & Prince, C. (1995). Enhancing transfer of training: Using role-play to foster teamwork in the cockpit. *The International Journal of Aviation Psychology*, *5*(2), 131–143. doi:10.120715327108ijap0502_1 PMID:11540253

Bobbit, L. M., Inks, S. A., Kemp, K. J., & Mayo, D. T. (2000). Integrating marketing courses to enhance team-based experiential learning. *Journal of Marketing Education*, *22*(1), 15–24. doi:10.1177/0273475300221003

Brown, C. L., Comunale, M. A., Wigdahl, B., & Urdaneta-Hartmann, S. (2018). Current climate for digital game-based learning of science in further and higher education. *FEMS Microbiology Letters*, *365*(21), fny237. Advance online publication. doi:10.1093/femsle/fny237 PMID:30260380

Chang, C.-Y., & Hwang, G.-J. (2019). Trends in digital game-based learning in the mobile era: Asystematic review of journal publications from 2007 to 2016. *Int. J. Mobile Learning and Organisation*, *13*(1), 68–90. doi:10.1504/IJMLO.2019.096468

Chang, M., Lachance, D., Lin, F., Al-Shamali, F., & Chen, N. S. (2015). Enhancing Orbital Physics Learning Performance through a Hands-on Kinect Game. *Egitim ve Bilim, 40*(180).

Chye, C., & Nakajima, T. (2012). Game based approach to learn martial arts for beginners. *18th IEEE International Conference on Embedded and Real-Time Computing Systems and Applications*, 482-485. 10.1109/RTCSA.2012.37

Clark, K. R. (2015). The effects of the flipped model of instruction on student engagement and performance in the secondary mathematics classroom. *The Journal of Educators Online*, *12*(1), 91–114. doi:10.9743/JEO.2015.1.5

Cummings, Mason, & Baur. (2017). Active Learning Strategies for Online and Blended Learning Environments. Flipped Instruction: Breakthroughs in Research and Practice, 88–116.

Deterding, S., Dixon, D., Khaled, R., & Nacke, L. (2011, September). From game design elements to gamefulness: defining "gamification". In *Proceedings of the 15th international academic MindTrek conference: Envisioning future media environments* (pp. 9-15). 10.1145/2181037.2181040

Dhamija, A., & Dhamija, D. (2020). Impact of Innovative and Interactive Instructional Strategies on Student Classroom Participation. In M. Montebello (Ed.), Handbook of Research on Digital Learning (pp. 20-37). IGI Global. doi:10.4018/978-1-5225-9304-1.ch002

Dhamija, A., Sharma, R., & Dhamija, D. (2020). Emergence of EdTech Products in South Asia: A Comparative Analysis. In S. Ikuta (Ed.), *Handbook of Research on Software for Gifted and Talented School Activities in K-12 Classrooms* (pp. 303–327). IGI Global. doi:10.4018/978-1-7998-1400-9.ch014

Dias, J. (2017). Teaching operations research to undergraduate management students: The role of gamification. *International Journal of Management Education*, *15*(1), 98–111. doi:10.1016/j.ijme.2017.01.002

Ding, D., Guan, C., & Yu, Y. (2017). Game-based learning in tertiary education: A new learning experience for the generation Z. *International Journal of Information and Education Technology (IJIET)*, *7*(2), 148–152. doi:10.18178/ijiet.2017.7.2.857

Esteves, M., Pereira, A., Veiga, N., Vasco, R., & Veiga, A. (2018). The Use of New Learning Technologies in Higher Education Classroom: A Case Study. In M. Auer, D. Guralnick, & I. Simonics (Eds.), *Teaching and Learning in a Digital World. ICL 2017. Advances in Intelligent Systems and Computing* (Vol. 715). Springer., doi:10.1007/978-3-319-73210-7_59

Forbes. (2019). *Research Report Shows How Much Time We Spend Gaming*. Retrieved from https://www.forbes.com/sites/kevinanderton/2019/03/21/research-report-shows-how-much-time-we-spend-gaming-infographic/#1a9602d13e07

Gee, J. P. (2007). *Good Video Games and Good Learning: Collected Essays on Video Games, Learning and Literacy*. P. Lang. doi:10.3726/978-1-4539-1162-4

Gilboy, M. B., Heinerichs, S., & Pazzaglia, G. (2015). Enhancing student engagement using the flipped classroom. *Journal of Nutrition Education and Behavior*, *47*(1), 109–114. doi:10.1016/j.jneb.2014.08.008 PMID:25262529

Gündüz, A. Y., & Akkoyunlu, B. (2020). Effectiveness of Gamification in Flipped Learning. *SAGE Open*, *10*(4). doi:10.1177/2158244020979837

Habershon, N. (1993). Metaplan (R): Achieving Two-way Communications. *Journal of European Industrial Training*, *17*(7). doi:10.1108/03090599310042528

Hosseini, H., Hartt, M., & Mostafapour, M. (2019). Learning is child's play: Game-based learning in computer science education. *ACM Transactions on Computing Education*, *19*(3), 1–18. doi:10.1145/3282844

Hussein, G. (2010). The Attitudes of Undergraduate Students towards Motivation and Technology in a Foreign Language Classroom. *International Journal of Learning and Teaching*, *2*(2), 14–24.

Jin, G., Tu, M., Kim, T. H., Heffron, J., & White, J. (2018). Evaluation of game-based learning in cybersecurity education for high school students. [EduLearn]. *Journal of Education and Learning*, *12*(1), 150–158. doi:10.11591/edulearn.v12i1.7736

Johnson, D. W., & Johnson, F. P. (1997). *Joining Together: Group Theory and Group Skills* (6th ed.). Allyn & Bacon.

Kahoot! for schools - choose plan for higher education. (2021, September 16). *Kahoot!* Retrieved September 11, 2021 from https://kahoot.com/register/pricing-higher-ed/

Kamarudin, N., Halim, L., Osman, K., & Meerah, T. S. M. (2009). Pengurusan Penglibatan Pelajar dalam Amali Sains [Management of Students' Involvement in Science Practical Work]. *Jurnal Pendidikan Malaysia*, *34*(1), 205–217.

Kinect for Windows. (2016). Retrieved September 11, 2021 from http://kinectforwindows.org/

Lee, W. J., Huang, C. W., Wu, C. J., Huang, S. T., & Chen, G. D. (2012). The effects of using embodied interactions to improve learning performance. *2012 IEEE 12th international conference on advanced learning technologies (ICALT)*, 557-559.

Li, Z., Zou, D., Xie, H., Wang, F.-L., & Chang, M. (2018). Enhancing Information Literacy in Hong Kong Higher Education through Game-based Learning. *Proceedings of 22nd Global Chinese Conference on Computers in Education (GCCCE 2018)*, 595-598.

Lin, C. J., & Hwang, G. J. (2018). A flipped classroom approach to supporting gamebased learning activities for EFL business writing course. In *3rd Annual International Seminar on Transformative Education and Educational Leadership (AISTEEL 2018).* Atlantis Press

Majid, S., Yeow, C. W., Audrey, C. S. Y., & Shyong, L. R. (2010). *Enriching learning experience through class participation: A students' perspective. 76th IFLA General Conference and Assembly: Satellite Meeting on Cooperation and Collaboration in Teaching and Research*, Gothenburg, Sweden.

Mavromihales, M., Holmes, V., & Racasan, R. (2019). Game-based learning in mechanical engineering education: Case study of games-based learning application in computer aided design assembly. *International Journal of Mechanical Engineering Education*, *47*(2), 156–179.

Miller, A. (2012). *Kinect in the Classroom.* Retrieved September 15, 2021 from https://www.edutopia.org/blog/kinect-classroom-andrew-miller

Mustapha, S. M., Abd Rahman, N. S. N., & Yunus, M. M. (2010). Factors influencing classroom participation: A case study of Malaysian undergraduate students. *Procedia: Social and Behavioral Sciences*, *9*, 1079–1084.

Pho, A., & Dinscore, A. (2015). *Game-based learning. Tips and Trends.* https://acrl.ala.org/IS/wp-content/uploads/2014/05/spring2015.pdf

Rao, D., & Stupans, I. (2012). Exploring the potential of role play in higher education: Development of a typology and teacher guidelines. *Innovations in Education and Teaching International*, *49*(4), 427–436.

Rosa, J. A. (2012). Marketing education for the next four billion: Challenges and innovations. *Journal of Marketing Education*, *34*(1), 44–54.

Ryan, R. M., Rigby, C. S., & Przybylski, A. (2006). The motivational pull of video games: A self-determination theory approach. *Motivation and Emotion*, *30*(4), 344–360.

Sailer, M., Hense, J. U., Mayr, S. K., & Mandl, H. (2017). How gamification motivates: An experimental study of the effects of specific game design elements on psychological need satisfaction. *Computers in Human Behavior*, *69*, 371–380.

Silva, R., Rodrigues, R., & Leal, C. (2019). Play it again: How gamebased learning improves flow in Accounting and Marketing education. *Accounting Education*. Advance online publication. doi:10.1080/09639284.2019.1647859

Socrative. (2021, September 2). *Higher Ed.* Retrieved September 12, 2021 from https://www.socrative.com/higher-ed/

Socrative. (2021a, August 26). *Plans.* Retrieved September 12, 2021 from https://www.socrative.com/plans/

Sogunro, O. A. (2004). Efficacy of role-playing pedagogy in training leaders: Some reflections. *Journal of Management Development*, *23*(4), 355–371.

Stansbury, J. A., & Earnest, D. R. (2017). Meaningful gamification in an industrial/organizational psychology course. *Teaching of Psychology*, *44*(1), 38–45.

Talib, C. A., Aliyu, F., & Siang, K. H. (2019). Enhancing students' reasoning skills in engineering and technology through game-based learning. *International Journal of Emerging Technologies in Learning*, *14*(24), 69-80. doi:10.3991/ijet.v14i24.12117

Tan Ai Lin, D., Ganapathy, M., & Kaur, M. (2018). Kahoot! It: Gamification in Higher Education. *Pertanika Journal of Social Science & Humanities*, *26*(1).

Tate, M. (2013). *Worksheets don't grow dendrites: 20 instructional strategies that engaged the brain.* Corwin.

Vásquez. (2017). *Maria & Peñafiel, Myriam & Cevallos Cevallos, Andrés & Zaldumbide, Juan & Vásquez, Diego.* Impact of Game-Based Learning on Students in Higher Education. doi:10.21125/edulearn.2017.1942

Wade, R. (1994). Teacher education students' views on class discussion: Implications for fostering critical thinking. *Teaching and Teacher Education, 10*(2), 231–243. doi:10.1016/0742-051X(94)90015-9

Wang, A. I. (2020, April 17). *Impact of Kahoot! in higher education – research roundup.* Kahoot! Retrieved September 11, 2021 from https://kahoot.com/blog/2020/04/08/kahoot-impact-higher education-research/

Wardoyo, C., Satrio, Y. D., & Ma'ruf, D. (2020). Effectiveness of Game-Based Learning – Learning in Modern Education. *3rd International Research Conference on Economics and Business*, 81–87. 10.18502/kss.v4i7.6844

Westrup, U. & Planander, A. (2013). Role-play as a pedagogical method to prepare students for practice: The students' voice. *Ogre utbildning, 3*(3), 199-210.

Yang, Y. H., Xu, W., Zhang, H., Zhang, J. P., & Xu, M. L. (2014). The application of KINECT motion sensing technology in game-oriented study. *International Journal of Emerging Technologies in Learning, 9*(2), 59–63.

Yukselturk, E., Altıok, S., & Başer, Z. (2018). Using game-based learning with kinect technology in foreign language education course. *Journal of Educational Technology & Society, 21*(3), 159–173.

Yusof, M. (2011). *The Dynamics of Student Participation in Classroom: Observation on level and forms of participation.* Paper presented at Learning and Teaching Congress of UKM, Penang, Malaysia.

Chapter 4
A Systematic Review on the Neuro-Cognitive Correlates of Game-Based Learning in Higher Education Learning Environments

Smitha Baboo
CHRIST University (Deemed), India

Yogesh Kanna
CHRIST University (Deemed), India

Cathlyn Niranjana Bennett
CHRIST University (Deemed), India

ABSTRACT

Game-based learning is one of the sustainable education methods for future professionals from the higher education learning environment. To attain these innovative and sustainable teaching pedagogies, the components of games and simulations need to be incorporated into the teaching-learning content. The integration of neuroscience and cognitive concepts has become an essential feature in understanding various phenomena in game-based learning with regard to higher education learning environments. Several neural and cognitive processes are involved while engaging in such activities. These activities have played a pivotal role in the pedagogy and teachers had to think on their feet while engaging students in higher education as well. Game-based learning has proven to be a very effective method of engaging higher education students.

A Systematic Review on the Neuro-Cognitive Correlates of Game-Based Learning in Higher Education

INTRODUCTION

Game-based learning (GBL) is a new mass medium with many games that allow learners to interact, participating actively and not just passively receiving information (Lytras et al., 2018). Over the past decade, the popularity of game-based learning has led to an explosion of numerous genres of game research and development. Despite the increasing interest in games and gamification in recent years, games in general still suffer from the prevalent public perception that gameplay is merely an entertainment medium (Jeong so & Minhwi, 2018). Game is defined as any mental and physical activity which is characterized by goals, rules, challenges, having a feedback system, voluntary participation (Game & Mcgonical, 2011; Prensky; 2001) and videogame is a complex digital medium with gaming properties that requires active interaction with the human and the computers (Galloway, 2006; Wadrip-Fruin, 2009). The pandemic pedagogy has even made game-based learning more relevant as most of the teaching fraternity has used this platform in the teaching-learning process.

The use of game-based learning in education has recently received everyone's attention, but games have always been available in the teaching-learning process. Education is one of the fields to test newly emerging technologies (Cantoni & Blas, 2006). Game-based learning is one of the technologies that started widely grabbing the interest of various learners (Miller, 2008). In the Indian higher education learning environment, the teaching fraternity has incorporated GBL into every subject. The critical component is that the learners, even though they also need some fun, adventurous and competitive environment at an adolescent level. The learners are getting more engaged during GBL, and understanding the subject is also remarkable.

Years back, there was a negative approach to game-based learning as the game was not well designed, which affected the reputation of the game learning. The literature suggests that there have been three generations of educational games distinctively designed by the underlying pedagogical practices in game design and purpose (Egenfeldt-Nielsen, 2007; Ulicsak, 2010). The first generation is broadly termed edutainment which included education and entertainment elements leveraging various media and technology. There was a strong influence of behaviourism using the reward system for a correct response, drill and practice games, and brain training games fall into this. In the second generation, education games began to employ more cognitive and constructivist approaches in the gameplay. The players experience a multimodal interactive experience during this game-based learning. Simulation games and micro-worlds characterize this generation of games. The teaching was not linked with a simple reward pathway, instead of through scaffolding, exploration and problem-solving. Scaffolding is a learning process, as mentioned by Lev Vygotsky. In the third generation, educational games are highly influenced by socio-cultural and constructivist perspectives. The role of social interaction and cultural processes plays a role in the game design and gameplay in a simulated virtual environment (Jeong so & Minhwi, 2018).The objective of this systematic review is to understand the changes observed in the neural and cognitive correlates while higher education students get engaged in game based learning and to give an overview of this understanding in further figuring out the usefulness of game based learning for sustainable education in future.

BACKGROUND OF THE STUDY

Most of the literature has theorized on the potential educational benefits of game-based learning in higher education. The effectiveness of games in the learning process has been a matter of debate for more than a decade. Several meta-review and meta-analyses have taken a step to answer the question by synthesizing a considerable amount of research in gaming and learning. In recent years, game-based learning has taken its prominence in the teaching-learning process of the Indian higher education system and educational research.

Game-based learning has increased engagement, enjoyment, higher-order thinking, increased attention, and resulted in lesser anxiety. Very few studies elaborate on the neuroscience and cognitive areas that affect game-based learning. The changes that happen to the neurotransmitters while involved in the game need to be analyzed. The usage of game-based learning in the higher education learning environment needs more attention, as this kind of pedagogy facilitates the learners to understand the importance of developing a sustainable future for themselves and the people around them. Prioritizing on the importance of having a neuro-cognitive base of game-based learning the researchers have consolidated these concepts into this study.

THEORETICAL FRAMEWORK

Educational games will increase motivation and improve the learning process, making the learners successful in the academic journey (Keller, 2008; Schrader & Bastiaens, 2012; Woo, 2014; Nebel et al., 2015). The main goal of game-based learning is learning and behavioural change (Connolly et al., 2012). Digital game-based learning environments are complex and demand the learners working memory processes (Norman, 2011). The working memory process is one of the four pillars of the cognitive load theory wherein the working memory has a limited capacity and allows the processing of a few information elements at each time. Cognitive load theory is implicitly connected to the motivation of learners, which enables them to attend to relevant information and to construct schemas (Moreno & Mayer, 2007; Schnotz et al.,2009). Intrinsic motivation is connected to high-quality learning (Ryan & Deci, 2000).

In game-based learning theory of social constructivism plays a pivotal role in providing necessary tools to the students to develop their own procedures to bring a solution to the given problem in the game. Safe practice, experience and interaction are the different pillars upon which the game based learning theory stands. The theory on cognitive evaluation (Deci & Ryan, 1985) elaborate on the social-contextual events that improves the intrinsic motivation and engagement among the learners (Deci & Ryan, 2010). One of the foundations of game-based learning methods is the transformation of experience (Kolb, 2005) supported by experiential learning theory, enhancing and completing learning in higher education. Irrespective of these theories, situated learning (Lave, 1991) and problem-based learning (Savin-Baden, 2004) also form the pedagogical background for using game-based learning methods.

ISSUES/PROBLEMS/TRENDS

The researchers have looked into the issues and trends that game-based learning brings changes in the neural and cognitive correlates of game-based learning and whether these changes have an effect on the higher education students.

NEURAL CORRELATES OF LEARNING

Fundamentals of Acquisition and Consolidation in Children and Young Adults

At least until 60 years of age, we encounter novel words and our vocabularies continue to grow (Hartshorne and Germine, 2015). This section focuses on understanding the underlying phenomenon of acquisition and consolidation in individuals engaged in school level and higher education. At a young age, in school and at home children grow and expand their vocabulary, it increases at different rates according to their ages and education levels. How do they retain and incorporate these newly learned words into their mental word bank? It is not known whether children learn differently from adults in the way they consolidate the newly learned words they learn (Landi et al., 2018, tested adolescents). In developmental populations, we are not yet sure if the same neural mechanisms that underpin behaviors at various ages (James et al., 2017). The same consolidation process appears likely to be taking place across ages according to behavioral and sleep studies of young adults and school-aged children. However, because children's brains are still in a state of long-term development that extends into puberty and beyond, also because certain brain structures mature in a different manner (Ghetti and Bunge, 2012; Menon et al., 2005; Paus, 2005; Schmithorst et al., 2007), then the pattern of responses to novel words could be entirely different than that observed in young adults. The hippocampus undergoes a prolonged development during middle childhood (ages 6–11 years) (Ghetti and Bunge, 2012). It is expected that school children show a weaker consolidation/integration effect compared to teenagers. Most critical questions have not been addressed to date, both in terms of understanding the neural basis of learning new words and remembering them. This is true both in terms of how they are remembered.

Multiple memory systems are predicted to be useful in supporting linguistic information acquisition in a declarative/procedural model (Ullman, 2016). Explicit instruction in the association between their meanings and forms is more likely to be used for vocabulary learning. Grammatical learning can also depend on the declarative system, especially for languages other than one's native tongue (Ullman and Lovelett, 2018). Young adults are considered to be in the process of forming and consolidating mental representations of words (Davis and Gaskell, 2009; Gaskell and Dumay, 2003). A novel approach called the Complementary Learning Systems (CLS) approach is thought to be involved in word learning (Davis and Gaskell, 2009). In which new words are initially encoded sparingly, independently of their lexical content, and are then gradually integrated with existing memory representations.

Emotional Engagement in Games in Children and Young Adults

The playing of digital games has become a very common phenomenon in today's society (Lenhart et al., 2008). Moreover, playing is a fundamental part of human nature (Huizinga et al., 2006; Gray, 2013; Panksepp, 2005). According to research, play is part of the list of emotional systems in the brain that are present from birth, just like anger, fear, lust, and grief (Panksepp, 2005). Children learn new skills by playing (Huizinga et al., 2006), it's the identified method for children to acquire new knowledge (Edwards, 2002) and generally serves evolutionary needs (Ryan & Deci, 2000). The concept of play is normally viewed today as an activity with intrinsic purpose (Wilkinson, 2016), which can be used to overcome obstacles, for instance (Krouse et al., 2011; Suits, 2005).

The experience of playing a game is often accompanied by enjoyment and emotions, making them an inseparable component of gaming (Yannakakis & Paiva, 2015). In addition to emotions being an integral part of our daily lives (Dixon et al., 2017), the way they affect our interactions with games is also likely to be a factor (Yannakakis & Paiva, 2015). It is only logical that they are acknowledged as essential elements in game design (Baharom, Tan, & Idris, 2014; Karpouzis & Yannakakis, 2016) since they play a central part in enhancing the gaming experience.

In educational games, similar mechanisms are recruited for more specific purposes. By maintaining motivation, effort, flow, or engagement when playing, for example, they facilitate learning. (Sabourin & Lester, 2014). It has been argued that positive affect has a positive impact on learning, motivation, and information processing not only in traditional learning settings (Pekrun & Linnenbrink-Garcia, 2014) as well as digital learning environments (Um et al., 2012). Gamification can however facilitate both positive and negative emotions as well (Ninaus et al., 2019). The stress of error can cause negative emotions, like frustration, to emerge (Kapoor et al., 2007), as well as being linked to improved learning (Shute et al., 2015). In this study, the authors argued that a learner must actually be engaged in the learning process to experience frustration, which is in line with previous research suggesting increased emotional engagement (both positive and negative emotions) among game-based learners (Ninaus et al., 2019). The key to an enjoyable and challenging overall gaming experience can indeed include negative effects such as frustration (Gee, 2007).

Psychologists have historically divided emotions from cognition (Y. Liu et al., 2009). We now understand them through their dynamic interaction (Pessoa, 2008). Emotions are widely believed to have an impact on human cognition, including perception, attention, and memory learning, memory, reasoning, and problem-solving (Barbas, 2000; Brosch et al., 2013; Y. Liu et al., 2009; Pessoa, 2008; Tyng et al., 2017). For example, adding positive or negative emotions when learning can improve memory consolidation (Nielson & Powless, 2007). Emotional targets are detected faster than neutral targets among distractors (Ohman et al., 2001; Hamann, 2001; Phelps, 2004). As a consequence, engaging the player emotionally influences their cognitive processes in a positive way (Greipl et al., 2020; Plass et al., 2015). A successful learning game will therefore be able to accommodate both emotional and cognitive resources that are constantly interacting (Greipl et al., 2020). Yet, a neurofunctional study has not yet proven that game-based learning is associated with higher emotional engagement.

Reward Circuitry and Mechanism May be Linked to Game-Based Learning

First, using fMRI Howard-Jones et al. (2016) found that when learning sessions included video game elements, fMRI activation of default-mode network hubs decreased but that activation of ventral striatum increased. In another study by Cole et al. (2012) tested the difference in brain activation between watching someone else play and actively participating in it. The anterior cingulate cortex, anterior insula, putamen, and thalamus were all activated more strongly during active play. The thalamus, anterior insula, and putamen were all active during active play, in contrast to rest.

The areas activated for game-based learning in both studies are well in line with expectations derived from the neuroscientific literature concerning reward-related activation, including both positive (win) and negative (loss) valences of reward processing. (Silverman et al., 2015; Sescousse et al., 2013). Additionally, the anterior insula and the nucleus accumbens, areas that are typically associated with experiences of emotion and pleasure (Kurth et al., 2010; Berridge & Kringelbach, 2015) seemed to be involved as well. Together, these findings suggest that gamified learning may be able to enhance educational outcomes by activating the reward system (Howard-Jones et al., 2016).

There seems to be a close relationship between reward and emotions (Rolls, 2005). However, systematizing research into whether gaming environments provide players with rewarding (and therefore emotional) feedback is still needed. In order to identify which areas of the brain are activated when these emotions and rewards are processed, there must be an evaluation of their activation in associated brain areas. It may be considered more rewarding and emotionally engaging to provide feedback embedded in the game (for a comprehensive review of how personal/contextual factors can be considered (Fishbach et al., 2010) when compared to its non-game-based equivalent. Differences in energy expenditure within these brain regions should be seen, which were areas of interest to us.

A number of subcortical areas have been shown to be involved in various types of emotional experience and/or pleasure (Sergerie et al., 2008), ventral pallidum (Johnston & Olson, 2015) as well as striatal areas including the nucleus accumbens (Berridge & Kringelbach, 2015), the putamen, and the caudate nucleus (Waraczynski, 2006; Silverman et al., 2015). In addition, we considered starting points of the dopaminergic pathway, such as the ventral tegmental cortex and the substantia nigra (pars reticulata) (Garris et al., 1993; Nieuwenhuys, 1985), crucially involved in reward processes (Knutson et al., 2000). It is important to note that some of those brain regions also process negative emotions. Specifically, positive and negative emotions are processed in several valence-insensitive brain regions, making it difficult to distinguish positive and negative emotions on the basis of brain activity (Lindquist et al., 2016).

Anterior insula and the frontal medial cortex are cortically associated with emotional processing (Phan et al., 2002; O'Doherty et al., 2001; Kurth et al., 2010; Lindquist et al., 2016) and medial orbital cortex activation has been demonstrated to be a predictor of pleasure (Berridge & Kringelbach, 2013). In addition, two parts of the cingulate cortex were frequently found to be associated with reward perception (Silverman et al., 2015).

Neurotransmitters Responsible for Game Based Learning

Playing games can stimulate several neurotransmitters, which will promote beneficial cognitive activities. The diagrammatic representation of neurotransmitters acting upon the game-based learning is as follows:

COGNITIVE CORRELATES OF GAME BASED LEARNING

Gamification in education enhances learning outcomes through emotional engagement and motivation of students (Barna & Fodor, 2017; S. Greipl et al., 2021; Hartt, Hosseini, & Mostafapour, 2020; Yang, 2012). Video gaming has been tied to a host of cognitive outcomes including processing speed, attention, memory, reasoning, and problem-solving abilities (Hisam et al., 2018; Pallavicini, Ferrari, & Mantovani, 2018). One of the key factors that determine the type of skill enhanced through the video game is the genre of the game. For instance, strategy-based games are associated with planning ability. Or speed games could be associated with better processing speeds and reaction times. However, one aspect of cognition that appears to be elementary to all forms of gaming appears to be attention.

Table 1. Stimulation of neurotransmitters during game-based learning

Neurotransmitters	Functions	Stimulation of Neurotransmitters during Game-based Learning
Dopamine	Released during the time of pleasure, satisfaction, addiction, movement, and motivation	Games that offer novelty and feedback
Serotonin	Released during the time of well-being and happiness	Games that offer recognition and praise
Endorphins	Range of compounds that are biologically active and formed from long-chain amino acids. Released during the time of exercise, excitement, pain, and well-being	Games that offer achievement of complex challenges
Oxytocin	Released during the time of feelings of contentment, trust, and altruism in individuals	Games that offer collaboration

Game Based Education and Attention

It stands to reason that game-based learning primarily targets attention circuits in the brain. Brain-based-attention circuits have been primarily implicated in forebrain activity (Knudsen, 2018). These networks have been implicated in several aspects of attention including the orienting aspect of attention, arousal, and the ability to sustain attention. A well-designed game-based learning curriculum therefore primarily appears to target specific attention circuits leading to better engagement in the classroom.

Attention circuits are typically engaged in the early phases of cognitive activity and serve as a precursor to several higher executive functions, learning, and memory (Conejero & Rueda, 2017). The cascading effect of attention enhancement into academic performance through higher-order functions such as planning, set shift, working memory, learning, and long-term memory is, therefore, a significant aspect to be explored. More specific targeting of game-based learning on specific cognitive functions can be achieved through the use of different gaming techniques. In this context, Game-based learning is found to be positively associated with vocabulary, problem-solving ability, and working memory (Alzubi, Fernández, Flores, Duran, & Cotos, 2018; Hartt et al., 2020; Yang, 2012).

Game Based Education and Higher Order Executive Functions

Cognition can be enhanced not only from action gamers but also from non-action gamers. Cognitive improvements were not limited to action game training alone and different games enhanced different aspects of cognition. Many video-games-related cognitive improvements may not be due to training of general broad cognitive systems such as executive attentional control, but instead due to frequent utilisation of specific cognitive processes during game play. Hence, many video game training related improvements to cognition may be attributed to near-transfer effects (Oei & Patterson, 2013). The video game experience is often associated with cognitive flexibility. Some of the executive functions cultivated through video gaming are shifting, inhibition and updating (Olfers & Band, 2019). Research also indicates that working memory plays an important role in education (Pickering, 2006). Working memory is the ability to hold information for a short term and manipulate that information in order to produce an output. This is an important cognitive function in the learning process. Gaming has also been found to be positively associated with working memory (Waris, 2019).

Game Based Education in Special Populations

Having established that game-based learning has positive associations with different aspects of cognition in the typically developing student, it becomes important to examine the ramifications of this mode of learning among students that have specific challenges in cognition. Game-based learning has been found to have positive implications for conditions that typically affect the teaching-learning process such as Specific Learning disability and attention deficit hyperactivity disorder (García-Redondo, García, Areces, Núñez, & Rodríguez, 2019; Sullivan-Carr, 2016). Interestingly enough game-based education also appears to have a positive impact on individuals with intellectual disabilities and those with associated sensory disturbances (Brown et al., 2013).

Future Directions for Cognitive Studies in Game Based Learning

Some additional factors to be considered while increasing the effectiveness of game-based learning on cognition should include the influence of the learning environment of the student as well as innate aspects of learning including intrinsic motivation. Some other considerations of future directions of study would include an assessment of the role of cognitive load on the outcome as well as the implication of cognitive styles on learning (Chang, Liang, Chou, & Lin, 2017; Milovanović, Minović, Kovačević, Minović, & Starčević, 2009). Functional Neuroimaging and Electrophysiological based studies, while the student is engaged in game based learning tasks can add great value to our understanding of this field.

HIGHER EDUCATION AND GAME BASED LEARNING

Game-based learning has recently received growing attention in higher education, promoting content knowledge and higher-order cognitive skills like communication, collaboration, and problem-solving (Belova & Zovada, 2020). In higher education, learners anticipate new techniques, assignments on information technology and challenging assessment patterns. Students got introduced to a new digital-based learning platform that motivates learners to engage and kindle the practice of self-learning, leading to the acquisition of high competency and skills (Priyaadarshini, 2020). Even though few studies have touted the potential benefits of game-based learning about content acquisition, deep learning, engagement, its effectiveness in practice remains an open question (Crocco et al., 2016).

Meta-analysis posits severe limitations and problems with studies in higher education that make it difficult to ascertain the efficacy of game-based learning. Some meta-analyses sought to clarify what advantages GBL affords educators over traditional curricula, which is inconclusive (Perotta et al., 2013). The influence of game-based learning methods on learning outcomes like cognition, knowledge acquisition, motivation, affection, learning, and social construction has been studied, but less evidence from the higher education learning environment (Young et al., 2012). The game environment facilitates managing connections between people and activities, integration, and uncertainty (Jaaska, 2021). Besides specific discipline-based skills, GBL improves students' generic skills like decision making, problem-solving and collaborative skills. Game-based learning in higher education can be achieved and enhanced by active experimentation, abstract conceptualization, reflective observation and systematic feedback (Kolb, 2005).

Playing games requires informed decisions, and the consequences are seen as the game proceeds further. Literature suggests that educational games positively affect decision making performance (Rumeser, 2019), challenge and engagement in play-based learning. Collaboration with team members is a beneficial aspect of game-based education. Attention is required to have an interest in learning the subject, and it helps in interacting with the course content, which improves learning (Antonaci et al., 2015; Hamari et al., 2016).Game mechanics is one of the powerful learning tools to promote and sustain learners' engagement and motivation. Gamification is a process of using game design elements in non-game contexts (Deterding et al., 2011). Nicholson (2012) elaborates the definition of gamification in education as a meaning-making process in ludic learning spaces focusing on the external motivation with reward-based systems in the use of game elements.

A meta-review by Young et al. (2012) found 300 articles that prove the effect of game-based learning on learners' academic achievement. Other meta-analysis studies have demonstrated the positive impact of serious games on the educational and cognitive dimensions (Wouters et al., 2013). The literature review done by Hamari et al. (2014) highlighted the efficacy of gamification, which depends highly on the context and users.Digital game-based learning has been in use for over three decades with advances in information technology and the internet, leading to increased popularity and usage (Brom et al., 2010). In the last 20 years, game-based learning has gained much interest (Conolly et al., 2012; Li and Tsai, 2013; All et al.,2014; Westera, 2015; Boyle et al., 2016; Mc Laren et al., 2017). There are many outcomes because of game-based learning in perceptual, cognitive, behavioural, affective and motivational areas of learners (Boyle et al.,2016; Clark, 2016; Parong et al., 2017).

Mcgonigal (2015) suggests that certain mainstream games like call of duty and other related videogames can be powerful tools to improve one's attention, mood, cognitive strengths and relationships. Many of the research findings slowly try to change people's conceptions about video games. The results mention the positive outcomes of game-based learning such as improvement in problem-solving skills, cognitive abilities, etc. Shute et al. (2014) found that educational games geared towards entertainment can improve attention, spatial orientation and problem-solving skills. The learners develop problem-solving skills as they play games more and more due to the simulation effects of the same, which give a real effect and help to gain mastery over it. The release of dopamine will be high for those who play games as it is reward-motivated. This is the reason why students play intending to gain reward, be its advancement in the game, rising a ranking board or badges and trophies (Baboo.S & Raja, 2017).

DISCUSSION

The beneficial contribution of game-based learning is about the cognitive, neural and affective outcomes. The research shows that game-based education can create positive effects such as joy, engagement, and excitement for learning (Sabourin & Lester, 2014). It has been found that positive effects positively impact learning, motivation, and information processing in traditional learning settings (Pekrun & Linnenbrink-Garcia, 2014) and digital learning environments (Um et al., 2012). The role of social interaction and cultural processes plays a role in the game design and gameplay in a simulated virtual environment (Jeong so & Minhwi, 2018). GBL resulted with a shred of empirical evidence that games are highly motivating and have natural ties with how people learn (Gee, 2003; Mcnamara, 2009; Kapp, 2012). Incorporating competition like features into the learning modules has increased drastically in students' engagement (Hallinen et al.,2009). Game-based learning can be aligned with the sustainability-related courses which are offered to higher education learners. Many pieces of research done in the area of sustainability have proven that games are effective in bringing a practical and attitude change among the learners (Knol & De Vries, 2011; Nordby et al.,2016; Tan & Biswas, 2007; Wu & Huang, 2015; Chien & Lieu, 2012).

LIMITATIONS AND RECOMMENDATIONS

The reviews related to the neural and cognitive areas of game-based learning in higher education are minimal. The researchers tried to establish the efficacy of GBL in bringing changes in the neural circuitry and the cognitive regions of higher education students who engage in gaming as a pedagogy in teaching and learning.

The upcoming research can continue empirically based, especially with the different groups of higher education students. When incorporated in the learning pedagogy in the longer run, various simulation games can establish the success of using game-based learning. Research using innovative technology like electroencephalogram and cognitive batteries can bring better results in understanding neural-cognitive aspects of learning.

CONCLUSION

Teaching and learning process has seen tremendous changes over the years. With the advent of multimedia learning, conventional pedagogy has taken a back seat. In the past few years, game-based learning has been gaining momentum in the higher education system. The emerging practice in game-based learning is the most recent expression of this millennium, incorporating the power of play to improve understanding. With the advent of new technology, games and simulations are already integrated into the traditional educational processes. Game-based learning is deployed widely in education, with existing research examining the relation of fun and education. Most research has been done primarily on school-based learning and fewer studies in the higher education system. There is a shortage of research to find the effectiveness of game-based learning, and its underlying correlates in the higher education environment. This gap is the focus of this research. The current study thus focuses on reviewing various literature to understand the neurocognitive correlates associated with higher education learners engaged in game-based learning.

Learning involves both focused and peripheral attention which is both conscious and unconscious. The ultimate goal of such pedagogy must be thorough immersion while learning and orchestrated immersion is advocated in education these days. To facilitate this immersion a lot of game-based pedagogical practices have emerged. Using rewarding methodologies strengthens learning pathways and also facilitates immersive engagement in class. Games-based activities are assumed to increase engagement in the task, positive affect, motivation, and consequently the learning outcome.

FUNDING INFORMATION

This research received no specific grant from any funding agency in the public, commercial, or not-for-profit sectors.

REFERENCES

All, A., Nunez Castellar, E. P., & Van Looy, J. (2014). Measuring effectiveness in digital game-based learning: A methodological review. *International Journal of Serious Games*, *1*(2), 3–20. doi:10.17083/ijsg.v1i2.18

Alzubi, T., Fernández, R., Flores, J., Duran, M., & Cotos, J. M. (2018). Improving the Working Memory During Early Childhood Education Through the Use of an Interactive Gesture Game-Based Learning Approach. *IEEE Access: Practical Innovations, Open Solutions*, *6*, 53998–54009. doi:10.1109/ACCESS.2018.2870575

Antonaci, A., Klemke, R., & Specht, M. (2019). The Effects of Gamification in Online Learning Environments: A Systematic Literature Review. *Informatics (MDPI)*, *6*(3), 32. doi:10.3390/informatics6030032

Baboo, S & Raja, V. (2017). Impact of playing and watching videogames on classroom attention, problem-solving and prosocial behavior of school children, *IDC International Journal, 4*(3).

Baharom, S. N., Tan, W. H., & Idris, M. Z. (2014). Emotional design for games: The roles of emotion and perception in game design process. *1st International Symposium on Simulation & Serious Games*, 978-981. 10.3850/978-981-09-0463-0_015

Barbas, H. (2000). Connections underlying the synthesis of cognition, memory, and emotion in primate prefrontal cortices. *Brain Research Bulletin*, *52*(5), 319–330. doi:10.1016/S0361-9230(99)00245-2 PMID:10922509

Barna, B., & Fodor, S. (2018). *An Empirical Study on the Use of Gamification on IT Courses at Higher Education. In Advances in Intelligent Systems and Computing* (Vol. 715). Springer. doi:10.1007/978-3-319-73210-7_80

Belova & Zomada. (2020). Innovating Higher Education via Game-Based Learning on Misconceptions. *Education Sciences*, (10), 221.

Boyle, E. A., Hainey, T., Connolly, T. M., Gray, G., Earp, J., Ott, M., Lim, T., Ninaus, M., Ribeiro, C., & Pereira, J. (2016). An update to the systematic literature review of empirical evidence of the impacts and outcomes of computer games and serious games. *Computer Education*, *94*, 178–192. doi:10.1016/j.compedu.2015.11.003

Bozarth, M. A. (1994). Pleasure systems in the brain. *Pleasure: The politics and the reality*, 5-14.

Brom, C., Preuss, M., & Klement, D. (2011). Are educational computer micro-games engaging and effective for knowledge acquisition at high schools? A quasi-experimental study. *Computer Education*, *57*(3), 1971–1988. Advance online publication. doi:10.1016/j.compedu.2011.04.007

Brosch, T., Scherer, K. R., Grandjean, D. M., & Sander, D. (2013). The impact of emotion on perception, attention, memory, and decision-making. *Swiss Medical Weekly, 143*, 13786. doi:10.4414mw.2013.13786 PMID:23740562

Brown, D., Standen, P., Saridaki, M., Shopland, N., Roinioti, E., Evett, L., & Smith, P. (2013). *Engaging Students with Intellectual Disabilities through Games Based Learning and Related Technologies.* Paper presented at the Universal Access in Human-Computer Interaction. Applications and Services for Quality of Life, Berlin, Germany. 10.1007/978-3-642-39194-1_66

Cantoni, L., & Di Blas, N. (2006). Comunicazione. *Teoria e pratiche*, 6.

Chang, C. C., Liang, C., Chou, P.-N., & Lin, G.-Y. (2017). Is game-based learning better in flow experience and various types of cognitive load than non-game-based learning? Perspective from multimedia and media richness. *Computers in Human Behavior, 71*, 218–227. doi:10.1016/j.chb.2017.01.031

Clark, D. B., Tanner-Smith, E. E., & Killingsworth, S. S. (2016). Digital games, design, and learning: A systematic review and meta-analysis. *Review of Educational Research, 86*(1), 79–122. doi:10.3102/0034654315582065 PMID:26937054

Cole, S. W., Yoo, D. J., & Knutson, B. (2012). Interactivity and reward-related neural activation during a serious videogame. *PLoS One, 7*(3), e33909. doi:10.1371/journal.pone.0033909 PMID:22442733

Conejero, A., & Rueda, M. (2017). Early Development of Executive Attention. *Journal of Child and Adolescent Behavior, 05*(02), 341. doi:10.4172/2375-4494.1000341

Connolly, T. M., Boyle, E. A., MacArthur, E., Hainey, T., & Boyle, J. M. (2012). A systematic literature review of empirical evidence on computer games and serious games. *Computers & Education, 59*(2), 661–686. doi:10.1016/j.compedu.2012.03.004

Connolly, T. M., Boyle, E. A., MacArthur, E., Hainey, T., & Boyle, J. M. (2012). A systematic literature review of empirical evidence on computer games and serious games. *Computer Education, 59*(2), 661–686. doi:10.1016/j.compedu.2012.03.004

Crocco, F., Offenholley, K., & Hernandez, C. (2016). A Proof-of-Concept Study of Game-Based Learning in Higher Education. *Simulation & Gaming, 47*(4), 403–422. doi:10.1177/1046878116632484

Davis, M. H., & Gaskell, M. G. (2009). A complementary systems account of word learning: Neural and behavioural evidence. *Philosophical Transactions of the Royal Society of London. Series B, Biological Sciences, 364*(1536), 3773–3800. doi:10.1098/rstb.2009.0111 PMID:19933145

Deterding, S., Dixon, D., Khaled, R., & Nacke, L. (2011). From game design elements to gamefulness: defining gamification. In *Proceedings of the 15th international academic MindTrek conference: Envisioning future media environments* (pp. 9–15). New York: ACM. 10.1145/2181037.2181040

Dixon, M. L., Thiruchselvam, R., Todd, R., & Christoff, K. (2017). Emotion and the prefrontal cortex: An integrative review. *Psychological Bulletin, 143*(10), 1033–1081. doi:10.1037/bul0000096 PMID:28616997

Edwards, C. P. (2002). Three approaches from Europe: Waldorf, Montessori, and Reggio Emilia. *Early Childhood Research & Practice, 4*(1), n1.

Egenfeldt-Nielsen, S. (2007). Third generation educational use of computer games. *Journal of Educational Multimedia and Hypermedia, 16*(3), 263–281.

Fishbach, A., Eyal, T., & Finkelstein, S. R. (2010). How positive and negative feedback motivate goal pursuit. *Social and Personality Psychology Compass, 4*(8), 517–530. doi:10.1111/j.1751-9004.2010.00285.x

Galloway, A. R. (2006). Protocol. *Theory, Culture & Society, 23*(2-3), 317–320. doi:10.1177/026327640602300241

García-Redondo, P., García, T., Areces, D., Núñez, J. C., & Rodríguez, C. (2019). Serious Games and Their Effect Improving Attention in Students with Learning Disabilities. *International Journal of Environmental Research and Public Health, 16*(14), 2480. doi:10.3390/ijerph16142480 PMID:31336804

Garris, P. A., Collins, L. B., Jones, S. R., & Wightman, R. M. (1993). Evoked extracellular dopamine in vivo in the medial prefrontal cortex. *Journal of Neurochemistry, 61*(2), 637–647. doi:10.1111/j.1471-4159.1993.tb02168.x PMID:8336146

Gee, J. P. (2003). *What Video Games Have to Teach Us about Learning and Literacy*. Palgrave Macmillan. doi:10.1145/950566.950595

Ghetti, S., & Bunge, S. A. (2012). Neural changes underlying the development of episodic memory during middle childhood. *Developmental Cognitive Neuroscience, 2*(4), 381–395. doi:10.1016/j.dcn.2012.05.002 PMID:22770728

Gray, P. (2013). Free to Learn: Why Unleashing the Instinct to Play Will Make Our Children Happier. *More Self-Reliant, and Better Students for Life, 141*.

Greipl, S., Klein, E., Lindstedt, A., Kiili, K., Moeller, K., Karnath, H. O., & Ninaus, M. (2021). When the brain comes into play: Neurofunctional correlates of emotions and reward in game-based learning. *Computers in Human Behavior, 125*, 106946. doi:10.1016/j.chb.2021.106946

Greipl, S., Moeller, K., & Ninaus, M. (2020). Potential and limits of game-based learning. *International Journal of Technology Enhanced Learning, 12*(4), 363–389. doi:10.1504/IJTEL.2020.110047

Hallinen, N., Walker, E., Wylie, R., Ogan, A., & Jones, C. (2009). I Was Playing When I Learned: A Narrative Game for French Aspectual Distinctions. *Proc. Workshop Intelligent Educational Games at the 14th Int'l Conf. Artificial Intelligence in Education*, 117-120.

Hamann, S. (2001). Cognitive and neural mechanisms of emotional memory. *Trends in Cognitive Sciences, 5*(9), 394–400. doi:10.1016/S1364-6613(00)01707-1 PMID:11520704

Hamari, J., Koivisto, J., & Sarsa, H. (2014, January). Does gamification work? - A literature review of empirical studies on gamification. In *2014 47th Hawaii International Conference on System Sciences* (pp. 3025–3034). New York: IEEE.

Hartshorne, J. K., & Germine, L. T. (2015). When does cognitive functioning peak. *The asynchronous rise and fall of different cognitive abilities across the life span, 26*, 433-443.

Hartt, M., Hosseini, H., & Mostafapour, M. (2020). Game On: Exploring the Effectiveness of Game-based Learning. *Planning Practice and Research, 35*(5), 589–604. doi:10.1080/02697459.2020.1778859

Hisam, A., Mashhadi, S. F., Faheem, M., Sohail, M., Ikhlaq, B., & Iqbal, I. (2018). Does playing video games effect cognitive abilities in Pakistani children? *Pakistan Journal of Medical Sciences, 34*(6), 1507–1511. doi:10.12669/pjms.346.15532 PMID:30559813

Howard-Jones, P. A., Jay, T., Mason, A., & Jones, H. (2016). Gamification of learning deactivates the default mode network. *Frontiers in Psychology, 6*, 1891. doi:10.3389/fpsyg.2015.01891 PMID:26779054

Huizinga, J., Nachod, H., & Flitner, A. (2006). *Homo ludens: vom Ursprung der Kultur im Spiel*. Rowohlt Taschenbuch Verlag.

Jaaska, E., Aaltonen, K., & Kujala, J. (2021). Game-Based Learning in Project Sustainability Management Education. *Sustainability, 13*(15), 15. doi:10.3390u13158204

James, E., Gaskell, M. G., Weighall, A., & Henderson, L. (2017). Consolidation of vocabulary during sleep: The rich get richer? *Neuroscience and Biobehavioral Reviews, 77*, 1–13. doi:10.1016/j.neubiorev.2017.01.054 PMID:28274725

Johnston, E., & Olson, L. (2015). *The feeling brain: The biology and psychology of emotions*. WW Norton & Company.

Karpouzis, K., & Yannakakis, G. N. (2016). *Emotion in Games*. Springer. doi:10.1007/978-3-319-41316-7

Keller, J. (2008). An integrative theory of motivation, volition, and performance. *Technol. Instr. Cogn. Learn., 6*, 79–104. https://www.oldcitypublishing.com/journals/ticl-home/ticl-issue-contents/ticl-volume-6-number-2-2008/ticl-6-2-p-79-104/

Kempson, E. (2009). *Framework for the development of financial literacy baseline surveys: A first international comparative analysis*. Academic Press.

Kiili, K., Moeller, K., & Ninaus, M. (2018). Evaluating a Game-Based Training of Rational Number Understanding-In-Game Metrics as Learning Indicators. *Computers & Education*, 13–28. doi:10.1016/j.compedu.2018.01.012

Knol, E., & De Vries, P. W. (2011). EnerCities, a serious game to stimulate sustainability and energy conservation: Preliminary results. *eLearning Papers, 25*, 1–10. Retrieved from https://papers.ssrn.com/sol3/papers.cfm?abstract_id=1866206

Knudsen, E. I. (2018). Neural Circuits That Mediate Selective Attention: A Comparative Perspective. *Trends in Neurosciences, 41*(11), 789–805. doi:10.1016/j.tins.2018.06.006 PMID:30075867

Knutson, B., Westdorp, A., Kaiser, E., & Hommer, D. (2000). FMRI visualization of brain activity during a monetary incentive delay task. *NeuroImage, 12*(1), 20–27. doi:10.1006/nimg.2000.0593 PMID:10875899

Kolb, A. Y., & Kolb, D. A. (2005). Learning Styles and Learning Spaces: Enhancing Experiential Learning in Higher Education. *Academy of Management Learning & Education, 4*(2), 193–212. doi:10.5465/amle.2005.17268566

Krouse, R. Z., Ransdell, L. B., Lucas, S. M., & Pritchard, M. E. (2011). Motivation, goal orientation, coaching, and training habits of women ultrarunners. *Journal of Strength and Conditioning Research, 25*(10), 2835–2842. doi:10.1519/JSC.0b013e318204caa0 PMID:21946910

Landi, N., Malins, J. G., Frost, S. J., Magnuson, J. S., Molfese, P., Ryherd, K., & Pugh, K. R. (2018). Neural representations for newly learned words are modulated by overnight consolidation, reading skill, and age. *Neuropsychologia*, *111*, 133–144. doi:10.1016/j.neuropsychologia.2018.01.011 PMID:29366948

Lenhart, A., Kahne, J., Middaugh, E., Macgill, A. R., Evans, C., & Vitak, J. (2008). *Teens, Video Games, and Civics: Teens' Gaming Experiences Are Diverse and Include Significant Social Interaction and Civic Engagement.* Pew internet & American Life Project.

Li, M. C., & Tsai, C.-C. (2013). Game-based learning in science education: A review of relevant research. *Journal of Science Education and Technology*, *22*(6), 877–898. doi:10.100710956-013-9436-x

Lindquist, K. A., Satpute, A. B., Wager, T. D., Weber, J., & Barrett, L. F. (2016). The brain basis of positive and negative affect: Evidence from a meta-analysis of the human neuroimaging literature. *Cerebral Cortex (New York, N.Y.)*, *26*(5), 1910–1922. doi:10.1093/cercor/bhv001 PMID:25631056

Liu, Y., Fu, Q., & Fu, X. (2009). The interaction between cognition and emotion. *Chinese Science Bulletin*, *54*(22), 4102–4116. doi:10.100711434-009-0632-2

Lopez Frias, F. J. (2019). Bernard Suits' Response to the Question on the Meaning of Life as a Critique of Modernity. *Sport, Ethics and Philosophy*, *13*(3-4), 406–418. doi:10.1080/17511321.2018.1550526

Lytras, M. D., Ruan, D., Tennyson, R. D., Ordonez De Pablos, P., García Peñalvo, F. J., & Rusu, L. (2013). Communications in Computer and Information Science. In Information Systems, E-learning, and Knowledge Management Research (vol. 278). doi:10.1007/978-3-642-35879-1

Marcos-García, J. A., Martínez-Monés, A., & Dimitriadis, Y. (2015). DESPRO: A method based on roles to provide collaboration analysis support adapted to the participants in CSCL situations. *Computers & Education*, *82*, 335–353. doi:10.1016/j.compedu.2014.10.027

McClelland, J. L., McNaughton, B. L., & O'Reilly, R. C. (1995). Why there are complementary learning systems in the hippocampus and neocortex: Insights from the successes and failures of connectionist models of learning and memory. *Psychological Review*, *102*(3), 419–457. doi:10.1037/0033-295X.102.3.419 PMID:7624455

McGonigal, J. (2011). *Reality is broken: Why games make us better and how they can change the world.* Penguin Press.

McLaren, B. M., Adams, D. M., Mayer, R. E., & Forlizzi, J. (2017). A computer-based game that promotes mathematics learning more than a conventional approach. *International Journal of Game-Based Learning*, *7*(1), 36–56. doi:10.4018/IJGBL.2017010103

McNamara, D. S., Jackson, G. T., & Graesser, A. C. (2009). Intelligent Tutoring and Games (ITaG). *Proc. Workshop Intelligent Educational Games at the 14th Int'l Conf. Artificial Intelligence in Education*, 1-10.

Menon, V., Boyett-Anderson, J. M., & Reiss, A. L. (2005). Maturation of medial temporal lobe response and connectivity during memory encoding. *Brain Research. Cognitive Brain Research*, *25*(1), 379–385. doi:10.1016/j.cogbrainres.2005.07.007 PMID:16122916

Miller, C.T. (2008). Games: Purpose and Potential in Education. *Springer Science*, 7.

Milovanović, M., Minović, M., Kovačević, I., Minović, J., & Starčević, D. (2009). *Effectiveness of Game-Based Learning: Influence of Cognitive Style.* Paper presented at the Best Practices for the Knowledge Society. Knowledge, Learning, Development and Technology for All, Berlin, Germany.

Moreno, R., & Mayer, R. (2007). Interactive multimodal learning environments: special issue on interactive learning environments: contemporary issues and trends. *Educational Psychology Review, 19*(3), 309–326. doi:10.100710648-007-9047-2

Nebel, S., Schneider, S., & Rey, G. D. (2015). From duels to classroom competition: Social competition and learning in educational videogames within different group sizes. *Computers in Human Behavior, 55*, 384–398. doi:10.1016/j.chb.2015.09.035

Nicholson, S. (2012). *Strategies for meaningful gamification: Concepts behind transformative play and participatory museums.* Presented at Meaningful Play 2012, Lansing, MI. Retrieved August 22, 2016, from https://scottnicholson.com/pubs/meaningfulstrategies.pdf

Nielson, K. A., & Powless, M. (2007). Positive and negative sources of emotional arousal enhance long-term word-list retention when induced as long as 30 min after learning. *Neurobiology of Learning and Memory, 88*(1), 40–47. doi:10.1016/j.nlm.2007.03.005 PMID:17467310

Nordby, A., Øygardslia, K., Sverdrup, U., & Sverdrup, H. (2016). The art of gamification; Teaching sustainability and system thinking by pervasive game development. *The Electronic Journal of e-Learning, 14*(3), 152–168.

Norman, K. L. (2011). *Assessing the Components of Skill Necessary for Playing Video Games.* Human-Computer Interaction Technical Report 11-11-11. University of Maryland. Available online at: http://hcil2.cs.umd.edu/trs/2011-27/2011-27.pdf

O'Doherty, J., Kringerlbach, M. L., Rolls, R. T., Hornak, J., & Andrews, C. (2001). Sažetak reprezentacije nagrade i kazne u ljudskoj orbitofrontalnoj korteksu. *Nature Neuroscience, 4*, 95–102. doi:10.1038/82959 PMID:11135651

Oei & Patterson. (2013). Enhancing cognition with video games: a multiple game training study. *Pubmed, 8*(3).

Ohman, A., Lundqvist, D., & Esteves, F. (2001). The face in the crowd effect: An anger superiority effect with schematic stimuli. *Journal of Personality and Social Psychology, 80*(3), 381–396. doi:10.1037/0022-3514.80.3.381 PMID:11300573

Olfers, K. J. F., & Band, G. P. H. (2018). Game-based training of flexibility and attention improves task-switch performance: Near and far transfer of cognitive training in an EEG study. *Psychological Research, 82*(1), 186–202. doi:10.100700426-017-0933-z PMID:29260316

Palaus, M., Marron, E. M., Viejo-Sobera, R., & Redolar-Ripoll, D. (2017). Neural basis of video gaming: A systematic review. *Frontiers in Human Neuroscience, 11*, 248. doi:10.3389/fnhum.2017.00248 PMID:28588464

Pallavicini, F., Ferrari, A., & Mantovani, F. (2018). Video Games for Well-Being: A Systematic Review on the Application of Computer Games for Cognitive and Emotional Training in the Adult Population. *Frontiers in Psychology*, *9*, 2127. doi:10.3389/fpsyg.2018.02127 PMID:30464753

Panksepp, J. (2004). *Affective neuroscience: The foundations of human and animal emotions*. Oxford University Press.

Parong, J., Mayer, R. E., Fiorella, L., MacNamara, A., Homer, B. D., & Plass, J. L. (2017). Learning executive function skills by playing focused video games. *Contemporary Educational Psychology*, *51*, 141–151. doi:10.1016/j.cedpsych.2017.07.002

Passarotti, A. M., Sweeney, J. A., & Pavuluri, M. N. (2009). Neural correlates of incidental and directed facial emotion processing in adolescents and adults. *Social Cognitive and Affective Neuroscience*, *4*(4), 387–398. doi:10.1093can/nsp029 PMID:20035016

Pekrun, R., & Linnenbrink-Garcia, L. (2014). Introduction to emotions in education. In R. Pekrun & L. Linnenbrink-Garcia (Eds.), International handbook of emotions in education (pp. 1–10). Routledge/Taylor & Francis Group.

Perrotta, C., Featherstone, G., Aston, H., & Houghton, E. (2013). Game-based learning: Latest evidence and future directions. Slough, UK: National Foundation for Educational Research (NFER).

Pessoa, L. (2008). On the relationship between cognition and emotion. *Nature Reviews. Neuroscience*, *9*(2), 148–158. doi:10.1038/nrn2317 PMID:18209732

Phan, K. L., Wager, T., Taylor, S. F., & Liberzon, I. (2002). Functional neuroanatomy of emotion: Embodied persuasion: Fundamental processes by which bodily responses can impact attitudes. *NeuroImage*, *16*, 331–348. doi:10.1006/nimg.2002.1087 PMID:12030820

Pickering, S. J., & Phye, G. D. (2006). *Working Memory and Education*. Elsevier.

Plass, J. L., Homer, B. D., & Kinzer, C. K. (2015). Foundations of game-based learning. *Educational Psychologist*, *50*(4), 258–283. doi:10.1080/00461520.2015.1122533

Polman, de Castro, B. O., & van Aken, M. A. G. (2008). Experimental study of the differential effects of playing versus watching violent video games on children's aggressive behaviour. *Aggressive Behavior*, *34*(3), 256–264. doi:10.1002/ab.20245 PMID:18161877

Prensky, M. (2001). *Digital Game-Based Learning*. McGraw hill.

Prensky, M. (2012). *From digital natives to digital wisdom: Hopeful essays for 21st century learning*. Corwin Press. doi:10.4135/9781483387765

Priyaadharshini, M., Natha Mayil, N., Dakshina, R., Sandhya, S., & Bettina Shirley, R. (2020). Author. *Procedia Computer Science*, *172*, 468–472. doi:10.1016/j.procs.2020.05.143

Rumeser, D., & Emsley, M. (2019). Can serious games improve project management decision making under complexity? *Project Management Journal*, *50*(1), 23–39. doi:10.1177/8756972818808982

Ryan, R. M., & Deci, E. L. (2000). Intrinsic and extrinsic motivations: Classic definitions and new directions. *Contemporary Educational Psychology*, *25*(1), 54–67. doi:10.1006/ceps.1999.1020 PMID:10620381

Ryan, W. S., & Ryan, R. M. (2019). Toward a social psychology of authenticity: Exploring within-person variation in autonomy, congruence, and genuineness using self-determination theory. *Review of General Psychology*, *23*(1), 99–112. doi:10.1037/gpr0000162

Sabourin, J., Rowe, J. P., Mott, B. W., & Lester, J. C. (2011). When Off-Task Is On-Task: The Affective Role of Off-Task Behavior in Narrative-Centered Learning Environments. *Proc. 15th Int'l Conf. Artificial Intelligence in Education*, 523-536.

Sabourin, J. L., & Lester, J. C. (2013). Affect and engagement in Game-BasedLearning environments. *IEEE Transactions on Affective Computing*, *5*(1), 45–56. doi:10.1109/T-AFFC.2013.27

Schmithorst, V. J., Holland, S. K., & Plante, E. (2007). Object identification and lexical/semantic access in children: A functional magnetic resonance imaging study of word-picture matching. *Human Brain Mapping*, *28*(10), 1060–1074. doi:10.1002/hbm.20328 PMID:17133401

Schnotz, W., Fries, S., & Horz, H. (2009). Some motivational aspects of cognitive load theory. In S. Wosnitza, S. A. Karabenick, A. Efklides, & P. Nenniger (Eds.), *Contemporary Motivation Research: From Global to Local Perspectives* (pp. 86–113). Hogrefe.

Schrader, C., & Bastiaens, T. (2012). Educational computer games and learning: The relationship between design, cognitive load, emotions and outcomes. *Journal of Interactive Learning Research*, *23*, 251–271. https://www.learntechlib.org/primary/p/36201/

Sescousse, G., Caldú, X., Segura, B., & Dreher, J. C. (2013). Processing of primary and secondary rewards: A quantitative meta-analysis and review of human functional neuroimaging studies. *Neuroscience and Biobehavioral Reviews*, *37*(4), 681–696. doi:10.1016/j.neubiorev.2013.02.002 PMID:23415703

Silverman, M. H., Jedd, K., & Luciana, M. (2015). Neural networks involved in adolescent reward processing: An activation likelihood estimation meta-analysis of functional neuroimaging studies. *NeuroImage*, *122*, 427–439. doi:10.1016/j.neuroimage.2015.07.083 PMID:26254587

So & Seo. (2018). *A systematic literature review of game-based learning and gamification*. Routledge.

Sullivan-Carr, M. (2016). *Game-based learning and children with ADHD* (10126186 Ed.D.), Drexel University. Retrieved from https://www.proquest.com/dissertations-theses/game-based-learning-children-with-adhd/docview/1797415951/se-2?accountid=38885

Tamminen, J., Payne, J. D., Stickgold, R., Wamsley, E. J., & Gaskell, M. G. (2010). Sleep spindle activity is associated with the integration of new memories and existing knowledge. *The Journal of Neuroscience: The Official Journal of the Society for Neuroscience*, *30*(43), 14356–14360. doi:10.1523/JNEUROSCI.3028-10.2010 PMID:20980591

Tan, J., & Biswas, G. (2007). Simulation-based game learning environments: Building and sustaining a fish tank. *IEEE Xplore Digital Library*, 73–80. . doi:10.1109/DIGITEL.2007.44

Taub, M., Sawyer, R., Smith, A., Rowe, J., Azevedo, R., & Lester, J. (2020). The agency effect: The impact of student agency on learning, emotions, and problem-solving behaviors in a game-based learning environment. *Computers & Education*, *147*, 103781. doi:10.1016/j.compedu.2019.103781

Tyng, C., Amin, H., Saad, M., & Malik, A. (2017). The Influences of Emotion on Learning and Memory. Front.Ullman, M. T. (2016). The declarative/procedural model: a neurobiological model of language learning, knowledge, and use. In *Neurobiology of language* (pp. 953–968). Academic Press.

Ullman, M. T., & Lovelett, J. T. (2018). Implications of the declarative/procedural model for improving second language learning: The role of memory enhancement techniques. *Second Language Research*, *34*(1), 39–65. doi:10.1177/0267658316675195

Um, E., Plass, J. L., Hayward, E. O., & Homer, B. D. (2012). Emotional design in multimedia learning. *Journal of Educational Psychology*, *104*(2), 485–498. doi:10.1037/a0026609

Van Eck, R. (2006). Digital Game-Based Learning: It's Not Just the Digital Natives Who Are Restless. *EDUCAUSE*, 17–30.

Waraczynski, M. A. (2006). The central extended amygdala network as a proposed circuit underlying reward valuation. *Neuroscience and Biobehavioral Reviews*, *30*(4), 472–496. doi:10.1016/j.neubiorev.2005.09.001 PMID:16243397

Wardrip-Fruin. (2009). Better Game Studies Education the Carcassonne Way. *2009 DiGRA '09 - Proceedings of the 2009 DiGRA International Conference: Breaking New Ground: Innovation in Games, Play, Practice and Theory.*

Waris, O., Jaeggi, S. M., Seitz, A. R., Lehtonen, M., Soveri, A., Lukasik, K. M., Söderström, U., Hoffing, R. A. C., & Laine, M. (2019). Video gaming and working memory: A large-scale cross-sectional correlative study. *Computers in Human Behavior*, *97*, 94–103. doi:10.1016/j.chb.2019.03.005 PMID:31447496

Westera, W. (2015). Games are motivating, aren't they? Disputing the arguments for digital game-based learning. *Int. J. Serious Games*, *2*(2), 4–17. doi:10.17083/ijsg.v2i2.58

Wilkinson, P. (2016). A brief history of serious games. *Entertainment computing and serious games*, 17-41.

Woo, J.-C. (2014). Digital game-based learning supports student motivation, cognitive success, and performance outcomes. *Journal of Educational Technology & Society*, *17*, 291–307. https://www.j-ets.net/ETS/issues3ebc.html?id=64

Wouters, P., Van Nimwegen, C., Van Oostendorp, H., & Van Der Spek, E. D. (2013). A meta-analysis of the cognitive and motivational effects of serious games. *Journal of Educational Psychology*, *105*(2), 249–265. doi:10.1037/a0031311

Wu, K., & Huang, P. (2015). Treatment of an anonymous recipient: Solid-waste management simulation game. *Journal of Educational Computing Research*, *52*(4), 568–600. doi:10.1177/0735633115585928

Wu, K., & Huang, P. (2015). Treatment of an anonymous recipient: Solid-waste management simulation game. *Journal of Educational Computing Research*, *52*(4), 568–600. doi:10.1177/0735633115585928

Yang, J. C., Chien, K. H., & Liu, T. C. (2012). A digital game-based learning system for energy education: An energy Conservation PET. *The Turkish Online Journal of Educational Technology*, *11*(2), 27–37.

Yang, Y.-T. C. (2012). Building virtual cities, inspiring intelligent citizens: Digital games for developing students' problem solving and learning motivation. *Computers & Education*, *59*(2), 365–377. doi:10.1016/j.compedu.2012.01.012

Young, M. F., Slota, S., Cutter, A. B., Jalette, G., Mullin, G., Lai, B., & Yukhymenko, M. (2012). Our princess is in another castle: A review of trends in serious gaming for education. *Review of Educational Research*, *82*(1), 61–89. doi:10.3102/0034654312436980

Chapter 5
Game-Based Teaching and Learning in Higher Education:
Challenges and Prospects

M. Mahruf C. Shohel
https://orcid.org/0000-0002-4048-0577
University of Surrey, UK

Iffat Naomee
https://orcid.org/0000-0002-8364-6581
University of Dhaka, Bangladesh

Md. Ashrafuzzaman
https://orcid.org/0000-0003-2100-9998
Bangabandhu Sheikh Mujibur Rahman Digital University, Bangladesh

Sanjida Akter Tanni
Jagannath University, Bangladesh

Farhan Azim
https://orcid.org/0000-0001-8011-1090
University of Melbourne, Australia

ABSTRACT

Game-based pedagogies use games for achieving learning outcomes by guiding the learners through specific tasks, which can be digital and/or non-digital and can promote deep meaningful learning. Therefore, the design of game-based learning helps learners to engage in the meaning-making process and ensure better participation. As the boundaries of classroom learning become blurred through blended or hybrid learning approaches, game-based learning enhances digital literacies for digital natives to prepare them for building a knowledge economy. By exploring existing literature, this chapter highlights how technology can support teachers and learners to go beyond their existing pedagogical boundaries by focusing on ways games may serve as digital sources of learning. It also explores the role game-based pedagogies and digital learning design frameworks play in enhancing learner engagement, collaboration, and cultural understanding.

DOI: 10.4018/978-1-7998-7271-9.ch005

Game-Based Teaching and Learning in Higher Education

INTRODUCTION

In game-based teaching and learning, purposefully designed and developed games are used to support the process of education where games become a powerful tool to assist teachers for enhancing the motivation of students to achieve expected learning outcomes (Thompson & von Gillern, 2020). Conversely, gamification is adapted in teaching and learning for using game design elements in non-gaming contexts as an innovative approach to motivate and engage learners so that they could have enjoyable and sustainable learning experiences (Bozkurt & Durak, 2018). However, game as a support tool is used in pedagogical approaches to develop the activities. Accordingly, digital games as a medium can certainly facilitate constructive learning in a variety of contexts (Clark et al., 2016; Wouters et al., 2013). There is a plethora of literature on using games for educational purposes (Sendra & Lozano-Monterrubio, 2021). Game-based teaching and learning approaches have been utilized in diverse fields of learning such as language (Li et al., 2021), information technology (Oliveira et al., 2013), physics and astronomy (Cardinot & Fairfield, 2019), chemistry (Chen et al., 2020), civil engineering (Taillandier & Micolier, 2021), natural risk management (Taillandier & Adam, 2018), fire safety (Rüppel & Schatz, 2011), research skills (Abbott, 2019) and cultural heritage (Malegiannaki, 2021).

When it is not forced upon them, children, like all people, like learning. Children's growth is inextricably linked to games, and they are constantly surrounded by toys (Chen, 2017). In the 21st century's changing landscape of education, teaching and learning approaches are shifting throughout the globe by embracing digital transition and transformation. Many higher education institutions have already adapted game-based pedagogies to teach 21st century's learners who are considered to be 'digital natives'. Computer games are becoming the most popular computer activity and give a new method of engagement by meeting the genuine requirements and interests of children. However, modern computer and video games present many learning opportunities for individuals (Prensky, 2003). Some of the benefits of games include their attractiveness, novelty, ability to create a better virtual learning environment, and ability to keep the learner focused on the task (Heinich et al., 2002), all of which point to games as excellent educational aids (Cheng & Su, 2012). According to Gee (2003), the real value of successful computer and video games is that they allow people to recreate themselves in new environments while also providing profound learning. Games have been identified as a useful strategy for encouraging students to actively participate in learning activities (Yien et al. 2011; Alessi & Trollip, 1984; Baid & Lambert, 2010; Kirikkaya et al., 2010; Huizenga et al., 2009).

The majority of teaching and learning methods still adhere to the conventional face-to-face delivery modality, and textbooks can often appear esoteric with their numerous phases, theories, and case studies, while lacking practical application. Several studies have revealed the applicability and effectiveness of computer games by using the game-based learning approach to a variety of learning activities (Bourgonjon et al., 2010; Warren et al., 2008). There are certain features of game-based learning that help students learn more effectively such as representation, fun, play, goals, outcomes, feedback, win states and others. In addition, competition/challenge, problem solving, task, and stories can make learning more viable (Felix & Johnson, 1993; Prensky, 2001a). An educational game places the learner at the center of the learning process, making learning easier, more enjoyable, and more successful (Cheng & Su, 2012).

A game-based learning environment is one in which specific learning objectives are accomplished through game play (Ennis, 2018). The majority of definitions of game-based learning emphasize that it is a sort of game play with specific learning outcomes (Shaffer et al., 2005). The assumption is that the game is digital, however this is not always the case. As a parallel to this concept, the design process for educational games entails balancing the necessity to cover subject information with the desire to prioritize game play (Plass et al., 2010). Gamification and game-based strategies, on the other hand, have distinct properties. Gamification incorporates components such as point-based systems, leaderboards, badges, and other elements, whereas game-based learning is training that incorporates game elements to teach a certain skill or accomplish a specific learning outcome (it takes core content and objectives and makes them fun). Games-based learning, such as virtual reality (VR), can be used in history classes to digitally visit and explore historical lands. For example, in Ubisoft's "Assassin's Creed: Odyssey," students can tour ancient Greece as well as various historical monuments (Ivus, 2021). This corollary emphasizes the distinction between gamification and game-based learning. Consider the gamification of math homework, which involves awarding points and stars to students for completing existing exercises that they would otherwise find tiresome. Game-based learning of the same math topic, on the other hand, would include restructuring homework activities, utilizing artificial conflict and rules of play to make them more exciting and engaging, even if it included points and stars (Plass et al., 2015).

Qian and Clark (2016) define game-based learning (GBL) as, "an environment where game content and game play enhance knowledge and skills acquisition, and where game activities involve problem solving spaces and challenges that provide players/learners with a sense of achievement" (p.51). Moreover, according to Tang, Hanneghan, and El Rhalibi (2009), game-based learning is an innovative learning approach derived from the use of computer games with educational value or various types of software applications that use games for learning and education purposes such as learning support, teaching enhancement, assessment, and evaluation of learners. As per Ebner and Holzinger (2007), game-based learning is comparable to problem-based learning in that the specific problem scenarios are embedded within a play framework. Duolingo[1], Minecraft[2], Second Life[3], Brainscape[4], Kahoot[5], Creadly[6], and Tophat[7] are examples of gamification and game-based learning applications.

The fact that games are not very trustworthy as teaching tools is a basic issue with game-based learning in formal education. Creating a technological infrastructure that allows digital games to run consistently and efficiently as well as performing regular maintenance to ensure that they do so for every classroom activity takes a significant amount of time and resources (Marklund & Taylor, 2016). As with any new teaching technique, there are a variety of obstacles to overcome while using games in the curriculum and classroom. Teachers are put under a lot of pressure in game-based learning because they must fulfill a variety of roles, each of which necessitates a particular set of skills. According to Jan and Chen (2015) pedagogical, technological, and logistical concerns are grade two challenges, which can be tackled when research and financial resources are in place and are more likely to be overcome. Grade one problems include curricular, performative, social, and temporal issues, which are more adaptable to change even when external resources are poured in. Moreover, Chee, Mehrotra, and Ong (2014) identify technological accessibility and literacy as a main barrier and guiding element in the integration of digital game-based learning in schools, claiming that "the key challenges teachers encounter are not technology oriented but practice centric" (p. 313).

Games are often used to improve a boring and difficult course, with course content corresponding to game levels and game-based learning providing access to the knowledge and expertise of the course instructor. People enjoy engaging with the digital game-based learning system, which uses different courses as activity content to allow students to achieve personalized learning through 'learning by doing', bringing game entertainment, fun, and interaction into education, and achieving the goal of edutainment (Cheng & Su, 2012). Some educators believe that game-based learning is an effective instructional strategy (Von Wangenheim & Shull, 2009). According to studies, game-based learning may be the most effective technique to motivate pupils to study (Provost, 1990; Papastergiou, 2009a; Dickey, 2010; Huang, 2010; Tüzün et al., 2009; Wang & Rao, 2020). Furthermore, it has been suggested that a game-based learning method could be a suitable way to engage children's abstract thinking during the cognitive development process, as well as encourage their higher order thinking ability (Carbonaro et al., 2010). Game-based learning increases learning performance and outcomes through affective (e.g., enjoyment), cognitive (e.g., cognitive load), and behavioral (e.g., intention to participate in learning) factors (Koivisto & Hamari, 2019; Sailer & Homner, 2019).

GOALS AND OBJECTIVES

In the context of the changing landscape of higher education, this chapter focuses on several aspects of game-based learning. Emerging technologies, digital skills, digital transformation and digital economy, digital native and 21st century skills, game-based pedagogical approaches and higher education, prospects of using game-based teaching and learning in higher education, and challenges of adapting game-based pedagogical approaches are also highlighted. To summarize, the purpose of this study was to achieve the following objectives:

1. To explore the use of game-based pedagogical approaches in higher education.
2. To identify the prospects of using game-based teaching and learning in higher education.
3. To discuss the difficulties associated with adapting game-based pedagogical approaches.

CHANGING LANDSCAPE OF HIGHER EDUCATION

Higher education has been expanding across national lines in recent years, both in terms of collaboration and competition. A large number of institutions, stakeholders, and students now have global access to advancements in this field in multiple sectors (Varghese, 2014). Advancements in technology and communication are impacting tertiary level learners in their personal, social, and economic life and many developments have emerged to fulfill their demand. For tertiary level students, institutions and employers now expect practical and skill-oriented education which will help to create human assets (Bengu et al., 2020). Students also believe that the goal of higher education is to help them with their personal and social development as well as to prepare them for the job market (Brooks et al., 2020). Hence, teachers' beliefs are constantly changing and moving towards constructivism (Azim & Ahmed, 2010). Teachers encourage experienced students to engage, participate and build rapport with peers and teachers which makes learning more dynamic and interesting (Fischer & Hänze, 2020).

Prior to World War II, the goal of higher education was to develop community leaders and create a better version of citizens to serve the society. However, the aim of higher education has shifted substantially as a result of changes in society. Instead of traditional qualities, novel aspects are emerging; traditionally, higher education was seen as a public good, but it has now evolved into a means of obtaining work. Furthermore, rather than being considered as curious learners, students at this level are now treated as customers, and professors are treated as service providers (Alemu, 2018). However, it is hoped that current higher education would also provide standardized education, globalized education, a large number of educational materials, a flexible education platform, and research-based education (Teichler,

2017). Higher education today is more adaptable, student-centered, and substantially more accessible, fostering an inclusive, equitable, and lifelong learning environment (Alexander, 2010).

Information and communication technology (ICT) has a huge impact on our day to day lives and in the past couple of decades it has brought great changes in our lifestyle. The biggest impact it has, is in the field of education as the learning landscape is continuously changing and new learning methods and techniques are emerging (Sharma et al., 2017). Massive open online courses (MOOCs) are now being offered to global students, traditional classrooms are being replaced by virtual classrooms and students are continuously looking for new and improved learning approaches.

In 21st century higher education, new teaching methods like flipped learning, project-based learning, cooperative learning, personalized learning, gamification, design thinking, thinking-based learning, and competency-based learning are encouraged (Mehta, 2020). Moreover, educational institutions are attempting to go beyond online education by developing a "metaverse" that aids in the delivery of classes and creates an immersive learning experience that encompasses all aspects of campus life while utilizing cutting-edge digital technologies such as virtual reality, augmented reality, image recognition and eye-tracking, and avatars (Lee, 2021). In these modern days, education is becoming more digitized and globalized. Therefore, learners' development is dependent on acquiring digital information and abilities. Students are always connected to mobile devices, using social media as the major medium of communication, and employing cloud computing skills to create new tools and products, while educational institutes are supposed to leverage technology to compete with online education alternatives. Higher education and academics are being impacted and changed as a result of this influence (Sergeant, 2021).

In the recent past, the COVID-19 pandemic has had a huge impact on the global education sector, causing the closure of the majority of educational institutions (Shohel et al., 2021b; Shohel et al., 2021c; Emon, Alif & Islam, 2020, Ratten, 2020). To combat the COVID-19 pandemic, most countries had to temporarily shut down educational institutions (Shohel et al., 2021a; Dutta & Smita, 2020) and teaching and learning shifted from the typical classroom setting to emergency remote teaching and learning. Most universities transitioned from face-to-face to online learning consequently (Shohel et al., 2021e) and are considering blended teaching and learning in the post-COVID or new normal era (Shohel et al., 2021d). It has been widely reported that, home-bound and deprived of any other activities, many students are spending time playing a wide variety of computer/mobile games during the pandemic. With the emergence of this newly established and much larger user-base of computer and mobile games, it is high time to consider how to transform learning materials and approaches into various game-based educational content and approaches for the near future when these students get back to formal learning.

Higher education today places a greater emphasis on skills compared to knowledge. Critical thinking, independent learning and active learning are all attainable in higher education. Its goal is to prepare students to participate in the economy and society as a whole (Mukwambo, 2019). Innovative teaching methods such as game-based teaching-learning are being utilized as technology and communication advance (Buckless, 2014). Through a game-based method, soft skills, managerial skills, self-evaluation, and leadership abilities can be acquired and utilized to meet the needs of the twenty-first century (Weng et al., 2016).

However, despite the development of digitization in higher education, it still has several drawbacks, such as lack of devices and connectivity, lack of resources, lack of skills, inequalities and lack of motivation on an individual level (Shohel et al., 2021a). Institutions are also dealing with budget issues and a lack of government assistance is a concern (Bond et al, 2018). While considering game-based teaching and learning in higher education, these issues need to be kept in mind and any development of such teaching learning strategies needs to have built-in measures within the design to address such limitations.

EMERGING TECHNOLOGIES

Technology encompasses far more than just computers, tablets, and the internet. Digital tools and media-rich resources are examples of technology-enabled learning; including computers, the internet, social media, mobile and tablet devices, open educational materials (OERs), online films and documents, to name a few (COL, 2017). Technology is a term that refers to a tool or system that is used to address problems. In education, this word refers to "things or tools used to support teaching and learning" (Bates, 2015, para. 7). Software (like word processors), systems (like learning management systems), services (like YouTube or Google Docs), and settings (like virtual worlds) are all examples of educational technologies, as are the hardware and networks that support them. Traditional "technologies" like blackboards and textbooks are also acceptable (Cleveland-Innes & Wilton, 2018).

Technologies help to solve challenges. When a tool is used with the objective of meeting a human need, it is called a technology; an educational technology's description will include its teaching or learning purpose. In many cases, this will entail delivering learning information in various kinds of media (e.g., text, image, audio, video, games), but it might also entail social or collaborative activities (such as discussion boards or videoconferencing) or learner-created artefacts (assessment and evaluation activities or e-portfolios) (Cleveland-Innes & Wilton, 2018). It is critical to realize that technology in education can be used in a variety of ways and for a variety of goals. The explosion of Web 2.0 or social media tools on the internet over the last several years is an illustration of this broad toolset (Ashrafuzzaman, 2021).

Regardless of the variety of tools, there are six key purposes for technology in education according to research and practice in the classroom. These are: communicating, searching, collaborating, creating, assessing, and developing utilizing technology (COL, 2017). Learning management systems, or LMSs, web conferencing, digital textbooks, blogs and wikis, social bookmarking, mashups and digital storytelling, e-portfolios and simulations, serious games, and virtual worlds and metaverse are all developing and effective technology for face-to-face, online, or blended teaching and learning.

Recent studies emphasize the potential of digital technologies as learning tools that can foster collaborative, creative, and authentic learning. Though higher education was mostly unaltered by technical advancements in the early 1900s, educational administrations, instruction processes, and teaching-learning had become increasingly linked to technology. With the advances in technology, computer-based and online-based new technologies are constantly moving towards a more collaborative and interactive learning environment. Teachers, in addition to learners, are now being exposed to technologies and benefiting from these digital breakthroughs (Staley & Trinkle, 2011). Gradually, e-learning is evolving and shaping higher education into more digitized versions. When it comes to e-learning, there are three different phases: e-learning 1.0 (1995–2005), e-learning 2.0 (2005–2015), and e-learning 3.0 (2015–present), all of which are used or have been used in education and the current phase involves cloud-based distributed computing, smart mobile technology, artificial intelligence, 3D visualization, and learning management systems (LMS).

Individuals are now encouraged to learn better through creative thinking, critical thinking, communicating, and collaborating using online platforms creating the e-learning trajectory. Universities are implementing new curricular and pedagogical approaches through impacting personal learning concepts

(Sharma et al., 2017). It has been established that the usage of developing technology in education can help educators and students be more creative and learn more effectively (Backhouse, 2013). Similarly, incorporating new technologies into the classroom might help teachers and students be more creative and learn more successfully (Backhouse, 2013). Education and higher education institutions can benefit by using technology to make things easier, more effective, interactive, and communicative. Technology can also help educational assessment systems, governance frameworks, and strategic plans (Azim & Rahman, 2015; Bozalek et al., 2013).

DIGITAL SKILLS, DIGITAL TRANSFORMATION AND DIGITAL ECONOMY

Digital skills are a set of capabilities that enable individuals to access and manage information through the use of digital devices, communication applications, and networks. These skills allow people to generate and connect digital information, interact and cooperate, and resolve issues in order to be more successful and creative in their lives, education, employment, and community engagements (UNESCO, 2018). Digital skills are a new type of literacy competency that consists of two parts: formal and substantial information abilities in the use of computers and the internet (Gui, 2007). Van Dijk created a model in 2005 to characterize the various components of digital skills, including operational skills, informational skills, formal, substantive, and strategic skills (Van Dijk, 2005).

UNESCO's Digital Literacy Global Framework defines Digital Literacy as: the ability to access, manage, understand, integrate, communicate, evaluate and create information safely and appropriately through digital technologies for employment, decent jobs, and entrepreneurship. It includes competences that are variously referred to as computer literacy, ICT literacy, information literacy, and media literacy (Digital Skills Country Action Plan Methodological Guidebook, Part 2, 2021).

According to DigComp 2.0 (Vuorikari, 2016) and DigComp 2.1 (Carretero et al., 2017) digital skills or competencies can be grouped into five categories which are:

1. Information and data literacy
    a. Browsing, searching, filtering data, information and digital content
    b. Evaluating data, information and digital content
    c. Managing data, information and digital content Competence area
2. Communication and collaboration
    a. Interacting through digital technologies
    b. Sharing through digital technologies
    c. Engaging in citizenship through digital technologies
    d. Collaborating through digital technologies
    e. Netiquette
    f. Managing digital identity Competence area
3. Digital content creation
    a. Developing digital content
    b. Integrating and re-elaborating digital content
    c. Copyright and licences
    d. Programming Competence area

4. Safety
   a. Protecting devices
   b. Protecting personal data and privacy
   c. Protecting health and well-being
   d. Protecting the environment Competence area
5. Problem solving
   a. Solving technical problems
   b. Identifying needs and technological responses
   c. Creatively using digital technologies
   d. Identifying digital competence gaps

The European Union's DigComp 2.0 and its more recent upgrade DigComp 2.1, which identifies five domains with 21 competencies, are the most comprehensive and extensively used frameworks for general digital skills. The five domains are as follows: (i) information and data literacy; (ii) communication and cooperation; (iii) digital content creation; (iv) safety; and (v) problem solving (Carretero et al. 2017). There are eight proficiency levels (in DigComp 2.1) for each competency, which are divided into four major categories: foundational, intermediate, advanced, and highly specialized.

ICTC also conducted primary research into the 21st century digital skills or core competencies that are fundamental for student success after graduation. According to respondents these are, critical thinking, communication (language/etiquette), adaptability, creativity (troubleshooting), learning autonomy (independence), collaboration, determination, computational thinking, problem solving, empathy, curiosity, confidence, resilience depiction of student competencies, categorized as "human" or "transferrable" skills and digital citizenship (data privacy, media literacy) digital fluency (knowledge/navigation/digital awareness), coding, information/data management, project coordination, marketing, financial literacy these are depiction of student competencies, categorized as "technical" or "academic" skills (Ivus et al., 2020).

Gamification and Game Based Learning (GBL) fosters the development of information and data literacy abilities, such as the capacity to explore and understand information and digital content. When there is a need to engage, communicate, and participate in "quests," especially as a team, communication and cooperation skills are also cultivated. When developing, constructing, or building within a game, strong digital content production and problem-solving skills are also essential. Furthermore, when utilized correctly, gamification and GBL have been shown to increase student engagement, motivation, flexibility, and collaboration while also establishing and promoting digital skills (Fortier, 2019).

DIGITAL NATIVE AND 21ST CENTURY'S SKILLS

Prensky (2001a) coined the terms "digital native" and "digital immigrant" in 2001. According to him, digital natives are those who were born during the technological revolution, whereas digital immigrants are people who were born before the technological era. Digital natives are pupils who were born and nurtured in a world where technology has become an integral part of their social, educational, and professional lives (Dingali & Scychell, 2015). They are referred to as the millennial generation or Generation Z. Individuals from the Z generation are thought to be digitally savvy and comfortable with technology. Furthermore, they spend considerable time engaging in digital activities, making life easier with digital abilities, and pursuing careers based on this (Gills, 2020). The Framework for the Twenty-First

Century defines 21st-century skills as those that aim to prepare learners for the twenty-first century. This consists of cognitive, problem-solving abilities, effective communication, teamwork, information and communications technologies for learning, and self-control (Partnership for 21st Century Learning, 2016). 21st century talents include certain critical knowledge and skills, according to the Framework for 21st Century Learning Definition.

The P21 framework's (Figure 1) theoretical foundation is that students should be provided the right opportunities and tools to acquire the skills that they will need for work and careers in today's world (Raymundo, 2020).

Figure 1. P21 framework for 21st century learning (P21 Framework Definitions, 2009, p.1; Erdem, 2019, p.7).

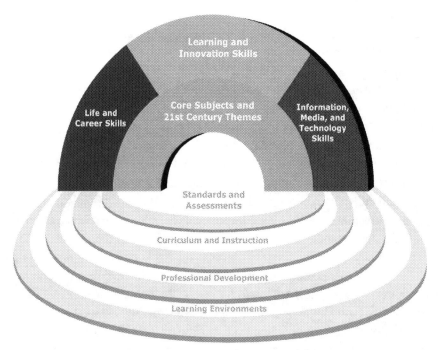

Mastery of basic disciplines and 21st century themes is required of all 21st century students. English, reading or language arts, world languages, arts, mathematics, economics, science, geography, history, government, and civics are all core disciplines. In addition to these subjects, P21 believes that schools should focus not only on mastery of core subjects, but also on promoting understanding of academic content at much higher levels by weaving 21st century interdisciplinary themes into core subjects: Global Awareness, Financial, Economic, Business, and Entrepreneurial Literacy, Civic Literacy, Health Literacy, and Environmental Literacy (P21 Framework Definitions, 2009).

Learning skills, literacy skills, and life skills are the three areas of 21st-century skills. Critical thinking, creativity, collaboration, and communication are the four Cs that make up learning skills (LCs). Information, media, and technological literacy are three literacy skills that focus on how students can understand facts, publishing outlets, credible sources, and the technology behind them. Life skills concern inner elements of individuals' day to day life at personal and professional level i. e. flexibility, leadership, initiative, productivity and social skills. (Partnership for 21st Century Learning, 2019). The Organisation for Economic Co-operation and Development (OECD) has defined 21st-century skills as the combination of three dimensions: information, communication and ethics & social impact (Ananiadou & Claro, 2009). The most crucial 21st-century (21C) learning abilities, critical thinking and problem-solving, can be improved by frequent exposure to computer games and other digital media (Day et al., 2001; Gee, 2003).

Figure 2. Framework for 21st century learning (©2019, Battelle for Kids. All Rights Reserved. www.bfk.org[8]).

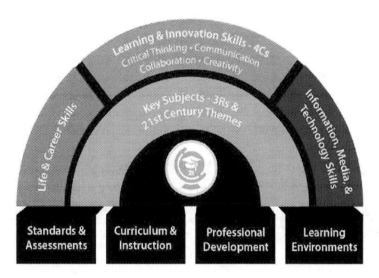

These digital natives are at ease in collaborative, interactive, participatory, and active learning environments. Furthermore, online platforms provide a flexible and resourceful environment because there are various sources for learning which are resulting in an experienced, independent, and inquisitive student (Barnes & Noble College, 2015). As a result, these natives learn in open, joyful, innovative, updated, smart, practical, and collaborative learning environments, although they often lose concentration (Kivunja, 2014). Students gain knowledge, but not in depth, and they are also overloaded with information, causing them to get disoriented (Scharton, 2019). So, in order to teach these digital natives, the teaching technique must be appropriate. Teachers should encourage them to engage in increasingly technology-based, activity-based, interactive, and collaborative pedagogies (UNESCO-IITE, 2011). Nowadays, digital immigrants are teaching digital natives, resulting in a digital gap that is already affecting teaching and learning (Chun & Evan, 2009). However, material-based, game-based, interactive, and up-to-date teaching should be used to accommodate digital natives (Bowman, 2020).

GAME-BASED PEDAGOGICAL APPROACHES AND HIGHER EDUCATION

The idea of using games in teaching-learning probably was first introduced by Socrates as 'law-abiding play', where he described that the play will direct towards learning the truth and useful things and not distract from it (Plato, 1943). Renowned psychologists such as Jean Piaget (1962) and Lev Vygotsky (1962) also argued that play is an important factor for cognitive development throughout life. From then till now a number of scholars have described the use of games as a powerful tool of instruction (Warren et al., 2009; Crocco et al., 2016) that have positive impacts on students' learning (Prensky, 2001b; Aldrich, 2003; Jenkins et al. 2003; Dickey, 2007). Game that involves learning has been defined as "a challenging activity, structured with rules, goals, progression and rewards, that is separate from the real world, and undertaken with a spirit of playfulness" (Moseley & Whitton, 2015, p. 3). Although this definition gives a clear idea about the games that are needed for game-based learning mechanisms in educational contexts, it is important to distinguish between game, simulation, serious game and gamification. Kapp (2012) argued that gamification is not simply adding game-like features in e-learning platforms, but rethinking the whole learning design.

Figure 3. Game thinking decision tree (Marczewski, 2015)

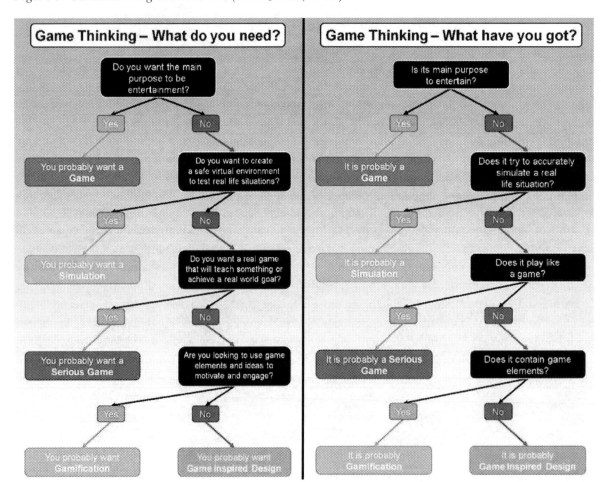

Game-Based Teaching and Learning in Higher Education

Designing a game-based instruction can be difficult and thus the decision chart by Marczewski (2015) can be a great starting point to understand different concepts related to games and gamification.

Game-based pedagogy allows learners to discover and engage in the decision-making process by creating opportunities for experiential learning spaces where learners can engage in rich collaborative interactions to develop complex problem-solving skills by using a variety of complex tools. However, meaningful learning, including critical thinking, decision-making, in video games may model engaging and effective instructional techniques for acquiring digital literacies through different multimodal learning experiences.

Plass, Homer, and Kinzer (2015) propose a simple model that describes the essential structure that practically all games appear to have, rather than a comprehensive theory of learning. A challenge, a response, and feedback are the three main components of this structure (see Figure 4). When the feedback creates a new challenge or leads the player to respond differently to the original task, a loop is created.

The model demonstrates how game design elements are at the heart of the learning process, influencing how challenges, responses, and feedback are created. The different types of interaction of each of these three crucial parts with the others alter the learning process in distinct ways. Challenges, for example, might be motivating when told in a compelling story. Game elements, such as tossing birds in Angry Birds, can make responses pleasurable. Game characters or a leaderboard, as in Little Big Planet, might provide amusing feedback.

Figure 4. Model of game-based learning (Plass, Homer & Kinzer, 2015).

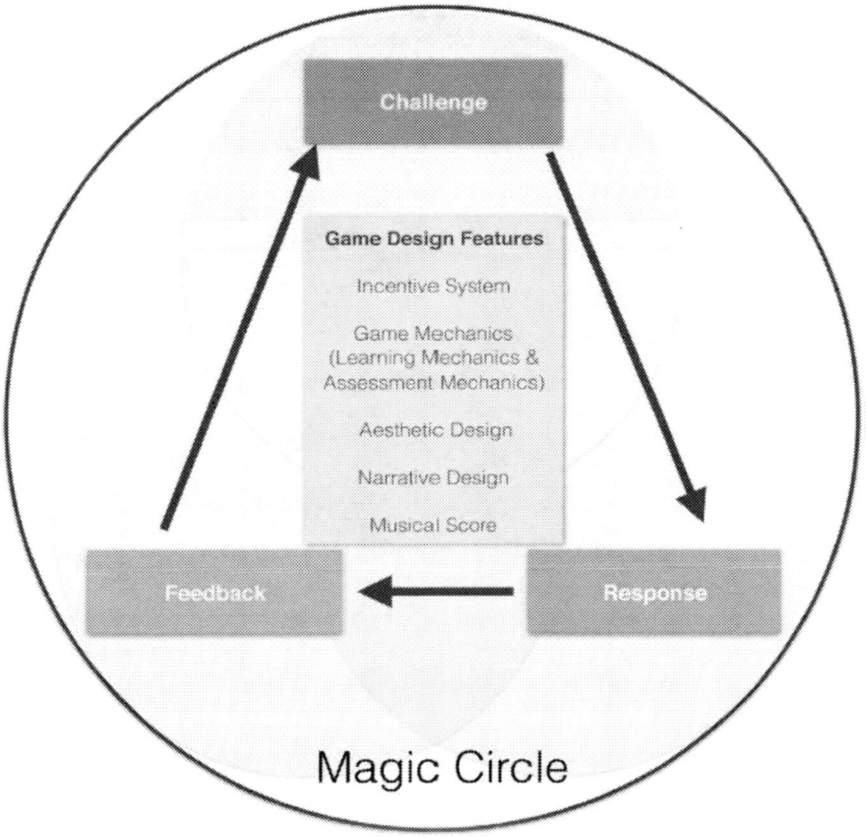

Figure 5 shows a design framework that suggests numerous study lines looking into how specific theories may be implemented through specific design elements, how these designs can lead to specific types of learner engagement, and how these sorts of engagement aid learning. Plass et al. (2015) advocate for a broad scope for this Integrated design framework of game-based and playful learning, including independent and dependent variables for cognitive, emotional, motivational, social, and cultural perspectives.

Figure 5. Integrated design framework of game-based and playful learning (Plass, Homer & Kinzer, 2015).

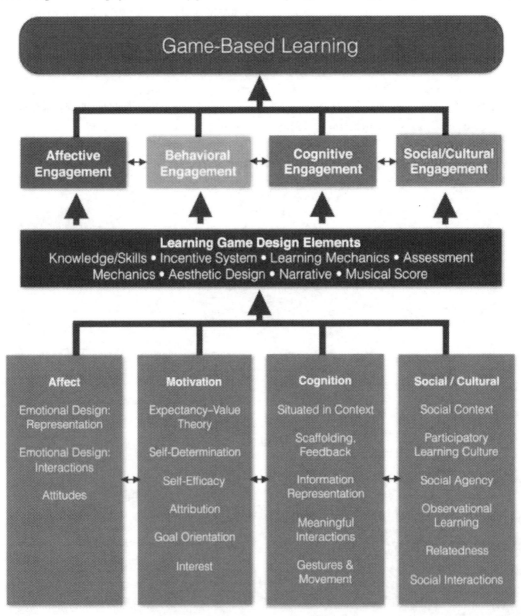

This carefully crafted learning experience integrates affective, behavioral, cognitive, and sociocultural engagement, resulting in a Magic Circle of fun learning (Plass et al., 2010). This type of learning experience is sometimes referred to as a flow experience (Csikszentmihalyi, 1990), but we prefer to think of it as optimal engagement, or engagement that is maximized for learning. In most other learning settings, taking into account numerous types of engagement is unusual: As indicated at the top of Figure 5, design aspects that result in a playful experience enable these various forms of involvement. In this way, games are a unique genre for implementing existing learning models, and playfulness gives these models a new dimension. This generates a learning environment that makes games a better genre to use for implementing these principles than other, more traditional genres (Plass et al., 2015).

CHALLENGES OF ADAPTING GAME-BASED PEDAGOGICAL APPROACHES

Despite its benefits, game-based learning pedagogy has certain difficulties. The teacher must be able to assess the circumstances of their school environment at the start of a game-based learning session. Before designing a game-based learning curriculum, institutional support systems, hardware and software availability, and the accessibility of other resources or obstacles must be considered (Marklund & Taylor, 2016). According to Kaimara et al. (2021), there are significant constraints in the game-based pedagogical approach. These are -

1. Financial constraints
2. The stick-on tendency for traditional teaching methods
3. Lack of ICT training
4. Lack of resources and
5. Lack of strategy and framework

Similarly, Spiegelman and Glass (2008) have pointed out several concerns regarding the design, development and implementation of game-based learning. Those are-

1. Game making is time consuming
2. Needs a lot of positive effort to develop and administrate
3. May involve expensive materials
4. Designing is expensive and a very complex procedure
5. A number of additional resources (pedagogical and technical) needed
6. Difficult to ensure access for everyone
7. Students' acceptance is crucial

Lack of funding is a major issue when it comes to implementing game-based pedagogy in teaching and learning (Mozelius et al., 2017). The majority of the time, teachers prefer using traditional teaching approaches. Because of their pre-assumptions about game-based learning (which often manifests some unfounded discomfort towards such approaches) and their preference for traditional teaching methods, most people do not explore game-based teaching methods (Ruggiero, 2013). Lack of ICT training and infrastructure are very common reasons behind the unwillingness to pursue game-based methods in the classroom (Hébert, 2021). Furthermore, in game-based teaching-learning, an ineffective assessment approach often works as a barrier (Marklund, 2015) because teachers do not use standard and structured teaching approaches in game-based learning, the strategy may not always produce the desired results (Epper et al., 2012). Apart from a lack of prior experience, learners and educators frequently face challenges when introducing game-based teaching methods, and the attitudes of both are critical for successful implementation (Allsop & Jesse, 2015).

Game-based teaching-learning is made easier by the motivation and mindset of the teachers. In addition, subject-based game credibility, exchangeability, and the social component can pose obstacles in game-based classroom instruction (Ney et al, 2012). Many obstacles, such as aimless game instruction, lack of interaction, lack of clarity, feedback, and monitoring, can lead to game-based classroom lessons being misinterpreted (Kevin et al., 2021). According to Mertala's (2019) results, students frequently lose attention and seriousness in game-based learning because they mistake it for meaningless play. Whitton and Moseley (2012) along with White and McCoy (2019) also agreed that students may not take game-based teaching-learning seriously at times. When it comes to adopting game-based learning in large classrooms, a lack of control is a major issue. Students are prone to be disorganized, causing confusion, and failing to meet their goals (Abbot, 2019). Moreover, according to Marklund and Taylor (2016), there is a shortage of reliable hardware in game-based technology. Besides, teachers do not have enough time to integrate game-based learning. While the infrastructure is challenging, teacher and student preparation is also expected to be important.

All these obstacles can be listed under logistic, technological and pedagogical challenges which according to Jan et al. (2015) are grade two challenges, which can be overcome with financial support and proper training. On the other hand, grade one challenges include curricular, performative, social, and temporal issues, which are more complex and need more time, effort, knowledge and understanding of game-based learning programs, in-depth knowledge of the content and subject matter and proper utilization of resources to overcome (Jan et al., 2015). Educause (2014) raised some concerns regarding game-based pedagogical approaches which are similar to the grade one challenges. Those are-

1. Pedagogically sound games might not be interesting to all
2. Students may take games as leisure activities and not as opportunities for learning
3. Games may increase self-consciousness among students
4. Aligning games with learning objectives and keeping them enjoyable at the same time might be difficult
5. Aligning the main focus of the game/games with the curriculum could be hard

Marklund and Taylor (2016) in their study also found that the most challenging parts of introducing game-based learning are designing the curriculum and aligning the learning outcomes with the game. Ifenthaler et al. (2012) identified evaluation and game instructions as the most significant issues in game-based classes. Watson et al. (2016) also identified a number of challenges for game-based teaching-learning. According to them, there are issues in organizing game-based learning to correspond with the course, certain games are extremely challenging for learners and students are sometimes unable to differentiate the value of games. Teachers don't have enough time for professional development on game utilization when there is a lack of administrative support for introducing this method in schools. Besides, some games aren't relevant to the real world, and delivering proper assessment and feedback on game-based learning becomes more difficult.

Game-Based Teaching and Learning in Higher Education

To incorporate game-based learning in higher education, the educators should cautiously keep all these challenges in mind and plan accordingly. Despite all the challenges, incorporating game-based pedagogy in higher education is highly desirable as different researchers have found that game-based instruction is generally more effective than nongame instructions (Vogel et al., 2006; Sitzmann, 2011; Wouters et al., 2013; Clark et al., 2016).

PROSPECTS OF USING GAME-BASED TEACHING AND LEARNING IN HIGHER EDUCATION

The new generation of young adults who have had access to advanced technological instruments, high-speed internet and social networking applications since birth, have a different perception of teaching-learning methods and techniques and thus game-based learning is gaining more popularity among them (Prensky, 2001b; Becker, 2008). Their venturesome attitude towards life, excellent ability to multitask and continuous enthusiasm for knowing and learning new things indicate that the future of education and learning approaches needs to improve to match their expectations (Ibrahim & Jaafar, 2009). Industry 4.0 concepts such as robotics, augmented reality and the internet have had a significant impact on transforming overall educational perspectives (James, 2019).

Higher education is becoming more concerned with innovation, as seen by new teaching-learning methods and personalized learning (Suvin, 2020). Teachers and students can use innovative tools and technology as part of Education 4.0 (Lawrence et al., 2019). Learning is more practical, motivating, personalized, and aligned with digital game-based learning, which creates pioneering, creative, and self-reliant learners (Crocco et al., 2016)

A number of researchers have thus argued that game-based learning or incorporating games in teaching-learning can elicit students' interest in learning the contents, create a joyful learning environment for them, match with their rapidly changing expectations and transform the process of instruction (Kiili, 2005; Oblinger, 2006; Teh, 2007; Gee, 2014). According to Grussendorf (2021) Game-based learning has some additional advantages. They are as follows:

1. Increase student engagement
2. Provide instant feedback
3. Motivate yourself from within
4. Enhance decision-making and problem-solving abilities
5. Prompt behavioral modification
6. Contribute to the development of skills
7. Capture theoretical notions and social occurrences that are complex.
8. Encourage knowledge application
9. Assist students in learning
10. Provide experiential learning

Focusing on the prospects of game-based learning, Oblinger (2004) identified six 'key learning functions' of games, which are:

1. Activation of prior learning

2. Fostering understanding of the relation between knowledge and practice within context
3. High quality 'feedback and assessment' facilities
4. Promoting application of prior knowledge in new setting
5. Accommodation of experience-based learning
6. Motivation and stimulation towards knowledge sharing

Games have a positive impact on students' attitude towards learning different subject matters and their attention and concentration on understanding the contents (Steinkuehler, 2004; Barab et al., 2006; Squire, 2006). In addition, games can create opportunities for the students to explore a wide range of areas of knowledge (Squire & Jenkins, 2003).

Game-based learning has a number of advantages including enhancing learners' performance and encouraging cognitive, behavioral and affective development (Plass et al., 2015; Howard-Jones & Jay, 2016; Koivisto & Hamari, 2019; Sailer & Homner, 2019). Game-based learning allows students to learn the same concepts as traditional lessons while also having fun. According to Connectivism ideals, Students learn using the knowledge and perspective gained through the inclusion of a personal network understanding (Siemens, 2004). It helps students with strategic thinking, systematic planning and problem-solving which in turn develop their logical thinking capabilities, improve their problem-solving accuracy and encourage creativity and innovative thinking (Kim, 2012; Hsiao et al., 2014; Chuang et al., 2015; Misra et al., 2019).

Game-based learning supplements traditional teaching and learning with a fun element (Ibrahim et al., 2017) which increases motivation, attention and enthusiasm of the students making learning more active and engaging (Spiegelman & Glass, 2008; Divjak & Tomic, 2011; Kim, 2012; Kurkovsky, 2013; Fahuzan & Santosa, 2018). As an alternative to worksheets, game-based learning enables students to present their knowledge, skills and understanding of a content in a stress-free manner which increases positive perception towards learning and gives students a sense of ownership of their learning (Kim, 2012; Wati & Yuniawatika, 2020). Nevertheless, the most important prospect for using game-based teaching-learning is that it increases the achievement of learning outcomes a lot more than traditional teaching-learning methods (Wati & Yuniawatika, 2020; Chan et al., 2021).

THE IMPLICATIONS OF GAME-BASED PEDAGOGICAL APPROACHES IN HIGHER EDUCATION

Game based teaching and learning give meaning to experiences by providing a set of boundaries within a safe environment in which to explore, think, and try things out. According to May (2021), game-based teamwork amongst students appears to promote student learning and engagement. However, while using game-based instructional practices, intense competition and timekeeping may become issues. Nonetheless, teachers should begin working on how they can incorporate game-based learning in the classroom for maximum impact. Game-based learning should especially be considered by instructors who are looking for a fresh approach to encourage and engage students in their classrooms.

Game-based learning can play a vital role in developing collaboration, which is a critical skill for tertiary level students. Collaboration is a crucial aspect of game-based learning, and it gives students an opportunity to feel significant to others. It also allows students to master problems they might not have been able to overcome on their own, leading to a sense of accomplishment.

While game-based pedagogy is unquestionably effective and impactful, educators must first consider the state standards or curriculum they are expected to teach in order to effectively use such tactics. When using game-based instructional strategies, care should be taken because it can be difficult to correlate learning objectives with educational models in game dynamics. They must meet the objectives and be properly aligned with the curriculum (Dadheech, undated). In addition, it is always preferable to make games that can be utilized again and again in teaching and learning (Omer, 2017). Designing and using upcycleable game-based pedagogies is also easier when existing standards and curriculum are closely followed.

Another important aspect to keep in mind while considering such pedagogies is that teachers must simultaneously use several game aspects that stimulate engagement, enjoyment, and student collaboration in order for game-based learning to be effective. Themes, leaderboards, and badges are examples of game aspects. In the classroom, these game features will enhance competition and student involvement.

Finally, professional development should enlighten and train educators about the resources available to assist them gamify their classrooms. Educators require time to plan and prepare how they will incorporate gamification and game-based learning in their classrooms in addition to professional development (May, 2021).

CONCLUSION

Teaching and learning are integrated processes where learners construct their required knowledge and understanding. There is evidence that game-based learning impacts on a learner's emotion, promotes collaborative learning and improves students' achievement (Chen et al., 2020). A recent systematic review of existing research shows that the majority of research related to game-based learning has been in the field of education (Bozkurt & Durak, 2018). Game-based collaborative learning assists learners to acquire essential skills for future workplaces. Higher order thinking skills such as collaboration, problem solving, communication, and critical thinking are twenty-first-century skills for Generations Y and Z[9]. In some cases, game-based teaching and learning approaches have been used for raising awareness and understanding of cultural heritage for promoting active citizenship and sustainable development (Malegiannaki, 2021). In the context of the global south, board and card games allow teachers to design and deliver creative instruction using minimum resources (Husnaini & Chen, 2019). Thus, the education system could benefit in a resource-constrained environment.

REFERENCES

P21 Framework Definitions. (2009). Retrieved from https://files.eric.ed.gov/fulltext/ED519462.pdf

Abbott, D. (2019). Game-based learning for postgraduates: An empirical study of an educational game to teach research skills. *Higher Education Pedagogies*, *4*(1), 80–104. doi:10.1080/23752696.2019.1629825

Aldrich, C. (2003). *Simulations and the future of learning*. Pfeiffer.

Alessi, S. M., & Trollip, S. R. (1984). *Computer-based instruction: Methods and development*. Prentice-Hall.

Alexander, S. (2010). *Flexible Learning in Higher Education*. International Encyclopedia of Education., doi:10.1016/B978-0-08-044894-7.00868-X

Allsop, Y., & Jesse, J. (2015). Teachers' Experience and Reflections on Game-Based Learning in the Primary Classroom: Views from England and Italy. *International Journal of Game-Based Learning*, 5(1), 1–17. doi:10.4018/ijgbl.2015010101

Ananiadou, K., & Claro, M. (2009). *21st Century Skills and Competences for New Millennium Learners in OECD Countries*. OECD Education Working Papers, 41. OECD Publishing. doi:10.1787/19939019

Ashrafuzzaman, M. (2021). *Impact of Facebook Usage on University Students' Academic Performance*. Unpublished Research Report, Bangabandhu Sheikh Mujibur Rahman Digital University, Bangladesh (BDU).

Azim, F., & Ahmed, S. S. (2010). Exploring mathematics teachers' beliefs in secondary schools of Bangladesh. *Teacher's World*, *35-36*, 41–53.

Azim, F., & Rahman, M. M. S. (2015). Mobile embedded self-study materials for CPD: The use of English language for teachers (EL4T) in Bangladesh. In G. Pickering & P. Gunashekar (Eds.), *Innovation in English Language Teacher Education*. British Council.

Backhouse, J. (2013). What makes lecturers in higher education use emerging technologies in their teaching? *Knowledge Management & E-Learning*, 5(3), 345–358. http://www.kmel-journal.org/ojs/index.php/online-publication/article/view/216/218

Baid, H., & Lambert, N. (2010). Enjoyable learning: The role of humour, games, and fun activities in nursing and midwifery education. *Nurse Education Today*, *30*(6), 548–552. doi:10.1016/j.nedt.2009.11.007 PMID:20044181

Barab, S. A., Warren, S. J., Zuiker, S., Hickey, D., Ingram-Goble, A., & Dodge, T. (2006). *Transfer of Learning in Complex Learning Environments*. Paper presented at the American Educational Research Association Annual Meeting, San Francisco, CA.

Barnes & Noble College. (2015). *Getting to Know Gen Z – Exploring Middle and High Schoolers' Expectations for Higher Education*. https://www.bncollege.com/wp-content/uploads/2015/10/Gen-Z-Research-Report-Final.pdf

Bates, T. (2015). *Teaching in the digital age*. BC Open Textbooks. Retrieved from https://opentextbc.ca/teachinginadigitalage/

Becker, K. (2008). *The invention of good games: Understanding learning design in commercial video games* (PhD thesis). University of Calgary.

Bengu, E., Abrignani, E., Sabuncuoglu, I., & Yilmaz, C. (2020). Rethinking higher education for the emerging needs of society. *Global Solutions Summit 2020 Edition*, 5(1), 178-187.

Bond, M., Marín, V. I., Dolch, C., Bedenlier, S., & Zawacki-Richter, O. (2018). Digital transformation in German higher education: Student and teacher perceptions and usage of digital media. *Int J Educ Technol High Educ*, *15*(1), 48. doi:10.118641239-018-0130-1

Bourgonjon, J., Valcke, M., Soetaert, R., & Schellens, T. (2010). Students' perceptions about the use of video games in the classroom. *Computers & Education*, *54*(4), 1145–1156. doi:10.1016/j.compedu.2009.10.022

Bowman, S. (2020). *Educating the Digital Native: Teaching Students in a Binge-Watching World*. Faculty Focus.

Bozalek, V., Ng'ambi, D., & Gachago, D. (2013). Transforming teaching with emerging technologies: Implications for higher education institutions. *South African Journal of Higher Education*, *27*(2), 419–436. https://open.uct.ac.za/handle/11427/9844

Bozkurt, A., & Durak, G. (2018). A Systematic Review of Gamification Research: In Pursuit of Homo Ludens. *International Journal of Game-Based Learning*, *8*(3), 15–33. doi:10.4018/IJGBL.2018070102

Brooks, R., Gupta, A., Jayadeva, S., & Abrahams, J. (2020). Students' views about the purpose of higher education: A comparative analysis of six European countries. *Higher Education Research & Development*, 1–14. Advance online publication. doi:10.1080/07294360.2020.1830039

Buckless, F. A., Krawczyk, K., & Showalter, D. S. (2014). Using virtual worlds to simulate real-world audit procedures. *Issues in Accounting Education*, *29*(3), 389–417. doi:10.2308/iace-50785

Carbonaro, M., Szafron, D., Cutumisu, M., & Schaeffer, J. (2010). Computer-game construction: A gender-neutral attractor to Computing Science. *Computers & Education*, *55*(3), 1098–1111. doi:10.1016/j.compedu.2010.05.007

Carretero, S., Vuorikari, R. & Punie, Y. (2017). *DigComp 2.1: The Digital Competence Framework for Citizens with eight proficiency levels and examples of use*. EUR 28558 EN, Publications Office of the European Union. doi:10.2760/38842

Carroll, J. M. (1982). The adventure of getting to know a computer. *IEEE Computer*, *15*(11).

Chan, K., Wan, K., & King, V. (2021). Performance Over Enjoyment? Effect of Game-Based Learning on Learning Outcome and Flow Experience. *Frontiers in Education*, *6*, 1–10. doi:10.3389/feduc.2021.660376

Chee, Y. S., Mehrotra, S., & Ong, J. C. (2014). Facilitating dialog in the game-based learning classroom: Teacher challenges reconstructing professional identity. *Digital Culture & Education*, *6*(4), 298–316.

Chen, S., Husnaini, S. J., & Chen, J.-J. (2020). Effects of games on students' emotions of learning science and achievement in chemistry. *International Journal of Science Education*, *42*(13), 2224–2245. doi:10.1080/09500693.2020.1817607

Chen, Y. C. (2017). Empirical Study on the Effect of Digital Game-Based Instruction on Students' Learning Motivation and Achievement. *Eurasia Journal of Mathematics, Science and Technology Education*, *13*(7). Advance online publication. doi:10.12973/eurasia.2017.00711a

Cheng, C. H., & Su, C. H. (2012). A Game-based learning system for improving student's learning effectiveness in system analysis course. *Procedia: Social and Behavioral Sciences*, *31*, 669–675. doi:10.1016/j.sbspro.2011.12.122

Chuang, T. Y., Liu, E. Z., & Shiu, W. Y. (2015). Game-based creativity assessment system: The application of fuzzy theory. *Multimedia Tools and Applications, 74*(21), 9141–9155. doi:10.100711042-014-2070-7

Chun, E., & Evans, A. (2009). Bridging the diversity divide: Globalization and reciprocal empowerment in higher education. *ASHE Higher Education Report, 35*(1). https://onlinelibrary.wiley.com/doi/10.1002/aehe.3501

Clark, D. B., Tanner-Smith, E. E., & Killingsworth, S. S. (2016). Digital Games, Design, and Learning. *Review of Educational Research, 86*(1), 79–122. doi:10.3102/0034654315582065 PMID:26937054

Cleveland-Innes, M., & Wilton, D. (2018). *Guide to Blended Learning*. Commonwealth of Learning. Retrieved from http://oasis.col.org/handle/11599/3095

Commonwealth of Learning (COL). (2017). *MOOC on Introduction to Technology-Enabled Learning*. Commonwealth of Learning and Athabasca University.

Crocco, F., Offenholley, K., & Hernandez, C. (2016). A Proof-of-Concept Study of Game-Based Learning in Higher Education. *Simulation & Gaming, 47*(4), 403–422. doi:10.1177/1046878116632484

Csikszentmihalyi, M. (1990). *Flow: The psychology of optimal experience*. Harper and Row.

Dadheech, A. (n.d.). *The Importance of Game Based Learning in Modern Education*. Knowledge Review. Retrieved from https://theknowledgereview.com/importance-game-based-learning-modern-education/

Day, E. A., Arthur, W. Jr, & Gettman, D. (2001). Knowledge structures and the acquisition of a complex skill. *The Journal of Applied Psychology, 86*(5), 1022–1033. doi:10.1037/0021-9010.86.5.1022 PMID:11596796

Dickey, M. D. (2007). Game design and learning: A conjectural analysis of how massively multiple online role-playing games (MMORPGs) foster intrinsic motivation. *Educational Technology Research and Development, 55*(3), 253–273. doi:10.100711423-006-9004-7

Dickey, M. D. (2010). Murder on Grimm Isle: The impact of game narrative design in an educational game-based learning environment. *British Journal of Educational Technology*. Advance online publication. doi:10.1111/j.1467-8535.2009.01032.x

Digital Skills Country Action Plan Methodological Guidebook Part 2. (2021). *Digital Skills: The Why, the What and the How*. Retrieved from https://thedocs.worldbank.org/en/doc/a4a6a0b2de23c53da91bf4f-97c315bee-0200022021/original/DSCAP-Guidebook-Part2.pdf

Dingli, A., & Seychell, D. (2015). Who Are the Digital Natives? In *The New Digital Natives*. Springer. doi:10.1007/978-3-662-46590-5_2

Divjak, B., & Tomic, D. (2011). The Impact of Game-Based Learning on the Achievement of Learning Goals and Motivation for Learning Mathematics - Literature Review. *Journal of Information and Organizational Sciences, 35*(1), 15–30.

Dutta, S., & Smita, M. K. (2020). The Impact of COVID-19 Pandemic on Tertiary Education in Bangladesh: Students' Perspectives. *Open Journal of Social Sciences, 8*(9), 53–68. doi:10.4236/jss.2020.89004

Educause. (2014). *7 things you should know about games and learning*. Retrieved from https://courses.dcs.wisc.edu/design-teaching/PlanDesign_Fall2016/2-Online-Course-Design/4_Instructional-Materials/resources/SevenThingsGames.pdf

Emon, E. K. H., Alif, A. R., & Islam, M. S. (2020). Impact of COVID-19 on the Institutional Education System and its Associated Students in Bangladesh. *Asian Journal of Education and Social Studies*, *11*(2), 34–46. doi:10.9734/ajess/2020/v11i230288

Ennis, L. (2018). *Game-Based Learning: An Instructional Tool, Digital repository*. Iowa State University.

Epper, R., Derryberry, A., & Jackon, S. (2012). *Game-Based Learning: Developing an Institutional Strategy*. EDUCAUSE Research. http://educause.edu/ecar

Erdem, C. (2019). *Introduction to 21st century skills and education*. Retrieved from https://www.researchgate.net/publication/336148206_Introduction_to_21st_century_skills_and_education

Fahuzan, K., & Santosa, R. H. (2018). Gender Differences in Motivation to Learn Math Using Role Play Game in Smartphone. *Journal of Physics: Conference Series*, *1097*(1), 1–7. doi:10.1088/1742-6596/1097/1/012130

Felix, J. W., & Johnson, R. T. (1993). Learning from video games. *Computers in the Schools*, *9*(2-3), 119–134. doi:10.1300/J025v09n02_11

Fischer, E., & Hänze, M. (2020). How do university teachers' values and beliefs affect their teaching? *Educational Psychology*, *40*(3), 296–317. doi:10.1080/01443410.2019.1675867

Fortier, M. (2019). *The Power of a Gamified Classroom, Technology and Curriculum*. Retrieved from https://techandcurr2019.pressbooks.com/chapter/gamified-classroom/

Gee, J. P. (2003). What video games have to teach us about learning and literacy. *ACM Computers in Entertainment*, *1*(1), 1–3. doi:10.1145/950566.950595

Gee, J. P. (2014). *What video games have to teach us about learning and literacy*. MacMillan.

Gills, A. S. (2020). *Definition: Digital native*. Teach Target. https://whatis.techtarget.com/definition/digital-native

Grussendorf, S. (2021). *Game-based Learning*. Retrieved from https://lse.atlassian.net/wiki/spaces/MG2/pages/1427144719/Game-based+learning#Benefits

Gui, M. (2007). Formal and substantial Internet information skills: The role of socio-demographic differences on the possession of different components of digital literacy. *First Monday*, *12*(9). Advance online publication. doi:10.5210/fm.v12i9.2009

Hébert, C., Jenson, J., & Terzopoulos, T. (2021). Access to technology is the major challenge: Teacher perspectives on barriers to DGBL in K-12 classrooms. *E-Learning and Digital Media*, *18*(3), 307–324. doi:10.1177/2042753021995315

Heinich, R., Molenda, M., Russell, J. D., & Smaldino, S. E. (2002). *Instructional media and technologies for learning*. Merrill Prentice Hall.

Howard-Jones, P. A., & Jay, T. (2016). Reward, Learning and Games. *Current Opinion in Behavioral Sciences*, *10*, 65–72. doi:10.1016/j.cobeha.2016.04.015

Hsiao, H.-S., Chang, C. S., Lin, C. Y., & Hu, P. M. (2014). Development of children's creativity and manual skills within digital game-based learning environment. *Journal of Computer Assisted Learning*, *30*(4), 377–395. doi:10.1111/jcal.12057

Huang, W. H. (2010). Evaluating learners' motivational and cognitive processing in an online game-based learning environment. *Computers in Human Behavior*. Advance online publication. doi:10.1016/j.chb.2010.07.021

Huizenga, J., Akkerman, S., Admiraal, W., & Dam, G. T. (2009). Mobile game-based learning in secondary education: Engagement, motivation and learning in a mobile city game. *Journal of Computer Assisted Learning*, *25*(4), 332–344. doi:10.1111/j.1365-2729.2009.00316.x

Husnaini, S. J., & Chen, S. (2019). Effects of guided inquiry virtual and physical laboratories on conceptual understanding, inquiry performance, inquiry self-efficacy, and enjoyment. *Physical Review. Physics Education Research*, *15*(1), 010119. doi:10.1103/PhysRevPhysEducRes.15.010119

Ibrahim, R., & Jaafar, A. (2009). Educational games (EG) design framework: Combination of game design, pedagogy and content modeling. *IEEE International Conference on Electrical Engineering and Informatics*, 293-298. 10.1109/ICEEI.2009.5254771

Ibrahim, R., Masrom, S., Yusoff, R. C. M., Zainuddin, N. M. M., & Rizman, Z. I. (2017). Students' acceptance of Educational Games in Higher Education. *Journal of Fundamental and Applied Sciences*, *9*(3S), 809–829. doi:10.4314/jfas.v9i3s.62

Ifenthaler, D., Eseryel, D., & Ge, X. (2012). Assessment for game-based learning. In *Assessment in game-based learning: Foundations, innovations, and perspectives*. Springer-Verlag. doi:10.1007/978-1-4614-3546-4_1

Ivus, M., Quan, T., & Snider, N. (2020). *Class, take out your tablets: The impact of technology on learning and teaching in Canada*. Information and Communications Technology Council.

Ivus, M., Quan, T., & Snider, N. (2021). *21st Century Digital Skills: Competencies, Innovations and Curriculum in Canada, Information and Communications Technology Council*. ICTC.

James, F. (2019). *Everything You Need to Know About Education 4.0*. QS. https://www.qs.com/everything-you-need-to-know-education-40/

Jan, M., Tan, E. M., & Chen, V. (2015). Issues and Challenges of Enacting Game-Based Learning in Schools. In T. B. Lin, V. Chen, & C. Chai (Eds.), *New Media and Learning in the 21st Century. Education Innovation Series*. Springer. doi:10.1007/978-981-287-326-2_5

Jenkins, H., Squire, K., & Tan, P. (2003). Entering the education arcade. *Computers in Entertainment*, *1*(1), 17. doi:10.1145/950566.950591

Kaimara, P., Fokides, E., & Oikonomou, A. (2021). *Potential Barriers to the Implementation of Digital Game-Based Learning in the Classroom: Pre-service Teachers' Views*. Tech Know Learn. doi:10.100710758-021-09512-7

Kapp, K. M. (2012). *The gamification of learning and instruction: game-based methods and strategies for training and education*. Pfeiffer.

Kevin, C., Kelvin, W. & Vivian, K. (2021). Performance Over Enjoyment? Effect of Game-Based Learning on Learning Outcome and Flow Experience. *Frontiers in Education, 6*, 185. doi:10.3389/feduc.2021.660376

Kiili, K. (2005). Content creation challenges and flow experience in educational games: The IT-Emperor case. *The Internet and Higher Education, 8*(3), 183–198. doi:10.1016/j.iheduc.2005.06.001

Kim, B. (2012). Harnessing the power of game dynamics: Why, how to, and how not to gamify the library experience. *College & Research Libraries News, 73*(8), 465–469. doi:10.5860/crln.73.8.8811

Kirikkaya, E. B., Işeri, Ş., & Vurkaya, G. (2010). A board game about space and solar system for primary school students. *The Turkish Online Journal of Educational Technology, 9*(2), 1–13.

Kivunja, C. (2014). Theoretical Perspectives of How Digital Natives Learn. *International Journal of Higher Education, 3*(1), 94–109. doi:10.5430/ijhe.v3n1p94

Koivisto, J., & Hamari, J. (2019). The Rise of Motivational Information Systems: A Review of Gamification Research. *International Journal of Information Management, 45*, 191–210. doi:10.1016/j.ijinfomgt.2018.10.013

Kurkovsky, S. (2013). Mobile game development: Improving student engagement and motivation in introductory computing courses. *Journal of Computer Science Education, 23*(2), 138–157. doi:10.1080/08993408.2013.777236

Lawrence, R., Ching, L. F., & Abdullah, H. (2019). Strengths and Weaknesses of Education 4.0 in the Higher Education Institution. *International Journal of Innovative Technology and Exploring Engineering, 9*(2), 511–519. Advance online publication. doi:10.35940/ijitee.B1122.1292S319

Lee, K. H. (2021). *The educational 'metaverse' is coming*. The Campus. Retrieved from https://www.timeshighereducation.com/campus/educational-metaverse-coming

Li, K., Peterson, M., & Wang, Q. (2021). Using Community of Inquiry to Scaffold Language Learning in Out-of-School Gaming: A Case Study. *International Journal of Game-Based Learning, 11*(1), 31–56. doi:10.4018/IJGBL.2021010103

Malegiannaki, I., Daradoumis, T., & Retalis, S. (2021). Using a Story-Driven Board Game to Engage Students and Adults With Cultural Heritage. *International Journal of Game-Based Learning, 11*(2), 1–19. doi:10.4018/IJGBL.2021040101

Marczewski, A. (2015). *Game Thinking Decision Tree*. Gamified UK. https://www.gamified.uk/gamification-framework/differences-between-gamification-and-games/game-thinking-decision-trees-small/

Marklund, B. B., & Taylor, A.-S. A. (2015). *Teachers' Many Roles in Game-Based Learning Projects*. The 9th European Conference on Games Based Learning (ECGBL'15), Steinkjer, Norway.

Marklund, B. B., & Taylor, A. S. A. (2016). Educational Games in Practice: The challenges involved in conducting a game-based curriculum. *Electronic Journal of e-Learning, 14*(2), 122-135.

May, A. (2021). *Gamification, Game-Based Learning, and Student Engagement in Education*. Leadership Education Capstones 55. Retrieved from https://openriver.winona.edu/leadershipeducationcapstones/55

Mehta, S. (2020). Modern teaching methods: Importance and application. *Eduvoice: The Voice of Education Industry*. Retrieved from https://eduvoice.in/modern-teaching-methods/

Mertala, P. (2019). Digital technologies in early childhood education – a frame analysis of preservice teachers' perceptions. *Early Child Development and Care, 189*(8), 1228–1241. doi:10.1080/03004430.2017.1372756

Misra, R., Eyombo, L. B., & Phillips, F. T. (2019). Benefits and Challenges of Using Educational Games. In *Digital Games for Minority Student Engagement: Emerging Research and Opportunities*. doi:10.4018/978-1-5225-3398-6.ch001

Moseley, A., & Whitton, N. (2015). Using games to enhance the student experience. York, UK: Higher Education Academy (HEA).

Mozelius, P., Hernandez, W., Sällström, J., & Hellerstedt, A. (2017). Teacher attitudes toward game-based learning in history education. *International Journal of Information and Communication Technology Education, 6*(4), 27–35. doi:10.1515/ijicte-2017-0017

Mukwambo, P. (2019). *Quality higher education means more than learning how to work*. The Conversation. https://theconversation.com/quality-higher-education-means-more-than-learning-how-to-work-122820

Ney, M., Emin, V., & Earp, J. (2012). Paving the Way to Game Based Learning: A Question Matrix for Teacher Reflection. *Procedia Computer Science, 15*, 17–24. doi:10.1016/j.procs.2012.10.053

Oblinger, D. G. (2004). The next generation of educational entertainment. *Journal of Interactive Media in Education, 8*(1), 1–18.

Oblinger, D. G. (2006). Games and learning: Digital games have the potential to bring play back to the learning experience. *EDUCAUSE Quarterly, 3*, 5–7.

Omer, A. H. (2017). *Implications And Importance Of Game-Based Learning For New Hires, elearning industry*. Retrieved from https://elearningindustry.com/game-based-learning-for-increased-learner-engagement-new-hires

Papastergiou, M. (2009a). Digital game-based learning in high school computer science education: Impact on educational effectiveness and student motivation. *Computers & Education, 52*(1), 1–12. doi:10.1016/j.compedu.2008.06.004

Partnership for 21st Century Learning. (2016). *Framework for 21st century learning*. www.p21.org/about-us/p21-framework

Partnership for 21st Century Learning. (2019). *Framework for 21st Century Learning Definitions*. http://static.battelleforkids.org/documents/p21/P21_Framework_DefinitionsBFK.pdf

Piaget, J. (1962). *Play Dreams and Imitation in Childhood*. WW Norton.

Plass, J. L., Homer, B. D., & Kinzer, C. K. (2015). Foundations of Game-Based Learning. *Educational Psychologist, 50*(4), 258–283. doi:10.1080/00461520.2015.1122533

Plass, J. L., Perlin, K., & Nordlinger, J. (2010). *The games for learning institute: Research on design patterns for effective educational games*. Paper presented at the Game Developers Conference, San Francisco, CA.

Plato. (1943). *The Republic* (R. E. Allen, Trans.). Yale University Press.

Prensky, M. (2001a). Digital natives, digital immigrants. *On the Horizon*, *9*(5), 1–6. doi:10.1108/10748120110424816

Prensky, M. (2001b). *Digital game-based learning*. McGraw-Hill.

Prensky, M. (2003c). Digital game-based learning. *ACM Computers in Entertainment*, *1*(1), 1–4. doi:10.1145/950566.950596

Provost, J. A. (1990). *Work, play and type: Achieving balance in your life*. Consulting Psychologist Press.

Raymundo, M. R. D. (2020). Fostering creativity through online creative collaborative group projects. *Asian Association of Open Universities Journal*, *15*(1), 97–113. doi:10.1108/AAOUJ-10-2019-0048

Ruggiero, D. (2013). Video games in the classroom: The teacher point of view. In *Games for learning workshop of the foundations of digital games conference*. http://fdg2013.org/program/workshops/papers/G4L2013/g4l2013_02.pdf

Sailer, M., & Homner, L. (2019). The Gamification of Learning: aMeta-Analysis. *Educational Psychology Review*, *32*(1), 77–112. doi:10.100710648-019-09498-w

Scharton, H. (2019). *Busting the Myths of the Digital Native*. https://ptaourchildren.org/busting-the-myths-of-the-digital-native/

Sendra, A., Lozano-Monterrubio, N., Prades-Tena, J., & Gonzalo-Iglesia, J. L. (2021). Developing a Gameful Approach as a Tool for Innovation and Teaching Quality in Higher Education. *International Journal of Game-Based Learning*, *11*(1), 53–66. doi:10.4018/IJGBL.2021010104

Sergeant, A. (2021). *Re: Higher Education's Changing Landscape*. Retrieved from https://www.equantiis.com/thinkslabs/higher-educations-changing-landscape/

Shaffer, D. W., Halverson, R., Squire, K. R., & Gee, J. P. (2005). *Video games and the future of learning* (WCER Working Paper No. 2005-4). University of Wisconsin–Madison, Wisconsin Center for Education Research (NJ1).

Sharma, S. K., Palvia, S. C. J., & Kumar, K. (2017). Changing the landscape of higher education: From standardized learning to customized learning. *Journal of Information Technology Case and Application Research*, *19*(2), 75–80. doi:10.1080/15228053.2017.1345214

Shohel, M. M. C., Ashrafuzzaman, M., Ahsan, M. S., Mahmud, A., & Alam, A. S. (2021a). Education in Emergencies, Inequities, and the Digital Divide: Strategies for Supporting Teachers and Students in Higher Education in Bangladesh. In L. Kyei-Blankson, J. Blankson, & E. Ntuli (Eds.), *Handbook of Research on Inequities in Online Education During Global Crises* (pp. 529–553). IGI Global. doi:10.4018/978-1-7998-6533-9.ch027

Shohel, M. M. C., Ashrafuzzaman, M., Alam, A. S., Mahmud, A., Ahsan, M. S., & Islam, T. M. (2021e). Preparedness of Students for Future Teaching and Learning in Higher Education: A Bangladeshi Perspective. In E. Sengupta & P. Blessinger (Eds.), *New Student Literacies amid COVID-19: International Case Studies, Innovations in Higher Education Teaching and Learning* (Vol. 41, pp. 29–56). Emerald Publishing Limited. doi:10.1108/S2055-364120210000041006

Shohel, M. M. C., Ashrafuzzaman, M., Islam, M. T., Shams, S., & Mahmud, A. (2021d). Blended Teaching and Learning in Higher Education: Challenges and Opportunities. In S. Loureiro & J. Guerreiro (Eds.), *Handbook of Research on Developing a Post-Pandemic Paradigm for Virtual Technologies in Higher Education* (pp. 27–50). IGI Global. doi:10.4018/978-1-7998-6963-4.ch002

Shohel, M. M. C., Mahmud, A., Urmee, M. A., Anwar, N., Rahman, M. M., Acharya, D., & Ashrafuzzaman, M. (2021b). Education in Emergencies, Mental Wellbeing and E-Learning. In M. M. C. Shohel (Ed.), *E-learning and digital education in the twenty-first century: Challenges and Prospects* (pp. 1–22). IntechOpen. doi:10.5772/intechopen.97425

Shohel, M. M. C., Sham, S., Ashrafuzzaman, M., Alam, A. T. M., Mamun, A. A., & Kabir, M. M. (2021c). Emergency Remote Teaching and Learning: Digital Competencies and Pedagogical Transformation in Resource-Constrained Contexts. In M. Islam, S. Behera, & L. Naibaho (Eds.), *Handbook of Research on Asian Perspectives of the Educational Impact of COVID-19*. IGI Global.

Siemens, G. (2005). Connectivism: A learning theory for the digital age. *International Journal of Instructional Technology and Distance Learning.*, *3*, 3–10.

Sitzmann, T. (2011). A meta-analytic examination of the instructional effectiveness of computer-based simulation games. *Personnel Psychology*, *64*(2), 489–528. doi:10.1111/j.1744-6570.2011.01190.x

Spiegelman, M., & Glass, R. (2008). Gaming and learning: Winning information literacy collaboration. *College & Research Libraries News*, *69*(9), 522–547. doi:10.5860/crln.69.9.8058

Squire, K. (2006). From Content to Context: Videogames as Designed Experience. *Educational Researcher*, *35*(8), 19–29. doi:10.3102/0013189X035008019

Squire, K., & Jenkins, H. (2003). Harnessing the power of games in education. *Insight (American Society of Ophthalmic Registered Nurses)*, *3*(1), 5–33. PMID:12703249

Staley, D., & Trikle, D. (2011). The Changing Landscape of Higher Education. *Educase Review*. Retrieved from https://er.educause.edu/articles/2011/2/the-changing-landscape-of-higher-education

Steinkuehler, C. (2004). *The literacy practices of massively multiplayer online gaming*. Paper presented at the American Educational Research Association, San Diego, CA.

Suvin, C. (2020). *Why should higher education institutions focus on Education 4.0?* Creatix Campus. https://www.creatrixcampus.com/blog/Education-4.0

Taillandier, F., Micolier, A., Sauce, G., & Chaplain, M. (2021). DOMEGO: A Board Game for Learning How to Manage a Construction Project. *International Journal of Game-Based Learning*, *11*(2), 20–37. doi:10.4018/IJGBL.2021040102

Teh, C. L., Fauzy, W. W., & Toh, S. C. (2007). Why use computer games for learning? *1st International Malaysian Educational Technology Convention*, 835-843.

Teichler, U. (2017). Internationalisation Trends in Higher Education and the Changing Role of International Student Mobility. *Journal of international Mobility, 5*, 177-216. doi:10.3917/jim.005.0179

Thompson, C. G., & von Gillern, S. (2020). Video-game based instruction for vocabulary acquisition with English language learners: A Bayesian meta-analysis. *Educational Research Review, 30*, 100332. doi:10.1016/j.edurev.2020.100332

Tüzün, H., Yılmaz-Soylu, M., Karakuş, T., İnal, Y., & Kızılkaya, G. (2009). The effects of computer games on primary school students' achievement and motivation in geography learning. *Computers & Education, 52*(1), 68–77. doi:10.1016/j.compedu.2008.06.008

UNESCO. (2018). *Digital skills critical for jobs and social inclusion*. https://en.unesco.org/news/digital-skills-critical-jobs-and-social-inclusion

UNESCO Institute for Information Technologies in Education (UNESCO-IITE). (2011). *Digital natives: How do they learn; How to teach them?* Retrieved from https://iite.unesco.org/files/policy_briefs/pdf/en/digital_natives.pdf

Van Dijk, J. A. G. M. (2005). *The deepening Divide: Inequality in the information society*. SAGE Publications. doi:10.4135/9781452229812

Varghese, N. V. (2014). Globalization and higher education: Changing trends in cross border education. *Analytical Reports in International Education, 5*(1), 7–20.

Vogel, J. J., Vogel, D. S., Cannon-Bowers, J., Bowers, C. A., Muse, K., & Wright, M. (2006). Computer gaming and interactive simulations for learning: A meta-analysis. *Journal of Educational Computing Research, 34*(3), 229–243. doi:10.2190/FLHV-K4WA-WPVQ-H0YM

Vuorikari, R. (2016). *DigComp 2.0: The Digital Competence Framework For Citizens. Update Phase 1: the Conceptual Reference Model*. European Commission, Retrieved from https://ec.europa.eu/jrc/en/publication/eur-scientificand-technical-research-reports/digcomp-20-digital-competence-framework-citizens-update-phase-1-conceptualreference-model

Vygotsky, L. (1962). *Thought and language* (E. Hanf-mann & G. Vakar, Trans.). MIT Press. doi:10.1037/11193-000

Wang, J., & Rao, N. (2020). What Do Chinese Students Say about Their Academic Motivational Goals-Reasons Underlying Academic Strivings? *Asia Pacific Journal of Education, 12*, 1–15. doi:10.1080/02188791.2020.1812513

Wang, L. C., & Chen, M. P. (2010). The effects of game strategy and preference-matching on flow experience and programming performance in game-based learning. *Innovations in Education and Teaching International, 47*(1), 39–52. doi:10.1080/14703290903525838

Warren, S. J., Dondlinger, M. J., & Barab, S. A. (2008). A MUVE towards PBL writing: Effects of a digital learning environment designed to improve elementary student writing. *Journal of Research on Technology in Education, 41*(1), 113–140. doi:10.1080/15391523.2008.10782525

Warren, S. J., Dondlinger, M. J., Stein, R., & Barab, S. A. (2009). Educational Game as Supplemental Learning Tool: Benefits, Challenges, and Tensions Arising from Use in an Elementary School Classroom. *Journal of Interactive Learning Research, 20*(4), 487–505.

Wati, I. F., & Yuniawatika. (2020). Digital Game-Based Learning as A Solution to Fun Learning Challenges During the Covid-19 Pandemic. *Advances in Social Science, Education and Humanities Research, 508*, 202–210. doi:10.2991/assehr.k.201214.237

Watson, W. R., Yang, S., & Dana, R. (2016). Games in Schools: Teachers' Perceptions of Barriers to Game-based Learning. *Journal of Interactive Learning Research, 27*(2). https://www.learntechlib.org/primary/p/151749/

White, K., & McCoy, L. P. (2019). Effects of Game-Based Learning on Attitude and Achievement in Elementary Mathematics Achievement in Elementary Mathematics. Networks. *An Online Journal for Teacher Research, 21*(1), 1–17. Advance online publication. doi:10.4148/2470-6353.1259

Whitton, N., & Moseley, A. (2012). *Using Games to Enhance Learning and Teaching: A Beginner's Guide*. Routledge. doi:10.4324/9780203123775

Wouters, P., van Nimwegen, C., van Oostendorp, H., & van der Spek, E. D. (2013). A meta-analysis of the cognitive and motivational effects of serious games. *Journal of Educational Psychology, 105*(2), 249–265. doi:10.1037/a0031311

Wu, M. L. (2015). *Teachers' experience, attitudes, self-efficacy and perceived barriers to the use of digital game-based learning: A survey study through the lens of a typology of educational digital games* [Michigan State University]. In ProQuest Dissertations and Theses. https://d.lib.msu.edu/etd/3754

Yien, J., Hung, C., Hwang, G., & Lin, Y. (2011). A game-based learning approach to improving students' learning achievements in a nutrition course. *The Turkish Online Journal of Educational Technology, 10*(2).

ENDNOTES

[1] https://www.duolingo.com/
[2] http://www.minecraft.com/
[3] https://www.secondlife.com/
[4] https://www.brainscape.com/
[5] https://kahoot.com/
[6] https://info.credly.com/
[7] https://tophat.com/
[8] http://static.battelleforkids.org/documents/p21/P21_Framework_Brief.pdf
[9] Generation Z (born after 2000 (Ozkan & Solmaz, 2015), like generation Y (born between 1980 and 1999 (Lissitsa & Kol, 2016)

Chapter 6
A Paradigm Shift in Higher Education:
Evidence-Based Cross-Sectional Study Conducted in South India

Vikas Salunkhe
https://orcid.org/0000-0002-1465-8888
CHRIST University (Deemed), India

Seena Thomas Kaithathara
CHRIST University (Deemed), India

Darshan S. M.
CHRIST University (Deemed), India

Gowri Shankar R.
CHRIST University (Deemed), India

Shabarisha N.
CHRIST University (Deemed), India

ABSTRACT

Game-based learning is widely followed at the school level in India, but the higher education system has been longer in adopting it. The pandemic situation has transformed teaching and learning processes from the traditional to the technical method, which requires a more versatile approach. Because of the rapid change from the offline mode to the online mode in higher education, there is little evidence available on the inefficiency of implementing the traditional system of teacher-centered education on online platforms. There comes a lot of the significance in of adapting technology-based games in order to engage and motivate students throughout their course of study. The aim of this chapter is to provide an overview of the effectiveness of game-based learning strategies over traditional learning methods. Moreover, the results of a cross-sectional study conducted by the authors in South Indian universities at the higher education level is included.

DOI: 10.4018/978-1-7998-7271-9.ch006

INTRODUCTION

"A university is not an information shop. It is a place where the students' will, intellect, and emotions are disciplined". - Dr. Sarvepalli Radhakrishnan.

1.8 billion Young Indians, between the ages of 10 to 24 contribute 20% global population. This unique demography is an opportunity in utilizing the country's socio-economic landscape. To overcome the need of youngsters like the expansion of learning, skill development, employment, and engagement opportunities in the process of creating change-makers in the form of national as well as international leaders.

This chapter revolves around online-game-based learning and teaching, while keeping in mind the availability, accessibility and affordability of tech-based gadgets which will be equipped with adequate sources of learning and teaching materials available for everyone in the era of skill based revolution in the 21st century during the challenging time of pandemic. Merits and demerits of adoption of game-based learning also are in the consideration in this study. Lifelong learning will be an integral part of the education system blended with game based learning. Creation of future centric leaders to give back to the society, is the ultimate goal. Fragmentation of the information: with the help of charts, key information can be stored in the blocks. At one glance through this chart, any topic can be taught, understood and remembered. Association and correlation can lead to accumulation of knowledge.

Background

Gamification is one of the techniques that can be used in higher education system, to increase the inquisitive learning of students. Many western universities have tried implementing gamification or game-based learning in their pedagogy to teach the relevant courses that support gamification. Effective game design will cater to the current challenging audiences and thereby facilitate and support their learning process. Pedagogically highly valued game-based products in learning have proven to be successful and most of the western universities have adopted them (Pivec, Dziabenko, & Schinnerl, 2003). Several elements that plays a vital role in designing games according to the requirements of a particular course to teach in higher education system viz., cognitive, motivational, affective, and socio-cultural elements that also facilitate effective learning among the students (Plass, Homer, & Kinzer 2015). Students' motivation, engagement and learning can be increased through designing various gamification ideas like digital badges and scavenger hunts etc. And it is highly essential to consider the learning principles while designing the games (Pho, Dinscore, & Badges, 2015). Computer and video games can be effectively used in the teaching-learning process. However, designing such games to instruct the learners should cover various aspects like playing time, integration of games with curricular objectives, external tasks and other aspects of cognitive learning process and effectiveness in the evaluation process (tobias, fletcher, & wind, 2014). Game based learning pedagogy can be employed to many relevant courses in the higher education system across different disciplines. Rui Pedro lopes and CristinaMesquita (2015) evaluated the application of the gamified pedagogical methodology in the course of the network and systems management of an informatics engineering Programme. The evaluation process adopted a three-instrument process viz., class observations, interviews, and a questionnaire. They observed that there was a change in the motivations of students, compared with their motivation in expositive class. Students demonstrated higher persistence in solving problems, higher levels of complexity, and creativity through the gamification strategy. Daniela Serra Castilhos (2018) conducted a case study to examine the application of

A Paradigm Shift in Higher Education

gamification in the discipline of constitutional law in a university. Their study focused on evaluating the usage of the Kahoot platform for teaching and learning. The study results showed a positive outcome of an increase in the students' motivation and engagement in academics. Further, the kahoot platform facilitated the use of game elements like feedback, clear rules, and students' demonstration of fun and motivation to perform better. Piroska szegedine lengyel (2020) investigated the potential and limitations of digital games through the instance of online learning management of accounting-related courses. They opined that the teaching-learning environment should provide an appropriate learning environment for students to acquire progressive knowledge and professional skills pertaining to accounting and auditing. The study results also show a positive change and response from the students' community in learning advanced knowledge in accounting courses and developing professional skills. Higher education institutions need to develop resilience in students by introducing gamification as a strategy for teaching and learning. The protective resilience factors have an association with the academic performance of the students and improvement in the student's grades and resilience can be expected with the adoption of gamification as a teaching resource (B. Villegas Aguilera and e. Alvarado Martinez, 2017). For the effective implementation of gamification in higher education system, it is necessary to design and implement a framework on gamification which includes students' engagement and motivation in the academic process. This may results in active engagement of learners and increase in the overall performance in their academic endeavor (Kavisha Duggal et. Al. 2021).

This pandemic has set a precedent for all of us to learn, re-learn and unlearn and upskill at the pace of thought. To manifest, the future is going to be equipped with a virtual and digital landscape, teachers and students have to adapt to the contemporary and 21st century upskilling (Mingfong Jan and Mathew Gaydos, 2016). Games and learning publishing council suggests that 55% of nearly 700 teachers have students play games at least weekly (Takeuchi and Vaala, 2014).

The revolution in information and communication technology (ICT) has facilitated symmetric information flow and greater connectivity to learning resources. Students can access information and learning resources through digital platforms, which has brought about a major transformation in the learning environment and also in the traditional role of teachers as subject experts and knowledge providers to facilitators of self-directed learning. To achieve active participation of learners in the dynamic socio-cultural and economic environment, facilitators are required to adopt innovative techniques that provoke learners' activity in the learning process. One such technique that can be adopted by facilitators is gamification.

Gamification is "the strategic attempt to enhance systems, services, organizations, and activities to create similar experiences to those experienced when playing games to motivate and engage users" (Hamari, 2019). This can also be defined as "a set of activities and processes to solve problems by using or applying the characteristics of game elements'' (Wikipedia). Implementing gamification at the school-level is easier than in higher-level education, as children are more inclined to be involved in games till adolescence. Moreover, teachers at the school level are trained in such a way that game-based learning is included in the curriculum of teacher-training programmes (Cózar-Gutiérrez & Sáez-López, 2016). In the higher education system also, it is possible to incorporate some strategies to develop game-based learning under various disciplines. It has already been proved by researchers that traditional teaching with games inside the classroom would improve students' ability to understand and analyse various concepts (Priyaadharshini, et. Al, 2020). Hence online teaching also has to be implemented in such a way that students attending online classes would get a chance to take part in the activity initiated by the instructors and thus the level of students would be improved (Abbott, 2019).

Researchers' observation, inquisitiveness or curiosity is one of the most important factors that stimulate learners to devote more time and efforts to explore, learn, and enhance expertise in new knowledge and experiences. Gamification is one such kind of teaching-learning technique that increases the inquisitive learning of students. Using gamification in higher education is logical, as it's learning objectives can be achieved by performing specific learning activities and interacting with educational content (glover, 2013). Gamification in higher education allows for student-centric flexible learning paths, and individualized learning rather than competition among students, which facilitates the opportunity to achieve greater scores by solving different tasks. It also motivates learners to enjoy autonomy and take responsibility for their learning process and leads to significant development of their careers (Katalin Nagy 2018). Further, gamification influences the behavior of learners, their commitment towards the learning process, and motivation that can lead to improvement of knowledge and skills required to meet current market requirements (W. Hsin-yuan huang, D. Soman, 2013).

Owing to various innovations, ICT makes it possible for HEIs to strengthen their position in the education landscape. With the various innovations in the ICT for higher education in India, game-based learning has evolved as one of the innovative teaching-learning strategies in various institutions. Specifically, during times of pandemic, it is a greater challenge for both the facilitators and learners of higher education to achieve quality and sustainable education. Game-based learning implies more participation in the learning process and stimulates the inquisitiveness of learners to study and understand concepts in a better way. In this regard, the application of game-based learning models in higher education institutions is required to create the conditions suitable for an effective teaching and learning environment. The study conducted by the authors is an attempt to find out how game-based learning and teaching can be a way forward to overcoming the challenges being faced by students, teachers and parents during the covid-19 pandemic. How to fill up the vacuum created by the closure of schools and colleges for more than 18 months? How can this ray of hope help students and teachers to sustain the process of teaching and learning with collaboration of game-based learning and teaching?

Provide broad definitions and discussions of the topic and incorporate views of others (literature review) into the discussion to support, refute, or demonstrate your position on the topic.

MAIN FOCUS OF THE CHAPTER

The research mainly aims to overcome the challenges of learning and teaching through educational institutions, individuals, and organizations. Game-based learning will help to create, enhance and make the educational system easy and interesting. The current challenging situations emerging due to covid-19 all over the world, with the help of game-based learning, will endeavor to overcome and set a unique precedent in education. The current study is focusing on creating awareness on game-based learning strategies and their effectiveness in the teaching-learning process for HEIs. The study will be endeavoring to reinvigorate and correlate with the science, technology, engineering, and mathematics (STEM) disciplines. For this purpose, the current study is planning to cover southern Indian higher educational institutions - both from the facilitators' and learners' perspectives. Motivation, rewards, and awards should be part of game-based learning to lure students and let them get involved instead of forcing them to do so.

How to involve all parts of the body in the teaching and learning process? How can the five sense organs viz touch, hearing, smell, sight, and taste store multi-dimensional information for long, which can be recalled easily? How to make learning and teaching crazy or funny? Game-based learning in collaboration with short stories or association with live examples helps a lot to store information. Even if the learner is alone or a self-learner, the learning process will lead towards a positive and productive outcome. The ability to convert words into pictures and numbers and vice versa is important. Authors are experiencing the learning process most of the time, loaded with theories and less with practical or application-based systems. After a short period, the ability to recall or memorize declines day by day, as authors are just mugging up only words or numbers as part of the syllabus. Our students with a score of 100 percentile are in the news for a while, but due to cutthroat competition, the implementation and reproduction of new knowledge is lacking, which is the need of the hour.

ISSUES, CONTROVERSIES, PROBLEMS

The oft-quoted dictum, 'one for all or all for one, would not be suitable for each and every student and teacher. Implementing the game-based learning and teaching process today is not very difficult but quite challenging. The new generation of the 21st century is well-equipped, with research developments in science and technology and the availability of basic infrastructures, such as smartphones, Internet, connectivity, and electronic gadgets, with full-time or adequate electricity supply. Getting familiar with the game-based gadgets and applications is a challenge for the old or individuals from the previous generation. The need of the hour is how authors should have hybrid models in this field of game-based learning, such as online and offline games and applications to create an eco-friendly environment suitable for all.

The contemporary issue is due to ambiguity in understanding basic concepts. Thousands of students are drifting away from acquiring advanced prowess despite having their high-class performance in academics. Unproductive or non-result oriented based teaching processes can be attributed to this. Most of the time, students are overburdened with lengthy assignments and lack application-based learning. Students apparently opt to have a middle path of buying readymade projects from the market and submit them as their bona fide projects. Projects and assignments must be a combination of a variety of skills and techniques, without drifting away from the core concepts. Students must be allowed to implement their own concepts to do their things in other ways too. Teachers should be well-versed, with advanced skills, to equip them with knowledge. To get involved with 21st-century skills and design educational games, students need to acquire some basic knowledge of coding languages. The Python programming language can be taught for beginners. Continuous learning and assignments based on this will be result-oriented.

Research is a continuous process, but the application of the results of the research is a tough task. How and where to implement the new ideas and skills is an outcome of our research. Now, this is a thousand-dollar opportunity to face the situation, learn from it, and use our ideas and research skills. Over a long period, authors came across various research and publications, and now is the time to recall our past activities on research, observe the present situation and implement it for a stable and sustainable future of game-based learning and teaching. Most of the well-researched and studied skills and new knowledge are eagerly awaiting to spread all over the world, but due to lack of opportunities and inadequate awareness of the results, most of them are under the shadow. This game-based learning will be a torchbearer to focus on the dark area of learning and teaching process towards a bright future.

Being the second most populated country in the world, India and Indian students can develop industry-academic partnerships, which will benefit both parties. Academic Research and Development will be able to solve real-life problems and provide advanced, skilled talent to the world market.

Present your perspective on the issues, controversies, problems, etc., as they relate to theme and arguments supporting your position. Compare and contrast with what has been, or is currently being done as it relates to the chapter's specific topic and the main theme of the book.

1. 21st Century Skills:
    a. 4 Cs:
        i. Communication
        ii. Creativity
        iii. Collaboration
        iv. Creative
2. Wellbeing of Mental Health:
    i. Spend some time with yourself once in a while regularly.
    ii. Talk to yourself to reproduce new thoughts.
    iii. Breaks during the study time to energies yourself.
    iv. Regular or at least three times in a week workout.

Research Objectives:
- To understand the importance of gamification in higher education.
- To understand the various aspects of game-based learning.
- To find out the relationships between gamification and the learning process.
- To study the impact of gamification in higher education.

Methodology

Step 1: How the gamification will impact on teaching-learning in the higher education institutions?

Step 2: A cross-sectional study was conducted among university students of South India, for which the sample size was estimated to be 375, with a confidence level of 95% and absolute precision 5% assuming a proportion of 50% variability in the attribute of interest and awareness about Gamification. The questionnaire used for the survey was the modified version of a standardized questionnaire, for which the reliability measure Cronbach's alpha was found to be 0.85, showing that the questionnaire was reliable. The questionnaire was divided into four sections. The first section contains demographic variables such as age, gender, educational level, place of residence, type of family, and a number of siblings. The second section contains questions related to awareness and the inclusiveness of games in the learning process. The third section includes the application of gamification in the learning process by using tools like Learning Management System (LMS), video games in education, mobile based learning etc for the adaptation. The other section includes statements relating to the impact and effectiveness of gamification in the learning process. The Likert Scale with responses, strongly disagree-1, Disagree-2, Neutral-3, Agree-4, strongly agree-5 were used for each of the domains. The higher the score, the higher the rate of agreement.

Table 1. Demographic characteristics

Variables (n=375)		n (%)
Age	15-18	25 (6.7)
	18-21	226 (60.3)
	21-24	114 (30.4)
	>24	10 (2.7)
Gender	Male	194 (51.7)
	Female	181 (48.3)
Place	Urban	263 (70.1)
	Sub-Urban	75 (20.0)
	Rural	37 (9.9)
Education	Less than degree	158 (42.1)
	Degree	138 (36.8)
	Masters	75 (20.0)
	Professional	4 (1.1)
Type of family	Nuclear	301 (80.3)
	Joint	74 (19.7)

Step 3: To test and analyze the same a multivariate analysis is used. The variable representing the total score of applications was categorized into two - lower and upper, based on the median score (18) and 58.3% of the subjects belonged to the lower category. A binary logistic regression analysis was performed to find out the predictors of application. The variables' age, gender, education, place of residence, and type of family were included in the logistic regression model. The backward LR method was applied and the final model included gender and level of education. The odds of application is more for males compared to females (OR=0.657, p=0.079). Similarly, the odds of application of degree level students are more compared to other groups (OR=0.752, p=0.059).

Table 2. Descriptive Statistics

	Mean	Std. Deviation
Gamebasedlearningis1Theadaptationofgamingelementsand	2.31	1.525
Gamebasedlearningis2Gamemechanicsappliedtobusinesspr	2.21	1.438
Gamebasedlearningis3Makingsomethingpotentiallytedious	2.85	1.323
Gamebasedlearningis3Moreappealingandprovidemotivation	2.86	1.352
Gamebasedlearningis4Theconceptofapplyinggamemechanic	2.71	1.385
Gamebasedlearningis5ConsideredasNonfictiongameplay	1.62	1.533
Gamebasedlearningis6Usinggametechniquestoincreaseeng	2.90	1.256
Gamebasedlearningis7Leadstoabetterunderstandingofth	2.78	1.357
Gamebasedlearningis8Changesthemotivationfromfinishing	2.66	1.399
Gamebasedlearningis9Usedtosupporteachother	2.48	1.500
Gamebasedlearningis10Usedtoimprovethelearningatmosph	2.84	1.337

Step 4: The domain Awareness included questions Descriptive statistics mean (SD) for continuous variables and numbers (%) were used to describe the sample characteristics. The Shapiro Wilk test was employed to check the normality of the data. It was found that the continuous variables were not normally distributed. Hence nonparametric tests were performed for various statistical analyses. Mann-Whitney U test was used to compare the median scores between two groups. The Kruskal Wallis test was used to compare the median score between more than two groups. Chi-square test was used to examine the association between categorical variables and Spearman's correlation coefficient was used to examine the relationship between continuous variables. A p-value less than 0.05 was considered to be statistically significant and all the analyses were performed using R software version 4.1.1.

Table 3 Descriptive statistics

My institution uses the following	Mean	Std. Deviation
Class room training	2.91	1.333
On the job learning	1.95	1.553
LMS Online courses	2.91	1.296
Mobile learning	2.11	1.504
Video training	2.26	1.494
Gamified learning	1.43	1.268
Virtual classrooms	3.01	1.267

Step 5: The respondents were given various statements regarding their awareness level of gamification and a descriptive statistical analysis such as Arithmetic Mean and Standard Deviation is used to analyze the same. From table 2a it is clear that the respondents most preferred statement is "gamification techniques to increase engagement, satisfaction and fun" with a highest mean score (2.9) and lowest standard deviation(1.256). Similarly table 2b shows that the virtual classrooms were the most desirable statement selected by the respondents with a highest mean score (3.01) and lowest standard deviation (1.26).

Table 4.

Variable	Median	(IQR)
Awareness	32	(27, 36)
Application	18	(15, 21)
Impact	14	(11, 18)
Effectiveness	18	(15, 21)

A Paradigm Shift in Higher Education

While comparing the average scores of awareness, application, impact, and effectiveness, the Mann-Whitney U test showed that there is a statistically significant difference between males and females in the application of Gamification (p=0.007). The boys were found to be ahead of girls in applying games in learning. Other variables were not statistically significant. The same test was performed for the comparison of average scores between two groups of Types of family and was not statistically significant. Kruskal Wallis test was performed to compare average scores between various age groups and it was found that the Application and Impact of game-based learning were statistically significant (p = 0.02 and p = 0.002 respectively). The post hoc analysis performed using pairwise comparison (Mann-Whitney U) showed that there were statistically significant differences between the lower age group and upper age group (p<0.05). The average scores were compared between the groups of places of residence and levels of education using the same test and were found to be not statistically significant.

Table 5.

Variable	Group	Median (IQR)	p-value
Application	Male	18 (15, 21.25)	0.007
	Female	17 (14.5, 20)	

Step 6: The survey sample of 376 participants from South India indicates that large age groups between 18 to 24 years are involved in our study, with a slight majority of males over females. The analyzed data shows that the gap between joint and nuclear families is widening gradually. The reach of technology in urban areas is much higher than in rural areas, which is impacting the process of delivering education during this challenging COVID-19 time.

Table 6.

Variable	Group	Median (IQR)	p-value
Application	15 - 18	21 (14, 24)	0.02
	18 - 21	18 (15, 21)	
	21 - 24	17 (15, 19)	
	>24	20 (19, 24)	
Impact	15 - 18	11 (8, 14)	0.002
	18 - 21	15 (11, 18)	
	21 - 24	14 (10, 17)	
	>24	22 (14, 23)	

Phase One: Kruskal Wallis test
Phase Two: The next objective of the study is to find out the relationship between Gamification and the learning processes.

Phase Three: Spearman's correlation test was performed to find the strength of correlation between continuous variables. The correlation between awareness and the remaining variables was found to be statistically significant. The correlation between application and effectiveness also was statistically significant. The correlation coefficients and the p-values are given in Table 6. So it is evident that there is a relation between gamification and the learning process.

Table 7.

	Awareness	Application	Impact	Effectiveness
Awareness	1	0.116 (0.050)	0.132 (0.015)	0.589 (<0.05)
Application		1	0.089 (0.138)	0.146 (0.024)
Impact			1	0.026 (0.662)
Effectiveness				1

Phase Four: The next objective of the study is to find the impact of Gamification in Higher Education.
Hypothesis One: There is no significant impact of Gamification on Higher Education.
Hypothesis Two: There is a significant impact of Gamification on Higher Education.

SOLUTIONS AND RECOMMENDATIONS

Higher education institutions (HEIs) in India are vested with providing quality education to the larger population and facilitating socio-economic development through research activities. These institutions are creating an appropriate learning environment for both learning and research in the country, thereby facilitating socio-economic cooperation and development. To achieve high-level academic performance in the higher education system, adequate student learning disposition is the key to success. But one of the major issues in higher education nowadays pertains to the lack of engagement and motivation of learners to actively participate in the learning process. Due to this, the facilitators are required to adapt and introduce a new teaching-learning pedagogy to stimulate active student engagement. Active participation of learners and their engagement in academic endeavors can be stimulated by both intrinsic and extrinsic motivation. The intrinsic motivation is purely derived from the core self and the extrinsic motivation is driven by the learning environment facilitated by the HEIs. If learners are motivated by their core self, they exhibit their active academic engagement and the expected outcome from learning activities. However, even if learners are motivated intrinsically, external motivation in terms of creating an appropriate learning environment is also the need of the hour.

FUTURE RESEARCH DIRECTIONS

Researcher's subsequent research study will be based on a combination of traditional and modern approaches to games. It will be a way forward for our article, which will culminate into a broad coverage of society. Traditional games have a huge impact on cultural and behavioral attitudes. It helps in alleviating consternation, enhancing relationships, promoting healthy competition, mutual tolerance, and critical thinking skills to overcome day-to-day life challenges. There should be the attitude to accept defeat and show dignity in victory. Being the second most populated country in the world, India and Indian students can develop industry-academic partnerships, which will benefit both parties. Academic research and development will be able to solve real-life problems and provide advanced, skilled talent to the world market.

CONCLUSION

This research started with few selected objectives with respect to gamification in the learning process. The objectives were tested and analysed with various statistical tools and finally understood that gamification as a concept which is widely accepted by the respondents but when it comes to the implementation of it, not all universities and affiliated colleges were having the modalities to execute the same. In many cases either the infrastructure is a limitation or the students' varied economic background or their level of exposure to such technological tools is a hurdle to execute the same. Interestingly it is also found in the course of research that demographic variables like age and gender play a vital role in the acceptance of gamification as a learning tool.

REFERENCES

Abbott, D. (2019). Game-based learning for postgraduates: an empirical study of an educational game to teach research skills. *Higher Education Pedagogies, 4*(1), 80–104. doi:10.1080/23752696.2019.1629825

Aguilera & Martínez. (2017). Gamification, a didactic strategy in higher education. *Edulearn17 Proceedings*, 6761-6771.

Castilhos, D. (2018). *Gamification and active methodologies at university: The case of teaching learning strategy in law.* doi:10.21125/iceri.2018.0220

Cózar-Gutiérrez, R., & Sáez-López, J. M. (2016). Game-based learning and gamification in initial teacher training in the social sciences: An experiment with minecraftedu. *International Journal of Educational Technology in Higher Education, 13*(1), 2. doi:10.118641239-016-0003-4

Duggal, Gupta, & Singh. (2021). Gamification and machine learning inspired approach for classroom engagement and learning. *Mathematical Problems in Engineering.* doi:10.1155/2021/9922775

Glover, I. (2013). Play as you learn: Gamification as a technique for motivating learners. In *Proceedings of World Conference on Educational Multimedia, Hypermedia and Telecommunications.* AACE.

Hamari, J. (2019). Gamification. *The Blackwell encyclopedia of sociology*, 1–3.

Huang, W. H.-Y., & Soman, D. (2013). *A practitioner's guide to gamification of education.* University of Toronto, Rotman School of Management.

Lopes & Mesquita. (2015). Evaluation of a gamification methodology in higher education. *Edulearn15 Proceedings*, 6996-7005.

Nagy, Molnár, Szenkovits, Horváth-Czinger, & Szűts. (2018). Gamification and microcontent orientated methodological solutions based on bring-your-own device logic in higher education. *2018 9th IEEE International Conference on Cognitive Infocommunications (Coginfocom)*, 385-388. doi:10.1109/CogInfoCom.2018.8639702

Pho, B. A., Dinscore, A., & Badges, D. (2015). *Game-based learning*. Academic Press.

Pivec, M., Dziabenko, O., & Schinnerl, I. (2003). *Aspects of game-based learning*. Academic Press.

Plass, L., Homer, B. D., & Kinzer, C. K. (2015). Foundations of game-based learning. *Educational Psychologist*, *50*(4), 258–283. doi:10.1080/00461520.2015.1122533

Priyadharshini, M., Nathamayil, N., Dakshina, R., Sandhya, S., & R, B. S. (2020). *Learning analytics : Game-based learning for programming course in higher education*. Academic Press.

Szegedine Lengyel, P. (2020). Can the game-based learning come? Virtual classroom in higher education of 21st century. *International Journal of Emerging Technologies in Learning*, *15*(112). doi:10.3991/ijet.v15i02.11521

Tobias, S., Fletcher, J. D., & Wind, A. P. (2014). *Game-based learning*. 5 doi:10.1007/978-1-4614-3185-

Wikipedia. (n.d.). Retrieved from https://en.wikipedia.org/wiki/gamification

Xiong, C., Ye, B., Mihailidis, A., Cameron, J. I., Astell, A., Nalder, E., & Colantonio, A. (2020). Sex and gender differences in technology needs and preferences among informal caregivers of persons with dementia. *BMC Geriatrics*, *20*(1), 176. https://www.jstor.org/stable/pdf/44430486.pdf?refreqid=excelsior%3a6a06f288b510b457d0a9c16f60991e8d

KEY TERMS AND DEFINITIONS

21st Century Skills: Skills which are highly advanced and sophisticated. The skills revolve around technology and scientific world and also critical thinking, advanced learning, and decision-making skills.

Cross-Sectional Study: The study involves interactions and evidence based analyzed observations of population participated.

Mugging Up: In this process learners just read the information without understanding the insights.

On-the-Job Learning: A method of providing practical training to the new or fresh learners at workplace.

Technological Tools: The gadgets designed to get connected and access around the world in search of information through internet. The tools are well versed with advanced information technology and automation.

Traditional Methods: This kind methods are well known to everyone but less equipped with advanced technology or non-tech based.

Visualization: The process of creating an image of particular thing in mind and designing thought process accordingly.

APPENDIX

Questionnaire

Game-Based Learning Acquiring 21st Century Literacy Skills

1. **My Age is:**
    a. 15-18 ☐
    b. 18-21 ☐
    c. 21-24 ☐
    d. 24-27 ☐
    e. >27 ☐
2. **Gender**
    a. Female ☐
    b. Male ☐
3. **Educational Qualification**
    a. Less than Degree ☐
    b. Degree ☐
    c. Masters ☐
    d. Professional ☐
4. **Type of Family**
    a. Nuclear ☐
    b. Joint ☐
5. **The number of siblings**
    a. Sisters ☐
    b. Brothers ☐
6. **Place**
    a. Urban ☐
    b. Suburban ☐
    c. Rural ☐
7. **I considered myself** as
    a. Slow learner ☐
    b. Average learner ☐
    c. Advanced learner ☐

Sci-Tech Information

8. **I feel more comfortable with**
    a. Laptop ☐
    b. Desktop ☐
    c. Mobile ☐
    d. iPad ☐
    e. Notebook ☐

    f.   Tablet ☐
    g.   iPhone ☐
    h.   Mac ☐

9. **Game-based learning is**

	Strongly Disagree	Disagree	Neutral	Agree	Strongly Agree
a. The adaptation of gaming elements and game mechanics to non-game contexts					
b. Game mechanics applied to business processes.					
c. Making something potentially tedious, fun.					
d. More appealing and provide motivation and excitement.					
e. The concept of applying game mechanics and game design techniques to engage and motivate people to achieve their goals.					
f. Considered as Non-fiction gameplay.					
g. Using game techniques to increase engagement, satisfaction, and fun.					
h. Leads to a better understanding of the curriculum through games.					
i. Changes the motivation from finishing a task to participating in the game.					
j. Used to support each other					
k. Used to improve the learning atmosphere					

10. **My institution uses the following**

	Very likely	Likely	Neutral	Not likely	Very unlikely
a. Classroom training					
b. On-the-job learning					
c. LMS/Online courses					
d. Mobile learning					
e. Video training					
f. Gamified learning					
g. Virtual classrooms					

11. **How strongly do you agree with the following statements about gamification?**

	Strongly Disagree	Disagree	Neutral	Agree	Strongly Agree
a. Game-based learning can help create more engaging experiences for learners					
b. Game-based learning can make learning more rewarding					
c. Online Game-based learning system improves my learning performance					
d. Online Game-based learning system increases my learning outcome					
e. Online Game-based learning enhances my desire to produce the desired result in my learning					
f. Online Game-based learning system is more useful in my learning then the other available options					

12. **Game-based learning helps me to Create and track levels of accomplishment.**

	Strongly Disagree	Disagree	Neutral	Agree	Strongly Agree
a. Perceived cost for developing gamified learning content					
b. Lack of cultural appetite, or scepticism from students/teachers					
c. Lack of suppliers/designers working in this area					
d. Can only be used for training small numbers of people					
e. Unsure of how to measure the effectiveness					
f. Not sure how it could be used in our subjects					
g. N/A - we already use gamification					

Adopting Game-based learning is difficult because Lack of knowledge of how to implement it.

*** *** ***

Chapter 7
Effectiveness of Game-Based Learning as a Pedagogy Among the MBA Students

Karthigai Prakasam Chellaswamy
CHRIST University (Deemed), India

Georgy P. Kurien
CHRIST University (Deemed), India

Nagarjuna Gururaj Rao
CHRIST University (Deemed), India

Sreedhara Raman
CHRIST University (Deemed), India

Sharon Varghese
CHRIST University (Deemed), India

Anand Shankar Raja Manivannan
CHRIST University (Deemed), India

ABSTRACT

Game-based learning is an exciting and interactive tool used by many teachers across the globe. This research aims to check whether any significant change is found in the learning of the student before and after introducing game-based learning in classroom teaching. MBA students were identified as the target group for this research. The production dice game was used for this experiment. The teacher engaged the first session traditionally and later with the production dice game. Student learning was captured through a Google form before and after the game. The Google form had questions ranging from understanding to analyzing to application-level to capture exactly the effectiveness of game-based learning, Paired sample t-test was applied to check the before and after test results, and it was found that there was a significant change in the learning among the identified target group. Through this study, the authors conclude that game-based learning provides better results in student learning as compared to regular classroom teaching.

DOI: 10.4018/978-1-7998-7271-9.ch007

Effectiveness of Game-Based Learning as a Pedagogy Among the MBA Students

INTRODUCTION

Educational institutions are working hard to provide a quality education through different means. Educational institutions try to arrange and organize Faculty Development Programs and Workshops to imbibe teachers the use technology in their routine teaching. On the other hand, students expect digital learning on online platforms and offline scenarios to get a better learning experience. In this regard, the role of game-based learning has become successful. However, game-based learning is more into experiments to find new ways to make teaching and learning more interesting it still has opportunities to be explored. Technological upgrades are very constant across the globe. Gamification, a boon in the technological era, has paved the way for educational institutions to break the mundane teaching pedagogy and impose learning with adventurous and exciting experiences. Game-based learning has focused goals that have to be accomplished by the players. It motivates the students to achieve success and experience a sense of accomplishment when they finish different stages. Moreover, the portions and syllabus which has to be completed by the concerned teachers are also accomplished. Game-based learning has helped the students and the teachers in different means. The system of education keeps changing from time to time. Different vendors who design and develop special software imbibing gamification have been vital contributors to the upliftment of quality education. On the other hand, the situational impact has also motivated researchers to research on game-based learning, which will be helpful for the teachers and learners. For example, the Covid-19 health crisis has devastated the entire educational structure where teaching and learning had to be facilitated on online platforms. In this regard, game-based learning has helped the stakeholders in several ways. Since the majority of the households have a basic phone, personal computer, and laptops with a decent internet connection game-based learning has become the spotlight during the Covid-19 crisis. Game-based learning has three core elements that highlight game-based learning, i.e., narrative-centered learning, combined-learning-context, problem-solving, and storytelling in an interactive format (Rowe, Mott, & Lester, 2012). Based on these core elements, game-based learning enjoys several benefits.

First and foremost, the users enjoy and can easily connect to the subject when learning pedagogy is more pleasant and attractive (Davis et al., 1992). Moreover, different software used for the game-based-learning is user-friendly and flexible. It provides the users a peaceful experience without leading to stress. Hence, game-based learning is suitable for the present age groups who are tech-savvy and prefer to learn using digital platforms. The third most important factor which has made game-based learning successful is customization. A class with different categories of students may not be over-familiar with technological usage. Thus, few concepts can be broken into simple blocks and can be customized. Therefore, game-based learning, a tailored learning mechanism, has helped educational institutions achieve the goal of facilitating quality education (Troussas et al., 2020). Various pedagogies are used to instill Learning among the students. One such popular and effective pedagogy is game-based learning. GBL has not been widely followed and practiced since many are not aware of it. In Game-based education, the course content is mapped into the game to provide a scenario environment of learning, repeated self-learning, and ongoing interaction and feedback to increase learning interest and motivation (Cheng & Su, 2012). In addition, gamification will also enhance students' cognitive abilities and skills as it gives them an opportunity to think and progress to achieve the goal (Guyton, 2011). Multiple researchers have found that game-based learning raised test scores, allowed for hands-on social skill lessons, and helped generate a positive student environment (McKenzi James, 2020). To measure the effectiveness of game-based learning, a group of post-graduate students were identified. A concept was taught using the traditional model "class lecture". Later, the same ideas were conveyed through a game to determine their level of understanding before and after the game-based learning pedagogy.

STATEMENT OF PURPOSE

MBA (Masters in Business Administration) becomes the base course across the globe helping individuals fetch a decent job or to pursue their passion. However, there are many educational institutions in Indian setup which offers MBA course in the Postgraduate level. There is a need to go with the basic anecdote mentioned by pioneers in management "Management is a Science and Art" because management has to be practiced to gain credits. In this regard, MBA students with expectations and keenness to learn and acquire new knowledge with practical exposure expect a new teaching and learning pedagogy. With the advancement in technology there are many digital tools and devices which are available to make learning more interesting and meaningful. Gamification has become popular as it improves the cognitive abilities and cognitive accuracy (Ahmad et al., 2021). Though there are many positive outcomes of Game-based-learning there is a need to explore the outcome which are analytical in nature with validated results. Hence, the purpose of this research is to measure the impact of GBL (Game-based-learning) on the students test scores, the application of the concepts and themes and level of understanding. This research aim is to conduct practical experiments to know the outcomes of game-based-learning. The outcomes and meaningful inferences will help the Indian educational institutions offering MBA program to make game-based-learning a compulsory component to facilitate better teaching and learning and to make students learning experience more meaningful.

Review of Literature

Game based learning makes the learner to experience the subject rather than studying it. When games are used for educational purposes, it supports the learners in terms of decision-making capability, effective solutions to the problems and encourages teamwork that often leads to improving their social skills (M. Pivec et al., 2003). The blend of both simulation game and offline classroom activities helps the teacher to exploit students' potential in specific parts of their traditional learning paths (La Guardia et al., 2014). The experiment was conducted between two students' groups to understand the effectiveness of game-based learning in system analysis course. One is experiential group and other is control group. The results proved that game-based learning enhance the learning achievements of the students compared to those who are under face-to-face teaching (Cheng & Su, 2012). Combining game elements in the course not only attracts the students towards course but also elevate the learning motivation among the students (Lai et al., 2012). Games based learning is very crucial to impart the 21st century skills such as analytical, critical, argumentation, communication, collaboration, reasoning, problem solving and decision-making skills among the students. Digital games such as Academic Talk, InterLoc and Computer-Based lab for Language Games in Education (College) proves to be powerful in enhancing argumentation skills among the students. (Noroozi et al., 2020). Collaborative game-based learning not only promote the learning attitudes and motivation of the students but also improves their learning achievement and self-efficacy (Sung & Hwang, 2013). To work at a global level, it is essential to impart foreign language skills among students. A game-based app is developed to involve the students in their learning process and to assess their foreign language skill (Palomo-Duarte et al., 2016). Effectiveness of digital game-based learning depends on intervention and methods dimensions. Intervention dimension consists of guidance from the instructor, substantial information about the game in terms of its procedure and proper training. Game based learning will be effective if; it assesses learners while playing the game by providing details insights on learning process, tracking motivational, emotional and metacognitive features to understand behaviour and final outcome, and immediate feedback based on embedded assessment to identify the areas of difficulties for learners to play the game (Ifenthaler et al., 2012). Creating challenging games is important since its not only has a positive impact on learning outcomes of the students but also helps them to be more involved and engage in the game. So educational games should develop games which are challenging in nature, keeping learners' growing abilities and supports continued learning (Hamari et al., 2016). Industry Giant II is a business simulation game that enables the learner ability in setting up new business that consists of construction of building, product transportation, development, resources collection and financial management. Zapitalism is another game-based learning that enhances the skills of learners in terms of understanding real world economics, actual business and sales cycles and competitive pricing structures. Virtual U, a management game-based learning is developed to impart management practices among learners. Through this game, the learners can enhance their problem solving, team building, leadership and communication skills (Blunt, n.d.). The game-based learning design model can be adopted to create educational games (Shi & Shih, 2015). The games should be designed in such a way that the learners should be able to acquire specific knowledge and skills. The game should also integrate motivational aspects along with instructional design to meet the learning objectives (Tobias et al., 2014). Learners who play educational games show more anxiety, challenges and interest in their learning process and also experience higher levels of cognitive load compared to learners who adopt hypertext instructions (Stiller & Schworm, 2019). The principles such as 'intrinsic motivation', 'intense enjoyment and fun', 'authenticity', 'self-reliance' and 'experiential learning' need to be considered while developing games-based learning. The game-based should adopt following mechanism; 'rules should be simple and binary', 'clear with challenging goals', 'a fictional setting', 'progressive difficulty levels', 'interaction and high degree of student control', 'immediate feedback', and 'a social element that allows to share experience and build bonds' (Perotta et al., 2013). Game-based learning will help in imparting leadership skills among students. Leadership skills. This approach helps in developing primary leadership skills such as motivation, facilitation, coaching, mindset changing and communication (Sousa & Rocha, 2019). To create interest in game-based learning one should need to be motivated, engaged and supported in the learning process. The game-based learning should address the learning outcome and it should be relevant to real-world context of practice. Game-based learning should adopt experiential, problem-based and exploratory learning approaches (Freitas, 2006). Game-based learning, especially location-based technology, helps students to acquire historical knowledge and create motivation towards history subjects compared to students who receive project-based instructions (Huizenga et al., 2009). Collaboration, choice, feedback and instructional design elements need to be incorporated while designing games, so that will create a positive impact on the students' engagement in the learning process (Serrano, 2019). The game which focuses on business strategy, advergaming and entertainment elements will be a future paradigm for e learning. These games develop problem solving skills among learners since it not only presents the facts but also makes them ways of seeing and understanding the problems (Squire, 2008).

Theoretical Underpinning

Experimental learning is very challenging and also gives an opportunity to discover new outcomes. The concept of experimental learning has been widely researched. However, David Allen Kolb is an American educational theorist has been instrumental in developing theories which has helped many researchers. In this research article for the theoretical underpinning, we have used the "Experimental Learning Theory". Learning should always happen through the process of discovery and search of knowledge which will help the learners achieve the desired outcomes. Thus, the Experimental Learning Theory has been instrumental in the field of education to be practically applied and researched. Though there are many other theories developed by various researchers, importance was not given to few important elements such as: Cognitive abilities, experience-based transformation and transformation of experience into knowledge and other utilities. In the research article by (McCarthy, 2016) it has been stated that, four learning elements are very important namely Concentrate experience, Active experiment, Reflective experiment and abstract conceptualization. These elements are the four basic elements of the experimental learning cycle and basic learning styles proposed by Kolb during the year 1994 (Kolb, 1984). This research conducted on the MBA students gives importance to the four basic elements. Hence, this theory is chosen to be the base theory in this research. In the later years post Kolb's theory was introduced other scholars have relooked into the theory and have proposed six propositions. These propositions are Learning is a process and not just an outcome, learning is re-learning, learning required resolution, learning is holistic, learning is a synergetic link between the learner and the environment and learning creates knowledge. In this research we have stressed on the importance of gaming in the learning process. The usage of games in education has been for many years, however the upgradation of technology creates new impacts. In this regard, when a student puts himself/herself into the learning process with gaming tools and devices they learn something new and get a very new exposure and experience. This provides an opportunity for the learners to go through a sequential process to attain the final goal. There is an interaction between the learner and the gaming platforms to acquire knowledge. The end-result is knowledge acquisition. The six propositions proposed by different researchers which stems from the original theory of Kolb is more suitable for this research. Even for conducting the experiments in this research we asked questions related to knowledge acquisition, environmental impact, process of learning and experience. On the other hand, the suitability of this theory for this research work is because of the practicality and applicability of the theory in the entire learning process (Kolb & Kolb, 2013). When the student is exposed to the game-based learning, they concentrate to know the learning task and work hard to achieve the desired goals. On the second stage based on their observations based on experience they are able to extract information and learn new concepts. In this regard, they get an opportunity to learn. Based on their learning they draw conclusions. The same has been explained by (Mcleod, 2013) in his article where he explains David Kolb's learning styles. In this research we have considered all the four stages and have conducted a systematic experiment and have drawn response based on the experience of the students who participated in the experiment. From the crux of the base theory the experiment has been designed and facilitated.

Effectiveness of Game-Based Learning as a Pedagogy Among the MBA Students

RESEARCH METHODOLOGY

Game-based learning is not much popular among Indian educational institutions. Though there are many positive impacts on students learning abilities and outcomes, educational institutions have not considered game-based learning seriously as they have not experimented and benefitted out of it. Hence, we have tested with post-Graduate students to observe and find the actual impact on students. The MBA program has been chosen because it is a cluster of students from different backgrounds and has vast subjects to learn during the program duration. Out of various topics which are offered to the MBA graduates, the focus has been placed on Lean Operation because it is complex in nature and needs more attentiveness to understand the core concepts. A predetermined game was used in the delivery of a concept to the control group. The experiment is conducted by using students as a control group who are studying MBA at Christ University, Bangalore. Though the University offers different MBA specializations to its students, we used judgmental sampling in choosing a sample of students studying Lean Operations and Systems specialization (control group), as they were already familiar with the basic concepts of production management. The sample size was 36 MBA students based on convenient sampling. Three significant variables are used to measure the outcome of the study. They are Students' *Understanding* of the concepts, *ability to apply* the concepts, and *Ability to analyze* the concepts. The experiment was conducted in two stages. In the first stage, the control group was taught a concept by the usual lecture method or pedagogy. Soon after the delivery of the lecture, the control group was assessed for their understanding, ability to apply and analyze the concepts. The assessment was carried out by using Multiple choice questions throughout the survey instrument. Based on the experience, the respondents responded to the questions on the survey instrument. The responses being a reflection on their expertise adds more value and transparency to the research work. To further experiment and have more clarity in the second stage, after a gap of around a week, the same concept was driven by using the predetermined game to the same control group. Again, the control group was assessed for their understanding, ability to apply and analyze the concepts. Same multiple-choice questions were used which were used in the first assessment. The difficulty level of the questions was intentionally maintained at a higher-order level. Paired sample t-tests were used to compare the test scores.

Hypotheses

Conducting a scientific experiment with experimental and control groups, it is important to develop certain meaningful assumptions and prove the same post-experiments with valid and reliable results. Game-based learning has several positive outcomes if proven true, can benefit the stakeholders. Hence, there is a need to develop a hypothesis before proceeding with the analysis. The following hypotheses are developed considering a few important variables: test scores, understanding capacity, and practical applications and tested against respective alternatives.

H_1: There is no significant effect of game-based learning on test scores
H_2: There is no significant effect of game-based learning on understanding concepts by the students.
H_3: There is no significant effect of game-based learning on application of concepts by students.
H_4: There is significant effect of game-based learning on analysing concepts by students

The Production Dice Game

The production dice game demonstrates the impact and the causes of dependency and variability in supply chains and production systems. In addition, the game can also familiarise students with assembly line production systems and demonstrate basic operations management concepts such as throughput, cycle time, bottleneck, process layouts, material requirements planning (MRP) and work in progress (WIP) inventory. The game's origin is traced back to the well-known novel 'The Goal' written by Eliyahu Goldratt (Gupta & Boyd, 2011). The classroom adaptation of the game is illustrated by many authors such as Johnson & Drougas (2002) and Umble & Umble (2005). Since then, many versions of the dice game have been extended to demonstrate lean manufacturing systems, supply chains, and different production layouts (Lambrecht et al., 2012). In addition, there are also variations in its execution, such as a physical lab setup, online played remotely or in a classroom setup (Cole & Snider, 2017; Manikas et al., 2015). The game played as part of the present study deals with an assembly line layout, in which the path of a product is a straight line. WIP moves from one workstation to the next along the assembly line. In this layout, the production system is dependent, meaning successive operations cannot start until the previous operations are completed. In addition, this system has variability in individual workstation outputs. The production system thus has bottlenecks and starvation, resulting in loss of production output (throughput) and increased costs due to larger WIPs. Game Instructions Each student in the game represents a workstation, so five players represent five successive workstations of the production line. The role of a dice (six-faced) will determine the production output of a workstation per day. The output is thus of uniform distribution with a mean of 3.5 and a standard deviation of 1.75. The experiment layout is shown in Fig. 1.

Figure 1. Experiment layout

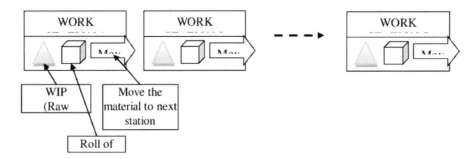

The game is played for ten consecutive days. Each worker will roll the dice once each day. Depending on the day's production (based on the dice roll), WIP is moved along the production chain. The last operator, representing workstation five, will deliver the finished products day wise. The simulation is run for ten consecutive days. We have modified the traditional production dice game for an online audience. Student groups of seven (five students representing five workstations, one supervisor and a scribe who do the data entry) played the game in online breakout rooms. The results were tabulated in a shared spreadsheet. The format of the spreadsheet is placed in Table 1.

Table 1. Format of the shared spreadsheet for data entry

Day	Work station 1		Workstation 2			Workstation 3			Workstation 4			Workstation 5			Day summary	
	Dice value	Prodn	WIP	Dice value	Prodn	WIP	Dice value	Prodn	WIP	Dice value	Prodn	WIP	Dice value	Prodn	Finished good	Total WIP
1																
2																
3																

Variations of the Game

After playing the game with high variability and dependence, the game is repeated with reduced variability and reduced dependency. Variability is reduced by replacing the dice with tossing of a coin with a 'head' equated to a production output of four and a 'tail' equated to a production output of 3. With ten days of play, the output seems to increase by a substantial amount (30% increase or more).

The third trial is done with reduced dependency. This is achieved by pre-stocking all the workstations with some amount of WIP. We have used four WIP pre-stock at each workstation. This inventory decouples processes and reduces dependency resulting in increased process outputs.

The game can be further played by asking students to find other ways to reduce variability and dependency. This exercise generates a good amount of brainstorming and discussions among the participating students. A detailed debriefing concludes the game.

RESULTS AND ANALYSIS

The control group consisted of 36 MBA students specializing in Lean and Operations Management. The students were evenly divided by gender, and their undergraduate degree was either a Bachelor of Technology or a Bachelor of Engineering. R-software was used perform all the analysis. Table 2 shows the students' scores before and after playing the game. The mean score for students after using the lecture method is 6.333, while the mean score for students after using the game as pedagogy is 7.833. Figure 2's box plot clearly shows that there are no outliers in the data.

Table 2. Summary for overall score before and after the game

	Scores before the game	Scores after the game
Minimum	3	2
1st Quartile	5	5.75
Median	6	8
Mean	6.333	7.833
3rd Quartile	7	10
Maximum	12	18

Figure 2. Box-plot for the difference of score for checking outliers

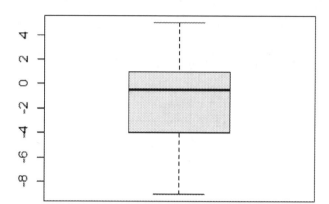

Checking Normality Assumption of Difference

The normality of the difference of scores is required to perform the paired t-test. The Shapiro-Wilk normality test was used to determine the normality of the difference of the test scores under consideration for analysis. The null hypothesis for the Shapiro-Wilk normality test is that the distribution of the data is not significantly different from the normal distribution. From Table 3, it is observed that the p-value is 0.1272 which is greater than 0.05. As a result, we cannot reject the null hypothesis and conclude that the data distribution is not different from the normal distribution at 5% level of significance and that the paired t-test can be performed for the analysis.

Table 3. Shapiro-Wilk's test results for overall scores

Test Statistic	p-value
0.9527	0.1272

Comparison of Overall Scores – Before and After the Usage of the Game

The paired sample t-test was performed to compare the overall scores of students before and after the game-based pedagogy was used. The following null hypothesis was being tested.

H_1 - There is no significant effect of the game-based learning on test scores against
H_1' – There is an improvement in scores after the game-based learning. The paired t-test results are summarized in the Table 4.

Table 4. Results of the paired t-test for overall scores

Mean difference	t-statistic	Degrees of freedom	p-value
-1.5	-2.4853	35	0.0089

The p-value is 0.0089 and H_1 is rejected in favor of H_1' hence there is a significant effect of the game-based learning on test scores at 5% level of significance. This means that the overall assessment scores of the students improved because of the usage of game-based pedagogy.

Checking the Effect of the Game-Based Pedagogy on the 3 Assessment Criteria of Variables

In this section, we wanted check the effect of game-based pedagogy on the 3 variables used for assessment of the students. These three variables are a) Understanding of the concepts b) Application of the Concepts and c) Analysis of the Concepts.

1. Checking the impact of game on Understanding of the concept

The scores of understanding level questions are analysed for checking the impact of game – based learning on understanding the concepts. The null hypothesis for the paired t-test is that

H_2 - There is no significant effect of game-based learning on understanding concepts by the students
against
H_2' – There is an improvement of scores of understanding level questions after the game-based learning. The test results are summarized in the Table 5.

Table 5. Results of the paired t-test for scores of understanding level questions

Mean difference	t-statistic	Degrees of freedom	p-value
-0.3889	-1.2369	35	0.1122

Since p-value is 0.1122 and we do not reject H_2 at the 5% significance level. The game has no significant impact on concept understanding at the 5% significance level. This means that the lecture method was sufficient to ensure that the students understood the concepts. The game-based pedagogy had no significant impact on concept understanding. From the above interpretations we can understand that the traditional lecture method is more sufficient enough for the students to understand the concepts. However, GBL are just an additional pedagogy used by the teachers to give adventurous exposure to the students. Few research also says that the traditional learning method helps in long-term knowledge retention (Rondon, 2013). However, there are also few studies which says that GBL are more effective and the student community enjoys learning. Hence, different researchers who have conducted research to know the difference between GBL and traditional learning method have got different opinion. Hence in this research we have proved that there is no impact on GBL and students understanding of the concepts.

2. Checking the impact of game on Application of the concept

The scores of application level questions are analysed for checking the impact of game – based learning on application of the concepts. The null hypothesis for the paired t-test is that

H_3 - There is no significant effect of game-based learning on application of concepts by students against
H_3' – There is an improvement in scores of application level questions after the game-based learning.

The corresponding paired t-test results are summarized in the Table 6.

Table 6. Results of the paired t-test for scores of application level questions

Mean difference	t-statistic	Degrees of freedom	p-value
-0.8056	-2.292	35	0.014

Since the p-value is 0.014, we reject H_3 at the 5% significance level. From the above results it is clear that, there is a significant difference in concept application before and after game-based learning at the 5% significance level. In other words, game-based learning has an effect on concept application. Through game-based learning, students can now apply concepts and solve problems. The aim of game-based learning is to enhance the student's analytical capacity and provide an opportunity to think logically. The assignments which are given through the GBL are chronological in nature and hence if an individual wants to clear all the levels and reach the final destination, he/she has to invest time and efforts. Only when the individuals are clear with the concepts and learn them with clarity they proceed towards the next stage. Education is not a problem to be solved however it is a source of knowledge to benefit. The key of GBL is to motivate the students to think differently and practically apply their cognitive abilities to understand a concept (Sartre, 2020). Moreover, GBL is a competitive exercise which enhances the thinking power of the students. From the teacher's perspective, GBL helps teachers to simplify a concept and deliver the same to the students with a visual treat and adventurous experience using the digital platform (Matthew, 2018).

3. Checking the impact of game on Analysing the concept

The scores of analysing level questions are analysed for checking the impact of game – based learning on analysing the concepts. The null hypothesis for the paired t-test is that

H_4 - There is significant effect of game-based learning on analysing concepts by students against
H_4' – There is an improvement in scores of analysing level questions after the game-based learning

The corresponding paired t-test results are summarized in the Table 7.

Table 7. Results of the paired t-test for scores of analysing level questions

Mean difference	t-statistic	Degrees of freedom	p-value
-0.4	-2.5624	35	0.007925

Since the p-value is 0.0079, we reject H_4 at the 5% significance level. There is a significant difference in concept analysis before and after game-based learning at the 5% significance level. That is, game-based learning has an effect on concept analysis. Students can now analyse concepts. This means that when game-based pedagogy is used, the students' analytical skills are best utilized. Being Tech-savvy is considered to be an important quality amongst the student community in the 21st century. For example, during the Covid-19 crisis many schools shut down and students had to learn through the online platform. Few concepts were taught to the students and few concepts were delivered to the students in form of games. These games help the students progress in academics and also enhances their thinking capacity. Since games are filled with suspense the students try hard to solve different problems and start to think from a different perspective (Hwang, 2020).

DISCUSSION

Education has not become very effective after the advent and upgradation of technology. Effective education changes the life of an individual which imposes more practical exposure. From the research it is understood that the skills of students enhances when they learn through Game-Based-Learning (GBL). Since every GBL has a defined outcome, it motivates students achieve the final goals. They solve problems, understand and apply cognitive skills to finish different levels and proceed to the final level. Moreover, GBL provides flexibility where students can learn from anywhere as per their comfort. In addition, teachers customize the assignments and concepts and deliver the same to the students in form of games. Different targets such as badges, credit points, stars, reward points etc. motivate the students to strike a healthy competition with other students. The success of learning can be measured when an individual uses his cognitive abilities to logically think, use cognitive skills, analyze and find meaningful solutions. Thus, few games are designed in such a way that there are high level of engagement and involvement. Even in this research we could find that GBL has a positive impact on the test scores. This means that students are able to learn and understand the concepts in a simple and better way. Moreover, since the MBA programs has a spread of different subjects which has to be taught with practical exposure GBL facilitates teaching as well. Certain subjects cannot be just explained verbally because students may not understand the concept. In this regard, the complex concepts are converted into assignments which becomes a part of the games and the same is exposed to the students. Hence, GBL has supported educational institutions to provide valuable and quality education for the student community.

SOLUTIONS AND RECOMMENDATIONS

The results of this research match and supports the existing studies. Games Based Learning as a pedagogy has proven to be an excellent tool for better learning among the students. The same has been witnessed in the previous studies which have been presented here. Gamification in education enables students' creativity, makes them work collaboratively, develop their communication skills, increase their competency, adopt innovative practices and increase their motivation in the learning process. Gamification in education also makes students active learners by creating more interest towards the subject and also brings exciting elements in the assessment that makes them enjoy the activity (Cózar-Gutiérrez & Sáez-López, 2016). Current employers give more importance to soft skills such as critical thinking, debating and decision making, ability to work, communicate and achieve set goals in teams. So, a game-based learning model that supports collaborative role play is essential to achieve the learning outcome (Paul, 2009). Game-based learning increases students' engagement and performances in their learning process (Polikov, 2017). Game-based learning can be used as an effective tool to assess the student skills, during the phase of instructional process but requires more time to explain, demonstrate, play, reflect and assess (Pinder, 2016). The integration of the game not only generates a positive attitude towards the subject but also improves the scientific knowledge of the students (Liu & Chen, 2013). To summaries, the benefits of a Game Based Learning is lot more when introduced among the students and needless to say that the loss would be much greater if an attempt is not made by the teaching fraternity to take it to the classroom.

CONCLUSION

The research results show a significant improvement in the students learning before and after the experiment. Game-Based learning facilitates the students to understand and remember the theoretical concepts with a practical approach. It ensures the students acquire the essential subject knowledge and move further to achieve higher-order thinking skills by expanding their thought process. Educators must introduce Game-Based Learning across all programmes and courses to ensure effective class engagement, active participation, and knowledge enhancement. Instructors need to remember that Game-Based learning is only a pedagogical tool that aids the learning process. Its application may not be sufficient. Still, it requires a mastery approach from the faculty side to get the best results out of it. The current research has been done with only 36 respondents and in particular the MBA students which is considered as a limitation to this research, Future researches can focus on the difference in the learning level among the UG students and other demographic differences.

REFERENCES

Ahmad, F., Ahmed, Z., & Muneeb, S. (2021). Effect of gaming mode upon the players' cognitive performance during brain games play: An exploratory research. *International Journal of Game-Based Learning*, *11*(1), 67–76. Advance online publication. doi:10.4018/IJGBL.2021010105

Blunt, R. (n.d.). *Does Game-Based Learning Work? Results from Three Recent Studies*. Academic Press.

Cheng, C.-H., & Su, C.-H. (2012). A Game-based learning system for improving student's learning effectiveness in system analysis course. *Procedia: Social and Behavioral Sciences*, *31*, 669–675. doi:10.1016/j.sbspro.2011.12.122

Cole, R., & Snider, B. (2017a). Rolling the Dice on Global Supply Chain Sustainability: A Total Cost of Ownership Simulation. *INFORMS Transactions on Education*, *20*(3), 165–176. doi:10.1287/ited.2019.0225

Cole, R., & Snider, B. (2017b). Rolling the Dice on Global Supply Chain Sustainability: A Total Cost of Ownership Simulation. *INFORMS Transactions on Education*, *20*(3), 165–176. doi:10.1287/ited.2019.0225

Cózar-Gutiérrez, R., & Sáez-López, J. M. (2016). Game-based learning and gamification in initial teacher training in the social sciences: An experiment with Minecraft Edu. *International Journal of Educational Technology in Higher Education, 13*(1), 2. doi:10.118641239-016-0003-4

Davis, F. (1989). Perceived usefulness, perceived ease of use, and user acceptance of information technology. *Management Information Systems Quarterly, 13*(3), 319–340. doi:10.2307/249008

Freitas, S. de. (2006). *Learning in Immersive worlds: A review of game-based learning*. Academic Press.

Gupta, M., & Boyd, L. (2011). An Excel-based dice game: An integrative learning activity in operations management. *International Journal of Operations & Production Management, 31*(6), 608–630. doi:10.1108/01443571111131962

Guyton, G. (2011). Using Toys to Support Infant-Toddler Learning and Development. *Young Children, 66*, 50.

Hamari, J., Shernoff, D. J., Rowe, E., Coller, B., Asbell-Clarke, J., & Edwards, T. (2016). Challenging games help students learn: An empirical study on engagement, flow and immersion in game-based learning. *Computers in Human Behavior, 54*, 170–179. doi:10.1016/j.chb.2015.07.045

Hsiao, H.-S., Chang, C.-S., Lin, C.-Y., & Hu, P.-M. (2014). Development of children's creativity and manual skills within digital game-based learning environment. *Journal of Computer Assisted Learning, 30*(4), 377–395. doi:10.1111/jcal.12057

Huizenga, J., Admiraal, W., Akkerman, S., & ten Dam, G. (2009). Mobile game-based learning in secondary education: Engagement, motivation and learning in a mobile city game. *Journal of Computer Assisted Learning, 25*(4), 332–344. doi:10.1111/j.1365-2729.2009.00316.x

Ifenthaler, D., Eseryel, D., & Ge, X. (2012). Assessment for Game-Based Learning. In D. Ifenthaler, D. Eseryel, & X. Ge (Eds.), *Assessment in Game-Based Learning: Foundations, Innovations, and Perspectives* (pp. 1–8). Springer., doi:10.1007/978-1-4614-3546-4_1

Johnson, A. C., & Drougas, A. M. (2002). *Using Goldratt's Game to Introduce Simulation in the Introductory Operations Management Course*. Https://Doi.Org/10.1287/Ited.3.1.20

Kolb, D. A. (1984). Experiential learning: Experience as the source of learning and development, David A. Kolb, Prentice-Hall International, Hemel Hempstead, Herts., 1984. No. of pages: xiii + 256. Journal of Organizational Behavior.

Kolb, D. A., & Kolb, A. Y. (2013). Research on Validity and Educational Applications. *Experience Based Learning Systems, 5*.

La Guardia, D., Gentile, M., Dal Grande, V., Ottaviano, S., & Allegra, M. (2014). A Game based Learning Model for Entrepreneurship Education. *Procedia: Social and Behavioral Sciences, 141*, 195–199. doi:10.1016/j.sbspro.2014.05.034

Lai, C.-H., Lee, T.-P., Jong, B.-S., & Hsia, Y.-T. (2012). A Research on Applying Game-Based Learning to Enhance the Participation of Student. In Embedded and Multimedia Computing Technology and Service (pp. 311–318). Springer Netherlands. doi:10.1007/978-94-007-5076-0_36

Lambrecht, M., Creemers, S., Boute, R., & Leus, R. (2012). Extending the production dice game. *International Journal of Operations & Production Management*, *32*(12), 144–3577. doi:10.1108/01443571211284197

Liu, E. Z. F., & Chen, P.-K. (2013). The Effect of Game-Based Learning on Students' Learning Performance in Science Learning – A Case of "Conveyance Go." *Procedia: Social and Behavioral Sciences*, *103*, 1044–1051. doi:10.1016/j.sbspro.2013.10.430

Manikas, A., Gupta, M., & Boyd, L. (2015). Experiential exercises with four production planning and control systems. *International Journal of Production Research*, *53*(14), 4206–4217. doi:10.1080/00207543.2014.985393

McCarthy, M. (2016). Experiential Learning Theory: From Theory To Practice. *Journal of Business & Economics Research*, *14*(3), 91–100. doi:10.19030/jber.v14i3.9749

Mcleod, S. (2013). *Kolb-Learning Styles.* simplypsychology.org/learning-kolb.html

Noroozi, O., Dehghanzadeh, H., & Talaee, E. (2020). A systematic review on the impacts of game-based learning on argumentation skills. *Entertainment Computing*, *35*, 100369. doi:10.1016/j.entcom.2020.100369

Palomo-Duarte, M., Berns, A., Cejas, A., Dodero, J. M., Caballero, J. A., & Ruiz-Rube, I. (2016). Assessing Foreign Language Learning Through Mobile Game-Based Learning Environments. *International Journal of Human Capital and Information Technology Professionals*, *7*(2), 53–67. doi:10.4018/IJHCITP.2016040104

Paul, P. (2009). *Game-based Learning or Game-based Teaching?* Academic Press.

Perotta, C., Featherstone, G., Aston, H., & Houghton, E. (2013). *Game-based learning: Latest evidence and future directions*. Academic Press.

Pinder, D. P. J. (2016). Exploring the Effects of Game Based Learning in Trinidad and Tobago's Primary Schools: An Examination of In-Service Teachers'. *Perspectives*, 17.

Pivec, M., Dziabenko, O., & Schinnerl, I. (2003). Aspects of Game-Based Learning. *Proceedings of I-KNOW3*, 11.

Polikov, V. (2017, March 6). *New Research Proves Game-Based Learning Works—Here's Why That Matters—EdSurge News*. EdSurge. https://www.edsurge.com/news/2017-03-06-new-research-proves-game-based-learning-works-here-s-why-that-matters

Rowe, J. P., Shores, L. R., Mott, B. W., & Lester, J. C. (2011). Integrating learning, problem solving, and engagement in narrative-centered learning environments. *International Journal of Artificial Intelligence in Education*, *21*(1-2), 115–133.

Serrano, K. (2019). *The effect of digital game-based learning on student learning: A literature review.* Academic Press.

Shi, Y.-R., & Shih, J.-L. (2015). Game Factors and Game-Based Learning Design Model. *International Journal of Computer Games Technology*, *11*, 11. doi:10.1155/2015/549684

Shi, Y.-R., & Shih, J.-L. (2015). *Game factors and game-based learning design model*. Academic Press.

Sousa, M. J., & Rocha, Á. (2019). Leadership styles and skills developed through game-based learning. *Journal of Business Research*, *94*, 360–366. doi:10.1016/j.jbusres.2018.01.057

Squire, K. D. (2008). Video game–based learning: An emerging paradigm for instruction. *Performance Improvement Quarterly*, *21*(2), 7–36. doi:10.1002/piq.20020

Stiller, K. D., & Schworm, S. (2019). Game-Based Learning of the Structure and Functioning of Body Cells in a Foreign Language: Effects on Motivation, Cognitive Load, and Performance. *Frontiers in Education*, *4*, 18. doi:10.3389/feduc.2019.00018

Sung, H.-Y., & Hwang, G.-J. (2013). A collaborative game-based learning approach to improving students' learning performance in science courses. *Computers & Education*, *63*, 43–51. doi:10.1016/j.compedu.2012.11.019

Tobias, S., Fletcher, J. D., & Wind, A. P. (2014). Game-Based Learning. In J. M. Spector, M. D. Merrill, J. Elen, & M. J. Bishop (Eds.), *Handbook of Research on Educational Communications and Technology* (pp. 485–503). Springer. doi:10.1007/978-1-4614-3185-5_38

Troussas, C., Krouska, A., & Sgouropoulou, C. (2020). Collaboration and fuzzy-modeled personalization for mobile game-based learning in higher education. *Computers & Education*, *144*, 103698. doi:10.1016/j.compedu.2019.103698

Umble, E. J., & Umble, M. (2005). The Production Dice Game: An Active Learning Classroom Exercise and Spreadsheet Simulation. *Operations Management Education Review*, *1*, 105–122.

Chapter 8
Game-Based Learning in Higher Education:
An Effective Pedagogical Tool for Enhanced Competency Building

Sunitha Abhay Jain
https://orcid.org/0000-0002-8367-8014
CHRIST University (Deemed), India

Sunil John
https://orcid.org/0000-0002-5544-3306
CHRIST University (Deemed), India

Nilofer Hussaini
https://orcid.org/0000-0002-6092-5203
CHRIST University (Deemed), India

Daisy Alexander
https://orcid.org/0000-0001-6971-7737
CHRIST University (Deemed), India

Bidisha Sarkar
CHRIST University (Deemed), India

ABSTRACT

The technological developments and innovations have thrown open many challenges in the field of higher education. We are growing up in a society of digital natives who are exposed to the digital environment from their birth. Of late, the focus has shifted from traditional teaching methods to finding innovative ways and means to engage the students. Competence building instead of rote learning is the need of the hour. In order to prepare the students to face the challenges of the real world and make them future ready, it is important for higher educational institutions to focus on imparting to learners 21st century skill sets such as creativity, problem solving, and critical thinking, amongst others. Game-based learning is gaining momentum and is becoming a popular pedagogical tool as it is learner-centric and fosters creativity.

DOI: 10.4018/978-1-7998-7271-9.ch008

GAME-BASED LEARNING - A PEDAGOGICAL TOOL

Technological innovations, development and digital revolution have impacted the lives of people around the world. It has changed the way various sectors function and carry on their activities in the digital era be it business, banking, tourism, trading and education. Many of these activities have moved to the online platforms. Educational sector is no exception to this paradigm shift. The changing technological landscape has opened up new avenues and has also posed various challenges. Higher educational institutions need to gear up to meet these challenges. The teaching and learning process in higher educational institutions is undergoing an unprecedented transformation. Today the way knowledge is imparted is no more limited to the class room lectures. Online teaching has become the new normal especially owing to the Covid-19 pandemic. Advances in digital technologies, penetration of internet and affordable smartphones have facilitated digital learning. Various new trends can be witnessed in the world of education in the form of adoption of game-based learning, gamification, video-based learning, adaptive learning, micro-learning and so on. Many higher educational institutions are also adopting virtual and augmented reality in order to make the teaching learning process interactive, participatory and immersive. Innovative pedagogical tools are being explored and adopted by higher educational institutions of several developed and developing countries to engage the learners for a fruitful learning experience. One such pedagogical tool that is gaining popularity especially in the higher educational sector is Game-based Learning [GBL].

In the light of the above, the authors have given an overview of the concept of game-based learning as an instructional tool in higher education along with case studies. Competence building & skill development through game-based learning both from the teacher's and the learner's perspective is highlighted in the chapter. Further, the authors have also discussed the advantages, disadvantages and challenges involved in implementing game-based learning and the solutions to overcome the same. The authors have proposed a 360 degree approach to facilitate the effective implementation of game-based learning in curriculum and assessment.

Objectives of the Chapter

1. To provide an insight to the concept of game-based learning as an instructional tool in higher education.
2. To provide a theoretical framework of game-based learning.
3. To distinguish game-based learning from gamification.
4. To differentiate game-based learning from traditional learning.
5. To understand the competence building process through game-based learning.
6. To understand the implementation process of game-based learning and to offer solutions.
7. To highlight the benefits, drawbacks and challenges of game-based learning.

CONCEPT OF GAME-BASED LEARNING

Game-based learning has grabbed the attention of various educational institutions and researchers world-wide. The game-based learning market is projected to grow at an annual compound growth rate of 20.07% and is expected to reach a market size of US$17.09 billion in 2026 (Research and Market, 2021). Many factors have contributed to the growth of game-based learning market such as the increase in the number of smart phone users, improvement in internet connectivity, the growing popularity of online games and e-learning amongst others. A large number of companies are investing huge amount in research and development for the purpose of designing new and innovative game-based learning solutions. Further, researchers and academicians are also focusing on designing and integrating games to supplement their teaching.

Now-a-days, game-based learning is increasingly becoming popular as a pedagogical tool to impart to the learners new skill sets which are popularly termed as the new age 21st century competencies. According to Charles Fadel and Bernie Trilling, the twenty first century skills include - learning and innovation, digital literacy and life skills. Further there is a need to engage the learners in problem solving, critical and creative thinking which is at the heart of innovation and learning (Fadel & Trilling, 2012). It is also important that the educational institutions must emphasize and develop these competencies and include it in their curriculum and pedagogy. To make the learners ready to face the challenge of today's globally connected, competitive and technologically intensive world, it is very important to focus on competence building. This will prepare the students to tackle complex problems and also address issues that might arise in the future. Games have been used from time immemorial for the purpose of entertainment as well as for imparting knowledge and skills to the learners. Games are usually structured and have a set of rules to be followed for the purpose of achieving the set goals. McGonigal (McGonigal, 2011) identifies four fundamental features of the game namely clearly defined goals, rules, a steady feedback system and a free will to participate in the game.

Game-based learning can be defined as the learning that is facilitated by the use of a game (Whitton, 2012). Qian and Clark have defined game-based learning, "as an environment in which the game content and game play are involved in the learning process and also aid in the enhancement of knowledge, acquisition of skills and involve problem solving spaces and challenges that provide the player and learners with a sense of achievement." (Qian & Clark, 2016). Game-based learning is an innovative learning approach which is used now-a-days to support learning that helps in enhancing teacher's and learner's competence. It is an effective tool to assess and evaluate the learners. (Tang, Hanneghan, & Rhalibi, 2009).

Game-based learning can also take place either in the classroom setting/off-line mode as well as in the online mode. It is often assumed that the game-based pedagogy is adopted only in the online mode. But this is not the case. Even in the classroom setting traditional games are used to impart the knowledge to the students. Usually in the online mode, when game-based learning is integrated into the curriculum digital games are preferred. A teacher's role becomes very important in game-based learning as the teachers need to design the game-based curriculum content in such a manner that it caters to the diverse needs of the learners. The effectiveness of game-based learning depends on the type of the game that has been designed, the stage at which it is introduced and the learning outcomes that are to be achieved. Further the efficacy of a game-based learning also depends on the level of student participation. Figure.1 describes game-based learning.

GAME-BASED LEARNING VS. GAMIFICATION

Game-based learning involves the use of games to impart and deliver the curriculum in higher education. It is useful as it focuses on learning through a problem solving approach. The learners can be given instant feedback to rectify their mistakes and this can prove to be helpful in understanding the concept.

Game-Based Learning in Higher Education

It also fosters collaborative learning and is helpful in boosting the confidence of the learners as they achieve their goals through game-based learning. At the core of game-based learning is the fact that the learners can learn from their mistakes as they explore different solutions.

Figure 1. Game-based learning
Source: Self-constructed

In gamification, the mechanics which are involved in a game are added to a non-game scenario. Game mechanics involves exploring the different design possibilities to be integrated so as to influence the motivation and the participation of the learner. For example, it is usually used for the purpose of encouraging a change in behavior and attitudes which is essential in various fields. The cultural dimension, the social context, behavioral changes, motivation are the key drivers in gamification. Game mechanics, design and dynamics are an integral part of gamification. In order to motivate the learners, triggers such as points, leader boards, badges or other elements are integrated in the teaching process and to involve the students as well. Table-1 highlights the distinction between game-based learning and gamification.

GAME BASED APPROACH VS. TRADITIONAL APPROACH

Traditional learning involves a teacher-centric rather than student-centric approach. In a traditional approach the role of a teacher is limited to dissemination of knowledge rather than acting as a facilitator. The mode of teaching is usually the chalk and talk method in which more emphasis is placed on theoretical understanding. The assessments revolve around rote learning rather than competence building. There is limited collaboration and peer learning with no proper alignment of objectives, activities and assessments. Studies have found that traditional classroom learning does not work well with young minds. According to a research study by Massachusetts Institute of Technology (Plass, Mayer, & Homer, 2020), brain behaviour of a young nineteen year old boy was found to be zero while attending traditional classroom learning which was similar to watching television.

On the other hand, game-based learning involves a student-centric approach wherein a teacher uses games as teaching tools for better student engagement. This has a significant impact on the students' performance as it involves 'learning by doing' at their own pace which is beneficial to both slow learners and fast learners. Students can move to advanced levels of problem solving only after mastering the basic level of understanding in the game based approach. Immediate and continuous feedback on their performance enables them to rectify their mistakes and helps them improve their performance. A study conducted by Traci Sitzmann (Sitzmann, 2011) proves that GBL increases self-confidence of learners by 20%, improves concept related knowledge by 11%, learning retention up to 90% and generated task completion by 30%. Table-2 highlights the distinction between Game-based learning and Traditional learning.

Table 1. Distinction between game-based learning and gamification

Parameters	Game-based Learning	Gamification
Concept	• Games are used and integrated into the curriculum to enhance the learning experience. • Used as an additional tool to supplement the curriculum.	• The mechanics of a game are added to a non-game environment like a website or online learning platforms like Learning Management System (LMS) to motivate and engage the learners and to increase participation. • Game mechanics, game dynamics, and design are the key drivers in gamification.
Triggers	• Games are used to trigger curiosity and learning. • Knowledge gap can be bridged through experiential learning.	• Levels are used - Until one level is completed, the learner is not allowed to move to another level. • Turns - a segment of the game wherein a certain action needs to be completed before moving to next segment. • Time-limit - Time is fixed to complete the tasks.
Reward	• Compliments e.g., Stickers	• Points- When a specific task is done by a learner points are awarded. • Badges are given to the players when they reach a certain goal. • Leaderboards- Ranking of learners according to their achievements can be displayed to the other participants. • Progress bars- are used for the learners to track their progress. • Feedback- instant feedback is given to the learners to check their progress.
Learning and Outcome	• Learning takes place through failures • Growth mind-set to reach their goals	• Extrinsic motivation to learn • Accomplishment of tasks
Examples	• Kahoot • Quizlet • Gimkit • Board games-Offline mode	• Nick Russell • Life saver • Christina Stephenson • Sim City 4

GAME-BASED LEARNING - A THEORETICAL FRAMEWORK

With the emergence of sophisticated and immersive technologies, games can be an effective learning tool The foundation of the game-based learning is based on four underlying theories and these are cognitive, behavioural, affective, and socio-cultural engagement.

1. Cognitive Theory

In this theory, learners initially try to understand what the game is all about. Then the process of organizing verbal and visual information begins. At the end, the visuals are integrated based on the previous understanding and perception. There are different ways through which cognitive processing can be done and those are 'Scaffolding and Feedback', 'Situatedness Learning', 'Dynamic Assessment', 'Interaction Design' and so on (Plass, Homer, & Kinzer, 2015).

Table 2. Game-based learning vs. traditional learning

Criteria	Game-Based Learning	Traditional Learning
Learning by doing	Learners learn through action while playing. New concepts learnt are applied immediately in the gaming environment.	Learners learn theoretically. They apply knowledge after they are out of classroom.
Creativity	Encourages learners to think differently.	May not inspire learners to think out of the box.
Innovation	It does have a fixed set of rules but scope for innovation is much higher.	It usually has a fixed structure which reduces innovation considerably.
Engagement Level	Fun in learning increases the attention span of learners. Game based learners get completely engrossed in games.	It is difficult to keep the engagement level up because of fun element missing in this approach.
Retention and recall	Faster	Slower
Assessment	It is easy to record and analyse learners reaction in Game-based Learning	Assessment in traditional approach cannot gauge learner's understanding very well.
Feed back	Immediate & Continuous feedback	Delayed feedback
Competence building	Helps in developing real life competence building involving critical thinking and problem solving skills	Emphasis is on rote learning rather than skill development.
Learner's styles	Suited to all learner types such as slow learners and fast learners	Less suited to slow learners
Cost	Requires high investment initially but its cost is written off over the long term. It is more environmentally friendly as it reduces the use of paper.	Requires recurring investment over a long period as printed materials are used throughout learning by learner and mentor.

2. Behavioural Theory

Behavioural theory is effective when game based learning mechanisms are viewed from a motivational perspective. It focuses on the ability of the game to occupy and motivate the students by providing experiences that would develop the sense of enjoyment and want to continue the game. It has been observed that during the academic games if participants are interacting with each other and try to understand the challenges faced by others, it fosters and improves the learning process (Zusho, Anthony, Hashimoto, & Robertson, 2014)

3. Affective Theory

This theory focuses on the experienced emotions, beliefs and aims to understand how game environments influence the affective state of the learners through affective engagement. There are several ways through which affects can be incorporated into games and those are aesthetic design, musical score and so on. Emotion can be induced in players with the help of the ability of specific games. The objective of the affective theory is to influence the learner's experience of different emotions such as boredom, fear, happiness, frustration, anxiety and so on (Craig, Graesser, Sullins, & Gholson, 2004).

4. Socio-Cultural Theory

The social and cultural perspective is not much different from the other theories discussed above. However, the objective of social and cultural attributes is to develop opportunities for these factors to influence learning through creating a socially enriched and a meaningful activity. In the real world, game play is embedded with observations based on social actions. Here, design principles emphasize more on motivational and empathetic opportunities than the specific instructions (Plass, Homer, & Kinzer, 2015). Figure.2 describes the theoretical framework of Game-based learning.

Figure 2. Theoretical framework of game-based learning
Source: Self-constructed

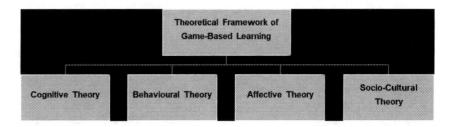

GAME-BASED PEDAGOGY FOR COMPETENCE BUILDING IN HIGHER EDUCATION

The most significant change in the curriculum of higher education in recent times worldwide has been the introduction of competence based curriculum. Competence based education, which is commonly understood as the learning based outcome, describes the competency and proficiency of a graduating student (Choudaha, 2008). It specifies what a graduate is expected to know, understand and would be able to do at the end of his/her program of study. These expected competencies are used as reference points to establish the relationship between education and the world (Kouwenhoven, Howie, & Plomp, 2003). When specific competencies such as innovation, creativity, problem solving, critical thinking, collaboration and self-management among others are developed through the curriculum design, students after graduating from college and universities are considered better 'work-ready' and are readily accepted by the industry. So occupation-specific competencies in the curriculum design reduces the unemployment and under-employment gap (Sudsomboon, 2007). The importance of implementing competency-based curriculum in universities serves two purposes: (i) competencies that are linked with an academic degree become the basis of assessment of the course. (ii) Linking specific competencies to a program helps faculty, students, employers and other international institutions understand the specific skills and knowledge acquired by the students as a result of their learning experience.

Amongst several pedagogical approaches used for teaching learning in higher education, the application of game based pedagogy cannot be ignored. Game based education not only addresses higher-order cognitive skills but also promotes creativity, innovation, critical thinking and problem-solving skills among students to a great extent. In traditional classroom settings, especially in developing countries such as India, not much attention is paid to building non-cognitive skills like patience, motivation, self-control and perseverance. However, for students to succeed in life, these non-cognitive competencies are just as important as their cognitive competencies. Game based pedagogy as a tool encourages self-directed learning amongst students. It further helps them acquire and improve upon the skills and competencies required to adopt the right approach. Several research studies conducted have confirmed the positive effect of game based learning on building various cognitive and non-cognitive competencies of students in higher education. (Vogel, Greenwood-Ericksen, Cannon-Bowers, & Bowers, 2006), (Clark, Nelson, Sengupta, & Angelo, 2009), (Gillispie, Martin, & Parker, 2009), (Hickey, Goble, & Jameson, 2012), (Papastergiou, 2009). Figure-3 deals with the key highlights of the game-based pedagogical tool.

Figure 3. Key highlights of the game-based pedagogical tool
Source: Self-constructed

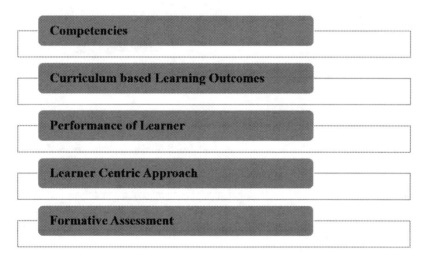

The competencies built through game based learning can be divided into domain-specific competencies or generic competencies (Troitschanskaia, et al., 2017). Domain specific competencies mainly relate to domain specific cognitive skills such as knowledge, critical thinking, problem solving of a specific subject such as economics, mathematics. Another set of competencies are called 'generic' and are needed in all content domains, that can be utilized in real life situations for collaboration or teamwork, self-motivation, and conscientiousness. Figure-4 deals with competence building through game-based pedagogy.

While teaching adult learners, it is often observed that student apply the knowledge in a way that they feel fits the situation, not how they are told to apply (Schneider & Preckel, 2017). This is because unlike school learners, learners at higher education have more life experiences on which they can base important decisions and how information can be applied. Game based pedagogy helps students to simulate, interact, and imitate real life situations. Table-3 deals with different types of competencies built through game-based learning.

Figure 4. Competence building through game-based pedagogy
Source: Self-constructed

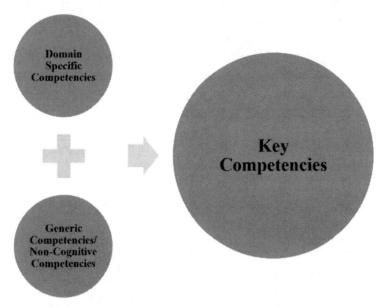

Table 3. Description of different types of competencies built through game-based learning

Domain Specific Competencies	Description
Discipline specific knowledge	To demonstrate in depth knowledge and understanding on various discipline
Critical thinking	Ability to evaluate knowledge based on evidence, identify the assumptions and critically evaluate arguments
Problem Solving	Ability to apply what has been learned in order to solve different kinds of non-familiar problems
Generic Competencies	**Description**
Attention Building	Ability to process necessary information from environment
Collaboration and Teamwork	Ability to work effectively with diverse groups and work together in their best interest.
Reflective thinking	To reflect on life experience and society for better awareness
Leadership skill	Ability to set direction, formulate vision, map tasks for the team
Communication Skill	To be able to express ideas and thoughts effectively and confidently read and write one's views.

LEARNER SPECIFIC COMPETENCY

It is important to understand students learning style component because the games have to be adopted according to their preferred learning (Sajjadi, Broeckhoven, & Troyer, 2014), (Ozdamar-Keskin, Ozata, Banar, & Royle, 2015). VARK learning style viz. visual, auditory, kinesthetic, and reading/writing learning styles developed by Fleming and Mill (Fleming & Mills, 1992) is a popular model in this regard. According to this classification, visual learners are those who absorb more information when they visualize relationships and ideas. Diagrams, charts, graphs, hierarchies, flowchart, arrows, maps, diagrams help them to retain and remember information better. Auditory learners are those learners who prefer listening to information rather than reading or visualizing it. When it comes to studying, an auditory learner might remember material best if they talk about it with someone else, since it will be easier to recall a conversation than a visual image of words on a page (Byun & Loh, 2015). Reading and writing learners are those who read and write comfortably. They prefer to consume information by reading texts and can further absorb information by condensing and rephrasing it. Kinesthetic learners are the most hands-on learning type. They learn best by doing and may get fidgety if forced to sit for long period of time. Kinesthetic learners do best when they can participate in activities or solve problems in a hands-on manner. Being physically engaged help retain information better. They tend to remember what they do best. Another category of learners often found in higher education are advanced learners and slow learners. Slow learner is a term often used for those learners who compared to advanced learners takes more time to engage with the learning content and have a slower speed of learning process. They also lack motivation for the same reason. Slow learners require more engagement, motivation and attention to learn complex content and higher order skills. Game based learning helps slow learners adapt challenging concepts more quickly, with greater retention by making their participation pleasurable through active games than by traditional ways (Humphrey & Sullivan, 1970).

Following are some of the specific competencies build through game based pedagogy among different types of learners:

1. **Reflective Thinking:** Students in higher education learn much faster when there is a shorter time interval between their action and feedback. It is encouraging for students to learn from their mistakes if feedback is shared for their action immediately rather than receiving a comment or a red mark on a paper assignment a few days later. Feedback in the game based pedagogy is a very relevant feature in building this competence as immediate scoring and feedback facilitates comparison and correction.
2. **Attention Building:** Rewards, incentives and bonuses keeps a student glued to the game who often comes back for more. This feature of game in the learning pedagogy helps students stay alert and attentive throughout. Since each learning outcome is tied to a series of challenges continued and in diverted attention is rewarding to level the play field.
3. **Teamwork and Collaboration**: Games are fun to play and this feature of game significantly helps to improve learning performance of a student in higher education. When students have fun, the pressure of learning is reduced that allows them to freely interact without any bias as participants or opponents in the game and can strategize towards achieving their goal.
4. **Motivation:** The competitive element of a game is generally missing in the traditional mode like a classroom lecture or discussion. Competition motivates the students to engage in the game from start to finish. Competition need not be against another participant every time. It could be an attempt to improve one's highest score or outdoing one's self performance. This intrinsic motivation in learning activity is strongly correlated with the outcome of the learning process.
5. **Self-Control:** In a traditional learning process the learners may not reveal the true behavior. However through a game based learning, as the learner interacts in the game the behavior is revealed. For instance, a student who reacts quickly in a game is more likely to be an impulsive or high anxiety learner. Game based learning helps them to control their emotions and impulses to sustain in the game for long, hence building better self-control. Table-4 is about game-based learning tools appropriate for different types of learners.

Table 4. Game-based learning tools appropriate for different types of learners

Game-Based Learning Tool	Visual	Auditory	Reading & Writing	Kinesthetic	Slow Learners
Chessboard	Yes			Yes	
Card games	Yes	Yes			Yes
Digital video games	Yes	Yes		Yes	Yes
Case Study	Yes		Yes		
Role Play		Yes		Yes	Yes
Real life Industry projects/Project based learning				Yes	Yes
Debates		Yes	Yes		Yes
Simulation	Yes			Yes	Yes

TEACHERS' COMPETENCE IN BUILDING AN EFFECTIVE GAME-BASED PEDAGOGY

The teacher competence and a good pedagogical model will be integral in implementing game-based learning. It is important for a teacher to use game based pedagogy, an unconventional model which is an effective and an integral way to identify the competence area. The challenges are that the teachers' competence in the game-based pedagogy is rare and are underrepresented. During the pandemic, assessment of the students was done through boring quizzes and tests which focused more on recalling information and hence it is important to design strategies to develop teacher's competence. More time was expended on monitoring the students through the camera, wherein privacy, equity and efficacy issues popped in. In a game-based learning activity an inter-disciplinary approach needs to be well coordinated and adopted. These competencies can relate to the abilities to acknowledge the requirement of the student towards reception to knowledge. Further a teacher has to interact and tutor the student for a better learning process and to acquire an in depth understanding of the topic and proceedings of the game. It is also pertinent to develop the teacher competence in the digital context and must have the attitude to embrace technical expertise and possess digital self-efficacy. The teacher should engage students using various skills sets (refer figure no.5) into the game play to align with the learning goals and have the ability to control the content. The expectation of the student centric learning should be fulfilled through game play. Figure-5 deals with teacher's competence & skill sets.

Game Based Pedagogy Approach for Teachers' Competence

The above competencies are increasingly important for a teacher especially with respect to research, development and policy making. It is pertinent to make performance based education and application of the knowledge skills in practical situations and authentic contexts to be imparted to students. In this context game based learning plays a vital role. Hence the teacher has to adopt multi-pronged approach for students to hone their skills and at the same time care has to be taken to retain their alignment to the core values. Table-5 deals with the pedagogical approaches for teacher's competence.

Figure 5. Teacher's competence and skill sets
Source: htttps://www.prodigygame.com/in-en/blog/competency-based-education/

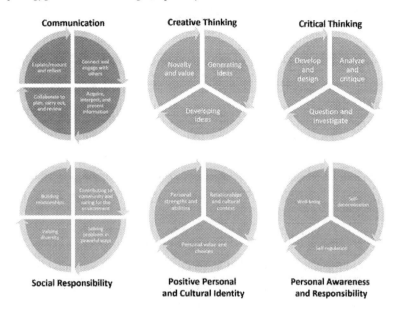

Table 5. Pedagogical approaches for teacher's competence

Pedagogy	Technology	Collaboration	Creativity
Curriculum Planning	Selection of games and technological tools	Mutual Collaboration within Institution	Experiential learning
Tutoring	Overcoming technology-related obstacles	Inter-University Networking	Experimentation
Assessment and Evaluation	Learning Management System	Self-development	Innovation

1. Curriculum Planning

In a game based learning it is important for a teacher to have competence in integrating games into the curriculum planning to achieve the desired learning outcomes. A teacher must develop a course plan with respect to the elements of the game in the content of the course. The main competence should be acquired from the reflections and the ability to apply the game based pedagogy to support the curriculum. The other dimension of the teachers' competence required is the involvement of students in defining and formulating the curriculum related goals and orient towards these goals. The students then will be able to demonstrate and orient themselves with such an activity.

2. Tutoring

The teachers' tutoring competencies refers to guiding the learning process during game based activity. It also includes applying motivational techniques, personalizing activities, regulating flexibility and encouraging student responsibility. The teaching and learning process in game based learning involves varied competencies from curriculum to assessment planning. If the students are motivated and work in a self-directed manner, the teacher's tutoring role will only be limited to observing the activities and ensuring smooth learning within the general pedagogical framework. In such a scenario it is crucial for a teacher to identify and react to student's required performance (Peddycord-Liu, et al., 2019).

3. Assessment and Evaluation

Another necessary component for teacher's competence is the assessment and evaluation of students' learning and reflection. Teachers should have the competence to understand and relate domain specific concepts to the game based activity for effective assessment. Games do provide relevant data which a teacher needs to utilize efficiently to assess and evaluate the students. They need to monitor and evaluate the students carefully taking into consideration the content of the subject and competencies of the students. This will help them to identify different ways in which the student may demonstrate their learning during the activity. In some situations, it will be useful if a set of good assessment criteria is developed. The assessment has to be done throughout with careful instructions. Teachers must maintain game reports in which they could record performance of students. They should organize team games and class discussions to share difficulties and accomplishments. This will help the teacher to adjust the units and activities, address the problems and create new knowledge in the course of adopting game based learning.

4. Selection of Games and Technological Tools

Teachers are required to develop competence in selecting digital games and technological tools for their courses and integrate it with the curriculum. In practice, technological competencies include the ability to select and combine appropriate games and tools (Foster & Shah, 2015). They can also combine non-digital tools in their pedagogy to engage the students in a meaningful manner. It is also important that trainings and workshop are organized to up skill the teachers' competence for better implementation of game based learning. Further it is important to explore the students and peer expertise as resources in using technologies and overcoming obstacles (Cachia, Ferrari, & Punie, 2010). If the teachers are technologically competent they can understand specific games and digital tools as flexible learning environments to adapt to students' knowledge and skill levels.

5. Technology-Related Obstacles

Before engaging students in a game-based learning it is important for a teacher to run a trial and error cycle to ensure smooth conduct of the activity and factor in the technological glitches that might arise during the course of the activity. Teachers avoid using new tools because they are not confident and are not well-trained to use them. It is observed that where hands-on collaboration between teachers was adopted it worked well in boosting confidence and competence in game based learning (Nousiainen, Kangas, Rikala, & Vesisenaho, 2018). Teachers' technological competence is closely linked with the collaborative and creative areas. One of the difficulties is the uncertainty related to identifying when a problem is solvable by the teacher on the spot and when it is not? For instance, the problem of network connectivity, a missing component such as a SIM card or device malfunctions and so on can hinder the smooth flow of the running a game. Students get frustrated when the network or the devices don't work

Game-Based Learning in Higher Education

and are not able to complete their tasks. In order to handle such situations the teacher should undergo basic training in technology related areas.

6. Learning Management System

This platform allows teachers to organize resources such as online quiz, audio –video files, discussion boards, grading tools to facilitate game based learning.

7. Mutual Collaboration Within Institution

Mutual collaboration should be encouraged in game based learning environment. Sharing of ideas and practices would help in building teachers' competence. Collaborative efforts must be done on a routine basis in order to improve the competency of teachers. Innovative teaching ideas flourish when the culture in an institution is collaborative and supportive. Peer support, sharing, direct involvement of teachers in practicing new teaching methods and a common vision encouraging novel approaches are some of the ways in which mutual collaboration can be encouraged (Shear, et al., 2014). This kind of mutual development and collaboration provide teachers with opportunities to identify and link tacit knowledge for new openings and ideas (Vesisenaho, Dillon, & Sari, 2017).

8. Inter-University Networking

Networking and collaboration amongst faculty from other universities plays a vital role in exchange of ideas and challenges faced during the adoption and implementation of game based pedagogy. This will help in devising ways and means to overcome the challenges and in turn necessitates a broader culture of sharing and willingness. When collaboration is robust it will be a rewarding to build a teacher's competence.

9. Experiential Learning

Another approach towards building teachers' competence is to convert learning activity into a game by using game mechanics. Playful stance motivates the students and engages them effectively. In order to have pedagogical and emotional engagement with students teacher should adopt playful learning creatively. This will help in building personal entrepreneurship skills of the teachers and help them to engage learners effectively (Kangas, 2017).

10. Experimentation

Teachers should have the ability to experiment novel teaching methods with new tools and techniques so as to venture and explore the unknown areas. They must work in such a way that these practices turn into established practices (Sawyer, 2012).

11. Self-Development

Self-development is important for a teacher to gain expertise in adopting game learning. The importance of continuously developing their competency in game based pedagogy cannot be undermined as it reflects and reshapes their identity. The game based pedagogy does challenge the teachers' competence to reflect and hone their skills in designing meaningful game based activities.

12. Innovative Assessment

Innovative assessments and evaluation should be adapted to grade students towards encouraging active participated and self-directed learning.

UNDERSTANDING GAME-BASED LEARNING THROUGH CASE STUDIES

In order to understand the relevance and application of game-based learning in different domain, a few case studies have been explored below.

Case Study-1: Physics and Engineering Domain

Game Name: Racing Academy

Racing academy is designed for the science and engineering students. This game will enable the students to understand the effect of their choices, its interventions and actions. It is based on the vehicle dynamics simulation system which assists to recreate the driving experience. It is important to mention that the racing academy is an independent organization that provides gaming solutions to educational institutions. It had been implemented at Barnfield Further Education College (IMI Nationals: Motor Vehicle Engineering Course) and Penwith Further Education College. The first step of the implementation process was to conduct a design workshop. Racing academy design team and lecturers from the client colleges were the targeted participants. The implementation process was followed by an experimentation process wherein both pre-test and post-test had been administered. The pre-test was conducted a week before students started playing with it and the post-test was taken up by the students one week after the completion of using the racing academy. The assessments of pre-test and post-test were based on three motivational aspects of physics and engineering and those were as follows.

1. Perceived Competence
2. Enjoyment
3. Importance of physics and engineering at personal level.

A five-point likert scale was adopted for the assessment. The implementation process also considered few observations and modified it accordingly. The observations were as follows:

1. How frequently students were engaging themselves with racing academic game?
2. Whether they are comfortable playing it at home or in college?

3. How much did students learn from the game?

The college authority measured the motivation which the students had to complete the game. They found a significant improvement in terms of learning experience and motivation towards physics and engineering (Baek & Whitton, 2013).

Case Study-2: Finance Domain

Game Name: e-Finance Game

In most of the countries, finance is not taught at secondary level. In universities, students come from diverse backgrounds and find it challenging to pursue the course. Hence, to ensure that students are learning, teachers are moving towards activity oriented approach. The educators designed a digital game for the introductory course in finance which is known as 'e-Finance Game' (e-FG). This game tries to capture the students' previous knowledge and experience in finance. The preliminary phase of any implementation process is the designing part and e-FG was not an exception. The developing and designing process had been done with the collaboration of experienced professors from ESADE Law and Business School (Department of Finance). The aim of the game was to frame a relevant and authentic finance related activity and develop the confidence of the professors to adopt and implement game-based learning in their respective classrooms. It had been observed by the designer that few students were active when any finance related questions were asked and they didn't perform properly in a collaborative manner. This observation was the foundation of designing the game. The paper-based game had four phases. In the first phase students play alone. However, in the second and third phases students are asked to participate in collaboration with other students. The fourth phase is the evaluation phase where students will be given feedback about their performances within a team and ranked them in the scoreboard. The other part of e-FG was a computer-based game where students' experience was mapped through the TAM Questionnaire. This mechanism was intended to understand the acceptability of the computer based environment based on the User Perceived Ease of Use (PEU) and User Perceived Usefulness (PU). With the help of e-FG, finance students learned to perform in a real time scenario (Baek & Whitton, 2013).

Case Study-3: Information Literacy Domain

Game Name: Non-Digital Information Classes

Digital games have been getting prominence since last decade and presently it is one of the widely adopted class activities. However, non-digital analog games are equally competent. Librarians often use games during information literacy sessions. The question-answer game at Georgia State University was famous for understanding students' information literacy skills. On the other hand, librarians of University of Notre Dame adopted pen and paper games such as Word Find, Tic-Tac-Toe, puzzles and crossword for the same purpose. The noteworthy aspect is, these games were reward based which enabled them to motivate the students. In this field, the most innovative approach was implemented by the Nassau Community College where the librarians devised a game imitating Reality TV show mechanism. The game had been implemented in three stages. At the first stage, librarians had to frame a set of questions. Students had to find out the answers collaboratively and needed to present the answers in-front of the peers, at the second stage. The final stage included the voting system where students have to vote for the best answers. The University of Florida devised a campus wide game called Zombies Versus Humans. This was a part of the University's library mission where students had to get acquainted with the library. The aforementioned instances justify the fact that game-based learning can motivate the students to acquire non-conventional skills (University of Toronto Libraries, 2021).

Case Study-4: Introductory Philosophy Domain

Game Name: Appalachian State University Game-Based Learning

The game-based learning system in Appalachian State University is one of the prominent mechanisms in this field. The researchers of Appalachian State University, found correlation between the game-based learning experience and effective educational experiences. Scott-Rice, an Associate Professor of the university, had adopted GBL to improve the classroom experience. He applied games like simulations and puzzles for his introductory philosophy course. Professor Rice, who was heading a course, entitled 'The Study of Games' brought an innovative way of implementation of game-based learning. The students of the 'The Study of Games' course had to design their own game as a part of their final evaluation. All the games designed by the students would be examined in detail. This practice enabled the students to innovate games which would have proper application and eventually, they could patent it (Rice).

360 DEGREE APPROACH TO IMPLEMENT GAME-BASED LEARNING IN HIGHER EDUCATION

A holistic development is not possible without scientific progression. A 360 Degree implementation approach can be proposed for effective game-based learning by engaging all the important stakeholders into the process. Administrators and IT Personnel are two major participants who should be part of the implementation process. Game-based learning could be offline or online and IT plays a major role in it. Game-based Learning would not be effective in the online context without the support of certain platforms such as Moodle and Gaming apps. Hence, involvement of administrators is crucial. Under a 360-degree approach we can consider both internal and external stakeholders. Teachers, students, administrators and IT personnel could be the internal stakeholders whereas external stakeholders like educators, companies and game designers are amongst those who use the online education platform to launch games especially designed for a particular age group of students. Thus, an effective implementation process can be ensured. Figure-6 deals with internal and external stakeholders in proposed 360 degree approach.

Based on the aforementioned case analysis, certain steps can be proposed for an effective implementation. It had been observed that most of the cases started with a designing process. However, before designing, a proper planning and approval is required where the target participants, aim of the game and nature of the game should be decided. Next step that could be proposed is the creation or design of the game, based on the requirement of the participants. At the same time, the game should also be incorporated in the curriculum. After designing it should be approved by the management or a panel of experts. It could be done through a trial-and-error process. Before applying the game in the classroom, it should be evaluated and the criterion of evaluation should be usability, relevance and difficulty. Once it satisfies all the criteria, students can start using the game. After completion of the session, the entire

Game-Based Learning in Higher Education

system should be evaluated. The evaluation can be done in terms of students' participation, motivation towards the game and content, improved performance and overall academic result. In most of the cases, it has been observed that the assessment of game-based learning was conducted either through a pre and post-test or through the feedback analysis. Figure-7 deals with implementation process of game-based learning.

The below-mentioned Table-6 deals with the implementation process and involvement of stakeholders in Game-based learning.

Figure 6. Internal and external stakeholders in proposed 360 degree approach
Source: Self-constructed

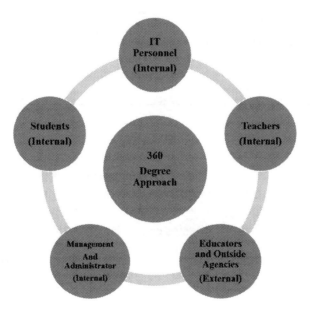

Figure 7. Implementation process of game-based learning
Source: Self-constructed

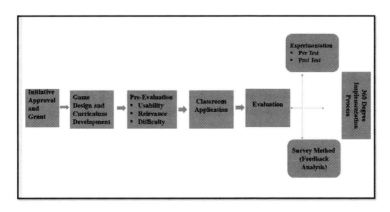

Table 6. Implementation process and involvement of stakeholders

Stakeholders	Initiative Approval and Grant	Game Design and Curriculum Development	Pre-Evaluation	Classroom Application	Post Evaluation
Administrators And Management	Yes	Yes (Partial)			
Teachers	Yes (Initiative)	Yes	Yes	Yes	Yes
Students			Yes	Yes	Yes
IT Personnel	Yes (Feasibility)	Yes	Yes	Yes	Yes
External Educators and Agencies		Yes	Yes	Yes	Yes

BENEFITS OF GAME-BASED LEARNING

The discussions have often revolved around understanding the intrinsic educational value of game-based learning to develop the inter-personal and analytical skills of students. It has also enabled them to combat absenteeism, boredom and reluctance, leading to academic achievement. However, it is found that while game based learning exhibit certain positive effects in the learning experience of the students, they also helps instructors to gain substantial teaching experience. Games have high educational potential, and studies have shown a positive correlation between gaming activities and learning. Researchers have studied and described games based on their qualities as situated activities rather than artefacts of how it is applied. All discussions on the topic related to the potential educational value in using game based education as a pedagogy has frequently highlighted games' intrinsic educational value and its experiential nature and their ability to encourage players to master certain domains through games design framework (Egenfeldt Nielsen, 2008).

When students participate in a web-based simulation game there is a deeper cognitive understanding of the subject related content. It enables them to reflect and get actively involved which in turn leads to faster and better retention. A web-based simulation also helps students to have better learning experience and help them strategize their learning efficiently. Game based learning will help an average student to become an advanced learner as it provides him/her a better learning experience. Teacher must take into consideration the requirements of the slow learners and accordingly design games by reducing the challenge perception or promoting the skill perception.

The teachers attain learning outcome by correlating the concepts with games in order to achieve not only the higher order learning but also attitude building and generic skill development. This would enable students to face the real world challenges. The role of the instructor is to act as a facilitator and foster learning particularly where higher order skill development is involved. (Rutten, Joolingen, & Veen, 2012). When teachers adopt game based learning strategy, it helps in improved student's engagement and involvement, building greater interest in the course. Such flexible learning environment created by the faculty encourages peer interaction, better motivation towards learning, supporting pedagogy and autonomy and self-directed learning amongst students.

As aforementioned the pedagogical shift from teacher-centric to the student centric active learning through web-simulation and other game based activities helps in achieving greater engagement to both student and instructors. Students are better equipped to handle their emotions, nervousness, uncertainty and so in through gaming experience. On the other hand faculty as motivators and continuous mentors are able to transfer the knowledge in a more rewarding way to the students which leads to an improved learning experience.

DRAWBACKS OF GAME-BASED LEARNING

In most cases, teachers are not so techno-savvy and may lack game based literacy, that makes it highly unfeasible for them to adopt game-based learning. Another difficulty faced by teachers is the time constraint in preparing for classroom gaming sessions. Similarly individual students have their own learning styles, preferences, subject matter knowledge, motor-skills and motivation to engage in the learning process leading to reluctance amongst students towards online gaming.

While discussing the viability and efficacy of digital games as tools for learning, games as an educational tool has heavily emphasized on their artefacts and the relationship between players. Hence the games' ability to produce learning outcomes, do not reveal much about their viability and usefulness as teaching tools in formal settings. It is used as a tool for the fulfilment of pre-defined learning objectives as an effectiveness parameter but this does not allow developers and researchers to see unexpected and unintended changes in practice that occur as a result of the e-learning program.

There has been several attempts to examine how e-learning and games affect teachers' and students' processes of working and learning. It is very rare to find any empirical work undertaken to analyse the practical situations involved in using educational games including the kind of appropriate tasks that teachers need to perform while integrating games into formal educational contexts. (Alkind Taylor & Backlund, 2012)

It would be a misnomer to consider that students always prefer virtual learning to a traditional classroom setting. Varying results have shown that the cognitive perceptions relating to simulations presents a difference in comprehending and application of knowledge relating to serious gaming. (Riemer & Schrader, 2015). It is true that game based learning provides a stimulating and fun-filled experience. However, there is a lack of consistent evidence to show that games lead to efficacious results. Studies have also shown that students do not view the integration of online games as an effective learning method (Bolliger, Mills, White, & Kohyama, 2015). Research has shown that many students and educator have expressed uncertainty over the use of virtual simulations, games as tools for learning. A stronger connection needs to be established between the curricula and games, even when the benefits of a gaming have been highlighted (Pløhn, 2013).

CHALLENGES OF GAME-BASED LEARNING

One of the challenges of game based learning is to address the affective outcomes which involve attitudes, motivation and values. Online players would look for a 'challenge' in game based learning as a top-ranked motivation. In doing so they have no concern for gender or number of players in the game. In spite of the advantages of the implementation of games and simulations effective and positive outcomes, there exists a doubt regarding motivation as the only contributing factor for a game based learning environment. There is no significant difference when it comes to motivation being used in either solitary or a team environment while approaching gaming as an experience (Chen, Wang, & Lin, 2015).

Students who have used online gaming have constantly attained high scores when compared to students who do not use gaming as a learning tool. It is noticed that female students do not display the same enthusiasm as their male counterparts while spending more time playing digital game (Hainey, Connolly, Stansfield, & Boyle, 2011). The reason for this is that the male students are more inclined and familiar with computers and web-based technologies, while female students have less interest towards digital game based learning methods due to gender bias leading to poor scores. Further, professional experience of the player's matters when it comes to high scores in any game based application (Riemer & Schrader, 2015). Learners with no gaming experience have shown that they could achieve high test scores when they used a web-based gaming tool because of their familiarity with modern technological tools. Inclusion of certain features which would enable learners to instantly process the educational content in a game can motivate students to view gaming as positive tool. The major factors in enhancing higher education learning objectives are engagement and motivation. To realise the potential of the game based learning to be part of higher level Bloom's taxonomy, a combination of elements such as confidence and relevance has to be in-built as a cognitive mechanism (Connolly, Boyle, MacArthur, Hainey, & Boyle, 2012).

A shift has started to emerge in educational games research, where the structures and components that surround the game artefact are getting more attention. They have started to focus more on the understanding as to how organizational cultures and teachers' literacies needs to be supported if game-based learning and other e-learning solutions are to be seen as accessible for all teachers and institutions. It is pertinent that educators have to seek a game-based learning project which should discuss what kinds of gaming sessions their schedule and curriculum would allow for. The demands and the availability of hardware would determine both the choice of game and the plans of how gaming sessions could be scheduled.

There is an increasing need to address the knowledge gap, and provide a pragmatic explanation of the lack of widespread game integration in the education sector since games are laborious and resource intensive to use. There are hardly any few standards which have been established to guide through the complex process of integrating games into working environments. It is a challenge to examine the roles that teachers have performed in order to implement and using computer games in their course activities in the classroom. This would also include creating an educational environment and processes, implementing the chosen game into their environment, and conducting maintenance between and during gaming sessions. Each of these phases consisted of several smaller activities such as maintaining software and hardware equipment.

CONCLUSION

Competence building is one of the key indicators of an effective learning mechanism. Game-based pedagogy can be adopted as an effective tool for competence building in higher education institutions. In this chapter the concept and related aspects of game based learning has been delved into. The distinction between game-based learning, gamification and traditional learning has also been drawn out to adduce clarity. The theoretical framework of game-based learning has been explored to understand its importance as a pedagogical tool for competence building both from the teachers and learners perspective. In order to understand the implementation of game-based learning in different subject domains, case studies involving digital and non-digital game based learning techniques have been discussed. In this context, a

360 Degree implementation process has been proposed and discussed where equal weightage has been given to both internal and external stakeholders. The benefits, drawbacks and challenges of game-based learning in higher education have also been highlighted.

REFERENCES

Alkind Taylor, A. S., & Backlund, P. (2012). Making the Implicit Explicit: Game-based Training Practices from an Instructor Perspective. In *6th European Conference on Games Based Learning (ECGBL'12)* (pp. 1-10). Cork, Ireland: European Conference on Games Based Learning.

Baek, Y., & Whitton, N. (2013). *Digital Game Based Learning: Methods, Models and Strategies*. IGI Global. doi:10.4018/978-1-4666-2848-9

Bolliger, D. U., Mills, D., White, J., & Kohyama, M. (2015). Japanese Students' Perceptions of Digital Game Use for English-Language Learning in Higher Education. *Journal of Educational Computing Research*, *53*(3), 384–408. doi:10.1177/0735633115600806

Bourgonjon, J., De Grove, F., De Smet, C., Van Looy, J., Soetaert, R., & Valcke, M. (2013). Acceptance of Game-Based Learning by Secondary School Teachers. *Computers & Education*, *67*, 21–35. doi:10.1016/j.compedu.2013.02.010

Byun, J., & Loh, C. S. (2015). Audial engagement: Effects of game sound on learner engagement in digital game-based learning environments. *Computers in Human Behavior*, *46*, 129–138. doi:10.1016/j.chb.2014.12.052

Cachia, R., Ferrari, A., & Punie, Y. (2010). Creative Learning and Innovative Teaching. Final Report on the Study on Creativity and Innovation in Education in the EU Member States. *JRC Scientific Technical Reports*, 1-55.

Chen, C. H., Wang, K. C., & Lin, Y. H. (2015). The Comparison of Solitary and Collaborative Modes of Game-Based Learning on Students' Science Learning and Motivation. *Journal of Educational Technology & Society*, *18*(2), 237–248.

Choudaha, R. (2008). *Competency-based curriculum for a master's program in Service Science, Management and Engineering (SSME): An online Delphi study* [Dissertation Thesis]. University of Denver, Proquest Dissertation Publishing.

Clark, D., Nelson, B., Sengupta, P., & Angelo, C. D. (2009). *Rethinking science learning through digital games and simulations: Genres, examples, and evidence*. Academic Press.

Connolly, T. M., Boyle, E. A., MacArthur, E., Hainey, T., & Boyle, J. M. (2012). A systematic literature review of the empirical evidence on computer games and serious game. *Computers & Education*, *59*(2), 661–686. doi:10.1016/j.compedu.2012.03.004

Craig, S. D., Graesser, A. C., Sullins, J., & Gholson, B. (2004). Affect and Learning: An Exploratory Look into the Role of Affect in Learning with AutoTutor. *Journal of Educational Media*, *29*(3), 241–250. doi:10.1080/1358165042000283101

Egenfeldt Nielsen, S. (2008). Practical Barriers in Using Educational Computer Games. In D. Drew (Ed.), Beyond Fun (pp. 20-26). ETC Press.

Fadel, C., & Trilling, B. (2012). *21st Century Skills, Learning for Life in our Times*. Wiley.

Fleming, N. D., & Mills, C. (1992). Not Another Inventory, Rather a Catalyst for Reflection. *To Improve the Academy, 11*(1), 137-144.

Foster, A., & Shah, M. (2015). The Play Curricular Activity Reflection Discussion Model for Game-Based Learning. *Journal of Research on Technology in Education, 47*(2), 71–88. doi:10.1080/15391523.2015.967551

Gillispie, L., Martin, F., & Parker, M. (2009). Effects of the Dimension-M 3D Video Gaming Experience on Middle School Student Achievement and Attitude in Mathematics. In *Society for Information Technology & Teacher Education International Conference*. Society for Information Technology & Teacher Education.

Hainey, T., Connolly, T. M., Stansfield, M., & Boyle, E. A. (2011). Evaluation of a Game to Teach Requirements Collection and Analysis in Software Engineering at Tertiary Education Level. *Computers & Education, 56*(1), 21–35. doi:10.1016/j.compedu.2010.09.008

Hamari, J., & Nousiainen, T. (2015). Why Do Teachers Use Game-Based Learning Technologies? The Role of Individual and Institutional ICT Readiness. *Hawaii International Conference on System Sciences*. 10.1109/HICSS.2015.88

Hickey, D., Goble, A. I., & Jameson, E. (2012). Designing Assessments and Assessing Designs in Virtual Educational Environments. *Journal of Science Education and Technology, 18*(2), 187–208. doi:10.100710956-008-9143-1

Humphrey, J. H., & Sullivan, D. D. (1970). *Teaching Slow Learners through Active Games*. Academic Press.

Kangas, A. (2017). Global Cities, International Relations and the Fabrication of the World. *Global Society, 31*(4), 531–550. doi:10.1080/13600826.2017.1322939

Kiili, K. (2005). Digital Game-Based Learning: Towards an Experiential Gaming Model. *The Internet and Higher Education, 81*(1), 13–24. doi:10.1016/j.iheduc.2004.12.001

Kouwenhoven, W., Howie, S. J., & Plomp, T. (2003). The Role of Needs Assessment in Developing Competence-Based Education in Mozambican Higher Education. *Perspectives in Education, 21*(1), 34–154.

McGonigal, J. (2011). *Reality is Broken: Why Games make us Better and How they can Change the World*. Penguin.

Nousiainen, T., Kangas, M., Rikala, J., & Vesisenaho, M. (2018). Teacher Competencies in Game-Based Pedagogy. *Teaching and Teacher Education, 74*, 85–96. doi:10.1016/j.tate.2018.04.012

Ozdamar-Keskin, N., Ozata, F. Z., Banar, K., & Royle, K. (2015). Examining Digital Literacy Competences and Learning Habits of Open and Distance Learners. *Contemporary Educational Technology, 6*(1), 74–90. doi:10.30935/cedtech/6140

Papastergiou, M. (2009). Digital Game-Based Learning in high school Computer Science education: Impact on educational effectiveness and student motivation. *Computers & Education*, *52*(1), 1–12. doi:10.1016/j.compedu.2008.06.004

Peddycord-Liu, Z., Cateté, V., Vandenberg, J., Barnes, T., Lynch, C. F., & Rutherford, T. (2019). A Field Study of Teachers Using a Curriculum-integrated Digital Game. In *Proceedings of the 2019 CHI Conference on Human Factors in Computing Systems* (pp. 1-12). CHI Conference. 10.1145/3290605.3300658

Plass, J. L., Homer, B. D., & Kinzer, C. K. (2015). Foundations of Game-Based Learning. *Educational Psychologist*, *50*(4), 258–283. doi:10.1080/00461520.2015.1122533

Plass, J. L., Mayer, R. E., & Homer, B. D. (2020). *Handbook of Game-based Learning*. MIT Press.

Pløhn, T. (2013). Nuclear Mayhem-A Pervasive Game Designed to Support Learning. *Proceedings of the 7th European Conference on Games Based Learning ECGBL 2013, 2*.

Qian, M., & Clark, K. R. (2016). Game-Based Learning and 21st Century Skills: A Review of Recent Research. *Computers in Human Behavior*, *63*, 50–58. doi:10.1016/j.chb.2016.05.023

Redecker, C. (2017). *European Framework for the Digital Competence of Educators*. European Commission.

Research and Market. (2021, June 23). *World Game-Based Learning Market Report 2021-2026*. Retrieved September 4th, 2021, from Globe Newswire: https://www.globenewswire.com/en/news-release/2021/06/23/2251646/28124/en/World-Game-Based-Learning-Market-Report-2021-2026.html

Rice, S. (n.d.). *Game-Based Learning*. Retrieved September 5, 2021, from College STAR: https://www.collegestar.org/modules/game-based-learning

Riemer, V., & Schrader, C. (2015). Learning with quizzes, simulations, and adventures: Students' attitudes, perceptions and intentions to learn with different types of serious games. *Computers & Education*, *88*, 160–168. doi:10.1016/j.compedu.2015.05.003

Rutten, N., Joolingen, W., & Veen, J. T. (2012). The Learning Effects of Computer Simulations in Science Education. *Computers & Education*, *58*(1), 136–153. doi:10.1016/j.compedu.2011.07.017

Sajjadi, P., Broeckhoven, F. V., & Troyer, O. D. (2014). Dynamically Adaptive Educational Games: A New Perspective. *International Conference on Serious Games*. 10.1007/978-3-319-05972-3_8

Sawyer, R. K. (2012). *Explaining Creativity: The Science of Human Innovation*. Oxford University Press.

Schneider, M., & Preckel, F. (2017). Variables Associated With Achievement in Higher Education: A Systematic Review of Meta-Analyses. *Psychological Bulletin*, *143*(6), 565–600. doi:10.1037/bul0000098 PMID:28333495

Seeney, M., & Routledge, H. (2009). Drawing Circles in the Sand: Integrating Content into Serious Games. Games-Based Learning Advancements for Multi-Sensory Human Computer Interfaces.

Shear, L., Tan, C. K., Patel, D., Trinidad, G., Koh, R., & Png, S. (2014). ICT and Instructional Innovation; The Case of Crescent Girls' School in Singapore. *International Journal of Education and Development Using Information and Communication Technology, 10*(2), 77–88.

Sitzmann, T. (2011). A Meta-Analytic Examination of the Instructional Effectiveness of Computer-Based Simulation Games. *Personnel Psychology, 64*(2), 489–528. doi:10.1111/j.1744-6570.2011.01190.x

Sudsomboon, W. (2007). Construction Of a Competancy Based Curriculum Content Framework For Mechanical Technology Education Program on Automotive Technology Subjects. *Proceedings of the ICASE Asian Symposium.*

Tang, S., Hanneghan, M., & Rhalibi, A. (2009). *Introduction to Games-Based Learning*. IGI Global. doi:10.4018/978-1-60566-360-9.ch001

Troitschanskaia, Z. O., Pant, H., Lautenbach, C., Molerov, D., Toepper, M., & Brückner, S. (2017). *Modeling and Measuring Competencies in Higher Education: Approaches to Challenges in Higher Education Policy and Practice*. Springer. doi:10.1007/978-3-658-15486-8

University of Toronto Libraries. (2021, August 25). *Research Guides.* Retrieved September 6, 2021, from https://guides.library.utoronto.ca/c.php?g=448614&p=3508116

Vesisenaho, M., Dillon, P., & Sari, H.-N. (2017). Creative Improvisations with Information and Communication Technology to Support Learning: A Conceptual and Developmental Framework. *Journal of Teacher Education and Educators, 6*(3), 229–250.

Vogel, J. J., Greenwood-Ericksen, A., Cannon-Bowers, J., & Bowers, C. A. (2006). Using Virtual Reality with and without Gaming Attributes for Academic Achievement. Journal of Research on Technology in Education, 39(1), 105-118.

Whitton, N. (2012). Game Based Learning. In *Encyclopedia of the Sciences of Learning*. Springer. doi:10.1007/978-1-4419-1428-6_437

Youngkyun, B., & Nicola, W. (2013). *Cases on Digital Game Based Learning: Methods, Models & Strategies*. IGI Global.

Zusho, A., Anthony, J. S., Hashimoto, N., & Robertson, G. (2014). Do video games provide motivation to learn? In ILearning by playing: Video gaming in education (pp. 69-86). Oxford, UK: Oxford University Press. doi:10.1093/acprof:osobl/9780199896646.003.0006

KEY TERMS AND DEFINITIONS

Competence: A generic or specific skill, attribute or knowledge acquired in the learning process.

Games: An activity which is structured and has a set of rules. It can be digital and non-digital. Usually used for entertainment but of late it is being used for educational purposes.

Gamification: Game mechanics applied to a non-game environment for increased participation and engagement.

Higher Education: Post secondary or degree level education provided by universities or similar level of institutions.

Learning Outcome: A statement that describes clearly what a student is expected to acquire at the completion of a course or a program.

Pedagogical Tools: A set of instruments or techniques used by teachers to execute their theoretical and practical content.

Skills: The learned ability to use knowledge in good execution or performance of a task within the given time.

Chapter 9
Gamification Strategies for Higher Education Student Worker Training

Emily Guetzoian
https://orcid.org/0000-0003-1553-8236
Anderson School of Management, UCLA, USA

ABSTRACT

This chapter discusses gamification strategies in the context of higher education student worker training. Specifically, it builds on the concepts of gamification in corporate training contexts and gamification in the academic classroom environment. It also considers various options to support gamified training content and methods to support student worker engagement and knowledge retention. It explains how these strategies relate to the concept of information literacy for an adult, higher education population. This chapter is ideal for higher education staff, faculty, or administrators who design training curricula for student workers.

INTRODUCTION

The term gamification has been in use since approximately 2003 (Dale, 2014). Although there is no uniform definition, gamification is generally the use of game-like components employed in a situation that is not traditionally game based. The general goal of using these game-like strategies "is to motivate people to change behaviours or develop skills, or to drive innovation" (Dale, 2014, p. 84). The growth of technology has encouraged this rise in gamification, and "Internet-accessible digital tools have made gaming a mobile learning tool that can accommodate many participants in a single game, via a single platform" (Lin et al., 2018, p. 569). Using technology to enact gamification strategies does not mean that the strategies need to use video games or computer games specifically. Strategies could include board games, word games, card games, or even things that do not require equipment, such as charades. Some gamified applications include having participants earn points, complete missions, or compete with others in contests or leaderboards (Dale, 2014).

DOI: 10.4018/978-1-7998-7271-9.ch009

Although Nick Pelling is cited as having first used the term gamification to describe making hardware more fun in 2002-2003, the concept itself can be traced back to at least the 1980s (Dale, 2014). Beginning in the 1980s, academic papers and books started focusing on gamification of learning. By the 1990s, an increase in computers in the classroom brought about some basic games like Math Blaster. By 2010, gamification had become a popular term, especially due to the rise of interest in the Internet. San Francisco held the first inaugural gamification summit in 2011, which was the same year the Oxford Dictionary officially added the word to its pages. It is safe to say that the concept of gamification is not just a fad and is not disappearing any time soon.

There are many benefits to including these game-like components in non-gaming situations. Gamification "develops learners' metacognitive abilities, promotes empathy, and builds teamwork skills" (Lin et al., 2018, p. 566). Additionally, "Game-based learning provides a thrill from the ordinary, a thrill which is absent from traditional instruction and everyday life" (Lin et al., 2018, p. 566). Although there are many benefits to gamification, some people actively avoid the term in favor of less trivial sounding phrases like employee engagement or motivation (Dale, 2014).

There are other terms associated with gamification that are often used in a related way. Game-based learning is commonly used as a substitution or synonymous term for gamification. Although gamification and game-based learning are similar, they have distinct common definitions and usages (Ritter, 2015). *Gamification* usually refers to making already-existing content more gamified in efforts to motivate people or help them achieve a learning goal more effectively. *Game-based learning*, by contrast, focuses more on the organization and delivery of the training content. Learning takes place during the game; thus, if you do not play, you will not learn. Although both gamification and game-based learning are applicable to the topic of this chapter, this chapter will reference and use the term gamification.

This chapter explores gamification strategies in the higher education realm. Specifically, it addresses how gamification strategies can be incorporated into a training curriculum for higher education student employees. It will also relate gamification to knowledge acquisition and literacy skills. The chapter is organized in the following sections: (a) an overview of how gamification has traditionally been used in the higher education classroom environment; (b) an overview of how gamification has been incorporated into corporate training programs; (c) a discussion of how higher education and corporate training program concepts can combine for student worker training; (d) tips for building a training program with gamification strategies, including ideas specific to various types of student workers; (e) the impact of COVID-19 on gamification; (f) a discussion of how information literacy and knowledge acquisition relate to gamification; and (g) how to measure the outcomes or success of gamification training strategies. The chapter concludes with an overview of information presented, a definition of terms used throughout the chapter, and a list of additional recommended readings.

GAMIFICATION IN HIGHER EDUCATION

Gamification is not a new concept to the realm of higher education. Because "teachers and instructors had often been struggling with keeping students' motivation and concentration to the course" (Šćepanović et al., 2015, p. 3), many faculty have incorporated gamification components into their courses. This incorporation of gamification in classroom education has many benefits. Gamification strategies can help develop lifelong learners who have more information literacy, which is "central to the mission of higher education institutions" (Information Literacy Competency Standards for Higher Education, 2000). The ties between information literacy, gamification, and training will be discussed in more detail later in this chapter. An additional benefit of gamification in the classroom environment is intrinsic motivation. Intrinsically, students who learn via gamification can feel more ownership over their own learning, experience a more relaxed and comfortable atmosphere for learning and failing, and it can serve as a visual indicator for learning (Witte et al., 2017). When students are not motivated, they may "not experience effective learning" (Lin et al., 2018, p. 567). Gamification helps to "[garner] learners' full attention and promotes knowledge retention due to its 'play nature'" (Lin et al., 2018, p. 566). Thus, gamification can be an important factor to motivate students.

Selected case studies show how gamification strategies have been employed successfully in various contexts, such as in different countries, in different fields of study, and with different types of students. One class of undergraduate students in Malaysia used *Kahoot!*, a gamified learning platform, during their weekly lectures for an entire semester (Lin et al., 2018). The students found the platform beneficial for inducing their motivation and engagement. Thus, Kahoot! has been "effective in terms of its ability to foster and reinforce learning" (Lin et al., 2018, p. 579) and is a tool that can help induce both intrinsic and extrinsic motivation in university students.

Another study examined students in a geography course (Witte et al., 2017). The students were split up into teams and acted as explorers of a certain region of the world; thus, they were engaged in the activity through game play. Students in another course could earn virtual currency, which they could then use to plant virtual flowers and trees to harvest and virtually trade with each other. This type of game play gave students a motivation to earn their virtual currency by completing tasks related to the assignments.

In an undergraduate engineering course in the United States, students participated in a modified version of an escape room (Leung & Pluskwik, 2018). In this activity, students solved problems and questions related to their course competencies such as economics, statistics, or electric machines. By solving the problem correctly, they could move on to another problem, until they were able to figuratively escape the room successfully.

Although the purpose of this chapter is not a full review of existing literature on higher education gamification strategies, located studies consisted of academic, classroom-based case studies, such as the ones mentioned previously. Located case studies examined faculty gamification strategies as they related to a particular course or field of study. Few studies that were located reviewed gamification strategies for student employees in the higher education environment specifically. This limitation will be addressed later in this chapter.

GAMIFICATION IN CORPORATE TRAINING

Numerous companies and corporations have used gamification in the training of their employees. Corporate training gamification really took off in 2011 when the gamified application, *FourSquare*, inspired other large corporations to gamify their products as well (Dale, 2014). Many companies who use gamification in their training generally do so for two reasons: (a) they are consumer or service-based organizations looking to implement rewards-based systems for consumer loyalty solutions, or (b) they are looking for tools to further engage their employees in their work (Dale, 2014). For example, some larger businesses, such as "Google, Microsoft, Cisco, Deloitte, Sun Microsystems, IBM, L'Oreal, Canon, Lexus, FedEx, UPS, Wells Fargo and others are using games to engage workers" (Witte et al., 2017, p. 56). These employees tend to be more satisfied with their jobs, better trained for their roles, more focused while at work, and

Gamification Strategies for Higher Education Student Worker Training

are also improving products and services for the company as a result of this gamified training strategy. Similarly, Ērgle and Ludviga (2018) found gamification had a significant positive impact on employee job satisfaction, and that the concepts of team building and internal communication in particular tend to respond well to gamification strategies.

Baxter et al. (2016) employed a gamified field experiment for employees at a large bank to examine the effectiveness of gamified anti-corruption and anti-fraud training. The trainers used a fictional story and fictional investigation to examine a large-scale bribery scenario. Employees enjoyed the gamified training and strongly preferred gamified training to traditional training, which they had often perceived as dull, especially for an anti-fraud topic. The gamified training program used realistic animations and audio components to increase the realistic nature of the scenario. This gamified training also modestly increased the employees' knowledge of the bank's policies. With corporate training, learning and knowledge retention are key goals; thus, employees need to be "in compliance and alignment with corporate policies and procedures" (Baxter et al., 2016, p. 6). The trainers asked many assessment questions afterward to test the employees' knowledge of the policies. These assessment results showed gamification strategies resulted in learning gains for all employees and resulted in greater learning gains for newer, less experienced employees in particular.

GAMIFICATION AND STUDENT WORKER TRAINING

This section describes the justification for combining the previous two sections, or combining the concept of corporate employee gamification training with higher education gamification in the classroom. It makes the case for using a gamification strategy as an effective way to structure student worker training in college environments. Specifically, this section overviews the types of student employees that may benefit the most from this type of gamified strategy, such as resident assistants, tutors, or library workers. This section also highlights how the COVID-19 global pandemic and learn-from-home environment have affected the possibilities for gamification, and whether this environment has expanded or reduced access to this type of training.

Gamification has wide applications, and "Gamification techniques can be applied to any learning application in any industry, from the military, to business, to education" (Witte et al., 2017, p. 56). These techniques are often used in simulation training, such as training for nurses and doctors, or training for pilots in the Federal Aviation Agency. Similarly, training student workers in the higher education environment is crucial (Connell & Mileham, 2006). Training can "empower the student assistants so that they are more confident answering questions" (Connell & Mileham, 2006, p. 82) and extensive training can help student workers "effectively answer the majority of questions received" (p. 81). Thus, student worker training in the higher education realm is another field where gamification strategies can apply.

A student employment position common to residential campuses is a resident advisor or resident assistant role. In this role, students typically live in on-campus housing and provide peer mentoring and guidance to residents in the halls. This role can be considered a student leader or peer mentor type of role, so effective training can be crucial for these students. California Polytechnic State University - San Luis Obispo used an activity with actual spoons to help their resident advisors in training understand how spoon theory may impact their resident populations. In another activity, trainees used a virtual dorm room layout to practice making furniture changes based on various student physical disability needs. Another activity allowed resident advisors in training to swipe left or swipe right on their phones as a

167

play on the interface of popular dating apps to indicate whether or not a dating behavior is problematic (Rahman et al., 2019).

Tutoring roles are also fairly common student worker roles at colleges and universities. Student workers in tutoring roles would usually need training on both the practice and process of tutoring, and the content knowledge of the subject they are tutoring. For learning about the process of tutoring and practicing tutoring skills, tutors in training can use the gamified concept of role playing. Miller (2013) discussed role play and encouraged educators to provide "a variety of interesting characters and roles" (p. 199) for learners. Tutors learning tutoring skills can use a role play scenario to practice their active listening skills, summarizing back to the student, handling challenging student scenarios, and much more. The role play environment allows the tutors in training a safer space to practice their skills and a safer space if they make a mistake. One undergraduate engineering program in Minnesota assessed several gamification strategies: three interactive online platforms (Plickers, Quizlet, and Kahoot!) and two physical games (immediate feedback assessment technique and a modified escape room) to cover course competencies such as economics, statistics, and electric machines (Leung & Pluskwik, 2018). Plickers, Quizlet, and Kahoot! use a mobile app where students can answer questions live and get real-time responses. The immediate feedback assessment technique game consists of paper cards where the students can scratch off boxes to reveal the correct answers and earn points for how few guesses it takes them to get to the right answer. Escape rooms involve a series of puzzles to escape in a specific time limit. Engineering students assessed core electrical and mechanical principles until they completed a certain number of activities and escaped. These strategies could all be helpful ways to train tutors on subject content, such as engineering.

Library student workers serve another important student employee role at colleges and universities. One library used a scavenger hunt with their student workers in training, which served as an introduction or orientation to the library (Wesley, 1990, as cited in Connell & Mileham, 2006). With a scavenger hunt, students had the opportunity to explore the library and organization of various library resources in a fun and hands-on way. These library workers also had weekly quiz questions to test the retention of their job knowledge. Students were even able to help create the quiz questions, which "gave their supervisor a break from quiz creation" (Connell & Mileham, 2006, p. 78) as an added bonus. These library student assistants found that the quizzes, and coming up with the quiz questions, helped improve their reference skills.

As evidenced by the case study examples provided in this section, gamification strategies can be applied to a wide variety of student worker training programs. These examples also demonstrated how the activity should be appropriate for the type of student worker and the knowledge that the student needs to learn during training to be successful in their role. A resident advisor may need to be able to recognize when one of their residents is suffering from an inappropriate dating relationship, so using a simulation app to swipe left or swipe right, similar to dating applications, is fitting for the role and the goal. That simulation or gamified strategy would not be as appropriate for the library student worker, who would generally not need to concern themselves with the dating relationships of library patrons. A tutor in training would need to ensure they have the content knowledge needed to be able to effectively tutor in that subject. Thus, a gamified escape room with engineering questions is appropriate for that role and goal. On the contrary, a resident advisor probably would not need to know about engineering principles to be successful in their role. A library student worker would likely need to be very familiar with where all of the materials and resources are located throughout the library, so a library scavenger hunt is a very fitting activity to meet that role and goal. A student who works as a tutor would probably not need to know that much detail about library references, so that activity would likely not suffice for that position. Thus, it is important to consider first the role and goal of the position, and then assign an appropriate gamified strategy or activity to support it. Although a certain type of activity might be fun, it also needs to serve the purpose of educating and training the student worker on their task.

GAMIFICATION AND THE COVID-19 GLOBAL PANDEMIC

This section briefly highlights how the COVID-19 global pandemic and learn-from-home environment have affected the possibilities for gamification, and whether this environment has expanded or reduced access to this type of training. The COVID-19 global pandemic "enforced a shutdown of educative institutions of all levels" (Nieto-Escámez & Roldán-Tapia, 2021, p. 1). Thus, educators have needed educational tools compatible with distance learning and have turned to a variety of new or expanding online tools. However, simply switching to online content delivery using a particular technology tool does not equate to gamification; there also has to be a game component. For example, gamified videoconferences can help students connect with each other during times of isolation caused by work-from-home environments or pandemic quarantines.

In particular, "The COVID-19 pandemic learning disruption has seriously affected interactive and hands-on experiences in laboratories" (Nieto-Escámez & Roldán-Tapia, 2021, p. 3) such as Chemistry labs. Similarly, student employees who would normally be trained for hands-on activities such as desk assistant work or athletics student assistants may not have access to the type of hands-on training that would help them to effectively learn their role. One lab class used *Labventures* and mimicked the principles of escape rooms so students could complete laboratory tasks and learn proper techniques online. A biology class had students take photos of plants and animals around their house and upload the photos to a shared, online platform. These types of creative learning examples are good examples of how to infuse creativity into online teaching to help students learn when in-person options are not available. For example, a student assistant working as a personal trainer or weight room assistant in the campus gymnasium could record themselves demonstrating proper form and upload the video to a platform for their trainees to access. Likewise, the person training that student assistant could demonstrate proper form or proper ways to use athletic gear in the same virtual manner.

Unfortunately, the quick efforts to change teaching modality at the beginning of the COVID-19 global pandemic resulted in some educators poorly planning or implementing their gamified educational environment (Nieto-Escámez & Roldán-Tapia, 2021). These methods were ineffective in large part because they either added gamification elements on an ad hoc basis or they gave unclear directions to students about how to play the game or complete the activity. Nieto-Escamez and Roldán-Tapia (2021) shared that "Technology-enhanced learning initiatives will become more prominent as the education landscape is reorganized following COVID-19, and gamification may therefore be considered as an option to augment traditional learning" (p. 8). Thus, building an effective gamified training curriculum will be a critical skill for many educators to learn.

BUILDING A GAMIFIED TRAINING CURRICULUM

This section discusses how higher education staff members can build a gamified training curriculum for their student workers. It provides various tips for educators to consider, such as the type of activities that may be most successful, scalability based on the number of students they train, the functions and major job duties of the student worker's roles, and the type of student population they are training.

Similar to the concept that there is no universal definition of gamification, there is also "no universal list of game elements" (Werback, 2014, p. 410). Thus, it can be challenging to know where to start with crafting a gamified student worker training curriculum. Some of the more common game mechanics include achievements, exercises, community, results, time, and luck (Dale, 2014). Achievement components include things such as giving participants experience points or bonuses, or having students progress through levels. Exercise components include activities such as challenges, discoveries, or quests that students can go on to achieve a goal. The community component includes synchronizing with other students, such as by collaborating on a team game or activity, or progressing on a leaderboard with other students in the group or class. The results component includes transparency in how students are progressing through the game or activity, such as by having viewable experience bars or using real-time feedback on their success with the activity. Including time as a component can mean using a countdown timer for students to progress through their activity in a certain amount of time, or using speed challenges as a way to acquire additional points or benefits. Finally, components of luck include benefits not based on skill, such as a lottery component or being selected for random achievements. All of these components are things to consider when building a gamified training curriculum.

Gamification in training curricula must be done carefully. If not implemented correctly, or if implemented without effective game design, it can have negative outcomes (Ērgle & Ludviga, 2018). Unfortunately, "There are many more ways to do it wrong than right" (Dale, 2014, p. 88). Additionally, "Good gamification design should be user-centric and not mechanism-centric" (Dale, 2014, p. 85). There may be temptation to use gamification strategies simply because they are trendy or fun, and "One of the dangers when considering [game components] is the compulsion to design the game around features available, rather than thinking first about the user and the behavior that is to be encouraged (or discouraged)" (Dale, 2014, p. 85). Thus, the student and their training needs and knowledge acquisition needs should be first considered, and gamification strategies matched to those needs.

On the contrary, "Properly employed gamification can result in added learning value not realized in other teaching/learning settings" (Witte et al., 2017). For example, the lecture method is often an unfavored form of teaching because it does not typically employ gamification (Lin et al., 2018). Proper gamification tactics and platforms should effectively motivate students to pay attention and learn (Lin et al., 2018). In one study, university instructional designers helped introduce some faculty members to online game tools that could be set up and implemented in a relatively short and easy way (Leung & Pluskwik, 2018). Similarly, this chapter provides several tips and strategies to help educators find online game tools and implement their own gamified educational environment and student worker training program.

Tips and Strategies

Dale (2014) provided several tips for building gamification training. The first tip is to plan everything out before implementing it. This includes considering the goal of the training, the institution culture, and what behaviors you are seeking to change. Additionally, do not use money as a motivator, as it can make the goals purely about money and intrinsic motivations will get set aside. Another tip is to make the gamification platforms look professional. Bright colors or a cutesy animal theme are okay for children, but not as well received for the adult, college aged population, or for the workplace. Also, find the right balance of measuring behaviors. Do not reward or measure weak behaviors, such as rewarding employees just for sending emails or for leaving an arbitrary number of comments on a discussion board post. Either use existing games to help teach content or build a custom game from scratch. Finally, Dale (2014) stated "Involving the users in the gamification design is essential" (p. 87). Thus, consider how students can help build or frame training content. Student workers of traditional college age may be more up-to-date on the newest technologies or trends with gaming applications. Another way to include students is to have returning student workers help craft and lead gamified training activities for the new student workers being trained. If there are returning student workers, the activities selected may also need to be carefully considered so they are not a duplicate of the previous training that the student received the prior year. Thus, it is also recommended to change the gamification system periodically so students do not become bored (Dale, 2014).

Several other authors provided tips and strategies in implementing gamification strategies. An important tip is that "Learning by game should always be optional, not mandatory" (Šćepanović et al., 2015, p. 5). Not every student will be excited to participate in an escape room or a competition, so having an option to opt-out for more traditional or passive learning can be helpful to those students. Additionally, it is important to remember the main goal of gamification "is to increase students' motivation and to add value to traditional teaching and learning - not to play" (Šćepanović et al., 2015, p. 5). The objectives of the game or strategy should always be at the forefront of the activity. Training activities are important because they help students learn how to do their job correctly; fun can be a part of that, but should not be so fun that students cannot articulate what they learned from the activity or learning cannot be measured.

Gamifying student training activities can also be done through smaller efforts that do not require a ton of prep. Šćepanović et al. (2015) recommended using specific vocabulary during educational activities. Some classes went on *side quests*, which were really just bonus activities to learn more and get additional points. Assignments or learning objectives could be *missions*. Students could pick a nickname and character or avatar for themselves, or even use popular culture references in activity phrasing, like a Star Wars theme. Letting students have some say in their theme or what popular culture reference they want to use to gamify their content can also help make them more engaged.

Another recommendation is to carefully consider points systems or scoreboard systems if used. There should be a careful balance between the student's effort and the amount of points or badges they get for a particular activity (Šćepanović et al., 2015). Students who earn points too easily may become unmotivated because there is no challenge. Students who have a challenging time earning points can also become unmotivated because it is hard for them to visualize the end goal. In the student employee curriculum, this can be seen depending on the length of the training program. For multi-day training, students may benefit from having a points goal per day, and overall goal. Šćepanović et al. (2015) also recommended being cautious when using scoreboards or leaderboards that show results transparently. Some students might not be happy knowing people can see their individual score, including students who might not enjoy a competition based game. This issue could be remedied by having students pick their own usernames where they can choose to use their own name or pick a fun pseudonym for more anonymity. Additionally, results could be displayed by teams or groups instead of by individuals.

Some authors highlighted the importance of creating a coherent narrative to increase the engagement of the gamification process (Iacono et al., 2020). This could be accomplished by including a narrative story about who the people are that the student workers are supporting with their work. A resident advisor could benefit from examples provided in training related to the population that they will be overseeing in their assigned residence hall. For example, if they are assigned to a floor of transfer students, training could include important stories and narratives about real transfer students and the experience of being a transfer student. Simulations, role-plays, and other scenario-based activities can incorporate these narratives as well. Likewise, tutor training can include narrative examples throughout the gamification process that help tutors understand who their constituents are. A way to gamify this type of activity could be to do some sort of 20 questions activity where students ask questions with the goal of figuring out who the main populations are that are served by the tutoring center.

Although there are many more tips to consider when planning gamified training activities, Grafstein (2002) is the final tip for this section. Grafstein (2002) recommended placing emphasis "on the process of locating and retrieving information" (p. 200), and not on memorization, because "the specific content of any subject is constantly changing" (p. 200). For example, it might be more important for a student assistant working as a desk attendant to know how to problem solve and use common sense to answer a variety of questions over the phone rather than to memorize individual responses to dozens of questions. Likewise, a library student worker does not need to memorize where every single book or resource is, just how to use the search functions to locate the books. The concept of information retrieval will be further discussed in the information literacy and knowledge acquisition section.

Scalability Considerations

Similarly to how no two institutions are created equal, no two student worker training programs are created equal either. How educators decide to structure their training, and what activities they choose to offer in a gamified way, will depend heavily on things such as institutional context, department context, resources available for training, the nature of the student role, and a variety of other factors. Some student workers, such as resident advisors, may require longer training time, training that is more likely to be in person, and group-based training, due mainly to the nature of the role and how it interacts with a residence hall community on a university campus. Tutoring, by contrast, is a much more individual role by nature and could reasonably be done online or in person. Thus, training modality and activities can be adjusted to reflect those differences. Although training tactics and gamification strategies will differ due to the aforementioned reasons, there are some general ways to scale gamified training by the amount of student workers that would need to be trained at one time.

Some large institutions or large departments may have a lot of student employees that they need to train, making large group training sessions the most practical. For these types of large groups, group-based gamified activities could work well, especially if the nature of the student worker role involves building collaborative working relationships with other student workers. Examples of group-based gamified training activities could include team scavenger hunts, escape rooms, or a team role-play activity. Unless a department has a good amount of funding and/or resources, activities that tend to use existing materials or very few, if any, materials, could be easier and more cost effective for a large number of students. For training a large group of students online, using the campus's already-existing learning management system to set up a gamified training module can be helpful. These platforms can generally hold a large number of students and the campus likely has templates or instructional designers to help get the module started. Another consideration for using gamified training with large groups is to allow activities to occur simultaneously so students do not become disengaged while waiting for their turn. For example, instead of splitting up 100 students into groups of two and having each pair present a role-play scenario to the other 98 people, training facilitators could consider putting students into 20 groups of five, and having two groups present to each other.

There are also several strategies for scaling gamified student worker training for a smaller group of students. Small is a relative term, but a small group of students could include about 10 or fewer students that need to be trained at the same time. A smaller group could be easier to train in person, although that would depend on the nature of the training and role. It could also be easier to use gamified strategies requiring materials or prep work for a smaller group of people. For example, it may be easier to train athletics student workers on setting up gym equipment if they are a smaller group. Otherwise, it may be impractical to set up hands-on training activities like balls, nets, cones, and other athletic gear for activities with a group of 100 student trainees. Smaller groups of students have the benefit of perhaps providing more input and personalization for their gamified training. If there are only four student workers to train, they could be surveyed in advance of their training to find out their favorite popular culture references or favorite phone apps or gamified activities they have benefitted from in the past. Gamified activities that tend to work well in smaller groups could be role-play activities in teams of two, or hands-on activities like setting up equipment or practicing setting up signage. One category of gamified training activities to avoid with smaller groups would be any tools that rely on anonymity, such as polling or quiz games. These tend not to work as well for smaller groups of students because it may be more obvious who provided what response, which defeats the anonymity purpose.

INFORMATION LITERACY AND KNOWLEDGE ACQUISITION

This section addresses how gamification supports information literacy and knowledge acquisition for student workers. Information literacy is another widely researched and broadly defined area of education. The term has been used widely but not always consistently (Bawden & Robinson, 2002). In general, information literacy is not skill-based literacy; it is an ability to use information in a multitude of areas in everyday life. It grew as a concept in education as a response to increasing types of information formats available to students, especially online sources (Grafstein, 2002). Quick advances in digital technologies have increased the quantity of information available, but it has also increased the different ways and options for thinking about and packaging that information. Additionally, there are many ways to approach information literacy from a training perspective, because information literacy principles "must be contextualized, illustrated with very different examples, and presented in a very different way, to meet the needs of different groups of learners" (Bawden & Robinson, 2002, p. 30). This chapter does not go into detail about the principles and applications of information literacy; however, it relates information literacy to the concept of gamification and ties it in with the goal of knowledge acquisition that often coincides with gamification goals.

Grafstein (2002) posited there is a reason why people say we live in the age of information and not in the age of knowledge; information and knowledge are distinctly different. Information does not need a specific context because it "is certainly a skill, features of which are transferable across disciplines and applications" (Grafstein, 2002, p. 200). Likewise, "Information literacy forms the basis of lifelong learning. It is common to all disciplines, to all learning environments, and to all levels of education" (Information Literacy Competency Standards for Higher Education, 2000). By contrast, knowledge exists within a certain context (Grafstein, 2002). To be able to locate knowledge or information, "students must have the ability to understand and formulate the nature of their information need" (Grafstein, 2002, p. 201). One way to help student workers improve their information literacy skills during training is to present the content to them in a linear way. Learning is a linear process; thus, students should only see the next step of their training once they complete the previous one (Šćepanović et al., 2015). This is especially helpful for training that is module based with multiple modules. Information can be packaged logically into each module to help student workers learn the material in a linear manner. Students can also take some type of gamified checkpoint or knowledge acquisition quiz at the end of each module to ensure they understood that content before moving on to more detailed or more involved content in the next module.

One of the goals of student worker training should be to encourage workers to become more information literate. A student worker who is information literate "is able to determine the extent of information needed, access needed information effectively and efficiently, [and] evaluate information and its sources critically" (Information Literacy Competency Standards for Higher Education, 2000, pp. 2-3). Especially in departments that have a large number of student workers to the ratio of staff supervisors, having student workers with the skill to evaluate information and make critical decisions can help save the manager time in hand-holding the student employee and allows the employee to be more autonomous and empowered in their role. Additionally, "gaining skills in information literacy multiplies the opportunities for students' self-directed learning" (Information Literacy Competency Standards for Higher Education, 2000, p. 4). A student employee who has the skill to self-direct their learning in the classroom would likely also be able to do so in their role as a student employee. Student workers who have a less clear-cut or defined role can use their self-directing skills to determine the best tasks to work on and independently initiate those tasks. Gamified training can help two-fold in this scenario: (a) gamified training could increase the student's excitement for their role, making them more likely to initiate additional, independent tasks; and (b) gamification can help students acquire more knowledge about their position, allowing them to have a greater understanding of what tasks may need to be done.

Information literacy emphasizes broad learning skills and not necessarily the acquisition of specific pieces of knowledge. However, Grafstein (2002) demonstrated information literacy can be seen as a way of thinking about discipline-specific information, and it equips students with both subject knowledge and broader principles about information retrieval. This could include skills not related to a specific discipline, such as critical thinking or lifelong learning. These concepts of information literacy should be at the forefront of student worker training curriculum. Instead of providing gamified training activities that allow students to learn a very particular skill or piece of knowledge, it can be more helpful to think about gamified training activities that give students a way of thinking or learning, which can then be translated to a variety of different contexts. For example, instead of purely content-based training for chemistry tutors where they would memorize the periodic table of the elements, a gamified training strategy could focus more on learning the patterns in the table, and why elements are arranged in their specific way. Thus, when a chemistry tutor looks at the periodic table of elements after that training, they do not see dozens of squares as individual pieces of knowledge; they see a cohesive table and can think of how squares relate to their rows, columns, or colors. Tutors do not necessarily need to memorize the atomic number of each element, just how to locate that information from the table.

MEASURING OUTCOMES

To ensure gamification strategies are having their intended outcome or meeting their intended objectives, it is important to use assessment efforts to analyze their effectiveness. One of the first steps is to determine what construct you are seeking to measure, and this construct can be based on your learning objectives. For example, if "Researchers and practitioners argue that engaged employees are better performers" (Ērgle & Ludviga, 2018, p. 411), then measuring engagement levels and productivity levels are important constructs to measure. These could be measured in a pre-assessment and post-assessment method or measured at one point in time during or after the gamification activities. Once you have the constructs you would like to measure, it is also important to use consistent definitions of terms. In the example of the word engagement, it is important to clarify if more engagement means students have decreased burnout, have higher retention levels, are more satisfied, or if it has some other meaning (Ērgle & Ludviga, 2018).

Practitioners interested in implementing and assessing gamification strategies in student worker training can rely on both objective and subjective measurements. Although students in training are not in an academic, classroom environment, they still can take learning assessments at the end of their training to ensure they have retained the information they have learned. Objective measurements can be based more on quantitative scoring, such as points in learning games. For example, "Learning games such as Kahoot! are channels to evaluate whether learning objectives have been achieved" (Lin et al., 2018, p. 571). These quiz-based games can provide an objective score that can be compared to other student scores or compared against a maximum total or baseline total. The other benefit of games that score participants is that it provides immediate feedback to the student on whether or not they have answered the question correctly. Šćepanović et al. (2015) recommended this type of feedback where students can see a progress bar and track their progress or status instantaneously.

In one study, student workers took quizzes at the beginning of the year, weekly, and then a cumulative one at the end of the year to see how much knowledge had remained with them (Connell & Mileham, 2006). This same concept can be applied to student worker training. Students could take a pre-assessment prior to the training to gauge their knowledge on the job responsibilities and functions, and then take the same quiz at the end of training to see if the gamification strategies improved their scores from point A to point B. To make this a really effective analyzation tool, those scores could be compared to scores from a group of students who went through a traditional, non-gamified training program.

Subjective measures can also be used to assess the effectiveness of gamified training. Students can self report if they felt the game play helped with their learning (Lin et al., 2018). This could be done by answering survey questions in a Likert-scale format, for example, or by having the students write up some sort of narrative reflection on their training experience. In a study with undergraduate engineering students, the students wrote reflections on how useful the gamification tools were toward their learning and "completed paper and pencil surveys, which included questions on enjoyment, engagement, and value of the games played" (Leung & Pluskwik, 2018, p. 9). Students also had a section in their end-of-term course evaluations that specifically asked about the gamification tools used. Students self reported they enjoyed the games and also had high engagement levels. In addition to student self-report feedback, the staff or administrators who plan and administer the training could also assess the success of the training from their perspective. Although it is not a formal, objective measurement, staff who are actively involved in the training can probably gain a general perspective of how students are engaging or enjoying the training based on the student's nonverbal cues and expressions. Staff can also consider how much time, effort, and resources went into planning a particular activity, and whether they felt the time and effort was worth the result (Leung & Pluskwik, 2018). Thus, it can be important to measure specific activities or gamified sessions in addition to the gamified training as a whole. Students can self report which session(s) they enjoyed the most or least, and which session(s) prepared them the best for their role.

Another way to measure the success of your gamification strategies is through performance indicators. Many higher education institutions, or individual departments and programs, will have learning objectives or goals, and higher education training programs should be no different. This can be as simple as making a list of what you want the students to gain from the training. Or, practitioners can use more formal indicators, such as the Information Literacy Competency Standards for Higher Education (2000). Although there are many standards to serve as guiding posts for creating your own performance indicators, the first two standards (1.1 and 1.2) serve as good examples. Standard 1.1 indicated "The information literate student defines and articulates the need for information" (Information Literacy Competency Standards for Higher Education, 2000, p. 8). Essentially, this standard could represent that a student employee should be able to formulate appropriate questions based on information that they need to do a function of their job, and are able to combine existing information with their own ideas to form a coherent idea. Standard 1.2 stated "The information literate student identifies a variety of types and formats of potential sources for information" (Information Literacy Competency Standards for Higher Education, 2000, p. 8). If this standard is placed in the context of student employee training, students would be able to leave their training and be able to see the value of different types of resources, such as audio or visual, and be able to identify the audience or population they are serving. For example, a math tutor who exhibits mastery of this standard may be able to explain a complicated math problem both verbally and by drawing out the problem. Additionally, they would be able to tailor their approach and appropriately choose which method(s) to use depending on the student they are tutoring.

CONCLUSION

The purpose of this chapter was to examine gamification strategies in the context of higher education student employee training. It provided a basic overview of gamification and its historical context, and then examined gamification's use in higher education classrooms and in corporate training. It then discussed how strategies from corporate training and classroom gamification can merge to support gamification for student employee training at the college level. Additionally, this chapter briefly examined how the COVID-19 global pandemic has impacted current and future potential uses of gamification in the learning environment. It ended with an overview of how information literacy relates to gamification and training, and suggestions for gamification training assessment.

This chapter served as more of a practical guide or "tips and tricks" style resource for providing gamification ideas and strategies for student employee training. Thus, future work examining gamification can specifically tie in theoretical frameworks in further detail, such as game theory. Although there is ample research on gamification, information about using gamification for student worker training was sparse. Thus, this is an area where future studies could be conducted.

REFERENCES

Bawden, D., & Robinson, L. (2002). Promoting literacy in a digital age: Approaches to training for information literacy. *Learned Publishing*, *15*(4), 297–301. doi:10.1087/095315102760319279

BaxterR. J.HoldernessD. K.JrWoodD. A. (2016). The effects of gamification on corporate compliance training: A field experiment of true office anti-corruption training programs. *Social Science Research Network*. doi:10.2139/ssrn.2766683

Connell, R. S., & Mileham, P. J. (2006). Student assistant training in a small academic library. *Public Services Quarterly*, *2*(2–3), 69–84. doi:10.1300/J295v02n02_06

Dale, S. (2014). Gamification: Making work fun, or making fun of work? *Business Information Review*, *31*(2), 82–90. doi:10.1177/0266382114538350

Ērgle, D., & Ludviga, I. (2018). Use of gamification in human resource management: Impact on engagement and satisfaction. *Contemporary Business Management Challenges and Opportunities*, 409–417. doi:10.3846/bm.2018.45

Grafstein, A. (2002). A discipline-based approach to information literacy. *Journal of Academic Librarianship*, *28*(4), 197–204. doi:10.1016/S0099-1333(02)00283-5

Iacono, S., Vallarino, M., & Vercelli, G. (2020). Gamification in corporate training to enhance engagement: An approach. *International Journal of Emerging Technology in Learning*, *15*(17), 69–84. doi:10.3991/ijet.v15i17.14207

Information Literacy Competency Standards for Higher Education. (2000). [Brochure]. *Association of College & Research Libraries*. http://hdl.handle.net/10150/105645 https://www.ala.org/ala/acrl/acrlstandards/informationliteracycompetency.htm

Leung, E., & Pluskwik, E. (2018, June). *Effectiveness of gamification activities in a project-based learning classroom* [Classroom paper presentation]. 2018 ASEE Annual Conference & Exposition, Salt Lake City, UT. https://peer.asee.org/30361

Lin, D. T. A., Ganapathy, M., & Kaur, M. (2018). Kahoot! it: Gamification in higher education. *Social Sciences & Humanities*, *26*(1), 565–582. https://www.researchgate.net/profile/Debbita-Tan/publication/320182671_Kahoot_It_Gamification_in_Higher_Education/links/5ab3757aa6fdcc1bc0c288fe/Kahoot-It-Gamification-in-Higher-Education.pdf

Miller, C. (2013). The gamification of education. *Developments in Business Simulation and Experiential Learning*, *40*, 196–200. https://absel-ojs-ttu.tdl.org/absel/index.php/absel/article/view/40

Nieto-Escamez, F. A., & Roldán-Tapia, M. D. (2021). Gamification as online teaching strategy during COVID-19: A mini-review. *Frontiers in Psychology*, *12*(648552), 648552. Advance online publication. doi:10.3389/fpsyg.2021.648552 PMID:34093334

Rahman, I. S., Falkenthal, E., Holzner, L., & Lozano, A. A. (2019). *Studentaffairs.com 2019 virtual case study* [Powerpoint slides]. https://www.studentaffairs.com/Customer-Content/www/CMS/files/VCS/2019/CalPolySanLuisObispo_rahman.pdf

Ritter, J. (2015, June 25). Gamification or game-based learning? What's the difference? *Knowledge Direct: A Learning Management Platform.* https://www.kdplatform.com/gamification-game-based-learning-whats-difference/

Šćepanović, S., Žarić, N., & Matijević, T. (2015, September 24-25). *Gamification in higher education learning - state of the art, challenges and opportunities.* The Sixth International Conference on e-Learning, Belgrade, Serbia. https://elearning.metropolitan.ac.rs/files/pdf/2015/23-Snezana-Scepanovic-Nada-Zaric-Tripo-Matijevic-Gamification-in-higher-education-learning-state-of-the-art-challenges-and-opportunities.pdf

Witte, J., Westbrook, R., & Witte, M. M. (2017). *Proceedings of the Global Conference on Education and Research.* 10.5038/2572-6374-v1

ADDITIONAL READING

Buckley, P., & Doyle, E. (2014). Gamification and student motivation. *Interactive Learning Environments, 24*(6), 1162–1175. doi:10.1080/10494820.2014.964263

Cope, W., & Kalantzis, M. (2009). "Multiliteracies": New literacies, new learning. *Pedagogies, 4*(3), 164–195. doi:10.1080/15544800903076044

Fotaris, P., Mastoras, T., Leinfellner, R., & Rosunally, Y. (2016). Climbing up the leaderboard: An empirical study of applying gamification techniques to a computer programming class. *Electronic Journal of e-Learning, 14*(2), 94-110. https://eric.ed.gov/?id=EJ1101229

Hanghøj, T. (2013). Game-based teaching: Practices, roles, and pedagogies. In S. de Freitas, M. Ott, M. M. Popescu, & I. Stanescu (Eds.), *New Pedagogical Approaches in Game Enhanced Learning: Curriculum Integration* (pp. 81–101). doi:10.4018/978-1-4666-3950-8.ch005

Hung, A. C. Y. (2017). A critique and defense of gamification. *Journal of Interactive Online Learning, 15*(1), 57–72. www.ncolr.org/jiol/issues/pdf/15.1.4.pdf

KEY TERMS AND DEFINITIONS

Engagement: A subjective measurement of the degree to which a student employee is interested in, and participating actively in, a training session or activity.

Game-Based Learning: A learning strategy or pedagogy that focuses on the broad organization and delivery of training content. The game is a crucial piece of how learning takes place.

Gamification: Using game-based strategies to teach students or employees tasks that otherwise may be relatively mundane, with the goal of increasing motivation, knowledge retention, engagement, and/or satisfaction.

Information Literacy: A type of skill that students build and develop over time. A student's ability to think critically about a decision when specific directives or precedence may not exist.

Knowledge Retention: An objective-leaning measurement to examine how well student workers were able to grasp and remember learning content during their training sessions.

Satisfaction: A subjective measurement for examining how content students are with their training sessions.

Student Assistant/Student Worker: A student enrolled at a university and simultaneously working in an on-campus job that is available to them due to their student status.

Chapter 10
Interactive Multimedia Experiences in Higher Education:
Gaming, Augment and Virtual Reality, and Research

Patrícia Gouveia
LARSyS, Interactive Technologies Institute (ITI), Faculdade de Belas-Artes, Universidade de Lisboa (FBAUL), Portugal

Luciana Lima
LARSyS, Interactive Technologies Institute (ITI), Faculdade de Belas-Artes, Universidade de Lisboa (FBAUL), Portugal

Anna Unterholzner
LARSyS, Interactive Technologies Institute (ITI), Faculdade de Belas-Artes, Universidade de Lisboa (FBAUL), Portugal

ABSTRACT

This chapter presents experiences in using gaming and interactive media in higher education environments since 2017 culminating in the 2020/21 years when the COVID-19 pandemic forced teachers and students to adopt different work methodologies. Participatory design strategies merged with a tradition of critical and interdisciplinary studies in humanities mediated by online technologies helped shape these strategies enhanced by the cooperation from three different faculties from Lisbon University in Portugal (Universidade de Lisboa, UL), namely FBAUL, IST, and IGOT. The aim of these experiments was to augment the potential for innovation and research taking advantage of gaming research methodologies to involve teachers and students in a common context. This chapter also shows research done in interactive media, augmented and virtual reality, game art, and gender equity. The year 2020 showed how institutional collaboration can open learning spaces to a more focused approach on the interests of young people and to promote a more sustainable and dynamic future.

DOI: 10.4018/978-1-7998-7271-9.ch010

INTRODUCTION AND BACKGROUND

A Holistic Systemic Participatory Design and Interdisciplinary Strategy

The complexity of the year 2020 leads us to reflect on various factors far beyond the COVID 19 pandemic. Since March 2020, confined at home, disoriented higher education teachers and students worked together to make the health situation a little less overwhelming. In our country, some people mastered digital technologies enough not to be excluded from the unsettling present that was felt on television, newspapers, radio, and other traditional media. On the internet, conspiracy theory flourished at toxic levels in social media, but escape was possible after all. Armed with time, due to the mandatory confinement, we could play, watch movies and series, read, and work together in a renewal way, to take the opportunity to do things differently. We received books in PDF format through the web to distribute, we attended online free conferences from around the world, we could play games, see movies on free streaming platforms, but outside the screen, the world had never been so grey.

This situation was the trigger for thinking about the ongoing processes of digital change in the country. Some took the opportunity to do what they had been postponing for years (i.e., Digital Transition Action Plans), accelerated by a time of rush that turned into a pandemic context into something else, another world that claimed slowness and delicacy. Stopping was possible for some, but not all. On the one hand, the COVID-19 pandemic has caused many people to strive to use different digital technologies, so it has been a catalyst in the widespread use of technological resources, making it an immediate priority to ensure the maintenance and continuity of educational, labour, health, and training processes. On the other hand, the pandemic has revealed the gap between those who have technological resources and digital skills and those who did not have these capacities. This gap is even greater if we consider factors such as gender, age, and socio-economic conditions (UN, 2020, online). The evident contrasts between those who had access to digital technologies and those who did not, between those who could work from home and those who could not do it, dismantled, and awakened old ideologies and dogmatic ways of thinking. The discrepancies in accessing technological possibilities that have been going on for decades have made it evident how Portugal needed changes.

Participatory and slow design merge real and imagined spaces that bring artists, designers, researchers, and participants together in defence of six principles: to reveal spaces and experiences that may be forgotten, including materials and processes; to expand, taking into account the potential of artificially produced artefacts and environments, leading to more balanced consumption; to engage in open and collaborative processes based on information sharing, cooperation, and transparency; to encourage people to become active participants in design processes, strengthening a sense of community and social value; to evolve, from experiences, artefacts and reflected environments (Correia, 2017). Participatory design is crucial to understand the role of technological mediated participation supported by digital media. Looking beyond the immediate needs of everyday life participatory design is nothing new. It evolved from the seventies Nordic cooperative design systemic processes and the firsts attempts, in 1971, from the Design Research Society in the United Kingdom. The field was defined in a conference named "Design Participation" (Correia, 2017). In this context, "arts and design merge the creation and solving of problems in a holistic manner incorporating systemic ideas and emergent behaviour" (Gouveia, 2018). We can also consider that the "goal of participatory design is to include all stakeholders in each step of the design process. Such stakeholders include designers, clients, users, the community, and others. Users are especially valuable stakeholders when it comes to designing for the public" (Kang, Choo, &

Watters, 2014, online). Tendencies that incorporate participatory strategies, drawing on the perspectives of the humanities and sciences are not new (Bianchini & Verhagen, 2016) and we should also be aware of the influence of the digital interactive transition since the end of last century.

Grounded in a tradition of critical and interdisciplinary studies in humanities, enhanced by cooperation from three different faculties in **arts** (*Faculdade de Belas-Artes da Universidade de Lisboa*, FBAUL), **engineering** (*Instituto Superior Técnico*, IST) and **geography** (*Instituto de Geografia e Ordenamento do Território*, IGOT) from the University of Lisbon (*Universidade de Lisboa*, UL) we augmented the potential for innovation and research taking advantage of gaming research methodologies to involve teachers and students in a shared participatory environment. These experiences were built in an arts and design multimedia tradition previously developed by (Gouveia, 2010) and others (Manovich, 2001; Bogost, 2007; Flanagan, 2009; Deterding, 2014). Gaming processes interconnect various communities, countries, city spaces, and people in a hybrid fashion creating a *gameful* world where teachers and students can learn together in a shared environment.

The Use of Digital Games and Interactive Media in Higher Education

The creation and development of digital games in higher education allow students to acquire communication skills, teamwork capabilities, organizational competencies, and ability in task planning. It can also enhance integrative knowledge from various fields and stimulate a holistic perspective on knowledge acquisition. As David Skorton and Ashley Bear state these integrative strategies are essential for the twenty first century academic learning environment (Skorton and Bear, 2018). Together students can test different research methodologies in arts, design, and engineering. Thus, some of the most basic work skills are simulated in a safe learning context, whose applicability is fundamental for the insertion of young people in the labour market. Antonio Figueiredo, an expert on higher education mediated technological environments for the European higher education space, suggests how project-based or studio practice can contribute to pedagogical development in various areas. In the author's pedagogical map for 2020, the main set of skills, abilities, and competencies are project oriented and emancipatory research methodologies connected with social and collaborative skills (Figueiredo, 2020).

Serious gaming and games-based learning can help change the higher education environment in multiple ways (Gouveia, 2015) and promote transmedia knowledge acquisition (Gouveia, 2018; 2020). Taylor Kubota suggests that the University aims to embrace and pursue the study of games and interactive media to promote interdisciplinary abilities and social skills (Kubota, 2017). In addition, Stuart Brown, from the National Institute of Play at Stanford University, advert that play is more than just fun and can be a trigger to innovation and creativity (Brown, 2008), and António Damásio suggests that creativity is the capacity of creating future scenarios and the ability to plan (Damásio, 2021). Therefore, many of the future uncertainties related to public health and education can be anticipated by promoting work environments that do not make binary cleavages between the real and online worlds. Other examples of recent literature using game theory and practice as a source of knowledge creation and production in higher education could be found in the work of Shira Chess (2020). The author highlights the interplay of oppressive systems within culture speaking about inequalities such as gender, ethnicity, social class, sexuality, and disability (Chess, 2020, p. 54). Kishonna L. Gray (2020) uses transmedia studies to focus on intersectional tech to examine systemic legal exclusions (Gray, 2020, p. 27). As Amanda C. Cote suggests, the "consistent representation of gamers as male in news, marketing, and other media presents for men a simple point of identification where they can see themselves taking on the identity of a gamer (and a game developer). This same representational trend can exclude women by making their connection to that identity harder do envision" (Cote, 2020, p. 16). Our five-year academic exchange of teachers and students worked on these problematics to stimulate an inclusive workspace without social, racial, ethnic or gender discrimination in a broad perspective.

MAIN FOCUS OF THE CHAPTER: THE STORY OF AN INSTITUTIONAL PARTNERSHIP AT THE UNIVERSITY OF LISBON (UL) FACULTIES

Faculdade de Belas-Artes da Universidade de Lisboa (FBAUL) and Instituto Superior Técnico (FBAUL + IST, 2017-2021) and Faculdade de Belas-Artes da Universidade de Lisboa (FBAUL) and Instituto de Geografia e Ordenamento do Território (FBAUL + IGOT, 2019-21).

At the Fine Arts Faculty at the University of Lisbon (FBAUL), and other Faculties and Institutes of the same institution, online classes were the possible alternative at an unknown and complex moment. We could not stop, because that would limit students' future. Together, we were finding solutions that, in some way, reduced the difficult moment that we are still going through. In our concrete context, 2020 turned out to be the time when the work of the last five years became visible and started to make sense, a path that we should continue to explore in the future. It was the moment when the contamination of educational practices and strategies in higher education between three institutions of the **University of Lisbon** (*Universidade de Lisboa,* **UL**), namely, the **Fine Arts Faculty** (*Faculdade de Belas-Artes da Universidade de Lisboa,* **FBAUL**), the **Engineer Institute** (*Instituto Superior Técnico,* **IST**) and the **Geography Institute** (*Instituto de Geografia e Ordenamento do Território,* **IGOT**), has been emancipated in a student's project recognized internationally (please see online resources: *Sea of Roses* **links 2021**), showing how these initiatives are forms of relevant innovation and development in higher education that is urgent to support.

This story began in 2017 (please see online resources: **Student's blog link 2017**), when an exchange of Multimedia Art, Communication Design and Engineering bachelor and master students from FBAUL and IST began, within the scope of an informal partnership between the two institutions. Arts and Engineering students began to collaborate annually in the creation of digital games for one semester. In the five editions of this partnership more than 300 students of both institutions were involved. In the subsequent years of 2018, 2019, 2020 and 2021 (please see online resources: **Student's blog link 2018, 2019, 2020 and 2021**), this partnership continued. However, in 2020 and 2021, the exhibition of the final works, which takes place annually in late May, migrated entirely to the online modality due to the pandemic. Other collaborations, between professors and students from FBAUL and IST, were emerging. Annually, both institutions collaborate on Global Game Jams, based at IST, and in the creation of augmented reality projects for the University of Lisbon IST Faraday Museum (please see online resources: **Faraday Museum augmented reality app** *Extended Play at Faraday Museum*).

The partnership between FBAUL and IST has brought visible gains to both the teachers and the students involved, enabling a new culture of collaboration between Arts & Design and Computer Engineering students. The students recorded their testimonies and experiences in their public blogs, and all the digital games produced under these initiatives are available on the project's websites (Please see online resources: **Game Lab IST**).

Student's Public Blogs Testimonies

To better illustrate how this collaboration develops, a student from FBAUL who participated in this interdisciplinary proposal describes how this experience was: "Participation is part of the Game Design course we have in the Master's program. We have the option not to choose. For example, people who work and do not have so much free time to have collaborative and constant work may choose not to do it. However, most of them like to have this experience because we can understand how our working relationship with engineers is, right? What they ask us, how they ask us, the communication itself, how it is done, I think it is always an added value. And it was also a bit around that time that I decided to be part of and experience the partnership between the two schools, FBAUL and IST, the IST students start early on working on concepts and ideas of the games they will develop and we get a synopsis (...) with those synopsis of the works they want to develop and, as a rule, we try to see what we more or less identify with and stay with that group" (female, 25 years old, Master in Communication Design). In their public blogs, students describe the step-by-step development of the games they are making and the positives and negatives of this collaborative work. Some student accounts show what it was like to work in a diverse team: "In my opinion, the whole idea of this collaboration is fantastic. We, as artists, were able to experience a new kind of art that I had never tried before. We also got to understand better how the work environment functions. Since the first time that I heard about this project, I considered it a great and innovative opportunity, even after the 'not so great personal experience that I had, I still think the same about it (...)" (female, 20 years old, Bachelor in Multimedia Art). Another student considers "I'll be honest, during my academic career, I did a lot of group work, and I hated almost all of it (laughs), not because I have any difficulty getting along with people. However, it was very difficult because as we were all informatics, it was complicated to have a division of labour that was equal, that was well divided, so there was always that feeling that sometimes one person did everything or sometimes nobody did anything, it was very complicated to manage that, and I speak against myself, we informatics people are also a little difficult to manage. When I started working with the FBAUL students, I realized that we were able to fit in very well, from the perspective that, where there is respect, there is respect for the capacities and limitations of other people" (male, 31 years old, Master in Computer Engineering).

Finally, this pedagogical strategy can encourage students from different areas of knowledge to share experiences and, especially, to work collaboratively, promoting high-quality games such as, for example, the game *Sea of Roses* (Batista, Fidalgo & Parrilha, FBAUL/IST, 2021) that won second place in the international contest *Video Games exploring Culture's Influence on Dating 2020*. This contest was promoted and sponsored by the American organization Jennifer Ann's Group. After the award, and with the help of Jennifer Ann's Group, students developed their prototype which ended as a final game product available for free at STEAM. *Sea of Roses* was also a finalist for 2021 James Paul Gee Learning Games Award ("informal learning" category).

We can also consider that these academic higher education partnerships encourage equal participation of men and women, making it possible to deconstruct the gender stereotypes still very present in our educational institutions and in our society (please see online resources: Gender Action, 2021). In 2019, a FBAUL student joined, within the scope of her master's research, Prof. Dr. Margarida Queirós IGOT research group for the creation and development of a web documentary on the life experiences of University of Lisbon students in the public space (please see online resources: **web documentary with student's testimonies**). Mobility among FBAUL students expanded to another institution and opened

Interactive Multimedia Experiences in Higher Education

new horizons for collaboration. Today, other FBAUL Ph.D. and master students work with Prof. Dr. Margarida Queirós in other IGOT research projects as, for example, *Vivido*, Management Platform of the National Support Network for Victims of Domestic Violence, Working together for an INCLUSIVE Europe, EEA Grants Portugal 2020 (please see online resources: *Vivido*).

The Contribution of the Game Lab for the Creation of a Student's Club (2020)

The collaboration between Ph.D. students from FBAUL and IST began in 2019 with the help of Anna Unterholzner from FBAUL. At the Global Game Jam 2020, the first ideas for the creation of a student club were outlined. The club was named GameDevTécnico and has been an official association since September 2020 (please see online resources: **GameDevTecnico 2020**). This club aims to promote the value of games by supporting students to create and develop their projects, encouraging the final work distribution, and promoting a learning-based environment that allows them to acquire professional experience at an early stage of the academic path. For that purpose, Anna Unterholzner recruited, coordinated, and supported FBAUL students, mostly women, gathering signatures and promoting youth associations between FBAUL and IST. In this context, it was possible to conclude that institutional collaboration in game and playful multimedia creation and development is very stimulating for students. Through these partnerships students access work experiences in a multifaceted team in the field of game and playful creation and production, creating practical works together, learning to present them, discuss them critically, and exchange ideas for upcoming projects. In addition, it allows an integrated understanding of the relevance of different knowledge areas, for example, the connection between arts and design and programming and its articulation.

The Games Laboratory is an IST facility for students to connect, have fun, exchange ideas, participate in Global Game Jams, and show their games and playful applications at MOJO, *Montra de Jogos*, an annual Games Window (please see online resources: **MOJO,** *Montra de Jogos* **IST: 2021, 2020, 2019, 2018 & 2017**). The games presented are created together to promote teamwork, the relevance of meeting deadlines, and fluid learning based on the creation and development of projects.

Both, in the Games Laboratory as well as in the students' club, people were using technologies for creating collaborative game projects such as, for instance, Unity, Godot Engine, Unreal Engine, and Buildbox, amongst others. On the side of the students more involved in the technical parts of the games, programming languages such as C++, C#, Javascript, HTML5, UnrealScript and Python were used frequently. On the side of the students more involved in the artistic part (be it visual or auditive), programs such as, for example, Adobe Creative Apps, Asesprite, Affinity, Audacity, Blender, Maya, Houdini, Gimp, Krita, Paint, Pyxel Edit, and Zbrush were applied often. The choices of programs were depended on each one's abilities and individual learning ambition or common vision of the outcome within a project.

Since March 2020, all collaborative work among students has been carried out online via Skype, Zoom, WhatsApp, Discord, email, and Slack, among other possibilities. These platforms were used to recruit and interview students since the institutions have different geographical locations, and restrictions on mobility have been very significant. Although with some communication problems that would be more easily solved through physical presence, the general challenge, from an academic point of view, of the COVID-19 phase requires that we find the balance between being online and offline.

The choice of the communication channels such as WhatsApp, email, Slack, Skype, and Zoom were used primarily since these were the channels that had already been implemented within the collaborative work since the beginning. All these communication tools were used by students and staff depending on their working methods. Even though these interfaces fortunately made it possible to maintain the workflow within the different faculties during the COVID-19 phase, the team realized that the communication channels were too many, resulting in non-efficacy. Therefore, the switch to Discord was ideal, since the platform is one that is primarily used within the gaming community, making it possible to host large-scale meetings and set up rooms for teamwork and projects using any device. Additionally, Notion was implemented as a seamless tool for the administrative, organizational, and accounting tasks within the gaming club. With these two interfaces applied, the collaborative work has maintained to be an efficient and playful one on the one side while structured and transparent to each team member on the other side.

Anna Unterholzner from FBAUL was often the only female student with the contentment that there is more diversity within the club after the recruitment phase. Not only are there more female students, but also more artists and people with diverse backgrounds (Please see online resources: **GameDevTecnico Students Twitter and Instagram links**). Both in the association named Game Dev Student Club and in the IST Games Laboratory (*Laboratório de Jogos* do IST) the most used language was English.

In the 2020 autumn, Prof. Dr. Patrícia Gouveia's research group at Interactive Technologies Institute (ITI/LARSyS), a research centre and associate lab for interdisciplinary studies in human computer interaction, created and developed another experiment in higher education and interactive media. Two of the group members participated in a two-month online residency named RAUM Residencies for the research and development of an artwork named *Speak Out!* (Gouveia & Martilla, 2020). The artist and the curator of the online exhibition worked together with an interaction designer to present an interactive work for the world wide web about speech recognition, migration, and decolonial studies. The exhibition opened on December 28 and is now available online until digital oblivion (please see online resources: *Speak Out!* **RAUM Residency 2020)**.

Besides these projects, the research group in general (involving 8 master's, 6 doctoral and 1 post-doctoral students) and Dr. Luciana Lima in particular is carrying out research to identify and analyse gender issues in higher education for the creation and production of games and in the gaming industry (Lima and Gouveia, 2020). As interactive media and technological products promoting sociability, digital games are an essential means of discussing gender equality/equity. The gaming industry has been expanding along with the training offer in design, art, and digital game programming in our country. However, there is no consistent scientific research on gender parity in this sector. Thus, we created the project named *Game Art and Gender Equality/Equity* (GAGE) to fill this gap and continue ongoing national research on this issue (Lima, Gouveia, Pinto and Cardoso, 2021). In 2019, we started GAGE with the aim to provide a comprehensive assessment of the gaps and challenges of gender equity in the national gaming sector and foster diversity and change values and behaviours through inclusive practices that encourage the participation of women in this economic and cultural sector. Some results will be presented in the next section.

Game Art and Gender Equity Research Initiatives (2019-2021)

Worldwide, many educational programs in design, art and development of digital games have emerged since the late 90s of the 20th century, particularly in North America and Europe (Aarseth, 2015; Fachada, 2018). Although Portugal only started to follow this trend almost a decade later, the training offered in digital games increased significantly in the country, going from a degree in 2009 to fifteen educational programs in 2020, including six degrees, four Master's degrees, and five vocational/professional technical

Interactive Multimedia Experiences in Higher Education

programs in higher education (Romero, Nunes, Santos and Pinto, 2020). If we count on post-graduate and vocational/professional education courses and not higher education, this number will probably increase.

Following an international trend of creating gaming courses, driven mainly by the emergence of the academic and scientific field called Game Studies (Aarseth, 2001; 2002; Mäyrä, 2008) and by the guidelines of the International Game Developers Association (IGDA), which developed a model of a study plan program for digital games, the awakening to the creation of degrees focused exclusively in this area was also driven by the opening of new educational new study plans in Portuguese educational institutions after the Bologna Process became official (Decree-Law 74 / 2006 of March 24), and for changes in the level of development and consolidation of the professional community of developers throughout the first decade of the 21st century (Zagalo, 2013).

As an interdisciplinary area, which aggregates content and knowledge from different fields of study (communication sciences, computer sciences, digital humanities, arts and design, social sciences, and technologies), national academic training in digital games is linked to the area of computer sciences, electronics, and automation, as well as the audio visual and media creation and production areas, so people can take degrees that are more focused on computer engineering and programming, as well as degrees more focused on design, communication, and arts of digital games, digital animation, and production of multimedia content. The emphasis on programming and the erasure of arts and design contributions can create the idea that women are not suited for gaming industry (Lima, Gouveia, Pinto and Cardoso, 2021). Critics about a national tendency to forget women's integration in the national videogame history were made (Gouveia, 2014) and a lack of awareness between the connection of digital emancipation and women's integration in technological areas seems evident when we analyse what happened to women working in gaming industry during the COVID 19 lookdown (Lima, L. Gouveia, P. and Pinto, C., 2021).

One of the results of our research refers to the number of students enrolled in the following academic years (2016/2017 to 2018/2019) in higher education institutions that offer degrees in the field of digital games. In eleven educational programs analysed in Portugal, the total enrolled went from 651 in 2017 to 793 students in 2019, an increase of about 22% (Lima and Gouveia, 2020), which shows a growing interest in young people in the gaming field. However, when focusing on the number of boys and girls enrolled in these courses, we found that the female audience enrolled is significantly smaller: 793 enrolments, only 121 are women (15.2%). Taking into consideration that gaming is an interdisciplinary area related to a playful and technological environment highly consumed by girls and women worldwide the question arises: why there is not a greater presence of the female audience in digital games degrees in Portugal (Lima and Gouveia, 2020)?

Although a large body of research has examined the perpetuation of gender stereotypes in online games (Linda and Pennington, 2016; Vermeulen, Bauwel, and Looy, 2017), the same spirit of scientific production does not exist when it comes to studies that focus on the professional choice in the area of digital games, with many questions still to be explored, such as, for example, the impact of toxic gamer culture in the choice of that professional area or how gender inequality and discrimination against non-normative groups are being fought by the global digital games industry (Consalvo, 2012; Shaw, 2013; Lima and Gouveia, 2020).

The most recent IGDA survey on the satisfaction of digital game developers indicated that only 24% of professionals who took up positions as game developers were women IGDA, 2019). This survey revealed that 33% of producers affirm that this industry does not offer equal treatment or opportunities for all. The data shows that these professionals are primarily young, male, white, and childless or have any elderly care responsibilities. In addition, they are highly qualified, and most have training in specialized programs relevant to game design or development. As such, important representation challenges remain. These include immediate negative effects, such as inequality and discrimination for women, members of other raciaiized ethnic groups, and older workers, but also have implications for career plans and development, innovation in game content, art, and design, perpetuating occupational norms with long hours of work and precarious working conditions.

Given that the digital games sector has a long history of male predominance, both in online games (Vermeulen, Bauwel and Looy, 2017), and in e-sports (Ruotsalainen and Friman, 2018), it is likely that perceptions that narratives potentially guide boys and girls about this field focused on male geek culture so that it can influence the professional choice in that area. In addition, the cultural belief that the player's identity is intrinsically linked to normative gender models, creating a relatively intimidating environment for players, men, and women, who do not meet this criterion (Vermeulen, Bauwel and Looy, 2017; Consalvo, 2012), it is likely that such threatening and stigmatizing experiences will prevent girls from seeing this area as a promising and safe professional locus. Our research aims to expose asymmetries and lack of equity in gaming environments.

FUTURE RESEARCH AND CONCLUSION

In future our aim is to develop further our research in game art and gender equity in Portugal promoting gaming practices that foster diversity and inclusion. In a recent published paper (Lima, Gouveia, Pinto and Cardoso, 2021) we advise for the necessity of creating in Portugal a more mixed environment where people shared the creation and development of game-based projects and we emphasize how the myth pf programming, that is, the persistent belief that you can only work on games through programming, is somehow responsible for a deeper escape of women from gaming environments. For that purpose, we quote interviews with Portuguese professional women who belong to the gaming industry. We are convinced that in higher education we can use other strategies besides asking women to attend programming courses. Gaming is an interdisciplinary field where learning moving image creation software like, for example, the Adobe Creative Cloud, among many other possibilities, could be instrumental to engage people in a less deterministic manner where programming is the default educational mode. Another possible solution could be, for example, creative *do-it-yourself* and *do-it-with-others* or *together* methodologies that take advantage of analogic materials and digital sensors. Nowadays, this integrative educational model could challenge the hegemonic assertion that the knowledge of programming languages is the major area in gaming environments. When the emphasis is placed on programming and not on the artistic creation, production, and dissemination of playful artefacts, we tend to forget that games are above all cultural products and not just technological objects or programming software artefacts. In our present moment where technological apparatus merge and overlap with human sensibility (Peraica, 2019; Bridle, 2019; Gouveia, Lima, Unterholzner & Carvalho, 2021) we might avoid focusing on technologies instead of ideas. Enhancing the ability to think about complex systems taking advantage of gaming methodologies and procedures can help us project and develop a more sustainable future.

There is a tradition of multimedia arts that we can duplicate in gaming fields where women teamwork with other people for the creation of complex interactive projects if they are not familiar with programming languages but only with moving image software. The idea is to develop learning environments where we learn how to work together and how to develop further these interactive art and design partnerships to gain sophistication in gaming environments. Such initiatives emphasize the creation and development of creative ethical stories, non-stereotypical visuals, videos, and animations, to promote the engaging of women and people, normally excluded from these initiatives, in game arts and design fields. In this case, people can work in other areas such as game design, game environment design, character creation and animation, narrative and content development (script creation and research), among other possibilities, with an emphasis in ethical and social aspects. For that purpose, we will continue to develop, in future, as we did in the past five years, project-based gaming workshops that engage students in a shared environment for the development of game art and design with inclusive perspectives.

In 2020 the COVID-19 pandemic caused many people to strive to use different digital technologies, so it was a catalyst in the widespread use of technological resources, becoming an immediate priority to ensure the maintenance and continuity of educational, labour, and health processes worldwide. This context showed us in an expressive way how institutional collaborations and partnerships can open learning spaces to be more focused on the interests of young people and promote a more sustainable and dynamic future. This chapter is an overview of a series of pedagogical and research projects done in interactive media, augmented and virtual reality, game art, and gender equity. Finally, integrative educational models are essential to fight populism and ignorance (Rosling, 2020). The challenges of education are not to divide but to unite, overcoming social inequalities and cultural integration. Learning should combine presential and online resources mediated by digital technologies to attract the attention of a broader audience.

ACKNOWLEDGMENT

This work was financially supported by: ARDITI - Regional Agency for the Development of Research, Technology, and Innovation, for the support given in the scope of Project M1420-09-5369-FSE-000002-Post-Doctoral Fellowship, co-funded by the Madeira 14-20 Program-European Social Fund (Dr. Luciana Lima, FBAUL post doc). This work was also financially supported by a three-month grant: ITI-LX UIDB/50009/2020 - (99/2021-IST-ID) (Anna Unterholzner, FBAUL PhD candidate).

REFERENCES

Aarseth, E. (2001). Computer Game Studies, Year One. *Game Studies Journal, 1*(1). Retrieved from http://www.gamestudies.org/0101/editorial.html

Aarseth, E. (2002). The Dungeon and the Ivory Tower: Vive La Difference ou Liaison Dangereuse? *Game Studies Journal, 2*(1). Retrieved from http://www.gamestudies.org/0102/editorial.html

Aarseth, E. (2015). Meta-Game Studies. *Game Studies Journal, 15*(1). Retrieved from http://gamestudies.org/1501/articles/editorial

Barreto, J. (2018). *Faraday Museum augmented reality app Extended Play at Faraday Museum*. Retrieved October 4, 2021, from, https://joxnds4.wixsite.com/jbarretoportefolio/copia-leapmotion-game-for-kids

Bianchini, S., & Verhagen, E. (Ed.). (2016). Practicable, From Participation to interaction in Contemporary Art. MIT Press.

Bogost, I. (2007). *Persuasive Games: The Expressive Power of Videogames*. MIT Press. doi:10.7551/mitpress/5334.001.0001

Bridle, J. (2019). *New Dark Ages, Technology and the End of the Future*. Verso.

Brown, S. (2008). *Play is More Than Just Fun*. Retrieved January 18, 2020, from https://www.ted.com/talks/stuart_brown_play_is_more_than_just_fun

Chess, S. (2020). *Play Like a Feminist*. MIT Press. doi:10.7551/mitpress/12484.001.0001

Consalvo, M. (2012). Confronting toxic gamer culture: a challenge for feminist game studies scholars. Ada: A Journal of Gender, New Media, and Technology, 1. doi:10.7264/N33X84KH

Correia, V. (2017). *Design and the Culture of Participation in the Era of Digital Media* (PhD Thesis). Faculdade de Ciências Sociais e Humanas (FCSH), Universidade Nova de Lisboa, Lisbon, Portugal.

Cote, A. C. (2020). *Gaming Sexism, Gender and Identity in the Era of Casual Video Games*. New York University Press. doi:10.18574/nyu/9781479838523.001.0001

Damásio, A. (2021). *Deus Cérebro. Maquinaria das emoções*. Retrieved January 18, 2020, from https://www.rtp.pt/play/p8309/deus-cerebro

Deterding, S. (2014). The Ambiguity of Games: Histories and Discourses of a Gameful World. In S. P. Walz & S. Deterding (Eds.), *The Gameful World: Approaches, Issues, Applications* (pp. 23–64). MIT Press.

Fachada, N. (2018). Teaching database concepts to video game design e development students. *Revista Lusófona de Educação*, *40*(40), 151–165. doi:10.24140/issn.1645-7250.rle40.10

Faculdade de Belas-Artes da Universidade de Lisboa. (2021). Retrieved October 4, 2021, from, http://www.belasartes.ulisboa.pt/

Figueiredo, A. D. (2020). *Which School for Citizenship?* Retrieved January 14, 2020, from https://adfig.com/pt/?p=630

Flanagan, M. (2009). *Critical Play, Radical Game Design*. MIT Press. doi:10.7551/mitpress/7678.001.0001

Game Lab. Laboratório de Jogos. (2021). Retrieved October 4, 2021, from, https://labjogos.tecnico.ulisboa.pt/en https://www.facebook.com/LabJogosIST/

GameDevTecnico. (2021). Retrieved October 4, 2021, from, https://gamedev.tecnico.ulisboa.pt/ https://gamedevtecnico.itch.io/

GameDevTecnico Students Twitter and Instagram links. (2021). Retrieved October 5, 2021, from, https://twitter.com/gamedevtecnico https://www.instagram.com/p/CGpvQ24KJKM/

Gender Action, Mutual Learning Workshop on Gender and Digitalization. (2021). *Interactive Multimedia Experiences in Higher Education: Gaming, Augmented and Virtual Reality, and Research*. Retrieved October 4, 2021, from https://genderaction.eu/exploratory-mutual-learning-workshop-on-gender-and-digitalization/

Gouveia, P. (2010). Artes e Jogos Digitais, Estética e Design da Experiência Lúdica. Universitárias Lusófonas.

Gouveia, P. (2014). A possible narration about Portuguese videogames creation. Critical book review: *Videogames in Portugal: History, Technology and Art*, Nelson Zagalo, 2013. *Aniki, Portuguese Journal of the Moving Image, 1*(2), 369-74. doi:10.14591/aniki.v1n2.69

Gouveia, P. (2015). Serious gaming: how gamers are solving real world problems. In *Proceedings of Artech 2015, Seventh International Conference on Digital Arts (Creating Digital e-motions)*. Óbidos

Gouveia, P. (2018). Transmedia experiences that blur the boundaries between the real and the fictional world. In Trends, Experiences, and Perspectives on Immersive Multimedia Experience and Augmented Reality. IGI Global.

Gouveia, P. (2020). The New Media vs. Old Media Trap: How Contemporary Arts Became Playful Transmedia Environments. In Multidisciplinary Perspectives on New Media Art. IGI Global. doi:10.4018/978-1-7998-3669-8.ch002

Gouveia, P., Lima, L., Unterholzner, A., & Carvalho, D. (2021). *O mundo expandido das imagens invisíveis*. Instituto de Estudos Filosóficos, Faculdade de Letras da Universidade de Coimbra.

Gray, K. L. (2020). *Intersectional Tech, Black Users in Digital Gaming*. Louisiana State University Press.

IGDA. (2019). *Developer Satisfaction Survey 2019*. International Game Developers Association.

Instituto de Geografia e Ordenamento do Território. (2021). Retrieved October 4, 2021, from, http://www.igot.ulisboa.pt/

Instituto Superior Técnico. (2021). Retrieved October 4, 2021, from, https://tecnico.ulisboa.pt/en/

Interactive Technologies Institute. (2021). Retrieved October 5, 2021, from, https://iti.larsys.pt/

Kang, M., Choo, P., & Watters, C. E. (2015). Design for experiencing: Participatory design approach with multidisciplinary perspectives. *Procedia: Social and Behavioral Sciences, 174*, 830–833. doi:10.1016/j.sbspro.2015.01.676

Kubota, T. (2017). *Faculty and students at Stanford argue for increased study of games and interactive media*. Retrieved January 14, 2020, from https://news.stanford.edu/2017/05/03/interest-grows-study-games-interactive-media/

Lima, L., Gouveia, P., Pinto, C., & Cardoso, P. (2021). I Never Imagined That I Would Work in The Digital Game Industry. In *CoG 2021 Proceedings: 3rd IEEE Conference on Games*. University of Copenhagen.

Lima, L., Gouveia, P., & Pinto, C. (2021). *Gaming in Portugal 2020: Women in Digital Games and the Impact of Covid-19*. Retrieved October 4, 2021, from, https://icswac.weebly.com/program.html

Lima, L., & Gouveia, P. (2020). Gender Asymmetries in the Digital Games Sector in Portugal. *DIGRA 2020 Tampere Conference Proceedings*, 1-16.

Linda, K., & Pennington, C. (2016). "Girls Can't Play": The effects of Stereotype Threat on Females' Gaming Performance. *Computers in Human Behavior, 59*, 202–209. doi:10.1016/j.chb.2016.02.020

Manovich, L. (2001). *The Language of New Media*. MIT Press.

Mäyrä, F. (2008). *An introduction to Game Studies: Games in Culture*. Sage.

Mojo, *Montra de Jogos* IST. (2017). Retrieved October 5, 2021, from, https://tecnico.ulisboa.pt/en/events/mojo-montra-de-jogos/

Mojo, *Montra de Jogos* IST. (2018). Retrieved October 5, 2021, from, https://tecnico.ulisboa.pt/en/events/mojo-11th-edition/

Mojo, *Montra de Jogos* IST. (2019). Retrieved October 5, 2021, from, https://tecnico.ulisboa.pt/en/events/mojo-2019-12th-edition/

Mojo, *Montra de Jogos* IST. (2020). Retrieved October 5, 2021, from, https://tecnico.ulisboa.pt/en/events/mojo-2020-13th-edition/

Mojo, *Montra de Jogos* IST. (2021). Retrieved October 5, 2021, from, https://labjogos.tecnico.ulisboa.pt/mojo/2021/

Peraica, A. (2019). The age of total images: disappearance of a subjective viewpoint in post-digital photography. Amsterdam University Institute of Network Cultures.

Romeiro, P., Nunes, F., Santos, P., & Pinto, C. (2020). Atlas do Setor dos Videojogos em Portugal. Edição Sociedade Portuguesa para a Ciência dos Videojogos.

Rosling, H. (2020). Factfulness. Edições Círculo de Leitores: Temas e Debates, Lisboa.

Ruotsalainen, M., & Friman, U. (2018). "There Are No Women and They All Play Mercy": Understanding and Explaining (the Lack of) Women's Presence in Esports and Competitive Gaming. *Proceedings of Nordic DIGRA 2018*. http://www.digra.org/wp-content/uploads/digital-library/DiGRA_Nordic_2018_paper_31.pdf

Sea of Roses Game. (2021). Retrieved October 4, 2021, from, https://tecnico.ulisboa.pt/en/news/campus-community/sea-of-roses-wins-second-place-in-international-game-design-contest/ https://store.steampowered.com/app/1581940/Sea_of_Roses/

Shaw, A. (2013). On Not Becoming Gamers: Moving Beyond the Constructed Audience. *Ada: A Journal of Gender, New Media and Technology*, (2).

Skorton, D., & Bear, A. (2018). *The Integration of the Humanities and Arts with Sciences, Engineering, and Medicine in Higher Education: Branches from the Same Tree*. The National Academies Press. doi:10.17226/24988

Speak Out! RAUM Residency. (2020). Retrieved October 5, 2021, from, https://raum.pt/en/terhi-marttila https://www.academia.edu/44788195/Speak_Out_a_playful_interactive_artwork_about_migration_with_a_radical_openness_to_the_World

Student's blog link. (2017). Retrieved October 4, 2021, from, https://fbaulgaming.wixsite.com/gaming2017

Student's blog link. (2018). Retrieved October 4, 2021, from, https://fbaulistgaming2018.wixsite.com/fbaul-istgaming2018

Student's blog link. (2019). Retrieved October 4, 2021, from, https://fbaulistgaming2019.wixsite.com/fbaulistgaming2019

Student's blog link. (2020). Retrieved October 4, 2021, from, https://fbaulistgaming2020.wixsite.com/fbaulistgaming2020

Student's blog link. (2021). Retrieved October 4, 2021, from, https://fbaulistgaming2021.wixsite.com/fbaulistgaming2021

Students' testimonies web documentary. (2019). *Mobility and Permanence in Public Space. Narratives of University Students with Different Self-Determination of Gender and Sexual Orientation.* Retrieved October 4, 2021, from http://www.ceg.ulisboa.pt/mpps/#3

United Nations. (2020). *UN Secretary-General's policy brief: The impact of COVID-19 on women.* Retrieved January 18, 2020, from https://www.unwomen.org/en/digital-library/publications/2020/04/policy-brief-the-impact-of-covid-19-on-women

University of Lisbon. (2021). Retrieved October 4, 2021, from https://www.ulisboa.pt/en

Vermeulen, L., Bauwel, S. V., & Looy, J. V. (2017). Tracing Female Gamer Identity: An Empirical Study Into gender and Stereotype Threat Perceptions. *Computer in Human Behavior, 71,* 90-98. doi:10.1016/j.chb.2017.01.054

Vivido. (2021). *Management Platform of the National Support Network for Victims of Domestic Violence.* Working together for an Inclusive Europe, EEA Grants Portugal 2020. Retrieved October 4, 2021, from https://vividoproject.wixsite.com/vivido?lang=en

Zagalo, N. (2013). *Videojogos em Portugal: História, Tecnologia e Arte.* FCA Editora.

Chapter 11
Live Long and Educate:
Adult Learners and Situated Cognition in Game-Based Learning

Samantha Taylor
Dalhousie University, Canada

Binod Sundararajan
Dalhousie University, Canada

Cora-Lynn Munroe-Lynds
Dalhousie University, Canada

ABSTRACT

Using the lenses of Vygotskian constructivism, situated cognition, the antecedents of flow, and a pedagogy interwoven with the multiliteracy framework, the authors present a COVID-19 simulation game. The game has multiple levels, challenges, disrupters, and allows for student player groups to work together (i.e., collaborate within and across player groups) to achieve the strategic objectives of the game. The player groups have an overall goal to minimize loss of life, while other parameters need to be optimized, depending on the stakeholder group that the player group is role-playing. While the game can be digitized, it is presented in a manner that allows instructors to implement the game simulation right away in their classrooms. Assessment rubrics, decision matrix templates, and debriefing notes are provided to allow for student learners to reflect on their decisions (based on course concepts) both individually and as a player group.

ANOTHER 'WICKED PROBLEM' IN EDUCATION

Effective March 2020, our world entered a new state of being. Cruise ships parked, flights grounded, national leaders called for residents abroad to return home immediately. Schools directed students of all ages home, sending educators into a tailspin. What once seemed implausible, a pandemic soon found

DOI: 10.4018/978-1-7998-7271-9.ch011

Live Long and Educate

students either attending Zoom (or similar) lessons or ceasing their studies altogether. In rather simplistic terms, COVID-19 disrupted education as we once knew it.

Borko and Listen (2009) detailed the barriers for educators to accept technology, once referring to the adoption of wide-scaled technology as its own 'wicked' problem. Jordan, Kleinsasser, and Roe (2014) discuss the issues present in the paradox of wicked problems in higher education. Adopting these so-called "wicked problems" often created unexpected issues for which educators must solve. Not only are educators required to adapt their teaching strategies to online formatting, but they are also required to troubleshoot any problems that may arise from transitioning to online learning.

Wicked problems which – if at all possible to resolve – are difficult to mitigate. We have seen such problems in various forms of popular culture. The cinematic treasures created in the last century have engaged and entertained spectators. Perhaps lessons gleaned from popular cultures, like the story of Captain Kirk in Star Trek, may be used to parallel real-life or simulated solutions to complex problems, encouraging students to leverage existing skills and knowledge and apply them in new and novel ways. In the next section, we describe the Kobayashi Maru simulation game that Star Fleet Academy cadets in the Star Trek Movies, must play to train before embarking on actual starships. These are not any different from flight simulators that pilots train on before actually getting to fly real planes.

A NO-WIN INTRODUCTION

As a cadet in the Starfleet Academy, Captain James T. Kirk had to beat the no-win simulation, Kobayashi Maru (KM), in the movie Star Trek (2009). The choice of saving a disabled freighter while not entering the neutral zone and not alerting the Klingons (and subsequently losing the starship to them) appeared impossible. Kirk reprogrammed the game simulation and inserted himself as the Human-in-the-Loop. This adaptation allowed him to win the unwinnable simulation.

The Starfleet Academy commends Kirk's innovative choice; by design, the game was no doubt challenging. Also, by design, the game was not winnable, which wrested control from the players (Starfleet Academy cadets). While the game simulation was a collaboration among the cadets (role-playing as Starfleet crew on the starship's bridge), the decision-making rested on the captain's shoulder. Kirk's confidence (likely borne from successfully reprogramming KM) was indicative of the construction of meaning or sense-making around the simulation, particularly around the need to prove himself and demonstrate "leadership ability". Given that KM was a simulation, Kirk was not particularly worried about the consequences of his actions.

MODELLING MOTIVATION

The C's underlined are the 6 C's of Motivation (Turner & Paris, 1995) and used to understand learners and instructional design (Wang & Han, 2010). Looking at the antecedents of Flow State (or Flow Experience) in the context of game-based learning, KM had a challenge, a clear set of rules (save the freighter, do not alert the Klingons, do not enter the neutral zone, etc.), relied on learner characteristics to follow their training, appeared to provide a sense of control (the captain could fire torpedoes at the Klingon warbirds, take other evasive action, listen to the crew for suggestions, make a choice or a set of choices), and provided feedback during the simulation (for example, visual, audio, crew feedback).

In essence, KM was an ideal game simulation whose primary objective was to teach cadets they could not win every battle situation.

The KM simulation required its participants to work collaboratively, utilizing strengths and current knowledge, then applying that knowledge in new and novel ways. Applying current skills in fun and engaging ways may have encouraged learners to enter a state of focus, thus heightening the learning experience.

THE FOCUS FRONTIER

Looking from the perspective of some of the dimensions of the Flow State/Experience, the game was engaging, required concentration, provided intrinsic rewards (because of the challenge associated with the game), while performing well (or winning) it provided high outcomes or prestige (Kiili, Lainema, de Freitas, and Arnab, 2014). In the case of the KM simulation, it is unknown whether players lost consciousness (went into the zone) while playing the simulation. As with any simulated learning exercise (gaming or role-playing in the classroom), the experiential learning cycle or model (Kolb,1984), described the experiential learning process as iterative: starting from abstract conceptualization, moving to active experimentation, gaining the experience, and undergoing critical reflection necessary to absorb the concepts.

Disrupting the Experience

Oxendine, Robinson, & Wilson (2010) added to this model by introducing the concept of disruptive experience into the cycle, where the unexpected experience triggers emotional responses (which they call emotional inventory) collected by the players because of the disruptive experience. When players (learners) critically reflect on their experiences, the **c**hoices they make (**c**ollaboratively or individually), and the **c**onsequences of their decisions when faced with **c**hallenges in the simulation, the level of **c**ontrol (or lack thereof) will theoretically move them to **c**onstruct meaning and hence learn. The supposed "aha moments" come much later during a debriefing session or studying for an exam.

Facilitating Flow

For educators, learners, and instructional designers of learning games, the question is whether this state of flow during learning can occur? When playing games for entertainment, the loss of consciousness indicative of experiencing a flow state can happen (Kiili et al., 2014). If learning happens (ways to beat the game high scores because of continuous practice), can this be translated into higher education classrooms?

Educators are likely to observe several instances of the 6 C's occurring in classrooms; video-game aficionados lose themselves in "for-pleasure" video game simulations. In short, can the flow state be induced in game simulations designed for learning environments?

Live Long and Educate

VYGOTSKIAN CONSTRUCTIVISM, SITUATED COGNITION AND FLOW

Table 1 summarizes the various aspects of Situated Cognition or Learning (Brown et al., 1989) combined with Vygotskian constructivism (1978), instructional design considerations for game-based learning (devised for E-Learning by Hung and Chen, 2001, in Taylor 2002), and the antecedents and dimensions of Flow State of Experience (Kiili et al., 2014).

When considering Vygotskian constructivism and peer-learning, and what happens when combining the concept of situated cognition or learning, it is understood that learning is a process. When learners are connected to social peers, learning may become reflective, deliberative, and create deep understanding at the cognitive levels because of the situatedness that accompanies such social interactions. From there, the learners can tap into their nascent or dominant characteristics, further impelling the learning effort.

Further commonalities are found when looking at the antecedents and dimensions of flow, particularly when the learner and their social peers are engaged in challenging game-based learning scenarios requiring collaboration, thought, initiative, and a deliberative approach to solving the game-related challenges. Experiential learning ranges from job shadowing to work-integrated learning, with learning from cases, simulations, and role-playing occupying a space midway in the spectrum. The effort of any educator using such experiential learning approaches is to move the learner from point A in their learning to point B, described as the Zone of Proximal Development (ZPD) (Vygotsky, 1978).

Table 1.

Principles of situated cognition and Vygotskian thought #	Instructional design considerations for game-based learning **	Antecedents of Flow State/Flow Experience $	Dimensions of Flow State Flow Experience $
Sense-making: learning is a process in which learners are active sense makers who seek to construct coherent and organized knowledge. $	Game-based Learning environments will provide learners with the opportunity for exploration, allowing them to develop a knowledge representation of their experience or discover an inconsistency between their current knowledge representation and their experience. $	Clear Goals – Set of rules	Concentration, Intrinsic Rewards
Commonality: Learning is a social act leading to identity formation and associated membership of a community of practice. **	Game-based Learning environments should capitalize on social and collaborative communication with others who have shared interests. **	Learner Characteristics	Fun – engagement
Situatedness: Learning is reflective, metacognitive, and embedded in rich socio-cultural contexts. **	Game-based Learning environments should enable students to account for disruptive and constructive experiences and take stock of their emotional inventory. $	Challenge	Intrinsic Rewards
Interdependency: Learning is socially mediated and facilitated through engagement in practice with others. **	Game-based Learning environments should generate interdependencies that benefit from the diverse expertise in the learning community. **	Sense of Control – intense practice	Loss of Consciousness
Infrastructure: Learning is facilitated by activity, accountability, and associated support mechanisms. *	Game-based Learning environments should incorporate facilitating structures, accountability mechanisms, and associated rules of engagement. *	Feedback	High Score – outcomes -prestige

** Taylor (2002).
$ Adapted from Kiili, Lainema, de Freitas, and Arnab (2014).
# Oxendine, C., Robinson, J., and Willson, G. (2010); Experiential learning. In M. Orey (Ed.), Emerging perspectives on learning, teaching, and technology.

Multidisciplinary Pedagogy

Each type of experiential learning activity is an effort to create an interdisciplinary approach to learning, particularly in Management Education and Psychology (Bevan & Kipka, 2012). Sundararajan (2020) found that students get eased into experiential learning activities by discussing organizational scenarios and mini cases in the early years of their academic study. However, as they head into the higher 3rd/4th years of their undergraduate programs, they are better able to grapple with more complex organizational scenarios and simulations.

The use of simulations for learning has had a rich history across various disciplines and with multiple layers of student benefits in international development studies (Chasek, 2005; Schnurr, De Santo, Green, and Taylor, 2015), in political science (Asal & Blake, 2006; Shellman & Turan, 2006), in medicine (Schroedl et al., 2012; Sheakley et al., 2016), and physics education (Martinez et al., 2013). These approaches to using simulations as a technique to engage learners in multiple academic disciplines is an indicator that such an approach, combined with a game-based learning approach where a real-life scenario is converted into a challenging game, has repeatedly found the learners to be engaged in the course material (Chasek, 2005; Martinez et al., 2013), accelerate situational awareness and knowledge acquisition (Schnurr et al., 2015), hones skill development (Schroedl et al., 2012), and gain the ability to apply course concepts in a real-world situation (Asal & Blake, 2006; Shellman & Turan, 2006).

The authors of this chapter have additionally used simulations in their classrooms for several years, where case-based learning was combined with role-playing, with students taking on roles of organizational stakeholders and simulating the organizational crises and demonstrate ways to solve the organizational issues presented in the case. Anecdotal evidence about students' engagement in the simulations, subsequent learning demonstrated in classroom performance, and end-of-term teaching evaluations further indicate the efficacy of using role-play simulations as an effective way to engage classroom learners. These, however, were short cases and student groups often had two to three such cases to work on during the course of the academic term. While the simulations proved to be effective, it would have been difficult for students to enter into the flow state, mainly because of the short duration of these case-based, role-play simulation games.

Pedagogical Preparedness for a 'Wicked' Problem

We have used the following theoretical lenses – social constructivism, the 6Cs of Motivation, problem-based learning, Kolb's Experiential Learning Model, and the multiliteracy framework. There are other learning frameworks like scaffolding, collaborative & cooperative learning, resource-based learning, creativity, information processing approaches to learning, and Piaget's learning models. However, with the theoretical lenses we have adopted to view our game-based COVID19 simulation, we subsume scaffolding (the game administrator provides increasing levels of support to allow learners to move from one learning place to the next – ZPD). Since student learners will have to work in groups, this again subsumes collaborative and cooperative learning approaches. We have however not addressed the concept of resource-based learning in this simulation, but solutions to the complex problems presented in the COVID19 game simulation would also require student learners to demonstrate their ability to process the information provided and come up with creative solutions to the issues faced by the stakeholders in the game. Piaget's learning models have centered mostly around child developmental and learning stages and since we are dealing with adult learners, we have not adopted Piaget's learning approaches.

Live Long and Educate

In addition to using the above-mentioned theoretical lenses, this chapter will look to delve into the question of how best to introduce flow states when learners in higher education classrooms are engaging in game-based learning simulations or scenarios. Using the context of the COVID-19 pandemic, the COVID-19 Simulation (the "Simulation") lays out elements of a supra-simulation to involve role-playing and is used directly in classroom groups and forms the core ideas behind designing a learning game simulation. The Simulation could involve multiple players from multiple disciplines across any higher ed campus. One key aspect of the simulation being described next is that it runs throughout the semester, providing increasingly challenging situations for learners to engage in, and possibly enter into the flow state, i.e., multiple instances of reviewing their decisions (practice) and having the opportunity to refine their decision-making at each progressive step.

SIMULATED DISRUPTION

Stanford Professor, neurobiologist, and podcast host Dr. Andrew Huberman (2021) separated flow state from learning; Huberman requires base-level knowledge as a pre-requisite to flow, where flow is achievable through *applying or revisiting* that knowledge. The objective of simulations is to allow learners to express, interact, and apply their knowledge in new and novel ways, much like employees would need to utilize concepts mastered in the classroom to solve new problems in the workplace.

Former University of Toronto business dean Roger Martin (2020) likened business silos (e.g., accounting, marketing, operations) to tools, where management education trains students to "tool match" a scenario to a single model without consideration for the impact on other silos (let alone any internal or external stakeholders). A game-based simulation is an integrative, transdisciplinary, immersive experience disrupting traditional silos. The combination of flow state earned through expressing knowledge mastery and intrinsic motivation from peer-based learning is anything but "tool matching". The Simulation will guide learners confidently towards applying knowledge necessary to "educate *for* practice, not just *about* practice" (Brook & Pedler, 2020, pp 1).

ADULT LEARNERS AND HIGHER EDUCATION

The National Center for Education Statistics reported an increase of eight percent fall enrollment in degree-granting institutions from 2007 to 2017, while the number of "mature" students (those classified as aged twenty-five and older) increased at the same time by eleven percent (para. 6). Huberman (2021) separates learners as young (ages twenty-five and under) and mature (twenty-five and older) based on neuroplasticity (the ability to learn and retain new information), where young brains are pre-wired to learn, while mature brains require a sequence of events, including moments of frustration, to induce neuroplasticity.

Engagement produced by game-based learning positively affects learning, while the game's challenge itself was a predictor of learning outcomes (Hamari et al., 2016). Incorporating a "bottoms-up" approach to learning, where learners take ownership of the simulation to build and present solutions, results in efficient and effective decision-making (Orey, 2010).

By taking existing knowledge from pre-requisite courses and events mature learners have experienced and exposing them to concurrent lessons of in-class learning (including the Simulation), the expression of mastery (flow state) could facilitate the inherent peer-based learning. Further, the natural frustration through the Simulation can provide the neurobiology necessary for adult learners to "stack" the incremental benefits of acquired and applied knowledge, thus providing an environment for learning.

PEDAGOGY

The Simulation provides upper-level rules of engagement, challenge levels, pedagogical aspects, describe a few scenarios, and how post-game debriefing (i.e., critical reflection in the form of verbal dialogue in the classroom and written, submitted work) can form the basis of a renewed effort to better integrate game-based learning simulations in higher ed classrooms. While no game would need to be unwinnable like the Kobayashi Maru simulation in Star Trek, the COVID-19 Simulation will be surfeit with several dilemmas requiring students from all disciplines to test their conceptual understanding of the subject matter under discussion. Pedagogical elements include (considering the multiliteracy framework — Cazden, C., Cope, B., Fairclough, N., Gee, J., et al., 1996):

1. Learning is expected to be both overt and subliminal. As will the teaching (***Overt and subliminal instruction***, Cazden et al., 1996).
2. Each player group needs to outline their strategy to tackle their problem and layout an implementation plan (***Transformed Practice***, Cazden et al., 1996).
3. Feedback is critical at each stage.
    a. Peer feedback (on decisions made).
    b. Peer feedback (on group member participation in or contribution to decision-making).
    c. Instructor feedback.
4. Course learning objectives need to be matched with each stage/level of the game (***Situated Practice***, Cazden et al., 1996).
5. Reflection pieces to be submitted by members of each player group or produced collectively by the group after advancing to the next level in the Simulation will form the basis of course learning concepts learners can study from for midterm and final exams (***Critical Framing***, Cazden et al, 1996; ***Reflection***, Kolb, 1984).
6. Prior to the end of the semester, the game operator (course instructor) uses class time to debrief collectively. Much learning will occur during this time.
    a. Debriefing is a process that involves each player group reviewing their notes and reflections from the semester and making a presentation to the class, outlining their strategies and how well they did or could have done. If they achieved a target score, what worked, what did not. The key is to identify what did not and what they would do differently.
    b. Debriefing allows all player groups to listen to and share ideas behind the approaches they took to achieve the set target (***Critical Framing***, Cazden et al., 1996).
    c. Debriefing allows individual learners to reflect on their contribution to the decision-making in their player group, recognizing their understanding of the course concepts and the context of the problem/issues faced by the group.
7. Debriefing will need to result in final individual submissions of student reflections when they look back at how they contributed to their player group's performance in the game (***Transformed Practice***, Cazden et al., 1996).

Live Long and Educate

COVID19 SIMULATION

Player Groups

Table 2.

Player Group	Description
Government	Municipal, Provincial (State), Federal
Governmental Organizations	Health Authority, Emergency Services (Ambulance, Fire, Police), Medical Services (Hospitals, Pharmacies etc.)
Transportation and Logistics	Goods, medical products, hospital needs (equipment, disposables), testing facilities (collection and analysis labs) etc.
Non-governmental organizations	Watchdog organizations, FDA, others, EPA
Businesses	For profit and not-for-profit
	Goods – capital goods, consumables, perishables
	Services – tourism, consultancies, daycare, long-term care, etc.
	Food, restaurants, cafes, etc.
	Pharmaceutical companies – vaccines, other medicines, healthcare
	Supply chains
	Sanitation, water, utilities, internet providers, garbage collection/disposal
	Realtors, contractors, household and building maintenance and services, other small businesses
	Staffing – when to hire, when to let go of staff, when to resume normal business operations etc.
Education	K-12, Higher Ed, colleges, polytechnics, private institutes etc.
Legal	legal issues can occur at all levels and will be an important stakeholder as individuals, organizations, and governments make decisions that impact communities (marginalized or the majorities).

Rules of Engagement

1. Each player group will need to have between 3-5 people (learners).
2. Each player group needs to take a set of optimal decisions to:

a. Minimize loss of life – higher the loss of life, lower the score – a greater number of lives saved – higher the score – hospitals, EMTs, long-term care facilities (based on their containment and hygiene practices).
b. Minimize errors – labs, testing facilities (collection protocols) – fewer errors lead to a higher score and vice versa.
c. Minimize errors in messaging and reporting – External and internal communication, media messaging, clarity in message, tone, legibility/readability etc. Clarity of messages lead to higher scores and vice versa.
d. Minimize contamination – all public and private spaces where people can gather – decisions on how many people can gather and when is it safe to increase numbers, etc. more people in potential exposure sites lead to lower scores (which impacts government decisions on when to remove mask mandates, increase number of people gathering at events etc.).
e. Ensure reasonable flow of goods – supply chain operating well – better flow of goods lead to higher scores and vice versa.
f. Have a clear strategy for next steps for each organization to emerge with surplus – lower the surplus (or deficit) will lead to a lower score and vice versa. The surplus need not only be a financial one, but it can also be about other resources (more healthcare workers leaving their jobs because of exhaustion etc.).
3. Each player group will use course concepts to devise their approaches to solving the problem faced by the group, with the overall context being to enable all player groups (in the municipality/state/province) to emerge with minimal loss of life and a reasonable chance of survival of their organization, post-pandemic.
4. Each player group will adopt a consultative approach within the group and with other player groups in the Simulation.

Challenge Levels

1. The game operator (course instructor) can change the difficulty levels, increase the constraints, and adjust the optimal outcomes.
2. The game operator can determine the correct sequence of events and deviations can result in the group having to restart the game/simulation resulting in a loss of time (unless the deviations can be clearly explained with evidence supporting such decisions).
3. The game operator can determine the optimal time by which decisions need to be submitted, acted upon, and outcomes measured.
4. The game operator needs to ensure that the game is playable and can determine the levels that each player group can pass or advance. Getting to each stage or past each stage, can be phased to match with the course progression in the semester.
5. The game operator maintains a leaderboard throughout the semester.

Playability

1. The Simulation and game are designed to be playable, i.e., the right set of decisions will lead each player group to advance to the next level.

2. The game will have increasingly harder levels to ascend and scores to achieve to proceed to the next level.
3. The game will arrive at a set of rational conclusions, determining that the game has been successfully completed.

With the overall goal of "minimizing the loss of life", we present the stakeholder map in Figure 1 for all the player groups.

Figure 1. Stakeholder Map

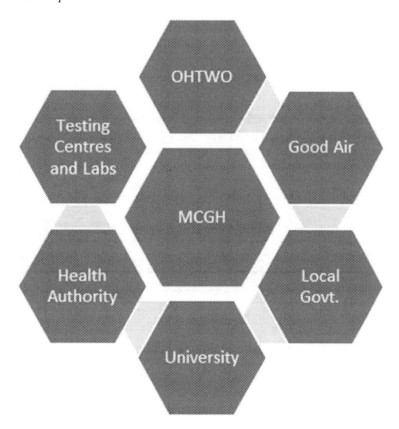

The player groups will have to pass three levels before it can be considered complete. The game is winnable when loss of life has been minimized when optimum levels for:

- a reduction in revenue for the organizations concerned,
- workload management (morale
- testing centres and labs to produce continuous results,
- healthcare for COVID19 and non-COVID 19 patients,
- an environment where classes can continue in some fashion and learning can occur in classrooms,
- local businesses continuing to stay operational and possibly survive,
- confidence in the collective effort of the health authority and the local government.

Optimum levels can be determined by the game moderator (Instructor) based on real city data, which can be superimposed on this scenario (around cases, business data, etc.).

For each player group, the assessment rubric can be used as a guide to determine whether they did not meet, met, or exceeded expectations around their analysis of the situation faced by the stakeholder of that player group. The assessment rubric is provided below (an adaptation from an AACSB Assurance of Learning assessment rubric).

Each level of the game will consist of two challenge questions. Upon the satisfactory completion of each challenge question (response by way of a set of decisions arrived at by the player group), the player group can proceed to the next level. The challenge questions in levels 2 and 3 will increase in difficulty and complexity, requiring the students in the player groups to research, understand course concepts, and collaborate (within and across stakeholder groups).

Work produced will be assessed for quality of the work (written, the sophistication of the decision-making process, and correctness of the decisions) and the depth of the reflection around the case and the course concepts. One standard technique of deciding the right course of action has been to use a decision matrix or a weighted decision matrix which has a set of criteria and decisions in rows and columns. The aim is to arrive at a rating (say from 1-3 or 1-5) for each criterion to support a decision. A sample decision matrix is provided in table 3. The decision with the highest score in all the criteria is often chosen. The decisions are often based on course concepts and a good understanding/reading of the main issue and consequences of the decisions.

Table 3.

	Decision 1	Decision 2	Decision 3	Decision 4
Criteria 1				
Criteria 2				
Criteria 3				
Criteria 4				
Total				

Debriefing

For any case, simulation, or game, debriefing is the phase where learning often occurs. The instructor can debrief midway through the game and scaffold struggling groups, following Vygotsky's constructivist paradigm (1978) of the Most Knowledgeable Other (MKO) and guiding learners to move from point A to point B. It also follows the multiliteracy approach to overt instruction (Cazden et al., 1996) and is also known as the Zone of Proximal Distance (ZPD). Debriefing can also occur at the end of the game, when all player groups have completed level 3 or when time runs out. The end-of-game debrief can be done with the entire class dropping out of their assumed stakeholder roles or just after all player groups have made their final presentations.

Player groups can provide the witness how other groups had approached the problems faced by these groups and pose questions to clarify why certain decisions were made (Critical Framing and Transformed

Live Long and Educate

Practice, Cazden et al., 1996). At this time, questions that typically go beyond just financial or resources related issues can be posed by the instructor or the students. Questions surrounding ethical dilemmas when one group of patients get attention before another group, the impact of supplying oxygen cylinders in a rationed way or raising prices to make short-term profits or denying or reducing access to marginalized communities can all allow students to get multiple perspectives and move them towards a greater understanding of the course concepts (key elements of the multiliteracy framework, Cazden et al., 1996).

THE NEXT FRONTIER

In subsequent sections, scenarios for in-person classroom role-play simulations will provide a game environment used by instructors and game developers. The simulation starts with an overview which may be shared with learners at the start of the simulation. Immediately thereafter, the simulation commences, and learners receive the information for Level 1.

There are three levels for this simulation. The game operator may choose the timing (guidance is to engage in the simulation alongside regular class material, so a progression from Level 1 to Level 2 is suggested to happen after Week 4 of a 12-week course) when to stop and debrief each level, and when to progress to the next level.

During two of the levels (Level 1 and Level 2) there are "Disrupters"; while the simulation is able to be played on occasion concurrently with current lesson planning, the "Disrupters" are meant to be intensive learning opportunities contained to one class without a concurrent learning activity that day. Figure 2 outlines a suggested schedule for the Simulation, its various levels, including disrupters.

Figure 2. Suggested 12-week schedule

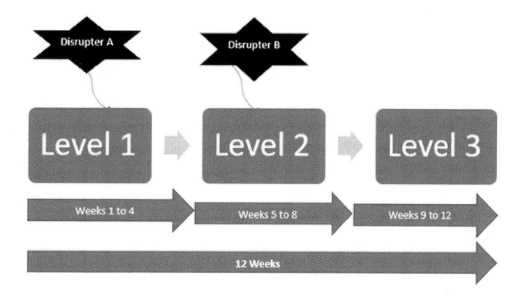

Points will accumulate throughout the and will be captured using a leaderboard. Points will be awarded at the end of each level, and for each disrupter stage. Points will be awarded for each imperative as listed above in the rules of engagement.

Teaching notes, evaluation and a sample assessment outline will assist instructors in evaluating in-game individual student and group performance. For students to achieve a "flow state", formal and informal debriefing notes will provide a framework for instructors to identify critical in-game areas to intervene and assist. What follows is a description of the game, the scenarios within the game, the challenge levels and questions, and a set of assessment rubrics and tables that will allow educators to use this simulation in their classrooms. This chapter will end by discussing options for future evolutions of this game and offer concluding remarks.

THE COVID-19 PANDEMIC SIMULATION

Introduction[1]

A joint statement by the International Labour Organization (ILO), the Food and Agricultural Organization (FAO), the International Fund for Agricultural Development (IFAD), and the World Health Organization (WHO), sheds light on the direct and potential impact of COVID-19 on world populations.

The COVID-19 pandemic has led to a dramatic loss of human life worldwide and presents an unprecedented challenge to public health, food systems, and the world of work. The economic and social disruption caused by the pandemic is devastating, tens of millions of people are at risk of falling into extreme poverty, while the number of undernourished people, currently estimated at nearly 690 million, could increase by up to 132 million by the end of the year. Millions of enterprises face an existential threat. Nearly half of the world's 3.3 billion global workforce are at risk of losing their livelihoods. Informal economy workers are particularly vulnerable because the majority lack social protection and access to quality health care and have lost access to productive assets. Countries dealing with existing humanitarian crises or emergencies are particularly exposed to the effects of COVID-19. Responding swiftly to the pandemic, while ensuring that humanitarian and recovery assistance reaches those most in need, is critical.

Assembly of Representatives

A team of representing Government Officials, Governmental Organizations, Transportation and Logistics, Non-governmental Organizations, Businesses, and Education (the "Representatives") have been gathered in a top-secret location.

Shortly, Representatives will receive information and need to make decisions that will impact their country. Representatives are encouraged to consider how their recommendations will impact their direct stakeholders, the direct stakeholders of their fellow representatives, the elected official reviewing the recommendations, and international implications impacting both developed and developing countries.

Level 1 – Brace for Impact

Middle City General Hospital (MCGH) is one of the three medium-sized hospitals in Middle City. Serving a population of around 500,000 that includes many surrounding towns, MCGH, a multi-care facility, is a 225-bed hospital with several special wards for acute care, ophthalmology, children's wing, cancer treatment facilities, and many others. The city had generally survived the COVID-19 pandemic quite well. The positive cases had been steady during the third wave, in the low 200s, and MCGH staff (doctors, nurses, and all healthcare professionals) were able to manage their workload, as well as attend to COVID-19 cases and other general (and special) cases and had done well to minimize loss of life. When things started looking up, news of the Delta variant filtered through and suddenly, without warning, the number of cases started to spike, among both vaccinated and unvaccinated patients. This appeared to be a national event and the need for PPE (personal protective equipment), ventilators, and oxygen cylinders rose steeply.

OHTWO Specialists Pvt. Ltd, is the Middle City distributor of oxygen cylinders and supplied them to all the medical and healthcare facilities in Middle City. They had a local production unit, but sourced many of their large and small, industrial and hospital grade cylinders from other national and overseas suppliers. Due to the global supply chain disruption caused by reduced production worldwide, the shortage of shipping containers, and a host of other logistics issues, the supply of oxygen cylinders was now going to be disrupted. Long delays are likely to occur before normal supplies could resume.

Good Air Systems LLC, a national manufacturer of ventilators and other medical equipment with a national and regional network of distributors, was facing similar challenges with procuring raw materials for their ventilator systems, many components of which needed to be imported from overseas. With a reduction in overall ventilator supplies, things turned critical, both internally and for their reputation.

Middle City's Mayoral office was working furiously with the provincial (state) government and the Health Authority to plan their responses to the shortage in supplies, manage to keep local businesses afloat. They were all staring at the start of the fall academic semesters for the two local universities and several community colleges and schools (with unvaccinated children under the age of 12). Pressure from local businesses was intense, as after a year and a half of no students in the city (numbering up to 30,000 or more), lack of tourism revenues, and the need to gently get the economy moving again, political careers were in jeopardy impacting the reputations of the current government and the question of whether anything the government does will be enough. With the increase in cases, the testing centres, which depended on volunteers, were also feeling the pressure, as were the testing labs.

The universities and colleges, which had been conducting online classes for over a year and half, with mixed success, also needed to ensure the safe arrival of students on campus and in residences, with the assumption that most classes would be offered face-to-face, possibly without masking mandates and no distancing requirements. The universities and colleges were struggling with the messaging around guidelines and mandates, as nervous faculty members and frontline staff were seeking consistency and clarity in what they could and could not do.

Questions/Challenges

1. What are the options available for MCGH, because of the disruption in the supply of oxygen cylinders and ventilators? What trade-offs do they need to make around attending to COVID19 patients vs. patients requiring other kinds of treatments? What are the workload implications for

the healthcare professionals, when there is a general shortage of physicians, nurse practitioners, and other healthcare professionals?
2. What are the options available to OHTWO Specialists? What sources can they tap to get the supply of oxygen cylinders restarted?
3. What are the options available to Good Air Systems? How can they restart the manufacture and supply of ventilator systems?
4. What can the municipal and state (provincial) government do to address this crisis? Calling for another lockdown can save lives, but can be devastating for the local economy, so what trade-offs can they decide on and how will that affect policy and governance?
5. How can testing centres and testing labs improve their productivity and sustain the turnaround time for generating test results? What are they going to do about the huge increase in plastic and other medical waste? The environmental fallout will be substantial, and this can become a municipal, national, global issue?
6. How can the universities and colleges manage their messaging to their students, staff, and faculty, while allowing for the resumption of normal, face-to-face classes? While moving back online would be one way to manage, the fact that students are likely to arrive on campus soon, faculty members may or may not wish to teach online, and anecdotal information indicated that this way of continuously learning online were causing many difficulties and not particularly indicative whether learning occurred.
7. What were the potential legal implications of failed policies, increased infections, reduction in care for non-COVID19 cases, loss of revenue etc.?

Requirements

Each Representative is responsible for preparing a presentation which will be shared with the Country's Elective Official, who will then deliberate and decide what steps the stakeholder will take to move forward. Each ten-minute presentation must take into consideration, at a minimum, the following elements: minimization of loss of life, errors (collection), errors (communication), contamination, and to ensure the flow of goods, all to be addressed with a clear strategy.

DISRUPTER A – SHORTAGE OF PPE[2]

The World Health Organizations (WHO) has further commented on the lack availability or even access to personal protective equipment (PPE) for health care workers and how this could impact the responses to the steep rise in COVID19 cases worldwide.

Since the start of the COVID-19 outbreak, prices have surged. Prices for surgical masks have seen a sixfold increase and prices for N95 respirators have trebled, and those for gowns have doubled. Supplies can take months to deliver and market manipulation is widespread, with stocks frequently sold to the highest bidder. The WHO has so far shipped nearly half a million sets of personal protective equipment to 47 countries, but supplies are rapidly depleting. Based on WHO modelling, an estimated 89 million medical masks are required for the COVID-19 response each month. For examination gloves, that figure goes up to 76 million, while international demand for goggles stands at 1.6 million per month. Recent

Live Long and Educate

WHO guidance calls for the rational and appropriate use of PPE in healthcare settings, and the effective management of supply chains. WHO is working with governments, industry and the Pandemic Supply Chain Network to boost production and secure allocations for critically affected and at-risk countries. To meet rising global demand, WHO estimates that industry must increase manufacturing by 40 per cent.

Requirements

You open your email and find that in exactly one-hour from now, you have a maximum two-minute phone call scheduled with the top elected official to advise them how to address the PPE shortage. Considerations should be made to ensure the minimization of loss of life, errors (collection), errors (communication), contamination, and to ensure the flow of goods, all to be addressed with a clear strategy.

LEVEL 2 – DEVELOPING A VACCINE[3]

The Centers for Disease Control and Prevention (CDC), issued a briefing describing the vaccine approval process and what were the implications around Emergency Use Authorizations, so the public could be informed about the efficacies of the protocols and the effectiveness of the process.

Bringing a new vaccine to the public involves many steps, including vaccine development, clinical trials, US Food and Drug Administration (FDA) authorization or approval, manufacturing, and distribution. Many different public organizations and private companies have worked together to make COVID-19 vaccines available to the public. While COVID-19 vaccines have been developed rapidly, all steps have been taken to ensure their safety and effectiveness.

The Vaccine Process: From the Lab to You

Initial Development

New vaccines are first developed in laboratories. The virus that causes COVID-19 is related to other coronaviruses that cause diseases such as severe acute respiratory syndrome (SARS) and Middle East respiratory syndrome (MERS). Scientists have been studying these other coronaviruses to develop vaccines against them for many years, long before SARS-COV-2 was identified. The knowledge gained through past research on coronavirus vaccines helped to accelerate the initial development of the current COVID-19 vaccines.

Clinical Trials

After initial development, vaccines go through three phases of clinical trials to make sure they are safe and effective. For other vaccines routinely used in the United States, the three phases of clinical trials are performed one at a time. During the development of COVID-19 vaccines, these phases have overlapped to speed up the process so the vaccines can be used as quickly as possible to control the pandemic. No trial phases have been skipped.

The clinical trials for COVID-19 vaccines have involved tens of thousands of volunteers of different ages, races, and ethnicities. Clinical trials for vaccines compare outcomes (such as how many people get sick) between people who are vaccinated and people who are not.

Because COVID-19 continues to be widespread, the vaccine clinical trials have been conducted more quickly than if the disease were less common. Results from these trials have shown that COVID-19 vaccines are effective. They have also shown no serious safety concerns after more than 8 weeks following vaccination. This is an important milestone, as it is unusual for adverse effects caused by vaccines to appear after this amount of time.

Emergency Use Authorization

Before vaccines are made available to people in real-world settings, FDA assesses the findings from clinical trials. So far, they have determined that three COVID-19 vaccines meet FDA's safety and effectiveness standards and have granted those vaccines Emergency Use Authorizations (EUAs)external icon. The EUAs have allowed the vaccines to be quickly distributed for use while maintaining the same high safety standards required for all vaccines.

The US government has invested substantial resources for both manufacturing and distribution of COVID-19 vaccines. This has allowed manufacturing to begin when the vaccines are still in the third phase of clinical trials so that distribution can begin as soon as the FDA has authorized each vaccine.

Questions/Challenges

1. What are the options available for MCGH now, given the change in circumstance (US FDA approval and the surging Delta variant, with a possible Mu variant rapidly appearing on the horizon)? What trade-offs do they need to make around attending to COVID19 patients vs. patients requiring other kinds of treatments, given the change in circumstance? What are the workload implications for the healthcare professionals, when there is a general shortage of physicians, nurse practitioners, and other healthcare professionals?
2. What are the options available to OHTWO Specialists, given the change in circumstance? What sources can they tap to get the supply of oxygen cylinders restarted?
3. What are the options available to Good Air Systems, given the change in circumstance? How can they restart the manufacture and supply of ventilator systems?
4. What can the municipal and state (provincial) government do to address this crisis, given the change in circumstance? Calling for another lockdown can save lives, but can be devastating for the local economy, so what trade-offs can they decide on and how will that affect policy and governance?
5. How can testing centres and testing labs improve their productivity and sustain the turnaround time for generating test results, given the change in circumstance? What are they going to do about the huge increase in plastic and other medical waste (per WHO's estimate, if 89 million units of PPE will be required per month, the amount of post-use hazardous plastic will be immense)? The environmental fallout will be substantial, and this can become a municipal, national, global issue?
6. How can the universities and colleges manage their messaging to their students, staff, and faculty, while allowing for the resumption of normal, face-to-face classes, given the change in circumstance? While moving back online would be one way to manage, the fact that students are likely to arrive on campus soon, faculty members may or may not wish to teach online, and anecdotal informa-

Live Long and Educate

tion indicated that this way of continuously learning online were causing many difficulties and not particularly indicative whether learning occurred.

Requirements

Each Representative is responsible for preparing a presentation which will be shared with the Country's Elective Official, who will then deliberate and decide what steps the country will take to move forward. Each ten-minute presentation must address, at a minimum, supported (through external research, facts and figures) consideration of the following elements: minimization of loss of life, errors (collection), errors (communication), contamination, and to ensure the flow of goods, all to be addressed with a clear strategy.

DISRUPTER B – INTERNATIONAL RELATIONS[4]

In 2020, many countries that had the ability and expertise to develop and produce vaccines to protect people against the COVID19 virus, worked jointly to create a Covax scheme to those countries that did not enjoy such access or have the affluence could have at least 20% of their healthcare and frontline workers get vaccinated.

What is the Covax Scheme?

Covax was created last year to ensure Covid vaccines were made available around the world, with richer countries subsidising costs for poorer nations. The scheme hopes to distribute enough vaccines to protect at least 20% of the population in 92 low- or medium-income countries - starting with healthcare workers and the most vulnerable groups. Globally, more than two billion doses of coronavirus vaccines have now been administered, in over 190 countries. However, while some countries have fully vaccinated a large amount of their population, many others have only just begun, or in some cases are still waiting for their first doses to arrive. Covax aims to close that gap. "With a fast-moving pandemic, no one is safe, unless everyone is safe," the WHO says on its website.

Requirements

You open your email and find that in exactly one-hour from now, you have a maximum two-minute phone call scheduled with the top elected official to advise them on how many, if any, vaccines should be donated to the Covax scheme. Considerations should be made to ensure the minimization of loss of life, errors (collection), errors (communication), contamination, and to ensure the flow of goods, all to be addressed with a clear strategy.

Level 3 – Re-entry: Planning for the New Normal[5]

Over the last year and a half, the world has been reacting and responding to the constantly changing and evolving situations around COVID19 cases, healthcare needs of communities and populations, restoring some semblance of normalcy, and keeping a wary eye on variants of the virus. However, as people start learning to "live with the virus", the prospect of resuming life in a "normal, pre-pandemic way", is quite daunting. The 2021 McKinsey report indicates what could be in our foreseeable futures.

Among high-income countries, cases caused by the Delta variant reversed the transition toward normalcy first in the United Kingdom, during June and July of 2021, and subsequently in the United States and elsewhere. "Our own analysis supports the view of others that the Delta variant has effectively moved overall herd immunity out of reach in most countries for the time being". The United Kingdom's experience nevertheless suggests that once a country has weathered a wave of Delta-driven cases, it may be able to resume the transition toward normalcy. Beyond that, a more realistic epidemiological endpoint might arrive not when herd immunity is achieved but when COVID-19 can be managed as an endemic disease. The biggest overall risk would likely then be the emergence of a significant new variant.

Questions/Challenges

1. What are the options available for MCGH now, given the change in circumstance? What trade-offs do they need to make around attending to COVID19 patients vs. patients requiring other kinds of treatments, given the change in circumstance? What are the workload implications for the healthcare professionals, when there is a general shortage of physicians, nurse practitioners, and other healthcare professionals?
2. What are the options available to OHTWO Specialists, given the change in circumstance? What sources can they tap to get the supply of oxygen cylinders restarted?
3. What are the options available to Good Air Systems, given the change in circumstance? How can they restart the manufacture and supply of ventilator systems?
4. What can the municipal and state (provincial) government do to address this crisis, given the change in circumstance? Calling for another lockdown can save lives, but can be devastating for the local economy, so what trade-offs can they decide on and how will that affect policy and governance?
5. How can testing centres and testing labs improve their productivity and sustain the turnaround time for generating test results, given the change in circumstance? What are they going to do about the huge increase in plastic and other medical waste? The environmental fallout will be substantial, and this can become a municipal, national, global issue?
6. How can the universities and colleges manage their messaging to their students, staff, and faculty, while allowing for the resumption of normal, face-to-face classes, given the change in circumstance? While moving back online would be one way to manage, the fact that students are likely to arrive on campus soon, faculty members may or may not wish to teach online, and anecdotal information indicated that this way of continuously learning online were causing many difficulties and not particularly indicative whether learning occurred.

Requirements

Each Representative is responsible for preparing a presentation which will be shared with the Country's Elective Official, who will then deliberate and decide what steps the country will take to move forward. Each ten-minute presentation must address, at a minimum, supported (through external research, facts and figures) consideration of the following elements: minimization of loss of life, errors (collection),

Live Long and Educate

errors (communication), contamination, and to ensure the flow of goods, all to be addressed with a clear strategy.

Next, we present two tables that will help educators and administrators evaluate the game as played in the classroom. The Simulation Evaluation Grid (Table 4) will allow the game administrator to keep track of key metrics for each player group, while the scoreboard (Table 5) will allow player groups to see their progress through the various challenge levels and the game disrupter stages. Following these two tables, we present a Simulation Assessment Rubric (adapted from AACSB Assurance of Learning rubrics) that will again help the administrator to grade player group performances, for the purpose of course grade.

Table 4.

Objective/ Player Group	Minimize loss of life	Minimize errors (collection)	Minimize errors (communication)	Minimize contamination	Ensure flow of goods	Clear strategy
1. Government						
2. Governmental Organizations						
3. Transportation and Logistics						
4. Non-governmental organizations						
5. Businesses						
6. Education						
7. Legal						

Instructions: For each Level (1 through 3) and separately for each Disrupter (A and B), the instructor is to record the results for each group for each category, rank each group relative to their performance in that category, and give the highest-ranking group 60 points, the second highest ranking group 50 points, continuing to decrease the points awarded by 10 points until the group ranked last receives 10 points.

For example, if the objective is to minimize the loss of life, the group with the lowest number of lives lost would be ranked the highest and would receive 60 points. Another example for the objective is to ensure flow of goods, the group with the highest flow of goods would also be ranked the highest, so a group who had the least amount of goods shipped would receive 10 points.

Table 5.

Score / Player Group	Level 1	Disrupter A	Level 2	Disrupter B	Level 3	Total Score
1. Government						
2. Governmental Organizations						
3. Transportation and Logistics						
4. Non-governmental organizations						
5. Businesses						
6. Education						

Instructions: Place the score from the Simulation (Level/Disrupter) Evaluation Grids. Note, each column represents one Level (1 through 3) and one Disrupter (A and B) for each stage of the simulation.

COVID19 GAME SIMULATION ASSESSMENT RUBRIC (CAN VARY BY STAKEHOLDER)

Semester:
Course:
Learning Outcomes:

Measure: Individual student assignment required students to complete a case analysis. This included identification of the issues, analysis and recommendation. This can be done at the player group level also.

Expectation:

Criteria	Does Not Meet Expectations 1 Approached the challenge questions well. < 10	Meets Expectations 2 Had a better understanding of the challenge questions. 11 < Marks < 20	Exceeds Expectations 3 Great understanding of the challenge questions and the consequences of the decisions 21 < Marks < 30
Issues	Entirely ignored/none of the important problems/issues identified.	Most of the important problems/ issues identified with moderate back-up.	All important problems/ issues are identified and brilliantly backed up.
Analysis	Analysis is not supported by concepts or frameworks or materials from class lectures or readings or analysis of table(s)/ figure(s)/ information in the appendix. Underlying causes of the issues are not analyzed, and alternative actions are not considered.	Analysis is somewhat supported by concepts/ frameworks/ materials from class lectures/ readings/analysis of able(s)/ figure(s)/ information in the appendix, but further insight could be included. Underlying causes of the issues are adequately analyzed, and alternative actions are considered.	Analysis is concisely supported by concepts/ frameworks/ materials from class lectures/ readings/ analysis of table(s)/figure(s)/ information in the appendix and it also presents insight for the decision maker. Underlying causes of the issues are brilliantly analyzed, and alternative actions are considered.
Recommendations for actions to be taken by the stakeholder	Recommendations are not clear and not supported by the analysis.	Recommendations are adequately clear and/or moderately supported by or connected to the analysis; further insight is required.	Recommendations are very clear and strongly supported by the analysis.
Quality of the Presentation	Did not reach the level of meeting expectations.	The Presentation considers the intellectual tools to incorporate research, where research inquiry and analysis are substantially demonstrated.	The Presentation supports the intellectual tools to incorporate research, where research inquiry and analysis are skillfully demonstrated.
Audience engagement	Did not reach the level of meeting expectations.	The Presentation is simplistically presented; is simplistically engaging; and partially incorporates reasoned judgments based on relevant criteria.	The Presentation is skillfully presented; is highly engaging; and overtly invites reasoned judgments based on relevant criteria.

continues on following page

Criteria	Does Not Meet Expectations 1 Approached the challenge questions well. < 10	Meets Expectations 2 Had a better understanding of the challenge questions. 11 < Marks < 20	Exceeds Expectations 3 Great understanding of the challenge questions and the consequences of the decisions 21 < Marks < 30
Simulation Group Performance	Received one of the two lowest total scores	Received one of the two middle total scores	Received one of the two highest total scores
Formatting, Grammar, Spelling, etc.	Many grammatical/ spelling errors and is very poorly written.	A few grammatical/ spelling errors and is moderately written.	No grammatical/ spelling errors and is superbly well-written.
Total Group Score			/ 210 (A)
Individual Performance Multiplier: 100% less Cumulative Minor/Major Individual Deductions			% (B)*
Total Individual Score			/ 210 (A x B)

* Deductions are at the discretion of the instructor; suggested deductions are as follows:

- 1% deduction from 100% of the Group Score for minor infractions (e.g., unexcused absence, lack of participation);
- 3+% deduction from 100% of the Group Score for major infractions (e.g., poor attitude impacting the simulation).

FUTURE EVOLUTIONS FOR THE SIMULATION

The Simulation can have several iterations and variations; COVID-19 is alive and current in our collective memories, and conditions are rapidly changing, requiring constant reflection of decisions and the need for organizations to respond to newer challenges. This Simulation also illustrates the concepts of VUCA (Volatility, Uncertainty, Complexity, and Ambiguity), which requires all actors (physicians, politicians, government servants, businesspeople, citizens) to learn to be agile, adapt, and be ready to modify decisions that impact not just themselves, but everyone around them (Bennett & Lemoine, 2014).

As this simulation has yet to take place in a classroom, future research incorporating teaching notes and anecdotes from student experience with this simulation could provide insights relevant to improving our simulation. Similarly, a longitudinal study of students who were involved in this study and subsequently were employed could provide insights into the pedagogical effectiveness of our simulation. Feedback from educators who use this simulation will further enhance the usefulness of the game, particularly if it is developed as a software or online game. Where possible, if we can detect or discern whether student learners were able to enter into the flow state, then we can continue to refine the game for not just higher education learners, but variations can be used to teach K-12 learners as well.

CONCLUSION

The chapter began by looking at how game-based learning can be used more effectively in Higher Ed classrooms and provide the requisite challenge to facilitate neuroplasticity for mature learners. Through Vygotskian constructivism and situated cognition lenses, learners engage in the 6 C's of Motivation. By incorporating pedagogical elements of the multiliteracy framework, learners benefit from social (classroom) peers through gameplay. The COVID-19 Simulation (game) has both macro-level entities and micro-level issues impacting small and medium-sized organizations in a city and large governments across countries.

While it may take a company time to develop this game into a digital simulation, instructors in Higher Ed classrooms can use this layout and levels of the simulation right away, having their students role-play as the stakeholder groups in the simulations. Instructors can look at what is currently happening in their cities, bring those elements into the game, and use real data to guide students towards understanding the course concepts. Such variations will continue to challenge students and prevent standard answers. Each time the simulation is run, a different set of questions/challenges can be provided for each level, or a different set of disruptions can be generated. Since standard answers are not likely to be available, this may motivate learners to engage with the game, enter the flow state, and learn.

To paraphrase the ending words from most Star Trek episodes or movies, "COVID19 has taken the world to a new frontier. The variations in the pandemic simulation as described, to explore new ways to make effective decisions, to seek out better ways to distribute resources while reducing the environmental fallout, will allow learners to boldly go where no learner has gone before."

REFERENCES

Asal, V., & Blake, E. (2006). Creating simulations for political science education. *Journal of Political Science Education*, *2*(1), 1–18. doi:10.1080/15512160500484119

Bennett, N., & Lemoine, G. J. (2014). What a difference a word makes: Understanding threats to performance in a VUCA world. *Business Horizons*, *57*(3), 311–317. doi:10.1016/j.bushor.2014.01.001

Bevan, D., & Kipka, C. (2012). Experiential learning and management education. *Journal of Management Development*, *31*(3), 193–197. doi:10.1108/02621711211208943

Borko, H., Whitcomb, J., & Liston, D. (2009). Wicked Problems and Other Thoughts on Issues of Technology and Teacher Learning. *Journal of Teacher Education*, *60*(1), 3–7. doi:10.1177/0022487108328488

Brook, C., & Pedler, M. (2020). Action learning in academic management education: A state of the field review. *International Journal of Management Education*, *18*(3), 100415. doi:10.1016/j.ijme.2020.100415

Brown, J. S., Collins, A., & Duguid, P. (1989). Situated Cognition and the Culture of Learning. *Educational Researcher*, *18*(1), 32–42. doi:10.3102/0013189X018001032

Cazden, C., Cope, B., Fairclough, N., & Gee, J. (1996). A pedagogy of multiliteracies: Designing Social Futures. *Harvard Educational Review*, *66*(1), 60–92. doi:10.17763/haer.66.1.17370n67v22j160u

CDC. (2020, February 11). *COVID-19 Vaccination*. Centers for Disease Control and Prevention. https://www.cdc.gov/coronavirus/2019-ncov/vaccines/distributing/steps-ensure-safety.html

Chasek, P. S. (2005). Power politics, diplomacy and role playing: Simulating the UN Security Council's response to terrorism. *International Studies Perspectives*, 6(1), 1–19. doi:10.1111/j.1528-3577.2005.00190.x

Covax: How many Covid vaccines have the US and the other G7 countries pledged? (2021, June 11). *BBC News*. https://www.bbc.com/news/world-55795297

Hamari, J., Shernoff, D. J., Rowe, E., Coller, B., Asbell-Clarke, J., & Edwards, T. (2016). Challenging games help students learn: An empirical study on engagement, flow and immersion in game-based learning. *Computers in Human Behavior*, 54, 170–179. doi:10.1016/j.chb.2015.07.045

Huberman, A. (Host). (2021, February 15). Using Failures, Movement & Balance to Learn Faster. *Huberman Lab* [Audio podcast episode]. https://hubermanlab.com/using-failures-movement-and-balance-to-learn-faster/

Impact of COVID-19 on people's livelihoods, their health and our food systems. (n.d.). Retrieved September 2, 2021, from https://www.who.int/news/item/13-10-2020-impact-of-covid-19-on-people's-livelihoods-their-health-and-our-food-systems

Jordan, M. E., Kleinsasser, R. C., & Roe, M. F. (2014). Wicked problems: Inescapable wickedity. *Journal of Education for Teaching*, 40(4), 415–430. doi:10.1080/02607476.2014.929381

Kiili, K., Lainema, T., de Freitas, S., & Arnab, S. (2014). Flow framework for analyzing the quality of educational games. *Entertainment Computing*, 4(4), 367–377. doi:10.1016/j.entcom.2014.08.002

Kolb, D. (1984). *Experiential learning: Experience as the source of learning and development*. Prentice-Hall.

Martínez Muñoz, M., Jiménez Rodríguez, M. L., & Gutiérrez de Mesa, J. A. (2013). Electrical storm simulation to improve the learning physics process. *Informatics in Education*, 12(2), 191–206. doi:10.15388/infedu.2013.13

Orey, M. (2010). *Emerging perspectives on learning, teaching, and technology*. Academic Press.

Oxendine, C., Robinson, J., & Willson, G. (2010). Experiential learning. In M. Orey (Ed.), Emerging perspectives on learning, teaching, and technology. Global Text Project, funded by the Jacob Foundation, Zurich, Switzerland. Creative Commons 3.0 Attribution Licence.

Parrish, S. (Host) (2020, November 24). Forward thinking with Roger Martin. *The Knowledge Project* [Audio podcast episode]. https://www.youtube.com/watch?v=gmn2c5hrUmI&t=1345s

Schnurr, M. A., De Santo, E., Green, A., & Taylor, A. (2015). Investigating student perceptions of learning within a role-play simulation of the Convention on Biological Diversity. *The Journal of Geography*, 114(3), 94–107. doi:10.1080/00221341.2014.937738

Schroedl, C. J., Corbridge, T. C., Cohen, E. R., Fakhran, S. S., Schimmel, D., McGaghie, W. C., & Wayne, D. B. (2012). Use of simulation-based education to improve resident learning and patient care in the medical intensive care unit: A randomized trial. *Journal of Critical Care*, *27*(2), 219.e7–219.e13. doi:10.1016/j.jcrc.2011.08.006 PMID:22033049

Sheakley, M. L., Gilbert, G. E., Leighton, K., Hall, M., Callender, D., & Pederson, D. (2016). A brief simulation intervention increasing basic science and clinical knowledge. *Medical Education*, *21*(1), 30744. Advance online publication. doi:10.3402/meo.v21.30744 PMID:27060102

Shellman, S. M., & Turan, K. (2006). Do simulations enhance student learning? An empirical evaluation of an IR simulation. *Journal of Political Science Education*, *2*(1), 19–32. doi:10.1080/15512160500484168

Shortage of personal protective equipment endangering health workers worldwide. (n.d.). Retrieved September 2, 2021, from https://www.who.int/news/item/03-03-2020-shortage-of-personal-protective-equipment-endangering-health-workers-worldwide

Sundararajan, B. (2020). Role Play Simulation: Using Cases to Teach Business Concepts - Simulations and Student Learning: A transdisciplinary perspective. University of Toronto Press.

Taylor. (2002). *Teaching & learning online: The workers, the lurkers and the shirkers*. USQ.

The NCES fast facts tools provides quick answers to many education questions. (n.d.). *National Center for Education Statistics*. Retrieved September 2, 2021, from https://nces.ed.gov/fastfacts/display.asp?id=98

Tsai, M.-J., Huang, L.-J., Hou, H.-T., Hsu, C.-Y., & Chiou, G.-L. (2016). Visual behavior, flow and achievement in game-based learning. *Computers & Education*, *98*, 115–129. doi:10.1016/j.compedu.2016.03.011

Vygotsky, L. (1978). *Mind in society*. Harvard University Press. (Original work published 1930)

Wang, S.-K., & Han, S. (2010). Six C's of motivation. In M. Orey (Ed.), Emerging perspectives on learning, teaching, and technology. Global Text Project, funded by the Jacob Foundation, Zurich, Switzerland. Creative Commons 3.0 Attribution Licence.

When will the COVID-19 pandemic end? (n.d.). *McKinsey*. Retrieved September 2, 2021, from https://www.mckinsey.com/industries/healthcare-systems-and-services/our-insights/when-will-the-covid-19-pandemic-end

ENDNOTES

[1] From the joint statement by ILO, FAO, IFAD and WHO: *Impact of COVID-19 on people's livelihoods, their health and our food systems*. (2020). Retrieved September 2, 2021, from https://www.who.int/news/item/13-10-2020-impact-of-covid-19-on-people's-livelihoods-their-health-and-our-food-systems

[2] From the World Health Organization: *Shortage of personal protective equipment endangering health workers worldwide*. (n.d.). Retrieved September 2, 2021, from https://www.who.int/news/item/03-03-2020-shortage-of-personal-protective-equipment-endangering-health-workers-worldwide

[3] From the Centers for Disease Control and Prevention: CDC. (2020, February 11). *COVID-19 Vaccination*. Centers for Disease Control and Prevention. https://www.cdc.gov/coronavirus/2019-ncov/vaccines/distributing/steps-ensure-safety.html

[4] From BBC.com news: Covax: How many Covid vaccines have the US and the other G7 countries pledged? (2021, June 11). *BBC News*. https://www.bbc.com/news/world-55795297

[5] From McKinsey & Company: *When will the COVID-19 pandemic end? | McKinsey*. (2021). Retrieved September 2, 2021, from https://www.mckinsey.com/industries/healthcare-systems-and-services/our-insights/when-will-the-covid-19-pandemic-end

Chapter 12
Worldbuilding, Gaming, and Multiliteracies in an Online First-Year Seminar

Brian Angus McKenzie
Maynooth University, Ireland

ABSTRACT

This chapter provides a case study of the use of worldbuilding for role-playing games as the foundation for a first year multiliteracies seminar. The author provides an overview of teaching and learning during the pandemic in the Irish context. The chapter provides practical advice on using a MediaWiki installation as the infrastructure for worldbuilding projects. The author shows how this imparts important digital literacies and allows for a critical apprehension of Wikipedia itself. The author argues that online learning and professional development benefit from a multiliteracies approach and, furthermore, that worldbuilding is a useful strategy for overcoming the limitations of online learning while at the same time achieving rigorous learning outcomes.

"*Every great or even every very good writer makes the world over according to his own specifications. It's akin to style, what I'm talking about, but it isn't style alone. It is the writer's particular and unmistakable signature on everything he writes. It is his world and no other.*"

Raymond Carver, On Writing

DOI: 10.4018/978-1-7998-7271-9.ch012

Worldbuilding, Gaming, and Multiliteracies in an Online First-Year Seminar

INTRODUCTION

In the wake of the global pandemic the "Near Futures" related to work, citizenship, and personhood that Bill Cope and Mary Kalantzis identified (2013) have arrived sooner and with more immediacy than perhaps we expected. Individuals and communities confronted important questions about inequality, governance, personal agency, and the nature and conditions of work.

The pandemic created acute conditions for teaching and learning. As Kurt Squire remarks, the pandemic "laid bare the thin veneer masking existing educational inequities" (Squire 2021, p. 2). Even where digital capacity existed, Squire points out that traditional educational paradigms proved incapable of overcoming isolation, providing a sense of place, or offering collaborative, social learning experiences in the context of the pandemic (Squire 2021). As practitioners and officials assess and plan post-pandemic educational policy, Vygotsky's argument for the fundamental importance of social interaction as precondition for learning is important to remember (Ramirez and Squire, 2015).

This chapter offers a case study of online learning that used worldbuilding for gaming as its foundation. The context was a first-year online seminar in an Irish university delivered during the Covid-19 pandemic. The objective of this chapter is to offer an example of how this pedagogy works in practice to build community and support students while achieving key multiliteracies learning outcomes relating to research, writing, teamwork, and information and digital literacies. The conceptualization of multiliteracies by Cope and Kalantzis (2013) is, I argue, a compelling critical premise for instructional design, one that opens creative spaces for instructors. This chapter shows the utility and success of pairing worldbuilding for gaming as a mode of teaching with a multiliteracies as a course outcome in an online educational context.

FIRST-YEAR SEMINARS: BACKGROUND

Access to higher education in Ireland is granted through a terminal written state examination, the Leaving Certificate. This exam focuses on prescribed content, for example *King Lear* for English. Students spend the final two years of secondary school preparing for the exam which is characterized by "banking" of content rather than dialogical education (Freire, 1996). Although more research is needed, at the conclusion of their first year of university study one cohort of Irish students reported that the Leaving Certificate had failed to prepare them for university work (O'Leary & Scully, 2018). The study notes that students expressed frustration that the strategies for a successful Leaving Certificate center on rote learning and memorization which did not transfer to university assessments that required the ability to evaluate and analyze information (O'Leary & Scully, 2018).

Many higher education institutions have created first-year seminars to promote student success and help students transition to higher education. By design these small classes help with peer group formation, academic socialization, and the development of information literacy, writing, and research skills. Research indicates that robust, credit-bearing seminars have a positive impact on student retention as well as students' feelings of success and satisfaction (Keup & Barefoot, 2005; Padgett et al., 2013; Starke et al., 2001).

In developing Critical Skills, the first-year seminar at Maynooth University, I adopted a multiliteracies approach to its curriculum. This was a result of the tension between an institutional view which saw the programme as a means of reforming the under-graduate curriculum to impart "employability" skills and the desire of academic staff to impart a critical literacy to students (See Gee et al., 2019, for a comprehensive discussion of the alignment between neo-liberalism and educational reform). The multiliteracies approach provides a way for instructors to embrace the "emancipatory views of education's possibilities" while rhetorically satisfying a political-educational context that emphasizes personal "capacities" and the "knowledge economy" (Cope & Kalantzis, 2013, p. 115). Crucially, this approach offers an alternative to the "tyranny of content" and allows for the creation of a student-centered curriculum (Petersen et al., 2020). Critical Skills has increased participating Bachelor of Arts student retention by 7% to 13% per year since its creation in 2015 (Nestor, 2019). Its success is a result of a community of practice dedicated to the program, an emphasis on peer group formation, and the teaching of multiliteracies with wide academic, personal, and professional applicability.

Critical Skills uses a multiliteracies approach informed by the Association of College and Research Library's *Framework for Information Literacy in Higher Education* (ACRL, 2015). Both the ACRL and the multiliteracies approach emphasize the recognition and development of learner dispositions. Take, for example, the "microdynamics of pedagogy," to use Cope and Kalantzis's felicitous phrasing (2013, p. 128), involved in a first-year student learning how to find a peer-reviewed journal article on a university library search engine. The ACRL encourages students to view searching as "strategic exploration." As a starting point, therefore, we approach this as a novel class activity and experience for students. We devote a class to this metaphor that unpacks both elements—strategic searching and discovery—in the context of hands-on use of our library's federated search engine as well as Google Scholar. The ACRL frame "Information Has Value" is also a powerful way for students to understand the nature of information privilege as they explore expensive databases. Thus, even before students get to the mechanics of setting date ranges on the search engine, the Critical Skills class has used a multiliteracies approach to frame this new experience as rewarding, exciting, empowering, and creative.

The ACRL framework itself can be difficult for students to engage with (Hsieh et al., 2021). However, it is a powerful approach for instructors in higher education who are interested in achieving literacies skills transfer between the academic, personal, and civic life of learners (Kuglitsch, 2015). In my years of using the framework I have found that an effective strategy is to introduce a frame conceptually and at a high level, and then immediately provide a practical application for students. For example, I use examples of different waves of feminism to illustrate Scholarship as Conversation. Another example of this frame is Charles Darwin's use of the work of Charles Lyell and Thomas Malthus to develop the theory of natural selection, and Darwin's own correspondence with Alfred Wallace. These examples can be given practical application for students in their own writing through discussions of paraphrasing, quoting, the value of referencing, and "They Say/I Say" exercises.

In terms of written texts, the multiliteracies emphasis on meaning-making is also a powerful way to understand academic genres such as the monograph or journal article. As students learn to see the meaning in and of texts, they become better able to produce meaning by the rules and constraints of specific genres and rhetorical situations (Zawilski, 2020).

PANDEMICAL TEACHING AND LEARNING

The pandemic upended our approach. Maynooth University transitioned from in-person teaching to online delivery overnight on March 13, 2020. At the conclusion of the semester, it was clear that achieving the class goals, especially those relating to socialization and peer group formation, would be difficult in an online context. Student access to the necessary hardware and broadband infrastructure was inconsistent; domestic situations were conducive to study for some students but not for others; access to supports—learning but also mental health and student services broadly—was difficult (Maynooth Students' Union, 2020). The challenges of online learning were exacerbated by personal losses, illness, and the stringent conditions of Ireland's lock down. In short, the pandemic's effects on the well-being of students (Grubic et al., 2020) added an urgency to the goals of the class while making them much harder to achieve.

As a result, for the summer 2020 iteration of Critical Skills I used worldbuilding as the basis for a complete redesign of the class. Central to my thinking was the idea that the pandemic, the sacrifices demanded by the state of its citizens, and the so-called digital transformation of the workplace and university make the teaching of multiliteracies an imperative. Recognizing that the aftermath of the pandemic will occasion serious debates about the nature of the status quo, any graduate can benefit professionally, civically, and personally by possessing multimodal writing, numeracy, and ICT skills. The ACRL's 2015 articulation of the importance this approach is even more compelling now, "Students have a greater role and responsibility in creating new knowledge, in understanding the contours and the changing dynamics of the world of information, and in using information, data, and scholarship ethically" (ACRL, 2015). Having decided an approach, I promoted the class through social media using memes and short videos. Figure 1 and Figure 2 are examples of social media promotion for the class.

Figure 1. Script and screen-capture of promotional video

Figure 2. Example of meme used to promote worldbuilding class

WORLDBUILDING FOR GAMING AND LEARNING

Redesigning Critical Skills around worldbuilding and gaming offered an innovative solution to the challenges of delivering a first-year seminar online in the context of a global pandemic. Worldbuilding is an ideal digital writing project for promoting critical literacy and critical reflections on contemporary issues (Tomin & Jenson, 2021). Worldbuilding also can build disciplinary expertise in writing transfer and digital literacies. In the context of the global Covid-19 pandemic where isolation and loss characterized the student experience, collaborative worldbuilding offered a powerful means of building solidarity and community. Worldbuilding gave students the agency to imagine and articulate a speculative setting that was personal and meaningful. Through worldbuilding they reflected on their roles as citizens and scholars in our crisis-stricken world.

I structured the class around the collaborative worldbuilding framework of Trent Hergenrader (2018). A key requirement of the students' speculative fiction was that it apply academic research. Individual learning journals afforded a formal space for students to record and reflect on their academic research. The academic content was a blend of synchronous seminars and asynchronous recordings used primarily to offer instructions on software. Students used Microsoft Teams to hold meetings and plan their worldbuilding. I marked students on their speculative fiction writing, academic research, teamwork, and low-risk ACRL frames quizzes.

Setting is fundamental to games. In addition to providing the mechanical, rule-bound possibilities, settings offer the narrative context and the space in which players together construct meaning and experience agency. The settings created by students for this course were suitable for use with fantasy RPGs such as *Dungeons & Dragons* or science fiction RPGs such as *Starfinder* or *Traveller*. "Fictive worlds" are one of two components (the other being events) that make up a game narrative (Salen et al., 2004, p. 402). Setting makes the game; it is arguably so important that a compelling setting allows a game to transcend media. Games which began as computer-based, the *Fallout* franchise for example, are now successful as board games or RPGs. The award-winning book and television series *The Expanse* began as a setting for a science fiction RPG (Orbit Books, 2011). For a class that uses writing for gaming as its starting point, worldbuilding is an effective pedagogical strategy. It is a core activity of gaming whether a student is studying computer science and wants to make a digital game or a student wants to make a table-top RPG. Examples of the primacy of setting are plentiful which makes convincing students of its importance an easy task.

"Worldbuilding," explains Trent Hergenrader (2018, p. 18), "Is the process by which an author creates an imaginary world that takes into account the varied social and cultural forces at play, how these forces work in concert as a coherent system, and how in a work of fiction the details of the imaginary world often emerge by way of narrative". Worldbuilding is compelling as an assessed academic exercise because of the opportunities speculative fiction offers for deploying disciplinary knowledge. Students as authors use fictional worlds to imagine, explore, and extrapolate the consequences of contemporary issues and social forces (Hergenrader, 2018; Tomin & Jenson, 2021). Worldbuilding is so effective at promoting critical thinking about contemporary issues that it can be regarded as a "strategic tool" for instructors (Martin & Sneegas, 2020, p. 20).

The collaborative worldbuilding model created by Hergenrader is particularly robust and tailor-made for classroom adoption. He provides detailed suggestions for class design, resources, and numerous examples of student work at each stage. A short but lively theoretical introduction makes a compelling case for worldbuilding and addresses pedagogical skeptics (Hergenrader, 2018).

Students start with foundational work. They determine the genre of their world fiction. My students chose to create classical science fiction and fantasy worlds. In our discussions about genre students expressed a desire to avoid post-apocalyptic or dystopian worlds because they felt as if this would too closely mirror their ongoing experience of living through a pandemic. They wanted their worlds to provide an imaginative escape.

After deciding genre, students determine their world's scope. Scope can be small—think of the garden as an entire world in *Mrs. Frisby and the Rats of NIMH*—or large, the solar system of *The Expanse* series. The worlds are made manageable by using focal points—important locations where the action takes place. Regardless of the scope of the world, the number of focal points will be the same to make the assignment achievable over a series of weeks not months or years. For example, in *The Expanse* not every space station of settlement on the moon or Mars is detailed. Conversely, a garden can have dozens of focal points: the vegetable patch, the half-buried bucket, the bird feeder, the shed, etc.

The sequence or timeline of the world is another important decision at this early stage. As Hergenrader explains, "Collaborative worldbuilders must contemplate not only how their world works in the present, but how it came to be, and to consider different directions in which it may be heading in the future" (Hergenrader, 2018, p. 36). Students conceptualize a beginning to their world, a "point of present," and indicate possible futures. My students were initially intimidated by this but a few examples can show that sequence does not entail a Big Bang to Heat Death timeline. The opening crawl of the first the first Star Wars movie, *A New Hope*, is an easy way to illustrate sequence to players. Figure 3 shows the opening crawl for *A New Hope*.

Figure 3. The Opening Crawl from Star Wars Episode 4 ("Star Wars Opening Crawl," 2021)

Worldbuilding, Gaming, and Multiliteracies in an Online First-Year Seminar

The beginning of this world is literally "a long time ago." We learn that the point of present the characters find themselves in is a civil war between rebels and the Galactic Empire, that there is a Death Star weapon, and that Princess Leia is racing home with its plans. Speculation about the future is easy. Will Leia get away? Will the rebels win? Will the Death Star destroy planets?

One group of students creating a sci-fi world decided that its beginning would be the day it was colonized by intergalactic settlers, that its point of present would involve a political conflict between an autocratic ruler and revolutionaries, and that future concerns for characters in this world revolve around the economic exploitation of a resource that is a galactic commodity. A group of students creating a fantasy world decided that it started in the aftermath of a war between gods, that the point of present is centuries after this war when the defeated gods are re-emerging, and that the future would be determined by how humans, who were not involved in the initial war of the gods, aid the defeated gods.

Students also create a rough, tentative map of their world at this early stage. Mapping is an important but potentially difficult activity. Maps of fantasy worlds are notoriously unrealistic and geography as a discipline is now contributing greatly to worldbuilding as a critical exercise (Acks, 2017; Martin & Sneegas, 2020). The scope of the class will determine how deeply an instructor can engage with the geography of worlds. In fact, for some worlds the issue will not arise at all. A garden like the one of the *Rats of NIMH* or the bedroom in *Toy Story* that is the heart of the fantasy world can be mapped realistically with ease. Similarly, a map that uses our or another known solar system as a model is straightforward. Where a student has a specific academic interest in mapping physical worlds then the instructor should make room for this. Indeed, making maps of fantasy worlds can provide hours of enjoyment. There is a risk that the map becomes a focus of student work and the instructor must be careful that they do not neglect other work by falling into a map-making rabbit hole.

Hergenrader offers some useful tips on mapping (2018, pp. 118–119). I devoted a single online seminar to mapping using Google Earth/Maps and the free version of the software Inkarnate. I made it clear to students that maps would not be assessed but that one was required. Some of the students were already familiar with map making software from previous gaming experience. I asked students to content themselves with using the maps generated in this seminar and explained that they could return to it at the conclusion of the class if they wanted to delve deeper into fantasy map making. Figure 4 and Figure 5 are examples of the maps made for the class.

The final stage in the foundational work is for students to write a short "metanarrative lead." This is a short paragraph that describes the genre, scope, and sequence of the world. It is explicitly a draft that will be revised as more details of their worlds emerge.

Worldbuilding is profoundly engaging and empowering. As the *Dungeon Master's Guide* reminds us, "Your world is more than just a backdrop for adventures…it's a place to which you can escape and witness fantastic stories unfold" (Wizards of the Coast, 2015, p. 4). This echoes the perspective Gary Alan Fine presented in his landmark book on RPGs:

Fantasy role-playing games are cultural systems. They are finely woven worlds of magic and belief. They have structure, norms, values, and a range of cultural artifacts, which if not physically real, are real to those who participate in them, and presumably (if I can stretch the metaphor) are real to the characters that inhabit these worlds. (2002, p. 123)

Figure 4. Map of the student world Atlas

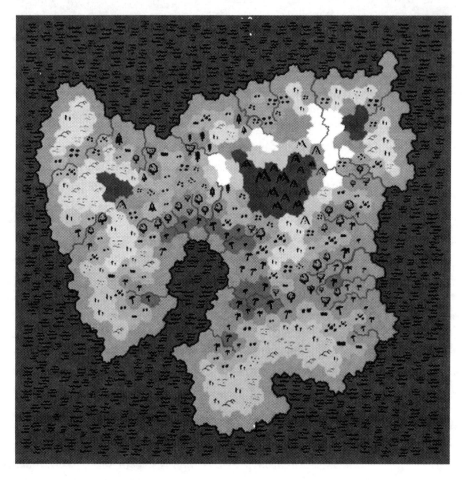

Worldbuilding allows students to create a world of their own imagining; it allows them to write with their own voice about issues important and relevant to them. And it does so as part of an academic activity that achieves "classic" learning outcomes in research, writing, information literacy, and teamwork skills.

Agency, Social Structures, and Frameworks for Fictional Worlds

Hergenrader's randomization mechanic provides the engine for writing and academic speculation. He provides a worldbuilding card deck that can be downloaded (https://www.collaborativeworldbuilding.com/). You lay out individual cards for each substructure. You then deal one numeric card to each substructure card, and then one trending card to each substructure. Numeric values indicate the prevalence or presence of the substructure in that society. A "1" indicates that there is a low level (either in terms of abundance or tolerance) of this substructure and a "5" indicates a high level. Trending cards indicate if that structure is stable or undergoing a change in a society. The deck is constituted to created "balanced" worlds which nevertheless possess some clear points of tension (Hergenrader, 2018).

Figure 5. Map of the student world Brodewell

Table 1. Trent Hergenrader's structures for fictional worlds (2018, p. 11)

Governance	Economics	Social Relations	Cultural Influences
Government presence Rule of law Social services	Economic strength Wealth distribution Agricultural production and trade	Race relations Class relations Gender relations Sexual orientation relations	Military influence Religious influence Technology influence Influence of arts and culture

A significant portion of a class should be used to discuss and interpret the results of the worldbuilding deck with students. A fun activity is to ask the class to generate a worldbuilding deck result that reflects their own university, locality, and country. For example, my Irish students gave Ireland a "3" in sexual orientation relations but indicated that it was trending up. They gave religious influence a "4," trending down. Students can also discuss the nature of their favorite fictional worlds for inspiration. Figure 6 shows the results of a random world generated by the worldbuilding deck.

To Hergenrader's structures I added an optional characteristic based on discussions with a student: notable physical or ecological aspects of the world. This trait should be used with caution and only after explaining, critiquing, and discussing examples of environmental determinism with students. In other words, physical or ecological features of the world should be used critically. For example, the desert nature of Frank Herbert's Arrakis or the low-gravity vacuum-precarity of the Belters in *The Expanse* open the door for a powerful look at how social structures influence and affect resource scarcity. Nevertheless, the temptation of a vulgar determinism can be compelling to students so unless a student articulates a specific academic interest in emphasizing an environmental aspect of the world this characteristic need not be emphasized.

Figure 6. Worldbuilding deck results

Van Richten's Guide to Ravenloft, a recent *Dungeons & Dragons* book, provides excellent writing prompts relating to the culture of fictional worlds. Although intended for the creation of horror genre worlds, these questions will generate interesting content for any world (Wizards of the Coast, 2021, p. 43):

- What does the culture fear?
- What does the culture consider taboo?
- What is scarce, and how do inhabitants compensate for this scarcity?
- Who or what does the culture inflict harm upon?
- How does the culture treat outsiders?
- What values does the culture hold that not everyone abides by?
- How does the culture prevent change?

This early stage of worldbuilding is enjoyable and shows students the rich potential for bringing academic interests to bear on speculative fiction writing. Hergenrader's process is also accessible, and students found his text to be clear and engaging.

Worldbuilding in the context of the pandemic was a way for students to express agency. Civic participation in the pandemic was characterized by a distinct lack of agency. Opportunities to volunteer were non-existent unless you possessed specialized skills. "Doing your part" involved staying in your home and avoiding other people. Worldbuilding allowed students to create characters who were agentic, who were able to play an active role in the crises and events unfolding in their fantasy worlds. Indeed, worldbuilding allowed for a fascinating exploration of the tensions between structure and agency. Students frame the actions of institutions and individuals in their worlds in relation to its cultural and societal structures. This in turn presents an opportunity for an awakening of their critical consciousness. In other words, a student's critical-speculative worldbuilding provides an invitation to reflect on their own lived experience. The psychologist Anna Stetsenko (2020) characterizes personal agency as actual worldbuilding: "We do not passively dwell in the world, but instead co-create and co-author it together with other people—thus simultaneously realizing the world and ourselves" (p. 53).

Class Logistics and Infrastructure

Before going into more detail of my adaptation of Hergenrader's framework it is useful to review the teaching infrastructure of the class. The transition of Irish universities to online teaching was done with short notice in March 2020 and again in September 2020. The loss of revenue from international students decimated Irish universities (McMorrow, 2020). Because the move to online teaching on both occasions was seen as a "temporary" and "emergency" measure and as a result of fiscal constraints, the government made very few additional resources available to instructors. In an effort to close the digital divide the Irish government did increase funding to students to purchase computers and broadband. In practical terms this resulted in being limited to the use of Microsoft Teams for online teaching supplemented with the Moodle virtual learning environment. Production of high-quality asynchronous content was particularly challenging given the lack of resources.

Nevertheless, the nature of the summer Critical Skills class mitigated these constraints. The class was small, twelve students. Teamwork is a key learning goal of Critical Skills and unlike my less fortunate colleagues who were forced to deliver lectures with Microsoft Teams, I was able to use it on this occasion for its intended purpose: the management and development of team projects. This presented an opportunity for students to develop teamwork skills in a digital environment. I used the Comprehensive Assessment of Team Member Effectiveness (CATME) developed and hosted by Purdue University to scaffold student teamwork and its assessment. Student groups of four created their own Microsoft Teams pages. The use of Microsoft Teams contributed to the development of students' digital literacies and opened a conversation about employer-gathered data analytics and the right to disconnect.

If innovative pedagogy allows for an ascent into the higher realms of student engagement and creativity one still travels there on class structure and logistics. The scaffolding of the worldbuilding assignment was, therefore, one of the most important aspects of the class design. Moodle possesses useful tools for promoting student engagement and allowing instructors to identify where support is needed. Here too, I had an important conversation about how I would use Moodle's data analytics. I organized the Moodle page with an introductory section, two content sections—one for information literacy the other for teamwork skills, and then by week according to the stages of the worldbuilding project. Students initially had access only to the class syllabus and unlocked the rest of the Moodle page by completing a short unassessed syllabus quiz. Each week included a checklist for the student to complete in line with the pace and intended progression of the worldbuilding project. An anonymous Padlet (this is akin to virtual post-it notes) wall on Moodle served as an open FAQ. I emailed students in advance of the first class and asked them to post a response to the following question to the Moodle discussion forum:

"What does 'online learning community' mean to you and how can the instructor and students support each other in building one?"

Weekly individual learning journals and articles produced for the team's world were the primary basis for the course grade. The latter grade was adjusted up or down based on an assessment of teamwork skills as evidenced through documentation (primarily minutes of meetings) on Microsoft Teams and a peer survey through CATME. Each team was required to produce a 4000-word metanarrative of their world which served as an overview of the history and current issues of their worlds. In addition, students wrote eight individual articles to contribute to their team's world. Figure 7 shows the guidelines provided to students for the Learning Journal assessment.

Figure 7. Guidelines for learning journal

Critical Skills Learning Journal

The Critical Skills Learning Journal serves three important functions:

1. It is an individual summary and record of your daily learning for the class. You use the learning journal to record what you have done and how much time you spent doing it.
2. It provides evidence of the application of your academic research—crucially, how you applied your academic interest to the worldbuilding project.
3. It provides an opportunity for reflective learning.

We will use a Moodle Learning Journal starting Week 2. This is a private journal that only your instructor can view. Each week's entry should have three components that reflect the three functions of the journal.

Reflective components serve as place where you write about what you are doing well in the class and what you are struggling with or need to improve. What is working well for you that you should keep doing? Is there something you need to start or stop doing to improve your learning? Another way to think about reflective writing is as a three-step process: a description of a learning experience, an analysis of it, and plans going forward based on the experience. Like Application entries, you need to complete a Reflective entry once a week, and the word count is the same, 250-500 words.

Record components are a short statement of what you did, how much time it required, and why you did it. Some examples:

"July 31. Spent an hour reading Alicia Garza on BLM so that I can better represent police brutality and racism in my world."

"August 2. Spent an hour looking for sources on creatures that live in aquatic cave systems to get ideas for animals in our world. Found two good sources and added them to MS Teams site."

"August 3. Worked at Tesco today—no formal work on the world but thought about it a lot."

There should be a record entry for every day of the group project. This should not be retroactively completed.

No word count—bullet point your efforts for the week.

Application of Research components detail how you have applied your academic knowledge to world building. These are longer, more substantive entries, but you only must complete one at the end of each week. An application of research entry should be between 250 and 500 words. It is *crucial* that these reflective entries provide a clear explanation of how you have applied your academic research to the project. Refer to the exemplar document.

The instructor will give you feedback on entries throughout the course.

Exemplars are powerful tools for helping students. They are especially important in the Irish context because the rote learning and narrow preparation of the Leaving Certificate leaves students unprepared for assessments that are not exams (O'Leary & Scully, 2018). However, in my experience Irish students conditioned for exams by years of studying prescribed content can too closely mimic an exemplar, not only in structure but style and content. Years of preparation for the Leaving Certificate also produce risk-averse students. This disposition limits creativity. Even worse, however, these students may react with anxiety and frustration to an "atypical" form of assessment. It is essential to be transparent about every aspect of the assignment, from the learning goals and the premises and assumptions of the instructor to the specifics of how a final grade will be assessed. Given these considerations I typically do provide exemplars for students, either student or instructor-created exemplars. Figure 8 provides an example of a Learning Journal exemplar. Figure 9 is an example of a student article informed by academic research.

Collaboration and Peer Group Formation

A key goal of the class was to help students form meaningful bonds and share rewarding experiences through collaborative worldbuilding. As a matter of necessity the class focused on the development of digital literacies. Digital communication and digital collaboration became foundational skills for participation. Recent research shows the potential of technology and digital literacy instructional design to contribute to social-emotional literacies (Blau et al., 2020).

Each worldbuilding team created a dedicated project site on Microsoft Teams. I provided recorded tutorial screencasts to teach the basics of the application. I also assigned required readings on professional boundaries and the "right to disconnect."

The temptation for students to collaborate through pre-existing social media channels or messaging applications was strong. However, compulsory use of Teams provided me with empirical evidence to assess collaboration. It also offered a practical space to create shared content through Microsoft Word and host project files. For example, CATME provides template documents for team charters, roles, and meeting minutes. Student teams worked on these through their Teams sites. The calendar function allowed for the scheduling of team meetings that were integrated with students' university emails. Students used the Planner and To Do applications to track project deadlines and milestones. Achieving student "buy in" on the use of Teams was a challenge. However, students ultimately accepted the importance of offering empirical evidence of collaboration as well as my arguments concerning the transferability and future applicability of proficiency with Microsoft Teams. Student frustration with Teams centered on perceptions of its mobile functionality as poor.

MS Teams was important as an official, assessable space. However, it is also important to afford students an informal, private space to discuss a class among themselves. I openly acknowledged this but implored students to respect privacy if they did create such a space. Privacy expectation is an important area of research (Miltgen & Peyrat-Guillard, 2014); my students certainly did not possess the level of privacy concerns I expressed. For example, I pointed out that sharing personal phone numbers was a breach of professional boundaries. What if someone in the class is not comfortable sharing their number? How will a student be perceived if they do not want to join an informal group? I reminded students that the Padlet wall on Moodle was anonymous. The use of breakout rooms during class was another strategy I used to provide students with informal spaces to discuss the class.

Figure 8. Exemplar for an "Application of Research" Learning Journal entry

> This week I read Burrin, P., 1996. *France under the Germans: Collaboration and Compromise*. New Press.
>
> This is a great book that will definitely help a lot with our speculative fiction. Burrin provides several case studies that investigate and illustrate the difference and nature of 'accommodation' vs 'collaboration' with the German occupation of France in the Second World War.
>
> Burrin distinguishes between Accommodation and Collaboration. Accommodation is more than adaptation but less than collaboration. Accommodation at the most basic level was doing what a person had to do not to starve. However, accommodation can also involve political and economic opportunism. For example, Burrin provides a scathing analysis of how French publishers accommodated themselves to the policies of the German occupiers: they agreed not to publish certain texts and pushed forward other texts that the Germans viewed favorably (324-341).
>
> Burrin shows how Frederic Joliot-Curie, the 1935 Nobel Laureate and France's most advanced researcher in nuclear technology, accommodated German rule. He agreed to work 'alongside' a group of German scientists as a condition of keeping his lab open. He continued his research even after Paul Langevin, his boss, was arrested for being an outspoken critic of Vichy, Nazism, and fascism. Joliot-Curie eventually changed his mind, but the Germans benefitted immensely from his work (317).
>
> Collaboration was easily defined and 'recognizable' in the aftermath of liberation when trials and purges occurred. However, collaboration does not capture the complexity of living under occupation. It is easier to single out collaboration, but any occupation depends on accommodation.
>
> Burrin concludes that three factors determine the extent of accommodation and collaboration. If the occupation policy is harsh then both will be minimal. However, if the occupation policy allows a semblance of normality then the likelihood of accommodation increases. The second factor is the existence of alternatives, or expectations about the future. If people think that nothing will change going forward, then they are more likely to collaborate. In the case of France, Germany seemed invincible through 1941. The final factor is social cohesion. Where there is strife collaboration is likely. French society before the war was deeply divided. People used the occupation as a chance to 'settle scores' with their political opponents.
>
> Our world involves an occupation by a group called the 'Anguses' who remain behind the scenes as much as possible. I'm going to use the Burrin analysis to develop my characters. I'm particularly interested in showing how a judge could easily switch from enforcing one set of laws to another—the 'rule of law' is a principle of authority but the content is arbitrary.

Our use of Microsoft Teams was nearly comprehensive in terms of using it to work collaboratively and generate significant content. Although its use was incidental to worldbuilding, student engagement and "take up" of this digital tool was commensurate with their investment in the assignment for which the tool was used. Because collaborative worldbuilding is so powerfully engaging it resulted in students acquiring a high degree of familiarity with Microsoft Teams as a tool for digital collaboration. Figure 10 is an example of minutes from a student team meeting.

Worldbuilding, Gaming, and Multiliteracies in an Online First-Year Seminar

Figure 9. Student article influenced by academic research on surveillance and social credit

Gods-Eye

"G0ds-Eye" is Brodewells highly advanced surveillance system, its headquarters is located inside Brodewells main government buildings in a restricted underground level, It is said that this building is once of the most well gauded and secretive buildings in the whole world, at its fingertips is one of the most advanced surveillance and defence systems in the world, storing Yottabytes of data on its citizens.

military personnel can monitor the day to day life of every citizen, by utilising their advanced CCTV system, fake birds, drones and UAV's which are all equipped with highly advanced facial recognition software which automatically logs and flags any potential cases of misbehaviour or suspicious activities for analysis by military personnel. At a click of a button, every single detail of a person can be pulled up, including their name and address, movements, social interactions, conversations, travel history and work performance.

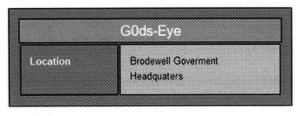

Previously before brodewells advancements in technology old green watchtowers were scattered throughout the city which were manned 24/7, however, these eventually became obsolete as technology advanced and could easily outperform any watch guard, who were also frequently bribed to turn a blind eye. The last remaining guard tower can be seen in the high peaks of the eastern mountains beside Lake Louise which was once used as a place of worship before the civil war. This was the last operational watchtower which purposely stayed opened until only recently due to defectors using this area to preach Peroganism, it was later decommissioned and replaced with orbital UAV's.

BrodeEye226

BrodeEye226 is a remotely piloted aircraft developed by Brode research inc, The highly advanced highflying UAV is designed for reconnaissance, surveillance, target recognition, and detection. it is equipped with state of the art surveillance and defence payload including camera platforms, synthetic aperture radar (SAR), sonar, communication relay systems, GM-114 Hellfire missiles, GBU-12 Paveway II bombs, Brode 237B missiles. The first flight of the aircraft was conducted on December 8th 2002 marking the event of Charles Brode birthday. The combat drone has a maximum take-off weight of 8,255kg.

The drone is capable of reaching altitudes up to 90,000ft. It has a maximum speed of 700k and endurance of 8760.01 hours. At its core is a small Brode nuclear reactor which can power the drone for up to 12 months, making it one of the highest endurance UAV's ever built.

In the end-of-class survey I asked an open-ended question: "What is the most important thing that you learned in this course." One student wrote, "Communicating completely online." Another simply wrote "teamwork." Although the class was small—twelve students—and six students participated in the survey it is, nevertheless, significant that two of these students identified collaboration skills as the primary learning outcome for them in a class where they created fictional worlds for use in RPGs. This speaks to the importance in instructional design of understanding that innovative pedagogy need not obfuscate "traditional" learning outcomes. Just as the map is not the territory, a specific learning outcome hardly prescribes a pedagogical design or approach. A student-centered approach requires a time commitment by a teacher to instructional design but it also requires creativity, flexibility, and empathy.

Figure 10. Example of student meeting minutes recorded on MS Teams

Meeting Date: 30/07/20	Start Time: 7 pm End Time: 7.40 pm Summary of Meeting
1. Attendance	*Full attendance:* [redacted]
2. Purpose of Meeting	*To talk about the team contract and meta-narrative.*
3. Discuss work completed since last meeting.	*Small blurb written that can now be expanded and be the metanarrative. Learning journals started.*
4. Summarize work completed during meeting	1. *Discussed the different topics: gender relations, art and culture etc.* 2. *Decided where the world was located and what it was called and what the race of the people were called.* 3. *[redacted] took on the responsibility to detail the world map.* 4. *Everyone gave ideas about the world. However, [redacted] took the responsibility to write it up. All said that each person would make small edits to it too.* 5. *The next meeting was then scheduled for Monday at 10 am.*
5. Review action items to be completed after meeting	1. *Meeting minutes to be uploaded by [redacted].* 2. *[redacted] to schedule the next meeting on Microsoft Teams.* 3. *[redacted] to start on the meta-narrative.* 4. *[redacted] to expand the map.* 5. *All to complete learning journals.*
6. Schedule next meeting	*10 am Monday 03/08* *Duration: 1 hour*
7. Recording secretary	*[redacted] 30/07*

DIGITAL COMPETENCE, MEDIAWIKI, AND CRITICAL LITERACY

Students coordinated their work through Microsoft Teams. However, we created the worlds on a MediaWiki installation on a subdomain of our program's website. MediaWiki is an outstanding platform for worldbuilding. In addition to this practical application, the use of MediaWiki also offers:

- An opportunity to critically reflect on issues of content creation, systemic bias, and hegemony on Wikipedia itself while students write the content of their own worlds;
- A means of developing ICT skills and important digital literacies;
- A piece of software that is recognizable, professional, and tailor-made in functionality for encyclopedic content.

In the past I have successfully used Wikipedia for class activities to promote information literacies and writing skills (McKenzie et al., 2018). Although I still have students engage critically with Wikipedia, I now avoid having students directly edit it. The negative aspects of the Wikipedia community are well-established: misogyny, perverse hierarchy, and an intolerance of newcomers (Ford & Wajcman, 2017; Halfaker et al., 2011; Jemielniak, 2014; Peake, 2015; Wagner et al., 2016). In addition to the factors which affect the student experience of editing Wikipedia, the content of Wikipedia itself is profoundly affected by systemic bias (Kumar, 2017; Menking & Rosenberg, 2021). Given the hegemonic presence

Worldbuilding, Gaming, and Multiliteracies in an Online First-Year Seminar

of Wikipedia in information searches and its widespread use by students, it is important that students have a critical understanding of the encyclopedia (Todorinova, 2015; McMahon et al., 2017).

At the same time, digital literacies, digital competencies, and digital writing and composition skills are now seen as fundamental (Baer, 2014; Fucci, 2015). Learning outcomes for this class referenced the five competencies of the European Digital Competence Framework: information and data literacy, communication and collaboration, digital content creation, safety, and problem solving (Carretero, Vuorikari, and Punie, 2017). Academic, class use of Wikipedia remains an important tool for achieving these objectives. The use of a private MediaWiki installation for digital writing offers students the experience of working work with a markup language (Wikitext) and digital composition (text and images); concurrent critical engagement with Wikipedia itself allows students to reflect on their own role as producers as well as users of information. This approach has distinct advantages over students editing actual Wikipedia: it still allows for a critical understanding of bias and systems of knowledge but in a safer (broadly construed) venue, and one that tolerates creativity, humor, and mistakes.

The installation of MediaWiki software was straightforward. I first used the web hosting control panel to create a new subdomain of the Critical Skills website. The web hosting control panel offered MediaWiki as an application to install. The software can be customized to restrict account creation and the visibility of student work. This was the only part of the process I found to be intimidating as an instructor. MediaWiki offers a useful guide to setting up a "simple private wiki" (*Manual*, n.d.). This required using the web hosting control panel to edit a file, LocalSettings.php, in the MediaWiki folder. This proved no more difficult than making changes to a document using a basic text editor. Figure 11 shows the front page of the MediaWiki installation.

Figure 11. Front page of the worldbuilding MediaWiki installation

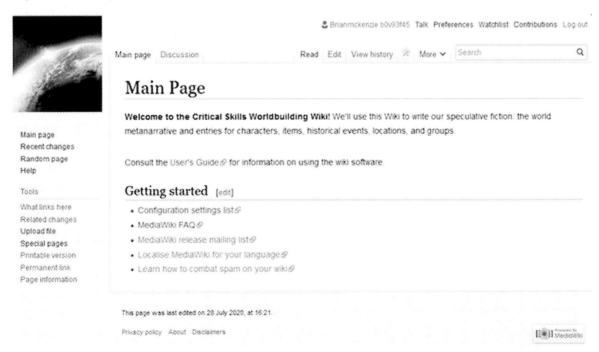

A basic MediaWiki installation such as I used for the class lacks the user-friendly, WYSIWYG editor of Wikipedia (referred to there as its "visual editor"). However, my students had no trouble using the "cheatsheet" provided by MediaWiki to format text (*Cheatsheet - MediaWiki*, n.d.). Students and I were able to incorporate more advanced Wikitext styles and formatting. The website Tables Generator generates the required Wikitext for complex tables (*Generate Tables in MediaWiki Format - Tables-Generator.Com*, n.d.).

The inclusion of infoboxes was a more challenging addition. On Wikipedia infoboxes are a type of table that provide a summary of important information. For example, the infobox of a famous person will tell when and where they were born; the infoboxes for mountains provide location and height information. I decided to limit the types of infoboxes to the main article categories used by Hergenrader: locations, groups, items, events, and characters. I then created a template page for each type of infobox using instructions I found on stackoverflow (*Sidebar - How Do You Make "Infoboxes" in Mediawiki?*, n.d.). This requires that the "ParserFunctions extension" is installed as part of MediaWiki. This appears to have been part of my default installation of MediaWiki because the instructions worked. Once one infobox template is set up the others can be generated from it by changing the parameters (e.g., changing "age" in a character infobox template to "date" for an event infobox). My Wikitext for the Infobox Historical Event Template is presented below. To create an infobox you first create the template by making a page called "Template: Infobox [insert type]". Once the template is set up, in this case for a historical event, a student need only insert the following as Wikitext: {{Infobox historical event | Event name = | Date = | Location = | Type of event = | Major figures = | Related events = }} and add the details after each "=". Table 2 provides the Wikitext to create an infobox.

Table 2. Wikitext for the Historical Event infobox

```
<div class="infobox">
<div class="infobox-title">{{{title|{{PAGENAME}}}}}</div>{{#if:{{{image|}}}|<div class="infobox-image">[[File:{{{image}}}|300px]]</div>}}
<table>
{{#if:{{{Event name|}}}|<tr>
<th>Event name</th>
<td>{{{Event name}}}</td>
</tr>}}
{{#if:{{{Date|}}}|<tr>
<th>Date</th>
<td>{{{Date}}}</td>
</tr>}}
{{#if:{{{Location|}}}|<tr>
<th>Location</th>
<td>{{{Location}}}</td>
</tr>}}
{{#if:{{{Type of event |}}}|<tr><th>Type of event</th>
<td>{{{Type of event}}}</td>
</tr>}}
{{#if:{{{Major figures|}}}|<tr>
<th>Major figures</th>
<td>{{{Major figures}}}</td>
</tr>}}
{{#if:{{{Related events|}}}|<tr>
<th>Related events</th>
<td>{{{Related events}}}</td>
</tr>}}
</table>
</div>
```

Infoboxes are a nice cosmetic feature on a worldbuilding wiki but can be difficult to implement. They lend an air of formality and professionalism to the articles that students seemed to appreciate. Their use was optional for our worldbuilding, but most students used them once I set them up and helped students insert them during classes. Figure 12 is an example of an infobox in a student article.

Figure 12. Example of an infobox used in an article for a fictional element

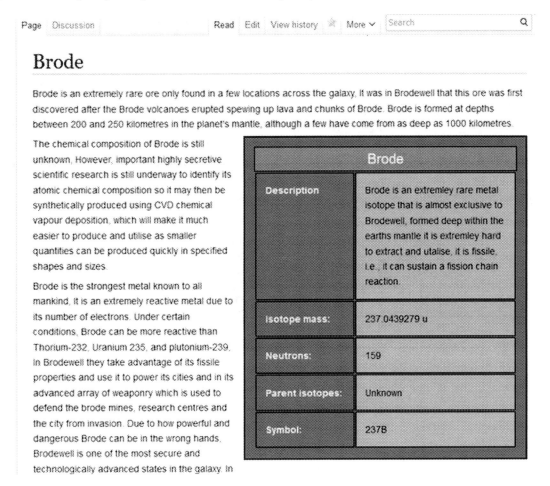

Objectivity and "Neutral Point of View"

An important decision occurred in the foundational stage: the choice of perspective. This is a crucial moment in the class for the pedagogy of critical literacy. The core work of the class entailed students writing a long "metanarrative" article on their world as a team and then contributing eight individual articles relating to historical events, items, locations, characters, and groups in the world. As they develop their own voice as writers it is important that students learn to recognize and analyze the voices of others. Students learn how tone and style aid in the construction of authority.

Wikipedia is a fascinating and engaging tool for teaching critical literacy. As students wrote their own Wiki for a world we engaged critically with Wikipedia. Hergenrader suggests that students adopt Wikipedia's "neutral point of view (NPOV)" in their own writing, but allow for "competing viewpoints and perspectives" (Hergenrader, 2018, p. 38). The actual Wikipedia policy on NPOV is: "All encyclopedic content on Wikipedia must be written from **neutral point of view** (**NPOV**), which means representing fairly, proportionately, and, as far as possible, without editorial bias, all the significant views that have been published by reliable sources on a topic" ("Wikipedia," 2019b).

The idea of a "neutral point of view" was refuted decades ago following the postmodern turn. As Menking and Rosenberg argue, "Embracing the thesis that knowledge (and knowers) are situated requires us to abandon the idea that points of view can be neutral" (Menking & Rosenberg, 2021, p. 470). Scholars of Wikipedia argue that the primary function and benefit of Wikipedia's NPOV policy is to manage editor conflict, a task that it has largely achieved (Rijshouwer, 2019, pp. 178, 182; Tkacz, 2007, p. 14).

The NPOV policy includes "proportionately" and "significance" as a condition of inclusion. In practice these subcategories of NPOV, referred to jointly as "undue weight," are used tactically by editors to push their own points of view. Content that an editor wants removed can be labelled as "undue" and the onus is on the editor who wants to include the material to provide evidence. Groups of editors form "Wikiprojects" to coordinate editing on topics of shared interest. Wikiprojects can be powerful tools to mobilize editors to enforce consensus and silence opposition on Wikipedia.

I introduce students to the controversy of the "clean Wehrmacht" on Wikipedia to illustrate important information literacy concepts from the ACRL framework: Information Creation as a Process and Authority is Constructed and Contextual. An important disposition of the creation frame is that learners "are inclined to seek out characteristics of information products that indicate the underlying creation process." Wikipedia editors' authority is based not on academic content but edit count, familiarity with its bureaucracy, and the facility with which they can deploy Wikipedia policies in content disputes (Al-Khatib et al., 2018; Peake, 2015). This prompts students to think about how authority can be context-specific but also how Wikipedia editors challenge traditional academic authority on topics with a construction of their own that reflects the norms of their community.

The myth of the "clean Wehrmacht" refers to the dominate historiographical perspective from 1958, the publication date of the convicted war criminal Erich von Manstein's memoirs, until the 1980s when it was comprehensively discredited by German historians (Stahel, 2018). Proponents of the myth downplay the role of the German army in the atrocities of World War Two, in general, and the actions of specific individuals in particular. The historian David Stahel identifies the Wikiproject Military History as the main promulgator of the clean Wehrmacht myth on Wikipedia (Stahel, 2018). Independent of Stahel's research, one Wikipedia editor, K.e.coffman, began trying to address the clean Wehrmacht myth in Wikipedia articles (Cohen, 2021). The efforts of the editor were initially blocked and the editor was subjected to harassment. The dispute eventually reached Wikipedia's highest "court," the Arbitration Committee. They ruled in favour of K.e.coffman, banned some editors, and issued a rare rebuke to the leader of a powerful Wikiproject: "project coordinators have no special roles in a content dispute" ("Wikipedia," 2019a). It is important to point out that K.e.coffman was successful only because of her vast experience as a Wikipedia editor and her familiarity with Wikipedia's bureaucracy.

The myth of the clean Wehrmacht on Wikipedia makes for a nice, short introduction to ACRL frames and Wikipedia itself. Other examples of Wikipedia's bias can be easily found. For example, one editor recently accused WikiProject Firearms of scrubbing gun violence from Wikipedia articles (Dlthewave, 2019). Instructors should use their own disciplinary interests to find examples on Wikipedia that illus-

Worldbuilding, Gaming, and Multiliteracies in an Online First-Year Seminar

trate not mere factual inaccuracies, which are actually not a significant weakness of the encyclopedia, but how systems of knowledge privilege certain voices and strategies used, in the name of "objectivity" and "neutrality," to silence others.

A critical apprehension of Wikipedia is valuable preparation for students as they begin to plan their own encyclopedia. I required students to adopt a third-person omniscient point of view because of the importance of having students use academic research to create speculative fiction. In a fiction writing class it would perhaps be useful to have students write articles from a different perspective. Nevertheless, student articles displayed a high degree of nuance and understanding regarding the production and consumption of knowledge. Figure 13 is a student article that demonstrates an awareness of the social construction of knowledge.

Figure 13. Example of a student article illustrating an awareness of systems of knowledge

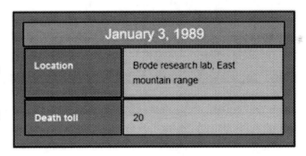

WORLDBUILDING AS AN ACADEMIC ASSESSMENT

Fantasy worlds to serve as the settings for RPGs were the "product" of student work in this class. However, the class was premised on achieving broad multiliteracies learning outcomes, particularly as related to navigating a digital, remote context for research, writing, and collaboration. As such, I embedded key digital and critical literacy instruction in the more traditionally understood—by students and institutionally—learning outcomes of improving research, writing, and teamwork skills.

Research was the most straightforward outcome to assess. Students watched two recorded lectures on the ACRL frames "Searching as Strategic Exploration" and "Research as Inquiry" and completed two short Moodle quizzes. I provided the above exemplars for research learning journal entries and how applied research might look in an actual wiki article. The learning journal provided evidence of engagement with and understanding of academic sources, and effective library research.

I assessed writing and teamwork outcomes through the content produced for the worlds' wikis. I assigned an individual grade to each world based on an assessment of its metanarrative article and every other article created for that world. I then adjusted individual marks of students up or down based on an assessment of teamwork learning outcomes. Embedding a grade for teamwork in a project rather than assessing it separately is an effective strategy made easier with the CATME software. At the completion of a team project students take an anonymous survey. They rate themselves and their teammates in five categories: 1. Contributing to the Team's Work 2. Interacting with Teammates 3. Keeping the Team on Track 4. Expecting Quality 5. Having Related Knowledge, Skills, Abilities. CATME tells students how they rated themselves, how the team rated them, and what the average of the team was for the category. CATME also flags, for student and instructors, instances where students rate themselves lower or higher than their peers rated them. The algorithm behind the survey also identifies if a team developed cliques, e.g., two students rate each other high and other students low, and vice versa. Students also have the option to provide typed comments for the instructor.

Ideally, a CATME peer evaluation should be done early in the project as a formative assessment. However, the timeline of the summer class did not allow this. Instead, I assigned readings on teamwork and held numerous "check in" meetings with teams to assess dynamics. I maintained an active presence on the MS Teams site for each worldbuilding team. Students did receive CATME feedback in time for their final piece of reflective writing. Based on a review of the CATME survey and evidence offered through documentation and activity on the MS Teams site I adjusted students' marks up or down within 15% of the over-arching mark assigned to the world. Where a team evidenced particularly strong collaboration everyone received an adjustment up.

The mark for the world itself was the primary means of capturing the writing learning outcome. Between the weekly learning journals, the metanarrative, and eight individual articles, students in this class produced more writing than in other iterations of Critical Skills I have taught. Interestingly, they did so with gusto, a fact which I attribute to the engagement offered by worldbuilding for gaming. Hergenrader writes of the "lure of endless worldbuilding" (Hergenrader, 2018, p. 131). The metanarrative suggests myriad other topics, individual articles indicate the existence of other important topics, and maps suggest their own articles—a famous battle at a bottleneck between mountain ranges, or the existence of a thriving city in a bay.

Quality of writing is a straightforward assessment based on organization, style, grammar, and ideas (my requirement that students ground their speculative fiction in academic research). Coherence and consistency are also important factors to consider when assessing writing for collaborative worldbuilding. Here again, Hergenrader's framework provides useful guidance. Articles should not contradict other articles, nor should they change the narrative of other characters or events without a detailed discussion between authors. Articles should, however, relate to each other and contribute to an immersive world for a RPG. Each team of four students produced thirty-two articles divided as equally as possible among Hergenrader's categories. The results were settings that made effective starting points for two *Dungeons*

& *Dragons* campaigns and one *Traveller* campaign. In the end-of-class survey two students identified writing benefits ("improved my confidence as a writer," "improved my writing") as the most important learning outcomes for them.

CONCLUSION

Qualitative feedback from students shows that the class achieved its key learning outcomes. More importantly, student engagement during the class and their feedback also indicates that collaborative worldbuilding was a powerful means of building connections and empathy between students in the context of isolation amid a global pandemic.

Hergenrader's worldbuilding framework is highly adaptable but its most straightforward use is in a creative writing or game design class. My use of it therefore offers some insights into the viability of worldbuilding as an approach to teaching first-year seminars. Worldbuilding takes a class out of the mold of a traditional first-year seminar or writing class.

Perhaps most significantly, my class did not teach the academic essay genre, an assignment model that students will be subjected to repeatedly during their university career. Kelly Schrum advocates digital storytelling (DST) as a replacement for the traditional academic essay: "DST challenged students to think in new ways, to ask new questions, and to interrogate the sources and ideas they were reading, researching, and developing" (Sample & Schrum, 2013, p. 95). Mark Sample, Schrum's co-author, points out the narrow, self-referential nature of the traditional essay: "I don't believe my mission as a professor is to turn my students into miniature versions of myself or of any other professor, yet that is the only function that the traditional student essay serves" (Sample & Schrum, 2013, p. 87).

Nevertheless, there is an element of university service for a first-year seminar; students expect the class to prepare them for work in other classes, and some faculty have an expectation that a first-year seminar will obviate the need to teach "remedial" content such as referencing in their own classes. My solution is to use the ACRL framework to embed a range of practical skills, such as paraphrasing, in a broader understanding of and experience with genres and multimodal composition. Devoting a first-year seminar to worldbuilding exclusively may be difficult where composition features in the learning outcomes. However, if the focus on the first-year seminar is that of "extended orientation" (Keup & Barefoot, 2005) then worldbuilding for gaming should be considered as the focus, and Hergenrader's model can be embraced. As a programmatic approach, adopting a worldbuilding approach would likely necessitate a significant amount of training for contributing faculty.

A significant question here is the importance of creating meaningful assessments, and the extent to which students will challenge themselves as writers, researchers, and members of a project team based on the meaning to which they attach to assessments. In other words, to what extent does an assignment give agency to students; to what extent does an assignment allow for meaning making by our learners? High stakes examinations are certainly meaningful, primarily punitively, but the learning outcomes achievable through them are narrow and even secondary to an exam's function of establishing rank order. In the context of a pandemic, collaborative worldbuilding resulted in a class that was engaging and empowering. Worldbuilding offers the chance for a transformative pedagogy (Cope & Kalantzis, 2013) that is experientially rich and fosters analysis and reflection. Integration of research, writing, and teamwork learning outcomes resulted in a corpus of student work that was academically rigorous and relevant to future learning.

REFERENCES

Acks, A. (2017, August 1). *Tolkien's Map and The Messed Up Mountains of Middle-earth*. https://www.tor.com/2017/08/01/tolkiens-map-and-the-messed-up-mountains-of-middle-earth/

Al-Khatib, K., Wachsmuth, H., Lang, K., Herpel, J., Hagen, M., & Stein, B. (2018). *Modeling Deliberative Argumentation Strategies on Wikipedia*. https://scholar.googleusercontent.com/scholar?q=cache:sOSvXuDA-IAJ:scholar.google.com/&hl=en&as_sdt=2005&sciodt=0,5

Arbitration/Requests/Case/German war effort. (2019a). In *Wikipedia*. https://en.wikipedia.org/w/index.php?title=Wikipedia:Arbitration/Requests/Case/German_war_effort&oldid=886462669

Association of College and Research Libraries (ACRL). (2015, February 9). *Framework for Information Literacy for Higher Education*. Association of College & Research Libraries (ACRL). https://www.ala.org/acrl/standards/ilframework

Baer, A. (2014, April 15). *Keeping Up With... Digital Writing in the College Classroom*. Association of College & Research Libraries (ACRL). https://www.ala.org/acrl/publications/keeping_up_with/digital_writing

Blau, I., Shamir-Inbal, T., & Avdiel, O. (2020). How does the pedagogical design of a technology-enhanced collaborative academic course promote digital literacies, self-regulation, and perceived learning of students? *The Internet and Higher Education, 45*, 100722. doi:10.1016/j.iheduc.2019.100722

Carretero Gomez, S., Vuorikari, R., & Punie, Y. (2017). *DigComp 2.1: The Digital Competence Framework for Citizens with eight proficiency levels and examples of use. EUR 28558 EN*. Publications Office of the European Union.

Cheatsheet—MediaWiki. (n.d.). Retrieved June 1, 2021, from https://www.mediawiki.org/wiki/Cheatsheet

Cohen, N. (2021, September 7). One Woman's Mission to Rewrite Nazi History on Wikipedia. *Wired*. https://www.wired.com/story/one-womans-mission-to-rewrite-nazi-history-wikipedia/

Cope, B., & Kalantzis, M. (2013). "Multiliteracies": New Literacies, New Learning. In M. Hawkins (Ed.), *Framing Languages and Literacies: Socially Situated Views and Perspectives* (pp. 115–145). Routledge. doi:10.4324/9780203070895-13

Dlthewave. (2019). Pro and Con: Has gun violence been improperly excluded from gun articles? In *Wikipedia*. https://en.wikipedia.org/w/index.php?title=Wikipedia:Wikipedia_Signpost/2019-03-31/Op-Ed&oldid=969726090

Fine, G. A. (2002). *Shared Fantasy*. University of Chicago Press. https://press.uchicago.edu/ucp/books/book/chicago/S/bo5949823.html

Ford, H., & Wajcman, J. (2017). 'Anyone can edit', not everyone does: Wikipedia's infrastructure and the gender gap. *Social Studies of Science, 47*(4), 511–527. doi:10.1177/0306312717692172 PMID:28791929

Freire, P. (1996). *Pedagogy of the oppressed* (New rev. ed). Penguin Books.

Fucci, M. (2015, July 9). *The Digital Competence Framework 2.0*. EU Science Hub - European Commission. https://ec.europa.eu/jrc/en/digcomp/digital-competence-framework

Gee, J. P., Hull, G., & Lankshear, C. (2019). *The New Work Order: Behind the Language of the New Capitalism*. Routledge. doi:10.4324/9780429496127

Generate tables in MediaWiki format—TablesGenerator.com. (n.d.). Retrieved June 1, 2021, from https://www.tablesgenerator.com/mediawiki_tables

Grubic, N., Badovinac, S., & Johri, A. M. (2020). Student mental health in the midst of the COVID-19 pandemic: A call for further research and immediate solutions. *The International Journal of Social Psychiatry*, *66*(5), 517–518. doi:10.1177/0020764020925108 PMID:32364039

Halfaker, A., Kittur, A., & Riedl, J. (2011). Don't bite the newbies: How reverts affect the quantity and quality of Wikipedia work. *Proceedings of the 7th International Symposium on Wikis and Open Collaboration - WikiSym '11*, 163. 10.1145/2038558.2038585

Hergenrader, T. (2018). *Collaborative Worldbuilding for Writers and Gamers*. Bloomsbury Publishing.

Hsieh, M. L., Dawson, P. H., & Yang, S. Q. (2021). The ACRL Framework successes and challenges since 2016: A survey. *Journal of Academic Librarianship*, *47*(2), 102306. doi:10.1016/j.acalib.2020.102306

Jemielniak, D. (2014). *Common Knowledge? An Ethnography of Wikipedia*. Stanford University Press. https://ebookcentral.proquest.com/lib/nuim/detail.action?docID=1680678

Keup, J., & Barefoot, B. (2005). Learning How to be a Successful Student: Exploring the Impact of First-Year Seminars on Student Outcomes. *Journal of the First-Year Experience & Students in Transition*, *17*(1), 11–47.

Kuglitsch, R. Z. (2015). Teaching for Transfer: Reconciling the Framework with Disciplinary Information Literacy. *Portal (Baltimore, Md.)*, *15*(3), 457–470. doi:10.1353/pla.2015.0040

Kumar, S. (2017). A river by any other name: Ganga/Ganges and the postcolonial politics of knowledge on Wikipedia. *Information Communication and Society*, *20*(6), 809–824. doi:10.1080/1369118X.2017.1293709

Manual:Preventing access—MediaWiki. (n.d.). Retrieved June 1, 2021, from https://www.mediawiki.org/wiki/Manual:Preventing_access

Martin, J., & Sneegas, G. (2020). *Critical Worldbuilding: Toward a Geographical Engagement with Imagined Worlds*. /paper/Critical-Worldbuilding%3A-Toward-a-Geographical-with-Martin-Sneegas/8a8d4538706af65d8479b11cbd0fcb135c32ca44

Maynooth Students' Union. (2020). *COVID-19 Survey Results*. https://www.msu.ie/news/article/6013/COVID-19-Survey-Results/

McKenzie, B., Brown, J., Casey, D., Cooney, A., Darcy, E., Giblin, S., & Mhórdha, M. N. (2018). From Poetry to Palmerstown: Using Wikipedia to Teach Critical Skills and Information Literacy in A First-Year Seminar. *College Teaching*, *66*(3), 140–147. doi:10.1080/87567555.2018.1463504

McMahon, C., Johnson, I., & Hecht, B. (2017). The Substantial Interdependence of Wikipedia and Google: A Case Study on the Relationship Between Peer Production Communities and Information Technologies. *Proceedings of the International AAAI Conference on Web and Social Media, 11*(1), Article 1. https://ojs.aaai.org/index.php/ICWSM/article/view/14883

McMorrow, C. (2020). *Coronavirus plunges universities into funding crisis*. https://www.rte.ie/news/2020/0503/1136316-covid-19-universities/

Menking, A., & Rosenberg, J. (2021). WP:NOT, WP:NPOV, and Other Stories Wikipedia Tells Us: A Feminist Critique of Wikipedia's Epistemology. *Science, Technology & Human Values, 46*(3), 455–479. doi:10.1177/0162243920924783

Miltgen, C. L., & Peyrat-Guillard, D. (2014). Cultural and generational influences on privacy concerns: A qualitative study in seven European countries. *European Journal of Information Systems, 23*(2), 103–125. doi:10.1057/ejis.2013.17

Nestor, E. (2019). *Undergraduate Curriculum Evaluation*. Maynooth University.

Neutral point of view. (2019b). In *Wikipedia*. https://en.wikipedia.org/w/index.php?title=Wikipedia:Neutral_point_of_view&oldid=901367786

O'Leary, M., & Scully, D. (2018). *The Leaving Certificate programme as preparation for higher education: The views of undergraduates at the end of their first year in university*. The Centre for Assessment Research, Policy and Practice in Education.

Orbit Books. (2011, January 23). *Leviathan Wakes: Part One*. https://www.youtube.com/watch?v=Yu0xJpCy95o

Padgett, R. D., Keup, J. R., & Pascarella, E. T. (2013). The Impact of First-Year Seminars on College Students' Life-long Learning Orientations. *Journal of Student Affairs Research and Practice, 50*(2), 133–151. doi:10.1515/jsarp-2013-0011

Peake, B. (2015, April 1). WP:THREATENING2MEN: Misogynist Infopolitics and the Hegemony of the Asshole Consensus on English Wikipedia. *Ada New Media*. https://adanewmedia.org/2015/04/issue7-peake/

Petersen, C. I., Baepler, P., Beitz, A., Ching, P., Gorman, K. S., Neudauer, C. L., Rozaitis, W., Walker, J. D., & Wingert, D. (2020). The Tyranny of Content: "Content Coverage" as a Barrier to Evidence-Based Teaching Approaches and Ways to Overcome It. *CBE Life Sciences Education, 19*(2), ar17. doi:10.1187/cbe.19-04-0079 PMID:32412836

Ramirez, D., & Squire, K. (2015). Gamification and learning. In S. P. Walz & S. Deterding (Eds.), *The Gameful World: Approaches, Issues, Applications* (pp. 629–652). MIT Press.

Rijshouwer, E. (2019). *Organizing Democracy: Power concentration and self-organization in the evolution of Wikipedia*. https://repub.eur.nl/pub/113937

Salen, K., Tekinbaş, K. S., & Zimmerman, E. (2004). *Rules of Play: Game Design Fundamentals*. MIT Press.

Sample, M., & Schrum, K. (2013). What's Wrong with Writing Essays. In D. Cohen & J. Scheinfeldt (Eds.), *Hacking the Academy: New Approaches to Scholarship and Teaching from Digital Humanities*. University of Michigan Press. https://muse.jhu.edu/chapter/833166

sidebar—How do you make "infoboxes" in mediawiki? (n.d.). *Stack Overflow*. Retrieved June 1, 2021, from https://stackoverflow.com/questions/27801082/how-do-you-make-infoboxes-in-mediawiki

Squire, K. D. (2021). From virtual to participatory learning with technology during COVID-19. *E-Learning and Digital Media*. doi:10.1177/20427530211022926

Stahel, D. (2018). The Battle for Wikipedia: The New Age of 'Lost Victories'? *The Journal of Slavic Military Studies*, *31*(3), 396–402. https://doi.org/10.1080/13518046.2018.1487198

Star Wars opening crawl. (2021). In *Wikipedia*. https://en.wikipedia.org/wiki/Star_Wars_opening_crawl

Starke, M., Harth, M., & Sirianni, F. (2001). Retention, Bonding, and Academic Achievement: Success of a First-Year Seminar. *Journal of the First-Year Experience & Students in Transition*, *13*(2), 7–36.

Stetsenko, A. (2020). Radical-Transformative Agency: Developing a Transformative Activist Stance on a Marxist-Vygotskyan Foundation. In F. Liberali, M. Dafermos, & A. T. Neto (Eds.), *Revisiting Vygotsky for Social Change: Bringing Together Theory and Practice* (pp. 31–62). Peter Lang Inc.

Tkacz, N. (2007). Power, Visibility, Wikipedia. *Southern Review: Communication. Política y Cultura*, *40*(2), 5.

Todorinova, L. (2015). Wikipedia and undergraduate research trajectories. *New Library World*, *116*(3/4), 201–212. doi:10.1108/NLW-07-2014-0086

Tomin, B., & Jenson, J. (2021). Exploring Science Fictional Futures With Secondary Students: Practicing Critical Literacy. In *Disciplinary Literacy Connections to Popular Culture in K-12 Settings*. IGI Global. doi:10.4018/978-1-7998-4721-2.ch005

Wagner, C., Graells-Garrido, E., Garcia, D., & Menczer, F. (2016). Women through the glass ceiling: Gender asymmetries in Wikipedia. *EPJ Data Science*, *5*(1), 5. https://doi.org/10.1140/epjds/s13688-016-0066-4

Wizards of the Coast. (2015). *Dungeons & Dragons Core Rulebook: Dungeon Master's Guide* (1st ed.). Dungeons & Dragons.

Wizards of the Coast. (2021). *Van Richten's Guide to Ravenloft* (1st ed.). Dungeons & Dragons.

Zawilski, B. (2020, August 31). *Rhetoric and Situations; Like Peanut Butter and Jelly*. Medium. https://medium.com/@bzawilski/rhetoric-and-situations-like-peanut-butter-and-jelly-ddb0d64e8b6c

Section 2
Exploring Literacy in Game-Based Learning

Chapter 13
Using Game-Based Learning to Improve Boys' Literacy

Minda Marshall
Lectorsa, South Africa

Marinda Marshall
Lectorsa, South Africa

ABSTRACT

This chapter foregrounds an online gamified visual intelligence innovation (eyebraingym) developed to enhance visual processing skills, improve memory and vocabulary, and increase reading fluency. The explicit aim of the innovation is to improve comprehension towards visual intelligence. Ninety-eight Grade 8 learners at a South African Boy's School completed their online development during the 2021 academic year. These learners were part of a group of students participating in a whole school reading and literacy intervention program. The innovation is an integral part of this ongoing project. Their interaction with the innovation consists of 15 sessions completed once or twice a week for 20 – 40 minutes over five months. The results of the project are positive. It shows that most participating students improved their perceptual development and reading speed (VPF) and cognitive development and comprehension skills (CDF). In addition, these outcomes transferred to improved relative efficiency when working with information (AIUF).

INTRODUCTION

Visual intelligence is the ability to find, process, understand and express or use visual information. One of the foundations of visual intelligence is reading with adequate comprehension. If then reading takes up this important role, it means that basic literacy skills are one of the foundation walls of visual intelligence. However, reading is not a natural process. Authors of reading research postulate that reading skills are not hard-wired into the human brain, and thus, every sub-skill has to be explicitly taught (Noble, Wolmetz, Ochs, Farah & McCandliss, 2006). The current understanding of reading development is that students will likely struggle throughout their school career if they cannot obtain adequate literacy skills

DOI: 10.4018/978-1-7998-7271-9.ch013

by Grade 4. These students are also more than likely to end up leaving school without the skills needed for further study or the ability to function in a decent job. In addition, they are most likely to drop out of school without completing their final schooling exam.

There is much public interest in how children learn to read and how to best teach them this foundational skill. Unfortunately, despite much financial investment and hours of research, combined with the outstanding efforts of teachers, parents, and students, the gaps in literacy levels continue to increase. Recently, research by Boakye and Linden (2018) found that students' limited reading proficiency negatively affects their academic performance. In addition, it is generally understood that poor reading skills lead to high learning poverty levels.

When we consider everything, literacy rates are globally much lower than the accepted levels. Learners in Secondary schools need to be able to read fluently at an appropriate speed with good comprehension. Therefore, it is safe to argue that reading fluency is a significant key when reading for comprehension. When students struggle to move their eyes rhythmically and fluently across the page, they will likely experience challenges because they will have to decipher a jumbled message. If they struggle to recognize and use words to give meaning to the text, they will also experience challenges understanding what they are reading. The theoretical support for reading fluency as a prerequisite for comprehension is advocated for in the automaticity theory, as explained by Samuels, Rasinski, and Hiebert (2013). Taylor (2013) also explains the importance of visual/ functional competence in silent reading fluency. He states that the lack of visual competence can make reading uncomfortable and result in poorer word perception, which leads to an increase in the number of eye-stops (fixations) and regressions per word during a lesson. Students can also experience further challenges in silent reading fluency due to overemphasizing instructional styles such as oral reading, round-robin reading, and overstressing phonics training. Furthermore, students can also feel uncomfortable when reading silently if they struggle with comprehension and lack confidence.

New research and our understanding of neuroplasticity have changed the way teachers and reading facilitators understand reading and learning processes, directly impacting teaching and developing reading. According to Demarin and Morovic (2014), neuroplasticity depends on two basic processes, learning and memory. They confirm that the brain is a self-organizing creative system. During learning, permanent changes occur in synaptic relationships between neurons. As a result, the human brain is constantly making new connections. Continuous focus and use reinforce connections and cause these connections to become stronger. It takes between 8 – 12 weeks of focused interval training to re-wire the human brain. (Harvard Gazette, 2011).

On the other hand, connections that are neglected due to a lack of use become weaker. This, then, at a simplistic level, explains why repetition in any form of learning is valuable, irrespective of age. Repetition, as a strategy, can therefore augment the 'muscle-building' part of the brain; embedded within is a physical basis why repetition strengthens the power of choices and actions. Over time, these actions become automatic. (Marshall, Taukeni, Haihambo, Shihako, Muruti, Ligando, De Silva & Marshall, 2020). In short, we can continue to learn new things and improve on already learned skills. Therefore we can continue developing reading skills and learning new strategies to improve our literacy levels and visual intelligence throughout our lives.

This chapter will study the use of an online gamified visual intelligence innovation (eyebraingym) developed to improve visual skills, reading, and comprehension as implemented at a South African Boy's School during the 2021 academic year. According to the latest statistics in South Africa, boys are more at risk than ever before to fail in developing these foundational skills and to leave school without completing their final year.

Outcomes achieved during this project to develop visual processing, reading, and comprehension to enhance visual intelligence when schools were part of the lockdowns in the pandemic are giving us hope. The project results show that when students improve their visual processing in reading, they also increase the mental energy they can devote to understanding complex ideas.

BACKGROUND

International figures indicate that 1.6 billion students in 195 countries worldwide were out of school at the peak of the COVID-19 lockdown in April 2020. The World Bank (2020) indicates that the learning loss caused by the lockdown will impact two areas. First, an estimated loss of 10 trillion dollars in earnings over time for this generation of students; secondly, many countries will be severely challenged to achieve their Learning Poverty goals. Global data indicates that 91.3% of students have been adversely impacted in some way or another during the Covid-19 pandemic. In addition, the expected results of these Covid-19 lockdowns are that 100 million children will fall below the minimum proficiency level in reading, according to a United Nations News article (2021).

Moreover, the article points out that the number of children lacking basic reading skills was on a downward curve before the pandemic. However, the downward trend was negatively impacted by the lockdown of schools. As a result, the number of children who are challenged in the area of literacy development jumped to 584 million in 2020, increasing by more than 20% and wiping out gains made over the past two decades through education efforts. (UNESCO, 2021).

Reading and literacy rates, which is the foundation of academic learning, have been a challenge before the learning losses of the Covid-19 lockdowns. Nel, Dreyer, and Klopper (2004) indicate that one of the most challenging aspects of preparing students for the demands of further studies is the problem of reading. This unpreparedness is much more evident within the context of reading, and more specifically, academic reading. Layton and Brown (2012) and Chaudhury and Karim (2014) advocate that academic reading is the primary means of academic learning and that inadequate reading skills will impair the learning process.

Academic reading is silent fluency reading, incorporating a variety of reading skills and comprehension strategies. There are various relevant areas in understanding silent reading fluency and its importance towards improved academic outcomes. First, students should be skillful in the foundational building blocks of reading. These include phonological awareness, phonics, vocabulary, and fluency. Students will struggle to understand what they read if their skills in one of these areas are not developed to expected levels. Fluency in reading is critical when comprehension is the goal. Taylor (2000:1) states that many students fail to make the transition to fluent reading. Subsequently, they encounter significant difficulties in contracting meaning from text.

Jean Chall's model (1993) explains the phases or stages of reading development. It gives us the understanding that we should continue to develop reading skills beyond primary school years. Visual skills, reading, and cognitive development are not a 'Junior Primary' task but are part of lifelong learning. The model proposed by Jean Chall clearly shows that reading development is not completed at the end of Primary School years. Even up to the end of the final year of schooling and further into tertiary studies and in the modern-day work environment, it is essential to develop visual skills, reading skills and strategies, cognitive strategies, and visual intelligence.

Secondary schools are responsible for improving more advanced comprehension skills and supporting students in attaining study skills, an increase in silent fluency reading rate, and the achievement of flexibility in reading for different purposes. Also, secondary school years are when we require more extended periods of concentrated reading. Likewise, it is during extended periods of concentrated reading when many readers begin to fail. Reading skills are never completely perfected; even into college and adult life, developing advanced and different visual processing, reading, and cognitive skills and strategies to improve visual intelligence is vital.

Automaticity

As students continue to develop their reading skills, one aims to achieve automaticity in decoding. When words and word parts are automatically recognized as visual orthographic images from the declarative and procedural memory, the working memory can be utilized for comprehension purposes. This type of development should then develop students' skills to see more, see faster, remember better, and reason clearer. Samuels, Rasinski, and Hiebert (2013) explain the automaticity theory's importance in realizing reading fluency.

Cognitive Load Theory

Sweller explains in his Cognitive Load Theory (1994) that the capacity of the working memory influences our intellectual abilities. When the cognitive load exceeds the working memory, our intellectual abilities decrease. The decrease of intellectual abilities impacts directly on silent reading fluency. Working memory has two significant limitations. First, it can grasp only approximately seven items of distinct bits of information at a time. Secondly, it can hold this information for roughly ten seconds. If then, when reading, this critical moment in the working memory must be applied for decoding, no time is available for comprehension (Marshall, 2020.) This explains why poor readers spend hours reading and rereading to properly decode what they are reading and then adding meaning to the text. Finally, to ensure readers achieve competence, the distinct bits of information must be constructed into a schema of understanding to achieve convergent and divergent comprehension outcomes.

Fundamental Reading Process

The fundamental reading process is comprised of the most basic functions of reading, oral or silent. According to Taylor (2016), the reader should be able to see clearly, use both their eyes as a team, easily rotate the eyes – not the head, and accurately track the text that they read. These factors influence the clarity of print, the ability to read rhythmically and fluently from left to right, and therefore the ability to decode the text coherently. We can conclude that visual efficiency is, therefore, a key in developing reading fluency. Secondly, readers must be perceptually accurate to grasp the orthography (letters, letter order, and letter cluster awareness of words) quickly and efficiently. This skill combined with automaticity in word recognition and the ability to retain word images for a reasonable time during the realization of syntax directly affects comprehension and rate of reading (Taylor, 2016).

Taylor further suggests that training practices involving the flashing of groups of letters, numbers, and core vocabulary words can improve orthographic awareness, increase automaticity in word recognition, and develop improved visual memory. In addition, these improvements will lead to a more significant amount of time available during each eye stop or fixation that can be devoted to understanding and comprehending what they are reading.

Language occurs in units, such as phrases, sentences, and paragraphs. Readers must process these units in rhythm, similar to the way we communicate in oral language. Thus, reading must 'flow' just as talking flows if we want to understand what is communicated in the reading text.

Incorporating these aspects into a structured, comprehensive reading program would be greatly beneficial in supporting and developing visual intelligence. However, the challenge also remains to achieve interest from students when developing these skills. For years scientists stated that we could use online media as a cognitive tool for learning. Can online learning be used to improve literacy levels? Can students improve their reading, comprehension, and visual intelligence when playing games? Will we achieve greater interest when improving these skills and strategies through online gamified means?

The South African Context

Tertiary institutions in South Africa accept 13% of matriculants yearly for further study. Of these, 47% will drop out due to poor academic literacy rates. Completion rates from the first year to the completion of degrees are among the lowest in the world. Male students dominated Higher Education in South Africa for many years, but the number of male students registered at Higher Education Institutions is less every year. For instance, one million thirty-six thousand nine hundred eighty-four million students registered for tertiary study in South Africa during the 2017 academic year. Of these, 606,898 were female and 444,000 male students. One boy's school in South Africa concluded that fewer boys are entering Higher Education because of poor literacy levels. Therefore, they planned an intervention to support their students with the development of foundational skills in reading, namely visual processing, silent fluency reading, and comprehension development. The aim is to ensure these students are better prepared for their High School academic pursuits. Improved skills in these areas would also expand their chances of successful further study.

The school had a screening process for boys entering the boy's college that was functional for many years. However, the data of these screenings showed that literacy rates of adolescent boys were declining year on year and came to a point where it was severely lacking. Furthermore, the school acknowledged that literacy demands are growing with every school year. Reading is also a critical component to giving boys access to university. Therefore, the school believed that the importance of literacy development could no longer be overlooked.

Students need to be proficient in reading when entering higher education as this is an important indicator of academic success. This has been confirmed by a study conducted by Maree, Fletcher, and Sommerville (2011), who found that both aspects of language (including vocabulary and reasoning ability), as well as reading ability, are strong predictors of academic success. Consequently, many students often discontinue their studies as a result of their poor reading proficiency. This boy's school wanted to ensure every effort was made to increase their students' opportunity for further study as well as the completion of said studies.

Many schools, specifically in Africa, could not successfully implement online learning during the Covid-19 pandemic due to a lack of resources, data, and devices. Nevertheless, some institutions were able to advance learning through using online means. Schools that were able to opt for online training used new methods of supporting students and continued learning online.

During the school lockdowns in the 2020 and 2021 academic years, the boy's school where the project with eyebraingym was completed used the opportunity to continue training for improved literacy using the online game-based innovation(eyebraingym). The school implemented a deliberate, targeted, whole school reading and literacy intervention program. To ensure student participation, the school formalized a reading development lesson on the timetable. The online innovation (eyebraingym) is one of the components of this program. It is compulsory for all Grade 6, 7, 8, and 9 learners to complete this program. By the time these boys reach the FET phase, they have had 60 personalized, targeted reading interventions. The innovation allows students online access to various games gauged at their skill levels and is designed to develop visual processing, vocabulary, various reading skills, reading, comprehension, and learning strategies.

The online gamified visual intelligence innovation (eyebraingym) focuses on improving three measurable factors, gauged against international norms and standards, namely the visual processing factor (VPF) and cognitive development factor (CDF). The innovation measures VPF as words per minute (wpm) read within the parameters of the readability of the material. The percentage of comprehension gauged against the complexity of content is represented as the CDF. The combined VPF and CDF confirm the third - AIU-factor (action-interpret-understand factor).

STUDY METHOD

This study used a quantitative descriptive research design as one of the most fitting to meet the study's objective. Participants were randomly selected from the list of students completing the online intervention at a South African Boys School. A sample of 180 Grade 8 learners took part in the project. All selected respondents were subjected to the Placement module in the innovation (eyebraingym) to determine visual processing proficiency, language proficiency, and reading with comprehension outcomes. After they completed the placement, participants were ready to start the program.

Of the 180 learners, 121 completed their 15 sessions at the cut-off time for this research project. Their data is included in the outcomes of this study. The eyebraingym innovation gave students access to 15 sessions with compilations of games and exercises—students assigned to the project aimed to complete the 15 sessions in the six months from March to September in 2020 and March to September in 2021.

Students were further asked to complete a questionnaire to ascertain their personal experience when playing the games and doing the exercises on the eyebraingym innovation. Thirty-nine (39) students were able to complete the online questionnaire to give feedback on their experience. The results of this questionnaire are also included in the outcomes of this study.

THE EYEBRAINGYM PROCESS

Improving visual intelligence gives us the opportunity to develop our mental agility. When you are mentally agile, you are curious, always looking for new connections, you can move between concepts, and you can find connections between new and existing information quickly. The creators of the eyebraingym innovation postulate that using the system to prescribed guidelines will help students improve problem-

Using Game-Based Learning to Improve Boys' Literacy

solving skills and their ability to reason and plan. The battery of games is developed to strengthen brain functions, increase mental acuity and vitality. Exercises in the system assist the brain in finding a way to be successful and connecting background knowledge to current information.

Games and online games are a widely acknowledged component of the life of teenage boys. Using an online, gamified system should create an environment that would encourage boys to participate towards improving their literacy levels. This online gamified visual intelligence innovation(eyebraingym) endeavors to develop and upscale visual skills, reading abilities, and comprehension outcomes through individualized games and activities. The exercises fluctuate between fun games and more demanding exercises that challenge students at various levels to see faster and interpret what you see just as fast. Individualized algorithms ensure the intervals and speed of each exercise are targeted to ensure specific modulations to assist individual users in achieving improved visual perception and accuracy. The different modules in the innovation include, among others, the following games, and exercises:

1. Eye-Gym module
    a. Perceptual Accuracy area: FrameFlash, ObjectMesh, Repeater
    FrameFlash is geared towards improving the span of recognition as well as the duration of fixation of students. These exercises develop how fast and how much you see in a fun way. In addition, the exercises are functional in developing visual analysis and visual discrimination. Object mesh helps the brain to learn how to complete an incomplete picture. Students must distinguish differences in the outline shape of the configuration and distinguish a complete object from an incomplete image.
    In Repeater, students must quickly view the objects, numbers, or letters and identify the repeat ones.
    b. Visual Efficiency area: FollowMe, FocusOut, CountMe
    FollowMe targets the development of visual scanning skills and develops visual efficiency. Students must follow the images, shapes, numbers, and letters in a circle, determining how many times the example is flashed on the screen.
    FocusOut is the exercise for developing peripheral vision. This is an aspect of vision that is integrally part of visual scanning. We use our whole visual field to find information pertinent to the task at hand. Peripheral vision also enables the eye to find the next fixation point while moving from one fixation to the next. It is a crucial skill when developing silent reading fluency. Peripheral vision is also an aspect of vision that is integrally part of visual scanning. CountMe is an exercise that helps to improve various ocular-motor skills specifically geared towards visual scanning. Students must identify and remember how many times the example is flashed rhythmic across the screen from left to right. Targeted difficulty levels challenge the visual system and brain constantly. This exercise helps students improve their visual and cognitive processing abilities using shapes, images, numbers, letters, and combinations.
    c. Visual Accuracy area: BlockFlash, JumbleMatch, BlockMatch
    This is a fundamental skill in the visual system. It is the ability to look for relevant information quickly and efficiently in your environment. We use our vision to find something specific. BlockFlash and BlockMatch challenge and develop visual scanning in a variety of ways. First, you need to quickly identify the object and remember where it was displayed within the given timeframe. The ability to discriminate between detail is also developed with this exercise. Complete the game by choosing the option that indicates the correct position.

JumbleMatch assists students in developing visual scanning. Students must quickly and accurately discriminate between sizes, patterns, words and word shapes, classification of items, connections between names and formulae, etc., in a fun and interactive way.
   d. Visual Memory area: MemoryBlocks, ObjectMemory, FindMyFriend
   MemoryBlocks one of the most challenging exercises in the eyebraingym innovation gives students the challenge to remember 4 – 12 pictures in their exact positions within the timeframe given.
   ObjectMemory is a fun way to practice visual discrimination. Visual discrimination is the ability to recognize details in visual images. It allows students to identify and recognize the likeness and differences of shapes/forms, colors, and position of objects, people, and printed materials. In Object Memory, students must use visual memory to differentiate between what was and what was not displayed in the first picture.
   FindMyFriend is a fun game of remembering where the same image is hiding. Students turn the blocks and remember where the image was displayed.
2. Vocabulary development module
   a. Mind-activation exercises
   MindActivation trains your brain to ask the right questions to find the information you need to succeed in the visual task at hand. The exercises aim to develop the brain to see the 'bigger picture' when looking at new information, ask the right questions to find what you need, and develop vocabulary and language strategies.
   b. WordFlash
   WordFlash is part of a detailed sequence of exercises within the innovation geared towards building and developing Visual Sequential Memory. This is the ability to remember visual details in the correct sequence. It is an essential skill needed in spelling and reading, where you need to remember the sequence of letters to spell the word correctly.
   c. Build the word
   WordBuild is an exercise focused on developing spelling through visual memory. First, you have to build a keyword from the passage you read through, ordering the letters in the correct sequence.
   d. PhraseFlash
   This exercise can be quite demanding. However, it aims to assist students in reading more than one word at a time to develop improved fundamental reading skills.
3. Silent reading fluency training module
Reading with comprehension develops the 'flow of reading' or reading fluency, giving students a strategy and the skill to work coherently with visual information. As a result, the message you receive will make more sense and allow your brain to allocate more resources to critical thinking skills while processing information when interacting with the text you are reading fluently from left to right.
   a. Paragraph reading word-by-word projection (slot-reading)
   b. Paragraph reading line-by-line (line-reading)
   c. Paragraph reading full page with pacer
4. Comprehension skills development module

Using Game-Based Learning to Improve Boys' Literacy

These exercises include pre-, in-, and post-reading strategy training.

    a.   Answer the questions

The aim is to allows students to develop reading comprehension. Reading comprehension is the ability to read, understand, process, and recall what was just read. Having excellent reading comprehension skills is crucial. It increases the enjoyment and effectiveness of reading and helps academically, professionally, and in a person's personal life.

    b.   Complete the sentence

Complete the sentence allows students to place words from the passage they have read correctly within a sentence. This exercise helps students to improve various visual and cognitive skills to achieve improved visual intelligence.

    c.   Put in order

PutInOrder is focused on developing sequential memory. Students are expected to remember and place random sentences in the correct order from the story they have read.

    d.   MatchUs

MatchUs is an exercise where students must link a sight word from the passage to the description in the FlashPhrase exercise. Visual memory and language skills will assist them in reaching the goal to complete the exercise as quickly as possible.

    e.   Skimming, Scanning, Summary

Skimming will allow them to look at a few sentences from a passage and develop their prediction skills. Next, students write a few sentences on what they expect will happen in the passage. This exercise takes visual scanning to the next level by learning how to interact quickly and creatively with visual information.

Scanning will test their visual scanning capabilities. Students are trained to move their eyes quickly and rhythmically over the passage as they search and point out specific sight words indicated at the top of the screen.

    f.   Meta-cognition worksheets to develop thinking about learning strategies

Various of these exercises are focused on training the brain to recognize patterns. For instance, visual exploration tasks are part and parcel of the Meta-cognition exercises. Meta-cognition exercises train the eyes and the brain to explore visual information in new and exciting ways. They learn to ask the right questions to be able to find the information they need. They are also able to develop strategies to improve their exploration skills. Using clues to predict and infer more than what the information is telling you, evaluate information and decide what is important, and draw conclusions faster and more efficiently are a few.

Meta-cognitive exercises also teach students to think about the way they achieved outcomes of previous games. In addition, to discern what type of strategy works best for them personally and learn new ways of reading, learning, and working with information.

5.   Downloadable resources

These resources are available from the student dashboard as printable worksheets. Teachers often use these worksheets to support small-group instruction. However, it is accepted that most of the students participating in this project did not use these downloadable worksheets.

    a.   Language development
    b.   Comprehension skills and strategy training
    c.   Study skills

Most perceptual, visual efficiency, visual accuracy, and visual memory exercises develop visual skills in fun and accelerating ways. The games challenge students at various levels to see faster, see more and interpret what they see at a faster speed. The innovation (eyebraingym) aims to develop these skills to enable students to see and interpret what they see in less than 250 milliseconds. Aiming for faster than 250 milliseconds is based on research done by Taylor and Robinson (1963) that indicates school-aged children tend to move their eyes over visual material at a rate of three movements per second (eye stops). As children in the study began to read, this fixation duration was inadequate to identify and recognize a word. All the children in the Taylor and Robinson study resorted to making two or more fixations for each word encountered. This reading habit slows down the reading speed and can impede further advances in silent reading fluency, especially if the "learning to read" instruction overemphasize phonics in primary grades. The influence is evident in secondary school students who continue to sub-vocalize when reading silently.

The time to see and say typically exceeds the usual time of one-third of a second to fixate, see and interpret during silent reading fluency. Additionally, norms and standards defined by Taylor, Frackenpohl, and Pettee indicate 250 milliseconds as the target for an eye stop at the end of schooling. Thus, incorporating games that train students to see more and see faster is one of the ways the innovation leverage skills needed in silent reading fluency to improve automaticity in the fundamental reading process.

The innovation (eyebraingym) assists students in working through the process of attention using the working memory when mastering new information. Working memory is our operational memory. It has been defined as a cluster of processes that allows us to store and manipulate information temporarily. It also carries out complex cognitive tasks when reading, comprehending, learning, and reasoning with information. It is a type of short-term memory that can be likened to the RAM of a computer. The capacity of the working memory is limited, and it is an active memory – therefore, not only temporarily storing but also transforming our memory. (Eyebraingym website, 2021). The content within the working memory is constantly being updated. The fluid availability of information gives us the ability to keep information within reach while carrying out a task. We can integrate new and known information because of our working memory. It is a cognitive skill used in the majority of daily tasks.

Skills and strategies built into the innovation support and develop students to follow an information process by interpreting new knowledge with logic through previously known information from long-term memory. Games and exercises also develop skills and strategies for understanding and comprehension. Comprehension outcomes are measured throughout student interaction in the innovation as the cognitive development factor. Thus, the innovation focuses on improving cognitive skills through developing and training students in skills and strategies to remember, understand, apply, analyze, evaluate, and create new knowledge. These skills and strategies should then enable the student to arrive at a place of competence in the different levels of educational expectations and outcomes.

The innovation (eyebraingym) measures development and improvement through three factors, gauged against international norms and standards, namely the visual processing factor (VPF) and cognitive development factor (CDF), and the third - AIU-factor (action-interpret-understand). System guidelines indicate that these three factors incorporate identified values, marking the minimum and advanced processing skills and abilities required to meet the expected level of operation in the different stages. Thus, students should achieve the expected minimum levels to interact with information on their relevant levels.

1. The **VPF factor** calculates the wpm achieved and considers the complexity or difficulty level of the information the student engages. This outcome measures the student proficiency against the industry norm for the expected skill levels of the specific user.
2. The **CDF factor** regards the complexity or difficulty level of the information the user is engaging with, apart from the comprehension outcomes achieved by the student. The respective scores also identify the processing of convergent and divergent abilities.
3. The **AIUF** combines the VPF and CDF to determine the student's relative efficiency and ability to function meaningfully and intelligently with the visual information in their respective levels and environments.

The above outcomes calculate student progress against the industry norms & standards expected to operate with visual information meaningfully and successfully at a specific level or in a specific environment.

Figure 1 below indicates the flow of information process that the innovation utilizes. Through repetitive games and exercises, students are developing their skills and learning new strategies. The innovation leverages the aspects of muscle training through the processes of reading and the science of neuromodulation to advance students' visual processing, reading, comprehension skillsets, and strategies. These new skill levels enable students to action new information whilst interpreting it against known information and bring them to improved competence when understanding the information they must study.

Figure 1. The eyebraingym information flow process

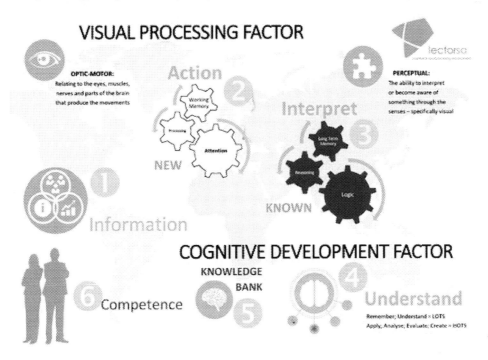

Students complete their exercises by playing the games, all the while developing their skills and learning new strategies. For brain exercises to be successful, scholars have noted the following aspects to be important:

1. Exercises are most effective when they include challenging high-level tasks (like exercises that require a high degree of speed and accuracy) while also including low-level exercises that improve our ability to perceive similar images more distinctly (Ahissar, Nahum, Nelken, & Hochstein, 2009).
2. Exercises should increase or decrease in difficulty based on performance. Therefore, it is proficient to continuously adapt to the new skill level (Roelfsema, 2010).
3. The relevant 'skills' must be identified, isolated, then practiced through hundreds if not thousands of trials on an intensive (i.e., quasi-daily) schedule (Roelfsema, 2010).
4. The games or exercises in each learning event should grab the student's attention to maximize enduring plastic changes in the cortex.
5. A very high proportion of the learning trials must be rewarded as soon as possible. (Roelfsema, 2010).

The above authors (Ayres, & Narum, L., 2019) comment that brain changes will enhance higher-level skills if the exercises have sufficient intensity and duration on specific sets of activities that focus on lower-level (perceptual) and middle-level stimuli (attention, memory, and language) tasks. As a result, learning will be easier and more advanced. It is evident in the outcomes achieved during this project that students did experience improved reading and learning when studying their schoolwork.

By taking advantage of the above aspects, the innovation is structured as a customized eye-brain training course with an individualized specific game plan to assist students in staying on track with their scheduled games.

Once registered, the system takes each student through an online assessment module (the Placement). This Placement combines a visual processing, reading, and cognitive assessment in which it measures processing speed, visual skills, language proficiency, and silent reading fluency outcomes. The innovation provides each user with a targeted set of personalized games and exercises based on individual results. The games are given in a specific sequence with targeted intervals and researched weights and timeslots to achieve particular visual processing and cognitive skills development outcomes. After each activity and lesson, learners have access to their infographic report of progress. In addition, learners achieve badges as they progress through the games.

The developers state that the aim is to develop a coherent mind to improve interaction with visual information through improved visual processing and cognitive skills.

RESULTS AND DISCUSSION

Taylor, Frackenpohl, and Pettee (1960) established the norms incorporated in the innovation in their research regarding the Fundamental Reading Process. These norms were reaffirmed in a study by Spichtig et al. (2016) wherein the decline of silent fluency reading in the United States was studied. The innovation uses an index to compile a level of proficiency expressed as a Grade level. This level is calculated as the AIU factor. The comprehension outcomes indicate the CDF (Cognitive Development Factor),

Using Game-Based Learning to Improve Boys' Literacy

which is directly dependent on the VPF (Visual Processing Factor). If students struggle with their visual processing, they will continue to experience challenges when trying to understand what they are reading.

Based on the normative rates, in combination with fluency development technology (Taylor, Frankenpohl & Pettee, 1960; Taylor, 2000), a Grade 8 student (aged 14 – 15) should read 204 w.p.m. with a minimum of 70% comprehension without any effort. However, students at the boy's college were reading approximately 155 w.p.m. (grade 4 level) before participating in the eyebraingym project. This is four grade levels below the expected normative rates.

The data in this project was sampled from the results of two groups of Grade 8 boys (121) who were able to complete their eyebraingym sessions during the 2020 and 2021 academic years. The final results, included in Table 1, reveal that the students improved their reading speed from 155 words per minute to 283 words per minute. These results translate to an improvement of 128 words per minute, a relative improvement of 8 years achieved within the five months that the students played games and completed exercises on the innovation.

Furthermore, students were also able to improve their VPF from 108 to 241, their CDF from 42 to 85, and their AIUF from 62 to 112. These results translate to an improvement of 8 years relative efficiency when working with visual information on a Grade 8 level.

Table 1. Final results eyebraingym

	Pre-eyebraingym	Final eyebraingym results
Visual Processing Factor	108	241
Reading speed – words per minute	155	283
Cognitive Development Factor	42	85
Action-Interpret-Understand Factor	62	112
Grade level efficiency	5	12

The two population means tested were the S 1 Wpm and S 15 Wpm populations of Grade 8 Students for the 2020-2021 year. We used the S 1 Wpm population as the control group and the S 15 Wpm population as the test group for this project. S 1 Wpm group completed their placement and only session one within the eyebraingym innovation to confirm their scores. S 15 Wpm includes the 121 students who completed 15 sessions on eyebraingym.

The null hypothesis is a statement of "no effect" or "no difference." And the alternative hypothesis is a statement that there is a significant difference of (125.0331 words per minute) in the means of the two populations. The calculated Variance for the two populations were 950,2363 for S 1 Wpm and 3186,735 for S 15 Wpm, respectively.

As P = 0.000000, it is less than the significance level of 0.05. This determines that we can reject the null hypothesis in favor of the alternative hypothesis that there is a significant difference in the means of the two populations tested.

Figure 2 illustrates the distribution curve of the S 1 Wpm and the S 15 Wpm populations in terms of the students' wpm results, respectively.

Table 2. Z-test outcomes

If Hypothesized Mean Difference is 125,0331		
	S 1 Wpm	**S 15 Wpm**
Mean	157,9421488	282,9752066
Known Variance	950,2363	3186,735
Observations	121	121
Hypothesized Mean Difference	125,0331	
z	-42,76676031	
P(Z<=z) one-tail	0,000000	
z Critical one-tail	1,644853627	
P(Z<=z) two-tail	0,000000	
z Critical two-tail	1,959963985	

Figure 2. S 1 Wpm and S 15 Wpm distribution

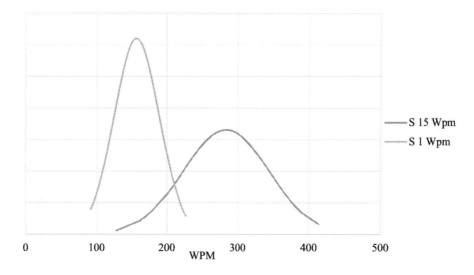

Figure 3 indicates the Wpm scores distribution comparison between the S 1 Wpm and the S 15 Wpm populations. Notice the consistency in the distribution of the population included before and after participation in eyebraingym.

Figure 4 illustrates the relative improvement of the S 1 Wpm and S15 Wpm populations in regard to the Placement wpm scores of the respective populations. Note the correlation in the polynomial trendlines of the respective populations, which indicates a proportional individual increase of their wpm scores.

Grade 8 students who completed a 15 session eyebraingym course achieved significantly higher wpm scores than those who did not complete a 15 session eyebraingym course. Thus, it can be stated that completing an eyebraingym course of 15 sessions will significantly improve students' words per minute scores.

Figure 3. S 1 Wpm and S 15 Wpm distribution comparison

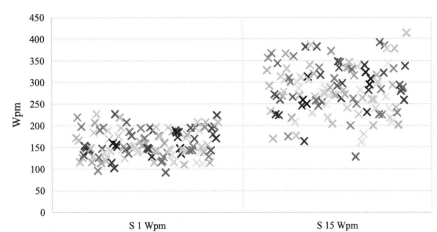

Figure 4. S 1 Wpm and S 15 Wpm relative improvement

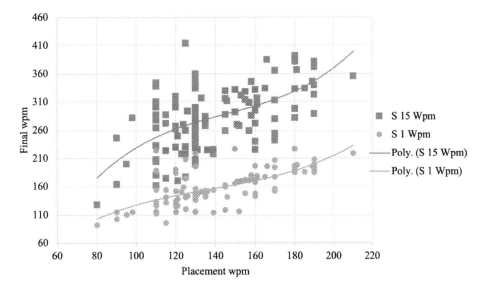

In addition, the general data indicates that the lowest improvement achieved with this group of students was 29 words per minute, while the best improvement was 211 words per minute. These results collaborate with projects done at the University of Namibia (Marshall, Taukeni, Haihambo, Shihako, Muruti, Likando, De Silva, & Marshall, 2020) and the University of Pretoria (Lombard, 2018).

Thirty-nine students completed a questionnaire to reference their experience on the innovation. The following cursory feedback was received:

1. How did eyebraingym impact your academic performance?
    a. It has become a bit easier with memorizing work.
    b. I used to struggle with English. I used to get 60%. Now I am at 70%.
    c. It has not improved my academics, but I do feel like I have a better memory.

d. My marks stayed almost the same.
   e. I improved my grades in English from 72 to 80 and Math from 68 to 78.
   f. Geography was less than 50%, but now I got 76%.
2. What impact did eyebraingym have on your reading, comprehension, and vocabulary?
   a. I can read faster.
   b. I can read faster and more accurately.
   c. It helped with my comprehension.
   d. My reading speed increased from 256 wpm to 300 wpm.
   e. I feel I read a little bit faster.
   f. It did not help.
   g. It made my memory clearer and more focused.

In rating the system, students gave eyebraingym an average of 60

- 62% rated eyebraingym above 50
- 39% rated eyebraingym below 50

The system facilitator and educational psychiatrist at the Boy's School indicated to the research team that the school had seen the impact in all marks of the boys participating in this project across the grades.

SOLUTIONS AND RECOMMENDATIONS

The outcomes of the system showed that accurate and precise communication when on-boarding students on a new project is a key factor in the way students perceive their time spent. Evidence from the student feedback form indicated that students expected their sessions to be shorter and wanted an opportunity to complete more than the two sessions allocated in their Gameplan. These references indicate that some students did not understand intervals chosen for their interaction with the innovation. In addition, they did not receive information regarding the impact on the neuromodulation that was taking place while they were playing the games and completing the exercises. Students who wanted to complete more exercises but could not do more than the expected two sessions a week rated the system lower than their peers. Also, the more support students receive, the more motivated they are.

Despite these challenges, due to school lockdowns during the 2020 and 2021 academic years, the system has seen students increase their visual processing, reading, comprehension, and visual intelligence skills by a good measure.

It is recommended that the system be used as an activator or a co-activator with existing literacy programs to advance students' visual processing, comprehension, learning, and visual intelligence skills to the expected norm and standard faster. In addition, due to the increase in learning poverty due to poor literacy rates, more students should have access to technology-driven innovations that can help them overcome the more significant challenges they now face in the education journey.

FUTURE RESEARCH DIRECTIONS

It will be advantageous to, by way of future research, follow the students who participated in this project to ascertain the results of the impact this development had on their academic studies throughout their High School years.

It will also be beneficial to see the impact of this development on the National Benchmark Tests outcomes. The National Benchmark Test (NBT) is part of the university entrance exams in South Africa. The NBTs are designed to provide criterion-referenced information to supplement the NSC results and help institutions meet the educational needs of their incoming students as effectively as possible. The NBT includes The Academic and Quantitative Literacy Test, which evaluates students' capacity to engage successfully with the demands of academic study in the medium of instruction provided. It also provides outcomes to ascertain students' ability to manage situations or solve problems in a real context relevant to higher education, using basic quantitative information presented verbally, graphically, in tabular or symbolic form.

A third area to be looked at for further research could be teachers' perspectives and their insights into the changes regarding the socio-emotional development of boys during their participation in this project.

CONCLUSION

During the COVID-19 lockdowns, educators worldwide were thrown into the deep end to continue teaching their students online. This situation culminated in being an opportunity to change how they taught their students for many years. Educators faced many challenges while having to cope with several ineffective strategies. Notwithstanding, numerous opportunities emerged that affords the chance to build an education system that is more resilient, adaptable to student needs, equitable, and inclusive. Technology will play an increasingly important role in this area of education development. Therefore, the possibility to support and improve foundational skills for reading and learning online through gamified systems, such as eyebraingym, should receive the attention it deserves.

Secondly, COVID-19 has, in a sense, highlighted gaps and challenges that already existed in the education and training sector. The lockdown of schools and training institutions has placed at-risk students at greater risk and exacerbated existing learning gaps. The gains made in literacy development during the previous two decades were destroyed due to schools' lockdowns. Furthermore, keeping in mind that the Fourth Industrial Revolution is placing a higher demand on learning, unlearning, and relearning, we need now, more than before, to achieve higher, develop more, read faster, think more intelligent, and learn better. Even students that were doing good will not be doing well enough going forward. In his Cognitive load theory (1994), Sweller explains that intellectual abilities decrease when the cognitive load exceeds the working memory capacity. If then students do not have the opportunity to develop the fundamental aspects of the reading process and continue towards efficient, silent reading fluency and visual intelligence development, they will surely not be able to function adequately in the economies of the future workplace. If students struggle with the visual processing aspects of the reading action, they will continuously wrestle with cognitive overload. They will not know how to find pertinent information, process it, and use it to make better choices. Students in previous decades were taught to remember facts, but now students are faced with oceans of information. Today, the challenge is finding the appropriate information and deciding how to interact with it to achieve the results they need for their studies.

Incorporating new technologies and innovations like eyebraingym into the learning environment makes it possible for teachers to continue to assist their students either on-campus or off-campus, if necessary. In addition, teachers should be empowered to use these technologies to continue developing and improving the skills and strategies needed to achieve improved visual intelligence and better education outcomes.

Thirdly all stakeholders in the education sector should pursue access to data, the internet, and devices for students of all demographics. Giving access to these three levels is essential in fighting the learning loss experienced globally because of the school lockdowns during the Covid-pandemic. It should be of even greater importance in poorer countries. New technology and innovations, such as eyebraingym, have the potential to bridge gaps and leap-frog students to develop crucial skills that will enable them to achieve more, think higher, and advance exponentially. Educators and students can face learning poverty head-on. Learning losses can be reversed and overcome by empowering teachers and giving students access to these types of innovations and technology. When foundational skills for reading and learning are in place, students can continue their development towards advanced literacy levels and become lifelong learners.

ACKNOWLEDGMENT

This research was approved and funded by M3line (Research, and Development Company, South Africa).

REFERENCES

Ahissar, M., Nahum, M., Nelken, I., & Hochstein, S. (2009). Reverse hierarchies and sensory learning. *Philosophical Transactions of the Royal Society of London. Series B, Biological Sciences*, *364*(1515), 285–299. doi:10.1098/rstb.2008.0253 PMID:18986968

Ayres, L., & Narum, L. (2019). The promise of brain plasticity – overcoming language, learning and reading problems. *The Promise of Brain Plasticity-Overcoming Language*. Retrieved from: https://www.tarnowcenter.com/tarnow-articles/28-tarnow-articles/article-desc/584-the-promise-of-brain-plasticity-overcoming-language,-learning,-and-reading-problems.html

Boakye, N. A., & Linden, M. M. (2018). Extended strategy-use instruction to improve students' reading proficiency in a content subject. *Reading and Writing*, *9*(1), 1–9.

Chall, J. S. (1996). *Stages of Reading Development*. Harcourt Brace College Publishers.

Chaudhury, T. A., & Karim, Z. (2014). CLT approach in developing English reading skills in tertiary levels in Bangladesh. *Asian Journal of Education and e-Learning*, *2*(1), 47-55.

Demarin, V., & Morovic, S. (2014). Neuroplasticity. *Periodicum Biologorum*, *116*(2), 209–211. https://hrcak.srce.hr/126369

Eyebraingym. (2021). *Key Science*. eyebraingym. Retrieved from: https://www.eyebraingym.com/key-science/

Layton, L., & Brown, E. (2012, Sept. 24). SAT Reading Scores Hit a Four-Decade Low. *The Washington Post*, p. 1.

Lombard, P. J. P. (2018). *Factors influencing the transition from high school to higher education: a case of the JuniorTukkie programme* [Doctor of Philosophy, University of Pretoria]. https://repository.up.ac.za/bitstream/handle/2263/67771/Lombard_Factors_2018.pdf?sequence=1&isAllowed

Maree, J. G., Fletcher, L., & Sommerville, J. (2011). Predicting success among prospective first-year students at the University of Pretoria. *South African Journal of Higher Education, 25*(6), 1125–1139.

Marshall, M. B. (2020). *White paper: Finding the way through the waves*. Retrieved from: https://www.eyebraingym.com/wp-content/uploads/2021/03/WHITEPAPER-Finding-the-way-through-the-waves-1.0_compressed.pdf

Marshall, M. B., Taukeni, S. G., Haihambo, C. K., Shihako, M., Muruti, R. D., Ligando, G., De Silva, C. & Marshall, M. (2020). Maximizing student's learning success through Lab-on-line. *Addressing multicultural needs in school guidance and counselling*, 262-276.

McGreevy, S. (2011). Eight weeks to a better brain. *The Harvard Gazette*. https://news.harvard.edu/gazette/story/2011/01/eight-weeks-to-a-better-brain/

Nel, C., Dreyer, C., & Klopper, M. (2004). An analysis of the reading profiles of first-year students at Potchefstroom University: A cross-sectional study and a case study. *South African Journal of Education, 24*(1), 95–103.

Noble, K. G., Wolmetz, M. E., Ochs, L. G., Farah, M. J., & McCandliss, B. D. (2006). Brain behavior relationships in reading acquisition are modulated by socio-economic factors. *Developmental Science, 9*(6), 642–654. doi:10.1111/j.1467-7687.2006.00542.x PMID:17059461

Roefsema, P. R., Van Ooyen, A., & Watanabe, T. (2010, February). Perceptual learning rules based on reinforcers and attention. *Trends in Cognitive Sciences, 14*(2), 64–71. doi:10.1016/j.tics.2009.11.005 PMID:20060771

Samuels, S. J., Rasinski, T. V., & Hiebert, E. H. (2011). Eye movements and reading: What teachers need to know. In A. Farstrup & S. J. Samuels (Eds.), *What research has to say about reading instruction* (4th ed.). IRA. doi:10.1598/0829.02

Spichtig, A. N., Hiebert, E. H., Vorstius, C., Pascoe, J. P., Pearson, D. P., & Radach, R. (2016). The Decline of Comprehension-Based Silent Reading Efficiency in the United States: A Comparison of Current Data With Performance in 1960. *Reading Research Quarterly, 51*(2), 239–259. doi:10.1002/rrq.137

Sweller, J. (1994). Cognitive load theory, learning difficulty, and instructional design. *Learning and Instruction, 4*(4), 295–312. doi:10.1016/0959-4752(94)90003-5

Taylor, S.E., Frackenpohl, H. & Pettee, J.L. (1960). Grade level norms for the Components of the Fundamental Reading skill. *EDL Research Information Bulletin, 3*.

Taylor, S. E., & Robinson, H. A. (1963). *The relationship of oculomotor efficiency of the beginning reader to his success in learning to read.* Paper presented at the meeting of the American Educational Research Association, Chicago, IL.

The World Bank. (2020). *Pandemic Threatens to Push 72 Million More Children into Learning Poverty—World Bank outlines a New Vision to ensure that every child learns, everywhere* [Press release]. https://www.worldbank.org/en/news/press-release/2020/12/02/pandemic-threatens-to-push-72-million-more-children-into-learning-poverty-world-bank-outlines-new-vision-to-ensure-that-every-child-learns-everywhere

UNESCO. (2021). *100 million more children under the minimum reading proficiency level due to COVID-19 – UNESCO convenes world education ministers.* Retrieved September 16, 2021 from https://en.unesco.org/news/100-million-more-children-under-minimum-reading-proficiency-level-due-covid-19-unesco-convenes

United Nations. (2021). *100 million more children fail basic reading skills because of COVID-19.* UN News. Retrieved September 16, 2021, from https://news.un.org/en/story/2021/03/1088392

ADDITIONAL READING

Koenig, L., Du Plessis, A., & Viljoen, M. (2015). The Effect of a Reading Program on the Reading Performance of First-Year Students at a Higher Education Institution. *International Journal of Educational Sciences, 10*(2), 297–305. doi:10.1080/09751122.2015.11917660

Marshall, M. B. (2016). Accurate Online Intervention Practices for Efficient Improvement of Reading Skills in Africa. *The Universal Journal of Educational Research., 4*(8), 1764–1771. doi:10.13189/ujer.2016.040804

Taylor, S. E. (2000). *Visagraph eye-movement recording system.* Taylor Associates.

Taylor, S. E. (2006). *Fluency in silent reading.* Retrieved November 15, 2018, from http://www.readingplus.com/schools/pdfs/FluencyInSilentReading.pdf

Chapter 14
Game-Based Pedagogy:
Educate, Collaborate, and Engage

Carol-Ann Lane
University of Western Ontario, Canada

ABSTRACT

Interpretations of the cultural meanings made by each of the boys in the study, based on their individual unique experiences engaging with video games, can provide readers with insights into how to approach adolescent aged boys' literacy development through game-based pedagogy. In this chapter the author describes how these four boys developed their multimodal ways of learning by engaging with visual perspectives of video games. The methodological approach documented what boys are saying, as much as possible, which is currently understudied in the literature surrounding boys and their video gaming practices. This chapter addresses some boys' out-of-school video gaming practices for meaning-making and gaining cultural knowledge. Studying the ways in which boys make meanings through multimodal ways of learning can offer insights into strategies for cyber culture that can potentially reinvent traditional literacy pedagogical boundaries and establish new ways and practices for building knowledge.

INTRODUCTION

Scholars have acknowledged the potential contribution of video gaming to complex forms of learning, identifying links between gaming and engagement, experiential learning spaces, problem-solving, strategies, transliteracy reflectivity, critical literacy, and metacognitive thinking. Using a multiliteracies lens, this multi-case study examined the experiences of four boys engaged with video gaming in two different contexts: a community centre and an after-school video club.

Implementing game-based pedagogy, with the focus of video games, as an alternative classroom multiliteracies resource is acknowledged in technology and multiliteracies discourses as a strategy for meaning-making and developing cultural knowledge (Cope & Kalantzis, 2009; The New London Group, 2000). Video games include complex forms of interactive visuals, both intertextual and multimodal. Decades of scholarly research has shown that these complex forms of interactive visuals, specifically in

DOI: 10.4018/978-1-7998-7271-9.ch014

video games, are key to inviting players to understand a variety of texts in a variety of circumstances. This chapter provides an overview of a multi-case study I conducted about four boys' out-of-school video gaming practices which may support their cultural knowledge meaning-making. There were a number of findings emanating from this study, including the following: (i) boys use their video gaming practices for meaning-making and collaborative efforts in order to gain an understanding of several knowledge processes (such as decision-making, predicting, analysing, strategizing, etc.), (ii) boys extend and apply their cultural knowledge as creative innovators, producing and publishing YouTube instructional videos for video game players and designing video games for a history project, (iii) boys demonstrate peer mentoring through storytelling, face-to-face interactions or in their online community of practice, (iv) boys make meanings using metacognitive literacy skills in a variety of ways, and (v) boys focus on cultural preservation and narrative storytelling. The use of video games in game-based learning continues to evolve, representing many forms of literacy, yet video games are met often with concerns when introduced as a pedagogical strategy. While acknowledging concerns related to video gaming, such as negative identity construction, violence, distraction, and time commitment for integration, this chapter seeks to contribute to the scholarly discussion about the use of video games in classrooms by explicitly considering the ways in which gaming may support boys' meaning-making and cultural knowledge.

BACKGROUND

Using a multiliteracies lens, this multi-case ethnographic study examined the experiences of four boys engaged with video gaming in two different contexts: a community centre (Albert & Jeffrey) and an after-school video club (Mike & Brian). The case study helped me to gain an understanding of the nature of boys' behavior and learning in social settings while they engage in video game play. Studying the ways in which boys make meanings through multimodal ways of learning can offer insights into strategies that can potentially reinvent traditional literacy pedagogical boundaries and establish new ways and practices for building knowledge. which can offer insights to how they constructed cultural knowledge and meaning-making.

THE BOYS IN MY STUDY

Four boys participated in my multi-site study of two ethnographic cases. First, I briefly describe two of the boys who were included in the community centre case; second, I describe the other two boys who were included in the after-school video club case.

Upon meeting Albert (the community centre case), I observed that his behavior appeared to be very quiet, never seeming to talk to anyone. Albert, a 14-year-old adolescent, was tall and had a thin physical stature. I observed him to be very courteous and respectful to me and to other students. The other students, not part of the study, I observed as being loud and very boisterous; at times, I noticed them pushing each other and yelling. I observed Albert, who was generally focused on his video gameplay and tended not to mix with the other youth at the centre. Albert's meaning-making, such as problem-solving and analysing, generally occurred in his independent play and use of online surrounding networks. Even if other youth were conversing with him, I observed he would maintain his concentration on his video gameplay, nod or talk to them, but without moving his eyes away from the computer screen. Albert maintained a

Game-Based Pedagogy

consistent routine. Albert explained to me that he would often play certain video games to practice his problem-solving and analytical skills and then access surrounding online networks to interact with other gamers or peers by demonstrating what he had learned independently. I observed that he did not share these designing and redesigning (Cope & Kalantzis, 2009; The New London Group, 1996) knowledge processes with peers at the community centre.

The second participant in the community centre case was Jeffrey. When I first met Jeffrey, a 15-year-old adolescent, I noticed that he was slightly shorter, but larger in physical stature than Albert. I observed that Jeffrey, like Albert, did not seem to be social with the other individuals at the community centre. I observed Jeffrey to be very quiet and introspective in his actions. Although observations of Jeffrey's personality would be difficult to justify and would require further investigation for a future study, I frequently noticed in later observations and casual conversations with him that he preferred not to interact much with others. The community centre did not seem to offer Jeffrey opportunities for the ways he made meanings during his learning processes. During observations and conversations, Jeffrey revealed aspects of his mastery of several video games, practices, and particular discourses such as storytelling—an example of oral language (Cope & Kalantzis, 2009).

During my fieldwork, Jeffrey only engaged in conversation with me when other students were not in the video games room area. I was not aware of any particular reason and wanting to be sensitive and at the same time objective, I listened to him. Early in my fieldwork, Jeffrey requested, as a participant in my study, that if I was willing to listen to him, he would prefer to talk with me about video games, rather than play the games. One of the reasons he explained to me was that the available games on the video games room computers were not the narrative-driven video games which he preferred to play at home, where likely most of his meaning-making occurred. Jeffrey was highly articulate in his conversations with me, often telling stories about the video games he played, demonstrating an example of drawing on the oral language representation (Cope & Kalantzis, 2009). The community centre setting became an important factor for Jeffrey's behaviours. He always appeared to be conscious of his surroundings (Wolcott, 1987)—the room, its function and people interacting around him. He would often take up gestural representations with his abrupt body language of walking into the video games room, turning his body, and then leaving if other kids were in the room. At the post observation interview, Jeffrey shared that he had autism, which may have accounted for this behavior, although I did not make previous connections between his autism and his lack of success in engaging with others. Moreover, it also did not appear to impact the way that he provided thoughtful descriptions and stories about the games he played, often talking for long periods with me. Neither Albert nor Jeffrey interacted socially with peers or each other at the community centre.

The third participant, Mike (after-school video club), was a tall 15-year-old adolescent, with a thin physical stature. Mike was the president of the after-school video club. I observed him as friendly and respectful to me and to other students in the club. Mike chatted with everyone, ensuring all were enjoying playing the games. During my observations, Mike generally focused on his gameplay but still found time to bond with other players. He also appeared to be interested in mentoring other players. He would frequently pause a video game sequence during a competition to instruct other players on gameplay functions, strategies, or problem-solving. In doing so, Mike demonstrated his knowledge and willingness to share his experiences and meaning-making with others, and to place less emphasis on competitive goals. Mike's meaning-making also emerged from his rich collaborative interactions in the online surrounding networks and communities of practice (Alexander, 2009; Squire, 2013). He constantly exchanged strategies, ideas, and best practices with others who shared a connection and common video gaming goal with him (Gee, 2007).

The fourth participant, Brian (after-school video club), a 15-year-old adolescent, was shorter and slightly larger in physical stature than Mike. I observed Brian to be friendly and respectful to the other students, but he did not appear as talkative as Mike. During video gaming experiences, Brian was quick to share his meaning-making experiences with fellow peers by explaining certain gameplay sequences. Although some of these observations would be difficult to explain without further probing in a planned future study, Brian appeared to be conscious of the high-energy surroundings in the ways he demonstrated his gestural, visual and spatial representations (Cope & Kalantzis, 2009; Wolcott, 1987). During his game playing experiences, he would draw on video game characters' functionality to jump, dance, and perform acrobatic movements on the computer screen. Some of these actions represented ways that Brian showed mastery of his skills in the video game, but they also demonstrated Brian's' ability to navigate the various interplay of visuals while playing the game. Additionally, these action sequences represented for Brian some of his emotional gestures, feelings, and emotions. He would sometimes physically perform these same movements in the classroom in front of his peers, and did not appear inhibited by the surroundings, peers, or the space he occupied. In some ways, Brian demonstrated weaving his experiences with peers (Cope & Kalantzis, 2009), by openly demonstrating unfamiliar actions and texts with others. Brian appeared to be an expert in video gaming, and he would often find ways to mentor other players and share experiences. Brian, like Mike, was less interested in video game competition, but rather focused on knowledge, collaboration, and engagement with peers. Like Mike, Brian frequently paused a video game sequence to guide his peers in the mechanics of characters and gameplay strategies.

GAME-BASED PEDAGOGY: CO-CONSTRUCTING KNOWLEDGE

The pattern among the boys, Albert, Mike, and Brian, revealed a strong interest in increasing aptitudes in decision-making, problem-solving, and strategy. These themes relate to how children focus their capabilities by hypothetical reasoning and concerning themselves with the aim of improving capabilities with new experiences in solving problems (Piaget, 1972). Albert specifically chose puzzle platformer video games, such as Minecraft, and Portal 2, by associating these game-playing experiences with new ways of meaningful learning and new ways of problem-solving and strategy. He would sometimes use Minecraft before he played a multiplayer competitive video game called Team Fortress, where other players would rely on his skills of building or helping the team. Choosing puzzle games, for example, was a way for Albert to problem solve while multiplayer competitive games provided a way for him to build by choosing certain characters and being part of a team. Rather than follow the game sequences, he concentrated his efforts on building and constructing. According to Albert, "you can build different things, portals and dispenser ... Ahhh 'cause when you're engineer, you can build different things." He explained this to me, ignored his train of thought, and then returned to the task at hand: "I was just gonna build almost at the wall."

Although Albert focused less on the setting or narrative plot events, being able to navigate multiple events, locations, and semiotics in a game enhanced his literacy skills to comprehend plot and characters (Gros, 2007). Albert consistently demonstrated the ways he organized his self-directed activities with persistence until he achieved his goal of learning a task (Aarsand, 2010).

Game-Based Pedagogy

Likewise, Mike, and Brian focused their efforts and interest on Super Smash Bros. Melee, which allowed them to build on their quick decision-making and strategic skills. For Mike, and Brian, cultural knowledge emerged from how they made sense of playing those specific video games. For example, Mike's cultural experiences connected to the ways he would improve his strategy and decision-making skills. Mike explained "the game has a lot of decision-making … it teaches you how to analyze things, say like Prisoner of Zelda … problem-solving."

Mike's clarification demonstrated his willingness to give up difficulty or challenge in a game if he could have a cultural game playing experience involving decision-making. His reasoning relates to assumptions made by Sanford and Madill (2006) that players will sometimes favour quick-paced decision-making games and forego playing games with rich embedded literacy content. For example, Mike explained how he developed his own learning strategies for better decision-making during Super Smash Bros. Melee tournaments: "But at the beginning like once you just like ahhh get assigned to your partners and you have like thirty seconds to quickly make a plan, we've kinda developed our own language." Mike's comment demonstrated the ways he used his video gaming experiences to learn actively and gain knowledge from peers by developing language codes and speech. Mike's language development is an example of Vygotsky's (1978) reasoning that children use signs and words as the most important means of their social contact to communicate with others. This also suggests Mike's flexibility and adaptability. In addition, he is highly responsive to video gaming tournaments, especially those involving high pressure, having only seconds to develop a plan and language in which to communicate. Mike's comments also illustrate the fact that his cultural gaming experiences involve resourcefulness, quick decision-making, and effective communication skills, utilizing his language development. This type of communication relates to Gee's (2009) argument that video games recruit a "specialized language" to promote learning "in and out of school" (p. 54). Mike's comment is a good example of his collaborative activities, often providing him opportunities to be creative and innovative with partners and reminding us of how children use surroundings to exchange information with others (Piaget, 1972). The university space for tournaments appeared to be an inviting social environment where Mike actively contributed as a member, which in turn provided him with positive reinforcement for developing his cultural knowledge (Gee, 2007; Lankshear, 1997; Steinkuehler, Squire & Barab, 2012). At the same time, Mike made meanings by reinforcing his own perspective and ideas (Cope & Kalantzis, 2009). His vocal actions related to sharing gameplay strategies and guiding peers, suggested ways in which he publicized his beliefs and values in a social setting. Thus, by providing feedback and suggestions about gameplay strategies Mike was allowing his cognition to be heard by others, creating a way for new concepts and new meanings to be developed (Cope & Kalantzis, 2009; Squire, 2013). Mike subvocalized and exhibited verbal activities to engage and interact with others in a way that allowed him a pathway to share his cultural knowledge.

Mike and Brian demonstrated experiencing the new by directly seeking collaborative opportunities in team related video games, such as Super Smash Bros. Melee. For Mike and Brian, experiences of collaborating with others became meaningful to them. They viewed human partners as the best training partners, demonstrating their awareness that experiencing the new involves exposing themselves to other learners' knowledge processes (Cope & Kalantzis, 2016). Their learning processes resembled Vygotsky's (1978) zone of proximal development, where social activity enhances learning. For instance, Mike privileged the social aspects of gaming by engaging with friends who had common affiliations with learning strategies, decision-making, and problem-solving with Super Smash Bros. Melee. His meaning-making suggests ways he developed out-of-school literacy practices, such as listening, responding, and reflecting on meanings with friends. Mike explained many details about the characters including strengths and weaknesses, and optimal choices to make for certain strategic moves. Mike commented, "Just playing we can practice so I talk about different strategies and stuff." His meaning-making helped him to develop out-of-school literacy practices, such as listening, responding, and reflecting about meanings with friends (Alexander, 2009; Beach et al., 2006; Beavis, 2012; Gee, 2003, 2007; Steinkuehler, Squire, & Barab, 2012).

The boys focused highly on improving their skills, and although Jeffrey did not focus on these abilities specifically for himself, he did recount cultural experiences of reasoning skills specific to analysing why historical events occurred in video game plots.

Mike actively engaged in online and face-to-face communities of practice. These online spaces are indicative of what Squire (2013) termed 'experiential learning spaces', where learners engage in rich collaborative interactions organized around a primary affiliation to their common goals (Gee, 2007). Mike demonstrated experiencing the known by contributing his values and ideas about strategies or video games to the online community of practice. Mike is a good example of Jansz' (2005) claim that players' social interest will influence them to "exchange information about (new) video games and gaming practices." By interacting with other online players and with peers at face-to-face university video game tournaments, he experienced his learning processes through his awareness of peers' knowledge and through building friendships. He exchanged ideas and posed questions about various strategies with others to develop his knowledge processes. In drawing from this diverse resource base of experts and novices, both online and face-to-face, Mike was experiencing the new by actively participating as a member within his community of practice (Cope & Kalantzis, 2009; Steinkuehler, Squire & Barab, 2012). Part of Mike's active engagement in the community of practice involved literacy practices referred to as metagaming (Steinkuehler, 2007) which involved his participation in peer-based discussion forums and chatrooms. This type of collaborative mentoring, Mike explained, manifested itself in the form of "reading your opponents … Predict what they're gonna do." More importantly, Mike explained that he used chatboards, which also support and confirm alternative forms of literacy (Lankshear, 1997). His reliance on smashboards, which is similar to a message chatroom, represented for him a form of collaboration and communication in literacy. This alternative form of communication parallels Lankshear's (1997) argument that "new forms of discourse is [are] especially evident in such forums as electronic journals, email, news groups, and a diverse array of MOOs, webpages, message boards and the like" (p. 153). For Brian, he preferred to collaborate and share ideas with peers, extending and communicating ideas such as plots, storylines, and strategies. This cooperative style of learning supports Vygotsky's (1978) theory of socialized learning; to learn by others or with others. Brian's learning development is highly reliant on collaboration and mentoring, which also echoes Lankshear's (1997) claim that the "hidden curriculum of gaming is an initiative into modes of practice that are characterized much more by learning, and self-collaborative direction and discovery than about whole sale exposure to teaching and instruction" (p. 151). Gee (2007), Vygotsky (1978), and Steinkuehler, Squire and Barab (2012) reiterated the importance of collaboration and mentoring, through the "depth of collaborative inquiry, complexity of gameplay, opportunities for consequentiality, rich perception – action cycles, exploration of situated identities and the complex forms of learning and participation that can occur during gameplay" (Steinkuehler, Squire & Barab, 2012, p. 271). He experienced the new by building his awareness of the differences among other players' theories and different strategies about gameplay (Kafai, Burke, & Steinkuehler, 2016). Mike maintained his online role consistently by demonstrating his commitment to his beliefs, reflections and play style, making his "cognition visible to participants" (Squire, 2013, p. 115), both with random players and with friends in the online community of practice.

Game-Based Pedagogy

Co-operating with friends and sharing ideas or gaming practices was important to Jeffrey, Mike, and Brian. Albert also interacted with online players but in a somewhat different way. His preference was to learn independently, then share his ideas through game walkthroughs. Different forms of communication also occurred during the boys' cultural experiences, which became meaningful for them. During my fieldwork, the boys shared ideas, interacted with each other and often recounted cultural experiences involving some form of social dynamics. In this way, they drew distinctions between their own gaming experience and their peers, given they played together and would exchange ideas and be exposed to others' views (Steinkuehler, Squire, & Barab, 2012). What became significant in these gaming activities was how they attributed meanings to these experiences. Some of these social interactions involved playing together (Mike and Brian), sharing directions (Albert and Jeffrey), having discussions (Mike and Brian), and telling stories and asking probing questions with friends (Jeffrey).

Mike and Brian would often seek gaming activities with peers, whereas Jeffrey and Albert appeared to be more independent in their knowledge processes. Most times, Albert engaged in self-initiated learning from puzzle platformer video games, but this was in preparation for his video gaming practices with multiple online players, whereby he acted as an interdependent team member. Albert's ability to play independently and as a team member reflects his flexibility and adaptability in his playing experiences. Jeffrey at one point played one of these multiplayer competitive video games, and during much of this gameplay sequence he would give directions to Albert, and then they would alternate these roles, warning each other of pending threats and best strategies (Alexander, 2009). Their communication represented strategic planning, interdependence on each other, and collaborating, but not specifically producing or extending new knowledge. When they collaborated using this form of oral and visual support, they demonstrated their gameplay activity with socialized speech patterns in the form of oral discussions (Vygotsky, 1978). Steinkuehler, Squire, and Barab (2012) have long argued that when players play together, they often exchanged ideas and are exposed to one another's thinking. Albert and Jeffrey shared and exchanged ideas about different strategies they used during the video game sequences, and also shared paratexts, such as developer information and references to comic book characters, referred to as "spontaneous knowledge" (Cope & Kalantzis, 2009) between learners who are active theory makers.

EDUCATE: SOCIAL SITUATION OF GAME-PLAY

One of the themes demonstrated by Albert, Jeffrey, Mike, and Brian was the way they applied their knowledge in real world situations, and shared their opinions reflectively (Cope & Kalantzis, 2009). Their reliance on intrapersonal abilities, relating to the individual's thoughts, became less important among friends when they openly guided peers and shared stories or strategies, demonstrating their seamless transition to interpersonal functioning (Vygotsky, 1978) in their cognitive development. Mike, Brian, and Jeffrey demonstrated informal techniques of building social dynamics, whether about strategies, competing against other opponents, or understanding the storylines. Jeffrey also distinguished his need to collaborate on stories or ideas with friends and individuals that he had established relationships with. Mike and Brian, however, were more flexible and willing to collaborate face-to-face (Finn, 1999) with random partners assigned to them in tournaments. Mike explained, "Ahhh I mean collaboration, ahhh strategy I guess ... it's a big part and gets other people to talk a lot about strategy an what we want to do next time ahh ... we go to weekly tournaments"

This also relates to some suggestions made by Gee (2010), who argued, "that participation in the practices of various social and cultural groups determines which experiences a person has and how they pay attention to the elements of these experiences" (p. 27).

Before continuing the discussion of my findings and linking them to research conducted by well-known psychologists Piaget (1972) and Vygotsky (1978), it is important to note a major gap in the literature. Both psychologists acknowledged the lack of studies in cultural knowledge, and cognitive development in adolescents, as their work concentrated efforts on children. Even though this gap exists, it is still useful to draw on their work. Although Piaget's (1972) was a boys' only study and is considered somewhat controversial now, his work sheds some light on how children use reasoning powers independently through experimentation prior to indulging in social interactions. Having said that, there were certain instances when Albert demonstrated a formal exchange of information through collaboration with Jeffrey when they played a video game together. This formal exchange resembled an interdependence or co-operation using simultaneous directions. Furthermore, Albert's and Jeffrey's mutual support for each other demonstrated the capacity to reach a semi-formal social dynamic, which helped to heighten their aptitude (Piaget, 1972) for playing the game, but lacked the social bonding aspect, which is a strong condition for collaboration. This mutual bonding was significant in the cultural experiences of gameplay sequences between Mike and Brian.

Social dynamics were demonstrated in my study, occurring in different forms with Jeffrey, Mike, and Brian. Recall Jeffrey who played video games online using surrounding networks of random players. He found that he could not work or co-operate with random players, even though he tried because the social aspect was missing. For Jeffrey, playing with friends was an important aspect to his cultural gaming experiences because he knew their play style and had fun sharing ideas and questions with them. Well-known clinical psychologists (Piaget, 1972; Vygotsky, 1978) have suggested that children develop certain behaviors to guide themselves. They organize their own activities, within a favourable environment, to fit a social form of behavior to succeed. Brian's approach to cultural knowledge was similar to Jeffrey's in the sense that he preferred sharing exciting moments with others during these social interactions. Brian called these moments positive fleeting interactions, found in the learning – sharing moments domain. He also explained that peers offer support and are the best training partners. Brian's demonstration of video gaming as having a social impact on his learning mirrors Steinkuehler, Squire, and Barab (2012) findings, advancing Vygotsky's (1978) movement about socialization, when they argued "consistent with the sociocultural approach, it's equally important for researchers and theorists to understand the socially situated nature of gameplay." This view coincides with Gee's (2007) perspective of building "affinity spaces" (p. 91). Although affinity spaces relate more specifically to online gaming, Gee's views also apply to video gaming in the same way, as evidenced by Brian's perspective about playing with a human, which provides more depth to learning rather than just playing against a computer. Gee (2007) argued,

Players can play alone against the computer or with and against other human players. Whether they play alone or together, the enterprise is social since almost all players need to get and share information about the games in order to become adept at playing them. (pp. 91-92)

These actions are echoed by Steinkuehler (2006) and Taylor (2006) when they identified video gaming "to be a deeply social enterprise" (p. 20). Peers supporting peers is congruent with Vygotsky's (1978) theory of the zone of proximal development, which relates to how children imitate each other in an activity or by following a demonstration. Brian and Mike both focused on working with peers and friends

Game-Based Pedagogy

to learn from each other, thus predicting or understanding psychological aspects by collaborating with more capable peers (Vygotsky, 1978). The zone of proximal development (Vygotsky, 1978) includes peer demonstrations, which is directly related to how Albert gained his social interaction through demonstrating video gameplays and strategies to surrounding network online players. According to Albert, he would play Minecraft, often "alone when my friends aren't on, because that way when they do get on I casually show them what I made." References to video demonstrations and game walkthroughs are examples of how he applied his theories by sharing them with others. Albert's willingness to show others what he learned demonstrated his confidence in his own skills and abilities.

Furthermore, social activity emerging as a cultural theme from this study parallels the collaborative, socialized activity of teams of over 200 students playing a video game for one day in an Amsterdam study (Huizenga et al., 2009), as they guided and collaborated with each other in order to actively learn.

The boys indicated that they preferred working with peers and friends they know, rather than with random online players. Moreover, Mike and Brian demonstrated this preference for bonding and socializing during their video game playing sequences, by physically sitting close together, cheering, dancing, clapping their hands, and encouraging each other. When Albert and Jeffrey recounted their video gaming experiences with friends, they also shared how they built relationships, helping the team and each other. These forms of social interaction support Vygotsky's (1978) theory that learning is an external process.

Prior studies also demonstrated that boys cultivate their cultural meanings through social dynamics. One such study determined how youth, particularly boys, are motivated socially to play video games (Olson, 2010). Jansz (2005) also found that adult males were significantly motivated to play in large-scale video game tournaments based on socially driven interests, rather than for competitive reasons. Although a literature gap exists with these studies in that Jansz (2005) did not focus on adolescent boys, it provides some insight into my study findings.

EXTENDING CULTURAL KNOWLEDGE

Albert and Mike chose the puzzle platformer video games to learn independently to improve their gaming practices. They were not competing against others to achieve higher points, but rather they were developing their own skills to share what they had learned with others. They demonstrated these skills and extended learning by showing others. For example, both Albert and Mike provided instruction to random online game players, friends, and peers through walkthroughs and gameplays. Albert would use YouTube to facilitate some of these demonstrations (Vygotsky, 1978), whereas Mike would solve problems using Legend of Zelda and share those strategies with others. What distinguishes Albert's and Mike's cultural knowledge from the other boys is their desire to use problem-solving skills, not just to problem solve and improve in a game but as a means to extend knowledge to others.

A commonality in the findings among Albert, Jeffrey, Mike, and Brian is their interactions with friends, other online gamers, and team members. Mike, Brian, and Jeffrey, interacted directly through peer-to-peer support activities, playing with each other to build and actively co-produce cultural knowledge. However, Albert's interactions differed from the others. As an interdependent team member, Albert often played Team Fortress, choosing characters such as medic or an engineer to help instruct the team. In addition, Albert built cultural knowledge through his video demonstrations, which involved a certain amount of collaboration. The transfer of knowledge is an indirect social method to exchange information with others who shared a common affiliation with the video games (Cope & Kalantzis, 2009; Gee,

2007). Therefore, Albert shared cultural experiences with others through these demonstrations (Vygotsky, 1978). Albert tended to focus on using online surrounding networks such as YouTube in order to facilitate these demonstrations, and often showed his friends different things he built when he played Minecraft. Albert's way of demonstrating his cultural knowledge about video games relates to the way both boys and girls can gain satisfaction from teaching others how to play (Olson, 2010).

Mike, Brian, and Jeffrey, and in some cases Albert, showed a continuous cultural pattern of social engagement with friends or peers. Researchers (Gee, 2007; Lankshear, 1997; Steinkuehler, Squire, & Barab, 2012) have suggested that positive reinforcement for learning can occur when individuals work together, socialize, receive feedback, or encouragement from peers or friends. The boys' communication pattern was consistent throughout their gameplay as they relied on each other to learn and exchange ideas. These actions are in agreement with Gee's (2007) findings that highlight the social aspect of video games, whereby players construct meaning. Gee (2007) also explained the social affinity of playing video games as "their characteristic social practices, and the sorts of identities people take on within these groups and practices" (p. 43). Gee (2010) argued that,

Knowing how to read or write a game faq (a strategy guide for a video game) requires knowing how game faqs are used in the social practices of gamers, practices that involve much more than just reading and writing. It requires knowing how gamers talk about, debate over, and act. (pp. 19-20)

The actions and responses demonstrated by Mike and Brian revealed an emerging theme of peer mentoring and collaboration. Although Brian and Mike were typical gamers, showing much enthusiasm, and even appearing, at times, to be in competition with each other during their tournaments, they always found the time to provide guidance, and peer-to-peer teaching to other players. In this way, Brian and Mike could help other players familiarize themselves with learning the game. Peer mentoring supports Steinkuehler, Squire and Barab's (2012) claim that, "people get encouragement from an audience and feedback from peers, although everyone plays both roles at different times" (p. 144).

Albert, however, appeared to be highly motivated by independent video gaming experiences, often playing Minecraft or Portal 2. Similarly, Jeffrey independently played Never Alone (Kisima Innitchuna) to learn about Alaskan heritage before suggesting that others play the game with him, so they could discuss ideas about it and share opinions about the stories or historical events. Both Jeffrey and Albert showed strength in developing their sense of cultural knowledge independently, before transitioning to a collaborative focus to share their thinking processes with others (Cope & Kalantzis, 2009). Independent learning prior to collaborative learning mimics how children acquire independence in cognitive development through internalizing practical steps, guiding themselves, then moving to an interpersonal function of organized activities in relation to another person (Vygotsky, 1978).

PEER-MENTORING AND SHARING CULTURAL MEANINGS

Mike, and specifically Brian, created cultural meanings by playing video games with peers who were perceived as the best training partners in the training partners' domain. Brian commented, "If I'm playing a game like Smash Brothers it's better to have, better to have a human, ummm another human to practice against where your peers are the best training partners." This phenomenon was also evident in Ito et al.'s (2008) study of 800 youth, which found that most youth engage in video gaming to connect with others as a means to socialize with friends and learn from peers. Mike and Brian would often disrupt tournament matches to give peers chances to learn new strategies. In this way, they transformed their video gaming practices into tangible ways of mentoring each other (Steinkuehler, Squire, & Barab, 2012). Their desire to facilitate and mentor others with their acquired knowledge demonstrated their active participation within their video gaming surroundings, such as the after-school video club. As active members, they found opportunities to produce their meanings and share with others (Alexander, 2009; Gee, 2003, 2007; Gros, 2007).

Mike and Brian privileged mentoring their peers over the actual competition, and their actions resembled those of students in Huizenga et al.'s (2009) study who worked together in teams in a virtual reality game. Mike and Brian's active theory making demonstrated their willingness to collaborate and socially interact with each other, thus contributing to the ways they actively learned and gained knowledge from each other (Vygotsky, 1978). They also demonstrated literacy skills associated with developing strategies and decision-making (Alexander, 2009). Mike and Brian's conceptualising highlighted them as resident experts (Cope & Kalantzis, 2009) who demonstrated their way of thinking to others (Steinkuehler, Squire, & Barab, 2012).

Mike specifically referred to the many times he would play video games at home with his friends, bonding and socializing with them, talking about different things, not just video game related. Engaging in conversations with friends while playing video games relates to Vygotsky's (1978) suggestion that in the first stage of cultural development, children create meanings through their own system of social behavior. Albert's cultural meanings represented his sense of flexibility and sensitivity to others' needs. Through his choices of video game characters, Albert helped the team when needed and in doing so, he showed a responsiveness to others. Albert interacted with team members in a helpful way, which relates to Vygotsky's (1978) theory of children planning their activities by enlisting the help of another person to solve problems. Jeffrey developed his cultural meanings from his experiences of playing video games mostly with friends. It was important for Jeffrey that his friends played the same video games with him in order to have conversations with them. Jeffrey felt that by sharing moments, such as talking about the games, plots, and characters, and expressing opinions with friends, he would know them well enough to share common goals or to use their cultural and social differences as strategic resources (Gee, 2007).

Jeffrey explained to me,

Yah, I'll talk about plot with friends. Especially if they played the game themselves, cause of course we'll both have ... we'll have questions about the game where always gonna be questions like why did this happen or why did this have to happen? Especially with very emotional events in the games. (Jeffrey, personal communication, community centre case, August 2015)

Both Mike and Brian exhibited cultural patterns of shared moments when they socialized at the after-school video club. The cultural theme of social dynamics also emerged when they attended Super Smash Bros. Melee tournaments. At these tournaments, they collaborated and experienced the socially situated nature of this type of video game to get better at their video game strategies and to learn from each other (Steinkuehler, Squire & Barab, 2012).

Jeffrey extended his cultural experiences by means of storytelling, which is a way of socializing his experiences through his narrative and socialized levels of speech (Piaget, 1972; Vygotsky, 1978). Similarly, Brian, and Mike shared this pattern of socialized talk about their video gaming experiences with whomever was willing to listen, relating to the ways that children use signs and words as a means of social contact with others (Vygotsky, 1978).

CO-CONSTRUCTING KNOWLEDGE

Jeffrey, Mike, and Brian all showed strong tendencies of co-constructing knowledge through their reliance on oral discussions, which does not entirely support the suggestions made by Blum (1997) that boys' brains crowd out verbal processing. It is important to note there is a literature gap in the age-level of the studies by Blum (1997), Gurian and Stevens (2010a, 2010b), and Sax (2005), which appear to focus on boys just prior to puberty. This may or may not be a factor, but it is interesting to recognize that my study involved adolescent-aged boys (14-15) and that they gained much of their cultural knowledge through verbal literacy skills and social dynamics while playing video games. Brian expressed his critical literacy skills by interpreting and sharing stories with peers. Brian took his literacy skills to another level by using his in-depth analytical skills to explore psychological or emotional concepts. He not only assessed game narratives, but also expanded on his own ideas to develop complex theoretical game concepts. Both Mike and Brian's co-construction of knowledge and exploration of psychological concepts demonstrated their awareness of the game and reflexivity, further validating claims made by Hommel (2010) and Van Sledright (2002) who argued that these, combined with other intertextual skills, validated subject criteria. Although Van Sledright's (2002) study involved fifth grade students, the findings revealed that "all appeared more adept at analyzing the documents and images ... Intertextual on-line comments regarding the documents and images increased from 17% of the total number of vocalizations in the initial task to 41% in the end-point task" (p. 143).

Mike played Undertale regularly to improve his literacy and decision-making skills. Mike explained that he read external resources to determine better decisions for outcomes. Mike's immersion with complex multimodal elements demonstrated his competency in terms of interacting with the storyline, characters, and strategic decision-making (Jenkins, 2002). He also transferred his experience with building skills to other problem-solving games, spatially understanding the complex layout designs of the different worlds, different frames, options, and outcomes (Cope & Kalantzis, 2009). Mike recognized how the immersive quality of the game created an emotional connection (Jenkins, 2002; Squire, 2013), thus enhancing his overall learning experience. Mike's meaning-making with this video game reflected an experiential approach to co-construct narratives by immersing himself in the video game design elements as he interacted with the characters, and deconstructed and reconstructed the game narrative plot (Jenkins, 2002; Squire, 2013). Mike's cultural associations reflect suggestions made by Squire (2013), Steinkuehler (2010), Gee (2007), and Jenkins, (2002), that popular games designed with storylines offer video game players experiential learning spaces to think with complex tools and resources for complex problem-solving (Squire, 2013). In addition, although Mike generally relied on speech and words for his learning processes, his listening skills were equally important and are a key part of the meaning-making process according to The New London Group's (1996) and Cope and Kalantzis' (2009) multiliteracies theory of redesigning processes. Mike made meanings based on the ways he organized ideas, thoughts, and critically reflected options when he interacted with the characters (Alexander, 2009). His actions suggest his overall ability and responsiveness to strategies and decision-making.

Game-Based Pedagogy

Mike recognized how the immersive quality of the game created an emotional connection (Jenkins, 2002; Squire, 2013), thus enhancing his overall learning experience. Undertale also includes multiliteracies interactive functionality, where players assume character roles and activate empathy for the other characters in the game. Meaningful learning experiences emerged for Mike through playing this video game when he made emotional and cultural associations with a character, he called mom. Mike recognized how the immersive quality of the game created an emotional connection (Jenkins, 2002; Squire, 2013), thus enhancing his overall learning experience. These game-based immersive approaches help to create "an emotionally compelling context for the player" (Squire, 2013, p. 110). Further to this point, Squire (2013) argued that good games connect players emotionally and invite them "into a world that is to be a learner" (p. 110). The way Mike interacted with the game's various embedded semiotics, such as sound, images, movement, and speech, demonstrated his ability to read, listen, choose, process information, and redesign his meanings (Cope & Kalantzis, 2009; Hommel, 2010; Rowsell & Walsh, 2011).

Many of Mike, Brian, and Jeffrey's cultural experiences, in the form of social dynamics and peer support or bonding with friends, were actively supplemented with socialized speech patterns in the form of oral discussions (Vygotsky, 1978). Such patterns challenge researchers' claims that boys rely less on verbal activities (Blum, 1997). Albert, Jeffrey, Mike, and Brian's reliance on oral discussions as a means of communicating and applying cultural knowledge is directly related to how children's intellectual development occurs when speech and activity are fused (Vygotsky, 1978). Mike and Brian used socialized language as a way to communicate (Vygotsky, 1978) and they shared video gameplay strategies by creatively applying their new ideas with others (Cope & Kalantzis, 2009). This externalized form of activity (Vygotsky, 1978) became a preferred way of increasing their culturally shared knowledge. While Mike and Brian spoke about strategies, video game plots, or characters with friends, Jeffrey was more sophisticated in his use of language through his storytelling capabilities. Jeffrey told stories and probed his friends with questions as cognitive and communicative functions of language (Vygotsky, 1978). The boys showed strong reliance on oral discourse to build and co-construct cultural knowledge (Gee, 2007). Jeffrey's primary borrowing of available designs was linguistic, generally oral storytelling, and auditory, with a secondary focus on visual, gestural, and spatial representations (Cope & Kalantzis, 2009). At times, the surrounding online communities of practice allowed Jeffrey to share his redesigned meanings with other players (Sanford & Madill, 2006; Steinkuehler, Squire, & Barab, 2012; Vygotsky, 1978). Jeffrey participated in these online communities of practice as online forums, chat sessions among online players occurring within a video game. For example, through his participation and membership in these various online spaces, Jeffrey actively built his literacy and discourse skills, such as storytelling, listening, critically reflecting and responding to others (Alexander, 2009; Beach et al. 2006; Beavis, 2012; Gee, 2003, 2007; Steinkuehler, Squire & Barab, 2012). The sociocultural context of online communities of practice invites players to engage in forms of multimodal textual play. Steinkuehler (2011) suggests that these online discourse communities provide players with opportunities for "interpreting and understanding print text" (p. 4). In this sense, higher reliance on visual spatial aspects of the game were apparent. Albert interacted with others in these surrounding online communities of practice to reinforce gameplay actions, explanations, and problem-solving with peers (Alexander, 2009; Gros, 2007), while Jeffrey focused more on the background context of the story, questioning why certain events occurred (Alexander, 2009, Hommel, 2010; Jenkins, 2006; Van Sledright, 2002).

Jeffrey connected meaning to his game playing experiences by classifying the culturally rich non-linear storyline (Jenkins, 2006) rather than the competitive strategic significance associated with Mike's and Brian's experiences.

Both Mike and Brian relied on exchanging ideas about those strategies by talking with partners, peers, and friends. The boys' cultural video game experiences became meaningful to their co-construction of knowledge. Their exchange of ideas about video games and gaming experiences was a method of communicating. This observation aligns with Jansz' (2005) finding that face-to-face exchanges of information about gaming experiences increased the motivation of players.

GENDER IN VIDEO GAMES: MULTIPLE MASCULINITIES

Connell (2000) defined masculinities as including patriarchal forms of dominance "while others are subordinated or marginalized" (p. 10). Although Connell (1996) often related to the "stereotypical images of violent masculinity" (p. 209) found in games, Connell (1996) also understood that "boys are not a homogeneous bloc, that masculinities vary and change" (p. 230). Connell (1996), also believed that boys are continuously exposed to social media, and because of this it is particularly difficult for them to navigate among school peers and micro cultures that shape identities. Connell (1996) argued that "schools are routinely blamed for social problems affecting boys. It is, therefore important to register the fact that the school is not the only institution shaping masculinities … the mass media are crammed with representations of masculinities" (p. 211). By conducting my study with adolescent boys who played video games outside of school, I attempted to limit any micro cultural influences from peers, to understand the ways boys would express their masculine identities, and to observe how they would approach learning using these video games. As multiple masculinities is a complex and broad topic in itself, I will limit my discussion in this section will touch briefly on my findings relating to how multiple masculinities were expressed by the boys. Future studies are planned for this topic.

Jeffrey, Mike, and Brian Toxic masculine behaviors were absent from the results as those behaviors were never exhibited by the boys. Mike and Brian preferred to use animal or non-masculine or feminine characters when they played video games. They explained how they made these choices on a regular basis and were quite open with peers in tournaments and/or public competitions. They provided context in their post-observation interviews by citing reasons for choosing feminine characters as stronger than masculine ones, and generally choosing non-violent options in video games. They also reasoned how their game choices were particular to not harming other characters during gameplay sequences. The only evidence emerging from this theme about gender was with Albert, who admitted to exploring feminine and masculine characters. He explained that he was interested in understanding the abilities of those characters and his understanding would help him to play the game differently or have different responses to the gameplay experiences. He admitted to selecting his gender first then transitioning to a female character. Albert's response challenges Sanford and Madill's (2006) claim that boys tend to "resist traditional school literacies, choosing instead modes of literacy to support the particular type of masculine persona they have selected for themselves, and make a commitment to that self-selected identity" (p. 299).

Jeffrey spoke more about the description of a virtual video game character rather than specific gender qualities. The only real reference that Jeffrey made about gender was when he responded to "Are there ways that you act as a boy at school (do you perform certain masculine traits) that you don't act at home or while playing video games?" Jeffrey's response to this question was "Ok … if something scares me in real life I'm not gonna scream like a little girl like I do in a video game with my friends." In this way, although Jeffrey did not display overall significance in his exploration of gender or multiple masculini-

Game-Based Pedagogy

ties, he did demonstrate other ways by resisting "toxic" (Connell, 1996) masculinity traits by resisting violence in games.

Neither Mike nor Brian explored different genders of characters; however, evidence suggests they consistently reversed their gender roles while playing video games. Therefore, it is apparent that the boys were exploring varying "modes of masculinity" (Skelton & Francis, 2011, p. 458). For the boys, expressing different forms of their masculinity continues to challenge claims made by scholars about video games influencing negative forms of identity (Alexander, 2009; Connell, 1996; Gros, 2007).

Similarly, neither Albert nor Jeffrey played video games selecting a different gender role from their own gender or expressing outward characteristics of a reverse gender role. Brian exhibited this pattern and consistently selected feminine characters during his gameplay sequences. He did so without any prompts and openly indicated his effeminate nature, suggesting that he did not privilege masculine gender or characters in a video game and did not put efforts into being masculine. Here, Brian defends his choices and behavior by providing context about his personal background. He further downplays any association with potential "toxic" (Mac an Ghaill, 1994) masculine behavior, such as aggression or competitiveness in playing games, which further challenges Sanford and Madill's (2006) findings. The researchers indicated that they, "did not find evidence that learners were thinking consciously and reflecting about cultural models of the world, or that they were consciously reflecting on the values that make up, their real or video game worlds" (p. 300). Brian continuously reinforced his position on gender by consciously reflecting on the lack of female representation and the need to promote this aspect in gaming. He referred to reading a documentary that was created about Super Smash Bros. Melee and noted that it did not do "a great job of representing its females players very well."

Similarly, Mike consistently chose animal characters, although not specific to reversing a gender role but still representing non-gendered characters, and indicated that he would not specifically choose a masculine gender. Mike explained that he preferred to choose gender-neutral characters such as animals. This does not really support a strong gender association either way, but he did provide context to these preferences, by indicating that masculinity did not influence his decisions. In this way, Mike was not attempting to use video games as a means to express his masculine identity. Mike and Brian's actions challenge Sanford and Madill's (2006) claim that video games provide players with opportunities "to resist connections to the feminine" (p. 297). He explained, "Well I'm say like, masculinity of a character again that stuff doesn't really affect me. Say like in Melee I don't play fox because he's a fox." Mike also provided a basis for exhibiting a sensitive form of masculinity by thoughtfully expressing the maternal aspects of a video game, when he stated, "So it's called Undertale, and it's just like a really good experience, because you get really emotionally attached to the creature. You call her mom afterwards … It's like really emotional."

These video game skills, actions, and behaviors are somewhat linked to the boys' subjectivity and forms of multiple masculinities, although these links are not conclusive. Their behaviors were not a defined rejection of the masculine 'self' but a self-awareness that was celebrated, weaknesses and all, especially in the ways they were inclined not to choose characters stereotypically masculine. Furthermore, the boys did not appear to use video games as a conscious effort to explore or understand their gender or stereotypical masculinity.

PLANNED FUTURE STUDIES AND CONCLUSION

There remains continued reluctance by educators to accept video games as an alternative pedagogical resource due to concerns such as time commitment and common themes of competition. However not all video games are alike and not all students respond to video game content in the same way as evidenced by my research (Lane, 2018). As findings indicated, participants habitually co-constructed knowledge, establishing new cultural and meaningful experiences. Many video games are narrative-driven with embedded storylines to engage learners to develop their critical perspectives about how the texts work, such as characters' roles within the storyline (Beavis, 2012; Cope & Kalantzis, 2009). Based on my research, educators may gain insight by exploring the benefits of incorporating game=based pedagogy and by fusing outside gaming practices with in-school learning.

I observed the boys' behavioral traits within the multiple sites, which resembled semi-regulated environments. A future study is planned to include observations inside and outside of the school, including the home. These extended observations may reveal their interactions with family or friends and confirm consistency of their behavioral traits present in the current findings. Additionally, Mike and Brian provided many insights about their experiences at university video gaming tournaments. They explained ways that they made meanings and built cultural knowledge by collaborating with peers, building relationships, and learning strategies during these tournament visits. To understand their unique experiences better, a future study is planned for attending these tournaments with them or others to observe how they interact with peers and make meanings in such contexts. Within the literature there are many contradictions and lack of empirical research regarding the perception of boys and their potential transference of critical literacy skills to the in-school practice. Therefore, future studies are required to investigate levels of content literacy of video games and boys' perception of how to use these skills to improve their literacy development for in-school practice. Because multiple masculinities presents a broad range of complexities in and of itself, and some of the boys in my study expressed different identities, I have planned a future study to explore this phenomena further. Although some of the boys in my study showed minor tendencies to explore gender and multiple masculinities, due to the complexity of this domain of research, a future study is planned in which I would draw specifically upon a multiple masculinities lens to make sense of the ways in which the boys constructed their gender while engaging in video gaming practices. Similarly, a gap exists in Dietz's (1998) study because no adolescent boys were identified as participants to express their masculinity in multiple ways through their character choices.

REFERENCES

Aarsand, P. (2010). Young boys playing digital games. *Nordic Journal of Digital Literacy*, 5(1), 38–55. doi:10.18261/ISSN1891-943X-2010-01-04

Alexander, J. (2009). Gaming, student literacies, and the composition classroom: Some possibilities for transformation. *College Composition and Communication*, 61(1), 35–63.

Beach, R., Appleman, D., Hynds, S., & Wilhelm, J. (2006). *Teaching literature to adolescents*. Lawrence Erlbaum Association.

Beavis, C. (2012). Video games in the classroom: Developing digital literacies. *Practically Primary, 17*(1), 17–20.

Blum, D. (1997). *Sex on the brain: The biological differences between men and women*. Viking.

Connell, R. (1996). Teaching the boys: New research on masculinity, and gender strategies for schools. *Teachers College Record, 98*(2), 206–235.

Connell, R. W. (2000). *The men and the boys*. Polity.

Cope, B., & Kalantzis, M. (Eds.). (2000). *Multiliteracies: Literacy learning and the design of social futures*. Routledge.

Cope, B., & Kalantzis, M. (2009). "Multiliteracies": New literacies, new learning. *Pedagogies, 4*(3), 164–195. doi:10.1080/15544800903076044

Cope, B., & Kalantzis, M. (2016). *A pedagogy of multiliteracies: Learning by design*. Palgrave Macmillan UK. Retrieved from https://books.google.ca/books?id=N6GkCgAAQBAJ

Finn, P. J. (1999). *Literacy with an attitude: Educating working-class children in their own self-interest*. State University of New York Press.

Gee, J. P. (2003). *What video games have to teach us about learning and literacy* (1st ed.). Palgrave Macmillan. doi:10.1145/950566.950595

Gee, J. P. (2007). *Good video games and good learning: Collected essays on video games, learning, and literacy*. P. Lang. doi:10.3726/978-1-4539-1162-4

Gee, J. P. (2009). *New digital media and learning as an emerging area and "worked examples" as one way forward*. MIT Press. doi:10.7551/mitpress/8563.001.0001

Gee, J. P. (2010). A situated-sociocultural approach to literacy and technology. *The New Literacies: Multiple Perspectives on Research and Practice*, 165–193.

Gros, B. (2007). Digital games in education: The design of games-based learning environments. *Journal of Research on Technology in Education, 40*(1), 23–38. doi:10.1080/15391523.2007.10782494

Gurian, M., & Stevens, K. (2010a). *Boys and girls learn differently! A guide for teachers and parents*. Jossey-Bass.

Gurian, M., & Stevens, K. (2010b). *The minds of boys: Saving our sons from falling behind in school and life*. Jossey-Bass.

Hommel, M. (2010). Video games and learning. *School Library Monthly, 26*(10), 37–40.

Huizenga, J., Admiraal, W., Akkerman, S., & Dam, G. (2009). Mobile game-based learning in secondary education: Engagement, motivation and learning in a mobile city game. *Journal of Computer Assisted Learning, 25*(4), 332–344. doi:10.1111/j.1365-2729.2009.00316.x

Ito, M. (2008). *Living and learning with new media: summary of findings from the digital youth project*. The John D. and Catherine T. MacArthur Foundation.

Jansz, J. (2005). The emotional appeal of violent video games for adolescent males. *Communication Theory, 15*(3), 219-241. Retrieved from https://onlinelibrary.wiley.com/doi/10.1111/j.1468-2885.2005.tb00334.x/abstract;jsessionid=797D278A2C3BFFD76C1E71DA17729991.f02t02

Jenkins, H. (2002). Game design as narrative architecture. In P. Harrington & N. Frup-Waldrop (Eds.), *First Person*. MIT Press.

Jenkins, H. (2006). *Convergence culture: Where old and new media collide*. New York University Press.

Kafai, Y. B., Burke, Q., & Steinkuehler, C. (2016). *Connected gaming: What making video games can teach us about learning and literacy*. MIT Press. Retrieved from https://books.google.ca/books?id=zPC7DQAAQBAJ

Kalantzis, M., & Cope, B. (2012). *Literacies*. Cambridge University Press. doi:10.1017/CBO9781139196581

Laboratory, H. A. L. (2014). *Super Smash Bros. Melee* [Video game]. Nintendo.

Lane, C. A. (2018). *Multiliteracies meaning-making: How four boys' video gaming experiences influence their cultural knowledge—Two ethnographic cases* (Doctoral Dissertation, Western University). Electronic Thesis and Dissertation Repository. 5303. https://ir.lib.uwo.ca/etd/5303

Lankshear, C. (1997). *Changing literacies*. McGraw-Hill Education.

Mac an Ghaill, M. (1994). *The making of men: Masculinities, sexualities and schooling*. Open University Press.

Olson, C. K. (2010). Children's motivations for video game play in the context of normal development. *Review of General Psychology, 14*(2), 180-187. Retrieved from http://psycnet.apa.org/?&fa=main.doiLanding&doi=10.1037/a0018984

Piaget, J. (2008). Intellectual evolution from adolescence to adulthood. *Human Development, 51*(1), 40–47. doi:10.1159/000112531

Rowsell, J., & Walsh, M. (2011). Rethinking literacy education in new times: Multimodality, multiliteracies, & new literacies. *Brock Education, 21*(1), 1. doi:10.26522/brocked.v21i1.236

Sanford, K., & Madill, L. (2006). Resistance through video game play: It's a boy thing. *Canadian Journal of Education, 29*(1), 287–306, 344–345. doi:10.2307/20054157

Sanford, K., & Madill, L. (2007). Understanding the power of new literacies through video game play and design. *Canadian Journal of Education, 30*(2), 432–455. doi:10.2307/20466645

Sax, L. (2005). *Why gender matters*. Doubleday.

Skelton, C., & Francis, B. (2011). Successful boys and literacy: Are "literate boys" challenging or repackaging hegemonic masculinity? *Curriculum Inquiry, 41*(4), 456–479. doi:10.1111/j.1467-873X.2011.00559.x

Spradley, J. P. (1979). *The Ethnographic Interview*. The University of Michigan: Holt, Rinehart and Winston.

Squire, K. D. (2013). Video game-based learning: An emerging paradigm for instruction. *Performance Improvement Quarterly, 26*(1), 101–130. doi:10.1002/piq.21139

Steinkuehler, C. (2006). The mangle of play. *Journal of Adolescent & Adult Literacy, 1*(3), 199–213.

Steinkuehler, C. (2007). Massively multiplayer online gaming as a constellation of literacy practices. *E-Learning and Digital Media, 4*(3), 297–318. doi:10.2304/elea.2007.4.3.297

Steinkuehler, C. (2010). Video games and digital literacies. *Journal of Adolescent & Adult Literacy, 54*(1), 61–63. doi:10.1598/JAAL.54.1.7

Steinkuehler, C. (2011). *The mismeasure of boys: Reading and online videogames.* Wisconsin Center for Education Research, University of Wisconsin.

Steinkuehler, C., Squire, K., & Barab, S. A. (2012). *Games, learning, and society: Learning and meaning in the digital age.* Cambridge University Press. doi:10.1017/CBO9781139031127

Taylor, T. L. (2006). Does WoW change everything? How a PvP server, multinational player base, and surveillance mod scene caused me pause. *Games and Culture, 1*(4), 61–63. doi:10.1177/1555412006292615

The New London Group. (1996). A pedagogy of multiliteracies: Designing social futures. *Harvard Educational Review, 66*(1), 60–93. doi:10.17763/haer.66.1.17370n67v22j160u

The New London Group. (2000). A pedagogy of multiliteracies: Designing social futures. In B. Cope & M. Kalantzis (Eds.), *Multiliteracies: Literacy learning and the design of social futures.* Routledge.

VanSledright, B. A. (2002). Fifth graders investigating history in the classroom: Results from a researcher-practitioner design experiment. *The Elementary School Journal, 103*(2), 131–160. doi:10.1086/499720

Vygotsky, L. S. (1978). Readings on the development of children. In From Mind and Society (pp. 79-91). Cambridge, MA: Harvard University Press.

Wolcott, H. F. (1987). On ethnographic intent. In Interpretive Ethnography on Education: At Home and Abroad. Hillsdale, NJ: Erlbaum.

KEY TERMS AND definitions

Analysing: Is the part of the process in which learners establish relations between cause and effect and explain textual patterns and connections. It also adds a dimension to the knowledge process by extending the need for learners to constructively evaluate their learning and others' perspectives (Cope & Kalantzis, 2009).

Applying: Involves the learners demonstrating their acquired knowledge and applying it to real world situations. It represents how learners develop innovative and creative ways to demonstrate their meaning-making and knowledge (Cope & Kalantzis, 2009).

Available Designs: (Also known as metalanguages) are modes of meaning based on an individual's past and new experience of everyday life and how they apply it to their learning. These modes represent linguistic (written and oral language), visual, audio, tactile, gestural and spatial (Cope & Kalantzis, 2009; The New London Group, 1996, 2000).

Community of Practice: Represents an online network of video gaming participants that could involve virtual gaming through massively multiplayer online games (MMOG), peer-based forums, chatrooms, and other social media (Aarsand, 2010; Steinkuehler, 2006; Wenger, 1998).

Conceptualising: Represents learners' cultural meaning-making experiences and thinking or building knowledge within the community of learners (Cope & Kalantzis, 2009).

Cultural Knowledge: Includes multimodal forms of meanings and modes of learning (Cope & Kalantzis, 2009).

Cultural Meaning Systems: Are actions or ideas that are made up of different cultural terms that are meaningful to people (Spradley, 1979).

Experiencing: Represents the view that learners' cognition is situated, contextual and cultural. Learners immerse in meaningful practices within a community of other learners (Kalantzis & Cope, 2012).

Multiliteracies: Represents a concept that addresses literacy pedagogy as a design encompassing various interconnected systems, including environment, and people, which become part of the broader picture of cultural experiences. It involves teachers and learners using available resources to design activities of reading, seeing, speaking, writing, and listening (Cope & Kalantzis, 2009). Whenever this term is used, it is in reference to multiliteracies as articulated by Cope and Kalantzis, (2000, 2009), Kalantzis and Cope, (2012), and The New London Group (1996, 2000).

Operational Literacy: Represents how adolescents read both visual and print textual instructions and use and adapt semiotic systems to meet their needs (Sanford & Madill, 2007).

Chapter 15
Using Gamification to Improve Literacy Skills

Jamie Mahoney
https://orcid.org/0000-0003-4354-2339
Murray State University, USA

Kristina M. Buttrey
Murray State University, USA

ABSTRACT

Students in the 21st century are learning by doing and playing. Teachers need to incorporate technology into everyday tasks. Games assist students in the learning process. Once students have learned a task through the playing process, they will remember this much easier and longer than simply doing a worksheet. Research shows students enjoy interactive and engaging activities and will choose these types of activities over pencil and paper types of activities. Teachers must prepare students for the future which involves more critical thinking and technological types of skills. Traditional teaching methods and styles have underused technology tools and pedagogical methods. The 2020 Covid pandemic and remote learning delivery style assisted teachers in developing new tools and methods to reach and teach all students with various and diverse needs.

INTRODUCTION

Literacy instruction has come a long way since early colonial times. In New England in the eighteenth century, illiteracy was rampant and even higher for females than males. Some of this is documented through the lack of signatures and the use of marks or symbols in place of names (Monaghan, 1988). Early instruction was mostly for the purpose of learning to read the Bible and used texts that were simple scripture excerpts or a copy of the alphabet. Writing was valued less, so literacy instruction was not necessarily inclusive of writing instruction. In 1747, Ben Franklin is credited with popularizing a spelling primer after he reprinted Thomas Dilworth's *A New Guide to the English Tongue* and leading the way to more advanced literacy preparations (Monaghan, p. 22, 1988). From small home-schools, to

DOI: 10.4018/978-1-7998-7271-9.ch015

one room-school houses, to the advanced education systems of today, literacy instruction has drastically changed based on scientific studies, technological advances, and cultural differences.

Olson, Scarcella, and Matachniak offer the Common Core State Standards (CCSS), which were adopted by 46 states, changed the way schools viewed literacy in the the twenty-first century, expecting students to have more interaction with complex texts and to be able to write more critically about these texts. The researchers suggest the standards stress the importance of more practice with academic vocabulary (2015). Since the adoption of the CCSS many state education departments have changed the names of their standards to appease constituents who did not like the idea of a national standard. However, the adherence to critical thinking and academic vocabulary across the curriculum remains.

Currently, the infusion and advancements with technology in American classrooms allow students to more engaged in digital tools such as podcasts, Garageband, using animation, and multiple devices such as laptops, tablets, and cell phones, all loaded with multiple apps (or applications) capable of complex presentations, discussions, and multilingual literacies for innovative pedagogical practices (Price-Dennis, Holmes, & Smith, 2015). These 21st century student-led practices build communities of digitally literate and inclusively and multiculturally aware producers and consumers of knowledge of engaging practices of literacy (Price-Dennis, Holmes, & Smith). Teachers preparing students for future world pedagogical needs and practices consider how technological literacy enables students "to be proficient consumers, producers, and disseminators of a variety of print-based and digital texts" (Price-Dennis, Holmes, & Allen, 2015, p. 196). With these resources at their fingertips, teachers have to determine best practices for using the technology, especially for literacy instruction.

The International Literacy Association (ILA) and the National Council of Teachers of English (NCTE) "define 21st century literacies as abilities for teachers and students to: 1) develop fluency with technology tools; 2) build intentional relationships and problem-solve collaboratively; 3) design and share information for global communities" (Price-Dennis, et. al., 2015, p. 196). These 21st century paradigm shifts proposed in the new literacies elicit new collaborations between both general education and special education teachers in order to meet the needs of all students with varying abilities and needs. New pedagogical approaches and curriculum using technology will incorporate multifaceted approaches using multimodal and multimedia tools (Price-Dennis, et al., 2015). Technological tools will include Flipboard, Bitstrips, blogs, apps, Web 2.0 platforms and multimedia texts just to name a few. Learning will be student-centered and student-driven; no longer teacher-led and lecture-based.

LITERACY DEFINITIONS: BASIC TO EXTENDED USAGE

According to Hodges (1999) literacy refers to the ability of an individual to be able to read and write well. However, in his exploration of literacy, he furthers there are at least 38 different types of literacy, inferring different purposes and ways of thinking as criteria for some of the categories. A few of these include functional, academic, and computer literacies. Teachers in classrooms are very focused on academic literacy in part because of common core literacy demands for each subject area. While standards vary from state to state, most are generally consistent with the spirit of the common core standards. Within the Common Core Standards Initiative created in 2010, literacy standards play a prominent role in student learning and assessment, appearing as career and college ready anchor standards, specific reading standards, and embedded literacy standards in history/social studies, science, and technical subjects ("Read the Standards") For the purposes of this text, we will focus on academic literacy with the key components of writing, vocabulary, comprehension, and spelling, as well as, information literacy with an emphasis on critical thinking.

Informational literacy involves the abilities people utilize to search, locate, evaluate, comprehend, use, and apply knowledge to daily living and working experiences. Bruce (2002) described information literacy as "the personal empowerment learners engage in when independently pursuing lifelong learning" (p. 2). The more a learner knows and can apply the knowledge learned, the more power the learner has in making life decisions. Knowledge can no longer just be the ability to know information such as facts and trivia; students must be scholars able to apply this knowledge to daily life. Additionally, students must be able to evaluate information and determine the suitability of the knowledge for their current situation. Bruce added, the goal of every teacher should be to "transform dependent learners into independent, self–directed, lifelong learners" (2002, para. 16).

Content area or academic literacy is another form of literacy in which teachers must instruct students in the areas of vocabulary, comprehension, and writing skills associated with each discipline. This type of literacy involves vocabulary as well as the appropriate writing skills and structures related to the subject matter. Specifically, Baumann and Graves (2010) note two types of vocabulary that would be beneficial to teachers: "domain specific" and "general academic" vocabulary. The first refers to words that will help students understand the content being studied, while the latter refers to words used across multiple disciplines.

LITERACY AND GAMIFICATION

Gamification is a specific strategy in which teachers incorporate games into lesson plans to teach skills and objectives. While this concept is not new-innovative teachers have been finding ways to use games to teach students for centuries-the advancements in technology have taken gamification to new levels. Teachers can turn the entire class into a thematic quest with characters and storylines (Fulks & Lord, 2016) or simply add games throughout the traditional lesson plan to intensify engagement and promote more intense learning. This can include video or computer games because as Squire (2003) proposed, video games "elicit emotional reactions in their players, such as fear, power, wonder or joy" (p. 49). Creating games, video or board-based, allowing students to interact with characters, obstacles, risks, rewards, problem-solving, collaboration with others, and developing attributes related to the narrative characters provides students opportunities to learn in real-life game simulations (Squire, 2003).

Gamification can be especially helpful in promoting informational literacy skills practice within the classroom. Bruce (2002) suggested the best practices approach to creating a more informational literate society. Teachers with learning-centered programs should realize information literacy is imperative to the learning process, be student guided to reflect on what has been learned, be collaboratively implemented, and be partnered with other community organizations. By allowing students some choice in what they will learn, students will make more connections and see more relevance in the lessons presented. The use of games in the classroom aids teachers in allowing students to explore information in a forum that provides student choice, real-life connections, and application.

Gaming also provides teachers with a way to enhance academic literacy by allowing students to practice comprehension, vocabulary, communication, and writing skills in a way that is engaging, creative, and fun. Gamification can occur with or without technology. Using old-fashioned board games, everyday objects, and a good imagination can help all students to learn new vocabulary words to improve literacy skills and become better readers. Students want and need to be engaged in the learning process and have interactive activities involving all areas of their brain. Multisensory learning activities and multiple opportunities to demonstrate their knowledge are necessary for developing reading, writing, speaking, listening, and language skills, making students literate participants in all content areas.

THE TECHNOLOGY-GAME CONNECTION

Students of the 21st-century use technology to learn and do everyday tasks. These students have had technological devices in their hands almost since birth. The Apple Macintosh II with a hard drive was used in classrooms in the late 1980s early 1990s for students to practice academic skills by playing games. Today's students have more gigabytes and RAM in their cell phones and can not only play games but can access the Internet while carrying them in their back pockets. According to Squire (2003), classroom teachers have traditionally underused technology; however, with the 2020 Covid pandemic, remote learning became the new standard method for course delivery, requiring students to use multiple devices for learning. Consequently, teachers are more able and willing to explore new technology for classroom instruction and assessment, especially for literacy instruction.

Kolb (2020) examined the best practices of how children learn in technology-based and interactive research-based classrooms. Highlights of this research include but are not limited to the following: "active, hands-on and minds-on activities through social learning while working in their Zone of Proximal Development and connected to prior knowledge using real-world situations" (p. 185). What better way to incorporate all these elements but to use technology and games! Games provide students with hands-on experiences while using critical thinking and problem-solving fun and repetitive learning activities. Games are socially interactive experiences for students to learn the soft skills of turn-taking, sharing, getting along with others, and following instructions.

Merrill and Merrill (2019) explain: "the importance of {interactive} learning happening in a way that allows students to be responsive rather than reactive" (p. 11). The Merrills also discuss the differences between a responsive classroom environment and a reactive one. They note, "Teachers in a responsive-thinking environment offer student choice, use music, movement, novelty, actively challenge ideas, show gratitude, and have a sense of optimism" (p. 12). Digital tools provide many of these responsive environment processes and procedures without adding to the teacher workload.

The Merrills offer that strategically scaffolding learning activities provide students with choices and opportunities to be successful throughout their day (2019). Kolb furthers that scaffolding assists students in understanding the requirements of assignments and helps students meet their goals in achieving completion of those assignments (2020). The Merrills suggest the digital use of QR codes, hyperdocs, and hyperlinks, can assist in more easily giving students a choice for tasks (2019).

With technology, music can also be added for transitions, timers, and to teach content Researchers also highlighted the importance of movement for students of all ages, and game usage is a great way to get students moving and help students to practice and retain information (Merrill & Merrill, 2019).

Using Gamification to Improve Literacy Skills

GAMIFICATION AND DIFFERENTIATION

One of the critical qualities of a successful classroom is how lessons are differentiated for all students. Differentiation focuses on a student's readiness or ability level, interests, learning profiles, or preferred methods to approach learning activities. For example, some learners are better at using visual skills, auditory skills, or blended skills. Teachers should present lessons in various methods that allow students to access materials; gamification can play a vital role. Instructional strategies that help with differentiation can include learning centers, graphic organizers, scaffolded reading/writing, and tiered assignments; games provide the means to incorporate these strategies in a fun, engaging way. Because good teaching uses best practices and careful planning (Tomlinson, 2001), the intentional incorporation of games and activities to teach literacy skills is a potent combination.

DIGITAL GAMES FOR LITERACY LEARNING

Teachers today have a variety of choices to incorporate digital games into lesson planning. The following is a list of some of the more popular games being used by teachers in classrooms all over the world.

Digital Scoot is the old task card game with a new name using technology. Students would go from desk to desk, answering questions on cards placed on each desk. Now teachers load up digital devices with various activities, surveys, response questions and turn them into digital scoot. Each computer screen has something different, and each student will move "scoot" from one to the next- be sure you have more slide activities than you need so no student is waiting (Merrill & Merrill, 2019). This game can be used to practice grammar skills, vocabulary, writing, or comprehension skills but in a game-based or computerized manner, making the activity more engaging, interactive, and meaningful for students.

Kahoot is a web application that teachers can use to assess student progress through teacher-made quizzes and surveys informally. Once a teacher has made the "Kahoot," they are given a corresponding code that goes along with it. When students access the web application, they enter a username and the code given to them by the teacher, and they are then able to participate in the "Kahoot" the teacher has set up. As the quiz progresses, students must choose the answer they believe to be correct. After the end of each question, students receive real-time results, including whether they answered correctly and what place they are in. After the questions have all been asked, the application shows the results. Educators can use this information on a question-by-question basis to determine who knows the material and needs more time and assistance.Kahoot is another free website tool available for teachers to use as a review tool or an assessment tool with students in preparing for a test. Students see the tool as a game rather than as an assessment tool. Teachers can create a quiz, a discussion, or a survey. Kahoot questions are limited to 95 characters, and the answers are limited to 60 characters. Students respond using iPhones, Android phones, or computers. Kahoot is a competitive, fast-paced game in which the faster the student responds to the questions, the more points the student earns. Kahoot can be shared or made public on the website to enable students to visit and review the questions and answers as often as needed when studying before testing. Teachers use this tool to engage students in assessing areas learned versus areas needing more instruction based upon correct and incorrect responses. This tool also allows discussions between the teacher and each student related to differences of opinion (Learning Games, 2021)

Quizziz is a web-based resource and tool students and teachers can use to assist in learning vocabulary words. *Quizziz* can be used as an alternative to Kahoot. Students will be engaged and interactive using their own "self-paced questions, funny memes, and enjoy the competitive element" (Miller, Ridgway, & Ridgway, 2019, p. 30). According to Bal (2018), students using *Quizziz* performed better than students using the traditional paper-pencil worksheets or tests.

Quizlet: One technological resource students can use to assist their rate of processing is a website called *Quizlet*. The premise of *Quizlet* is an online flashcard system, but there are a variety of tools available for students to use. Students can make their online flashcards with the help of the auto-defined features or find other members' flashcard sets to supplement their own. Once the flashcards are created, the student can review the cards repeatedly with an optional speech setting, where the program will read the flashcard aloud to the student. As an added feature, there are review games available such as *Scatter* and *Gravity*. One of *Quizlet's* best features is a generated test based on flashcard information, which allows students to test their knowledge of the course content before testing it at school. *Quizlet* is free to use and has a mobile application available for on-the-go learning. Due to these various options, *Quizlet* may be a beneficial tool for students with Dyslexia ("Learning Tools")

Gimkit is a web-based application similar to Kahoot. This is an interactive digital quiz-style game where students answer questions earning money to purchase various powerup options depending on the mode chosen to play. The more questions answered correctly, the more money earned. Students are encouraged to collaborate with other students to problem solve to complete the mission. Gimkit provides teachers with formative assessment data to drive instructional lessons and review for tier 2 and 3 interventions. ("Live Learning")

Blooket is a web-based game-based learning review or assessment tool teachers use engaging students either as a pre-assessment or post-assessment activity. Students are actively involved in responding to the questions. If the student responds with the wrong answer, the game provides immediate feedback on the correct answer. This helps the student to learn from their mistakes. Blooket has several gaming formats in which students either work collaboratively or individually to accomplish a goal. Students can also earn points in which to purchase different characters called "blooks." After playing just one blooket game, students are hooked and will request to play Blooket repeatedly. Blooket is free for teachers and students to use. There are games such as "cafe" in which students fulfill orders with food items after earning points for each item, racing, gold quest, and the classic version (Blooket).

Breakout EDU provides students opportunities to work in an immersive learning game platform. These games consist of physical and digital puzzle formats to be solved within an established amount of time. All players' ages benefit from the challenges provided by the Breakout EDU critical thinking, collaboration, and creativity activities (Breakout Edu).

Goose Chase provides learners the opportunity to go on a digital and multimodal scavenger hunt. Hunters are provided the option to take videos or photos of the items on the checklist, solving riddles and solving word puzzles. Using the GPS locator, students can take pictures of themselves in different locations and tag themselves. Options include working individually or working collaboratively as a team. Every Goosechase mission has different point values, and everyone can see a live update on the leaderboard. Goosechase is a very competitive activity that provides an authentic learning experience related to accurate historical fiction exemplary texts ("Create").

Wakelet provides students the options and location to be creative. Wakelet is the hub where students can curate and customize their ideas into their own games and activities. This online tool allows students the privilege to save their work and to continue to save and share their work with others similar

Using Gamification to Improve Literacy Skills

to a portfolio or folder. Students can collaborate and research together on a project within the Wakelet framework. The interactivity and social aspects of Wakelet provide the perfect atmosphere for students to engage in higher-level critical thinking and problem-solving synthesis and application of content area ideas ("Bring Your Resources").

FROM GAME SHOWS TO LITERACY CLASSROOMS

Teachers can make real-world connections with students turning game shows from television into games for the classroom. Some enterprising teachers have created templates for many of these games and can be found with a simple internet search. With or without the ready-made resources, teachers can add fun and excitement to the classroom by providing the elements of competition and social engagement to the learning experience.

Jeopardy is a game perfect for assessing vocabulary comprehension. In this game show, participants are provided the answers and must come up with the questions (Griffin, 1964); students would do the same. If teachers want to use a technological version of Jeopardy, a quick internet search will provide many different downloads options for free. When students write the questions, it initiates higher-level thinking strategies, uses their abilities to synthesize and apply their content knowledge, and increases their creativity skills (Overturf, Montgomery, & Smith, 2013). If teachers want to truly add another buzzer-type atmosphere to their classroom, Overturf et al. suggested using a tool called Eggspert. This device provides students the opportunity to push one of the egg-shaped buzzers to indicate a student is ready to respond to a question, rather than just shouting out or raising their hand (p. 92).

The $100,000 or the $10,000 Pyramid is another example of a gameshow used to improve literacy skills in the classroom. In this strategy, students will be divided up into pairs and will mimic the game show (Stewart, et.al., 1964). The teacher makes a pyramid of ideas/concepts/themes/people and displays their pyramid on the smartboard. Student A sits with their back to the answers while Student B tries to get them to say the solution by giving them hints without saying the word. The team that correctly answers all of the items wins. Pyramid is a fun way for teachers to engage students in active learning. This strategy can be used to increase comprehension in any subject.

Are You Smarter than a Fifth Grader is a game show that quizzes contestants on subject matter commonly taught in 5th-grade classrooms (Burnett, Poxnick, and Stevens, 2007). This game could easily be adapted to fit the students' grade level in any classroom and could be based on vocabulary from a variety of subject areas. Students will enjoy "phoning a friend" in the school to get help on a word that has them stumped. Teachers can increase or decrease the complexity of the questions by choosing words and definitions from previous grades or preceding grades for differentiation of questioning for various student academic levels.

To Tell the Truth is a game show where one person is sworn to tell the truth, and the others can respond to the questions asked by the panel members. The panel members are trying to figure out who is telling the truth and not the others, trying to make everyone think they are "the one." (Stewart, 1956). This game can be adapted to the social studies content very quickly. Social Studies literacy content is difficult to comprehend; therefore, playing a game such as, To Tell the Truth, would bring History to life. Students could pretend to be the actual characters learned about in the pages of the chapters and could help the rest of the class to determine which contestant is telling the whole true story about the main character of the episode. Which contestant is the Real George Washington? Which contestant explained and answered the questions to help the classroom audience understand the characteristics? Another idea for the game, To Tell the Truth, is to use fictional characters from the stories being studied within the reading/ literature block of the day. Students can ask questions related to character traits, character's story elements, problems and solutions, and plots of the exemplar literature being studied.

Family Feud is a game show that can easily be adapted to a classroom setting. On this game show, two teams or families answer questions from surveys to earn points without getting three strikes. (Goodson, 1976). Teams can be formed within the classroom by mixed ability groups. Students can use google forms to poll their classmates and peers in other classrooms.

The "Amazing Race" is another television show that requires contestants to complete a series of challenges (Doganieri and Munster, 2001). This game can easily be incorporated into lessons by changing the types of challenges to meet the specific learning objectives of a subject area. Fulks and Lord (2016) note an example of the "Amazing Grammar Race," which has students complete grammar challenges throughout a lesson.

Game of Games- This game is based on *Ellen's Game of Games* which uses emoji or picture formats for contestants to determine the answer to specific questions (Leman, K., 2017). These types of visual cues help students to think outside the box about meanings and how pictures represent words. This type of activity helps students to understand vocabulary in multiple ways.

THE VOCABULARY CONNECTION: TIER 1,2 AND 3 VOCABULARY WORDS

Vocabulary words are multi-tiered, and teachers should consider the tier category of their chosen word list to determine suitability for gamification.

Tier 1 words are essential vocabulary words that do not have multiple meanings. These are words students already know and should not be chosen for vocabulary word study. An assessment for students would be to rate these words as either:

1. Don't know.
2. Have seen or heard but do not know the meaning.
3. I think I see the meaning.
4. I know the importance.

Group these words into these categories to help develop Tier 1 development.

Tier 2 words are general academic words students encounter across texts in all content areas or help them discuss in more detail. These vocabulary words are more challenging, and students will see these words most often in text. Examples include: analyze, diminish, and obscure.

Tier 3 words are domain-specific words such as isotope, Renaissance, or coefficient. Vocabulary words are related to content text areas such as Science, Social Studies, or Math. Choose specific Tier 3 words that are most vital for understanding the particular unit of study at that moment in time. Besides tier levels, teachers should consider specific purposes and differentiation when choosing word lists. Teachers can determine vocabulary based upon specific content areas, Greek or Latin roots being learned, and how affixes change those base words.

GAMING FOR VOCABULARY

Teachers use a variety of materials to promote vocabulary enrichment and attainment. These reading materials can be inserted into any game to provide practice and assessment. The following is another list of possibilities for teachers looking to make vocabulary lessons more engaging and fun.

Scattergories-to think of many things beginning with a particular letter in a specific category (Parker Brothers, 1988).Students compare vocabulary words to random objects that fit into that category. Making comparisons is a great way for students to identify similarities and differences. They share their scattergories sentences and see how many different connections they have made.

Headbanz: With the original game, players wear a picture card on a headband without looking at the picture. They are given a chance to ask questions about the image from the other players to try and guess the object on the picture (Spin Master Games, 1991). This could easily be adapted for any subject area vocabulary set. Students would have the written word instead of a photo and would ask a series of questions to try and guess the vocabulary word. It is a creative way to review, assess, and practice vocabulary. Teachers could ensure the differentiation of the game by creating rules to make it easier for some and more difficult for others.

Charades game is an excellent way for students to demonstrate their understanding of vocabulary words or literary information from fictional stories. Divide the class into small groups. Each small group will randomly choose one of the week's vocabulary words or fictional story elements to demonstrate to the rest of the class. The small group showing is allowed 5-10 minutes to prepare and present their version of the randomly chosen item. After the time is up, each member is provided an opportunity to guess using a marker and whiteboard. After the guessing is completed and the teams have explained their answers, each team reflects on how their knowledge of the information has improved (Overturf, Montgomery, & Smith, 2013). **Blank Slate** is the clever party game where participants try to predict what others are thinking. Everyone secretly writes a word that completes a phrase on the cue card and earns points for matching with others (Camp, 2018). Teachers can adjust this game by creating their own cards with phrases to use this game as a review or vocabulary practice.

Comic Books: Now even comic books can be turned into games. Students can use Google Forms to choose their own adventure stories and set them up into comic book formats using BookCreator. According to Miller (2015), "Set up the story for your students in Google Forms and then have them each write an alternate ending or a portion of the story. Using links, the readers click on and read different stories based on their choices:" (p. 136). Using https://www.storyboardthat.com/storyboard-creator students can turn their ideas for a comic into a real version online. Using Vocabulary words in comic books or graphic novels is another way for students to demonstrate comprehension and usage. Students can demonstrate abilities in developing higher-level vocabularies. Comic books and graphic novels have a complexity of language through pictures tied to the vocabulary. The complexity of language in comic books is even higher, with 53.5 rare words per thousand. A typical comic book has about 2 thousand words, and a student reading one comic book per day will read nearly 500,000 words per year. Comic books are a significant vehicle for vocabulary study for struggling readers (Overturf, Montgomery, & Smith, 2013). Students that have difficulties in putting their ideas on paper may find the online version is not only motivating but also accommodates their learning style using an assistive technology device and service. Teachers want the product from the students and this online version of the comic strip maker will produce that product for students with various disabilities.

FIGURATIVELY SPEAKING GAMES

One literary device known as figurative language can also be incorporated into classroom games. This is a fun and creative way to demonstrate the competent use of metaphors, similes, alliteration, hyperbole, analogies, as well as many others.

I Spy is an iconic car game with which students may be very familiar. Participants find an object around the space and say, "I spy something _____." Usually, the blank is filled with a color. However, for figurative language practice, the students can be required to reply with a simile or metaphor. For example, students may offer, "I spy something that is as yellow as the sun," or "I spy something that is as the sun," applying a skill that is generally only written. Teachers can increase the complexity level by providing the specific figurative element that must be demonstrated with each turn.

Matching Game: By creating cards matching the type of literary device with cards displaying either the definitions or specific examples. Students will get quick practice for understanding the different types of devices. Flippity.net provides teachers with the opportunity to make students a matching game of their own sight words, vocabulary words or special words related to word families, spelling words, or content-related words. This website provides multiple methods of working with the words but the matching game is the best interactive tool for students. Another website for teachers to explore and make other interactive games, try wordwall.net. This site provides a community of resources or teachers can build their own types of literature, word or content specific interactive and engaging games for students to practice or quiz themselves with instant feedback.

ADAPTING BOARD GAMES INTO DIGITAL GAMES

Traditional board games can be used to combine the advantages of digital technology with the tangible board games of the past. The following looks at how technology has enhanced these ideas and made literacy instruction more appealing to students.

Bingo: This game usually involves the use of numbers across a Bingo board. However, Bingo is easily adapted to vocabulary practice. Teachers can either read the definitions, with the students finding the word that matches the description, or vice versa. This strategy would require teachers to create their playing cards, but there are several Bingo card generators available online to teachers, such as bingobaker.com or https://www.canva.com/create/bingo-cards/.

Online bingo makers such as https://myfreebingocards.com/bingo-card-generator can help students of all abilities. Teachers can input any words into the generator therefore students learning any sight word or vocabulary can use this as an engaging and interactive activity. This can even be sent home for parents to use to practice words with their children at home rather than completing worksheets. Worksheets are not best practice methods to keep students engaged in the learning process.

Boggle is a 16 dice randomly selected game contained within a four-by-four cubic tray in which the players shake the game up pieces and have a 3-minute timer to build all the words possible. Each player searches for words constructed from the letters of sequentially adjacent cubes, where "adjacent" cubes are horizontally, vertically, and diagonally neighboring. Words must be at least three letters long, may include singular and plural (or other derived forms) separately, but may not use the same letter cube more than once per word. Each player records all the words they find by writing on a private sheet of paper. After three minutes have elapsed, all players must immediately stop writing and the game enters the scoring

Using Gamification to Improve Literacy Skills

phase (Turoff and Cook, 1974). Wordshake.com/boggle is a digital version of the old classic game of boggle. This online version provides students with the same opportunity to play boggle except now in a digital format. However, if students want another version try https://www.puzzle-words.com/boggle-4x4/. This online version provides multiple versions such as a 3X3 easy all the way up to 5X5 extreme. Students need to have choices and options. The online versions provide this for all types of learners.

Scrabble is a word game in which two to four players score points by placing tiles, each bearing a single letter, onto a game board divided into a 15×15 grid of squares. The tiles must form words that, in crossword fashion, read left to right in rows or downward in columns and be included in a standard dictionary or lexicon, (Butts, 1938). Teachers can use this online website to personalize the learning experience for students. This website https://www.edu-games.org/word-games/scrabble-word-maker.php provides letter games, word games such as Scrabble, and sentence games for students to improve their literacy skills. This amazing site has more than just Scrabble to meet the needs of various students. Crossword puzzles, Word ladders, word pyramids, bingos, and scrambles are just a few literacy games to engage students.

GAMIFY LESSONS/ PLANS

Although teachers may understand the benefits of gamifying lesson plans, they may be apprehensive about attempting it for a variety of reasons including a fear of behavioral issues, an uncertainty of how to begin, and a lack of resources. However, gamification can easily occur if the following specific steps are taken.

1. First, teachers need to determine the specific objectives to be practiced, assessed, or introduced.
2. Next, the location within the lesson plan needs to be determined. Is this an introductory activity, a review, or a main event activity?
3. Additionally, teachers need to decide the level of gamification for the lesson. Will this be an "all in" activity including characters, decorations, and themes or a "part" of the lesson as an additional strategy?
4. After researching the list of game ideas, choose the game that feels "right" for the lesson.
5. Consider your resources. Can you use the technologically enhanced version or the hands-on, physical version?
6. Prepare your materials.
7. Next, teachers should script the directions, class rules, and expectations (including transitions).
8. Finally, have fun with the new strategy and the students will "catch" your enthusiasm.

CONCLUSION

Teachers of the 21st century must find ways to engage and motivate students. Making lessons interactive and using games is one of the best ways to get students involved in learning and helping students to remember what has been taught and what has been learned. Students will forget what has been said but they will remember what they have done. Let students interact and play. The more they play the more repetitions with the information they will have and the more they will learn. Go make a game of it and watch students' progress grow!

REFERENCES

Bal, S. (2018). Using Quizziz.com to enhance pre intermediate students' vocabulary knowledge. *International Journal of Language Academy, 6*(3), 295–303. doi:10.18033/ijla.3953

Baumann, J., & Graves, M. (2010). What is academic vocabulary? *Journal of Adolescent & Adult Literacy, 54*(1), 4–12. doi:10.1598/JAAL.54.1.1

Blooket. (n.d.). Retrieved October 26, 2021, from https://www.blooket.com/play

Breakout edu. (n.d.). Retrieved October 26, 2021, from https://platform.breakoutedu.com/login

Bring your learning resources to life! (n.d.). *Wakelet for Educators*. Retrieved October 26, 2021, from https://learn.wakelet.com/

Bruce, C. (2002). Information literacy as a catalyst for educational change: A background paper. In P. Danahar (Ed), *Lifelong Learning: Whose responsibility and what is your contribution? Proceedings of The 3rd International Lifelong Learning Conference* (pp. 8-19). Queensland University of Technology. Retrieved from http://eprints.qut.edu.au/4977/1/4977_1.pdf

Burnett, M., Poxnick, B., & Stevens, J. (2007) *Are You Smarter Than a 5th Grader* [Game Show Series]. Fox.

Butts, A. (1938). *Scrabble* [Board Game]. Hasbro.

Camp, R. (2018). *Blank Slate* [Board Game]. USAopoly.

Create unforgettable experiences. (n.d.). *GooseChase*. Retrieved October 26, 2021, from https://www.goosechase.com/

Doganieri, E. & Munster, B. (2001). *The Amazing Race* [Game Show Series]. CBS.

Fulks, A., & Lord, B. (2016). Leveling up in a gamified classroom. *AMLE Magazine, 3*(6), 41.

Goodson, M. (1976). *Family Feud* [Game Show Series]. ABC.

Griffin, M. (1964). *Jeopardy!* [Game Show Series]. NBC.

Hodges, R. E. (2004). *What is literacy? Selected definitions and essays from "The literacy dictionary: The vocabulary of reading and writing"*. International Reading Assoc.

Kolb, L. (2020). *Learning first, Technology second in practice: New strategies, research and tools for student success*. International Society for Technology in Education.

Learning games: Make learning awesome! (2021, October 22). *Kahoot!* Retrieved October 26, 2021, from https://kahoot.com/

Learning tools & flashcards, for free. (n.d.). *quizlet*. Retrieved October 26, 2021, from https://quizlet.com/

Leman, K. (2017). *Ellen's Game of Games* [Game Show Series]. NBC.

Live learning game show. (n.d.). *Gimkit*. Retrieved October 26, 2021, from https://www.gimkit.com/

Merrill, J., & Merrill, K. (2019). *The Interactive Class*. Elevate Books Edu.

Miller, M. (2015). *Ditch that textbook*. Dave Burgess Consulting, Inc.

Miller, M., Ridgway, N., & Ridgway, A. (2019). *Don't ditch that tech: Differentiated instruction in a digital world*. Dave Burgess Consulting, Inc.

Monaghan, J. E. (1988). Literacy Instruction and Gender in Colonial New England. *American Quarterly, 40*(1), 18–41. https://doi.org/10.2307/2713140

Olson, C. B., Scarcella, R., & Matuchniak, T. (2015). English Learners, Writing, and the Common Core. *The Elementary School Journal, 115*(4), 570–592. https://doi.org/10.1086/681235

Overturf, B. J., Montgomery, L. H., & Smith, M. H. (2013). *Word nerds: Teaching all students to learn and love vocabulary*. Stenhouse Publishing.

Parker Brothers. (1988). *Scattergories*. Board Game.

Price-Dennis, D., Holmes, K. A., & Smith, E. (2015). Exploring digital literacy practices in an inclusive classroom. *The Reading Teacher, 69*(2), 195–205.

Read the standards. (n.d.). *Common Core State Standards Initiative*. Retrieved October 25, 2021, from http://www.corestandards.org/read-the-standards/

Spin Master Games. (1991). *Headbanz [Board Game]*. Spin Master Games.

Squire, K. (2003). Video games in education. *International Journal of Intelligent Simulations and Gaming, 2*(1), 49-62.

Stewart, B. (1956). *To Tell the Truth* [Game Show Series]. CBS.

Stewart, B., Rubino, V., Schwartz, C., & Strahan, M. (Producers). (1964). *100,000 Dollar Pyramid* [Game Show Series]. CBS.

Tomlinson, C. A. (2001). *How to differentiate instruction in mixed ability classrooms* (2nd ed.). ASCD.

Turoff, A., & Cooke, B. (1974). *Boggle [Board Game]*. Parker Brothers.

Chapter 16
Digital Storyworlds:
Transformative Ways to Play

Karen Le Rossignol
https://orcid.org/0000-0002-3826-1156
Deakin University, Australia

ABSTRACT

The digital storyworld model is conceptualised in this chapter as an innovative digital storytelling that incorporates both transmedia and meaning-making narrative approaches. Working with Aristotelian story elements in a non-linear digital series of mini-worlds, the higher education narrator-as-learner enters real-world situations mirrored in a fictional and fragmented environment. The model encourages a playful engagement in the experiential learning process through a range of points of view, encouraging empathy for differing perspectives that are transferable to real-life environments.

INTRODUCTION

Within a twenty first century higher education environment increasingly focused on student-centred learning principles and digital literacies (Coleman and Money, 2020), the platforms for games and simulations, digital scenarios and virtual worlds provide exciting digital learning environments. This chapter outlines a transformative digital narrative for learning, the digital storyworld model, which takes the principles of game-based learning or virtual worlds into a storytelling meaning-making. Transformative learning, a deep learning which can be applied or transferred to other situations, is the aim of the digital storyworld model. The educational philosopher John Dewey (1934) defined a transformative learning environment as entering 'through imagination and the emotions they evoke, into other forms of relationships and participation than [their] own' (p. 336). In this sense of an immersive (and transformative) learning environment this chapter explores an extended or augmented reality which parallels or mirrors the real and the virtual, where the learner moves imaginatively between the two. The real-world experience is the point of view the learner brings to the digital storyworld; and the virtual or digital storylines of character, plot and setting are provided as non-sequential, non-linear scenarios to stimulate

DOI: 10.4018/978-1-7998-7271-9.ch016

Digital Storyworlds

the imagination and engage the minds of learners. The playability of this storytelling centres on learners immersing themselves in the story that they synthesise for themselves as active agents. They engage for the purpose of developing their real-world skills through story.

Games and simulations are being adopted into educational resources and courses to support achievement of learning outcomes (Connolly, 2012). There is also a strong existing body of research examining the role of games within education (Yang, Chen, & Jeng, 2010; Vlachopoulos & Makri, 2017). Vlachopoulos and Makri have concerns in their review of the literature about the mixed effects in areas such as 'student performance, engagement, and learning motivation' (Vlachopoulos & Makri, 2017) as well as a gap in consideration of the framework of use across different disciplines. This chapter positions the digital storyworld (DSW) as a more niche narrative model of digital worlds and scenarios, to apply to discipline areas in arts and humanities in general, and professional writing and communication in particular. This model is infinitely flexible in terms of applications across different discipline areas, as it is low cost, easily accessible and based on tutor/learner engagement in the story 'game' or imaginative playful rendering of digitally based narrative worlds.

The DSW model is centred on the traditional role of storytelling as learning, indicated through Skain's (2021) belief that 'humans store (and use) knowledge implicit in stories' (p. 4). This model is an interactive digital narrative that scopes scenario-based experience within a 2D website as alternate 'real' world, not a separate fully functioning virtual world (Koenitz et al., 2015). The representations of a city office block, or a country town, or a Pacific island, are rendered through transmedia approaches such as video interviews, photographic slideshows, audio/podcasting and text to engage students' imaginations in a playful 'reality'.

Scenario-based learning works through approximating a real-life or situational experience, which will involve an emotional engagement or response. That response is strongly indicated by both individual and collective interactivity, where learners are immersed in both the tasks they are completing and the context or scenario for those tasks. Learners can be more motivated by the near-real world, work settings and situations as they get actively engaged and perceive relevance for their own life experience, while also acknowledging that this is not actually real, it is a narrative or story. The students are able to opt out at any level and in fact travel easily between their own real world and the storyworld, creating an exploratory liminal space. This is gamification of the imaginative narrative world rather than a game set apart as a separate world of set rules, levels and player roles.

The digital storyworld model integrates principles of transmedia narrative (Ryan, 2014) and the cognitive educational psychologist Bruner's narrative meaning-making (1986) into an innovative digital narrative approach. Moving beyond digital storytelling as a form of personalized and individualised digital narrative working across a range of media (for example Lambert, 2013), this virtual world model integrates Aristotelian story elements into a non-linear narrative ecosystem. The narrative eco-system is a form of interdisciplinary digital narrative (IDN), which combines entertaining and engaging narratives with educationally aligned tasks or inventions (Skain et al., 2021) and encourages play as a motivation to engage. Play in this chapter is aligned with Huizinga's (1949) ludic positioning as 'a free activity standing quite consciously outside "ordinary" life as being "not serious", but at the same time absorbing the player intensely and utterly' (p.13). The centrality of absorption in play encourages a transformative perspective because of the freedom and openness of the model to explore stories about social issues relevant and motivating to the learner.

The question posed here is whether this digital storyworld model and creative pedagogical design encourages higher education transformative learning through multiple points-of-view and perspectives as a playful learning approach to digital narratives.

DEFINING THE DIGITAL STORYWORLD

This chapter does not propose to review educational serious games (see for example De Gloria et al., 2014), game-based learning and gamification (Connolly, T. M. et al., 2012) or simulations (Sauve, L. et al., 2007). These indicate valuable contributions to game-based learning that are fully immersive, with multiplayer and single player interactivity as collaborative learning. However, games and virtual worlds also provide playful digital environments that establish transitions or bridges into real-world problems and skills, as stated by Gee (2014):

One of the promising things about games, simulations, and virtual worlds is that they allow us to create tools for foregrounding aspects of possible worlds (modelled usually on the real world in some sense) that can become niches for worlds. These worlds can then lead to debate about possibilities, innovation, transformation and change. (2014. p. 109)

Gee (2014) discusses video games as problem-solving spaces, aligned to a real world which 'is itself largely a set of problem-solving spaces, but much more "open-ended" (and consequential) than video games' (p. 100). There are many subcategories of online spaces, but the two most general are game and social virtual worlds. By defining the virtual worlds, I will more closely differentiate the digital world space of the *Deakinopolis* portfolio.

For games, the motivations and goals are to participate, to reach further levels of capacity, to find the end of the story/role playing game. Sauve et al. (2007) review identifying characteristics between games and simulations, differentiating games as artificial and pedagogical tools, applying conflict, rules and goals (Sauve et al., 2007). Simulations are contrasted as dynamic tools, representing reality. As Bell, Smith-Robbins and Withnail (2010) apply Koster (2004), 'the more limiting structure there is in a game, the sooner it will become stale ...the more open-ended a system is, the greater its longevity' (p. 184). A classic example of open-ended game system is chess. The social virtual world referred to by Bell, Smith-Robbins and Withnail emphasise not only this open-ended quality, but also the sense of fun. Bell et al. (2010) apply Castronova's definition of fun (2008) as a 'pleasurable sensation attributed to an activity' (p. 183). Fun is obvious in a role-playing game – it is a combination of subjective considerations of playability that emerge from the player experience combining motivation, meaningful choices, balance, usability and aesthetics (Eng, 2019). But what makes a social virtual world fun? Huizenger in *Homo Ludens* (1949) talks of the fun of playing as resisting 'an analysis, all logical interpretation' (p. 3) and delights in the English word fun and its untranslatability. He sees fun as central to or the essence of play (p. 3). With play as a voluntary activity (p. 7), as a 'stepping out of "real" life into a temporary sphere of activity with a disposition all of its own' (p. 8), Huizinga is aligning with my own sense of a social virtual narrative world.

Digital Storyworlds

The digital storyworld model, in some ways more akin to a social virtual world, requires a learner to have a motivation for moving from the concept of playing a game into social interaction with a common cause (problem-solving) and to develop the capacity to use innovative content creation tools, or narratives. Peachey et al.(2010) argue:

Rather than experiencing content created by game designers, users in a social virtual world create their own stories and their own interactions, even where they are unable to create or form the environment itself. (p. xx).

The *Deakinopolis* narrative worlds are about creating stories and interactions with the local communities created in them. There is a game-like fun element, but the key aspects that engage are the interpersonal relationships and characters' identity creation (Bell, Smith-Robbins and Withnail 2010, p. 186).

Wolf (2014) talks of humans as 'story-telling animals' with stories that 'can be transmitted by more media than verbal texts' (p. 216). He asks the question: 'how do we know ... that a text, an artefact, or, more precisely, a particularly represented world ... is a storyworld?' (2014, p. 126). Ryan (2014) elaborates on the term storyworld by allocating two types of narrative elements: 'intradiegetic elements, which exist within the storyworld, and extradiegetic elements, which are not literally part of the storyworld but play a crucial role in its presentation' (p. 37). She draws a distinction between 'the speech of the characters and the discourse of the narrator. The former always belongs to the storyworld while the latter may or may not belong to it' (2014, p. 37). The narrator, in the digital storyworld model, is the participant-learner who engages with the story.

The digital storyworld model deliberately does not present a completed narrative. This is play 'based on the manipulation of certain images, on a certain "imagination" of reality (i.e. its conversion into images)' (Huizinga, 1949, p. 4). The learner-as-narrator can move into and out of the storyworld. The characters, context and situation in the storyworld are activated by the agency of a learner/narrator who enters, constructs and transforms the story into relevance by having fun (in Huizinger's terms) with differing perspectives.

DESIGNING EXPERIENCE AS A CONSTRUCTIVIST MODEL

My focus on digital storyworlds has grown from my development of scenarios and role-plays as ways of engaging with experiential, active learning. Transferring print-based scenario and role-play learning approaches and resources to a digital world provides the possibility to engage with storytelling purposes and styles within a nontemporal and nonsequential environment. This digital storyworld grew or developed from issues for contemporary tertiary learners who are time-poor, just-in-time, digitally literate millennials. The portfolio work is based in a constructivist theoretical space, which is relevant to learners with a range of learning approaches and disciplinary areas. As a writer, I am interested in the power of storytelling to make learning relevant and motivational. As an educator, I find the constructivist experiential learning environment most compatible with my portfolio directions.

The digital storyworld or interactive digital narrative approach shares student-centred learning and a playful game-oriented quality to the storytelling which is its constructivist basis for learning. A constructivist-based approach incorporating innovative teaching methods aims to:

...promote learning in communication with teachers and other learners, taking students seriously as active participants in their own learning and fostering transferable skills such as problem-solving and critical/reflective thinking. (Attard et al., 2010, p. 4)

The areas of learner empowerment, problem solving and understanding provide an overarching definition of the links to student-centred learning central to both game-based learning and the digital storyworld model proposed in this chapter (Coleman and Money 2019, p. 419). Coleman and Money (2019) present Gee's thirteen design principles for digital game-based learning within a context of student-centred experience (p. 418). Key principles overlap in design with the digital storyworld model, particularly in learner empowerment with a focus on co-design and customisation, problem-solving as sandbox learning, and understanding through meaning from experience (Coleman and Money, 2019, p. 418). The driver for learning is empowering the learner through storytelling to understand the problems that are posed by social issues in that storyworld.

Piaget (1964) has a reputation for talking of learners constructing knowledge out of their experience. He defines knowledge as being able to modify, transform and 'operate on' an object or idea, to transform into understanding (Piaget, 1964). There are other forms of constructivism where collaboration or sharing is encouraged, such as within Vygotski's social constructivist argument (for example Vygotski, 1978). Many different learning theories such as discovery learning (Bruner), problem-based (Barrows) or inquiry-based learning (Dewey) and experiential learning (Kolb) have a similar constructivist teaching technique of learning by doing. My approach in designing the digital storyworld model is applying some aspects of the above constructivist theoretical frameworks, but as a constructivist practitioner.

Jonassen (1997) suggests that a well-designed and structured learning environment can support problem-solving, particularly related to the challenge of 'ill-structured problem solving' based on 'constructivist and situated cognition processes of learning' (1997, p. 94). This ill-structured problem solving, as Jonassen calls it, is also about 'learning by doing', taking Piaget's process of modifying, transforming and operating on ideas. The digital storyworld is a constructivist learning environment which illustrates Jonassen's (1991) criteria of 'the promotion of multiple perspectives of reality' through provision of 'appropriate interpretations and provision of the intellectual tools' and engagement within the environments (p. 12). These multiple perspectives of reality are related to entering the digital storyworld in a state of uncertainty, both of where to start and how to synthesise what is front of the learner.

Jonassen, Campbell and Davidson (1994) are interested in the application of a constructivist approach both to educational psychology and media technology, merging interests in constructivism with educational technology to learn with media, not from it (Jonassen, Campbell and Davidson 1994). The emphasis in a constructivist design process is, according to Jonassen (1994), on knowledge construction, a context for learning, and collaboration (p. 37). These three elements could be extrapolated out to: knowledge construction moving through internal working out of meaning; a context which uses scenarios based on authentic tasks; and a collaborative approach where there is social negotiation and the teacher emphasises the role of mentor or coach rather than the holder of knowledge. Duffy and Cunningham (1996) talk of design goals of a constructivist learning environment with seven points of context (p. 177). The key terms I have applied to my portfolio from these design goals have been providing a context and authentic tasks, constructing different world views and multiple perspectives, and encouraging learner agency through providing reflective tools for 'knowing how we know'.

Digital Storyworlds

Because my focus is on experiences which reflect the surrounding environment and its relevance to the learner, my development of digital storyworlds has been within a context of extensive social and cultural change across the previous twenty years or so. The first key component of change I have considered as a specific influence is a contemporary university sector which is subject to global as well as local pressures to prepare students for an uncertain future world of work (for example consider, Beetham & Sharpe 2007; Bellanca & Brandt 2010; Facer 2011; Kalantzis, Varnvava-Skoura & Cope 2002; Laurillard 2002). The second component is the effect of an information revolution which may lead to a potentially disruptive technology-driven state of change for the contemporary learner who has access to masses of information. Labelled as a range of variations on millennials or digital natives (see for example, Dede 2005; Prensky 2012), these learners are required to adapt to different forms of social community, knowledge building and the world of work.

Defining the limits of discussion on digital accessibility and contemporary social change is intertwined with my definition of experiential learning in a contemporary context, and this is the third area requiring consideration. The portfolio of digital storyworlds reflects my interest in a pedagogical practice exploring the interplay between knowledge acquisition, the role of the teacher, learner needs and the learning environment. The storyworld model invites the learner to 'form his or her own understandings' (Olsen 2007, p. 133), echoing Bruner's view as a pedagogy of thinking (Olsen 2007, p. 133ff). My pedagogical position across the portfolio explores the relationships between the learner and learning environment, which I interpret here as the higher education context, the digital world and their own social and cultural experiences. Other relationships include the knowledge acquisition inherent in the digital storyworld and the learner's relationship to knowledge acquisition through agency in their own learning. My pedagogical focus is on developing learning to form the tertiary learners' own understanding, thinking and reflective skills.

DIGITAL AND OTHER LITERACIES

I moved to a digital environment from print-based scenarios for several reasons, as has been emerging. One of these was to engage learners who had been assumed to be digitally literate because of their generational positioning. Prensky (2012) describes these as 'growing up in a digital country or culture, as opposed to coming to it as an adult' as a form of digital wisdom (p. 17). He is arguing for digital extensions and enhancements, and a homo sapiens digital who 'accepts digital enhancement as an integral fact of human existence', and is digitally wise in the way s/he 'uses enhancements to facilitate wiser decision making' (p. 204). He believes digital wisdom has leaped over the gap between native and immigrant, with enhancement and extension providing more sophistication. The digital wisdom is about selecting what is appropriate, whether it is a live simulation or a wearable device that improves receptors. Prensky is looking at a future of digital literacy that will be as overwhelming as the information superhighway, and that will require such digital wisdom. Digital literacies develop broader competencies, that enable people to 'meaningfully create and interact with complex practices that locate literacy within "cultural processes, personal circumstances and collective structures"' (UNESCO 2004, p. 6, in Sheridan & Rowsell 2010, p. 3).

Overarching these digital literacies is information literacy, incorporating new media literacy, which includes cultural media and communication media (Lorenzo & Dziuban 2006, p. 4). The literacies present for the digital learner also include silicon literacies, 'understanding how the different modalities are combined in complex ways to create meaning' (Snyder 2002, p. 3). Multiliteracies advance the silicon literacies further, assuming a multimodal approach to learning. These multiliteracies 'encompass the multiplicity of communications channels and media'; and 'the increasing salience of cultural and linguistic diversity (Cope & Kalantzis 2000, p. 5). As Carmen Luke (2000) sees multiliteracies, they are based on 'notions of hybridity and intertextuality' (p. 73), where:

an understanding of the relationship among ideas is as important as ... mastery of the ideas themselves. ...the expert is the one who sees and seeks the connection among related pieces of information, not the one who has the bare decontextualized facts. (2000, p. 73).

In 2005, Dede wrote of contemporary learners as having an information-age mindset, as millennials or part of that Echo Boomer generation. He speculates that there are what he calls neomillennial learning styles, which I believe could be more accurately termed neomillennial literacies. These are listed by Dede (2005a) as:

- Fluency in multiple media and in simulation-based virtual settings
- Communal learning involving diverse, tacit, situated experience, with knowledge distributed across a community and a context as well as within an individual
- A balance among experiential learning, guided mentoring, and collective reflection
- Expression through nonlinear, associational webs of representations
- Co-design of learning experiences personalized [sic] to individual needs and preferences. (p. 10)

Dede positions the digital world and learner most strongly within situated learning as 'virtual environments and ubiquitous computing can draw on the power of situated learning by creating immersive, extended experiences with problems and contexts similar to the real world' (Dede 2005b, p.15.5). Situated learning is important in part because of the crucial issue of transfer. Within the working-in-teams scenario of *Kaleidoscope Consulting* (a workplace mini-world within *Deakinopolis*), this concept of transfer has been demonstrated by ongoing participants over the more than ten years it has been utilised. This scenario is probably one of the most transferable, not just to real-world settings, but also as an interdisciplinary model – it has been implemented across multiple faculties, with relevant, transferable underpinning stories. Part of its popularity is that it is immediately identifiable both as a complex selection process task and a real-world application. The participants in these worlds, and in *Deakinopolis* as a whole, have demonstrated ease with the neomillennial 'literacies' Dede lists above.

THE DIGITAL STORYWORLD MODEL

The digital storyworld provides a multiplicity of scenarios/mini-worlds demonstrating the setting or landscape, the context, and also the characters and their narratives or backstories, but without specific plots or being set in a particular point in time. Figure 1 provides a visual summary of the story elements of *Deakinopolis*, incorporating not only businesses such as *Kaleidoscope Consulting* with conflict resolution and interview scenarios, but also trips to the Pacific Island of *Newlandia* to advocate for sustainable third world development, and the country town of *Bilby* to support regional development. The

Digital Storyworlds

participants are higher education (HE) learners studying in communications, creative and persuasive writing, incorporating work-integrated learning (WIL) and social advocacy in a multidisciplinary way, through narrative and play.

Figure 1. Deakinopolis digital storyworld portfolio – five 'worlds' and multiple embedded scenarios

There is no structure with plotpoints, or character quests and motivations as catalysts or themes. There is also no temporality, the various mini-worlds represented within Figure 1 above await activation while holding relevant scenarios in stasis. What the storyworld needs to animate it is not a brief navigational entry via a drop-down menu, or a game-based cut scene or dialogue suggesting the plot, but the narrator/learner exploring point of view. 'Point of view is the window that you …open on to your imaginary world. This all-important choice determines not only your story's tone, but also its characterization and plot' (Newman 2001, p. 141). The interactivity of the digital storyworld model encourages learner agency through role-playing points of view to encourage empathy for diverse perspectives.

In the concept of the portfolio containing a multiplicity of mini-worlds within *Deakinopolis*, point of view across all those mini-worlds is transferred into a broader concept of shifting learner perspective, dependent on the purpose of the role and writing. The learners are seeing situations from different perspectives, 'one of the pleasures of fiction' (Newman 2001, p. 146). They are synthesizing the story as it sits digitally and nonsequentially before them, into a temporal environment of engagement in the digital world's issues.

The narrative structural aspect of the digital storyworld concept or model is complex although the platform it is based on is simple. There are components of story – the setting, characters, contexts – within the digital world in no particular sequence or sense of time/temporality, other than being generally in-the-moment or present. Although the story components are based on real experience – that is, they have a work-related or general life experience relevance – they do not have built into them a plot sequencing or linear narrative meaning. The narrative process (leading to establishing point of view) is what will activate the stories into meaning for participants. The model encourages imaginative engagement in story through agency in the narration as learners take on different perspectives.

My concentration here is on a design model of a narrative process that will use plot and time – or a form of chronology and sequencing – to make meaning for the learner in working with the storyworld. The narrative process moves the storyworld into a temporal structure which enables meaning-making. This particularly represented storyworld (Wolf 2014) invites the learner to consider the past (the storyworld) of significant events, characters and contexts, with a present that searches out the value of the social interactions through changing perspectives, suggesting a future of possible actions and intentions.

THE CONNECTIVE PORTAL FOR CONTEMPORARY TERTIARY LEARNERS

Weller (2011) talks of the digital scholar being digital, networked and open. He calls openness a 'state of mind' (2011, pp. 6-7), with the technology as a set of tools provided to encourage a culture of openness. Digital flexibility is central to the use of this technology. This is where the portfolio sits, with technology or a platform that is fast, cheap and out of control, to quote Brian Lamb in Weller (2011, p. 9). The three characteristics, summarised from Weller (2011), that ensure the platform for my portfolio of digital storyworlds can work, are that the technology is fast, easy to learn and quick to set up, encouraging experimentation (p. 9). The tools are also free or readily accessible to a wide audience, and the technologies exist out of control of formal institutional structures, therefore are more flexible and personalised. Digital flexibility is central to the storyworld applications of this technology, which integrates a simple website portal, downloadable audio-visual files and podcasting of character situations.

In simple definitional terms, a portal is a doorway, gate, or other entrance, especially a large and imposing one. This model's portal is the nexus between the real and the virtual world, the point where learners enter a space, suspending disbelief and allowing the imagination to engage. The platform technology is simple and flexible, the portal into the story suggests the complexity the learner is about to explore. Laurillard (2007), in her foreword to *Rethinking Pedagogy for a Digital Age*, states, 'imaginative use of digital technologies could be transformational for teaching and learning, taking us well beyond the incremental value of more accessible lecture presentations' (p. xvi). Laurillard's statement is exploring value within both digital technologies and the transaction as transfer or transmission of knowledge. My interest is in how the digital technologies now available may be used to support a storytelling learning approach for contemporary learners. The focus is on the bridge between the imagination and the learning contexts, and the digital technologies are the interface or platform to play out these interrelationships.

Digital Storyworlds

Focusing on the learner skills, Oblinger and Oblinger (2005) turn the focus back to learners brought up with computers and technology, who have 'hypertext minds, they leap around' (Prensky 2001), and demonstrate a 'bricolage' thought process (Brown 2000), more than a linear thought process. Other relevant qualities identified by Oblinger and Oblinger (2005, p. 25) indicate learner interest in two-way fast response times and inductive discovery, learning from discovery more than being told. They are more likely to construct knowledge in a nonlinear way, starting from the known or concrete, then moving informally through more lateral mosaic-style developments (Marquardt, 2007). These learners, according to Oblinger and Oblinger (2005), are prone to take a digital path towards information, filtering what they need through 'attentional deployment', where 'they are able to 'shift their attention rapidly from one task to another, and may choose not to pay attention to things that don't interest them' (pp. 2.2, 2.5).

Dede (2005a) describes neomillennial learners as fluent in multiple media and simulation-based virtual settings, with their learning communal and situated in experience. Dede (2005a) argues that neomillennials' education is shaped by 'learning based on seeking, sieving, and synthesizing, rather than on assimilating a single "validated" source of knowledge as from books, television, or a professor's lectures' (p. 7). The digital storyworld model is particularly focused on Dede's consideration of the web of nonlinear and associational links to be made in exploring an immersive imaginative interrelationship, as well as the linkages between the experience, mentoring or facilitation, and reflection. The world is also built with a capacity to entertain and persuade, an interactive digital narrative (IDN) similar to the case studies Skains (2021) describes, as utilising 'strong entertainment narratives whose underlying informative and persuasive themes regarding climate change and AMR [anti-microbial resistance] could affect audiences' perceptions and subsequent behaviours regarding these issues' (p. 3).

NARRATIVES AS MEANING-MAKING

Rutton and Soetaert (2012) argue that narratives are 'not to be understood as a literal prescription, but as an orientation to a situation, providing assistance in adjusting to it', through 'opening up a narrative to multiple perspectives' (p. 337). These multiple perspectives require learners to face the challenge of synthesising a mass of situational events into some sort of meaning for themselves.

The digital storyworld has a portal of story, an imaginative leap into what presents as a somewhat chaotic or incoherent world. The learner enters through the portal to synthesise the stories within the digital world into responses to the structural situations given as plot from an external stimulus. The platform remains separate to time, only existing if someone enters it, and although the platform is multiplayer in the sense that unlimited numbers can enter, there is no interaction between the players in story development within the digital world. The movement between the real and near-real digital world is fluid and two-way, with no barriers to multiple entry and exit.

When I developed the portfolio initially, one of my major intentions was to develop summary and synthesis skills in a relevant context. The concept was to be able to move between different audiences and purposes, to change from an employee of a social advocacy organisation in a virtual world writing a media release, to working as an individual character in that world writing a letter to the editor complaining about windfarms and the new multinational *TrustWind* organisation. The context grew through my practice-led research into an imaginatively conceived world of overlapping stories, interrelated characters – a series of relationships between the key characters in the town for instance – and search across at least four different areas of the digital world for the tasks to be imaginatively conceived.

This led to some frustrated students wanting to be directed to the specific place for the information – a bookmarked page, an information sheet – but the exploration across the worlds became a vital element of the digital world model.

The total context of a learning space, in Raschke's (2003) view, involves a sense of digital culture 'which by its very character involves constant experimentation and exploratory activity' (p. 59). The portfolio is embedded in that digital culture and is open to exploration and risk. Because it is an open space, learners are encouraged to bring other knowledge and information to the tasks. There is no right answer or key content deliverable to respond to the tasks, as they are structured for the learner to become immersed and engaged in the uncertainty of story narrative, to discover their own unique voice and agency through participation.

Narrative is explored by Bruner (1986) as 'how we come to endow experience with meaning' (p. 12). Bruner details narrative as combinations of plot linking events together, action and interaction, character itself. The portfolio's storytelling sets up the events seemingly without an organised pattern or consecutiveness, leaping between incidents in mimicry of human memory and its associative patterns. These are spiral forms of narrative, circling around the central web or revisiting digressively the multiple paths of digital storytelling. Spiralling is described by Gingerich (2012) as 'the idea of exploring a story's prevailing theme from as many different angles and perspectives in the narrative as possible' (para. 4). He calls spiralling 'the idea of repeating a story's thematic meaning by taking occurrences in the foreground — in plot, dialogue and characters — and mirroring them in the background: in symbols, imagery, and suggestions'(para. 4). In the digital world environment, there are countless story paths, and, as in real experience, the endings are transitory and dependent on decisions made and adjusted by those involved. They are ongoing in a continuous present. The multitudinous ways into these storylines invoke an exploration of themes or resonances; they are forms of spiral narrative.

The other major skill that is central to the digital storyworld model is extending learner capacities to move imaginatively into other perspectives. Transformation is the process, as Mezirow (2009) describes,

...by which we transform problematic frames of reference (mindsets, habits of mind, meaning perspectives) – sets of assumption and expectation – to make them more inclusive, discriminatory, open, reflective and emotionally able to change. (p. 92)

When they are first introduced to the digital storyworld as part of their learning, learners initially look for a map or how-to guide. This is a challenge because there is no simple option. The world they face has possibilities for the learners to create a different reality. Bruner (1986) suggests that:

...many worlds are possible, that meaning and reality are created and not discovered, that negotiation is the art of constructing new meanings by which individuals can regulate their relations with each other. (p. 149)

Integrated into the storyworld model is the need to leap between materials, to use imagination to create different perspectives on the stories/narratives required. Bruner (1979) talks of this as 'an act that produces effective surprise' in his essay 'Conditions of Creativity' (p. 21).

I propose that the digital storyworld model is moving through a narrative textual discourse within the story towards a narrative mode of knowing for the learner as narrative agent. Bruner (1986) compares a narrative mode of knowing to a paradigmatic mode as being a good story or well-formed argument:

Digital Storyworlds

Both can be used as means for convincing another. Yet what they convince of is fundamentally different: arguments convince one of their truth, stories of their lifelikeness. The one verifies by eventual appeal to procedures for establishing formal and empirical proof. The other establishes not truth but verisimilitude. (p. 11)

Verisimilitude and lifelikeness are linked to finding open-ended options or perspectives in the narrative for the learner, being able to explore the unexpected or the effective surprise of disrupted or changed situations. Bruner also discusses narratives as structures 'in terms of which people interpret the world and explain their actions to themselves and to each other' (in Olson 2007, p. 27).

Disruption, uncertainty and interruption are a part of the storyworld model of narrative. Managing these as potentially transformative experiences is made possible through the agency of the learner/narrator. Bruner (1996) believes skilled agency in studying the human condition will 'achieve not unanimity, but more consciousness. And more consciousness always implies more diversity' (p. 97). Olson (2007) felt Bruner settled for 'a variety of ways of knowing, for entertaining possibilities, and for judging the value of knowledge on the basis that it opened up new views rather than that it settled old questions' (p. 134).

There is an uncertainty, as well as knowledge acquisition, in opening up new possibilities and diverse ways of knowing. Part of the destabilising effect of the nonsequential presentation of the digital portfolio is the uncertainty for the learner of knowing where to start the investigation. This is a deliberate part of the model, as a disruptive function of encouraging the learner's agency to move through the uncertainty and explore the possibilities. Being in charge of the narrative's point of view, the learner has engaged in a praxical exercise to integrate perspectives into the plot structure given, within the storyworld context. The further aim of the model is to transform this into learning through the uncertainty, embracing new views. Bruner's (1979) effective surprise 'takes one beyond common ways of experiencing the world' (p. 22). Engaging the learner's imagination through the storyworld is central to the model.

TRANSFORMATIVE LEARNING

To be transformative in developing connections from seemingly unrelated sequences in the digital storyworlds requires an imaginative leap. This is in part the leaps that learners have been making between the real and the digital worlds, a form of play in the digital space. They are, as Greene (1995) notes, 'about openings, about possibilities, about moving in quest and in pursuit' (p. 15).

Greene (2001) talks of imagination, the capacity to change things from as they are as 'the mode of grasping, of reaching out that allows what is perceived to be transformed' (p. 31). She believes imagination is able to shape experience into something new, to create surprise. Built into the word itself is its capacity to create image, but imagination also provides the power to 'put oneself in another's place' (Greene 2001, p. 30). This educational focus is about seeing alternatives, connections, moving from the known or leaving something behind, while reaching towards something new. Dewey (1934) saw this as 'the conscious adjustment of the new and the old' (p. 272), while Bruner saw it as effective surprise. Greene is concerned about learners being petrified, which entails being incapable of learning, and shut off from change. She makes a strong case for engaging with possibilities, which will 'add to the multiplicity of our realities' (2001, p. 132).

Like Greene (1995), I am interested in extending the imaginative capacities of the learners to 'work for the ability to look at things as if they could be otherwise' (p. 19). When students are within their just-in-time, earn-and-learn ways of thinking, I believe the storytelling of the portfolio can enlarge and transform their sense of self and identity into consideration of other points of view. As Greene (1995) states, '[o]ne of the reasons I have come to concentrate on imagination as a means through which we can assemble a coherent world is that imagination is what, above all, makes empathy possible' (p. 3).

English (2016) focuses on the twinned concepts of empathy and imagination as points of contemporary relevance. There is what English (2016) calls an '*in-between* realm of learning' (original emphasis), a space between the old and new ideas and beliefs, a twilight zone (p. 1050). My research into that in-between realm is centred on the digital storyworld and its capacity to transform. English (2016) believes it is the capacity for imagination that

...allows us to dwell in the space of the in-between because it facilitates our ability to extend our thinking beyond the known, and allows alternative ways of seeing and being in the world to emerge in our minds. (p. 1051)

There are echoes of the differing perspectives of the narrator's imaginative engagement in the portfolio digital worlds, and this seeing and being as an emergent process depends on imagination which can handle the initial doubts and uncertainties experienced. Weible (2015) particularises imagination as 'putting emphasis alternatively on two complementary aspects; that is, particular form and universal content' (p. 88).

English (2016) differentiates between imaginary, daydreaming or escape from experience, and imagination, which can perceive the full scope, integrating the unexpected or habits of resistance. She argues for rich experiences in educative learning environments (p. 1055) so that learners may 'enter, through imagination and the emotions they evoke, into other forms of relationships and participation than our own' (Dewey 1934, p. 336).

CONCLUSION

The digital storyworld provides a multiplicity of scenarios/mini-worlds demonstrating the setting or landscape, the context, and also the characters and their narratives or backstories. What the storyworld needs to animate it is entry into an exploration of point of view by a narrator playing within that virtual world. The model encourages exploration of situations from different perspectives, with learner-participants synthesising the story as it sits digitally and nonsequentially before them. The storyworld model plays with what is real to encourage learner engagement in a world not necessarily their own, although recognisable for having close or parallel to real experiences. This present continuous world then enables learners to experience developing further their own understanding of perspectives within that world through narrative.

Deakinopolis, as a digital storyworld model, is about imaginatively entering a fictional storyworld that largely presents as factual, experientially mirroring reality. The digital world, apparently chaotic and nonsequential, requires the narrator-as-learner to find their own order. They become active agents or players in searching out the meaning via their own narratives. The storyworld model is a concept within which sit nonsequential story sequences, awaiting narration for meaning by participants who enter this digital space. The learners activate their immersive engagement in this digital story narrative through praxical experience leading to, and concurrent with, transformative immersion of imagination encouraging empathy across perspectives.

REFERENCES

Attard, A., Di Iorio, E., Geven, K., & Santa, R. (2010). Time for a new paradigm in education: student-centred learning. In A. Attard (Ed.), *Student-centred Learning Toolkit* (pp. 1-4). European Students Union. https://www.esu-online.org/wp-content/uploads/2016/07/100814-SCL.pdf

Beetham, H., & Sharpe, R. (Eds.). (2007). *Rethinking pedagogy for a digital age: Designing and delivering e-learning.* Routledge., doi:10.4324/9780203961681

Bell, M., Smith-Robbins, S., & Withnail, G. (2010). This is not a game – Social virtual worlds, fun, and learning. In *Researching learning in virtual worlds* (pp. 177–191). Springer., doi:10.1007/978-1-84996-047-2_10

Bellanca, J., & Brandt, R. (Eds.). (2010). *21st Century skills: Rethinking how students learn.* Solution Tree Press.

Brown, J. S. (2000). Growing Up Digital. *Change, 32*(2), 10–11. http://www.johnseelybrown.com/Growing_up_digital.pdf

Bruner, J. (1979). On knowing: Essays for the left hand (expanded edition). Harvard University Press.

Bruner, J. (1986). *Actual minds, possible worlds.* Harvard University Press. doi:10.4159/9780674029019

Bruner, J. (1996). *The culture of education.* Harvard University Press.

Castronova, E. (2008). *Exodus to the virtual world: How online fun is changing reality.* Palgrave Macmillan.

Coleman, T. E., & Money, A. G. (2020). Student-centred digital game–based learning: A conceptual framework and survey of the state of the art. *Higher Education, 79*(3), 415–457. doi:10.100710734-019-00417-0

Connolly, T. M., Boyle, E. A., MacArthur, E., Hainey, T., & Boyle, J. M. (2012). A systematic literature review of the empirical evidence on computer games and serious games. *Computers & Education, 59*(2), 661–686. doi:10.1016/j.compedu.2012.03.004

Cope, B., & Kalantzis, M. (Eds.). (2000). *Multiliteracies: Literacy learning and the design of social futures.* Macmillan. doi:10.1080/10572250701372847

De Gloria, A., Bellotti, F., & Berta, R. (2014). Serious games for education and training. *International Journal of Serious Games, 1*(1). Advance online publication. doi:10.17083/ijsg.v1i1.11

Dede, C. (2005a). Planning for neomillennial learning styles: Shifts in students' learning style will prompt a shift to active construction of knowledge through mediated immersion. *EDUCAUSE Quarterly, 28*(1), 7–12. https://er.educause.edu/-/media/files/article-downloads/eqm0511.pdf

Dede, C. (2005b). Planning for neomillennial learning styles: Implications for investments in technology and faculty. In *Educating the net generation*. EDUCAUSE. https://www.educause.edu/research-and-publications/books/educating-net-generation/planning-neomillennial-learning-styles-implications-investments-tech

Dewey, J. (1934). *Art as Experience*. Capricorn Books.

Duffy, T. M., & Cunningham, D. J. (1996). Constructivism: Implications for the design and delivery of instruction. In D. H. Jonassen (Ed.), *Handbook of research for educational communications and technology*. Macmillan Library Reference. doi:10.4324/9781410609519

Eng, D. (2019). *The player experience*. https://www.universityxp.com/blog/2019/9/10/the-player-experience

English, A. R. (2016). John Dewey and the role of the teacher in a globalised world: Imagination, empathy, and "third voice". *Educational Philosophy and Theory*, *48*(10), 1046–1064. doi:10.1080/00131857.2016.1202806

Facer, K. (2011). *Learning futures: Education, technology and social change*. Routledge. doi:10.4324/9780203817308

Gee, J. P. (2014). *Collected essays on learning and assessment in the digital world. The Learner series*. Common Ground. doi:10.18848/978-1-61229-424-7/CGP

Gingerich, J. (2012). The *spiraling narrative*. Litreactor LLC. https://litreactor.com/columns/the-spiraling-theme

Greene, M. (1995). *Releasing the imagination: Essays on education, the arts, and social change*. Jossey-Bass. doi:10.1080/14452294.2011.11649524

Greene, M. (2001). *Variations on a blue guitar: The Lincoln Centre Institute lectures on aesthetic education*. Teachers College Press.

Huizinga, J. (1949). *Homo Ludens Ils 86* (1st ed.). Routledge. doi:10.4324/9781315824161

Jonassen, D., Campbell, J., & Davidson, M. (1994). Learning with media: Restructuring the debate. *Educational Technology Research and Development*, *42*(2), 31–39. doi:10.1007/BF02299089

Jonassen, D. H. (1994). Thinking technology: Toward a constructivist design model. *Educational Technology*, *34*(4), 34–37. https://www.learntechlib.org/p/171050/

Jonassen, D. H. (1997). Instructional design models for well-structured and ill-structured problem-solving learning outcomes. *Educational Technology Research and Development*, *45*(1), 65–94. doi:10.1007/BF02299613

Kalantzis, M., Varnvava-Skoura, G., & Cope, B. (2002). *Learning for the future: New worlds, new literacies, new learning, new people*. Common Ground Publishing. http://www.thelearner.com

Koenitz, H., Ferri, G., Haahr, M., Sezen, D., & Sezen, T. I. (Eds.). (2015). *Interactive digital narrative: History, theory and practice*. Routledge. doi:10.4324/9781315769189

Koster, R. (2004). *Theory of fun for game design*. Paraglyph.

Lambert, J. (2013). *Digital storytelling: Capturing lives, creating community* (4th ed.). Routledge. doi:10.4324/9780203102329

Laurillard, D. (2002). *Rethinking university teaching: a framework for the effective use of learning technologies* (2nd ed.). Routledge Falmer. doi:10.4324/9780203160329

Lorenzo, G., & Dziuban, C. (2006). *Ensuring the Net Generation is net savvy*. Educause Learning Initiative Paper 2, September 2006 EDUCAUSE Learning Initiative. https://understandingxyz.com/index_htm_files/Net%20Gen%20paper.pdf

Luke, C. (2000). Cyber-schooling and technological change: Multiliteracies for new times. In B. Cope & M. Kalantzis (Eds.), 2009 Multiliteracies (pp. 69–91). Macmillan.

Marquardt, M. (2007). Action learning: resolving real problems in real time. In M. Silberman (Ed.), *The handbook of experiential learning* (pp. 94–110). Pfeiffer.

Mezirow, J. (2009). An overview on transformative learning. In K. Illeris (Ed.), *Contemporary Theories of Learning* (pp. 90–105). Routledge. doi:10.4324/9781315147277

Newman, J. (2001). Eye level. In J. Bell & P. Magrs (Eds.), *The creative writing coursebook* (pp. 141–147). Macmillan.

Oblinger, D., & Oblinger, J. (Eds.). (2005). *Educating the net generation*. EDUCAUSE. https://www.educause.edu/ir/library/PDF/pub7101.PDF

Olson, D. (2007). *Jerome Bruner: The cognitive revolution in educational theory*. Continuum International Publishing Group.

Peachey, A., Gillen, J., Livingstone, D., & Smith-Robbins, S. (Eds.). (2010). *Researching learning in Virtual Worlds*. Springer. doi:10.1007/978-1-84996-047-2

Piaget, J. (1964). Cognitive development in children: Development and learning. *Journal of Research in Science Teaching*, *2*(3), 176–186. doi:10.1002/tea.3660020306

Prensky, M. (2001). Digital datives, digital immigrants, Part II: Do they really think differently? *On the Horizon*, *9*(6), 15–24. doi:10.1108/10748120110424843

Prensky, M. (2012). *From digital natives to digital wisdom: Hopeful essays for 21st century learning*. Corwin. doi:10.4135/9781483387765

Raschke, C. A. (2003). *The digital revolution and the coming of the postmodern university*. Routledge. doi:10.4324/9780203451243

Rutten, K., & Soetaert, R. (2012). Narrative and rhetorical approaches to problems of education: Jerome Bruner and Kenneth Burke revisited. *Studies in Philosophy and Education*, *32*(4), 327–343. doi:10.100711217-012-9324-5

Ryan, M. (2014). Story/Worlds/Media: Tuning the instruments of a media-conscious narratology. In M. Ryan & J. Thon (Eds.), *Storyworlds across media: Toward a media-conscious narratology* (pp. 25–49). University of Nebraska Press. doi:10.2307/j.ctt1d9nkdg.6

Sauve, L., Renaud, L., Kaufman, D., & Marquis, J. S. (2007). Distinguishing between games and simulation: A systematic review. *Journal of Educational Technology & Society*, *10*(3), 247–256. http://citeseerx.ist.psu.edu/viewdoc/download?doi=10.1.1.169.5559&rep=rep1&type=pdf

Sheridan & Rowsell. (2010). Design literacies: Learning and innovation in the digital age. Routledge.

Skains, L., Rudd, J. A., Casaliggi, C., Hayhurst, E. J., Horry, R., Ross, H., & Woodward, K. (2021). *Using interactive digital narrative in science and health education.* Emerald Publishing Ltd. doi:10.1108/9781839097607

Snyder, I. (Ed.). (2002). *Silicon literacies*. Routledge.

Vlachopoulos, D., & Makri, A. (2017). The effect of games and simulations on higher education: A systematic literature review. *International Journal of Educational Technology in Higher Education*, *14*(22), 22. Advance online publication. doi:10.118641239-017-0062-1

Vygotski, L. (1978). *Mind in society: The development of higher psychological processes*. Harvard University Press.

Weller, M. (2011). *The digital scholar: How technology is transforming scholarly practice*. Bloomsbury Academic. https://www.open.edu/openlearn/ocw/pluginfile.php/731937/mod_resource/content/1/The%20Digital%20Scholar_%20How%20Technology%20Is%20T%20-%20Martin%20Weller.pdf

Wolf, W. (2014). Framings of narrative in literature and the pictorial arts. In M. Ryan & J. Thon (Eds.), *Storyworlds across media: Toward a media-conscious narratology* (pp. 126–150). University of Nebraska Press. doi:10.2307/j.ctt1d9nkdg.10

ADDITIONAL READING

Biddiss, E., & Howcroft, J. (2010). Active Video Games to Promote Physical Activity in Children and Youth A Systematic Review. *Archives of Pediatrics & Adolescent Medicine*, *164*(7), 664–672. doi:10.1001/archpediatrics.2010.104 PMID:20603468

Çankaya, S., & Karamete, A. (2009). The effects of educational computer games on students' attitudes towards mathematics course and educational computer games. *Procedia: Social and Behavioral Sciences*, *1*(1), 145–149. doi:10.1016/j.sbspro.2009.01.027

De Gloria, A., Bellotti, F., & Berta, R. (2014). Serious Games for education and training. *International Journal of Serious Games*, *1*(1). Advance online publication. doi:10.17083/ijsg.v1i1.11

Kampmann Walther, B., & Larsen, L. J. (2021). Reflections on Ludification: Approaching a Conceptual Framework – And Discussing Inherent Challenges. *International Journal of Serious Games*, *8*(3), 115–127. doi:10.17083/ijsg.v8i3.436

Roessel, L. & Mastrigt-Ide, J. (2011). Collaboration and Team Composition in Applied Game Creation Processes. . doi:10.13140/2.1.1454.4009

Ryan, M.-L., Foote, K., & Azaryahu, M. (2016). *Narrating Space/Spatializing Narrative: Where Narrative Theory and Geography Meet*. Ohio State University Press.

Staiano, A. E., & Calvert, S. L. (2011). Exergames for Physical Education Courses: Physical, Social, and Cognitive Benefits. *Child Development Perspectives*, *5*(2), 93–98. doi:10.1111/j.1750-8606.2011.00162.x PMID:22563349

Woo, J.-C. (2014). Digital Game-Based Learning Supports Student Motivation, Cognitive Success, and Performance Outcomes. *Journal of Educational Technology & Society*, *17*(3), 291–307.

Yang, J., Chen, C., & Jeng, M. (2010). Integrating video-capture virtual reality technology into a physically interactive learning environment for English learning. *Computers & Education*, *55*(3), 1346–1356. doi:10.1016/j.compedu.2010.06.005

KEY TERMS AND DEFINITIONS

Digital Storytelling: Combination of digitised media with the art of telling stories.

Digital Storyworld: A fictional world described in a narrative using digitised media.

Experiential Learning: Learning through reflection on the process of taking active part in a task, activity, or experience.

Game Simulation: A game representing reality, dynamic and encouraging interaction.

Game-Based Learning: The use of game-based technology to deliver, support, and enhance teaching, learning, assessment, and evaluation.

Interactive Digital Narrative: A storytelling where users create or influence a storyline through their actions using digital platforms/tools.

Serious Games: Games designed for a primary goal different from pure entertainment, may be produced by the video game industry, with connection to the acquisition of knowledge.

Chapter 17
Minecraft and Elementary Literacy Learning:
The Perspectives and Ideas of Preservice Teachers

Sam von Gillern
University of Missouri, USA

Carolyn Stufft
Berry College, USA

Rick Marlatt
https://orcid.org/0000-0002-2182-1655
New Mexico State University, USA

Larysa Nadolny
Iowa State University, USA

ABSTRACT

This research examines the perceptions and instructional ideas of preservice teachers as relates to using Minecraft, a popular video game, to facilitate game-based learning opportunities in their future elementary classrooms. The participants were 21 preservice teachers who played Minecraft as part of a teacher preparation program course and then completed essays on their experiences with the game and its potential to support student learning in the elementary English language arts classroom. These essays were coded and analyzed for themes. Three primary results were found in data analysis. First, three groups emerged from the data with each group indicating either no interest, some interest, or high interest in using Minecraft in their future teaching. Second, the preservice teachers illustrated various potential instructional strategies for integrating the game into the classroom, and third, participants identified a variety of ways that Minecraft integration can support English language arts instruction and learning.

DOI: 10.4018/978-1-7998-7271-9.ch017

INTRODUCTION

Literacy is a social, connective practice (Wolfe & Flewitt, 2010). This inherent connectivity has only expanded in response to technological development, such as the advent of Web 2.0 tools, as teachers continue to incorporate technology into their K-12 classrooms at an increasing rate (Alhassan, 2017). In order for teachers to become familiar with the use of technology for teaching and learning, it is helpful for them to experience technology use as preservice teachers (PSTs) during their teacher preparation program. Scholars have provided support regarding the positive outcomes associated with using digital literacies with PSTs (Bonk & Zhang, 2006; Hramiak et al., 2009). In particular, it is important for teacher preparation programs to introduce and model educational approaches to integrating technological tools, as doing so increases the likelihood that PSTs will incorporate technology into their own teaching practices (Larose et al., 2009).

Research has shown that game-based learning (GBL) is a valuable approach to utilizing technology in educational contexts (Clark et al., 2016). While literacy is a content area that has received less scholarly attention with GBL than other disciplines (Wouters et al., 2013), scholars who have examined GBL in literacy contexts have found that playing video games and engaging in game-related activities can support students' literacy and learning in a variety of ways (Gee, 2007; Squire, 2014; von Gillern et al., 2021). Playing video games requires people to interpret multimodal symbols and make decisions that impact how the game unfolds (Alberti, 2008; von Gillern, 2016a, 2016b). These are complex processes that represent a "constellation of literacy practices" (Steinkuehler, 2007, p. 297).

Thus, video games can serve as a medium for student learning. Students can engage in a variety of literacy practices in which they not only "read" and explore digital worlds but can also read, create, and share game-related texts, teaching and learning from one another in the process (Schreyer, 2012; Stufft & von Gillern, 2021). Given the potential for video games to promote learning, it is important to understand how games can be integrated in educational contexts, and *Minecraft*, one of the most popular and child-friendly games in the world, is a valuable game to examine for integrating in educational and literacy settings. *Minecraft* is a popular video game for people across ages in which the player explores a large 3D virtual world, collects/mines resources, and then crafts tools and structures. While *Minecraft* came out a decade ago in 2011, the number of active players has been trending upwards ever since and reached 140 million active players in 2021 (Sinclair, 2021). Thus, the game is as popular and relevant as ever.

The purpose of this research was to investigate the perspectives of preservice elementary teachers as relates to the value of using *Minecraft* in educational and English language arts (ELA) settings, which would addresses a gap in the research. This study utilizes a GBL perspective that recognizes that people can learn valuable information and skills through gameplay (Troppo, 2015). Thus, as game-based approaches and *Minecraft*, more specifically, can facilitate learning (Marlatt, 2018; Nebel et al., 2016), it is important to understand the perspective of PSTs as their attitudes and plans ultimately impact whether or not and how GBL approaches and video games such as *Minecraft* are utilized in educational and ELA settings. Thus, this study aims to develop an understanding of PSTs perspectives on instructional ideas and the value of incorporating *Minecraft* via GBL in elementary classrooms.

LITERATURE REVIEW

Digital Literacies

The National Council of Teachers of English (NCTE, 2019) recently revised its definition of literacy in a digital age, positing that literates command diverse collections of dispositions and competencies that constantly evolve alongside technology and society and "are inextricably linked with histories, narratives, life possibilities, and social trajectories of all individuals and groups" (para. 2). To this end, practitioners and scholars alike, who are committed to affording students a culturally-responsive literacy learning experience (Gay, 2010), recognize that literacy practices are embedded in fluid sociocultural contexts and are inseparable from the rapidly expanding, increasingly ubiquitous digitization of meaning-making (Harvey & Marlatt, 2020). NCTE is joined by numerous other professional educational organizations whose leaders advocate for the consistent integration of digital literacies, which Lankshear and Knobel (2011) argue, comprise the multiple, multimodal ways in which learners generate meaning via technology and texts.

The field of digital literacies has evolved as an important branch of the New London Group's Multiliteracies framework (1996), whose collective authors posited that a successful future for education would involve representation, in theory and practice, of the digital society for which it would serve. New London's early foundation has set forth a new generation of researchers who prioritized digital literacies as a vital component of learning in and out of academic spaces, and this work has resulted in new landmark texts which extol the possibilities of digitized teaching and learning (Alvermann, 2005), conceptualize social semiotics as central to classroom-based communication (Kress, 2010), and situate digital literacies as a centerpiece of reflective pedagogy (Cope & Kalantzis, 2015).

Early iterations of digital literacies studies at the turn of the century focused on substituting traditional print-based texts and operations for digitized means including internet applications and social media platforms and have since exploded into numerous offshoots in line with a digital revolution (Collins & Halverson, 2009). Recent scholarship has carved new pathways for socio-spatial conceptions and other lenses pertinent for the digital age (Mills, 2015), produced explorations of the affect turn in literacy education (Leander & Ehret, 2019), and leveraged digital literacies toward equity-driven teaching and learning (Rybakova et al., 2019). The field has also proved to be a sprawling playground for the incorporation of video games across multiple contexts and interdisciplinary settings (von Gillern et al., 2021; Squire, 2011). As Gee (2003) argued, video games support many processes undertaken by learners at all ages and developmental stages, including comprehension and response, adaption, decision-making, critical thinking, and more. Video games can be meaningfully integrated into English language arts instruction for educators in their aims to promote student participation and interaction (von Gillern et al., 2021); further, video games allow for students to engage in a variety of textual modes and positions as they construct knowledge and generate content through digital platforms and discourses (Marlatt, 2019).

For many digital literacies scholars, video games can help educators answer the call from Rowsell et al. (2016) for schools to reconceptualize their inclusivity for students from diverse cultural and linguistic backgrounds. Video games demonstrate how multimodal play can be integral to academic growth and development (Lewis Ellison & Solomon, 2018) because they offer learners innovative onramps to interact with texts and translate socially-based literacy practices into meaningful learning opportunities (Harvey & Marlatt, 2020). Video games also help students link subject matter with contemporary real-world news and events (Price-Dennis et al., 2015), can support English language learners (Thompson

& von Gillern, 2020; Lee & Gerber, 2013), and can support teachers to reimagine pedagogies in the age of high-stakes testing (Portier, et al., 2019).

Game-Based Learning

The role of play within society has long been recognized (Huizinga, 1955). More recently, video gameplay has received attention in regard to its possible applications in the classroom. GBL involves the use of commercial video games to teach classroom content (Shapiro, 2014). GBL typically focuses on commercial-off-the-shelf (COTS) video games that were not created for educational purposes (Connolly et al., 2012); these types of games differ from serious games and edutainment, which involves video games specifically designed to teach concepts such as math, science, or history (Egenfeldt-Nielsen, 2018). For example, scholars have examined how the video game *Civilization III* can support history learning (Squire, 2004) and *Age of Mythology* can help players learn about ancient Greek, Egyptian, and Norse civilizations (Gee & Hayes, 2010). In these instances, the video games were created as commercial products but are able to be applied to content areas standards in support of student learning.

At its core, GBL centers around the use of video games to help students learn knowledge and skills in ways that support educational learning goals (Alaswad & Nadolny, 2015; Nadolny et al., 2020; von Gillern, 2018). Students learn the specified content standards/topics from their video gameplay. The video games that students play are intended to promote students' ability to engage in critical thinking and to solve problems encountered in gameplay that also have applications to course content. GBL can be used for any subject area and is effective in meeting the needs of different learning styles (Prensky, 2001; von Gillern & Alaswad, 2016). Further, the use of video games can promote general cognition beyond a specific topic, such as through the development of skills related to inductive reasoning (Greenfield, 2014).

Video games have demonstrated applications for learning (Beavis, 2013; Nadolny et al., 2017; Steinkuehler, 2010). Many teachers recognize that video games relate to desirable skills, such as problem-solving (Gros, 2007). While some educators express interest in considering the use of video games in their classrooms, few actually integrate video games into their teaching (Gerber et al., 2014; Mifsud et al., 2013; Silva Dos Santos et al., 2020). In some cases, teachers express concern related to negative perceptions of video games or possible lack of support regarding training and resources even if they want to use video games for teaching and learning (Gerber & Price, 2013). The lack of knowledge and support on effectively integrating GBL in the classroom constricts teachers' abilities to innovate and support student learning by harnessing the power of video games, one of the most popular forms of media today, which approximately 90% of school-age children in the United States engage with (NPD Group, 2020), underscoring the relevance of introducing video games for teaching and learning as part of PSTs' educational preparation program experiences.

Video Games in Literacy Learning

In order for school literacy activities to make an impact on students, these activities must connect in some way with capital available to students (Carrington & Luke, 1997; von Gillern, 2021). Cultural and social capital (Bourdieu, 1986) may relate to students' videogame experiences as they have opportunities to showcase their expertise with other avid gamers; such capital specific to videogame play experiences can be referred to as gaming capital (Walsh, 2010). By acknowledging students' capital, teachers are able to empower students as experts. GBL provides an avenue for teachers to connect student interests with classroom concepts. As Abrams (2009) demonstrates, students can learn vocabulary terms and historical information from their video gameplay, later connecting this content with material discussed/taught in K-12 classrooms; specifically, Abrams suggests that when students encounter information in video games, they may develop schemas that they can connect to classroom material. Through the case study examples of high school gamers included in her article, Abrams (2009) builds the case that video games can promote "authentic, meaningful learning" in that students engaged in video gameplay outside of school and were able to connect information from the video games to content taught in school to support literacy learning (p. 338). As teachers consider ways to connect out of school video gameplay with in-school materials, GBL provides an option for bridging student interests and educational standards and goals.

Not only can teachers incorporate video game paratexts as part of literacy instruction (Stufft, 2016), but they also can engage students in video game literature circles, writing game reviews, and creating how-to guides (von Gillern et al., 2021). Teachers can provide opportunities for students to engage in video gameplay as part of instructional time by using video games as texts for reading and writing workshops (Gerber et al., 2014), utilizing video games as literature (Harvey, 2018), and integrating video games to foster critical thinking and reflective writing (Stufft & von Gillern, 2021). Teachers can support students' video gameplay-related learning by providing debriefing opportunities after gameplay sessions, which can occur through discussions and written reflections (Hsu & Wang, 2010). Debriefing after video gameplay allows educators to scaffold students' learning; during debriefing is when students connect their video gaming activities with classroom content (Peters & Vissers, 2009).

As teachers consider which games to use in English language arts settings, it is important to bear in mind that "not all games and gamers are created equal" and that it is important to consider the individual "gamer's experience with the game rather than just the content of the game itself" (Abrams, 2009, p. 337). For example, at first glance *Minecraft* may appear to lack educational content. However, the game lends itself to a variety of content applications, ranging from connections with science (Short, 2012) to geography (Scarlett, 2015) to art (Overby & Jones, 2015). Not only can students play *Minecraft* as part of learning, but they also can engage in book groups using *Minecraft* paratexts (Stufft, 2018). In short, *Minecraft* has made its ways into a variety of educational settings (Bilton, 2013; Jenkins, 2014; Tromba, 2013) and English language arts learning more specifically (Barack, 2013; Brownell, 2021; Daly, 2012; Gauquier & Schneider, 2013

THEORETICAL PERSPECTIVE

Over the past couple decades scholars have recognized the value of games as tools that can facilitate learning experiences (Gee, 2007; Prensky, 2005; Squire, 2011). Scholars have examined serious games, which are games that are designed for educational and training purposes (Michael & Chen, 2005), and commercial-off-the-shelf games, which are designed primarily for entertainment purposes that can still be used in educational contexts (Sandford et al., 2006). Thus, GBL has shown potential in a variety of contexts, and this study utilizes GBL as a theoretical framework that recognizes games often enhance student motivation and engagement, two factors that impact learning (Hattie, 2009), and can lead to meaningful learning outcomes.

Furthermore, it is important to recognize how teachers conceptualize and utilize GBL in their teaching, which has led scholars to investigate educators' instructional approaches to GBL (Sitzmann, 2011). This study recognizes the value of investigating how educators conceptualize methods for integrating GBL approaches into their teaching. Thus, this study utilizes the concept of GBL, particularly as relates to how educators conceptualize methods for effectively integrating video games into their instruction, which complements existing work in the field (Gerber et al., 2014; Gerber & Price, 2013; Sandford et al., 2006;). The following research questions guided the study:

Table 1. Research questions

Research Question 1	What beliefs and experiences influence preservice elementary teacher's intentions to integrate *Minecraft* in their teaching?
Research Question 2	What instructional strategies do preservice elementary teachers select when designing educational lessons incorporating *Minecraft*?
Research Question 3	How do preservice teachers envision *Minecraft* facilitating learning in English language arts instruction?

METHODS

This is a qualitative case study that seeks to understand the perceptions of the participants (Creswell & Poth, 2017). Case studies examine a bounded system (Merriam & Tisdell, 2015), which, in the case of this research, is a set of essays from 21 preservice elementary school teachers (18 female, 3 male) who were enrolled in a teacher preparation program at a large research university in the Midwest and taking a course on integrating technology into literacy instruction. Throughout the semester PSTs learned a variety of concepts related to and strategies for promoting literacy engagement and development using technology. Towards the end of the semester, they engaged in a unit on GBL in which they read about and discussed concepts related to GBL and brainstormed ideas for integrating games (both digital and non-digital) into their literacy instruction. As part of this unit, the 21 participants each played *Minecraft* for approximately two hours, and during this process reflected upon the game, its content, and how they learned to play. Participants then wrote essays approximately 2-3 double-spaced pages in length in which in response to writing prompts they reflected on *Minecraft*, their learning processes during gameplay, and opportunities to integrate the game in elementary classrooms and literacy instruction.

Essays were then coded for segments of text that were potentially relevant to the research questions (Merriam & Tisdell, 2015). The coding process included first- and second-level coding by the researchers of the study. First-level coding involved both descriptive and process codes (Saldaña, 2016). Descriptive codes involved generating words or short phrases that described the passage's topic, and process codes involved labeling passage segments with gerunds (i.e., "-ing" words) that demonstrated the actions and planned actions of the participants (Saldaña, 2016). These codes were then analyzed via pattern coding that led to the formation of themes addressed the research questions (Miles et al., 2014).

RESULTS

The data analysis revealed patterns in the perceptions of preservice elementary teachers related to their intention to use *Minecraft* in their future teaching, instructional strategies they believe might be helpful for integrating *Minecraft* in their classroom, and potential educational activities that may facilitate literacy learning through *Minecraft*. The results of this research are presented below with each of the three research questions being examined in turn.

Research Question 1: What beliefs and experiences influence preservice elementary teacher's intentions to integrate *Minecraft* in their teaching?

Three groups of participants emerged from the data (see Table 2). Their responses illustrated issues such as their perceived value of using *Minecraft* in their future teaching as well as opportunities and barriers to implementation, including their own levels of technological self-efficacy. Each of the three groups and their responses are examined below to illustrate patterns among group members.

Table 2. Groups of participants

Group Number	Group Description	Number of Participants
Group 1	Preservice teachers who have no interest in using *Minecraft* in their teaching	n=5
Group 2	Preservice teachers who had some interest in using *Minecraft*	n=11
Group 3	Preservice teachers who showed substantial interest in using *Minecraft*	n=5

Group 1: No Interest in using *Minecraft*. The participants in this group (n=5) were characterized by barriers to integration and negative perceptions of classroom technologies. The major barrier to the inclusion of *Minecraft* in the classroom centered on the comfort level of the participants with the technology itself, describing themselves as not confident or not knowledgeable and frequently indicating a need to master the technology in order to introduce students to the game. Bailey (note: all names are pseudonyms) would not consider using *Minecraft* because she feels "as if I would never feel confident enough in my own game skills as a teacher to then transfer these skills to my students."

Other barriers to integration included perceptions of the game being too difficult for younger students to master, concerns regarding the potential for game addiction, perceptions of the use of video games for teaching being too time consuming for the teacher, and concerns regarding frightening content with the zombies in *Minecraft* and the ability for gamers to engage in violence during gameplay, such as by attacking/being attacked by zombies. Although the other two groups did mention barriers occasionally, there was a strong focus on the potential negative aspects of *Minecraft* by this particular group. Although the participants in this group do not have future plans to use *Minecraft* in the classroom, some did indicate an openness to learning more. For example, one student mentioned that "even though I personally would not incorporate *Minecraft* into my classroom based on my first-hand experience, I would not completely rule it out until more research and gameplay is conducted."

Group 2: Some Interest in using *Minecraft*. The majority of the class (n=11) are considering using *Minecraft* in their future classrooms but are not firm in their beliefs. They recognize that video games can provide a valuable way to promote motivation, engagement, and learning. Many participants indicated that they are interested in using *Minecraft* in the classroom, but they would want to learn more about *Minecraft* and its potential educational applications before making a final decision. For example, one participant wrote "I think I could see myself using *Minecraft* in my future teaching. I would want to have a better understanding of the game and how it works, but from my very limited understanding, I think it could be a useful tool."

This group is also more comfortable with not needing to be the expert in the room when it comes to that game. This group's responses illustrated hesitancies to using *Minecraft* in the classroom, such as acknowledging their own limited understanding of *Minecraft* and potential educational applications, but their hesitancies were accompanied by an open-mindedness that recognize some value and potential for learning as well.

Group 3: Substantial Interest in using *Minecraft*. Participants in this group showed significant interest in using *Minecraft* in their future teaching. One participant wrote "I am interested in using *Minecraft* in my teaching because I know how engaging it is for students and can see from my own experiences the potential that it has in the classroom." These participants identified relatively few barriers to integration, and they recognized positive educational opportunities for *Minecraft* in English language arts, often connecting *Minecraft* related activities to current educational standards. One participant, Nikki (all names pseudonyms), wrote:

I could definitely see myself using Minecraft in my future classroom...Students also have a lot of freedom when using Minecraft, and I think it could be an excellent way to develop students' storytelling skills and help give them real experiences to reflect on as they are going to write.

Furthermore, these participants see integrating *Minecraft* as a way to engage students and connect to their personal lives. Yessica wrote:

Teachers can succeed in using this in their classrooms as students' motivation to learn rises, connecting in school activities to students out of school activities they participate in.

Overall, most participants (including those from Groups 2 & 3) demonstrated a level of comfort with not needing to be the expert in the room when it comes to the integration of this video game, which provides opportunities for students to teach one another. For example, Tasha noted *Minecraft* provides opportunities for student-led learning. She described that as many students already have experience with *Minecraft*, these students could teach students who were less familiar with the game about the game, how it works, and gameplay strategies. In this sense, students would provide scaffolding to one another, rather than relying on teacher scaffolding.

Research Question 2: What Instructional Strategies do Preservice Elementary Teachers Select when Designing Educational Lessons Incorporating *Minecraft*?

The participants highlighted various educational strategies for integrating *Minecraft* into their teaching. A common theme was recognizing the importance of reflective experience surrounding game play, as Ana stated, "the best times to incorporate instruction with *Minecraft* is before and after game play, which requires students to prepare, organize, problem-solve, and reflect upon their processes." The participants highlighted instructional strategies for before, during, and after gameplay, and these strategies are illustrated below.

Instructional Strategies for before Gameplay: Participants recognized that there were multiple opportunities to utilize instructional strategies before the students even begin to play *Minecraft* (see Table 3). For example, the participants recognized the importance of discussing the purpose of playing the game as well as setting expectations for students before the students began playing. This is particularly important given that many students are not used to playing video games in their classrooms, and this game, in particular, is typically played for entertainment purposes rather than for educational ones. Thus, the teachers recognize value in helping students understand how the *Minecraft* activity connects to more traditional educational topics and activities as well as the benefit of providing directions and creating warm-up activities in advance of gameplay.

Table 3. Instructional strategies before gameplay.

Instructional Strategy	Sample Quote
Discuss purpose of and expectations for gameplay with students	"First, I would want to have a purpose for having the students play the game and I would want to make this purpose very clear to them."
Open-ended play time to introduce the game to students	"I might design a lesson around *Minecraft* in my literacy teaching by first introducing the game and allowing students to have 90 minutes to learn to navigate the game."
Pre-writing activity	"To begin, I would give students a list of questions that I have created to prompt them on their writing. These questions might include; "Who are the main characters in your story, what is the setting, and what events will take place in your story?" Prompting students with these type of questions will get their brains thinking so that they can begin the writing process for their imaginative story." (Note: after prewriting, the students would then recreate their story in *Minecraft* by building settings, creating characters, and incorporating text.)

Instructional Strategies during Gameplay: A common theme that emerged for instructional strategies during gameplay was student-to-student interaction, teaching, and mentoring. The participants recognized potential collaborative and social benefits to help students engage and learn during gameplay. Tasha noted "it would be easy to have students teach one another about new concepts that they've learned or help struggling students develop throughout the game," and Yessica wrote "This game also allows students to engage with each other in a variety of ways. These include: building projects together, competing against one another, and inviting their friends into virtual worlds and be invited as well." Katie also reflected on opportunities for peer teaching and mentorship. She wrote:

Students would be able to teach each other how to play and help each other. When students are able to help each other they gain confidence and it really helps them feel good, and what kid doesn't like to help their friend? Not only can they help one another play, but they can play with each other. Minecraft is a very social game, where students can rely on other players for help. When students work together it helps build a positive classroom climate

Overall, the participants recognized the value of the students' social interactions, collaborative learning, and mentorship, and the teacher can facilitate opportunities for these interactions to unfold during gameplay

Instructional Strategies for after Gameplay: The instructional strategies that participants identified for after gameplay were largely reflective activities in which students discussed and analyzed their gameplay experiences (see Table 4). For example, students could engage in a whole-class discussion and reflect on their experiences and the decisions they made. Alternatively, students could write about their experiences or create graphic organizers that help them analyze their experiences and the game. Such collaborative efforts can occur in game circles, similar to literature circles, in which students engage deeply with a game, such as *Minecraft*, and critically reflect on the game's content and their learning and decision-making processes in the game. In such experiences, *Minecraft* serves as a platform that can be deeply interesting, engaging, and motivating for the children, and more traditional educational activities, such as writing, discussing, and creating graphic organizers, can be coupled with *Minecraft* to draw students in and facilitate learning.

Table 4. Instructional strategies after gameplay.

Instructional Strategy	Sample Quote
Student reflective writing after playing the game	"Students could simply reflect on their experiences with *Minecraft* after playing while practicing their writing skills at the same time."
Whole class discussion after gameplay	"They could come back together as a class after…playing *Minecraft* and discuss the experiences they had and the reasoning behind the decisions that they made during play."
Graphic organizers after playing the game	"I would have students spend some time playing the game. This would allow for the students to get a sense of the environment and even make changes to that environment. Once the students had played the game, I would have them create a chart that compiles all of the characteristics of the world where they were playing. Then I would have them use those charts to compare and contrast with their peers who sit in the same pod. After comparing their characteristics, I will have students write a story in which the character is living in the world where they explored during *Minecraft*."

Research Question 3: How do Preservice Teachers Envision *Minecraft* Facilitating Learning in English Language Arts?

The participants conceptualized a variety of *Minecraft* activities they could use to promote literacy learning (see Table 5 for overview). Writing was a prominent area that participants saw could be used to engage students via *Minecraft*-related activities. Potential writing activities included having students create an informational text about *Minecraft* (e.g., a description of the game or how to play it). Children could also journal about their *Minecraft* experiences for the day or write opinion pieces on why (or why not) it's a high-quality game or whether or not it should be incorporated into classroom instruction. These types of writing experiences, at the teacher's discretion, could potentially be posted on the class website or in online *Minecraft* forums to promote participatory literacies.

Reading and comprehension activities also were illustrated in participants' responses. Many participants wrote how students could interpret and read multimodal symbols in the game (e.g., written language, numbers, sounds, and visuals), skills they noted were highly valuable in the 21st century. These multimodal reading skills can be modeled in advance of gameplay by teachers to guide the students' focus and thinking. The participants also noted how there is a wide variety of *Minecraft* texts available to students, including published books and an endless supply of online tutorials and commentary, that students can read and view before, during, or after gameplay to support their understanding and develop their *Minecraft* knowledge and abilities.

Table 5. Minecraft and literacy learning according to preservice teachers

Literacy Concept	Supporting Quotes from Preservice Teachers
Writing	Have students write an informational text about what *Minecraft* is or how to use it. Have students explain in detail in their journals what they learned and did in their *Minecraft* game on this day. Have students write an opinion piece about why they think *Minecraft* is the best/worst videogame or have students write and opinion piece about why you should use *Minecraft* in school. With either writing prompt, they would have to support their position using reasons.
Storytelling	I could have students write a story and create it on *Minecraft*. They could write an outline for what they want their story to be about, for example a zombie apocalypse, and then try and recreate that story on *Minecraft*. They could record themselves narrating their story while playing the game and acting it out. *Minecraft* can be used for students to tell and write stories using characters, setting, plot, locations, choices, and motivations. Students could either build a world first and then write about it or write a story and then build their *Minecraft* world. I think the teacher could use either way for students to write a story or use being able to write or create first based on students' needs.
Multimodality	Students would gain navigation skills regarding the multimodal symbols provided in the game. I could incorporate it in my literacy instruction as a way to give students practice with interpreting multimodal symbols.
Digital Stories	[Students] could write a narrative story based off of the experiences that they had while playing the game. They could use the characters, setting, and events that took place while they played. Similarly, they could play the game and take screenshots throughout. They could use these screenshots to create a digital story about what happened while they played the game. I would design my lesson around a standard dedicated to mastering how to produce and publish writing through technology. My students would create a script of a movie of their own choosing, or a movie they have made up including a plot and a solution. The students would then create a *Minecraft* world they would model after their movie scripts and would have the ability to use a voice-over app to create audio over the images they have taken from their *Minecraft* world. The audio would depict the movie script the students have created, and would allow the students freedom to express their ideas through audio and visuals rather than through traditional paper and pencil.
Reading and Comprehension	I have tutored many students and been in plenty of classrooms where students have [and use] *Minecraft* tutorial handbooks, and they cannot get enough of them. Their reading of these informational texts fulfills Common Core Standard CCSS.ELA-LITERACY.RI.5.7, which has students "draw on information from multiple print or digital sources, demonstrating the ability to locate an answer to a question quickly or to solve a problem efficiently." Assigning students a block of time to work on their *Minecraft* [worlds] and do the necessary research [to construct their world] not only increase their motivation in the classroom and gets them reading for a purpose, but it allows them to engage in a wide variety of resources. Having students respond to what they have read, what they learned, and the changes they made would all make for a great reading response. A specific lesson idea I have for this is giving students various settings from a text they have read, and they would use *Minecraft* to re-create those settings and different events from the text to show their understanding. *Minecraft* also would be a useful tool when teaching how to make inferences, point of view, new vocabulary, and analyzing text/data. Overall, *Minecraft* would be a great guiding tool when teaching reading comprehension strategies in the classroom.
Speaking and Listening	Students could work together or individually to report on the game *Minecraft*. It could be a research project and students would have to find information about the game and interview peers about why they like the game. [During conferences, students] could vocally tell me what they did in Minecraft on that day and how it helped them, what they liked about it, and what their goal for the next *Minecraft* time is.

Minecraft and Elementary Literacy Learning

Storytelling was another area in which participants saw opportunities. Given the wide latitude of opportunities *Minecraft* provides users, participants thought that students could write a story, and then create that story in *Minecraft* (see Figures 1-4, a sample treasure hunting story in *Minecraft*, which includes a variety of multimodal symbols and demonstrates how students can create stories and worlds for their peers to explore). Alternatively, students could first build a world in *Minecraft*, and then write a story about their world including information about the setting, characters, ideas, and objects within their story. Participants recognized opportunities to engage students in multimodality and storytelling with *Minecraft*. Several participants envisioned their students creating digital stories using *Minecraft*. Jordan wrote:

My students would create a script of a movie of their own choosing, or a movie they have made up including a plot and a solution. The students would then create a Minecraft world they would model after their movie scripts and would have the ability to use a voice-over app to create audio over the images they have taken from their Minecraft world. The audio would depict the movie script the students have created, and would allow the students freedom to express their ideas through audio and visuals rather than through traditional paper and pencil

Participants also identified opportunities for developing speaking and listening skills through *Minecraft*-related activities. Digital storytelling, as noted above, provides opportunities for creators to engage in speaking via voiceovers and readers/viewers to engage in listening. Through such activities, students can engage in creativity, self-expression, speaking, and listening through producing *Minecraft*-centered digital stories.

Figure 1.

Figure 2.

Figure 3.

Additionally, Kris mentioned that students could interview one another about their *Minecraft* experiences, and Tasha described that students could reflect on their experiences and learning in *Minecraft* and share goals for future *Minecraft* sessions during student-teacher conferences. These types of conversations demonstrate opportunities for metacognitive, reflective, and goal-driven learning that can occur in conjunction with *Minecraft* gameplay. Thus, overall, participants identified a wide variety of *Minecraft*-related activities to promote students' literacy engagement and learning.

Figure 4.

DISCUSSION

Overall, the majority of participants (16 of 21) showed interest in using *Minecraft* in their future elementary classrooms for literacy activities and instruction. They recognized the engaging nature of games and demonstrated a desire to connect to the play habits of the 21st century child. Our participants' reflections support the work and findings of scholars who have investigated video games, particularly *Minecraft*, and their abilities to promote student learning, in that students can engage in creative expression (Abrams, 2016) and a variety of literacy practices via *Minecraft* (Niemeyer & Gerber, 2015). Additionally, participants recognized that students can develop digital stories (Lewis Ellison, 2017) and demonstrate text comprehension using *Minecraft* (Stufft, 2016). Utilizing ideas such as these and developing new ideas for classroom uses provides students opportunities to creatively engage in valuable language and literacy practices.

Additionally, participants highlighted instructional strategies for before, during, and after gameplay, which supports the work of Kozdras et al. (2015) who noted the value of teacher support and scaffolding throughout gameplay processes in literacy contexts. Furthermore, participants illustrated how they could have students engage in traditional literacy skills by reading *Minecraft* texts before, during, or after gameplay to engage with *Minecraft*-related readings, which, particularly when accessing online forums and spaces, connects to the participatory literacies afforded by *Minecraft* noted by Rowsell and Wohlwend (2016) while also supporting traditional classroom approaches to comprehension and discussion of texts (Stufft, 2018).

This study's findings on approaches educators can use *Minecraft* to promote students' literacy development contributes to the literature on digital literacies as well (Lankshear & Knobel, 2011). This study recognizes video gaming as a digital literacy practice and also demonstrates that educators can meaningfully integrate *Minecraft*-related activities to promote traditional literacy skills as well, including reading, writing, and storytelling. In these ways, this research supports the findings of Abrams (2016), who investigated how allowing students to create and explain digital worlds using *Minecraft* "can spur ingenuity and discovery as students layer their literacies in meaningful and nuanced ways" (p. 506). Additionally, this study complements classroom-based empirical studies that have shown how *Minecraft* has supported video game book groups (Author, 2018); helped personalize curriculum via problem-solving (Risberg, 2015); reinvigorated curricular units with group learning (Kenkel, 2015); translated multimodal analysis into reflective writing exercises (Author, 2021b); guided diverse students to explore their literacy identities (Author, 2018); and enabled students to respond to their literacy learning experiences through gaming (Stufft, 2016). The high levels of agency and choice triggered in students sustain *Minecraft*'s longevity despite newer systems and devices constantly being introduced (Lewis Ellison, 2017). As indicated, researchers have given initial attention to ways that *Minecraft* can become part of K-12 classrooms; additionally, through the advent of online resources housed at the Minecraft Education Edition website (education.minecraft.net), classroom application ideas have become more accessible.

While Minecraft has shown great potential for supporting students learning and literacy, effective integration of GBL in lesson planning is likely influenced by the individual teacher's beliefs and experiences with games. In this study, participants with negative perceptions of technology in the classroom and lack of comfort with playing video games were not interested in using *Minecraft* in their future classrooms. These participants focused on both the lack of perceived value of integrating *Minecraft* as well as the challenges that accompany integrating the game. They believed that effectively integrating the game would take substantial time and effort and that parents and administrators may object to integrating video games into their instruction. These concerns are not unfounded. Effectively integrating a variety of educational technologies can be challenging, and utilizing video games may attract negative or unwanted attention from parents and administrators. However, given that research has shown GBL can positively and substantially impact student learning (Clark et al., 2016; Wouters et al., 2013), it is important for educators to develop their knowledge of the effectiveness of GBL, strategies for effective implementation and talking points for communicating with parents and administrators on their activities and pedagogical rationale.

While five students focused on such challenges, the majority of the class was somewhat or strongly interested in the potential impacts of *Minecraft* on student motivation, engagement, and learning. In particular, those with substantial interest in integrating *Minecraft* were able to come up with creative solutions to technical barriers and innovative opportunities to promote ELA learning. Additionally, while many students were initially hesitant to use *Minecraft* in their teaching, these hesitancies were often overcome through participants' spending time with the video game and reflecting on how it can facilitate learning opportunities for their future students, as illustrated by Haleigh's reflection:

As I started the game of Minecraft, I did not see any reason why I would ever use this game in my teaching. Even though I am a big advocate for incorporating technology into the classroom in order to benefit student learning, I did not think this game would be useful in that way. I was quick to turn this game down for any use in my classroom, but have slowly seen ways that it might be beneficial for growing students thinking and decision making…The more I played Minecraft, the more opportunities I saw for using the game in my classroom.

These ideas relate to the technology acceptance model (TAM), which identifies a variety of issues that influence decisions related to people's adoption of technology and teachers' integration of technology into educational settings (Yuen & Ma, 2008). For example, this model recognizes the importance of teachers' perceived usefulness, perceived ease of use, and their own self-efficacy with the technology as factors that influence their decision about if and how they may integrate technology into their teaching (Scherer et al., 2019). The participants self-efficacy was a mediating factor in their perspectives on whether or not they planned to include *Minecraft* in their future teaching. Most of the participants who indicated they did not plan on including *Minecraft* in their teaching (Group 1), as well as some who were interested in using the game (Group 2), reflected on their own lack of knowledge and skills about the game, which connected to their concerns about being able to effectively integrate *Minecraft* into their instruction and TAM's ease of use. What separated many Group 1 participants from Group 2 and 3 participants was that the latter groups tended to perceive *Minecraft* as useful for promoting student learning while Group 1 did not. This perceived usefulness, aligning with TAM, led Groups 2 and 3 to think deeply on ways to overcome barriers to integration given they thought *Minecraft* had substantial learning benefits. These findings build upon those of Robinson and Mackey (2006), who found that among the technologies PSTs used, games rarely were considered; further, PSTs indicated varied levels of confidence with particular digital literacies. Additionally, this work expands upon that of Burnett (2010), who investigated the ways PSTs used technology both as part of school and in their home lives, focusing on their experiences with technology and the value that PSTs place on technology as a way to consider possible future integration of technology for teaching as well as perceived barriers to such integration.

There are a few implications from the TAM for teacher educators who want to encourage their PSTs to use *Minecraft* and/or other GBL approaches in their future classrooms. First, it is important to explicitly highlight and demonstrate the value of integrating games into their teaching, including their capacity to promote student motivation, engagement, and learning (Clark et al., 2016). Second, teacher educators should scaffold and facilitate opportunities for their PSTs to engage with the target video games to increase the PSTs' self-efficacy and perceived ease of use with using the games themselves as well as teaching with the games. Such efforts can impact PSTs' thinking and plans for integrating GBL into their future classrooms, which in turn can lead to student learning (Thompson & von Gillern, 2020; Wouters et al., 2013).

The results of this study are significant in three ways. First, a thematic pattern emerged with a strong connection between positive beliefs around technology integration and positive intentions to integrate games-based learning activities and opportunities. Second, participants demonstrated an ability to apply general teaching strategies to the integration of *Minecraft*. Third, participants created a wide variety of instructional activities that can be used as part of elementary ELA instruction that promote student engagement and learning with both traditional literacy and digital literacy skills, including reading, writing, collaboration, storytelling, and interpreting and creating multimodal texts. Overall, these findings contribute to the literature on integrating technology, *Minecraft*, and GBL into elementary ELA education.

While this study makes unique contributions to the literature and demonstrates practical ideas for integrating *Minecraft* and GBL into elementary literacy instruction, it is not without its limitations. First, this was a study conducted with a single class of preservice elementary teachers, and having a broader participant pool that included more participants or included preservice secondary teachers as well may have illuminated instructional opportunities further and provided greater clarity about which activities may work best at different grade levels. It would also be helpful to specifically measure the teachers' competencies related to educational technology and gaming, which may have provided additional insights. Additionally, while the perspectives of PSTs are valuable and can illustrate what their plans and ideas are for their future classrooms, further research should continue to investigate how in-service teachers use *Minecraft* in their ELA instruction to see how GBL can support the development of students' literacy and digital literacy skills (Abrams, 2016; Marlatt OR Stufft, 2018; Lewis Ellison, 2018). It also is of interest to conduct longitudinal research regarding PSTs who were exposed to GBL as part of their teacher preparation who then did/did not go on to use GBL in their own classroom in order to better understand the ways that experiences with GBL during a preparation program can impact in-service teachers' use of video games for teaching and learning. Finally, given the potential for *Minecraft* and GBL to provide motivating and engaging opportunities for children's literacy development, additional research that examines how students participate in such activities to learn specific skills and students' perspectives on using GBL and *Minecraft* to learn would be valuable.

CONCLUSION

In this study, the PSTs saw a variety of opportunities to promote language and literacy development through *Minecraft*-related activities. They believed that *Minecraft* would promote motivation and engagement, two factors that impact learning (Hattie, 2009) and could engage in both traditional ELA activities (such as reading, writing, speaking, listening, and storytelling) as well as digital literacy practices that integrate traditional literacy practices with digital technologies (such as digital storytelling and multimodal reading and composition). Thus, there are substantial opportunities for thoughtful integration that promote student motivation, engagement, and ultimately, learning through GBL.

Ultimately, GBL has shown to be effective at promoting student learning in a variety of contexts and content areas (Clark et al., 2016; Wouters et al., 2013). Thus, it is critical for teacher educators to help PSTs develop their understanding of GBL as well as specific strategies for implementation. This may occur in educational technology classroom and/or different content area methods courses. Through understanding the value and potential of GBL as well as learning pedagogical strategies for integrating video games effectively into their classrooms, teacher educators can help prepare their PSTs for effective and innovative instruction in the future.

REFERENCES

Abrams, S. S. (2009). A gaming frame of mind: Digital contexts and academic implications. *Educational Media International*, *46*(4), 335–347. doi:10.1080/09523980903387480

Abrams, S. S. (2016). Emotionally crafted experiences: Layering literacies in Minecraft. *The Reading Teacher*, *70*(4), 501–506. doi:10.1002/trtr.1515

Alaswad, Z., & Nadolny, L. (2015). Designing for game-based learning: The effective integration of technology to support learning. *Journal of Educational Technology Systems*, *43*(4), 389–402. doi:10.1177/0047239515588164

Alberti, J. (2008). The game of reading and writing: How video games reframe our understanding of literacy. *Computers and Composition*, *25*(3), 258–269. doi:10.1016/j.compcom.2008.04.004

Alhassan, R. (2017). Exploring the relationship between Web 2.0 tools self-efficacy and teachers' use of these tools in their teaching. *Journal of Education and Learning*, *6*(4), 217–228. doi:10.5539/jel.v6n4p217

Alvermann, D. E. (Ed.). (2005). *Adolescents and literacies in a digital world* (3rd ed.). Peter Lang.

Barack, L. (2013). A Minecraft library scores big. *School Library Journal, 59*(9), 14.

Beavis, C. (2013). Multiliteracies in the wild: Learning from computer games. In G. Merchant, J. Gillen, J. Marsh, & J. Davies (Eds.), *Virtual literacies: Interactive spaces for children and young people* (pp. 57–74). Routledge.

Bilton, N. (2013, September 16). Minecraft, a child's obsession, finds use as an educational tool. *The New York Times, 162*(56261), B8.

Bonk, C. J., & Zhang, K. (2006). Introducing R2D2 model: Online learning for the diverse learners of this world. *Distance Education, 27*(2), 249–264. doi:10.1080/01587910600789670

Bourdieu, P. (1986). The forms of capital. In J. Richardson (Ed.), *Handbook of theory and research for the sociology of education* (pp. 241–258). Greenwood Press.

Brownell, C. J. (2021). Writing as a Minecrafter: Exploring How Children Blur Worlds of Play in the Elementary English Language Arts Classroom. *Teachers College Record, 123*(3), 1–19. doi:10.1177/016146812112300306

Burnett, C. (2010). Personal digital literacies versus classroom literacies: Investigating pre-service teachers' digital lives in and beyond the classroom. In V. Carrington & M. Robinson (Eds.), *Digital literacies: Social learning and classroom practices* (pp. 115–129). SAGE.

Carrington, V., & Luke, A. (1997). Literacy and Bourdieu's sociological theory: A reframing. *Language and Education, 11*(2), 96–112. doi:10.1080/09500789708666721

Clark, D. B., Tanner-Smith, E. E., & Killingsworth, S. S. (2016). Digital games, design, and learning: A systematic review and meta-analysis. *Review of Educational Research, 86*(1), 79–122. doi:10.3102/0034654315582065 PMID:26937054

Collins, A., & Halverson, R. (2009). *Rethinking education in the age of technology: The digital revolution and schooling in America*. Teachers College Press.

Connolly, T. M., Boyle, E. A., MacArthur, E., Hainey, T., & Boyle, J. M. (2012). A systematic literature review of empirical evidence on computer games and serious games. *Computers & Education, 59*(2), 661–686. doi:10.1016/j.compedu.2012.03.004

Cope, B., & Kalantzis, M. (2015). *The things you do to know: An introduction to the pedagogy of multiliteracies*. Springer.

Creswell, J. W., & Poth, C. N. (2017). *Qualitative inquiry and research design: Choosing among five approaches*. Sage.

Cushen, W. E. (1955). War games and operations research. *Philosophy of Science, 2*(4), 309–320. doi:10.1086/287446

Daly, E. (2012). Explore, create, survive. *School Library Journal, 58*(5), 24–25.

Egenfeldt-Nielsen, S. (2018). *Making sweet music: The educational use of computer games*. Center for Computer Games Research: University of Copenhagen. Retrieved from https://www.cs.swarthmore.edu/~turnbull/cs91/f09/paper/MakingSweetMusic.pdf

Gauquier, E., & Schneider, J. (2013). Minecraft programs in the library: If you build it they will come. *Young Adult Library Services, 11*(2), 17–19.

Gay, G. (2010). *Culturally responsive teaching: Theory, research, and practice*. Teachers College Press.

Gee, J. P. (2003). *What video games have to teach us about learning and literacy*. Palgrave MacMillan. doi:10.1145/950566.950595

Gee, J. P. (2007). *Good video games and good learning: Collected essays on video games, learning, and literacy*. Peter Lang. doi:10.3726/978-1-4539-1162-4

Gee, J. P., & Hayes, E. R. (2010). *The Sims and 21st century learning*. Palgrave Macmillan., doi:10.1057/9780230106734

Gerber, H. R. (2012). *Can education be gamified? Examining gamification, education, and the future*. Charles Town, WV: White paper for the American Public University System (APUS).

Gerber, H. R., Abrams, S. S., Onwuegbuzie, A. J., & Benge, C. L. (2014). From Mario to FIFA: What qualitative case study research suggests about games-based learning in a US classroom. *Educational Media International, 51*(1), 16–34. doi:10.1080/09523987.2014.889402

Gerber, H. R., & Price, D. P. (2013). Fighting baddies and collecting bananas: Teachers' perceptions of games-based literacy learning. *Educational Media International, 50*(1), 51–62. doi:10.1080/09523987.2013.777182

Gough, C. (2019, August 9). *Number of active players of Minecraft worldwide as of October 2018 (in millions)*. Retrieved from https://www.statista.com/statistics/680139/minecraft-active-players-worldwide/

Gros, B. (2007). Digital games in education: The design of games-based learning environments. *Journal of Research on Technology in Education, 40*(1), 23–38. doi:10.1080/15391523.2007.10782494

Group, N. P. D. (2020, December 7). *Evolution of entertainment: Spotlight on video games* [Video]. YouTube. https://youtu.be/lrPiK506umQ

Harvey, M. M. (2018). *Video games and virtual reality as classroom literature: Thoughts, experiences, and learning with 8th grade middle school students* (Doctoral dissertation). https://digitalrepository.unm.edu/educ_llss_etds/90/

Harvey, M. M., & Marlatt, R. (2020). That was then, this is now: Literacies for the 21st Century classroom. In E. Podovšovnik (Ed.), *Examining the roles of teachers and students in mastering new technologies* (pp. 164–183). IGI Global. doi:10.4018/978-1-7998-2104-5.ch008

Hattie, J. (2009). *Visible learning: A synthesis of over 800 meta-analyses relating to achievement*. Routledge.

Hramiak, A., Boulton, H., & Irwin, B. (2009). Trainee teachers' use of blogs as private reflections for professional development. *Learning, Media and Technology, 34*(3), 259–269. doi:10.1080/17439880903141521

Hsu, H., & Wang, S. (2010). Using gaming literacies to cultivate new literacies. *Simulation & Gaming*, *41*(3), 400–417. doi:10.1177/1046878109355361

Huizinga, J. (1955). *Homo ludens: A study of the play element in culture.* Routledge.

Jenkins, B. (2014). Don't quit playing: Video games in the STEM classroom. *Techniques*, *89*(1), 60–61.

Jenkins, H. (2006). *Fans, Bloggers, and Gamers: Exploring Participatory Culture.* New York University Press.

Kapp, K. (2012). *The gamification of learning and instruction.* Pfeiffer Press.

Kozdras, D., Joseph, C., & Schneider, J. J. (2015). Reading Games: Close Viewing and Guided Playing of Multimedia Texts. *The Reading Teacher*, *69*(3), 331–338. doi:10.1002/trtr.1413

Kress, G. R. (2010). *Multimodality: A social semiotic approach to contemporary communication.* Routledge.

Lankshear, C., & Knobel, M. (2011). *New literacies: Everyday practices and social learning* (3rd ed.). McGraw-Hill.

Larose, F., Grenon, V., Morin, M. P., & Hasni, A. (2009). The impact of pre-service field training sessions of the probability of future teachers using ICT in school. *European Journal of Teacher Education*, *32*(3), 289–303. doi:10.1080/02619760903006144

Leander, K., & Ehret, C. (Eds.). (2019). *Affect turn in literacy learning and teaching: Pedagogies, politics, and coming to know.* Routledge. doi:10.4324/9781351256766

Lederman, L. C. (1984). Debriefing: A critical re-examination of the post-experience analytic process and implications for effective use. *Simulation & Games*, *15*(4), 415–431. doi:10.1177/0037550084154002

Lee, Y. J., & Gerber, H. (2013). It's a WoW World: Second language acquisition and massively multiplayer online gaming. *Multimedia-Assisted Language Learning*, *16*(2), 53–70. doi:10.15702/mall.2013.16.2.53

Lewis Ellison, T. (2017). Digital participation, agency, and choice: An African American youth's digital storytelling about Minecraft. *Journal of Adolescent & Adult Literacy*, *61*(1), 25–35. doi:10.1002/jaal.645

Marlatt, R. (2019). Fortnite and the next level discourse: Understanding how gamers cultivate pedagogy in teacher education. *Proceedings from SITE '19: Society for Information Technology and Teacher Education Annual Conference.*

Merriam, S. B., & Tisdell, E. J. (2015). *Qualitative research: A guide to design and implementation* (4th ed.). Jossey-Bass.

Michael, D., & Chen, S. (2006). *Serious games: Games that educate, train, and inform.* Thomson Course Technology.

Mifsud, C. L., Vella, R., & Camilleri, L. (2013). Attitudes toward and effects of the use of video games in classroom learning with specific reference to literacy attainment. *Research in Education*, *90*(1), 32–52. doi:10.7227/RIE.90.1.3

Miles, M. B., Huberman, A. M., & Saldaña, J. (2014). *Qualitative data analysis.* Sage.

Mills, K. A. (2015). *Literacy theories for the digital age: Social, critical, multimodal, spatial, material, and sensory lenses*. Multilingual Matters. doi:10.21832/9781783094639

Nadolny, L., Alaswad, Z., Culver, D., & Wang, W. (2017). Designing with game-based learning: Game mechanics from middle school to higher education. *Simulation & Gaming*, *48*(6), 814–831. doi:10.1177/1046878117736893

NCTE. (2019). *Definition of Literacy in a Digital Age*. National Council of Teachers of English Position Statements. https://ncte.org/statement/nctes-definition-literacy-digital-age/

Nebel, S., Schneider, S., & Rey, G. D. (2016). Mining learning and crafting scientific experiments: A literature review on the use of Minecraft in education and research. *Journal of Educational Technology & Society*, *19*(2), 355–366.

New London Group. (1996). A pedagogy of multiliteracies: Designing social futures. *Harvard Educational Review*, *66*(1), 60–92. doi:10.17763/haer.66.1.17370n67v22j160u

Niemeyer, D., & Gerber, H. R. (2015). Maker culture and *Minecraft*: Implications for the future of learning. *Educational Media International*, *52*(3), 216–226. doi:10.1080/09523987.2015.1075103

Overby, A., & Jones, B. L. (2015). Virtual LEGOs: Incorporating Minecraft into the art education curriculum. *Art Education*, *68*(1), 21–27. doi:10.1080/00043125.2015.11519302

Peters, V. A. M., & Vissers, G. A. N. (2009). A simple classification model for debriefing simulation games. *Simulation & Gaming*, *35*(1), 70–84. doi:10.1177/1046878103253719

Petranek, C. F. (2000). Written debriefing: The next vital step in learning with simulations. *Simulation & Gaming: An Interdisciplinary Journal*, *31*(1), 108–118. doi:10.1177/104687810003100111

Portier, C., Friedrich, N., & Peterson, S. S. (2019). Play(ful) pedagogical practices for creative collaborative literacy. *The Reading Teacher*, *73*(1), 17–27. doi:10.1002/trtr.1795

Prensky, M. (2001). *Digital game-based learning*. McGraw-Hill.

Prensky, M. (2005). Computer games and learning: Digital game-based learning. In J. Raessens & J. Goldstein (Eds.), *Handbook of computer game studies* (pp. 97–122). MIT Press.

Robinson, M., & Mackey, M. (2006). Assets in the classroom: Comfort and competence with media among teachers present and future. In J. Marsh & E. Millard (Eds.), *Popular literacies, childhood and schooling* (pp. 200–220). Routledge.

Rowsell, J., Burke, A., Flewitt, R., Liao, H.-T., Lin, A., Marsh, J., Mills, K., Prinsloo, M., Rowe, D., & Wohlwend, K. (2016). Humanizing digital literacies: A road trip in search of wisdom and insight. Digital Literacy Column. *The Reading Teacher*, *70*(1), 121–129. doi:10.1002/trtr.1501

Rowsell, J., & Wohlwend, K. (2016). Free play or tight spaces? Mapping participatory literacies in apps. *The Reading Teacher*, *70*(2), 197–205. doi:10.1002/trtr.1490

Rybakova, K., Rice, M., Moran, C., Zucker, L., McGrail, E., McDermott, M., Loomis, S., Piotrowski, A., Garcia, M., Gerber, H., & Gibbons, T. (2019). A long arc bending towards equity: Tracing almost 20 years of ELA teaching trends. *Contemporary Issues in Technology and Teacher Education, 19*(4), 549-604. https://citejournal.org/volume-19/issue-4-19/english-language-arts/a-long-arc-bending-toward-equity-tracing-almost-20-years-of-ela-teaching-with-technology/

Saldaña, J. (2016). *The coding manual for qualitative researchers* (3rd ed.). Sage.

Sandford, R., Ulicsak, M., Facer, K., & Rudd, T. (2006). *Teaching with games: Using commercial off-the-shelf computer games in formal education*. Futurelab.

Scarlett, J. (2015). Gaming geography: Using Minecraft to teach essential geography skills. In D. Rutledge & D. Slykhuis (Eds.), *Proceedings of SITE 2015 – Society for Information Technology & Education International Conference* (pp. 838-840). Association for the Advancement of Computing in Education (AACE).

Scherer, R., Siddiq, F., & Tondeur, J. (2019). The technology acceptance model (TAM): A meta-analytic structural equation modeling approach to explaining teachers' adoption of digital technology in education. *Computers & Education, 128*, 13–35. doi:10.1016/j.compedu.2018.09.009

Schifter, C., & Cipollone, M. (2013). Minecraft as a teaching tool: One case study. In R. McBride & M. Searson (Eds.), *Proceedings of Society for Information Technology & Teacher Education International Conference 2013* (pp. 2951-2955). Chesapeake, VA: Association for the Advancement of Computing in Education (AACE).

Schreyer, J. (2012). Adolescent literacy practices in online social spaces. In New media literacies and participatory culture: Popular culture across borders. Routledge.

Shapiro, J. (2014). *MindShift guide to digital games + learning*. Retrieved from https://a.s.kqed.net/pdf/news/MindShift-GuidetoDigitalGamesandLearning.pdf

Short, D. (2012). Teaching scientific concepts using a virtual world—Minecraft. *Teaching Science-the Journal of the Australian Science Teachers Association, 58*(3), 55–58.

Silva Dos Santos, L., von Gillern, S., Lockwood, J., & Geluso, J. (2020). Digital mindsets: College-level ESL instructors' perceptions of multimodal technologies and video games for language instruction. *The European Journal of Applied Linguistics and TEFL, 9*(1), 131–152.

Sinclair, B. (2021). *Microsoft game revenues up 50% in Q3*. Gameindustry.biz. https://www.gamesindustry.biz/articles/2021-04-27-microsoft-game-revenues-up-50-percent-in-q3

Sitzmann, T. (2011). A meta-analytic examination of the instructional effectiveness of computer-based simulation games. *Personnel Psychology, 64*(2), 489–528. doi:10.1111/j.1744-6570.2011.01190.x

Squire, K. (2004). *Replaying history: Learning world history through playing Civilization III* [Unpublished doctoral dissertation]. Indiana University. Retrieved from https://www.academia.edu/1317076/Replaying_history_Learning_world_history_through_playing_Civilization_III

Squire, K. (2011). *Video games and learning: Teaching and participatory culture in the digital age*. Teachers College Press.

Squire, K. D. (2014). Video-Game Literacy - a Literacy of Expertise. In J. Coiro, M. Knobel, C. Lankshear, & D. Leu (Eds.), The Handbook of Research in New Literacies (pp. 635-670). Routledge.

Steinkuehler, C. (2007). Massively multiplayer online gaming as a constellation of literacy practices. *E-learning*, *4*(3), 297–318. doi:10.2304/elea.2007.4.3.297

Steinkuehler, C. (2010). Video games and digital literacies. *Journal of Adolescent & Adult Literacy*, *54*(1), 61–83. doi:10.1598/JAAL.54.1.7

Stufft, C. (2016). Videogames and YA literature: Using book groups to layer literacies. *The ALAN Review*, *43*(3), 96–102.

Stufft, C., & von Gillern, S. (2021). Fostering Multimodal Analyses of Video Games: Reflective Writing in the Middle School. *Journal of Adolescent & Adult Literacy*, jaal.1198. doi:10.1002/jaal.1198

Stufft, C. J. (2018). Engaging students in literacy practices through video game book groups. *Literacy Research: Theory, Method, and Practice*, *67*(1), 195–210. doi:10.1177/2381336918787191

Thompson, C., & von Gillern, S. (2020). Video-game based instruction for vocabulary acquisition with English language learners: A Bayesian meta-analysis. *Educational Research Review*, *30*(100332), 1–23. doi:10.1016/j.edurev.2020.100332

Tromba, P. (2013). Build engagement and knowledge one block at a time with Minecraft. *Learning and Leading with Technology*, *40*(8), 20–23.

Troppo, G. (2015). *The game believes in you: How digital play can make our kids smarter*. St. Martin's Press.

von Gillern, S. (2016a). The gamer response and decision framework: A tool for understanding video gameplay experiences. *Simulation & Gaming*, *47*(5), 666–683. doi:10.1177/1046878116656644

von Gillern, S. (2016b). Perceptual, decision-making, and learning processes during video gameplay: An analysis of *Infamous - Second Son* with the Gamer Response and Decision Framework. *Games and Learning Society 2016 Conference Proceedings*.

von Gillern, S. (2018). Games and their embodied learning principles in the classroom: Connecting learning theory to practice. In M. Khosrow-Pour (Ed.), *Gamification in Education: Breakthroughs in Research and Practice* (pp. 554–582). IGI Global. doi:10.4018/978-1-5225-5198-0.ch029

von Gillern, S. (2021). Communication, cooperation, and competition: Examining the literacy practices of esports teams. In M. Harvey & R. Marlatt (Eds.), *Esports research and its integration in education* (pp. 148–167). IGI Global. doi:10.4018/978-1-7998-7069-2.ch009

von Gillern, S., & Alaswad, Z. (2016). Games and game-based learning in instructional design. *The International Journal of Technologies in Learning*, *23*(4), 1–7. doi:10.18848/2327-0144/CGP/v23i04/1-7

von Gillern, S., Stufft, C., & Harvey, M. (2021). Integrating video games into the ELA classroom. *Literacy Today*, *38*(6), 64–65.

Walsh, C. (2010). Systems-based literacy practices: Digital games research, gameplay and design. *Australian Journal of Language and Literacy*, *33*(1), 24–40.

Wolfe, S., & Flewitt, R. (2010). New technologies, new multimodal literacy practices and young children's metacognitive development. *Cambridge Journal of Education*, *40*(4), 387–399. doi:10.1080/0305764X.2010.526589

Wouters, P., Van Nimwegen, C., Van Oostendorp, H., & Van Der Spek, E. D. (2013). A meta-analysis of the cognitive and motivational effects of serious games. *Journal of Educational Psychology*, *105*(2), 249–265. doi:10.1037/a0031311

Yuen, A. H. K., & Ma, W. W. K. (2008). Exploring teacher acceptance of e-learning technology. *Asia-Pacific Journal of Teacher Education*, *36*(3), 229–243. doi:10.1080/13598660802232779

Zichermann, G. (2011). *Gamification by design: Implementing game mechanics in web and mobile apps*. O'Reilly Media.

KEY TERMS AND DEFINITIONS

Digital Literacies: Practices in which people utilize, learn from, and communicate using digital technologies.

Digital Storytelling: An approach to telling stories through multimodal digital media, such as images, videos, written text, oral narrations, and sound effects.

Game-Based Learning: The use of games to help individuals, such as students, learn content and skills.

Gaming Pedagogy: An approach to teaching that utilizes games, including video games, to promote student motivation, engagement, and learning.

Multimodality: The use and integration of multiple communicative modes in media and human communication, such as visual, oral, and written information.

Technology Acceptance Model: A theoretical approach for understanding if and how people are likely to utilize a technology based on different factors such as ease of use, perceived usefulness, and self-efficacy.

Video Game Literacies: Skills and processes in which players interpret, analyze, make decisions, and learn during video gameplay.

Chapter 18
Play Is the Game:
Literacy Learning Through Game-Based Instruction

Sharon Peck
State University of New York College at Geneseo, USA

ABSTRACT

Drawing on a multimodal framework, this chapter looks at the ways engagement and embodiment of learning are mediated through play as sixth graders learn to skin or repurpose board games to represent the story of The Lightning Thief. Studying game design for the purpose of skinning, that is, applying a new theme or skin to a game, provides a literacy learning process that can foster collaborative, creative, and authentic learning. Outcomes demonstrated gains in social skills and interactions, critical thinking, reading comprehension, visual representation, graphic design, and writing for specific purposes. Analysis revealed that students were immersed in the learning process to the extent that they felt comfortable acting informally, responding in the moment, and being playful. This chapter shows a way to foster academic growth, engagement in learning, and collaboration is to engage students in skinning games based on literature and integrated a playful learning environment.

INTRODUCTION

The shifting nature of literacy and definitions of "text" call for educators to redefine the way we teach literacy (American Library Association, n.d.). Without responding to these shifts, we will continue to lose students who are not engaged in their learning, who don't see their instruction as relevant, and who don't see themselves as successful consumers and creators of texts (Bruns, 2008). One response to this need is the incorporation of multimodal game-based pedagogies (deJaan, 2019). Games, regardless of type, require critical thinking, interpretation of directions and other literacy tasks. Ultimately, games "encompass and look well beyond the forms of literacy that are defined by existing school and library standards, combining computational fluency, mathematics, logic, storytelling, sound and graphic design..." and many more literacies depending on the game (ALA, n.d).

DOI: 10.4018/978-1-7998-7271-9.ch018

Play Is the Game

This chapter explores the outcomes of engaging urban sixth grade students in playing and creating tabletop games. After studying game design and mechanics, students created their own skin of a game by changing the theme of the game to the book, *The Lightning Thief* by Rick Riordan (2006). This is supported by New Literacy studies (Lankshear & Knobel, 2006) which call for the incorporation of multiple modalities in student performance tasks. There are benefits to playing video games as students engage in collaboration in critical thinking while engaging in simulated collaboration with either a digital avatar or another player. Yet, multimodality includes more than just video consoles. This work centers around the medium of tabletop games. Tabletop games are accessible for students, do not require wi-fi and are inexpensive to acquire or create. Tabletop games provide a way of knowing game literacy. Many video game developers use tabletop games as a mode of teaching and learning game design, elements and mechanics (Wawro, 2017). Immersing students in game play and game creation as an instructional strategy for multimodal reader response yields many outcomes. These include ownership of learning, increased use of purposeful and playful discourse, deeper understandings of game design and mechanics, and ultimately, deeper understandings of the myths, symbolism, characters and plot lines of *The Lightning Thief* (Jackson, 2007).

In his work on gaming, Toppo asks, "Can we make the learning so engaging and so interesting and so hands-on that you have the feeling that you lose yourself in it? (2015, p.6)." The following scene suggests that we can.

Giavanna and three friends are playing a skinned version of Love Letter. This card game engages players in using deduction to eliminate players from the game. A peer asks "Giavanna, Do you have Percy?" She reacted by standing up and throwing her cards across the table, exclaiming "I thought I had you girl!" The whole table erupts in shouts. The teacher looks over to the group with a knowing smile as Giavanna walks away and then returns to the table with a dramatic pout.

This outburst was evidence of her investment in the game. It was a powerful moment. Giavanna was invested in learning. She was in the moment, responding honestly with her surprise at being caught. She was focused on the game, using logic to help her succeed. And she thought she had succeeded until her friend called her. And in this context, of game play in the classroom, her actions were accepted. She was allowed to stand up, to stomp away, to speak out. And, she was able to then regain her composure despite her disappointment. A few minutes later the table was laughing and recalling the steps of their game. Then they realized they had time for one more round before the bell rang. This shows us a bit about what happens when preteens are engaged in tabletop games. But this wasn't just a game, it was a game that Giavanna and her friends had created themselves. The students in this study did lose themselves for a bit as they became immersed in game design and game play. Work on multiliteracies (Lankshear and Knobel, 2006), game-based pedagogy (deJaan, 2019, Kangas, 2010) and playful literacy instruction (Wohlwend, 2008) support the questions of: How does playing tabletop games impact literacy learning? How does skinning games impact literacy learning? What factors should be considered when engaging in game-based pedagogy?

The present study contributes to the knowledge base growing around the impact of game-based pedagogies, multimodal engagement and ownership of literacy learning.

BACKGROUND

This work is informed by multiliteracies, 21st Century Skills, and game-based pedagogy to explore the possibilities afforded through playful literacy instruction. New literacies studies (Lankshear & Knoble, 2006, ALA, n.d) call for an interaction and meaning making with a variety of texts through multiple modes. Multiliteracies pedagogy, which stemmed from the work by The New London group as they explored the needs that new literacies require, diverges from a focus on digital literacy to present a framework for incorporating multiple types of literacy. It is marked by honoring the multimodal meaning systems inherent in all types of texts, connecting older and new forms of literacy (New London Group, 1996, Cope & Kalantzis, 2009).

Due to the fast pace of changes in technology and media, "Teachers must recognize the new literacy demands of the 21st century and, most important, must transform their programs to meet these demands with timely literacy instruction (Karmeicher-Klein & Shinas, 2012, p. 289)." Such literacies provide opportunities for multiple ways of meaning making from a wide variety of texts and media. As students learn to negotiate a variety of texts, encompassing multiple modalities, they also become both consumers of content, and producers (Bruns, 2008). This participatory literacy (Wohlwend, 2017) helps students use the media to represent knowledge and author all types of texts. "Students must be encouraged to use the capabilities technology affords them to develop rich, dynamic, forward-thinking presentations of their knowledge (Karmeicher-Klein & Shinas, 2012, p. 292)." For teachers this meets the goals of providing relevant, authentic learning experiences which break out of the traditional school literacy to help students situate themselves as authors and content creators.

In *Gaming and Literacy* (ALA, n.d.), the ALA describes 21st century literacy as a space where reading and understanding information is still vital, but so, too, is evaluating and thinking critically in order to draw conclusions and make informed decisions. 21st century literacy relies on the production of new knowledge and sharing that knowledge (ALA, n.d.). The ALA argues that gaming is a way to further develop these new manner of literacies because gaming and literacy go hand-in-hand. Games, regardless of type and modality, require critical thinking, interpretation of directions and other literacy tasks. Ultimately, games require literacy abilities including those defined in school and library standards, and more, depending on the game and the way it is incorporated into instruction (ALA, n.d.).

Game-Based Pedagogy and Tabletop Games

Game-based pedagogy focuses on games in digital and non-digital contexts. It can include using educational games, using entertainment games, learning by making games, and using game elements in non-game contexts, as in gamification (Van Eck, 2006, Kapp, 2012, Nousiainen, et al., 2015). This inquiry takes up two of these approaches. First, students learned from games used purely for entertainment how to make new, educational games based on the content being covered in ELA. Second, this work focused on tabletop games, whereas much of the work on game-based pedagogy focuses solely on technology and media, while acknowledging that it does include other forms of games. Games in this study centers around the medium of tabletop games. Tabletop games are accessible for students, do not require wi-fi and are inexpensive to acquire or create. And, tabletop games provide rich affordances for face-to-face interactions, discourse, cognitive embodiment of concepts, and physical engagement. Multimodal tabletop games for popular use that may or may not have educational goals or content, termed entertainment games, were used. However, through modifying or skinning games, such games move from entertainment to educational or serious games. The referent of entertainment games is a misnomer, for all games are iterative. Each game play provides insights for the next game play. This makes tabletop games effective learning tools. They promote creativity, concentration, and confidence and appeal to students who expect learning tasks to be fast, active, and exploratory (Sardon & Devlin- Sherer, 2016, Kirriemuir & McFarlane 2004). Tabletop games differ from video games in that the rules are always explicit. This allows students to easily understand the mechanics and the way aspects of the game work together. It also makes these games easy to modify and skin for the classroom (Castronova, & Knowles, 2015). "Board games in particular are an under-appreciated medium for teaching through games. Especially when the educator's goal is to teach players about a complex system, the transparency of a board game's rules can make them exceptional teaching aids (Castronova, & Knowles, 2015, p. 42)."

Many teachers are not familiar with the value of using games. They may not enjoy games themselves, or don't feel that their students couldn't participate without becoming off task. Some may even feel that games are only for indoor recess. However, affordances of tabletop include- clear directions, breadth of topics, low technology, small groups, student to student, easy to see design options, limited the breadth of the game, and virality. Additionally, students become authors and developers, putting out products of their learning that are taken up outside of school. Students can take their newly created games home and share them.

In this study, students did not have access to video games or tablets. However, they came together in the library after lunch by choice to explore games together. Seeing this interest, the librarian developed this extended unit on game design and skinning. While video games provide a powerful medium for game design and exploration, the students in this study began with tabletop games as a means of understanding game design. And, they ultimately added to their literacy learning through the process of participating and interacting with and around the game (Gee & Hayes, 2012).

Toppos (2015) suggests that what makes games so successful is that students have opportunities to practice or demonstrate their learning through games. Features of physical and video games offer students the ability to fail and try again, to have immediate and interactive feedback, to work in a system that is fair to all players, to lose themselves in the work and take on aspirational roles, to find their own path to proficiency, and to collaborate and share successes. These traits highlight the stark contrast between common instructional methods and game-based learning. The role of the student is that of the active learner who has control over their outcomes, is allowed to freely interact, to take on the role of being successful, and feel supported. "Traditional instructional methods may have a harder time meeting the expectations of today's learners whereas gaming adds energy to a class and encourages student learning in unique ways (Sardon & Devlin- Sherer, 2016, p.221)." Additionally, tabletop games create spaces for students to interact face to face in small groups in acceptable ways within school settings. This style of games require students to be actively focused on the game play even when it isn't their turn. The games are inherently inclusive, and foster authentic connections (Kangas, 2010a). These connections and ways of interacting are often different from traditional and permissible ways of collaborating in the classroom.

Game Design: Through skinning games and studying game design, students gain an enhanced understanding of specific academic content, in this case, deeper comprehension of the book *The Lightning Thief* (Riordan, 2006). Kafia (2006) suggests that designing and building a game creates a different experience than solely playing a game. Designing leads learners to effectively construct new relationships with knowledge and learn new things, and to take different viewpoints into consideration (Randolph et al., 2016). Creating games also extends the student development of 21st century skills, creative expression and thinking skills (Rotherham, & Willingham, 2010).

In projects where students collaborate to design a game that incorporates new learning in the form of targeted content and concepts, utilizing familiar board game formats can make the learning task less intimidating. The familiarity of the game structure facilitates creativity and critical thinking as it serves as a scaffold that mediates learning by holding part of the cognitive load so that students can use more critical and analytical thinking.

An interesting consideration in the work on game-based pedagogy is the notion of playfulness, which is defined as a mindset and stance that cross-cuts all game-based approaches (Nousainen et al, 2015). This stance contributes to the creation of a safe space for students to try on different roles, take risks, let their guard down, and become immersed in learning. In his seminal work on play, Huizinga (1938) reminds us that enjoyment, freedom and having fun are central to play and playfulness. He reminds us that these traits have always been central to animals and humans. He also suggests that these elements should be safeguarded when play is used with educational goals (Singer, 2013).

A playful stance is central to playful literacy instruction, in which the use of play, exploration, engagement, games and game elements can enhance the outcomes of instruction. This mindset though, may help us understand why play and game-based pedagogies are resisted. It does take a flexible stance to trust that the engagement of games will yield the outcomes that teachers are pressured to create.

Often teachers will treat game-based applications as the fun that students are allowed to have when other work is completed. Or, games are allowed to be played on Friday afternoons for twenty minutes. This unfortunate view conveys to students that learning should not be fun. This overlooks the powerful outcomes of games for learning, cognitive development and social development.

Games and Literacy Learning: Essentially a reader must become "literate" in the language and ideals of the games they play in order to be successful The ALA (n.d) supports the notion that standards and modes of literacy instruction need to change at the same rate that literacy does. Ultimately, including multimodal or "new literacies" as a method of instruction is something that reflects the shifting demands of education. This move promotes critical thinking, problem solving, and a number of other reading skills. Koster reminds us that through the appropriate level of challenge and fun, games become "deliberate practice machines" (Koster, 2004, p. 100). Literacy learning through game play makes the purpose of literacy skill applications tangible and authentic for students.

MAIN FOCUS: THE GAME PLAY

This study centered on two groups of sixth graders in an urban northeastern city ranked among the top five highest poverty rates of all US cities. The school, located just southwest of the city center, recently went into receivership. This means that the school state test scores did not reflect demonstrable gains in achievement. This led to a coalition with a local college School of Education to address educational needs and offerings.

This project followed a collaboration between the school librarian and the sixth grade teachers. In this school, during the afternoon, classes are split into two smaller groups. One group attends the library while the other goes to the art room. Throughout the three months of observation the librarian worked with groups of ten to fourteen students. The students read *Percy Jackson and The Lightning Thief* (Riordan, 2005) in their classrooms. In the library they set off on the challenge of studying game design with the ultimate goal of skinning a game based on the book. The students stated that they enjoy coming to the library where learning is more active and less scripted.

Play Is the Game

Kangas (2010b) suggests creative and playful learning for designing game-based teaching and learning. In this view, teachers engage in framing, organization, implementation, facilitation, and assessment. The creative and playful learning processes for students includes knowledge co-creation through *orientation*, *creation*, *play*, and *elaboration*. Each of these aspects were evident in the process initiated by the librarian, who had a history of embracing gaming in and out of the classroom.

The librarian wanted the games inquiry to address state curriculum goals of providing instruction in using a research plan and creating a timeline. Other goals included supporting students in identifying primary and secondary sources, engaging in note taking and understanding the difference between plagiarism and and paraphrasing. Additionally, the goals supported the International Society for Technology in Education (ISTE, 2016), standards for technology, to create empowered learners, innovative designers and creative communicators. She had a background in playing games and attending annual gaming conventions. She frequently invited students to eat in the library and play games together.

In initiating game play with the sixth graders though, most of the students admitted that they preferred video games, however their game awareness was low. Students stated that they played games such as Uno and Connect Four. They hadn't experienced other types of board games, even random games like Chutes and Ladders, or games like Monopoly. They professed little understanding of game mechanics. This provided an additional goal of introducing different game mechanics and game designs. The students had never experienced collaborative games before. They were challenged by the concept of an entire team attempting to reach a goal together, rather than one person winning and all others losing. Their lack of awareness of games also impacted their ability to make sense of game directions.

Board games were selected with the goal of including a variety of mechanisms. The mechanism is how the game progresses. Does it rely on dice? Cards? A spinner? Placement of tiles? Trading? Since the students had such little experience with board games, three types of games with different goals and mechanisms were selected. A goal was to include games that could be played in a short amount of time, each game selected takes 15- 20 minutes to play. Rather than modifying a game to fit into the school time constraints, shorter games allowed for authentic experiences with the game play.

Many serious or educational games focus on roll and move mechanics. These keep the outcomes of play completely random. Engaging with games that have more deliberate ways to control game play builds student agency. They are in control of their own success or failure. Key aspects of games include having a clear purpose or goal. This can include the win condition, so that students know how to be successful. It should have simple clearly communicated rules. Games have immediate rewards, the feedback students receive as they play is instant. It should have continuous challenges. As with any type of instruction, the level of challenge is key; if it is too easy or too hard, students won't want to play. Games have an engaging story line, creating the genre of the game, and can be easily skinned. Games provide opportunities for meaningful choices. Games have complex implications and ramifications for student choices. And, in a well developed game, all players are involved until the end. This aspect adds to engagement and focus as students have to be mindful of the actions of their fellow players.

During the orientation phase (Kangas, 2010a), students researched game design, met with game designers, and studied game mechanics. Students generated questions including: What's the background story or theme of the game? How do you win? What pieces or materials do you need and what do they do? How many people can play and how old could they be? How do you set it up? What are the steps or mechanics to play?

For each of the games explored, students worked to understand the rules of game play from both the printed rules provided with the game and an online video tutorial provided by *Rules Girl* (2017). Students found the videos helpful but ultimately relied on the details in the written directions.

The central games in their inquiry focused on three different game mechanics. They studied card game mechanics, playing the game *Love Letter* (Kenai, 2012). They learned about dice game mechanics with the game *Catan Dice,* a condensed version of the popular board game, Settlers of Catan, and uses dice as the mechanic (Tuber, 2007). And they explored collaborative games with the game *Hoot, Owl, Hoot* (McKinley Ross, 2010). Despite being a roll and move game, this is a cooperative game. All players work together to either achieve the end goal and win, or fail together.

Board Game Geek, a popular game website, explains *Love Letter* as a game of risk, deduction, and luck for 2–4 players. Your goal is to get your love letter into Princess Annette's hands while deflecting the letters from competing suitors. From a deck with only sixteen cards, each player starts with only one card in hand; one card is removed from play. On a turn, you draw one card, and play one card, trying to expose others and knock them from the game. Powerful cards lead to early gains, but make you a target. Rely on weaker cards for too long, however, and your letter may be tossed in the fire! (BGG, 2021).

For *Catan Dice* BGG suggests that like all the other games of the "Settlers of Catan'' series, this game is about building settlements, roads, cities and hiring knights. This time, there is no board on which to place little figures: Every player has his own scorecard called the *building sheet*, which depicts a mini Catan. You build by drawing the settlements and roads on your scorecard. To build you still require resources. These are collected by a Yahtzee-like mechanism that involves throwing six special dice (depicting the different resource symbols) up to three times. After each roll, the player can select which dice to keep and which to roll again. In the end, he may build using the thusly determined resources, and is awarded victory points for any finished buildings, which are recorded on the scorecard. The game lasts fifteen turns or about 15-30 minutes, after which the player with the most victory points wins (BGG, 2021).

And BGG describes that in *Hoot Owl Hoot!* (McKinley, 2010) the players want to move all the owls back to their nest before the sun rises and the new days begin. To set up the game, place the sun token on the first place of the sun track, place three owls on the starting spaces of the owl track, and give three cards to each player; the fifty-card deck includes 36 color cards (six each in six colors) and 14 sun cards. Players keep their cards face up in front of them so that they can work together to strategize how to move. If a player has a sun card, on her turn she must discard the sun and move the sun token to one space; if she has all color cards, she discards any one color card, then moves any owl to the next open space of that color. If an owl "flies" over an owl on a space of that color on its way to the next open space, all players make a hooting sound! (BGG, 2021).

After spending time playing each of the three games, and reflecting on the merits of the mechanics, students chose one game to skin based on The Lightning Thief (Riordan, 2005). The *creation* phase (Kangas, 2010a) focused on the method of skinning. Skinning is a term that comes from the online video game genre, and it refers to changing the look and feel (which includes the game characters, artwork, background, theme and story etc.) but not the game play. For instance, the most commonly skinned game is *Monopoly* with over 2500 versions of the game. Chances are you've seen a version of Monopoly where the properties reflect your city, region or hobby. You may have seen themed versions of Sorry, Bingo, Yahtzee or Fluxx.

Engaging students in skinning a game has benefits of helping students understand aspects of game development, without having to create a whole new game. Rather, they can grapple with the connections between the story and characters in their reading with the story and key elements of the game play.

Play Is the Game

The students began by choosing the game that they wanted to skin. Students chose to work in pairs and analyze the game to determine what they would have to create as they changed the context or theme of each game to the context of the book *The Lightning Thief*. This process engaged students in a deep dive into the characters from Greek Mythology as they worked to make comparisons between characters in each game.

For instance, in Love Letter, there are eight types of cards representing various characters, each with a different ability. So students aligned the cards in the game with characters from *The Lightning Thief*. This was very revealing, and did call for many students to revisit the book to ensure they understood the nuances of each character.

Then they spent time looking up image depictions of the characters to adapt for their games. This was interesting to see the variety of preferred characters' images. The creation of the pieces also involved finding open source imagery to add to the game cards. Using the free graphic design website Pixelmator, the Librarian helped the students create game cards. The students got their feet wet with digital design and graphic arts as they learned to create layered images. (Figure 1)

Figure 1. This is an image of the student created game Lightning Bolt

The process of developing rules was consuming for the students. They began by reading and rereading the rules provided in the game, and reviewing the video directions. They worked together to determine the key rules in each game. Then, they began the task of rewriting the rules in the voice and context of their version. Here they grappled with language choices, voice and style. And, with little experience with game directions, this task seemed to provide a good level of challenge.

For example, in skinning Love Letter into Lightning Bolt, students recreated the following rules, demonstrating their understanding of the characters and motivations from *The Lightning Thief* (Jackson, 2006). Students worked hard to match the effects and traits of each character card with the characters from the novel. (Box 1)

Students then worked to create comparisons between design mechanisms: In *Hoot Owl Hoot!* (McKinley, 2010) the design lent itself to the book well. In the original game the owls have to work together to get back to the nest before sunrise. The students adapted this to the amount of days that Percy had to complete his journey. They chose to design a path to Mt. Olympus rather than a path to a nest. (Figure 2)

Play Is the Game

Box 1. Directions for the student developed game Lightning Bolt

Someone stole the lightning bolt from Zeus and Percy, Grover and Annabeth are trying to get it back. The game has 16 cards. Each card's name represents a character from the lightning thief.
8: Zeus is the sky god and the leader of the olympians. His symbol of power is the lightning bolt. You will lose the round if you draw this card. 7: Hades is the god of the underworld. Initially Percy thought that Hades stole the lightning bolt. Discard this card if you have Poseidon or Percy. 6: Poseidon is the sea god/ Percy's father . He is one of the three sons of Kronos. Trade this card with another player of your choice. 5: Percy is the son of Poseidon. He is a hero of the lightning thief. He has a great sense of humor. His best friend is Grover. Choose a player to discard their hand. Choose any player to discard their hand. 4: Dionysus is the irritable director of camp half-blood and he is also the god of wine. His father, Zeus, has sentenced him to centuries of servitude at camp half-blood for bad behavior. Ignore effects until the next round. 3: Ares is the God of War, and he is Zeus's son. We first met him at Denver when he rode up on a Harley outside of the diner where Percy, Grover, and Annabeth are about to eat. Compare hands with another player the player with the lower card is out. 2: Luke has been the best swordsman for the last three hundred years. He is the counselor in Hermy's cabin, and he helps Percy. Look at another player's hand. 1: Grover is a satyr, he is half man half goat. He helps Percy because he is his protector. When you play this card you can choose another player. You'll have to guess what card they have. If they have it they are out.
Each card has a value in the upper left corner-the higher the number, the closer that person gets to zeus. At the bottom of each card, a text box describes the effect when the card is discarded.

Figure 2. An example of a student made game board for Mt. Olympus.

Play Is the Game

In the Catan dice group, the task was to recreate the dice and change the icons from wheat, sheep, rock, wheat and gold. They settled on armour, wood nymphs, water, goats, gold and a lightning bolt. They enjoyed determining which symbols to draw with sharpies on wooden dice. The challenging task was to develop symbols which matched the reasoning of the novel to create the trading rules. Then they recreated the individual game boards for recording progress, using just what was available in google docs. (Figures 3 and 4)

Figure 3. This is the student created image guide for the Percy's Lightning Bolt Trouble Game

Armour	 ♕	Goat	 🍭
Wood Nymphs	 W	Water	)
Gold	 OOO	Lightning bolt	 ⚡

Trading:

Road	Armour ♕ + Wood Nymphs W
Settlement	Armour ♕ + Wood Nymphs W + Goat 🍭 + Water)
Temples	3 Gold OOO + 2 Water)
Knight	Gold OOO + Goat 🍭 + Water)

The *play phase* (Kangas, 2010) focused on the very important step of play testing the new games. The students had confidence that the games would work since they didn't change the methods of game play, just the setting. They practiced playing their games together. They were able to revise rules for clarity as they taught their classmates their new games.

Figure 4. This is the student created game Percy's Lightning Trouble.

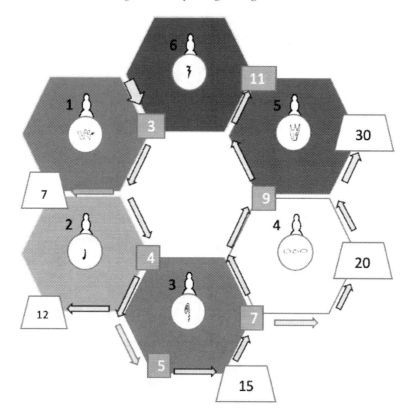

It was during the play phase that students grappled with their individual abilities to enact the game play. They struggled at times to play the games strategically. However, when one student struggled, others came to the rescue. It became common for them to collaboratively support each other to make sound choices during the game play. Despite the fact that two of the games were not collaborative in nature, students playing Percy's Lightning Trouble (Catan Dice) in particular, offered suggestions, questioned each other's choices, and pointed out better plays.

In Lightning Bolt (*Love Letter*) students readily embraced the competitive nature of the game. The game also asks players to use a "game face" so their mannerisms and responses don't offer hints to the cards that they are holding. This was interesting as students learned not to exclaim or grin upon seeing their cards, which was against their initial instincts.

In the Mt. Olympus Adventure (*Hoot, Owl, Hoot!*) group, students eagerly negotiated together the best ways to ensure success. They were able to disagree, argue for their suggestions, and come to a shared understanding. They also responded to the ever present pacing of the game as they drew sun cards to shorten the remaining play time. The "oohs" and "no way" exclamations resounded across the library.

The final phase is *elaboration* (Kangas, 2010a), where students reflect upon their learning. Students took time to celebrate their connections as they invited their classroom teachers and other classes to play their games.

Play Is the Game

The library had represented an alternate learning space where students could relax, play around more in their interactions, and get to the work of play. Their individual classrooms however were marked by whole group lessons, where students were expected to remain quiet until called upon. When students did bring the games to the classrooms to play with the students who had been studying art, they beamed. They became experts as they explained the game. They did not hold back in attempting to beat their new opponents. And they brought the volume and joy of the library to the classroom interactions.

METHODS

This study centered on participant observation. The researcher attended the library classes daily for four months to observe, support instruction, and ultimately coach the players in game development. The details of this project were documented over the course of four months using field notes, transcripts of the video recordings of small group interactions, textual products (student work samples), and transcripts of teacher interviews. Data was used to gather a close look at student learning, the mediation of technology, and the social interactions that ensued.

This methodology assisted in understanding literacy as a social practice and how students produced their own meanings (Jewitt et al, 2016). The nature of the tasks of inquiry, game creation, and game play placed students as active creators of meaning and interactive dialogue. Initially, the data were analyzed in grounded theory (Glaser & Strauss, 1967) to gain insight into the emerging data. This approach allowed for the discovery of the data that led to open coding and weekly memos. This first layer of data analysis afforded opportunities to see the overlapping of codes, the need for new codes, and eventually larger themes (Saldaña, 2015).

Cross case analysis and coding of videos, interviews and student surveys brought out the way in which the game play was more than engagement but positioned the students differently, gave them agency in a place where they often don't feel it. It uncovered the ways in which the creative inquiry and creation process immersed students in taking responsibility for their learning. And, through game creation and playing of their own games, students demonstrated that it was acceptable to be fully engaged, to feel challenged, and to respond authentically as they experienced the possibility of winning and disappointment of defeat.

OUTCOMES

The engagement was different from their classroom experiences and called upon multimodal learning in powerful ways - the students were able to critically think, draw upon their understandings of the book and grapple with their newer understandings of the games. They were able to build off of the story of the game to apply the theme of *The Lightning Thief* (Riordan, 2005). They explored graphic representations of character traits as they designed symbols on their game pieces. They were challenged to create game pieces, maps and game boards. They used technology including Pixlr.com to create their own character cards for *Love Letter* (Kenai, 2012).

Analysis suggested that the act of creating games led to increased student engagement and ownership of both games and knowledge. Students gained specific knowledge of game design, and deepened their understanding of the initial text that became the theme for the game they chose to skin. Throughout the process students continually referred back to the text to clarify their understanding.

While students explored games, they unknowingly improved their social skills and interactions, practiced critical thinking, made deeper connections to text, expressed their understandings through visual representation matching imagery, matched content representation, experienced graphic design, took on writing for specific purposes (directions for game play and game story), experienced pride in authoring a text and seeing others engage in said text, ultimately producing a text to be used by others.

Students were successful as they inquired into the nature of the game design and mechanics. They eagerly took on the challenge of authoring new games based on their understanding of the novel. The day that they were able to bring their games home the excitement was evident. Additionally, students who normally interrupted, offered inappropriate outbursts and often teased each other, changed their demeanors. They let go of the mantle of student and became players and authors. The teasing remained, but through the lens of their game play. They enacted turn taking. They explored the nuances of the game play, supporting each other through each challenge.

What became evident through review of the video data is the ways in which students become immersed in the play. They took on stances that are inherent to game play but not to classroom learning. They engaged in informal discourse and interactions as they negotiated knowledge, and as they engaged in game play. The library was not a quiet space during the game testing phase. Rather, students felt comfortable raising their voices, responding in earnest to their peers, and reacting to good and bad plays. This freedom to interact in ways not usually allowed in the library or classroom adds to student engagement and the social nature of literacy learning. This reinforces the notion that when engaged in play, participants may feel permission to "behave in new ways" (Harrison & West, 2014, p. 75). Students may be more comfortable engaging in novel behavior and courageous about opening themselves up to variation (Statler, Heracleous, & Jacobs, 2011).

These students demonstrated that they felt safe taking risks, and were able to let go of social stances and outlooks that they brought with them as they entered the room. These students continually navigated their social stances as they worked, researched, struggled, collaborated and played. As deJaan (2019) asserts, "multimodality and affinity spaces contribute to broad linguistic exploration and better understandings."

A final aspect of this experience was the pride evident as students brought the games back to the classroom. The stern and controlled space became animated and active as students asked peers in different groups to engage in game play. Throughout the play testing and play periods students demonstrated extenuation desire (Brown, 2009). They did not want to stop playing and continually tried to play extra rounds of their games despite the clock.

In summary, outcomes highlight not only the curricular gains afforded through game play, but also, the ways in which the social nature of the play supported student identity, confidence and motivation.

CONSIDERATIONS

This work explores the affordances of engaging in game-based pedagogy (Kangas, 2010a) through studying game design and skinning games. Outcomes demonstrated many gains in social skills and interactions, critical thinking, reading comprehension, visual representation, graphic design, and writing for specific purposes. Students engaged in participatory literacies as they created a product for others to consume,

Play Is the Game

rather than passively reading texts. Analysis revealed that students were immersed in the learning process to the extent that they felt comfortable acting informally, responding in the moment, and being playful.

Tabletop games are consistently rising in popularity. The global board games market is over $3.2 billion and continues to rise (Sargeantston, 2021). Game play has increased in homes, in communities and in classrooms. Game conventions are well attended and on the rise. Popular websites provide information, ratings, descriptions and forums for gamers to connect. With sources like Kickstarter and Maker Spaces, more board games are being designed and marketed by independent creators. Even mainstream vendors like Barnes and Noble now carry a full range of board game options. Yet, we see few games included in school classrooms. We see students who aren't aware of games that use critical thinking and strategy rather than random outcomes. We don't see comprehensive inclusion of game making in preservice teacher programs and professional development.

This chapter shares more ways to integrate tabletop games into the classroom and curriculum. "You can use authentic board games to assist in teaching curricular concepts, but the point is to let them have fun while they are playing and learning (Crews, 2011, p.13)." Fun and playfulness is central to learning for all ages. However, we see less and less inclusion of "fun" in schools today. Yet, if we integrate a game-based pedagogy, students can engage in a motivating and consuming way to learn, work collaboratively in groups, and collaborate creatively for a common goal (Kangas, 2010a). The playful stance enhances the learning experience for students and teachers.

Here are ideas for exploring the power of games for literacy learning in your classroom:

- Make games of all kinds available to students
- Let them find tutorials on YouTube to pair with the directions.
- Make a few extra copies of game directions so more students can review them at once.
- After students have familiarity with the game, offer the option to skin, modify, mash or create a new game.
- Try games to help students master content or to focus on specific skills and critical thinking. Games can serve as a way to introduce topics, practice skills, and even as assessments.
- Engaging students in game creation is a good way to transfer the novelty and engagement of game play to support student ownership of knowledge and abilities.
- Recognize that many second-hand stores sell next to new tabletop games for $4 or less.
- Ask the community to donate old (or new) games.
- Connect with local game stores, game designers and developers.
- Reach out to the gaming community - they are eager to share.
- Look at BoardGameGeek (http://www.boardgamegeek.com) and ShutUp and Sit Down (https://www.shutupandsitdown.com/games/) for more information.
- Consider attending a game convention near you, or an online gaming community.
- Be flexible. Sit back and notice the ways students engage with games.
- Keep a playful mindset.

FUTURE RESEARCH DIRECTIONS

This work suggests many areas for future research. There are so many rich possibilities of game-based learning in literacy instruction. More work is needed to explore the impact of board game play for learning (Bayeck, 2020) at the elementary, intermediate and high school levels. Work at the college level has demonstrated that use of board games increases student motivation to learn Gonzalo-Iglesia et. al., 2018, Taspinar et al., 2016).

We see more and more state curriculum initiatives implementing play and games, yet not more support for teachers on how to develop games. To avoid a run of random games, work should focus on exposing teachers and students to more skill based forms of game design. Within the framework then of game play, and of game creation, students can demonstrate their understanding and application of content knowledge.

Future work on the impact and affordances of tabletop games will support populations without digital access. Tabletop games have shown to improve social interactions (Fang, Chen & Huang, 2016). Studies have compared board game and digital board gameplay of the same games, to see that the tabletop players demonstrated a higher level of connection and satisfaction than those playing the same game through a digital medium. There is more to learn about developing emotional intelligence through the social expectations of tabletop game play.

There is a rich dichotomy to explore between learning from engaging in game play (Gee & Hayes, 2012) to learning from skinning, modding, mashing and creating games. The affordances of each process lead back to the query of why we aren't seeing more of this in classrooms of all ages.

Research should extend the work on designing tabletop games based on literature. Students can look at popular games that have been emerging recently based on books, movies and genres. Research can address the ways in which skinning a game draws on literary understandings, as well as multimodal learning.

Exploration of the outcomes of engaging middle schoolers in skinning, modding, mashing and creating their own games is needed. And game development can easily fit into most curricular areas.

There is a real need for teachers to use relevant, engaging and motivational strategies to engage learners (ALA, n.d). Current work shows that board games can enable participation in diverse practices that are creative, fun, and engaging (Carter, Gibbs & Harrock, 2014, Sharp, 2012). However games are not frequently included in preservice teacher training and the professional development offered to teachers. While play and games are encouraged through state standards, 21st century education and lines of research, many administrators still question the use of games and fun during educational time. More research is needed to help educators of all levels understand the possibilities which games offer (Bayeck, 2020). While there are some studies addressing the role of the teacher (Nousiainen, Kangas, Rikala, Vesisenaho, 2018), more work is needed to develop teachers competence and confidence in integrating games into their instruction. Research focusing on pedagogical aspects of using play, games and a playful stance in teaching and learning has the potential to transform instruction in powerful ways.

LIMITATIONS

This study was limited to one urban school and two sixth grade classes. The work took place in the library because the librarian had experience with games. The work was coordinated by the librarian with support from the researcher. It would be worth identifying settings with teachers who are using game-based pedagogy in the literacy classroom. However, even though the data is limited, the experience can be helpful in understanding the ways it was implemented and the outcomes for students.

An additional limitation of this research is that the focus centered on tabletop games. It would be very interesting to extend this work and engage students in playing the same games through a digital format.

However, it might not be feasible for them to skin the games in a digital format, based on limited access to technology and game design software.

CONCLUSION

With such a resurgence in board game play, and more compelling research detailing the ways that they can be used in the classroom, it is time to ensure that teachers have the support to successfully integrate games into their playful instruction, and to feel confident leading students to create, modify and skin games.

This chapter reminds us of what the ALA (n.d.) suggests: "Games, regardless of type, require critical thinking, interpretation of directions and other literacy tasks. Ultimately, games "encompass and look well beyond the forms of literacy that are defined by existing school and library standards, combining computational fluency, mathematics, logic, storytelling, sound and graphic design..." and many more literacies depending on the game (ALA, n.d). Ultimately, game-based pedagogies that immerse students in play, and engage students in creating their own games, develop not only multiple literacies, and multimodal ways of meaning making, skills, but also serve to change the learners stance from passive to fully engaged.

REFERENCES

American Library Association. (n.d.). *Games and literacy: the connection between literacy and gaming*. Games & Gaming Round Table: A Round Table of the American Library Association. Retrieved from https://www.ala.org/gamert/games-

And-literacy. (n.d.). https://www.ala.org/gamert/games-and-literacy

Bayeck, R. Y. (2020). Examining board gameplay and learning: A multidisciplinary review of recent research. *Simulation & Gaming*, *51*(4), 411–431. doi:10.1177/1046878119901286

Board Game Geek. (n.d.). https://boardgamegeek.com/boardgame/27710/catan-dice-game

Brown, S. L. (2009). *Play: How it shapes the brain, opens the imagination, and invigorates the soul*. Penguin.

Bruns, A. (2008). *Blogs, Wikipedia, Second Life, and beyond: From production to produsage* (Vol. 45). Peter Lang.

Carter, M., Gibbs, M., & Harrop, M. (2014). Drafting an army: The playful pastime of warhammer 40,000. *Games and Culture*, *9*(2), 122–147. doi:10.1177/1555412013513349

Castronova, E., & Knowles, I. (2015). Modding board games into serious games: The case of Climate Policy. *International Journal of Serious Games*, *2*(3), 41–62.

Cope, B., & Kalantzis, M. (2009). "Multiliteracies": New literacies, new learning. *Pedagogies*, *4*(3), 164–195. doi:10.1080/15544800903076044

Crews, A. (2011). Getting Teachers on" Board. *Knowledge Quest*, *40*(1), 10.

Darrow, C.D. (2006). *Monopoly: the property trading board game* [Board Game]. Hasbro/Parker.

deHaan, J. (2019). Teaching language and literacy with games: What? How? Why? *Ludic Language Pedagogy*, *1*, 1–57.

Fang, Y., Chen, K., & Huang, Y. (2016). Emotional reactions of different interface formats: Comparing digital and traditional board games. *Advances in Mechanical Engineering*, *8*(3), 1–8. doi:10.1177/1687814016641902

Gee, J., & Hayes, E. (2012). Nurturing affinity spaces and game-based learning. In C. Steinkuehler, K. Squire, & S. A. Barab (Eds.), *Games, learning, and society: Learning and meaning in the digital age* (pp. 129–153). Cambridge University Press. doi:10.1017/CBO9781139031127.015

Girl, R. (2017, February 14). *How to play Love Letter in 3 minutes* [Video]. YouTube. https://www.youtube.com/watch?v=WAiI7G3QdOU

Gonzalo-Iglesia, J. L., Lozano-Monterrubio, N., & Prades-Tena, J. (2018). Non Educational board games in university education. Perceptions of students experiencing game-based learning methodologies. *Revista Lusófona de Educação*, *41*(41), 45–62. doi:10.24140/issn.1645-7250.rle41.03

Hinebaugh, J. P. (2009). *A board game education*. R&L Education.

International Society for Technology in Education. (2016). *Essential Conditions for Teaching ISTE Standards*. Author.

Jewitt, C., Bezemer, J., & O'Halloran, K. (2016). *Introducing multimodality*. Routledge.

Kanai, S. (2012). *Lover Letter* [Board Game]. Alderac Entertainment Group.

Kangas, M. (2010a). Creative and playful learning: Learning through game co-creation and games in a playful learning environment. *Thinking Skills and Creativity*, *5*(1), 1–15. doi:10.1016/j.tsc.2009.11.001

Kangas, M., Koskinen, A., & Krokfors, L. (2017). A qualitative literature review of educational games in the classroom: The teacher's pedagogical activities. *Teachers and Teaching*, *23*(4), 451–470.

Karchmer-Klein, R., & Shinas, V. H. (2012). Guiding principles for supporting new literacies in your classroom. *The Reading Teacher*, *65*(5), 288–293. doi:10.1002/TRTR.01044

Koster, R. (2013). *Theory of fun for game design*. O'Reilly Media, Inc.

Lankshear, C., & Knobel, M. (2006). *New literacies: Everyday practices and classroom learning*. Open University Press.

McKinley Ross, S. (2010). *Hoot Owl Hoot*. Peaceable Kingdom.

Nousiainen, T., Kangas, M., Rikala, J., & Vesisenaho, M. (2018). Teacher competencies in game-based pedagogy. *Teaching and Teacher Education*, *74*, 85–97. doi:10.1016/j.tate.2018.04.012

Pixlr. (n.d.). https://pixlr.com/. *Free photo editor online graphic design*. Academic Press.

Randolph, J. J., Kangas, M., Ruokamo, H., & Hyvönen, P. (2016). Creative and playful learning on technology-enriched playgrounds: An international investigation. *Interactive Learning Environments*, *24*(3), 409–422. doi:10.1080/10494820.2013.860902

Riordan, R. (2005). *The Lightning Thief*. Hyperion Books for Children.

Rotherham, A. J., & Willingham, D. T. (2010). 21st-century" skills. *American Educator*, *17*(1), 17–20.

Sardone, N. B., & Devlin-Scherer, R. (2016). Let the (Board) Games Begin: Creative Ways to Enhance Teaching and Learning. *The Clearing House: A Journal of Educational Strategies, Issues and Ideas*, *89*(6), 215–222. doi:10.1080/00098655.2016.1214473

Sargeantston, E. (2021). Why boardgames are so popular. *Mykindofmeeple*. Accessed August 28, 202. https://mykindofmeeple.com/why-are-board-games-popular

Sharp, L. A. (2012). Stealth learning: Unexpected learning opportunities through games. *Journal of Institutional Research*, *1*, 42–48. doi:10.9743/JIR.2013.6

Shut Up and Sit Down. (n.d.). *Shut Up and Sit Down*. https://www.shutupandsitdown.com/games/

Singer, E. (2013). Play and playfulness, basic features of early childhood education. *European Early Childhood Education Research Journal*, *21*(2), 172–184. doi:10.1080/1350293X.2013.789198

Statler, M., Heracleous, L., & Jacobs, C. D. (2011). Serious play as a practice of paradox. *The Journal of Applied Behavioral Science*, *47*(2), 236–256. doi:10.1177/0021886311398453

Taspinar, B., Schmidt, W., & Schuhbauer, H. (2016). Gamification in education: A board game approach to knowledge acquisition. *Procedia Computer Science*, *99*, 101–116. https://doi.org/10.1016/j.procs.2016.09.104

Toppo, G. (2015). *The game believes in you: How digital play can make our kids smarter*. Macmillan.

Tuber, K. (2007). *Catan Dice* [Board Game]. CatangmbH.

Wawro, A. (2017). Why video game devs don't get 'board' of learning from tabletop games. *Game Developer*. https://www.gamedeveloper.com/design/why-video-game-devs-don-t-get-board-of-learning-from-tabletop-games

Wohlwend, K. E. (2008). *Play as a literacy of possibilities: Expanding meanings in practices, materials, and spaces*. Academic Press.

Wohlwend, K. E. (2017). Who gets to play? Access, popular media and participatory literacies. *Early Years*, *37*(1), 62–76. doi:10.1080/09575146.2016.1219699

KEY TERMS AND DEFINITIONS

Game Mechanics: Game design mechanics refer to the mechanisms that guide game play. Common mechanisms include cards, dice, spinners, trading, commodity building.

Mashing: Mashing refers to the popular action of mash up, where a new game is created by putting together aspects of two or more other games. For example, one could play Monopoly Jenga, or Guess Who Clue.

Modding: Modding refers to modifying a game. In tabletop settings this could include changing a game mechanic, or even the win condition so that the game will fit time constraints.

Play-Based Pedagogy: Play based pedagogy refers to teaching using multimodal games, it can include educational or serious games, entertainment games, game creation and gamification.

Playful Stance: Having a playful stance is a construct for educators to take on to enhance learning. It can include flexibility, being open to new ideas, problem solving, reflecting, and engaging in physical movement and play.

Skinning: Skinning is a term that comes from the online video game genre, and it refers to changing the look and feel (which includes the game characters, artwork, background, theme and story etc.) but not the game play.

Tabletop Games: Tabletop games refer to board games, and can include cards and puzzles. tabletop games are interactive and focus on small group play.

Chapter 19
The Transformation of Literacy and Media Literacy

Hacer Dolanbay
Muş Alparslan University, Turkey

ABSTRACT

Whether we call it the age of information, the age of digitalization, or the informatics, this century is an era in which rapid technological developments are taking place and will continue without stopping. The importance of using the media consciously and appropriately is increasing by reducing the effects of the media on individuals with many positive and negative characteristics. Having media literacy skills, which is one of the basic skills of the new century, is important in learning how tool live with the media. Becoming a conscious media consumer and producer, the way to realize the reality in the media is to have media literacy skills which is one of the basic skills of the new century. This chapter is mainly aimed at studying the dynamics that makeup media literacy and media literacy skills. How the century has transformed to meet the needs of its students will be highlighted within the context of media literacy. Then, the chapter will be completed by explaining how media literacy is reflected in pedagogy with examples suitable for different courses and levels.

INTRODUCTION

Rapid developments in information communication technologies are enabling the globalization of information, while diversifying the forms and environments of people's communication, creating a new world for them that is decorated with mass media. This world, which has been separated from traditional media by its increasingly digital evolution, is a new media world. This new order, which increases the interaction of people with each other and keeps the far corners of the world informed about each other with the information it spreads, is increasingly surrounding us. Face-to-face studies, meetings began to be held online using digital tools. People create social media accounts to socialize, and meet new people. Research reports that media use is increasing rapidly to include social media, and the number of individuals dependent on vehicles is multiplying significantly.

DOI: 10.4018/978-1-7998-7271-9.ch019

Whether we call it the age of information, the age of digitalization, or the age of informatics, this century is an era in which rapid technological developments are taking place and will continue without stopping. It seems impossible to stay away from all kinds of media surrounding us and their effects. The content presented through media channels become a force that deeply affects perceptions, beliefs, attitudes and preferences (Kelner & Share, 2005). Technological developments in the economic, social and, cultural areas of personal or social life have transformed people's habits in an unprecedented way in the last century. Thus, it causes the differentiation of the knowledge and skills that should be possessed by the individual in particular (Ananiadou ve Claro, 2009). For these reasons, reading and writing are no longer enough for life. Individuals need the ability to critically interpret the powerful images of multimedia culture and express themselves in different media forms (Thoman ve Jolls, 2003).

The importance of using the media consciously and appropriately is increasing by reducing the effects of the media on individuals with many positive and negative characteristics. Having media literacy skills, which is one of the basic skills of the new century, is important in learning how tool live with the media, becoming a conscious media consumer and producer, the way to realize the reality in the media is to have a "media literacy skill" which is one of the basic skills of the new century.

Media literacy involves individuals taking a critical, questioning approach to hidden and explicit messages from different types of media and asking questions about the message by thinking about it. Messages that are analyzed using different methods are evaluated with their hidden and explicit meanings and meaning is created about the message. Media literacy supports individuals who use media not only to become consumers but also to produce and share in different environments. In this aspect, media literacy is a 21st-century technology that allows individuals to be active against written, visual, and auditory messages by removing them from passivity (Baker, 2010). In particular, production, critical thinking and creative thinking skills are media literacy skills that lay the foundation for the formation of active and participatory citizenship ((European Commission, 2009). Although different models have been developed related to media literacy, it is possible to mention three models as a basis. These are James W. Potter's cognitive media literacy model, Rick Shepherd's critical media education model, and J. It is Francis Davis' model of the theoretical origins of media education programs. Potter's cognitive media literacy model consists of the responsibility axiom, effect axiom, the interpretation axiom, the importance of shared meaning axiom, and the power and purpose axioms. Shepherd's model of media literacy is based on the fact that teachers can use a critical point of view in media education together with students. In Davis's model, the view that television does not do anything to people the opinion that people do something with television is effective (Sezer, 2009).

In particular, globalization and the widespread introduction of the Internet into circulation lead to the fact that the media are more involved in our lives due to the effect of digitalization. Due to this important effect, media literacy has been increasingly turned into a course that is placed in curricula as a separate course in more and more countries, at different grade levels in educational institutions, sometimes in other courses, sometimes as a separate course. This chapter is mainly aimed at studying the dynamics that makeup media literacy and media literacy skills. For this purpose, first of all, it will be emphasized how traditional and new media are changing and developing. What is the concept of media literacy, including social media, will be explained with the support of national and international literature. What are the differences between traditional literacy and 21 st literacies? How the century has transformed to meet the needs of its students will be highlighted within the context of media literacy. Then, the section will be completed by explaining how media literacy is reflected in pedagogy with examples suitable for different courses and levels.

The Transformation of Literacy and Media Literacy

TRADITIONAL MEDIA AND NEW MEDIA

The media encountered intensively every day and form a unique cultural industry includes many products ranging from print publications to digital resources; from books to newspapers, from television to computers, from movies to photographs, from billboards to CDs. There have been innovative developments in media since the end of the 20 century, which have changed our point of view towards the world, our awareness, and how we perceive the life. The tools in traditional print media have changed at a dizzying speed, and new computer and network-supported tools have begun to enter into our lives. Digital-based media that are allow two-way communication is called new media and are separated from traditional media in these aspects. Media used to interactively convert existing media into digital data and providing production, distribution, and sharing through computers is defined as new media (Manovich, 2001: 19).

The new media is a bidirectional structure that includes both computing, that is, computer-specific operations, and structures specific to communication tools such as communication, publishing. In this context, it's used to indicate that new media communication tools will be constantly updated and will cover future systems (Yolcu, 2020: 42). Since the 1990s, with the use of the Internet, television can watch on the same medium, newspapers, books could be read, or radio could be listened to. In addition to the rapid introduction of the Internet into all spheres of life, globalization and large-scale international companies are among the elements that accelerate the development of new media (Baudrillard, 2004: 19).

Marshall McLuhan says that the form of technological tools is important, in the words of which the famous *medium is the message*. It is the medium that determines and shapes people's relationships, actions, behavior (Güngör, 2018: 190). The medium states that with a message, the media itself can be a message. Harold Laswell emphasizes that content is just as important as the medium itself in the Theory of Influence. Technology offers people many ways to create, edit and share products using the internet and social media (Chayko, 2018: 85). Messages formatted on these paths serve their users in different formats in parallel with the differentiation of the tools used. As a matter of fact, mediums such as newspapers, televisions continue to present the content they produce without changing with the current features brought about by technological developments and especially digitalization. The main issue that distinguishes new media from traditional media is the content offered by the tools, the format of the content, and the content production process. The channels and content it uses distinguish new media from traditional ones. Achieving the goal of a message in traditional media occurs unilaterally, without allowing any interaction. However, most of the new media technologies are digital, interactive, and hyper-textual (Rozario, 2013), and they are usually digitally, can be connected to a network, has the characteristics of being neutral and interactive (Krishnaswamy, 2011).

On the other hand, unlike traditional media, almost all of the content published on social media platforms are created by users. That's why mass initiatives through social media platforms and mobile technologies such as mobile phones can be used by people of different age groups and genders without limits, as far as the application allows (Mihailidis, 2011).Digitizing technology is causing a rapid spread of the event that occurs anywhere in the world. In this form, the time and location difference disappears. Relationships have been replaced by virtual relationships, and with the transformation of the world into a global village, the cultures have become interacting. Especially in communication environments, the inclusion of visual elements such as photos and videos next to written texts and their convenient sharing has changed the concept of literacy in the classical sense. So much so that literacy, as before, does not cover only listening, speaking, writing, and reading. Now all these skills have become embedded in symbolic systems, such as music and sound, moving and images (Hobbs, 2010: 17). The text is not just text, and the visual does not just point to the visual. Although it retains its traditional meaning, this structure is a website, video, Photoshop, blog. Wikis or Web 2.0 tools can be in environments such as social media platforms such as Facebook, Twitter (Khadka, 2014: 27).

THE TRANSFORMATION OF TRADITIONAL LITERACY AND THE MEDIA LITERACY

This century is a period during which information is produced and consumed very quickly, and a large number and variety of information sources open their doors to the fullest. By its general definition, literacy is the ability to read and write various texts that carry different messages (Cameron, 2008: 124). Along with technological developments, the concept of literacy has changed by new literacies. Literacy is the ability to effectively use communicative symbols that are meaningful for society (Kellner, 2001).

Before the 21st century, being able to read and write was perceived only as knowing how to read and write something. After this century, there was a revolutionary change in the meaning of literacy, and new ones were added to the meanings it covers when defining literacy. These new meanings relate to how to rearrange, make sense and create the acquired information (Real, 2008). Various theories have been developed for the deciphering and rearrangement of the acquired by Shannon-Weaver Transition Theory, Schramm model, Game theory and Expectation-Value theory are among them (Black, Bryant ve Thompson, 1997). In this context, the concept of text has moved away from its traditional meaning and has turned into different media such as the Internet, television (TV), and film (Considine, Horton & Moorman, 2009: 471). Visual images that require the correct interpretation of not only written but also visual and digital messages have entered our lives. For this reason, literacies have changed, and the act of reading has ceased to be just messages created by letters. It has been expanded metaphorically in the sense of reading all kinds of messages in print, visual and oral, that is, "reading the world (Freire & Macedo, 1987). The definition of literacy has also expanded to improve electronic, digital, and visual expressions. In particular, after the entry of Web 2.0 to the user service, bidirectional and simultaneous information sharing has begun. Thus, computer literacy, internet literacy, network literacy, technology literacy, digital literacy, media literacy, social literacy, and new literacies, such as cyber literacy has emerged (Livingstone, 2003; Gentry & McAdams, 2013).

In the century we live in, the progress of technology is at a breakneck pace, and this sudden change in literacy obliges us to have many different skills than before. It's important that individuals who come into contact with different mediums in different formats every day, adapt to this new world. The skill required to correctly detect, identify, analyze and evaluate messages from all types of media, written, auditory, visual, is the media literacy skill.

The Internet is no longer as expensive as it used to be. This situation allows individuals to effortlessly share their own generated content with mobile applications. Especially when social media supports participatory citizenship with this feature, unfortunately, it can lead to the problem of internet or technology addiction (RobbGrieco & Hobbs, 2013: 4). As students connect to communication tools, they break away from social life and increasingly become lonely. In addition to print publications, especially Internet resources and the increase of other digital resources, individuals are almost bombarded with information. Incomplete, biased, or incorrect messages received from the source can directly affect the lives of individuals. The problem of accessing the right information makes the ability to analyze, evaluate and reproduce information through the filter of critical thinking a necessity. The rapid distribution

The Transformation of Literacy and Media Literacy

of information, on the other hand, leads to rapid consumption. Due to commercial concerns, the content offered by the media to individuals has started to carry more and more entertainment elements for the sake of getting a rating. The main task of the media is to provide information and news to the public. In place of this function, the media began to take on the main task of producing the entertainment industry. For this reason, the main agendas that concern people can ignore when creating artificial agendas. Advertising, which is a fairly powerful source of persuasion, promotion, and propaganda ((Laughey, 2010: 42) it can affect the consumer behavior of individuals and push them to consumerism. Due to its cultural effects, violence, and hate speech that it sometimes creates, the correct reading and interpretation of the media are becoming increasingly important (Dolanbay, 2018). For all these reasons, and for more, media literacy skills and training are very important.

BASIC APPROACHES IN MEDIA LITERACY

In media literacy education, the attitude of educators towards the media is usually divided into three parts. The first is the anti-media approach, which aims to protect the consumer against media messages. This approach, which considers the media to be the devil, has no effect today. The second is the "about the media" approach, which aims to explain and teach the media and focuses on media systems, tools, messages (Fedorov, 2003: 10). But telling only about what the media is insufficient for media literacy. The third approach advocates that media education can be done by using media power such as media technologies and creating media products (Fedorov, 2003: 6). Although this is the most appropriate attitude to the understanding of media literacy, it is difficult to have a critical attitude to the media when you are with the media. Apart from these three attitudes towards media literacy education, there are various approaches. Critical thinking, critical democratic approach, cultural approaches, semiotic approach, aesthetic and popular arts approach, ideological approach, use, and satisfaction approaches widely used. Less commonly used are vaccination, protectionist, hypodermic needle theory, social defense approaches (Bilici, 2010: 48).

In the 1950s and '60s, the vaccination approach was seen as a tabula rasa. On this blank sheet, that is, the media, the audience would write powerful messages. In this approach, which is also referred to by names Hypodermic needle theory and Magic bullet, the media is seen as a potential danger. The media is a microbe that tries to disrupt the patient's system, and therefore people should be vaccinated against this microbe. This approach was developed to protect children against the excesses of the media and to ensure the continuation of cultural values, to distinguish between good and bad media (Thoman, 1990: 2).When used in education, some media materials are brought to the classroom to vaccinate make students aware of the possible harmful effects of the media. Thus, they are informed about the harmful aspects of the media. The protectionist approach (mainstream media literacy) emphasizes that children should be protected to prevent harm from the media. According to the approach, for children to be protected, the media content they will watch should be selected by adults. According to this approach, if the media is a cultural disease, media education should be designed to ensure protection against it (Masterman, 1993:6).

The empowerment approach; In the 1960s and 70s, the view that students are active and not passive was brought to the fore. According to this approach, which can be considered as the opposite of the protectionist approach, students should be empowered in the face of the media. The student who learns the preparation processes of media messages, why and how they are prepared will gain strength against the media. Thanks to this, students increase their own strength, participate in social networks and protect themselves from online threats by following ethical rules. In the 1970s and 80s, media literacy began to be recognized in the form of critical thinking as a result of civic responsibility, the need for citizenship, and democratic rights (Hobbs & Jensen, 2009: 3). According to the approach, the purpose of media literacy is to create critical awareness. The student knows that the information in the media messages presented can be criticized (Bilici, 2010: 53). The approach defined by such concepts as critical reading, critical research, and critical pedagogy emphasizes critical analysis. The information in the message given in the critical analysis should be compared by investigating it from other sources. Apart from these approaches, mass society theory, cultural studies theory, impact approach, and analysis approach can be mentioned for media literacy.

WHAT IS MEDIA LITERACY? WHAT ARE ITS GENERAL GOALS?

Definitions of media literacy vary according to content levels such as knowledge, skills, attitude, according to the context of whether it is educational, commercial, and social, and according to the layout provider and developer actors. Some experts describe media literacy as "critical analysis" (Wood, 2009). In the most basic sense, media literacy is active questioning and critical thinking, as well as critical thinking about the messages created (Hobbs & Jensen,2009). In 1992, however, held at the National Leadership Conference on media literacy in the United States defined and accepted according to extensive definition in the literature, media literacy; access to the media in its various forms of analysis (analyzing how the message occurs), evaluation (evaluation according to the democratic principles of overt and covert messages) and product (using different types of media materials is the skill of creating new media (Considine, Horton & Moorman, 2009; Kellner & Share, 2005; Thoman & Jolls, 2003). The concept means that individuals can access all kinds of messages, evaluate and share them after analyzing them. In short, media literacy is a skill that provides the correct understanding and interpretation of all kinds of messages encountered. In this context, the concept supports the cultural and social participation of individuals. Hence enables them to become participating citizens.

Media literacy education is based on "learning through research "and Freire's"critical pedagogy"(Auderfheide, 1992: 10; Scheibe, 2009: 68). The theorists of the Frankfurt School, one of the great supporters of critical pedagogy, have defined media as a cultural industry by studying cultural products that turn into media messages within the concept of mass culture. According to Adorno, cultural industry refers to the manipulation of the masses through the transformation of cultural diversity in society into a single popular culture. Media literacy provides a perspective that sees the differences between the actual world and the fictional world (Potter, 2011: 9). There are five key questions that an individual who encounters any media message, whether written, auditory or visual, should ask. 1. Who/who created this message? *All media posts are created.* 2. What creative techniques are used to interest me? *Media messages are created according to their own rules, using creative language.* 3. How can other people understand this message differently from what I understand? *Different people can understand the same message differently.* 4. What values, lifestyles, and perspectives are reflected in this message, and which ones are omitted? *The media has its unique point of view and values.* 5. Why was this message sent? *Most of the media posts create to get profit and power* (Thoman & Jolls, 2008: 23).

These questions are aimed at individuals in a general sense and students in an essential sense to get in the habit of asking questions to the media when they encounter media messages. Teachers should know these basic questions that provide students with learning opportunities to ask critical questions to

The Transformation of Literacy and Media Literacy

the media throughout their lives connect with classroom activities (Share & Thoman, 2007: 13). When the students encounter a written, auditory, visual, or digital media message should ask these questions. Students who have asked these questions will have received the answers by asking critical questions to the media. Students investigate and question what purpose, which audiences are targeted, who/who is creating the incoming message. To attend to the message, the media interprets the components that make up the format of the message, such as music, sound, words, light, lighting, images. The students solve symbols and images by understanding the methods used to attract their attention. They understand that different people can interpret the same message differently because their characteristics, such as life experience, age, and socio-cultural values, are different. They learn that all media messages give an idea. Who produce them are shaped by value, point of view, and so on, and that the purpose of most messages is to provide commercial profit to the media (Kellner & Share, 2005: 374-377; Dolanbay, 2018).

The purpose of media literacy education is to explain some unknown features of the media, to encourage students to independently criticize the role of the media in society, and to make them realize the inevitable dangers of manipulation and bias through the media. Media literacy is the ability to interpret what we see and hear. In this way, it helps students and teachers to develop critical autonomy (Steinbrick & Cook, 2003: 285). The media literate person is expected to interpretivism after analyzing the message he encounters, investigating, and evaluating. So, what are the characteristics of a media literate individual? The features of a media literate person can be listed with the following items (Hobbs, 1998: 21):

- Ability to use the media consciously and effectively,
- Decertifying the accuracy of information from various information sources using technology,
- Who is aware that media messages are produced in social, political, moral, economic contexts,
- Who knows that the media has its own unique, creative language,
- People who have a critical point of view towards the media.
- Why is there a need for media literacy based on research and inquiry? What are the reasons for media literacy?

WHAT ARE THE REASONS FOR MEDIA LITERACY EDUCATION, OR WHY DO WE NEED A MEDIA LITERACY EDUCATION?

Nowadays, new communication technologies have caused social transformation and changed the basic structure of society. The new media has shifted the social structure to a new level by changing the economic, moral, and political order as well as the social structure. It's a question of transferring popular culture products to wide audiences with the content created by the media. This artificial commercial culture can even change the habits of daily life. Media literacy is interested in especially the non-need consumption desire that the media creates on the masses using ads and the fact that media content carries more and more entertainment elements. Even today's news programs have sections devoted to entertaining videos. Many mass media, especially television, are seen as a means of entertainment. Postman emphasizes that the problem is not that television offers entertaining content, but that all themes are presented as entertainment (Postman, 2004: 101).

People use the media for different purposes such as education, entertainment, information, socializing, spending time playing games. Internet browsers that we use in the media are an indispensable element for social life, make an impression that they dominate everything. Media contents effect of directing and changing the emotions, behaviors, habits, and attitudes of individuals towards an object. The media, which sharply affects public opinion, plays an active role in the processes of representing events by creating the truth rather than reflecting or transmitting it as it is (Masterman, 2005: 20).

Individuals can be exposed to millions of messages from different mediums. Media that addresses needs such as informing people, informing them about the order, social communication; performs all this at minimal cost with the help of developing technologies. However, the media, which has the power to give, has unofficial sovereignty over individuals. So, it can create public opinion by influencing the masses Simons, Meeus ve T'Sas, 2017: 99). The use of popular language, which is especially influential on the younger generation, the creation of craving for other cultures, and the uncared behavior of media companies that do not take any responsibility in return are media-related problems that for society today (Paluck & Green, 2009: 637). It should be discussed to what extent the media assumes the responsibility for bringing culture and values to the younger generations. Especially children and young people who are convinced through advertising can be exposed to a large number of messages from the media. The media makes the depiction of reality in the virtual world, which is created for children who are moving away from creating their own experiences. However, children who have taken the media literacy course will become not only passive consumers of the media but also active producers. On the other hand, the media no longer only shapes the lives of individuals. The media is our culture anymore (Thoman & Jolls, 2004:18).

The students who create soap operas, movies, newspapers, and TV programs, must be informed well about how their goals within the period of producing these publications are going to evolve that must be explained to the students in this new culture, New media has facilitated the flow of information with the introduction of the Internet and has introduced various applications and especially social media into our lives that its users cannot give up.Facebook, WeChat, Whatsapp, Instagram, Youtube, Messenger, WeChat, and Twitter are social media platforms that lock individuals of all ages on the screen and attract attention with their large number of users. According to the 2021 data published on the website of We Are Social, an organization that attracts attention with its research conducted in various countries around the world, the number of social media users worldwide has reached 4.66 billion. In other words, one out of every two people worldwide is a social media user (We Are Social, 2021). Among the problems that media literacy is trying to solve is the trouble of long-term media consumption of children and young people and how to address the addiction that arises after it.

As it can be seen, the media surrounds our lives. It affects the individual and society in social, economic, moral, psychological, and political terms. That is why the importance of consciously controlling it has increased, rather than running away from the media. For this reason, individuals of all ages should give media literacy skills. Media literacy allows people to make their own choices and evaluate the media at will. The media offers us a variety of content, and we choose the one that best meets our needs, in other words, the one that best suits our purposes (Potter, 2004: 57). The media that determine our order of the day can deliver the message it wants to its target audience secretly (implicitly) or openly with its propaganda and persuasion techniques. It is media that can change people's perceptions of a topic, event, or situation. In this century, when it is impossible to avoid the media, to integrate new skills into life and adapt to the digitizing world, an individual at any age should have media literacy skills (Krumsvik, 2008; Hobbs, 2010: 15).

The ability of media literacy plays an active role in the acquisition of skills such as digital literacy by the students of this century. Students benefit from e-books, e-school, virtual libraries, virtual museums in their classrooms. Free books, online e-books, and digital books can be accessed information effort-

The Transformation of Literacy and Media Literacy

lessly. With the COVID pandemic, students have moved away from classes and started to participate in virtual environments. Students who have started to use technology more and more have used various learning teaching management systems and software to maintain distance learning. Virtual classes have been created using this software. Simultaneous (synchronous) classes can be held in these virtual classrooms. Software systems such as Advancity, Canvas, Moddle, Adobe Connect, Perculus, Balckboard, Google products, and Microsoft products are used. Various software is used to create simultaneous virtual classes in these learning teaching systems. Google Microsoft software systems Classroom and Meet, and Microsoft creates live lessons using Teams software. Similarly, Zoom, Big Blue Button is used. Students can prepare PowerPoint presentation files, course videos, and questionnaires within the distance learning system. Assignments can also be shared with teachers using these tools as exams are conducted (Durak, Çankaya ve İzmirli, 2020: 801).

Along with digitalization, education systems have also changed from traditional to digital. Digital games have started to be used especially to provide classroom motivation for students at an early age. Gamification is a technique to use game-based mechanics, aesthetics, and game thinking to engage people, motivate action, promote learning, and solve problems (Kapp, 2012). In addition these in cases where it is not possible to visit, virtual trip-like educational technologies are used. A media literate individual has all these systems and software with the ability to have access and they have the ability to use different resources when accessing information. Even accessible from mobile phones, 3D spaces, 3D printers, and Google Maps – Google Earth applications are other elements that lead students from traditional literacy to digital literacy. Like Google Drive, Yandex Disk, Dropbox, Evernote, Onenote, iCloud the use of cloud systems also brings students closer to digital culture. It is one of the innovations brought about by digitalization that students shoot videos, remix an existing video, and publish it in appropriate environments. Also, an individual's ability to read, write, do problem-solve, think critically, and use the information and communications technologies is essential to education and workforce preparation, as well as civic participation (Spires, 2012: 6). These abilities support the civic participation and digital citizenship of today's students.

HOW IS MEDIA LITERACY EDUCATION PROVIDED?

At the heart of media literacy education is to ask critical questions to the media. In addition to the visible meaning of media messages, there are also invisible, hidden (implicit) meanings. An individual who is media literate is expected to be in an interpretive structure after analyzing the message she/he encounters, investigating, and evaluating As media-consuming individuals, it is a skill that allows us to become more active individuals, manage the data flow we encounter every day, and make informed decisions about the importance of the message we encounter (Gilmor, 2008: 4).

Media literacy skills have been remarkable for educators, students, and policymakers in recent years.. However, there are still some difficulties, especially in the training of the skill. The fact that not everyone has access to the internet and technology on equal terms is one of the problems. At what age should children and young people be in digital environments in terms of their cognitive and moral development in the digital world, it is a problem for them to interact with media tools from an early age. In particular, their active use of social networks leads to the conclusion that they should combat problems such as online ethics, the threat of personal security, the privacy of private life, cyberbullying, etc. (Graber, 2012:85). Against all this, it should be planned at what grade levels, which content, and how to conduct a media education. Educators should teach digital media tools to improve students' media proficiency. For them to understand technology, they should use Socratic interrogations and encourage critical thinking. Similarly, especially in the first grades, the game design supports participation and critical thinking and improves digital and media literacy skills (Hobbs, 2010: 27). Popular social network games such as FarmVille, CityVille, and Gardens of Time allow players of different demographics to design games and create successful systems. In addition to traditional games, these digital games are also turning into new applications like sports, puzzles, and competitions, increasing social sharing between players.

The training of this skill, which ensures adaptation to life, is extremely significant. Interestingly, research suggests that while they are frequent users of technology tools, students often their critical thinking skills are often weak (Oblinger & Oblinger, 2005). For this reason, students should inform about the political, commercial, social, psychological, and moral effects of the media. The efforts of the media industries to stimulate the masses to buy should explain to the students with the best examples. The representations, use of language, emphasis, and intonations in the news, which are shaped according to the wishes of media bosses and political decision-makers, can create doubts about whether the news is real. It's the media literacy skill that allows you to decipher the difference between real and fake news. Because journalists and media producers manipulate the news and interpret events from their point of view. Advertising companies, on the other hand, try to convince the masses that the product or service they want to sell is needed (Potter, 2011:10). However, a media literate person will be able to grasp these facts by gaining awareness.

In this context, teachers should include five key questions in their lessons to teach students to ask critical questions about the media. Watching some TV shows or movies together in the classroom, starting a discussion about the watched program can speed up the process of mental questioning in students. Current news that will be brought to the classroom will improve the media literacy skills of students, as well as contribute to citizenship education issues such as connecting freedom of expression and civil decencies. Commenting on media texts/images, applying the basic principles of criticism also reveal student opinions (Westbrook, 2011:158). According to Burn and Durran who are media education experts (2007), Media Literacy has the characteristics of culturally, criticality, and creativity. The acquisition of these characteristics is directly proportional to the quality of education provided to individuals. According to the European Charter for Media Literacy (The European Charter for Media Literacy), there are seven basic competencies for media literacy skills (Bachmair & Bazalgette, 2007):

1. Using the media effectively,
2. Conscious access to media content,
3. Understanding the creation of media content,
4. Analysis of media techniques and messages,
5. Using the media for communication,
6. Avoiding harmful media content,
7. Using the media for democratic rights and civil purposes,

Countries that want to integrate this into their education systems have understood the importance of media literacy and added it to their education systems. Acquire these competencies have understood the importance of media literacy and added it to their education systems. However, the history of the development of media literacy education has taken a different course in each country. It's possible to start this process from the 1920s when the first films launched in the UK and France in the film industry.

The Transformation of Literacy and Media Literacy

Media literacy has developed primarily in countries such as the United Kingdom, the United States, Australia and Canada. After that, it developed in other countries like Russia, the Netherlands, and Brazil. The concept of media literacy education and curriculum started in the 1970s an emphasis on protecting children from the harmful effects of the media (Buckingham, 2013:1). Later, an understanding focused on critical thinking was switched to media literacy. This understanding was called the empowering or empowering understanding. In the 1980s, UNESCO drew attention to media literacy and education with the following sentences: *"Rather than condemn or endorse the undoubted power of the media, we need to accept their significant impact and penetration throughout the world as an established fact, and also appreciate their importance as an element of culture in today's world."* (UNESCO, 1990).

Media literacy integrates into education in two ways. In some countries, it's put directly into the curriculum or interspersed with related courses such as social studies, language, citizenship, and art. For example, the media literacy course in Turkey was prepared according to the constructivist approach. Accordingly, students will create their information through the information they observe in their close and distant surroundings as the discoverer of information. The course was accepted in 2006. It conducted selectively, separately held since the 2018-2019 academic year. It's taught once a week in the classrooms for two hours (MoNE, 2018).

In the classes, media and technology are used for both purposes by many teachers. .as a means to ensure and support effective teaching in classrooms and as an issue and subject area in itself. News, competition programs, cartoons, and games are topics that can be used to explain media literacy in classrooms. Auxiliary sites can be used to provide media literacy education. The sites can provide information about the concept of media literacy as well as information about the activities & projects that have been and can be carried out. Topics such as the distinction between false and true news, cyberbullying, technology or media addiction, safe internet use can be explained. Links that will be useful for media literacy can be included. For instance medialit.org, CML has created a *mediaLit* Kit. This series contains resources that will be useful for students, educators, and families. Especially evidence-based curricula framework is very helpful for students and others (medialit.org, 2021).

The Media Literacy Resource Guide, published by the Ontario Ministry of Education of Canada, is an important resource book that has been translated into many languages. The National Film Board of Canada has provided content that complements the curriculum of this guide (Sezen, 2011: 146). UNESCO has been supported media literacy for many years with publications and funds such as Youth Media Education (unesco.org). CLEMI (Centre de Liasion de l'Enseignement et des Moyen d'Information), an organization that supports the planning and promotion of media education in schools in France, and Canada's Centre for Digital and Media Literacy continues to support media literacy. OFCOM (Communications Office), located in the United Kingdom, is the National Association for media literacy education (NAMLE), which aims to improve the implementation of media literacy education in the United States and conducts work media literacy. The purpose of the activities carried out in all these organizations is to create a map of media literacy education and try to create policies for the development of media literacy.

Teacher training, doing different levels of appropriate teaching programs, the establishment of partnerships that allows you to collaborate with schools and other public institutions are among the activities that take. Programs, magazines, newspapers, advertisements in the courses; evaluating media representations by examining media biases; analyzing the mass communication industries and media processes that shape the media economy (Hobbs, 1994). The use of Facebook and similar social networks in education, the use of technology, trying to stay out of the classroom more than the length of the school day can also provide media literacy training (Griffith, 2014). Students use various tools and social media, including Facebook, Twitter, video games, instant messaging, wikis, and blogs, to discuss problems, spread their ideas and entertain themselves. However, classes rarely use these resources for teaching. It is difficult to say that students use them in a way that encourages higher-level think (Spires, 2012: 6). For this reason, it is possible to use these resources as aids that facilitate teaching, especially in undergraduate courses of university students.

While conducting media literacy training, activities should promote to the media literacy competencies and skills. Especially in undergraduate courses, films or short films and camera shots and angles can teach. Students can also learn scriptwriting, digital story writing, scanning, and using web resources. Media literacy awareness can be gained by conducting skills such as Access, Analysis, Evaluation, Production, Sharing, Activism/ Act (Aufderheide,1993; Silverblatt and all, 2014). According to Hobbs (2010), access is finding the appropriate media tools and using them. For this skill, mediums such as mobile phones, computers, and tablets can be used. The students must be able to use these tools, and the knowledge of technology should also have. An individual who is trying to find the right and reliable sources using the appropriate strategies should make choices at this stage. To get the true information, important to determine which source is reliable. For example, it is difficult for students who cannot distinguish between fake websites and sites that provide real information to access a reliable source. The use of multiple resources is significant for the ability to access.

Media analysis, on the other hand, improves the students ' critical thinking skills. It includes all the competencies of Bloom's taxonomy, which we'll rank as information, comprehension, application, analysis, evaluation, synthesis. In this aspect, it forms an important element of media literacy and its education (Share &Thoman, 2007: 24). When analyzing a media message, the message is first asked "what did you notice?" What is being analyzed should be a movie scene, a commercial film much deeper than the meaning in a novel. For example; "What does the camera angle tell us about the person seen on the screen? Would showing injured people in accident news be a deterrent or an annoyance for accidents? Does the music in the movie I watched give the appropriate mood to the topic being watched?" similar questions will allow you to get meaningful answers about the message. Representations such as media industries, media types and related problems, the process of production and consumption of media technologies, media languages, techniques, and codes used in the media, media viewers, text, and reality in the media can be analyzed (Livingstone, 2003: 10). After a message has been analyzed by asking various questions, it should evaluate according to criteria such as ethics, children's rights, human rights, publication principles in the context in which the message is produced, and interpretation (MoNE, 2018). For example, actions such as determining the conformity of characters in a watched movie with traditions, making a decision about the accuracy of news published on social media, exposing persuasion techniques used in advertising, or expressing the effects of social media applications on young people will improve the ability to evaluate.

On the other hand, today it is important to be a good media producer rather than a media consumer, that is, to create original media messages (Considine, Horton & Moorman, 2009: 75). In the generated texts, each medium or information source generates meanings using unique codes and techniques. It is important to understand how the environment or form formats the content, as well as to be able to analyze the texts (Wilson, 2012: 17). For example, students can prepare a PowerPoint presentation for any course or create a poster about mobile phone addiction. All these actions develop the ability to think creatively and can help students express themselves. Media literacy emphasizes being active. The ability to act refers to the talent of individuals to react appropriately in the face of situations that they like or are uncomfortable about the media they follow and their content. According to the skills of media activism, media literacy educators should try to spread democratic processes in a real sense by staying away from political and ideological understanding. For example, responses to issues such as drug and substance abuse, consumption frenzy, violence, and cyberbullying are cover by activism.

While providing qualified media education, the participation of young people in media-related activities should be increased. Because the fact that media literacy is a course in which only theoretical information is conveyed through narration will not create the desired awareness on individuals. Instead of memorizing the relationship between subjects and concepts, students should be provided with correct examples for practice.

Applied, experimental, democratic, and process-oriented media literacy education emphasizes critical thinking. However, its basis is "research-based learning" (Auderfheide, 1992: 10). Therefore, to improve media literacy in classrooms, it is important to ask critical questions to the media and analyze the message. The students learn to film analyze that film by utilizing specific vocabulary, discussing camera angles, lighting, music, and composition. Media literacy education, which includes understanding the hidden meanings behind media messages, has been part of school curricula in countries such as Canada, Australia, and New Zealand for many years (Domingo & Mashiko, 2013: 13).

To improve media literacy in their classrooms, teachers should first teach the media to ask critical questions. Documentaries and TV Shows for students are also convenient resources for analyzing. Below are two examples of activities that can use directly in a media literacy course. Also in social studies, health information, language programs that media literacy can take part in:

Table 1.

Activity 1	
Application: Students will look at a news story taken from a national newspaper. The following questions will ask to this news	• Who was this message written to reach? Who constitutes the target audience? • What is the purpose of the message? • Does the visuals, language, message in the news try to impress me, or does it just want to inform me? • What did you find yourself in the news? • Have you caught hints about prejudices and stereotypes? Do you think it's neutral? • Would it have the same effect if you had seen the same news on TV or social media?
Activity 2:	
Application: Students are given visuals. Students ask the following questions:	• Is the visual taken from an animated movie? • How does media affect the purchase? • Do you think that the transformation of animation into a toy and a game did consciously?

continues on following page

Globalization and technological innovations have brought digitalization to the classrooms. During the last two years of the pandemic, teachers have discovered how to conduct classroom learning online in the most successful way. The education of media literacy, the ability to adapt to life, is very significant. To develop skills, the role played by media organizations and the media industries should be explained.

Table 1. Continued

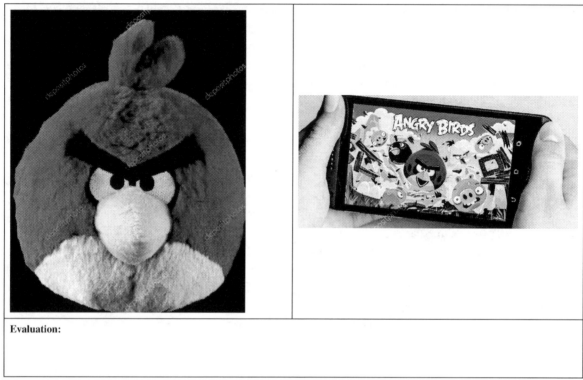

Evaluation:	

The visual 1: https://tr.depositphotos.com/stock-photos/angry-birds.html?filter=all

RESULT

As a result, literacies in the developing world have also experienced a transformation by shifting towards digital. More and more visual elements have entered our lives, literacy has abandoned its traditional form. Nowadays, being literate is defined not as being able to read and write, but as being able to rearrange and interpret the information we have acquired through the media it is being evaluated (Real, 2008). Media literacy, which can state as an umbrella concept, reveals to us the importance of reading the media correctly. Thanks to this skill, they will learn how advertising encourages people to buy, the role of propaganda in changing the fate of countries, as well as the ability to read safe news and access reliable sites. Media, which is the basis of media literacy, can facilitate game learning by providing new and powerful environments with social network games, digital games, and alternative reality games. The media literacy skill, which requires understanding the implicit meanings of messages additional their explicit meanings, is a skill that every living person should have. There are many ways to improve media literacy to be given to the university from preschool to university. Educational programs should prepare from kindergarten to university level. In order to achieve the goal of interrogative education, broad-based, committed, and realistic civilian support is needed. In-service training programs for teachers, summer semester courses should plan. Not only teachers and students, but also parents should provide with media training.

REFERENCES

Ananiadou, K., & Claro, M. (2009). 21st century skills and competences for new millennium learners in OECD countries. *OECD Education Working Papers, 4*.

Aufderheide, P. (1993). *Media literacy: A report of the national leadership conference on media literacy*. Aspen Institute.

Bachmair, B., & Bazalgette, C. (2007). The European Charter for media literacy: Meaning and potential. *Research in Comparative and İnternational Education, 2*(1), 80-87.

Milli Eğitim Bakanlığı. (2018). *Medya Okuryazarlığı Dersi Öğretim Programı (Ortaokul ve İmam Hatip Ortaokulu 7 veya 8. Sınıflar)*. Temel Eğitim Genel Müdürlüğü.

Baker, F. (2010). Media literacy: 21 st century literacy skills. In H. H. Jacobs (Ed.), Curriculum 21 essential education for a changing world (pp. 133–152). Academic Press.

Baudrillard, J. (2004). Full Screen. İstanbul: Yapı Kredi Yayınları.

Bilici, İ. E. (2011). *Türkiye'de ortaöğretimde medya okuryazarlığı dersi için bir model önerisi*. Erciyes Üniversitesi. Doktora Tezi.

Black, J., Bryant, J., & Thompson, S. (1997). *Introduction to Media Communication* (5th ed.). Mc Grw Hill Company.

Buckingham, D. (2013). Challenging concepts: Learning in the media classroom. In Current Perspectives on Media Education (pp. 1-14). London: Routledge.

Burn, A., & Durran, J. (2007). *Media Literacy in Schools: Practice, Production and Progression*. Paul Chapman Publishing.

Chayko, M. (2018). Süper Bağ(lantı)lı. Çev. Berkan Bayındır, Deniz Yengin ve Tamer Bayrak. İstanbul: Der Kitabevi.

Comeron, L. (2008). *Teaching Languages to Young Learners* (10th ed.). Cambridge Universty Press.

Considine, D., Horton, J., & Moorman, G. (2009). Teaching And Reaching The Millenial Generation Through Media Literacy. *Journal of Adolescent and Adult Literacy, 52*(6), 471-481.

Dolanbay, H. (2018). *Sosyal Bilgiler Öğretmen Adaylarına Yönelik Medya Okuryazarlığı Eğitimi Modeli*. Doktora Tezi. Marmara Üniversitesi.

Dolanbay, H. (2018). Günümüz dünya sorunları bağlamında medya ve etkileri. In Günümüz Dünya Sorunları. Pegem akademi.

Domingo, H., & Mashiko, N. (2013). Media literacy education (MLE) in the classroom: A descriptive case study of one exemplary Japanese teacher's mle practices, attitude and perception. Gifu University Curriculum Development Research, 30(1), 13-29.

Durak, G., Çankaya, S., & İzmirli, S. (2020). Examining the Turkish universities' distance education systems during the COVID-19 pandemic. *Necatibey Eğitim Fakültesi Elektronik Fen ve Matematik Eğitimi Dergisi.*, *14*(1), 787–809. doi:10.17522/balikesirnef.743080

European Commission (EC) & Gabinete de Comunicacion. (2009). *Study on the current trends and approaches to media literacy in Europe*. Authors.

Fedorov, A. (2003). Media Education and Media Literacy: Experts' Opinions. A Media Education Curriculum for Teachers in the Mediterranean, UNESCO.

Freire, P., & Macedo, D. (1987). *Literacy: Reading the Word and the World*. Bergin Garvey.

Gentry, J., & McAdams, L. (2013). Digital Story Expressions: Blending Best Practices in Literacy and Technology with Middle School Students. In *Proceedings of Society for Information Technology and Teacher Education International Conference* (pp.4253-4257). Chesepake, VA: AACE. http://www.editlib.org/p/48794

Graber, D., & Mendoza, K. (2012). New Media Literacy Education: A Developmental Approach The national association for media literacy education. *The Journal of Media Literacy Education*, *4*(1), 82–92.

Griffith, J. (2014). *Teaching Literacy in the Digital Age: İnspiration For All Levels And Literacies* (M. Gura, Ed.). İnternational Society for Technology in Education.

Güngör, N. (2018). İletişim Kuram ve Yaklaşımlar. Ankara: Siyasal Kitabevi.

Hobbs, R. (1994, Winter). Teaching Media Literacy—Are you hip to this? *Media Studies Journal*, 135-145.

Hobbs, R. (2010). *Digital and Media Literacy: A Plan of Action*. The Aspen Institute.

Hobbs, R. & Jensen, A. (2009). The past, present and future of media literacy education. *Journal of Media Literacy Education*, *1*, 1-11.

Kapp, K. M. (2012). *The gamification of learning and instruction: game-based methods and strategies for training and education*. John Wiley & Sons.

Kellner, D. (2001). New Technologies/New Literacies: Reconstructing Education for the new millennium. *International Journal of Technology and Design Education*, *11*, 67–81.

Kellner, D., & Share, J. (2005). Toward critical media literacy: Core concepts, debates, organizations, and policy. *Discourse (Abingdon)*, *26*(3), 369–386.

Khadka, S. (2014). *New Media Multiliteracies, and the globalized classroom*. Syracuse University. Dissertations. https://surface.syr.edu/cgi/viewcontent.cgi?article=1055&context=etd

Krishnaswamy. (2011). *New media vs traditional media*. Retrieved in Sept 2021, from https://www.scribd.com/document/397697219/New-Media-vs-Traditional-Media

Laughey, D. (2010). Medya calışmaları, teoriler ve yaklaşımlar. İstanbul: Kalkedon.

Livingstone, S. (2003). The Changing Natüre and Uses of Media Literacy. *European-mediaculture.org*, (4), 1-37.

Manovich, L. (2001). *The Language of New Media*. Massachusetts Institute of Technology.

Masterman, L. (1993). The Media Education Revolution. *Canadian Journal of Educational Communication*, 22(1), 5–14.

Masterman, L. (2005). *Teaching the Media*. Taylor and Francis.

Mentor Gilmor, D. (2008). *Principles for a new media literacy*. Berkman Center for Internet & Society at Harvard University.

Mihailidis, P. (2011). New Civic Voices & Emerging Media Literacy Landscape. *The Journal of Media Literacy Education*, 3(1), 4–5.

Oblinger, D. G., & Oblinger, J. L. (Eds.). (2005). Educating the net generation. Boulder, CO: Educause.

Paluck, E. L., & Green, D. P. (2009). Deference, Dissent, and Dispute Resolution: An Experimental Intervention Using Mass Media to Change Norms and Behavior in Rwanda. *The American Political Science Review*, 103(4), 622-644.

Postman, N. (2004). Televizyon Öldüren Eğlence. İstanbul: Ayrıntı.

Potter, W. J. (2004). *Theory of Media Literacy A Cognitive Approach*. Sage Publications.

Potter, W. J. (2011). Media Literacy (5th ed.). Sage Publication.

Real, Y. M. (2008). *An assessment of the relationship between creativity and information and media literacy skills of community college students for a selected major* (PhD Thesis). Pepperdine University Graduate School of Education and Psychology.

Rozario, R. B. (2013). New Media and the Traditional Media Platforms: Introspection on the Differences in Technical and Ideological Factors and Audience-integration Patterns between New Media and Traditional Media. *The Arab Journal of the Social Sciences*, 12(3), 43–61.

Sezen, D. (2011). *Katılımcı Kültürün Oluşumunda Yeni Medya Okuryazarlığı: ABD ve Türkiye Örnekleri* (PhD thesis). İstanbul Üniversitesi Sosyal Bilimler Enstitüsü.

Share, J., & Thoman, E. (2007). Teaching Democracy a media literacy approach: A media literacy educators' Guide for dilemma decisions. National Center for the Preservation Democracy.

Silverblatt, A. (Ed.). (2014). The Praeger Handbook of Media Literacy. Praeger.

Simons, M., & Meeus, W., & Sas, J. T. (2017). Measuring media literacy for media education: Development of a questionnaire for teachers competencies. *The Journal of Media Literacy Education*, 9(1), 99–115.

Spires, H. A. (2012). Digital literacies and learning: Designing a path forward. NC State University.

Steinbrick, J. E., & Cook, J. W. (2003). Media literacy skills and the "war on terrorism". *The Clearing House*, 76(6), 284-288. https://www.jstor.org/stable/30189852

Thoman, E. (1990, July). New Directions in Media Education. In *An International Conference at the University of Toulouse*. BFI, CLEMI and UNESCO.

UNESCO. (1990). http://www.unesco.org/new/fileadmin/MULTIMEDIA/HQ/CI/CI/pdf/youth_media_education.pdf

We are Social. (2021). *Digital 2021. Global Digital Overview*. https://dijilopedi.com/2021-dunya-internet-sosyal-medya-ve-mobil-kullanim-istatistikleri/

Westbrook, N. (2011). Media literacy pedogog: Critical and new /twenty first centries instructions. *E-Learning and Digital Media*, *8*(2), 154–164.

Wilson, C. (2012). Media and İnformation Literacy: Pedogogy and Possibilities. *Comunicar*, *39*, 15–22.

Wood, E. (2009). Media literacy education: Evaluating media literacy education in Colorado Schools (Master's thesis). Faculty of Social Sciences, University of Denver.

Yolcu, Ö. (2020). *Yeni medya*. İstanbul Üniversitesi AUZEF. http://auzefkitap.istanbul.edu.tr/kitap/medyaveiletisim_ue/yenimedya.pdf

Chapter 20
The Application of AI Teachers in Facilitating Game-Based Literacy Learning:
An Introduction to Theories and Evidence-Based Tools

Yixun Li
https://orcid.org/0000-0003-2193-6126
The Education University of Hong Kong, Hong Kong

Lin Zou
Primary School Affiliated to South China Normal University, China

ABSTRACT

This chapter discusses the theoretical frameworks for artificial intelligence (AI) teachers and how AI teachers have been applied to facilitate game-based literacy learning in existing empirical studies. While the application of artificial intelligence (AI) in education is a relatively emerging research area, it has received increasing attention in the scientific community. In the future, AI teachers are likely to be able to serve as powerful supplementary tools in classroom teaching in support of human teachers. The main goal here is to provide the readers with new insights on promoting game-based literacy learning from the perspectives of AI teachers. To this end, the authors introduce the readers to the key concepts of AI teachers, the merits and demerits of AI teachers in education, scientific research on AI teachers in literacy learning, and some highlighted examples of AI teachers in literacy classrooms for practical concerns.

DOI: 10.4018/978-1-7998-7271-9.ch020

INTRODUCTION

The advent of modern technology brings a substantial impact on the whole world, including educational practice. Such advances enrich game-based learning with digital platforms. Artificial Intelligence (AI) technology stands out as one of the most profound techniques to customize the learning needs of different learners and teachers. AI could have many benefits in education, as suggested as early as in Papert's (1980) theory of constructivism, which argues that robotics activities can engage children to learn and construct objects more effectively, especially in language learning. Among others, educational robots (e.g., AI teacher) have become very popular due to their positive effects on students' learning outcomes indicated by a meta-analysis of 49 empirical studies (Shan et al., 2019), and thus have been used to assist children in learning, especially in the K-12 learning environment (Mubin, Stevens et al., 2013).

To date, researchers have developed and applied AI teacher to facilitate literacy learning and teaching in many countries across continents. The present chapter aims to introduce professionals and scholars to AI teacher regarding the extent to which AI teacher works for literacy learning. First, the present chapter introduces the theoretical background of AI teacher in general, including their merits and the respective challenges to human teacher and students. Second, this chapter discusses empirical work on AI teacher in literacy learning, linking to game-based literacy learning. In this part, we also provide a detailed illustration of some representative, evidenced-based AI teacher for literacy learning for readers' references. Lastly, we reflect on the current advancement of AI teacher in literacy learning and point out the future directions.

Background of AI Teacher in Education

The current application of AI technology mainly includes three aspects: adaptive learning, intelligent tutoring systems, and educational robots (Zhu & Ma, 2019). Previous studies indicate that educational robots have become very popular and have a positive effect on students' learning outcomes in different stages (Shan et al., 2019). Huang et al. (2017) classified educational robot products into 12 categories. Among them, classroom robot assistants and robot teachers are mainly used in teaching. Robot as Teacher is also known as AI teacher. AI teacher has the function of assisting teachers to complete classroom teaching and achieve certain teaching effects (Huang et al., 2017).

AI teacher is an educational service robot, which can directly carry out intelligent auxiliary service in the teaching process. Its application process is often classified into three basic roles, namely mentor, student companion, and supervisor. Many studies have tested the role of AI teacher in supporting educational classroom activities. Technically, oral dialogue technology systems or other scripted programming technology systems allow AI agents to take on more important tasks than accessibility tools. It reduces the burden on human teachers and improves the quality of student learning (Edwards et al., 2016).

In the course of the operation of AI teacher, AI can obtain subjective cognitive ability and creativity similar to teachers' learning, which solves the problem of an insufficient number of human teachers and uneven professional level to a certain extent. For instance, AI teachers such as the Korean white oval telepresence robot *Eng Key*, the Japanese humanoid robot *Saya*, and the Israeli humanoid robot *Robo Thespian* have learned to elaborate concepts, explain cases, assign homework, and announce answers to students (Chen et al., 2019).

Yu and Wang (2019) indicated that there are four steps in the basic workflow using deep learning for AI teacher. First, the machine-based perceptual intelligence collects and extracts learners' and teachers' problems and their operational behavior in the process of teaching and learning. Second, the computational intelligence processes the collected data, and then establishes learners' and teachers' problem behavior patterns. Third, cognitive intelligence calculates a large-scale knowledge base to obtain the adaptive reference for behavior patterns in the current situation. Lastly, AI teacher compares and analyzes the problem behavior patterns, identify the shortcomings of learners, and recommend resources and programs for improving learning.

AI Teacher as a Supporting Tool for Human Teacher

To date, AI teacher has been mainly used to provide language, science, or technical education (Sharkey, 2016). In educational practice, more and more K-12 schools have introduced AI teacher to optimize the traditional teaching model, making classroom teaching more interesting and efficient (Chen et al., 2019). Notice that the incorporation of AI teacher into traditional classrooms is one way to empower human teachers' teaching practice, similar to utilizing multimedia, digital devices, or games in teaching. In this regard, AI teacher functions as a supporting tool for a human teacher in a teaching context (i.e., a dual-teacher classroom). Through human-robot collaboration (e.g., a case of Human-Robot Interaction when both are teachers), AI teacher will assist human teachers in completing their daily work to achieve efficient teaching (Yu, 2018) and serve as an important part of the campus smart learning environment. They can be tutors, teacher assistants, or learning partners, thereby forming a new type of teaching (Huang et al., 2017).

When both AI teacher and human teacher teach in the classroom (i.e., dual-teacher classroom), it is no surprise that human teacher takes the lead. Human teachers need to distinguish which tasks are repeatable and linear so that they can be conducted by AI teacher instead and which need to be undertaken by themselves. That said, AI teacher is not designed to take over the human teacher's role. Teaching is a highly complex, creative, and adaptive work that heavily relies on human teachers' planning, management, monitor, decision-making, and implementation. AI teacher can help with the implementation of teaching instead of replacing the human teacher. For instance, Wang et al. (2019) compared the teaching design of the new "dual-teacher classroom" with the traditional teaching design, and found that the three basic characteristics needed for organizing teaching in a dual-teacher classroom: data analysis, refined activities, and human-computer collaboration.

More specifically, in the environment of e-whiteboard and digital tablets, students transfer questions to AI teacher via smart mobile terminals (Wang et al., 2019). For the questions that can be answered by AI teacher, different answering ways are randomly chosen by AI teacher to respond to students. By contrast, for other questions that cannot be recognized or answered by AI teacher, they are forwarded to the human teacher terminal. In this process, data of students' learning profiles keep being collected and analyzed by AI teacher in real-time. After class, AI teacher gathers an evaluation report on individual learners and the learning situation of the whole class, and presents it to the human teacher, which is the critical step for the collaboration between AI teacher and human teacher. Then, the human teacher processes such reports to better understand students' learning progress, and adjust the teaching design of the next teaching session accordingly (i.e., refined activities).

AI Teacher's Advantages over Other Technologies

Clarifications are needed in terms of how AI teacher outperforms other technologies in supporting learning and teaching. First of all, with the use of robots, AI teacher is a three-dimension existence that is visible and tangible and often could serve as a social partner for human teachers and students. For instance, the sociable robots (e.g., Tega robots with cartoon face from MIT Media Lab: https://www.media.mit.edu) have shown to be able to modulate Israelis preschoolers' affective state throughout the tutoring sessions on learning English as a second langue, and thus maximize long-term learning gains (Gordon et al., 2016). AI teacher can interact with learners physically and provide feedback through facial expressions and body movements. This is very different from other forms such as PowerPoints, videos, or even digital learning games that could only show students two-dimension information. The embodiment of AI teacher could have a profound impact on especially young children, who do rely on their perception a lot to explore the world and often face challenges in understanding abstract learning materials from the textbook.

Furthermore, the element of Human-Robot Interaction within AI teacher distinguishes itself from other technologies. AI teacher considers psychological aspects to work as naturally as possible in order to be accepted by young students. In addition to presenting stored information (e.g., teaching materials and corresponding feedback) to students as other technologies capable of, AI teacher could learn ethics in teaching students, such as elementary students, including using correct words and providing clear and understandable feedback on student's responses based on students' existing levels. Research suggests that AI teacher is more friendly than other media and is especially effective in motivating students to learn a language (e.g., Pegrum et al., 2015).

Challenges to Human Teacher with Regard to AI Teacher

Despite the aforementioned advantages of AI teacher in facilitating teaching and learning, AI teacher raise considerable challenges to human teacher that must be recognized and carefully evaluated. There have been serval empirical studies seeking to identify such challenges through a survey (e.g., Xia & LeTendre, 2021), interviews (e.g., Serholt et al., 2014), and focus group sessions (e.g., Ewijk et al., 2020). Here we summarize the three overarching challenges identified in this line of work.

The first major challenge relates to human teacher's technology experiences and competency. The interaction with AI teacher is, at least currently, a new experience for most human teachers worldwide (e.g., Xia & LeTendre, 2021). As elucidated above, human teacher direct the socio-technical learning environments involving AI teacher, and must be prepared for different scenarios such as the potential breakdown of AI teacher (e.g., Alhashmi et al., 2021; Sharkey, 2016). As of now, little has been known from empirical research regarding how to prepare human teacher to work with AI teacher. Consequently, very little attention has been paid to incorporating AI into teacher education or professional development programs. Xia and LeTendre (2021) conducted a survey among pre-service teachers in the U.S. and reported that increased exposure to AI teacher in teacher education might be an effective way to improve educators' positive attitudes toward AI teacher. On the one hand, it could be very demanding to expect human teacher with insufficient AI experiences and competency to work with AI teacher. On the other hand, providing necessary AI training and workshops to human teacher on large scale requires substantial recourses (e.g., experts and AI teacher) and manpower, which could be too expensive in many contexts and regions.

The Application of AI Teachers in Facilitating Game-Based Literacy Learning

Relatedly, the second main challenge is about human teacher's emotions regarding working with AI teacher. Xia and LeTendre (2021) suggested that human teachers who lack AI experiences are likely to demonstrate negative attitudes toward AI teacher. In addition, it could be challenging for human teacher to figure out how they should perceive AI teacher, such as what role they would give to AI teacher in the classroom (Serholt et al., 2014), and to what extent they could trust AI teacher regarding the data privacy (Ewijk et al., 2020). There are other anxieties about the use of data collected by AI teacher, such as the fear that parents would not understand the data, the fear of being blamed by parents due to reasons such as not immediately helping a child (Serholt et al., 2014). All in all, working with AI teacher has the possibility to become a stress factor for human teacher.

Lastly, AI teacher may lead to the additional workload of human teacher beyond technology competency. In Serholt et al.' (2014) teacher interview conducted across several European countries, some participating teachers reported that they perceived AI teacher to bring in an extra burden. For instance, human teacher need to involve in the process of instructional design for AI teacher, since it is essential to ensure that AI teacher will fit well into the classroom situation. Also, AI teacher create administrative overhead on a daily basis for the teacher. For example, human teacher need to keep track of each student's time spent with AI teacher, such as revisiting the data collected by AI teacher.

Challenges to Students with Regard to AI Teacher

It should be noted that AI teacher also introduce challenges to students in many aspects, and some major challenges have been identified across empirical studies (e.g., Lin et al., 2009; Mubin and Shahid et al., 2013). First of all, learning from AI teacher is also a new experience for most students across countries. Students are likely to be more motivated and interested in classroom learning with the presence of AI teacher, particularly in the beginning sessions due to the novelty factor; such novelty factor may diminish from the third session if the AI teacher do not adapt (Ahmad et al., 2019). Meanwhile, students' attention to AI teacher due to novelty may distract their attention from the teaching and learning content (e.g., Alhashmi et al., 2021). Relatedly, it is possible that students have high expectations for AI teacher, which would lead to disappointment whenever AI teacher reach their technical limitations as they can only address questions that have been programmed (Lin et al., 2009).

Furthermore, students' data privacy is a critical issue, especially when AI teacher interact with multiple children (Ewijk et al., 2020), which is a typical scenario in the classroom. Mubin and Shahid et al. (2013) reviewed empirical work on AI teacher in education and found that having small groups of students working together in a learning activity with AI teacher has great pedagogical value. But as Cappuccio et al. (2021) noted, there are always concerns that AI teacher may influence the positive values they have. The challenge to data privacy is not only those obvious such as students' learning progress and behavior in the classroom, but also more broadly including students' friendship, attachment, and safety. In addition, it remains a huge challenge for AI teacher to detect the value of human emotion in real-time, and thus AI teacher are not able to perceive and react to students' emotions as human teacher (Ahmad et al., 2019). Especially for young students, it could be challenging for them to realize that AI teacher is not human, which may invoke some negative emotions due to AI teacher's limitations of emotional function.

The aforementioned merits and demerits of AI teacher apply to education in general. Bearing this information in mind, in this chapter, we concentrate on AI teacher in literacy learning. In the next section, we will then showcase a couple of evidence-based AI teacher proven to be fruitful for literacy teaching. Naturally, the elements of game-based learning in AI teacher will be covered and discussed.

AI TEACHER IN LITERACY LEARNING AND ITS GAME-BASED ELEMENTS

Literacy learning could be viewed as a four-level hierarchy in children's development, ranging from sub-word, word, clause to discourse/text, and educational robots have been used to facilitate students' literacy learning at all levels (Chen et al., 2011). Under the big umbrella of educational robots, robot-assisted language learning (RALL) is a subdomain referring to the use of robots to support language learning. Randall (2019) provides a thorough review and synthesis of theories and empirical studies of RALL and found that robots appear to aid in language production beyond other technologies and provide unique advantages in increasing learning motivation and engagement as well as decreasing anxiety. Our focus here is AI teacher for literacy learning, which is a specific case of robot-assisted language learning (RALL). In particular, this chapter centers on AI teacher that illustrates game-based elements in promoting literacy learning.

Here we provide an overview of evidence-based AI teacher for literacy learning that more or less contains game-based instructional designs. This section summarizes the empirical findings of studies on the applications of such AI teacher. Similar to other intervention studies in education and psychology, in this line of work, a study typically consists of a pre-test phase, an intervention phase, and a post-test phase. The effectiveness of the intervention is estimated by student's improvement from pre-test to post-test, compared to that in a control condition without intervention. Qualitatively, some studies also evaluate the usability, feasibility, and effectiveness of the intervention through analysis of video recordings and interviews. The use of AI teacher is incorporated in the intervention phase. Across studies, the specific type of AI teacher varies, so does the instructional design. The type of AI teacher could vary in many ways, such as the physical appearance (e.g., whether or not it's a humanoid robot whose body shape is built to resemble the human body), the mode of operation (e.g., whether or not it carries a touchable screen, or if it supports remote control), and the ways of providing feedback (e.g., whether or not it has a variety of facial expressions and body movement in response to learners' and teachers' questions). The technical details of AI teacher will not be targeted here. We would like to make it clear that AI teacher is a platform that should be able to accommodate different kinds of instructional designs in various disciplines. Our major interest is thus in the instructional design of AI teacher, which could provide actual educational implications.

As for the instructional design, it concerns the actual content in a teaching session, mainly including teaching materials and activities. As Wu et al. (2015) justified, without a well-developed instructional design, AI teacher's advantages likely would be limited to their novelty in attracting students' attention at the surface level. The instructional design clearly relies on considerable work by content experts (e.g., experienced teachers). Since AI teacher is a developing area including the technology aspect, not all of the good instructional designs available in traditional teaching are feasible to function in AI teacher. More collaborations between researchers in AI teacher and content experts (e.g., experienced teachers and educational psychologists) are warranted to advance this field and eventually make an impact on the educational practice. At this point, we argue that introductory pieces such as the present chapter serve as critical ways in facilitating such potential collaborations. Meanwhile, due to the relative infancy of AI teacher in literacy learning, we fully acknowledge that the present review must be selective, and we spotlight the game-based elements as much as possible. To showcase representative studies, we sought to cover a variety of types of AI teacher and instructional designs, as well as different age groups as participants and different countries and regions.

The Application of AI Teachers in Facilitating Game-Based Literacy Learning

Validation of AI Teacher

In this subsection, we review empirical work that focuses on the development and validation of AI teacher for literacy learning. In this line of work, researchers do not yet compare students' literacy learning outcomes between different instructional designs of AI teacher or that between with versus without the help of AI teacher.

AI teacher may be an effective and low-cost technology to enrich early childhood education environments. As Movellan et al. (2009) suggest, AI teacher significantly improved the vocabulary skills of English-speaking toddlers aged18-24 months in the United States. In this work, a RUBI-4 robot (https://rubi.ucsd.edu/) with a touch screen served as AI teacher and operated fully autonomously during the intervention period. AI teacher did not explicitly teach the children any words. Instead, AI teacher played games with the children that contained target novel words. Game-based elements include the use of songs and educational games presented on the touch-screen. AI teacher sang a song and meanwhile physically danced while presenting a relevant video clip on the screen. In addition, flash-based educational games targeting vocabulary development were conducted through AI teacher. In one game, for instance, the AI teacher asked the children to touch a particular image (e.g., the orange) when presenting four alternative images on the screen and responded to the children's choices with its physical actuators. In physical games, AI teacher played with the children in the way that they took and gave back physical objects using their two arms/hands.

Similarly, Kim et al. (2014) found that English-speaking, 3- to 5-year-old children's play with AI teacher significantly facilitated their learning of vocabulary. The ATTI robot (Korea & USA SK-Telecom, http://www.sktelecom.com) served as an AI teacher, which is a humanoid robot that targets preschool or kindergarten-aged children. A robot-based curricular app was designed in this study, guided by psychological theories and developmentally appropriate and engaging for 3- to 5-year-olds' learning and motivation. AI teacher did learning activities with the children either one-on-one or in small groups of two to three children, and study length ranged from 30 minutes to one hour. The activities and resources were intentionally chosen to balance the familiar and the new, such as familiar educational tools (songs and the accompanying book and cards) and new educational tools (AI teacher), as well as familiar content (identifiable and easily recognizable such as items from home, simple colors, and shapes) and new, imaginative content (e.g., spaceships, secret labs). Game-based elements were nicely embedded in the activities: (1) introduction: songs that are familiar to the children are played to expose them to target vocabulary, and then AI teacher invites children to repeat target vocabulary or sounds multiple times; (2) reinforcement: games are played to help the children to practice newly acquired vocabulary by ways such as asking them to find the correct matching card for a word; (3) extending: built upon children's newly learned vocabulary, new content is introduced by AI teacher through conversations with the children (e.g., AI teacher asks for children's help with finding an object).

Efforts also have been devoted to integrating AI teacher into familiar educational tools (e.g., books and digital devices) to support primary school students beyond their learning of native language. For instance, Chen et al. (2011) investigated the integration of books, computers, and AI teacher to create a novel and joyful English learning environment for fifth-grade Chinese-speaking children in Taiwan. They sought to link books with digital learning content on the computer and AI teacher, so as to allow students to obtain supplementary learning content, including motions performed by AI teacher to enhance learning outcomes. Learning activities included vocabulary, single sentence read-along, full article read-along, conversation, singalong, and dancing. The results suggest that this system did enrich students' learning experience and enhance their motivation and engagement.

The benefit of AI teacher could go beyond vocabulary and conversation. In Switzerland, Hood et al. (2015) develop a novel AI teacher that supports 6- to 8- year-old children's learning of handwriting. In this work, a humanoid robot with a tablet, NAO V4, was used as an AI teacher. The learning by teaching paradigm was used in the way that children engage with AI teacher by teaching AI teacher handwriting. Results indicate that AI teacher significantly supported children's engagement and improvement in handwriting. The interaction sequence between the child and the robot consists of four stages: (1) the child shows the robot some words to write; (2) the robot responds to the word request verbally and writes the letters; (3) the robot asks for feedback from the child, and the child demonstrates how to write the letter that needs to be corrected. (4) the robot writes an adapted letter based on the child's feedback and the interaction iterates. Note that such learning by teaching paradigm has also been used in AI teacher to promote children's second language learning (e.g., Japanese 3-to 6-year-olds learning English, Tanaka & Matsuzoe, 2012).

Effective Use of AI Teacher

In this subsection, we review empirical work that moves a step forward compared to studies reviewed previously. With the use of AI teacher, researchers further ask how to make the application more effective by experimentally manipulating different instructional designs of the same AI teacher. In this line of work, AI teacher is used independently without investigating their collaboration with human teacher.

Balkibekov et al. (2016) conducted a study among 6- to 10-year-olds in Kazakhstan to examine whether AI teacher who always win or those who always lose could better support children's learning of English vocabulary. A humanoid robot with an Android application, NAO, was used as an AI teacher who played games with the children approximately 10 minutes per day over a week. In the game, the AI teacher and the child take turns and answer five questions each. Each question has a displayed letter (e.g., "A") and images of three fruits (e.g., apple, pear, and banana). Depending on the turn, either a child or the AI teacher needs to select their answer (e.g., apple because it starts with the letter "A") on the screen. Then, either of them gets the same letter but different fruits (e.g., avocado, orange, and peach). The difficulty of words is in increasing order from one question to the next. Upon completion of 10 questions, results for each letter are displayed, and the winner is either AI teacher (in the AI win condition) or the child (in the AI lose condition).

All children were assigned to one of the four conditions in the combination of 2 (play strategy: win versus lose) × 2 (child gender: boys versus girls). Results indicate that all children improve their English vocabulary significantly more when playing with the losing AI teacher than that with the winning AI teacher, regardless of child gender. Furthermore, girls rated playing with the AI teacher significantly higher than boys did regardless of playing strategy. Thus, the results of gameplay appear to affect children's learning outcomes in game-based instructions, at least in the current case of using AI teacher to play games with children in learning English vocabulary.

The type of emotional feedback provided by AI teacher also influences children's engagement and learning outcomes; positive emotional feedback appears to better support children's learning. In Australia, Ahmad et al. (2019) examined the impact of the positive, negative, and neutral emotional feedback of AI teacher on children's vocabulary learning. A humanoid robot, NAO, was used as an AI teacher, along with a Samsung tablet. The key instructional design was that AI teacher teaches vocabulary to

The Application of AI Teachers in Facilitating Game-Based Literacy Learning

children while playing the popular game "Snakes and Ladders," which has been updated and adapted into a game to facilitate vocabulary learning (Ahmad et al., 2015). The game is designed to be played by two players. As the game begins, the child rolls the dice by tapping on their dice displayed on the screen. The child then moves the number of steps equal to the number on the dice on the game board. On each snake appearance on the game board, the AI teacher is programmed to teach a new word to the child. Once the snake appeared, the word was shown with an image-based description on the screen to the child. Meanwhile, the AI teacher explained the meaning of that word. Afterward, the AI teacher asked the child to press the back arrow to return to the game. The same process was repeated on each snake.

In this work, 10- to 12-year-old children at a primary school participated, and all of them were assigned into one of the three groups in which the AI teacher provided positive, neutral, or negative feedback during the activities. The children interacted with the AI teacher on four separate occasions over the course of two school weeks. Results show that the condition where AI teacher displayed positive emotional feedback significantly facilitated children's vocabulary learning performance more than the two other conditions.

Some researchers have incorporated AI teacher into storytelling activities and suggest that strategically matching and mismatching AI teacher's language ability to the child's could improve their language learning outcomes. Children appear to learn more from AI teacher that adapts to maintain an equal or greater ability than the children, whereas playing with AI teacher of less ability could prompt teaching or mentoring behavior from children. In the United Kingdom, Kory and Breazeal (2014) recruited 4- to 6-year-olds and randomly assigned them to either playing with the adaptive AI teacher or the non-adaptive AI teacher. The DragonBot robot was used to implement a storytelling game. The adaptive AI teacher acted as a slightly older peer growing with the child during the storytelling game (e.g., learning new vocabulary), whereas the non-adaptive AI teacher remained at its level as the child progressed, thus becoming a younger peer as the child develops. Children played with the AI teacher once per week for a total of eight weeks. The storytelling game was situated on a tablet computer on a table, and both the child and AI teacher played. They took turns telling stories about characters on the tablet screen, and each told three different stories in total. During the game, the AI teacher introduced new vocabulary words and modeled good story narration skills, such as including a beginning, middle, and end; varying sentence structure; and keeping cohesion across the story. Such storytelling game appears to support socially-situated interaction, rooted in free play, allowing creative conversation and space for learning topics such as new words, metalinguistic knowledge about language patterns and structure, and decontextualized language.

Interestingly, adapting educational theories in game-based AI teacher could further improve its effectiveness of promoting students' learning motivation, learning performance, and continuance intention. In a case that uses AI teacher to promote adult learners' second language learning, Hung et al. (2013) compared student's improvement through learning activities with AI teacher with versus without being guided by the ARCS model (The Attention, Relevance, Confidence, and Satisfaction model). Chinese-speaking undergraduate and postgraduate students in Taiwan were recruited and divided into a test (AI teacher with the ARCS model) and a control group (AI teacher without ARCS model) to learn English reading skills. A humanoid robot developed by the researchers served as an AI teacher in this work. The key instructional design here is the application of the ARCS model. First, a 5-min instruction stage was designed to attract learners' Attention. Second, in a 20-min case simulation stage, the AI teacher presented the learning content and guided students to immerse themselves in the learning scenario. Group-based learning activities and interactive Q&As were used in this stage to fulfill Relevance and Confidence.

Third, a 25-min quiz game stage was implemented to promote students' feeling of Satisfaction through complimentary and encouraging feedback.

Dual-Teacher Classroom

In this subsection, we review empirical work that examined how AI teacher facilitate literacy teaching through human-computer interaction in the dual-teacher classroom, in which both AI teacher and human teacher teach, thus called dual-teacher classroom. Unlike the studies reviewed in the previous subsections, this line of work tested and supported the effectiveness of AI teacher as a supplementary tool for human teacher by comparing students' learning outcomes between the condition that they learn from both AI teacher and human teacher versus that from human teacher only. In a dual-teacher classroom, there could be a variety of modes for AI teacher to instruct language teaching, such as "story-telling mode," "oral reading mode," "cheering mode," "action command mode," and "question and answer mode" in Chen and Chung (2008).

A dual-teacher approach appears to be fruitful for teaching preschoolers' language, such as young Iranian 3- to 6-year-olds who learn English as a foreign language (Alemi & Haeri, 2017). In Alemi and Haeri's (2017) work, AI teacher was applied to teach greetings to young EFL (English as Foreign Language) students in Tehran, Iran. A humanoid robot, NAO, was used in the dual teacher group to support a human teacher. In the game-based group, however, no AI teacher was present; game-based instruction was implemented based on gaming methods such as command, mystery bag, and pass the ball. The teaching materials were exactly the same, but it only took eight hours for the dual teacher group to cover all materials, whereas it took 32 hours for the game-based group. Results suggest that the dual teacher method outperformed the game-based method in improving children's language performance.

Similarly, in primary schools, Alemi et al. (2015) used a humanoid robot, NAO, as an AI teacher to support a human teacher in teaching English as a foreign language to Iranian 7-9-year-old children with autism in a school classroom. Children's English skills were assessed before and after ten teaching lessons. The findings suggest fairly persistent benefits of having an AI teacher: children who learned from an AI teacher, and a human teacher gained significantly more vocabulary than children who only had a human teacher. As for young middle-school students, Alemi et al. (2014) suggest that the use of AI teacher in addition to human teacher enhanced the quality of English vocabulary learning and increased interest among young Iranian learners at middle schools. A humanoid, cartoon-like robot, NAO, was used as AI teacher, and a video projector equipped with a laptop computer was used to show pictures of various items when necessary. Note that Alemi's lab has conducted rich research in this line, and here we further introduce the game-based elements in AI teacher from their group.

In Alemi et al. (2014), for instance, for each session, a lesson plan was designed to focus on vocabulary for the teaching session. The human teacher started a conversation with AI teacher and then with the students. Students were also asked to talk to AI teacher with their own words and repeat after the AI teacher to practice new words and vocabulary. AI teacher was pre-programmed to explain each vocabulary item by pictures, pantomime actions, sounds, and their usage, and taught each vocabulary item as the picture showed on the computer screen and then asked the students to repeat the phrase. Sometimes, AI teacher would make mistakes intentionally, and thus provided the students with opportunities to learn from AI teacher's mistakes and feel less anxious when being called upon to answer. Immediate feedback was provided by both human teacher (e.g., verbal compliments) and AI teacher (e.g., singing and dancing) in real-time to reward, encourage, and motivate students in the learning process.

Other research groups made similar efforts and support the significant benefits of using AI teacher in a dual-teacher classroom to promote students' language learning across age groups. Kennedy et al. (2016) used a humanoid NAO robot as an AI teacher delivering all lessons through speech and moving words on a touch screen to primary school students and found similar results as Alemi et al. (2015). In Korea, Yun et al. (2011) developed an AI teacher for English education (Engkey, namely English jockey) using a teleoperated robot controlled by a native human teacher in a remote site. This is different from the dual-teacher method reviewed in the aforementioned studies, in that while both AI teacher and human teacher collaboratively teach at the same time, the AI teacher implements the teaching in the front whereas the human teacher is not physically present in the classroom. Empirical evidence supports the effectiveness of Engkey, and the participating elementary students achieved good improvements on standardized tests after receiving intervention by Engkey in the study. In the class, the AI teacher provides educational supplement through conversation and practice such as pronunciation practice, sing-alongs, and robotic games, as well as dynamic behavior on its arms, various emotional expressions on its avatar lip-syncing and LED, and free movement with its wheels, which easily help students be more focused and memorize an English song or rhyme and sing along.

Beyond the language itself, in Australia, Pegrum et al. (2015) also found that the dual-teacher classroom mode could significantly promote undergraduate students' knowledge acquisition and thinking development and further enhance their sense of self-efficacy, learning attitude, and motivation.

FUTURE DIRECTIONS

Until this point, we would like to reiterate that AI teacher is designed to assist human teachers as a supplementary tool in completing their daily work so as to better achieve efficient teaching through human-computer collaboration (Yu, 2018). But AI teacher themselves is not necessarily helpful for classroom teaching unless the human teacher is equipped with sufficient knowledge to make good use of AI teacher flexibly. To maximize the positive effects of AI teacher in future classrooms, systematic AI training in teacher education would be a must in the future, which is not an easy task. Toward this goal, more scientific research is warranted to identify the efficient approaches to guide the human teacher in working with AI teacher.

Furthermore, as introduced and illustrated in this chapter, the instructional design of AI teacher is the key. The development and implementation of AI teacher rely on human teachers' creative work and careful monitor. It is still controversial regarding teachers' opinions on the applicability of AI teacher, specifically on the level of education that AI teacher are able to offer (Ewijk et al. 2020). At least in the case of literacy teaching, as we reviewed here, AI teacher indeed appear to deliver relatively superficial levels of education involving giving the solution to an exercise instead of deeper levels of education, including insights into the problem-solving process (Ewijk et al. 2020). We view this not merely as a technical concern but also a theoretical and practical question, since the instructional design, by large, determines the maximum level of education that AI teacher may offer. In the future, more efforts will be called for both theoretical and empirical research on the instructional design of AI teacher.

CONCLUSION

The present piece focuses on introducing Artificial Intelligence (AI) teacher for game-based literacy learning. As an introductory piece, our goal is to provide the readers with some insights on promoting game-based literacy learning from the perspectives of AI teacher. In the above review, we introduced AI teacher in education in general, regarding its advantages and challenges, followed by a particular analysis on AI teacher in literacy learning. As technology keeps advancing, AI teacher is likely to be an organic part of future teachers' work. But based on what have been known in the literature to date, it is concluded that while the application of AI teacher provides fruitful insights to education, there are good reasons to stay cautious about welcoming AI teacher to classroom teaching in the short term.

REFERENCES

Ahmad, M., Mubin, O., & Escudero, P. (2015, October). Using adaptive mobile agents in games-based scenarios to facilitate foreign language word learning. In *Proceedings of the 3rd International Conference on Human-Agent Interaction* (pp. 255-257). 10.1145/2814940.2814990

Ahmad, M. I., Mubin, O., Shahid, S., & Orlando, J. (2019). Robot's adaptive emotional feedback sustains children's social engagement and promotes their vocabulary learning: A long-term child–robot interaction study. *Adaptive Behavior*, 27(4), 243–266. doi:10.1177/1059712319844182

Alemi, M., & Haeri, N. S. (2017, October). How to Develop Learners' Politeness: A Study of RALL's Impact on Learning Greeting by Young Iranian EFL Learners. In *2017 5th RSI International Conference on Robotics and Mechatronics (ICRoM)* (pp. 88-94). IEEE. 10.1109/ICRoM.2017.8466206

Alemi, M., Meghdari, A., Basiri, N., & Taheri, A. (2015). The Effect of Applying Humanoid Robots as Teacher Assistants to Help Iranian Autistic Pupils Learn English as a Foreign Language. In *Social Robotics* (pp. 1–10). Lecture Notes in Computer Science. Springer International Publishing.

Alemi, M., Meghdari, A., & Ghazisaedy, M. (2014). Employing humanoid robots for teaching English language in Iranian junior high-schools. *International Journal of HR; Humanoid Robotics*, 11(03), 1450022. doi:10.1142/S0219843614500224

Alhashmi, M., Mubin, O., & Baroud, R. (2021). Examining the use of robots as teacher assistants in UAE classrooms: Teacher and student perspectives. *Journal of Information Technology Education*, 245–261. https://doi-org.ezproxy.uws.edu.au/10.28945/4749

Balkibekov, K., Meiirbekov, S., Tazhigaliyeva, N., & Sandygulova, A. (2016, August). Should robots win or lose? Robot's losing playing strategy positively affects child learning. In *2016 25th IEEE International Symposium on Robot and Human Interactive Communication (RO-MAN)* (pp. 706-711). IEEE. 10.1109/ROMAN.2016.7745196

Cappuccio, M. L., Sandoval, E. B., Mubin, O., Obaid, M., & Velonaki, M. (2021). Robotics Aids for Character Building: More than Just Another Enabling Condition. *International Journal of Social Robotics*, 13, 1–5. doi:10.100712369-021-00756-y

Chen, C. M., & Chung, C. J. (2008). Personalized mobile English vocabulary learning system based on item response theory and learning memory cycle. *Computers & Education*, *51*(2), 624–645. doi:10.1109/ICSMC.2006.384727

Chen, N. S., Quadir, B., & Teng, D. C. (2011). Integrating book, digital content and robot for enhancing elementary school students' learning of English. *Australasian Journal of Educational Technology*, *27*(3). Advance online publication. doi:10.14742/ajet.960

Chen, S., Huang, F., Zeng, W., Dong, N., Wu, X., & Tang, Y. (2019). Robots can teach knowledge but can't cultivate values? *China Educational Technology*, (2), 29-35.

Edwards, A., Edwards, C., Spence, P., Harris, C., & Gambino, A. (2016). Robots in the classroom: Differences in students' perceptions of credibility and learning between "teacher as robot" and "robot as teacher." *Computers in Human Behavior*, *65*, 627–634. doi:10.1016/j.chb.2016.06.005

Gordon, G., Spaulding, S., Westlund, J. K., Lee, J. J., Plummer, L., Martinez, M., . . . Breazeal, C. (2016, March). Affective personalization of a social robot tutor for children's second language skills. In *Proceedings of the AAAI conference on artificial intelligence* (Vol. 30, No. 1). https://ojs.aaai.org/index.php/AAAI/article/view/9914

Hood, D., Lemaignan, S., & Dillenbourg, P. (2015, March). When children teach a robot to write: An autonomous teachable humanoid which uses simulated handwriting. In *Proceedings of the Tenth Annual ACM/IEEE International Conference on Human-Robot Interaction* (pp. 83-90). 10.1145/2696454.2696479

Huang, R., Liu, D., Xu, J., Chen, N., Fan, L., & Zeng, H. (2017). The development status and trend of educational robots. *Modern Educational Technology*, *27*(1), 13–20.

Hung, I. C., Chao, K. J., Lee, L., & Chen, N. S. (2013). Designing a robot teaching assistant for enhancing and sustaining learning motivation. *Interactive Learning Environments*, *21*(2), 156–171. doi:10.1080/10494820.2012.705855

Kennedy, J., Baxter, P., Senft, E., & Belpaeme, T. (2016). Social Robot Tutoring for Child Second Language Learning. *The Eleventh ACM/IEEE International Conference on Human Robot Interaction*, 231-238. 10.1109/HRI.2016.7451757

Kim, Y., Smith, D., Kim, N., & Chen, T. (2014). Playing with a robot to learn English vocabulary. In *KAERA. Research Forum*, *1*(2), 3–8.

Kory, J., & Breazeal, C. (2014, August). Storytelling with robots: Learning companions for preschool children's language development. In *The 23rd IEEE international symposium on robot and human interactive communication* (pp. 643-648). IEEE. 10.1109/ROMAN.2014.6926325

Lin, Y. C., Liu, T. C., Chang, M., & Yeh, S. P. (2009, August). Exploring children's perceptions of the robots. In *International Conference on Technologies for E-Learning and Digital Entertainment* (pp. 512-517). Springer. 10.1007/978-3-642-03364-3_63

Movellan, J., Eckhardt, M., Virnes, M., & Rodriguez, A. (2009). Sociable robot improves toddler vocabulary skills. *Proceedings of the 4th ACM/IEEE International Conference on Human Robot Interaction*, 307-308. 10.1145/1514095.1514189

Mubin, O., Shahid, S., & Bartneck, C. (2013). Robot Assisted Language Learning through Games: A Comparison of Two Case Studies. *Australian Journal of Intelligent Information Processing Systems*, *13*(3), 9–14.

Mubin, O., Stevens, C. J., Shahid, S., Al Mahmud, A., & Dong, J. J. (2013). A review of the applicability of robots in education. *Journal of Technology in Education and Learning, 1*(209). doi:10.2316/Journal.209.2013.1.209-0015

Papert, S. A. (1980). *Mindstorms: Children, computers, and powerful ideas*. Basic books.

Pegrum, M., Bartle, E., & Longnecker, N. (2015). Can creative podcasting promote deep learning? The use of podcasting for learning content in an undergraduate science unit. *British Journal of Educational Technology, 46*(1), 142–152. doi:10.1111/bjet.12133

Randall, N. (2019). A survey of robot-assisted language learning (RALL). *ACM Transactions on Human-Robot Interaction, 9*(1), 1–36. doi:10.1145/3345506

Serholt, S., Barendregt, W., Leite, I., Hastie, H., Jones, A., Paiva, A., . . . Castellano, G. (2014, August). Teachers' views on the use of empathic robotic tutors in the classroom. In *The 23rd IEEE International Symposium on Robot and Human Interactive Communication* (pp. 955-960). IEEE. https:// doi:10.1109/ROMAN.2014.6926376

Shan, J., Gong, L., Li, Y., & Yan, H. (2019). The impact of educational robots on student learning outcomes—Based on a meta-analysis of 49 experimental or quasi-experimental research papers. *China Educational Technology*, (5), 76–83.

Sharkey, A. (2016). Should we welcome robot teachers? *Ethics and Information Technology, 18*(4), 283–297. doi:10.100710676-016-9387-z

Tanaka, F., & Matsuzoe, S. (2012). Children teach a care-receiving robot to promote their learning: Field experiments in a classroom for vocabulary learning. *Journal of Human-Robot Interaction, 1*(1), 78–95. doi:10.5898/JHRI.1.1.Tanaka

van Ewijk, G., Smakman, M., & Konijn, E. A. (2020, June). Teachers' perspectives on social robots in education: an exploratory case study. In *Proceedings of the Interaction Design and Children Conference* (pp. 273-280). 10.1145/3392063.3394397

Wang, S., Fang, H., Zhang, G., & Ma, T. (2019). Research on a new type of "dual-teacher classroom" supported by artificial intelligence educational robots & on the teaching design and future prospects of "human-machine collaboration". *Journal of Distance Education, 37*(2), 25–32.

Wu, W. C. V., Wang, R. J., & Chen, N. S. (2015). Instructional design using an in-house built teaching assistant robot to enhance elementary school English-as-a-foreign-language learning. *Interactive Learning Environments, 23*(6), 696–714. doi:10.1080/10494820.2013.792844

Xia, Y., & LeTendre, G. (2021). Robots for future classrooms: A cross-cultural validation study of "negative attitudes toward robots scale" in the US context. *International Journal of Social Robotics, 13*(4), 703–714. doi:10.100712369-020-00669-2

Yu, S. (2018). The future role of AI teachers. *Open Education Research, 24*(1), 6-28.

Yu, S. & Wang, Q. (2019). Analysis of Collaborative Path Development of "AI+Teachers." *e-EducationResearch*, (4), 14-29.

Yun, S., Shin, J., Kim, D., Kim, C. G., Kim, M., & Choi, M. T. (2011, November). Engkey: Tele-education robot. In *International Conference on Social Robotics* (pp. 142-152). Springer. 10.1007/978-3-642-25504-5_15

Zhu, W., Ma, A. (2019). The application status and development path analysis of domestic AI education. *Primary and Middle School Educational Technology, 8*, 99-102.

KEY TERMS AND DEFINITIONS

AI Teacher: An educational robot that serves the role of teacher.

Artificial Intelligence: The intelligence demonstrated by machines, in contrast to the natural intelligence displayed by humans or animals.

Dual-Teacher Classroom: A classroom setting in which both a human teacher and an AI teacher teach.

Educational Robot: A robot that is used for educational purposes.

Human-Robot Interaction: An interdisciplinary research field that concerns the dynamic interaction between humans and robots.

Humanoid Robot: A robot with its body shape built to resemble the human body.

Robot-Assisted Language Learning (RALL): The use of robots in supporting language learning.

Section 3
Culturally-Based Game-Based Pedagogy

Chapter 21
Enhancing Literacy Skills Using Indigenous Games

Rendani Tshifhumulo
https://orcid.org/0000-0003-4133-3656
University of Venda, South Africa

Livhuwani Daphney Tshikukuvhe
University of Venda, South Africa

Talifhani Trevor Ramatswi
University of Venda, South Africa

ABSTRACT

This chapter explores the possibility of enhancing literacy skills using indigenous games played by Vhavenda children at foundation phase. It critically analyses different types of Vhavenda games played by children which are ndode, mufuvha, muravharavha, and tsetsetse or trere-tsere to solicit the possibility to enhance literacy skills. Methodologically, this study aligns with the use of qualitative approach where researchers collected data using interviews and observations. The focus is on Vhavenda indigenous games that can be adopted by other cultures to enhance learning inside and outside the classroom environment. The results found that indigenous games develop several literacy skills inclusive of school, arithmetic, communication, cultural, emotional, and physical literacies which are very important for total development of children. Games are enjoyable and interesting and as such make learning fun.

BACKGROUND OF THE STUDY

Let us take a picture of a real story where a teacher decided to cut a piece of paper and write a simple statement that says I will go to Botswana during December holidays. The paper was given to one student and the student was asked to tell the next learner what was written in the paper. The information rotated and the 10th person was asked to tell the class the story she was told by the student sited next to her. Students were given a chance to view the original message, to their surprise, the original message

DOI: 10.4018/978-1-7998-7271-9.ch021

written was very different to words uttered by the last speaker. Students were surprised to realise that in the process of passing the information from one student to another, a lot of information was lost and distorted before it reached the next person. The teacher used a simple game to let the students learn critical skills pertaining to passing information. The teacher may have used talk and chalk to tell the students not to take everything they hear as concrete truth, to evaluate information, may be not to take things they hear on face value, may be to learn to listen carefully and report information accurately, but he used a game to enhance the knowledge. The class was so amazed to learn that not everything they hear from people will be accurate information and the fact that it is important to listen and report on information as accurately as possible. The game was so exciting that information was learned in a comical way and it is impossible for children to forget what was taught in this manner. In this statement, we introduce game based learning and our aim in this chapter is to assess the practicality of indigenous games in enhancing literacy skills.

Van Mele and Renson (1990: 16) mention that traditional games are recreational activities with local and cultural dimensions, having roots in traditional life of people. The 'traditional' label represents a time dimension of being preserved and transmitted from one generation to the next among a group (Van der Merwe, 1999), in this case, traditional games or what we refer to in this chapter as Indigenous games. Indigenous knowledge and games within the South African context, reflect the circumstances, traditions and cultures of the various population groups and communities which have been identified by the people as being part of their cultural heritage (Corlett & Mokgwathi, 1986). The Afro-centric nature of knowledge and games form an integral part of the Nguni, Sotho and Venda-speaking peoples as they originally migrated from the central lakes of Africa and settled in the southernmost end of Africa, during the 12th century (Junod, 1927; Schapera, 1966) as cited by (Bunnert & Holander, 2004).

Alegi (2004: 10) alluded that examples of indigenous games that were played in pre-colonial times includes among others stick-fighting as one of the popular indigenous game that was played in some parts of Zululand. Even though stick-fighting was considered rough play, it was nonetheless a play which had its own rules. It was prohibited to use a short spear. Further, stabbing was also prohibited and other dangerous war techniques designed to ensure fairness and avert severe injuries. Cattle raiding, racing and hunting also formed part of the popular indigenous games amongst men particularly between the ages of eighteen and forty. For example, cattle racing (uleqo) among the Xhosa speaking people provided both ritual and competitive entertainment. Both the Xhosa and Basotho men raced specialised oxen (Alegi, 2004: 11).

Previous studies found that games play a significant role in the socialisation of children (Potgieter & Malan, 1987). Several researchers (Honeyford & Boyd, 2015, Martlew, Stephen & Ellis, 2011) have documented the significant role of learning through play for children especially in the foundational level. In this regard, games can be adapted to suit a variety of social, cognitive and affective needs of children. Example is given to a game called masekitlane game that was successfully used as a therapeutic tool (Dipale, 2013). In the African context, indigenous games are symbolic representations of cultural expression from a specific society and children are bearers of cultural expression through these games (Burnette & Sierra, 2003).

Enhancing Literacy Skills Using Indigenous Games

PROBLEM IDENTIFIED

The school curriculum in many African countries and more specifically in South Africa has been dominated by eurocentric knowledge, and most of the games used for learning and teaching also followed suit. Indigenous games were marginalised and resulted in a devastating effect on indigenous cultures and knowledge. The contestation is that operative education and learning could be enabled, transmitted and articulated through indigenous games including *ndode, muravharavha, tsetsetse* and *mufuvha*. Previous studies found that incorporating of indigenous games into learning and teaching in the classroom could develop level of self-confidence, identity and in quickening active participation, healthy living and higher academic achievement of indigenous children in most school subjects especially Mathematics and Physical Education (Burnette & Sierra, 2003).

To enhance the structure of education, it is essential to introduce contemporary and advanced methods, strategies and approaches towards teaching and learning even at foundational phase. In the quest to be innovative, we should not renounce traditional strategies that formed the foundation of learning for centuries. It is for this purpose that we seek to explore the possible contribution of Vhavenda traditional games in enhancing literacies that improves development on growing children. We believe that in under developed countries they can be very helpful where children lack technology apparatus but they can be easily adopted by developed countries as they offer physical and health benefits that cannot be afforded by using computers. There are several games that are played within the Vhavenda cultural group but for this chapter we focused on four games, *ndode, mufuvha, muravharavha* and *tsetsetse*. These games are played by children and at various ages. Previous research alluded that games usually involve materials (game boards, dice, cards, computers, etc.) that may range from those that are inexpensive to those that requires expensive materials. (de Freitas, 2006, p. 16). In this study, all games are cheap and accessible to children and mostly played outdoors although they can be designed for indoor as well.

What are we looking for? Literacy skills were previously confined to the ability to speak and write (Mirenda,2002); (Cope & Keefa,2007) & UNESCO (2008) where illiterate people are defined as those people who cannot read or write, and focus here is on skills, functionality and individualism. This definition is very limited in scope as deduced by critics alluding that the former is limiting people with cognate disabilities in spaces where literacy skills is said to be a human right. This lead to many scholars engaging in the broadening of the definitions to include many other literacy skills which are of utter most important to the fully functioning of the human being. For this chapter our scope will fall under the latter inclusive types of literacy.

It is out of this quest that our definitions of literacy will not be limited to reading, writing and arithmetic skills but will solicit other literacy skills including those definitions that emanate from a functionalist perspective with emphasize on (school) teaching skills that individuals need for daily living as well as complex demands of a changing technological and economic environment, computer, vernacular, digital, visual, media, health, emotional, cultural and moral. In the present existence, apart from getting enrolled in educational institutions and training centres to acquire academic knowledge and develop competencies and abilities, the individuals, belonging to all age groups, categories and backgrounds are augmenting their knowledge and skills in terms of all the above stated literacy skills.

Just to give a glimpse of the picture of our explanations on different literacies, Knoblauch (1990) alluded that cultural literacy is embedded on of cultural heritage, a capacity of higher order thinking, even some aesthetic discernment (Knoblauch, 1990, p. 77). Digital literacy defined by Downing's (2005) as literacy which includes activities involving accessing, using, and communicating about anything in print or image media format and which is not limited to material accessed through sight or hearing.

Our aim of this project then is to explore how *ndode, mufuvha, muravharavha* and *tsetsetse/tseretsere* may enhance different types of literacies and the possibility of future use in the learning environment. The use of games to enhance learning is not a new phenomenon. Scholars like James Paul Gee, Presidential Professor of Literacy Studies in Education at Arizona State University played a vital role as a pioneer of discussions into games-based learning. Gee (2005) observes that many of today's video games are "hard, long, and complex," yet still immensely enjoyable which lead to gamers playing for hours and extremely focused on the game. On the other hand, in learning the concertation span cannot be sustained for longer hours and a dull classroom is not conducive for learning. If games can engage learners for a long period while learning is fun, they are then a good instrument that should not be ignored in developing literacy skills. According to (Gee, 2005, pp. 34-37) there are many features of games that facilitate learning and in his example, he mentioned that games allow players to take on a new identity, which enables learners to make "an extended commitment of self." Games are interactive, and players must perform some action to receive feedback.

LITERATURE

The assessment of weather physical and web-based games can enhance learning is not a new phenomenon. Several studies were previously conducted to test weather games can enhance learning where learning is merged with fun to make it interesting. Shan (2021) experimented about web-based games to identify the possibility of promoting reading and pre-reading skills. In the study 136 pre-schoolers and kindergarteners were randomly assigned to play literacy-focused games as an intervention group and puzzle- and arts-themed computer games as a control for 8 weeks at home. Pre- and post-interventions thru 12 literacy assessments were evaluated to determine children's early literacy skills. Children in the intervention group outperformed control group peers on eight different outcomes. Learning was most pronounced for alliteration and phonics, which are important early predictors of later reading abilities. A similar study was done by Feng Liua,b*& Po-Kuang Chena (2011) who investigated the perceptions of students regarding the integration of the game into science learning as well as the educational benefits of the game with regard to learning performance. The main purpose of the study was to help elementary school students to learn science-related concepts by participating in an educational card game, named Conveyance Go. Results emanating from a one-group pre-test post-test design used with eighteen 5th grade students from a single elementary school in northern Taiwan demonstrated positive attitudes toward the use of the educational card game in science learning. They also found that Game-based learning can instill significant motivation in students and offer a practical learning experience to enhance effective learning. Lastly, they alluded that game based learning helps to transform dull, dry classroom learning into an enjoyable, engaging experience that motivates students to participate in an absorbing learning process. They concluded that people are motivated to learn in exciting environments than when teaching is boring. Smale (2011) from the study exploring the use of games in library instruction found that game based learning can be employed in many disciplines including psychology, education, science etc. Although it was found that there are obstacles that can be anticipated in using game based learning approach it is said that the promising benefits of the approach outweigh the obstacles. Using games in library instruction capitalizes on the many similarities between games and the way that students do research, and has the strong potential to increase student engagement in information literacy training.

POSITIVE ATTRIBUTES ON GAME BASED LEARNING

It is deduced that game-based learning offer multiple ways to learn, provide an opportunity for active learning, and encourage experimentation and discovery (Gee, 2007, pp. 221-227). Shaffer, Squire, Halverson, and Gee (2005) stress one benefit of games-based learning as the fact that game-based learning immerse players in a community of practice (2005, p. 107). It was found that using games can enhance content knowledge because words that are difficult to memorize through rote learning "comes easily if learners are immersed in activities and experiences that use these facts for plans, goals, and purposes within a coherent domain of knowledge" (Shaffer et al., 2005, p. 109).

Researchers have studied differences in the ways that learning was structured in the past compared to the preferences of current students. For example, learner's may master a task by reading the manual rather than if the interface will teach how to use it, as is standard in most video games (Prensky, 2001, p. 2). Social interactions are not the only skills occurring when using game-based learning within the classroom. There is a direct correlation to academic scores heightening through game-based learning, especially for struggling students. Students with disabilities have a more difficult time connecting with traditional approaches, as discussed before, which is why game-based learning can help alleviate some of the labor students feel from academics (Rominus, 2019). Researchers found another direct correlation between higher academic outcomes using game-based learning (Spires, 2015; Hamari et al., 2015; El Mawas et al., 2019). In mathematics, specifically division and multiplication, students who were in the experimental group played games focused on multiplication and division while the control group was taught with a traditional approach. At the end of the experiment, the experimental In a nutshell, the link between games and literacies is the bigger question in this chapter. Ours is to bring learning closer to fun by assessing the potential of using game based learning method as a strategy to enhance learning.

LIMITATIONS AND PROBLEMS ANTICIPATED ON GAME BASED LEARNING

A criticism frequently voiced about games-based learning arises from the notion that playing games is strictly a leisure activity, while education is (or should be) serious work. As Rieber, Smith, and Noah (1998) note: "The common-sense tendency to define play as the opposite of work makes it easy to be sceptical that play is a valid characterization for adult behaviors" (para. 8). However, there is a large and growing body of research that supports the efficacy of games in teaching and learning. Games can "provide structure and organization to complex domains" (Rieber et al., para. 21), and "create intrinsic motivation [emphasis in original] through fantasy, control, challenge, curiosity, and competition" (Squire, 2005, para. 5). These elements of games are also critical components of learning Smale (2011).

Games usually involve materials (game boards, dice, cards, computers, etc.) that may range from inexpensive to costly (de Freitas, 2006, p. 16). There are also the costs of game development (deWinter et al., 2010, para. 5-6). Instructors interested in using games in teaching must also consider issues of access to required game materials and supplies. Will students play games in a traditional classroom, a computer lab, at home, or outside of school, and will materials be available in those locations (de Freitas,

2006, p. 16)? Again, access may be particularly problematic for digital games, which could ostensibly be played on a game console, computer, handheld system, or cell phone. While common, these technologies are still unevenly distributed throughout the college and university student population (deWinter et al., 2010) with the content to be explored and learned through the game.

Indeed, many of the information literacy video games discussed above required significant financial investment and were often funded via grants (Beck et al., 2008; Markey et al., 2008a, 2010; Thistlethwaite, 2001). Pedagogical and technical support may be necessary for both instructors and students (de Freitas, 2006, p. 16), which carries additional costs. While relatively inexpensive and user-friendly applications for developing, digital games do exist,10 issues of time and technical skill may limit opportunities for many librarians to use them. As Martin and Ewing (2008) suggested, "creating digital games for library instruction may not be feasible with tight budgets and limited staff" (p. 212).

Games can be time consuming as teachers also faces a lot of administration work like planning for lessons and assessments on top of teaching. Choosing games, creation and making resources available is a tremendous but demanding and tiring work. Extra efforts are required for teachers not used to including games as part of their teaching and knowledge construction. Teaching large classes is challenging on its own and adding game based learning will require organization especially where games will need materials like papers and the accompanying resources, such as print-outs, game boards, and game cards can be damaged or lost, which results in a need for replacement. von Gillern& Alaswad (2016) alludes that although non-digital games often need to be maintained and/or reproduced over time, the benefits they can confer often outweigh such a cost.

Lastly it is contested that prior to the use of game-based learning, educators should be taught how to use certain game design framework to help form games creating positive learning outcomes. Educators should also play these games prior to having students play the games to have a better understanding of what the students are doing and why. Two other important concepts prior to using game-based learning in a classroom include preaching students with disabilities how to appropriately use technology for digital games and training for the teachers on technology and digital gaming (Wajiuhullah et al.,2018) McKenzi (2020).

MATERIALS AND METHODS

Study Area

The study is based on fieldwork conducted around Thohoyandou community in the Limpopo Province, South Africa. The community falls within Thulamela district under Vhembe municipal area. The population is dominated by Venda speaking people and very few Tsonga and Sotho speaking people. There are other tribes like Indians, other Africans and Chinese who arrived in the area to seek business opportunities. Thohoyandou is the major town in the municipality. The municipality is situated in the eastern subtropical region of the province, and is categorised as falling within the hot semi-arid region (Kottek et al., 2006).

Study Design

A qualitative study was conducted to assess the potential enhancement of different literacies that emanates from playing indigenous and the feasibility to introduce them to learning environment. Data was collected directly by interactions with participants. 12 different groups of children were observed while playing different games. In each game 3 groups were observed to familiarise researchers with the games and interviews were done using a checklist of different forms of literacies to identify relevancy. Different groups of children participated in different games and they were observed from the natural environment. Parents were asked to allow the children to participate in the study and they were very happy that the children were part of the games. Permission was sought from the chief as the gate keeper of the community and it was through him that the parents were asked to allow the children to participate in the study. All children speak Tshivenda and the interviews were done in their language. The themes were developed using content analysis and different types of literacies came out during interviews and observations. Completeness and consistency of collected data were obtained through quick evaluation of data through informal discussions with the participants.

Brown (2010) alluded that game based learning allow students to engage in various types of play which includes social play, imaginative and pretend play, storytelling and narrative play and creative play.

RESULTS AND DISCUSSIONS

To address the aim of this chapter, we observed 5 groups of children playing different games and interviewed key informants within the communities to identify weather the games enhance literacies when children performs them. The first game that we shall discuss is *tsetsetse,* followed by *muravharavha* then *ndonde* and *mufuvha*. In our discussions, we address the different literacies that align to a specific game. Hayes and Gee (2010, p. 67) asserted that, 'Game literacy is itself multiple, embedded in different practices and fully sociocultural situated.

Tsetsetse

Tsetsetse has different categories but our presentation is limited to two types. The first type is the one which uses alphabetical order and the second one uses numbers. The game is played by girls and boys together. Children starts by drawing a box with ten blocks. Each block is assigned a different alphabet. As an example, a category of alphabets displayed will be: B- which stand for a boys, G- stand for girls, F- stand for Fruits, V- stand for vegetables, C- stand for colors, A- stand for animals, D -stand for domestic animals, B -stand for birds, T- stand for trees, Z- stand for zoo. .

To play this game one person stands in a first block, she or he must be able to jump from the first block to the next until they cover all the blocks at the same time shouting the names of boys, in this example the child can use the following names as example: Liam, Noah, Olive, Elijah., William, James, Benjamin, Lucas, Paul. Because the player will be standing in block number 1, 9 blocks will be left and the player should jump from one block to another 9 times. In case the player miss to mention a name in a block, they have failed and the next person will replace the player.

Figure 1. Tsetsetse game, picture taken by authors

The next person will come and start from the first box and mention names of boys. In case they manage to recall all names jumping from one block to another they have passed and they can go to the next level which is the second block with a G- standing for girls. Just like in the previous one, the child will jump within the blocks mentioning names of girls until they arrive at the tenth box but this time the player remains with 8 blocks instead of 9 as the G is on the second in the box. The player can use the following names as examples: Olivia, Emma, Ava, Charlotte, Sophia., Amelia, Isabella, Mia.The third block is written F and the F stands for different kind of fruits. Starting from the third block the players will be expected to mention 7 different types of fruits until they finish and again with reduction of boxes, examples will be apple, pear, mango, banana, litchis, pineapple, pawpaw & oranges. When they pass, the next level is easier as blocks are reduced. The next box may require the player to mention different colours if written C, then a player will name different cloulours as they jump from one block to another like blue, green, yellow, red, white, orange, black, purple, grey, brown etc.

In the next level the player will be expected to mention different types of animal in the same manner, then move to letter A for animals she/he can be able to mention the wild animals, in D they will mention domestic animals only, T for different trees, B for birds, Z for different types of ZOOs they know. In case a player finishes all the boxes without skipping, the player wins a crown and become the champion. A champion is expected write new letters for the boxes, for example F- for flowers, P for pets, etc. The next player must name them as they continue to play.

The second type do not use alphabets but they replace alphabets with numbers. The players draw two rows with 5 boxes on each row and a big circle on top, the players number the boxes from number 1 up to 10. The first player will put the flat stone on the block move it with one leg while jumping, the trick for the player is that they make it a point that that the stone should be inserted inside block and if a stone stop on top of a line, the player is out. A player who manage to pass in all this stages and win they crown her/him and a champion who is expected to lead by inserting numbers the way they deem fit.

Enhancing Literacy Skills Using Indigenous Games

Figure 2. Tsetsetse using numbers, picture taken by authors

Table 1. Check list of literacy skills observed from tsetsetse

Literacy skill	Examples	Checklist
Vernacular literacy	• Writing skills • Oral skills	X
Visual literacy	• discriminate and • interpret the visible actions, • objects and • symbols that are natural and man-made	X
School literacy	• effective communication skills, • manners and etiquettes, • morals, values, standards, principles and ethics • *Academic Concepts* • *Peaceful Conflict Resolution Methods*	X

continues on following page

405

Table 1. Continued

Literacy skill	Examples	Checklist
Health literacy	• decisions in one's daily life in terms of health care, disease prevention, health promotion • using medication	x
Numerical literacy	• Understanding charts, diagrams and data • Solve problems • Check answers • Explain solutions • Use logic	X
Digital literacy	• critically use technology, • to navigate through various online forums and devices, • understanding how technology works, and • being able to creatively and inventively manipulate technology to solve problems	
Financial literacy	• Understanding how finance work and applying them in one's life • Managing personal funds • Confidence in making decisions • Using resources constructively	
Media literacy	• understand the messages you are being told on television, radio, video games, movies, news programs, social media, and more	
Cultural literacy	• language, • methods, • assumptions, • and unstated ideas that make up a way to behave and communicate	X
Emotional literacy	• Identifying, validating, and expressing your feelings, as well as • recognizing and responding to the feelings	X
Physical literacy	• The development and repeated use of fine motor skills, balance, confident movement, and the enjoyment of being able to move with skill	X

As literature indicated, using games can enhance content knowledge because words that are difficult to memorize through rote learning "comes easily if learners are immersed in activities and experiences that use these facts for plans, goals, and purposes within a coherent domain of knowledge" (Shaffer et al., 2005, p. 109). Tsetsetse teaches children literacy skills because through the game children learn to read and write numbers and alphabets, this skill falls under vernacular literacy. This game is played by both sexes together which teaches children cooperation and working together. Playing the game requires the children to be able to think quickly as they are jumping from different blocks and they should be able to memorize words. Children learn different categories of things which is helpful at their level for cognitive development, e.g. players will be required to mention the names of different vegetables by listing them one can be able to know the types of vegetables such as black jack, okra, pumpkins etc. by doing so the children's will be learning relevant information for food security. Children learn different colours, animals and their differences as different animals and makes them to differentiate between wild animals such as wolf, tigers, cheetah etc. and domestic animals such as dogs, cat, cows, goats etc. the game also teaches this children's to differentiate the animals that live in water such as hippopotamus, crocodiles, fish, crabs etc. and in a land, also birds that birds are something that fly on air with different names such as owl, swallows, doves etc. ., animal live on land, to animals they are those live in a zoo where people can go and see them such as Zebra, Lion, Giraffe, chimpanzee etc., because they are not anywhere. They also learn the different types of trees that trees such as Marula tree, Pine tree, oak etc. The game will teach players to count and add through blocks. The children also develop their physical and emotional literacy while jumping. They learn to cooperate and work in groups. Lastly the players advance school literacy through playing *tsetsetse*. Players can develop knowledge and understanding in terms of other aspects such as, effective communication skills, manners and etiquettes, morals, values, standards, principles and ethics. The school literacy is regarded as an instrument that helps the individuals to achieve their personal and professional goals (Blikstad - Balas, 2013). School literacy is regarded as a social activity. From this perspective, literacy is no longer framed as the discrete set of individual cognitive skills. In conclusion, physical literacy and health are added because the play itself carries health benefits which is crucial for children who usually uses transport with less walking and physical activities especially in developed areas where children will not be expected to go out and carry water, wood or go to the fields to farm. Children can also learn different types of diseases if D is ascribed to a block and they should name different types of diseases.

Muravharavha

Muravharavha is a game that is being played by both girls and boys. *Muravharavha* is played on a special board with 24 cells connected with lines indicating valid movements as in the diagram. The players are divided into two groups and they use two different colour of stones. One group can use smooth white stones while another group play with brown stones/ black stones of the average size. The board is empty when the game begins. Each player has 12 pieces of stones. The player with dark stones will be the one to make a first move. Each turn consists of placing a stone on an empty intersection on the board or a ground where it is drawn. The aim is to create a row of three stones on any line drawn on the board. If a player forms a row, he or she may remove or "shoot" one of the opponent's stones. The lost stones are removed from the board and not placed again. A stone in a row may not be taken unless all the opponent's stones are in row, in which case any stone may be lost. Even if a move creates more than one row, only one stone can be taken in a single move.

Players can "break" their own raw. A row may be broken and remade repeatedly by shuffling stones back and forth. Each time the row is remade, one of the opponent's stones are shot. Of course, by breaking the row the player exposes the stones which were in a row to the risk of being taken by the opponent on his or her next turn.

A player who is left with only three stones remaining can be allowed to take frantic measures where the player's stones "fly" to any empty intersection. If one player has three stones and the other player has more than three stones, only the player with three stones can fly. When one opponent is left with two stones or cannot move further, the other player wins. If one player picks up all stones while the play is still on, the player whose stones are on the board wins by default. As part of the rules if one cheats the other one wins by default. Playing twice as well gives the other an opportunity to win by default. Beck and Wade (2006) mention that game based playing encourages players 'cognitive, language, emotional and social engagement in a social/cultural environment for collaborative play. This is easily traced from *muravharavha* players. They proposition here is that game based learning provides a context that allows students to immerse themselves in complex, problem tasks which requires expertise, social networking and collaboration where gamers can rapidly analyse new situations, interact with other people of different characteristics from theirs, solve problems quickly and independently, think strategically in a chaotic world and collaborate effectively in teams (Beck & Wade, (2006)

Figure 3. Children drawing muravharavha board on the ground

Players of this game, *Muravharavha* learns to solve problems and to plan to avoid loss. Players should make sure that when playing *Muravharavha*, they strategize to have same colour stones in a raw to win or at least block the opponent so that the opponent may fail to move to any direction. Arithmetic skills are integral when playing this game. Good moral behaviour helps players not to lose by default in case they cheat. Drawing skills are very critical today for technology students and planners. When children draw the board, they get to learn how to draw at an early age and it may influence the love to design as they grow.

Figure 4. Children playing muravharavha

Enhancing Literacy Skills Using Indigenous Games

It should be noted that this is one game that was found to be very popular in many cultures in our study and researchers believe that the game is helpful in developing arithmetic skills. Previous research on *muravhravha* thou using different names from the Venda articulations includes the work of Dunne (2014) and Knight (2003) from Moloi (2021), who suggests that incorporating indigenous games into the teaching and learning of mathematics is significant because learners in elementary grades learn through playing. In acknowledging the importance of decolonisation in mathematics education, Nkopodi and Mosimege (2009) incorporated (morabaraba) translated to be *muravharavha in Tshivenda*, an indigenous game, in the learning of mathematics, and presented information on relevant skills and indigenous knowledge that could be linked with the game.

Nkopodi and Mosimege (2009) cited that *morabaraba* (board game) and *diketo* (coordination game) as examples of indigenous games that could assist learners to learn mathematics word problems better and with deeper understanding. In support of this view, Dziva, Mpofu and Kusure (2011) state that using indigenous games to teach mathematics gives learners the opportunity to learn how to link their everyday experiences with mathematics. Cognisant of the foregoing, the researchers confirm that children learn mathematical word problems optimally when their learning is deep-rooted in playful activities, thus using play to learn (Imray & Hinchcliffe, 2013; Young & Murray, 2017; Moro, 2020). In agreement with previous research we found that school literacy, visual literacy, financial, arithmetic, cultural and physical literacy was observable skills that *muravharavha* contributed to as children were playing the games. Through playing *muravharavha* children could learn to solve problems, check answers and explain solutions while using logic to make sure they win against the opponents. *Muravharavha* teaches financial management because a child needs to keep the stones safe and they need to spend those available wisely targeting needs. They acquire a skill to understand how finance work and applying them in one's life, helping them to learn managing personal funds, confidence in making decisions and using resources constructively. The other literacies and explanations are ticked in the table below.

Table 2. Check list of literacy skills observed from muravharavha

Literacy skill	Examples	checklist
Vernacular literacy	• Writing skills • Oral skills	
Visual literacy	• discriminate and • interpret the visible actions, • objects and • symbols that are natural and man-made	X
School literacy	• effective communication skills, • manners and etiquettes, • morals, values, standards, principles and ethics • *Academic Concepts* • *Peaceful Conflict Resolution Methods*	X
Health literacy	• decisions in one's daily life in terms of health care, disease prevention, health promotion • using medication	
Numerical literacy	• Understanding charts, diagrams and data • Solve problems • Check answers • Explain solutions • Use logic	X

continues on following page

Table 2. Continued

Literacy skill	Examples	checklist
Digital literacy	• critically use technology, • to navigate through various online forums and devices, • understanding how technology works, and • being able to creatively and inventively manipulate technology to solve problems	
Financial literacy	• Understanding how finance work and applying them in one's life • Managing personal funds • Confidence in making decisions • Using resources constructively	X
Media literacy	• understand the messages you are being told on television, radio, video games, movies, news programs, social media, and more	
Cultural literacy	• language, • methods, • assumptions, • and unstated ideas that make up a way to behave and communicate	X
Emotional literacy	• Identifying, validating, and expressing your feelings, as well as • recognizing and responding to the feelings	X
Physical literacy	• The development and repeated use of fine motor skills, balance, confident movement, and the enjoyment of being able to move with skill	X

Ndode

Ndode is a game that is usually played by Vhavenda girls. Girls collect 48 small stones of the same size and the stones must be put in a small circle or small hole. There is one big stone that is used to play with. The players sit around the hole while the first player hold the big stone, she throws it up, quickly scoop some small stones from the circle while the big stone is still rolling up on the air, hold the big one, throw it on the air again while taking back small stones into the circle, leaving one stone. The process is repeated until all stones are collected and there will be no stone left in the circle. The players are expected to count verbally while playing. The player can fail if the big stoned fall or if they leave more than two small stones out of the circle or if on returning small stones they fail to be inserted in the whole or inside the circle. The layers must monitor the big stone thrown to the air and small stones on the ground.

When players finish the first round in the second round they remain with two small stones outside the circle instead of one. This continues until they remain with three, four, five conservatively. The process happens very fast to an extent that coordination is needed. In the last round the player scoop all small stones from the circle and return them at ones. The following skills are of imperative during the game, it helps children to develop the hand, eyes and memory coordination. *Ndode* teaches children arithmetic 'skills as they learn to read and count. In this game, more than one child can play in one circle at a go depending on the space. In doing so they learn to work together in a group. The check list assist us to see some of the skills developed during *ndode* game.

Enhancing Literacy Skills Using Indigenous Games

Figure 5. Taken by the authors

Table 3. Check list of literacy skills observed from ndode

Literacy skill	Examples	Checklist
Vernacular literacy	• Writing skills • Oral skills	
Visual literacy	• discriminate and • interpret the visible actions, • objects and • symbols that are natural and man-made	X
School literacy	• effective communication skills, • manners and etiquettes, • morals, values, standards, principles and ethics • *Academic Concepts* • *Peaceful Conflict Resolution Methods*	X
Health literacy	• decisions in one's daily life in terms of health care, disease prevention, health promotion • using medication	
Numerical literacy	• Understanding charts, diagrams and data • Solve problems • Check answers • Explain solutions • Use logic	X
Digital literacy	• critically use technology, • to navigate through various online forums and devices, • understanding how technology works, and • being able to creatively and inventively manipulate technology to solve problems	

continues on following page

Table 3. Continued

Literacy skill	Examples	Checklist
Financial literacy	• Understanding how finance work and applying them in one's life • Managing personal funds • Confidence in making decisions • Using resources constructively	X
Media literacy	• understand the messages you are being told on television, radio, video games, movies, news programs, social media, and more	
Cultural literacy	• language, • methods, • assumptions, • and unstated ideas that make up a way to behave and communicate	X
Emotional literacy	• Identifying, validating, and expressing your feelings, as well as • recognizing and responding to the feelings	X
Physical literacy	• The development and repeated use of fine motor skills, balance, confident movement, and the enjoyment of being able to move with skill	X

Mufuvha/ Mutoga

Mufuvha is a Vhavenda game that is also called mutoga in other areas. The game dated from many years as holes for mutoga were also found craved on stones in mapungubwe area. To play the game depending on weather is a small one or a big one a set of holes are prepared. It may be 4 rows, each row with 12 small holes. To set the players may decide to put 3 or 4 stones in each hole. Two players engage in a game while others will be spectators. The stones that are used to play mufuvha are assigned different names which are: *ndomo, thoga, khasha as well as mboho. Mboho is the main character/* the main stone. Players of Mufuvha move a stone *ndomo* to the relevant hole if he/ she wins the player take the stones for his opponent, he will move the stones until they form *mboho*, even the opponents play and if he/she wins, the player must take the opponents stones. By doing that they do counter plays while in alternates between the players, with each choosing one of their holes to move the stones from, dropping a stone in each hole, moving clockwise around the board, and skipping the opponent's store. If the last stone ends in the player's store, the player may take another turn. Play ends when all the holes on one side of the board are empty, and the winner is the one with the most stones in their store. If the number of stones in each store is equal, the game is a tie. Assuming standard intelligence, a new player should be able to understand the game and begin playing strategically within just a few games. When they add stones to the holes the remaining one will be called *khasha,* it goes like that but a person who is playing can be someone who is intelligent and able to know where to go which stone to move when playing, When a game is over we call it *mufuvha woxa* .

Mufuvha has been found to encourage literacy skills especially mathematics. The calculations involved can help players to be financially smart. A lot of other literacies include moral behavior and working with others in a group, critical thinking, creativity, self-control, empathy, negotiation, communication, collaboration, problem solver, open-minded, flexibility, and organizational skills. The table easily shows all the literacy skills observed from children while playing the game.

Figure 6. Children playing Mufuvha, picture taken by authors

Table 4. Checklist Observed for Mufuvha

Literacy skill	Examples	Checklist
Vernacular literacy	• Writing skills • Oral skills	
Visual literacy	• Discriminate and • interpret the visible actions, • objects and • symbols that are natural and man-made	X
School literacy	• effective communication skills, • manners and etiquettes, • morals, values, standards, principles and ethics • *Academic Concepts* • *Peaceful Conflict Resolution Methods*	X
Health literacy	• decisions in one's daily life in terms of health care, disease prevention, health promotion • using medication	
Numerical literacy	• Understanding charts, diagrams and data • Solve problems • Check answers • Explain solutions • Use logic	X
Digital literacy	• critically use technology, • to navigate through various online forums and devices, • understanding how technology works, and • being able to creatively and inventively manipulate technology to solve problems	
Financial literacy	• Understanding how finance work and applying them in one's life • Managing personal funds • Confidence in making decisions • Using resources constructively	X
Media literacy	• understand the messages you are being told on television, radio, video games, movies, news programs, social media, and more	
Cultural literacy	• language, • methods, • assumptions, • and unstated ideas that make up a way to behave and communicate	X

continues on following page

Table 4. Continued

Literacy skill	Examples	Checklist
Emotional literacy	• Identifying, validating, and expressing your feelings, as well as • recognizing and responding to the feelings	X
Physical literacy	• The development and repeated use of fine motor skills, balance, confident movement, and the enjoyment of being able to move with skill	X

CONCLUSION

The beauty of games from Vhavenda context is based on unity, sharing, working together, cultural and social expressions. In addition, games, can build mental skills and help in physical development. The inclusion of games as a method in teaching is doable and can be done with targeted outcomes. As cultural practices gradually erode, it is imperative that we look at those cultural aspects that can develop our nation and preserve them. The study shows that games can enhance learning, the fact that children spends more time at schools make it important to revive them by incorporating them into the curriculum as we decolonize education, in so doing our cultural heritage as Africans will be preserved as well. Governments and private sectors may also play a role by encouraging competitions based on cultural heritage games to popularise them again as children today spend much of their times on media. In a nutshell, the importance of using games carries the possibility of positive contributions to teaching and learning as others researchers contemplates that contemporary education should focuses on assisting learners in reaching their full potential in all developmental domains (cognitive, affective, psychomotor and social) (Gallahue & Donnelly, 2003). Curriculum design and development is said to be an urgent priority in addressing the unique needs of the learners in a culturally diverse society. Physical activity is a crucial component in the school curriculum which focuses on the holistic development of learners (Davis et al., 2000). Being said, Indigenous games can enrich the school curriculum and provide meaningful means for education in promoting ethnic understanding as well as in providing an opportunity in all developmental domains. The multi-faceted development is therefore aided by exposure to cultural and game content that is acted out on the field of play. Inclusion of indigenous games in a school curriculum can develop a sense of community and therefore demonstrates acceptable social values, contributing towards nation building. Learners participating in organized sessions of indigenous games can foster a positive self-concept within their own cultural heritage, as well as among the various ethnic groups within a multicultural society (Roux, Burnett & Hollande,2008).

REFERENCES

Blikstad-Balas, M. (2013). *Redefining School Literacy. Prominent Literacy Practices. Across Subjects in Upper Secondary School*. University of Oslo. Retrieved May 01, 2019 from https://www.duo.uio.no/bitstream/handle/10852/38160/1/dravhandling-blikstad-balas.pdf

Bogopa, D. L. (2012). The importance of indigenous games: The selected cases of indigenous games in South Africa. *Indilinga, 11*(2), 245–256.

Brown, C. L., Comunale, M. A., Wigdahl, B., & Urdaneta-Hartmann, S. (2018). Current climate for digital game-based learning of science in further and higher education. *FEMS Microbiology Letters*, *365*(21), fny237. doi:10.1093/femsle/fny237 PMID:30260380

Brundha, M. P., & Akshaya, K. (n.d.). *Use of crazy card games in understanding pathology-research*. Academic Press.

Burnett, C., & Hollander, W. J. (2004). The South African indigenous games research project of 2001/2002. *S.A. Journal for Research in Sport Physical Education and Recreation*, *26*(1), 9–23. doi:10.4314ajrs.v26i1.25873

Campbell, B. (1990). What is literacy? Acquiring and using literacy skills. *Australasian Public Libraries and Information Services*, *3*(3), 149–152.

Catts, R., & Lau, J. (2008). *Towards information literacy indicators*. Academic Press.

Chapter 6. (2006). *Understandings of Literacy*. Education for All Global Monitoring Report. Retrieved May 02, 2019 from http://www.unesco.org/education/GMR2006/full/chapt6_eng.pdf

Computer Literacy Skills. (n.d.). Retrieved May 01, 2019 from https://mdk12.msde.maryland.gov/instruction/curriculum/technology_literacy/computerliteracyskills.pdf

Corlett, J. T., & Mokgwathi, M. M. (1986). Play, games, sport preferences of Tswana children. In *Sport, culture, society. International historical and sociological perspectives. Proceedings of the VIII Commonwealth and International Conference on Sport, Physical Education, Dance, Recreation and Health. Conference'86 Glasgow, 18-23 July* (pp. 253-261). E. & FN Spon.

De Freitas, S. (2006). *Learning in immersive worlds: A review of game-based learning*. Academic Press.

Digital Literacy. (n.d.). Retrieved May 01, 2019 from https://www.deakin.edu.au/__data/assets/pdf_file/0008/1237742/digital-literacy.pdf

Dinan Thompson, M., Meldrum, K., & Sellwood, J. (2014). '… it is not just a game': Connecting with culture through Traditional Indigenous Games. *American Journal of Educational Research*, *2*(11), 1015–1022.

Ding, J., Shan, R., Chenmeng, M., Tu, M., Yu, Q., Kong, F., & Zhao, Q. (2021). Are online games a blessing or evil? The moderating role of self-worth. *Thinking Skills and Creativity*, *41*, 100915. doi:10.1016/j.tsc.2021.100915

Downing, S. (2005). The social construction of entrepreneurship: Narrative and dramatic processes in the coproduction of organizations and identities. *Entrepreneurship Theory and Practice*, *29*(2), 185–204. doi:10.1111/j.1540-6520.2005.00076.x

Edlund, A. C., Edlund, L. E., & Haugen, S. (Eds.). (2014). *Vernacular Literacies – Past, Present and Future*. Umea University and Royal Skyttean Society. Retrieved May 01, 2019 from http://umu.diva-portal.org/smash/get/diva2:738154/FULLTEXT01.pdf

Felten, P. (2008). *Visual Literacy*. Retrieved May 02, 2019 from http://one2oneheights.pbworks.com/f/Felten,P.(2008).Visual%20Literacy.pdf

Franklin, R. M. (2004). *Moral Literacy: The Knowledge of Truth, Justice, Goodness and Interdependence*. Retrieved May 02, 2019 from https://c.ymcdn.com/sites/www.sais.org/resource/resmgr/imported/HC%2004%20Franklin.pdf

Gallahue, D. L., & Donnelly, F. C. (2003). Movement skill acquisition. In *Developmental Physical Education for all Children* (4th ed.). Human Kinetics.

Hayes, E. R., & Gee, J. P. (2010). No selling the genie lamp: A game literacy practice in The Sims. *E-Learning and Digital Media*, 7(1), 67–78. doi:10.2304/elea.2010.7.1.67

Imray, P., & Hinchcliffe, V. (2013). *Curricula for teaching children and young people with severe or profound and multiple learning difficulties: Practical strategies for educational professionals*. Routledge. doi:10.4324/9781315883298

James, M. (2020). *The Impact of Game-Based Learning in a Special Education Classroom*. Academic Press.

Kapur, R. (n.d.). *Significance and Meaning of Academic Literacy*. https://www.researchgate.net/profile/Radhika_Kapur/publication/336982773_Significance_and_Meaning_of_Academic_Literacy/links/5dbd1fc4a6fdcc2128f8ff82/Significance-and-Meaning-of-Academic-Literacy

Katz, J., & Mirenda, P. (2002). Including students with developmental disabilities in general education classrooms: Educational benefits. *International Journal of Special Education*, 17(2), 14–24.

Keefe, E. B., & Copeland, S. R. (2011). What is Literacy? The Power of a Definition. *Research and Practice for Persons with Severe Disabilities*, 36(3-4), 92–99. doi:10.2511/027494811800824507

Kickbusch, I., Pelikan, J. M., Apfel, F., & Tsouros, A. D. (Eds.). (2013). *Health Literacy. The Solid Facts*. World Health Organization. Retrieved May 03, 2019 from http://www.euro.who.int/__data/assets/pdf_file/0008/190655/e96854.pdf

Kottek, M., Grieser, J., Beck, C., Rudolf, B., & Rubel, F. (2006). *World map of the Köppen-Geiger climate classification updated*. Academic Press.

Liu, E. Z. F., & Chen, P. K. (2013). The effect of game-based learning on students' learning performance in science learning–A case of "conveyance go". *Procedia: Social and Behavioral Sciences*, 103, 1044–1051. doi:10.1016/j.sbspro.2013.10.430

Livingstone, S. (2004). What is media literacy? *Intermedia*, 32(3), 18-20. Retrieved May 03, 2019 from http://eprints.lse.ac.uk/1027/1/What_is_media_literacy_(LSERO).pdf

Moloi, T. J. (2015). Using indigenous games to teach problem-solving in mathematics in rural learning ecologies. *Journal of Higher Education in Africa/Revue de l'enseignement supèrieur en Afrique*, 13(1-2), 21-32.

Moloi, T. J., Mosia, M. S., Matabane, M. E., & Sibaya, K. T. (2021). The Use of Indigenous Games to Enhance the Learning of Word Problems in Grade 4 Mathematics: A Case of Kgati. *International Journal of Learning, Teaching and Educational Research*, 20(1), 240–259.

Mweli, P. (2018). Indigenous stories and games as approaches to teaching within the classroom. *Understanding Educational Psychology*, 94-101.

Nkopodi, N., & Mosimege, M. (2009). Incorporating the indigenous game of morabaraba in the learning of mathematics. *South African Journal of Education*, *29*(3), 377–392. doi:10.15700aje.v29n3a273

Nxumalo, S. A., & Mncube, D. W. (2018). Using indigenous games and knowledge to decolonise the school curriculum: Ubuntu perspectives. *Perspectives in Education*, *36*(2), 103–118. doi:10.18820/2519593X/pie.v36i2.9

Pinard, R., de Winter, A., Sarkis, G. J., Gerstein, M. B., Tartaro, K. R., Plant, R. N., Egholm, M., Rothberg, J. M., & Leamon, J. H. (2006). Assessment of whole genome amplification-induced bias through high-throughput, massively parallel whole genome sequencing. *BMC Genomics*, *7*(1), 1–21. doi:10.1186/1471-2164-7-216 PMID:16928277

Polistina, K. (n.d.). *Cultural Literacy. Understanding and Respect for the Cultural Aspects of Sustainability*. Retrieved May 02, 2019 from http://arts.brighton.ac.uk/__data/assets/pdf_file/0006/5982/Cultural-Literacy.pdf

Roux, C. J., Burnett, C., & Hollander, W. J. (2008). Curriculum enrichment through indigenous Zulu games. *S.A. Journal for Research in Sport Physical Education and Recreation*, *30*(1), 89–103. doi:10.4314ajrs.v30i1.25985

Shaffer, D. W., Squire, K. R., Halverson, R., & Gee, J. P. (2005). Video games and the future of learning. *Phi Delta Kappan*, *87*(2), 105–111. doi:10.1177/003172170508700205

Smale, M. A. (2011). *Learning through quests and contests: Games in information literacy instruction*. Academic Press.

Steiner, C. (2003). *Emotional Literacy: Intelligence with a Heart*. Retrieved May 03, 2019 from http://emotional-literacy-training.com/wp-content/uploads/2015/09/Steiner-Emotional-Literacy.pdf

Tillman, A. (2012). *What We See and Why It Matters: How Competency in Visual Literacy Can Enhance Student Learning*. Retrieved May 03, 2019 from https://digitalcommons.iwu.edu/cgi/viewcontent.cgi?article=1008&context=education_honproj

Vandercruysse, S., Vandewaetere, M., & Clarebout, G. (2012). Game-based learning: A review on the effectiveness of educational games. Handbook of research on serious games as educational, business and research tools, 628-647.

von Gillern, S., & Alaswad, Z. (2016). Games and game-based learning in instructional design. *International Journal of Technologies in Learning*, *23*(4), 1–7. doi:10.18848/2327-0144/CGP/v23i04/1-7

Chapter 22
Exploring the Use of African Indigenous Games in Teaching Critical Thinking Skills

Hulisani Mulaudzi
University of Venda, South Africa

Rendani Tshifhumulo
https://orcid.org/0000-0003-4133-3656
University of Venda, South Africa

Tshimangadzo J. Makhanikhe
University of Venda, South Africa

ABSTRACT

Critical thinking skills are fundamental for both undergraduate and postgraduate students in the academic environment. These skills allow students to question and reflect on the knowledge and information presented to them. These skills can be learned differently through various instruments. This chapter explores how this game can contribute towards teaching critical thinking skills. There are various indigenous games played in Vhavenda culture. The researchers focus on an indigenous game, Duvheke. The chapter employs game-based pedagogy as a theory that underpins this study. Methodologically, the chapter assumes a qualitative complexion because it seeks to collect in-depth information about Duvheke and how it can be used in teaching critical thinking skills first entering students in a rural university. The data collection method used is interviews which were collected from first entering students. Preliminary findings suggest that critical thinking is needed to play Duvheke. The chapter suggests that Duvheke can be a valuable tool in teaching critical thinking skills.

DOI: 10.4018/978-1-7998-7271-9.ch022

Exploring the Use of African Indigenous Games in Teaching Critical Thinking Skills

INTRODUCTION

Critical thinking is a cognitive action which is connected to the ability to use the mind effectively. Learning to think critically, analyse and evaluate ways is interpreted as the demonstration of mental processing of attention, categorisation, selection and judgment (Cotrell, 2017). Critical thinking (CT) is an operative example of higher order thinking that can be accounted for due to reliable and validated tests. In the literature, CT has been defined as a skill of taking responsibility and control of our own mind (Paul, 1996), or as a logical and reflective thought which focuses on a decision in what to believe and what to do (Ennis, 1985). Linn (2000) mentions that critical thinking skills include the individual 'ability to identify the source of information, analysing its credibility, reflecting on whether that information is consistent with their prior knowledge, and drawing conclusions based on their critical thinking. University of Venda in its mission aims to produce students that are globally competitive future citizens and to achieve this aim, the University should be able to build students with high cognitive skills who can think critically, make decisions and solve problems. Ben-Chaim, Ron, & Zoller, 2000 alluded that in order to develop higher-order thinking skills, or higher order cognitive skills, there should be students' transmission of knowledge and skills into responsible action, regardless of their particular future role in society. Meeting this challenge requires, among others, the development of students' capacities of critical thinking (CT), which is necessary for the analysis of unfamiliar situations, so that their question-asking, problem-solving, and decision-making capabilities will be based on a framework of rational thinking (Ennis, 1989; Zoller, Ben-Chaim, Ron, Pentimalli, & Borsese, 2000).

Students with critical thinking skills can use scepticism and doubt constructively to analyse that which is before them(Cotrell,2017). In other words, they do not take information at face value but pound over it before they can digest information for use. Critical thinkers can make informed decisions based on rationality, judging its truthfulness and worth unlike acting on their first thought as the brain may assume that whatever comes is right. Critical thinker's reasons and make conclusion based on reasons (Kahneman, 2011). In doing so they do not miss relevant information nor omit it. A person who reasons makes conclusions based on facts that should support the concluded evidence.

In this study, we want to explore the possibility of using indigenous games to a teach high ordered skill which is critical thinking. We assume that there is rich knowledge hidden in one indigenous game, *duvheke* as we advocate for its use to enhance critical thinking skills. Critical thinking skills that we are interested in are based on the work of Cotrell (2017) which includes:

1. The ability to identify other people's position, arguments and conclusion,
2. To identify evidence for alternative points of view,
3. Weigh up the opposing arguments and evidence in a fair manner,
4. The ability to read between lines while searching behind surfaces, identify false and unfair assumptions,
5. The ability to recognise techniques used to make certain positives more appealing than others such as false issues and percussive devices,
6. Reflecting on issues in a structured way, bringing logic and insight,
7. The ability to draw conclusions about weather arguments are valid and justifiable based on good evidence and visible assumption and lastly,
8. The ability to synthesising information, drawing together own judgements of the evidence, synthesising false from own new position.

LITERATURE REVIEW

Optimistic Traits Proceeding Game Based Learning

According to Prensky (2001) a game must have the following six structural elements: (a) rules; (b) goals and objectives; (c) outcomes and feedback; (d) conflict, competition, challenge, or opposition; (e) interaction; and (f) representation or story. Compared to traditional learning methods such as listening to lectures, students are often more active during GBL (Kiili, 2005). Positive attributes from scholars on game based learning (GBL) includes the fact that GBL promote not only academic achievement but also critical thinking, according to both *problem-based learning* and *social conflict* theories (Noroozi et al., 2020; Wu et al., 2012). It is assumed that GBL can simulate real-world problems without perfect information in a safe environment, allowing students to try to solve them with different strategies over time, receive feedback, evaluate their information use and decisions, and thereby improve their future critical thinking. (Hwang & Chang, 2020).

Some games provide rich conflicting information and perspectives about a controversial topic (Noroozi et al., 2016), and students constructing games might create and resolve character and plot conflicts (Yang & Wu, 2012). Thoughtful and reconciling conflicting interpretations to make superior decisions advances students' beliefs about knowledge from absolutism to multiplism to evaluativism (Kuhn, 2020), providing the epistemic basis for critical thinking (Kuhn, 1999). In addition, storyline, incentives, or other game design elements can engage students to enhance their critical thinking and eloquent scientific argumentation over period of time(Bonney & Sternberg, 2011; Squire & Jan, 2007).

Limitations Raised

From a negative point of view Turkle, 2003; West et al., 2008; Wouters & van Oostendorp, 2013 is of the opinion that GBL might aid critical thinking and again foster intuitive learning and simple heuristics, which drive cognitive biases in judgment or reasoning and hinder critical thinking (Also, some game features unrelated to learning can distract students, increase their extraneous cognitive processing, and decrease available cognitive processing for critical thinking (Mayer, 2014). For example, an intensive high school course with digital game construction created a high cognitive load that hindered students' critical thinking skills (Chen & Zhuang, 2018)

Game Based Learning as an Instructional Tool

Cahill (2021) indicates that games have been used as a learning tool for centuries. The prevalence of games coupled with their motivational power has led renowned scholars to suggest that they will revolutionize education (Gee,2007; Prensky, 2008; Squire & Jenkins, 2003). While Cahill (2021) cites chess as game, this chapter focusses on an indigenous game, *duvheke*. Cahill says that the main idea behind game-based learning is teaching through repetition, failure and the accomplishment of goals. He further highlights that with game-based learning, students learn and practice the right way to do things. This aligns with the purpose of this chapter, which is to establish how *duvheke* can be used to teach critical thinking skills.

Globalization and digitization have reshaped the communication landscape, affecting how and with whom we communicate and deeply altering the terrain of language and literacy education (Lothering & Jenson. 2011). This coupled with the emergence of covid-19 has forced us to rethink and evaluate how we do things. That the world is changing it is undisputable and children do not want to be stuck in the classroom. (Cahill. 2021) shows that instead of education based on rote memorization, students learn through experimentation, trial and error. Discussions about modernizing the curriculum need to include solutions for keeping the students engaged and making sure that they learn how to be critical, confident and creative which are abilities they will need to succeed in the workplace (Cahill. 2021). We propose that *duvheke* can assist in instilling these abilities in students.

Mao et al. (2021) shows that game-based learning has a significant positive overall effect on students' critical thinking. Advocates of game-based learning argue that it increases critical thinking, however some studies show mixed results (Mao et al., 2021). In recent years, several literature review studies have attempted to summarize the collective body of knowledge that has been generated in the field of game based leaning with the hope of providing a sense of direction to the field (Bado, Franklin.,2014) Several studies focused on the outcome of game-based learning higher education (Subhash & Cudney, 2018; Tan et al., 2017). This supports the gap identified by the researchers that more research needs to be done on game-based learning. There have been studies conducted on game based leaning, but as a relatively new field of research, conducting more studies will allow us to arrive at better results and conclusions on how game-based learning can assist in teaching critical thinking skills.

Game Based Leaning and Critical Thinking Skills

The large positive game-based learning effect on critical thinking is consistent with two theories (problem-based learning, socio-conflict) and related studies (Mao et al. 2021). (Hwang & Chang, 2020; Wu et al., 2012) agree that the game-based learning effect is consistent with problem-based learning theory and the view that game-based learning's complex problems with imperfect information lets students try different strategies to solve them, give feedback to help them evaluate their information use and make decisions, which improves their critical thinking. This positive game-based learning effect is also consistent with the benefits of storyline and other game elements that engage students to sustain their critical thinking (Bonney & Sternberg, 2011; Squire & Jan, 2007). Evidence abounds that there are many benefits of using games in the classroom and importantly on critical thinking. This study will contribute positively by using an indigenous game(*duvheke*) to teach critical thinking skills to children and it is assumed that this will also contribute to other desirable academic outcomes such as mathematics (Tokac et al., 2019) creativity, communication and collaboration (Qian & Clark, 2016).

Vygotsky's Learning Theory

Vygotsky (2016) argued that when children play, they try to think with superior knowledge and skills, allowing them to perform at higher levels than otherwise. Vygotsky advocates for the superiority of play in children's learning of higher psychological skills such as critical thinking. Vygotsky operating in the education and early childhood education realm has contributed significantly to how children learn and this study. He conducted contextualizes the relevance of this chapter not only in the game-based learning environment but in the broader context of education and indigenous knowledge systems which this chapter assumes.

Superior critical thinking is related to better learning outcomes (Fong et al., 2017). Game design elements can engage students to sustain their critical thinking and meaningful scientific argumentation over time (Bonney & Sternberg, 2011; Squire & Jan, 2007). If games (*duvheke*) are to reach their full potential as a tool for teaching critical thinking skills, more research needs to be done on teachers' instructional practices in the classroom. (Garris, Ahles, & Driskell, 2002; Gunter, Kenny, & Vick, 2008) have conducted research on game-based learning, however the academic community needs more research that can aid in the teaching of critical thinking skills and how *duvheke* can facilitate that process. This is supported by Mao et.al (2021) who says that future studies of game-based learning should consider the impact of their specific game type. The insight that will be contributed by this chapter will bring depth to the teaching of critical teaching skills and to the entire academic community. Whilst there has been a lot of research conducted on game-based learning (Gee,2007; Prensky, 2008; Squire & Jenkins, 2003) most literature available focuses on digital games and how they can be developed and used in the classroom. There are no studies that have been done on *duvheke* as a game and how it can be used to teach critical thinking. This study therefore establishes the unique link between *duvheke* and teaching critical teaching skills.

The Difference between Digital and Non-Digital Games

Games originated as face to face social interaction with benefits of different literacy skills including physical development, social development and communication skills. People have been playing with and learning from games long before the personal computers (Avedon & Sutton-Smith, 1971; Juul, 2011). Researchers on game based learning believed that learning is an intrinsic component of games and the instructional design procedure. In relation to academic environments, educators have habitually used non-digital games to indorse learning in different disciplines for many years (Author, 2016; Kamii & DeVries, 1980; Zuckerman & Horn, 1973). Teachers realized that students enjoy playing games and these influenced teachers to pay their attention and got satisfaction with the activities, aligning with the ARCS model to include games in education through their instructional design (Keller, 1987). Different games can be useful for instructional subjects including math and physical science.

(Kapp, 2012; Prensky, 2005) agree on the definition of digital game-based learning, which they believe refers to the meaningful use of digital technological tools to facilitate actual games or a collection of digital gaming elements in an educational environment to enhance student learning through increasing student motivation and engagement. It comes with advantages to teaching and learning as results from a survey indicate that digital game-based learning often facilitates better attitudes towards learning, increases student motivation, fosters higher-order thinking, influence personal real-life perceptions, impacts decision-making processes, and aides students learning achievement, and these affordances align well with the four elements of the ARCS instructional design model. Games have been found to be better than conventional teaching as they are always enjoyable. Digital game based learning allows instructors to reach a comfortable medium where today's learners can engage and become educated in a manner that fits their learning processes and speaks their language (Prensky and Berry, 2001).

Griffiths (2003) alludes that educational video games are helpful when children have attention and impulsive disorders and through game based learning they gain social, instructional and organizational benefits. Floyd (2008) added that games that are designed properly provide authentic learning opportunities which can add to sense of relevance to instructional materials.

Digital game based learning is limited because they require instructors to be cautious to avoid overlooking opportunities that apply learning in life contexts. Digital game-based learning can be a valuable approach to simulate life applications when actual involvement in life activities is not possible or feasible, but it does not necessarily replace physical involvement. In conclusion, digital games often require players to look at computer screens for extended periods of time, but non-digital games often incorporate verbal interaction, eye-contact, and body language, which are valuable social skills to be developed in conjunction with the content to be explored and learned through the game.

METHODOLOGY

Babbie and Mouton (2014) says that qualitative research is based on studying human action from the perspectives of social actors which is an emic perspective. It is made of a pool of methodological approaches which studies social action. It is from this stand point that our research is based on, building on the natural setting of social actors to understand social action in terms of its specific context. We used interviews to get the insider perspective in trying to find if critical thinking is achievable by using d*uvheke*, an indigenous game played by Vhavenda children. Children were observed in their natural settings without any intervention or interference. Interviews were done using a checklist to find the type of critical thinking skills that are generated during the game based on Cotrell, 2017's lists of critical thinking skills.

STUDY AREA

The study was conducted in Makonde village which is in Thulamela Local Municipality under Vhembe District Municipality which is in Limpopo province in South Africa. Vhembe District Municipality consists of significant biodiversity and rich heritage (Stats SA, 2012). The heritage in Vhembe District Municipality includes tangible and intangible heritage this study is focusing on the intangible heritage which include indigenous games such as Duvheke, proverbs and idioms to name but a few. Makonde village is occupied by Vhavenda people and it was chosen because it is one of the areas in Venda where Duvheke is still played. The other reason was that because the area is occupied by Vhavenda people it was easier for the authors to observe and interview all the participants because they are all Tshivenda speaking. The individuals in the study area belong to the Vhavenda ethnic group. Population can be defined as a group or individuals from which the sample for research purposes is to be derived from and findings of research are to be extrapolated (Saunders et al., 2012). The population for this study in this area were children between the ages 10 and 16 who still play Duvheke game. To gain deeper understanding of *Duvheke* game authors saw it important to include knowledge holders who know more about *Duvheke* in that area.

Sampling Methods

Merrian (2009) defines sampling as a process or technique of selecting a representative part of a population for purposes of determining parameters or characteristics of a whole population. Non-probability sampling methods such as purposive and Snowball were adopted for this study. According to Lincon & Guba, (1985) purposive sampling is known as judgmental sampling which requires specific people to be selected and interviewed. For this study 10 children who play Duvheke and who usually take responsibilities of being team leaders were sampled to participated in this study using purposive sampling. Due to the difficulty of finding knowledge holders who have deeper knowledge and understanding about

Duvheke game, snowball sampling method was used. Snowball sampling method is a non-random sampling strategies, which gathers participants through referrals. In this study two knowledge holders with more knowledge about Duvheke game were identified and they helped to identify there more for them to be five. This was because people who possess specialised knowledge are likely to know other people with similar specialisations (Breweston & Millward, 2001).

Observation

Authors used non-participant observation for data collection purposes. Non-participant observation was preferred because it allowed authors of this chapter to study children playing *Duvheke* game in a natural setting without authors alteration, contribution or influence (Griffiths, 2008:65). Children where the only ones that were observed playing *Duvheke* and knowledge holders only participated through interviews and that has been discuss in the section below. Observing children playing Duvheke allowed authors to gain better understanding of the game. It was interesting to see how they selected players, how they positioned themselves as well as how they changed strategies as the game progressed. It is this kind of information which made the study to be interesting and important.

INTERVIEWS

Interviews have been used for data collection in qualitative research for ages and there are different types of interviews including structured, semi structured, unstructured interviews to name but a few. Semi structured interviews were preferred for data collection purposes. Semi structured interviews were chosen mainly because it is a data collection method known to collect more and in-depth information from participants. The authors used questions which allowed them to probe and get deeper understanding of *Duvheke* game. It is critical to note that semi structured interviews were used to complement data that was collected through observation. 10 children between the ages of 10 and 16 were interviewed. In addition, 5 knowledge holders who are known *Duvheke* game were also asked some questions for data collection purposes using the same method of semi structured interviews. It is important to note that these 10 children who participated in the interviews are known to play *Duvheke* game and they are usually team leaders during the play of such game. It is these important elements that made them to be selected to participate in this study because the authors felt that they are more relevant to provide important information about *Duvheke* game. Knowledge holders were also involved in this study because of their knowledge about *Duvheke* game and they were interviewed individually and in the comfort of their homes. All the views, perceptions, knowledge and feelings of the participants were captured and analyzed to arrive at the findings and conclusion.

ETHICAL CONSIDERATION

All research ethics were observed in this study. Since the study involved children, parents/guardians were informed about the study topic, objectives and the purpose and they were asked for the permission to allow their children to participate in the study. Parents were told that they must be present during this data collection processes and whenever they feel like withdrawing their children from participating in the study, they are free to do that and they do not have to give reasons for their withdrawal if they do not want to do that. This implies that participation in this study was purely voluntary. In addition, data for this study was collected during Covid-19 alert level 2 lock down restrictions in South Africa. Considering that, all Covid-19 protocols such as wearing of face masks, social distancing, sanitizing were always adhered to during data collection. This was to avoid and assist the country in preventing the spread of Covid-19.

FINDINGS AND DISCUSSION

This section discusses what the researchers found when they were engaging participants regarding an indigenous game called duvheke. The section of the chapter focusses on the following themes that emerged from the data collected; explaining duvheke as a game, positioning, choosing of players, team work, observing rules of the game, individual player's creativity and how all these can contribute in developing and sharpening critical thinking skills.

DUVHEKE GAME

Duvheke is a game that was popular in the late sixties and during seventies especially in Limpopo province. The game was played by both boys and girls of different ages; they could play the game separately or together. Duvheke was not unique to Vhavenda people and it was enjoyed by various communities in Limpopo and it was called in different names by different communities. For instance, VaTsonga people called it Luveke and Bapedi people called it Dibeke. The name duvheke came from the addictive nature of the game in that the game can be played for days and weeks. The game was considered as one of the cheapest games a child in a rural area could play, this is because it only required a stick to draw the defining border lines on the ground and a ball made of wrapped plastic bags or a tennis ball were possible and children to play.

There are several rules that are observed when the game is played, and these rules differ from community to community. Some of the rules of the game include among others that for a ball shooter/kicker to be disqualified they must have done a number of things; one of the things is that if they kick the ball and the ball does not cross the line drown between the two circles that player is disqualified; if a person is hit with a ball before they reach a circle while making runs that person is disqualifies; there are clearly designed and agreed upon borders of the game and if a shooter kicks a ball beyond such borders that player is disqualified; and if a person kicks a ball which does not touch the ground and the ball is caught before it touches the ground that person is disqualified; lastly if the shooter misses the ball three times when it is thrown to them to kick, that person is disqualified. This means that ball shooters/kickers must avoid all these things at all costs to play longer and be the winning team. Ball kickers must think critically and kick the ball in a way that will cross the line, the ball must run on the group and not go up to avoid being caught and run faster to avoid being hit by the ball before reaching a circle.

Participants also indicated that the game is still played even in various communities, but it is not as popular as it was in the sixties, seventies and early eighties. This could be because of various computer games which are preferred by many children. One of the participants said that:

During the sixties, seventies and eighties most families in the rural communities where not exposed to computer games and as such many children did not have such exposure and resorted to playing indigenous games such as duvheke at the time. Children enjoy this game and they learn various skills through playing this game.

It is within this context that the game is still important for children all over the world as they can learn various skills including critical thinking which are critical for the development of a child. Cahill (2021) shows that instead of education based on rote memorization, students learn through experimentation, trial and error and duvheke game provides such opportunity for experiential learning.

SELECTION OF PLAYERS

Participants indicated that players are selected by two team leaders. One will go first and call upon a name of the person to be part of their team, then another team leader follows and call upon the team member with their name. The teams are complete when all players have been selected and all the teams have equal members in terms of the number. One of the participants voiced that:

Selection of players is not done just for the sake of forming a team but is done with the idea of forming a very strong team considering several things. Both team leaders who select players must consider that for their teams to be strong and be the winning team they must have runners, brilliant ball collectors and shooters/kickers as well as catchers. Team leaders must think critically about who must be included in their teams considering different skills and contributions members of the teams that are selected will bring in the team for it to be a winning team.

This means that team leaders must know the strength and the weaknesses of all the players to select the best possible players to their teams. All teams will get an opportunity to be ball shooters/kickers and ball collectors, members of the team must be suitable for both tasks so that when they are shooters/kickers the team can excel on that and can play longer than the other team. Interestingly, the same team must be also good in collecting the ball when it is their turn to collect the ball. They must collect and catch the balls quicker and make the ball shooting team spend as little time as possible in shooting the ball so that their team can go back to shoot the ball once more. It should be noted that critical thinking skills are essential in the selection process and a lack of these skills may lead to a team leader selecting the weakest team and a team leader who is critical and considers having players that have different abilities will have a strongest team. It is within this context that the authors in this chapter argue that this game can be used inside the classroom to teach critical thinking skills not only to undergraduate students in the institution of higher learning, but also in primary and secondary schools. This will allow students to learn their surroundings especially regarding how to constitute the best groups where group work is a required. Students who are undertaking their undergraduate qualifications always form groups and do certain tasks as a team to promote and build team work. Duvheke game becomes an important instrument students can use to form a strong team that will perform well and achieve great results and grades on given tasks.

POSITIONING OF PLAYERS (BALL COLLECTORS)

When playing the game, ball collectors are expected to position themselves in a manner that will allow them to quickly disqualify all the members of the ball shooting/kicking team so that the collecting team can become the shooting/kicking team and the shooting/kicking becomes the collecting team. One participant specifically mentioned that:

The team leader must know the strength and weaknesses of all his/her team players and this will assist him/her in positioning all the team members when the team is the one collecting balls. Those who are good in catching the ball must be positioned in areas where they will be able to catch all the balls, those who are runners must be positioned in places where they will be able to chase the balls and bring the ball back quicker so that the runners must not make more runs. A person who is good in catching and throwing the ball must be given a responsibility of throwing the ball to shooters/kickers.

The authors found that positioning of players requires serious critical thinking skills because all the players must be positioned properly and strategically. For instance, a ball thrower must be good in throwing, catching the ball and know the best and weak shooters so that they can target the best shooters first and disqualify them quickly so that the team can be left dealing with weak shooters/kickers. This will allow the ball collecting team to spend very little time collecting and then become the ball shooting team. Students can use this game in allocating responsibilities to each other when it comes to group tasks. For example, if the task is a group assignment, students can assign each other roles on the bases of their strength and their weaknesses. Those who are strong in research can be given tasks relating information gathering, those with superb writing skills can be the writers and those who are good in language can proof read and edit the work. This will ensure full and equal participation and enable the team to achieve great results and grades on the task given to them. It has been established that Duvheke can be used to teach critical thinking skill inside the classroom and it can be very beneficial to undergraduate students as well as children in primary and secondary schools.

BALL SHOOTING/KICKING SKILLS

Important to note is that for a ball shooter/kicker to be disqualifies they must have done a number of things; one of the things is that if they kick the ball and it does not cross the line drawn between the two circles that player is disqualified; if a person is hit with a ball before they reach a circle while making runs that person is disqualified; there are clearly designed and agreed upon borders of the game and if a shooter kicks a ball beyond such borders that player is disqualified; and if a person kicks a ball which does not touch the ground and the ball gets caught before it touches the ground that person is disqualified; lastly if the shooter misses the ball three times when it is thrown to him/her to kick that person is disqualified. This means that ball shooters/kickers must avoid all these things at all costs to play longer and be the winning team. Ball kickers must think critically and kick the ball in a way that it will cross the line, the ball must run within the group and not go up to avoid being caught and run faster to avoid being hit by the ball before reaching a circle.

The shooter must also make sure that they kick the ball in a manner that the ball must not go beyond the agreed upon borders of the game to avoid being disqualified. This requires serious critical thinking skills because the shooter should take all these things into consideration when shooting the ball. In terms of undergraduate students, they are exposed to different texts from different authors in different subjects. This game can assist students to critically think about the text they read, who wrote it, why it was written at the time it was written and how the author expects the reader to act and react after reading the text. These skills are important because they allow the students to understand the context of the text and the contexts in which the text and arguments may not apply. This makes students to challenge ideas and develop new ideas from old ones and push boundaries and frontiers of knowledge, thereby developing new knowledge. This was supported by Bonney & Sternberg, (2011) who argued that game design elements can engage students to sustain their critical thinking and meaningful scientific argumentation over time. Although these authors did not write about duvheke or indigenous game, they bring out an interesting relationship between games and the acquisition of critical skills.

TEAM WORK

Duvheke game is not an individualistic game and it requires two teams to play. Duvheke game teaches players indispensable communication and social skills, such as active listening and effective speaking. In the process of playing duvheke players within the same team are required to speak to each other and listen to each other. They may need to change positions, coach each other and even change strategies and tactics. Students are also required to work as a team to do different task and when they work as a team, students learn how to listen to their leaders and coaches to perform their individual roles. Students learn how to listen to one another to function as an interconnected unit. It is within this context that if duvheke game can be used inside the class room, students can learn effective listening and speaking effectively. Students can also learn respect for each other and everyone around them through this game. The way in which team members speak to each other when they are playing duvheke can assist students to be critical about how they speak with a purpose of communicating to various audiences and in different context and platforms. Moli et al (2021) conducted a study focusing on the Use of Indigenous Games to Enhance the Learning of Word Problems in Grade 4 Mathematics: A Case of Kgati. The findings of this study revealed that learners can use the indigenous knowledge gained by playing and observing moves of kgati to interpret and understand mathematics word problems relating to the geometrical shapes that they observed from the kgati moves. Although this study does not necessarily teach leaners team work, it talks to the relevance and importance of indigenous knowledge inside the classroom.

SELF-CONFIDENCE

Duvheke is played within the context of a team. Team member talk and listen to each other. This two-way communication builds the confidence of all players as they start to feel valued and that their opinion matters. Teamwork teaches students that their voices are respected and valued. When students know that their counterparts and their lecturers listen to them and value their contributions in discussions, debates and arguments, students develop self-confidence. Self-confidence is crucial for students because it allows them to participate and contribute in class and in other academic activities. It is therefore, clear that duvheke game can be an important tool to teach students critical thinking skills thereby contributing to both their academic and professional development. This finding is in line with the study conducted by Tachie and Galawe (2021) who looked at the value of incorporating Indigenous Games in the teaching of number sentences and geometric patterns. Their findings confirmed that the use of indigenous games was good for teaching number sentences and geometric geometry patterns. This highlights the importance of indigenous games in teaching and learning. It boosts students' confidence because indigenous games forms part of the knowledge they bring to the classroom and teaching them using this kind of knowledge gives them a better chance of performing well in their academic endeavors and increases their participation and improves their grades. We believe that using duvheke even those students who do not participate inside the classroom or in academic activities can reflect and be critical about their none participation and they may become the most vocal students in class and in other academic activities.

CONCLUSION

In summation, this chapter found that duvheke can be used as a tool to inculcate critical thinking skills based of the nature of the game, how the game is played and rules that need to be observed when the game is being played. The positioning of players in the game needs serious critical thinking skills as there are a lot of things to consider when players are positioned, especially on the team that is collecting/catching balls. In addition, critical thinking skills are involved when team leaders engage in the process of players' selection. Team leaders should consider having diverse players in terms of catchers, runners, ball throwers who are good in hitting the targeted objects using a ball. It necessitates for the team leaders to know all the players to select only the best to have a winning and powerful team. The chapter also concluded that self-confidence and team work can also be built and developed in students using duvheke game. Recommendations are that lecturers in the higher education institutions should adopt duvheke game as a tool to teach students critical thinking skills. Another recommendation is that duvheke is an important indigenous game which is common in many South African communities especially in Limpopo province and this game must be preserved, promoted and developed. Duvheke game could also be introduced in the school curriculum in both basic and higher education institutions so that children can develop critical thinking skills at a young age. There is a serious need to research more about the use of indigenous games to impart knowledge at various levels and angles.

REFERENCES

Bado, N., & Franklin, T. (2014). Cooperative Game-based Learning in the English as a Foreign Language Classroom. *Issues and Trends in Educational Technology*, 2(2). Advance online publication. doi:10.2458/azu_itet_v2i2_bado

Boney, C. R., & Sternberg, R. J. (2011). Learning to think critically. In R. E. Mayer & P. A. Alexander (Eds.), *Handbook of research on learning and instruction* (pp. 166–196). Routledge., doi:10.4324/9780203839089

Breweston, P., & Millward, L. (2001). *Organizational research methods*. Sage. doi:10.4135/9781849209533

Fong, C. J., Kim, Y., Davis, C. W., Hoang, T. V., & Kim, Y. W. (2017). A meta-analysis on critical thinking and community college student achievement. *Thinking Skills and Creativity*, *26*, 71-83. .2017.06.002 doi:10.1016/j.tsc

Garris, R., Ahlers, R., & Driskell, J. E. (2002). Games, motivation and learning: A research and practice model. *Simulation & Gaming*, *33*(4), 441–467. doi:10.1177/1046878102238607

Gee, J. P. (2007). *What video games have to teach us about learning and literacy?* Palgrave Macmillan.

Gunter, G. A., Kenny, R. F., & Vick, E. H. (2008). Taking educational games seriously: Using the RETAIN model to design endogeneous fantasy into standalone educational games. *Educational Technology Research and Development*, *56*(5-6), 511–537. doi:10.100711423-007-9073-2

Hwang, G. J., & Chang, C. Y. (2020). Facilitating decision-making performances in nursing treatments: A contextual digital game-based flipped learning approach. *Interactive Learning Environments*, 1–16. Advance online publication. doi:10.1080/10494820.2020.1765391

Lincoln, Y., & Guba, G. (1985). *Naturalistic inquiry*. Sage. doi:10.1016/0147-1767(85)90062-8

Moloi, T. J., Mosia, M. S., Matabane, M. E., & Sibaya, K. T. (2021). The Use of Indigenous Games to Enhance the Learning of Word Problems in Grade 4 Mathematics: A Case of Kgati. *International Journal of Learning. Teaching and Educational Research*, *20*(1), 240–259.

Presnsky, M. (2008). Students as designers and creators of educational computer games: Who else? *British Journal of Educational Technology*, *39*(6), 1004–1019. doi:10.1111/j.1467-8535.2008.00823_2.x

Qian, M., & Clark, K. R. (2016). Game based leaning and 21st century skills: A review of recent research. *Computers in Human Behavior*, *63*, 50–58. doi:10.1016/j.chb.2016.05.023

Saunders, M., Lewis, P., & Thornhill, A. (2012). *Research methods for business students*. Peason Education.

Squire, K., & Jenkins, H. (2003). Harnessing the power of games in education. *Insight (American Society of Ophthalmic Registered Nurses)*, *3*(1), 3–33. PMID:12703248

Squire, K. D., & Jan, M. (2007). Mad city mystery: Developing scientific argumentation skills with a place-based augmented reality game on handheld computers. *Journal of Science Education and Technology*, *16*(1), 5-29. doi:10.1007/s10956-006-9037-z

Stats, S. A. (2012). *Census 2011 statistical release*. Statistics South Africa.

Subhash, S., & Cudney, E. A. (2018). Gamified learning in higher education: A systematic review of literature. *Computers in Human Behavior*, *87*, 192–206. doi:10.1016/j.chb.2018.05.002

Tachie, S. A., & Galawe, B. F. (2021). The Value of Incorporating Indigenous Games in the Teaching of Number Sentences and Geometric Patterns. *International Journal for Cross-Disciplinary Subjects in Education*, *12*(1), 4350–4361. doi:10.20533/ijcdse.2042.6364.2021.0533

Chapter 23
GraphoGame:
A Computer–Assisted Reading Acquisition Tool – An Enabling Support to Reading in the African Classroom

Pamela Jennifer February
https://orcid.org/0000-0003-1736-6642
University of Namibia, Namibia

ABSTRACT

This chapter investigates the effectiveness of a digital reading tool, called GraphoGame, that could be employed as one of the solutions to the poor reading results of learners that have been revealed in both national and international assessments in Namibia, specifically, and Sub-Saharan Africa in general. Following a research study, this chapter sets out to demonstrate that, through pre-and post-tests, GraphoGame Afrikaans improved the initial reading skills of Grade 1 learners. The results have implications for the utilization of computer-assisted tools to support reading acquisition in the lower grades. As GraphoGame employs a scaffolded approach by presenting learners with letters and words, it can be utilized to support learners individually in classes with large numbers, as is typical in Africa.

INTRODUCTION

Namibia is typical of many African countries where the inability of learners to read is still a major problem. This chapter introduces the reader to the reading situation that has been revealed through both national and international assessments in Namibia, specifically, and Sub-Saharan Africa, in general. The poor reading results are highlighted not as a learner problem, but as a socioeconomic issue that impacts effective teaching and learning. Based on the current economic climate, it will be many years before classes larger than 40 learners are resolved to more manageable sizes. In the meantime, many learners fail to learn to read and, consequently, fail to read to learn. This, in turn, could lead to poor academic performance and learners possibly dropping out of school later (Chinyoka, 2014; Nekongo-Nielsen et al.,

DOI: 10.4018/978-1-7998-7271-9.ch023

2015). For most Africans, education may be the only route to avoid poverty and gain financial security. "According to UNESCO, if all students in low-income countries had just basic reading skills (nothing else), an estimated 171 million people could escape extreme poverty" (Giovetti, 2020).

This chapter examines an alternative to the more unlikely scenario of employing more teachers and reducing class sizes as a possible measure that could lead to initial reading acquisition. It investigates the effectiveness of a digital reading tool, called GraphoGame, and discusses the origin of GraphoGame and its nature as an adaptive tool for reading instruction. It reviews studies that were conducted globally with GraphoGame and investigates GraphoGame Afrikaans as a possible reading acquisition support tool for Namibia and other African countries, such as South Africa, where Afrikaans is offered as a medium of instruction. The use of GraphoGame is discussed against Vygotsky's theory of proximal development and scaffolded learning as a dynamic, computer-assisted, adaptive, intervention tool that could play a role in mimicking the scaffolding a learner may need in reading acquisition.

The main focus of the chapter is a detailed presentation of a study conducted in Namibia in a setting where all the learners were from previously disadvantaged communities. They were taught through the medium of Afrikaans, which was the home language of the majority of the learners. The background to the study will briefly examine the history of Afrikaans that was foisted upon Namibians as part of the apartheid ideology of the then South African government. As a result, Afrikaans became the *lingua franca* of the Namibian people until Namibia's political independence from South Africa.

The research methodology presents the research design, the participants of the study, the measures to assess the learners in pre-and post-tests, and the procedures utilized in the study. This section describes how GraphoGame Afrikaans was developed and piloted. The study set out to prove that GraphoGame Afrikaans improved the reading skills of Grade 1 learners. The results of the study also demonstrate how GraphoGame affected reading skills development in a relatively short time. The findings, furthermore, indicate that GraphoGame could be utilized effectively in a regular classroom in Namibian schools, with very little need for teacher input, except for the monitoring of the process of play. GraphoGame takes into consideration the individual levels of the players by presenting them with 20% of the letters or words with which they are struggling, as well as 80% of those letters or words with which they are comfortable. Thus, the learning opportunities are scaffolded with a high rate of success that ensures that there is a high probability that the learner will continue the engagement.

In conclusion, the chapter discusses how GraphoGame can be utilized in large classes as a teaching and learning tool. The ease of downloading and employing GraphoGame is elaborated. Thus, this chapter examines the viability of utilizing a computer-assisted tool that supports reading acquisition in typical African countries comprising large classes.

BACKGROUND

Reading Situation

According to international and national assessments, learners' competence in reading at the primary school level is not at the desired level. Evidence shows that this is also the case with Namibian learners. The Southern and Eastern African Consortium for Monitoring Educational Quality (SACMEQ) Reports show poor English reading levels in Grade 6 (Hungi et al., 2010; Spaull & Taylor, 2012). In addition, the

Early Grade Reading Assessment scores (EGRA) reveal poor reading performance in mother tongue and English as a second language in the lower primary grades (i.e. Grades 1 to 3) (Gains & Parkes, 2012). These results resonate with those provided by the Namibian National Standardized Achievements Test (NSAT) for Grades 5 and 7 in English (Hanse-Himarwa, 2015). Specifically, of the 8 levels classified by SACMEQ, ranging from *pre-reading* (level 1) to *critical reading* (level 8), three-quarters of the Namibian Grade 6 learners were only able to read at level 3, which comprises *basic reading*. Ideally, it is expected that learners should at least be able to *read for meaning* (level 4).

Several Sub-Saharan African countries are in a similar or worse situation. To date, there have been 4 SACMEQ assessments at approximately 5-year periods (starting in 1995). The benchmark assessment for reading (and mathematics) is set at 500. Although there has been an improvement over the 4 SACMEQ assessments for most countries, only 7 of the 15 countries that are now part of the consortium have consistently achieved the benchmark of 500 (Botswana, Kenya, Mauritius, Seychelles, Swaziland Tanzania (Mainland), and Zimbabwe). Countries, such as Namibia and South Africa, have had only one reading assessment above the 500 benchmark score based on the available SACMEQ reports (such as Dwarkan, 2017; Shigwedha et al., 2015; Spaull & Taylor, 2012).

To put these poor results in reading in perspective, the aim of this chapter is not just to focus on learner issues, but to provide a broader description of the African classroom in which the learners find themselves. Thus the aspects that constitute the classroom need to be examined. Research studies indicate that low socioeconomic status has an impact on academic performance, in general (Daniele, 2021; Glock & Kleen, 2020;), and reading achievement, specifically (Dwarkan, 2017; Kruger, 2012; Zuze & Reddy, 2014). Low socioeconomic status has implications for classroom resources and home literacy such as access to adequate reading materials (Kirchner et al., 2014; Ministry of Education Arts and Culture & UNICEF Namibia, 2016; Ninnes, 2011). It also has implications for the teacher-learner ratio. SACMEQ and other cross-national studies call for reduced class sizes as an aspect related to reading improvement (Benbow et al., 2007; Dwarkan, 2017). Based on the current economic climate which also takes into account COVID-19, this may not happen for many years. This chapter, thus, examines an alternative to the more unlikely scenario of employing more teachers and reducing class sizes and so improve the quality of reading, with a more likely solution that could lead to initial reading acquisition.

MAIN FOCUS OF THE CHAPTER

The main focus of the chapter is to illustrate the viability of employing a computer-assisted tool, called GraphoGame, to enhance initial reading acquisition, especially in large African classes. This section examines computer-assisted reading intervention tools, the origin of GraphoGame, the nature of GraphoGame as an adaptive tool for reading instruction, and studies conducted globally with GraphoGame. The utilization of GraphoGame is discussed from the social constructivism theoretical perspective of Vygotsky's theory of proximal development and scaffolded learning. The research study that investigated the utilization of GraphoGame Afrikaans is presented, and the concluding remarks for its viability are discussed.

Computer-Assisted Reading Interventions

Studies in computer-assisted reading intervention have documented their effectiveness in supporting at-risk children (e.g., Magnan & Ecalle, 2006; Nicolson & Fawcett, 2000; Regtvoort & van der Leij, 2007; Torgesen et al., 2010). This type of intervention provides more individualized programming and allows the child the needed time on the intervention. In addition, there is recognition that computer-assisted applications are beneficial in teaching literacy skills to children with reading disabilities in kindergarten and primary school (e.g. Elbro et al., 1996; van Daal & Reitsma, 2000; Wise et al., 2000) as well as in secondary school (e.g., Lynch, Fawcett, & Nicolson, 2000; Potocki, Magnan, & Ecalle, 2015). These findings are supported by reviews and meta-analyses (Blok, Oostdam, Otter, & Overmaat, 2002; Hall, Hughes, & Filbert, 2000; Hattie, 2008; Maddux & Lamont, 2013; Stetter & Hughes, 2010)

GraphoGame

The Origin of GraphoGame

A study conducted by the University of Jyväskylä, Finland (Jyväskylä Longitudinal Study of Dyslexia) initially aimed at early identification of children who were at familial risk for dyslexia, and followed children from birth (Lyytinen et al., 2007; Puolakanaho, 2007). Results indicate that children at risk for dyslexia demonstrated problems in either phonological awareness, naming speed, or letter knowledge (Lyytinen et al., 2006). Conversely, research indicates that phonological awareness, letter knowledge, and RAN (Rapid Autonomised Naming) were strong predictors of success in reading (Torppa, 2007). Having identified those children at risk for dyslexia at an early stage, as well as identifying those aspects that played a role in reading success, the researchers felt obligated to develop prevention and intervention tools that could mitigate the effect of dyslexia on reading acquisition in these children. A computer game was devised as a possible intervention (Eklund et al., 2013; Lyytinen et al., 2007).

The original Finnish game that was devised at the University of Jyväskylä was called 'Ekapeli' (*First Game*) (Lyytinen et al., 2007). It was later renamed 'GraphoGame' for the English and other international language versions (Ojanen et al., 2015). GraphoGame is a mobile learning game that teaches the basics of reading by focusing on the phonics approach. The player sees a written stimulus or stimuli (letters or words) while hearing an auditory stimulus simultaneously through headphones, and has to select the correct letter or word to match the auditory stimulus. The game starts with letters and increases in difficulty in subsequent levels; this engages the players' interest. The teacher or parent only needs to introduce children aged 5 to 8 years to the game before they can play the game independently.

According to Lyytinen et al. (2007), after playing the game in 10 to 20 minutes sessions, 3 to 4 times a week for a total of 1 to 4 hours, children aged 6 to 7 years, who were initially non-readers, acquired basic reading skills. Children who are at risk may need more playing time for effective reading acquisition. The game is construed in such a way that children are constantly exposed to the same letters and words in various formats; they grasp more quickly and learn to recognize these letters and words accurately. Thus, the game can also be employed as a predictive, dynamic test of reading acquisition (Lyytinen et al., 2007; Ronimus et al., 2014). As the focus of GraphoGame is on recognizing letters and words, reading practice with texts will eventually automatize the skills and lead to reading fluency as well as better comprehension of the content of texts (Lyytinen et al., 2007).

GraphoGame

The Nature of GraphoGame

Currently, GraphoGame can be played on computers, tablets, and mobile phones. By utilizing headphones, each child can focus on his or her playing time without disturbing others or being disturbed by external noises. Children are logged in as players with their name, age, and gender, and they have a choice of 20 characters (robots, animals, and fairy-type characters). Their name appears when they click on their character. By clicking on their name, the game continues from where they have last stopped. The game keeps track of the time for each 'Session', as well as the overall 'Exposure time' (time from the stimulus onset to the child's reaction). The child plays the game by listening to letter sounds and words and responds by clicking on the correct letter or word. If the answer is correct, the letter or word is highlighted in green. If the child's response is incorrect, the correct answer is shown alone, and the letter sound or word is repeated in order for the child to make the connection. Through a series of rewards, the learner stays potentially motivated to the task for at least 20 minutes (Kyle, Kujala, Richardson, Lyytinen, & Goswami, 2013; Lyytinen et al., 2007).

The game monitors each child's progress and, thus, ensures that the game is played at the literacy level of that particular child. Once the child has mastered the letters and word patterns of the first level, the game switches to the next level. However, the letters and word patterns that the child is struggling with are presented in a variety of forms to keep the child engaged. For example, if the child chooses the correct letter or word on a fish, that fish is caught but when the child chooses the incorrect fish, the fish swims away. The letters and words could also be related to cars that race or balloons that float, among other animations. Thus, although letters and words are repeated for the child, it is done in different ways to keep her or his attention.

This computer-assisted device aids the teacher whose time is limited regarding the amount of attention that can be provided to individual learners. When a learner plays GraphoGame, there is no limit to the number of exposures that the adaptive game will present to a struggling learner. A teacher, especially in large classes, is not always able to do this. Thus, as a supportive reading tool, GraphoGame can be utilized in large classes to tailor individual support. This frees up some time for teachers to attend to children who desperately need individual attention. This kind of repetition that struggling children need is not always possible in African classrooms where teachers have large classes and cannot always provide the attention that the child needs. In the Namibian schools where a Grade 1 teacher may have more than 40 learners in the class, GraphoGame can become a useful tool to assist with learning and practicing reading skills. This makes GraphoGame an invaluable scaffolding tool for teachers and learners alike.

Global Studies with GraphoGame

Since its inception, GraphoGame (GG) has expanded globally to assist children with reading difficulties. As a result, the GraphoWorld Network of Excellence (https://info.grapholearn.com/partners/) was created. Several research studies have been conducted around the world to ascertain the benefits of utilizing GraphoGame. Each country involved in the GraphoGame project developed its own content in a local language. Table 1 displays some of the countries that have developed GraphoGame in a local language and, subsequently, conducted research studies regarding its impact. The overall results of these specific studies show that GraphoGame has shown positive results in improving the reading skills of early Grade learners (aged 6 to 9 years).

Table 1. Research using GraphoGame (GG)

Language	Country	Study	Age (yrs/Grade)	Number of participants in the study	Playing time (PT) and/or Exposure time (ET) as provided
Finnish	Finland	Saine et al (2010)	7-8 yrs	n = 166: CARRI=25 and RRI=25; Control=116	4x45 mins per week/28 weeks
German	Switzerland	Brem et al (2010)	6-6.9 yrs	ERP group=32:GG=15, Control (Number-knowledge)=17 fMRI group=16:GG=8; Control (Number-knowledge)=8	PT=+/-3.6h
English (GG Phoneme, GG Rime)	U.K.	Kyle, Kujala, Richardson, Lyytinen, & Goswami (2013)	6-7 yrs	n = 31: *GG Phoneme=10; *GG Rime=11; *Control=10	PT = 10-15 mins/5 sessions per week/12 weeks (+/-60 sessions) No ET provided
Polish	Poland	Kamykowska, Haman, Latvala, Richardson, & Lyytinen (2014)	6-7 yrs	n = 62 *Intervention Crossover (lowest pre-test scores)=24 (GG=12; GM=12 and vice-versa) *Reference/Control (next results higher than intervention group)=24 *Deleted from study (highest results, ceiling results)=14	PT=15 mins per day Early GG group (M= 57.4 min); Late GG group (M=48.9 min)
Swedish	Sweden	von Mentzer et al. (2014)	5-7 yrs	n = 48: *CI=17; * HA=15; NH=16	PT: 10 mins/day/4 weeks; M=3h20min
Norwegian	Norway	Kyle, Lundetræ, Schwippert, Solheim, & Uppstad (2014)	6-7 yrs	n = 1024 (17 schools): *Intervention-Grade 1=9 schools (lowest 20%; n = 92) *Intervention-Grade 2=4 schools (lowest 20%; n = 34) *Control=4 schools	1/hr intervention/ 4 days per week / 25 weeks (4 intervention elements: Letter knowledge (GG or OnTrack); guided reading; spelling; and shared reading)
Cinyanja	Zambia	Jere-Folotiya et al (2014)	5-9yrs	Pre-T, 573 (Post-T 314) learners:*No GG; *Learners GG *Learners/Teachers GG; *Teachers GG	M=94 min (between 50-190 mins)
Kiswahili Kikuyu	Kenya	Puhakka (2015)	Gr 1	196 participants: *111 Kiswahili (n = 18 GG) *85 Kikuyu (n = 11 GG)	15 mins/4 times per day/5 days Min = 4hrs playing time
Greek	Cyprus	Ktisti (2015)	6-7yrs	n = 56 with RD: 4 experimental groups- GG, PREP, GGtoPREP, PREPtoGG plus Control (n = 17)	PT/ET not specified
Portuguese	Portugal	Sucena, Filipa, & Viana (2016)	Gr. 1	n = 57 participants: *Grp 1 (mixed intervention-daily GG + weekly promotion of reading skills)=24; *Grp 2 (GG)=20;*Grp 3 (Control)=13	No available info on playing time
Spanish	Chile	Rosas, Escobar, Ramírez, Meneses, & Guajardo (2017)	Gr.1	n = 48: *Low SES=56 (GG=28; Control=28) *High SES=31 (GG=16; Control=15)	30 mins per day x 5days (+/-3 months)
Spanish	USA	Luft Baker et al. (2017)	Gr.1	n = 78(5 classes): GG=3 classes; Control=2 classes	10 min/day/16 weeks

Theoretical Framework: GraphoGame and Social Constructivism

This study was based on the assumption that, with adequate support and facilitation, Namibian learners could gain the necessary level of reading skills to ensure the attainment of an education that would eventually enable them to earn a good living. Vygotsky's (1978) socio-cultural theory posits that the interactions within the socio-cultural environment provide much-needed support and facilitation for learning. This interdependent relationship between a child and his or her environment, that promotes the child's development, is encaptured in the concept of the zone of proximal development (ZPD). It is within this zone that the child learns best. The support that the child receives is termed scaffolding and, although Vygotsky did not coin the term, the concept fits in naturally with the concept of ZPD (Fani & Ghaemi, 2011; Stone, 1998).

Vacca and Levitt (2008), as literacy teachers working in the field of special education, claim that, when teachers employ scaffolding as an instructional tool in literacy learning, they model good learning strategies, and ensure that each learner comprehends successfully the desired learning outcomes at all levels. This ideal instructional methodology aimed at individual potential is not easy to maintain optimally in typically large African classes; therefore, a dynamic, computer-assisted, adaptive intervention tool could play a role in mimicking the scaffolding a learner may need. It could also play a role in extending the support that a special education teacher can provide. Typically, a special education teacher scaffolds the learning process by providing the work in chunks or components that a learner can cope with successfully. In the same vein, GraphoGame, comprising these features, has the potential to do scaffold the learning of letters and words in the same way.

Research Employing GraphoGame Afrikaans

This section examines in detail a study conducted in Namibia in a setting where all the learners were from previously disadvantaged communities. They were taught through the medium of Afrikaans, which was the home language of the majority of the learners. As part of the background to the study, this section will briefly elaborate on the history of Afrikaans that was foisted upon the then South West Africa (now Namibia) as part of the South African apartheid ideology. As a result, Afrikaans became the *lingua franca* of the Namibian people until Namibia's political independence from South Africa.

This section, furthermore, discusses in detail the research methodology employed in terms of the research design, the participants of the study, the measures to assess the learners in pre-and post-tests, and the procedures utilized in the study. This section also describes how GraphoGame Afrikaans was developed and piloted. It introduces GraphoMath as one of the two control measures in this experimental study. The second control measure was another class group that did not participate in the intervention. The study set out to confirm that GraphoGame Afrikaans improved the reading skills (letter sounds, phonological awareness, reading, and spelling) of Grade 1 learners when compared to the two control measures in the study.

Background to the Study: Afrikaans as a Namibian Language

Namibia, a country of 825 000 km^2 in southwest Africa, has a relatively small population of 2.5 million people, making it one of the most sparsely populated countries in the world. Namibian schools offer 16 languages, of which 15 are regarded as first languages. French is offered as a foreign language. English is the official language of the country, adopted as such at Independence in 1990. According to the Namibian language policy, all children should ideally be taught in their mother tongue from pre-primary to Grade 3 (Ministry of Education Arts and Culture, 2015), with English as the second language. From Grade 4 onwards, English becomes the medium of instruction.

According to the 2011 Population and Housing Census (Namibia Statistics Agency, 2013), Afrikaans is the third most spoken language in Namibia. In the Khomas Region, where the research study was undertaken, Afrikaans is either the medium of instruction or the second language that is offered at 38 of the 54 primary schools (i.e. 70.4%). Oshiwambo, the language most spoken in Namibia (Oshiwanyama and Oshindonga), is offered at 10 schools in the region.

Historically, Afrikaans was foisted on Namibians as part of the South African apartheid ideology. As a result, Afrikaans became the *lingua franca* of the Namibian people. However, like most complicated issues, the history of Afrikaans is not as simple as stated above. Historically, the languages that the colonialists brought into a country remained relatively the same. Consider, for example, English, French and Portuguese brought to Africa. When the German colonialists occupied then South West Africa and were forced out of power at the end of World War I, the German language remained constant, even during the ensuing South African rule. Germans visiting Namibia have no problem conversing with German-speaking Namibians. Conversely, the question of why the Dutch language imposed by the Dutch colonizers in the 1650s, when they occupied South Africa, eventually changed to Afrikaans can be posed. Van Rensburg (2013) believes that, because the focus has largely been on the similarities between Dutch and Afrikaans, there was little attention to the external influences of indigenous languages on Dutch. He cites Den Besten (1987, 24) who states "… were it not for the agentivity of indigenous Khoekhoen and imported African and Asian slave labor … there would be no 'Afrikaans.'" Currently, there is a movement afoot in South Africa to claim Afrikaans as belonging to the "Camissa People" (the so-called Coloured people) who stem from the "Khoena" (Khoi) and include the Nama from Namibia. It is against this milieu that the study was set.

Research Methodology

Participants

This experimental study was conducted in four schools in a suburb of Windhoek, the capital city of Namibia. These 4 schools were purposively sampled as they offered Afrikaans as the medium of instruction in Grade 1. For most learners at these schools, Afrikaans was their first language. These schools were situated in one of the largest Afrikaans-speaking communities in Windhoek. Because the children in these schools were living in the same suburb, they were likely to have a similar socioeconomic status, although this variable was not controlled. All learners were from previously disadvantaged communities.

Consent and assent were provided through the approved channels of the Ministry of Education, Arts and Culture, and specifically at the schools. Learners had a choice to participate; however, one learner did not participate in the assessment tests but played one of the games. He did not form part of the study.

A total of five Grade 1 classes in 4 schools formed the population as well as the sample (N = 202). Four classes formed the experimental group (n = 162) and the fifth class formed the control group (n = 40). In each of the four classes of the experimental group, the learners were randomly divided into GraphoGame Afrikaans (n = 82) and GraphoMath (n = 80) groups. GraphoGame Afrikaans and GraphoMath are digital games that will be described in detail under *Measures* in the next section. Henceforth, the groups will be termed GraphoGame (GG), GraphoMath (GM), and Control (C). All the learners completed pre-tests (n = 202) and post-tests (n = 197) in phonological awareness, letter knowledge, word reading, spelling, counting, and mathematical operations.

Five learners moved to other parts of the country and dropped out of the study early (Little's MCAR test: Chi-Square = 16.5, DF = 11, Sig. = .241). As the result is not significant, it can be concluded that the missing data were likely to be completely random. Consequently, cases can be excluded listwise when running analyses without biasing the estimates (Enders, 2011).

Measures

GraphoGame Afrikaans

GraphoGame Afrikaans was developed by employing the syllabus for teaching Afrikaans literacy in Grades 1 and 2. Although Afrikaans has a fairly regular orthography, there are instances where letters or the combination of letters are not typically transparent. To minimize the confusion of learners, these combinations of letters were presented to learners in a rime format. For example, a single 'o' is pronounced /ɔ/ as in 'mot' (moth), the 'o' sounding similar to *awe* (English). The double 'oo' (/uə̯/) sound, however, sounds similar to *moor* (English). In GraphoGame, children were introduced to the sound, and presented with words that contained this sound in rime format, for example, 'loop' (walk), 'room' (cream), and 'boot' (boat) for them to make the connection between phoneme and orthography.

The sounds for GraphoGame Afrikaans were recorded in Windhoek, Namibia, at a radio station, and the graphics and technology were created and developed at the Agora Centre at the University of Jyväskylä, Finland. The piloting of GraphoGame Afrikaans was undertaken during the GraphoLearn project by five teacher educators from the University of Namibia, involving ten Grade 3 learners who were struggling to learn to read. During this project, GraphoGame Afrikaans was employed as an intervention tool to improve these learners' reading skills (letter sounds, phonological awareness, reading, and spelling). Pre- and post-test assessments were conducted, and the learners played GraphoGame for an average exposure time of 180 minutes (3 hours) (*Adapted from February, 2018*).

GraphoMath Afrikaans

GraphoMath is a computer-assisted tool that was developed at the Agora Centre at the University of Jyväskylä, Finland. The focus of the tool is to support the acquisition of initial numeracy. The number concepts from zero (0) to ten (10) form the target of the game. This is in line with the mathematics taught in Grade 1 in Namibia. The game was translated from English to Afrikaans and, hence, the name GraphoMath Afrikaans. The rationale for employing GraphoMath was for it to serve as a control measure in the study.

Pre-and Post Assessment Tests

Pre- and post-assessment tests in reading and numeracy skills were utilized to assess the learners' skill levels in Afrikaans reading and mathematics before and after the intervention. These tests included the assessment of phonological awareness, letter knowledge, word reading, spelling, counting, and simple mathematical operations. The same tools and procedures were employed in both the pre-and post-tests.

Letter-sound connection. The 23 letters of the Afrikaans alphabet (minus C, Q, and X in the English alphabet) were randomly presented on flashcards to individual learners, and they had to respond by providing the correct letter sounds (Ketonen, Salmi, & Krimark, 2015). Each learner's response to each letter was recorded with a tick or a cross to indicate correct or incorrect responses respectively. The total score was calculated out of 23. Cronbach's alphas were .93 and .91 for the pre-and post-tests respectively.

Phonological Awareness. Learners were individually assessed on their ability to identify expressively (1) the number of syllables in two words of varying length, (2) the initial letter sound in three words, (3) the final letter sound in three words, and (4) two items each of syllable deletion, phoneme identification, phoneme addition and phoneme deletion (Ketonen, et al., 2015). Each learner's expressive response was reported and recorded to indicate correct or incorrect responses. The total score was calculated out of 16. Cronbach's alphas were .84 and .79 for the pre-and post-tests respectively.

Word Reading. Twenty listed words were presented to learners individually (Ketonen, et al., 2015). The child's task was to read as many words correctly as possible within one minute. The words ranged from easy (i.e. two letters/one-syllable words) to more difficult (i.e. ten letters/four-syllable words). Each learner's response was reported and recorded to indicate correct or incorrect responses. The total score was calculated out of 20. Cronbach's alphas were .89 and .86 for the pre-and post-tests respectively.

Spelling skills. Twenty words were dictated as a group test (Ketonen, et al., 2015). The learners were required to write down these words, spelled correctly. The words ranged from easy (i.e. two letters/one-syllable words) to more difficult (i.e. ten letters/four-syllable words). The total score was calculated out of 20. Cronbach's alphas were .83 and .82 for the pre-and post-tests respectively.

Mathematics skills. Learners were individually assessed on their ability to count, add, subtract and solve mathematical problems (Bridges in Mathematics, 2012; Ministry of Education, 2005). The counting tasks involved counting from 1 to 30, counting forward, counting backward, and counting in twos, both forwards and backward. The addition and subtraction tasks (three tasks each) involved simple operations up to 10. Two problem-solving word tasks involved a combination of addition and subtraction. Each learner's response was reported and recorded to indicate correct or incorrect responses. The total score was calculated out of 17. Cronbach's alphas were .86 and .83 for the pre-and post-tests, respectively.

The coefficients for Cronbach's alpha show that all the assessments (both pre-and post-intervention tests) were suitably reliable as their items demonstrated a relatively high internal consistency with the lowest at .79 and the highest at .93. Thus, instrumental reliability was consistent for all the assessment tests (*Adapted from February, 2018*).

Procedures

Following the pre-assessment tests, the four classes that had been randomly divided into GraphoGame Afrikaans or GraphoMath Afrikaans played for a period of two months. The study utilized 41 tablets (with their headphones) containing the content of either GraphoGame Afrikaans or GraphoMath Afrikaans, as the largest class comprised 41 learners; the other classes comprised 40 learners each. Each tablet was assigned to four learners (i.e. one learner for each class). A profile was created for each learner containing details of her or his first name and surname, date and place of birth, as well as the name of the school. Learners chose a character or avatar to accompany their name. Two classes played per day. This meant that learners played every second day. They played +/-40 minutes in two sessions of 20 minutes each. The playing continued until an exposure time of about 5 hours (+/-300 minutes) was reached for each player. Exposure time commenced when a learner heard the letter sound, syllable, or word and ended

GraphoGame

when he or she had selected the corresponding written letter sound, syllable, or word, whether correct or incorrect. The time when learners were not focused on the game and doing something else was not calculated as part of the exposure time. The class designated as the control group did not play any game. Except for playing time for GraphoGame Afrikaans and GraphoMath groups, teaching took place as usual in all the classes. During this period, GraphoGame Afrikaans and GraphoMath Afrikaans data were routinely uploaded to the server in Finland.

Results of the Study

This study examined the hypothesis that the mean gain scores of the assessment tests for GraphoGame were equal to the mean gain scores of the two control measures (GraphoMath and Control), i.e. H_0: $\mu GG = \mu GM = \mu C$.

Comparison of GraphoGame Afrikaans and control measures regarding reading and spelling skills

The means and standard deviations for the three groups (GraphoGame Afrikaans, GraphoMath, and Control) in letter-sound connections, phonological awareness, word reading, spelling, and mathematics, both pre-test and post-test scores are presented in Table 2.

Table 2. Means and standard deviations of assessment scores across sample groups

Measure		GraphoGame (n = 81)	GraphoMath (n = 77)	Control (n = 39)
Letter Sounds (Pre-Test) (max 23)	M	15.4	16.09	18.69
	SE	0.75	0.71	0.74
	SD	6.62	6.23	4.61
	Range	0-23	0-23	7-23
Letter Sounds (Post-Test) (max. 23)	M	19	18.57	19.72
	SE	0.55	0.61	0.56
	SD	4.94	5.31	3.51
	Range	4-23	3-23	7-23
Phonological Awareness (Pre-Test) (max. 16)	M	9.07	9.19	11.69
	SE	0.40	0.45	0.47
	SD	3.63	3.93	2.95
	Range	0-16	1-16	4-16
Phonological Awareness (Post-Test) (max. 16)	M	12	9.68	10.46
	SE	0.34	0.37	0.51
	SD	3.02	3.25	3.19
	Range	2-16	0-15	3-16

continues on following page

Table 2. Continued

Measure		GraphoGame (n = 81)	GraphoMath (n = 77)	Control (n = 39)
Reading (Pre-Test) (max. 16)	M	2.6	2.87	4.56
	SE	0.3	0.35	0.52
	SD	2.7	3.05	3.27
	Range	0-11	0-10	0-10
Reading (Post-Test) (max. 16)	M	4.73	3.92	5.92
	SE	0.31	0.35	0.50
	SD	2.78	3.06	3.15
	Range	0-12	0-10	0-10
Spelling (Pre-Test) (max. 20)	M	3.17	3.45	5.97
	SE	0.30	0.34	0.48
	SD	2.69	2.99	3.01
	Range	0-11	0-11	0-11
Spelling (Post-Test) (max. 20)	M	7.17	6.94	7.69
	SE	0.41	0.37	0.42
	SD	3.66	3.26	2.62
	Range	0-18	0-16	1-12
Mathematics (Pre-Test) (max. 17)	M	8.49	9.12	10.64
	SE	0.43	0.44	0.60
	SD	3.88	3.81	3.75
	Range	0-17	2-17	3-17
Mathematics (Post-Test) (max. 17)	M	11.48	12.08	12.44
	SE	0.39	0.36	0.58
	SD	3.5	3.19	3.65
	Range	3-17	1-17	2-17

The mean assessment scores increased for all three groups (GraphoGame, GraphoMath, and Control) after the intervention, except for phonological awareness in the control group. The increase in mean scores shows that, in general, learners had improved their skills in these areas between the time-points 1 and 2 (September to November). However, the means of the three groups in the pre-test assessments were not equivalent. The control group had higher means in all the pre-test assessments.

Due to the differences across the means in the pre-test assessments, the gain scores had to be calculated. To determine whether the increase in the means of the assessment tests was the same across the groups, the difference between the pre-and post-intervention scores of letter-sound connections, phonological awareness, word reading, spelling, and mathematics were calculated. The means and standard deviations for the gain scores between the pre-and post-test scores were computed (Table 3), and then multiple group comparisons of the gain scores were conducted. As the main aim of this study was to investigate the effectiveness of GraphoGame Afrikaans in Grade 1 as a supporting tool, the focus of this section of the study was the comparison of GraphoGame Afrikaans to both the control measures (GraphoMath and Control). The results are presented in Table 3.

Table 3. Means and standard deviations of gain scores across sample groups

Gain Scores for assessments		Groups		
		GraphoGame (n = 81)	GraphoMath (n = 77)	Control (n = 39)
Letter Sound	Mean	3.60	2.48	1.03
	SD	3.26	2.93	2.42
	SE	0.36	0.33	0.39
Phonological Awareness	Mean	2.93	0.48	-1.23
	SD	2.53	2.60	1.77
	SE	0.28	0.30	0.28
Word Reading	Mean	2.12	1.05	1.36
	SD	1.61	1.56	1.41
	SE	0.18	0.18	0.23
Spelling	Mean	4.00	3.38	1.72
	SD	2.93	2.50	2.51
	SE	0.33	0.28	0.40
Mathematics	Mean	2.99	2.96	1.79
	SD	2.48	2.76	2.45
	SE	0.28	0.31	0.39

The ANOVA F-test was employed to determine whether any of the treatments (GraphoGame, GraphoMath, and Control) was superior, inferior, or equal, as per the null hypothesis, i.e. H_0: $\mu GG = \mu GM = \mu C$. The results reveal that, in general, there was a significant effect in all three groups on the gain scores of all five assessments at the p < .05 level for the three conditions:

- Letter-sound connections: $F(2, 194) = 10.061$; $p < .001$; $\eta_p^2 = .094$,
- Phonological awareness: $F(2, 194) = 43.266$; $p < .001$; $\eta_p^2 = .308$,
- Word reading: $F(2, 194) = 9.784$; $p < .001$; $\eta_p^2 = .092$,
- Spelling: $F(2, 194) = 9.560$; $p < .001$; $\eta_p^2 = .092$, and
- Mathematics: $F(2, 194) = 3.255$; $p = .041$; $\eta_p^2 = .032$.

Additionally, the partial eta square values indicate that the effect sizes, that is the variation of the dependent variable (the assessment tests), ranged from 3% in mathematics, 9% in letter-sound connections, word reading, and spelling to 31% in phonological awareness for the grouping. The conclusion is that the *F*-test proved that the null hypothesis could be rejected because of the variation, that is, H₀: µGG ¹ µGM ¹ µC.

The *F*-test, however, does not indicate which treatment (group) is superior to the other. Thus, a comparison of gain means was made between the three groups' scores on each of the assessment tests using a one-way ANOVA including post hoc multiple comparisons using Games-Howell, which is recommended by Field (2013) for unequal group variances and sample sizes to avoid a family-wise error (Type I error) (see Table 4).

Table 4. Multiple variable pairwise group comparisons of the mean gain scores

Measures	Groups		Mean difference in gain scores	SE	Sig.	95%CI for the mean difference in gain scores	Effect Size (Cohen's d)	95% CI for ES
Letter Sounds	GG	GM	1.12	.49	.061	-.04 - 2.29	.36	.046 – .68
	GG	C	2.58*	.53	.000	1.32 - 3.84	.85	.46 – 1.25
	GM	C	1.46*	.51	.015	.24 - 2.67	.52	.13 – .92
Phonological Awareness	GG	GM	2.45*	.41	.000	1.48 - 3.41	.96	.63 – 1.28
	GG	C	4.16*	.40	.000	3.21 - 5.11	1.797	1.35– .24
	GM	C	1.71*	.41	.000	.74 - 2.69	.73	.33 – 1.12
Reading	GG	GM	1.07*	.25	.000	.47 - 1.67	.67	.35 – 1.00
	GG	C	.76*	.29	.025	.08 - 1.45	.49	.11 – .88
	GM	C	-.31	.29	.535	-.99 - .38	-.21	-.59 – .18
Spelling	GG	GM	.62	.43	.322	-.40 - 1.64	.23	-.09 – .54
	GG	C	2.28*	.52	.000	1.05 - 3.52	.81	.42 – 1.21
	GM	C	1.66*	.49	.003	.49 - 2.84	.66	.27 – 1.1
Math	GG	GM	.03	.42	.998	-.96 - 1.02	.01	-.30 – .32
	GG	C	1.19*	.48	.040	.05 - 2.34	.49	.10 – .87
	GM	C	1.17	.50	.058	-.03 - 2.37	.44	.051 – .83

Notes. (1) GG = GraphoGame, GM = GraphoMath, C = Control, E.S. = Effect Size, C.I. = Confidence Interval.
(2) Determining specific effect size for the 3 groups, Cohen's *d* was computed using an online calculator *(Psychometrica; Lenhard & Lenhard, 2016)*.
(3) *The mean difference is significant at the 0.05 level.

The results specifically show that the gain scores for the GraphoGame group (GG) were higher than those for the two control measures (GM and C) in all the assessment tests. Significant differences were attained between GraphoGame (GG) and Control (C) in all the assessment tests. Significant differences between GraphoGame (GG) and GraphoMath (GM) occurred in phonological awareness and reading but not in spelling and mathematics. In letter-sound connections, the result could be considered marginally significant between GG and GM.

When comparing the effect sizes of GraphoGame to Control only, according to Cohen (1992), large effect sizes were found in letter-sound connections, phonological awareness, and spelling (0.8 £ *d*< 0.8). Small to moderate effect sizes were found in reading and mathematics (*d* < 0.5).

GraphoGame

When interpreting the effect sizes, there was a large effect size in phonological awareness ($d \geq 0.8$) between GraphoGame and GraphoMath, with a medium effect size in reading ($0.5 \leq d < 0.8$), and small effect sizes in letter-sound connections and spelling ($0.2 \leq d < 0.5$). These results reflect marginal significance.

In summary, these results indicate that GraphoGame could be an effective tool for improving Grade 1 learners' reading skills, such as phonological awareness, as well as play a role in improving letter-sound connections, word reading, and spelling.

Discussion of the Study

The study aimed to investigate to what extent the utilization of GraphoGame Afrikaans in a regular Grade 1 classroom supports reading skills. The results reveal, firstly, that the gain scores among the learners playing GraphoGame Afrikaans were higher than for the learners in the two control measures (i.e. the GraphoMath Afrikaans and no-treatment control groups). Except for mathematics and spelling, significance was gained in the other areas. The results are in line with several previous studies which indicate that learners who played GraphoGame had improved their letter-sound skills and phonological awareness from the pre- to the post-intervention tests (Richardson, 2011; Sucena et al., 2016)

Consequently, GraphoGame is associated with increased scores on post-intervention assessment tests in aspects contributing to reading and spelling. Research has indicated how these aspects are linked to reading (Ehri & McCormick, 1998; Georgiou et al., 2011) it can be assumed that, as GraphoGame has been proven to increase these aspects, it also directly improves reading. The results of the study also demonstrate how GraphoGame affects reading skills development in a relatively short time (5 hours of playing time), and that it could be employed effectively in a regular classroom in Namibian schools with very little need for teacher input, except for monitoring the playing process. GraphoGame takes into consideration the individual level of the player by presenting the learners with 20% of letters or words with which they are struggling and 80% of letters or words with which they are successful. Thus, the learning opportunities are scaffolded with a high rate of success that ensures that there is a high probability that the learner will continue the engagement.

SOLUTIONS AND RECOMMENDATIONS

GraphoGame will repeat learning opportunities in a variety of ways without the learner being aware of being drilled. This repetition is important for all learners, especially those learners who struggle. The dynamic and adaptive nature of GraphoGame ensures that it follows the ability of the learner because 80% of the letters or words shown to learners are already known to them. As a result, they experience success. Because GraphoGame is dynamic in catering to the individual level of the learner, it is a good scaffolding tool (Ojanen et al., 2015). As a teaching tool that could be employed in classrooms where the emphasis should be learner-centered, as prescribed by the Namibian education curriculum, the GraphoGame could be invaluable in small group activities within large class groups. Learners who would typically be unable to receive the necessary attention from their teachers could be provided with appropriate repetition in learning letter sounds and words during GraphoGame play. Furthermore, they are also being occupied appropriately while the teacher provides attention to those learners who need more individualized attention.

As several learners can play on the same tablet, each with his or her own name and a distinctive character, only a few tablets in a classroom will suffice. The Grade 1 teacher can also arrange group work to provide each learner with the opportunity to play daily for 10 to 20 minutes to support her or his initial reading skills. For struggling readers, this opportunity may be provided twice a day.

Currently, GraphoGame Afrikaans is free in developing countries through the appropriate channels. The license for GraphoGame Afrikaans is shared between the University of Jyväskylä and the University of Namibia. GraphoGame is also easily downloadable to an android device, and since many Namibians, indeed many Africans, utilize mobile phones to communicate, even parents can download GraphoGame for their children. The game can be played offline; therefore, except for downloading, parents need not be connected to the internet for their child to make use of GraphoGame.

As a tool, teachers can check game logs to determine areas with which learners are struggling. It can, thus, also be a good diagnostic tool. GraphoGame could also be employed as an assessment tool as GraphoGame Afrikaans version regularly assesses learners' letter, word, and pseudo-word knowledge. The data for these assessments could be downloaded from the server and analyzed diagnostically for typical problem areas. These problem areas could be addressed during classroom teaching to provide further support to learners.

In summary, the relevance of a digital tool such as GraphoGame for African schools is three-fold. It can serve as a breakthrough into ICT in African classrooms, something that is currently unattainable for most African learners. Furthermore, the game demonstrates several learning and teaching advantages in promoting initial reading acquisition, and, finally, the ease with which it can be downloaded on Android devices and played offline makes the transfer from school to home more seamless. The last aspect became more relevant during the 2019 COVID pandemic when learners missed many school days due to the unexpected closing of schools.

FUTURE RESEARCH DIRECTIONS

The current study compares the progress of learners playing GraphoGame (a reading-based game) with those learners who played GraphoMath (a mathematics-based game) and those who did not play any game. Future research could compare GraphoGame with another reading-based game. The results of such a research design could be more comparable as the focus of such a design would be on two reading programs instead of only comparing a computer-assisted reading program with a computer-assisted mathematics program.

The version of GraphoGame Afrikaans employed in this study focuses on the initial reading acquisition that involves acquiring knowledge of letters and words. Consequently, it has limitations in aspects such as sentence reading, reading comprehension, and fluency. Future research could investigate the transition from GraphoGame's letter and word reading to the complex process of reading in order to determine the success rate of this transition.

To minimize the possibility of the Hawthorne effect, where participants in a study change their behavior because they are being studied, an intervention crossover study could be a better research design for learners involved in the study as this research design first selects one group as the experimental group and a second group as control. At a later stage, the groups, switch and the previous control group becomes the experimental group.

GraphoGame

Technology is not readily available and/or utilized in African classrooms. It often rather becomes a limitation to teachers who have been grounded in traditional modes of teaching and learning modes, contrasting the readiness of young learners to use technology; therefore, research to investigate ways in which teachers utilize tools, such as GraphoGame, organically would be of interest. Such a study could be aimed at determining which of the methods produce better learning results.

CONCLUSION

This chapter has highlighted how technology which may still be considered a "luxury" in the majority of African school settings, given the overall low socioeconomic status of such schools, can be utilized. Most African schools comprise large classes, and this phenomenon may be contributing to learners receiving insufficient, individual attention from the teacher to ensure that each one has grasped the basic reading skills necessary to move from learning to read to reading to learn. The research study involving GraphoGame has shown that with a simple android device that is becoming more inexpensive these days and that can be shared by many (each with their own name and character/avatar), the teacher can track the individual progress of the learners in the class. This frees up the teacher to attend to those learners who are more in need of individual attention. Due to the nature of GraphoGame that scaffolds the learning experience, this has implications for learners who are struggling to "crack the code" to initial reading acquisition. Unlike a teacher that may not have the time to repeat *ad infinitum*, for example, letter sounds to enable each learner to make the connection in their own time, GraphoGame provides such support at the learner's own pace and ability.

Support tools, such as GraphoGame, may be the ideal introduction of ICT into African classrooms and advance 21st-century skills for which learners are possibly more ready than their teachers. As this research indicates, learners who had never had access to a tablet, grasped the game easily after only the initial introduction to it. Since GraphoGame can also be played on phones, on- and offline, the transition from school to home and vice-versa can serve as an additional connection between the two settings that have been plagued with a divide for so long. This could have positive connotations for continued learning in instances such as the lockdowns during the COVID-19 pandemic that have had a dire impact on education in African countries where internet connectivity is sadly lacking for most.

There have been discussions surrounding the development of GraphoGame in other Namibian languages. The next language that is targeted is Oshikwanyama, spoken by one of the majority language groups in Namibia. In addition, there is a research plan to introduce the GraphoGame English Rime version (developed in the UK) to assist in the transition from mother-tongue to English in Grade 4. These are exciting developments and show promise of a positive move in bringing Namibia, and other African countries into the 21st century as far as more progressive education is concerned.

REFERENCES

Aguiar, A. L., & Aguiar, C. (2020). Classroom composition and quality in early childhood education: A systematic review. *Children and Youth Services Review, 115*(May), 105086. doi:10.1016/j.childyouth.2020.105086

Benbow, J., Mizrachi, A., Oliver, D., & Said-Moshiro, L. (2007). *Large Class Sizes in the Developing World : What Do We Know and What Can We Do?* (Cooperative Agreement No. GDG-A_00-03-00006-00; Issue October). https://pdf.usaid.gov/pdf_docs/PNADK328.pdf

Blok, H., Oostdam, R., Otter, M. E., & Overmaat, M. (2002). Computer-assisted instruction in support of beginning reading instruction: A review. *Review of Educational Research, 72*(1), 101–130. doi:10.3102/00346543072001101

Bridges in Mathematics. (2012). *Grade 1 Assessments and Scoring Checklists, Common Core State Standards*. Bridges in Mathematics. https://bridges1.mathlearningcenter.org/files/media/Bridges_GrK-5_Assmnt/GR1-YearlongAssessment-0512w.pdf

Chang, M., & Gu, X. (2018). The role of executive function in linking fundamental motor skills and reading proficiency in socioeconomically disadvantaged kindergarteners. *Learning and Individual Differences, 61*(December), 250–255. doi:10.1016/j.lindif.2018.01.002

Chinyoka, K. (2014). Causes of school drop-out among ordinary level learners in a resettlement area in Masvingo, Zimbabwe. *Journal of Emerging Trends in Educational Research and Policy Studies, 5*(3), 294–300.

Cohen, J. (1992). A power primer. *Psychological Bulletin, 112*(1), 155–159. doi:10.1037/0033-2909.112.1.155 PMID:19565683

Daniele, V. (2021). Socioeconomic inequality and regional disparities in educational achievement: The role of relative poverty. *Intelligence, 84*(October), 101515. doi:10.1016/j.intell.2020.101515

Davidson, M., & Hobbs, J. (2013). Delivering reading intervention to the poorest children: The case of Liberia and EGRA-Plus, a primary grade reading assessment and intervention. *International Journal of Educational Development, 33*(3), 283–293. doi:10.1016/j.ijedudev.2012.09.005

Department of Basic Education. (2017). *SACMEQ IV project in South Africa: A study of the conditions of schooling and quality of education*. http://www.sacmeq.org/sites/default/files/sacmeq/publications/sacmeq_iv_project_in_south_africa_report.pdf

Department of Educational Planning and Research Services. (2017). *SACMEQ IV project in Botswana: A study of the conditions of schooling and quality of education*. http://www.sacmeq.org/sites/default/files/sacmeq/publications/final_saqmeq_iv_report_botswana-compressed.pdf

Dolean, D., Melby-Lervåg, M., Tincas, I., Damsa, C., & Lervåg, A. (2019). Achievement gap: Socioeconomic status affects reading development beyond language and cognition in children facing poverty. *Learning and Instruction, 63*(June), 101218. doi:10.1016/j.learninstruc.2019.101218

Dwarkan, L. (2017). *SACMEQ IV project in Mauritius: A study of the conditions of schooling and quality of education*. http://www.sacmeq.org/sites/default/files/sacmeq/publications/final_sacmeq_4_report_mauritius.pdf

Ehri, L. C., & McCormick, S. (1998). Phases of word learning: Implications for instruction with delayed and disabled readers. *Reading & Writing Quarterly, 14*(April), 135–163. doi:10.1080/1057356980140202

Eklund, K. M., Torppa, M., & Lyytinen, H. (2013). Predicting reading disability: Early cognitive risk and protective factors. *Dyslexia (Chichester, England)*, *19*(1), 1–10. doi:10.1002/dys.1447 PMID:23297103

Elbro, C., Rasmussen, I., & Spelling, B. (1996). Teaching reading to disabled readers with language disorders: A controlled evaluation of synthetic speech feedback. *Scandinavian Journal of Psychology*, *37*(2), 140–155. doi:10.1111/j.1467-9450.1996.tb00647.x PMID:8711453

Enders, C. K. (2011). Analyzing longitudinal data with missing values. *Rehabilitation Psychology*, *56*(4), 267–288. doi:10.1037/a0025579 PMID:21967118

Fani, T., & Ghaemi, F. (2011). Implications of Vygotsky's Zone of Proximal Development (ZPD) in Teacher Education: ZPTD and Self-scaffolding. *Procedia: Social and Behavioral Sciences*, *29*, 1549–1554. doi:10.1016/j.sbspro.2011.11.396

February, P. J. (2018). *Teaching and learning to read in Afrikaans: Teacher competence and computer-assisted support*. University of Jyväskylä. http://urn.fi/URN:ISBN:978-951-39-7515-9

Field, A. (2013). *Discovering statistics using IBM SPSS Statistics: And sex and drugs and rock 'n' roll* (4th ed.). Sage Publications.

Gains, P., & Parkes, A. (2012). *Report on the development, implementation and findings of the EGRA pilot in Hardap, Kavango and Oshikoto regions: November 2011-May 2012*. Academic Press.

Georgiou, G. K., Hirvonen, R., Liao, C.-H., Manolitsis, G., Parrila, R., & Nurmi, J.-E. (2011). The role of achievement strategies on literacy acquisition across languages. *Contemporary Educational Psychology*, *36*(2), 130–141. doi:10.1016/j.cedpsych.2011.01.001

Giovetti, O. (2020). *How does education affect poverty? It can help end it*. Concern Worldwide. https://www.concernusa.org/story/how-education-affects-poverty/

Glock, S., & Kleen, H. (2020). Preservice teachers' attitudes, attributions, and stereotypes: Exploring the disadvantages of students from families with low socioeconomic status. *Studies in Educational Evaluation*, *67*(October), 1–9. doi:10.1016/j.stueduc.2020.100929

Hall, T. E., Hughes, C. A., & Filbert, M. (2000). Computer assisted instruction in reading for students with learning disabilities: A research synthesis. *Education & Treatment of Children*, *23*(2), 173–193. http://eric.ed.gov.ezp-prod1.hul.harvard.edu/ERICWebPortal/search/detailmini.jsp?_nfpb=true&_&ERICExtSearch_SearchValue_0=EJ611303&ERICExtSearch_SearchType_0=no&accno=EJ611303

Hanse-Himarwa, K. (2015). *State of Education*. Arts and Culture Address.

Hattie, J. A. C. (2008). *Visible Learning: A synthesis of over 800 meta-analyses relating to achievement*. Routledge. doi:10.4324/9780203887332

Hungi, N., Makuwa, D., Ross, K., Saito, M., Dolata, S., van Capelle, F., Paviot, L., & Vellien, J. (2010). SACMEQ III Project Results: Pupil achievement levels in reading and mathematics. Southern and Eastern African Consortium for Monitoring Educational Quality. doi:10.100711125-005-6819-7

Ketonen, R., Salmi, P., & Krimark, P. (Eds.). (2015). Namibia: Literacy Assessment Tools for Grades 1-3 and Special Education. Namibia: Literacy Assessment Tools for Grades 1-3 and Special Education. Grapho Learning training Programme (2012-2014). Niilo Mäki Institute.

Kirchner, E., Alexander, S., & Tötemeyer, A.-J. (2014). The reading habits / behaviour and preferences of African children : The Namibian chapter in collaboration with UNISA. Academic Press.

Krstic, K., Stepanovic-Ilic, I., & Videnovic, M. (2017). Student dropout in primary and secondary education in the Republic of Serbia. *Psiholoska Istrazivanja*, *20*(1), 27–50. doi:10.5937/PsIstra1701027K

Kruger, W. (2012). *Learning to read Afrikaans*. www.homeschooling-curriculum-guide.com

Kyle, F., Kujala, J., Richardson, U., Lyytinen, H., & Goswami, U. (2013). Assessing the effectiveness of two theoretically motivated computer-assisted reading interventions in the United Kingdom: GG rime and GG phoneme. *Reading Research Quarterly*, *48*(1), 61–76. http://www.learntechlib.org/p/91905. doi:10.1002/rrq.038

Lenhard, W., & Lenhard, A. (2016). *Calculation of Effect Sizes*. Psychometrica., doi:10.13140/RG.2.1.3478.4245

Lynch, L., Fawcett, A. J., & Nicolson, R. I. (2000). Computer-assisted reading intervention in a secondary school: An evaluation study. *British Journal of Educational Technology*, *31*(4), 333–348. doi:10.1111/1467-8535.00166

Lyytinen, H., Erskine, J., Kujala, J., Ojanen, E., & Richardson, U. (2009). In search of a science-based application: A learning tool for reading acquisition. *Scandinavian Journal of Psychology*, *50*(6), 668–675. doi:10.1111/j.1467-9450.2009.00791.x PMID:19930268

Lyytinen, H., Erskine, J., Tolvanen, A., Torppa, M., Poikkeus, A.-M., & Lyytinen, P. (2006). Trajectories of reading development: A follow-up from birth to school age of children with and without risk for dyslexia. *Merrill-Palmer Quarterly*, *52*(3), 514–546. doi:10.1353/mpq.2006.0031

Lyytinen, H., Ronimus, M., Alanko, A., Poikkeus, A., & Taanila, M. (2007). Early identification of dyslexia and the use of computer game-based practice to support reading acquisition. *Nordic Psychology*, *59*(2), 109–126. doi:10.1027/1901-2276.59.2.109

Maddux, C. D., & Lamont, J. D. (2013). *Technology in Eduction: A Twenty-Year Retrospective*. Taylor and Francis. doi:10.4324/9781315821245

Magnan, A., & Ecalle, J. (2006). Audio-visual training in children with reading disabilities. *Computers & Education*, *46*(4), 407–425. doi:10.1016/j.compedu.2004.08.008

Makuwa, D., Amadhila, L., Shikongo, S., & Dengeinge, R. (2011). Trends in achievement levels of grade 6 Learners in Namibia. *Policy Brief*, *1*.

Maswahu, I. L. (2012). *Grade 10 dropout predisposition and resilience in one rural and one urban secondary school in the Kizito cluster of the Caprivi education region in Namibia*. University of the Western Cape. http://etd.uwc.ac.za/handle/11394/4494

Ministry of Education. (2005). *Curriculum for the Lower Primary Phase: English Version*. Windhoek: Ministry of Education.

Ministry of Education Arts and Culture. (2015). *Final Draft Language Policy for Schools in Namibia: Pre-primary, Grade 1-12*. Windhoek: Ministry of Education Arts and Culture.

Ministry of Education Arts and Culture & UNICEF Namibia. (2016). *We are the architects of our destiny: Study of positive deviant schools in Namibia*. https://www.unicef.org/namibia/na.MoEAC_-_Positive_Deviant_Schools_Report_(2016)_-_web_quality(1).pdf

Namibia Statistics Agency. (2013). *Namibia 2011 Population & Housing Census - Main Report*. http://www.nsa.org.na/files/downloads/Namibia 2011 Population and Housing Census Main Report.pdf

Nekongo-Nielsen, H., Mbukusa, N. R., & Tjiramba, E. (2015). Investigating factors that lead to school dropout in Namibia. *Namibia CPD Journal for Educators, 2*(1), 99–118. http://journals.unam.edu.na/index.php/NCPDJE/article/view/1282/1109

Nhongo, K. (2014, March 19). Grade 5 NSAT results depressing. *Windhoek Observer*. http://www.observer.com.na/national/3131-grade-5-nsat-results-depressing#

Nicholson, R. I., & Fawcett, A. J. (2000). Long-term learning in dyslexic children. *The European Journal of Cognitive Psychology, 12*(3), 357–393. doi:10.1080/09541440050114552

Ninnes, P. (2011). *Improving Quality and Equity in Education in Namibia: A Trend and Gap Analysis*. Academic Press.

Ojanen, E., Ronimus, M., Ahonen, T., Chansa-Kabali, T., February, P., Jere-Folotiya, J., Kauppinen, K.-P., Ketonen, R., & Ngorosho, D., Pitknen, M., Puhakka, S., Sampa, F., Walubita, G., Yalukanda, C., Pugh, K., Richardson, U., Serpell, R., & Lyytinen, H. (2015). GraphoGame-A catalyst for multi-level promotion of literacy in diverse contexts. *Frontiers in Psychology, 6*(May). Advance online publication. doi:10.3389/fpsyg.2015.00671 PMID:26113825

Potocki, A., Magnan, A., & Ecalle, J. (2015). Computerized trainings in four groups of struggling readers: Specific effects on word reading and comprehension. *Research in Developmental Disabilities, 45–46*(April), 83–92. doi:10.1016/j.ridd.2015.07.016

Puolakanaho, A. (2007). Early prediction of reading and related language and cognitive skills in children with a familial risk for dyslexia. *Jyväskylä Studies in Education, Psychology and Social Research 317*. https://jyx.jyu.fi/dspace/bitstream/handle/123456789/13367/9789513929985.pdf?sequence=1

Regtvoort, A., & van der Leij, A. (2007). Early intervention with children of dyslexic parents: Effects of computer-based reading instruction at home on literacy acquisition. *Learning and Individual Differences, 17*(1), 35–53. doi:10.1016/j.lindif.2007.01.005

Richardson, U. (2011). *GRAPHOGAME Report Summary*. European Commission, Community Research and Development Information Service (CORDIS). https://cordis.europa.eu/result/rcn/48026_en.html

Ronimus, M., Kujala, J., Tolvanen, A., & Lyytinen, H. (2014). Children's engagement during digital game-based learning of reading: The effects of time, rewards, and challenge. *Computers & Education, 71*, 237–246. doi:10.1016/j.compedu.2013.10.008

Saine, N. L., Lerkkanen, M.-K., Ahonen, T., Tolvanen, A., & Lyytinen, H. (2010a). Predicting word-level reading fluency outcomes in three contrastive groups: Remedial and computer-assisted remedial reading intervention, and mainstream instruction. *Learning and Individual Differences*, *20*(5), 402–414. doi:10.1016/j.lindif.2010.06.004

Saine, N. L., Lerkkanen, M. K., Ahonen, T., Tolvanen, A., & Lyytinen, H. (2010b). Predicting word-level reading fluency outcomes in three contrastive groups: Remedial and computer-assisted remedial reading intervention, and mainstream instruction. *Learning and Individual Differences*, *20*(5), 402–414. doi:10.1016/j.lindif.2010.06.004

Shigwedha, A. N., Nakashole, L., Auala, H., Amakutuwa, H., & Ailonga, I. (2015). *The SACMEQ IV project in Namibia: A study of the conditions of schooling and the quality of primary education in Namibia*. http://www.sacmeq.org/sites/default/files/sacmeq/publications/final_sacmeq_iv_report_namibia-compressed-compressed.pdf

Spaull, N., & Taylor, S. (2012). SACMEQ at a glance series. In *Research on Socio-economic Policy (RESEP)*. https://resep.sun.ac.za/index.php/projects

Stetter, M. E., & Hughes, M. T. (2010). Computer-Assisted Instruction to Enhance the Reading Comprehension of .... *Journal of Special Education Technology*, *25*(5), 1–16. doi:10.1177/016264341002500401

Stone, C. A. (1998). The Metaphor of Scaffolding: Its Utility for the Field of Learning Disabilities. *Journal of Learning Disabilities*, *31*(4), 344–364. doi:10.1177/002221949803100404 PMID:9666611

Sucena, A., Filipa, A. S., & Viana, F. L. (2016). Early intervention in reading difficulties using the Graphogame software. *Letronica*, *9*(2).

Taylor, S., & Yu, D. (2009). The importance of socio-economic status in determining educational achievement in South Africa. *Stellenbosch Economic Working Papers*, 1–65.

Thomson, S. (2018). Achievement at school and socioeconomic background—An educational perspective. *NPJ Science of Learning*, *3*(1), 5. Advance online publication. doi:10.103841539-018-0022-0 PMID:30631466

Torgesen, J. K., Wagner, R. K., Rashotte, C. A., Herron, J., & Lindamood, P. (2010). Computer assisted instruction to prevent early reading difficulties in students at risk for dyslexia: Outcomes from two instructional approaches. *Annals of Dyslexia*, *60*(1), 40–56. doi:10.100711881-009-0032-y PMID:20052566

Torppa, M. (2007). *Pathways to Reading Acquisition: effects of early skills, learning environment and familial risk for dyslexia*. University of Jyväskylä.

UNESCO. (2006). *Cross-national studies of the quality of education: Planning their design and managing their impact* (K. N. Ross & I. J. Genevois, Eds.). International Institute for Educational Planning.

Vacca, J. S., & Levitt, R. (2011). Using Scaffolding Techniques to Teach a Lesson about the Civil War. *International Journal of Humanities and Social Science*, *1*(18), 150–161. www.ijhssnet.com

Valsiner, J. (1987). *Culture and the Development of Children's Action: A cultural-historical theory of developmental psychology*. John Wiley & Sons.

van Daal, V., & Reitsma, P. (2000). Computer-assisted learning to read and spell: Results from two pilot studies. *Journal of Research in Reading*, *23*(2), 181–193. doi:10.1111/1467-9817.00113

Van Rensburg, C. (2013). 'n Perspektief op 'n periode van kontak tussen Khoi en Afrikaans. *Literator*, *34*(2), 1–11. doi:10.4102/lit.v34i2.413

Vygotsky, L. S. (1978). *Mind in Society: The Development of Higher Psychological Processes (M. Cole, V. John-Steiner* (S. Scribner & E. Souberman, Eds.). Havard University Press.

Wise, B. W., Ring, J., & Olson, R. K. (2000). Individual differences in gains from computer-assisted remedial reading. *Journal of Experimental Child Psychology*, *77*(3), 197–235. doi:10.1006/jecp.1999.2559 PMID:11023657

Zakharov, A., Tsheko, G., & Carnoy, M. (2016). Do "better" teachers and classroom resources improve student achievement? A causal comparative approach in Kenya, South Africa, and Swaziland. *International Journal of Educational Development*, *50*, 108–124. doi:10.1016/j.ijedudev.2016.07.001

Zuze, T. L., & Reddy, V. (2014). School resources and the gender reading literacy gap in South African schools. *International Journal of Educational Development*, *36*, 100–107. doi:10.1016/j.ijedudev.2013.10.002

ADDITIONAL READING

Ahmed, H., Wilson, A., Mead, N., Noble, H., Richardson, U., Wolpert, M. A., & Goswami, U. (2020). An Evaluation of the Efficacy of GraphoGame Rime for Promoting English Phonics Knowledge in Poor Readers. *Frontiers in Education*, *5*(July), 1–12. doi:10.3389/feduc.2020.00132

Hsin, C., Li, M., & Tsai, C. (2014). The influence of young children's use of technology on their learning: A review. *Journal of Educational Technology & Society*, *17*, 85–99.

Jere-Folotiya, J., Chansa-Kabali, T., Munachaka, J. C., Sampa, F., Yalukanda, C., Westerholm, J., Richardson, U., Serpell, R., & Lyytinen, H. (2014). The effect of using a mobile literacy game to improve literacy levels of grade one students in Zambian schools. *Educational Technology Research and Development*, *62*(4), 417–436. doi:10.100711423-014-9342-9

Kreskey, D. D., & Truscott, S. D. (2016). Is Computer-Aided Instruction an Effective Tier-One Intervention for Kindergarten Students at Risk for Reading Failure in an Applied Setting? *Contemporary School Psychology*, *20*(2), 142–151. doi:10.100740688-015-0056-8

Lyytinen, H., Ojanen, E., Jere-Folotiya, J., Ngorosho, S. D., Sampa, F., February, P., Malasha, F., Munachaka, J., Pugh, K., & Serpell, R. (2019). Challenges associated with reading acquisition in Sub-Saharan Africa: Promotion of literacy in multilingual contexts. In *Improving early literacy outcomes* (pp. 119–132). Brill Sense., doi:10.1163/9789004402379_007

Nshimbi, J. C., Serpell, R., & Westerholm, J. (2020). Using a phone-based learning tool as an instructional resource for initial literacy learning in rural African families. *South African Journal of Childhood Education*, *10*(1), 1–9. doi:10.4102ajce.v10i1.620

KEY TERMS AND DEFINITIONS

First Language: This term indicates the advanced level at which a language is offered at school. It is expected that the child who takes a language at this level in school either has this language as a mother tongue or home language.

Foreign Language: This is a language that a child will not know and is typically not a language that is native to Namibia. French is an example of a foreign language in Namibia. German is the exception as it is a national language and the home language for almost 1% of the Namibian population, but is regarded as a foreign language for other Namibians. In the state schools, foreign languages are offered from Grades 8 to 12.

Home Language: The language that is used in the home, usually the mother tongue.

Mother Tongue: The language that a child acquires in the home.

National Language: In the Language Policy for Schools in Namibia, a national language is regarded as a language spoken by Namibians as a mother tongue. The Namibian school curriculum offers 15 national languages.

Official Language: The language used in government and for official purposes. For Namibia, English is the official language.

Second Language: As Namibia is a multilingual society, most Namibians speak two or more languages. It is expected that the second language is familiar to the child, a language of the community. English is usually offered as the second language in Namibian schools.

Chapter 24
Educational Video Games for Learning English Vocabulary:
Methodology of Empirical Research

Jianshu Qiao
Queen Mary University of London, UK

John R. Woodward
Queen Mary Univeristy of London, UK

Atm S. Alam
 https://orcid.org/0000-0002-8299-754X
Queen Mary University of London, UK

ABSTRACT

Researchers have been exploring the potential of educational video games for learning English vocabulary. The primary focus is on two questions: (1) Can educational video games motivate students to learn English vocabulary (which explores students' attitudes)? and (2) Are educational video games effective in acquiring English vocabulary (which explores learning outcomes)? Good quality empirical research on this is rare because of the shortage of games specific to educational purposes. In addition, although some researchers have contributed to answering these two questions, their methodology is not convincing. Therefore, this chapter aims to provide an overview of their methodologies by introducing participant groups, popular educational video games, pre-test, post-test, and data analysis. Finally, this chapter will inspire researchers to conduct more reliable empirical research, thereby making better-found contributions to the field.

DOI: 10.4018/978-1-7998-7271-9.ch024

INTRODUCTION

Learning English is crucial in schools in most non-speaking English countries (Hu, 2005; Yeşilbağ et al., 2020). Learning English is a difficult and time-consuming process requiring master English vocabulary, grammar, and pronunciation, etc. While vocabulary plays a fundamental role in effective communication, reading, and writing, students[1] struggle to remember English vocabulary because they lack an English-speaking environment and the fade of remembered vocabulary over time.

With the advancement of smart mobile devices, the Internet, and computing technologies, students aspire to a novel, motivating, and effective way of learning vocabulary. Digital games (DGs) could be a potential platform for students to acquire vocabulary. DGs are engaging, appealing, and exciting, and have greatly improved in terms of interactivity and visual performance (Franciosi et al., 2016). More importantly, DGs are capable of maintaining students' attention for long periods. For example, the attention span for learning is higher when DGs are involved in the learning process (Huang et al., 2017). Leveraging this feature of DGs to engage students in acquiring skills is called educational video games (EVGs) in this chapter.

There are two focuses as to the acquisition of learning English in EVGs. Firstly, researchers focus on whether students have positive attitudes towards learning vocabulary through EVGs. Secondly, researchers also concentrate on whether EVGs can help students acquire vocabulary. Empirical research on these two topics is scarce mainly for the two reasons; there are few EVGs designed specifically for learning vocabulary, and researchers do not have the time and money to develop such EVGs (Chen & Yang, 2013).

In addition, the methodology in empirical research is not appropriate enough to obtain reliable results. For example, some researchers (Azman & Farhana Dollsaid, 2018; Ebrahimzadeh & Alavi, 2016) use commercial-off-the-shelf games designed for entertainment. Since these games are not purpose-built, they are inappropriate to answer questions about the full potential of EVGs designed for education. Besides, some researchers (Janebi Enayat & Haghighatpasand, 2019; Oberg, 2011) only consider how the English proficiency of participants can impact the results. However, the prior gaming experience has a significant influence on learning outcomes (Yang & Quadir, 2018). Therefore, when choosing participants, researchers should consider both their English proficiency and their experience with video games.

Based on the above discussions, this chapter has two aims. The first objective is to introduce review the primary elements of research methodology, which helps researchers have a basic understanding of the methodology. The second objective is to provide researchers with insights on each of the elements of the methodology of empirical research, which facilitates the reliability of future empirical research.

The remainder chapter includes five sections: background, methodology of empirical research, future research directions, discussion, conclusion. This chapter finally provides a comprehensive overview of methodology to assist further empirical research including the breakdown of the methodological approach of empirical research. These contents will help researchers conduct reliable empirical research, and contribute to this field.

BACKGROUND

This section gives the importance of defining participants and selecting appropriate EVGs, and the inadequate research on the maximum effectiveness of EVGs.

There are three types of English language learners: (a) native language learners; (b) second language learners; and (c) foreign language learners. The crucial difference between these types is the frequency of English usage, which leads to different levels of English proficiency. Second language learners occasionally communicate in English in some special situations. Foreign language learners, apart from English classes, often do not have English environments in which to practice English vocabulary. Researchers often mix the three types of English language learners. Consequently, it is a common mistake to use EVGs designed for native language learners, to teach foreign language learners with less English knowledge.

Nevertheless, research has found benefits of EVGs ranging from increasing motivation and gaining English vocabulary (Camacho Vásquez & Ovalle, 2019; Sandberg et al., 2014; Subhash & Cudney, 2018; Thompson & von Gillern, 2020). In addition, EVGs expand opportunities for communicative competence in an online interactive setting (Azman & Farhana Dollsaid, 2018). For an instance, students can chat with English native speakers in an online virtual setting, which facilitates the usage of English vocabulary in authentic dialogue (Milton et al., 2012). EVGs also have a positive impact on the spelling of words with silent letters and the spelling of English homophones (Mehrpour & Ghayour, 2017).

However, it is difficult to conclude how effective EVGs are and if there is more potential. Although motivating students, EVGs achieve only a few learning outcomes at the cost of much time. The main reason is that EVGs often contain information and complex scenarios irrelevant to the learning objectives, misleading and distracting participants[2] from the educational task (Milton et al., 2012). Therefore, EVGs used in empirical research should carefully be selected so that students can get the maximum benefit of using EVGs for their learning success.

Moreover, students are the target group who are expected to learn English with purposes (e.g., pass examinations). Students primarily remember English vocabulary with pencil and paper in a rote memory method, which is called the traditional method in this chapter. Although the traditional method is boring, mundane, and self-obliged, it is a popular and practical way of learning English vocabulary. Therefore, researchers and teachers primarily are concerned about the question that whether EVGs are as effective as the traditional method.

To answer this question, researchers often need to conduct a comparative experiment. Students learn English vocabulary with EVGs in the experimental group, while they learn English vocabulary in the traditional method in the control group. Although some researchers concluded that EVGs are more effective than the traditional method (Janebi Enayat & Haghighatpasand, 2019; Yeşilbağ et al., 2020), another researcher (Franciosi et al., 2016) concluded that there is no difference in short-term retention of vocabulary.

Researchers still do not reach an agreement because the types of participants (e.g., primary students, middle students, university students) and the types of EVGs (e.g., board games, simulation games, card games, etc.) vary in their research. Therefore, it is pressing to conduct more appropriate experiments by taking various participant groups and EVGs into account.

METHODOLOGY OF EMPIRICAL RESEARCH

The methodology of empirical research includes some primary elements. Researchers need to recruit participants and choose appropriate EVGs which will be utilized in the empirical research. Next, researchers test how many English vocabulary participants know in the pre-test, followed by the experiment, and followed by the post-test whose method is the same as the pre-test. Last but not least, a reasonable data analysis to get reliable research results.

Participants

Before conducting any empirical research, researchers must have an overview of the participants. This is an important aspect because the target participants for empirical research can vary. For example, only male students could be recruited as participants due to educational policies in Iran (Ebrahimzadeh & Alavi, 2016). As a result, it is impractical to explore the gender difference in empirical research. Researchers can propose research aims according to the type of participants available. Regardless of the research aims, three important things should be clearly defined before conducting empirical research.

Firstly, it is significant to understand the target participants because it will help researchers choose appropriate EVGs. Complex grammar can hinder the learning process of participants with limited vocabulary (Cobb, 2007). For example, Ever Quest 2 is a game consisting of complicated grammar and vocabulary. Consequently, foreign language learners with inadequate English vocabulary often cannot catch up with the information displayed on screen (Rankin et al., 2006). EVGs designed for native language learners generally contain slang, complex vocabulary, and complicated grammar. As a result, it is unreasonable to choose such EVGs for foreign language learners in empirical research. Therefore, it would be acceptable to choose popularly local EVGs that are appropriate to the participants.

Secondly, researchers should know the educational background of the participants. In most cases, students in universities have more English proficiency compared with high school students while students from developed districts are better than students from developing districts. Similarly, city students have better English proficiency than rural students. Therefore, researchers should choose appropriate EVGs according to different situations. If the EVGs are too easy, students feel bored, while if the EVGs are too difficult, students will quit. Both situations will influence participants' attitudes toward EVGs, which further impacts the research results.

Thirdly, researchers need to know the prior gaming experience of participants. With the development of mobile games, most students more or less have the experience of playing DGs. The prior gaming experience can influence the acquisition of English vocabulary in EVGs (Yang & Quadir, 2018). Therefore, in the comparative experiment, it is better to assure the prior gaming experience of participants in each group does not influence the results. Researchers can judge the prior gaming experience of participants based on the amount of time they spent on DGs per week.

Educational Video Games

After knowing the background of participants, it is also important for empirical research to select appropriate EVGs. There are various genres of EVGs such as board games, massively multiplayer online games (MMOGs), web-based games, etc. This section provides a comprehensive discussion on different types of DGs that are used in previous EVGs research even though some DGs are not intended for educational purposes. Meanwhile, critical analysis with a constructive conclusion for each game type is also presented, which will facilitate the wide research community to choose and design EVGs in their research.

Massively Multiplayer Online Games

MMOGs are persistent virtual worlds, where players control different virtual avatars which have different occupations (e.g., mage, cleric, swordsman, archer, etc.). The virtual avatars gain knowledge and skills as the players conquer thousands of quests and levels (Azman & Farhana Dollsaid, 2018). More importantly, players can share knowledge while playing. Therefore, The learning mechanism of MMOGs is that students intangibly gain vocabulary knowledge as they seek to work together to accomplish tasks (Rama et al., 2012). MMOGs provide contextualized and authentic language interaction opportunities. Therefore, students can acquire English through communicating with online multilingual speakers (Azman & Farhana Dollsaid, 2018; Peterson, 2016). Apart from online multilingual speakers, non-playing characters (NPCs) also play an important role in improving English knowledge. By interacting with NPCs, students not only gain English vocabulary but also can infer the accurate meaning of English words when NPCs frequently use the same words (Rankin et al., 2006).

Three different MMOGs have been used in previous research. (a) World of Warcraft (WoW) (Ebrahimzadeh & Alavi, 2016) is a commercial-off-shelf game with complex operations and scenarios; (b) Second Life (SL) (Milton et al., 2012) is a simulations game, where players can control an avatar to move around in the virtual world. For example, players can have a virtual house and visit virtual shops. (c) 3rd World Farmer game (Franciosi et al., 2016) is a simpler simulation game than WoW and SL. All three games are commercial-off-the-shelf games, and available online.

Disadvantages

1. Researchers need to spend lots of time training participants before conducting empirical research. Since MMOGs have complex operations and complex scenarios, participants frequently complained about the unfamiliar things in Second Life, and the avatars often did not act as expected (Milton et al., 2012). In addition, participants without prior gaming experience cannot catch up with MMOGs. Consequently, participants receive few benefits from MMOGs.
2. MMOGs are not practical in schools. Firstly, MMOGs require high-quality computers and a stable internet connection, schools with a little budget cannot afford it. Secondly, MMOGs are not designed to achieve educational purposes. Therefore, even if schools can afford expensive devices, MMOGs cannot meet the pedagogical objectives. Finally, MMOGs generally require high-level gaming knowledge (Rama et al., 2012). Therefore, MMOGs cannot achieve effective teaching and learning because teachers and students lack training for such knowledge (Ariffin, 2012).
3. Enormous information and scenarios in MMOGs distract students. MMOGs offer a high degree of realism and immersion in lots of fantasy scenarios (Peterson, 2016). Immersed participants focus on the MMOGs instead of English vocabulary (Ebrahimzadeh & Alavi, 2016), which results in MMOGs losing their educational purposes. Therefore, there is little chance for vocabulary improvement without the teacher's control in MMOGs (Milton et al., 2012).
4. Researchers cannot alter the contents of MMOGs, which causes two limitations. (a) they are not able to alter MMOGs to meet educational purposes; and (b) they have to use the complex English vocabulary embedded in MMOGs.
5. Students have to spend much time to gain little vocabulary. In 3rd World Farmer game research, for example, the researchers allowed more than 5 hours to remember 29 unfamiliar words.

Advantages

1. Although designed for entertainment purposes, MMOGs can offer students significant motivational incentives in learning English vocabulary. From the viewpoints of the MMOGs mentioned above, there is no doubt that MMOGs can simultaneously achieve slightly learning performance and motivate students.
2. MMOGs provided an engaging, low-pressure, and low-anxiety context where students were able to explore and slightly improve vocabulary knowledge. Most participants could recognize and produce most of the vocabulary in SL (Milton et al., 2012), and the 3rd World Farmer game improved long-term retention of vocabulary (Franciosi et al., 2016).
3. MMOGs can be used to explore that which element of games (e.g., reward, feedback, challenge, vivid picture, and audio, etc.) mostly motivate the participants. It is helpful to help researchers create more qualified EVGs. Researchers can mostly decrease the learning period by cutting down most irrelevant information that distracts participants.

Compared to other types of EVGs, the distinct advantage of MMOGs is that they offer an immersed environment. However, immersion not only hardly achieves learning outcomes but also sometimes distracts participants' attention from learning. The disadvantages far more outweigh the advantages. Therefore, mobile applications with less immersion also have been used by current researchers.

Mobile Applications

There are lots of commercial-off-the-shelf applications that have been invented to help students learn English vocabulary. These applications are the combination of mobile devices, game features of DGs, and English vocabulary. Due to the recent advancement of the Internet and smart mobile devices, the learning environments becomes more flexible and convenient while more advanced game features (e.g., missions, score, rank, feedback, reward, etc.) can be implemented for such smart devices. Based on the recent trend, it is found that young people are always fascinated and inspired by new game features that can be leveraged to motivate students. These applications are often enriched with thousands of English vocabularies for students. Besides learning English vocabulary, some applications also offer additional learning space such as the ability to recognize alphabets, characters, or other images. In other words, students can match picture or mother tongue words with English vocabulary.

The followings are some of the applications that are commonly used to learn English vocabulary. (a) Super Word King (SWK) (Huang et al., 2017) provides various missions and levels for learners to accomplish; (b) Connecting English Word Game (CEWG) (Hung & Young, 2015) is a competitive game, which requires participants to work together to build a word map; and (c) Adapted Monopoly (Wei et al., 2018): the difference between adapted monopoly and traditional Monopoly is: players roll a dice to decide the steps of moving forward, while players answer questions to decide steps in adapted Monopoly.

Disadvantages

1. Mobile applications cannot engage students as much as MMOGs because mobile applications merely include some reduced game elements.

2. Cooperation setting in EVGs is harmful to participants with low English proficiency. English beginners are more or less possibly overlooked because they hardly contribute to competitive EVGs (Hung & Young, 2015).

Advantages

1. Mobile devices can offer better enjoyment and active interactions than offline devices. In CEWG research, compared to the offline approach, participants using tablets had better motivation and focus (Hung & Young, 2015).
2. Mobile applications can support learning outcomes. Participants had an obvious improvement after playing SWK (Huang et al., 2017). Unlike MMOGs, mobile application does not have much distracting information, which can keep participants concentrating on learning vocabulary.
3. Mobile applications are affordable and acceptable for most students. The English vocabulary in mobile applications is common and easy than those in MMOGs.
4. Participants can learn and share knowledge in competition and cooperation contexts (Chen & Chang, 2020).

Web-Based Games

Web-based games do not need to download the client, and any devices connecting to the Internet can play this type of EVGs. Compared with MMOGs and mobile applications, web-based games have the feature of low hardware and software requirements. Mingoville is an online web-based English learning program, for students aged between 5 to 15 years old. Students can learn English knowledge through completing different missions embedded in Mingoville (Anyaegbu et al., 2012).

Both mobile applications and web-based games are comprised of small challenges and tasks. These EVGs can both motivate participants and achieve learning outcomes in a low degree of immersion. Moreover, participants do not feel bored, even though both of them stress the same continuous repetition exercising as the traditional method. Therefore, the two types of EVGs are more practical in a classroom setting.

Pre-Test

Before conducting empirical research, researchers should assure their research has been approved by the research ethics committee of related institutions if applicable. To scale the improvement of participants in quantitative research, researchers are supposed to score every participant. Therefore, every participant will have a pre-test score before the experiment and a post-test score after the experiment. Finally, researchers can evaluate the effectiveness of EVGs by comparing the pre-test score and post-test score.

Binary Method

The binary method is often used to score the participant because it is simple, easy, and saves time. Researchers have already prepared some English words which will be learned in EVGs. If correctly spell the English word, participants can obtain one point, otherwise, they obtain zero points. After attempting to spell all prepared English words, researchers count all the points as their pre-test score. This method is a radical way because it does not consider the difficulty of each English word. Therefore, it is acceptable only if participants remember a few vocabularies in a long period. For example, participants remember 20 words in five days. In this case, any mistake cannot be tolerated.

However, researchers, sometimes, allow participants a short time (e.g., 45 minutes) to remember many words (e.g., 20). In this situation, it is unfair that 'elephant' and 'hen' are worth one point separately because 'elephant' has more letters than 'hen'. Participants spell 'elephant' as 'alephant', which does not mean the method (traditional memory, game method) does not work. After all, participants have already remembered 7 out of 8 letters.

Experiment

To make sure the process of the experiment proceeds smoothly, researchers should take some preparations:

1. Recruit a few more participants than expected in case some of the participants cannot attend.
2. Check whether EVGs can be executed on the platform especially if EVGs are self-designed.
3. No matter if EVGs are easy to understand or not, researchers must train participants in the operations of EVGs.
4. Experiment should not last a long time in one session because participants may lose patience.

In the middle of playing EVGs, observation can be leveraged to subjectively examine the degree of enjoyment of participants. The observer should be trained to focus on recording the information related to research objectives. After the experiment, the results of observation can be supplementary evidence to support research results.

Apart from the above preparations, researchers should consider more detailed measurements according to their research aims. A reasonable method is to conduct a pilot study, which will ensure the quality of the main study. Moreover, a pilot study probably helps researchers find out more potential problems and valuable research objectives.

Post-Test

In quantitative research, the binary method is also used in the post-test to get the post-test score of each participant. Researchers generally classified the post-test into short-term memory and long-term memory according to the time of doing the post-test. In qualitative research, researchers usually focus on the degree of motivation of participants so that they only need to conduct a post-test after the experiment.

Short-Term Memory

The researcher can either immediately do the post-test or one day after the experiment, which is to test the participants' short-term memory. It would be better to have an interval after the experiment because instant memory may have a huge influence on immediate post-test scores.

Long-Term Memory

It is hard to define the time scale of the long-term. The authors do not suggest that researchers do a delayed post-test after a far longer time (e.g., four weeks). The reason is participants may learn the same English vocabulary from other resources (e.g., textbooks, movies, games, etc.) as in their EVGs.

Since the short-term memory and long-term memory cannot precisely be defined, it would be acceptable to simply describe the interval in research (e.g., 15 minutes delayed post-test and four weeks delayed post-test). Some researchers aim to evaluate the effectiveness of EVG at different times. In this case, researchers should leave a time gap (e.g., two weeks) between the two post-tests because the first post-test reinforces the memory of remembered vocabulary, which further affects the results of the later post-test.

Qualitative Research

Questionnaires and interviews are the common methods when conducting a post-test in qualitative research. These two methods can be used alone or together. Moreover, these two methods can be used to understand the background of participants (e.g., prior gaming experience, computer skills, and gender, etc.).

Questionnaire

The questionnaire is easier than an interview. Researchers firstly conceive some questions according to their research objectives. It could be either open-end questions or set a Likert questionnaire or a combination of both ways. For example, a format of a typical five-level Likert item could be: 1: Strongly disagree; 2: Disagree 3: Neither agree nor disagree; 4: Agree; 5: Strongly agree. It would be better to do a pilot experiment that makes sure the questions in the questionnaire are clear and understandable for participants.

Interview

Although the interview usually costs more time than a questionnaire, researchers can get valuable information from participants. In addition, researchers can have a chance to instantly ask participants whenever they conceive new questions. Researchers firstly should prepare some open-end questions related to research objectives for participants. Then, researchers ask kinds of participants, which facilitates getting more opinions from different participants in line with the research aims. Due to participants usually respond lots of information, researchers need to extract useful information from their answers sentence by sentence.

Data Analysis

After obtaining the data, a serious data analysis will be essential to make convincing conclusions. Therefore, this section summarizes some common statistical methods, and how they can be used in empirical research. Researchers can use the combinations of some of the proposed methods below in their research.

Statistical Package for the Social Sciences (SPSS)

SPSS is a software package used for statistical analysis. The SPSS has been used in marketing, health, education research, and data mining. However, researchers can choose their most familiar tools, such as Microsoft Excel and Python, for data analysis.

Average

The average reflects the central tendency of the data set. Researchers initially calculate all participants' average scores of the pre-test and the post-test separately. Then, they can decide that whether participants made progress in English vocabulary by comparing the post-test score with the pre-test score. When it comes to questionnaire with the Likert scale, researchers can use the average score to explore the preference of participants.

Variance

Variance is a measure of the degree of discreteness when measuring a set of data. The combination of average and variance is the common and easy way to analyze the data. Researchers can evaluate the effectiveness of EVGs by comparing the average and variance of pre-test and post-test.

Cronbach Alpha

Cronbach alpha is used to measure the internal consistency or stability of the results obtained from the scaled questionnaire. Generally, the response of participants is acceptable when alpha is above 0.7.

Analysis of Variance (ANOVA)

Both the average and variance are not enough to tell whether EVGs help participants make progress or not. Therefore, ANOVA is used for the significance test of the difference between two or more samples. Whether EVGs help participants acquire English vocabulary? Within-group ANOVA can answer this question by calculating the significant difference between pre-test score and post-test score. When the experiment has a control group and an experimental group, there will be two groups of participants. Between-group ANOVA can calculate whether there is a significant difference in the English proficiency of participants by testing the pre-test scores in each group. The participants in each group are at the same English level if the analysis shows no significant difference. Moreover, in most cases, researchers need to know if the experimental group can have a bigger improvement of English vocabulary than the control group. Between-group ANOVA can solve this problem by analyzing the post-test scores in each group.

Chi-Square Test

The Chi-Square test applies to the data that do not obey any distribution. The Chi-Square test can be used to test whether there is a big difference between the control group and the experimental group. For example, researchers randomly divide the whole participants into two groups. However, either the number of female students and male students, or the English proficiency, or gaming experience is different in each group. How can researchers know the three differences cannot influence their research results? Chi-Square test can be used to answer this question if it shows no significant difference in each group.

T-Test

T-test assume the data to follow a normal distribution, and it is appropriate when the participants are small size. One-sample T-test is to compare whether there is a difference between the sample data and a specific value. Therefore, it can analyze the preference of participants in Likert-scale questionnaires. For example, the answer of participants on one question varies in the Likert-scale questionnaire. Instead of using the average score, one sample T-test examine the preference of participants by comparing the expectation of all answers with the target value.

The function of the paired-sample T-test is the same as the within-group ANOVA, except it requires the samples to be paired and has the same sample size. The function of independent-sample T-test is the same as between-group ANOVA, apart from it requires the variances of the two sets of data are equal. Therefore, F-test can be a supplement method before using the independent-sample T-test because the function of the F-test is to test whether the variances of the two sets of data are equal.

Figure 1. Generic methodology of empirical research

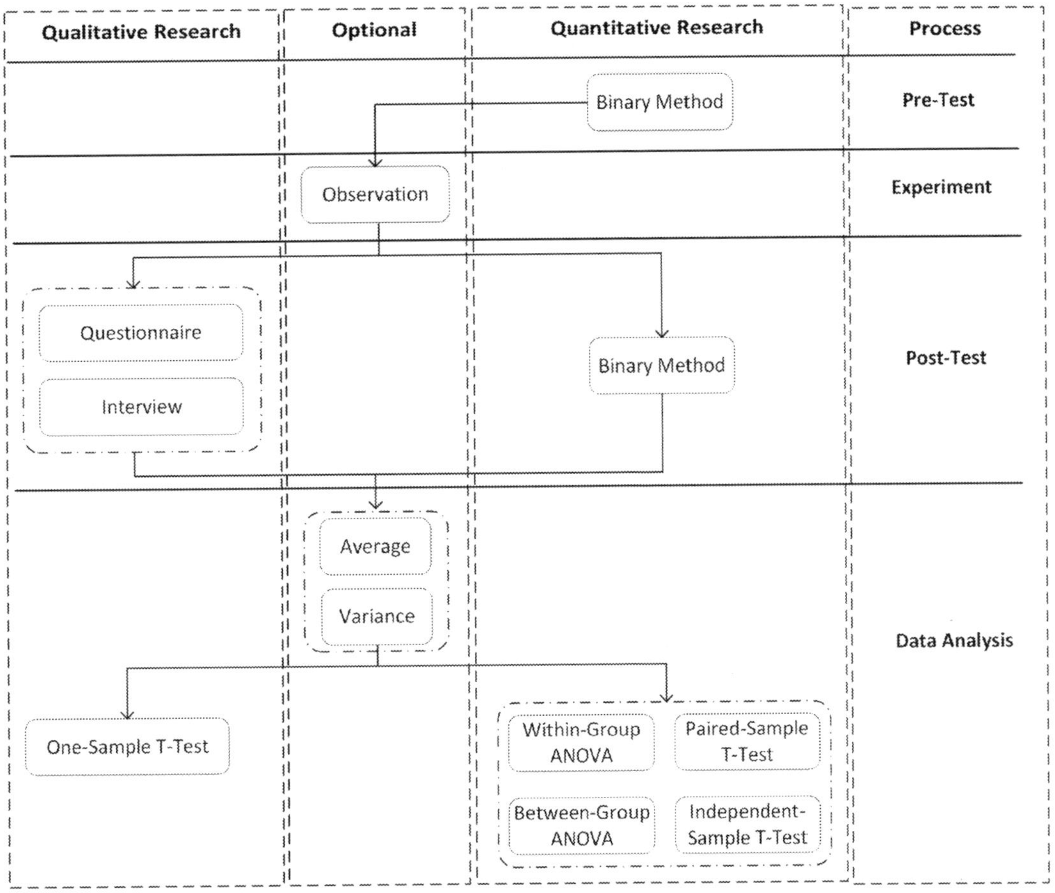

Based on the above discussion, there are some common aspects that are used in almost all types of EVGs. For simplicity, a generic methodology of empirical research is illustrated in Figure 1. The process column shows the common steps of empirical research. The qualitative research column and quantitative research column show the general method in each step. The optional column shows methods that are optional in qualitative and quantitative research.

FUTURE RESEARCH DIRECTIONS

EVGs have recently been attracting researchers' attention, and have been applied to learning English vocabulary. However, there are two matters that limit future research.

Firstly, there is a great lack of pedagogical elements with giving more emphasis on game settings for enhancing motivation, which is often unrelated to learning and giving less focus on achieving learning outcomes. As future work, one should consider implementing EVGs with a personalized assistance strategy (e.g., creating personalized game contents), which makes students pay more attention to their individually unknown words (Wei et al., 2018). Personalized strategy not only enhance short-term and long-term memory but also reduce the anxiety of learning English vocabulary. Therefore, useful game settings must be chosen with giving greater focus on pedagogical elements in order to gain the maximum potential of EVGs.

Secondly, a plausible method measuring the improvement of participants is necessary for empirical research. The binary method is radical and does not consider the length of the English vocabulary. Therefore, it is unfair that a long word is worth the same point as a short word. Researchers can work on the way of defining the difficulty of English vocabulary, which facilitates giving a reliable score in pre-test and post-test. Moreover, in the current research, researchers need to keep participants with the same English proficiency. If the difficulty of English vocabulary is defined, researchers can use the same participants in the experimental group and control group, but keep English vocabulary in each group at the same difficulty level to conduct the empirical research.

In the future, augmented reality (AR) and virtual reality (VR) are promising technologies to strengthen the experience of EVGs in the future. Computers and mobile devices are the common and convenient tools nowadays to play EVGs. However, it is students in the real world that interact with the items in the virtual world. On the other hand, AR and VR can simulate students' physical presence in a virtual world by generating realistic images, sounds, and other sensations. AR and VR make students feel that they are interacting with other players and NPCs, which offer students a more relaxing, flexible, and authentic English setting than mobile devices. With the development of advanced technologies, the necessary equipment will be available and affordable for most students. Therefore, AR and VR will bring up the revolutionary reform of EVGs for acquiring English vocabulary.

DISCUSSION

Vocabulary is key to mastering any language. However, students only use English in English lessons where learning vocabulary takes up little time in the precious lesson time. Consequently, students always struggle with learning English vocabulary. On the other hand, students play DGs in their own volition and they can be utilized for educational purposes, such as learning English vocabulary. However, it is important to find the nexus between the EVGs and the student' motivation of learning English vocabulary by using EVGs.

According to the previous research, there is no doubt that students became motivated and were willing to spend more time using EVGs (Huang et al., 2017; Janebi Enayat & Haghighatpasand, 2019). After all, EVGs are more interesting and attractive than the traditional method. Additionally, it is also important to understand the efficacy of EVGs in terms of achieving learning outcomes. Again, it is found that EVGs improve students' vocabulary size after playing WoW (Ebrahimzadeh & Alavi, 2016) and SL (Milton et al., 2012). However, it takes much time to acquire English vocabulary by WoW and SL. Therefore, these conclusions raise the question that can EVGs be effective as the traditional method? To answer the question, researchers are supposed to design the experimental group where students learn English vocabulary in EVGs, and the control group where students learn English vocabulary in the traditional method. Therefore, it is necessary to keep the English proficiency and prior gaming experience of participants in each group at the same level (Yang & Quadir, 2018). The Chi-Square test can help researchers statistically examine the influence of prior gaming experience. In addition, choosing appropriate EVGs that match students' English proficiency facilitates fully maximizing the advantages of EVGs to get reliable data.

Next, to measure the improvement of participants in each group, researchers are supposed to score every participant in the pre-test and post-test by examining the prepared English vocabulary. After obtaining the scores for each group, researchers can evaluate the improvement of EVGs by comparing the average and variance of pre-test and post-test. However, average and variance are not reasonable enough to express reliable results because the improvement of participants in each group may not be statistically different. Therefore, the independent-sample T-test or between-group ANOVA can be used to complement the drawback of average and variance. Finally, researchers can draw reliable results, and facilitate exploring the maximum effectiveness of EVGs.

CONCLUSION

This chapter provides a comprehensive process of empirical research by explaining each step. Researchers initially should have an understanding of the participants' English competence and previous experience with EVGs, which helps researchers propose research objectives, appropriate target vocabulary, and choose appropriate EVGs. Moreover, different types of EVGs are also presented and critically analyses to discuss the advantages and disadvantages. It is found that MMOGs need a long time to achieve the desired outcome due to the presence of irrelevant information distracting students' attention from learning English vocabulary. Therefore, future research should focus on what specific features of EVGs (e.g., scores, feedback, reward, etc.) motivate students and facilitate learning outcomes. As a result, researchers should look beyond commercial-off-the-shelf EVGs and design simple, effective, and practical EVGs that can be used in educational settings.

To measure the effectiveness of participants, researchers usually are supposed to do the pre-test and the post-test. In quantitative research, the binary method is leveraged to score participants in the pre-test and the post-test. However, the binary method does not consider the length of English vocabulary, leading to the unfair points of each English vocabulary. Therefore, a fair score standard that considers the difficulty of each English vocabulary is pressing in EVGs field. To make sure the quality of the empirical research, it would be better to conduct a pilot experiment to discover any potential problems when conducting an experiment. When it comes to qualitative research, researchers usually do not need to do a pre-test because the main objective of qualitative research is to explore the perspective of participants after playing EVGs. Therefore, the questionnaire and interview that are frequently used in the current research were summarized in the post-test section. After getting the data from the pre-test and post-test, the application of ANOVA, T-test, and Chi-Square test is described to help researchers get reasonable conclusions by analyzing the collected data. However, researchers should notice that the size of the data sample is important to achieve appropriate results. The chapter finally helps other researchers have a basic understanding of the methodology of empirical research and make substantial contributions to EVGs in future research.

There are two limitations in this chapter. Firstly, this chapter only focuses on the research about EVGs on English vocabulary, and it can be more comprehensive if EVGs on other knowledge (e.g., math, history, energy, etc.) are included. Secondly, the authors simply concentrate on MMOGs, mobile applications, and web-based games, and it can rich the research results if considering console games and arcade games.

ACKNOWLEDGMENT

This research was supported by the China Scholarship Council with the Queen Mary University of London [grant number 202006930007].

REFERENCES

Anyaegbu, R., Ting, W., & Li, Y. (2012). Serious game motivation in an EFL classroom in Chinese primary school. *The Turkish Online Journal of Educational Technology*, *11*(1), 154–164.

Ariffin, M. M. (2012). Towards digital game-based learning (DGBL) in higher education (HE): The educators' perception. *Developing Country Studies*, *2*(11), 228–236.

Azman, H., & Farhana Dollsaid, N. (2018). Applying Massively Multiplayer Online Games (MMOGs) in EFL Teaching. *Arab World English Journal*, *9*(4), 3–18. doi:10.24093/awej/vol9no4.1

Camacho Vásquez, G., & Ovalle, J. C. (2019). The Influence of Video Games on Vocabulary Acquisition in a Group of Students from the BA in English Teaching. *GIST Education and Learning Research Journal*, *19*, 172–192. doi:10.26817/16925777.707

Chen, H. J. H., & Yang, T. Y. C. (2013). The impact of adventure video games on foreign language learning and the perceptions of learners. *Interactive Learning Environments*, *21*(2), 129–141. doi:10.1080/10494820.2012.705851

Chen, S. Y., & Chang, Y. M. (2020). The impacts of real competition and virtual competition in digital game-based learning. *Computers in Human Behavior*, *104*(2), 106171. doi:10.1016/j.chb.2019.106171

Cobb, T. (2007). Computing the vocabulary demands of L2 reading. *Language Learning & Technology*, *11*(3), 38–63.

Ebrahimzadeh, M., & Alavi, S. (2016). Motivating EFL students: E-learning enjoyment as a predictor of vocabulary learning through digital video games. *Cogent Education*, *3*(1), 1255400. doi:10.1080/2331186X.2016.1255400

Franciosi, S. J., Yagi, J., Tomoshige, Y., & Ye, S. (2016). The effect of a simple simulation game on long-term vocabulary retention. *CALICO Journal*, *33*(3), 355–379. doi:10.1558/cj.v33i2.26063

Hu, G. (2005). English language education in China: Policies, progress, and problems. *Language Policy*, *4*(1), 5–24. doi:10.100710993-004-6561-7

Huang, Y. L., Chang, D. F., & Wu, B. (2017). Mobile game-based learning with a mobile app: Motivational effects and learning performance. *Journal of Advanced Computational Intelligence and Intelligent Informatics*, *21*(6), 963–970. doi:10.20965/jaciii.2017.p0963

Hung, H. C., & Young, S. S. C. (2015). An Investigation of Game-Embedded Handheld Devices to Enhance English Learning. *Journal of Educational Computing Research*, *52*(4), 548–567. doi:10.1177/0735633115571922

Janebi Enayat, M., & Haghighatpasand, M. (2019). Exploiting adventure video games for second language vocabulary recall: A mixed-methods study. *Innovation in Language Learning and Teaching*, *13*(1), 61–75. doi:10.1080/17501229.2017.1359276

Mehrpour, S., & Ghayour, M. (2017). The effect of educational computerized games on learning English spelling among Iranian children. *The Reading Matrix: An International Online Journal*, *17*(2), 165–178.

Milton, J., Jonsen, S., Hirst, S., & Lindenburn, S. (2012). Foreign language vocabulary development through activities in an online 3D environment. *Language Learning Journal*, *40*(1), 99–112. doi:10.1080/09571736.2012.658229

Oberg, A. (2011). Comparison of the effectiveness of a call-based approach and a card-based approach to vocabulary acquisition and retention. *CALICO Journal*, *29*(1), 118–144. doi:10.11139/cj.29.1.118-144

Peterson, M. (2016). The use of massively multiplayer online role-playing games in CALL: An analysis of research. *Computer Assisted Language Learning*, *29*(7), 1181–1194. doi:10.1080/09588221.2016.1197949

Rama, P. S., Black, R. W., Van Es, E., & Warschauer, M. (2012). Affordances for second language learning in World of Warcraft. *ReCALL*, *24*(3), 322–338. doi:10.1017/S0958344012000171

Rankin, Y., Gold, R., & Gooch, B. (2006). 3D Role-Playing Games as Language Learning Tools. *Eurographics*, *25*(3), 33–38.

Sandberg, J., Maris, M., & Hoogendoorn, P. (2014). The added value of a gaming context and intelligent adaptation for a mobile learning application for vocabulary learning. *Computers & Education*, *76*, 119–130. doi:10.1016/j.compedu.2014.03.006

Subhash, S., & Cudney, E. A. (2018). Gamified learning in higher education: A systematic review of the literature. *Computers in Human Behavior*, *87*, 192–206. doi:10.1016/j.chb.2018.05.028

Thompson, C. G., & von Gillern, S. (2020). Video-game based instruction for vocabulary acquisition with English language learners: A Bayesian meta-analysis. *Educational Research Review*, *30*(2), 100332. doi:10.1016/j.edurev.2020.100332

Wei, C. W., Kao, H. Y., Lu, H. H., & Liu, Y. C. (2018). The effects of competitive gaming scenarios and personalized assistance strategies on English vocabulary learning. *Journal of Educational Technology & Society*, *21*(3), 146–158.

Yang, J. C., & Quadir, B. (2018). Effects of prior knowledge on learning performance and anxiety in an English learning online role-playing game. *Journal of Educational Technology & Society*, *21*(3), 174–185.

Yeşilbağ, S., Korkmaz, Ö., & Çakir, R. (2020). The effect of educational computer games on students' academic achievements and attitudes towards English lesson. *Education and Information Technologies*, *25*(2), 1–18. doi:10.100710639-020-10216-1 PMID:32837235

ADDITIONAL READING

Abt, C. C. (1987). *Serious games*. University Press of America.

AlNatour, A. S., & Hijazi, D. (2018). The impact of using electronic games on teaching English vocabulary for kindergarten students. *US-China Foreign Language*, *16*(4), 193–205. doi:10.17265/1539-8080/2018.04.001

Furtado, P. G. F., Hirashima, T., & Yusuke, H. (2018). A serious game for improving inferencing in the presence of foreign language unknown words. *International Journal of Advanced Computer Science and Applications*, *9*(2), 7–14. doi:10.14569/IJACSA.2018.090202

Gee, J. P. (2014). *What Video Games Have to Teach Us About Learning and Literacy*. Macmillan.

Jassim, L. L., & Dzakiria, H. (2019). A Literature Review on the Impact of Games on Learning English Vocabulary to Children. *International Journal of Language and Literary Studies*, *1*(1), 47–53. Advance online publication. doi:10.36892/ijlls.v1i1.22

Klimesch, W. (2013). *The structure of long-term memory: A connectivity model of semantic processing*. Psychology Press. doi:10.4324/9780203773239

Nation, I. S. P. (2001). *Learning Vocabulary in Another Language*. Cambridge University Press. doi:10.1017/CBO9781139524759

Tang, J. T. (2020). Comparative study of game-based learning on preschoolers' English vocabulary acquisition in Taiwan. *Interactive Learning Environments*, 1–16. doi:10.1080/10494820.2020.1865406

Tsai, Y. L., & Tsai, C. C. (2018). Digital game-based second-language vocabulary learning and conditions of research designs: A meta-analysis study. *Computers & Education*, *125*, 345–357. doi:10.1016/j.compedu.2018.06.020

Zohud, N. W. (2019). Exploring palestinian and Spanish teachers' perspectives on using online computer games in learning english vocabulary. *Publicaciones de La Facultad de Educacion y Humanidades Del Campus de Melilla, 49*(2), 93–115. doi:10.30827/publicaciones.v49i2.11346

KEY TERMS AND DEFINITIONS

Binary Method: Researchers define the score of every prepared English vocabulary. If participants correctly spell a word, they obtain scores, otherwise, they obtain zero.

Educational Video Games: EVGs mean the games mainly for educational purposes when having fun. There are lots of interchangeable terms such as game-based learning and serious games.

Foreign Language Learners: Students do not use English in their daily life. English language exposure is limited to the English classroom.

Native Language Learners: Students who are born in English-speaking countries learn English knowledge from their environment. Namely, English is their mother tongue.

Non-Playing Characters: Non-playing characters are controlled by the computer programmer that has predetermined behaviors to respond to players' actions.

Second Language Learners: Students have a chance to learn and speak English in some specific situations, while they use their mother tongue in most cases.

Traditional Method: Students learn and reinforce English vocabulary according to vocabulary lists in English textbooks. Students remember and reinforce English vocabulary with pencil and paper in a rote memory fashion.

ENDNOTES

[1] Students: Students present primary students, middle students, and university students in non-speaking English countries in this chapter.

[2] Participants: The subjects are recruited by researchers in empirical research.

Compilation of References

Aarsand, P. (2010). Young boys playing digital games. *Nordic Journal of Digital Literacy*, *5*(1), 38–55. doi:10.18261/ISSN1891-943X-2010-01-04

Aarseth, E. (2001). Computer Game Studies, Year One. *Game Studies Journal*, *1*(1). Retrieved from http://www.gamestudies.org/0101/editorial.html

Aarseth, E. (2002). The Dungeon and the Ivory Tower: Vive La Difference ou Liaison Dangereuse? *Game Studies Journal*, *2*(1). Retrieved from http://www.gamestudies.org/0102/editorial.html

Aarseth, E. (2015). Meta-Game Studies. *Game Studies Journal*, *15*(1). Retrieved from http://gamestudies.org/1501/articles/editorial

Abadia Correa, J., Ortiz Paez, L., & Peña Castiblicanco, N. (2021). *Development of a Training Game to Provide Awareness in Cybersecurity to the Staff of the Aviation Military School "Marco Fidel Suárez" of the Colombian Air Force in the city of Cali*. Academic Press.

Abbitt, J. T. (2011). An Investigation of the Relationship between Self-Efficacy Beliefs about Technology Integration and Technological Pedagogical Content Knowledge (TPACK) among Preservice Teachers. *Journal of Digital Learning in Teacher Education*, *27*(4), 134–143. doi:10.1080/21532974.2011.10784670

Abbott, D. (2019). Game-based learning for postgraduates: An empirical study of an educational game to teach research skills. *Higher Education Pedagogies*, *4*(1), 80–104. doi:10.1080/23752696.2019.1629825

Abrams, S. S. (2009). A gaming frame of mind: Digital contexts and academic implications. *Educational Media International*, *46*(4), 335–347. doi:10.1080/09523980903387480

Abrams, S. S. (2016). Emotionally crafted experiences: Layering literacies in Minecraft. *The Reading Teacher*, *70*(4), 501–506. doi:10.1002/trtr.1515

Abt, C. (1970). *Serious Games*. The Viking Press.

Acker, A., & Pecker, J. C. (1990). Public misconceptions about astronomy. In *International Astronomical Union Colloquium* (Vol. 105, pp. 229-238). Cambridge University Press. 10.1017/S025292110008684X

Acks, A. (2017, August 1). *Tolkien's Map and The Messed Up Mountains of Middle-earth*. https://www.tor.com/2017/08/01/tolkiens-map-and-the-messed-up-mountains-of-middle-earth/

Adachi, P. J. C., & Willoughby, T. (2011). The effect of violent video games on aggression: Is it more than just the violence? *Aggression and Violent Behavior*, *16*(1), 55–62. doi:10.1016/j.avb.2010.12.002

Adams, C. (2017). *The Disadvantages of using games as a Learning tool*. Academic Press.

Adams, E. (2010). *Fundamentals of game design*. New Riders.

Compilation of References

Adjibolosoo, S. (2000). *Pillars of economic growth and sustained human-centred development*. Paper presented at the International Institute for Human Factor Development Conference, Harare, Zimbabwe.

Adjibolosoo, S. (1993). The human factor in development. *Scandinavian Journal of Development Alternatives*, *12*(4), 139–149.

Adjibolosoo, S. (1994). The human factor and the failure of economic development and policies in Africa. In F. Ezeala-Harrison & S. Adjibolosoo (Eds.), *Perspectives on Economic Development in Africa*. Praeger Publishers.

Adjibolosoo, S. (1995). *The significance of the human factor in African economic development*. Praeger.

Adjibolosoo, S. (1998). *Global development the human factor way*. Praeger.

Adjibolosoo, S. (1999). *Rethinking development theory and policy. A human factor critiques*. Praeger.

Adom, D., Hussain, E. K., & Joe, A. A. (2018). Theoretical and Conceptual Framework: Mandatory Ingredients. *International Journal of Scientific Research*, *7*(1), 93–98.

Adorno, T., & Horkheimer, M. (1972). *The dialectic of the enlightenment*. Herder and Herder.

Aggarwal, C. C. (2018). Neural networks and deep learning. Springer, 10, 978-973.

Aghlara, L., & Tamjid, N. H. (2011). The effect of digital games on Iranian children's vocabulary retention in foreign language acquisition. *Procedia: Social and Behavioral Sciences*, *29*, 552–560. doi:10.1016/j.sbspro.2011.11.275

Aguiar, A. L., & Aguiar, C. (2020). Classroom composition and quality in early childhood education: A systematic review. *Children and Youth Services Review*, *115*(May), 105086. doi:10.1016/j.childyouth.2020.105086

Aguilera & Martínez. (2017). Gamification, a didactic strategy in higher education. *Edulearn17 Proceedings*, 6761-6771.

Agustin-Llach, M. P., & Canga Alonso, A. (2016). Vocabulary growth in young CLIL and traditional EFL learners: Evidence from research and implications for education. *International Journal of Applied Linguistics*, *26*(2), 211–217. doi:10.1111/ijal.12090

Ahissar, M., Nahum, M., Nelken, I., & Hochstein, S. (2009). Reverse hierarchies and sensory learning. *Philosophical Transactions of the Royal Society of London. Series B, Biological Sciences*, *364*(1515), 285–299. doi:10.1098/rstb.2008.0253 PMID:18986968

Ahmad, F., Ahmed, Z., & Muneeb, S. (2021). Effect of gaming mode upon the players' cognitive performance during brain games play: An exploratory research. *International Journal of Game-Based Learning*, *11*(1), 67–76. Advance online publication. doi:10.4018/IJGBL.2021010105

Ahmad, M. I., Mubin, O., Shahid, S., & Orlando, J. (2019). Robot's adaptive emotional feedback sustains children's social engagement and promotes their vocabulary learning: A long-term child–robot interaction study. *Adaptive Behavior*, *27*(4), 243–266. doi:10.1177/1059712319844182

Ahmad, M., Mubin, O., & Escudero, P. (2015, October). Using adaptive mobile agents in games-based scenarios to facilitate foreign language word learning. In *Proceedings of the 3rd International Conference on Human-Agent Interaction* (pp. 255-257). 10.1145/2814940.2814990

Ahsan, M. T., Sharma, U., & Deppeler, J. M. (2012). Challenges to prepare pre-service teachers for inclusive education in Bangladesh: Beliefs of higher educational institutional heads. *Asia Pacific Journal of Education*, *32*(2), 241–257. doi:10.1080/02188791.2012.655372

Airaksinen, T., Halinen, I., & Linturi, H. (2016). Futuribles of learning 2030 - Delphi supports the reform of the core curricula in Finland. *European Journal of Futures Research*, *5*(1), 2. doi:10.1007/s40309-016-0096-y

Aires, L. (2015). *Paradigma Qualitativo e Práticas de Investigação Educacional*. Universidade Aberta.

Akçayır, M., Dündar, H., & Akçayır, G. (2016). What makes you a digital native? Is it enough to be born after 1980? *Computers in Human Behavior, 60*, 435–440. doi:10.1016/j.chb.2016.02.089

Aktinson, P., & Hammersley, M. (1998). Ethnography and participant observation. In *Strategies of Qualitative Inquiry* (pp. 248–261). Sage.

Al Bailey Apps. (2021). *Phonics town* (Version1.01) [Mobile app]. http://itunes.apple.com

Al Fatta, H., Maksom, Z., & Zakaria, M. H. (2019). Game-based learning and gamification: Searching for definitions. *International Journal of Simulation: Systems, Science & Technology, 19*, 10–5013.

Alabdulakareem, E., & Jamjoom, M. (2020). Computer-assisted learning for improving ADHD individuals' executive functions through gamified interventions: A review. Entertainment Computing. doi:10.1016/j.entcom.2020.100341

Al-Alwani, A. E. (2010, August). Barriers to effective use of information technology in science education. *International Conference on Enterprise Information Systems and Web Technologies (EISWT)*, 42–49.

Alam, M. J. (2019). Dilemma of Parental Aspiration for Children with Special Needs in Early Childhood Education (ECE) Settings: The Case of Bangladesh. *Asia-Pacific Journal of Research in Early Childhood Education, 13*(3), 25–43. doi:10.17206/apjrece.2019.13.3.25

Alam, M. J. (2020). Who Chooses School? Understanding Parental Aspirations for Child Transition from Home to Early Childhood Education (ECE) Institutions in Bangladesh. In S. Tatalović Vorkapić & J. LoCasale-Crouch (Eds.), *Supporting Children's Well-Being During Early Childhood Transition to School* (pp. 85–107). IGI Global. doi:10.4018/978-1-7998-4435-8

Alaswad, Z., & Nadolny, L. (2015). Designing for game-based learning: The effective integration of technology to support learning. *Journal of Educational Technology Systems, 43*(4), 389–402. doi:10.1177/0047239515588164

Alberti, J. (2008). The game of reading and writing: How video games reframe our understanding of literacy. *Computers and Composition, 25*(3), 258–269. doi:10.1016/j.compcom.2008.04.004

Albirini, A. (2006). Teachers' attitudes toward information and communication technologies: The case of Syrian EFL teachers. *Computers & Education, 47*(4), 373–398. doi:10.1016/j.compedu.2004.10.013

Aldabbus, S. (2018). Project-based learning: Implementation & challenges. *International Journal of Education, Learning and Development, 6*(3), 71–79.

Aldemir, T., Celik, B., & Kaplan, G. (2018). A qualitative investigation of student perceptions of game elements in a gamified course. *Computers in Human Behavior, 78*, 235–254. doi:10.1016/j.chb.2017.10.001

Aldosemani, T. (2019). Inservice Teachers' Perceptions of a Professional Development Plan Based on SAMR Model: A Case Study. *The Turkish Online Journal of Educational Technology, 18*(3), 46–53.

Aldrich, C. (2003). *Simulations and the future of learning*. Pfeiffer.

Alemi, M., & Haeri, N. S. (2017, October). How to Develop Learners' Politeness: A Study of RALL's Impact on Learning Greeting by Young Iranian EFL Learners. In *2017 5th RSI International Conference on Robotics and Mechatronics (ICRoM)* (pp. 88-94). IEEE. 10.1109/ICRoM.2017.8466206

Alemi, M., Meghdari, A., Basiri, N., & Taheri, A. (2015). The Effect of Applying Humanoid Robots as Teacher Assistants to Help Iranian Autistic Pupils Learn English as a Foreign Language. In *Social Robotics* (pp. 1–10). Lecture Notes in Computer Science. Springer International Publishing.

Compilation of References

Alemi, M., Meghdari, A., & Ghazisaedy, M. (2014). Employing humanoid robots for teaching English language in Iranian junior high-schools. *International Journal of HR; Humanoid Robotics, 11*(03), 1450022. doi:10.1142/S0219843614500224

Alessi, S. M., & Trollip, S. R. (1984). *Computer-based instruction: Methods and development.* Prentice-Hall.

Alessi, S. M., & Trollip, S. R. (2001). *Multimedia for learning: Methods and development.* Allyn & Bacon.

Alexander, A., & Ho, T. (2015). Gaming worlds: Secondary students creating an interactive Video game. *Art Education, 68*(1), 28–36. doi:10.1080/00043125.2015.11519303

Alexander, B. (2008). *The globalization of addiction: A study in poverty of the spirit.* Oxford University Press.

Alexander, J. (2009). Gaming, student literacies, and the composition classroom: Some possibilities for transformation. *College Composition and Communication, 61*(1), 35–63.

Alexander, S. (2010). *Flexible Learning in Higher Education.* International Encyclopedia of Education., doi:10.1016/B978-0-08-044894-7.00868-X

Alhashmi, M., Mubin, O., & Baroud, R. (2021). Examining the use of robots as teacher assistants in UAE classrooms: Teacher and student perspectives. *Journal of Information Technology Education*, 245–261. https://doi-org.ezproxy.uws.edu.au/10.28945/4749

Alhassan, R. (2017). Exploring the relationship between Web 2.0 tools self-efficacy and teachers' use of these tools in their teaching. *Journal of Education and Learning, 6*(4), 217–228. doi:10.5539/jel.v6n4p217

Alismail, H. A., & McGuire, P. (2015). 21st century standards and curriculum: Current research and practice. *Journal of Education and Practice, 6*(6), 150–154.

Al-Khatib, K., Wachsmuth, H., Lang, K., Herpel, J., Hagen, M., & Stein, B. (2018). *Modeling Deliberative Argumentation Strategies on Wikipedia.* https://scholar.googleusercontent.com/scholar?q=cache:sOSvXuDA-IAJ:scholar.google.com/&hl=en&as_sdt=2005&sciodt=0,5

Alkind Taylor, A. S., & Backlund, P. (2012). Making the Implicit Explicit: Game-based Training Practices from an Instructor Perspective. In *6th European Conference on Games Based Learning (ECGBL'12)* (pp. 1-10). Cork, Ireland: European Conference on Games Based Learning.

All, A., Nunez Castellar, E. P., & Van Looy, J. (2014). Measuring effectiveness in digital game-based learning: A methodological review. *International Journal of Serious Games, 1*(2), 3–20. doi:10.17083/ijsg.v1i2.18

All, A., Nuñez Castellar, E. P., & Van Looy, J. (2015). Assessing the effectiveness of digital game-based learning: Best practices. *Computers & Education, 92-93*, 90–103. doi:10.1016/j.compedu.2015.10.007

Allal-Chérif, O., & Makhlouf, M. (2016). Using serious games to manage knowledge: The SECI model perspective. *Journal of Business Research, 69*(5), 1539–1543. doi:10.1016/j.jbusres.2015.10.013

Allery, L. (2014). Make use of educational games. *Education for Primary Care, 25*(1), 65–66. doi:10.1080/14739879.2014.11494245 PMID:24423808

Alligator Apps. (2014). *Preschool matching game: Rhyming Words* [Mobile app]. http://itunes.apple.com

Alloway, N., Freebody, P., Gilbert, P., & Muspratt, S. (2002). *Boys, literacy and schooling: Expanding the repertoires of practice.* Commonwealth of Australia, Department of Education, Science and Training.

Allsop, Y., & Jesse, J. (2015). Teachers' Experience and Reflections on Game-Based Learning in the Primary Classroom: Views from England and Italy. *International Journal of Game-Based Learning, 5*(1), 1–17. doi:10.4018/ijgbl.2015010101

Almeida, F. (2020). Adoption of a Serious Game in the Developing of Emotional Intelligence Skills. *European Journal of Investigation in Health, Psychology and Education*, *10*(1), 30–43. doi:10.3390/ejihpe10010004 PMID:34542467

Almeida, F., & Simoes, J. (2019). The role of serious games, gamification and Industry 4.0 tools in the Education 4.0 paradigm. *Contemporary Educational Technology*, *10*(2), 120–136. doi:10.30935/cet.554469

Al-Qallaf, C. L., & Al-Mutairi, A. S. (2016). Digital literacy and digital content supports learning: The impact of blogs on teaching English as a foreign language. *The Electronic Library*.

Alqithami, S. (2021). A serious-gamification blueprint towards a normalized attention. *Brain Informatics*, *8*(1), 6. Advance online publication. doi:10.118640708-021-00127-3 PMID:33856585

Al-Samarraie, H., Teo, T., & Abbas, M. (2013). Can structured representation enhance students' thinking skills for better understanding of E-learning content? *Computers & Education*, *69*, 463–473. doi:10.1016/j.compedu.2013.07.038

Alsawaier, R. S. (2018). The effect of gamification on motivation and engagement. *International Journal of Information and Learning Technology*, *35*(1), 56–79. doi:10.1108/IJILT-02-2017-0009

Al-Senaidi, S., Lin, L., & Poirot, J. (2009). Barriers to adopting technology for teaching and learning in Oman. *Computers & Education*, *53*(3), 575–590. doi:10.1016/j.compedu.2009.03.015

AlShaiji, O. A. (2015). Video games promote Saudi children's English vocabulary retention. *Education*, *136*(2), 123–132.

Alt, D., & Raichel, N. (2020). Enhancing perceived digital literacy skills and creative self-concept through gamified learning environments: Insights from a longitudinal study. *International Journal of Educational Research*, *101*, 101561.

Alvermann, D. E. (Ed.). (2005). *Adolescents and literacies in a digital world* (3rd ed.). Peter Lang.

Alvermann, D., & Xu, S. (2003). Children's everyday literacies: Intersections of popular culture and language arts instruction. *Language Arts*, *81*(2), 145–154.

Alves, F. (2014). *Gamification - Como criar experiências de aprendizagem engajadoras. Um guia completo*. DVS Editora.

Alyaz, Y., & Genc, Z. S. (2016). Digital game-based language learning in foreign language teacher education. *Turkish Online Journal of Distance Education*, *17*(4), 130–146. doi:10.17718/tojde.44375

Alzubi, T., Fernández, R., Flores, J., Duran, M., & Cotos, J. M. (2018). Improving the Working Memory During Early Childhood Education Through the Use of an Interactive Gesture Game-Based Learning Approach. *IEEE Access: Practical Innovations, Open Solutions*, *6*, 53998–54009. doi:10.1109/ACCESS.2018.2870575

American Educational Research Association, American Psychological Association, & National Council on Measurement in Education. (2014). *Standards for educational and psychological testing*. American Educational Research Association.

American Library Association. (2000). *Information literacy competency standards for higher education*. https://repository.arizona.edu/handle/10150/105645

American Library Association. (n.d.). *Games and literacy: the connection between literacy and gaming*. Games & Gaming Round Table: A Round Table of the American Library Association. Retrieved from https://www.ala.org/gamert/games-

Amirnuddin, P. S., Mohamed, A. A. A., & Ahmad, M. H. (2020). Transforming Legal Education In The Era Of Fourth Industrial Revolution. *Current Law Journal*, *2*, ix–xxiv.

Amirnuddin, P. S., & Turner, J. T. (2020). Learning Law using Augmented Reality and Neuro-Linguistic Programming. In P. Kumar, M. J. Keppell, & C. L. Lim (Eds.), *Preparing 21st Century Teachers for Teach Less, Learn More (TLLM) Pedagogies* (pp. 259–278). IGI Global. doi:10.4018/978-1-7998-1435-1.ch015

Compilation of References

An Educator's Guide to Cyberbullying. (2011, Apr. 10). Senate.gov

Ananiadou, K., & Claro, M. (2009). 21st century skills and competences for new millennium learners in OECD countries. *OECD Education Working Papers, 4.*

Ananiadou, K., & Claro, M. (2009). *21st Century Skills and Competences for New Millennium Learners in OECD Countries.* OECD Education Working Papers, 41. OECD Publishing. doi:10.1787/19939019

Anastasiadis, T., Lampropoulos, G., & Siakas, K. (2018). Digital game-based learning and serious games in education. *International Journal of Advances in Scientific Research and Engineering, 4*(12), 139–144. doi:10.31695/IJASRE.2018.33016

Anazifa, R. D., & Djukri, S. (2017). Project-based learning and problem-based learning: Are they effective to improve student's thinking skills? *Journal Pendidikan IPA Indonesia, 6*(2), 346–355. doi:10.15294/jpii.v6i2.11100

Anderson, A., Barham, N., & Northcote, M. (2013). Using the TPACK framework to unite disciplines in online learning. *Australasian Journal of Educational Technology, 29*(4), 549–565. doi:10.14742/ajet.24

Anderson, J. L., & Barnett, M. (2013). Learning physics with digital game simulations in middle school science. *Journal of Science Education and Technology, 22*(6), 914–926. doi:10.100710956-013-9438-8

And-literacy. (n.d.). https://www.ala.org/gamert/games-and-literacy

Andone, D., Dron, J., Boyne, C., & Pemberton, L. (2005). Digital Students and Their Use Of Elearning Enviroments. *IADIS International Conference on WWW/Internet.*

Angeli, C., & Valanides, N. (2009). Epistemological and methodological issues for the conceptualization, development, and assessment of ICT-TPCK: Advances in technological pedagogical content knowledge (TPCK). *Computers & Education, 52*(1), 154–168. doi:10.1016/j.compedu.2008.07.006

Angell, C., Guttersrud, Ø., Henriksen, E. K., & Isnes, A. (2004). Physics: Frightful, but fun. Pupils' and teachers' views of physics and physics teaching. *Science Education, 88*(5), 683-706.

Anniroot, J., & De Villiers, M. R. (2012). *Study of Alice: A visual environment for teaching object-oriented programming.* Academic Press.

Antonaci, A., Klemke, R., & Specht, M. (2019). The Effects of Gamification in Online Learning Environments: A Systematic Literature Review. *Informatics (MDPI), 6*(3), 32. doi:10.3390/informatics6030032

Anwar, Z., Kahar, M. S., Rawi, R. D. P., Nurjannah, N., Suaib, H., & Rosalina, F. (2020). Development of interactive video based powerpoint media In mathematics learning. *Journal of Educational Science and Technology, 6*(2), 167–177. doi:10.26858/est.v6i2.13179

Anyaegbu, R., Ting, W., & Li, Y. (2012). Serious game motivation in an EFL classroom in Chinese primary school. *The Turkish Online Journal of Educational Technology, 11*(1), 154–164.

Araiza, P., Keane, T. L., Beaudry, J., & Kaufman, J. (2020). Immersive Virtual Reality Implementations in Developmental Psychology. *The International Journal of Virtual Reality: a Multimedia Publication for Professionals.* Advance online publication. doi:10.20870/IJVR.2020.20.2.3094

Arango-Lopez, J., Collazos, C. A., Velas, F. L. G., & Moreira, F. (2018). Using pervasive games as learning tools in educational contexts: A systematic review. *International Journal of Learning Technology, 13*(2), 93–114. doi:10.1504/IJLT.2018.092094

Arbitration/Requests/Case/German war effort. (2019a). In *Wikipedia.* https://en.wikipedia.org/w/index.php?title=Wikipedia:Arbitration/Requests/Case/German_war_effort&oldid=886462669

Archambault, L. M., & Barnett, J. H. (2010). Revisiting technological pedagogical content knowledge: Exploring the TPACK framework. *Computers & Education*, *55*(4), 1656–1662. doi:10.1016/j.compedu.2010.07.009

Ariffin, M. M. (2012). Towards digital game-based learning (DGBL) in higher education (HE): The educators' perception. *Developing Country Studies*, *2*(11), 228–236.

Armstrong, S. J. (2011). From the editors: Continuing our quest for meaningful impact on management practice. Academy of Management Learning & Education, 10(2), 181-7.

Arnab, S., Clarke, S., & Morini, L. (2019). Co-creativity through play and game design thinking. *Electronic Journal of E-Learning*, *17*(3), 184–198. doi:10.34190/JEL.17.3.002

Arnett, J. (2002). The psychology of globalization. *The American Psychologist*, *57*(10), 774–783. doi:10.1037/0003-066X.57.10.774 PMID:12369500

Artigue, M. (2002). Learning mathematics in a CAS environment: The genesis of a reflection about instrumentation and the dialectics between technical and conceptual work. *International Journal of Computers for Mathematical Learning*, *7*(3), 245–274. doi:10.1023/A:1022103903080

Asadullah, M., & Chaudhury, N. (2015). The Dissonance between schooling and learning: Evidence from rural Bangladesh. *Comparative Education Review*, *59*(3), 447–472. doi:10.1086/681929

Asai, K., Sugimoto, Y., & Billinghurst, M. (2010). Exhibition of lunar surface navigation system facilitating collaboration between children and parents in science museum. In *Proceedings of the 9th ACM SIGGRAPH Conference on Virtual-Reality Continuum and its Applications in Industry* (pp. 119-124). 10.1145/1900179.1900203

Asal, V., & Blake, E. (2006). Creating simulations for political science education. *Journal of Political Science Education*, *2*(1), 1–18. doi:10.1080/15512160500484119

Asay, M. (2009, 14 January). *Shirky: Problem is filter failure, not info overload*. c|net. Accessed from https://www.cnet.com/news/shirky-problem-is-filter-failure-not-info-overload/

Asch, F. (2015). *Popcorn*. Aladdin.

Ashkanasy, N. M. (2006). Introduction: Arguments for a more grounded approach in management education. *Academy of Management Learning & Education*, *5*(2), 207–208. doi:10.5465/amle.2006.21253785

Ashrafuzzaman, M. (2021). *Impact of Facebook Usage on University Students' Academic Performance*. Unpublished Research Report, Bangabandhu Sheikh Mujibur Rahman Digital University, Bangladesh (BDU).

Aslan, S., & Reigeluth, C. M. (2013). Educational technologists: Leading change for a new paradigm of education. *TechTrends*, *57*(5), 18–24. doi:10.100711528-013-0687-4

AssistiveWare. (2020). *Pictello* (Version 3.7.2) [Mobile app]. http://itunes.apple.com

Association of College and Research Libraries (ACRL). (2015, February 9). *Framework for Information Literacy for Higher Education*. Association of College & Research Libraries (ACRL). https://www.ala.org/acrl/standards/ilframework

Ataíde, A., Souto, I., & Pereira, A. (2019). School Problems and Teachers' Collaboration: Before a Collaborative Problem Solving Program. *Education and New Developments*, *1*(July), 222–226. doi:10.36315/2019v1end047

Atashrouz, B., Pakdaman, S. H., & Asgari, A. (2008). Prediction of academic achievement from attachment rate. *ZtF. Zeitschrift für Familienforschung*, *4*(2), 193–203.

Compilation of References

Attard, A., Di Iorio, E., Geven, K., & Santa, R. (2010). Time for a new paradigm in education: student-centred learning. In A. Attard (Ed.), *Student-centred Learning Toolkit* (pp. 1-4). European Students Union. https://www.esu-online.org/wp-content/uploads/2016/07/100814-SCL.pdf

Aufderheide, P. (1993). *Media literacy: A report of the national leadership conference on media literacy*. Aspen Institute.

Avizov, S. R., Atamuratova, T. I., Holova, S. A., Kamalova, F. R., Akobirova, L. H., & Oltiev, A. T. (2020). Traditional requirements and innovative learning models in the higher education context. *European Journal of Molecular & Clinical Medicine*, *7*(2), 872–885.

Axelrod, L., & Hone, K. (2006). Affectemes and allaffects: A novel approach to coding user emotional expression during interactive experiences. *Behaviour & Information Technology*, *25*(2), 159–173. doi:10.1080/01449290500331164

Ayastuy, M. D., Torres, D., & Fernández, A. (2021). Adaptive Gamification in Collaborative systems, a systematic mapping study. *Computer Science Review*, *39*, 100333.

Ayres, L., & Narum, L. (2019). The promise of brain plasticity – overcoming language, learning and reading problems. *The Promise of Brain Plasticity-Overcoming Language*. Retrieved from: https://www.tarnowcenter.com/tarnow-articles/28-tarnow-articles/article-desc/584-the-promise-of-brain-plasticity-overcoming-language,-learning,-and-reading-problems.html

Azam, A., Qiang, F., Abbas, S. A., & Abdullah, M. I. (2013). Structural equation modeling (SEM) based trust analysis of Muslim consumers in the collective religion affiliation model in e-commerce. *Journal of Islamic Marketing*, *4*(2), 134–149. doi:10.1108/17590831311329278

Azevedo, J., Padrão, P., Gregório, M. J., Almeida, C., Moutinho, N., Lien, N., & Barros, R. (2019). A web-based gamification program to improve nutrition literacy in families of 3-to 5-year-old children: The Nutriscience Project. *Journal of Nutrition Education and Behavior*, *51*(3), 326–334. doi:10.1016/j.jneb.2018.10.008 PMID:30579894

Azim, F., & Ahmed, S. S. (2010). Exploring mathematics teachers' beliefs in secondary schools of Bangladesh. *Teacher's World*, *35-36*, 41–53.

Azim, F., & Rahman, M. M. S. (2015). Mobile embedded self-study materials for CPD: The use of English language for teachers (EL4T) in Bangladesh. In G. Pickering & P. Gunashekar (Eds.), *Innovation in English Language Teacher Education*. British Council.

Azman, H., & Farhana Dollsaid, N. (2018). Applying Massively Multiplayer Online Games (MMOGs) in EFL Teaching. *Arab World English Journal*, *9*(4), 3–18. doi:10.24093/awej/vol9no4.1

Azuma, R. T. (1997). A survey of augmented reality. *Presence (Cambridge, Mass.)*, *6*(4), 355–385. doi:10.1162/pres.1997.6.4.355

Baboo, S & Raja, V. (2017). Impact of playing and watching videogames on classroom attention, problem-solving and prosocial behavior of school children, *IDC International Journal*, *4*(3).

Bachmair, B., & Bazalgette, C. (2007). The European Charter for media literacy: Meaning and potential. *Research in Comparative and International Education*, *2*(1), 80-87.

Backhouse, J. (2013). What makes lecturers in higher education use emerging technologies in their teaching? *Knowledge Management & E-Learning*, *5*(3), 345–358. http://www.kmel-journal.org/ojs/index.php/online-publication/article/view/216/218

Baden, D., & Higgs, M. (2015). Challenging the perceived wisdom of management theories and practice. *Academy of Management Learning & Education*, *14*(4), 539–555. doi:10.5465/amle.2014.0170

Bado, N. (2019). Game-based learning pedagogy: A review of the literature. *Interactive Learning Environments*, 1–13. doi:10.1080/10494820.2019.1683587

Bado, N., & Franklin, T. (2014). Cooperative Game-based Learning in the English as a Foreign Language Classroom. *Issues and Trends in Educational Technology*, 2(2). Advance online publication. doi:10.2458/azu_itet_v2i2_bado

Baek, Y., & Touati, A. (2017). Exploring how individual traits influence enjoyment in a mobile learning game. *Computers in Human Behavior*, 69, 347–357. doi:10.1016/j.chb.2016.12.053

Baek, Y., & Whitton, N. (2013). *Digital Game Based Learning: Methods, Models and Strategies*. IGI Global. doi:10.4018/978-1-4666-2848-9

Baer, A. (2014, April 15). *Keeping Up With... Digital Writing in the College Classroom*. Association of College & Research Libraries (ACRL). https://www.ala.org/acrl/publications/keeping_up_with/digital_writing

Baharom, S. N., Tan, W. H., & Idris, M. Z. (2014). Emotional design for games: The roles of emotion and perception in game design process. *1st International Symposium on Simulation & Serious Games*, 978-981. 10.3850/978-981-09-0463-0_015

Baid, H., & Lambert, N. (2010). Enjoyable learning: The role of humour, games, and fun activities in nursing and midwifery education. *Nurse Education Today*, 30(6), 548–552. doi:10.1016/j.nedt.2009.11.007 PMID:20044181

Bainbridge, W. S. (2018). Computer Simulation for Space-Oriented Strategic Thinking. In *Computer Simulations of Space Societies* (pp. 113–139). Springer. doi:10.1007/978-3-319-90560-0_5

Baker, F. (2010). Media literacy: 21 st century literacy skills. In H. H. Jacobs (Ed.), Curriculum 21 essential education for a changing world (pp. 133–152). Academic Press.

Baldy, E. (2007). A new educational perspective for teaching gravity. *International Journal of Science Education*, 29(14), 1767–1788. doi:10.1080/09500690601083367

Balkibekov, K., Meiirbekov, S., Tazhigaliyeva, N., & Sandygulova, A. (2016, August). Should robots win or lose? Robot's losing playing strategy positively affects child learning. In *2016 25th IEEE International Symposium on Robot and Human Interactive Communication (RO-MAN)* (pp. 706-711). IEEE. 10.1109/ROMAN.2016.7745196

Ballard, J., & Butler, P. (2011). Personalised Learning: Developing a Vygotskian Framework for E-learning. *International Journal of Technology, Knowledge and Society*, 7(2), 21–36. doi:10.18848/1832-3669/CGP/v07i02/56198

Bal, S. (2018). Using Quizziz.com to enhance pre intermediate students' vocabulary knowledge. *International Journal of Language Academy*, 6(3), 295–303. doi:10.18033/ijla.3953

Bampasidis, G. (2019). Ψηφιακά παιχνίδια σε συσκευές κινητής τεχνολογίας και κίνδυνοι δημιουργίας επιστημονικών παρανοήσεων: Παραδείγματα από την Αεροδιαστημική Επιστήμη και την Τεχνολογία [Digital games in portable devices and the dangers of creating misconceptions: Examples from Aerospace science and Technology]. *Astrolavos*, 32.

Banfield, J., & Wilkerson, B. (2014). Increasing student intrinsic motivation and self-efficacy through gamification pedagogy. *Contemporary Issues in Education Research (Online)*, 7(4), 291–298. doi:10.19030/cier.v7i4.8843

Baptista, G., & Oliveira, T. (2019). Gamification and serious games: A literature meta-analysis and integrative model. Computers in Human Behavior. doi:10.1016/j.chb.2018.11.030

Barab, S. A., Warren, S. J., Zuiker, S., Hickey, D., Ingram-Goble, A., & Dodge, T. (2006). *Transfer of Learning in Complex Learning Environments*. Paper presented at the American Educational Research Association Annual Meeting, San Francisco, CA.

Compilation of References

Barab, S. A., Scott, B., Siyahhan, S., Goldstone, R., Ingram-Goble, A., Zuiker, S. J., & Warren, S. (2009). Transformational play as a curricular scaffold: Using videogames to support science education. *Journal of Science Education and Technology*, *18*(4), 305–320. doi:10.100710956-009-9171-5

Barab, S., Ingram-Goble, A., & Warren, S. (2009). Conceptual play spaces. In R. E. Ferdig (Ed.), *Hand-book of Research on Effective Electronic Gaming in Education* (pp. 989–1009). IGI Global. doi:10.4018/978-1-59904-808-6.ch057

Barack, L. (2013). A Minecraft library scores big. *School Library Journal*, *59*(9), 14.

Barba, M. C., Covino, A., de Luca, V., De Paolis, L. T., D'Errico, G., Di Bitonto, P., Di Gestore, S., Magliaro, S., Nunnari, F., Paladini, G. I., Potenza, A., & Schena, A. (2019). *BRAVO: A gaming environment for the treatment of ADHD*. Lecture Notes in Computer Science. doi:10.1007/978-3-030-25965-5_30

Barbas, H. (2000). Connections underlying the synthesis of cognition, memory, and emotion in primate prefrontal cortices. *Brain Research Bulletin*, *52*(5), 319–330. doi:10.1016/S0361-9230(99)00245-2 PMID:10922509

Bardin, L. (2011). *Análise de conteúdo*. Coimbra: Edições 70.

Barfield, W., & Blitz, M. J. (2018). Research handbook on the law of virtual and augmented reality. In Research Handbook on the Law of Virtual and Augmented Reality. doi:10.4337/9781786438591

Barkley, J. E., Lepp, A., & Glickman, E. L. (2017). "Pokémon Go!" may promote walking, discourage sedentary behavior in college students. *Games for Health Journal*, *6*(3), 165–170. doi:10.1089/g4h.2017.0009 PMID:28628384

Barko, T., & Sadler, T. D. (2013). Practicality in virtuality: Finding student meaning in video game education. *Journal of Science Education and Technology*, *22*(2), 124–132. doi:10.100710956-012-9381-0

Barlett, C. P., Anderson, C. A., & Swing, E. L. (2009). Video game effects—Confirmed, suspected, and speculative: A review of the evidence. *Simulation & Gaming*, *40*(3), 377–403. doi:10.1177/1046878108327539

Barna, B., & Fodor, S. (2018). *An Empirical Study on the Use of Gamification on IT Courses at Higher Education. In Advances in Intelligent Systems and Computing* (Vol. 715). Springer. doi:10.1007/978-3-319-73210-7_80

Barnes & Noble College. (2015). *Getting to Know Gen Z – Exploring Middle and High Schoolers' Expectations for Higher Education*. https://www.bncollege.com/wp-content/uploads/2015/10/Gen-Z-Research-Report-Final.pdf

Barnett, L., Harvey, C., & Gatzidis, C. (2018). First Time User Experiences in mobile games: An evaluation of usability. *Entertainment Computing*, *27*, 82–88. doi:10.1016/j.entcom.2018.04.004

Barnett, T., Bass, K., & Brown, G. (1996). Religiosity, ethical ideology, and intentions to report a peer's wrongdoing. *Journal of Business Ethics*, *15*(11), 1161–1174. doi:10.1007/BF00412815

Barreto, J. (2018). *Faraday Museum augmented reality app Extended Play at Faraday Museum*. Retrieved October 4, 2021, from, https://joxnds4.wixsite.com/jbarretoportefolio/copia-leapmotion-game-for-kids

Bar-Tal, D., & Raviv, A. (1982). A cognitive-learning model of helping behavior development: Possible implications and applications. In N. Eisenberg (Ed.), *The development of prosocial behavior* (pp. 199–217). Academic Press. doi:10.1016/B978-0-12-234980-5.50013-4

Bas, G. (2010). effects of multiple intelligences instruction strategy on students achievement levels and attitudes towards English lesson. *Cypriot Journal of Educational Sciences*, *5*(3).

Bates, T. (2015). *Teaching in the digital age*. BC Open Textbooks. Retrieved from https://opentextbc.ca/teachinginadigitalage/

Bateson, G. (1955). A theory of play and fantasy. *Psychiatric Research Reports*, 2, 39–51. PMID:13297882

Battle for Kids. (2019). *Framework for 21st Century Learning*. http://static.battelleforkids.org/documents/p21/P21_Framework_Brief.pdf

Baudrillard, J. (2004). Full Screen. İstanbul: Yapı Kredi Yayınları.

Baumann, J., & Graves, M. (2010). What is academic vocabulary? *Journal of Adolescent & Adult Literacy*, 54(1), 4–12. doi:10.1598/JAAL.54.1.1

Bawden, D., & Robinson, L. (2002). Promoting literacy in a digital age: Approaches to training for information literacy. *Learned Publishing*, 15(4), 297–301. doi:10.1087/095315102760319279

BaxterR. J.HoldernessD. K.JrWoodD. A. (2016). The effects of gamification on corporate compliance training: A field experiment of true office anti-corruption training programs. *Social Science Research Network*. doi:10.2139/ssrn.2766683

Bayeck, R. Y. (2020). Examining board gameplay and learning: A multidisciplinary review of recent research. *Simulation & Gaming*, 51(4), 411–431. doi:10.1177/1046878119901286

Beach, R., Appleman, D., Hynds, S., & Wilhelm, J. (2006). *Teaching literature to adolescents*. Lawrence Erlbaum Association.

Beard, C., & Wilson, J. P. (2013). *Experiential learning: a handbook for education, training and coaching* (3rd ed.). Kogan Page Limited.

Beard, R. L., Salas, E., & Prince, C. (1995). Enhancing transfer of training: Using role-play to foster teamwork in the cockpit. *The International Journal of Aviation Psychology*, 5(2), 131–143. doi:10.120715327108ijap0502_1 PMID:11540253

Beavis, C. (2012). Video games in the classroom: Developing digital literacies. *Practically Primary*, 17(1), 17–20.

Beavis, C. (2013). Multiliteracies in the wild: Learning from computer games. In G. Merchant, J. Gillen, J. Marsh, & J. Davies (Eds.), *Virtual literacies: Interactive spaces for children and young people* (pp. 57–74). Routledge.

Beavis, C. (2014). Games as text, games as action: Video games in the English classroom. *Journal of Adolescent & Adult Literacy*, 57(6), 433–439. doi:10.1002/jaal.275

Beavis, C., Dezuanni, M., & O'Mara, J. (Eds.). (2017). *Serious Play: Literacy, Learning and Digital Games*. Routledge. doi:10.4324/9781315537658

Beavis, C., Muspratt, S., & Thompson, R. (2015). 'Computer games can get your brain working': Student experience and perceptions of digital games in the classroom. *Learning, Media and Technology*, 40(1), 21–42. doi:10.1080/17439884.2014.904339

Beavis, C., & O'Mara, J. A. (2010). *Computer games–pushing at the boundaries of literacy. Australian Journal of Language and Literacy, 33(1), 65-76.* http://hdl.handle.net/10072/37372

Becker, K. (2008). *The invention of good games: Understanding learning design in commercial video games* (PhD thesis). University of Calgary.

Becker, K. (2007). Digital game - based learning once removed : Teaching teachers. *British Journal of Educational Technology. SIG-GLUE Special Issue on Game-Based Learning*, 38(3), 478–488. doi:10.1111/j.1467-8535.2007.00711.x

Beck, I., McKeown, M., & Kucan, L. (2013). *Bringing Words to Life: Robust Vocabulary Instruction* (2nd ed.). Guilford Press.

Beck, J. C., & Wade, M. (2004). *Got game: How the gamer generation is reshaping business forever*. Harvard Business Press.

Beetham, H., & Sharpe, R. (Eds.). (2007). *Rethinking pedagogy for a digital age: Designing and delivering e-learning*. Routledge., doi:10.4324/9780203961681

Beetham, H., & Sharpe, R. (Eds.). (2013). *Rethinking pedagogy for a digital age: Designing for 21st century learning* (Vol. 711). Routledge. doi:10.4324/9780203078952

Beggs, T. (2000). Influences and Barriers to the Adoption of Instructional Technology. *Mid-South Instructional Technology Conference*, 14.

Begum, M., & Farooqui, S. (2008). School based assessment: Will it really change the education scenario in Bangladesh? *International Education Studies*, *1*(2), 45–53. doi:10.5539/ies.v1n2p45

Behnke, K. A. (2015). *Gamification in Introductory Computer Science* (Doctoral dissertation). University of Colorado Boulder.

Bell, T., Witten, I., & Fellows, M. (1998). Computer science unplugged … off-line activities and games for all ages. Academic Press.

Bellanca, J., & Brandt, R. (Eds.). (2010). *21st Century skills: Rethinking how students learn*. Solution Tree Press.

Bell, M., Smith-Robbins, S., & Withnail, G. (2010). This is not a game – Social virtual worlds, fun, and learning. In *Researching learning in virtual worlds* (pp. 177–191). Springer., doi:10.1007/978-1-84996-047-2_10

Bellotti, F., Kapralos, B., Lee, K., Moreno-Ger, P., & Berta, R. (2013). Assessment in and of serious games: An overview. *Advances in Human-Computer Interaction*, *2013*, 1–11. Advance online publication. doi:10.1155/2013/136864

Belova & Zomada. (2020). Innovating Higher Education via Game-Based Learning on Misconceptions. *Education Sciences*, (10), 221.

Benbow, J., Mizrachi, A., Oliver, D., & Said-Moshiro, L. (2007). *Large Class Sizes in the Developing World : What Do We Know and What Can We Do?* (Cooperative Agreement No. GDG-A_00-03-00006-00; Issue October). https://pdf.usaid.gov/pdf_docs/PNADK328.pdf

Benford, S., Magerkurth, C., & Ljungstrand, P. (2005). Bridging the physical and digital in pervasive gaming. *Communications of the ACM*, *48*(3), 54–57. doi:10.1145/1047671.1047704

Bengu, E., Abrignani, E., Sabuncuoglu, I., & Yilmaz, C. (2020). Rethinking higher education for the emerging needs of society. *Global Solutions Summit 2020 Edition*, *5*(1), 178-187.

Bennani, S., Maalel, A., & Ben Ghezala, H. (2020). Age-learn: Ontology-based representation of personalized gamification in e-learning. In Procedia Computer Science (Vol. 176, pp. 1005–1014). doi:10.1016/j.procs.2020.09.096

Bennett, D., Yábar, D. P. B., & Saura, J. R. (2017). University Incubators May Be Socially Valuable, but How Effective Are They? A Case Study on Business Incubators at Universities. In *Entrepreneurial Universities* (pp. 165–177). Springer International Publishing. doi:10.1007/978-3-319-47949-1_11

Bennett, N., & Lemoine, G. J. (2014). What a difference a word makes: Understanding threats to performance in a VUCA world. *Business Horizons*, *57*(3), 311–317. doi:10.1016/j.bushor.2014.01.001

Bereczki, E. O., & Kárpáti, A. (2021). Technology-enhanced creativity: A multiple case study of digital technology-integration expert teachers' beliefs and practices. *Thinking Skills and Creativity*, *39*, 39. doi:10.1016/j.tsc.2021.100791

Bergstrom, I., & Lotto, R. B. (2015). Code Bending: A new creative coding practice. *Leonardo*, *48*(1), 25–31. doi:10.1162/LEON_a_00934

Berkling, K., & Neubehler, K. (2019). Boosting Student Performance with Peer Reviews; Integration and Analysis of Peer Reviews in a Gamified Software Engineering Classroom. In *2019 IEEE Global Engineering Education Conference (EDUCON)* (pp. 253-262). IEEE. 10.1109/EDUCON.2019.8725247

Berland, M., & Lee, V. R. (2011). Collaborative strategic board games as a site for distributed computational thinking. *International Journal of Game-Based Learning*, *1*(2), 65–81. doi:10.4018/ijgbl.2011040105

Bermingham, N., Prendergast, M., Boland, T., O'Rawe, M., & Ryan, B. (2016). Developing mobile apps for improving the orientation experience of first-year third-level students. *Proceedings of 8th Annual International conference on Education and New Learning Technologies*. 10.21125/edulearn.2016.0137

Bernik, A., Vusić, D., & Milković, M. (2019). Evaluation of Gender Differences Based on Knowledge Adaptation in the Field of Gamification and Computer Science. *International Journal of Emerging Technologies in Learning*, *14*(8), 220. doi:10.3991/ijet.v14i08.9847

Besser, A., Flett, G. L., & Zeigler-Hill, V. (2020). Adaptability to a Sudden Transition to Online Learning During the COVID-19 Pandemic: Understanding the Challenges for Students. *Scholarship of Teaching and Learning in Psychology*. Advance online publication. doi:10.1037tl0000198

Bevan, D., & Kipka, C. (2012). Experiential learning and management education. *Journal of Management Development*, *31*(3), 193–197. doi:10.1108/02621711211208943

Bhatia, H. K., & Ilyas, Z. (2016). Barriers of ICT Integration in Teaching Learning. *Jamia Journal of Education*, *3*(1). Retrieved from https://www.researchgate.net/profile/Harjeet_Bhatia/publication/319272961_Jamia_Journal_of_Education_An_International_Biannual_Publication_Volume_3_Number_1_November_2016

Bhatti, N. (2019). CAI and conventional method for retention of mathematics: An experimental study. *Journal of Physics: Conference Series*, *1157*(3), 032079. doi:10.1088/1742-6596/1157/3/032079

Bianchini, S., & Verhagen, E. (Ed.). (2016). *Practicable, From Participation to interaction in Contemporary Art*. MIT Press.

Bicen, H., & Kocakoyun, S. (2018). Perceptions of Students for Gamification Approach. *International Journal of Emerging Technologies in Learning*, *13*(02), 72–93. doi:10.3991/ijet.v13i02.7467

Bignoux, S., & Sund, K. J. (2018). Tutoring executives online: What drives perceived quality? *Behaviour & Information Technology*, *37*(7), 703–713. doi:10.1080/0144929X.2018.1474254

Bilici, İ. E. (2011). *Türkiye'de ortaöğretimde medya okuryazarlığı dersi için bir model önerisi*. Erciyes Üniversitesi. Doktora Tezi.

Bilton, N. (2013, September 16). Minecraft, a child's obsession, finds use as an educational tool. *The New York Times*, *162*(56261), B8.

Bingimlas, K. A. (2009). Barriers to the successful integration of ICT in teaching and learning environments: A review of the literature. *Eurasia Journal of Mathematics, Science and Technology Education*, *5*(3), 235–245. doi:10.12973/ejmste/75275

Binkley, M., Erstad, O., Herman, J., Raizen, S., Ripley, M., Miller-Ricci, M., & Rumble, M. (2012). Defining twenty-first century skills. In P. Griffin & E. Care (Eds.), *Assessment and Teaching of 21st Century Skills: Methods and Approach* (pp. 17–66). Springer. doi:10.1007/978-94-007-2324-5_2

Compilation of References

Bíró, G. I. (2014). Didactics 2.0: A pedagogical analysis of gamification theory from a comparative perspective with a special view to the Components of Learning. *Procedia: Social and Behavioral Sciences*, *141*, 148–151. doi:10.1016/j.sbspro.2014.05.027

Bissoloti, K., Nogueira, H. G., & Pereira, A. T. C. (2014). *Potencialidades das mídias sociais e da gamificação na educação a distância*. Available at: https://seer.ufrgs.br/renote/article/view/53511/33027

Bista, S. K., Nepal, S., Colineau, N., & Paris, C. (2012). Using Gamification in an online community. In *Collaborative Computing: Networking, Applications, and Worksharing (CollaborateCom), 2012 8th International Conference on* (pp. 611-618). IEEE.

Black, P., & Wiliam, D. (2009). Developing the theory of formative assessment. *Educational Assessment, Evaluation and Accountability*, *21*(1), 5-31.

Black, J., Bryant, J., & Thompson, S. (1997). *Introduction to Media Communication* (5th ed.). Mc Grw Hill Company.

Black, P. (2015). Formative assessment – an optimistic but incomplete vision. *Assessment in Education: Principles, Policy & Practice*, *22*(1), 161–177. doi:10.1080/0969594X.2014.999643

Black, P., & Wiliam, D. (2006). Developing a Theory of Formative Assessment. In J. Gardner (Ed.), *Assessment and Learning* (pp. 81–100). SAGE.

Black, P., & Wiliam, D. (2018). Classroom assessment and pedagogy. *Assessment in Education: Principles, Policy & Practice*, *25*(6), 551–575. doi:10.1080/0969594X.2018.1441807

Blanco-Herrera, J. A., Gentile, D. A., & Rokkum, J. N. (2019). Video games can increase creativity, but with caveats. *Creativity Research Journal*, *31*(2), 119–131. doi:10.1080/10400419.2019.1594524

Blau, I., Shamir-Inbal, T., & Avdiel, O. (2020). How does the pedagogical design of a technology-enhanced collaborative academic course promote digital literacies, self-regulation, and perceived learning of students? *The Internet and Higher Education*, *45*, 100722. doi:10.1016/j.iheduc.2019.100722

Blickle, G. (1998). Personality traits, learning stratigies, and performance. *European Journal of Personality*, *10*(5), 337–352. doi:10.1002/(SICI)1099-0984(199612)10:5<337::AID-PER258>3.0.CO;2-7

Blikstad-Balas, M. (2013). *Redefining School Literacy. Prominent Literacy Practices. Across Subjects in Upper Secondary School*. University of Oslo. Retrieved May 01, 2019 from https://www.duo.uio.no/bitstream/handle/10852/38160/1/dravhandling-blikstad-balas.pdf

Blikstein, P., Kabayadondo, Z., Martin, A., & Fields, D. (2017). An assessment instrument of technological literacies in makerspaces and FabLabs. *Journal of Engineering Education*, *106*(1), 149–175. doi:10.1002/jee.20156

Blismas, N. G., & Dainty, A. R. (2003). Computer-aided qualitative data analysis: Panacea or paradox? *Building Research and Information*, *31*(6), 455–463. doi:10.1080/0961321031000108816

Blok, H., Oostdam, R., Otter, M. E., & Overmaat, M. (2002). Computer-assisted instruction in support of beginning reading instruction: A review. *Review of Educational Research*, *72*(1), 101–130. doi:10.3102/00346543072001101

Blooket. (n.d.). Retrieved October 26, 2021, from https://www.blooket.com/play

Blum, D. (1997). *Sex on the brain: The biological differences between men and women*. Viking.

Blunch, N. H., & Das, M. B. (2015). Changing norms about gender inequality in education: Evidence from Bangladesh. *Demographic Research*, *32*(6), 183–218. doi:10.4054/DemRes.2015.32.6

Blunt, R. (n.d.). *Does Game-Based Learning Work? Results from Three Recent Studies*. Academic Press.

Boakye, N. A., & Linden, M. M. (2018). Extended strategy-use instruction to improve students' reading proficiency in a content subject. *Reading and Writing*, *9*(1), 1–9.

Board Game Geek. (n.d.). https://boardgamegeek.com/boardgame/27710/catan-dice-game

Bobbit, L. M., Inks, S. A., Kemp, K. J., & Mayo, D. T. (2000). Integrating marketing courses to enhance team-based experiential learning. *Journal of Marketing Education*, *22*(1), 15–24. doi:10.1177/0273475300221003

Boekaerts, M. (2010). The crucial role of motivation and emotion in classroom learning. In H. Humont, D. Istance, & F. Benavides (Eds.), *The Nature of Learning: Using Research to Inspire Practice* (pp. 91–112). Centre for Educational Research and Innovation. doi:10.1787/9789264086487-6-en

Bogdan, R., & Biklen, S. (1994). *Investigação Qualitativa em Educação*. Porto Editora.

Bögels, S. M., van Oosten, A., Muris, P., & Smulders, D. (2001). Familial correlates of social anxiety in children and adolescents. *Behaviour Research and Therapy*, *39*(3), 273–287. doi:10.1016/S0005-7967(00)00005-X PMID:11227809

Bogliolo, A. (2018). *Coding in your classroom now*. Giunti.

Bogopa, D. L. (2012). The importance of indigenous games: The selected cases of indigenous games in South Africa. *Indilinga*, *11*(2), 245–256.

Bogost, I. (2007). *Persuasive Games: The Expressive Power of Videogames*. MIT Press. doi:10.7551/mitpress/5334.001.0001

Boller, S. (2017). "Appily ever after": How to create your own library mobile app through easy to use, low cost technology. *Library Hi Tech News*, *34*(10), 7–10. doi:10.1108/LHTN-09-2017-0069

Bolliger, D. U., Mills, D., White, J., & Kohyama, M. (2015). Japanese Students' Perceptions of Digital Game Use for English-Language Learning in Higher Education. *Journal of Educational Computing Research*, *53*(3), 384–408. doi:10.1177/0735633115600806

Bond, L. (2015). *Mathimagicians Quest: Applying game design concepts to Education to increase school engagement for students with emotional and behavioral disabilities* (Doctoral dissertation).

Bond, M., Marín, V. I., Dolch, C., Bedenlier, S., & Zawacki-Richter, O. (2018). Digital transformation in German higher education: Student and teacher perceptions and usage of digital media. *Int J Educ Technol High Educ*, *15*(1), 48. doi:10.118641239-018-0130-1

Boney, C. R., & Sternberg, R. J. (2011). Learning to think critically. In R. E. Mayer & P. A. Alexander (Eds.), *Handbook of research on learning and instruction* (pp. 166–196). Routledge., doi:10.4324/9780203839089

Bong, S. A. (2002). *Debunking myths in qualitative data analysis*. Paper presented at the Forum Qualitative Sozialforschung/Forum: Qualitative Social Research.

Bonk, C. J., & Zhang, K. (2006). Introducing R2D2 model: Online learning for the diverse learners of this world. *Distance Education*, *27*(2), 249–264. doi:10.1080/01587910600789670

Book Creator. (2021). *Book creator* [Online software]. https://bookcreator.com/2021/07/

Boonsamuan, S., & Nobaew, B. (2016). Key factor to improve Adversity Quotient in children through mobile game-based learning. In *2016 International Symposium on Intelligent Signal Processing and Communication Systems (ISPACS)* (pp. 1-6). IEEE. 10.1109/ISPACS.2016.7824759

Compilation of References

Borko, H., Whitcomb, J., & Liston, D. (2009). Wicked Problems and Other Thoughts on Issues of Technology and Teacher Learning. *Journal of Teacher Education, 60*(1), 3–7. doi:10.1177/0022487108328488

Bottentuit, J. B. Jr. (2012). Do Computador ao Tablet: Vantagens Pedagógicas na Utilização de Dispositivos Móveis na Educação. *Revista Educaonline, 6*, 125–149.

Boukhechba, H., & Bouhania, B. (2019). Adaptation of instructional design to promote learning in traditional EFL classrooms: Adobe Captivate for e-learning content. *International Journal of Education and Development Using Information and Communication Technology, 15*(4), 151–164.

Bourdieu, P. (1986). The forms of capital. In J. Richardson (Ed.), *Handbook of theory and research for the sociology of education* (pp. 241–258). Greenwood Press.

Bourgonjon, J., De Grove, F., De Smet, C., Van Looy, J., Soetaert, R., & Valcke, M. (2013). Acceptance of Game-Based Learning by Secondary School Teachers. *Computers & Education, 67*, 21–35. doi:10.1016/j.compedu.2013.02.010

Bourgonjon, J., & Hanghoi, T. (2011). What does it mean to be a game literate teacher? Interviews with teachers who translate games into educational practice. *Proceedings of the European Conference on Games-Based Learning*, 67–73.

Bourgonjon, J., Valcke, M., Soetaert, R., & Schellens, T. (2010). Students' perceptions about the use of video games in the classroom. *Computers & Education, 54*(4), 1145–1156. doi:10.1016/j.compedu.2009.10.022

Bovermann, K., Weidlich, J., & Bastiaens, T. (2018). Online learning readiness and attitudes towards gaming in gamified online learning – a mixed methods case study. *International Journal of Educational Technology in Higher Education, 15*(1), 0–17. doi:10.1186/s41239-018-0107-0

Bovermann, K., & Bastiaens, T. J. (2020). Towards a motivational design? Connecting gamification user types and online learning activities. *Research and Practice in Technology Enhanced Learning, 15*(1), 1–18. doi:10.118641039-019-0121-4

Bowman, S. (2020). *Educating the Digital Native: Teaching Students in a Binge-Watching World*. Faculty Focus.

Boxer, P., Groves, C. L., & Docherty, M. (2015). Video games do indeed influence children and adolescents' aggression, prosocial behavior, and academic performance: A clearer reading of Ferguson (2015). *Perspectives on Psychological Science, 10*(5), 671–673. doi:10.1177/1745691615592239 PMID:26386004

Boyd, D. (2008). *Taken out of context: American teen sociality in networked publics* (PhD Dissertation). University of California-Berkeley.

Boyd, D., & Ellison, N. (2007). Social network sites: Definition, history, and scholarship. *Journal of Computer-Mediated Communication, 13*(1), 210–230. doi:10.1111/j.1083-6101.2007.00393.x

Boydell, K. (2007). *Ethical issues in conducting qualitative research. Research ethics lecture series. Department of psychiatry*. University of Toronto.

Boyle, E. A., Hainey, T., Connolly, T. M., Gray, G., Earp, J., Ott, M., Lim, T., Ninaus, M., Ribeiro, C., & Pereira, J. (2016). An update to the systematic literature review of empirical evidence of the impacts and outcomes of computer games and serious games. *Computer Education, 94*, 178–192. doi:10.1016/j.compedu.2015.11.003

Bozalek, V., Ng'ambi, D., & Gachago, D. (2013). Transforming teaching with emerging technologies: Implications for higher education institutions. *South African Journal of Higher Education, 27*(2), 419–436. https://open.uct.ac.za/handle/11427/9844

Bozarth, M. A. (1994). Pleasure systems in the brain. *Pleasure: The politics and the reality*, 5-14.

Bozkurt, A., & Durak, G. (2018). A Systematic Review of Gamification Research: In Pursuit of Homo Ludens. *International Journal of Game-Based Learning*, *8*(3), 15–33. doi:10.4018/IJGBL.2018070102

Braßler, M. (2020). The Role of Interdisciplinarity in Bringing PBL to traditional Universities: Opportunities and Challenges on the Organizational, Team and Individual Level. *The Interdisciplinary Journal of Problem-Based Learning*, *14*(2). Advance online publication. doi:10.14434/ijpbl.v14i2.28799

Breakout edu. (n.d.). Retrieved October 26, 2021, from https://platform.breakoutedu.com/login

Bree, R. T., & Gallagher, G. (2016). Using Microsoft Excel to code and thematically analyse qualitative data: A simple, cost-effective approach. *All Ireland Journal of Higher Education, 8*(2).

Breweston, P., & Millward, L. (2001). *Organizational research methods*. Sage. doi:10.4135/9781849209533

Bridges in Mathematics. (2012). *Grade 1 Assessments and Scoring Checklists, Common Core State Standards*. Bridges in Mathematics. https://bridges1.mathlearningcenter.org/files/media/Bridges_GrK-5_Assmnt/GR1-YearlongAssessment-0512w.pdf

Bridget, B., & Andrea, T. (2011). Do avatars dream of electronic picket lines?: The blurring of work and play in virtual environments. *Information Technology & People*, *24*(1), 26–45. doi:10.1108/09593841111109404

Bridle, J. (2019). *New Dark Ages, Technology and the End of the Future*. Verso.

Brin, P., Krasnokutska, N., Polančič, G., & Kous, K. (2020). Project-Based Intercultural Collaborative Learning for Social Responsibility: The Ukrainian-Slovenian Experience. In Handbook of Research on Enhancing Innovation in Higher Education Institutions (pp. 566-586). IGI Global. doi:10.4018/978-1-7998-2708-5.ch024

Bring your learning resources to life! (n.d.). *Wakelet for Educators*. Retrieved October 26, 2021, from https://learn.wakelet.com/

Brom, C., Preuss, M., & Klement, D. (2011). Are educational computer micro-games engaging and effective for knowledge acquisition at high schools? A quasi-experimental study. *Computer Education*, *57*(3), 1971–1988. Advance online publication. doi:10.1016/j.compedu.2011.04.007

Brook, C., & Pedler, M. (2020). Action learning in academic management education: A state of the field review. *International Journal of Management Education*, *18*(3), 100415. doi:10.1016/j.ijme.2020.100415

Brooker, P. D. (2019). Programming with Python for Social Scientists. *Sage (Atlanta, Ga.)*.

Brooker, P. D., Sharrock, W., & Greiffenhagen, C. (2019). Programming visuals, visualising programs. *Science & Technology Studies*, *32*(1), 21–42.

Brooks, R., Gupta, A., Jayadeva, S., & Abrahams, J. (2020). Students' views about the purpose of higher education: A comparative analysis of six European countries. *Higher Education Research & Development*, 1–14. Advance online publication. doi:10.1080/07294360.2020.1830039

Brosch, T., Scherer, K. R., Grandjean, D. M., & Sander, D. (2013). The impact of emotion on perception, attention, memory, and decision-making. *Swiss Medical Weekly*, *143*, 13786. doi:10.4414mw.2013.13786 PMID:23740562

Brown, D., Standen, P., Saridaki, M., Shopland, N., Roinioti, E., Evett, L., & Smith, P. (2013). *Engaging Students with Intellectual Disabilities through Games Based Learning and Related Technologies*. Paper presented at the Universal Access in Human-Computer Interaction. Applications and Services for Quality of Life, Berlin, Germany. 10.1007/978-3-642-39194-1_66

Compilation of References

Brown, S. (2008). *Play is More Than Just Fun*. Retrieved January 18, 2020, from https://www.ted.com/talks/stuart_brown_play_is_more_than_just_fun

Brown, A., & Whiteside, S. (2008). Relations among perceived parental rearing behaviors, attachment style, and worry in anxious children. *Journal of Anxiety Disorders*, *22*(2), 263–272. doi:10.1016/j.janxdis.2007.02.002 PMID:17383852

Brown, C. L., Comunale, M. A., Wigdahl, B., & Urdaneta-Hartmann, S. (2018). Current climate for digital game-based learning of science in further and higher education. *FEMS Microbiology Letters*, *365*(21), fny237. Advance online publication. doi:10.1093/femsle/fny237 PMID:30260380

Brownell, C. J. (2021). Writing as a Minecrafter: Exploring How Children Blur Worlds of Play in the Elementary English Language Arts Classroom. *Teachers College Record*, *123*(3), 1–19. doi:10.1177/016146812112300306

Brown, J. S. (2000). Growing Up Digital. *Change*, *32*(2), 10–11. http://www.johnseelybrown.com/Growing_up_digital.pdf

Brown, J. S. (2000, March/April). Growing up digital: How the web changes work, education, and the ways people learn. *Change*, *32*(2), 10–20. doi:10.1080/00091380009601719

Brown, J. S., Collins, A., & Duguid, P. (1989). Situated Cognition and the Culture of Learning. *Educational Researcher*, *18*(1), 32–42. doi:10.3102/0013189X018001032

Brown, S. L. (2009). *Play: How it shapes the brain, opens the imagination, and invigorates the soul*. Penguin.

Bruce, C. (2002). Information literacy as a catalyst for educational change: A background paper. In P. Danahar (Ed), *Lifelong Learning: Whose responsibility and what is your contribution? Proceedings of The 3rd International Lifelong Learning Conference* (pp. 8-19). Queensland University of Technology. Retrieved from http://eprints.qut.edu.au/4977/1/4977_1.pdf

Brull, S., & Finlayson, S. (2016). Importance of gamification in increasing learning. *Journal of Continuing Education in Nursing*, *47*(8), 372–375. doi:10.3928/00220124-20160715-09 PMID:27467313

Brundha, M. P., & Akshaya, K. (n.d.). *Use of crazy card games in understanding pathology-research*. Academic Press.

Bruner, J. (1979). On knowing: Essays for the left hand (expanded edition). Harvard University Press.

Bruner, J. K. (1976). Play, Thought and Language. *Peabody Journal of Education*, *60*(3), 60-69.

Bruner, J. (1986). *Actual minds, possible worlds*. Harvard University Press. doi:10.4159/9780674029019

Bruner, J. (1996). *The culture of education*. Harvard University Press.

Bruner, J. S. (1961). The act of discovery. *Harvard Educational Review*, *31*(1), 21–32.

Bruns, A. (2008). *Blogs, Wikipedia, Second Life, and beyond: From production to produsage* (Vol. 45). Peter Lang.

Bryce, J. (1921). *Modern democracies*. Macmillan and Co., Ltd.

Buabeng-Andoh, C. (2012, Apr 30). Factors influencing teachers' adoption and integration of information and communication technology into teaching: A review of the literature. *International Journal of Education and Development using ICT*, *8*(1), 136–155. Retrieved from https://www.learntechlib.org/p/188018/

Buabeng-Andoh, C. (2019). Factors that influence teachers' pedagogical use of ICT in secondary schools: A case of Ghana. *Contemporary Educational Technology*, *10*(3), 272–288. doi:10.30935/cet.590099

Bubou, G. M., & Job, G. C. (2020). Individual innovativeness, self-efficacy and e-learning readiness of students of Yenagoa study centre, National Open University of Nigeria. *Journal of Research in Innovative Teaching & Learning*. doi:10.1108/JRIT-12-2019-0079

Buchner, J., & Zumbach, J. (2020). Augmented Reality in Teacher Education. a Framework To Support Teachers' Technological Pedagogical Content Knowledge. *Italian Journal of Educational Technology, 28*(2), 106–120. doi:10.17471/2499-4324/1151

Buckingham, D. (2013). Challenging concepts: Learning in the media classroom. In Current Perspectives on Media Education (pp. 1-14). London: Routledge.

Buckingham, D. (2016). Defining digital literacy. *Nordic Journal of Digital Literacy*, 21-34.

Buckingham, D. (2007). *Beyond technology: Children's learning in the age of digital culture*. Polity.

Buckingham, D. (2008). *Youth, identity, and digital media (The John D. and Catherine T. MacArthur Foundation series on digital media and learning)*. The MIT Press.

Buckingham, D. (2010). Defining digital literacy. In *Medienbildung in neuen Kulturräumen* (pp. 59–71). VS Verlag für Sozialwissenschaften. doi:10.1007/978-3-531-92133-4_4

Buckless, F. A., Krawczyk, K., & Showalter, D. S. (2014). Using virtual worlds to simulate real-world audit procedures. *Issues in Accounting Education, 29*(3), 389–417. doi:10.2308/iace-50785

Buckley, P., & Doyle, E. (2017). Individualising Gamification: An investigation of the impact of learning styles and personality traits on the efficacy of Gamification using a prediction market. *Computers & Education, 106*, 43–55. doi:10.1016/j.compedu.2016.11.009

Burianová, M., & Turčáni, M. (2016). Non-traditional education using smart devices. *DIVAI, 2016*.

Burke, Q., O'Byrne, W. I., & Kafai, Y. B. (2016). Computational participation: Understanding coding as an extension of literacy instruction. *Journal of Adolescent & Adult Literacy, 59*(4), 371–375. doi:10.1002/jaal.496

Burn, A., & Durran, J. (2007). *Media Literacy in Schools: Practice, Production and Progression*. Paul Chapman Publishing.

Burnett, M., Poxnick, B., & Stevens, J. (2007) *Are You Smarter Than a 5th Grader* [Game Show Series]. Fox.

Burnett, C. (2010). Personal digital literacies versus classroom literacies: Investigating pre-service teachers' digital lives in and beyond the classroom. In V. Carrington & M. Robinson (Eds.), *Digital literacies: Social learning and classroom practices* (pp. 115–129). SAGE.

Burnett, C., & Hollander, W. J. (2004). The South African indigenous games research project of 2001/2002. *S.A. Journal for Research in Sport Physical Education and Recreation, 26*(1), 9–23. doi:10.4314ajrs.v26i1.25873

Burns, B. (2008). Teaching the computer science of computer games. *Journal of Computing Sciences in Colleges, 23*(3), 154–161.

Bushman, B. J., & Anderson, C. A. (2002). Violent video games and hostile expectations: A test of the General Aggression Model. *Personality and Social Psychology Bulletin, 28*(12), 1679–1686. doi:10.1177/014616702237649

Butcher, C., Davies, C., & Highton, M. (2019). *Designing learning: From module outline to effective teaching*. Routledge. doi:10.4324/9780429463822

Butler, M. (2006). *Unlocking the groove: Rhythm, meter, and musical design in electronic dance music*. Indiana University Press.

Butts, A. (1938). *Scrabble* [Board Game]. Hasbro.

Compilation of References

Buyuksalih, I., Bayburt, S., Buyuksalih, G., Baskaraca, A. P., Karim, H., & Rahman, A. A. (2017). 3D modelling and visualization based on the unity game engine—advantages and challenges. *ISPRS Annals of Photogrammetry, Remote Sensing & Spatial Information Sciences*, 4.

Bwire, A. M., Nyagisere, M. S., Masingila, J. O., & Ayot, H. (Eds.). (2015). *Proceedings of the 4th International Conference on Education*. Academic Press.

Byrne, B. M. (2016). *Structural equation modeling with AMOS: Basic concepts, applications, and programming*. Routledge. doi:10.4324/9781315757421

Byun, J., & Loh, C. S. (2015). Audial engagement: Effects of game sound on learner engagement in digital game-based learning environments. *Computers in Human Behavior*, *46*, 129–138. doi:10.1016/j.chb.2014.12.052

C21 Canada. (2017). *The Spiral Playbook. Leading with an inquiring mindset in school systems and schools*. Canadians for 21st Century Learning and Innovation.

Cachia, R., Ferrari, A., & Punie, Y. (2010). Creative Learning and Innovative Teaching. Final Report on the Study on Creativity and Innovation in Education in the EU Member States. *JRC Scientific Technical Reports*, 1-55.

Cagiltay, N. E., Ozcelik, E., & Ozcelik, N. S. (2015). The effect of competition on learning in games. *Computers & Education*, *87*, 35–41. doi:10.1016/j.compedu.2015.04.001

Cahill, G. (n.d.). *Why game-based learning?* The Learning Counsel.

Caillois, R. (1990). *Man, play and games* (M. Tada & M. Tsukazaki, Trans.). Kodansha. (Original work published 1958)

Callaghan, N. (2016). Investigating the role of Minecraft in educational learning environments. *Educational Media International*, *53*(4), 244–260. doi:10.1080/09523987.2016.1254877

Calleja, G. (2007). Revising immersion: A conceptual model for the analysis of digital game involvement. *Situated Play, Proceedings of DiGRA 2007 Conference*, 83-90.

Call, K., Riedel, A., Hein, K., McLoyd, V., Petersen, A., & Kipke, M. (2002). Adolescent health and well-being in the twenty first century: A global perspective. *Journal of Research on Adolescence*, *12*(1), 69–98. doi:10.1111/1532-7795.00025

Calvo-Ferrer, J. R. (2017). Educational games as stand-alone learning tools and their motivational effect on L 2 vocabulary acquisition and perceived learning gains. *British Journal of Educational Technology*, *48*(2), 264–278. doi:10.1111/bjet.12387

Cam, L., & Tran, T. M. T. (2017). An evaluation of using games in teaching English grammar for first year English-majored students at Dong Nai Technology University. *International Journal of Learning, Teaching and Educational Research*, *16*(7), 55-71.

Camacho Vásquez, G., & Ovalle, J. C. (2019). The Influence of Video Games on Vocabulary Acquisition in a Group of Students from the BA in English Teaching. *GIST Education and Learning Research Journal*, *19*, 172–192. doi:10.26817/16925777.707

Cameron, K. E., & Bizo, L. A. (2019). Use of the game-based learning platform KAHOOT! To facilitate learner engagement in Animal Science students. *Research in Learning Technology*, *27*(0), 27. doi:10.25304/rlt.v27.2225

Cameron, S. (2011). Whether and where to enroll? Choosing a primary school in the slums of urban Dhaka, Bangladesh. *International Journal of Educational Development*, *31*(4), 357–366. doi:10.1016/j.ijedudev.2011.01.004

Camp, R. (2018). *Blank Slate* [Board Game]. USAopoly.

Campbell, B. (1990). What is literacy? Acquiring and using literacy skills. *Australasian Public Libraries and Information Services*, *3*(3), 149–152.

Campbell, D. T., & Stanley, J. C. (1963). *Experimental and quasi-experimental design for research*. Cengage Learning.

Campbell, H. (2013). *Digital religion: Understanding religious practice in new media worlds*. Routledge Taylor and Francis Group.

Camp, R. J., & Wheaton, J. M. (2014). Streamlining field data collection with mobile apps. *Eos (Washington, D.C.)*, *95*(49), 453–454. doi:10.1002/2014EO490001

CananA. (2014) *Philosophy of new media*. Accessed from http://philosophyofnewmedia.com/

Cankaya, S., & Karamete, A. (2009). The effects of educational computer games on students' attitudes towards mathematics course and educational computer games. *Procedia: Social and Behavioral Sciences*, *1*(1), 145–149. doi:10.1016/j.sbspro.2009.01.027

Cantoni, L., & Di Blas, N. (2006). Comunicazione. *Teoria e pratiche*, 6.

Cappuccio, M. L., Sandoval, E. B., Mubin, O., Obaid, M., & Velonaki, M. (2021). Robotics Aids for Character Building: More than Just Another Enabling Condition. *International Journal of Social Robotics*, *13*, 1–5. doi:10.100712369-021-00756-y

Carbonaro, M., Szafron, D., Cutumisu, M., & Schaeffer, J. (2010). Computer-game construction: A gender-neutral attractor to Computing Science. *Computers & Education*, *55*(3), 1098–1111. doi:10.1016/j.compedu.2010.05.007

Cardador, T. M., Northcraft, B. G., & Whicker, J. (2016). A theory of work gamification: Something old, something new, something borrowed, something cool? *Human Resource Management Review*.

Cardinot, A., & Fairfield, J. A. (2019). Game-based learning to engage students with physics and astronomy using a board game. *International Journal of Game-Based Learning*, *9*(1), 42–57. doi:10.4018/IJGBL.2019010104

Carenys, J., & Moya, S. (2016). Digital game-based learning in accounting and business education. *Accounting Education*, *25*(6), 598–651. doi:10.1080/09639284.2016.1241951

Carlo, G., Hausmann, A., Chritiansen, S., & Randall, B. A. (2003). Sociocognitive and behavioral correlates of a measure of prosocial tendencies for adolescents. *The Journal of Early Adolescence*, *23*(1), 107–134. doi:10.1177/0272431602239132

Carretero Gomez, S., Vuorikari, R., & Punie, Y. (2017). *DigComp 2.1: The Digital Competence Framework for Citizens with eight proficiency levels and examples of use. EUR 28558 EN*. Publications Office of the European Union.

Carretero, S., Vuorikari, R. & Punie, Y. (2017). *DigComp 2.1: The Digital Competence Framework for Citizens with eight proficiency levels and examples of use*. EUR 28558 EN, Publications Office of the European Union. doi:10.2760/38842

Carrington, V. (2001). Literacy instruction: A Bourdieuian perspective. In P. Freebody, S. Muspratt, & B. Dwyer (Eds.), *Difference, silence, and textual practice: Studies in critical literacy* (pp. 265–285). Hampton Press, Inc.

Carrington, V., & Luke, A. (1997). Literacy and Bourdieu's sociological theory: A reframing. *Language and Education*, *11*(2), 96–112. doi:10.1080/09500789708666721

Carroll, J. M. (1982). The adventure of getting to know a computer. *IEEE Computer*, *15*(11).

Carter, L. (2006). Why students with an apparent aptitude for computer science don't choose to major in computer science. *ACM SIGCSE Bulletin*, *38*(1), 27–31. doi:10.1145/1124706.1121352

Carter, M. S., & Mahoney, M. C. (2020). Gamification and Training the Technical Workforce. *The Marine Corps Gazette*.

Compilation of References

Carter, M., Gibbs, M., & Harrop, M. (2014). Drafting an army: The playful pastime of warhammer 40,000. *Games and Culture*, 9(2), 122–147. doi:10.1177/1555412013513349

Carvajal, D. (2002). *The artisan's tools. Critical issues when teaching and learning CAQDAS*. Paper presented at the Forum Qualitative Sozialforschung/Forum: Qualitative Social Research.

Carvalho, L. F. S. (2015). *Utilização de Dispositivos Móveis na aprendizagem da Matemática no 3o Ciclo*. Dissertação de Mestrado em Tecnologias de Informação e Comunicação na Educação. Universidade Portucalense. Departamento de Inovação, Ciência e Tecnologia.

Carvalho, L., & Yeoman, P. (2018). Framing learning entanglement in innovative learning spaces: Connecting theory, design and practice. *British Educational Research Journal*, 44(6), 1120–1137. doi:10.1002/berj.3483

Casañ-Pitarch, R. (2018). An approach to digital game-based learning: Video-games principles and applications in foreign language learning. *Journal of Language Teaching and Research*, 9(6), 1147–1159. doi:10.17507/jltr.0906.04

Castaneda, D. A., & Cho, M. H. (2016). Use of a game-like application on a mobile device to improve accuracy in conjugating Spanish verbs. *Computer Assisted Language Learning*, 29(7), 1195–1204. doi:10.1080/09588221.2016.1197950

Castells, M. (1999). *La Era de la información: economiá, sociedad y cultura*. Siglo Veintiuno Editores.

Castells, M. (2010). *The rise of the network society. The Information age: Economy, society, and culture* (2nd ed., Vol. 1). Wiley-Blackwell.

Castilhos, D. (2018). *Gamification and active methodologies at university: The case of teaching learning strategy in law*. doi:10.21125/iceri.2018.0220

Castro, K. A. C., Sibo, Í. P. H., & Ting, I. (2018a). Assessing gamification effects on E-learning platforms: An experimental case. *Communications in Computer and Information Science*, 870, 3–14. doi:10.1007/978-3-319-95522-3_1

Castronova, E. (2008). *Exodus to the virtual world: How online fun is changing reality*. Palgrave Macmillan.

Castronova, E., & Knowles, I. (2015). Modding board games into serious games: The case of Climate Policy. *International Journal of Serious Games*, 2(3), 41–62.

Catts, R., & Lau, J. (2008). *Towards information literacy indicators*. Academic Press.

Cavallo, A., Robaldo, A., Ansovini, F., Carmosino, I., & De Gloria, A. (2017). *Gamification of a System for Real-Time Monitoring of Posture. In eHealth 360*. Springer International Publishing.

Cazden, C. (1981). Performance before competence: Assistance to child discourse in the zone of proximal development. *The Quarterly Newsletter of the Laboratory of Comparative Human Cognition*, 3, 5–8.

Cazden, C., Cope, B., Fairclough, N., & Gee, J. (1996). A pedagogy of multiliteracies: Designing Social Futures. *Harvard Educational Review*, 66(1), 60–92. doi:10.17763/haer.66.1.17370n67v22j160u

CCSS. (2010). *Common core state standards initiative*. Retrieved May 6, 2015, from http://www.corestandards.org/the-standards

CDC. (2020, February 11). *COVID-19 Vaccination*. Centers for Disease Control and Prevention. https://www.cdc.gov/coronavirus/2019-ncov/vaccines/distributing/steps-ensure-safety.html

Celik, I., Sahin, I., & Akturk, A. O. (2014). Analysis of the relations among the components of technological pedagogical and content knowledge (TPACK): A structural equation model. *Journal of Educational Computing Research*, 51(1), 1–22. doi:10.2190/EC.51.1.a

Center for Media Literacy. (n.d.). *CML MediaLit Kit.* Retrieved May 15, 2011 from http://www.medialit.org/bp_mlk.html

Chafouleas, S. M., Riley-Tillman, T. C., & Christ, T. J. (2009). Direct Behavior Rating (DBR): An emerging method for assessing social behavior within a tiered intervention system. *Assessment for Effective Intervention, 34*(4), 201–213. doi:10.1177/1534508409340391

Chai, C. S., Koh, J. H., & Tsai, C. C. (2011). Exploring the factor structure of the constructs of technological, pedagogical, content knowledge (TPACK). *The Asia-Pacific Education Researcher, 20*(3), 595–603.

Chai, C. S., Koh, J. H., Tsai, C. C., & Tan, L. L. (2011). Modeling primary school pre-service teachers' Technological Pedagogical Content Knowledge (TPACK) for meaningful learning with information and communication technology (ICT). *Computers & Education, 57*(1), 1184–1193. doi:10.1016/j.compedu.2011.01.007

Chall, J. S. (1996). *Stages of Reading Development.* Harcourt Brace College Publishers.

Chambers, J. H., & Ascione, F. R. (1987). The effects of prosocial and aggressive videogames on children's donating and helping. *The Journal of Genetic Psychology, 148*(4), 499–505. doi:10.1080/00221325.1987.10532488 PMID:3437274

Chan, K. H. W., Wan, K., & King, V. (2021). *Performance over enjoyment? Effect of game-based learning on learning outcome and flow experience.* doi:10.3389/feduc.2021.660376

Chang, M., & Gu, X. (2018). The role of executive function in linking fundamental motor skills and reading proficiency in socioeconomically disadvantaged kindergarteners. *Learning and Individual Differences, 61*(December), 250–255. doi:10.1016/j.lindif.2018.01.002

Chang, M., Lachance, D., Lin, F., Al-Shamali, F., & Chen, N. S. (2015). Enhancing Orbital Physics Learning Performance through a Hands-on Kinect Game. *Egitim ve Bilim, 40*(180).

Chang, C. C., Liang, C., Chou, P.-N., & Lin, G.-Y. (2017). Is game-based learning better in flow experience and various types of cognitive load than non-game-based learning? Perspective from multimedia and media richness. *Computers in Human Behavior, 71*, 218–227. doi:10.1016/j.chb.2017.01.031

Chang, C.-Y., & Hwang, G.-J. (2019). Trends in digital game-based learning in the mobile era: Asystematic review of journal publications from 2007 to 2016. *Int. J. Mobile Learning and Organisation, 13*(1), 68–90. doi:10.1504/IJMLO.2019.096468

Chang, Y.-H., Hwang, J.-H., Fang, R.-J., & Lu, Y.-T. (2017). A Kinect- and Game-Based Interactive Learning System. *Journal of Mathematics Science and Technology Education, 13*(8), 4897–4914. doi:10.12973/eurasia.2017.00972a

Chapman, J. R., & Rich, P. J. (2018). Does educational gamification improve students' motivation? If so, which game elements work best? *Journal of Education for Business, 93*(7), 314–321. doi:10.1080/08832323.2018.1490687

Chapter 6. (2006). *Understandings of Literacy.* Education for All Global Monitoring Report. Retrieved May 02, 2019 from http://www.unesco.org/education/GMR2006/full/chapt6_eng.pdf

Chasek, P. S. (2005). Power politics, diplomacy and role playing: Simulating the UN Security Council's response to terrorism. *International Studies Perspectives, 6*(1), 1–19. doi:10.1111/j.1528-3577.2005.00190.x

Chatzimichali, E. (2020). *A comparative analysis between science curricula for primary school from 17 countries regarding the subject of astronomy* [Συγκριτική μελέτη της παρουσίας της αστρονομίας στα αναλυτικά προγράμματα της πρωτοβάθμιας εκπαίδευσης 17 χωρών προερχομένων από τις 5 ηπείρους] (Master's thesis). National & Kapodistrian University of Athens. Retrieved from https://pergamos.lib.uoa.gr/uoa/dl/frontend/el/browse/2916920

Compilation of References

Chaudhary, A. G. (2010). Educational gaming: An effective tool for learning and social change in India. *Journal of Creative Communications*, *5*(3), 135–152. doi:10.1177/0973258612471244

Chaudhury, T. A., & Karim, Z. (2014). CLT approach in developing English reading skills in tertiary levels in Bangladesh. *Asian Journal of Education and e-Learning*, *2*(1), 47-55.

Chaves, M. (2010). SSSR Presidential Address Rain Dances in the Dry Season: Overcoming the Religious Congruence Fallacy. *Journal for the Scientific Study of Religion*, *49*(1), 1–14. doi:10.1111/j.1468-5906.2009.01489.x

Chavez, V., & Soep, E. (2005). Youth radio and the pedagogy of collegiality. *Harvard Educational Review*, *75*(4), 409–434. doi:10.17763/haer.75.4.827u365446030386

Chayko, M. (2018). Süper Bağ(lantı)lı. Çev. Berkan Bayındır, Deniz Yengin ve Tamer Bayrak. İstanbul: Der Kitabevi.

Cheatsheet—MediaWiki. (n.d.). Retrieved June 1, 2021, from https://www.mediawiki.org/wiki/Cheatsheet

Checa-Romero, M., & Pascual Gómez, I. (2018). Minecraft and machinima in action: Development of creativity in the classroom. *Technology, Pedagogy and Education*, *27*(5), 625–637. doi:10.1080/1475939X.2018.1537933

Chee, Y. S., Mehrotra, S., & Ong, J. C. (2014). Facilitating dialog in the game-based learning classroom: Teacher challenges reconstructing professional identity. *Digital Culture & Education*, *6*(4), 298–316.

Chen, D., & Wu, J. (2010). *Deconstructing new media: From computer literacy to new media literacy.* Paper presented at the 8th international conference on education and information systems, Technologies and Applications, Orlando, FL.

Chen, D., Wu, J., & Wang, Y. (2011). *Unpacking new media literacy.* Retrieved on December 3, 2012, from www.iiisci.org/journal/CV$/sci/pdfs/OL508KR.pdf

Chen, S., Huang, F., Zeng, W., Dong, N., Wu, X., & Tang, Y. (2019). Robots can teach knowledge but can't cultivate values? *China Educational Technology*, (2), 29-35.

Chen, C. H., Huang, K., & Liu, J. H. (2020). Inquiry-Enhanced Digital Game-Based Learning: Effects on Secondary Students' Conceptual Understanding in Science, Game Performance, and Behavioral Patterns. *The Asia-Pacific Education Researcher*, *29*(4), 319–330. doi:10.100740299-019-00486-w

Chen, C. H., Liu, G. Z., & Hwang, G. J. (2016). Interaction between gaming and multistage guiding strategies on students' field trip mobile learning performance and motivation'. *British Journal of Educational Technology*, *47*(6), 1032–1050. doi:10.1111/bjet.12270

Chen, C. H., Wang, K. C., & Lin, Y. H. (2015). The Comparison of Solitary and Collaborative Modes of Game-Based Learning on Students' Science Learning and Motivation. *Journal of Educational Technology & Society*, *18*(2), 237–248.

Chen, C. M., & Chung, C. J. (2008). Personalized mobile English vocabulary learning system based on item response theory and learning memory cycle. *Computers & Education*, *51*(2), 624–645. doi:10.1109/ICSMC.2006.384727

Cheng, C. W. (2012). The system and self-reference of the app economy: The case of angry birds. *Westminster Papers in Communication & Culture*, *9*(1).

Cheng, M. T., Chen, J. H., Chu, S. J., & Chen, S. Y. (2015). The use of serious games in science education: a review of selected empirical research from 2002 to 2013. *Journal of Computers in Education*, *2*(3), 353-375.

Cheng, C. H., & Su, C. H. (2012). A Game-based learning system for improving student's learning effectiveness in system analysis course. *Procedia: Social and Behavioral Sciences*, *31*, 669–675. doi:10.1016/j.sbspro.2011.12.122

Chen, H. J. H., & Yang, T. Y. C. (2013). The impact of adventure video games on foreign language learning and the perceptions of learners. *Interactive Learning Environments*, *21*(2), 129–141. doi:10.1080/10494820.2012.705851

Chen, N. S., Quadir, B., & Teng, D. C. (2011). Integrating book, digital content and robot for enhancing elementary school students' learning of English. *Australasian Journal of Educational Technology*, *27*(3). Advance online publication. doi:10.14742/ajet.960

Chen, S. W., Yang, C. H., Huang, K. S., & Fu, S. L. (2019). Digital games for learning energy conservation: A study of impacts on motivation, attention, and learning outcomes. *Innovations in Education and Teaching International*, *56*(1), 66–76. doi:10.1080/14703297.2017.1348960

Chen, S. Y., & Chang, Y. M. (2020). The impacts of real competition and virtual competition in digital game-based learning. *Computers in Human Behavior*, *104*(2), 106171. doi:10.1016/j.chb.2019.106171

Chen, S., Husnaini, S. J., & Chen, J.-J. (2020). Effects of games on students' emotions of learning science and achievement in chemistry. *International Journal of Science Education*, *42*(13), 2224–2245. doi:10.1080/09500693.2020.1817607

Chen, S., Zhang, S., Qi, G. Y., & Yang, J. (2020). Games Literacy for Teacher Education : Towards the Implementation of Game-based Learning. *Journal of Educational Technology & Society*, *23*(2), 77–92.

Chen, Y. C. (2017). Empirical Study on the Effect of Digital Game-Based Instruction on Students' Learning Motivation and Achievement. *Eurasia Journal of Mathematics, Science and Technology Education*, *13*(7). Advance online publication. doi:10.12973/eurasia.2017.00711a

Chess, S. (2020). *Play Like a Feminist*. MIT Press. doi:10.7551/mitpress/12484.001.0001

Chetouani, M., Vanden Abeele, V., Leuven, K., Carmen Moret-Tatay, B., Lopes, S., Magalhães, P., Pereira, A., Martins, J., Magalhães, C., Chaleta, E., & Rosário, P. (2018). Games Used With Serious Purposes: A Systematic Review of Interventions in Patients With Cerebral Palsy. *Frontiers in Psychology*, *9*, 1712. doi:10.3389/fpsyg.2018.01712 PMID:30283377

Cheung, G. W., & Rensvold, R. B. (2002). Evaluating goodness-of-fit indexes for testing measurement invariance. *Structural Equation Modeling*, *9*(2), 233–255. doi:10.1207/S15328007SEM0902_5

Chien-Pen, C., Neien-Tzu, H., & Yi-Jeng, H. (2004). *Life education based on game learning strategy for vocational education students in Taiwan*. http://163.21.114.214/ezfiles/0/1000/img/4/20130527-d17.pdf

Childs, M. (2010). *Learners' experience of presence in virtual worlds* (Doctoral dissertation). University of Warwick.

Chinaka, G. (2017). *Factors affecting the adoption and integration of ICT as a pedagogical tool in rural primary schools* (Dissertation). Midlands State University.

Chinyoka, K. (2014). Causes of school drop-out among ordinary level learners in a resettlement area in Masvingo, Zimbabwe. *Journal of Emerging Trends in Educational Research and Policy Studies*, *5*(3), 294–300.

Chiong, C., Ree, J., Takeuchi, L., & Erickson, I. (2012). *Print books vs e-books. Comparing parent-child co-reading on print, basic and enhanced e-book platforms*. The Joan Ganz Cooney Center at Sesame Workshop. http://www.joanganzcooneycenter.org/wp-content/uploads/2012/07/jgcc_ebooks_ quickreport.pdf

Chiruguru, S. (2018). *The Essential Skills of 21st Century Classroom (4Cs)*. Louisiana Computer Using Educators.

Chivaura, V., & Mararike, C. (1998). *The human factor approach to development in Africa*. University of Zimbabwe Publications.

Cho, M. H., & Castañeda, D. A. (2019). Motivational and affective engagement in learning Spanish with a mobile application. *System*, *81*, 90–99. doi:10.1016/j.system.2019.01.008

Compilation of References

Chong, D. Y. K. (2019). Benefits and challenges with gamified multimedia physiotherapy case studies: A mixed-method study. *Archives of Physiotherapy*, *9*(1), 7. doi:10.118640945-019-0059-2 PMID:31139434

Chou, Y-k. (n.d.) *Wordpress*. Retrieved from https://yukaichou.com/gamification-examples/octalysis-complete-gamification-framework/

Choudaha, R. (2008). *Competency-based curriculum for a master's program in Service Science, Management and Engineering (SSME): An online Delphi study* [Dissertation Thesis]. University of Denver, Proquest Dissertation Publishing.

Chowdhury, F. D. (2010). Dowry, women, and law in Bangladesh. *International Journal of Law, Policy and the Family*, *24*(2), 198–221. doi:10.1093/lawfam/ebq003

Chowdhury, R., & Sarkar, M. (2018). Education in Bangladesh: Changing contexts and emerging realities. In R. Chowdhury, M. Sarkar, F. Mojumder, & M. M. Roshid (Eds.), *Engaging in Educational Research: Revisiting Policy and Practice in Bangladesh* (Vol. 44, pp. 1–18). Springer. doi:10.1007/978-981-13-0708-9_1

Chu, S. K. W., Tang, Q., Chow, K., & Tse, S. K. (2007). *A study on inquiry-based learning in a primary school through librarian-teacher partnerships*. Academic Press.

Chuang, T. Y., Liu, E. Z., & Shiu, W. Y. (2015). Game-based creativity assessment system: The application of fuzzy theory. *Multimedia Tools and Applications*, *74*(21), 9141–9155. doi:10.100711042-014-2070-7

Chun, E., & Evans, A. (2009). Bridging the diversity divide: Globalization and reciprocal empowerment in higher education. *ASHE Higher Education Report*, *35*(1). https://onlinelibrary.wiley.com/doi/10.1002/aehe.3501

Chung-Yuan, H., Meng-Jung, T., Yu-Hsuan, C., & Liang, J. C. (2017). Surveying in-service teachers' beliefs about game-based learning and perceptions of technological pedagogical and content knowledge of games. *Journal of Educational Technology & Society*, *20*(1), 134.

Chu, S. K. W., & Kennedy, D. M. (2011). Using online collaborative tools for groups to co-construct knowledge. *Online Information Review*, *35*(4), 581–597. doi:10.1108/14684521111161945

Chu, S. K. W., Reynolds, R. B., Tavares, N. J., Notari, M., & Lee, C. W. Y. (2017). *Assessment Instruments for Twenty-First Century Skills. In 21st Century Skills Development Through Inquiry-Based Learning*. Springer Singapore.

Chye, C., & Nakajima, T. (2012). Game based approach to learn martial arts for beginners. *18th IEEE International Conference on Embedded and Real-Time Computing Systems and Applications*, 482-485. 10.1109/RTCSA.2012.37

Cintang, N., Setyowati, D. L., & Handayani, S. S. D. (2018). The Obstacles and Strategy of Project Based Learning Implementation in Elementary School. *Journal of Education and Learning*, *12*(1), 7–15. doi:10.11591/edulearn.v12i1.7045

Clapper, T. C. (2018). Serious games are not all serious. *Simulation & Gaming*, *49*(4), 375–377. doi:10.1177/1046878118789763

Clark, D., Nelson, B., Sengupta, P., & Angelo, C. D. (2009). *Rethinking science learning through digital games and simulations: Genres, examples, and evidence*. Academic Press.

Clark, D. B., Sengupta, P., Brady, C. E., Martinez-Garza, M. M., & Killingsworth, S. S. (2015). Disciplinary integration of digital games for science learning. *International Journal of STEM Education*, *2*(1), 1–21. doi:10.118640594-014-0014-4

Clark, D. B., Tanner-Smith, E. E., & Killingsworth, S. S. (2016). Digital games, design, and learning: A systematic review and meta-analysis. *Review of Educational Research*, *86*(1), 79–122. doi:10.3102/0034654315582065 PMID:26937054

Clarke, S., Peel, D. J., Arnab, S., Morini, L., Keegan, H., Wood, O., Morini, L., & Wood, O. (2017). *escapED : A Framework for Creating Educational Escape Rooms and Interactive Games For Higher / Further Education*. Academic Press.

Clark, J. W., & Dawson, L. E. (1996). Personal religiousness and ethical judgements: An empirical analysis. *Journal of Business Ethics*, *15*(3), 359–372. doi:10.1007/BF00382959

Clark, K. R. (2015). The effects of the flipped model of instruction on student engagement and performance in the secondary mathematics classroom. *The Journal of Educators Online*, *12*(1), 91–114. doi:10.9743/JEO.2015.1.5

Claymier, B. (2014). Integrating stem into the elementary curriculum. *Children's Technology & Engineering*, *18*(3), 5.

Cleveland-Innes, M., & Wilton, D. (2018). *Guide to Blended Learning*. Commonwealth of Learning. Retrieved from http://oasis.col.org/handle/11599/3095

Cobb, T. (2007). Computing the vocabulary demands of L2 reading. *Language Learning & Technology*, *11*(3), 38–63.

Cobo, C., Zucchetti, A., Kass-Hanna, J., & Lyons, A. (2019). *Leaving no one behind: Measuring the multidimensionality of digital literacy in the age of AI and other transformative technologies*. Academic Press.

Cohen, N. (2021, September 7). One Woman's Mission to Rewrite Nazi History on Wikipedia. *Wired*. https://www.wired.com/story/one-womans-mission-to-rewrite-nazi-history-wikipedia/

Cohen, J. (1992). A power primer. *Psychological Bulletin*, *112*(1), 155–159. doi:10.1037/0033-2909.112.1.155 PMID:19565683

Cojocariu, V. M., & Boghian, I. (2014). Teaching the relevance of game-based learning to preschool and primary teachers. *Procedia: Social and Behavioral Sciences*, *142*, 640–646. doi:10.1016/j.sbspro.2014.07.679

Cole, H., & Griffiths, M. D. (2007). Social interactions in massively multiplayer online role-playing gamers. *Cyberpsychology & Behavior*, *10*(4), 575–583. doi:10.1089/cpb.2007.9988 PMID:17711367

Coleman, T. E., & Money, A. G. (2020). Student-centred digital game–based learning: A conceptual framework and survey of the state of the art. *Higher Education*, *79*(3), 415–457. doi:10.100710734-019-00417-0

Cole, R., & Snider, B. (2017a). Rolling the Dice on Global Supply Chain Sustainability: A Total Cost of Ownership Simulation. *INFORMS Transactions on Education*, *20*(3), 165–176. doi:10.1287/ited.2019.0225

Cole, S. W., Yoo, D. J., & Knutson, B. (2012). Interactivity and reward-related neural activation during a serious videogame. *PLoS One*, *7*(3), e33909. doi:10.1371/journal.pone.0033909 PMID:22442733

Collins, A., & Halverson, R. (2009). *Rethinking education in the age of technology: The digital revolution and schooling in America*. Teachers College Press.

Combefis, S., Beresnevicius, G., & Dagiene, V. (2016). Learning programming through games and contests: Overview, characterization, and discussion. *Olympiads in Informatics*, *10*(1), 39–60. doi:10.15388/ioi.2016.03

Comber, B., & Nixon, H. (2005). Children re-read and re-write their neighbourhoods: Critical literacies and identity work. In J. Evans (Ed.), *Literacy moves on: Using popular culture, new technologies and critical literacy in the primary classroom* (pp. 127–148). Heinemann.

Comeron, L. (2008). *Teaching Languages to Young Learners* (10th ed.). Cambridge Universty Press.

Common Sense Media. (2021). *Introduction to the TPACK model*. https://www.commonsense.org/education/videos/introduction-to-the-tpack-model

Commonwealth of Learning (COL). (2017). *MOOC on Introduction to Technology-Enabled Learning*. Commonwealth of Learning and Athabasca University.

Compilation of References

Computer Literacy Skills. (n.d.). Retrieved May 01, 2019 from https://mdk12.msde.maryland.gov/instruction/curriculum/technology_literacy/computerliteracyskills.pdf

Conejero, A., & Rueda, M. (2017). Early Development of Executive Attention. *Journal of Child and Adolescent Behavior*, *05*(02), 341. doi:10.4172/2375-4494.1000341

Conger, S. (2016). Gamification of Service Desk Work. *The Impact of ICT on Work*, (November), 1–220. doi:10.1007/978-981-287-612-6

Connell, R. (1996). Teaching the boys: New research on masculinity, and gender strategies for schools. *Teachers College Record*, *98*(2), 206–235.

Connell, R. S., & Mileham, P. J. (2006). Student assistant training in a small academic library. *Public Services Quarterly*, *2*(2–3), 69–84. doi:10.1300/J295v02n02_06

Connell, R. W. (2000). *The men and the boys*. Polity.

Connolly, T. M., Boyle, E. A., Macarthur, E., Hainey, T., & Boyle, J. M. (2012). A systematic literature review of empirical evidence on computer games and serious games. *Computers & Education*, *59*(2), 661–686. doi:10.1016/j.compedu.2012.03.004

Conroy, S. J., & Emerson, T. L. N. (2004). Business ethics and religion: Religiosity as a predictor of ethical awareness among students. *Journal of Business Ethics*, *50*(4), 383–396. doi:10.1023/B:BUSI.0000025040.41263.09

Consalvo, M. (2012). Confronting toxic gamer culture: a challenge for feminist game studies scholars. Ada: A Journal of Gender, New Media, and Technology, 1. doi:10.7264/N33X84KH

Considine, D., Horton, J., & Moorman, G. (2009). Teaching And Reaching The Millenial Generation Through Media Literacy. *Journal of Adolescent and Adult Literacy*, *52*(6), 471-481.

Cope, B., & Kalantzis, M. (2016). *A pedagogy of multiliteracies: Learning by design*. Palgrave Macmillan UK. Retrieved from https://books.google.ca/books?id=N6GkCgAAQBAJ

Cope, B., & Kalantzis, M. (2000). Introduction: Multiliteracies: the beginnings of an ideas. In B. Cope & M. Kalantzis (Eds.), *Multliteracies: Literacy learning and the design of social futures* (pp. 3–8). MacMillan Publishers.

Cope, B., & Kalantzis, M. (2009). "Multiliteracies": New literacies, new learning. *Pedagogies*, *4*(3), 164–195. doi:10.1080/15544800903076044

Cope, B., & Kalantzis, M. (2013). "Multiliteracies": New Literacies, New Learning. In M. Hawkins (Ed.), *Framing Languages and Literacies: Socially Situated Views and Perspectives* (pp. 115–145). Routledge. doi:10.4324/9780203070895-13

Cope, B., & Kalantzis, M. (2015). *The things you do to know: An introduction to the pedagogy of multiliteracies*. Springer.

Cope, B., & Kalantzis, M. (Eds.). (2000). *Multiliteracies: Literacy learning and the design of social futures*. Routledge.

Cope, B., Kalantzis, M., & Smith, A. (2018). Pedagogies and Literacies, Disentangling the Historical Threads: An Interview with Bill Cope and Mary Kalantzis. *Theory into Practice*, *57*(1), 5–11. doi:10.1080/00405841.2017.1390332

Corlett, J. T., & Mokgwathi, M. M. (1986). Play, games, sport preferences of Tswana children. In *Sport, culture, society. International historical and sociological perspectives. Proceedings of the VIII Commonwealth and International Conference on Sport, Physical Education, Dance, Recreation and Health. Conference'86 Glasgow, 18-23 July* (pp. 253-261). E. & FN Spon.

Cornellà, P., Estebanell, M., & Brusi, D. (2020). Gamificación y aprendizaje basado en juegos. Consideraciones generales y algunos ejemplos para la Enseñanza de la Geología. *Enseñanza de las Ciencias de la Tierra, 28*(1), 5–19.

Correia, V. (2017). *Design and the Culture of Participation in the Era of Digital Media* (PhD Thesis). Faculdade de Ciências Sociais e Humanas (FCSH), Universidade Nova de Lisboa, Lisbon, Portugal.

Costa, M. C., Manso, A., & Patrício, J. (2020). Design of a mobile augmented reality platform with game-based learning purposes. *Information (Basel), 11*(3), 127. doi:10.3390/info11030127

Costello, R. (2020). Gamification Strategies for Retention, Motivation, and Engagement in Higher Education: Emerging Research and Opportunities. IGI Global.

Costello, R., & Shaw, N. (2014). Personalised Learning Environments, HEA STEM (Computing): Learning Technologies Workshop. University of Hull.

Costello, R. (2017). *Research on Scientific and Technological Developments in Asia. In Socio-economic challenges facing the Asia and Pacific region in Higher Education.* IGI Global.

Costello, R., & Lambert, M. (2018). Motivational influences for Higher Education (HE) Students. *International Journal of Online Pedagogy and Course Design, 9*(1), 3.

Costello, R., & Lambert, M. (2019). Pokémon GO as a Cognitive and Societal Development Tool for Personalised Learning. *International Journal of End-User Computing and Development, 8*(1), 1–30. doi:10.4018/IJEUCD.2019010101

Costello, R., Lambert, M., & Smith, L. (2021). An innovative approach of using Mobile Gaming to bridge, anxiety, depression & isolation. *International Journal of Adult Vocational Education and Technology*.

Cote, A. C. (2020). *Gaming Sexism, Gender and Identity in the Era of Casual Video Games.* New York University Press. doi:10.18574/nyu/9781479838523.001.0001

Cotton, V., & Patel, M. S. (2019). Gamification use and design in popular health and fitness mobile applications. *American Journal of Health Promotion, 33*(3), 448–451. doi:10.1177/0890117118790394 PMID:30049225

Couse, L. J., & Chen, D. W. (2010). A Tablet Computer for Young Children? Exploring Its Viability for Early Childhood Education. *Journal of Research on Technology in Education, 43*(1), 75–98. doi:10.1080/15391523.2010.10782562

Covax: How many Covid vaccines have the US and the other G7 countries pledged? (2021, June 11). *BBC News.* https://www.bbc.com/news/world-55795297

Cowan, K. (2017). Digital Languages: Multimodal meaning-making in Reggio-inspired early years education. In DigiLitEY: The Digital and Multimodal Practices of Young Children, Short Term Scientific Mission—Final Report. Academic Press. http://digilitey.eu/wp-content/uploads/2015/09/ElisabeteBarros-STSM-FinalReport_FI-1.pdf

Cowan, K. (2019). Digital meaning making: Reggio Emilia-inspired practice in Swedish preschools. *Media Education Research Journal, 8*(2), 11–29.

Cowen, T. (2013). *Average is over: Powering America beyond the age of the great stagnation.* Dutton.

Coyle, D. (2007). Content and language integrated learning: Towards a connected research agenda for CLIL pedagogies. *International Journal of Bilingual Education and Bilingualism, 10*(5), 543–562. doi:10.2167/beb459.0

Coyle, D., Hood, P., & Marsh, D. (2010). *CLIL - content and language integrated learning.* Cambridge University Press. doi:10.1017/9781009024549

Compilation of References

Coyne, S. M., & Smith, N. J. (2014). Sweetness on the screen: A multidimensional view of prosocial behavior in media. In L. M. Padilla-Walker & G. Carlo (Eds.), *Prosocial development: A multidimensional approach* (pp. 156–177). Oxford University Press. doi:10.1093/acprof:oso/9780199964772.003.0008

Cózar-Gutiérrez, R., & Sáez-López, J. M. (2016). Game-based learning and gamification in initial teacher training in the social sciences: An experiment with minecraftedu. *International Journal of Educational Technology in Higher Education*, *13*(1), 2. doi:10.118641239-016-0003-4

Craft, J. L. (2013). A Review of the Empirical Ethical Decision-Making Literature: 2004–2011. *Journal of Business Ethics*, *117*(2), 221–259. doi:10.100710551-012-1518-9

Craig, S. D., Graesser, A. C., Sullins, J., & Gholson, B. (2004). Affect and Learning: An Exploratory Look into the Role of Affect in Learning with AutoTutor. *Journal of Educational Media*, *29*(3), 241–250. doi:10.1080/1358165042000283101

Create unforgettable experiences. (n.d.). *GooseChase*. Retrieved October 26, 2021, from https://www.goosechase.com/

Creswell, J. W. (2003). *Research design: qualitative, quantitative, and mixed method approaches.* Sage Publications.

Creswell, J. W. (2007). *Qualitative inquiry & research design: Choosing among five approaches.* Sage Publications.

Creswell, J. W. (2014). *Research design: qualitative, quantitative, and mixed methods approaches* (4th ed.). SAGE Publications.

Creswell, J. W., & Poth, C. N. (2017). *Qualitative inquiry and research design: Choosing among five approaches.* Sage.

Crews, A. (2011). Getting Teachers on" Board. *Knowledge Quest*, *40*(1), 10.

Crocco, F., Offenholley, K., & Hernandez, C. (2016). A Proof-of-Concept Study of Game-Based Learning in Higher Education. *Simulation & Gaming*, *47*(4), 403–422. doi:10.1177/1046878116632484

Crookall, D. (2010). Serious games, debriefing, and simulation/gaming as a discipline. *Simulation & Gaming*, *41*(6), 898–920. doi:10.1177/1046878110390784

Croxton, D., & Kortemeyer, G. (2018). Informal physics learning from video games: A case study using gameplay videos. *Physics Education*, *53*(1), 015012. doi:10.1088/1361-6552/aa8eb0

Csikszentmihalyi, M. (1975). *Beyond boredom and anxiety. Experiencing flow in work and play.* Jossey-Bass.

Csikszentmihalyi, M. (1990). *Flow.* Harper & Row.

Csikszentmihalyi, M. (1990). *Flow: The psychology of optimal experience.* Harper and Row.

Csikszentmihalyi, M. (1990). *Flow: The Psychology of Optimal Experience.* Harper.

Csikszentmihalyi, M. (1996). *Creativity. Flow and the psychology of discovery and invention.* Harper Perennial.

Csikszentmihalyi, M. (1997). *Finding flow.* Basic Books.

Csikszentmihalyi, M. (2000). Positive psychology: An introduction. *The American Psychologist*, *55*(1), 5–14. doi:10.1037/0003-066X.55.1.5 PMID:11392865

Csikszentmihalyi, M. (2013). *Flow: The psychology of happiness.* Random House.

Csikszentmihalyi, M., & Csikszentmihalyi, I. (1988). *Optimal experience: Psychological studies of flow in consciousness.* Cambridge University Press. doi:10.1017/CBO9780511621956

Csikszentmihalyi, M., Rathunde, K., & Whalen, S. (1993). *Talented teenagers.* Cambridge University Press.

Cudeck, R., & Browne, M. W. (1983). Cross-validation of covariance structures. *Multivariate Behavioral Research*, *18*(2), 147–167. doi:10.120715327906mbr1802_2 PMID:26781606

Culatta, B., Hall-Kenyon, K., & Bingham, G. (2016). *Five Questions Everyone Should Ask Before Choosing Early Literacy Apps*. The Joan Ganz Cooney Center at Sesame Workshop. https://www.joanganzcooneycenter.org/2016/01/07/five-questions-everyone-should-ask-before-choosing-early-literacy-apps/

Culatta, B., Black, S., & Hall-Kenyon, K. (2013). *Systematic and Engaging Early Literacy: Instruction and intervention*. Plural Publishing, Inc.

Culatta, B., Hall, K., Kovarsky, D., & Theodore, G. (2007). Contextualized approach to language and literacy instruction. *Communication Disorders Quarterly*, *28*(4), 216–235. doi:10.1177/1525740107311813

Culatta, R. (2021). *Digital for Good: Raising Kids to Thrive in an Online World*. Harvard Business Review Press.

Culatta, R., Culatta, B., Frost, M., & Buzzell, K. (2004). Project SEEL: Part II. Using technology to enhance early literacy instruction in Spanish. *Communication Disorders Quarterly*, *25*(2), 89–96. doi:10.1177/15257401040250020601

Cummings, Mason, & Baur. (2017). Active Learning Strategies for Online and Blended Learning Environments. Flipped Instruction: Breakthroughs in Research and Practice, 88–116.

Cushen, W. E. (1955). War games and operations research. *Philosophy of Science*, *2*(4), 309–320. doi:10.1086/287446

Cutrer, W. B., Miller, B., Pusic, M. V., Mejicano, G., Mangrulkar, R. S., Gruppen, L. D., & Moore, D. E. Jr. (2017). Fostering the development of master adaptive learners: A conceptual model to guide skill acquisition in medical Education. *Academic Medicine*, *92*(1), 70–75. doi:10.1097/ACM.0000000000001323 PMID:27532867

Dabbagh, N., Benson, A. D., Denham, A., Joseph, R., & Zgheib, M. A. G. (2015). *Learning Technologies and Globalization Pedagogical Frameworks and Applications*. Academic Press.

Dabbagh, N., Benson, A. D., Denham, A., Joseph, R., Al-Freih, M., Zgheib, G., Fake, H., & Guo, Z. (2016). *Learning Technologies and Globalization; Pedagogical Frameworks and Applications*. Springer. https://link.springer.com/10.1007/978-3-319-22963-8

Dadheech, A. (n.d.). *The Importance of Game Based Learning in Modern Education*. Knowledge Review. Retrieved from https://theknowledgereview.com/importance-game-based-learning-modern-education/

Dahlgren, P. (2007). *Young citizens and new media: Learning from democratic participation*. Routledge.

Dale, L., & Tanner, R. (2012). *CLIL activities: A resource for subject and language teachers*. Cambridge University Press.

Dale, S. (2014). Gamification: Making work fun, or making fun of work? *Business Information Review*, *31*(2), 82–90. doi:10.1177/0266382114538350

Dalton, B., & Proctor, C. P. (2007). Reading as thinking: Integrating strategy instruction in a universally designed digital literacy environment. *Reading comprehension strategies: Theories, interventions, and technologies*, 423-442.

Dalton-Puffer, C. (2007). *Discourse in content and language integrated learning (CLIL) classrooms*. John Benjamins Publishing Company. doi:10.1075/lllt.20

Daly, E. (2012). Explore, create, survive. *School Library Journal*, *58*(5), 24–25.

Damásio, A. (2021). *Deus Cérebro. Maquinaria das emoções*. Retrieved January 18, 2020, from https://www.rtp.pt/play/p8309/deus-cerebro

Compilation of References

Daniele, V. (2021). Socioeconomic inequality and regional disparities in educational achievement: The role of relative poverty. *Intelligence, 84*(October), 101515. doi:10.1016/j.intell.2020.101515

Danka, I. (2020). Motivation by gamification: Adapting motivational tools of massively multiplayer online role-playing games (MMORPGs) for peer-to-peer assessment in connectivist massive open online courses (cMOOCs). *International Review of Education, 66*(1), 75–92. doi:10.100711159-020-09821-6

Darling-Hammond, L., Schachner, A., & Edgerton, A. K. (2020). Restarting and reinventing school: Learning in the time of COVID and beyond. Palo Alto, CA: Learning Policy Institute.

Darrow, C.D. (2006). *Monopoly: the property trading board game* [Board Game]. Hasbro/Parker.

Daspit, J. J., & D'Souza, D. E. (2012). Using the community of inquiry framework to introduce wiki environments in blended-learning pedagogies: Evidence from a business capstone course. *Academy of Management Learning & Education, 11*(4), 666–683. doi:10.5465/amle.2010.0154

Davidson, M., & Hobbs, J. (2013). Delivering reading intervention to the poorest children: The case of Liberia and EGRA-Plus, a primary grade reading assessment and intervention. *International Journal of Educational Development, 33*(3), 283–293. doi:10.1016/j.ijedudev.2012.09.005

Davis, F. D. (1993). *User acceptance of information technology: system characteristics, user perceptions and behavioral impacts*. Academic Press.

Davis, F. (1989). Perceived usefulness, perceived ease of use, and user acceptance of information technology. *Management Information Systems Quarterly, 13*(3), 319–340. doi:10.2307/249008

Davis, F. D., Bagozzi, R. P., & Warshaw, P. R. (1989). User Acceptance of Computer-Technology - A Comparison of 2 Theoretical-Models. *Management Science, 35*(8), 982–1003. doi:10.1287/mnsc.35.8.982

Davis, F. D., Bagozzi, R. P., & Warshaw, P. R. (1992). Extrinsic and intrinsic motivation to use computers in the workplace. *Journal of Applied Social Psychology, 22*(14), 1111–1132. doi:10.1111/j.1559-1816.1992.tb00945.x

Davis, M. H., & Gaskell, M. G. (2009). A complementary systems account of word learning: Neural and behavioural evidence. *Philosophical Transactions of the Royal Society of London. Series B, Biological Sciences, 364*(1536), 3773–3800. doi:10.1098/rstb.2009.0111 PMID:19933145

Dawson, S. (2008). A study of the relationship between student social networks and sense of community. *Journal of Educational Technology & Society, 11*(3), 224–238.

Day, E. A., Arthur, W. Jr, & Gettman, D. (2001). Knowledge structures and the acquisition of a complex skill. *The Journal of Applied Psychology, 86*(5), 1022–1033. doi:10.1037/0021-9010.86.5.1022 PMID:11596796

De Coninck, K., Valcke, M., Ophalvens, I., & Vanderlinde, R. (2019). Bridging the theory-practice gap in teacher education: The design and construction of simulation-based learning environments. In *Kohärenz in der Lehrerbildung* (pp. 263–280). Springer VS. doi:10.1007/978-3-658-23940-4_17

De Freitas, S. (2006). *Learning in immersive worlds: A review of game-based learning*. Academic Press.

De Freitas, S. (2006). *Learning in immersive worlds: A review of game-based learning*. IJSC.

De Freitas, S. (2018). Are games effective learning tools? A review of educational games. *Journal of Educational Technology & Society, 21*(2), 74–84.

De Freitas, S., & Neumann, T. (2009). The use of 'exploratory learning' for supporting immersive learning in virtual environments. *Computers & Education, 52*(2), 343–352. doi:10.1016/j.compedu.2008.09.010

De Gloria, A., Bellotti, F., & Berta, R. (2014). Serious games for education and training. *International Journal of Serious Games*, *1*(1). Advance online publication. doi:10.17083/ijsg.v1i1.11

de Jong, M. T., & Bus, A. G. (2002). Quality of book-reading matters for emergent readers: An experiment with the same book in a regular or electronic format. *Journal of Educational Psychology*, *94*(1), 145–155. doi:10.1037/0022-0663.94.1.145

De Kort, Y. A. W., Ijsselsteijn, W. A., & Poels, K. (2007). Digital games as social presence technology: Development of the Social Presence in Gaming Questionnaire (SPGQ). *Presence (Cambridge, Mass.)*, *2007*, 1–9.

de Sousa Borges, S., Durelli, V. H., Reis, H. M., & Isotani, S. (2014). A systematic mapping on Gamification applied to Education. In *Proceedings of the 29th Annual ACM Symposium on Applied Computing* (pp. 216-222). ACM. 10.1145/2554850.2554956

de Temple, J. M., & Snow, C. E. (2001). Conversations about literacy: Social mediation of psycholinguistic activity. In L. Verhoeven & C. Snow (Eds.), *Literacy and motivation: Reading engagement in individuals and groups* (pp. 71–94). Lawrence Erlbaum Associates.

DeCoito, I., & Richardson, T. (2016). Focusing on integrated STEM concepts in a digital game. In M. Urban & D. Falvo (Eds.), *Improving K-12 STEM Education* (pp. 1–23).

Dede, C. (2005b). Planning for neomillennial learning styles: Implications for investments in technology and faculty. In *Educating the net generation*. EDUCAUSE. https://www.educause.edu/research-and-publications/books/educating-net-generation/planning-neomillennial-learning-styles-implications-investments-tech

Dede, C. (2005a). Planning for neomillennial learning styles: Shifts in students' learning style will prompt a shift to active construction of knowledge through mediated immersion. *EDUCAUSE Quarterly*, *28*(1), 7–12. https://er.educause.edu/-/media/files/article-downloads/eqm0511.pdf

deHaan, J. (2019). Teaching language and literacy with games: What? How? Why? *Ludic Language Pedagogy*, *1*, 1–57.

DeHaan, J., Reed, W. M., & Kuwanda, K. (2010). The effect of interactivity with a music video game on second language vocabulary recall. *Language Learning & Technology*, *14*(2), 74–94.

deLaet, V., Kuffner, J., Slattery, M., & Sweedyk, E. (2005). *Computers games and CS education: Why and How*. Paper presented at SIGCSE, St. Louis, MO.

Dellos, R. (2015). *Kahoot! A digital game resource for learning*. Academic Press.

Delors, J. (1996). *Learning: The treasure within*. Paris: UNESCO. Retrieved May 11, 2015 from https://unesdoc.unesco.org/images/0010/001095/109590eo.pdf

de-Marcos, L., Domínguez, A., Saenz-de-Navarrete, J., & Pagés, C. (2014). An empirical study comparing gamification and social networking on e-learning. *Computers & Education*, *75*, 82–91. doi:10.1016/j.compedu.2014.01.012

Demarin, V., & Morovic, S. (2014). Neuroplasticity. *Periodicum Biologorum*, *116*(2), 209–211. https://hrcak.srce.hr/126369

Demkah, M., & Bhargava, D. (2019, February). Gamification in Education: A Cognitive Psychology Approach to Cooperative and Fun Learning. In *2019 Amity International Conference on Artificial Intelligence (AICAI)* (pp. 170-174). IEEE. 10.1109/AICAI.2019.8701264

Deng, L., & Liu, Y. (2018). *Deep learning in natural language processing*. Springer. doi:10.1007/978-981-10-5209-5

Compilation of References

Denning, P. J., Flores, F., & Flores, G. (2011). Pluralistic coordination. In M. M. Cruz-Cunha, V. H. Varvalho, & P. Tavares (Eds.), *Business, technological, and social dimensions of computer games: Multidisciplinary developments* (pp. 416–431). Information Science Reference. doi:10.4018/978-1-60960-567-4.ch025

Department of Basic Education. (2017). *SACMEQ IV project in South Africa: A study of the conditions of schooling and quality of education.* http://www.sacmeq.org/sites/default/files/sacmeq/publications/sacmeq_iv_project_in_south_africa_report.pdf

Department of Education. (2004, September 2). White Paper on e-Education: Transforming Learning and Teaching through Information and Communication Technologies (ICTs). *Government Gazette,* (26734), 3 - 46.

Department of Educational Planning and Research Services. (2017). *SACMEQ IV project in Botswana: A study of the conditions of schooling and quality of education.* http://www.sacmeq.org/sites/default/files/sacmeq/publications/final_saqmeq_iv_report_botswana-compressed.pdf

Derboven, J., Zaman, B., Geerts, D., & De Grooff, D. (2016). Playing educational math games at home: The Monkey Tales case. *Entertainment Computing, 16,* 1–14. doi:10.1016/j.entcom.2016.05.004

Deterding, S. (2014). The Ambiguity of Games: Histories and Discourses of a Gameful World. In S. P. Walz & S. Deterding (Eds.), *The Gameful World: Approaches, Issues, Applications* (pp. 23–64). MIT Press.

Deterding, S., Dixon, D., Khaled, R., & Nacke, L. (2011, September). From game design elements to gamefulness: defining "gamification". In *Proceedings of the 15th international academic MindTrek conference: Envisioning future media environments* (pp. 9-15). 10.1145/2181037.2181040

Deterding, S., Sicart, M., Nacke, L., O'Hara, K., & Dixon, D. (2011). Gamification using game-design elements in non-gaming contexts. In *CHI'11 Extended Abstracts on Human Factors in Computing Systems* (pp. 2425–2428). ACM. doi:10.1145/1979742.1979575

Dewar, T. (1996). *Adult learning online.* http://www.cybercorp.net/ ~tammy/lo/oned2.html

Dewey, J. (1934). *Art as experience.* Academic Press.

Dewey, J. (1934). *Art as Experience.* Capricorn Books.

Dewey, J. (1963). *Experience and education.* Collier Books.

Dhamija, A., & Dhamija, D. (2020). Impact of Innovative and Interactive Instructional Strategies on Student Classroom Participation. In M. Montebello (Ed.), *Handbook of Research on Digital Learning* (pp. 20-37). IGI Global. doi:10.4018/978-1-5225-9304-1.ch002

Dhamija, A., Sharma, R., & Dhamija, D. (2020). Emergence of EdTech Products in South Asia: A Comparative Analysis. In S. Ikuta (Ed.), *Handbook of Research on Software for Gifted and Talented School Activities in K-12 Classrooms* (pp. 303–327). IGI Global. doi:10.4018/978-1-7998-1400-9.ch014

Dias, J. (2017). Teaching operations research to undergraduate management students: The role of gamification. *International Journal of Management Education, 15*(1), 98–111. doi:10.1016/j.ijme.2017.01.002

DiasSoeiro, J. (2021). Studying Wine in Non-Wine-Producing Countries: How Are Southeast Asian Students Coping With Their Learning? In C. Kahl (Ed.), *Higher Education Challenges in South-East Asia* (pp. 99-117). IGI Global. doi:10.4018/978-1-7998-4489-1.ch005

Dicheva, D., Dichev, C., Agre, G., & Angelova, G. (2015). Gamification in education: A systematic mapping study. *Journal of Educational Technology & Society, 18*(3), 75–88. https://www.jstor.org/stable/jeductechsoci.18.3.75

Dickey, M. D. (2007). Game design and learning: A conjectural analysis of how massively multiple online role-playing games (MMORPGs) foster intrinsic motivation. *Educational Technology Research and Development*, *55*(3), 253–273. doi:10.100711423-006-9004-7

Dickey, M. D. (2010). Murder on Grimm Isle: The impact of game narrative design in an educational game-based learning environment. *British Journal of Educational Technology*. Advance online publication. doi:10.1111/j.1467-8535.2009.01032.x

Diedrich, J., Benedek, M., Jauk, E., & Neubauer, A. (2015). Are Creative Ideas Novel and Useful? *Psychology of Aesthetics, Creativity, and the Arts*, *9*(1), 35–40. doi:10.1037/a0038688

Dietz, T. L. (1998). An examination of violence and gender role portrayals in video games: Implications for gender socialization and aggressive behavior. *Sex Roles*, *38*(5/6), 425–442. doi:10.1023/A:1018709905920

Digital Literacy. (n.d.). Retrieved May 01, 2019 from https://www.deakin.edu.au/__data/assets/pdf_file/0008/1237742/digital-literacy.pdf

Digital Skills Country Action Plan Methodological Guidebook Part 2. (2021). *Digital Skills: The Why, the What and the How*. Retrieved from https://thedocs.worldbank.org/en/doc/a4a6a0b2de23c53da91bf4f97c315bee-0200022021/original/DSCAP-Guidebook-Part2.pdf

Dill, K. E., & Dill, J. C. (1998). Video game violence: A review of the empirical literature. *Aggression and Violent Behavior*, *3*(4), 407–428. doi:10.1016/S1359-1789(97)00001-3

Dillon, J. D. (2020). More than netflix: The real potential of personalised learning. *Training & Development*, *47*(2), 20–23.

Dillon, L., & Dillon, D. (2002). *Rap a tap tap: Here's Bojangles—Think of that!* Blue Sky Press.

Dinan Thompson, M., Meldrum, K., & Sellwood, J. (2014). '… it is not just a game': Connecting with culture through Traditional Indigenous Games. *American Journal of Educational Research*, *2*(11), 1015–1022.

DiNardo, C. O., & Broussard, M. J. S. (2019). Commercial tabletop games to teach information literacy. *RSR. Reference Services Review*, *47*(2), 106–117. doi:10.1108/RSR-10-2018-0066

Ding, D., Guan, C., & Yu, Y. (2017). Game-based learning in tertiary education: A new learning experience for the generation Z. *International Journal of Information and Education Technology (IJIET)*, *7*(2), 148–152. doi:10.18178/ijiet.2017.7.2.857

Ding, J., Shan, R., Chenmeng, M., Tu, M., Yu, Q., Kong, F., & Zhao, Q. (2021). Are online games a blessing or evil? The moderating role of self-worth. *Thinking Skills and Creativity*, *41*, 100915. doi:10.1016/j.tsc.2021.100915

Dingli, A., & Seychell, D. (2015). Who Are the Digital Natives? In *The New Digital Natives*. Springer. doi:10.1007/978-3-662-46590-5_2

Divjak, B., & Tomic, D. (2011). The Impact of Game-Based Learning on the Achievement of Learning Goals and Motivation for Learning Mathematics - Literature Review. *Journal of Information and Organizational Sciences*, *35*(1), 15–30.

Dixon, M. L., Thiruchselvam, R., Todd, R., & Christoff, K. (2017). Emotion and the prefrontal cortex: An integrative review. *Psychological Bulletin*, *143*(10), 1033–1081. doi:10.1037/bul0000096 PMID:28616997

Dlthewave. (2019). Pro and Con: Has gun violence been improperly excluded from gun articles? In *Wikipedia*. https://en.wikipedia.org/w/index.php?title=Wikipedia:Wikipedia_Signpost/2019-03-31/Op-Ed&oldid=969726090

Doganieri, E. & Munster, B. (2001). *The Amazing Race* [Game Show Series]. CBS.

Compilation of References

Dolanbay, H. (2018). Günümüz dünya sorunları bağlamında medya ve etkileri. In *Günümüz Dünya Sorunları*. Pegem akademi.

Dolanbay, H. (2018). *Sosyal Bilgiler Öğretmen Adaylarına Yönelik Medya Okuryazarlığı Eğitimi Modeli*. Doktora Tezi. Marmara Üniversitesi.

Dolean, D., Melby-Lervåg, M., Tincas, I., Damsa, C., & Lervåg, A. (2019). Achievement gap: Socioeconomic status affects reading development beyond language and cognition in children facing poverty. *Learning and Instruction*, *63*(June), 101218. doi:10.1016/j.learninstruc.2019.101218

Dolgopolovas, V., Jevsikova, T., & Dagiene, V. (2018). From Android games to coding in C—An approach to motivate novice engineering students to learn programming. *Computer Applications in Engineering Education*, *26*(1), 75–90. doi:10.1002/cae.21862

Domingo, H., & Mashiko, N. (2013). Media literacy education (MLE) in the classroom: A descriptive case study of one exemplary Japanese teacher's mle practices, attitude and perception. Gifu University Curriculum Development Research, 30(1), 13-29.

Donahue, M. J. (1985). Intrinsic and extrinsic religiousness: Review and meta-analysis. *Journal of Personality and Social Psychology*, *48*(2), 400–419. doi:10.1037/0022-3514.48.2.400

Donohue, C., & Schomburg, R. (2017). Technology and interactive media in early childhood programs. *Young Children*, *72*(4), 72–78.

Donovan, L., Green, T. D., & Mason, C. (2014). Examining the 21st century classroom: Developing an innovation configuration map. *Journal of Educational Computing Research*, *50*(2), 161–178. doi:10.2190/EC.50.2.a

Down's Syndrome Association. (2008). *Incidence of Down's Syndrome in the UK*. DSA.

Downing, S. (2005). The social construction of entrepreneurship: Narrative and dramatic processes in the coproduction of organizations and identities. *Entrepreneurship Theory and Practice*, *29*(2), 185–204. doi:10.1111/j.1540-6520.2005.00076.x

Draper, S. (2004). *Learning Styles*. www.psy.gla.ac.uk/~steve/lstyles.html

Driver, R. (1989). The construction of scientific knowledge in school classrooms. In R. Millar (Ed.), *Doing science: Images of science in science education* (pp. 83–106). Falmer Press.

Driver, R., Squires, A., Rushworth, P., & Wood-Robinson, V. (2014). *Making sense of secondary science: Research into children's ideas*. Routledge. doi:10.4324/9781315747415

Droogers, A. F., van Harskamp, A., Clarke, P. B., Davie, G., & Versteeg, P. (2006). Playful Religion: Challenges for the Study of Religion. Uitgeverij B.V.

Duffy, T. M., & Cunningham, D. J. (1996). Constructivism: Implications for the design and delivery of instruction. In D. H. Jonassen (Ed.), *Handbook of research for educational communications and technology*. Macmillan Library Reference. doi:10.4324/9781410609519

Duggal, Gupta, & Singh. (2021). Gamification and machine learning inspired approach for classroom engagement and learning. *Mathematical Problems in Engineering*. doi:10.1155/2021/9922775

Duit, R. (1987). Research on students' alternative frameworks in science - topics, theoretical frameworks, consequences for science teaching. In J. Novak (Ed.), *Proceedings of the 2nd International Seminar on Misconceptions and Educational Strategies in science and Mathematics* (pp. 151–162). Ithaca, NY: Cornell University.

Duke, B., Harper, G., & Johnston, M. (1966). *Connectivism as a Learning Theory for the Digital Age*. Academic Press.

Duncan, J. (2019). Tech with a twist. Innovative youth programming combines coding with dance. *CBS News*. Retrieved 9/13/21 from https://www.cbsnews.com/news/dancelogic-innovative-youth-program-combines-coding-and-dance-2019-06-20/

Dunning, J. H. (2000). Regions, globalization, and the knowledge economy: Issues stated. In J. H. Dunning (Ed.), *Regions, globalization, and the knowledge-based economy* (pp. 7–41). Oxford University Press.

Dunn, J., Gray, C., Moffett, P., & Mitchell, D. (2018). 'It's more funner than doing work': Children's perspectives on using tablet computers in the early years of school. *Early Child Development and Care*, *188*(6), 819–831. doi:10.1080/03004430.2016.1238824

Dunn, R., Cavanaugh, D., Eberle, B., & Zenhausern, R. (1982). Hemispheric preference: The newest element of learning style. *The American Biology Teacher*, *44*(5), 291–294. doi:10.2307/4447506

Dunn, R., Della Valle, J., Dunn, K., Geisert, G., Sinatra, R., & Zenhausern, R. (1986). 'The effects of matching and mismatching students' mobility preferences on recognition and memory tasks'. *The Journal of Educational Research*, *79*(5), 267–272. doi:10.1080/00220671.1986.10885690

Dunn, R., Dunn, K., & Price, E. (1989). *The learning style inventory*. Price Systems.

Durak, G., Çankaya, S., & İzmirli, S. (2020). Examining the Turkish universities' distance education systems during the COVID-19 pandemic. *Necatibey Eğitim Fakültesi Elektronik Fen ve Matematik Eğitimi Dergisi.*, *14*(1), 787–809. doi:10.17522/balikesirnef.743080

Duret, C., & Pons, C. M. (Eds.). (2016). *Contemporary research on intertextuality in video games*. IGI Global. doi:10.4018/978-1-5225-0477-1

Dutta, S., & Smita, M. K. (2020). The Impact of COVID-19 Pandemic on Tertiary Education in Bangladesh: Students' Perspectives. *Open Journal of Social Sciences*, *8*(9), 53–68. doi:10.4236/jss.2020.89004

Dwarkan, L. (2017). *SACMEQ IV project in Mauritius: A study of the conditions of schooling and quality of education*. http://www.sacmeq.org/sites/default/files/sacmeq/publications/final_sacmeq_4_report_mauritius.pdf

Dzansi, D. Y., & Amedzo, K. (2014). Integrating ICT into Rural South African Schools: Possible Solutions for Challenges. *International Journal of Educational Sciences*, *6*(2), 341–348. doi:10.1080/09751122.2014.11890145

Dzimiri, C., & Mapute, L. (2013). Integration of Information and Communication Technology (ICT) with pedagogy. *IOSR Journal of Humanities and Social Science*, *16*(3), 86–92. doi:10.9790/0837-1638692

Eastwood, J. L., & Sadler, T. D. (2013). Teachers' implementation of a game-based biotechnology curriculum. *Computers & Education*, *66*(0), 11–24. doi:10.1016/j.compedu.2013.02.003

Ebrahimzadeh, M. (2017). Readers, players, and watchers: EFL students' vocabulary acquisition through digital video games. *English Language Teaching*, *10*(2), 1–18. doi:10.5539/elt.v10n2p1

Ebrahimzadeh, M., & Alavi, S. (2016). Motivating EFL students: E-learning enjoyment as a predictor of vocabulary learning through digital video games. *Cogent Education*, *3*(1), 1255400. doi:10.1080/2331186X.2016.1255400

Eck, R. V. (2006). Digital Game-Based Learning: It's Not Just the Digital Natives Who Are Restless. *EDUCAUSE Review*, *41*(2), 16–30.

Edlund, A. C., Edlund, L. E., & Haugen, S. (Eds.). (2014). *Vernacular Literacies – Past, Present and Future*. Umea University and Royal Skyttean Society. Retrieved May 01, 2019 from http://umu.diva-portal.org/smash/get/diva2:738154/FULLTEXT01.pdf

Compilation of References

Educause. (2014). *7 things you should know about games and learning*. Retrieved from https://courses.dcs.wisc.edu/design-teaching/PlanDesign_Fall2016/2-Online-Course-Design/4_Instructional-Materials/resources/SevenThingsGames.pdf

Edwards, A., Edwards, C., Spence, P., Harris, C., & Gambino, A. (2016). Robots in the classroom: Differences in students' perceptions of credibility and learning between "teacher as robot" and "robot as teacher." *Computers in Human Behavior*, *65*, 627–634. doi:10.1016/j.chb.2016.06.005

Edwards, B., Edwards, B. B., Griffiths, S., Reynolds, F. F., Stanford, A., & Woods, M. (2021). The Bryn Celli Ddu Minecraft Experience: A Workflow and Problem-Solving Case Study in the Creation of an Archaeological Reconstruction in Minecraft for Cultural Heritage Education. *Journal on Computing and Cultural Heritage*, *14*(2), 1–16. doi:10.1145/3427913

Edwards, C. P. (2002). Three approaches from Europe: Waldorf, Montessori, and Reggio Emilia. *Early Childhood Research & Practice*, *4*(1), n1.

Egenfeldt Nielsen, S. (2008). Practical Barriers in Using Educational Computer Games. In D. Drew (Ed.), Beyond Fun (pp. 20-26). ETC Press.

Egenfeldt-Nielsen, S. (2018). *Making sweet music: The educational use of computer games*. Center for Computer Games Research: University of Copenhagen. Retrieved from https://www.cs.swarthmore.edu/~turnbull/cs91/f09/paper/MakingSweetMusic.pdf

Egenfeldt-Nielsen, S. (2006). Overview of research on the educational use of video games. *Nordic Journal of Digital Literacy*, *1*(03), 184–214. doi:10.18261/ISSN1891-943X-2006-03-03

Egenfeldt-Nielsen, S. (2007). Third generation educational use of computer games. *Journal of Educational Multimedia and Hypermedia*, *16*(3), 263–281.

Egenfeldt-Nielsen, S., Smith, J. H., & Tosca, S. P. (2013). *Understanding video games: the essential introduction* (2nd ed.). Routledge. doi:10.4324/9780203116777

Eggs, R. (2021). *Fast phonics* (Version 3.0.4) [Mobile app]. https://readingeggs.com/fast-phonics-games/

Egri, C. P. (2013). From the editors: Context matters in management education scholarship. Academy of Management Learning & Education, 12(2), 155-7. doi:10.5465/amle.2013.0140

Ehri, L. C., & McCormick, S. (1998). Phases of word learning: Implications for instruction with delayed and disabled readers. *Reading & Writing Quarterly*, *14*(April), 135–163. doi:10.1080/1057356980140202

Eisenberg, N. (Ed.). (1982). *The development of prosocial behavior*. Academic Press.

Eklund, K. M., Torppa, M., & Lyytinen, H. (2013). Predicting reading disability: Early cognitive risk and protective factors. *Dyslexia (Chichester, England)*, *19*(1), 1–10. doi:10.1002/dys.1447 PMID:23297103

Elbro, C., Rasmussen, I., & Spelling, B. (1996). Teaching reading to disabled readers with language disorders: A controlled evaluation of synthetic speech feedback. *Scandinavian Journal of Psychology*, *37*(2), 140–155. doi:10.1111/j.1467-9450.1996.tb00647.x PMID:8711453

Eleftheria, C. A., Charikleia, P., Iason, C. G., Athanasios, T., & Dimitrios, T. (2013). An innovative augmented reality educational platform using Gamification to enhance lifelong learning and cultural education. In *Information, Intelligence, Systems and Applications (IISA), 2013 Fourth International Conference on* (pp. 1-5). IEEE. 10.1109/IISA.2013.6623724

Elkins, A. J. (2015). Lets Play: Why School Librarians Should Embrace Gaming in the Library. *Knowledge Quest*, *43*(5), 58–63.

Elkins, D. N., Hedstrom, L. J., Hughes, L. L., Leaf, J. A., & Saunders, C. (1988). Toward a humanistic-phenomenological spirituality: Definition, description, and measurement. *Journal of Humanistic Psychology*, *28*(4), 5–18. doi:10.1177/0022167888284002

Elliot, A. J. (1999). Approach and avoidance motivation and achievement goals. *Educational Psychologist*, *34*(3), 169–189. doi:10.120715326985ep3403_3

Elliott, E. (2019). *Composing software: An exploration of functional programming and object composition in JavaScript*. Leanpub.

Elliott, J., & Tsai, C. T. (2008). What might Confucius have to say about action research? *Educational Action Research*, *16*(4), 569–578. doi:10.1080/09650790802445759

Emon, E. K. H., Alif, A. R., & Islam, M. S. (2020). Impact of COVID-19 on the Institutional Education System and its Associated Students in Bangladesh. *Asian Journal of Education and Social Studies*, *11*(2), 34–46. doi:10.9734/ajess/2020/v11i230288

Enakrire, T. R., & Onyenania, O. G. (2007). Causes inhibiting the growth or development of information transfer in Africa: A contextual treatment. *Library Hi Tech News*, *24*(4), 20–28. doi:10.1108/07419050710778491

Encheva, M., Tammaro, A. M., & Kumanova, A. (2020). Games to improve students information literacy skills. *The International Information & Library Review*, *52*(2), 130–138. doi:10.1080/10572317.2020.1746024

Enders, C. K. (2011). Analyzing longitudinal data with missing values. *Rehabilitation Psychology*, *56*(4), 267–288. doi:10.1037/a0025579 PMID:21967118

Eng, D. (2019). *The player experience*. https://www.universityxp.com/blog/2019/9/10/the-player-experience

English, A. R. (2016). John Dewey and the role of the teacher in a globalised world: Imagination, empathy, and "third voice". *Educational Philosophy and Theory*, *48*(10), 1046–1064. doi:10.1080/00131857.2016.1202806

Ennis, L. (2018). *Game-Based Learning: An Instructional Tool, Digital repository*. Iowa State University.

Epic! Creations. (2021). *Epic books for kids* (version 5.31) [Mobile app]. https://www.getepic.com

Epper, R., Derryberry, A., & Jackon, S. (2012). *Game-Based Learning: Developing an Institutional Strategy*. EDUCAUSE Research. http://educause.edu/ecar

Epstein, E. M. (2002). Religion and business–the critical role of religious traditions in management education. *Journal of Business Ethics*, *38*(1-2), 91–96. doi:10.1023/A:1015712827640

Erdem, C. (2019). *Introduction to 21st century skills and education*. Retrieved from https://www.researchgate.net/publication/336148206_Introduction_to_21st_century_skills_and_education

Ērgle, D., & Ludviga, I. (2018). Use of gamification in human resource management: Impact on engagement and satisfaction. *Contemporary Business Management Challenges and Opportunities*, 409–417. doi:10.3846/bm.2018.45

Erickson, F. (1986). Qualitative Methods in Research on Teaching. In M. C. Wittrock (Ed.), *Handbook of Research on Teaching* (pp. 119–161). Macmillan.

Ermi, L., & Mäyrä, F. (2005). Fundamental components of the gameplay experience: Analysing immersion. *Proceedings of DiGRA 2005 Conference: Changing Views – Worlds in Play*.

Ernest, P. (1988). What's the use of LOGO? *Mathematics in School*, *17*(1), 16–20.

Erwig, M. (2017). *Once upon an algorithm: How stories explain computing*. MIT Press. doi:10.7551/mitpress/10786.001.0001

Compilation of References

Eryansyah, E., Erlina, E., Fiftinova, F., & Nurweni, A. (2019). EFL Students' Needs of Digital Literacy to Meet the Demands of 21stCentury Skills. *Indonesian Research Journal of Education*, 442–460.

Escudeiro, P., & de Carvalho, C. V. (2013). Game-based language learning. *International Journal of Information and Education Technology (IJIET)*, *3*(6), 643–647. doi:10.7763/IJIET.2013.V3.353

Eseryel, D., Law, V., Ifenthaler, D., Ge, X., & Miller, R. (2014). An investigation of the interrelationships between motivation, engagement, and complex problem solving in game-based learning. *Journal of Educational Technology & Society*, *17*(1), 42–53.

Esmaeili, H., & Woods, P. C. (2016). Calm down buddy! it's just a game: Behavioral patterns observed among teamwork MMO participants in WARGAMING's world of tanks. In *2016 22nd International Conference on Virtual System & Multimedia (VSMM)* (pp. 1-11). IEEE.

Esteves, M., Pereira, A., Veiga, N., Vasco, R., & Veiga, A. (2018). The Use of New Learning Technologies in Higher Education Classroom: A Case Study. In M. Auer, D. Guralnick, & I. Simonics (Eds.), *Teaching and Learning in a Digital World. ICL 2017. Advances in Intelligent Systems and Computing* (Vol. 715). Springer., doi:10.1007/978-3-319-73210-7_59

ET. (2008). 21st century learning: Research, innovation and policy. directions from recent OECD analyses. *OECD/CERI International Conference*.

EU Lifelong Learning Programme. (2011). *Production of Creative Game-Based Learning Scenarios: A Handbook for Teachers*. ProActive. https://bit.ly/3tJVKbq

European Commission (EC) & Gabinete de Comunicacion. (2009). *Study on the current trends and approaches to media literacy in Europe*. Authors.

Evoh, C. (2007). Policy networks and the transformation of secondary education through ICTs in Africa: The prospects and challenges of the NEPAD e-schools initiative. *International Journal of Education and Development Using Information and Communication Technology*, *3*(1), 64–84.

Eyebraingym. (2021). *Key Science*. eyebraingym. Retrieved from: https://www.eyebraingym.com/key-science/

Facer, K. (2011). *Learning futures: Education, technology and social change*. Routledge. doi:10.4324/9780203817308

Fachada, N. (2018). Teaching database concepts to video game design e development students. *Revista Lusófona de Educação*, *40*(40), 151–165. doi:10.24140/issn.1645-7250.rle40.10

Faculdade de Belas-Artes da Universidade de Lisboa. (2021). Retrieved October 4, 2021, from, http://www.belasartes.ulisboa.pt/

Fadel, C. (2008). *21st century skills: How can you prepare students for the new global economy?* https://www.oecd.org/site/educeri21st/40756908.pdf

Fadel, C., & Trilling, B. (2012). *21st Century Skills, Learning for Life in our Times*. Wiley.

Fahuzan, K., & Santosa, R. H. (2018). Gender Differences in Motivation to Learn Math Using Role Play Game in Smartphone. *Journal of Physics: Conference Series*, *1097*(1), 1–7. doi:10.1088/1742-6596/1097/1/012130

Fandiño Parra, Y. (2013). 21st century skills and the English foreign language classroom: A call for more awareness in Colombia. *Gist Education and Learning Research Journal*, *7*, 190–208.

Fang, X. Y., Dai, L. Q., Fang, C., & Deng, L. (2006). The relationship between parent-adolescent communication problems and adolescents' social adjustments. *Xinli Fazhan Yu Jiaoyu*, 2247–2252.

Fang, Y., Chen, K., & Huang, Y. (2016). Emotional reactions of different interface formats: Comparing digital and traditional board games. *Advances in Mechanical Engineering*, *8*(3), 1–8. doi:10.1177/1687814016641902

Fani, T., & Ghaemi, F. (2011). Implications of Vygotsky's Zone of Proximal Development (ZPD) in Teacher Education: ZPTD and Self-scaffolding. *Procedia: Social and Behavioral Sciences*, *29*, 1549–1554. doi:10.1016/j.sbspro.2011.11.396

Farber, M. (2015). *Gamify your classroom: A field guide to game-based learning*. Peter Lang. doi:10.3726/978-1-4539-1459-5

Favia, A., Comins, N. F., Thorpe, G. L., & Batuski, D. J. (2014). A direct examination of college student misconceptions in astronomy: A new instrument. *J. Rev. Astron. Educ. Outreach*, *1*(1), A21–A39.

February, P. J. (2018). *Teaching and learning to read in Afrikaans: Teacher competence and computer-assisted support*. University of Jyväskylä. http://urn.fi/URN:ISBN:978-951-39-7515-9

Federici, S., Molinas, J., Sergi, E., Lussu, R., & Gola, E. (2019). Rapid and easy prototyping of multimedia tools for education. *Proceedings of the World Conference on Media and Mass Communication*. 10.17501/24246778.2019.5102

Fedorov, A. (2003). Media Education and Media Literacy: Experts' Opinions. A Media Education Curriculum for Teachers in the Mediterranean, UNESCO.

Felix, J. W., & Johnson, R. T. (1993). Learning from video games. *Computers in the Schools*, *9*(2-3), 119–134. doi:10.1300/J025v09n02_11

Felten, P. (2008). *Visual Literacy*. Retrieved May 02, 2019 from http://one2oneheights.pbworks.com/f/Felten,P.(2008).Visual%20Literacy.pdf

Felton, E. L., & Sims, R. R. (2005). Teaching business ethics: Targeted outputs. *Journal of Business Ethics*, *60*(4), 377–391. doi:10.100710551-004-8206-3

Ferguson, C. J. (2015). Do Angry Birds make for angry children? A meta-analysis of video game influences on children's and adolescents' aggression, mental health, prosocial behavior, and academic performance. *Perspectives on Psychological Science*, *10*(5), 646–666. doi:10.1177/1745691615592234 PMID:26386002

Fernández-Batanero, J. M., Montenegro-Rueda, M., Fernández-Cerero, J., & García-Martínez, I. (2020). Digital competences for teacher professional development. Systematic review. *European Journal of Teacher Education*, 1–19. doi:10.1080/02619768.2020.1827389

Fernández, E., Ordóñez, E., Morales, B., & López, J. (2019). *La competencia digital en la docencia universitaria*. Octaedro.

Fernando, M., & Chowdhury, R. M. M. I. (2010). The relationship between spiritual well-being and ethical orientations in decision making: An empirical study with business executives in Australia. *Journal of Business Ethics*, *95*(2), 211–225. doi:10.100710551-009-0355-y

Ferreiro-González, M., Amores-Arrocha, A., Espada-Bellido, E., Aliano-Gonzalez, M. J., Vázquez-Espinosa, M., González-De-Peredo, A. V., Sancho-Galán, P., Álvarez-Saura, J. Á., Barbero, G. F., & Cejudo-Bastante, C. (2019). Escape ClassRoom: Can You Solve a Crime Using the Analytical Process? *Journal of Chemical Education*, *96*(2), 267–273. doi:10.1021/acs.jchemed.8b00601

Fhkps, B., Ho, W., Leung, E., Li, P., Mok, B., Shek, V., & Shek, E. (2021). Nurturing leadership qualities under COVID-19: Student perceptions of the qualities and effectiveness of online teaching and learning on leadership development. *International Journal of Child and Adolescent Health*, *14*(1), 89–100.

Compilation of References

Fichten, C. S., Asuncion, J., & Scapin, R. (2014). Digital Technology, Learning, and Postsecondary Students with Disabilities: Where We've Been and Where We're Going. *Journal of Postsecondary Education and Disability, 27*(4), 369–379.

Field, A. (2013). *Discovering statistics using IBM SPSS Statistics: And sex and drugs and rock 'n' roll* (4th ed.). Sage Publications.

Figueiredo, A. D. (2020). *Which School for Citizenship?* Retrieved January 14, 2020, from https://adfig.com/pt/?p=630

Filipe, A. (2019). Design of a Learning Framework for Open Mobile Applications. *Educ. foco. Juiz de Fora, 24*(1), 529-530.

Fine, G. A. (2002). *Shared Fantasy*. University of Chicago Press. https://press.uchicago.edu/ucp/books/book/chicago/S/bo5949823.html

Fine, G. A. (1983). *Shared fantasy: Role-playing games as social worlds*. The University of Chicago Press.

Finn, P. J. (1999). *Literacy with an attitude: Educating working-class children in their own self-interest*. State University of New York Press.

Fischer, H., Heinz, M., Schlenker, L., & Follert, F. (2016). Gamifying higher education. beyond badges, points and leaderboards. *Knowledge Communities in Online Education and, Visual Knowledge Management - Proceedings of 19th Conference GeNeMe 2016, as Part of IFKAD 2016*, 93–104.

Fischer, E., & Hänze, M. (2020). How do university teachers' values and beliefs affect their teaching? *Educational Psychology, 40*(3), 296–317. doi:10.1080/01443410.2019.1675867

Fishbach, A., Eyal, T., & Finkelstein, S. R. (2010). How positive and negative feedback motivate goal pursuit. *Social and Personality Psychology Compass, 4*(8), 517–530. doi:10.1111/j.1751-9004.2010.00285.x

Fitzgerald, M., Danaia, L., & McKinnon, D. H. (2019). Barriers inhibiting inquiry-based science teaching and potential solutions: Perceptions of positively inclined early adopters. *Research in Science Education, 49*(2), 543–566. doi:10.100711165-017-9623-5

Fitz-Walter, Z. J. (2015). Achievement unlocked: Investigating the design of effective gamification experiences for mobile applications and devices. School of Information Systems; Science & Engineering Faculty, Queensland University of Technology.

Flanagan, M. (2009). *Critical Play, Radical Game Design*. MIT Press. doi:10.7551/mitpress/7678.001.0001

Fleming, N. D., & Mills, C. (1992). Not Another Inventory, Rather a Catalyst for Reflection. *To Improve the Academy, 11*(1), 137-144.

Fleming, T. M., Bavin, L., Stasiak, K., Hermansson-Webb, E., Merry, S. N., Cheek, C., Lucassen, M., Lau, H. M., Pollmuller, B., & Hetrick, S. (2017). Serious games and gamification for mental health: Current status and promising directions. *Frontiers in Psychiatry, 7*. Advance online publication. doi:10.3389/fpsyt.2016.00215 PMID:28119636

Flores-Morador, F. (2013). *The beam in the eye: ICT, school and broken technologies* [La viga en el ojo: los nuevos medios de comunicación, la escuela y las tecnologías rotas]. Academic Press.

Floridi, L. (2014). *The Fourth Revolution: How the infosphere is reshaping human reality*. Oxford University Press.

Fong, C. J., Kim, Y., Davis, C. W., Hoang, T. V., & Kim, Y. W. (2017). A meta-analysis on critical thinking and community college student achievement. *Thinking Skills and Creativity, 26*, 71-83. .2017.06.002 doi:10.1016/j.tsc

Forbes. (2019). *Research Report Shows How Much Time We Spend Gaming*. Retrieved from https://www.forbes.com/sites/kevinanderton/2019/03/21/research-report-shows-how-much-time-we-spend-gaming-infographic/#1a9602d13e07

Ford, H., & Wajcman, J. (2017). 'Anyone can edit', not everyone does: Wikipedia's infrastructure and the gender gap. *Social Studies of Science*, *47*(4), 511–527. doi:10.1177/0306312717692172 PMID:28791929

Forsyth, D. R., O'Boyle, E. H. Jr, & McDaniel, M. A. (2008). East meets west: A meta-analytic investigation of cultural variations in idealism and relativism. *Journal of Business Ethics*, *83*(4), 813–833. doi:10.100710551-008-9667-6

Fortier, M. (2019). *The Power of a Gamified Classroom, Technology and Curriculum*. Retrieved from https://techandcurr2019.pressbooks.com/chapter/gamified-classroom/

Foster, A., & Shah, M. (2015). The Play Curricular Activity Reflection Discussion Model for Game-Based Learning. *Journal of Research on Technology in Education*, *47*(2), 71–88. doi:10.1080/15391523.2015.967551

Foster, A., & Shah, M. (2020). Principles for Advancing Game-Based Learning in Teacher Education. *Journal of Digital Learning in Teacher Education*, *36*(2), 84–95. doi:10.1080/21532974.2019.1695553

Fraillon, J., Ainley, J., Schulz, W., Duckworth, D., & Friedman, T. (2019). *IEA international computer and information literacy study 2018 assessment framework*. Springer Nature. doi:10.1007/978-3-030-19389-8

Francescato, D., Porcelli, R., Mebane, M., Cuddetta, M., Klobas, J., & Renzi, P. (2006). Evaluation of the efficacy of collaborative learning in face-to-face and computer-supported university contexts. *Computers in Human Behavior*, *22*(2), 163–176. doi:10.1016/j.chb.2005.03.001

Franciosi, S. J., Yagi, J., Tomoshige, Y., & Ye, S. (2016). The effect of a simple simulation game on long-term vocabulary retention. *CALICO Journal*, *33*(3), 355–379. doi:10.1558/cj.v33i2.26063

Francis, M. K., Wormington, S. V., & Hulleman, C. (2019). The Costs of Online Learning: Examining Differences in Motivation and Academic Outcomes in Online and Face-to-Face Community College Developmental Mathematics Courses. *Frontiers in Psychology*, *10*(September), 1–12. doi:10.3389/fpsyg.2019.02054 PMID:31551886

Franklin, R. M. (2004). *Moral Literacy: The Knowledge of Truth, Justice, Goodness and Interdependence*. Retrieved May 02, 2019 from https://c.ymcdn.com/sites/www.sais.org/resource/resmgr/imported/HC%2004%20Franklin.pdf

Fred Rogers Center for Early Learning and Children's Media at Saint Vincent College. (2012). *A framework for quality in digital media for young children: Considerations for parents, educators, and media creators*. https://cmhd.northwestern.edu/wp-content/uploads/2015/10/Framework_Statement_2-April_2012-Full_Doc-Exec_Summary-1.pdf

Fredricks, J. A., Blumenfeld, P. C., & Paris, A. H. (2004). School engagement: Potential of the concept, state of the evidence. *Review of Educational Research*, *74*(1), 59–109. https://doi.org/10.3102/00346543074001059

Freeman, A., Adams Becker, S., Cummins, M., Davis, A., & Hall Giesinger, C. (2017). *New Media Consortium (NMC)/Consortium of School Networking (CoSN) Horizon Report: 2017 K–12*. The New Media Consortium.

Freire, P. (1996). *Pedagogy of the oppressed* (New rev. ed). Penguin Books.

Freire, P., & Macedo, D. (1987). *Literacy: Reading the word and the world*. Bergin and Garvey.

Freire, P., & Macedo, D. (1987). *Literacy: Reading the Word and the World*. Bergin Garvey.

Freitas, S. de. (2006). *Learning in Immersive worlds: A review of game-based learning*. Academic Press.

Friedman, T. (2007). *The world is flat: A brief history of the twenty-first century*. Picador.

Frossard, F. (2013). *Fostering teachers' creativity through the creation of GBL scenarios* [Doctoral thesis, Universitat de Barcelona]. Departament de Didàctica i Organizació Educativa. http://hdl.handle.net/10803/130831

Frost, J. L., Wortham, S. C., & Reifel, S. (2012). *Play and child development* (4th ed.). Pearson Education Inc.

Compilation of References

Fucci, M. (2015, July 9). *The Digital Competence Framework 2.0*. EU Science Hub - European Commission. https://ec.europa.eu/jrc/en/digcomp/digital-competence-framework

Fulks, A., & Lord, B. (2016). Leveling up in a gamified classroom. *AMLE Magazine*, *3*(6), 41.

Fülöp, M. (2009). Happy and Unhappy Competitors: What Makes the Difference? *Psihologijske Teme*, *18*(2), 345–367.

Fundamentals of Management. (2021). *Students' reports on Fundamentals of Management* https://drive.google.com/drive/folders/1fhtTOTTeuWS-zzt7a31Eirbh7UQKQFsw?usp=sharing

Funk, J. B., Baldacci, H. B., Pasold, T., & Baumgardner, J. (2004). Violence exposure in real-life, video games, television, movies, and the internet: Is there desensitization? *Journal of Adolescence*, *27*(1), 23–39. doi:10.1016/j.adolescence.2003.10.005 PMID:15013258

Gainer, J. (2007). Social critique and pleasure: Critical media literacy with popular culture texts. *Language Arts*, *85*(2), 106–115.

Gains, P., & Parkes, A. (2012). *Report on the development, implementation and findings of the EGRA pilot in Hardap, Kavango and Oshikoto regions: November 2011-May 2012*. Academic Press.

Gallahue, D. L., & Donnelly, F. C. (2003). Movement skill acquisition. In *Developmental Physical Education for all Children* (4th ed.). Human Kinetics.

Galletta, D. F., Ahuja, M., Hartman, A., Teo, T., & Graham Peace, A. (1995). Social influence and end-user training. *Communications of the ACM*, *38*(7), 70–79. doi:10.1145/213859.214800

Galloway, A. R. (2006). Protocol. *Theory, Culture & Society*, *23*(2-3), 317–320. doi:10.1177/026327640602300241

Game Lab. Laboratório de Jogos. (2021). Retrieved October 4, 2021, from, https://labjogos.tecnico.ulisboa.pt/en https://www.facebook.com/LabJogosIST/

GameDevTecnico Students Twitter and Instagram links. (2021). Retrieved October 5, 2021, from, https://twitter.com/gamedevtecnico https://www.instagram.com/p/CGpvQ24KJKM/

GameDevTecnico. (2021). Retrieved October 4, 2021, from, https://gamedev.tecnico.ulisboa.pt/ https://gamedevtecnico.itch.io/

Garcia, M., Rabelo, D., Silva, D., & Amaral, S. (2011). Novas competências docentes frente às tecnologias digitais interativas. *Revista Teoria e Prática de Educação*, *14*(1), 79–87.

García-Redondo, P., García, T., Areces, D., Núñez, J. C., & Rodríguez, C. (2019). Serious Games and Their Effect Improving Attention in Students with Learning Disabilities. *International Journal of Environmental Research and Public Health*, *16*(14), 2480. doi:10.3390/ijerph16142480 PMID:31336804

Gardner, H., & Hatch, T. (1990). *Multiple intelligences go to school: educational implications of the theory of multiple intelligences*. Center for Children and Technology Technical Report. www.edc.org/cct/ccthome/reports/tr4.html

Gardner, H. (1983). *Frames of Mind: The Theory of Multiple Intelligences*. Basic Books.

Gardner, H. (1993). *Multiple Intelligences: The Theory in Practice*. Basic Books.

Garrido, P. C., Miraz, G. M., Ruiz, I. L., & Gomez-Nieto, M. (2011). *Use of NFC- based pervasive games for encouraging learning and student motivation*. doi:10.1109/NFC.2011.13

Garris, P. A., Collins, L. B., Jones, S. R., & Wightman, R. M. (1993). Evoked extracellular dopamine in vivo in the medial prefrontal cortex. *Journal of Neurochemistry*, *61*(2), 637–647. doi:10.1111/j.1471-4159.1993.tb02168.x PMID:8336146

Garris, R., Ahlers, R., & Driskell, J. E. (2002). Games, motivation and learning: A research and practice model. *Simulation & Gaming*, *33*(4), 441–467. doi:10.1177/1046878102238607

Garvey, C. (1990). *Play*. Harvard University Press.

Gatti, L., Ulrich, M., & Seele, P. (2019). Education for sustainable development through business simulation games: An exploratory study of sustainability gamification and its effects on students' learning outcomes. *Journal of Cleaner Production*, *207*, 667–678. doi:10.1016/j.jclepro.2018.09.130

Gauquier, E., & Schneider, J. (2013). Minecraft programs in the library: If you build it they will come. *Young Adult Library Services*, *11*(2), 17–19.

Gay, G. (2010). *Culturally responsive teaching: Theory, research, and practice*. Teachers College Press.

Geck, C. (2007). The generation Z connection: Teaching information literacy to the newest net generation. In E. Rosenfeld & D. V. Loertscher (Eds.), *Toward a 21st-century school library media program* (pp. 236–248). Scarecrow Press.

Gee, J. P. (2008). Learning and games. In K. Salen (Ed.) The Ecology of Games: Connecting Youth, Games, and Learning. John D. and Catherine T. MacArthur Foundation Series on Digital Media and Learning. Cambridge, MA: The MIT Press. 10.1162/dmal.9780262693646.021

Gee, J. P. (2010). A situated-sociocultural approach to literacy and technology. *The New Literacies: Multiple Perspectives on Research and Practice*, 165–193.

Gee, J. P., & Hayes, E. (2012). Nurturing affinity spaces and game-based learning. *Games, learning, and society: Learning and meaning in the digital age*, *123*, 1-40.

Gee, J. P., & Hayes, E. R. (2010). Passionate affinity groups. In Women and Gaming (pp. 105-123). Palgrave Macmillan. doi:10.1057/9780230106734_6

Gee, J. (1996). *Social linguistics and literacies: Ideology in discourses*. Falmer.

Gee, J. P. (2003). *What Video Games Have to Teach Us about Learning and Literacy*. Palgrave Macmillan. doi:10.1145/950566.950595

Gee, J. P. (2005). Learning by design: Good video games as learning machines. *E-Learning and Digital Media*, *2*(1), 5–16. doi:10.2304/elea.2005.2.1.5

Gee, J. P. (2007). *Good Video Games and Good Learning: Collected Essays on Video Games, Learning and Literacy*. P. Lang. doi:10.3726/978-1-4539-1162-4

Gee, J. P. (2007). *What video games have to teach us about learning and literacy?* Palgrave Macmillan.

Gee, J. P. (2009). *New digital media and learning as an emerging area and "worked examples" as one way forward*. MIT Press. doi:10.7551/mitpress/8563.001.0001

Gee, J. P. (2013). Games for learning. *Educational Horizons*, *91*(4), 16–20. doi:10.1177/0013175X1309100406

Gee, J. P. (2014). *Collected essays on learning and assessment in the digital world. The Learner series*. Common Ground. doi:10.18848/978-1-61229-424-7/CGP

Gee, J. P. (2014). *What video games have to teach us about learning and literacy*. MacMillan.

Gee, J. P. (2017). Affinity spaces and 21st-century learning. *Educational Technology*, 27–31.

Gee, J. P., & Hayes, E. R. (2010). *The Sims and 21st century learning*. Palgrave Macmillan., doi:10.1057/9780230106734

Compilation of References

Gee, J. P., Hull, G., & Lankshear, C. (2019). *The New Work Order: Behind the Language of the New Capitalism*. Routledge. doi:10.4324/9780429496127

Gee, J., & Hayes, E. (2012). Nurturing affinity spaces and game-based learning. In C. Steinkuehler, K. Squire, & S. A. Barab (Eds.), *Games, learning, and society: Learning and meaning in the digital age* (pp. 129–153). Cambridge University Press. doi:10.1017/CBO9781139031127.015

Gender Action, Mutual Learning Workshop on Gender and Digitalization. (2021). *Interactive Multimedia Experiences in Higher Education: Gaming, Augmented and Virtual Reality, and Research*. Retrieved October 4, 2021, from https://genderaction.eu/exploratory-mutual-learning-workshop-on-gender-and-digitalization/

Generate tables in MediaWiki format—TablesGenerator.com. (n.d.). Retrieved June 1, 2021, from https://www.tablesgenerator.com/mediawiki_tables

Genoni, M., Bhatta, S., & Sharma, U. (2019). Equity in education outcomes and spending in Bangladesh: Evidence from household income and expenditure surveys. *Bangladesh Development Studies*, *42*(2/3), 217–262. https://www.jstor.org/stable/27031112

Gentile, D. A., Anderson, C. A., Yukawa, S., Ihori, N., Saleem, M., Lim, K. M., Shibuya, A., Liau, A. K., Khoo, A., Bushman, B. J., Huesmann, L. R., & Sakamoto, A. (2009). The effects of prosocial video games on prosocial behaviors: International evidence from correlational, longitudinal, and experimental studies. *Personality and Social Psychology Bulletin*, *35*(6), 752–763. doi:10.1177/0146167209333045 PMID:19321812

Gentry, J., & McAdams, L. (2013). Digital Story Expressions: Blending Best Practices in Literacy and Technology with Middle School Students. In *Proceedings of Society for Information Technology and Teacher Education International Conference* (pp.4253-4257). Chesepake, VA: AACE. http://www.editlib.org/p/48794

Geo-politics and international power. (2017). *European Parliamentary Research Service European Parliament*. https://www.europarl.europa.eu/RegData/etudes/STUD/2017/603263/EPRS_STU(2017)603263_EN.pdf

Georgiou, G. K., Hirvonen, R., Liao, C.-H., Manolitsis, G., Parrila, R., & Nurmi, J.-E. (2011). The role of achievement strategies on literacy acquisition across languages. *Contemporary Educational Psychology*, *36*(2), 130–141. doi:10.1016/j.cedpsych.2011.01.001

Gerber, H. R. (2012). *Can education be gamified? Examining gamification, education, and the future*. Charles Town, WV: White paper for the American Public University System (APUS).

Gerber, H. R., Abrams, S. S., Onwuegbuzie, A. J., & Benge, C. L. (2014). From Mario to FIFA: What qualitative case study research suggests about games-based learning in a US classroom. *Educational Media International*, *51*(1), 16–34. doi:10.1080/09523987.2014.889402

Gerber, H. R., & Price, D. P. (2013). Fighting baddies and collecting bananas: Teachers' perceptions of games-based literacy learning. *Educational Media International*, *50*(1), 51–62. doi:10.1080/09523987.2013.777182

Geroimenko, V. (2019). Concluding Remarks: From Pokémon GO to Serious Augmented Reality Games. *Augmented Reality Games*, *2*, 305.

Ghavifekr, S., Razak, A. Z., Ghani, M. F., Ran, N. Y., Meixi, Y., & Tengyue, Z. (2014). ICT integration in education: Incorporation for teaching & learning improvement. *Malaysian Online Journal of Educational Technology*, *2*(2), 24–45.

Ghetti, S., & Bunge, S. A. (2012). Neural changes underlying the development of episodic memory during middle childhood. *Developmental Cognitive Neuroscience*, *2*(4), 381–395. doi:10.1016/j.dcn.2012.05.002 PMID:22770728

Giddens, A. (1991). *Modernity and self-identity: Self and society in the late modern age*. Stanford University Press.

Giddings, J., & Weinberg, J. (2020). Experiential Legal Education. Stepping Back to See the Future. In C. Denvir (Ed.), *Modernizing Legal Education* (pp. 38–56). Cambridge University Press. doi:10.1017/9781108663311.004

Gilbert, N. (2020). *Number of gamers worldwide: Demographics, statistics, and predictions*. Finances Online. Retrieved 9/14/21 from https://financesonline.com/number-of-gamers-worldwide/

Gilbert, A., Tait-MCutcheon, S., & Knewstubb, B. (2021). Innovative teaching in higher education: Teachers' perceptions of support and constraint. *Innovations in Education and Teaching International*, *58*(2), 123–134. doi:10.1080/14703297.2020.1715816

Gilboy, M. B., Heinerichs, S., & Pazzaglia, G. (2015). Enhancing student engagement using the flipped classroom. *Journal of Nutrition Education and Behavior*, *47*(1), 109–114. doi:10.1016/j.jneb.2014.08.008 PMID:25262529

Gillispie, L., Martin, F., & Parker, M. (2009). Effects of the Dimension-M 3D Video Gaming Experience on Middle School Student Achievement and Attitude in Mathematics. In *Society for Information Technology & Teacher Education International Conference*. Society for Information Technology & Teacher Education.

Gills, A. S. (2020). *Definition: Digital native*. Teach Target. https://whatis.techtarget.com/definition/digital-native

Gingerich, J. (2012). The *spiraling narrative*. Litreactor LLC. https://litreactor.com/columns/the-spiraling-theme

Giordano, V. A. (2007). A professional development model to promote Internet integration into p-12 teachers' practice: A mixed methods study. *Computers in the Schools*, *24*(3–4), 111–123. doi:10.1300/J025v24n03_08

Giovetti, O. (2020). *How does education affect poverty? It can help end it*. Concern Worldwide. https://www.concernusa.org/story/how-education-affects-poverty/

Girl, R. (2017, February 14). *How to play Love Letter in 3 minutes* [Video]. YouTube. https://www.youtube.com/watch?v=WAiI7G3QdOU

Glock, C. Y., & Stark, R. (1965). *Religion and Society in Tension, Rand McNally Sociology Series*. Rand McNally & Company.

Glock, S., & Kleen, H. (2020). Preservice teachers' attitudes, attributions, and stereotypes: Exploring the disadvantages of students from families with low socioeconomic status. *Studies in Educational Evaluation*, *67*(October), 1–9. doi:10.1016/j.stueduc.2020.100929

Glover, I. (2013). Play As You Learn: Gamification as a Technique for Motivating Learners. *Proceedings of World Conference on Educational Multimedia, Hypermedia and Telemcommunications*, 1999–2008. http://shura.shu.ac.uk/7172/

Glover, I. (2013). Play as you learn: Gamification as a technique for motivating learners. In *Proceedings of World Conference on Educational Multimedia, Hypermedia and Telecommunications*. AACE.

Goffman, E. (1974). *Frame analysis: An essay on the organization of experience*. Harper & Row.

Gomes, C., Pereira, A., & Nobre, A. (2018). *Gamificação no ensino superior online: dois exemplos. LE@D - Laboratório de Educação a Distância e Elearning*. Universidade Aberta.

Gómez-Gonzalvo, F., Molina Alventosa, P., & Devis, J. (2018). Los videojuegos como materiales curriculares: una aproximación a su uso en Educación Física / Video games as curriculum materials: an approach to their use in Physical Education. *Retos*, *34*(34), 305–310. doi:10.47197/retos.v0i34.63440

González, C. S., & Mora, A. (2014). Methodological proposal for Gamification in the computer engineering teaching. *Proceeding Computers in Education (SIIE), 2014 International Symposium on*, 29-34. 10.1109/SIIE.2014.7017700

Compilation of References

González-González, C., & Blanco-Izquierdo, F. (2012). Designing social video-games for educational uses. *Computers & Education*, *58*(1), 250–262. doi:10.1016/j.compedu.2011.08.014

Gonzalez, L., & Kardong-Edgren, S. (2017). Deliberate Practice for Mastery Learning in Nursing. *Clinical Simulation in Nursing*, *13*(1), 10–14. doi:10.1016/j.ecns.2016.10.005

Gonzalo-Iglesia, J. L., Lozano-Monterrubio, N., & Prades-Tena, J. (2018). Non Educational board games in university education. Perceptions of students experiencing game-based learning methodologies. *Revista Lusófona de Educação*, *41*(41), 45–62. doi:10.24140/issn.1645-7250.rle41.03

Gooch, D., Vasalou, A., & Benton, L. (2015). Exploring the use of a Gamification Platform to Support Students with Dyslexia. In *Information, Intelligence, Systems and Applications (IISA), 2015, 6th International Conference on* (pp. 1-6). IEEE. 10.1109/IISA.2015.7388001

Gooch, D., Vasalou, A., Benton, L., & Khaled, R. (2016). *Using Gamification to motivate students with dyslexia*. doi:10.1145/2858036.2858231

Goodman, S. (2003). *Teaching youth media: A critical guide to literacy, video production, and social change*. Teachers College Press.

Goodson, M. (1976). *Family Feud* [Game Show Series]. ABC.

Goosen, L. (2018a). Sustainable and Inclusive Quality Education Through Research Informed Practice on Information and Communication Technologies in Education. In L. Webb (Ed.), *Proceedings of the 26th Conference of the Southern African Association for Research in Mathematics, Science and Technology Education (SAARMSTE)* (pp. 215 - 228). Gabarone: University of Botswana.

Goosen, L. (2019c). Information Systems and Technologies Opening New Worlds for Learning to Children with Autism Spectrum Disorders. Smart Innovation, Systems and Technologies, 111, 134-143. doi:10.1007/978-3-030-03577-8_16

Goosen, L. (2019d). Innovative Technologies and Learning in a Massive Open Online Course. In L. Rønningsbakk, T.-T. Wu, F. E. Sandnes, & Y.-M. Huang (Eds.), Lecture Notes in Computer Science (Vol. 11937, pp. 653–662). Springer. doi:10.1007/978-3-030-35343-8_69

Goosen, L., & Van der Merwe, R. (2015). e-Learners, Teachers and Managers at e-Schools in South Africa. In C. Watson (Ed.), *Proceedings of the 10th International Conference on e-Learning (ICEL)* (pp. 127 - 134). Nassau: Academic Conferences and Publishing International.

Goosen, L., & Van der Merwe, R. (2017). Keeping ICT in Education Community Engagement Relevant: Infinite Possibilities? Communications in Computer and Information Science, 730, 113 - 127. doi:10.1007/978-3-319-69670-6_8

Goosen, L., & Van Heerden, D. (2013). Project-Based Assessment Influencing Pass Rates of an ICT Module at an ODL Institution. In E. Ivala (Ed.), *Proceedings of the 8th International Conference on e-Learning*. Academic Conferences and Publishing.

Goosen, L., & Van Heerden, D. (2017). Beyond the Horizon of Learning Programming with Educational Technologies. In U. I. Ogbonnaya, & S. Simelane-Mnisi (Ed.), *Proceedings of the South Africa International Conference on Educational Technologies* (pp. 78 - 90). Pretoria: African Academic Research Forum.

Goosen, L. (2008). A Brief History of Choosing First Programming Languages. In J. Impagliazzo (Ed.), *History of Computing and Education 3* (Vol. 269, pp. 167–170). Springer. doi:10.1007/978-0-387-09657-5_11

Goosen, L. (2018b). Trans-Disciplinary Approaches to Action Research for e-Schools, Community Engagement, and ICT4D. In T. A. Mapotse (Ed.), *Cross-Disciplinary Approaches to Action Research and Action Learning* (pp. 97–110). IGI Global. doi:10.4018/978-1-5225-2642-1.ch006

Goosen, L. (2018c). Ethical Data Management and Research Integrity in the Context of e-Schools and Community Engagement. In C. Sibinga (Ed.), *Ensuring Research Integrity and the Ethical Management of Data* (pp. 14–45). IGI Global. doi:10.4018/978-1-5225-2730-5.ch002

Goosen, L. (2018d). Ethical Information and Communication Technologies for Development Solutions: Research Integrity for Massive Open Online Courses. In C. Sibinga (Ed.), *Ensuring Research Integrity and the Ethical Management of Data* (pp. 155–173). IGI Global. doi:10.4018/978-1-5225-2730-5.ch009

Goosen, L. (2019a). Research on Technology-Supported Teaching and Learning for Autism. In L. Makewa, B. Ngussa, & J. Kuboja (Eds.), *Technology-Supported Teaching and Research Methods for Educators* (pp. 88–110). IGI Global. doi:10.4018/978-1-5225-5915-3.ch005

Goosen, L. (2019b). Technology-Supported Teaching and Research Methods for Educators: Case Study of a Massive Open Online Course. In L. Makewa, B. Ngussa, & J. Kuboja (Eds.), *Technology-Supported Teaching and Research Methods for Educators* (pp. 128–148). IGI Global. doi:10.4018/978-1-5225-5915-3.ch007

Goosen, L. (2022). Assistive Technologies for Children and Adolescents With Autism Spectrum Disorders. In F. Stasolla (Ed.), *Assistive Technologies for Assessment and Recovery of Neurological Impairments* (pp. 1–24). IGI Global. doi:10.4018/978-1-7998-7430-0.ch001

Goosen, L., Mentz, E., & Nieuwoudt, H. (2007). Choosing the "Best" Programming Language?! In E. Cohen (Ed.), *Proceedings of the 2007 Computer Science and IT Education Conference* (pp. 269-282). Informing Science Press.

Goradia, T. (2018). Role of educational technologies utilizing the TPACK framework and 21st century pedagogies: Academics' perspectives. *IAFOR Journal of Education, 6*(3), 43–61. doi:10.22492/ije.6.3.03

Gorbanev, I., Agudelo-Londoño, S., González, R. A., Cortes, A., Pomares, A., Delgadillo, V., Yepes, F. J., & Muñoz, Ó. (2018). A systematic review of serious games in medical education: Quality of evidence and pedagogical strategy. *Medical Education Online, 23*(1), 1438718. doi:10.1080/10872981.2018.1438718 PMID:29457760

Gordon, G., Spaulding, S., Westlund, J. K., Lee, J. J., Plummer, L., Martinez, M., . . . Breazeal, C. (2016, March). Affective personalization of a social robot tutor for children's second language skills. In *Proceedings of the AAAI conference on artificial intelligence* (Vol. 30, No. 1). https://ojs.aaai.org/index.php/AAAI/article/view/9914

Gough, C. (2019, August 9). *Number of active players of Minecraft worldwide as of October 2018 (in millions)*. Retrieved from https://www.statista.com/statistics/680139/minecraft-active-players-worldwide/

Gouveia, P. (2010). Artes e Jogos Digitais, Estética e Design da Experiência Lúdica. Universitárias Lusófonas.

Gouveia, P. (2014). A possible narration about Portuguese videogames creation. Critical book review: *Videogames in Portugal: History, Technology and Art*, Nelson Zagalo, 2013. *Aniki, Portuguese Journal of the Moving Image, 1*(2), 369-74. doi:10.14591/aniki.v1n2.69

Gouveia, P. (2015). Serious gaming: how gamers are solving real world problems. In *Proceedings of Artech 2015, Seventh International Conference on Digital Arts (Creating Digital e-motions)*. Óbidos

Gouveia, P. (2018). Transmedia experiences that blur the boundaries between the real and the fictional world. In Trends, Experiences, and Perspectives on Immersive Multimedia Experience and Augmented Reality. IGI Global.

Gouveia, P. (2020). The New Media vs. Old Media Trap: How Contemporary Arts Became Playful Transmedia Environments. In Multidisciplinary Perspectives on New Media Art. IGI Global. doi:10.4018/978-1-7998-3669-8.ch002

Gouveia, P., Lima, L., Unterholzner, A., & Carvalho, D. (2021). *O mundo expandido das imagens invisíveis*. Instituto de Estudos Filosóficos, Faculdade de Letras da Universidade de Coimbra.

Gozcu, E., & Caganaga, C. K. (2016). The importance of using games in EFL classrooms. *Cypriot Journal of Educational Sciences*, *11*(3), 126–135. doi:10.18844/cjes.v11i3.625

Graber, D., & Mendoza, K. (2012). New Media Literacy Education: A Developmental Approach The national association for media literacy education. *The Journal of Media Literacy Education*, *4*(1), 82–92.

Graddol, D. (2006). *English next*. British Council Publications.

Grafstein, A. (2002). A discipline-based approach to information literacy. *Journal of Academic Librarianship*, *28*(4), 197–204. doi:10.1016/S0099-1333(02)00283-5

Gray, P. (2013). Free to Learn: Why Unleashing the Instinct to Play Will Make Our Children Happier. *More Self-Reliant, and Better Students for Life*, *141*.

Gray, K. L. (2020). *Intersectional Tech, Black Users in Digital Gaming*. Louisiana State University Press.

Greco, A., & Morris, T. (2002). Parental child-rearing style and child social anxiety: Investigation of child perceptions and actual father behavior. *Journal of Psychopathology and Behavioral Assessment*, *24*(4), 259–267. doi:10.1023/A:1020779000183

Greene, M. (1995). *Releasing the imagination: Essays on education, the arts, and social change*. Jossey-Bass. doi:10.1080/14452294.2011.11649524

Greene, M. (2001). *Variations on a blue guitar: The Lincoln Centre Institute lectures on aesthetic education*. Teachers College Press.

Greenfield, P. M. (1994). Video games as cultural artefacts. *Journal of Applied Developmental Psychology*, *15*(1), 3–12. doi:10.1016/0193-3973(94)90003-5

Greenfield, P. M., Camaioni, L., Ercolani, P., Weiss, L., Lauber, B. A., & Perucchini, P. (1994). Cognitive socialization by computer games in two cultures: Inductive discovery or mastery of an iconic code. *Journal of Applied Developmental Psychology*, *15*(1), 59–85. doi:10.1016/0193-3973(94)90006-X

Greipl, S., Klein, E., Lindstedt, A., Kiili, K., Moeller, K., Karnath, H. O., & Ninaus, M. (2021). When the brain comes into play: Neurofunctional correlates of emotions and reward in game-based learning. *Computers in Human Behavior*, *125*, 106946. doi:10.1016/j.chb.2021.106946

Greipl, S., Moeller, K., & Ninaus, M. (2020). Potential and limits of game-based learning. *International Journal of Technology Enhanced Learning*, *12*(4), 363–389. doi:10.1504/IJTEL.2020.110047

Greitemeyer, T., & Osswald, S. (2009). Prosocial video games reduce aggressive cognitions. *Journal of Experimental Social Psychology*, *45*(4), 896–900. doi:10.1016/j.jesp.2009.04.005

Greitemeyer, T., & Osswald, S. (2010). Effects of prosocial video games on prosocial behavior. *Journal of Personality and Social Psychology*, *98*(2), 211–221. doi:10.1037/a0016997 PMID:20085396

Griffin, M. (1964). *Jeopardy!* [Game Show Series]. NBC.

Griffith, J. (2014). *Teaching Literacy in the Digital Age: İnspiration For All Levels And Literacies* (M. Gura, Ed.). İnternational Society for Technology in Education.

Griffiths, M. D. (2002). The educational benefits of videogames. *Education for Health, 20*(3), 47–51.

Gros, B. (2010). Game-based learning: A strategy to integrate digital games in schools. In J. Yamamoto, J. Kush, R. Lombard, & C. Hertzog (Eds.), Technology Implementation and Teacher Education: Reflective Models (pp. 365-379). doi:10.4018/978-1-61520-897-5.ch021

Gros, B. (2007). Digital games in education: The design of games-based learning environments. *Journal of Research on Technology in Education, 40*(1), 23–38. doi:10.1080/15391523.2007.10782494

Group, N. P. D. (2020, December 7). *Evolution of entertainment: Spotlight on video games* [Video]. YouTube. https://youtu.be/lrPiK506umQ

Grove, F. De, Cornillie, F., Mechant, P., & Looy, J. Van. (2013). *Tapping into the Field of Foreign Language Learning Games. April 2014.* doi:10.1504/IJART.2013.050690

Grover, S., & Pea, R. (2017). Computational Thinking: A Competency Whose Time Has Come. Computer science education: Perspectives on teaching and learning in school, 19.

Growth Engineering. (2021). *Growth Engineering.* Retrieved from https://www.growthengineering.co.uk/how-to-use-the-octalysis-framework-for-your-gamified-training-programme/

Grubic, N., Badovinac, S., & Johri, A. M. (2020). Student mental health in the midst of the COVID-19 pandemic: A call for further research and immediate solutions. *The International Journal of Social Psychiatry, 66*(5), 517–518. doi:10.1177/0020764020925108 PMID:32364039

Grussendorf, S. (2021). *Game-based Learning.* Retrieved from https://lse.atlassian.net/wiki/spaces/MG2/pages/1427144719/Game-based+learning#Benefits

Guigon, G., Humeau, J., & Vermeulen, M. (2018). A model to design learning escape games: SEGAM. *CSEDU 2018 - Proceedings of the 10th International Conference on Computer Supported Education, 2*(March), 191–197. 10.5220/0006665501910197

Guillemin, M., & Gillam, L. (2010). Ethics, reflexivity, and "ethically important moments" in research. *Qualitative Inquiry, 10*(2), 261–280. doi:10.1177/1077800403262360

Gui, M. (2007). Formal and substantial Internet information skills: The role of socio-demographic differences on the possession of different components of digital literacy. *First Monday, 12*(9). Advance online publication. doi:10.5210/fm.v12i9.2009

Gumulak, S., & Webber, S. (2011). Playing video games: Learning and information literacy. In *Aslib Proceedings.* Emerald Group Publishing Limited. doi:10.1108/00012531111135682

Gündüz, A. Y., & Akkoyunlu, B. (2020). Effectiveness of Gamification in Flipped Learning. *SAGE Open, 10*(4). doi:10.1177/2158244020979837

Güngör, N. (2018). İletişim Kuram ve Yaklaşımlar. Ankara: Siyasal Kitabevi.

Gunter, G. A., Kenny, R. F., & Vick, E. H. (2008). Taking educational games seriously: Using the RETAIN model to design endogeneous fantasy into standalone educational games. *Educational Technology Research and Development, 56*(5-6), 511–537. doi:10.100711423-007-9073-2

Compilation of References

Gupta, M., & Boyd, L. (2011). An Excel-based dice game: An integrative learning activity in operations management. *International Journal of Operations & Production Management*, *31*(6), 608–630. doi:10.1108/01443571111131962

Gurian, M., & Stevens, K. (2010a). *Boys and girls learn differently! A guide for teachers and parents*. Jossey-Bass.

Gurian, M., & Stevens, K. (2010b). *The minds of boys: Saving our sons from falling behind in school and life*. Jossey-Bass.

Guthrie, J. T., & Knowles, K. T. (2001). Promoting reading motivation. In L. Verhoeven & C. Snow (Eds.), *Literacy and motivation* (pp. 159–176). Erlbaum.

Guyton, G. (2011). Using Toys to Support Infant-Toddler Learning and Development. *Young Children*, *66*, 50.

Habershon, N. (1993). Metaplan (R): Achieving Two-way Communications. *Journal of European Industrial Training*, *17*(7). doi:10.1108/03090599310042528

Habgood, M. P. J., & Ainsworth, S. E. (2011). Motivating children to learn effectively: Exploring the value of intrinsic integration in educational games. *Journal of the Learning Sciences*, *20*(2), 169–206. doi:10.1080/10508406.2010.508029

Hackbarth, G., Grover, V., & Yi Mun, Y. (2003). Computer playfulness and anxiety: Positive and negative mediators of the system experience effect on perceived ease of use. *Information & Management*, *40*(3), 221–232. doi:10.1016/S0378-7206(02)00006-X

Hainey, T., Connolly, T. M., Stansfield, M., & Boyle, E. A. (2011). Evaluation of a Game to Teach Requirements Collection and Analysis in Software Engineering at Tertiary Education Level. *Computers & Education*, *56*(1), 21–35. doi:10.1016/j.compedu.2010.09.008

Haktanir, A., Watson, J. C., Ermis-Demirtas, H., Karaman, M. A., Freeman, P. D., Kumaran, A., & Streeter, A. (2018). Resilience, academic self-concept, and college adjustment among first-year students. *Journal of College Student Retention*, *38*, 286–297. doi:10.1177/1521025118810666

Hales, A. (2012). *Using Systematic and Engaging Early Literacy instruction and digital books to teach at-risk kindergarteners to read target words* [Unpublished master's thesis]. Brigham Young University, Provo, UT, United States.

Halfaker, A., Kittur, A., & Riedl, J. (2011). Don't bite the newbies: How reverts affect the quantity and quality of Wikipedia work. *Proceedings of the 7th International Symposium on Wikis and Open Collaboration - WikiSym '11*, 163. 10.1145/2038558.2038585

Halim, A., & Syukri, M. (2020). Integration of Problem Based Learning (PBL) and Engineering is Elementary (EiE) to improve students' creativity. *Journal of Physics: Conference Series*, *1460*(1), 012117.

Halinen, I. (2018). The new educational curriculum in Finland. In M. Matthes, L. Pulkkinen, C. Clouder, & B. Heys (Eds.), *Improving the quality of childhood in Europe* (Vol. 7, pp. 75–89). Alliance for Childhood European Network Foundation. https://www.allianceforchildhood.eu/files/Improving_the_quality_of_Childhood_Vol_7/QOC%20V7%20CH06%20DEF%20WEB.pdf

Hall, D., & Ames, R. (1987). *Thinking through Confucius. SUNY Series in Systematic Philosophy*. State University of New York Press.

Halliday, M., & Halliday, M. (1973). *Explorations in the functions of language*. Edward Arnold.

Hallifax, S., Serna, A., Marty, J. C., & Lavou, E. (2019). Adaptive gamification in education: A literature review of current trends and developments. *European Conference on Technology Enhanced Learning (EC-TEL)*, 294-307. 10.1007/978-3-030-29736-7_22

Hallinen, N., Walker, E., Wylie, R., Ogan, A., & Jones, C. (2009). I Was Playing When I Learned: A Narrative Game for French Aspectual Distinctions. *Proc. Workshop Intelligent Educational Games at the 14th Int'l Conf. Artificial Intelligence in Education*, 117-120.

Hall, S., & Gay, P. (1996). *Questions of cultural identity*. Sage.

Hall, T. E., Hughes, C. A., & Filbert, M. (2000). Computer assisted instruction in reading for students with learning disabilities: A research synthesis. *Education & Treatment of Children*, *23*(2), 173–193. http://eric.ed.gov.ezp-prod1.hul.harvard.edu/ERICWebPortal/search/detailmini.jsp?_nfpb=true&_&ERICExtSearch_SearchValue_0=EJ611303&ERICExtSearch_SearchType_0=no&accno=EJ611303

Halvorsen, A. (2018). *21st Century Skills and the "4Cs" in the English Language Classroom*, University of Oregon. https://creativecommons.org/licenses/by/4.0/

Hamann, S. (2001). Cognitive and neural mechanisms of emotional memory. *Trends in Cognitive Sciences*, *5*(9), 394–400. doi:10.1016/S1364-6613(00)01707-1 PMID:11520704

Hamari, J. (2019). Gamification. *The Blackwell encyclopedia of sociology*, 1–3.

Hamari, J., Koivisto, J., & Sarsa, H. (2014). Does gamification work? A literature review of empirical studies on gamification. *2014 47th Hawaii International Conference on System Sciences*, 3025-3034. 10.1109/HICSS.2014.377

Hamari, J., Koivisto, J., & Sarsa, H. (2014, January). Does gamification work? - A literature review of empirical studies on gamification. In *2014 47th Hawaii International Conference on System Sciences* (pp. 3025–3034). New York: IEEE.

Hamari, J., & Nousiainen, T. (2015). Why Do Teachers Use Game-Based Learning Technologies? The Role of Individual and Institutional ICT Readiness. *Hawaii International Conference on System Sciences*. 10.1109/HICSS.2015.88

Hamari, J., Shernoff, D. J., Rowe, E., Coller, B., Asbell-Clarke, J., & Edwards, T. (2016). Challenging games help students learn: An empirical study on engagement, flow and immersion in game-based learning. *Computers in Human Behavior*, *54*, 170–179. doi:10.1016/j.chb.2015.07.045

Hamburger, Y., & Ben-Artzi, E. (2003). Loneliness and Internet use. *Computers in Human Behavior*, *19*(1), 71–80. doi:10.1016/S0747-5632(02)00014-6

Hammerschall, U. (2019). A Gamification Framework for Long-Term Engagement in Education Based on Self Determination Theory and the Transtheoretical Model of Change. In *2019 IEEE Global Engineering Education Conference (EDUCON)* (pp. 95-101). IEEE. 10.1109/EDUCON.2019.8725251

Hamm, J. M., Perry, R. P., Chipperfield, J. G., Parker, P. C., & Heckhausen, J. (2019). A motivation treatment to enhance goal engagement in online learning environments: Assisting failure-prone college students with low optimism. *Motivation Science*, *5*(2), 116–134. doi:10.1037/mot0000107

Hammond, M., & Ross, M. (2014). *The Student Guide to Mooting*. Edinburgh University Press.

Hamzah, W. M., Ali, N., Saman, M., Yusoff, M. H., & Yacob, A. (2015). Influence of Gamification on Students' Motivation in using E-Learning Applications Based on the Motivational Design Model. *International Journal of Emerging Technologies in Learning*, *10*(2), 30–34. doi:10.3991/ijet.v10i2.4355

Hanbidge, A. S., Tin, T., & Sanderson, N. (2018). Information Literacy Skills on the Go: Mobile Learning Innovation. *Journal of Information Literacy*, *12*(1).

Hancock, D., Sirizzotti, M. S., Joe, R., & Martin, R. J. (2019). *Methods and systems for gamification*. U.S. Patent Application No. 15/466,379.

Compilation of References

Hanghøj, T., Nielsen, B. L., Skott, C. K., & Ejsing-Duun, S. (2020). Teacher agency and dialogical positions in relation to game-based design activities. *Proceedings of the European Conference on Games-Based Learning*, 234–241. 10.34190/GBL.20.033

Hanse-Himarwa, K. (2015). *State of Education*. Arts and Culture Address.

Hantzopoulos, M., Rivera-McCutchen, R. L., & Tyner-Mullings, A. R. (2021). Reframing School Culture Through Project-Based Assessment Tasks: Cultivating Transformative Agency and Humanizing Practices in NYC Public Schools. *Teachers College Record*, *123*(4), 1–38. doi:10.1177/016146812112300404

Hanus, M. D., & Fox, J. (2015). Assessing the effects of Gamification in the Classroom: A longitudinal study on intrinsic motivation, social comparison, satisfaction, effort, and academic performance. *Computers & Education*, *80*, 152–161. doi:10.1016/j.compedu.2014.08.019

Happ, C., Melzer, A., & Steffgen, G. (2014). Like the good or bad guy—Empathy in antisocial and prosocial games. *Psychology of Popular Media Culture*, *4*(2), 80–96. doi:10.1037/ppm0000021

Haque, M. S., & Akter, T. (2013). Cultural imperialism in English medium schools: A critical insight. *Stamford Journal of English*, *7*, 98–128. doi:10.3329je.v7i0.14468

Harada, V. H., & Yoshina, J. M. (2004). *Inquiry learning through librarian-teacher partnerships*. Linworth Publishing.

Hardy, C., & Tolhurst, D. (2014). Epistemological beliefs and cultural diversity matters in management education and learning: A critical review and future directions. *Academy of Management Learning & Education*, *13*(2), 265–289. doi:10.5465/amle.2012.0063

Harel, I. E., & Papert, S. E. (1991). *Constructionism*. Ablex Publishing.

Harman, K., Koohang, A., & Paliszkiewicz, J. (2014). Scholarly interest in gamification: A citation network analysis. *Industrial Management & Data Systems*, *114*(9), 1438–1452. doi:10.1108/IMDS-07-2014-0208

Harmer, N. (2014). *Project-based learning. Literature review. School of Geography, Earth and Environmental Sciences*. Plymouth University.

Harrop, M., Gibbs, M., & Carter, M. (2013). The pretence awareness contexts and oscillating nature of coaching frames. *Proceedings of DiGRA 2013 Conference: DeFragging Game Studies*.

Hart, A. (2013). *Kindergarteners' incidental learning of words during exposure to systematic and engaging early literacy instruction and digital books* [Unpublished honors thesis]. Brigham Young University, Provo, UT, United States.

Harteveld, C., Smith, G., Carmichael, G., Gee, E., & Stewart-Gardiner, C. (2013). A design- focused analysis of games that teach computer science. *Journal of Computing Sciences in Colleges*, *28*(6), 90–97.

Hartman, V. (1995). Teaching and learning style preferences: Transitions through technology. *VCCA Journal*, *9*(2), 18–20.

Hartshorne, J. K., & Germine, L. T. (2015). When does cognitive functioning peak. *The asynchronous rise and fall of different cognitive abilities across the life span*, *26*, 433-443.

Hartt, M., Hosseini, H., & Mostafapour, M. (2020). Game On: Exploring the Effectiveness of Game-based Learning. *Planning Practice and Research*, *35*(5), 589–604. doi:10.1080/02697459.2020.1778859

Harvey, M. M. (2018). *Video games and virtual reality as classroom literature: Thoughts, experiences, and learning with 8th grade middle school students* (Doctoral dissertation). https://digitalrepository.unm.edu/educ_llss_etds/90/

Harvey, M. M., & Marlatt, R. (2020). That was then, this is now: Literacies for the 21st Century classroom. In E. Podovšovnik (Ed.), *Examining the roles of teachers and students in mastering new technologies* (pp. 164–183). IGI Global. doi:10.4018/978-1-7998-2104-5.ch008

Hasana, S. N., & Alifiani, A. (2019). Multimedia development using visual basic for application (VBA) to improve students' learning motivation in studying mathematics of economics. *Indonesian Journal of Mathematics Education*, 2(1), 34–42. doi:10.31002/ijome.v2i1.1230

Hasan, K., Islam, M. S., Shams, A. T., & Gupta, H. (2018). Total quality management (TQM): Implementation in primary education system of Bangladesh. *International Journal of Research in Industrial Engineering*, 7(3), 370–380. doi:10.22105/RIEJ.2018.128170.1041

Hassan, L., Dias, A., & Hamari, J. (2019). How motivational feedback increases user's benefits and continued use: A study on Gamification, quantified-self and social networking. *International Journal of Information Management*, 46, 151–162. doi:10.1016/j.ijinfomgt.2018.12.004

Hassan, M. A., Habiba, U., Majeed, F., & Shoaib, M. (2021). Adaptive gamification in e-learning based on students' learning styles. *Interactive Learning Environments*, 29(4), 545–565. doi:10.1080/10494820.2019.1588745

Hattie, J. (2009). *Visible learning: A synthesis of over 800 meta-analyses relating to achievement*. Routledge.

Hattie, J. A. C. (2008). *Visible Learning: A synthesis of over 800 meta-analyses relating to achievement*. Routledge. doi:10.4324/9780203887332

Hawley, P. H. (2014). Evolution, prosocial behavior, and altruism: A roadmap for understanding where the proximate meets the ultimate. In L. M. Padilla-Walker & G. Carlo (Eds.), *Prosocial development: A multidimensional approach* (pp. 43–69). Oxford University Press. doi:10.1093/acprof:oso/9780199964772.003.0003

Hayak, M., & Avidov-Ungar, O. (2020). The Integration of Digital Game-Based Learning into the Instruction: Teachers' Perceptions at Different Career Stages. *TechTrends*, 64(6), 887–898. doi:10.100711528-020-00503-6

Hayes, E. (2008). Girls, gaming and trajectories of IT expertise. In Beyond Barbie and Mortal Kombat: New perspectives on gender and computer games (pp.138-194). Cambridge MA: The MIT Press.

Hayes, E. R., & Games, I. A. (2008). Making computer games and design thinking: A review of current software and strategies. *Games and Culture*, 3(3-4), 309–332. doi:10.1177/1555412008317312

Hayes, E. R., & Gee, J. P. (2010). No selling the genie lamp: A game literacy practice in The Sims. *E-Learning and Digital Media*, 7(1), 67–78. doi:10.2304/elea.2010.7.1.67

Hebert, C., & Jenson, J. (2019). Digital game-based pedagogies: Developing teaching strategies for game-based learning. *Journal of Interactive Technology and Pedagogy, 15*.

Hébert, C., Jenson, J., & Terzopoulos, T. (2021). Access to technology is the major challenge: Teacher perspectives on barriers to DGBL in K-12 classrooms. *E-Learning and Digital Media*, 18(3), 307–324. doi:10.1177/2042753021995315

Heeter, C. (1992). Being there: The subjective experience of presence. *Presence (Cambridge, Mass.)*, 1(2), 262–271. doi:10.1162/pres.1992.1.2.262

Heinich, R., Molenda, M., Russell, J. D., & Smaldino, S. E. (2002). *Instructional media and technologies for learning*. Merrill Prentice Hall.

Heintz, S., & Law, E. L. C. (2018). Digital educational games: Methodologies for evaluating the impact of game type. *ACM Transactions on Computer-Human Interaction*, 25(2), 1–47. doi:10.1145/3177881

Compilation of References

Hellerstedt, A., & Mozelius, P. (2019). *Game-based learning - a long history.* https://www.researchgate.net/publication/336460471_Game-based_learning_-_a_long_history

Hennessy, S., Harrison, D., & Wamakote, L. (2010). Teacher Factors Influencing Classroom Use of ICT in Sub-Saharan Africa. *Itupale Online Journal of African Studies, 2*(1), 39–54.

Hergenrader, T. (2018). *Collaborative Worldbuilding for Writers and Gamers.* Bloomsbury Publishing.

Herman, K. C., Prewett, S. L., Eddy, C. L., Savala, A., & Reinke, W. M. (2020). Profiles of middle school teacher stress and coping: Concurrent and prospective correlates. *Journal of School Psychology, 78,* 54–68. doi:10.1016/j.jsp.2019.11.003 PMID:32178811

Herman, S. W. (2015). Spirituality, Inc.: Religion in the American Workplace, by Lake Lambert III. New York: New York University Press, 2009. *Business Ethics Quarterly, 21*(3), 533–537. doi:10.5840/beq201121330

Herodotou, C. (2018). Mobile games and science learning: A comparative study of 4 and 5 years old playing the game Angry Birds. *British Journal of Educational Technology, 49*(1), 6–16. doi:10.1111/bjet.12546

Herodotou, C., Sharples, M., Gaved, M., Kukulska-Hulme, A., Rienties, B., Scanlon, E., & Whitelock, D. (2019, October). Innovative pedagogies of the future: An evidence-based selection. In *Frontiers in Education* (Vol. 4, p. 113). Frontiers. doi:10.3389/feduc.2019.00113

Heron, J., & Reason, P. (2006). The practice of co-operative inquiry: Research 'with'rather than 'on'people. In P. Reason & H. Bradbury (Eds.), *Handbook of action research: Participative inquiry and pratice.* Sage.

Herro, D. C., Lin, L., & Fowler, M. (2017). Meet the (Media) Producers: Artists, Composers, and Gamemakers. *Journal of Applied Research in Higher Education, 9*(1), 40–53. doi:10.1108/JARHE-04-2015-0029

Herzig, P., Strahringer, S., & Ameling, M. (2012). Gamification of ERP systems -Exploring gamification effects on user acceptance constructs. In *Multikonferenz Wirtschaftsinformatik* (pp. 793–804). GITO.

Hess, T., & Gunter, G. (2013). Serious game-based and nongame-based online courses: Learning experiences and outcomes. *British Journal of Educational Technology, 44*(3), 372–385. doi:10.1111/bjet.12024

Hewett, K. J. E. (2014). Jump in! A teacher's journey into Minecraft. *TechEdge Magazine, 2,* 14–17.

Hewett, K., Zeng, G., & Pletcher, B. (2020). The Acquisition of 21 st Century Skills Through Video Games: Minecraft Design Process Models and Their Web of Class Roles. *Simulation & Gaming, 51*(3). doi:10.1177/1046878120904976

Hickey, D., Goble, A. I., & Jameson, E. (2012). Designing Assessments and Assessing Designs in Virtual Educational Environments. *Journal of Science Education and Technology, 18*(2), 187–208. doi:10.100710956-008-9143-1

Higgins, S. (2014). Critical thinking for 21st century education: A cyber-tooth curriculum? *Prospects, 44*(4), 559–574. doi:10.100711125-014-9323-0

Hilton, M. (2015). Preparing students for life and work. *Issues in Science and Technology, 31*(4), 63.

Hinduja, S., & Patchin, J. (2009). *Bullying beyond the schoolyard: Preventing and responding to cyberbullying.* Corwin Press.

Hinebaugh, J. P. (2009). *A board game education.* R&L Education.

Hirsh-Pasek, K., Zosh, J. M., Golinkoff, R. M., Gray, J. H., Robb, M. B., & Kaufman, J. (2015). Putting education in educational apps: Lessons from the science of learning. *Psychological Science in the Public Interest, 16*(1), 3–34. https://doi.org/10.1177/1529100615569721

Hirumi, A., & Stapleton, C. (2009). Applying Pedagogy during Game Development to Enhance Game-Based Learning. *Games: Purpose and Potential in Education*, 127–162. doi:10.1007/978-0-387-09775-6_6

Hisam, A., Mashhadi, S. F., Faheem, M., Sohail, M., Ikhlaq, B., & Iqbal, I. (2018). Does playing video games effect cognitive abilities in Pakistani children? *Pakistan Journal of Medical Sciences*, *34*(6), 1507–1511. doi:10.12669/pjms.346.15532 PMID:30559813

Hmelo-Silver, C. E. (2004). Problem-based learning: What and how do students learn? *Educational Psychology Review*, *16*(3), 235–266. doi:10.1023/B:EDPR.0000034022.16470.f3

Hobbs, R. & Jensen, A. (2009). The past, present and future of media literacy education. *Journal of Media Literacy Education, 1*, 1-11.

Hobbs, R. (1994, Winter). Teaching Media Literacy— Are you hip to this? *Media Studies Journal,* 135-145.

Hobbs, R. (2010). *Digital and Media Literacy: A Plan of Action*. The Aspen Institute.

Hobbs, R. (2010). *Digital media literacy: A plan of action*. The Aspen Institute.

Hochleitner, C., Hochleitner, W., Graf, C., & Tscheligi, M. (2015). A Heuristic Framework for Evaluating User Experience in Games. In Game User Experience Evaluation. Bernhaupt.

Hodges, R. E. (2004). *What is literacy? Selected definitions and essays from "The literacy dictionary: The vocabulary of reading and writing"*. International Reading Assoc.

Hoel, T., & Jernes, M. (2020). Samtalebasert lesing av bildebok-apper: barnehagelærer versus hotspoter [Dialogue-Based Reading of Picture Book Apps: The Kindergarten Teacher Versus Hotspots]. *Norsk Pedagogisk Tidsskrift, 104*(2), 121–133. doi:10.18261/issn.1504-2987-2020-02-04

Hoffman, B., & Nadelson, L. (2010). Motivational engagement and video gaming: A mixed methods study. *Educational Technology Research and Development*, *58*(3), 245–270. doi:10.100711423-009-9134-9

Hofstede, G. (2011). Dimensionalizing cultures: The Hofstede model in context. *Online Readings in Psychology and Culture*, *2*(1). Advance online publication. doi:10.9707/2307-0919.1014

Hogg, M. A., Adelman, J. R., & Blagg, R. D. (2010). Religion in the face of uncertainty: An uncertainty-identity theory account of religiousness. *Personality and Social Psychology Review*, *14*(1), 72–83. doi:10.1177/1088868309349692 PMID:19855094

Ho, J. A. (2010). Ethical perception: Are differences between ethnic groups situation dependent? *Business Ethics (Oxford, England)*, *19*(2), 154–182. doi:10.1111/j.1467-8608.2010.01583.x

Holdcroft, B. (2006). What is religiosity. *Catholic Education: A Journal of Inquiry and Practice, 10*(1).

Holmes, W., Anastopoulou, S., Schaumburg, H., & Mavrikis, M. (2018). *Technology-enhanced personalised learning: Untangling the evidence*. Robert Bosch Stiftung GmbH.

Hommel, B. (2010). Grounding attention in action control: The intentional control of selection. In Effortless attention: A new perspective in the cognitive science of attention and action (pp. 121-140). Academic Press.

Hommel, M. (2010). Video games and learning. *School Library Monthly*, *26*(10), 37–40.

Hood, D., Lemaignan, S., & Dillenbourg, P. (2015, March). When children teach a robot to write: An autonomous teachable humanoid which uses simulated handwriting. In *Proceedings of the Tenth Annual ACM/IEEE International Conference on Human-Robot Interaction* (pp. 83-90). 10.1145/2696454.2696479

Hooshyar, D., Pedaste, M., Yang, Y., Malva, L., Hwang, G. J., Wang, M., Lim, H., & Delev, D. (2021). From gaming to computational thinking: An adaptive educational computer game-based learning approach. *Journal of Educational Computing Research*, *59*(3), 383–409. doi:10.1177/0735633120965919

Horkheimer, M. (1982). *Critical theory selected essays*. Continuum Pub.

Hossain, A., & Zeitlyn, B. (2010). *Poverty, equity and access to education in Bangladesh*. CREATE. https://files.eric.ed.gov/fulltext/ED517693.pdf

Hosseini, H., Hartt, M., & Mostafapour, M. (2019). Learning is child's play: Game-based learning in computer science education. *ACM Transactions on Computing Education*, *19*(3), 1–18. doi:10.1145/3282844

Howard-Jones, P. A., & Jay, T. (2016). Reward, Learning and Games. *Current Opinion in Behavioral Sciences*, *10*, 65–72. doi:10.1016/j.cobeha.2016.04.015

Howard-Jones, P. A., Jay, T., Mason, A., & Jones, H. (2016). Gamification of learning deactivates the default mode network. *Frontiers in Psychology*, *6*, 1891. doi:10.3389/fpsyg.2015.01891 PMID:26779054

Howard, T. C. (2001). Telling their side of the story: African-American students' perceptions of culturally relevant teaching. *The Urban Review*, *33*(2), 131–149. doi:10.1023/A:1010393224120

Howell, E. (2017). Pokémon GO: Implications for literacy in the classroom. *The Reading Teacher*, *70*(6), 729–732. doi:10.1002/trtr.1565

Hoyles, C., & Noss, R. (2003). What can digital technologies take from and bring to research in mathematics education? In A. J. Bishop, M. A. Clements, C. Keitel, J. Kilpatrick, & F. K. S. Leung (Eds.), *Second International Handbook of Mathematics Education* (Vol. 10, pp. 323–349). Springer. doi:10.1007/978-94-010-0273-8_11

Hramiak, A., Boulton, H., & Irwin, B. (2009). Trainee teachers' use of blogs as private reflections for professional development. *Learning, Media and Technology*, *34*(3), 259–269. doi:10.1080/17439880903141521

Hsiao, H.-S., Chang, C. S., Lin, C. Y., & Hu, P. M. (2014). Development of children's creativity and manual skills within digital game-based learning environment. *Journal of Computer Assisted Learning*, *30*(4), 377–395. doi:10.1111/jcal.12057

Hsieh, M. L., Dawson, P. H., & Yang, S. Q. (2021). The ACRL Framework successes and challenges since 2016: A survey. *Journal of Academic Librarianship*, *47*(2), 102306. doi:10.1016/j.acalib.2020.102306

Hsu, C. C., & Sandford, B. A. (2007). The Delphi technique: Making sense of consensus. *Practical Assessment, Research & Evaluation*, *12*(1), 1–8. doi:10.7275/pdz9-th90

Hsu, H., & Wang, S. (2010). Using gaming literacies to cultivate new literacies. *Simulation & Gaming*, *41*(3), 400–417. doi:10.1177/1046878109355361

Hu & Bentler. (1999). Cutoff criteria for fit indexes in covariance structure analysis: conventional criteria versus new alternatives. *Structural Equation Modeling, 6*(1), 1–55.

Huang, W. H. Y., & Soman, D. (2013). Gamification of education. *Report Series: Behavioural Economics in Action, 29*.

Huang, R., Liu, D., Xu, J., Chen, N., Fan, L., & Zeng, H. (2017). The development status and trend of educational robots. *Modern Educational Technology*, *27*(1), 13–20.

Huang, W. H. (2010). Evaluating learners' motivational and cognitive processing in an online game-based learning environment. *Computers in Human Behavior*. Advance online publication. doi:10.1016/j.chb.2010.07.021

Huang, W. H.-Y., & Soman, D. (2013). *A practitioner's guide to gamification of education*. University of Toronto, Rotman School of Management.

Huang, Y. L., Chang, D. F., & Wu, B. (2017). Mobile game-based learning with a mobile app: Motivational effects and learning performance. *Journal of Advanced Computational Intelligence and Intelligent Informatics*, *21*(6), 963–970. doi:10.20965/jaciii.2017.p0963

Huang, Y. L., Ho, Y. S., & Chuang, K. Y. (2006). Bibliometric analysis of nursing research in Taiwan 1991-2004. *The Journal of Nursing Research*, *14*(1), 75–81. doi:10.1097/01.JNR.0000387564.57188.b4 PMID:16547908

Huang, Y. M., Liang, T. H., Su, Y. N., & Chen, N. S. (2012). Empowering personalized learning with an interactive e-book learning system for elementary school students. *Educational Technology Research and Development*, *60*(4), 703–722. doi:10.100711423-012-9237-6

Huber, G. P., & Lewis, K. (2010). Cross-understanding: Implications for group cognition and performance. *Academy of Management Review*, *35*(1), 6–26.

Huberman, A. (Host). (2021, February 15). Using Failures, Movement & Balance to Learn Faster. *Huberman Lab* [Audio podcast episode]. https://hubermanlab.com/using-failures-movement-and-balance-to-learn-faster/

Huertas-Abril, C. A. (2020). *Tecnologías para la educación bilingüe*. Peter Lang.

Hu, G. (2005). English language education in China: Policies, progress, and problems. *Language Policy*, *4*(1), 5–24. doi:10.100710993-004-6561-7

Huizenga, J. C., ten Dam, G. T. M., Voogt, J. M., & Admiraal, W. F. (2017). Teacher perceptions of the value of game-based learning in secondary education. *Computers & Education*, *110*, 105–115. doi:10.1016/j.compedu.2017.03.008

Huizenga, J., Akkerman, S., Admiraal, W., & Dam, G. T. (2009). Mobile game-based learning in secondary education: Engagement, motivation and learning in a mobile city game. *Journal of Computer Assisted Learning*, *25*(4), 332–344. doi:10.1111/j.1365-2729.2009.00316.x

Huizinga, J. (1950). *Homo ludens, a study of the play-element in culture*. Oxford, UK: Roy. (Original work published 1938)

Huizinga, J. (1955/2006). Nature and significance of play as a cultural phenomenon from Homo Ludens: A study of the play element in culture. In The Game Designer Reader: A Rules of Play Anthology (pp. 96-120). Cambridge, MA: MIT Press.

Huizinga, J. (1949). *Homo Ludens Ils 86* (1st ed.). Routledge. doi:10.4324/9781315824161

Huizinga, J. (1955). *Homo ludens: A study of the play element in culture*. Routledge.

Huizinga, J., Nachod, H., & Flitner, A. (2006). *Homo ludens: vom Ursprung der Kultur im Spiel*. Rowohlt Taschenbuch Verlag.

Hulpuş, I., Hayes, C., & Fradinho, M. O. (2014). A framework for personalised Learning-plan recommendations in Game-based learning. In *Recommender Systems for Technology Enhanced Learning* (pp. 99–122). Springer. doi:10.1007/978-1-4939-0530-0_5

Humphrey, J. H., & Sullivan, D. D. (1970). *Teaching Slow Learners through Active Games*. Academic Press.

Hung, H. C., & Young, S. S. C. (2015). An Investigation of Game-Embedded Handheld Devices to Enhance English Learning. *Journal of Educational Computing Research*, *52*(4), 548–567. doi:10.1177/0735633115571922

Compilation of References

Hung, H. T., Yang, J. C., Hwang, G. J., Chu, H. C., & Wang, C. C. (2018). A scoping review of research on digital game-based language learning. *Computers & Education*, *126*, 89–104. doi:10.1016/j.compedu.2018.07.001

Hung, H. T., Yang, J. C., & Tsai, Y. C. (2020). Student Game Design as a Literacy Practice. *Journal of Educational Technology & Society*, *23*(1), 50–63.

Hungi, N., Makuwa, D., Ross, K., Saito, M., Dolata, S., van Capelle, F., Paviot, L., & Vellien, J. (2010). SACMEQ III Project Results: Pupil achievement levels in reading and mathematics. Southern and Eastern African Consortium for Monitoring Educational Quality. doi:10.100711125-005-6819-7

Hung, I. C., Chao, K. J., Lee, L., & Chen, N. S. (2013). Designing a robot teaching assistant for enhancing and sustaining learning motivation. *Interactive Learning Environments*, *21*(2), 156–171. doi:10.1080/10494820.2012.705855

Hunter, J. (2020). *STEAM games are good for learning: A study of teacher professional development in the Philippines.* New orleans, LA: SITE 2020.

Hunt, M. W. (2013). (APP) elite for instruction: 21st-century learners in a video and audio production classroom. *Techniques - American Vocational Association*, *88*(8), 36.

Hurtado, M. F., & González, J. (2017). Necesidades formativas del profesorado de Secundaria para la implementación de experiencias gamificadas en STEM. *Revista de Educación a Distancia*, *54*(8), 30–36. https://www.um.es/ead/red/54/fuentes_gonzalez.pdf

Husnaini, S. J., & Chen, S. (2019). Effects of guided inquiry virtual and physical laboratories on conceptual understanding, inquiry performance, inquiry self-efficacy, and enjoyment. *Physical Review. Physics Education Research*, *15*(1), 010119. doi:10.1103/PhysRevPhysEducRes.15.010119

Hussein, G. (2010). The Attitudes of Undergraduate Students towards Motivation and Technology in a Foreign Language Classroom. *International Journal of Learning and Teaching*, *2*(2), 14–24.

Hutchison, A., Beschorner, B., & Schmidt-Crawford, D. (2012). Exploring the use of the iPad for literacy learning. *The Reading Teacher*, *66*(1), 15–23. https://doi.org/ 10.1002/TRTR.01090

Hwang, D., Staley, B., Te Chen, Y., & Lan, J.-S. (2008). Confucian culture and whistle-blowing by professional accountants: An exploratory study. *Managerial Auditing Journal*, *23*(5), 504–526. doi:10.1108/02686900810875316

Hwang, G. J., & Chang, C. Y. (2020). Facilitating decision-making performances in nursing treatments: A contextual digital game-based flipped learning approach. *Interactive Learning Environments*, 1–16. Advance online publication. doi:10.1080/10494820.2020.1765391

Hwang, G. J., Chiu, L. Y., & Chen, C. H. (2015). A contextual game-based learning approach to improving students' inquiry-based learning performance in social studies courses. *Computers & Education*, *81*, 13–25. doi:10.1016/j.compedu.2014.09.006

Hwang, G. J., & Wu, P. H. (2012). Advancements and trends in digital game-based learning research: A review of publications in selected journals from 2001 to 2010. *British Journal of Educational Technology*, *43*(1), E6–E10. doi:10.1111/j.1467-8535.2011.01242.x

Hwang, G. J., Wu, P. H., & Chen, C. C. (2012). An online game approach for improving students' learning performance in web-based problem-solving activities. *Computers & Education*, *59*(4), 1246–1256. doi:10.1016/j.compedu.2012.05.009

Iacobucci, D., Posavac, S. S., Kardes, F. R., Schneider, M. J., & Popovich, D. L. (2015). The median split: Robust, refined, and revived. *Journal of Consumer Psychology*, *25*(4), 690–704. doi:10.1016/j.jcps.2015.06.014

Iacono, S., Vallarino, M., & Vercelli, G. (2020). Gamification in corporate training to enhance engagement: An approach. *International Journal of Emerging Technology in Learning, 15*(17), 69–84. doi:10.3991/ijet.v15i17.14207

IbanezF. C. (2018). https://elearningindustry.com/elearning-authors/felipe-casajus-ibanez

Ibrahim, N. A., Howard, D. P., & Angelidis, J. P. (2008). The relationship between religiousness and corporate social responsibility orientation: Are there differences between business managers and students? *Journal of Business Ethics, 78*(1-2), 165–174. doi:10.100710551-006-9321-0

Ibrahimoglu, N., Unaldi, I., Samancioglu, M., & Baglibel, M. (2013). The relationship between personality traits and learning styles: A cluster analysis. *Asian Journal of Management Sciences and Education, 2*(3), 93–108.

Ibrahim, R., & Jaafar, A. (2009). Educational games (EG) design framework: Combination of game design, pedagogy and content modeling. *IEEE International Conference on Electrical Engineering and Informatics*, 293-298. 10.1109/ICEEI.2009.5254771

Ibrahim, R., Masrom, S., Yusoff, R. C. M., Zainuddin, N. M. M., & Rizman, Z. I. (2017). Students' acceptance of Educational Games in Higher Education. *Journal of Fundamental and Applied Sciences, 9*(3S), 809–829. doi:10.4314/jfas.v9i3s.62

Ibrahim, R., Rahim, N. Z. A., Ten, D. W. H., Yusoff, R., Maarop, N., & Yaacob, S. (2018). Student's opinions on online educational games for learning programming introductory. *International Journal of Advanced Computer Science and Applications, 9*(6), 332–340. doi:10.14569/IJACSA.2018.090647

Ifenthaler, D., Eseryel, D., & Ge, X. (2012). Assessment for game-based learning. In *Assessment in game-based learning: Foundations, innovations, and perspectives*. Springer-Verlag. doi:10.1007/978-1-4614-3546-4_1

IGDA. (2019). *Developer Satisfaction Survey 2019*. International Game Developers Association.

Immordino-Yang, M. H. (2016). *Emotions, Learning, and the Brain*. W. W. Norton & Company.

Impact of COVID-19 on people's livelihoods, their health and our food systems. (n.d.). Retrieved September 2, 2021, from https://www.who.int/news/item/13-10-2020-impact-of-covid-19-on-people's-livelihoods-their-health-and-our-food-systems

Imray, P., & Hinchcliffe, V. (2013). *Curricula for teaching children and young people with severe or profound and multiple learning difficulties: Practical strategies for educational professionals*. Routledge. doi:10.4324/9781315883298

Information Literacy Competency Standards for Higher Education. (2000). [Brochure]. *Association of College & Research Libraries*. http://hdl.handle.net/10150/105645 https://www.ala.org/ala/acrl/acrlstandards/informationliteracycompetency.htm

Ingram, R. (1990). Self-focused attention in clinical disorders: Review and a conceptual model. *Psychological Bulletin, 107*(2), 156–176. doi:10.1037/0033-2909.107.2.156 PMID:2181521

Instituto de Geografia e Ordenamento do Território. (2021). Retrieved October 4, 2021, from, http://www.igot.ulisboa.pt/

Instituto Superior Técnico. (2021). Retrieved October 4, 2021, from, https://tecnico.ulisboa.pt/en/

INTEF. (2017). *Common Digital Competence Framework for Teachers*. National Institute of Educational Technologies and Teacher Training, Spanish Ministry of Education, Culture and Sport. https://bit.ly/3pkRJdh

Interactive Technologies Institute. (2021). Retrieved October 5, 2021, from, https://iti.larsys.pt/

International Society for Technology in Education. (2016). *Essential Conditions for Teaching ISTE Standards*. Author.

Compilation of References

Iosup, A., & Epema, D. (2014). *An Experience Report on Using Gamification in Technical Higher Education.* Conference paper SIGCSE, Atlanta, GA. 10.1145/2538862.2538899

Irmade, O., & Anisa, N. (2021, March). Research trends of serious games: Bibliometric analysis. []. IOP Publishing.]. *Journal of Physics: Conference Series, 1842*(1), 012036. doi:10.1088/1742-6596/1842/1/012036

Israel, M. (2017) *Game-based learning and gamification. Guidance from the experts.* White paper.

Israel, M., Marino, M., Delisio, L., & Serianni, B. (2014, September). *Supporting content learning through technology for K-12 students with disabilities* (Document No. IC-10). Retrieved from University of Florida, Collaboration for Effective Educator, Development, Accountability, and Reform Center: https://ceedar.education.ufl.edu/tools/innovation-configurations/

Ito, M., Gutierrez, K., Livingstone, S., Penuel, B., Rhodes, J., Salen, K., & Schor, J. (2010). Living and learning with new media: Summary of findings from the digital youth project (The John D. and Catherine T. MacArthur Foundation reports on digital media and learning). MIT Press.

Ito, M. (2008). *Living and learning with new media: summary of findings from the digital youth project.* The John D. and Catherine T. MacArthur Foundation.

Ivus, M., Quan, T., & Snider, N. (2020). *Class, take out your tablets: The impact of technology on learning and teaching in Canada.* Information and Communications Technology Council.

Ivus, M., Quan, T., & Snider, N. (2021). *21st Century Digital Skills: Competencies, Innovations and Curriculum in Canada, Information and Communications Technology Council.* ICTC.

Jaaska, E., Aaltonen, K., & Kujala, J. (2021). Game-Based Learning in Project Sustainability Management Education. *Sustainability, 13*(15), 15. doi:10.3390u13158204

Jackson, E. (2013). Choosing a methodology: philosophical underpinning. *Practitioner Research in Higher Education Journal, 7*(1), 49-62.

Jackson, G.T., & McNemara, D. (2013). *Motivation and Performance in a Game-Based Intelligent Tutoring System.* Academic Press.

Jackson, K. (2003). Blending technology and methodology: A shift toward creative instruction of qualitative methods with NVivo. *Qualitative Research Journal.*

Jackson, K., & Bazeley, P. (2019). Qualitative data analysis with NVivo. *Sage (Atlanta, Ga.).*

Jackson, L. C., O'Mara, J., Moss, J., & Jackson, A. C. (2018). A critical review of the effectiveness of narrative-driven digital educational games. *International Journal of Game-Based Learning, 8*(4), 32–49. doi:10.4018/IJGBL.2018100103

Jagger, S., Siala, H., & Sloan, D. (2015). It's All in the Game: A 3D Learning Model for Business Ethics. *Journal of Business Ethics, 137*(2), 383–403. doi:10.100710551-015-2557-9

Jaipal, K., & Figg, C. (2009). Using video games in science instruction: Pedagogical, social, and concept-related aspects. *Canadian Journal of Science Mathematics and Technology Education, 9*(2), 117–134. doi:10.1080/14926150903047780

Jamaludin, A., & Hung, D. (2017). Problem-solving for STEM learning: Navigating games as narrativized problem spaces for 21st. *Research and Practice in Technology Enhanced Learning, 12*(1), 1–14. doi:10.118641039-016-0038-0 PMID:30613250

Jamaludin, N. F., Wook, T. S. M. T., Noor, S. F. M., & Qamar, F. (2021). Gamification Design Elements to Enhance Adolescent Motivation in Diagnosing Depression. *International Journal of Interactive Mobile Technologies*, *15*(10), 154. doi:10.3991/ijim.v15i10.21137

James, F. (2019). *Everything You Need to Know About Education 4.0*. QS. https://www.qs.com/everything-you-need-to-know-education-40/

James, E., Gaskell, M. G., Weighall, A., & Henderson, L. (2017). Consolidation of vocabulary during sleep: The rich get richer? *Neuroscience and Biobehavioral Reviews*, *77*, 1–13. doi:10.1016/j.neubiorev.2017.01.054 PMID:28274725

James, M. (2020). *The Impact of Game-Based Learning in a Special Education Classroom*. Academic Press.

Jan, M. (2009). *Designing an augmented reality game-based curriculum for argumentation* (Unpublished doctoral dissertation). University of Wisconsin-Madison.

Jan, M., & Tan, E. (2013). Learning in and for the 21st century. Professorial Lecture Series, 4, 13-22.

Jan, M., Chee, Y. S., & Tan, E. M. (2010). Learning science via a science-in-the-making process: The design of a game-based learning curriculum. In S. Martin (Ed.), *iVERG 2010 Proceedings - International Conference on Immersive Technologies for Learning: A multi-disciplinary approach* (pp. 13-25). Stockton, CA: Iverg Publishing.

Jana, M. (2016). Teachers' Views on Game-based Learning (GBL) as a Teaching Method in Elementary Level Education. *Global Journal for Research Analysis*, *5*(1).

Janebi Enayat, M., & Haghighatpasand, M. (2019). Exploiting adventure video games for second language vocabulary recall: A mixed-methods study. *Innovation in Language Learning and Teaching*, *13*(1), 61–75. doi:10.1080/17501229.2017.1359276

Jang & Ryu. (2011). Exploring game experiences and game leadership in massively multiplayer online role-playing games. *British Journal of Educational Technology, 42*(4), 616-23. . doi:10.1111/j.1467-8535.2010.01064.x

Jan, M., Tan, E. M., & Chen, V. (2015). Issues and Challenges of Enacting Game-Based Learning in Schools. In T. B. Lin, V. Chen, & C. Chai (Eds.), *New Media and Learning in the 21st Century. Education Innovation Series*. Springer. doi:10.1007/978-981-287-326-2_5

Jansz, J. (2005). The emotional appeal of violent video games for adolescent males. *Communication Theory, 15*(3), 219-241. Retrieved from https://onlinelibrary.wiley.com/doi/10.1111/j.1468-2885.2005.tb00334.x/abstract;jsessionid=797D278A2C3BFFD76C1E71DA17729991.f02t02

Jarvis, P. (2009). Learning from everyday life. In P. Jarvis (Ed.), *The Routledge international handbook of lifelong learning* (pp. 19–30). Routledge. doi:10.4324/9780203870549

Jasperson, J. S., Carter, & Zmud. (2005). A comprehensive conceptualization of post-adoptive behaviors associated with information technology enabled work systems. *Management Information Systems Quarterly*, *29*(3), 525–557. doi:10.2307/25148694

Jemielniak, D. (2014). *Common Knowledge? An Ethnography of Wikipedia*. Stanford University Press. https://ebookcentral.proquest.com/lib/nuim/detail.action?docID=1680678

Jenkins, B. (2014). Don't quit playing: Video games in the STEM classroom. *Techniques*, *89*(1), 60–61.

Jenkins, H. (2002). Game design as narrative architecture. In P. Harrington & N. Frup-Waldrop (Eds.), *First Person*. MIT Press.

Jenkins, H. (2006). *Convergence culture: Where old and new media collide*. New York University Press.

Compilation of References

Jenkins, H. (2006). *Fans, Bloggers, and Gamers: Exploring Participatory Culture*. New York University Press.

Jenkins, H. (2009). *Confronting the challenges of participatory culture: Media education for the 21st century*. MacArthur Foundation.

Jenkins, H., Squire, K., & Tan, P. (2003). Entering the education arcade. *Computers in Entertainment, 1*(1), 17. doi:10.1145/950566.950591

Jewitt, C., Bezemer, J., & O'Halloran, K. (2016). *Introducing multimodality*. Routledge.

Jiang, X., Huang, X., Harteveld, C., & Fung, A. (2019). *The Computational Puzzle Design Framework*. Presented at the Association for Computing Machinery, San Luis Obispo, CA.

Jin, D. Y. (2017). The Emergence of Asian Mobile Games: Definitions, Industries, and Trajectories. *Mobile Gaming in Asia: Politics, Culture and Emerging Technologies*, 3-20.

Jin, G., Tu, M., Kim, T. H., Heffron, J., & White, J. (2018). Evaluation of game-based learning in cybersecurity education for high school students. [EduLearn]. *Journal of Education and Learning, 12*(1), 150–158. doi:10.11591/edulearn.v12i1.7736

Johnson, A. C., & Drougas, A. M. (2002). *Using Goldratt's Game to Introduce Simulation in the Introductory Operations Management Course*. Https://Doi.Org/10.1287/Ited.3.1.20

Johnson, D. W., & Johnson, F. P. (1997). *Joining Together: Group Theory and Group Skills* (6th ed.). Allyn & Bacon.

Johnson, S. (2005). *Everything bad is good for you: How today's popular culture is actually making us smarter*. Riverhead Books.

Johnston, E., & Olson, L. (2015). *The feeling brain: The biology and psychology of emotions*. WW Norton & Company.

Johnston, P. (2012). *Opening minds: Using language to change lives*. Stenhouse.

Jonassen, D. H. (2007). Engaging and supporting problem solving in online learning. *Online Learning Communities*, 109-127.

Jonassen, D. H. (1994). Thinking technology: Toward a constructivist design model. *Educational Technology, 34*(4), 34–37. https://www.learntechlib.org/p/171050/

Jonassen, D. H. (1997). Instructional design models for well-structured and ill-structured problem-solving learning outcomes. *Educational Technology Research and Development, 45*(1), 65–94. doi:10.1007/BF02299613

Jonassen, D. H., & Hung, W. (2012). Problem Solving. In N. M. Seel (Ed.), *Encyclopedia of the Sciences of Learning*. Springer. doi:10.1007/978-1-4419-1428-6_208

Jonassen, D., Campbell, J., & Davidson, M. (1994). Learning with media: Restructuring the debate. *Educational Technology Research and Development, 42*(2), 31–39. doi:10.1007/BF02299089

Jones, A. (2004). *A review of the research literature on barriers to the uptake of ICT by teachers*. London, UK: British Educational Communications and Technology Agency (BECTA). Retrieved from www.becta.org.uk

Jones, V. R. (2014). Teaching STEM: 21st century skills. *Children's Technology & Engineering, 18*(4), 11–13.

Jordan, M. E., Kleinsasser, R. C., & Roe, M. F. (2014). Wicked problems: Inescapable wickedity. *Journal of Education for Teaching, 40*(4), 415–430. doi:10.1080/02607476.2014.929381

Jouriles, E. N., McDonald, R., Kullowatz, A., Rosenfield, D., Gomez, G. S., & Cuevas, A. (2009). Can virtual reality increase the realism of role plays used to teach college women sexual coercion and rape-resistance skills? *Behavior Therapy*, *40*(4), 337–345. doi:10.1016/j.beth.2008.09.002 PMID:19892079

Jude, L. T., Kajura, M. A., & Birevu, M. P. (2014). Adoption of the SAMR model to asses ICT pedagogical adoption: A case of Makerere University. *International Journal of e-Education, e-Business, e- Management Learning*, *4*(2), 106–115.

Juul, J. (2005). Half-real: Video games between real rules and fictional worlds. Cambridge, MA: The MIT Press.

Juul, J. (2005). *Half-real: Video games between real rules and fictional worlds*. MIT Press.

Kader, M. A., & Salam, M. A. (2018). A comprehensive study on service quality and satisfaction level to the English medium education system in Bangladesh. *International Journal of Contemporary Research and Review*, *9*(7), 20850–20866. doi:10.15520/ijcrr/2018/9/07/541

Kafai, Y. B., Burke, Q., & Steinkuehler, C. (2016). *Connected gaming: What making video games can teach us about learning and literacy*. MIT Press. Retrieved from https://books.google.ca/books?id=zPC7DQAAQBAJ

Kafai, Y. B. (1995). *Minds in play: Computer game design as a context for children's learning*. Routledge.

Kahl, C. (2013). A deeper lecturer and student view of a sustainable learning requirement in tertiary education in Malaysia. *International Journal for Cross-Disciplinary Subjects in Education*, *4*(2), 1144–1152. doi:10.20533/ijcdse.2042.6364.2013.0161

Kahoot! for schools - choose plan for higher education. (2021, September 16). *Kahoot!* Retrieved September 11, 2021 from https://kahoot.com/register/pricing-higher-ed/

Kaimara, P., Fokides, E., & Oikonomou, A. (2021). *Potential Barriers to the Implementation of Digital Game-Based Learning in the Classroom: Pre-service Teachers' Views*. Tech Know Learn. doi:10.100710758-021-09512-7

Kalantzis, M., Varnvava-Skoura, G., & Cope, B. (2002). *Learning for the future: New worlds, new literacies, new learning, new people*. Common Ground Publishing. http://www.thelearner.com

Kalantzis, M., & Cope, B. (2012). *Introducing the Learning by Design Project*. University of Illinois.

Kalantzis, M., & Cope, B. (2012). *Literacies*. Cambridge University Press. doi:10.1017/CBO9781139196581

Kalantzis, M., & Cope, B. (2020). After the COVID-19 crisis: Why higher education may (and perhaps should) never be the same. *Access: Contemporary Issues in Education*, *40*(1), 51–55. doi:10.46786/ac20.9496

Kali, Y., McKenney, S., & Sagy, O. (2015). Teachers as designers of technology enhanced learning. *Instructional Science*, *43*(2), 173–179. doi:10.100711251-014-9343-4

Kamarudin, N., Halim, L., Osman, K., & Meerah, T. S. M. (2009). Pengurusan Penglibatan Pelajar dalam Amali Sains [Management of Students' Involvement in Science Practical Work]. *Jurnal Pendidikan Malaysia*, *34*(1), 205–217.

Kamisah, O., Zanaton, H. L., & Lilia, H. (2007). Sikap terhadap sains dan sikap saintifik di kalangan pelajar sains. *Jurnal Pendidikan*, *32*(3), 39–60.

Kamışlı, H. (2019). On primary school teachers' training needs in relation to game-based learning. *International Journal of Curriculum and Instruction*, *11*(2), 285–296.

Kamunya, S., Mirirti, E., Oboko, R., & Maina, E. (2020b). An Adaptive Gamification Model for E-Learning. *2020 IST-Africa Conference, IST-Africa 2020*. https://api.elsevier.com/content/abstract/scopus_id/85094323708

Compilation of References

Kamunya, S., Mirirti, E., Oboko, R., & Maina, E. (2020a). An Adaptive Gamification Model for E-Learning. *2020 IST-Africa Conference. IST-Africa, 2020,* 1–10.

Kanai, S. (2012). *Lover Letter* [Board Game]. Alderac Entertainment Group.

Kangas, A. (2017). Global Cities, International Relations and the Fabrication of the World. *Global Society, 31*(4), 531–550. doi:10.1080/13600826.2017.1322939

Kangas, M. (2010a). Creative and playful learning: Learning through game co-creation and games in a playful learning environment. *Thinking Skills and Creativity, 5*(1), 1–15. doi:10.1016/j.tsc.2009.11.001

Kangas, M., Koskinen, A., & Krokfors, L. (2017). A qualitative literature review of educational games in the classroom: The teacher's pedagogical activities. *Teachers and Teaching, 23*(4), 451–470.

Kang, M., Choo, P., & Watters, C. E. (2015). Design for experiencing: Participatory design approach with multidisciplinary perspectives. *Procedia: Social and Behavioral Sciences, 174,* 830–833. doi:10.1016/j.sbspro.2015.01.676

Kankanhalli, A., Taher, M., Cavusoglu, H., & Kim, S. H. (2012). Gamification: A new paradigm for online user engagement. *Thirty Third International Conference on Information Systems,* 1-10.

Kaplan, A., & Haenlein, M. (2010). "Users of the world, unite! The challenges and opportunities of social media" (PDF). *Business Horizons, 53*(1), 61. doi:10.1016/j.bushor.2009.09.003

Kapp, K. (2012). *The gamification of learning and instruction.* Pfeiffer Press.

Kapp, K. (2012). *The Gamification of Learning and Instruction: Game-based Methods and Strategies for Training and Education.* Pfeiffer.

Kapp, K. (2012). *The Gamification of Learning and Instruction: Game-Based Methods and Strategies for Training and Education.* Pfeiffer.

Kapp, K. M. (2012). *The gamification of learning and instruction: game-based methods and strategies for training and education.* Pfeiffer.

Kapur, R. (n.d.). *Significance and Meaning of Academic Literacy.* https://www.researchgate.net/profile/Radhika_Kapur/publication/336982773_Significance_and_Meaning_of_Academic_Literacy/links/5dbd1fc4a6fdcc2128f8ff82/Significance-and-Meaning-of-Academic-Literacy

Karacalli, S., & Korur, F. (2014). *The Effects of project-based learning on students' academic achievement, attitude, and retention of knowledge: The subject of electricity in our lives.* https://onlinelibrary.wiley.com/doi/abs/10.1111/ssm.12071

Karagiannis, S., & Magkos, E. (2021). Engaging Students in Basic Cybersecurity Concepts Using Digital Game-Based Learning: Computer Games as Virtual Learning Environments. In *Advances in Core Computer Science-Based Technologies.* Springer., doi:10.1007/978-3-030-41196-1_4

Karaman, M. A., Vela, J. C., Aguilar, A. A., Saldana, K., & Montenegro, M. C. (2019). Psychometric properties of U.S.-Spanish versions of the grit and resilience scales with a Latinx population. *International Journal for the Advancement of Counseling, 41*(1), 125–136. doi:10.100710447-018-9350-2

Karchmer-Klein, R., & Shinas, V. H. (2012). Guiding principles for supporting new literacies in your classroom. *The Reading Teacher, 65*(5), 288–293. doi:10.1002/TRTR.01044

Karen, H. (1939). *New ways in psychoanalysis.* Norton.

Karpouzis, K., & Yannakakis, G. N. (2016). *Emotion in Games.* Springer. doi:10.1007/978-3-319-41316-7

Kasasa. (2021, July). Boomers, Gen X, Gen Y, Gen Z, and Gen A Explained. *Kasasa.* https://bit.ly/3Bm4x5Z

Katada, H. (2019, March 1). *Interview.* Retrieved from https://www.famitsu.com/news/201903/01172506.html

Kathrani, P. (2020). The Gamification of Written Problem Questions in Law. Reflections on the "Serious Games at Westminster's Project. In C. Denvir (Ed.), *Modernizing Legal Education* (pp. 186–203). Cambridge University Press. doi:10.1017/9781108663311.012

Katz, J., & Mirenda, P. (2002). Including students with developmental disabilities in general education classrooms: Educational benefits. *International Journal of Special Education, 17*(2), 14–24.

Kaushik, V., & Walsh, C. A. (2019). Pragmatism as a research paradigm and its implications for Social Work research. *Social Sciences, 8*(9), 255. Advance online publication. doi:10.3390ocsci8090255

Kay, R. H. (2006). Evaluating strategies used to incorporate technology into preservice education: A review of the literature. *Journal of Research on Technology in Education, 38*(4), 383–408. doi:10.1080/15391523.2006.10782466

Keefe, E. B., & Copeland, S. R. (2011). What is Literacy? The Power of a Definition. *Research and Practice for Persons with Severe Disabilities, 36*(3-4), 92–99. doi:10.2511/027494811800824507

Keesey, C. (2011). Engagement, immersion, and learning cultures: Project planning and decision making for virtual world training programs. In *Global Business: Concepts, Methodologies, Tools and Applications* (pp. 121–134). IGI Global. doi:10.4018/978-1-60960-587-2.ch109

Keeshin, J. (2021). *Read, write, code. A friendly introduction to the world of coding and why it's the new literacy.* Lioncrest Publishing.

Ke, F. (2008). Computer games application within alternative classroom goal structures: Cognitive, metacognitive, and affective evaluation. *Educational Technology Research and Development, 56*(5-6), 539–556. doi:10.100711423-008-9086-5

Ke, F. (2016). Designing and integrating purposeful learning in gameplay: A systematic review. *Educational Technology Research and Development, 64*(2), 219–244. doi:10.100711423-015-9418-1

Keller, J. (2008). An integrative theory of motivation, volition, and performance. *Technol. Instr. Cogn. Learn., 6*, 79–104. https://www.oldcitypublishing.com/journals/ticl-home/ticl-issue-contents/ticl-volume-6-number-2-2008/ticl-6-2-p-79-104/

Keller, J. M. (1998). Using the ARCS process in CBI and distance education. In M. Theall (Ed.), *Motivation in teaching and learning: New directions for teaching and learning.* Jossey-Bass.

Kelley, & Knowles, Han, & Sung. (2019). Creating a 21st century skills survey instrument for high school students. *American Journal of Educational Research, 7*(8), 583–590. doi:10.12691/education-7-8-7

Kellinger, J. J. (2017). Let the Games Begin! Teaching Your Game. In *A Guide to Designing Curricular Games* (pp. 271-311). Springer International Publishing. doi:10.1007/978-3-319-42393-7_8

Kellinger, J. (2017). *A guide to designing curricular games: How to 'game' the system.* Springer.

Kellner, D. (2001). New Technologies/New Literacies: Reconstructing Education for the new millennium. *International Journal of Technology and Design Education, 11*, 67–81.

Kellner, D. (2002). New media and new literacies: Reconstructing education for the new millennium. In L. Lievrouw & S. Livingston (Eds.), *The handbook of new media* (pp. 90–104). Sage.

Compilation of References

Kellner, D., & Share, J. (2005). Toward critical media literacy: Core concepts, debates, organizations, and policy. *Discourse (Abingdon)*, *26*(3), 369–386.

Kempson, E. (2009). *Framework for the development of financial literacy baseline surveys: A first international comparative analysis*. Academic Press.

Kennedy, E. J., & Lawton, L. (1998). Religiousness and business ethics. *Journal of Business Ethics*, *17*(2), 163–175. doi:10.1023/A:1005747511116

Kennedy, J., Baxter, P., Senft, E., & Belpaeme, T. (2016). Social Robot Tutoring for Child Second Language Learning. *The Eleventh ACM/IEEE International Conference on Human Robot Interaction*, 231-238. 10.1109/HRI.2016.7451757

Keppell, M. (2014). Personalised learning strategies for higher education. In *The future of learning and teaching in next generation learning spaces*. Emerald Group Publishing Limited. doi:10.1108/S1479-362820140000012001

Kerim, A., & Genc, B. (2020). Mobile Games Success and Failure: Mining the Hidden Factors. In *2020 7th International Conference on Soft Computing & Machine Intelligence (ISCMI)* (pp. 167-171). IEEE.

Kervin, L., Mantei, J., & Herrington, J. (2009). Using technology in pedagogically responsive ways to support literacy learners. In T. Wee & R. Subramaniam (Eds.), *Handbook on new media literacy at the K-12 level: Issues and Challenges* (pp. 203–215). IGI Global.

Ketonen, R., Salmi, P., & Krimark, P. (Eds.). (2015). Namibia: Literacy Assessment Tools for Grades 1-3 and Special Education. Namibia: Literacy Assessment Tools for Grades 1-3 and Special Education. Grapho Learning training Programme (2012-2014). Niilo Mäki Institute.

Kétyi, A. (2013). Using smart phones in language learning – A pilot study to turn CALL into MALL. In L. Bradley & S. Thouësny (Eds.), *20 Years of EUROCALL: Learning from the Past, Looking to the Future. Proceedings of the 2013 EUROCALL Conference*, Évora, Portugal (pp.129-134). Research-publishing.net. 10.14705/rpnet.2013.000150

Keup, J., & Barefoot, B. (2005). Learning How to be a Successful Student: Exploring the Impact of First-Year Seminars on Student Outcomes. *Journal of the First-Year Experience & Students in Transition*, *17*(1), 11–47.

Khadka, S. (2014). *New Media Multiliteracies, and the globalized classroom*. Syracuse University. Dissertations. https://surface.syr.edu/cgi/viewcontent.cgi?article=1055&context=etd

Khan, A., Ahmad, F. H., & Malik, M. M. (2017). Use of digital game based learning and gamification in secondary school science: The effect on student engagement, learning and gender difference. *Education and Information Technologies*, *22*(6), 2767–2804. doi:10.100710639-017-9622-1

Khan, M. N. U., Rana, E. A., & Haque, M. R. (2014). Reforming the education system in Bangladesh: Reckoning a knowledge-based society. *World Journal of Education*, *4*(4), 1–11. doi:10.5430/wje.v4n4p1

Kickbusch, I., Pelikan, J. M., Apfel, F., & Tsouros, A. D. (Eds.). (2013). *Health Literacy. The Solid Facts*. World Health Organization. Retrieved May 03, 2019 from http://www.euro.who.int/__data/assets/pdf_file/0008/190655/e96854.pdf

Kietzmann, J., & Kristopher, H. (2011). Social media? Get serious! Understanding the functional building blocks of social media. *Business Horizons*, *54*(3), 241–251. doi:10.1016/j.bushor.2011.01.005

Kiili, K., Kiili, C., Ott, M., & Jönkkäri, T. (2012). Towards creative pedagogy: Empowering students to develop games. In *6th European Conference on Games Based Learning*. Academic Press.

Kiili, K. (2005). Content creation challenges and flow experience in educational games: The IT-Emperor case. *The Internet and Higher Education*, *8*(3), 183–198. doi:10.1016/j.iheduc.2005.06.001

Kiili, K. (2005). Digital game- based learning: Towards an experiential gaming model. *The Internet and Higher Education*, *8*(1), 13–24. doi:10.1016/j.iheduc.2004.12.001

Kiili, K., Lainema, T., de Freitas, S., & Arnab, S. (2014). Flow framework for analyzing the quality of educational games. *Entertainment Computing*, *4*(4), 367–377. doi:10.1016/j.entcom.2014.08.002

Kiili, K., Moeller, K., & Ninaus, M. (2018). Evaluating a Game-Based Training of Rational Number Understanding-In-Game Metrics as Learning Indicators. *Computers & Education*, 13–28. doi:10.1016/j.compedu.2018.01.012

Kim, B. (2012). Harnessing the power of game dynamics: Why, how to, and how not to gamify the library experience. *College & Research Libraries News*, *73*(8), 465–469. doi:10.5860/crln.73.8.8811

Kim, S. S., & Malhotra, N. K. (2005). A longitudinal model of continued IS use: An integrative view of four mechanisms underlying postadoption phenomena. *Management Science*, *51*(5), 741–755. doi:10.1287/mnsc.1040.0326

Kim, S., Song, K., Lockee, B., & Burton, J. (2018). *Gamification in learning and education: enjoy learning like gaming*. Springer. doi:10.1007/978-3-319-47283-6

Kim, Y., Smith, D., Kim, N., & Chen, T. (2014). Playing with a robot to learn English vocabulary. In *KAERA. Research Forum*, *1*(2), 3–8.

Kinect for Windows. (2016). Retrieved September 11, 2021 from http://kinectforwindows.org/

King, D. L., Delfabbro, P. H., Billieux, J., & Potenza, M. N. (2020). Problematic online gaming and the COVID-19 pandemic. *Journal of Behavioral Addictions*, *9*(2), 184–186. doi:10.1556/2006.2020.00016 PMID:32352927

King, D., Greaves, F., Exeter, C., & Darzi, A. (2013). 'Gamification': Influencing health behaviours with games. *Journal of the Royal Society of Medicine*, *106*(3), 76–78. doi:10.1177/0141076813480996 PMID:23481424

Kipping, P. (2004). Media literacy-An important strategy for building peace. *Peace Magazine*. Retrieved on December 3, 2012, from homes.ieu.edu.tr

Kirchner, E., Alexander, S., & Tötemeyer, A.-J. (2014). The reading habits / behaviour and preferences of African children : The Namibian chapter in collaboration with UNISA. Academic Press.

Kirikkaya, E. B., Işeri, Ş., & Vurkaya, G. (2010). A board game about space and solar system for primary school students. *The Turkish Online Journal of Educational Technology*, *9*(2), 1–13.

Kirriemuir, J. (2006). A history of digital games. In J. Rutter & J. Bryce (Eds.), *Understanding Digital Games* (pp. 21–36). Sage Publications. doi:10.4135/9781446211397.n2

Kirriemuir, J., & McFarlane, A. (2004). *Literature review in games and learning* (Vol. 8). Futurelab.

Kirschner, P. A. (2005). Learning in innovative learning environments. *Computers in Human Behavior*, *21*(4), 547–554. doi:10.1016/j.chb.2004.10.022

Kiryakova, G., Angelova, N., & Yordanova, L. (2014). Gamification in education. *Proceedings of 9th International Balkan Education and Science Conference*.

Kivunja, C. (2014). Theoretical Perspectives of How Digital Natives Learn. *International Journal of Higher Education*, *3*(1), 94–109. doi:10.5430/ijhe.v3n1p94

Kivunja, C. (2018). Distinguishing between theory, theoretical framework, and conceptual framework: A systematic review of lessons from the field. *International Journal of Higher Education*, *7*(6), 44–53. doi:10.5430/ijhe.v7n6p44

Compilation of References

Klaassen, R., Bul, K. C. M., Op Den Akker, R., Van Der Burg, G. J., Kato, P. M., & Di Bitonto, P. (2018). *Design and evaluation of a pervasive coaching and gamification platform for young diabetes patients*. Sensors. doi:10.339018020402

Klein, A. (2021). There aren't enough computer science classes for all the kids who want to take them. *Education Week*. Retrieved (from https://www.edweek.org/teaching-learning/there-arent-enough-computer-science-classes-for-all-the-kids-who-want-to-take-them/2021/09

Kler, S. (2014). ICT Integration in Teaching and Learning: Empowerment of Education with Technology. *Issues and Ideas in Education*, *2*(2), 255–271. doi:10.15415/iie.2014.22019

Klock, A. C. T., Gasparini, I., Pimenta, M. S., & Hamari, J. (2020). Tailored gamification: A review of literature. *International Journal of Human-Computer Studies*, *144*, 102495. Advance online publication. doi:10.1016/j.ijhcs.2020.102495

Klopfer, E., Osterweil, S., & Salen, K. (2009). *Moving learning games forward: Obstacles, opportunities, and openness*. The Education Arcade at MIT.

Klopfer, E., & Squire, K. (2008). Environmental Detectives—The development of an augmented reality platform for environmental simulations. *Educational Technology Research and Development*, *56*(2), 203–228. doi:10.100711423-007-9037-6

Knauf, H. (2016). Interlaced social worlds: exploring the use of social media in the kindergarten. *Early Years*, *36*(3), 254-270. doi:10.1080/09575146.2016.1147424

Knautz, K., Orszullok, L., & Soubusta, S. (2013). Game-based IL instruction–A journey of knowledge in four acts. In *European Conference on Information Literacy* (pp. 366-372). Springer International Publishing. 10.1007/978-3-319-03919-0_48

Knezek, G., & Christensen, R. (2002). Impact of new information technologies on teachers and students. *Education and Information Technologies*, *7*(4), 369–376. doi:10.1023/A:1020921807131

Knol, E., & De Vries, P. W. (2011). EnerCities, a serious game to stimulate sustainability and energy conservation: Preliminary results. *eLearning Papers*, *25*, 1–10. Retrieved from https://papers.ssrn.com/sol3/papers.cfm?abstract_id=1866206

Knudsen, E. I. (2018). Neural Circuits That Mediate Selective Attention: A Comparative Perspective. *Trends in Neurosciences*, *41*(11), 789–805. doi:10.1016/j.tins.2018.06.006 PMID:30075867

Knutson, B., Westdorp, A., Kaiser, E., & Hommer, D. (2000). FMRI visualization of brain activity during a monetary incentive delay task. *NeuroImage*, *12*(1), 20–27. doi:10.1006/nimg.2000.0593 PMID:10875899

Kocaman, O., & Cumaoglu, G. K. (2014). The effect of educational software (DENIS) and games on vocabulary learning strategies and achievement. *Eğitim ve Bilim*, *39*(176), 305–316. doi:10.15390/EB.2014.3704

Koehler, M. J., Mishra, P., & Cain, W. (2013). What is Technological Pedagogical Content Knowledge (TPACK)? *Journal of Education*, *193*(3), 13–19. doi:10.1177/002205741319300303

Koehler, M. J., Mishra, P., Kereluik, K., Shin, T. S., & Graham, C. R. (2014). The technological pedagogical content knowledge framework. In J. M. Spector, M. D. Merrill, J. van Merrienboer, & M. P. Driscoll (Eds.), *Handbook of research on educational communications and technology* (pp. 101–111). Springer. doi:10.1007/978-1-4614-3185-5_9

Koenitz, H., Ferri, G., Haahr, M., Sezen, D., & Sezen, T. I. (Eds.). (2015). *Interactive digital narrative: History, theory and practice*. Routledge. doi:10.4324/9781315769189

Kogan, L., Hellyer, P., Duncan, C., & Schoenfeld-Tacher, R. (2017). A pilot investigation of the physical and psychological benefits of playing Pokémon GO for dog owners. *Computers in Human Behavior*, *76*, 431–437. doi:10.1016/j.chb.2017.07.043

Koivisto, J., & Hamari, J. (2014). Demographic differences in perceived benefits from Gamification. Computers in Human Behavior, 35, 179-188.

Koivisto, J., & Hamari, J. (2019). The Rise of Motivational Information Systems: A Review of Gamification Research. *International Journal of Information Management*, *45*, 191–210. doi:10.1016/j.ijinfomgt.2018.10.013

Kolb, D. A. (1984). Experiential learning: Experience as the source of learning and development, David A. Kolb, Prentice-Hall International, Hemel Hempstead, Herts., 1984. No. of pages: xiii + 256. Journal of Organizational Behavior.

Kolb, D. A., & Kolb, A. Y. (2013). Research on Validity and Educational Applications. *Experience Based Learning Systems*, *5*.

Kolb, A. Y., & Kolb, D. A. (2005). Learning Styles and Learning Spaces: Enhancing Experiential Learning in Higher Education. *Academy of Management Learning & Education*, *4*(2), 193–212. doi:10.5465/amle.2005.17268566

Kolb, D. (1984). *Experiential learning as the science of learning and development*. Prentice Hall.

Kolb, D. (1984). *Experiential learning: Experience as the source of learning and development*. Prentice-Hall.

Kolb, L. (2020). *Learning first, Technology second in practice: New strategies, research and tools for student success*. International Society for Technology in Education.

Kong, S. C. (2014). Developing information literacy and critical thinking skills through domain knowledge learning in digital classrooms: An experience of practicing flipped classroom strategy. *Computers & Education*, *78*, 160–173. doi:10.1016/j.compedu.2014.05.009

Korn, O. (2012). Industrial playgrounds: how Gamification helps to enrich work for elderly or impaired persons in production. In *Proceedings of the 4th ACM SIGCHI symposium on Engineering interactive computing systems* (pp. 313-316). ACM. 10.1145/2305484.2305539

Kory, J., & Breazeal, C. (2014, August). Storytelling with robots: Learning companions for preschool children's language development. In *The 23rd IEEE international symposium on robot and human interactive communication* (pp. 643-648). IEEE. 10.1109/ROMAN.2014.6926325

Koster, R. (2004). *Theory of fun for game design*. Paraglyph.

Kotilainen, S. (2009). Promoting youth civic participation with media production: The case of youth choice editorial board. In D. Frau-Meigs & J. Torrent (Eds.), Mapping media education policies in the world: Vision, programmes and challenges. New York: UN-Alliance of Civilization.

Kottek, M., Grieser, J., Beck, C., Rudolf, B., & Rubel, F. (2006). *World map of the Köppen-Geiger climate classification updated*. Academic Press.

Koutromanos, G. (2020). Primary School Students' Perceptions About the Use of Mobile Games in the Classroom. In Mobile Learning Applications in Early Childhood Education (pp. 230-250). IGI Global.

Koutromanos, G., & Avraamidou, L. (2014). The use of mobile games in formal and informal learning environments: A review of the literature. *Educational Media International*, *51*(1), 49–65. doi:10.1080/09523987.2014.889409

Kouwenhoven, W., Howie, S. J., & Plomp, T. (2003). The Role of Needs Assessment in Developing Competence-Based Education in Mozambican Higher Education. *Perspectives in Education*, *21*(1), 34–154.

Compilation of References

Kozdras, D., Joseph, C., & Schneider, J. J. (2015). Reading Games: Close Viewing and Guided Playing of Multimedia Texts. *The Reading Teacher*, *69*(3), 331–338. doi:10.1002/trtr.1413

Krathwohl, D. R., & Anderson, L. W. (2010). Merlin C. Wittrock and the revision of Bloom's taxonomy. *Educational Psychologist*, *45*(1), 64–65. doi:10.1080/00461520903433562

Kress, G. R. (2010). *Multimodality: A social semiotic approach to contemporary communication*. Routledge.

Krishnaswamy. (2011). *New media vs traditional media*. Retrieved in Sept 2021, from https://www.scribd.com/document/397697219/New-Media-vs-Traditional-Media

Kritzinger, E., Loock, M., & Goosen, L. (2019). Cyber Safety Awareness – Through the Lens of 21st Century Learning Skills and Game-Based Learning. *Lecture Notes in Computer Science*, *11937*, 477–485. doi:10.1007/978-3-030-35343-8_51

Krouse, R. Z., Ransdell, L. B., Lucas, S. M., & Pritchard, M. E. (2011). Motivation, goal orientation, coaching, and training habits of women ultrarunners. *Journal of Strength and Conditioning Research*, *25*(10), 2835–2842. doi:10.1519/JSC.0b013e318204caa0 PMID:21946910

Krstic, K., Stepanovic-Ilic, I., & Videnovic, M. (2017). Student dropout in primary and secondary education in the Republic of Serbia. *Psiholoska Istrazivanja*, *20*(1), 27–50. doi:10.5937/PsIstra1701027K

Kruger, W. (2012). *Learning to read Afrikaans*. www.homeschooling-curriculum-guide.com

Kubota, T. (2017). *Faculty and students at Stanford argue for increased study of games and interactive media*. Retrieved January 14, 2020, from https://news.stanford.edu/2017/05/03/interest-grows-study-games-interactive-media/

Kucirkova, N. (2018). *How and why to read and create digital books: A guide for primary practitioners*. UCL Press.

Kuglitsch, R. Z. (2015). Teaching for Transfer: Reconciling the Framework with Disciplinary Information Literacy. *Portal (Baltimore, Md.)*, *15*(3), 457–470. doi:10.1353/pla.2015.0040

Kuglitsch, R. Z., & Burge, P. (2016). Beyond the first year: Supporting sophomores through information literacy outreach. *College & Undergraduate Libraries*, *23*(1), 79–92. doi:10.1080/10691316.2014.944636

Kuhlthau, C. C., Caspari, A. K., & Maniotes, L. K. (2007). *Guided inquiry: Learning in the 21st century*. Libraries Unlimited.

Kuhn, J. (2017). Minecraft: Education edition. *CALICO Journal*, *35*(2), 214–223. doi:10.1558/cj.34600

Kuhn, J., & Stevens, V. (2017). Participatory culture as professional development: Preparing teachers to use Minecraft in the classroom. *TESOL Journal*, *8*(4), 753–767. doi:10.1002/tesj.359

Kumar, S. (2017). A river by any other name: Ganga/Ganges and the postcolonial politics of knowledge on Wikipedia. *Information Communication and Society*, *20*(6), 809–824. doi:10.1080/1369118X.2017.1293709

Küng, H. (2015). A Global Ethic in an Age of Globalization. *Business Ethics Quarterly*, *7*(3), 17–32. doi:10.2307/3857310

Kurkovsky, S. (2013). Mobile game development: Improving student engagement and motivation in introductory computing courses. *Journal of Computer Science Education*, *23*(2), 138–157. doi:10.1080/08993408.2013.777236

Kyle, F., Kujala, J., Richardson, U., Lyytinen, H., & Goswami, U. (2013). Assessing the effectiveness of two theoretically motivated computer-assisted reading interventions in the United Kingdom: GG rime and GG phoneme. *Reading Research Quarterly*, *48*(1), 61–76. http://www.learntechlib.org/p/91905. doi:10.1002/rrq.038

La Guardia, D., Gentile, M., Dal Grande, V., Ottaviano, S., & Allegra, M. (2014). A Game based Learning Model for Entrepreneurship Education. *Procedia: Social and Behavioral Sciences*, *141*, 195–199. doi:10.1016/j.sbspro.2014.05.034

Laboratory, H. A. L. (2014). *Super Smash Bros. Melee* [Video game]. Nintendo.

Laborde, C., Kynigos, C., Hollebrands, K., & Strässer, R. (2006). Teaching and learning geometry with technology. In A. Guitiérrez & P. Boero (Eds.), *Handbook of Research on the Psychology of Mathematics Education: Past, Present and Future* (pp. 275–304). Sense Publishers.

Lai, C.-H., Lee, T.-P., Jong, B.-S., & Hsia, Y.-T. (2012). A Research on Applying Game-Based Learning to Enhance the Participation of Student. In Embedded and Multimedia Computing Technology and Service (pp. 311–318). Springer Netherlands. doi:10.1007/978-94-007-5076-0_36

Lai, N. K., Ang, T. F., Por, L. Y., & Liew, C. S. (2018). The impact of play on child development - a literature review. *European Early Childhood Education Research Journal, 26*(5), 625–643. doi:10.1080/1350293X.2018.1522479

Lambert, J. (2013). *Digital storytelling: Capturing lives, creating community* (4th ed.). Routledge. doi:10.4324/9780203102329

Lambrecht, M., Creemers, S., Boute, R., & Leus, R. (2012). Extending the production dice game. *International Journal of Operations & Production Management, 32*(12), 144–3577. doi:10.1108/01443571211284197

Lam, C. M. (2016). Fostering rationality in Asian education. In C. M. Lam & J. Park (Eds.), *Sociological and philosophical perspectives on education in the Asia-Pacific region: issues, concerns and prospects* (Vol. 29, pp. 9–22). Springer. doi:10.1007/978-981-287-940-0_2

Landers, R. N. (2014). Developing a Theory of Gamified Learning:Linking Serious Games and Gamification of Learning. *Simulation & Gaming, 45*(6), 752–768. doi:10.1177/1046878114563660

Landi, N., Malins, J. G., Frost, S. J., Magnuson, J. S., Molfese, P., Ryherd, K., & Pugh, K. R. (2018). Neural representations for newly learned words are modulated by overnight consolidation, reading skill, and age. *Neuropsychologia, 111*, 133–144. doi:10.1016/j.neuropsychologia.2018.01.011 PMID:29366948

Landow, G. (1997). *The convergence of contemporary critical theory and technology*. The Johns Hopkins University Press.

Lane, C. A. (2018). *Multiliteracies meaning-making: How four boys' video gaming experiences influence their cultural knowledge—Two ethnographic cases* (Doctoral Dissertation, Western University). Electronic Thesis and Dissertation Repository. 5303. https://ir.lib.uwo.ca/etd/5303

Lane, C. A. (2018). *Multiliteracies meaning-making: How four boys' video gaming experiences influence their cultural knowledge—Two ethnographic cases*. The University of Western Ontario. Retrieved from https://ir.lib.uwo.ca/cgi/viewcontent.cgi?article=7128&context=etd

Lane, C.-A. (2014, March). How video games affect boys' literacy practices. In *The Robert MacMillan Graduate Research in Education Symposium - Theory to Practice*. Western University.

Lane, C.-A. (2019a). Digitizing Learning: How Video Games Can Be Used as Alternative Pathways to Learning. In Innovative Trends in Flipped Teaching and Adaptive Learning (pp. 138-161). IGI Global.

Lane, C.-A. (2019b). Video Games Support Alternative Classroom Pedagogies to Support Boys' Meaning-Making. In Integrating Digital Technology in Education: School-University-Community Collaboration (pp. 199-224). Information Age.

Lane, C.-A. (2021). Using Digital Technologies in the 21st Century Classroom: How Video Games Support Dynamic Learning Opportunities. In Present and Future Paradigms of Cyberculture in the 21st Century (pp. 109-134). IGI Global.

Compilation of References

Lane, C. A. (2021). Using Digital Technologies in the 21st Century Classroom: How Video Games Support Dynamic Learning Opportunities. In C. A. Lane (Ed.), *Present and Future Paradigms of Cyberculture in the 21st Century* (pp. 109–134). IGI Global. doi:10.4018/978-1-5225-8024-9.ch007

Lane, C.-A. (2013). Using Video Technology to Address Boys' Literacy Gap and Connect the Male Voice in Gender Dynamics. *International Journal of Technology and Inclusive Education*, *2*(1), 139–150. doi:10.20533/ijtie.2047.0533.2013.0020

Lane, C.-A. (2016). 'Play, Score, Engage': Finding Ways for Boys to Make the Grade! *Literacy Information and Computer Education Journal*, *7*(4), 2461–2467. doi:10.20533/licej.2040.2589.2016.0327

Lane, H. C., & Yi, S. (2017). Playing with virtual blocks: Minecraft as a learning environment for practice and research. In *Cognitive development in digital contexts* (pp. 145–166). Academic Press. doi:10.1016/B978-0-12-809481-5.00007-9

Langat, A. C. (2015). Barriers Hindering Implementation, Innovation and Adoption of ICT in Primary Schools in Kenya. *International Journal of Innovative Research and Development*, *4*(2), 1–11.

Lankshear, C. (1997). *Changing literacies*. McGraw-Hill Education.

Lankshear, C., & Knobel, M. (2006). *New literacies: Everyday practices and classroom learning*. Open University Press.

Lankshear, C., & Knobel, M. (2011). *New literacies: Everyday practices and social learning* (3rd ed.). McGraw-Hill.

Lan, Y. J., Botha, A., Shang, J., & Jong, M. S. Y. (2018). Guest editorial: Technology enhanced contextual game-based language learning. *Journal of Educational Technology & Society*, *21*(3), 86–89.

Larmer, J. (2015). *Project-Based Learning vs. Problem-Based Learning vs. X-BL*. https://www.edutopia.org/blog/pbl-vs-pbl-vs-xbl-john-larmer

Larose, F., Grenon, V., Morin, M. P., & Hasni, A. (2009). The impact of pre-service field training sessions of the probability of future teachers using ICT in school. *European Journal of Teacher Education*, *32*(3), 289–303. doi:10.1080/02619760903006144

Larson, L. C. (2010). Digital readers: The next chapter in ebook reading and response. *The Reading Teacher*, *64*(1), 15–22. https://doi.org/10.1598/RT.64.1.2

Lasagabaster, D. (2008). Foreign language competence in content and language integrated courses. *The Open Applied Linguistics Journal*, *1*(1), 31–42. doi:10.2174/1874913500801010030

Latorre-Cosculluela, C., Suárez, C., Quiroga, S., Sobradiel-Sierra, N., Lozano-Blasco, R., & Rodríguez-Martínez, A. (2021). Flipped Classroom model before and during COVID-19: Using technology to develop 21st century skills. *Interactive Technology and Smart Education*, *18*(2), 189–204. Advance online publication. doi:10.1108/ITSE-08-2020-0137

Laughey, D. (2010). *Medya calışmaları, teoriler ve yaklaşımlar*. İstanbul: Kalkedon.

Lauricella, A. R., Robb, M. B., & Wartella, E. (2007). Challenges and suggestions for determining quality in children's media. In D. Lemish (Ed.), The Routledge international handbook of children, adolescents, and media (pp. 425–432). https://doi.org/10.4324/9780203366981.CH52

Laurillard, D. (2002). *Rethinking university teaching: a framework for the effective use of learning technologies* (2nd ed.). Routledge Falmer. doi:10.4324/9780203160329

Lavender, T. J. (2008). *Homeless: It's no game-measuring the effectiveness of a persuasive videogame*. School of Interactive Arts & Technology-Simon Fraser University.

Lawrence, R., Ching, L. F., & Abdullah, H. (2019). Strengths and Weaknesses of Education 4.0 in the Higher Education Institution. *International Journal of Innovative Technology and Exploring Engineering*, *9*(2), 511–519. Advance online publication. doi:10.35940/ijitee.B1122.1292S319

Layton, L., & Brown, E. (2012, Sept. 24). SAT Reading Scores Hit a Four-Decade Low. *The Washington Post*, p. 1.

Leadership Project. (1995). *Adult Learning Principles & Practice*. Sheridan College.

Leander, K., & Ehret, C. (Eds.). (2019). *Affect turn in literacy learning and teaching: Pedagogies, politics, and coming to know*. Routledge. doi:10.4324/9781351256766

Learning games: Make learning awesome! (2021, October 22). *Kahoot!* Retrieved October 26, 2021, from https://kahoot.com/

Learning tools & flashcards, for free. (n.d.). *quizlet*. Retrieved October 26, 2021, from https://quizlet.com/

Leary, M., & Tangney, J. (2003). *Handbook of self and identity*. Guilford Press.

Lederman, L. C. (1984). Debriefing: A critical re-examination of the post-experience analytic process and implications for effective use. *Simulation & Games*, *15*(4), 415–431. doi:10.1177/0037550084154002

Ledward, B. C., & Hirata, D. (2011). *An overview of 21st century skills. Summary of 21st century skills for students and teachers*. Kamehameha Schools–Research & Evaluation.

Lee, Cheung, & Chen. (2005). Acceptance of Internet-based learning medium: the role of extrinsic and intrinsic motivation. *Information & Management*, *42*(8), 1095-104.

Lee, K. H. (2021). *The educational 'metaverse' is coming*. The Campus. Retrieved from https://www.timeshighereducation.com/campus/educational-metaverse-coming

Lee, V., Poole, F., Clarke-Midura, J., Recker, M., & Rasmussen, M. (2020). *Introducing coding through tabletop board games and their digital instantiations across elementary classrooms and school libraries*. Paper presented at SIGCSE, Portland. OR.

Lee, W. J., Huang, C. W., Wu, C. J., Huang, S. T., & Chen, G. D. (2012). The effects of using embodied interactions to improve learning performance. *2012 IEEE 12th international conference on advanced learning technologies (ICALT)*, 557-559.

Leemkuil, H., & De Jong, T. O. N. (2012). Adaptive advice in learning with a computer-based knowledge management simulation game. *Academy of Management Learning & Education*, *11*(4), 653–665. doi:10.5465/amle.2010.0141

Lee, T. Y., Mauriello, M., Ahn, J., & Bederson, B. (2014). CTArcade: Computational thinking with games in school-aged children. *International Journal of Child-Computer Interaction*, *2*, 26–33.

Lee, Y. J., & Gerber, H. (2013). It's a WoW World: Second language acquisition and massively multiplayer online gaming. *Multimedia-Assisted Language Learning*, *16*(2), 53–70. doi:10.15702/mall.2013.16.2.53

Legaki, N. Z., Xi, N., Hamari, J., & Assimakopoulos, V. (2019, January). Gamification of The Future: An Experiment on Gamifying Education of Forecasting. *Proceedings of the 52nd Hawaii International Conference on System Sciences*. 10.24251/HICSS.2019.219

Leman, K. (2017). *Ellen's Game of Games* [Game Show Series]. NBC.

Lemmon, P. (1985). A school where learning styles make a difference. *Principal*, *64*, 26–29.

Lenhard, W., & Lenhard, A. (2016). *Calculation of Effect Sizes*. Psychometrica., doi:10.13140/RG.2.1.3478.4245

Compilation of References

Lenhart, A., Kahne, J., Middaugh, E., Macgill, A. R., Evans, C., & Vitak, J. (2008). *Teens, Video Games, and Civics: Teens' Gaming Experiences Are Diverse and Include Significant Social Interaction and Civic Engagement.* Pew internet & American Life Project.

Lenoir, T. (2004). Foreword. In *M.B.N. Hansen, New Philosophy for New Media.* The MIT Press.

Lenormand, M. (2019). The importance of not being Ernest: An archaeology of child's play in Freud's writings (and some implications for psychoanalytic theory and practice). *The International Journal of Psycho-Analysis*, *100*(1), 52–76. doi:10.1080/00207578.2018.1489708 PMID:33945712

Leont'ev, A. (1981). The problem of activity in psychology. In J. Wertsch (Ed.), *The concept of activity in Soviet psychology.* Sharpe.

Leung, E., & Pluskwik, E. (2018, June). *Effectiveness of gamification activities in a project-based learning classroom* [Classroom paper presentation]. 2018 ASEE Annual Conference & Exposition, Salt Lake City, UT. https://peer.asee.org/30361

Lewin, K. M. (2007). *Improving access, equity and transitions in Education: Creating a research agenda.* Centre for International Education. http://www.create-rpc.org/pdf_documents/PTA1.pdf

Lewis Ellison, T. (2017). Digital participation, agency, and choice: An African American youth's digital storytelling about Minecraft. *Journal of Adolescent & Adult Literacy*, *61*(1), 25–35. doi:10.1002/jaal.645

Li, C. (2017). *Attitudes towards Digital Game-based Learning of Chinese Primary School English Teachers* [Master's thesis]. University of Edinburgh. https://bit.ly/3yew4UR

Li, Z., Zou, D., Xie, H., Wang, F.-L., & Chang, M. (2018). Enhancing Information Literacy in Hong Kong Higher Education through Game-based Learning. *Proceedings of 22nd Global Chinese Conference on Computers in Education (GCCCE 2018)*, 595-598.

Lichty, P. (2019). The Gamification of Augmented Reality Art. In *Augmented Reality Games II* (pp. 225–246). Springer. doi:10.1007/978-3-030-15620-6_10

Liesa-Orús, M., Latorre-Cosculluela, C., Vázquez-Toledo, S., & Sierra-Sánchez, V. (2020). The Technological Challenge Facing Higher Education Professors: Perceptions of ICT Tools for Developing 21st Century Skills. *Sustainability*, *12*(13), 5339. doi:10.3390u12135339

Li, K., Peterson, M., & Wang, Q. (2021). Using Community of Inquiry to Scaffold Language Learning in Out-of-School Gaming: A Case Study. *International Journal of Game-Based Learning*, *11*(1), 31–56. doi:10.4018/IJGBL.2021010103

Li, M. C., & Tsai, C.-C. (2013). Game-based learning in science education: A review of relevant research. *Journal of Science Education and Technology*, *22*(6), 877–898. doi:10.100710956-013-9436-x

Lima, L., & Gouveia, P. (2020). Gender Asymmetries in the Digital Games Sector in Portugal. *DIGRA 2020 Tampere Conference Proceedings*, 1-16.

Lima, L., Gouveia, P., & Pinto, C. (2021). *Gaming in Portugal 2020: Women in Digital Games and the Impact of Covid-19*. Retrieved October 4, 2021, from, https://icswac.weebly.com/program.html

Lima, L., Gouveia, P., Pinto, C., & Cardoso, P. (2021). I Never Imagined That I Would Work in The Digital Game Industry. In *CoG 2021 Proceedings: 3rd IEEE Conference on Games.* University of Copenhagen.

Lin, C. J., & Hwang, G. J. (2018). A flipped classroom approach to supporting gamebased learning activities for EFL business writing course. In *3rd Annual International Seminar on Transformative Education and Educational Leadership (AISTEEL 2018)*. Atlantis Press

Lin, D. T. A., Ganapathy, M., & Kaur, M. (2018). Kahoot! it: Gamification in higher education. *Social Sciences & Humanities, 26*(1), 565–582. https://www.researchgate.net/profile/Debbita-Tan/publication/320182671_Kahoot_It_Gamification_in_Higher_Education/links/5ab3757aa6fdcc1bc0c288fe/Kahoot-It-Gamification-in-Higher-Education.pdf

Lin, Y., & Nguyen, H. (2021). International Students' Perspectives on e-Learning During COVID-19 in Higher Education in Australia: A Study of an Asian Student. *The Electronic Journal of e-Learning, 19*(4), 241-251. doi:10.34190/ejel.19.4.2349

Lincoln, Y., & Guba, G. (1985). *Naturalistic inquiry*. Sage. doi:10.1016/0147-1767(85)90062-8

Linda, K., & Pennington, C. (2016). "Girls Can't Play": The effects of Stereotype Threat on Females' Gaming Performance. *Computers in Human Behavior, 59*, 202–209. doi:10.1016/j.chb.2016.02.020

Linderoth, J., & Sjöblom, B. (2019). Being an Educator and Game Developer: The Role of Pedagogical Content Knowledge in Non-Commercial Serious Games Production. *Simulation & Gaming, 50*(6), 771–788. doi:10.1177/1046878119873023

Lindquist, K. A., Satpute, A. B., Wager, T. D., Weber, J., & Barrett, L. F. (2016). The brain basis of positive and negative affect: Evidence from a meta-analysis of the human neuroimaging literature. *Cerebral Cortex (New York, N.Y.), 26*(5), 1910–1922. doi:10.1093/cercor/bhv001 PMID:25631056

Lingard, B., Martino, W., Mills, M., & Bahr, M. (2002). Addressing the educational needs of boys. Commonwealth of Australia, Department of Education, Science and Training.

Lin, T. J., & Lan, Y. J. (2015). Language learning in virtual reality environments: Past, present, and future. *Journal of Educational Technology & Society, 18*(4), 486–497.

Lin, Y. C., Liu, T. C., Chang, M., & Yeh, S. P. (2009, August). Exploring children's perceptions of the robots. In *International Conference on Technologies for E-Learning and Digital Entertainment* (pp. 512-517). Springer. 10.1007/978-3-642-03364-3_63

Liou, H. H., Yang, S. J., Chen, S. Y., & Tarng, W. (2017). The influences of the 2D image-based augmented reality and virtual reality on student learning. *Journal of Educational Technology & Society, 20*(3), 110–121.

Li, S. C. S., & Huang, W. C. (2016). Lifestyles, innovation attributes, and teachers' adoption of game-based learning: Comparing non-adopters with early adopters, adopters and likely adopters in Taiwan. *Computers & Education, 96*, 29–41. doi:10.1016/j.compedu.2016.02.009

Litzinger, T. A., Lee, S. H., Wise, J. C., & Felder, R. M. (2007). A psychometric study of the index of learning styles. *Journal of Engineering Education, 96*(4), 309–319. doi:10.1002/j.2168-9830.2007.tb00941.x

Liu, Li, & Santhanam. (2013). Digital Games and Beyond: What Happens When Players Compete. *MIS Quarterly, 37*(1), 111-24.

Liu, E. Z. F., & Chen, P.-K. (2013). The Effect of Game-Based Learning on Students' Learning Performance in Science Learning – A Case of "Conveyance Go." *Procedia: Social and Behavioral Sciences, 103*, 1044–1051. doi:10.1016/j.sbspro.2013.10.430

Liu, S. H. (2011). Factors related to pedagogical beliefs of teachers and technology integration. *Computers & Education, 56*(4), 1012–1022. doi:10.1016/j.compedu.2010.12.001

Compilation of References

Liu, Y., Fu, Q., & Fu, X. (2009). The interaction between cognition and emotion. *Chinese Science Bulletin*, *54*(22), 4102–4116. doi:10.100711434-009-0632-2

Liu, Z., Moon, J., Kim, B., & Dai, C. P. (2020). Integrating additivity in educational games: A combined bibliometric analysis and meta-analysis review. *Educational Technology Research and Development*, *68*(4), 1931–1959. doi:10.100711423-020-09791-4

Live learning game show. (n.d.). *Gimkit*. Retrieved October 26, 2021, from https://www.gimkit.com/

Livingstone, S. (2003). The Changing Nature and Uses of Media Literacy. *European-mediaculture.org*, (4), 1-37.

Livingstone, S. (2004). What is media literacy? *Intermedia*, *32*(3), 18-20. Retrieved May 03, 2019 from http://eprints.lse.ac.uk/1027/1/What_is_media_literacy_(LSERO).pdf

Livingstone, S. (2009). *Children and the internet: Great expectations, challenging realities*. Polity Press.

Livstrom, I. C., Szostkowski, A. H., & Roehrig, G. H. (2019). Integrated STEM in practice: Learning from Montessori philosophies and practices. *School Science and Mathematics*, *119*(4), 190–202. doi:10.1111sm.12331

Li, Y., Garza, V., Keicher, A., & Popov, V. (2019). Predicting high school teacher use of technology: Pedagogical beliefs, technological beliefs and attitudes, and teacher training. *Technology. Knowledge and Learning*, *24*(3), 501–518. doi:10.100710758-018-9355-2

Lo, C. K., & Hew, K. F. (2017). A critical review of flipped classroom challenges in K-12 education: Possible solutions and recommendations for future research. *Research and Practice in Technology Enhanced Learning*, *12*(1), 1–22. doi:10.118641039-016-0044-2 PMID:30613253

LOGO Foundation. (2015). *Logo History*. https://el.media.mit.edu/logo-foundationl

Lombard, P. J. P. (2018). *Factors influencing the transition from high school to higher education: a case of the JuniorTukkie programme* [Doctor of Philosophy, University of Pretoria]. https://repository.up.ac.za/bitstream/handle/2263/67771/Lombard_Factors_2018.pdf?sequence=1&isAllowed

Lombardi, G. (2020). The role of unplugged coding activity in developing computational thinking in ages 6-11. In Handbook of Research on tools for teaching computational thinking in P-12 education (pp.184-199). Information Science Publishing.

Longenecker, J. G., McKinney, J. A., & Moore, C. W. (2004). Religious intensity, evangelical Christianity, and business ethics: An empirical study. *Journal of Business Ethics*, *55*(4), 371–384. doi:10.100710551-004-0990-2

Lopes & Mesquita. (2015). Evaluation of a gamification methodology in higher education. *Edulearn15 Proceedings*, 6996-7005.

Lopez Frias, F. J. (2019). Bernard Suits' Response to the Question on the Meaning of Life as a Critique of Modernity. *Sport, Ethics and Philosophy*, *13*(3-4), 406–418. doi:10.1080/17511321.2018.1550526

Lorås, M., Sindre, G., Trætteberg, H., & Aalberg, T. (2022). Study Behavior in Computing Education-A Systematic Literature Review. *ACM Transactions on Computing Education*, *22*(1), 1–28. doi:10.1145/3469129

Lorenzo, G., & Dziuban, C. (2006). *Ensuring the Net Generation is net savvy*. Educause Learning Initiative Paper 2, September 2006 EDUCAUSE Learning Initiative. https://understandingxyz.com/index_htm_files/Net%20Gen%20paper.pdf

Lotherington, H., & Jenson, J. (2011). Teaching multimodal and digital literacy in L2 settings: New literacies, new basics, new pedagogies. *Annual Review of Applied Linguistics*, *31*, 226–246. doi:10.1017/S0267190511000110

Lot, M., & Salleh, S. M. (2016). Game-based learning as a platform for formative assessment in principles of account. *Information (Japan), 19*(9B), 3971–3976.

Love, K., & Hamston, J. (2003). Teenage boys' leisure reading dispositions: Juggling male youth culture and family cultural capital. *Educational Review, 55*(2), 161–177.

Loveless, A., & Williamson, B. (2013). *Learning identities in a digital age: Rethinking creativity, education and technology*. Routledge. doi:10.4324/9780203591161

Lowyck, J., Elen, J., & Clarebout, G. (2004). Instructional conceptions: Analysis from an instructional design perspective. *International Journal of Educational Research, 41*(6), 429–444. doi:10.1016/j.ijer.2005.08.010

Lui, R., & Au, C. H. (2018). IS educational game: Adoption in teaching search engine optimization (SEO). *Journal of Computer Information Systems*.

Luke, C. (2000). Cyber-schooling and technological change: Multiliteracies for new times. In B. Cope & M. Kalantzis (Eds.), 2009 Multiliteracies (pp. 69–91). Macmillan.

Luke, A., & Elkins, J. (2002). Towards a critical, worldly, literacy. *Journal of Adolescent & Adult Literacy, 45*(18), 668–674.

Lu, L.-C., & Lu, C.-J. (2010). Moral Philosophy, Materialism, and Consumer Ethics: An Exploratory Study in Indonesia. *Journal of Business Ethics, 94*(2), 193–210. doi:10.100710551-009-0256-0

Luterbach, K. J., & Hubbell, K. R. (2015). Capitalizing on app development tools and technologies. *TechTrends, 59*(4), 62–70. doi:10.100711528-015-0872-8

Lyman, S. (2017). *Comparison of early literacy iPad applications: Children's engagement* [Unpublished master's thesis]. Brigham Young University, Provo, UT, United States.

Lynch, L., Fawcett, A. J., & Nicolson, R. I. (2000). Computer-assisted reading intervention in a secondary school: An evaluation study. *British Journal of Educational Technology, 31*(4), 333–348. doi:10.1111/1467-8535.00166

Lytras, M. D., Ruan, D., Tennyson, R. D., Ordonez De Pablos, P., García Peñalvo, F. J., & Rusu, L. (2013). Communications in Computer and Information Science. In Information Systems, E-learning, and Knowledge Management Research (vol. 278). doi:10.1007/978-3-642-35879-1

Lyytinen, H., Erskine, J., Kujala, J., Ojanen, E., & Richardson, U. (2009). In search of a science-based application: A learning tool for reading acquisition. *Scandinavian Journal of Psychology, 50*(6), 668–675. doi:10.1111/j.1467-9450.2009.00791.x PMID:19930268

Lyytinen, H., Erskine, J., Tolvanen, A., Torppa, M., Poikkeus, A.-M., & Lyytinen, P. (2006). Trajectories of reading development: A follow-up from birth to school age of children with and without risk for dyslexia. *Merrill-Palmer Quarterly, 52*(3), 514–546. doi:10.1353/mpq.2006.0031

Lyytinen, H., Ronimus, M., Alanko, A., Poikkeus, A., & Taanila, M. (2007). Early identification of dyslexia and the use of computer game-based practice to support reading acquisition. *Nordic Psychology, 59*(2), 109–126. doi:10.1027/1901-2276.59.2.109

Mac an Ghaill, M. (1994). *The making of men: Masculinities, sexualities and schooling*. Open University Press.

Mac Callum, K., Jeffrey, L., & Na, K. (2014). Factors impacting teachers' adoption of mobile learning. *Journal of Information Technology Education, 13*. doi:10.28945/1970

MacKay, K. (2015). *Does an iPad change the experience? A look at mother-child book reading interactions* [Unpublished doctoral dissertation]. Brigham Young University, Provo, UT, United States.

Compilation of References

MacMurren, H. (1985). *A comparative study of the effects of matching and mismatching sixth-grade students with their learning style preferences for the physical element of intake and their subsequent reading speed and accuracy scores and attitudes* (Doctoral dissertation). St. John's University.

MacQueen, K. M., & Milstein, B. (1999). A systems approach to qualitative data management and analysis. *Field Methods, 11*(1), 27–39. doi:10.1177/1525822X9901100103

Maddux, C. D., & Lamont, J. D. (2013). *Technology in Eduction: A Twenty-Year Retrospective*. Taylor and Francis. doi:10.4324/9781315821245

Magnan, A., & Ecalle, J. (2006). Audio-visual training in children with reading disabilities. *Computers & Education, 46*(4), 407–425. doi:10.1016/j.compedu.2004.08.008

Mahar, D., Henderson, R., & Deane, F. (1997). The effects of computer anxiety, state anxiety, and computer experience on users' performance of computer based tasks. *Personality and Individual Differences, 22*(5), 683–692. doi:10.1016/S0191-8869(96)00260-7

Maican, C., Lixandroiu, R., & Constantin, C. (2016). Interactive.ro – A study of a gamification framework using zero-cost tools. *Computers in Human Behavior, 61*, 186–197. doi:10.1016/j.chb.2016.03.023

Majid, S., Yeow, C. W., Audrey, C. S. Y., & Shyong, L. R. (2010). *Enriching learning experience through class participation: A students' perspective. 76th IFLA General Conference and Assembly: Satellite Meeting on Cooperation and Collaboration in Teaching and Research*, Gothenburg, Sweden.

Majuri, J., Koivisto, J., & Hamari, J. (2018). Gamification of education and learning: A review of empirical literature. *Proceedings of the 2nd International GamiFIN Conference*. Retrieved from: http://ceur-ws.org/Vol-2186/paper2.pdf

Makuwa, D., Amadhila, L., Shikongo, S., & Dengeinge, R. (2011). Trends in achievement levels of grade 6 Learners in Namibia. *Policy Brief, 1*.

Malak, M. S. (2013). Inclusive education in Bangladesh: Are pre-service teachers ready to accept students with special educational needs in regular classes? *Disability, CBR and Inclusive Development, 24*(1), 56–81. doi:10.5463/dcid.v24i1.191

Malegiannaki, I., Daradoumis, T., & Retalis, S. (2021). Using a Story-Driven Board Game to Engage Students and Adults With Cultural Heritage. *International Journal of Game-Based Learning, 11*(2), 1–19. doi:10.4018/IJGBL.2021040101

Malhotra, N. K., Kim, S. S., & Patil, A. (2006). Common method variance in IS research: A comparison of alternative approaches and a reanalysis of past research. *Management Science, 52*(12), 1865–1883. doi:10.1287/mnsc.1060.0597

Mallory, S. (2019). To the Mun: Kerbal Space Program as Playful, Educational Experience. In *International Conference on Human-Computer Interaction* (pp. 320-332). Springer. 10.1007/978-3-030-22602-2_24

Malone, T. W., & Lepper, M. R. (1987). Making learning fun: A taxonomy of intrinsic motivations for learning. In R.E. Snow & M.J Farr (Eds.), Aptitude, learning, and instruction volume 3: Conative and affective process analyses (pp. 223-253). Lawrence Erlbaum Associates, Publishers.

Mandel, M., & Long, E. (2017). *A Economia de Aplicativos no Brasil*. Washington, DC: PPI Progressive Policy Institute.

Manikas, A., Gupta, M., & Boyd, L. (2015). Experiential exercises with four production planning and control systems. *International Journal of Production Research, 53*(14), 4206–4217. doi:10.1080/00207543.2014.985393

Manovich, L. (2001). *The Language of New Media*. MIT Press.

Manovich, L. (2001). *The Language of new media*. The MIT Press.

Mantiri, O., Hibbert, G. K., & Jacobs, J. (2019). Digital literacy in ESL classroom. *Universal Journal of Educational Research*, *7*(5), 1301–1305. doi:10.13189/ujer.2019.070515

Manual:Preventing access—MediaWiki. (n.d.). Retrieved June 1, 2021, from https://www.mediawiki.org/wiki/Manual:Preventing_access

Manurung, K. (2012). Creative teachers and effective teaching strategies that motivates learners to learn. *Indonesian Journal of Science Education, 2*(1), 1-8.

Manzano-León, A., Camacho-Lazarraga, P., Guerrero, M. A., Guerrero-Puerta, L., Aguilar-Parra, J. M., Trigueros, R., & Alias, A. (2021). Between Level Up and Game Over: A Systematic Literature Review of Gamification in Education. *Sustainability*, *13*(4), 2247. doi:10.3390u13042247

Maqsood, S. (2020). *The Design, Development and Evaluation of a Digital Literacy Game for Preteens* (Doctoral dissertation). Carleton University.

Marcos-García, J. A., Martínez-Monés, A., & Dimitriadis, Y. (2015). DESPRO: A method based on roles to provide collaboration analysis support adapted to the participants in CSCL situations. *Computers & Education*, *82*, 335–353. doi:10.1016/j.compedu.2014.10.027

Marcovitz, D. M. (2012). *Powerful PowerPoint for educators: Using Visual Basic for applications to make PowerPoint interactive*. Abc-Clio.

Marczewski, A. (2015). *Game Thinking Decision Tree*. Gamified UK. https://www.gamified.uk/gamification-framework/differences-between-gamification-and-games/game-thinking-decision-trees-small/

Marczewski, A. (2013). *Gamification: A Simple Introduction*. Andrzej Marczewski.

Maree, J. G., Fletcher, L., & Sommerville, J. (2011). Predicting success among prospective first-year students at the University of Pretoria. *South African Journal of Higher Education*, *25*(6), 1125–1139.

Maree, K. (2020). Planning a research proposal. In K. Maree (Ed.), *First steps in research* (3rd ed., pp. 25–53). Van Schaik.

Marklund, B. B., & Taylor, A. S. A. (2016). Educational Games in Practice: The challenges involved in conducting a game-based curriculum. *Electronic Journal of e-Learning*, *14*(2), 122-135.

Marklund, B. B., & Taylor, A.-S. A. (2015). *Teachers' Many Roles in Game-Based Learning Projects*. The 9th European Conference on Games Based Learning (ECGBL'15), Steinkjer, Norway.

Marklund, B. B., & Alklind Taylor, A. S. (2016). Educational games in practice: The challenges involved in conducting a game-based curriculum. *Electronic Journal of E-Learning*, *14*(2), 121–135.

Marklund, B. B., & Taylor, A. S. A. (2015). Teachers' many roles in game-based learning projects. *Proceedings of the European Conference on Games-Based Learning*, 350–367.

Marlatt, R. (2019). Fortnite and the next level discourse: Understanding how gamers cultivate pedagogy in teacher education. *Proceedings from SITE '19: Society for Information Technology and Teacher Education Annual Conference*.

Marone, V. (2016). Playful constructivism: Making sense of digital games for learning and creativity through play, design, and participation. *Journal of Virtual Worlds Research*, *9*(3), 1–18. doi:10.4101/jvwr.v9i3.7244

Marquardt, M. (2007). Action learning: resolving real problems in real time. In M. Silberman (Ed.), *The handbook of experiential learning* (pp. 94–110). Pfeiffer.

Compilation of References

Marr, B. (2018). *7 Job Skills of The Future (That AIs And Robots Can't Do Better Than Humans)*. Retrieved from: https://www.forbes.com/sites/bernardmarr/2018/08/06/7-job-skills-of-the-future-that-ais-and-robots-cant-do-better-than-humans/#7c1894496c2e

Marshall, M. B. (2020). *White paper: Finding the way through the waves*. Retrieved from: https://www.eyebraingym.com/wp-content/uploads/2021/03/WHITEPAPER-Finding-the-way-through-the-waves-1.0_compressed.pdf

Marshall, M. B., Taukeni, S. G., Haihambo, C. K., Shihako, M., Muruti, R. D., Ligando, G., De Silva, C. & Marshall, M. (2020). Maximizing student's learning success through Lab-on-line. *Addressing multicultural needs in school guidance and counselling*, 262-276.

Marsh, J., & Yamada-Rice, D. (2013). Early literacy in the digital age. In D. Barone & M. Mallette (Eds.), *Best Practices in Early Literacy Instruction* (pp. 79–95). Guilford Press.

Martín del Pozo, M., Gómez-Pablos, V. B., Sánchez-Prieto, J. C., & García-Valcárcel Muñoz-Repiso, A. (2019). Review of Game-Based Learning in Secondary Education: Considering the Types of Video Games. Analysis. *Claves de Pensamiento Contemporáneo, 22*, 1–10.

Martin, J., & Sneegas, G. (2020). *Critical Worldbuilding: Toward a Geographical Engagement with Imagined Worlds*. /paper/Critical-Worldbuilding%3A-Toward-a-Geographical-with-Martin-Sneegas/8a8d4538706af65d8479b11cbd0f-cb135c32ca44

Martin, C. (2012). Video games, identity, and the constellation of information, video games, identity, and the constellation of information. *Bulletin of Science, Technology & Society, 32*(5), 384–392. doi:10.1177/0270467612463797

Martínez Muñoz, M., Jiménez Rodríguez, M. L., & Gutiérrez de Mesa, J. A. (2013). Electrical storm simulation to improve the learning physics process. *Informatics in Education, 12*(2), 191–206. doi:10.15388/infedu.2013.13

Martinez-Garza, M., Clark, D. B., & Nelson, B. C. (2013). Digital games and the US National Research Council's science proficiency goals. *Studies in Science Education, 49*(2), 170–208. doi:10.1080/03057267.2013.839372

Martino, J. C. R. (2019). *Hands-on machine learning with Microsoft Excel 2019: Build complete data analysis flows, from data collection to visualization*. Packt Publishing Ltd.

Martins, A., & Oliveira, L. (2019). Teachers' experiences and practices with game-based learning. *Proceedings of INTED2019 Conference*, 8575-8583. https://bit.ly/3guwMrd

Martin, W., Silander, M., & Rutter, S. (2019). Digital games as sources for science analogies: Learning about energy through play. *Computers & Education, 130*, 1–12. doi:10.1016/j.compedu.2018.11.002

Martí-Parreño, J., Méndez-Ibáñez, E., & Alonso-Arroyo, A. (2016). The use of gamification in education: A bibliometric and text mining analysis. *Journal of Computer Assisted Learning, 32*(6), 663–676. doi:10.1111/jcal.12161

Martí-Parreño, J., Seguí-Mas, D., & Seguí-Mas, E. (2016). Teachers' attitude towards and actual use of gamification. *Procedia: Social and Behavioral Sciences, 228*, 682–688. doi:10.1016/j.sbspro.2016.07.104

Marwick, A., & Ellison, N. (2012). "There isn't wifi in heaven!" Negotiating visibility on Facebook memorial pages. *Broadcast Education Association of Journal of Broadcasting and Electronic Media, 56*(3), 378–400. doi:10.1080/08838151.2012.705197

Massimino, P., Costa, A., Becciani, U., Krokos, M., Bandieramonte, M., Petta, C., Pistagna, C., Riggi, S., Sciacca, E., & Vitello, F. (2013). Learning astrophysics through mobile gaming. *Astronomical Data Analysis Software and Systems XXII, 475*, 113.

Massung, E., Coyle, D., Cater, K. F., Jay, M., & Preist, C. (2013). Using crowdsourcing to support pro-environmental community activism. In *Proceedings of the SIGCHI Conference on Human Factors in Computing Systems* (pp. 371-380). ACM. 10.1145/2470654.2470708

Masterman, L. (2005). *Teaching the Media*. Taylor and Francis.

Masterman, L. (1993). The Media Education Revolution. *Canadian Journal of Educational Communication, 22*(1), 5–14.

Maswahu, I. L. (2012). *Grade 10 dropout predisposition and resilience in one rural and one urban secondary school in the Kizito cluster of the Caprivi education region in Namibia*. University of the Western Cape. http://etd.uwc.ac.za/handle/11394/4494

Matheson, V. A., Abt-Perkins, D., & Snedden, D. (2002). *Making PowerPoint interactive with hyperlinks*. Paper presented at the poster session presented at the annual American Economic Association Convention, Atlanta, GA.

Mathevula, M. D., & Uwizeyimana, D. E. (2014). The challenges facing the integration of ICT in teaching and learning activities in South African Rural Secondary Schools. *Mediterranean Journal of Social Sciences, 5*(20), 1087–1097. doi:10.5901/mjss.2014.v5n20p1087

Mathrani, A., Christian, S., & Ponder-Sutton, A. (2016). PlayIT: Game based learning approach for teaching programming concepts. *Journal of Educational Technology & Society, 19*(2), 5–17.

Mattis, J. S. (2000). African American women's definitions of spirituality and religiosity. *The Journal of Black Psychology, 26*(1), 101–122. doi:10.1177/0095798400026001006

Mavromihales, M., Holmes, V., & Racasan, R. (2019). Game-based learning in mechanical engineering education: Case study of games-based learning application in computer aided design assembly. *International Journal of Mechanical Engineering Education, 47*(2), 156–179.

May, A. (2021). *Gamification, Game-Based Learning, and Student Engagement in Education*. Leadership Education Capstones 55. Retrieved from https://openriver.winona.edu/leadershipeducationcapstones/55

May, E. L., & Abreh, M. K. (2017). Strategies for Achieving ICT Literacy & Proficiency in the Rural Primary and Secondary Schools in Ghana. *Journal of Education & Social Sciences, 5*(2), 114–126. doi:10.20547/jess0521705203

Mayer, R. E. (2002). Multimedia learning. *Psychology of Learning and Motivation, 41*, 85–139. doi:10.1016/S0079-7421(02)80005-6

Mayer, R. E. (2020). Cognitive foundations of game-based learning. In J. L. Plass, R. E. Mayer, & B. D. Homer (Eds.), *Handbook of game-based learning* (pp. 83–110). The MIT Press.

Maynooth Students' Union. (2020). *COVID-19 Survey Results*. https://www.msu.ie/news/article/6013/COVID-19-Survey-Results/

Mayo, M. (2009). Video games: A route to large-scale STEM education? *Science, 323*(5910), 79–82. doi:10.1126cience.1166900 PMID:19119223

Mäyrä, F. (2008). *An introduction to Game Studies: Games in Culture*. Sage.

Mc Gregor, S. L. T., & Murnane, J. A. (2010). Paradigm, methodology and method: Intellectual integrity in consumer scholarship. *International Journal of Consumer Studies, 34*(4), 419–427. doi:10.1111/j.1470-6431.2010.00883.x

McCallum, S. (2012). Gamification and serious games for personalized health. *Studies in Health Technology and Informatics*. Advance online publication. doi:10.3233/978-1-61499-069-7-85 PMID:22942036

Compilation of References

McCarthy, M. (2016). Experiential Learning Theory: From Theory To Practice. *Journal of Business & Economics Research*, *14*(3), 91–100. doi:10.19030/jber.v14i3.9749

McCarthy, S. (2001). Identity construction in elementary readers and writers. *Reading Research Quarterly*, *36*(12), 122–134. doi:10.1598/RRQ.36.2.2

McCauley, V., Davison, K., McHugh, P., Domegan, C., & Grehan, A. (2021). Innovative Education Strategies to Advance Ocean Literacy. In *Ocean Literacy: Understanding the Ocean* (pp. 149–168). Springer. doi:10.1007/978-3-030-70155-0_7

McClelland, J. L., McNaughton, B. L., & O'Reilly, R. C. (1995). Why there are complementary learning systems in the hippocampus and neocortex: Insights from the successes and failures of connectionist models of learning and memory. *Psychological Review*, *102*(3), 419–457. doi:10.1037/0033-295X.102.3.419 PMID:7624455

McCoy, L., Lewis, J. H., & Dalton, D. (2016). Gamification and multimedia for medical Education: A landscape review. *Journal of Osteopathic Medicine*, *116*(1), 22–34. doi:10.7556/jaoa.2016.003 PMID:26745561

McCreery, M. P., Schrader, P. G., & Krach, S. K. (2011). Navigating Massively Multiplayer Online Games: Evaluating 21st Century Skills for Learning within Virtual Environments. *Journal of Educational Computing Research*, *44*(4), 473–493. doi:10.2190/EC.44.4.f

McCrindle, M. (2021). Generation Alpha. Academic Press.

McDaniel, S. W., & Burnett, J. J. (1990). Consumer religiosity and retail store evaluative criteria. *Journal of the Academy of Marketing Science*, *18*(2), 101–112. doi:10.1007/BF02726426

McGonigal, J. (2011). *Reality is broken: Why games make us better and how they can change the world*. Penguin Press.

McGonigal, J. (2011). *Reality is Broken: Why Games make us Better and How they can Change the World*. Penguin.

McGonigal, J. (2011). *Reality is Broken: Why Games Make Us Better and How They Can Change the World*. Penguin.

McGonigal, J. (2015). *SuperBetter: A revolutionary approach to getting stronger, happier, braver and more resilient*. Penguin.

McGreevy, S. (2011). Eight weeks to a better brain. *The Harvard Gazette*. https://news.harvard.edu/gazette/story/2011/01/eight-weeks-to-a-better-brain/

McKenney, S. (2005). Technology for curriculum and teacher development: Software to help educators learn while designing teacher guides. *Journal of Research on Technology in Education*, *38*(2), 167–190. doi:10.1080/15391523.2005.10782455

McKenzie, B., Brown, J., Casey, D., Cooney, A., Darcy, E., Giblin, S., & Mhórdha, M. N. (2018). From Poetry to Palmerstown: Using Wikipedia to Teach Critical Skills and Information Literacy in A First-Year Seminar. *College Teaching*, *66*(3), 140–147. doi:10.1080/87567555.2018.1463504

McKinley Ross, S. (2010). *Hoot Owl Hoot*. Peaceable Kingdom.

McKnight, K., O'Malley, K., Ruzic, R., Horsley, M. K., Franey, J. J., & Bassett, K. (2016). Teaching in a digital age: How educators use technology to improve student learning. *Journal of Research on Technology in Education*, *48*(3), 194–211. doi:10.1080/15391523.2016.1175856

McLaren, B. M., Adams, D. M., Mayer, R. E., & Forlizzi, J. (2017). A computer-based game that promotes mathematics learning more than a conventional approach. *International Journal of Game-Based Learning*, *7*(1), 36–56. doi:10.4018/IJGBL.2017010103

McLellan, S., Muddimer, A., & Peres, S. (2012). The effect of experience on system usability scale ratings. *Journal of Usability Studies*.

Mcleod, S. (2013). *Kolb-Learning Styles.* simplypsychology.org/learning-kolb.html

McLoughlin, C., & Lee, M. J. (2010). Personalised and self regulated learning in the Web 2.0 era: International exemplars of innovative pedagogy using social software. *Australasian Journal of Educational Technology, 26*(1). Advance online publication. doi:10.14742/ajet.1100

McMahon, C., Johnson, I., & Hecht, B. (2017). The Substantial Interdependence of Wikipedia and Google: A Case Study on the Relationship Between Peer Production Communities and Information Technologies. *Proceedings of the International AAAI Conference on Web and Social Media, 11*(1), Article 1. https://ojs.aaai.org/index.php/ICWSM/article/view/14883

McMorrow, C. (2020). *Coronavirus plunges universities into funding crisis.* https://www.rte.ie/news/2020/0503/1136316-covid-19-universities/

McNamara, D. S., Jackson, G. T., & Graesser, A. C. (2009). Intelligent Tutoring and Games (ITaG). *Proc. Workshop Intelligent Educational Games at the 14th Int'l Conf. Artificial Intelligence in Education*, 1-10.

Mehra, V., & Omidina, F. (2010). Predicting Factors Affecting University Students' Attitudes To Adopt E-Learning in India Using Technology Acceptance Model. *International Journal on New Trends in Education and Their Implications, 1*(June), 33–43.

Mehrpour, S., & Ghayour, M. (2017). The effect of educational computerized games on learning English spelling among Iranian children. *The Reading Matrix: An International Online Journal, 17*(2), 165–178.

Mehta, S. (2020). Modern teaching methods: Importance and application. *Eduvoice: The Voice of Education Industry*. Retrieved from https://eduvoice.in/modern-teaching-methods/

Mehtab, F. H. (2019). *Constitutional responsibility of the Government of Bangladesh for implementing compulsory primary education: Issues and challenges* [Doctoral dissertation, University of Dhaka]. Dhaka University Institutional Repository.

Mehtälä, S. (2018). *User interface design for children and youth: websites and applications to promote mental health and wellbeing*. Academic Press.

Melzer, P. (2019). Personalising the IS classroom–insights on course design and implementation. In *A conceptual framework for personalised learning* (pp. 77–100). Springer Gabler. doi:10.1007/978-3-658-23095-1_4

Mendez, M., & Boude, O. (2021). Uso de los videojuegos en básica primaria: Una revisión sistemática. *Espacios, 42*(1), 66–80. doi:10.48082/espacios-a21v42n01p06

Menking, A., & Rosenberg, J. (2021). WP:NOT, WP:NPOV, and Other Stories Wikipedia Tells Us: A Feminist Critique of Wikipedia's Epistemology. *Science, Technology & Human Values, 46*(3), 455–479. doi:10.1177/0162243920924783

Menon, D., Romero, M., & Viéville, T. (2019). Computational thinking development and assessment through tabletop escape games. *International Journal of Serious Games, 6*(4), 3–18.

Menon, V., Boyett-Anderson, J. M., & Reiss, A. L. (2005). Maturation of medial temporal lobe response and connectivity during memory encoding. *Brain Research. Cognitive Brain Research, 25*(1), 379–385. doi:10.1016/j.cogbrainres.2005.07.007 PMID:16122916

Mentor Gilmor, D. (2008). *Principles for a new media literacy*. Berkman Center for Internet & Society at Harvard University.

Mentz, E., & Goosen, L. (2007). Are groups working in the Information Technology class? *South African Journal of Education, 27*(2), 329–343.

Compilation of References

Merriam, S. (1988). *Case study research in education. A qualitative approach*. Jossey-Bass.

Merriam, S. B., & Tisdell, E. J. (2015). *Qualitative research: A guide to design and implementation* (4th ed.). Jossey-Bass.

Merrill, J., & Merrill, K. (2019). *The Interactive Class*. Elevate Books Edu.

Mertala, P. (2019). Digital technologies in early childhood education – a frame analysis of preservice teachers' perceptions. *Early Child Development and Care, 189*(8), 1228–1241. doi:10.1080/03004430.2017.1372756

Mesko, B., Győrffy, Z., & Kollár, J. (2015). Digital literacy in the medical curriculum: A course with social media tools and Gamification. *JMIR Medical Education, 1*(2), e4411. doi:10.2196/mededu.4411 PMID:27731856

Meyer, D. Z., & Avery, L. M. (2009). Excel as a qualitative data analysis tool. *Field Methods, 21*(1), 91–112. doi:10.1177/1525822X08323985

Meyer, M., & Wood, L. (2017). A critical reflection on the multiple roles required to facilitate mutual learning during service-learning in Creative Arts education. *Teaching in Higher Education, 22*(2), 158–177. doi:10.1080/13562517.2016.1221808

Mezirow, J. (2009). An overview on transformative learning. In K. Illeris (Ed.), *Contemporary Theories of Learning* (pp. 90–105). Routledge. doi:10.4324/9781315147277

Michael, D., & Chen, S. (2006). *Serious games: Games that educate, train, and inform*. Thomson Course Technology.

Michaelson, C. (2016). A novel approach to business ethics education: Exploring how to live and work in the 21st century. *Academy of Management Learning & Education, 15*(3), 588–606. doi:10.5465/amle.2014.0129

Michalos, A. C. (1982). Purpose and policy. *Journal of Business Ethics, 1*(4), 331.

Michalos, A. C., & Simon, H. A. (1970). The Sciences of the Artificial. *Technology and Culture, 11*(1), 118. Advance online publication. doi:10.2307/3102825

Mifsud, C. L., Vella, R., & Camilleri, L. (2013). Attitudes toward and effects of the use of video games in classroom learning with specific reference to literacy attainment. *Research in Education, 90*(1), 32–52. doi:10.7227/RIE.90.1.3

Mihailidis, P. (2011). New Civic Voices & Emerging Media Literacy Landscape. *The Journal of Media Literacy Education, 3*(1), 4–5.

Mikre, F. (2011). The Roles of Information Communication Technologies in Education: Review Article with Emphasis to the Computer and Internet. *Ethiopian Journal of Education and Sciences, 6*(2), 109–126.

Miles, M. B., Huberman, A. M., & Saldaña, J. (2014). *Qualitative data analysis*. Sage.

Milgram, P., & Kishino, F. (1994). A taxonomy of mixed reality visual displays. *IEICE Transactions on Information and Systems, 77*, 1321–1329.

Milgram, P., Takemura, H., Utsumi, A., & Kishino, F. (1995, December). Augmented reality: A class of displays on the reality-virtuality continuum. In *Telemanipulator and telepresence technologies* (Vol. 2351, pp. 282–292). International Society for Optics and Photonics. doi:10.1117/12.197321

Miller, A. (2012). *Kinect in the Classroom*. Retrieved September 15, 2021 from https://www.edutopia.org/blog/kinect-classroom-andrew-miller

Miller, C. (2013). The gamification of education. *Developments in Business Simulation and Experiential Learning, 40*, 196–200. https://absel-ojs-ttu.tdl.org/absel/index.php/absel/article/view/40

Miller, C. (2013). The gamification of education. *Developments in Business Simulation and Experiential Learning, 40*. https://absel-ojs-ttu.tdl.org/absel/index.php/absel/article/view/40/38

Miller, C.T. (2008). Games: Purpose and Potential in Education. *Springer Science*, 7.

Miller, J. Y. (2021). *Digital Literacy: The Impact of a Blended Learning Model on Student Motivation and Achievement* (Doctoral dissertation). Gardner-Webb University.

Miller, M. (2015). *Ditch that textbook*. Dave Burgess Consulting, Inc.

Miller, M., Ridgway, N., & Ridgway, A. (2019). *Don't ditch that tech: Differentiated instruction in a digital world*. Dave Burgess Consulting, Inc.

Milli Eğitim Bakanlığı. (2018). *Medya Okuryazarlığı Dersi Öğretim Programı (Ortaokul ve İmam Hatip Ortaokulu 7 veya 8. Sınıflar)*. Temel Eğitim Genel Müdürlüğü.

Mills, K. A. (2015). *Literacy theories for the digital age: Social, critical, multimodal, spatial, material, and sensory lenses*. Multilingual Matters. doi:10.21832/9781783094639

Milovanović, M., Minović, M., Kovačević, I., Minović, J., & Starčević, D. (2009). *Effectiveness of Game-Based Learning: Influence of Cognitive Style*. Paper presented at the Best Practices for the Knowledge Society. Knowledge, Learning, Development and Technology for All, Berlin, Germany.

Miltgen, C. L., & Peyrat-Guillard, D. (2014). Cultural and generational influences on privacy concerns: A qualitative study in seven European countries. *European Journal of Information Systems, 23*(2), 103–125. doi:10.1057/ejis.2013.17

Milton, J., Jonsen, S., Hirst, S., & Lindenburn, S. (2012). Foreign language vocabulary development through activities in an online 3D environment. *Language Learning Journal, 40*(1), 99–112. doi:10.1080/09571736.2012.658229

Minishi-Majanja, M. K. (2007). Integration of ICTs in library and information science education in sub-Saharan Africa. *World library and information congress: 73rd IFLA general conference and council, 19*.

Ministry of Education Arts and Culture & UNICEF Namibia. (2016). *We are the architects of our destiny: Study of positive deviant schools in Namibia*. https://www.unicef.org/namibia/na.MoEAC_-_Positive_Deviant_Schools_Report_(2016)_-_web_quality(1).pdf

Ministry of Education Arts and Culture. (2015). *Final Draft Language Policy for Schools in Namibia: Pre-primary, Grade 1-12*. Windhoek: Ministry of Education Arts and Culture.

Ministry of Education Bangladesh (MoE). (2004). *National Education Commission Report 2003*. http://lib.banbeis.gov.bd/pdf_view.php?book=National%20education%20Commission%20report-2003.pdf

Ministry of Education Bangladesh (MoE). (2010). National. *Educational Policy, 2010*. https://moedu.gov.bd/sites/default/files/files/moedu.portal.gov.bd/page/ad5cfca5_9b1e_4c0c_a4eb_fb1ded9e2fe5/National%20Education%20Policy%202010%20final.pdf

Ministry of Education. (2005). *Curriculum for the Lower Primary Phase: English Version*. Windhoek: Ministry of Education.

Miri, D. H., & Macke, J. (2021). Gamification, Motivation, and Engagement at Work: A Qualitative Multiple Case Study. *European Business Review*. Advance online publication. doi:10.1108/EBR-04-2020-0106

Mishra, P., & Koehler, M. (2009). Too cool for school? No way! Using the TPACK framework: you can have your hot tools and teach with them, too. *Learning & Leading with Technology, 36*(7), 14+. link.gale.com/apps/doc/A199794723/AONE?u=byuprovo&sid=bookmark-AONE&xid=6b0decfc

Compilation of References

Mishra, P. (2019). Considering contextual knowledge: The TPACK diagram gets an upgrade. *Journal of Digital Learning in Teacher Education*, *35*(2), 76–78. doi:10.1080/21532974.2019.1588611

Mishra, P., & Koehler, J. (2006). Technological pedagogical content knowledge: A new framework for teacher knowledge. *Teachers College Record*, *108*(6), 1017–1054. doi:10.1111/j.1467-9620.2006.00684.x

Mishra, P., & Koehler, M. (2006). Technological pedagogical content knowledge: A framework for integrating technology in teachers' knowledge. *Teachers College Record*, *108*(6), 1017–1054. https://doi.org/10.1111/j.1467-9620.2006.00684.x

Misra, R., Eyombo, L. B., & Phillips, F. T. (2019). Benefits and Challenges of Using Educational Games. In *Digital Games for Minority Student Engagement: Emerging Research and Opportunities*. doi:10.4018/978-1-5225-3398-6.ch001

Mohamad, A. (2021). The Impact of Project-Based Learning on Students' Cultural Awareness. *International Journal of Language and Literary Studies*, *3*(2), 54–80. Advance online publication. doi:10.36892/ijlls.v3i2.601

Mohamad, A. A. A., Amirnuddin, P. S., Ahmad, M. H., & Ramalingam, C. L. (2021). Transforming Legal Education Teaching and Learning: The Remote Communication Technology. *Malayan Law Journal*, *2*, cxxxvii.

Mohamad, A., & Tamer, Y. (2021). A review of literature on Project-Based Learning inside language education. *Turkish Online Journal of English Language Teaching*, *6*(2), 79–105.

Moher, D., Liberati, A., Tetzlaff, J., & Altman, D. G. (2009). Preferred reporting items for systematic reviews and meta-analyses: The PRISMA statement. *International Journal of Surgery*, *8*(5), 336–341. doi:10.1016/j.ijsu.2010.02.007 PMID:20171303

Mojo, *Montra de Jogos* IST. (2017). Retrieved October 5, 2021, from, https://tecnico.ulisboa.pt/en/events/mojo-montra-de-jogos/

Mojo, *Montra de Jogos* IST. (2018). Retrieved October 5, 2021, from, https://tecnico.ulisboa.pt/en/events/mojo-11th-edition/

Mojo, *Montra de Jogos* IST. (2019). Retrieved October 5, 2021, from, https://tecnico.ulisboa.pt/en/events/mojo-2019-12th-edition/

Mojo, *Montra de Jogos* IST. (2020). Retrieved October 5, 2021, from, https://tecnico.ulisboa.pt/en/events/mojo-2020-13th-edition/

Mojo, *Montra de Jogos* IST. (2021). Retrieved October 5, 2021, from, https://labjogos.tecnico.ulisboa.pt/mojo/2021/

Molderez, I., & Fonseca, E. (2018). The efficacy of real-world experiences and service learning for fostering competences for sustainable development in higher education. *Journal of Cleaner Production*, *172*, 4397–4410. doi:10.1016/j.jclepro.2017.04.062

Molin, G. (2017). The Role of the Teacher in Game-Based Learning: A Review and Outlook. Serious Games and Edutainment Applications, 649-674. doi:10.1007/978-3-319-51645-5_28

Moloi, T. J. (2015). Using indigenous games to teach problem-solving in mathematics in rural learning ecologies. *Journal of Higher Education in Africa/Revue de l'enseignement supèrieur en Afrique*, *13*(1-2), 21-32.

Moloi, T. J., Mosia, M. S., Matabane, M. E., & Sibaya, K. T. (2021). The Use of Indigenous Games to Enhance the Learning of Word Problems in Grade 4 Mathematics: A Case of Kgati. *International Journal of Learning, Teaching and Educational Research*, *20*(1), 240–259.

Mølstad, C. E. (2015). State-based curriculum-making: Approaches to local curriculum work in Norway and Finland. *Journal of Curriculum Studies*, *47*(4), 441–461. doi:10.1080/00220272.2015.1039067

Monaghan, J. E. (1988). Literacy Instruction and Gender in Colonial New England. *American Quarterly*, *40*(1), 18–41. https://doi.org/10.2307/2713140

Monsoï, K. C. (2017). Information Communication and Technology (ICT) diffusion and inequality in Africa. *Journal of Internet and Information Systems*, *7*(1), 1–7. doi:10.5897/JIIS2016.0090

Monteiro, T. B. P. (2017). "História Go": O contributo dos dispositivos móveis para o ensino-aprendizagem nas visitas de estudo. Relatório realizado no âmbito do Mestrado em Ensino de História no 3.o Ciclo do Ensino Básico e Ensino Secundário. Faculdade de Letras da Universidade do Porto.

Montessori, M. (1948). *The discovery of the child*. Kalakshetra.

Moon, J.-W., & Kim, Y.-G. (2001). Extending the TAM for a World-Wide-Web context. *Information & Management*, *38*(4), 217–230. doi:10.1016/S0378-7206(00)00061-6

Moran, J. (2013). A integração das tecnologias na educação. In A Educação que desejamos: novos desafios e como chegar lá (5th ed.). Campinas: Papirus.

Moreno, R., & Mayer, R. (2007). Interactive multimodal learning environments: special issue on interactive learning environments: contemporary issues and trends. *Educational Psychology Review*, *19*(3), 309–326. doi:10.100710648-007-9047-2

Morris, B. J., Croker, S., Masnick, A., & Zimmerman, C. (2012). *The emergence of scientific reasoning. In Trends in Cognitive Development*. InTech.

Morris, B. J., Croker, S., Zimmerman, C., Gill, D., & Romig, C. (2013). Gaming science: The "Gamification" of scientific thinking. *Frontiers in Psychology*, *4*, 607. doi:10.3389/fpsyg.2013.00607 PMID:24058354

Morris, T. H., & Rohs, M. (2021). The potential for digital technology to support self-directed learning in formal education of children: A scoping review. *Interactive Learning Environments*, 1–14. doi:10.1080/10494820.2020.1870501

Moschovaki, E., Meadows, S., & Pellegrini, A. (2007). Teachers' affective presentation of children's books and young children's display of affective engagement during classroom book reading. *Instituto Superior de Psicologia Aplicada*, *22*(4), 405-420. doi:10.1007/BF03173463

Moseley, A., & Whitton, N. (2015). Using games to enhance the student experience. York, UK: Higher Education Academy (HEA).

Moses, A. (2013). What, when, and how electronic media can be used in an early literacy classroom. In D. Barone & M. Mallette (Eds.), *Best Practices in Early Literacy Instruction* (pp. 96–118). Guilford Press.

Moura, A. (2009). *Geração móvel: um ambiente de aprendizagem suportado por tecnologias móveis para a "Geração Polegar"*. Universidade do Minho, Centro de Competência.

Mou, S. (2016). Possibilities and challenges of ICT integration in the Bangladesh education system. *Educational Technology*, *56*(2), 50–53. http://www.jstor.org/stable/44430461

Mousumi, M. A., & Kusakabe, T. (2017). Proliferating English-Medium schools in Bangladesh and their educational significance among the "Clientele". *Journal of International Development and Cooperation*, *23*(1), 1–13. https://ir.lib.hiroshima-u.ac.jp/files/public/4/42488/20170215110511630423/JIDC_23-1_1.pdf

Movellan, J., Eckhardt, M., Virnes, M., & Rodriguez, A. (2009). Sociable robot improves toddler vocabulary skills. *Proceedings of the 4th ACM/IEEE International Conference on Human Robot Interaction*, 307-308. 10.1145/1514095.1514189

Compilation of References

Mozelius, P., & Olsson, M. (2017, October). Learning to program by building learning games. In *European Conference on Games Based Learning* (pp. 448-455). Academic Conferences International Limited.

Mozelius, P., Fagerström, A., & Söderquist, M. (2017). Motivating factors and tangential learning for knowledge acquisition in educational games. *Electronic Journal of e-Learning, 15*(4), 343-354.

Mozelius, P., Hernandez, W., Sällström, J., & Hellerstedt, A. (2017). Teacher attitudes toward game-based learning in history education. *International Journal of Information and Communication Technology Education, 6*(4), 27–35. doi:10.1515/ijicte-2017-0017

Mubin, O., Stevens, C. J., Shahid, S., Al Mahmud, A., & Dong, J. J. (2013). A review of the applicability of robots in education. *Journal of Technology in Education and Learning, 1*(209). doi:10.2316/Journal.209.2013.1.209-0015

Mubin, O., Shahid, S., & Bartneck, C. (2013). Robot Assisted Language Learning through Games: A Comparison of Two Case Studies. *Australian Journal of Intelligent Information Processing Systems, 13*(3), 9–14.

Mukwambo, P. (2019). *Quality higher education means more than learning how to work*. The Conversation. https://theconversation.com/quality-higher-education-means-more-than-learning-how-to-work-122820

Mulhall, A. (2003). In the field: Notes on observation in qualitative research. *Journal of Advanced Nursing, 41*(3), 306–313. doi:10.1046/j.1365-2648.2003.02514.x PMID:12581118

Mumtaz, S. (2000). Factors affecting teachers' use of information and communications technology: A review of the literature. *Journal of Information Technology for Teacher Education, 9*(3), 319–342. doi:10.1080/14759390000200096

Mun, Y. (2003). Predicting the use of web-based information systems: Self-efficacy, enjoyment, learning goal orientation, and the technology acceptance model. *International Journal of Human-Computer Studies, 59*(4), 431–449. doi:10.1016/S1071-5819(03)00114-9

Muris, P., Meesters, C., Merckelbach, H., & Hulsenbeck, P. (2000). Worry in children is related to perceived parental rearing and attachment. *Behaviour Research and Therapy, 38*(5), 487–497. doi:10.1016/S0005-7967(99)00072-8 PMID:10816907

Musante, K., & DeWalt, B. R. (2010). *Participant observation: A guide for fieldworkers*. Rowman Altamira.

Mustapha, S. M., Abd Rahman, N. S. N., & Yunus, M. M. (2010). Factors influencing classroom participation: A case study of Malaysian undergraduate students. *Procedia: Social and Behavioral Sciences, 9*, 1079–1084.

Mustar, P. (2009). Technology management education: Innovation and entrepreneurship at MINES ParisTech, a leading French engineering school. *Academy of Management Learning & Education, 8*(3), 418–425.

Mutakinati L., Anwari I., & Yoshisuke K. (2018). Analysis of students' critical thinking skill of middle school through STEM education project-based learning. *Journal Pendidikan IPA Indonesia, 7*(1), 54-65. doi:10.15294/jpii.v7i1.10495

Muthuprasad, T., Aiswarya, S., Aditya, K. S., & Jha, G. K. (2021). Students' perception and preference for online education in India during COVID-19 pandemic. *Social Sciences & Humanities Open, 3*(1), 100101. Advance online publication. doi:10.1016/j.ssaho.2020.100101 PMID:34173507

Mutula, S. (2004). IT diffusion in Sub-Saharan Africa: Implications for developing and managing digital libraries. *New Library World, 105*(7/8), 281–289. doi:10.1108/03074800410551039

Mweli, P. (2018). Indigenous stories and games as approaches to teaching within the classroom. *Understanding Educational Psychology*, 94-101.

Myers, B. (2008). Minds at play. *American Libraries, 39*(5), 54–57.

Mystakidis, S., & Berki, E. (2018). The case of literacy motivation: Playful 3D immersive learning environments and problem-focused Education for blended digital storytelling. *International Journal of Web-Based Learning and Teaching Technologies*, *13*(1), 64–79. doi:10.4018/IJWLTT.2018010105

Nadolny, L., Alaswad, Z., Culver, D., & Wang, W. (2017). Designing with game-based learning: Game mechanics from middle school to higher education. *Simulation & Gaming*, *48*(6), 814–831. doi:10.1177/1046878117736893

Nagy, Molnár, Szenkovits, Horváth-Czinger, & Szűts. (2018). Gamification and microcontent orientated methodological solutions based on bring-your-own device logic in higher education. *2018 9th IEEE International Conference on Cognitive Infocommunications (Coginfocom)*, 385-388. doi:10.1109/CogInfoCom.2018.8639702

Nah, F. F.-H., Zeng, Q., Telaprolu, V. R., Ayyappa, A. P., & Eschenbrenner, B. (2014). Gamification of Education: A Review of Literature. Academic Press.

Nakamura, J., & Csikszentmihalyi, M. (2002). The concept of flow. In C. R. Snyder & S. J. Lopez (Eds.), Handbook of positive psychology (pp. 89–105). Academic Press.

Namibia Statistics Agency. (2013). *Namibia 2011 Population & Housing Census - Main Report*. http://www.nsa.org.na/files/downloads/Namibia 2011 Population and Housing Census Main Report.pdf

Naraghi-Taghi-Off, R., Horst, R., & Dörner, R. (2020). Gamification Mechanics for Playful Virtual Reality Authoring. In STAG (pp. 131-141). Academic Press.

Nath, S. R., & Chowdhury, M. A. R. (2019). *State of primary education in Bangladesh: Progress made, challenges remained*. Campaign for Popular Education.

National Association for the Education of Young Children. (2012). *Technology and interactive media as tools in early childhood programs serving children from birth through age 8*. http://www.naeyc.org/files/naeyc/file/positions/ PS_technology_ WEB2.pdf

National Early Literacy Panel. (2004, December). *The National Early Literacy Panel: Findings from a synthesis of scientific research on early literacy development* [Paper presentation]. The National Reading Conference, San Antonio, TX, United States.

National Education Association. (2010). *Preparing 21st century students for a global society: An educator's guide to the "Four Cs."* National Education Association.

National Governors Association Center for Best Practices & Council of Chief State School Officers. (2010). *Common Core State Standards (English Language Arts)*. http://corestandards.org/

National Research Council. (1997). *Science Teaching Reconsidered: A Handbook*. The National Academies Press. doi:10.17226/5287

National Research Council. (2010). *Exploring the Intersection of Science Education and 21st Century Skills: A Workshop Summary*. Washington, DC: National Academies Press.

National Research Council. (2012). *A Framework for K-12 Science Education: Practices, Crosscutting Concepts, and Core Ideas*. National Academies Press.

Navarrete, C. (2013). Creative thinking in digital game design and development: A case study. *Computers & Education*, *69*, 320–331. doi:10.1016/j.compedu.2013.07.025

NCTE. (2019). *Definition of Literacy in a Digital Age*. National Council of Teachers of English Position Statements. https://ncte.org/statement/nctes-definition-literacy-digital-age/

Compilation of References

NCTM. (2014). *Principles to Actions: Ensuring Mathematical Success For All*. NCTM.

Ndawi, V. E., Thomas, K. A., & Nyaruwata, T. L. (2013). Barriers to Effective Integration of Information and Communication Technology in Harare Secondary Schools. *International Journal of Scientific Research, 2*(9), 211–216.

Nebel, S., Schneider, S., & Rey, G. D. (2015). From duels to classroom competition: Social competition and learning in educational videogames within different group sizes. *Computers in Human Behavior, 55*, 384–398. doi:10.1016/j.chb.2015.09.035

Nebel, S., Schneider, S., & Rey, G. D. (2016). Mining learning and crafting scientific experiments: A literature review on the use of Minecraft in education and research. *Journal of Educational Technology & Society, 19*(2), 355–366.

Neidorf, T., Arora, A., Erberber, E., Tsokodayi, Y., & Mai, T. (2020). *Student misconceptions and errors in Physics and Mathematics: exploring Data from TIMSS and TIMSS Advanced*. Springer Nature. doi:10.1007/978-3-030-30188-0

Nekongo-Nielsen, H., Mbukusa, N. R., & Tjiramba, E. (2015). Investigating factors that lead to school dropout in Namibia. *Namibia CPD Journal for Educators, 2*(1), 99–118. http://journals.unam.edu.na/index.php/NCPDJE/article/view/1282/1109

Nel, C., Dreyer, C., & Klopper, M. (2004). An analysis of the reading profiles of first-year students at Potchefstroom University: A cross-sectional study and a case study. *South African Journal of Education, 24*(1), 95–103.

Nestor, E. (2019). *Undergraduate Curriculum Evaluation*. Maynooth University.

Neumann, M. M., & Neumann, D. L. (2014). Touch screen tablets and emergent literacy. *Early Childhood Education Journal, 42*(4), 231–239. https://www.learntechlib.org/p/152727/

Neutral point of view. (2019b). In *Wikipedia*. https://en.wikipedia.org/w/index.php?title=Wikipedia:Neutral_point_of_view&oldid=901367786

Neville, D. O. (2015). The story in the mind: The effect of 3D gameplay on the structuring of written L2 narratives. *ReCALL, 27*(1), 21–37. doi:10.1017/S0958344014000160

Newbery, R., Lean, J., & Moizer, J. (2016). Evaluating the impact of serious games: The effect of gaming on entrepreneurial intent. *Information Technology & People, 29*(4), 733–749. doi:10.1108/ITP-05-2015-0111

Newbery, R., Lean, J., Moizer, J., & Haddoud, M. (2018). Entrepreneurial identity formation during the initial entrepreneurial experience: The influence of simulation feedback and existing identity. *Journal of Business Research, 85*, 51–59. doi:10.1016/j.jbusres.2017.12.013

Newman, J. (2001). Eye level. In J. Bell & P. Magrs (Eds.), *The creative writing coursebook* (pp. 141–147). Macmillan.

Newton, L. D., & Newton, D. P. (2014). Creativity in 21st-century education. *Prospects, 44*(4), 575–589. doi:10.100711125-014-9322-1

Ney, M., Emin, V., & Earp, J. (2012). Paving the Way to Game Based Learning: A Question Matrix for Teacher Reflection. *Procedia Computer Science, 15*, 17–24. doi:10.1016/j.procs.2012.10.053

Nganji, J. T. (2018). Towards learner-constructed e-learning environments for effective personal learning experiences. *Behaviour & Information Technology, 37*(7), 647–657. doi:10.1080/0144929X.2018.1470673

Nhongo, K. (2014, March 19). Grade 5 NSAT results depressing. *Windhoek Observer*. http://www.observer.com.na/national/3131-grade-5-nsat-results-depressing#

Nicholson, S. (2012). *Strategies for meaningful gamification: Concepts behind transformative play and participatory museums*. Presented at Meaningful Play 2012, Lansing, MI. Retrieved August 22, 2016, from https://scottnicholson.com/pubs/meaningfulstrategies.pdf

Nicholson, R. I., & Fawcett, A. J. (2000). Long-term learning in dyslexic children. *The European Journal of Cognitive Psychology*, *12*(3), 357–393. doi:10.1080/09541440050114552

Nicholson, S. (2012). A user-centered theoretical framework for meaningful Gamification. *Games Learning Society*, *8*(1), 223–230.

Nicholson, S. (2018). Creating engaging escape rooms for the classroom. *Childhood Education*, *94*(1), 44–49. doi:10.1080/00094056.2018.1420363

Niederhauser, D. S., & Stoddart, T. (2001). Teachers' instructional perspectives and use of educational software. *Teaching and Teacher Education*, *17*(1), 15–31. doi:10.1016/S0742-051X(00)00036-6

Nielson, K. A., & Powless, M. (2007). Positive and negative sources of emotional arousal enhance long-term word-list retention when induced as long as 30 min after learning. *Neurobiology of Learning and Memory*, *88*(1), 40–47. doi:10.1016/j.nlm.2007.03.005 PMID:17467310

Niemeyer, D., & Gerber, H. R. (2015). Maker culture and *Minecraft*: Implications for the future of learning. *Educational Media International*, *52*(3), 216–226. doi:10.1080/09523987.2015.1075103

Nieto, J. J., Creus, R., & Giro-i-Nieto, X. (2021). *Unsupervised Skill-Discovery and Skill-Learning in Minecraft*. arXiv preprint arXiv:2107.08398.

Nieto-Escamez, F. A., & Roldán-Tapia, M. D. (2021). Gamification as online teaching strategy during COVID-19: A mini-review. *Frontiers in Psychology*, *12*(648552), 648552. Advance online publication. doi:10.3389/fpsyg.2021.648552 PMID:34093334

Ninnes, P. (2011). *Improving Quality and Equity in Education in Namibia: A Trend and Gap Analysis*. Academic Press.

Nkopodi, N., & Mosimege, M. (2009). Incorporating the indigenous game of morabaraba in the learning of mathematics. *South African Journal of Education*, *29*(3), 377–392. doi:10.15700aje.v29n3a273

Noble, K. G., Wolmetz, M. E., Ochs, L. G., Farah, M. J., & McCandliss, B. D. (2006). Brain behavior relationships in reading acquisition are modulated by socio-economic factors. *Developmental Science*, *9*(6), 642–654. doi:10.1111/j.1467-7687.2006.00542.x PMID:17059461

Nobre, A. (2020). The Pedagogy That Makes the Students Act Collaboratively and Open Educational Practices. In *Personalization and Collaboration in Adaptive E-Learning*. IGI Global. doi:10.4018/978-1-7998-1492-4.ch002

Nobre, A. (2021). Open Educational Practices and Resources in the Higher Education Learning Environment. In *Advancing Online Course Design and Pedagogy for the 21st Century Learning Environment*. IGI Global. doi:10.4018/978-1-7998-5598-9.ch006

Nobre, A., Mouraz, A., Goulão, M.F., Henriques, S., Barros, D., & Moreira, J. A. (2021). Processos de Comunicação Digital no Sistema Educativo Português em Tempos de Pandemia. *Revista Práxis Educacional, 17*(45), 1-19.

Nobre, A. (2021). Educational Practices Resulting From Digital Intelligence. In *Handbook of Research on Teaching With Virtual Environments and AI*. IGI Global., doi:10.4018/978-1-7998-7638-0.ch003.

Nonoo, S. (2019). *Playing Games Can Build 21st-Century Skills*. Research Explains How.

Nordby, A., Øygardslia, K., Sverdrup, U., & Sverdrup, H. (2016). The art of gamification; Teaching sustainability and system thinking by pervasive game development. *The Electronic Journal of e-Learning, 14*(3), 152–168.

Nor, E. B. A., & Eu, L. K. (2014). Hubungan antara sikap, minat, pengajaran guru dan pengaruh rakan sebaya terhadap pencapaian matametik tambahan tingkatan 4. *JuKu:Jurnal Kurikulum & Pengajaran Asia Pasifik, 2*(1), 1–10.

Norman, K. L. (2011). *Assessing the Components of Skill Necessary for Playing Video Games.* Human-Computer Interaction Technical Report 11-11-11. University of Maryland. Available online at: http://hcil2.cs.umd.edu/trs/2011-27/2011-27.pdf

Noroozi, O., Dehghanzadeh, H., & Talaee, E. (2020). A systematic review on the impacts of game-based learning on argumentation skills. *Entertainment Computing, 35*, 100369. doi:10.1016/j.entcom.2020.100369

North Carolina Foundations Task Force. (2013). *North Carolina foundations for early learning and development.* Author.

Northeastern University Innovation Survey. (2014). https://news.northeastern.edu/2014/11/18/generation-z-survey/

Northrop, L., & Killeen, E. (2013). A framework for using iPads to build early literacy skills. *The Reading Teacher, 66*(7), 531–537. https://doi.org/10.1002/TRTR.1155

Nouri, J., Norén, E., & Skog, K. (2018). Learning programming by playing and coding games in K-9. *INTED 2018 : Proceedings*, 7990–7995.

Nousiainen, T., Kangas, M., Rikala, J., & Vesisenaho, M. (2018). Teacher Competencies in Game-Based Pedagogy. *Teaching and Teacher Education, 74*, 85–96. doi:10.1016/j.tate.2018.04.012

Nunziati, G. (1990). Pour construire un dispositif d'évaluation formatrice. *Cahiers Pedagogiques, 280*, 47–62.

Nurazidawati, Tuan Mastura, & Kamisah. (2011). *Pengalaman pembelajaran melalui khidmat komuniti pelajar Sains: Tranformasi dan inovasi dalam pendidikan.* Bangi: Penerbit Universiti Kebangsaan Malaysia.

Nurtanto, M., Fawaid, M., & Sofyan, H. (2020). Problem Based Learning (PBL) in Industry 4.0: Improving Learning Quality through Character-Based Literacy Learning and Life Career Skill (LL-LCS). *Journal of Physics: Conference Series, 1573*, 012006. doi:10.1088/1742-6596/1573/1/012006

Nuutinen, M., Seppänen, M., Smedlund, A., & Kaasinen, E. (2017). *Seeking New Ways of Innovating in Industry-Research Collaboration Practice. Innovating in practice.* Springer International Publishing.

Nxumalo, S. A., & Mncube, D. W. (2018). Using indigenous games and knowledge to decolonise the school curriculum: Ubuntu perspectives. *Perspectives in Education, 36*(2), 103–118. doi:10.18820/2519593X/pie.v36i2.9

O'Bannon, B. W., & Thomas, K. (2014). Teacher perceptions of using mobile phones in the classroom: Age matters! *Computers & Education, 74*, 15–25. doi:10.1016/j.compedu.2014.01.006

O'Brolcháin, F., Jacquemard, T., Monaghan, D., O'Connor, N., Novitzky, P., & Gordijn, B. (2016). The convergence of virtual reality and social networks: Threats to privacy and autonomy. *Science and Engineering Ethics, 22*(1), 1–29. doi:10.100711948-014-9621-1 PMID:25552240

O'Connor, S., Hanlon, P., O'donnell, C. A., Garcia, S., Glanville, J., & Mair, F. S. (2016). Understanding factors affecting patient and public engagement and recruitment to digital health interventions: A systematic review of qualitative studies. *BMC Medical Informatics and Decision Making, 16*(1), 1–15. doi:10.118612911-016-0359-3 PMID:27630020

O'Doherty, J., Kringerlbach, M. L., Rolls, R. T., Hornak, J., & Andrews, C. (2001). Sažetak reprezentacije nagrade i kazne u ljudskoj orbitofrontalnoj korteksu. *Nature Neuroscience, 4*, 95–102. doi:10.1038/82959 PMID:11135651

O'Donnell, E., Lawless, S., Sharp, M., & Wade, V. P. (2015). A review of personalised e-learning: Towards supporting learner diversity. *International Journal of Distance Education Technologies*, *13*(1), 22–47. doi:10.4018/ijdet.2015010102

O'Leary, M., & Scully, D. (2018). *The Leaving Certificate programme as preparation for higher education: The views of undergraduates at the end of their first year in university*. The Centre for Assessment Research, Policy and Practice in Education.

Obar, J., & Wildman, S. (2015). Social media definition and the governance challenge: An introduction to the special issue. *Telecommunications Policy*, *39*(9), 745–750. doi:10.1016/j.telpol.2015.07.014

Oberg, A. (2011). Comparison of the effectiveness of a call-based approach and a card-based approach to vocabulary acquisition and retention. *CALICO Journal*, *29*(1), 118–144. doi:10.11139/cj.29.1.118-144

Oblinger, D. G., & Oblinger, J. L. (Eds.). (2005). Educating the net generation. Boulder, CO: Educause.

Oblinger, D., & Oblinger, J. (Eds.). (2005). *Educating the net generation*. EDUCAUSE. https://www.educause.edu/ir/library/PDF/pub7101.PDF

Oblinger, D. G. (2004). The next generation of educational entertainment. *Journal of Interactive Media in Education*, *8*(1), 1–18.

Oblinger, D. G. (2006). Games and Learning. Digital games have the potential to bring play back to the learning experience. *EDUCAUSE Quarterly*, 29.

Oblinger, D. G. (2006). Games and learning: Digital games have the potential to bring play back to the learning experience. *EDUCAUSE Quarterly*, *3*, 5–7.

OECD. (2019). *How much time do teachers spend teaching? In Education at a Glance 2019: OECD Indicators*. OECD Publishing. doi:10.1787/62fbb20d-

Oei & Patterson. (2013). Enhancing cognition with video games: a multiple game training study. *Pubmed*, *8*(3).

Offenholley, K. H. (2012). Gaming Your Mathematics Course: The Theory and Practice of Games for Learning. *Journal of Humanistic Mathematics*, *2*, 79–92. doi:10.5642/ jhummath.201202.07

Ofosu-Ampong, K. (2020). The Shift to Gamification in Education: A Review on Dominant Issues. *Journal of Educational Technology Systems*, *49*(1), 113–137. doi:10.1177/0047239520917629

Ohman, A., Lundqvist, D., & Esteves, F. (2001). The face in the crowd effect: An anger superiority effect with schematic stimuli. *Journal of Personality and Social Psychology*, *80*(3), 381–396. doi:10.1037/0022-3514.80.3.381 PMID:11300573

Oh, S., So, H. J., & Gaydos, M. (2017). Hybrid augmented reality for participatory learning: The hidden efficacy of multi-user game-based simulation. *IEEE Transactions on Learning Technologies*, *11*(1), 115–127. doi:10.1109/TLT.2017.2750673

Ojanen, E., Ronimus, M., Ahonen, T., Chansa-Kabali, T., February, P., Jere-Folotiya, J., Kauppinen, K.-P., Ketonen, R., & Ngorosho, D., Pitknen, M., Puhakka, S., Sampa, F., Walubita, G., Yalukanda, C., Pugh, K., Richardson, U., Serpell, R., & Lyytinen, H. (2015). GraphoGame-A catalyst for multi-level promotion of literacy in diverse contexts. *Frontiers in Psychology*, *6*(May). Advance online publication. doi:10.3389/fpsyg.2015.00671 PMID:26113825

Ojo, O., & Adu, E. (2019). The effectiveness of Information and Communication Technologies (ICTs) in teaching and learning in high schools in Eastern Cape Province. *South African Journal of Education*, *38*(Supplement 2), 1–11. doi:10.15700aje.v38ns2a1483

Compilation of References

Okoye, K., Nganji, J. T., & Hosseini, S. (2020). Learning analytics for educational innovation: A systematic mapping study of early indicators and success factors. *International Journal of Computer Information Systems and Industrial Management Applications*, *12*, 138–154.

Olfers, K. J. F., & Band, G. P. H. (2018). Game-based training of flexibility and attention improves task-switch performance: Near and far transfer of cognitive training in an EEG study. *Psychological Research*, *82*(1), 186–202. doi:10.100700426-017-0933-z PMID:29260316

Oliveira, L. R., Correia, A. C., Merrelho, A., Marques, A., Pereira, D. J., & Cardoso, V. (2009). Digital games: possibilities and limitations - The spore game case. In T. Bastiaens, J. Dron, & C. Xin (Eds.), *Proceedings of E-Learn: world conference on elearning in corporate, government, healthcare, and higher education* (pp. 3011-3020). Association for the Advancement of Computing in Education.

Olson, C. K. (2010). Children's motivations for video game play in the context of normal development. *Review of General Psychology*, *14*(2), 180-187. Retrieved from http://psycnet.apa.org/?&fa=main.doiLanding&doi=10.1037/a0018984

Olson, C. B., Scarcella, R., & Matuchniak, T. (2015). English Learners, Writing, and the Common Core. *The Elementary School Journal*, *115*(4), 570–592. https://doi.org/10.1086/681235

Olson, D. (2007). *Jerome Bruner: The cognitive revolution in educational theory*. Continuum International Publishing Group.

Olsson, M., & Mozelius, P. (2017). Learning to Program by Playing Learning Games. In *11th European Conference on Games Based Learning 2017, Graz, Austria, 5-6 October, 2017* (Vol. 11, pp. 498-506). Academic Conferences and Publishing International Limited.

Omer, A. H. (2017). *Implications And Importance Of Game-Based Learning For New Hires, elearning industry*. Retrieved from https://elearningindustry.com/game-based-learning-for-increased-learner-engagement-new-hires

Oprescu, F., Jones, C., & Katsikitis, M. (2014). I PLAY AT WORK—Ten principles for transforming work processes through Gamification. *Frontiers in Psychology*, *5*, 5. doi:10.3389/fpsyg.2014.00014 PMID:24523704

Orbit Books. (2011, January 23). *Leviathan Wakes: Part One*. https://www.youtube.com/watch?v=Yu0xJpCy95o

Orey, M. (2010). *Emerging perspectives on learning, teaching, and technology*. Academic Press.

Originator Inc. (2014). *Endless reader* (Version 2.3) [Mobile app]. http://itunes.apple.com

Osanloo, A., & Grant, C. (2016). Understanding, selecting, and integrating a theoretical framework in dissertation research: Creating the blueprint for your "house". *Administrative Issues Journal: Connecting Education, Practice, and Research*, *4*(2), 12-26.

Osatuyi, B. (2013). Information sharing on social media sites. *Journal of Computers in Human Behavior*, *29*(6), 2622–2631. doi:10.1016/j.chb.2013.07.001

Osborne, J. (2014). Teaching scientific practices: Meeting the challenge of change. *Journal of Science Teacher Education*, *25*(2), 177–196. doi:10.100710972-014-9384-1

Osman, K., & Marimuthu, N. (2010). Setting new learning targets for the 21st century science education in Malaysia. *Procedia: Social and Behavioral Sciences*, *2*(2), 3737–3741. doi:10.1016/j.sbspro.2010.03.581

Othman, M. N. A., Abdul Rashid, M. A., Ismail, I. R., Abd Aziz, M. F., Norizan, S., & Mohamad Saad, S. A. (2021). Predicting Preferred Learning Styles on Teaching Approaches Among Gen Z Visual Learner. *Turkish Journal of Computer and Mathematics Education*, *12*(9), 2969–2978.

Overby, A., & Jones, B. L. (2015). Virtual LEGOs: Incorporating Minecraft into the art education curriculum. *Art Education*, *68*(1), 21–27. doi:10.1080/00043125.2015.11519302

Overmars, M. (2004). Teaching computer science through game design. *Computer*, *37*(4), 81–83. doi:10.1109/MC.2004.1297314

Overturf, B. J., Montgomery, L. H., & Smith, M. H. (2013). *Word nerds: Teaching all students to learn and love vocabulary*. Stenhouse Publishing.

Oxendine, C., Robinson, J., & Willson, G. (2010). Experiential learning. In M. Orey (Ed.), Emerging perspectives on learning, teaching, and technology. Global Text Project, funded by the Jacob Foundation, Zurich, Switzerland. Creative Commons 3.0 Attribution Licence.

Oyshi, M. T., Saifuzzaman, M., & Tumpa, Z. N. (2018). Gamification in children education: Balloon shooter. *2018 4th International Conference on Computing Communication and Automation (ICCCA)*. 10.1109/CCAA.2018.8777534

Ozdamar-Keskin, N., Ozata, F. Z., Banar, K., & Royle, K. (2015). Examining Digital Literacy Competences and Learning Habits of Open and Distance Learners. *Contemporary Educational Technology*, *6*(1), 74–90. doi:10.30935/cedtech/6140

P21 Framework Definitions. (2009). Retrieved from https://files.eric.ed.gov/fulltext/ED519462.pdf

Padgett, R. D., Keup, J. R., & Pascarella, E. T. (2013). The Impact of First-Year Seminars on College Students' Life-long Learning Orientations. *Journal of Student Affairs Research and Practice*, *50*(2), 133–151. doi:10.1515/jsarp-2013-0011

Paiva, J. C., Leal, J. P., & Queirós, R. (2020). Fostering programming practice through games. *Information (Basel)*, *11*(11), 498. doi:10.3390/info11110498

Pala, Ş. M., & Başıbüyük, A. (2021). The Predictive Effect of Digital Literacy, Self-Control and Motivation on the Academic Achievement in the Science, Technology and Society Learning Area. *Technology, Knowledge and Learning*, 1-17.

Palaus, M., Marron, E. M., Viejo-Sobera, R., & Redolar-Ripoll, D. (2017). Neural basis of video gaming: A systematic review. *Frontiers in Human Neuroscience*, *11*, 248. doi:10.3389/fnhum.2017.00248 PMID:28588464

Pallavicini, F., Ferrari, A., & Mantovani, F. (2018). Video Games for Well-Being: A Systematic Review on the Application of Computer Games for Cognitive and Emotional Training in the Adult Population. *Frontiers in Psychology*, *9*, 2127. doi:10.3389/fpsyg.2018.02127 PMID:30464753

Palomo-Duarte, M., Berns, A., Cejas, A., Dodero, J. M., Caballero, J. A., & Ruiz-Rube, I. (2016). Assessing Foreign Language Learning Through Mobile Game-Based Learning Environments. *International Journal of Human Capital and Information Technology Professionals*, *7*(2), 53–67. doi:10.4018/IJHCITP.2016040104

Paluck, E. L., & Green, D. P. (2009). Deference, Dissent, and Dispute Resolution: An Experimental Intervention Using Mass Media to Change Norms and Behavior in Rwanda. *The American Political Science Review*, *103*(4), 622-644.

Panagiotarou, A., Stamatiou, Y. C., Pierrakeas, C., & Kameas, A. (2020). Gamification acceptance for learners with different E-skills. *International Journal of Learning. Teaching and Educational Research*, *19*(2), 263–278. doi:10.26803/ijlter.19.2.16

Pangrazio, L. (2016). Reconceptualising critical digital literacy. *Discourse (Abingdon)*, *37*(2), 163–174. doi:10.1080/01596306.2014.942836

Panksepp, J. (2004). *Affective neuroscience: The foundations of human and animal emotions*. Oxford University Press.

Papadakis, S., Kalogiannakis, M., & Zaranis, N. (2017). Designing and creating an educational app rubric for preschool teachers. *Education and Information Technologies*, *22*(6), 3147–3165. doi:10.100710639-017-9579-0

Compilation of References

Papastergiou, M. (2009a). Digital game-based learning in high school computer science education: Impact on educational effectiveness and student motivation. *Computers & Education*, *52*(1), 1–12. doi:10.1016/j.compedu.2008.06.004

Papert, S. A. (1980). *Mindstorms: Children, computers, and powerful ideas*. Basic books.

Pappas, S. (2020). What do we really know about kids and screens? *Monitor on Psychology*, *51*(3), 42.

Pariser, E. (2011). *The filter bubble: How the new personalized web is changing what we read and how we think*. Penguin Books.

Parker Brothers. (1988). *Scattergories*. Board Game.

Parong, J., Mayer, R. E., Fiorella, L., MacNamara, A., Homer, B. D., & Plass, J. L. (2017). Learning executive function skills by playing focused video games. *Contemporary Educational Psychology*, *51*, 141–151. doi:10.1016/j.cedpsych.2017.07.002

Parrish, S. (Host) (2020, November 24). Forward thinking with Roger Martin. *The Knowledge Project* [Audio podcast episode]. https://www.youtube.com/watch?v=gmn2c5hrUmI&t=1345s

Parry, E., & Urwin, P. (2017). The Evidence Base for Generational Differences: Where Do We Go from Here? *Work, Aging and Retirement*, *3*(2), 140–148. doi:10.1093/workar/waw037

Partnership for 21st Century Learning. (2016). *Framework for 21st century learning*. www.p21.org/about-us/p21-framework

Partnership for 21st Century Learning. (2019). *Framework for 21st Century Learning Definitions*. http://static.battelleforkids.org/documents/p21/P21_Framework_DefinitionsBFK.pdf

Partnership for 21st Century Skills. (2007). *Framework for 21stcentury learning*. Retrieved from: http://www.p21.org/documents/P21_Framework_Definitions.pdf

Partnership for 21st Century Skills. (2011). *21st century skills map*. Partnership for 21st Century Skills.

Parvin, N., & Alam, M. J. (2016). Empowerment of Women to alleviate Poverty through Education in Bangladesh. *Journal of Governance and Innovation*, *2*(2), 49–60. https://osderpublications.com/uploads/1597820877.pdf

Parvin, R., & Haider, M. Z. (2012). Methods and practices of English language teaching in Bangla and English medium schools. *Bangladesh Education Journal*, *11*(1), 51–63.

Pasquier, P., Mérat, S., Malgras, B., Petit, L., Queran, X., Bay, C., Boutonnet, M., Jault, P., Ausset, S., Auroy, Y., Perez, J. P., Tesnière, A., Pons, F., & Mignon, A. (2016). A serious game for massive training and assessment of french soldiers involved in forward combat casualty care (3d-sc1): Development and deployment. *JMIR Serious Games*, *4*(1), e5. Advance online publication. doi:10.2196/games.5340 PMID:27194369

Passarotti, A. M., Sweeney, J. A., & Pavuluri, M. N. (2009). Neural correlates of incidental and directed facial emotion processing in adolescents and adults. *Social Cognitive and Affective Neuroscience*, *4*(4), 387–398. doi:10.1093can/nsp029 PMID:20035016

Pastushenko, O., Hruška, T., & Zendulka, J. (2018). Increasing students' motivation by using virtual learning environments based on gamification mechanics. *ACM International Conference Proceeding Series*, 755–760. 10.1145/3284179.3284310

Patall, E. A., Cooper, H., & Robinson, J. C. (2008). The effects of choice on intrinsic motivation and related outcomes: A meta-analysis of research findings. *Psychological Bulletin*, *134*(2), 270–300. https://doi.org/10.1037/0033-2909.134.2.270

Patil, S. J., Chavan, R. L., & Khandagale, V. S. (2019). Identification of misconceptions in science: Tools, techniques & skills for teachers. *Aarhat Multidisciplinary International Education Research Journal*, *8*(2), 466–472.

Paul, P. (2009). *Game-based Learning or Game-based Teaching?* Academic Press.

Paul, J. (2015). Despite the terrors of typologies: The importance of understanding categories of difference and identity. *Interventions*, *17*(2), 174–195. doi:10.1080/1369801X.2014.993332

Payne, H. E., Moxley, V. B. A., & MacDonald, E. (2015). Health Behavior Theory in physical activity game apps: A content analysis. *JMIR Serious Games*, *3*(2), e4. doi:10.2196/games.4187 PMID:26168926

Pea, R. D., Kurland, D. M., & Hawkins, J. (1985). *Logo and the development of thinking skills*. Academic Press.

Peachey, A., Gillen, J., Livingstone, D., & Smith-Robbins, S. (Eds.). (2010). *Researching learning in Virtual Worlds*. Springer. doi:10.1007/978-1-84996-047-2

Peake, B. (2015, April 1). WP:THREATENING2MEN: Misogynist Infopolitics and the Hegemony of the Asshole Consensus on English Wikipedia. *Ada New Media*. https://adanewmedia.org/2015/04/issue7-peake/

Pedaste, M., Mäeots, M., Leijen, Ä., & Sarapuu, S. (2012). Improving students' inquiry skills through reflection and self-regulation scaffolds. *Technology, Instruction. Cognition and Learning*, *9*(1-2), 81–95.

Pedaste, M., Mäeots, M., Siiman, L. A., De Jong, T., Van Riesen, S. A., Kamp, E. T., Manoli, C. C., Zacharia, Z. E., & Tsourlidaki, E. (2015). Phases of inquiry-based learning: Definitions and the inquiry cycle. *Educational Research Review*, *14*, 47–61. doi:10.1016/j.edurev.2015.02.003

Peddycord-Liu, Z., Cateté, V., Vandenberg, J., Barnes, T., Lynch, C. F., & Rutherford, T. (2019). A Field Study of Teachers Using a Curriculum-integrated Digital Game. In *Proceedings of the 2019 CHI Conference on Human Factors in Computing Systems* (pp. 1-12). CHI Conference. 10.1145/3290605.3300658

Pedreira, O., García, F., Brisaboa, N., & Piattini, M. (2015). Gamification in software engineering–A systematic mapping. *Information and Software Technology*, *57*, 157–168. doi:10.1016/j.infsof.2014.08.007

Pegrum, M., Bartle, E., & Longnecker, N. (2015). Can creative podcasting promote deep learning? The use of podcasting for learning content in an undergraduate science unit. *British Journal of Educational Technology*, *46*(1), 142–152. doi:10.1111/bjet.12133

Peifer, J. L. (2015). The Inter-Institutional Interface of Religion and Business. *Business Ethics Quarterly*, *25*(3), 363–391. doi:10.1017/beq.2015.33

Pekrun, R., & Linnenbrink-Garcia, L. (2014). Introduction to emotions in education. In R. Pekrun & L. Linnenbrink-Garcia (Eds.), International handbook of emotions in education (pp. 1–10). Routledge/Taylor & Francis Group.

Pelgrum, W. J. (2001). Obstacles to the integration of ICT in education: Results from a worldwide educational assessment. *Computers & Education*, *37*(2), 163–178. doi:10.1016/S0360-1315(01)00045-8

Pellas, N., Fotaris, P., Kazanidis, I., & Wells, D. (2019). Augmenting the learning experience in primary and secondary school education: A systematic review of recent trends in augmented reality game-based learning. *Virtual Reality (Waltham Cross)*, *23*(4), 329–346. doi:10.100710055-018-0347-2

Pelletier, C., & Oliver, M. (2006). Learning to play in digital games. *Learning, Media and Technology*, *31*(4), 329–342.

Peraica, A. (2019). The age of total images: disappearance of a subjective viewpoint in post-digital photography. Amsterdam University Institute of Network Cultures.

Perotta, C., Featherstone, G., Aston, H., & Houghton, E. (2013). *Game-based learning: Latest evidence and future directions*. Academic Press.

Compilation of References

Perrotta, C., Featherstone, G., Aston, H., & Houghton, E. (2013). Game-based learning: Latest evidence and future directions. Slough, UK: National Foundation for Educational Research (NFER).

Perrotta, C., Featherstone, G., Aston, H., & Houghton, E. (2013). *Game-based Learning: Latest Evidence and Future Directions Innovation in Education*. NFER.

Perryer, C., Celestine, A. N., Scott-Ladd, B., & Leighton, C. (2016). Enhancing workplace motivation through Gamification: Transferrable lessons from pedagogy. *International Journal of Management Education*, *14*(3), 327–335. doi:10.1016/j.ijme.2016.07.001

Persson, M. (2014, February 25). *Minecraft user announcement* [Social media message]. Retrieved from https://twitter.com/notch/status/438444097141882880

Pessoa, L. (2008). On the relationship between cognition and emotion. *Nature Reviews. Neuroscience*, *9*(2), 148–158. doi:10.1038/nrn2317 PMID:18209732

Petersen, C. I., Baepler, P., Beitz, A., Ching, P., Gorman, K. S., Neudauer, C. L., Rozaitis, W., Walker, J. D., & Wingert, D. (2020). The Tyranny of Content: "Content Coverage" as a Barrier to Evidence-Based Teaching Approaches and Ways to Overcome It. *CBE Life Sciences Education*, *19*(2), ar17. doi:10.1187/cbe.19-04-0079 PMID:32412836

Peters, M. A., Besley, A. C., & Besley, T. (2006). *Building knowledge cultures: Education and development in the age of knowledge capitalism*. Rowman & Littlefield Education.

Peterson, A., Dumont, H., Lafuente, M., & Law, N. (2018). *Understanding innovative pedagogies: Key themes to analyse new approaches to teaching and learning*. Academic Press.

Peterson, M. (2012). Learner interaction in a massively multiplayer online role playing game (MMORPG): A sociocultural discourse analysis. *ReCALL*, *24*(3), 361–380. doi:10.1017/S0958344012000195

Peterson, M. (2016). The use of massively multiplayer online role-playing games in CALL: An analysis of research. *Computer Assisted Language Learning*, *29*(7), 1181–1194. doi:10.1080/09588221.2016.1197949

Peters, V. A. M., & Vissers, G. A. N. (2009). A simple classification model for debriefing simulation games. *Simulation & Gaming*, *35*(1), 70–84. doi:10.1177/1046878103253719

Petranek, C. F. (2000). Written debriefing: The next vital step in learning with simulations. *Simulation & Gaming: An Interdisciplinary Journal*, *31*(1), 108–118. doi:10.1177/104687810003100111

Pew Research Center. (2010). *Millennials: Confident. Connected. Open to change*. Retrieved August 15, 2011 from www.pewresearc.org/millennials

Pfeffer, J., & Fong, C. T. (2004). The business school 'business': Some lessons from the US experience. *Journal of Management Studies*, *41*(8), 1501–1520. doi:10.1111/j.1467-6486.2004.00484.x

Pham, H. H., Vuong, Q. H., Luong, D. H., Nguyen, T. T., Dinh, V. H., & Ho, M. T. (2021). A bibliometric review of research on international student mobility's in Asia with Scopus dataset between 1984 and 2019. *Scientometrics*, *126*(6), 5201–5224. doi:10.100711192-021-03965-4

Phan, K. L., Wager, T., Taylor, S. F., & Liberzon, I. (2002). Functional neuroanatomy of emotion: Embodied persuasion: Fundamental processes by which bodily responses can impact attitudes. *NeuroImage*, *16*, 331–348. doi:10.1006/nimg.2002.1087 PMID:12030820

Phellas, C. N., Bloch, A., & Seale, C. (2011). Structured methods: Interviews, questionnaires and observation. In C. Seale (Ed.), *Research Society and Culture* (3rd ed., pp. 181–205). SAGE.

Phelps, J. (2018, March 8). Trump turns spotlight on violent video games in wake of Parkland shootings. *ABC News*. Retrieved from https://abcnews.go.com/Politics/trump-turns-spotlight-violent-video-games-wake-parkland/story?id=53593714

Pho A & Dinscore A. (2015). *Game Based Learning*. Tips and Trends Instructional Technologies.

Pho, A., & Dinscore, A. (2015). *Game-based learning. Tips and Trends.* https://acrl.ala.org/IS/wp-content/uploads/2014/05/spring2015.pdf

Pho, B. A., Dinscore, A., & Badges, D. (2015). *Game-based learning*. Academic Press.

Piaget, J. (1951). *Play, dreams and imitation in childhood*. Heinemann.

Piaget, J. (1953). *Origins of intelligence in the child*. Routledge & Kegan Paul.

Piaget, J. (1954). *Construction of reality in the child*. Routledge & Kegan Paul. doi:10.1037/11168-000

Piaget, J. (1962). *Play Dreams and Imitation in Childhood*. WW Norton.

Piaget, J. (1964). Cognitive development in children: Development and learning. *Journal of Research in Science Teaching*, *2*(3), 176–186. doi:10.1002/tea.3660020306

Piaget, J. (2008). Intellectual evolution from adolescence to adulthood. *Human Development*, *51*(1), 40–47. doi:10.1159/000112531

Piccoli, G., Ahmad, R., & Ives, B. (2001). Web-based virtual learning environments: A research framework and a preliminary assessment of effectiveness in basic IT skills training. *Management Information Systems Quarterly*, *25*(4), 401–426. doi:10.2307/3250989

Pickering, S. J., & Phye, G. D. (2006). *Working Memory and Education*. Elsevier.

Pierce, R., & Stacey, K. (2013). Teaching with new technology: Four 'early majority' teachers. *Journal of Mathematics Teacher Education*, *16*(5), 323–347. doi:10.100710857-012-9227-y

Pietraß, M. (2009). Digital literacy as framing: Suggestions for an interactive approach based on E. Goffman s frame theory. *Nordic Journal of Digital Literacy, 4*(3-4), 131-142.

Pina, A. A., & Harris, B. R. (1993). *Increasing Teachers' Confidence in Using Computers for Education*. Paper presented at the annaul meeting of the Arizona Educational Research Organization, Tucson, AZ.

Pinard, R., de Winter, A., Sarkis, G. J., Gerstein, M. B., Tartaro, K. R., Plant, R. N., Egholm, M., Rothberg, J. M., & Leamon, J. H. (2006). Assessment of whole genome amplification-induced bias through high-throughput, massively parallel whole genome sequencing. *BMC Genomics*, *7*(1), 1–21. doi:10.1186/1471-2164-7-216 PMID:16928277

Pinder, D. P. J. (2016). Exploring the Effects of Game Based Learning in Trinidad and Tobago's Primary Schools: An Examination of In-Service Teachers'. *Perspectives*, 17.

Pink, D. H. (2006). *A whole new mind: Why right-brainers will rule the future*. Riverhead Books.

Pinto, M., & Ferreira, P. (2017). Use of Videogames in Higher Education in Portugal : A Literature Review. In Challenges 2017: Aprender nas nuvens, Learning in the clouds (pp. 605-620). Universidade do Minho – Centro de Competência.

Pirraglia, P., & Kravitz, R. (2012). Social media: New opportunities, new ethical concerns. *Journal of General Internal Medicine*, *28*(2), 165–166. doi:10.100711606-012-2288-x PMID:23225258

Pivec, M., Dziabenko, O., & Schinnerl, I. (2003). Aspects of Game-Based Learning. *Proceedings of I-KNOW3*, 11.

Compilation of References

Pivec, M. (2007). Editorial: Play and learn: potentials of game-based learning. *British Journal of Educational Technology*, *38*(3), 387–393. doi:10.1111/j.1467-8535.2007.00722.x

Pivec, M., Dziabenko, O., & Schinnerl, I. (2003). *Aspects of game-based learning*. Academic Press.

Pixlr. (n.d.). https://pixlr.com/. *Free photo editor online graphic design*. Academic Press.

Plass, J. L., Perlin, K., & Nordlinger, J. (2010). *The games for learning institute: Research on design patterns for effective educational games*. Paper presented at the Game Developers Conference, San Francisco, CA.

Plass, J. L., Homer, B. D., & Kinzer, C. K. (2015). Foundations of Game-Based Learning. *Educational Psychologist*, *50*(4), 258–283. doi:10.1080/00461520.2015.1122533

Plass, J. L., Mayer, R. E., & Homer, B. D. (2020). *Handbook of Game-based Learning*. MIT Press.

Plato. (1943). *The Republic* (R. E. Allen, Trans.). Yale University Press.

Pløhn, T. (2013). Nuclear Mayhem-A Pervasive Game Designed to Support Learning. *Proceedings of the 7th European Conference on Games Based Learning ECGBL 2013, 2*.

Plowman, L., McPake, J., & Stephen, C. (2010). The technologisation of childhood? Young Children and technology in the home. *Children & Society*, *24*, 63-74. http://dx.doi.org.erl.lib.byu.edu/10.1111/j.1099-0860.2008.00180.x

Podolefsky, N. S., Perkins, K. K., & Adams, W. K. (2010). Factors promoting engaged exploration with computer simulations. *Physical Review Special Topics. Physics Education Research*, *6*(2), 020117. doi:10.1103/PhysRevSTPER.6.020117

Podsakoff, P. M., MacKenzie, S. B., Lee, J.-Y., & Podsakoff, N. P. (2003). Common method biases in behavioral research: A critical review of the literature and recommended remedies. *The Journal of Applied Psychology*, *88*(5), 879–903. doi:10.1037/0021-9010.88.5.879 PMID:14516251

Poiroux, J., Dahl-Jørgensen, T., Løyland, M., & Rye, S. (2016). *Using Minecraft to Enhance Collaboration as a 21st Century Skill in Primary Schools*. University of Oslo.

Polikov, V. (2017, March 6). *New Research Proves Game-Based Learning Works—Here's Why That Matters—EdSurge News*. EdSurge. https://www.edsurge.com/news/2017-03-06-new-research-proves-game-based-learning-works-here-s-why-that-matters

Polished Play, L. L. C. (2021). *Puppet Pals* (Version 1.9.8) [Mobile app]. http://itunes.apple.com

Polistina, K. (n.d.). *Cultural Literacy. Understanding and Respect for the Cultural Aspects of Sustainability*. Retrieved May 02, 2019 from http://arts.brighton.ac.uk/__data/assets/pdf_file/0006/5982/Cultural-Literacy.pdf

Polman, de Castro, B. O., & van Aken, M. A. G. (2008). Experimental study of the differential effects of playing versus watching violent video games on children's aggressive behaviour. *Aggressive Behavior*, *34*(3), 256–264. doi:10.1002/ab.20245 PMID:18161877

Ponitz, C. C., & Rimm Kaufman, S. E. (2011). Contexts of reading instruction: Implications for literacy skills and kindergarteners' behavioral engagement. *Early Childhood Research Quarterly*, *26*(2), 157–168. https://doi.org/0.1016/j.ecresq.2010.10.002

Popat, S., & Starkey, L. (2019). Learning to code or coding to learn? A systematic review. *Computers & Education*, *128*, 365–376. doi:10.1016/j.compedu.2018.10.005

Portier, C., Friedrich, N., & Peterson, S. S. (2019). Play(ful) pedagogical practices for creative collaborative literacy. *The Reading Teacher*, *73*(1), 17–27. doi:10.1002/trtr.1795

Postman, N. (2004). Televizyon Öldüren Eğlence. İstanbul: Ayrıntı.

Potocki, A., Magnan, A., & Ecalle, J. (2015). Computerized trainings in four groups of struggling readers: Specific effects on word reading and comprehension. *Research in Developmental Disabilities, 45–46*(April), 83–92. doi:10.1016/j.ridd.2015.07.016

Potter, W. J. (2011). Media Literacy (5th ed.). Sage Publication.

Potter, W. J. (2004). *Theory of Media Literacy A Cognitive Approach*. Sage Publications.

Potts, R. (1991). Spirits in the bottle: Spirituality and alcoholism treatment in African-American communities. *Journal of Training & Practice in Professional Psychology*.

Prandi, C., Nisi, V., Salomoni, P., & Nunes, N. J. (2015). From Gamification to pervasive game in mapping urban accessibility. In *Proceedings of the 11th Biannual Conference on Italian SIGCHI Chapter* (pp. 126-129). ACM 10.1145/2808435.2808449

Prensky, M. (2001). *Digital Game-Based Learning*. McGraw hill.

Prensky, M. (2001). Digital Natives, Digital Immigrants. MCB University Press.

Prensky, M. (2001). Digital datives, digital immigrants, Part II: Do they really think differently? *On the Horizon, 9*(6), 15–24. doi:10.1108/10748120110424843

Prensky, M. (2001a). Digital natives, digital immigrants. *On the Horizon, 9*(5), 1–6. doi:10.1108/10748120110424816

Prensky, M. (2001b). *Digital game-based learning*. McGraw-Hill.

Prensky, M. (2003c). Digital game-based learning. *ACM Computers in Entertainment, 1*(1), 1–4. doi:10.1145/950566.950596

Prensky, M. (2005). Computer games and learning: Digital game-based learning. In J. Raessens & J. Goldstein (Eds.), *Handbook of computer game studies* (pp. 97–122). MIT Press.

Prensky, M. (2006). *Don't bother me Mom—I'm learning!* Paragon House.

Prensky, M. (2011). Comments on research comparing games to other instructional methods. In S. Tobias & J. D. Fletcher (Eds.), *Computer games and instruction* (pp. 251–280). Information Age.

Prensky, M. (2012). Aprendizagem Baseada. In *Jogos Digitais*. Senac São Paulo.

Prensky, M. (2012). *From digital natives to digital wisdom: Hopeful essays for 21st century learning*. Corwin Press. doi:10.4135/9781483387765

Presnsky, M. (2008). Students as designers and creators of educational computer games: Who else? *British Journal of Educational Technology, 39*(6), 1004–1019. doi:10.1111/j.1467-8535.2008.00823_2.x

Prestridge, S., & de Aldama, C. (2016). A Classification framework for exploring technology enabled practice-FramTEP. *Journal of Educational Computing Research, 54*(7), 901–921. doi:10.1177/0735633116636767

Price, P. C., Chiang, I.-C. A., Leighton, D. C., & Cutler, C. (2017). Reliability and validity of measurement. In R. Jhangiani (Ed.), Research methods in psychology. Pressbooks.

Price-Dennis, D., Holmes, K. A., & Smith, E. (2015). Exploring digital literacy practices in an inclusive classroom. *The Reading Teacher, 69*(2), 195–205.

Compilation of References

Priyaadharshini, M., Natha Mayil, N., Dakshina, R., Sandhya, S., & Bettina Shirley, R. (2020). Author. *Procedia Computer Science*, *172*, 468–472. doi:10.1016/j.procs.2020.05.143

Priyadharshini, M., Nathamayil, N., Dakshina, R., Sandhya, S., & R, B. S. (2020). *Learning analytics : Game-based learning for programming course in higher education*. Academic Press.

Provost, J. A. (1990). *Work, play and type: Achieving balance in your life*. Consulting Psychologist Press.

Pullano, G., Pinotti, F., Valdano, E., Boëlle, P. Y., Poletto, C., & Colizza, V. (2020). Novel coronavirus (2019-nCoV) early-stage importation risk to Europe, January 2020. *Eurosurveillance*, *25*(4), 2000057. doi:10.2807/1560-7917.ES.2020.25.4.2000057 PMID:32019667

Puolakanaho, A. (2007). Early prediction of reading and related language and cognitive skills in children with a familial risk for dyslexia. *Jyväskylä Studies in Education, Psychology and Social Research 317*. https://jyx.jyu.fi/dspace/bitstream/handle/123456789/13367/9789513929985.pdf?sequence=1

Putz, L. M., Hofbauer, F., & Mates, M. (2019). A vignette study among order pickers about the acceptance of Gamification. In GamiFIN (pp. 154-166). Academic Press.

Putz, L. M., Hofbauer, F., & Treiblmaier, H. (2020). Can Gamification help to improve Education? Findings from a longitudinal study. *Computers in Human Behavior*, *110*, 106392.

Qian, M., & Clark, K. R. (2016). Game-Based Learning and 21st Century Skills: A Review of Recent Research. *Computers in Human Behavior*, *63*, 50–58. doi:10.1016/j.chb.2016.05.023

Qualman, E. (2011). *Socialnomics: How social media transforms the way we live and do business*. John Wiley & Sons, Inc.

Quddus, M., Iii, H. B., & White, L. R. (2009). Business ethics: Perspectives from Judaic, Christian, and Islamic scriptures. *Journal of Management, Spirituality & Religion*, *6*(4), 323–334. doi:10.1080/14766080903290143

Rabone, D. (2013). How 'game mechanics" can revitalize education. *eSchoolNews*. http://www.eschoolnews.com/2013/02/12/how-game-mechanics-can-revitalize- education/3/

Raftopoulos, M. (2014). Towards gamification transparency: A conceptual framework for the development of responsible gamified enterprise systems. *Journal of Gaming & Virtual Worlds*, *6*(2), 159–178. doi:10.1386/jgvw.6.2.159_1

Rahman, I. S., Falkenthal, E., Holzner, L., & Lozano, A. A. (2019). *Studentaffairs.com 2019 virtual case study* [Powerpoint slides]. https://www.studentaffairs.com/Customer-Content/www/CMS/files/VCS/2019/CalPolySanLuisObispo_rahman.pdf

Raman, K., & Yamat, H. (2014). Barriers Teachers Face in Integrating ICT during English Lessons: A Case Study. *Malaysian Online Journal of Educational Technology*, *2*(3), 11–19.

Rama, P. S., Black, R. W., Van Es, E., & Warschauer, M. (2012). Affordances for second language learning in World of Warcraft. *ReCALL*, *24*(3), 322–338. doi:10.1017/S0958344012000171

Ramirez, D., & Squire, K. (2015). Gamification and learning. In S. P. Walz & S. Deterding (Eds.), *The Gameful World: Approaches, Issues, Applications* (pp. 629–652). MIT Press.

Ranalli, J., & Ritzko, J. (2013). Assessing the impact of video game based design projects in a first year engineering design course. In 2013 IEEE Frontiers in Education Conference (FIE) (pp. 530-534). IEEE. doi:10.1109/FIE.2013.6684880

Randall, N. (2019). A survey of robot-assisted language learning (RALL). *ACM Transactions on Human-Robot Interaction*, *9*(1), 1–36. doi:10.1145/3345506

Randolph, J. J., Kangas, M., Ruokamo, H., & Hyvönen, P. (2016). Creative and playful learning on technology-enriched playgrounds: An international investigation. *Interactive Learning Environments*, *24*(3), 409–422. doi:10.1080/10494820.2013.860902

Rankin, Y., Gold, R., & Gooch, B. (2006). 3D Role-Playing Games as Language Learning Tools. *Eurographics*, *25*(3), 33–38.

Rao, D., & Stupans, I. (2012). Exploring the potential of role play in higher education: Development of a typology and teacher guidelines. *Innovations in Education and Teaching International*, *49*(4), 427–436.

Rao, N., & Sun, J. (2010). Educating Asian adolescents: a developmental perspective. In L. F. Zhang, J. Biggs, & D. Watkins (Eds.), *Learning and development of Asian students: what the 21st Century teacher needs to think about* (pp. 37–59). Pearson.

Raschke, C. A. (2003). *The digital revolution and the coming of the postmodern university*. Routledge. doi:10.4324/9780203451243

Rasheed, R. A., Kamsin, A., & Abdullah, N. A. (2020). Challenges in the online component of blended learning: A systematic review. *Computers & Education*, *144*, 103701. doi:10.1016/j.compedu.2019.103701

Ratheeswari, K. (2018). Information Communication Technology in Education. *Journal of Applied and Advanced Research*, *3*(S1), 45. doi:10.21839/jaar.2018.v3iS1.169

Rauch, M. (2013). Best practices for using enterprise gamification to engage employees and customers. In *International Conference on Human-Computer Interaction* (pp. 276-283). Springer Berlin Heidelberg. 10.1007/978-3-642-39262-7_31

Raymundo, M. R. D. (2020). Fostering creativity through online creative collaborative group projects. *Asian Association of Open Universities Journal*, *15*(1), 97–113. doi:10.1108/AAOUJ-10-2019-0048

Raziunaite, P., Miliunaite, A., Maskeliunas, R., Damasevicius, R., Sidekerskiene, T., & Narkeviciene, B. (2018). Designing an educational music game for digital game based learning: A Lithuanian case study. *2018 41st International Convention on Information and Communication Technology, Electronics and Microelectronics, MIPRO 2018 - Proceedings*, 800–805. 10.23919/MIPRO.2018.8400148

Read the standards. (n.d.). *Common Core State Standards Initiative*. Retrieved October 25, 2021, from http://www.corestandards.org/read-the-standards/

Real, Y. M. (2008). *An assessment of the relationship between creativity and information and media literacy skills of community college students for a selected major* (PhD Thesis). Pepperdine University Graduate School of Education and Psychology.

Redecker, C. (2017). *European Framework for the Digital Competence of Educators*. European Commission.

Redecker, C. (2017). *European Framework for the Digital Competence of Educators: DigCompEdu*. Publications Office of the European Union., doi:10.2760/159770

Regtvoort, A., & van der Leij, A. (2007). Early intervention with children of dyslexic parents: Effects of computer-based reading instruction at home on literacy acquisition. *Learning and Individual Differences*, *17*(1), 35–53. doi:10.1016/j.lindif.2007.01.005

Reinders, H. (2012). *Digital games in language learning and teaching*. Palgrave Macmillan. doi:10.1057/9781137005267

Compilation of References

Reinhardt, J., & Sykes, J. M. (2012). Conceptualizing digital game-mediated L2 learning and pedagogy: Game-enhanced and game-based research and practice. In H. Reinders (Ed.), *Digital games in language learning and teaching* (pp. 32–49). Palgrave Macmillan. doi:10.1057/9781137005267_3

Resaba, M. L., & Gayeta, N. E. (2021). Utilization of Project - Based Learning (PBL) Resources in Senior High School. *International Multidisciplinary Research Journal*, *3*(2).

Research and Market. (2021, June 23). *World Game-Based Learning Market Report 2021-2026*. Retrieved September 4th, 2021, from Globe Newswire: https://www.globenewswire.com/en/news-release/2021/06/23/2251646/28124/en/World-Game-Based-Learning-Market-Report-2021-2026.html

Rest, J. R. (1986). *Moral development: Advances in research and theory*. Praeger publishers.

Reyes, D. L. Jr, & Gaston, T. W. K. (2017). Teaching ethics in business schools: A conversation on disciplinary differences, academic provincialism, and the case for integrated pedagogy. *Academy of Management Learning & Education*, *16*(2), 314–336. doi:10.5465/amle.2014.0402

Reynolds, R. (2016). Defining, designing for, and measuring "social constructivist digital literacy" development in learners: A proposed framework. *Educational Technology Research and Development*, *64*(4), 735–762. doi:10.100711423-015-9423-4

Reynolds, R., & Harel Caperton, I. (2011). Contrasts in student engagement, meaning-making, dislikes, and challenges in a discovery-based program of game design learning. *Journal of Educational Technology Research and Development*, *59*(2), 267–289. doi:10.100711423-011-9191-8

Rice, S. (n.d.). *Game-Based Learning*. Retrieved September 5, 2021, from College STAR: https://www.collegestar.org/modules/game-based-learning

Rice, J. (2007). Assessing higher order thinking in video games. *Journal of Technology and Teacher Education*, *15*(1), 87–100.

Richardson, U. (2011). *GRAPHOGAME Report Summary*. European Commission, Community Research and Development Information Service (CORDIS). https://cordis.europa.eu/result/rcn/48026_en.html

Rideout, V., & Robb, M. B. (2019). *The Common Sense census: Media use by tweens and teens*. Common Sense Media.

Rief, S. (2009). *Club cultures: Boundaries, identities and otherness*. Taylor and Francis.

Riemer, V., & Schrader, C. (2015). Learning with quizzes, simulations, and adventures: Students' attitudes, perceptions and intentions to learn with different types of serious games. *Computers & Education*, *88*, 160–168. doi:10.1016/j.compedu.2015.05.003

Rijshouwer, E. (2019). *Organizing Democracy: Power concentration and self-organization in the evolution of Wikipedia*. https://repub.eur.nl/pub/113937

Riordan, R. (2005). *The Lightning Thief*. Hyperion Books for Children.

Ritter, J. (2015, June 25). Gamification or game-based learning? What's the difference? *Knowledge Direct: A Learning Management Platform*. https://www.kdplatform.com/gamification-game-based-learning-whats-difference/

Roberts, L. D., Breen, L. J., & Symes, M. (2013). Teaching computer-assisted qualitative data analysis to a large cohort of undergraduate students. *International Journal of Research & Method in Education*, *36*(3), 279–294. doi:10.1080/1743727X.2013.804501

Robinson, K. (2006, June). *Ken Robinson: Do schools kill creativity?* [Video file]. Retrieved From https://www.ted.com/talks/ken_robinson_says_schools_kill_creativity?language=en#t201246

Robinson, K. (1998). National Advisory Council for creative and cultural education - NACCCE. *RSA Journal*, (5486), 20.

Robinson, K., & Aronica, L. (2006). *Creative schools: The grassroots revolution that is transforming education*. Penguin Books.

Robinson, M., & Mackey, M. (2006). Assets in the classroom: Comfort and competence with media among teachers present and future. In J. Marsh & E. Millard (Eds.), *Popular literacies, childhood and schooling* (pp. 200–220). Routledge.

Roca, J. C., & Gagné, M. (2008). Understanding e-learning continuance intention in the workplace: A self-determination theory perspective. *Computers in Human Behavior*, *24*(4), 1585–1604. doi:10.1016/j.chb.2007.06.001

Rodrigues, F. L., & Costa, C. J. O. A. (2016). Playing seriously – How gamification and social cues influence bank customers to use gamified e-business applications. *Computers in Human Behavior*, *63*, 392–407. doi:10.1016/j.chb.2016.05.063

Rodrigues, L. F., Costa, C. J., & Oliveira, A. (2017). How does the web game design influence the behavior of e-banking users? *Computers in Human Behavior*, *74*, 163–174. doi:10.1016/j.chb.2017.04.034

Roefsema, P. R., Van Ooyen, A., & Watanabe, T. (2010, February). Perceptual learning rules based on reinforcers and attention. *Trends in Cognitive Sciences*, *14*(2), 64–71. doi:10.1016/j.tics.2009.11.005 PMID:20060771

Rogers-Vaughn. (2012). The social trifecta of human misery and problematical constructions of the self: Implications for formation and supervision. *Reflective Practice (Decatur, Ga.)*, *32*, 206–223.

Rogoff, B. (1990). *Apprenticeship in thinking. Cognitive development in social context*. Oxford University Press.

Romeiro, P., Nunes, F., Santos, P., & Pinto, C. (2020). Atlas do Setor dos Videojogos em Portugal. Edição Sociedade Portuguesa para a Ciência dos Videojogos.

Ronimus, M., Kujala, J., Tolvanen, A., & Lyytinen, H. (2014). Children's engagement during digital game-based learning of reading: The effects of time, rewards, and challenge. *Computers & Education*, *71*, 237–246. doi:10.1016/j.compedu.2013.10.008

Rosa, J. A. (2012). Marketing education for the next four billion: Challenges and innovations. *Journal of Marketing Education*, *34*(1), 44–54.

Rosen, Y., Stoeffler, K., Yudelson, M., & Simmering, V. (2020). Towards Scalable Gamified Assessment in Support of Collaborative Problem-Solving Competency Development in Online and Blended Learning. In *Proceedings of the Seventh ACM Conference on Learning@ Scale* (pp. 369-372). 10.1145/3386527.3405946

Rosling, H. (2020). Factfulness. Edições Círculo de Leitores: Temas e Debates, Lisboa.

Rossi, M., & Scappini, E. (2014). Church Attendance, Problems of Measurement, and Interpreting Indicators: A Study of Religious Practice in the United States, 1975–2010. *Journal for the Scientific Study of Religion*, *53*(2), 249–267. doi:10.1111/jssr.12115

Rotherham, A. J., & Willingham, D. T. (2010). 21st-century" skills. *American Educator*, *17*(1), 17–20.

Roth, S., Schneckenberg, D., & Tsai, C. W. (2015). The ludic drive as innovation driver: Introduction to the Gamification of innovation. *Creativity and Innovation Management*, *24*(2), 300–306. doi:10.1111/caim.12124

Roux, C. J., Burnett, C., & Hollander, W. J. (2008). Curriculum enrichment through indigenous Zulu games. *S.A. Journal for Research in Sport Physical Education and Recreation*, *30*(1), 89–103. doi:10.4314ajrs.v30i1.25985

Compilation of References

Rowan, L., & Beavis, C. (2017). Serious outcomes from serious play: Teachers' beliefs about assessment of game-based learning in schools. In C. Beavis, M. Dezuanni, & J. O'Mara (Eds.), *Serious play: literacy, learning and digital games* (pp. 169–185). Routledge. doi:10.4324/9781315537658-16

Rowe, J. P., Shores, L. R., Mott, B. W., & Lester, J. C. (2011). Integrating learning, problem solving, and engagement in narrative-centered learning environments. *International Journal of Artificial Intelligence in Education, 21*(1-2), 115–133.

Rowsell, J., Burke, A., Flewitt, R., Liao, H.-T., Lin, A., Marsh, J., Mills, K., Prinsloo, M., Rowe, D., & Wohlwend, K. (2016). Humanizing digital literacies: A road trip in search of wisdom and insight. Digital Literacy Column. *The Reading Teacher, 70*(1), 121–129. doi:10.1002/trtr.1501

Rowsell, J., & Walsh, M. (2011). Rethinking literacy education in new times: Multimodality, multiliteracies, & new literacies. *Brock Education, 21*(1), 1. doi:10.26522/brocked.v21i1.236

Rowsell, J., & Wohlwend, K. (2016). Free play or tight spaces? Mapping participatory literacies in apps. *The Reading Teacher, 70*(2), 197–205. doi:10.1002/trtr.1490

Rozario, R. B. (2013). New Media and the Traditional Media Platforms: Introspection on the Differences in Technical and Ideological Factors and Audience-integration Patterns between New Media and Traditional Media. *The Arab Journal of the Social Sciences, 12*(3), 43–61.

Rozman, T., & Donath, L. (2019). The Current State of the Gamification in E-Learning. *Mednarodno Inovativno Poslovanje = Journal of Innovative Business and Management, 11*(3), 5–19. doi:10.32015/JIBM/2019-11-3-2

Roztocki, N., Soja, P., & Weistroffer, H. R. (2019). The role of information and communication technologies in socio-economic development: Towards a multi-dimensional framework. *Information Technology for Development, 25*(2), 171–183. doi:10.1080/02681102.2019.1596654

Ruggiero, D. (2013). Video games in the classroom: The teacher point of view. In *Games for learning workshop of the foundations of digital games conference*. http://fdg2013.org/program/workshops/papers/G4L2013/g4l2013_02.pdf

Ruggiero, T. E. (2000). Uses and gratifications theory in the 21st century. *Mass Communication & Society, 3*(1), 3–37. doi:10.1207/S15327825MCS0301_02

Rumeser, D., & Emsley, M. (2019). Can serious games improve project management decision making under complexity? *Project Management Journal, 50*(1), 23–39. doi:10.1177/8756972818808982

Ruotsalainen, M., & Friman, U. (2018). "There Are No Women and They All Play Mercy": Understanding and Explaining (the Lack of) Women's Presence in Esports and Competitive Gaming. *Proceedings of Nordic DIGRA 2018*. http://www.digra.org/wp-content/uploads/digital-library/DiGRA_Nordic_2018_paper_31.pdf

Rushkoff, D. (2011). *Program or be programmed: Ten commands for a digital age*. Soft Skull Press.

Rusman, E., Ternier, S., & Specht, M. (2018). Early second language learning and adult involvement in a real-world context: Design and evaluation of the "ELENA Goes Shopping" mobile game. *Journal of Educational Technology & Society, 21*(3), 90–103.

Russell, G., & Bradley, G. (1997). Teachers' computer anxiety: Implications for professional development. *Education and Information Technologies, 2*(1), 17–30. doi:10.1023/A:1018680322904

Rutten, K., & Soetaert, R. (2012). Narrative and rhetorical approaches to problems of education: Jerome Bruner and Kenneth Burke revisited. *Studies in Philosophy and Education, 32*(4), 327–343. doi:10.100711217-012-9324-5

Rutten, N., Joolingen, W., & Veen, J. T. (2012). The Learning Effects of Computer Simulations in Science Education. *Computers & Education*, *58*(1), 136–153. doi:10.1016/j.compedu.2011.07.017

Ryan, R. M., & Deci, E. L. (2000). *Self-Determination Theory and the Facilitation of Intrinsic Motivation, Social Development, and Well-Being.* *55*(1), 68–78. (https://www2.deloitte.com/us/en/insights/focus/behavioral-economics/gaming-away-leadership-gap-developing-leaders.html)

Ryan, M. (2014). Story/Worlds/Media: Tuning the instruments of a media-conscious narratology. In M. Ryan & J. Thon (Eds.), *Storyworlds across media: Toward a media-conscious narratology* (pp. 25–49). University of Nebraska Press. doi:10.2307/j.ctt1d9nkdg.6

Ryan, M., & Anstey, M. (2003). Identity and text: Developing self-conscious readers. *Australian Journal of Language and Literacy*, *26*(1), 9–22.

Ryan, R. M., & Deci, E. L. (2000). Intrinsic and extrinsic motivations: Classic definitions and new directions. *Contemporary Educational Psychology*, *25*(1), 54–67. doi:10.1006/ceps.1999.1020 PMID:10620381

Ryan, R. M., Rigby, C. S., & Przybylski, A. (2006). The motivational pull of video games: A self-determination theory approach. *Motivation and Emotion*, *30*(4), 344–360.

Ryan, W. S., & Ryan, R. M. (2019). Toward a social psychology of authenticity: Exploring within-person variation in autonomy, congruence, and genuineness using self-determination theory. *Review of General Psychology*, *23*(1), 99–112. doi:10.1037/gpr0000162

Rybakova, K., Rice, M., Moran, C., Zucker, L., McGrail, E., McDermott, M., Loomis, S., Piotrowski, A., Garcia, M., Gerber, H., & Gibbons, T. (2019). A long arc bending towards equity: Tracing almost 20 years of ELA teaching trends. *Contemporary Issues in Technology and Teacher Education*, *19*(4), 549-604. https://citejournal.org/volume-19/issue-4-19/english-language-arts/a-long-arc-bending-toward-equity-tracing-almost-20-years-of-ela-teaching-with-technology/

Saadé, R. G., & Kira, D. (2009). Computer anxiety in e-learning: The effect of computer self-efficacy. *Journal of Information Technology Education*, *8*.

Sabourin, J., Rowe, J. P., Mott, B. W., & Lester, J. C. (2011). When Off-Task Is On-Task: The Affective Role of Off-Task Behavior in Narrative-Centered Learning Environments. *Proc. 15th Int'l Conf. Artificial Intelligence in Education*, 523-536.

Sabourin, J. L., & Lester, J. C. (2013). Affect and engagement in Game-BasedLearning environments. *IEEE Transactions on Affective Computing*, *5*(1), 45–56. doi:10.1109/T-AFFC.2013.27

Sadler, D. R. (1989). Formative assessment and the design of instructional systems. *Instructional Science*, *18*(2), 119–144. doi:10.1007/BF00117714

Safapour, E., Kermanshachi, S., & Taneja, P. (2019). A review of nontraditional teaching methods: Flipped classroom, gamification, case study, self-learning, and social media. *Education Sciences*, *9*(4), 273. doi:10.3390/educsci9040273

Saia, S. M., Nelson, N. G., Young, S. N., Parham, S., & Vandegrift, M. (2021). *Ten simple rules for researchers who want to develop web apps*. Academic Press.

Sailer, M., Hense, J. U., Mayr, S. K., & Mandl, H. (2017). How gamification motivates: An experimental study of the effects of specific game design elements on psychological need satisfaction. *Computers in Human Behavior*, *69*, 371–380.

Sailer, M., Hense, J., Mandl, H., & Klevers, M. (2017). Fostering Development of Work Competencies and Motivation via Gamification. In *Competence-based Vocational and Professional Education* (pp. 795–818). Springer International Publishing. doi:10.1007/978-3-319-41713-4_37

Compilation of References

Sailer, M., & Homner, L. (2019). The Gamification of Learning: aMeta-Analysis. *Educational Psychology Review*, *32*(1), 77–112. doi:10.100710648-019-09498-w

Saine, N. L., Lerkkanen, M.-K., Ahonen, T., Tolvanen, A., & Lyytinen, H. (2010a). Predicting word-level reading fluency outcomes in three contrastive groups: Remedial and computer-assisted remedial reading intervention, and mainstream instruction. *Learning and Individual Differences*, *20*(5), 402–414. doi:10.1016/j.lindif.2010.06.004

Sajjadi, P., Broeckhoven, F. V., & Troyer, O. D. (2014). Dynamically Adaptive Educational Games: A New Perspective. *International Conference on Serious Games*. 10.1007/978-3-319-05972-3_8

Salajan, F. D., Schönwetter, D. J., & Cleghorn, B. M. (2010). Student and faculty inter-generational digital divide: Fact or fiction? *Computers & Education*, *55*(3), 1393–1403. doi:10.1016/j.compedu.2010.06.017

Salas, Wildman, & Piccolo. (2009). Using simulation-based training to enhance management education. *Academy of Management Learning & Education*, *8*(4), 559–573.

Saldaña, J. (2016). *The coding manual for qualitative researchers* (3rd ed.). Sage.

Salehi, H. (2017). Effects of using instructional video games on teaching English vocabulary to Iranian pre-intermediate EFL learners. *International Journal of Learning and Change*, *9*(2), 111–130. doi:10.1504/IJLC.2017.084609

Salem, J., & Fehrmann, P. (2013). Bibliographic management software: A focus group study of the preferences and practices of undergraduate students. *Public Services Quarterly*, *9*(2), 110–120. doi:10.1080/15228959.2013.785878

Salen, K., & Zimmerman, E. (2004). *Rules of Play - Game Design Fundamentals*. The MIT Press. https://gamifique.files.wordpress.com/2011/11/1-rules-of-play-game-design-fundamentals.pdf

Salen, K. (2007). Gaming literacies: A game design study in action. *Journal of Educational Multimedia and Hypermedia*, *16*(3), 301–322.

Salen, K., Tekinbaş, K. S., & Zimmerman, E. (2004). *Rules of Play: Game Design Fundamentals*. MIT Press.

Salen, K., & Zimmerman, E. (2004). *Rules of play: Game design fundamentals*. MIT Press.

Sallis, E. (2014). *Total quality management in education*. Routledge., doi:10.4324/9780203417010

Salvador, R. O., Merchant, A., & Alexander, E. A. (2014). Faith and fair trade: The moderating role of contextual religious salience. *Journal of Business Ethics*, *121*(3), 353–371. doi:10.100710551-013-1728-9

Samiee, S., & Chabowski, B. R. (2012). Knowledge structure in international marketing: A multi-method bibliometric analysis. *Journal of the Academy of Marketing Science*, *40*(2), 364–386. doi:10.100711747-011-0296-8

Sample, M., & Schrum, K. (2013). What's Wrong with Writing Essays. In D. Cohen & J. Scheinfeldt (Eds.), *Hacking the Academy: New Approaches to Scholarship and Teaching from Digital Humanities*. University of Michigan Press. https://muse.jhu.edu/chapter/833166

Sampson, D., & Karagiannidis, C. (2002). Personalised learning: Educational, technological and standarisation perspective. *Digital Education Review*, *4*(1), 24–39.

Samuels, S. J., Rasinski, T. V., & Hiebert, E. H. (2011). Eye movements and reading: What teachers need to know. In A. Farstrup & S. J. Samuels (Eds.), *What research has to say about reading instruction* (4th ed.). IRA. doi:10.1598/0829.02

Sánchez, A. D., Del Río, M. D. L. C., & García, J. Á. (2017). Bibliometric analysis of publications on wine tourism in the databases Scopus and WoS. *European Research on Management and Business Economics*, *23*(1), 8–15. doi:10.1016/j.iedeen.2016.02.001

Sánchez-Martín, J., Corrales-Serrano, M., Luque-Sendra, A., & Zamora-Polo, F. (2020). Exit for success. Gamifying science and technology for university students using escape-room. A preliminary approach. *Heliyon, 6*(7), e04340. doi:10.1016/j.heliyon.2020.e04340 PMID:32671257

Sandberg, J., Maris, M., & Hoogendoorn, P. (2014). The added value of a gaming context and intelligent adaptation for a mobile learning application for vocabulary learning. *Computers & Education, 76*, 119–130. doi:10.1016/j.compedu.2014.03.006

Sandford, R., Ulicsak, M., Facer, K., & Rudd, T. (2006). *Teaching with games: Using commercial off-the-shelf computer games in formal education.* Futurelab.

Sanford, K., & Madill, L. (2006). Resistance through video game play: It's a boy thing. *Canadian Journal of Education, 29*(1), 287–306, 344–345. doi:10.2307/20054157

Sanford, K., & Madill, L. (2007). Understanding the power of new literacies through video game play and design. *Canadian Journal of Education, 30*(2), 432–455. doi:10.2307/20466645

San-Martín, S., Jimenez, N., Camarero, C., & San-José, R. (2020). The path between personality, self-efficacy, and shopping regarding games apps. *Journal of Theoretical and Applied Electronic Commerce Research, 15*(2), 59–75. doi:10.4067/S0718-18762020000200105

Santos, E., & Santos, L. (2019). O papel do GeoGebra nas práticas de regulação do ensino da área do paralelogramo. Quadrante, 28(1), 6-26.

Santos, L. (2008). Dilemas e desafios da avaliação reguladora. In L. Menezes, L. Santos, H. Gomes & C. Rodrigues (Eds.), Avaliação em Matemática: Problemas e desafios, (pp. 11-35). Viseu: Secção de Educação Matemática da Sociedade Portuguesa de Ciências de Educação.

Santos, L. (2019). Reflexões em torno da avaliação pedagógica. In M. I. Ortigão, D. Fernandes, T. Pereira, & L. Santos (Orgs.), Avaliar para aprender no Brasil e em Portugal: Perspectivas teóricas, práticas e de desenvolvimento (pp. 165-190). Curitiba: Editora CRV.

Santos, L., & Cai, J. (2016). Curriculum and assessment. In A. Gutiérrez, G. Leder, & P. Boero (Eds.), *The Second Handbook in the Psychology of Mathematics Education* (pp. 153–185). Sense Publishers.

Santos, L., & Pinto, J. (2018). Ensino de conteúdos escolares: A avaliação como Fator estruturante. In *F. Veiga (Coord.), O Ensino como fator de envolvimento numa escola para todos* (pp. 503–539). Climepsi Editores.

Santos, S. A., Trevisan, L. N., Veloso, E. F. R., & Treff, M. A. (2021). Gamification In Training and Development Processes: Perception On Effectiveness And Results. *Revista de Gestão, 28*(2), 133–146. doi:10.1108/REGE-12-2019-0132

Saracho, O. N., & Spodek, B. (1995). Children's play and early childhood education: Insights from history and theory. *Journal of Education, 177*(3), 129–148. doi:10.1177/002205749517700308

Saraç, S., & Tarhan, B. (2021). Preschool teachers' promotion of self-regulated learning in the classroom and role of contextual and teacher-level factors. *International Electronic Journal of Elementary Education, 13*(2), 309–322. doi:10.26822/iejee.2021.192

Sardone, N. B., & Devlin-Scherer, R. (2010). Teacher candidate responses to digital games: 21st-century skills development. *Journal of Research on Technology in Education, 42*(4), 409–425. doi:10.1080/15391523.2010.10782558

Sardone, N. B., & Devlin-Scherer, R. (2016). Let the (Board) Games Begin: Creative Ways to Enhance Teaching and Learning. *The Clearing House: A Journal of Educational Strategies, Issues and Ideas, 89*(6), 215–222. doi:10.1080/00098655.2016.1214473

Compilation of References

Sargeantston, E. (2021). Why boardgames are so popular. *Mykindofmeeple*. Accessed August 28, 202. https://mykindofmeeple.com/why-are-board-games-popular

Sarkar, D. (2016). *Text analytics with python*. Springer. doi:10.1007/978-1-4842-2388-8

Saunders, M., Lewis, P., & Thornhill, A. (2012). *Research methods for business students*. Peason Education.

Saunders, M., Lewis, P., & Thornhill, A. (2019). *Research Methods for Business Students* (8th ed.). Pearson.

Sauro. (2012). *System Usability Scale. In Measuring Usability With The System Usability Scale*. SUS.

Sauve, L., Renaud, L., Kaufman, D., & Marquis, J. S. (2007). Distinguishing between games and simulation: A systematic review. *Journal of Educational Technology & Society*, *10*(3), 247–256. http://citeseerx.ist.psu.edu/viewdoc/download?doi=10.1.1.169.5559&rep=rep1&type=pdf

Sawyer, R. K. (2012). *Explaining Creativity: The Science of Human Innovation*. Oxford University Press.

Sax, L. (2005). *Why gender matters*. Doubleday.

Scarlett, J. (2015). Gaming geography: Using Minecraft to teach essential geography skills. In D. Rutledge & D. Slykhuis (Eds.), *Proceedings of SITE 2015 – Society for Information Technology & Education International Conference* (pp. 838-840). Association for the Advancement of Computing in Education (AACE).

Šćepanović, S., Žarić, N., & Matijević, T. (2015, September 24-25). *Gamification in higher education learning - state of the art, challenges and opportunities*. The Sixth International Conference on e-Learning, Belgrade, Serbia. https://elearning.metropolitan.ac.rs/files/pdf/2015/23-Snezana-Scepanovic-Nada-Zaric-Tripo-Matijevic-Gamification-in-higher-education-learning-state-of-the-art-challenges-and-opportunities.pdf

Scharton, H. (2019). *Busting the Myths of the Digital Native*. https://ptaourchildren.org/busting-the-myths-of-the-digital-native/

Schek, E. J., Mantovani, F., Realdon, O., Dias, J., Paiva, A., Schramm-Yavin, S., & Pat-Horenczyk, R. (2017). *Positive Technologies for Promoting Emotion Regulation Abilities in Adolescents. In eHealth 360*. Springer International Publishing.

Scherer, R., Siddiq, F., & Tondeur, J. (2019). The technology acceptance model (TAM): A meta-analytic structural equation modeling approach to explaining teachers' adoption of digital technology in education. *Computers & Education*, *128*, 13–35. doi:10.1016/j.compedu.2018.09.009

Scheuer, M. (2009). Foreword. In D. Frau-Meigs & J. Torrent (Eds.), Mapping media education policies in the world: Visions, programmes and challenges (pp. 7–8). New York: The United Nations-Alliance of Civilization.

Schifter, C., & Cipollone, M. (2013). Minecraft as a teaching tool: One case study. In R. McBride & M. Searson (Eds.), *Proceedings of Society for Information Technology & Teacher Education International Conference 2013* (pp. 2951-2955). Chesapeake, VA: Association for the Advancement of Computing in Education (AACE).

Schmidt, D. A., Baran, E., Thompson, A. D., Mishra, P., Koehler, M. J., & Shin, T. S. (2009). Technological Pedagogical Content Knowledge (TPACK): The development and validation of an assessment instrument for preservice teachers. *Journal of Research on Technology in Education*, *42*(2), 123–149. doi:10.1080/15391523.2009.10782544

Schmidt-Kraepelin, M., Thiebes, S., Stepanovic, S., Mettler, T., & Sunyaev, A. (2019). Gamification in health behavior change support systems-A synthesis of unintended side effects. In *Proceedings of the 14th International Conference on Wirtschaftsinformatik* (pp. 1032-1046). Academic Press.

Schmithorst, V. J., Holland, S. K., & Plante, E. (2007). Object identification and lexical/semantic access in children: A functional magnetic resonance imaging study of word-picture matching. *Human Brain Mapping*, *28*(10), 1060–1074. doi:10.1002/hbm.20328 PMID:17133401

Schneider, M., & Preckel, F. (2017). Variables Associated With Achievement in Higher Education: A Systematic Review of Meta-Analyses. *Psychological Bulletin*, *143*(6), 565–600. doi:10.1037/bul0000098 PMID:28333495

Schnotz, W., Fries, S., & Horz, H. (2009). Some motivational aspects of cognitive load theory. In S. Wosnitza, S. A. Karabenick, A. Efklides, & P. Nenniger (Eds.), *Contemporary Motivation Research: From Global to Local Perspectives* (pp. 86–113). Hogrefe.

Schnurr, M. A., De Santo, E., Green, A., & Taylor, A. (2015). Investigating student perceptions of learning within a role-play simulation of the Convention on Biological Diversity. *The Journal of Geography*, *114*(3), 94–107. doi:10.1080/00221341.2014.937738

Schöbel, S., Saqr, M., & Janson, A. (2021). Two decades of game concepts in digital learning environments–A bibliometric study and research agenda. *Computers & Education*, *173*, 104296. doi:10.1016/j.compedu.2021.104296

Schoepp, K. (2005). Barriers to Technology Integration in a Technology-Rich Environment. *Learning and Teaching in Higher Education: Gulf Perspectives*, *2*(1), 56–79. doi:10.18538/lthe.v2.n1.02

Schrader, C., & Bastiaens, T. (2012). Educational computer games and learning: The relationship between design, cognitive load, emotions and outcomes. *Journal of Interactive Learning Research*, *23*, 251–271. https://www.learntechlib.org/primary/p/36201/

Schreyer, J. (2012). Adolescent literacy practices in online social spaces. In New media literacies and participatory culture: Popular culture across borders. Routledge.

Schroedl, C. J., Corbridge, T. C., Cohen, E. R., Fakhran, S. S., Schimmel, D., McGaghie, W. C., & Wayne, D. B. (2012). Use of simulation-based education to improve resident learning and patient care in the medical intensive care unit: A randomized trial. *Journal of Critical Care*, *27*(2), 219.e7–219.e13. doi:10.1016/j.jcrc.2011.08.006 PMID:22033049

Schuytema, P. (2008). *Design de Games: uma abordagem prática*. Cengage Learning.

Sea of Roses Game. (2021). Retrieved October 4, 2021, from, https://tecnico.ulisboa.pt/en/news/campus-community/sea-of-roses-wins-second-place-in-international-game-design-contest/ https://store.steampowered.com/app/1581940/Sea_of_Roses/

Seaman, J. E., Allen, I. E., & Jeff Seaman, J. (2018). *Grade Increase: Tracking Distance Education in the United States*. Retrieved from Babson Survey Research Group: https://files.eric.ed.gov/fulltext/ED580852.pdf

Seeger, C. J. (2018). Open-source mapping: Landscape perception, participatory design and user-generated content; collecting user-generated walking and biking route preference data through repurposed apps, custom coding, and open-source mapping tools. In *Codify* (pp. 149–154). Routledge. doi:10.4324/9781315647791-14

Seele, P. (2018). What makes a business ethicist? A reflection on the transition from applied philosophy to critical thinking. *Journal of Business Ethics*, *150*(3), 647–656. doi:10.100710551-016-3177-8

Seele, P., & Lock, I. (2017). The game-changing potential of digitalization for sustainability: Possibilities, perils, and pathways. *Sustainability Science*, *12*(2), 183–185. doi:10.100711625-017-0426-4

Seemiller, C., & Grace, M. (2017). Generation Z: Educating and engaging the next generation of students. *About Campus: Enriching the Student Learning Experience*, *22*(3), 21–26. doi:10.1002/abc.21293

Compilation of References

Seeney, M., & Routledge, H. (2009). Drawing Circles in the Sand: Integrating Content into Serious Games. Games-Based Learning Advancements for Multi-Sensory Human Computer Interfaces.

Sefton-Green, J. (2003). *Digital diversions: Youth culture in the age of multimedia*. Routledge Tailor & Francis Group.

Segers, E., & Verhoeven, L. (2003). Effects of vocabulary training by computer in kindergarten. *Journal of Computer Assisted Learning*, *19*(4), 557–566. doi:10.1046/j.0266-4909.2003.00058.x

Seixas, L. R., Gomes, A. S., & Filho, I. J. M. (2016). Effectiveness of gamification in the engagement of students. *Computers in Human Behavior*, *58*, 48–63. doi:10.1016/j.chb.2015.11.021

Selwyn, N., & Bulfin, S. (2016). Exploring school regulation of students' technology use–rules that are made to be broken? *Educational Review*, *68*(3), 274–290. doi:10.1080/00131911.2015.1090401

Sendra, A., Lozano-Monterrubio, N., Prades-Tena, J., & Gonzalo-Iglesia, J. L. (2021). Developing a Gameful Approach as a Tool for Innovation and Teaching Quality in Higher Education. *International Journal of Game-Based Learning*, *11*(1), 53–66. doi:10.4018/IJGBL.2021010104

Sénéchal, M., LeFevre, J.-A., Smith-Chant, B. L., & Colton, K. V. (2001). On refining theoretical models of emergent literacy: The role of empirical evidence. *Journal of School Psychology*, *39*(5), 439–460. https://doi.org/10.1016/S0022-4405(01)00081-4

Sera, L., & Wheeler, E. (2017). Game on: The Gamification of the pharmacy classroom. *Currents in Pharmacy Teaching & Learning*, *9*(1), 155–159. doi:10.1016/j.cptl.2016.08.046 PMID:29180148

Sergeant, A. (2021). *Re:Higher Education's Changing Landscape*. Retrieved from https://www.equantiis.com/thinkslabs/higher-educations-changing-landscape/

Serholt, S., Barendregt, W., Leite, I., Hastie, H., Jones, A., Paiva, A., . . . Castellano, G. (2014, August). Teachers' views on the use of empathic robotic tutors in the classroom. In *The 23rd IEEE International Symposium on Robot and Human Interactive Communication* (pp. 955-960). IEEE. https:// doi:10.1109/ROMAN.2014.6926376

Serrano, K. (2019). *The effect of digital game-based learning on student learning: A literature review*. Academic Press.

Sescousse, G., Caldú, X., Segura, B., & Dreher, J. C. (2013). Processing of primary and secondary rewards: A quantitative meta-analysis and review of human functional neuroimaging studies. *Neuroscience and Biobehavioral Reviews*, *37*(4), 681–696. doi:10.1016/j.neubiorev.2013.02.002 PMID:23415703

Sezen, D. (2011). *Katılımcı Kültürün Oluşumunda Yeni Medya Okuryazarlığı: ABD ve Türkiye Örnekleri* (PhD thesis). İstanbul Üniversitesi Sosyal Bilimler Enstitüsü.

Shabalina, O., Malliarakis, C., Tomos, F., & Mozelius, P. (2017). Game-based learning for learning to program: from learning through play to learning through game development. In *11th European Conference on Games Based Learning 2017, Graz, Austria, 5-6 October 2017* (Vol. 11, pp. 571-576). Academic Conferences and Publishing International Limited.

Shabalina, O., Vorobkalov, P., Kataev, A., & Tarasenko, A. (2009). 3I-approach for IT educational games development. In *Proceedings of the European Conference on Games-based Learning* (pp. 339-344). Academic Press.

Shabalina, O., Malliarakis, C., Tomos, F., Mozelius, P., Balan, O. C., & Alimov, A. (2016) Game-Based Learning as a Catalyst for Creative Learning. *Proceedings of the 9th ECGBL*.

Shaban, A., & Pearson, E. (2019). A Learning Design Framework to Support Children with Learning Disabilities Incorporating Gamification Techniques. In *Extended Abstracts of the 2019 CHI Conference on Human Factors in Computing Systems* (p. LBW0284). ACM. 10.1145/3290607.3312806

Shafer, W. E., & Simmons, R. S. (2011). Effects of organizational ethical culture on the ethical decisions of tax practitioners in mainland China. *Accounting, Auditing & Accountability Journal, 24*(5), 647–668. doi:10.1108/09513571111139139

Shaffer, D. W., Halverson, R., Squire, K. R., & Gee, J. P. (2005). *Video games and the future of learning* (WCER Working Paper No. 2005-4). University of Wisconsin–Madison, Wisconsin Center for Education Research (NJ1).

Shaffer, D. W., Squire, K. R., Halverson, R., & Gee, J. P. (2005). Video games and the future of learning. *Phi Delta Kappan, 87*(2), 105–111. doi:10.1177/003172170508700205

Shaffer, D., & Kipp, K. (2010). *Developmental psychology: Childhood and adolescence* (8th ed.). Wadsworth Cengage Learning.

Shah, A., Kraemer, K. R., Won, C. R., Black, S., & Hasenbein, W. (2018). Developing digital intervention games for mental disorders: A review. *Games for Health Journal, 7*(4), 213–224. doi:10.1089/g4h.2017.0150 PMID:30106642

Shah, D., & McLeod, J. (2009). Communication and political socialization: Challenges and opportunities for research. *Political Communication, 26*(1), 1–10. doi:10.1080/10584600802686105

Shah, D., McLeod, J., & Lee, N. (2009). Communication competence as a foundation for civic competence: Process of socialization into citizenship. *Political Communication, 26*(1), 102–117. doi:10.1080/10584600802710384

Shah, M., & Foster, A. (2015). Developing and Assessing Teachers' Knowledge of Game-based Learning. *Journal of Technology and Teacher Education, 23*(2), 241–267.

Shan, J., Gong, L., Li, Y., & Yan, H. (2019). The impact of educational robots on student learning outcomes—Based on a meta-analysis of 49 experimental or quasi-experimental research papers. *China Educational Technology*, (5), 76–83.

Shapiro, J. (2014). *MindShift guide to digital games + learning*. Retrieved from https://a.s.kqed.net/pdf/news/MindShift-GuidetoDigitalGamesandLearning.pdf

Share, J., & Thoman, E. (2007). Teaching Democracy a media literacy approach: A media literacy educators' Guide for dilemma decisions. National Center for the Preservation Democracy.

Sharkey, A. (2016). Should we welcome robot teachers? *Ethics and Information Technology, 18*(4), 283–297. doi:10.100710676-016-9387-z

Sharma, K., Papavlasopoulou, S., & Giannakos, M. (2019). Coding games and robots to enhance computational thinking: How collaboration and engagement moderate attitudes. *International Journal of Child-Computer Interaction, 21*, 65–76.

Sharma, S. K., Palvia, S. C. J., & Kumar, K. (2017). Changing the landscape of higher education: From standardized learning to customized learning. *Journal of Information Technology Case and Application Research, 19*(2), 75–80. doi:10.1080/15228053.2017.1345214

Sharp, J. G., & Kuerbis, P. (2006). Children's ideas about the solar system and the chaos in learning science. *Science Education, 90*(1), 124–147. doi:10.1002ce.20126

Sharp, L. A. (2012). Stealth learning: Unexpected learning opportunities through games. *Journal of Institutional Research, 1*, 42–48. doi:10.9743/JIR.2013.6

Shaw, A. (2013). On Not Becoming Gamers: Moving Beyond the Constructed Audience. *Ada: A Journal of Gender, New Media and Technology*, (2).

Sheakley, M. L., Gilbert, G. E., Leighton, K., Hall, M., Callender, D., & Pederson, D. (2016). A brief simulation intervention increasing basic science and clinical knowledge. *Medical Education, 21*(1), 30744. Advance online publication. doi:10.3402/meo.v21.30744 PMID:27060102

Compilation of References

Shear, L., Tan, C. K., Patel, D., Trinidad, G., Koh, R., & Png, S. (2014). ICT and Instructional Innovation; The Case of Crescent Girls' School in Singapore. *International Journal of Education and Development Using Information and Communication Technology, 10*(2), 77–88.

Shellman, S. M., & Turan, K. (2006). Do simulations enhance student learning? An empirical evaluation of an IR simulation. *Journal of Political Science Education, 2*(1), 19–32. doi:10.1080/15512160500484168

Shen, C.-Y., & Chu, H.-P. (2014). *The relations between interface design of digital game-based learning systems and flow experience and cognitive load of learners with different levels of prior knowledge.* Paper presented at the International Conference on Cross-Cultural Design. 10.1007/978-3-319-07308-8_55

Shen, C., Sun, Q., Kim, T., Wolff, G., Ratan, R., & Williams, D. (2020). Viral vitriol: Predictors and contagion of online toxicity in World of Tanks. *Computers in Human Behavior, 108*, 106343. doi:10.1016/j.chb.2020.106343

Sheridan & Rowsell. (2010). *Design literacies: Learning and innovation in the digital age.* Routledge.

Shi, Y.-R., & Shih, J.-L. (2015). *Game factors and game-based learning design model.* Academic Press.

Shigwedha, A. N., Nakashole, L., Auala, H., Amakutuwa, H., & Ailonga, I. (2015). *The SACMEQ IV project in Namibia: A study of the conditions of schooling and the quality of primary education in Namibia.* http://www.sacmeq.org/sites/default/files/sacmeq/publications/final_sacmeq_iv_report_namibia-compressed-compressed.pdf

Shirky, C. (2009). *Here comes everybody: The power of organizing without organizations.* Penguin.

Shirky, C. (2010). *Cognitive surplus: Creativity and generosity in a connected age.* Penguin.

Shi, Y.-R., & Shih, J.-L. (2015). Game Factors and Game-Based Learning Design Model. *International Journal of Computer Games Technology, 11*, 11. doi:10.1155/2015/549684

Shmelev, V., Karpova, M., Kogtikov, N., & Dukhanov, A. (2016, October). Students' development of information-seeking skills in a computer-aided quest. In *2016 IEEE Frontiers in Education Conference (FIE)* (pp. 1-4). IEEE.

Shohel, M. M. C., Ashrafuzzaman, M., Ahsan, M. S., Mahmud, A., & Alam, A. S. (2021a). Education in Emergencies, Inequities, and the Digital Divide: Strategies for Supporting Teachers and Students in Higher Education in Bangladesh. In L. Kyei-Blankson, J. Blankson, & E. Ntuli (Eds.), *Handbook of Research on Inequities in Online Education During Global Crises* (pp. 529–553). IGI Global. doi:10.4018/978-1-7998-6533-9.ch027

Shohel, M. M. C., Ashrafuzzaman, M., Alam, A. S., Mahmud, A., Ahsan, M. S., & Islam, T. M. (2021e). Preparedness of Students for Future Teaching and Learning in Higher Education: A Bangladeshi Perspective. In E. Sengupta & P. Blessinger (Eds.), *New Student Literacies amid COVID-19: International Case Studies, Innovations in Higher Education Teaching and Learning* (Vol. 41, pp. 29–56). Emerald Publishing Limited. doi:10.1108/S2055-364120210000041006

Shohel, M. M. C., Ashrafuzzaman, M., Islam, M. T., Shams, S., & Mahmud, A. (2021d). Blended Teaching and Learning in Higher Education: Challenges and Opportunities. In S. Loureiro & J. Guerreiro (Eds.), *Handbook of Research on Developing a Post-Pandemic Paradigm for Virtual Technologies in Higher Education* (pp. 27–50). IGI Global. doi:10.4018/978-1-7998-6963-4.ch002

Shohel, M. M. C., Mahmud, A., Urmee, M. A., Anwar, N., Rahman, M. M., Acharya, D., & Ashrafuzzaman, M. (2021b). Education in Emergencies, Mental Wellbeing and E-Learning. In M. M. C. Shohel (Ed.), *E-learning and digital education in the twenty-first century: Challenges and Prospects* (pp. 1–22). IntechOpen. doi:10.5772/intechopen.97425

Shohel, M. M. C., Sham, S., Ashrafuzzaman, M., Alam, A. T. M., Mamun, A. A., & Kabir, M. M. (2021c). Emergency Remote Teaching and Learning: Digital Competencies and Pedagogical Transformation in Resource-Constrained Contexts. In M. Islam, S. Behera, & L. Naibaho (Eds.), *Handbook of Research on Asian Perspectives of the Educational Impact of COVID-19*. IGI Global.

Shopova, T. (2014). Digital literacy of students and its improvement at the university. *Journal on Efficiency and Responsibility in Education and Science*, 7(2), 26–32. doi:10.7160/eriesj.2014.070201

Shortage of personal protective equipment endangering health workers worldwide. (n.d.). Retrieved September 2, 2021, from https://www.who.int/news/item/03-03-2020-shortage-of-personal-protective-equipment-endangering-health-workers-worldwide

Short, D. (2012). Teaching scientific concepts using a virtual world—Minecraft. *Teaching Science-the Journal of the Australian Science Teachers Association*, 58(3), 55–58.

Shut Up and Sit Down. (n.d.). *Shut Up and Sit Down*. https://www.shutupandsitdown.com/games/

Shute, V. J., Rieber, L., & Van Eck, R. (2012). Games... and... learning. In R. A. Reiser & J. V. Dempsey (Eds.), Trends and issues in instructional design and technology (3rd ed., pp. 321–332). Academic Press.

Shute, V. (2011). Stealth assessment in computer-based games to support learning. In S. Tobias & J. D. Fletcher (Eds.), *Computer games and instruction* (pp. 503–524). Information Age Publishers.

Siala, H., Kutsch, E., & Jagger, S. (2019). Cultural influences moderating learners' adoption of serious 3D games for managerial learning. *Information Technology & People*, 33(2), 424–455. doi:10.1108/ITP-08-2018-0385

Siala, H., O'Keefe, R. M., & Hone, K. S. (2004). The Impact of Religious Affiliation on Trust in the Context of Electronic Commerce. *Interacting with Computers*, 16(1), 7–27. doi:10.1016/j.intcom.2003.11.002

Siddiquei, N. L., & Khalid, R. (2017). Emerging Trends of E- Learning in Pakistan: Past, Present and Future. *International Journal of Law, Humanities &. Social Science*, 2(1), 20–35.

sidebar—How do you make "infoboxes" in mediawiki? (n.d.). *Stack Overflow*. Retrieved June 1, 2021, from https://stackoverflow.com/questions/27801082/how-do-you-make-infoboxes-in-mediawiki

Sider, S., & Maich, K. (2014, February). Assistive technology tools: Supporting literacy learning for all learners in the inclusive classroom. *What Works? Research into Practice*, 50(1), 1-12. Retrieved from https://oere.oise.utoronto.ca/wp-content/uploads/2014/05/WW_TechnologyTools.pdf

Siemens, G. (2005). Connectivism: A learning theory for the digital age. *International Journal of Instructional Technology and Distance Learning.*, 3, 3–10.

Silseth, K. (2012). The multivoicedness of game play: Exploring the unfolding of a student's learning trajectory in a gaming context at school. *International Journal of Computer-Supported Collaborative Learning*, 7(1), 63–84. doi:10.100711412-011-9132-x

Silva Dos Santos, L., von Gillern, S., Lockwood, J., & Geluso, J. (2020). Digital mindsets: College-level ESL instructors' perceptions of multimodal technologies and video games for language instruction. *The European Journal of Applied Linguistics and TEFL*, 9(1), 131–152.

Silva, R. D. O. S., Pereira, A. M., Araújo, D. C. S. A. D., Rocha, K. S. S., Serafini, M. R., & De Lyra, D. P. Jr. (2021). Effect of digital serious games related to patient care in pharmacy education: A systematic review. *Simulation & Gaming*, 52(5), 104687812098889. doi:10.1177/1046878120988895

Compilation of References

Silva, R., Rodrigues, R., & Leal, C. (2019). Play it again: How gamebased learning improves flow in Accounting and Marketing education. *Accounting Education*. Advance online publication. doi:10.1080/09639284.2019.1647859

Silver, A. (2009). A European approach to media literacy: Moving toward an inclusive knowledge society. In D. Frau-Meigs & J. Torrent (Eds.), Mapping media education policies in the world: Visions, programmes and challenges (pp. 11–13). New York: The United Nations-Alliance of Civilization.

Silverblatt, A. (Ed.). (2014). The Praeger Handbook of Media Literacy. Praeger.

Silver, C., & Rivers, C. (2016). The CAQDAS Postgraduate Learning Model: An interplay between methodological awareness, analytic adeptness and technological proficiency. *International Journal of Social Research Methodology*, *19*(5), 593–609. doi:10.1080/13645579.2015.1061816

Silverman, M. H., Jedd, K., & Luciana, M. (2015). Neural networks involved in adolescent reward processing: An activation likelihood estimation meta-analysis of functional neuroimaging studies. *NeuroImage*, *122*, 427–439. doi:10.1016/j.neuroimage.2015.07.083 PMID:26254587

Simkins, D. W., & Steinkuehler, C. (2008). Critical ethical reasoning and role-play. *Games and Culture*, *3*(3-4), 333–355. doi:10.1177/1555412008317313

Simondon, G. (1989b). *L'individuation psychique et collective*. Aubier.

Simondon, G. (2005). *L'individuation à la lumière des notions de forme et d'information*. Jerome Million.

Simons, M., & Meeus, W., & Sas, J. T. (2017). Measuring media literacy for media education: Development of a questionnaire for teachers competencies. *The Journal of Media Literacy Education*, *9*(1), 99–115.

Sinclair, B. (2021). *Microsoft game revenues up 50% in Q3*. Gameindustry.biz. https://www.gamesindustry.biz/articles/2021-04-27-microsoft-game-revenues-up-50-percent-in-q3

Singer, N. (2012). You've won a badge (and now we know all about you). *New York Times*, 4.

Singer, E. (2013). Play and playfulness, basic features of early childhood education. *European Early Childhood Education Research Journal*, *21*(2), 172–184. doi:10.1080/1350293X.2013.789198

Singhapakdi, A., Marta, J. K., Rallapalli, K. C., & Rao, C. P. (2000). Toward an Understanding of Religiousness and Marketing Ethics: An Empirical Study. *Journal of Business Ethics*, *27*(4), 305–319. doi:10.1023/A:1006342224035

Singhapakdi, A., Vitell, S. J., Lee, D.-J., Nisius, A. M., & Yu, G. B. (2013). The influence of love of money and religiosity on ethical decision-making in marketing. *Journal of Business Ethics*, *114*(1), 183–191. doi:10.100710551-012-1334-2

Sipiyaruk, K., Gallagher, J. E., Hatzipanagos, S., & Reynolds, P. A. (2018). A rapid review of serious games: From healthcare education to dental education. *European Journal of Dental Education*, *22*(4), 243–257. doi:10.1111/eje.12338 PMID:29573165

Sitzmann, T., & Ely, K. (2009). A meta-analytic examination of the effectiveness of computer-based simulation games. Advanced Distributed Learning Technical Report.

Sitzmann, T. (2011). A meta-analytic examination of the instructional effectiveness of computer-based simulation games. *Personnel Psychology*, *64*(2), 489–528. doi:10.1111/j.1744-6570.2011.01190.x

Siu, Dickinson, & Lee. (2000). Ethical evaluations of business activities and personal religiousness. *Teaching Business Ethics*, *4*(3), 239-56.

Skains, L., Rudd, J. A., Casaliggi, C., Hayhurst, E. J., Horry, R., Ross, H., & Woodward, K. (2021). *Using interactive digital narrative in science and health education.* Emerald Publishing Ltd. doi:10.1108/9781839097607

Skarbez, R., Smith, M., & Whitton, M. C. (2021). Revisiting Milgram and Kishino's Reality-Virtuality Continuum. *Frontiers in Virtual Reality, 2*, 27. doi:10.3389/frvir.2021.647997

Skelton, C., & Francis, B. (2011). Successful boys and literacy: Are "literate boys" challenging or repackaging hegemonic masculinity? *Curriculum Inquiry, 41*(4), 456–479. doi:10.1111/j.1467-873X.2011.00559.x

Skinner, B. F. (1953). *Science and Human Behavior.* The Free Press.

Škorić, I., Pein, B., & Orehovački, T. (2016). *Selecting the most appropriate web IDE for learning programming using AHP.* Paper presented at the 39th International Convention on Information and Communication Technology, Electronics and Microelectronics (MIPRO). 10.1109/MIPRO.2016.7522263

Skorton, D., & Bear, A. (2018). *The Integration of the Humanities and Arts with Sciences, Engineering, and Medicine in Higher Education: Branches from the Same Tree.* The National Academies Press. doi:10.17226/24988

Slomka, J. (2014). *Toward transdisciplinary professionalism in the teaching of public health.* Establishing Transdisciplinary Professionalism for Improving Health Outcomes.

Smagorinsky, P. (2007). Vygotsky and the social dynamics of classrooms. *English Journal*, 61–66.

Smagorinsky, P. (2013). What does Vygotsky provide for the 21st-century language arts teacher? *Language Arts, 90*(3), 192–204.

Smale, M. A. (2011). *Learning through quests and contests: Games in information literacy instruction.* Academic Press.

Smiderle, R., Rigo, S.J., Marques, L.B., Coelho, J.A.P.D.M., & Jaques, P.A. (2020). *The impact of gamification on students' learning, engagement and behaviour based on their personality traits.* doi:10.1186/s40561-019-0098-x

Smith, E. M., & Holmes, N. G. (2021). Best practice for instructional labs. *Nature Physics, 17*(6), 662–663. doi:10.103841567-021-01256-6

Smith, K. (2012). Lessons learnt from literature on the diffusion of innovative learning and teaching practices in higher education. *Innovations in Education and Teaching International, 49*(2), 173–182. doi:10.1080/14703297.2012.677599

Smith, K., Mahdavi, J., Carvalho, M., Fisher, S., Russell, S., & Tippett, N. (2008). Cyberbullying: Its nature and impact in secondary school pupils. *Journal of Child Psychology and Psychiatry, and Allied Disciplines, 49*(4), 376–385. doi:10.1111/j.1469-7610.2007.01846.x PMID:18363945

Smith, N., Simpson, S. S., & Huang, C.-Y. (2007). Why managers fail to do the right thing: An empirical study of unethical and illegal conduct. *Business Ethics Quarterly, 17*(4), 633–667. doi:10.5840/beq20071743

Snelson, C. (2019). Teaching qualitative research methods online: A scoping review of the literature. *Qualitative Report, 24*(11), 2799–2814. doi:10.46743/2160-3715/2019.4021

Snoeyink, R., & Ertmer, P. A. (2001). Thrust into Technology: How Veteran Teachers Respond. *Journal of Educational Technology Systems, 30*(1), 85–111. doi:10.2190/YDL7-XH09-RLJ6-MTP1

Snyder, I. (Ed.). (2002). *Silicon literacies.* Routledge.

So & Seo. (2018). *A systematic literature review of game-based learning and gamification.* Routledge.

Socrative. (2021, September 2). *Higher Ed.* Retrieved September 12, 2021 from https://www.socrative.com/higher-ed/

Compilation of References

Socrative. (2021a, August 26). *Plans*. Retrieved September 12, 2021 from https://www.socrative.com/plans/

Sogunro, O. A. (2004). Efficacy of role-playing pedagogy in training leaders: Some reflections. *Journal of Management Development*, *23*(4), 355–371.

So, H. J., & Brush, T. A. (2008). Student perceptions of collaborative learning, social presence and satisfaction in a blended learning environment: Relationships and critical factors. *Computers & Education*, *51*(1), 318–336. doi:10.1016/j.compedu.2007.05.009

Sokal, R. R., & Rohlf, F. J. (2015). *Biometry: Principles and practice of statistics in biological research* (4th ed.). W. H. Freeman.

Sommers, C. (2013). *Primary education in rural Bangladesh: Degrees of access, choice, and participation of the poorest*. CREATE. http://www.create-rpc.org/pdf_documents/PTA75.pdf

Soulé, H., & Warrick, T. (2015). Defining 21st century readiness for all students: What we know and how to get there. *Psychology of Aesthetics, Creativity, and the Arts*, *9*(2), 178–186. doi:10.1037/aca0000017

Sousa, M. J., & Rocha, Á. (2019). Leadership styles and skills developed through game-based learning. *Journal of Business Research*, *94*, 360–366. doi:10.1016/j.jbusres.2018.01.057

Sousa, M., & Costa, E. (2014). Game based learning improving leadership skills. *EAI Endorsed Transactions on Serious Games*, *3*(3), e2. Advance online publication. doi:10.4108g.1.3.e2

Spaull, N., & Taylor, S. (2012). SACMEQ at a glance series. In *Research on Socio-economic Policy (RESEP)*. https://resep.sun.ac.za/index.php/projects

Speak Out! RAUM Residency. (2020). Retrieved October 5, 2021, from, https://raum.pt/en/terhi-marttila https://www.academia.edu/44788195/Speak_Out_a_playful_interactive_artwork_about_migration_with_a_radical_openness_to_the_World

Spector, J. M., Merrill, M. D., Elen, J., & Bishop, M. J. (Eds.). (2014). *Handbook of research on educational communications and technology*. Springer. doi:10.1007/978-1-4614-3185-5

Spichtig, A. N., Hiebert, E. H., Vorstius, C., Pascoe, J. P., Pearson, D. P., & Radach, R. (2016). The Decline of Comprehension-Based Silent Reading Efficiency in the United States: A Comparison of Current Data With Performance in 1960. *Reading Research Quarterly*, *51*(2), 239–259. doi:10.1002/rrq.137

Spiegelman, M., & Glass, R. (2008). Gaming and learning: Winning information literacy collaboration. *College & Research Libraries News*, *69*(9), 522–547. doi:10.5860/crln.69.9.8058

Spin Master Games. (1991). *Headbanz [Board Game]*. Spin Master Games.

Spires, H. A. (2012). Digital literacies and learning: Designing a path forward. NC State University.

Spradley, J. P. (1979). *The Ethnographic Interview*. The University of Michigan: Holt, Rinehart and Winston.

Squire, K. (2003). Video games in education. *International Journal of Intelligent Simulations and Gaming*, *2*(1), 49-62.

Squire, K. (2004). *Replaying history: Learning world history through playing Civilization III* [Unpublished doctoral dissertation]. Indiana University. Retrieved from https://www.academia.edu/1317076/Replaying_history_Learning_world_history_through_playing_Civilization_III

Squire, K. D. (2014). Video-Game Literacy - a Literacy of Expertise. In J. Coiro, M. Knobel, C. Lankshear, & D. Leu (Eds.), The Handbook of Research in New Literacies (pp. 635-670). Routledge.

Squire, K. D. (2021). From virtual to participatory learning with technology during COVID-19. *E-Learning and Digital Media*. doi:10.1177/20427530211022926

Squire, K. D., & Jan, M. (2007). Mad city mystery: Developing scientific argumentation skills with a place-based augmented reality game on handheld computers. *Journal of Science Education and Technology*, *16*(1), 5-29. doi:10.1007/s10956-006-9037-z

Squire, K. (2006). From Content to Context: Videogames as Designed Experience. *Educational Researcher*, *35*(8), 19–29. doi:10.3102/0013189X035008019

Squire, K. (2008). *Video games literacy: a literacy of expertise*. In J. Coiro, M. Knobel, C. Lankshear, & D. J. Leu (Eds.), *Handbook of Research on New Literacies* (pp. 639–673). Lawrence Erlbaum.

Squire, K. (2011). *Video games and learning: Teaching and participatory culture in the digital age*. Teachers College Press.

Squire, K. D. (2008). Video game–based learning: An emerging paradigm for instruction. *Performance Improvement Quarterly*, *21*(2), 7–36. doi:10.1002/piq.20020

Squire, K. D. (2013). Video game-based learning: An emerging paradigm for instruction. *Performance Improvement Quarterly*, *26*(1), 101–130. doi:10.1002/piq.21139

Squire, K., & Jenkins, H. (2003). Harnessing the power of games in education. *Insight (American Society of Ophthalmic Registered Nurses)*, *3*(1), 5–33. PMID:12703249

Stahel, D. (2018). The Battle for Wikipedia: The New Age of 'Lost Victories'? *The Journal of Slavic Military Studies*, *31*(3), 396–402. https://doi.org/10.1080/13518046.2018.1487198

Staley, D., & Trikle, D. (2011). The Changing Landscape of Higher Education. *Educase Review*. Retrieved from https://er.educause.edu/articles/2011/2/the-changing-landscape-of-higher-education

Stamper, L. J. (2015). The LandWarNet School, The Army Learning Model, and Appreciative Inquiry: How is a Centralized Training Organization Improved by Introducing Decentralization. Academic Press.

Stansbury, J. A., & Earnest, D. R. (2017). Meaningful gamification in an industrial/organizational psychology course. *Teaching of Psychology*, *44*(1), 38–45.

Star Wars opening crawl. (2021). In *Wikipedia*. https://en.wikipedia.org/wiki/Star_Wars_opening_crawl

Starke, M., Harth, M., & Sirianni, F. (2001). Retention, Bonding, and Academic Achievement: Success of a First-Year Seminar. *Journal of the First-Year Experience & Students in Transition*, *13*(2), 7–36.

Stark, R., & Glock, C. Y. (1968). *American Piety: The Nature of Religious Commitment*. University of California Press.

Statler, M., Heracleous, L., & Jacobs, C. D. (2011). Serious play as a practice of paradox. *The Journal of Applied Behavioral Science*, *47*(2), 236–256. doi:10.1177/0021886311398453

Stats, S. A. (2012). *Census 2011 statistical release*. Statistics South Africa.

Steinbrick, J. E., & Cook, J. W. (2003). Media literacy skills and the "war on terrorism". *The Clearing House*, *76*(6), 284-288. https://www.jstor.org/stable/30189852

Steiner, C. (2003). *Emotional Literacy: Intelligence with a Heart*. Retrieved May 03, 2019 from http://emotional-literacy-training.com/wp-content/uploads/2015/09/Steiner-Emotional-Literacy.pdf

Steinkuehler, C. (2004). *The literacy practices of massively multiplayer online gaming*. Paper presented at the American Educational Research Association, San Diego, CA.

Compilation of References

Steinkuehler, C. (2006). The mangle of play. *Journal of Adolescent & Adult Literacy, 1*(3), 199–213.

Steinkuehler, C. (2007). Massively multiplayer online gaming as a constellation of literacy practices. *E-Learning and Digital Media, 4*(3), 297–318. doi:10.2304/elea.2007.4.3.297

Steinkuehler, C. (2010). Video games and digital literacies. *Journal of Adolescent & Adult Literacy, 54*(1), 61–63. doi:10.1598/JAAL.54.1.7

Steinkuehler, C. (2011). *The mismeasure of boys: Reading and online videogames.* Wisconsin Center for Education Research, University of Wisconsin.

Steinkuehler, C., & Duncan, S. (2008). Scientific habits of mind in virtual worlds. *Journal of Science Education and Technology, 17*(6), 530–543. doi:10.100710956-008-9120-8

Steinkuehler, C., Squire, K., & Barab, S. A. (2012). *Games, learning, and society: Learning and meaning in the digital age.* Cambridge University Press. doi:10.1017/CBO9781139031127

Steinmaurer, A., Pirker, J., & Christian, G. (2020). sCool - Game Based Learning in STEM Education: A Case Study in Secondary Education. *The Challenges of the Digital Transformation in Education, 917*, 614–625. doi:10.1007/978-3-030-11932-4_58

Stetsenko, A. (2020). Radical-Transformative Agency: Developing a Transformative Activist Stance on a Marxist-Vygotskyan Foundation. In F. Liberali, M. Dafermos, & A. T. Neto (Eds.), *Revisiting Vygotsky for Social Change: Bringing Together Theory and Practice* (pp. 31–62). Peter Lang Inc.

Stetter, M. E., & Hughes, M. T. (2010). Computer-Assisted Instruction to Enhance the Reading Comprehension of .... *Journal of Special Education Technology, 25*(5), 1–16. doi:10.1177/016264341002500401

Stewart, B. (1956). *To Tell the Truth* [Game Show Series]. CBS.

Stewart, B., Rubino, V., Schwartz, C., & Strahan, M. (Producers). (1964). *100,000 Dollar Pyramid* [Game Show Series]. CBS.

Stewart, I., & McKee, W. (2009). Review of pedagogical research into technology to support inclusive personalised learning. *Engineering Education, 4*(2), 62–69. doi:10.11120/ened.2009.04020062

Stigler, J. W., & Hiebert, J. (2009). *The teaching gap: Best ideas from the world's teachers for improving education in the classroom.* Simon and Schuster.

Stiller, K. D., & Schworm, S. (2019). Game-Based Learning of the Structure and Functioning of Body Cells in a Foreign Language: Effects on Motivation, Cognitive Load, and Performance. *Frontiers in Education, 4*, 18. doi:10.3389/feduc.2019.00018

Stone, C. (1993). What is missing in the metaphor of scaffolding? In E. Forman, N. Minick, & C. Stone (Eds.), *Contexts for learning: Sociocultural dynamics in children's development* (pp. 169–183). Oxford University Press.

Stone, C. A. (1998). The Metaphor of Scaffolding: Its Utility for the Field of Learning Disabilities. *Journal of Learning Disabilities, 31*(4), 344–364. doi:10.1177/002221949803100404 PMID:9666611

Storch, S. A., & Whitehurst, G. J. (2002). Oral language and code-related precursors to reading: Evidence from a longitudinal structural model. *Developmental Psychology, 38*(6), 934–947. https://doi.org/10.1037/0012-1649.38.6.934

Storeygard, J., Hamm, J., & Fosnot, C. T. (2010). Determining what children know: Dynamic versus static assessment. In National Council of Teachers of Mathematics (Ed.), Models of Intervention in Mathematics: Reweaving the Tapestry (pp. 45-69). Reston, VA: NCTM.

Stork, M. G. (2020). Supporting twenty-first century competencies using robots and digital storytelling. *Journal of Formative Design in Learning, 4*(1), 43–50. doi:10.100741686-019-00039-w

Stott, A., & Neustadter, C. (2013). *Analysis of Gamification in Education*. Simon Fraser University.

Stoyanov, S. R., Hides, L., Kavanagh, D. J., Zelenko, O., Tjondronegoro, D., & Mani, M. (2015). Mobile app rating scale: A new tool for assessing the quality of health mobile apps. *JMIR mHealth and uHealth, 3*(1), e27. doi:10.2196/mhealth.3422 PMID:25760773

Student's blog link. (2017). Retrieved October 4, 2021, from, https://fbaulgaming.wixsite.com/gaming2017

Student's blog link. (2018). Retrieved October 4, 2021, from, https://fbaulistgaming2018.wixsite.com/fbaul-istgaming2018

Student's blog link. (2019). Retrieved October 4, 2021, from, https://fbaulistgaming2019.wixsite.com/fbaulistgaming2019

Student's blog link. (2020). Retrieved October 4, 2021, from, https://fbaulistgaming2020.wixsite.com/fbaulistgaming2020

Student's blog link. (2021). Retrieved October 4, 2021, from, https://fbaulistgaming2021.wixsite.com/fbaulistgaming2021

Students' testimonies web documentary. (2019). *Mobility and Permanence in Public Space. Narratives of University Students with Different Self-Determination of Gender and Sexual Orientation*. Retrieved October 4, 2021, from http://www.ceg.ulisboa.pt/mpps/#3

Stufft, C. (2016). Videogames and YA literature: Using book groups to layer literacies. *The ALAN Review, 43*(3), 96–102.

Stufft, C. J. (2018). Engaging students in literacy practices through video game book groups. *Literacy Research: Theory, Method, and Practice, 67*(1), 195–210. doi:10.1177/2381336918787191

Stufft, C., & von Gillern, S. (2021). Fostering Multimodal Analyses of Video Games: Reflective Writing in the Middle School. *Journal of Adolescent & Adult Literacy*, jaal.1198. doi:10.1002/jaal.1198

Su, A. Y. S., Huang, C. S. J., Yang, S. J. H., Ding, T. J., & Hsieh, Y. Z. (2015). Effects of annotations and homework on learning achievement: An empirical study of Scratch programming pedagogy. *Journal of Educational Technology & Society, 18*(4), 331–343.

Suarez-Orozco, M. M. (Ed.). (2007). *Learning in the global era: International perspectives on globalization and education*. University of California Press.

Subhash, S., & Cudney, E. A. (2018). Gamified learning in higher education: A systematic review of literature. *Computers in Human Behavior, 87*, 192–206. doi:10.1016/j.chb.2018.05.002

Subhash, S., & Cudney, E. A. (2018). Gamified learning in higher education: A systematic review of the literature. *Computers in Human Behavior, 87*, 192–206. doi:10.1016/j.chb.2018.05.028

Sucena, A., Filipa, A. S., & Viana, F. L. (2016). Early intervention in reading difficulties using the Graphogame software. *Letronica, 9*(2).

Sudsomboon, W. (2007). Construction Of a Competancy Based Curriculum Content Framework For Mechanical Technology Education Program on Automotive Technology Subjects. *Proceedings of the ICASE Asian Symposium*.

Suh, A., & Prophet, J. (2018). The state of immersive technology research: A literature analysis. *Computers in Human Behavior, 86*, 77–90. Advance online publication. doi:10.1016/j.chb.2018.04.019

Suh, S., Kim, S. W., & Kim, N. J. (2010). Effectiveness of MMORPG-based instruction in elementary English education in Korea. *Journal of Computer Assisted Learning, 26*(5), 370–378. doi:10.1111/j.1365-2729.2010.00353.x

Compilation of References

Sullivan-Carr, M. (2016). *Game-based learning and children with ADHD* (10126186 Ed.D.), Drexel University. Retrieved from https://www.proquest.com/dissertations-theses/game-based-learning-children-with-adhd/docview/1797415951/se-2?accountid=38885

Sundararajan, B. (2020). Role Play Simulation: Using Cases to Teach Business Concepts - Simulations and Student Learning: A transdisciplinary perspective. University of Toronto Press.

Sung, H.-Y., & Hwang, G.-J. (2013). A collaborative game-based learning approach to improving students' learning performance in science courses. *Computers & Education*, *63*, 43–51. doi:10.1016/j.compedu.2012.11.019

Sun, H., & Zhang, P. (2008). An exploration of affect factors and their role in user technology acceptance: Mediation and causality. *Journal of the Association for Information Science and Technology*, *59*(8), 1252–1263.

Sun, P.-C., Tsai, R. J., Finger, G., Chen, Y.-Y., & Yeh, D. (2008). What drives a successful e-Learning? An empirical investigation of the critical factors influencing learner satisfaction. *Computers & Education*, *50*(4), 1183–1202. doi:10.1016/j.compedu.2006.11.007

Surahman,, E., & Kuswandi,, D., Sulthoni, W. A., & Zufar, Z. (2019). Students' Perception of Project-Based Learning Model in Blended Learning Mode Using Sipejar. *Advances in Social Science, Education and Humanities Research*, 372.

Surendeleg, G., Murwa, V., Yun, H.-K., & Kim, Y. S. (2014). The role of gamification in education–a literature review. *Contemporary Engineering Sciences*, *7*(29), 1609–1616. doi:10.12988/ces.2014.411217

Susanti, N., Juandi, D., & Maximus Tamur, M. (2020). The Effect of Problem-Based Learning (PBL) Model On Mathematical Communication Skills of Junior High School Students – A Meta-Analysis Study. *Journal Theory dan Aplikasi Matematika*, *4*(2), 145-154. doi:10.31764/jtam.v4i2.2481

Susi, T., Johannesson, M., & Backlund, P. (2007). *Serious games: An overview.* DiVA.

Susman, K., & Pavlin, J. (2020). Improvements in Teachers' Knowledge and Understanding of Basic Astronomy Concepts through Didactic Games. *Journal of Baltic Science Education*, *19*(6), 1020–1033. doi:10.33225/jbse/20.19.1020

Suvin, C. (2020). *Why should higher education institutions focus on Education 4.0?* Creatix Campus. https://www.creatrixcampus.com/blog/Education-4.0

Sweller, J. (1994). Cognitive load theory, learning difficulty, and instructional design. *Learning and Instruction*, *4*(4), 295–312. doi:10.1016/0959-4752(94)90003-5

Swimberghe, K. R., Sharma, D., & Flurry, L. W. (2011). Does a consumer's religion really matter in the buyer–seller dyad? An empirical study examining the relationship between consumer religious commitment, Christian conservatism and the ethical judgment of a seller's controversial business decision. *Journal of Business Ethics*, *102*(4), 581–598. doi:10.100710551-011-0829-6

Swimberghe, K., Flurry, L. A., & Parker, J. M. (2011). Consumer religiosity: Consequences for consumer activism in the United States. *Journal of Business Ethics*, *103*(3), 453–467. doi:10.100710551-011-0873-2

Syed, J., & Van Buren, H. J. III. (2015). Global Business Norms and Islamic Views of Women's Employment. *Business Ethics Quarterly*, *24*(2), 251–276. doi:10.5840/beq201452910

Sylva, K., Melhuish, E., Sammons, P., Siraj-Blatchford, I., & Taggart, B. (Eds.). (2010). *Early childhood matters: Evidence from the effective pre-school and primary education project.* Routledge. doi:10.4324/9780203862063

Szegedine Lengyel, P. (2020). Can the game-based learning come? Virtual classroom in higher education of 21st century. *International Journal of Emerging Technologies in Learning*, *15*(112). doi:10.3991/ijet.v15i02.11521

Tachie, S. A., & Galawe, B. F. (2021). The Value of Incorporating Indigenous Games in the Teaching of Number Sentences and Geometric Patterns. *International Journal for Cross-Disciplinary Subjects in Education*, *12*(1), 4350–4361. doi:10.20533/ijcdse.2042.6364.2021.0533

Taillandier, F., Micolier, A., Sauce, G., & Chaplain, M. (2021). DOMEGO: A Board Game for Learning How to Manage a Construction Project. *International Journal of Game-Based Learning*, *11*(2), 20–37. doi:10.4018/IJGBL.2021040102

Takeuchi, L. M., & Vaala, S. (2014). *Level up learning: A national survey on teaching with digital games*. The Joan Ganz Cooney Center at Sesame Workshop. https://bit.ly/38cRQhp

Takeuchi, L., & Stevens, R. (2011). *The new coviewing: Designing for learning through joint media engagement*. The Joan Ganz Cooney Center at Sesame Workshop. https://www.joanganzcooneycenter.org/wp-content/uploads/2011/12/jgc_coviewing_desktop.pdf

Talib, C. A., Aliyu, F., & Siang, K. H. (2019). Enhancing students' reasoning skills in engineering and technology through game-based learning. *International Journal of Emerging Technologies in Learning*, *14*(24), 69-80. doi:10.3991/ijet.v14i24.12117

Tamminen, J., Payne, J. D., Stickgold, R., Wamsley, E. J., & Gaskell, M. G. (2010). Sleep spindle activity is associated with the integration of new memories and existing knowledge. *The Journal of Neuroscience: The Official Journal of the Society for Neuroscience*, *30*(43), 14356–14360. doi:10.1523/JNEUROSCI.3028-10.2010 PMID:20980591

Tan Ai Lin, D., Ganapathy, M., & Kaur, M. (2018). Kahoot! It: Gamification in Higher Education. *Pertanika Journal of Social Science & Humanities*, *26*(1).

Tan, J., & Biswas, G. (2007). Simulation-based game learning environments: Building and sustaining a fish tank. *IEEE Xplore Digital Library*, 73–80. . doi:10.1109/DIGITEL.2007.44

Tanak, A. (2020). Designing tpack-based course for preparing student teachers to teach science with technological pedagogical content knowledge. *Kasetsart Journal of Social Sciences*, *41*(1), 53–59.

Tanaka, F., & Matsuzoe, S. (2012). Children teach a care-receiving robot to promote their learning: Field experiments in a classroom for vocabulary learning. *Journal of Human-Robot Interaction*, *1*(1), 78–95. doi:10.5898/JHRI.1.1.Tanaka

Taneja, P., Safapour, E., & Kermanshachi, S. (2018). *Innovative higher education teaching and learning techniques: Implementation trends and assessment approaches*. Paper presented at the 2018 ASEE Annual Conference & Exposition. 10.18260/1-2--30669

Tang, S., Hanneghan, M., & El Rhalibi, A. (2007). *Describing games for learning: terms, scope and learning approaches*. https://www.academia.edu/25962572/Describing_Games_for_Learning_Terms_Scope_and_Learning_Approaches

Tang, S., Hanneghan, M., & Rhalibi, A. (2009). *Introduction to Games-Based Learning*. IGI Global. doi:10.4018/978-1-60566-360-9.ch001

Tanık Önal, N. (2020). Investigation of gifted students' environmental awareness. *International Journal of Curriculum and Instruction*, *12*(2), 95–107.

Tan, M., & Hew, K. F. (2016). Incorporating meaningful gamification in a blended learning research methods class: Examining student learning, engagement, and affective outcomes. *Australasian Journal of Educational Technology*, *32*(5). Advance online publication. doi:10.14742/ajet.2232

Tanouri, A., Mulcahy, R., & Russell-Bennett, R. (2019). Transformative gamification services for social behavior brand equity: A hierarchical model. *Journal of Service Theory and Practice*, *29*(2), 122–141. doi:10.1108/JSTP-06-2018-0140

Compilation of References

Tao, Z., Li, H., & Yong, L. (2010). The effect of flow experience on mobile SNS users' loyalty. *Industrial Management & Data Systems, 110*(6), 930–946. doi:10.1108/02635571011055126

Taspinar, B., Schmidt, W., & Schuhbauer, H. (2016). Gamification in education: A board game approach to knowledge acquisition. *Procedia Computer Science, 99*, 101–116. https://doi.org/10.1016/j.procs.2016.09.104

Tate, M. (2013). *Worksheets don't grow dendrites: 20 instructional strategies that engaged the brain*. Corwin.

Taub, M., Sawyer, R., Smith, A., Rowe, J., Azevedo, R., & Lester, J. (2020). The agency effect: The impact of student agency on learning, emotions, and problem-solving behaviors in a game-based learning environment. *Computers & Education, 147*, 103781. doi:10.1016/j.compedu.2019.103781

Taylor, S. E., & Robinson, H. A. (1963). *The relationship of oculomotor efficiency of the beginning reader to his success in learning to read*. Paper presented at the meeting of the American Educational Research Association, Chicago, IL.

Taylor, S., & Yu, D. (2009). The importance of socio-economic status in determining educational achievement in South Africa. *Stellenbosch Economic Working Papers*, 1–65.

Taylor, S.E., Frackenpohl, H. & Pettee, J.L. (1960). Grade level norms for the Components of the Fundamental Reading skill. *EDL Research Information Bulletin, 3*.

Taylor. (2002). *Teaching & learning online: The workers, the lurkers and the shirkers*. USQ.

Taylor, N. (2017). Monitoring, Accountability and Professional Knowledge. In *Monitoring the Quality of Education in Schools* (pp. 43–52). SensePublishers. doi:10.1007/978-94-6300-453-4_4

Taylor, T. L. (2006). Does WoW change everything? How a PvP server, multinational player base, and surveillance mod scene caused me pause. *Games and Culture, 1*(4), 61–63. doi:10.1177/1555412006292615

Tech4Learning. (n.d.). *Creating a 21st century classroom: combining the 3R's and the 4C's*. Author.

Teh, C. L., Fauzy, W. W., & Toh, S. C. (2007). Why use computer games for learning? *1st International Malaysian Educational Technology Convention*, 835-843.

Teichler, U. (2017). Internationalisation Trends in Higher Education and the Changing Role of International Student Mobility. *Journal of international Mobility, 5*, 177-216. doi:10.3917/jim.005.0179

Tejederas, M. (2020). Gamified methodologies in bilingual teacher training. *6th International Conference on Bilingual Education*. https://www.grupo-ebei.es/confbe/2020/

Tercanli, H., Martina, R., Dias, M. F., Wakkee, I., Reuter, J., Amorim, M., Madaleno, M., Magueta, D., Vieira, E., Veloso, C., Figueiredo, C., Vitória, A., Gomes, I., Meireles, G., Daubariene, A., Daunoriene, A., Mortensen, A. K., Zinovyeva, A., Trigueros, I. R., . . . Gutiérrez-Pérez, J. (2021). *Educational Escape Room in Practice: Research, experiences and recommendations*. Academic Press.

The City Reporters. (2013). *REVEALED! Govt plans to read your tweets, Facebook posts, possibly jail you*. Available at http://thecityreporters.com/revealed-govt-plans-to-readyour-tweets-facebook-posts-possibly-jail-you/

The NCES fast facts tools provides quick answers to many education questions. (n.d.). *National Center for Education Statistics*. Retrieved September 2, 2021, from https://nces.ed.gov/fastfacts/display.asp?id=98

The New London Group. (2000). A pedagogy of multiliteracies: Designing social futures. In B. Cope & M. Kalantzis (Eds.), *Multiliteracies: Literacy learning and the design of social futures*. Routledge.

The World Bank. (2020). *Pandemic Threatens to Push 72 Million More Children into Learning Poverty—World Bank outlines a New Vision to ensure that every child learns, everywhere* [Press release]. https://www.worldbank.org/en/news/press-release/2020/12/02/pandemic-threatens-to-push-72-million-more-children-into-learning-poverty-world-bank-outlines-new-vision-to-ensure-that-every-child-learns-everywhere

Theodoropoulos, A., & Lepouras, G. (2021). Augmented Reality and programming education: A systematic review. *International Journal of Child-Computer Interaction*, *30*, 100335. doi:10.1016/j.ijcci.2021.100335

Third Rail Games, L. L. C. (2014). *Flying kitchen* (Version 2.02) [Mobile app]. http://itunes.apple.com

Third Rail Games, L. L. C. (2014). *Hideout: Early reading* (Version 2.02) [Mobile app]. http://itunes.apple.com

Thoman, E. (1990, July). New Directions in Media Education. In *An International Conference at the University of Toulouse*. BFI, CLEMI and UNESCO.

Thomas, A. (2018). *TEDx Talk on The Effective Use of Game-Based Learning in Education*. https://www.youtube.com/watch?v=-X1m7tf9cRQ

Thompson, C. G., & von Gillern, S. (2020). Video-game based instruction for vocabulary acquisition with English language learners: A Bayesian meta-analysis. *Educational Research Review*, *30*, 100332. doi:10.1016/j.edurev.2020.100332

Thompson, K. M., & Haninger, K. (2001). Violence in E-rated video games. *Medicine and the Media*, *286*(5), 591–598. PMID:11476663

Thomson, S. (2018). Achievement at school and socioeconomic background—An educational perspective. *NPJ Science of Learning*, *3*(1), 5. Advance online publication. doi:10.103841539-018-0022-0 PMID:30631466

Threekunprapa, A., & Yasri, P. (2020). Unplugged Coding Using Flowblocks for Promoting Computational Thinking and Programming among Secondary School Students. *International Journal of Instruction*, *13*(3), 207–222. doi:10.29333/iji.2020.13314a

Tiba, C., Condy, J., & Tunjera, N. (2016). Re-examining factors influencing teachers' adoption and use of technology as a pedagogical tool. In *South Africa International Conference International Conference on Educational Technologies* (pp. 1-11). Pretoria: African Academic Research Forum.

Tillman, A. (2012). *What We See and Why It Matters: How Competency in Visual Literacy Can Enhance Student Learning*. Retrieved May 03, 2019 from https://digitalcommons.iwu.edu/cgi/viewcontent.cgi?article=1008&context=education_honproj

Tkacz, N. (2007). Power, Visibility, Wikipedia. *Southern Review: Communication. Política y Cultura*, *40*(2), 5.

Tobias, S., Fletcher, J. D., & Wind, A. P. (2014). *Game-based learning*. 5 doi:10.1007/978-1-4614-3185-

Tobias, S., Fletcher, J. D., & Wind, A. P. (2014). Game-Based Learning. In J. M. Spector, M. D. Merrill, J. Elen, & M. J. Bishop (Eds.), *Handbook of Research on Educational Communications and Technology* (pp. 485–503). Springer. doi:10.1007/978-1-4614-3185-5_38

Tobin, R., & McInnes, A. (2008). Accommodating differences: Variations in differentiated literacy instruction in grade 2/3 classrooms. *Literacy*, *42*(1), 3–9. doi:10.1111/j.1467-9345.2008.00470.x

Todorinova, L. (2015). Wikipedia and undergraduate research trajectories. *New Library World*, *116*(3/4), 201–212. doi:10.1108/NLW-07-2014-0086

Toh, W., & Kirschner, D. (2020). Self-directed learning in video games, affordances and pedagogical implications for teaching and learning. *Computers & Education*, *154*, 1–11. doi:10.1016/j.compedu.2020.103912

Compilation of References

Tolks, D., Sailer, M., Dadaczynski, K., Lampert, C., Huberty, J., Paulus, P., & Horstmann, D. (2019). ONYA—The Wellbeing Game: How to Use Gamification to Promote Wellbeing. *Information (Basel)*, *10*(2), 58. doi:10.3390/info10020058

Tomin, B., & Jenson, J. (2021). Exploring Science Fictional Futures With Secondary Students: Practicing Critical Literacy. In *Disciplinary Literacy Connections to Popular Culture in K-12 Settings*. IGI Global. doi:10.4018/978-1-7998-4721-2.ch005

Tomlinson, C. A. (2001). *How to differentiate instruction in mixed ability classrooms* (2nd ed.). ASCD.

Töremen, F., Karakuş, M., & Yasan, T. (2009). Total quality management practices in Turkish primary schools. *Quality Assurance in Education*, *17*(1), 30–44. doi:10.1108/09684880910929917

Torgesen, J. K., Wagner, R. K., Rashotte, C. A., Herron, J., & Lindamood, P. (2010). Computer assisted instruction to prevent early reading difficulties in students at risk for dyslexia: Outcomes from two instructional approaches. *Annals of Dyslexia*, *60*(1), 40–56. doi:10.100711881-009-0032-y PMID:20052566

Torppa, M. (2007). *Pathways to Reading Acquisition: effects of early skills, learning environment and familial risk for dyslexia*. University of Jyväskylä.

Torres-Toukoumidis, Á., Rodríguez, L. M. R., & Rodríguez, A. P. (2018). Ludificación y sus posibilidades en el entorno de blended learning: Revisión documental [Gamification and its possibilities in blended learning: Literature review]. *RIED. Revista Iberoamericana de Educación a Distancia*, *21*(1), 95–111. doi:10.5944/ried.21.1.18792

Tough, J. (1977). *The Development of Meaning*. George Allen & Unwin.

Tracey, D., & Morrow, L. (2009). *Best practices for phonics instruction in today's classroom. Sadlier Professional Development Series*, *13*, 1–22 .

Tractinsky, N., Katz, A. S., & Ikar, D. (2000). What is beautiful is usable. *Interacting with Computers*, *13*(2), 127–145. doi:10.1016/S0953-5438(00)00031-X

Trad, R. (2021). *Teachers' and students' experiences using social media as a pedagogical tool within classrooms: A systematic literature review* [Unpublished master's thesis]. https://ir.lib.uwo.ca/etd/7824

Trespalacios, J., Chamberlin, B., & Gallagher, R. R. (2011). Collaboration, engagement & fun: How youth preferences in video gaming can inform 21st century education. *TechTrends*, *55*(6), 49–54. doi:10.100711528-011-0541-5

Trilling, B., & Fidel, C. (2009). *21st Century skills: Learning for life in our times*. Jossey-Bass.

Trinidad, M., Ruiz, M., & Calderón, A. (2021). A bibliometric analysis of gamification research. *IEEE Access: Practical Innovations, Open Solutions*, *9*, 46505–46544. doi:10.1109/ACCESS.2021.3063986

Troitschanskaia, Z. O., Pant, H., Lautenbach, C., Molerov, D., Toepper, M., & Brückner, S. (2017). *Modeling and Measuring Competencies in Higher Education: Approaches to Challenges in Higher Education Policy and Practice*. Springer. doi:10.1007/978-3-658-15486-8

Tromba, P. (2013). Build engagement and knowledge one block at a time with Minecraft. *Learning and Leading with Technology*, *40*(8), 20–23.

Troppo, G. (2015). *The game believes in you: How digital play can make our kids smarter*. St. Martin's Press.

Troussas, C., Krouska, A., & Sgouropoulou, C. (2020). Collaboration and fuzzy-modeled personalization for mobile game-based learning in higher education. *Computers & Education*, *144*, 103698. doi:10.1016/j.compedu.2019.103698

Trundle, K. C., & Bell, R. L. (2010). The use of a computer simulation to promote conceptual change: A quasi-experimental study. *Computers & Education, 54*(4), 1078–1088. doi:10.1016/j.compedu.2009.10.012

Trybus, J. (2015). *Game-Based Learning: What it is, Why it Works, and Where it's Going*. New Media Institute. http://www.newmedia.org /game-based-learning--what-it-is-why-it -works-and-where-its-going.html

Tsai, M.-J., Huang, L.-J., Hou, H.-T., Hsu, C.-Y., & Chiou, G.-L. (2016). Visual behavior, flow and achievement in game-based learning. *Computers & Education, 98*, 115–129. doi:10.1016/j.compedu.2016.03.011

Tsay, C. H.-H., Kofinas, A., & Luo, J. (2018). Enhancing student learning experience with technology-mediated gamification: An empirical study. *Computers & Education, 121*, 1–17. doi:10.1016/j.compedu.2018.01.009

Tsekleves, E., Cosmas, J., & Aggoun, A. (2016). Benefits, barriers and guideline recommendations for the implementation of serious games in education for stakeholders and policymakers. *British Journal of Educational Technology, 47*(1), 164–183. doi:10.1111/bjet.12223

Tuber, K. (2007). *Catan Dice* [Board Game]. CatangmbH.

Tuomi, P., Multisilta, J., Saarikoski, P., & Suominen, J. (2018). Coding skills as a success factor for a society. *Education and Information Technologies, 23*(1), 419–434. doi:10.100710639-017-9611-4

Turgut, Y., & Irgin, P. (2009). Young learners' language learning via computer games. *Procedia: Social and Behavioral Sciences, 1*(1), 760–764. doi:10.1016/j.sbspro.2009.01.135

Turkle, S. (1995). *Life on the screen: Identity in the age of the Internet*. Touchstone.

Turner, J., Amirnuddin, P. S., & Singh, H. (2019). University Legal Learning Spaces Effectiveness in Developing Employability Skills of Future Law Graduates. *Malaysian Journal of Learning and Instruction, 16*(1), 49–79. doi:10.32890/mjli2019.16.1.3

Turoff, A., & Cooke, B. (1974). *Boggle [Board Game]*. Parker Brothers.

Tüzün, H., Yılmaz-Soylu, M., Karakuş, T., İnal, Y., & Kızılkaya, G. (2009). The effects of computer games on primary school students' achievement and motivation in geography learning. *Computers & Education, 52*(1), 68–77. doi:10.1016/j.compedu.2008.06.008

Tyng, C., Amin, H., Saad, M., & Malik, A. (2017). The Influences of Emotion on Learning and Memory. Front.Ullman, M. T. (2016). The declarative/procedural model: a neurobiological model of language learning, knowledge, and use. In *Neurobiology of language* (pp. 953–968). Academic Press.

Udara, S. W. I., & De Alwis, A. K. (2019). Gamification for Healthcare and Well-being. *Global Journal of Medical Research*, 25–29. doi:10.34257/GJMRKVOL19IS4PG25

Ullman, M. T., & Lovelett, J. T. (2018). Implications of the declarative/procedural model for improving second language learning: The role of memory enhancement techniques. *Second Language Research, 34*(1), 39–65. doi:10.1177/0267658316675195

Umble, E. J., & Umble, M. (2005). The Production Dice Game: An Active Learning Classroom Exercise and Spreadsheet Simulation. *Operations Management Education Review, 1*, 105–122.

Um, E., Plass, J. L., Hayward, E. O., & Homer, B. D. (2012). Emotional design in multimedia learning. *Journal of Educational Psychology, 104*(2), 485–498. doi:10.1037/a0026609

UNESCO Institute for Information Technologies in Education (UNESCO-IITE). (2011). *Digital natives: How do they learn; How to teach them?* Retrieved from https://iite.unesco.org/files/policy_briefs/pdf/en/digital_natives.pdf

Compilation of References

UNESCO. (1990). http://www.unesco.org/new/fileadmin/MULTIMEDIA/HQ/CI/CI/pdf/youth_media_education.pdf

UNESCO. (2006). *Cross-national studies of the quality of education: Planning their design and managing their impact* (K. N. Ross & I. J. Genevois, Eds.). International Institute for Educational Planning.

UNESCO. (2018). *Digital skills critical for jobs and social inclusion.* https://en.unesco.org/news/digital-skills-critical-jobs-and-social-inclusion

UNESCO. (2021). *100 million more children under the minimum reading proficiency level due to COVID-19 – UNESCO convenes world education ministers.* Retrieved September 16, 2021 from https://en.unesco.org/news/100-million-more-children-under-minimum-reading-proficiency-level-due-covid-19-unesco-convenes

United Nations. (2020). *UN Secretary-General's policy brief: The impact of COVID-19 on women.* Retrieved January 18, 2020, from https://www.unwomen.org/en/digital-library/publications/2020/04/policy-brief-the-impact-of-covid-19-on-women

United Nations. (2021). *100 million more children fail basic reading skills because of COVID-19.* UN News. Retrieved September 16, 2021, from https://news.un.org/en/story/2021/03/1088392

University of Lisbon. (2021). Retrieved October 4, 2021, from https://www.ulisboa.pt/en

University of Toronto Libraries. (2021, August 25). *Research Guides.* Retrieved September 6, 2021, from https://guides.library.utoronto.ca/c.php?g=448614&p=3508116

Unlock Creativity through game-based learning at higher education. (2021). https://www.un-lock.eu/

Urh, M., Vukovic, G., Jereb, E., & Pintar, R. (2015). The Model for Introduction of Gamification into E-learning in Higher Education. *Procedia - Social and Behavioral Sciences, 197*(March), 388–397. doi:10.1016/j.sbspro.2015.07.154

Uribe-Jongbloed, E., Espinosa-Medina, H. D., & Biddle, J. (2016). Cultural Transduction and intertextuality in video games: An analysis of three international case studies. In C. Duret & C. M. Pons (Eds.), *Contemporary research on intertextuality in video games* (pp. 143–161). IGI Global. doi:10.4018/978-1-5225-0477-1.ch009

Vaala, S., Ly, A., & Levine, M. H. (2015). Getting a read on the app stores: A market scan and analysis of children's literacy apps. *The Joan Ganz Cooney Center at Sesame Workshop.* https://www.joanganzcooneycenter.org/wp-ontent/uploads/2015/12/jgcc_gettingaread.pdf

Vacca, J. S., & Levitt, R. (2011). Using Scaffolding Techniques to Teach a Lesson about the Civil War. *International Journal of Humanities and Social Science, 1*(18), 150–161. www.ijhssnet.com

Vaidyanathan, S. (2016). What's the difference between coding and computational thinking? *EdSurge.* Retrieved 9/14/2021 from https://www.edsurge.com/news/2016-08-06-what-s-the-difference-between-coding-and-computational-thinking

Vaishnavi, V. & Kuechler, B. (2004). Design Science Research in Information Systems Overview of Design Science Research. *Ais.*

Valsiner, J. (1987). *Culture and the Development of Children's Action: A cultural-historical theory of developmental psychology.* John Wiley & Sons.

van Daal, V., & Reitsma, P. (2000). Computer-assisted learning to read and spell: Results from two pilot studies. *Journal of Research in Reading, 23*(2), 181–193. doi:10.1111/1467-9817.00113

Van der Heijden, H. (2004). User acceptance of hedonic information systems. *Management Information Systems Quarterly, 28*(4), 695–704. doi:10.2307/25148660

Van Der Maren, J. M. (1996). Méthodes de Recherche pour l'Education (2a ed.). Bruxelles: De Boeck Université.

Van Dijk, J. A. G. M. (2005). *The deepening Divide: Inequality in the information society.* SAGE Publications. doi:10.4135/9781452229812

Van Eck, R. (2006). Digital Game-Based Learning: It's Not Just the Digital Natives Who Are Restless. *EDUCAUSE*, 17–30.

Van Eck, N. J., & Waltman, L. (2010). Software survey: VOSviewer, a computer program for bibliometric mapping. *Scientometrics*, *84*(2), 523–538. doi:10.100711192-009-0146-3 PMID:20585380

van Ewijk, G., Smakman, M., & Konijn, E. A. (2020, June). Teachers' perspectives on social robots in education: an exploratory case study. In *Proceedings of the Interaction Design and Children Conference* (pp. 273-280). 10.1145/3392063.3394397

Van Heerden, D., & Goosen, L. (2012). Using Vodcasts to Teach Programming in an ODL Environment. *Progressio*, *34*(3), 144–160.

Van Laar, E., Van Deursen, A. J. A. M., Van Dijk, J. A. G. M., & De Haan, J. (2020). Determinants of 21st-Century Skills and 21st-Century Digital Skills for Workers: A Systematic Literature Review. *SAGE Open*, *10*(1), 1–14. doi:10.1177/2158244019900176

Van Rensburg, C. (2013). 'n Perspektief op 'n periode van kontak tussen Khoi en Afrikaans. *Literator*, *34*(2), 1–11. doi:10.4102/lit.v34i2.413

Van Roy, R., & Zaman, B. (2018). Need-Supporting Gamification In Education: An Assessment Of Motivational Effects Over Time. *Computers & Education*, *127*, 283–297. doi:10.1016/j.compedu.2018.08.018

Vandercruysse, S., Vandewaetere, M., & Clarebout, G. (2012). Game-based learning: A review on the effectiveness of educational games. Handbook of research on serious games as educational, business and research tools, 628-647.

Vandercruysse, S., Vandewaetere, M., Cornillie, F., & Clarebout, G. (2013). Competition and students' perceptions in a game-based language learning environment. *Educational Technology Research and Development*, *61*(6), 927–950. doi:10.100711423-013-9314-5

VanSledright, B. A. (2002). Fifth graders investigating history in the classroom: Results from a researcher-practitioner design experiment. *The Elementary School Journal*, *103*(2), 131–160. doi:10.1086/499720

Varghese, N. V. (2014). Globalization and higher education: Changing trends in cross border education. *Analytical Reports in International Education*, *5*(1), 7–20.

Vásquez. (2017). *Maria & Peñafiel, Myriam & Cevallos Cevallos, Andrés & Zaldumbide, Juan & Vásquez, Diego.* Impact of Game-Based Learning on Students in Higher Education. doi:10.21125/edulearn.2017.1942

Vasquez, V. (2003). What Pokemon can teach us about learning and literacy. *Language Arts*, *81*(2), 145–154.

Vaughn, P., & Turner, C. (2016). Decoding via coding: Analyzing qualitative text data through thematic coding and survey methodologies. *Journal of Library Administration*, *56*(1), 41–51. doi:10.1080/01930826.2015.1105035

Veldkamp, A., Daemen, J., Teekens, S., Koelewijn, S., Knippels, M. C. P. J., & van Joolingen, W. R. (2020). Escape boxes: Bringing escape room experience into the classroom. British Journal of Educational Technology, 51(4), 1220–1239. doi:10.1111/bjet.12935

Venkatesh, V. (2000). Determinants of perceived ease of use: Integrating control, intrinsic motivation, and emotion into the technology acceptance model. *Information Systems Research*, *11*(4), 342–365. doi:10.1287/isre.11.4.342.11872

Compilation of References

Venkatesh, V., & Bala, H. (2008). Technology acceptance model 3 and a research agenda on interventions. *Decision Sciences*, *39*(2), 273–315. doi:10.1111/j.1540-5915.2008.00192.x

Verhoeven, L., & Snow, C. (Eds.). (2001). *Literacy and motivation: Reading engagement in individuals and groups*. Lawrence Erlbaum Associates.

Vermeulen, L., Bauwel, S. V., & Looy, J. V. (2017). Tracing Female Gamer Identity: An Empirical Study Into gender and Stereotype Threat Perceptions. *Computer in Human Behavior, 71*, 90-98. doi:10.1016/j.chb.2017.01.054

Vesisenaho, M., Dillon, P., & Sari, H.-N. (2017). Creative Improvisations with Information and Communication Technology to Support Learning: A Conceptual and Developmental Framework. *Journal of Teacher Education and Educators*, *6*(3), 229–250.

Vial, M. (2001). *Se former pour évaluer. Pédagogies en développement*. De boeck Université.

Vicente, E., Verdugo, M. A., Gómez-Vela, M., Fernández-Pulido, R., Wehmeyer, M. L., & Guillén, V. M. (2019). Personal characteristics and school contextual variables associated with student self-determination in Spanish context. *Journal of Intellectual & Developmental Disability*, *44*(1), 23–34. doi:10.3109/13668250.2017.1310828

Vitell, S. J. (2009). The Role of Religiosity in Business and Consumer Ethics: A Review of the Literature. *Journal of Business Ethics*, *90*(2), 155–167. doi:10.100710551-010-0382-8

Vitell, S. J., & Paolillo, J. G. P. (2003). Consumer ethics: The role of religiosity. *Journal of Business Ethics*, *46*(2), 151–162. doi:10.1023/A:1025081005272

Vitos, B. (2014). *Experiencing electronic dance floors: A comparative research of techno and psytrance in Melbourne* (Unpublished PhD Thesis). Monash University, Clayton, Australia.

Vivido. (2021). *Management Platform of the National Support Network for Victims of Domestic Violence*. Working together for an Inclusive Europe, EEA Grants Portugal 2020. Retrieved October 4, 2021, from https://vividoproject.wixsite.com/vivido?lang=en

Vlachopoulos, D., & Makri, A. (2017). The effect of games and simulations on higher education: A systematic literature review. *International Journal of Educational Technology in Higher Education*, *14*(22), 22. Advance online publication. doi:10.118641239-017-0062-1

Vogel, J. J., Greenwood-Ericksen, A., Cannon-Bowers, J., & Bowers, C. A. (2006). Using Virtual Reality with and without Gaming Attributes for Academic Achievement. Journal of Research on Technology in Education, 39(1), 105-118.

Vogel, J. J., Vogel, D. S., Cannon-Bowers, J., Bowers, C. A., Muse, K., & Wright, M. (2006). Computer gaming and interactive simulations for learning: A meta-analysis. *Journal of Educational Computing Research*, *34*(3), 229–243. doi:10.2190/FLHV-K4WA-WPVQ-H0YM

von Gillern, S. (2016b). Perceptual, decision-making, and learning processes during video gameplay: An analysis of *Infamous - Second Son* with the Gamer Response and Decision Framework. *Games and Learning Society 2016 Conference Proceedings*.

von Gillern, S. (2016a). The gamer response and decision framework: A tool for understanding video gameplay experiences. *Simulation & Gaming*, *47*(5), 666–683. doi:10.1177/1046878116656644

von Gillern, S. (2018). Games and their embodied learning principles in the classroom: Connecting learning theory to practice. In M. Khosrow-Pour (Ed.), *Gamification in Education: Breakthroughs in Research and Practice* (pp. 554–582). IGI Global. doi:10.4018/978-1-5225-5198-0.ch029 von Gillern, S. (2021). Communication, cooperation, and competition: Examining the literacy practices of esports teams. In M. Harvey & R. Marlatt (Eds.), *Esports research and its integration in education* (pp. 148–167). IGI Global. doi:10.4018/978-1-7998-7069-2.ch009

von Gillern, S., & Alaswad, Z. (2016). Games and game-based learning in instructional design. *The International Journal of Technologies in Learning*, *23*(4), 1–7. doi:10.18848/2327-0144/CGP/v23i04/1-7

von Gillern, S., Stufft, C., & Harvey, M. (2021). Integrating video games into the ELA classroom. *Literacy Today*, *38*(6), 64–65.

Von Glasersfeld, E. (1995). *Radical constructivism: a way of knowing and learning. studies in mathematics education series: 6*. Falmer Press.

Voogt, J., & McKenney, S. (2017). TPACK in teacher education: Are we preparing teachers to use technology for early literacy? *Technology, Pedagogy and Education*, *26*(1), 69–83. https://doi.org/10.1080/1475939X.2016.1174730

Vorster, J., & Goosen, L. (2017). A Framework for University Partnerships Promoting Continued Support of e-Schools. In J. Liebenberg (Ed.), *Proceedings of the 46th Annual Conference of the Southern African Computer Lecturers' Association (SACLA)* (pp. 118 - 126). Magaliesburg: North-West University.

Vuorikari, R. (2016). *DigComp 2.0: The Digital Competence Framework For Citizens. Update Phase 1: the Conceptual Reference Model*. European Commission, Retrieved from https://ec.europa.eu/jrc/en/publication/eur-scientificand-technical-research-reports/digcomp-20-digital-competence-framework-citizens-update-phase-1-conceptualreference-model

Vygotski, L. (1978). *Mind in society: The development of higher psychological processes*. Harvard University Press.

Vygotsky, L. S. (1978). Readings on the development of children. In From Mind and Society (pp. 79-91). Cambridge, MA: Harvard University Press.

Vygotsky, L. (1962). *Thought and language* (E. Hanf-mann & G. Vakar, Trans.). MIT Press. doi:10.1037/11193-000

Vygotsky, L. (1966). Igra i ee rol v umstvennom razvitii rebenka [Play and its role in the mental development of the child]. *Voprosy Psihologii*, *12*(6), 62–76.

Vygotsky, L. (1978). *Mind in society*. Harvard University Press. (Original work published 1930)

Vygotsky, L. S. (1978). *Mind in society: Development of higher psychological processes*. Harvard UP.

Vygotsky, L. S. (1978). *Mind in Society: The development of higher mental processes* (M. Cole, V. John-Steiner, S. Scribner, & E. Souberman, Eds.). Harvard University Press.

Vygotsky, L. S. (1978). *Mind in Society: The Development of Higher Psychological Processes (M. Cole, V. John-Steiner* (S. Scribner & E. Souberman, Eds.). Havard University Press.

Wade, R. (1994). Teacher education students' views on class discussion: Implications for fostering critical thinking. *Teaching and Teacher Education*, *10*(2), 231–243. doi:10.1016/0742-051X(94)90015-9

Wafula-Kwake, A., & Ocholla, D. N. (2007). The Feasibility of ICT Diffusion amongst African Rural Women: A case study of South Africa and Kenya. *International Journal of Information Ethics*, *7*(2), 1–20.

Wagner, C., Graells-Garrido, E., Garcia, D., & Menczer, F. (2016). Women through the glass ceiling: Gender asymmetries in Wikipedia. *EPJ Data Science*, *5*(1), 5. https://doi.org/10.1140/epjds/s13688-016-0066-4

Wagner, S. C., & Lawrence Sanders, G. (2001). Considerations in ethical decision-making and software piracy. *Journal of Business Ethics*, *29*(1-2), 161–167. doi:10.1023/A:1006415514200

Compilation of References

Wagner, T. (2008). Rigor redefined: Even our "best" schools are failing to prepare students for 21st-century careers and citizenship. *Educational Leadership*, 2(66), 20–25.

Wahyuni, S., Mujiyanto, J., Rukmini, D., & Fitriati, S. W. (2020, June). Teachers' Technology Integration Into English Instructions: SAMR Model. In *International Conference on Science and Education and Technology (ISET)* (pp. 546-550). Atlantis Press. 10.2991/assehr.k.200620.109

Wallach, H. M., Murray, I., Salakhutdinov, R., & Mimno, D. (2009). Evaluation methods for topic models. *Proceedings of the 26th annual international conference on machine learning*. 10.1145/1553374.1553515

Walsh, C. (2010). Systems-based literacy practices: Digital games research, gameplay and design. *Australian Journal of Language and Literacy*, 33(1), 24–40.

Walsh, J. N., O'Brien, M. P., & Costin, Y. (2021). Investigating student engagement with intentional content: An exploratory study of instructional videos. *International Journal of Management Education*, 19(2), 100505. doi:10.1016/j.ijme.2021.100505

Wang, A. I. (2020, April 17). *Impact of Kahoot! in higher education – research roundup*. Kahoot! Retrieved September 11, 2021 from https://kahoot.com/blog/2020/04/08/kahoot-impact-higher education-research/

Wang, S.-K., & Han, S. (2010). Six C's of motivation. In M. Orey (Ed.), Emerging perspectives on learning, teaching, and technology. Global Text Project, funded by the Jacob Foundation, Zurich, Switzerland. Creative Commons 3.0 Attribution Licence.

Wang, J. Y., Wu, H. K., & Hsu, Y. S. (2017). Using mobile applications for learning: Effects of simulation design, visual-motor integration, and spatial ability on high school students' conceptual understanding. *Computers in Human Behavior*, 66, 103–113. doi:10.1016/j.chb.2016.09.032

Wang, J., & Rao, N. (2020). What Do Chinese Students Say about Their Academic Motivational Goals-Reasons Underlying Academic Strivings? *Asia Pacific Journal of Education*, 12, 1–15. doi:10.1080/02188791.2020.1812513

Wang, L. C., & Chen, M. P. (2010). The effects of game strategy and preference-matching on flow experience and programming performance in game-based learning. *Innovations in Education and Teaching International*, 47(1), 39–52. doi:10.1080/14703290903525838

Wang, L., Gunasti, K., Gopal, R., Shankar, R., & Pancras, J. (2017). The Impact of Gamification on Word-of-Mouth Effectiveness: Evidence from Foursquare. *Proceedings of the 50th Hawaii International Conference on System Sciences*. 10.24251/HICSS.2017.090

Wang, M., & Zheng, X. (2021). Using game-based learning to support learning science: A study with middle school students. *The Asia-Pacific Education Researcher*, 30(2), 167–176. doi:10.100740299-020-00523-z

Wang, S., Fang, H., Zhang, G., & Ma, T. (2019). Research on a new type of "dual-teacher classroom" supported by artificial intelligence educational robots & on the teaching design and future prospects of "human-machine collaboration". *Journal of Distance Education*, 37(2), 25–32.

Waraczynski, M. A. (2006). The central extended amygdala network as a proposed circuit underlying reward valuation. *Neuroscience and Biobehavioral Reviews*, 30(4), 472–496. doi:10.1016/j.neubiorev.2005.09.001 PMID:16243397

Wardoyo, C., Satrio, Y. D., & Ma'ruf, D. (2020). Effectiveness of Game-Based Learning – Learning in Modern Education. *3rd International Research Conference on Economics and Business*, 81–87. 10.18502/kss.v4i7.6844

Wardrip-Fruin. (2009). Better Game Studies Education the Carcassonne Way. *2009 DiGRA '09 - Proceedings of the 2009 DiGRA International Conference: Breaking New Ground: Innovation in Games, Play, Practice and Theory*.

Waris, O., Jaeggi, S. M., Seitz, A. R., Lehtonen, M., Soveri, A., Lukasik, K. M., Söderström, U., Hoffing, R. A. C., & Laine, M. (2019). Video gaming and working memory: A large-scale cross-sectional correlative study. *Computers in Human Behavior*, *97*, 94–103. doi:10.1016/j.chb.2019.03.005 PMID:31447496

Warren, S. J., Dondlinger, M. J., & Barab, S. A. (2008). A MUVE towards PBL writing: Effects of a digital learning environment designed to improve elementary student writing. *Journal of Research on Technology in Education*, *41*(1), 113–140. doi:10.1080/15391523.2008.10782525

Warren, S. J., Dondlinger, M. J., Stein, R., & Barab, S. A. (2009). Educational Game as Supplemental Learning Tool: Benefits, Challenges, and Tensions Arising from Use in an Elementary School Classroom. *Journal of Interactive Learning Research*, *20*(4), 487–505.

Wati, I. F., & Yuniawatika. (2020). Digital Game-Based Learning as A Solution to Fun Learning Challenges During the Covid-19 Pandemic. *Advances in Social Science, Education and Humanities Research*, *508*, 202–210. doi:10.2991/assehr.k.201214.237

Watson, W. R., Yang, S., & Dana, R. (2016). Games in Schools: Teachers' Perceptions of Barriers to Game-based Learning. *Journal of Interactive Learning Research*, *27*(2). https://www.learntechlib.org/primary/p/151749/

Wawro, A. (2017). Why video game devs don't get 'board' of learning from tabletop games. *Game Developer*. https://www.gamedeveloper.com/design/why-video-game-devs-don-t-get-board-of-learning-from-tabletop-games

We are Social. (2021). *Digital 2021. Global Digital Overview*. https://dijilopedi.com/2021-dunya-internet-sosyal-medya-ve-mobil-kullanim-istatistikleri/

Weaver, G. R., & Agle, B. R. (2002). Religiosity and ethical behavior in organizations: A symbolic interactionist perspective. *Academy of Management Review*, *27*(1), 77–97. doi:10.2307/4134370

Webb, M., & Cox, M. (2004). A review of pedagogy related to information and communications technology. *Technology, Pedagogy and Education*, *13*(3), 235–286. doi:10.1080/14759390400200183

Weber, S., & Mitchell, C. (2008). Imaging, keyboarding, and posting identities: Young people and new media technologies. In D. Buckingham (Ed.), Youth, identity, and digital media (pp. 25–48). The MIT Press.

WEF. (2020). *The Future of Jobs Report 2020*. Geneva: World Economic Forum. Retrieved from https://www3.weforum.org/docs/WEF_Future_of_Jobs_2020.pdf

Weibull, L. (1985). Structural factors in gratifications research. *Media gratifications research: Current perspectives*, 123-47.

Wei, C. W., Kao, H. Y., Lu, H. H., & Liu, Y. C. (2018). The effects of competitive gaming scenarios and personalized assistance strategies on English vocabulary learning. *Journal of Educational Technology & Society*, *21*(3), 146–158.

Weintrop, D., Holbert, N., Horn, M., & Wilensky, U. (2016). Computational thinking in constructionist video games. *International Journal of Game-Based Learning*, *6*(1), 1–17.

Weller, M. (2011). *The digital scholar: How technology is transforming scholarly practice*. Bloomsbury Academic. https://www.open.edu/openlearn/ocw/pluginfile.php/731937/mod_resource/content/1/The%20Digital%20Scholar_%20How%20Technology%20Is%20T%20-%20Martin%20Weller.pdf

Wells, S. H., Warelow, P. J., & Jackson, K. L. (2009). Problem based learning (PBL): A conundrum. *Contemporary Nurse*, *33*(2), 191–201. Advance online publication. doi:10.5172/conu.2009.33.2.191 PMID:19929163

Werbach, K. (2014). ReDefining Gamification: A Process Approach. In A. Spagnolli, L. Chittaro, & L. Gamberini (Eds.), *Persuasive Technology* (pp. 266–272). Springer. doi:10.1007/978-3-319-07127-5_23

Compilation of References

Werner, J. S., & James, W. T. Jr. (2001). *Communication Theories: Origins, Methods and Uses in the Mass Media*. Addison Wesley Longman, Inc.

Westbrook, N. (2011). Media literacy pedogog: Critical and new /twenty first centries instructions. *E-Learning and Digital Media*, 8(2), 154–164.

Westera, W. (2015). Games are motivating, aren't they? Disputing the arguments for digital game-based learning. *Int. J. Serious Games*, 2(2), 4–17. doi:10.17083/ijsg.v2i2.58

Westrup, U. & Planander, A. (2013). Role-play as a pedagogical method to prepare students for practice: The students' voice. *Ogre utbildning*, 3(3), 199-210.

When will the COVID-19 pandemic end? (n.d.). *McKinsey*. Retrieved September 2, 2021, from https://www.mckinsey.com/industries/healthcare-systems-and-services/our-insights/when-will-the-covid-19-pandemic-end

Whitaker, R. J. (1983). Aristotle is not dead: Student understanding of trajectory motion. *American Journal of Physics*, 51(4), 352–357. doi:10.1119/1.13247

White, K., & McCoy, L. P. (2019). Effects of Game-Based Learning on Attitude and Achievement in Elementary Mathematics Achievement in Elementary Mathematics. Networks. *An Online Journal for Teacher Research*, 21(1), 1–17. Advance online publication. doi:10.4148/2470-6353.1259

Whitton, N. (2012). Game Based Learning. In *Encyclopedia of the Sciences of Learning*. Springer. doi:10.1007/978-1-4419-1428-6_437

Whitton, N. (2014). *Digital games and learning: Research and theory*. Routledge. doi:10.4324/9780203095935

Whitton, N., & Moseley, A. (2012). *Using Games to Enhance Learning and Teaching: A Beginner's Guide*. Routledge. doi:10.4324/9780203123775

Wieringa, R. (2009). Design science as nested problem solving. *Proceedings of the 4th International Conference on Design Science Research in Information Systems and Technology, DESRIST '09*. 10.1145/1555619.1555630

Wikipedia. (n.d.). Retrieved from https://en.wikipedia.org/wiki/gamification

Wilkes, R. E., Burnett, J. J., & Howell, R. D. (1986). On the meaning and measurement of religiosity in consumer research. *Journal of the Academy of Marketing Science*, 14(1), 47–56. doi:10.1007/BF02722112

Wilkinson, P. (2015). *A Brief History of Serious Games*. https://core.ac.uk/download/pdf/157768453.pdf

Wilkinson, P. (2016). A brief history of serious games. *Entertainment computing and serious games*, 17-41.

Wilkinson, R., & Pickett, K. (2009). *The spirit level: Why greater equality makes societies stronger*. Bloomsbury Press.

Williams, J., Ritter, J., & Bullock, S. M. (2012). Understanding the complexity of becoming a teacher educator: Experience, belonging, and practice within a professional learning community. *Studying Teacher Education*, 8(3), 245–260. doi:10.1080/17425964.2012.719130

Wilson, C. (2012). Media and İnformation Literacy: Pedogogy and Possibilities. *Comunicar*, 39, 15–22.

Wing, J. M. (2006). Computational Thinking. *Communications of the ACM*, 49(3), 33-35. https://www.cs.cmu.edu/~15110-s13/Wing06-ct.pdf

Wing, J. M. (2008). Computational thinking and thinking about computing. *Philosophical Transactions Series A, Mathematical, Physical, and Engineering Sciences, 366*, 3717-25. . doi:10.1098/rsta.2008.0118

Wing, J. M. (2006). Computational thinking. *Communications of the ACM, 49*(3), 33–35. doi:10.1145/1118178.1118215

Wise, B. W., Ring, J., & Olson, R. K. (2000). Individual differences in gains from computer-assisted remedial reading. *Journal of Experimental Child Psychology, 77*(3), 197–235. doi:10.1006/jecp.1999.2559 PMID:11023657

Witte, J., Westbrook, R., & Witte, M. M. (2017). *Proceedings of the Global Conference on Education and Research*. 10.5038/2572-6374-v1

Wizards of the Coast. (2015). *Dungeons & Dragons Core Rulebook: Dungeon Master's Guide* (1st ed.). Dungeons & Dragons.

Wizards of the Coast. (2021). *Van Richten's Guide to Ravenloft* (1st ed.). Dungeons & Dragons.

Wohlwend, K. E. (2008). *Play as a literacy of possibilities: Expanding meanings in practices, materials, and spaces*. Academic Press.

Wohlwend, K. E. (2017). Who gets to play? Access, popular media and participatory literacies. *Early Years, 37*(1), 62–76. doi:10.1080/09575146.2016.1219699

Wolcott, H. F. (1987). On ethnographic intent. In Interpretive Ethnography on Education: At Home and Abroad. Hillsdale, NJ: Erlbaum.

Wolfe, S., & Flewitt, R. (2010). New technologies, new multimodal literacy practices and young children's metacognitive development. *Cambridge Journal of Education, 40*(4), 387–399. doi:10.1080/0305764X.2010.526589

Wolf, W. (2014). Framings of narrative in literature and the pictorial arts. In M. Ryan & J. Thon (Eds.), *Storyworlds across media: Toward a media-conscious narratology* (pp. 126–150). University of Nebraska Press. doi:10.2307/j.ctt1d9nkdg.10

Wolk, C., & Nikolai, L. A. (1997). Personality types of accounting students and faculty: Comparisons and implications. *Journal of Accounting Education, 15*(1), 1–17. doi:10.1016/S0748-5751(96)00041-3

Wong, Y. S., & Yatim, M. H. M. (2018, July). A Propriety Multiplatform Game-Based Learning Game to Learn Object-Oriented Programming. In *2018 7th International Congress on Advanced Applied Informatics (IIAI-AAI)* (pp. 278-283). IEEE. 10.1109/IIAI-AAI.2018.00060

Wong, E. M., & Li, S. C. (2008). Framing ICT implementation in a context of educational change: A multilevel analysis. *School Effectiveness and School Improvement, 19*(1), 99–120. doi:10.1080/09243450801896809

Wong, J. K. K. (2004). Are the Learning Styles of Asian International Students Culturally or Contextually Based? *International Education Journal, 4*(4), 154–166.

Wong, K. (1996). Video game effect on computer-based learning design. *British Journal of Educational Technology, 27*(September), 230–232. https://doi.org/10.1111/j.1467-8535.1996.tb00690.x

Wood, E. (2009). Media literacy education: Evaluating media literacy education in Colorado Schools (Master's thesis). Faculty of Social Sciences, University of Denver.

Wood, L. C., & Reiners, T. (2012). Gamification in logistics and supply chain education: Extending active learning. In P. Kommers, T. Issa, & P. Isaías (Eds.), *IADIS International Conference on Internet Technologies & Society*, (pp. 101–108). Academic Press.

Woods, M., Macklin, R., & Lewis, G. K. (2016). Researcher reflexivity: Exploring the impacts of CAQDAS use. *International Journal of Social Research Methodology, 19*(4), 385–403. doi:10.1080/13645579.2015.1023964

Compilation of References

Woo, J.-C. (2014). Digital game-based learning supports student motivation, cognitive success, and performance outcomes. *Journal of Educational Technology & Society*, *17*, 291–307. https://www.j-ets.net/ETS/issues3ebc.html?id=64

Workshop, S. (2021). *Art maker* [Online software]. https://www.sesamestreet.org/art-maker

World Health Organization. (2018, September). *Gaming disorder.* Retrieved from https://www.who.int/features/qa/gaming-disorder/en/

Wouters, Van der Spek, & Van Oostendorp. (2009). Current practices in serious game research: A review from a learning outcomes perspective. In Games-based learning advancements for multi-sensory human computer interfaces: techniques and effective practices. IGI Global.

Wouters, P., Paas, F., & van Merriënboer, J. J. G. (2008). How to optimize learning from animated models: A review of guidelines based on cognitive load. *Review of Educational Research*, *78*(3), 645–675. doi:10.3102/0034654308320320

Wouters, P., Van Nimwegen, C., Van Oostendorp, H., & Van Der Spek, E. D. (2013). A meta-analysis of the cognitive and motivational effects of serious games. *Journal of Educational Psychology*, *105*(2), 249–265. doi:10.1037/a0031311

Wozney, L., Venkatesh, V., & Abrami, P. C. (2006). Implementing computer technologies: Teachers' perceptions and practices. *Journal of Technology and Teacher Education*, *14*(1), 173.

Wu, M. L. (2015). *Teachers' experience, attitudes, self-efficacy and perceived barriers to the use of digital game-based learning: A survey study through the lens of a typology of educational digital games* [Michigan State University]. In ProQuest Dissertations and Theses. https://d.lib.msu.edu/etd/3754

Wu, K., & Huang, P. (2015). Treatment of an anonymous recipient: Solid-waste management simulation game. *Journal of Educational Computing Research*, *52*(4), 568–600. doi:10.1177/0735633115585928

Wu, W. C. V., Wang, R. J., & Chen, N. S. (2015). Instructional design using an in-house built teaching assistant robot to enhance elementary school English-as-a-foreign-language learning. *Interactive Learning Environments*, *23*(6), 696–714. doi:10.1080/10494820.2013.792844

Xia, Y., & LeTendre, G. (2021). Robots for future classrooms: A cross-cultural validation study of "negative attitudes toward robots scale" in the US context. *International Journal of Social Robotics*, *13*(4), 703–714. doi:10.100712369-020-00669-2

Xinogalos, S., & Tryfou, M. M. (2021). Using Greenfoot as a Tool for Serious Games Programming Education and Development. *International Journal of Serious Games*, *8*(2), 67–86. doi:10.17083/ijsg.v8i2.425

Xiong, C., Ye, B., Mihailidis, A., Cameron, J. I., Astell, A., Nalder, E., & Colantonio, A. (2020). Sex and gender differences in technology needs and preferences among informal caregivers of persons with dementia. *BMC Geriatrics*, *20*(1), 176. https://www.jstor.org/stable/pdf/44430486.pdf?refreqid=excelsior%3a6a06f288b510b457d0a9c16f60991e8d

Xu, F., Buhalis, D., & Weber, J. (2017). Serious games and the gamification of tourism. In *Tourism Management* (Vol. 60, pp. 244–256). 10.1016/j.tourman.2016.11.020

Yang, J. C., Chien, K. H., & Liu, T. C. (2012). A digital game-based learning system for energy education: An energy Conservation PET. *The Turkish Online Journal of Educational Technology*, *11*(2), 27–37.

Yang, J. C., & Quadir, B. (2018). Effects of prior knowledge on learning performance and anxiety in an English learning online role-playing game. *Journal of Educational Technology & Society*, *21*(3), 174–185.

Yang, Y. H., Xu, W., Zhang, H., Zhang, J. P., & Xu, M. L. (2014). The application of KINECT motion sensing technology in game-oriented study. *International Journal of Emerging Technologies in Learning*, *9*(2), 59–63.

Yang, Y.-T. C. (2012). Building virtual cities, inspiring intelligent citizens: Digital games for developing students' problem solving and learning motivation. *Computers & Education*, *59*(2), 365–377. doi:10.1016/j.compedu.2012.01.012

Yannakakis, G. N., & Togelius, J. (2018). Artificial intelligence and games. *Artificial Intelligence and Games*. doi:10.1007/978-3-319-63519-4

Yasin, A. I., Prima, E. C., & Sholihin, H. (2018). Learning Electricity Using Arduino-Android Based Game to Improve STEM Literacy. *Journal of science Learning*, *1*(3), 77-94.

Yee, N., Ducheneaut, N., Shiao, H. T., & Nelson, L. (2012). Through the azerothian looking glass: Mapping in-game preferences to real-world demographics. *Proceedings of the SIGCHI Conference on Human Factors in Computing Systems*, 2811-2814. 10.1145/2207676.2208683

Yeşilbağ, S., Korkmaz, Ö., & Çakir, R. (2020). The effect of educational computer games on students' academic achievements and attitudes towards English lesson. *Education and Information Technologies*, *25*(2), 1–18. doi:10.100710639-020-10216-1 PMID:32837235

Yeşilyurt, M., Özdemir Balakoğlu, M., & Erol, M. (2020). The impact of environmental education activities on primary school students' environmental awareness and visual expressions. *Qualitative Research in Education*, *9*(2), 188–216. doi:10.17583/qre.2020.5115

Yien, J., Hung, C., Hwang, G., & Lin, Y. (2011). A game-based learning approach to improving students' learning achievements in a nutrition course. *The Turkish Online Journal of Educational Technology*, *10*(2).

Yi, L., Zhou, Q., Xiao, T., Qing, G., & Mayer, I. (2020). Conscientiousness in Game-Based Learning. *Simulation & Gaming*, *51*(5), 712–734. doi:10.1177/1046878120927061

Yıldırım, İ., & Şen, S. (2019). The effects of gamification on students' academic achievement: A meta-analysis study. *Interactive Learning Environments*, 1–18. doi:10.1080/10494820.2019.1636089

Yin, R. (1989). *Case study research, design and methods*. Sage.

Yip, F. W. M., & Kwan, A. C. M. (2006). Online vocabulary games as a tool for teaching and learning English vocabulary. *Educational Media International*, *43*(3), 233–249. doi:10.1080/09523980600641445

Yolcu, Ö. (2020). *Yeni medya*. İstanbul Üniversitesi AUZEF. http://auzefkitap.istanbul.edu.tr/kitap/medyaveiletisim_ue/yenimedya.pdf

Youngkyun, B., & Nicola, W. (2013). *Cases on Digital Game Based Learning: Methods, Models & Strategies*. IGI Global.

Young, M. (2014). What is a curriculum and what can it do? *Curriculum Journal*, *25*(1), 7–13. doi:10.1080/09585176.2014.902526 PMID:6909418

Young, M. (2017). Quality of literature review and discussion of findings in selected papers on integration of ICT in teaching, role of mentors, and teaching science through science, technology, engineering, and mathematics (STEM). *Educational Research Review*, *12*(4), 189–201. doi:10.5897/ERR2016.3088

Young, M. F., Slota, S., Cutter, A. B., Jalette, G., Mullin, G., Lai, B., & Yukhymenko, M. (2012). Our princess is in another castle: A review of trends in serious gaming for education. *Review of Educational Research*, *82*(1), 61–89. doi:10.3102/0034654312436980

Young, S. S. C., & Wang, Y. H. (2014). The game embedded CALL system to facilitate English vocabulary acquisition and pronunciation. *Journal of Educational Technology & Society*, *17*(3), 239–251.

Compilation of References

Youniss, Bales, S., Christmas-Best, V., Diversi, M., McLaughlin, M., & Silbereisen, R. (2002). Youth Civic Engagement in the Twenty-First Century. *Journal of Research on Adolescence, 12*(1), 121–148. doi:10.1111/1532-7795.00027

You, Y. (2020). Learning experience: An alternative understanding inspired by thinking through Confucius. *ECNU Review of Education, 3*(1), 66–87. doi:10.1177/2096531120904247

Yu, S. & Wang, Q. (2019). Analysis of Collaborative Path Development of "AI+Teachers." *e-EducationResearch,* (4), 14-29.

Yu, S. (2018). The future role of AI teachers. *Open Education Research, 24*(1), 6-28.

Yuen, A. H. K., & Ma, W. W. K. (2008). Exploring teacher acceptance of e-learning technology. *Asia-Pacific Journal of Teacher Education, 36*(3), 229–243. doi:10.1080/13598660802232779

Yukselturk, E., Altıok, S., & Başer, Z. (2018). Using game-based learning with kinect technology in foreign language education course. *Journal of Educational Technology & Society, 21*(3), 159–173.

Yun, S., Shin, J., Kim, D., Kim, C. G., Kim, M., & Choi, M. T. (2011, November). Engkey: Tele-education robot. In *International Conference on Social Robotics* (pp. 142-152). Springer. 10.1007/978-3-642-25504-5_15

Yunus, M., & Shahana, S. (2018). New evidence on outcomes of primary education stipend programme in Bangladesh. *Bangladesh Development Studies, 41*(4), 29–55. https://www.jstor.org/stable/27031081

Yuratich, D. (2020). Ratio! A game of judgment: Using game-based learning to teach legal reasoning. *The Law Teacher*, 1–14.

Yusof, M. (2011). *The Dynamics of Student Participation in Classroom: Observation on level and forms of participation.* Paper presented at Learning and Teaching Congress of UKM, Penang, Malaysia.

Zagalo, N. (2013). *Videojogos em Portugal: História, Tecnologia e Arte.* FCA Editora.

Zakharov, A., Tsheko, G., & Carnoy, M. (2016). Do "better" teachers and classroom resources improve student achievement? A causal comparative approach in Kenya, South Africa, and Swaziland. *International Journal of Educational Development, 50*, 108–124. doi:10.1016/j.ijedudev.2016.07.001

Zakharov, W., & Maybee, C. (2019). Bridging the gap: Information literacy and learning in online undergraduate courses. *Journal of Library & Information Services in Distance Learning, 13*(1-2), 215–225. doi:10.1080/1533290X.2018.1499256

Zampa, M. P., & Felipe Mendes, L. C. (2016). Gamificação: uma proposta para redução da evasão e reprovação em disciplinas finais da graduação. *Caderno de estudos em sistemas de informação, 3*(2).

Zapata-Rivera, D., & Bauer, M. (2012). Exploring the Role of Games in Educational Assessment. In M. C. Mayrath, J. Clarke-Midura, D. H. Robinson, & G. Schraw (Eds.), *Technology-Based Assessments for Twenty-First-Century Skills: Theoretical and Practical Implications from Modern Research* (pp. 147–169). Information Age Publishing.

Zawilski, B. (2020, August 31). *Rhetoric and Situations; Like Peanut Butter and Jelly.* Medium. https://medium.com/@bzawilski/rhetoric-and-situations-like-peanut-butter-and-jelly-ddb0d64e8b6c

Zhang, Y. (2020). *Teach machine learning with Excel.* Paper presented at the 2020 ASEE Virtual Annual Conference Content Access. 10.18260/1-2--35268

Zhang, L. F., Biggs, J., & Watkins, D. (Eds.). (2010). *Learning and development of Asian students: what the 21st Century teacher needs to think about.* Pearson.

Zheng, Y. (2019). 3D Course Teaching Based on Educational Game Development Theory-Case Study of Game Design Course. *International Journal of Emerging Technologies in Learning, 14*(2), 54. doi:10.3991/ijet.v14i02.9985

Zhonggen, Y. (2019). A meta-analysis of use of serious games in education over a decade. *International Journal of Computer Games Technology, 17*, 1–8. doi:10.1155/2019/4797032

Zhu, W., Ma, A. (2019). The application status and development path analysis of domestic AI education. *Primary and Middle School Educational Technology, 8*, 99-102.

Ziadat, A. H. (2010). Major factors contributing to environmental awareness among people in a third world country/Jordan. *Environment, Development and Sustainability, 12*(1), 135–145. doi:10.100710668-009-9185-4

Zichermann, G. (2011). *Gamification by design: Implementing game mechanics in web and mobile apps.* O'Reilly Media.

Ziegler, N. (2016). Taking technology to task: Technology-mediated TBLT, performance, and production. *Annual Review of Applied Linguistics, 36*(1), 136–163. doi:10.1017/S0267190516000039

Zingaro, D. (2021). *Learn to code by solving problems: A Python programming primer.* No Starch Press.

Zinnbauer, B. J., Pargament, K. I., Cole, B., Rye, M. S., Butter, E. M., Belavich, T. G., Hipp, K. M., Scott, A. B., & Kadar, J. L. (1997). Religion and spirituality: Unfuzzying the fuzzy. *Journal for the Scientific Study of Religion, 36*(4), 549–564. doi:10.2307/1387689

Živkovi, Ł. (2016). A model of critical thinking as an important attribute for success in the 21st century. *Procedia: Social and Behavioral Sciences, 232*, 102–108. doi:10.1016/j.sbspro.2016.10.034

Zolyomi, A., & Schmalz, M. (2017). Mining for Social Skills: Minecraft in Home and Therapy for Neurodiverse Youth. *Proceedings of the 50th Hawaii International Conference on System Sciences.* 10.24251/HICSS.2017.411

Zubković, B. R., Pahljina-Reinić, R., & Kolić-Vehovec, S. (2017). Predictors of ICT Use in Teaching in Different Educational Domains. *European Journal of Social Sciences Education and Research, 11*(2), 145. doi:10.26417/ejser.v11i2.p145-154

Zupic, I., & Čater, T. (2015). Bibliometric methods in management and organization. *Organizational Research Methods, 18*(3), 429–472. doi:10.1177/1094428114562629

Zusho, A., Anthony, J. S., Hashimoto, N., & Robertson, G. (2014). Do video games provide motivation to learn? In I Learning by playing: Video gaming in education (pp. 69-86). Oxford, UK: Oxford University Press. doi:10.1093/acprof:osobl/9780199896646.003.0006

Zuze, T. L., & Reddy, V. (2014). School resources and the gender reading literacy gap in South African schools. *International Journal of Educational Development, 36*, 100–107. doi:10.1016/j.ijedudev.2013.10.002

About the Contributors

Carol-Ann Lane has a Ph.D. from the University of Western Ontario, in curriculum and applied linguistics, with a cross-disciplinary focus on science & innovation, multiliteracies, gender, and behavioral sciences. She has conducted Canadian studies about biotechnology among teacher candidates. Her master thesis examined impacts of distance learning on cognition and behaviors in higher education. Carol-Ann has taught elementary and secondary divisions for over 7 years and more than 4 years in university settings at the post-graduate level. She is the editor of an international Handbook of Research (two volumes), to be published in early 2022, she is co-authoring articles, she has published three chapters in 2019-20 (sole author) in global university research handbooks, and 13 sole-authored peer-reviewed journal articles. She is currently working on a series of creative nonfiction books. In the past years at UWO and UofT, Carol-Ann's faculty roles included research collaboration with various faculty members on matters such as instructional strategies, improving hybrid learner experiences, especially during the pandemic, addressing long-range program planning for teacher, master level and Phd level candidates. Furthermore, as a committee member, Carol-Ann collaborated on projects, such as program planning, and implementing an online course program for the Professional Education Doctorate degree; Carol-Ann has continued to work over a decade as a research committee member such as Online Teaching and Learning Group by collaborating and improving online pedagogy for higher education.

* * *

Yogendran Abrose is a post graduate student at Universiti Sains Malaysia. He is assisting the current project related with Minecraft-Game Based Learning.

Pedro B. Água is a Professor of General Management at the Portuguese Naval Academy. He has authored several articles and book chapters, while continuing his research in the field of cutting-edge technology, industrialization, innovation and business policy. Professor Água has over twenty-five years of experience across high technology endeavours, from defence to telecommunications and oil and gas industry, combining his extensive professional and business background with teaching. Professor Água holds an MBA from IESE Business School and a Ph.D. in Management and Engineering awarded by the University of Lisbon.

Nur Jahan Ahmad is a senior lecturer at the School of Educational Studies, Universiti Sains Malaysia (USM), Penang. Malaysia. She holds a B.Sc. in Biological Sciences (Hons) from the University of Pittsburgh, a Diploma in Education from the Universiti Sains Malaysia (USM), an M.Sc. in Chemistry from the Universiti Kebangsaan Malaysia (UKM), and a PhD. in Chemistry Education from the

University of Leeds. She was with the Southeast Asian Ministers of Education Organization Regional Centre for Education in Science and Mathematics (SEAMEO RECSAM) in the department of Research and Development. She also had experience working as a teacher in a secondary school and as a lecturer in Penang Teacher Education Institute. In addition, she had experience in training teachers from Southeast Asia, Asia Pacific, Africa, and Maldives. She has coordinated many workshops, capacity-building programs, Professional Learning Community (PLC) programs, and lesson study activities with the in-service teachers. She is an experienced researcher and involved in research related to chemistry education, science education, STEM Education, and curriculum development. She is the external board advisor for publication, editor, writer, and reviewer; and has published articles and books in science, chemistry, and STEM Education.

Atm S. Alam is currently an Assistant Professor at the School of Electronic Engineering and Computer Science, Queen Mary University of London, UK since 2019. He received his BSc (Hon's) degree with First Class in Information and Communication Engineering from the University of Rajshahi, Bangladesh, the M.Sc. degree with Distinction in Telecommunications and Computer Networks Engineering from the London South Bank University, UK, and the Ph.D. degree in Wireless Communications from The Open University, Milton Keynes, UK. Before joining at the Queen Mary University of London, he worked on several European and UK funded projects as a Research Fellow for the 5G Innovation Centre (5GIC), University of Surrey, UK, and University of Bradford, UK. His research interests include the areas of intelligent wireless communications and networks (5G/6G) and, the emerging applications of machine learning in wireless communications for verticals such as smart grids, intelligent transport systems, smart cities/homes, and industrial automation. Dr. Alam is also interested in technology-driven teaching and learning, and he is currently a Fellow of Higher Education Academy (FHEA).

Md Jahangir Alam is an Assistant Professor in the Department of Japanese Studies at University of Dhaka in Bangladesh. His research interest covers a broad spectrum of development discourses, focusing on the Political Economy of Education, International Education Cooperation, Global Cooperation Studies, and Japan-Bangladesh Relations. His experiences embrace collaborating with international and national organizations, especially International Labor Organization (ILO), International Organization for Migration (IOM), United Nations Development Programme (UNDP), The Japan Foundation (JF), and Bangladesh Consulting Services. He has received several international awards and scholarship from academic associations and government organizations, including the Comparative and International Education Society (CIES) and the Japanese Ministry of Education (MEXT), for his outstanding academic and research contributions to international education development. He has over 13 academic publications, including book chapters and journal articles. He holds his Ph.D. in Education Policy with focus on International Education Development from the Graduate School of International Cooperation Studies, Kobe University, Japan.

Daisy Alexander has completed her B.Sc.; LL.B.; LL.M. and PhD from University of Mumbai (formerly University of Bombay) India. She was also part 48th Graduate School of Ecumenical Studies at Bossey, Geneva affiliated to University of Switzerland in Religious Pluralism & Conflict Resolution on a full scholarship. Her Ph.D. was on Surrogacy seeking regulations for the same. She has 27 years of academic experience. She has been active in gender related issues. Her expertise is in Legal Language and Commercial laws.

About the Contributors

Menşure Alkış Küçükaydın, PhD, is an Associate Professor of Basic Education at Necmettin Erbakan University in Konya, Turkey. She received her undergraduate degree in Department of Primary Teacher Education from Gazi University, Faculty of Education in 2006. She received her Ph.D degrees in Department of Primary Teacher Education from Gazi University in 2017. Dr. Alkış Küçükaydın's scholarly work focuses on pedagogical content knowledge, the roles of educational technology in learners' scientific practices, use of technology in education, science and technology education in primary and science misconceptions. Alkış Küçükaydın has 3 books that are edited by her at national level. In addition, she has a book, book chapters, articles, papers and projects related to her study field.

Puteri Sofia Amirnuddin is a Senior Law Lecturer, Programme Director and Chief Project Officer for Centre of Industrial Revolution and Innovation (CIRI) at Taylor's University. Puteri Sofia Amirnuddin is a recipient of various awards and accolades for her teaching innovations in teaching law using AR, NLP, and Gamification.

Marlene Amorim is an Assistant professor at the Department of Economics Management and Industrial Engineering at the University of Aveiro and collaborates as an invited professor at the Catholic University in Porto in the field of Service Operations Management. She received her PhD degree in Management from IESE Business School of University of Navarra in Spain. Marlene serves on the editorial board of three international journals and publishes in leading journals in services operations management. She conducts research in the area of Service Operations and Quality, notably in topics related to service process design and customer participation in service delivery.

Daniela Andreini (PhD) is Associate Professor of Marketing and Management at the Department of Management of the University of Bergamo. Daniela's research focuses mainly on B2B and B2C marketing, branding, and consumer behavior. Her articles have appeared in highly ranked journals such as Organization Studies, Journal of Advertising, Family Business Review, Journal of Business Research, Industrial Marketing Management, Journal of Business Ethics, and Journal of Business & Industrial Marketing, Management Decision, Journal of Product & Brand Management, and other academic outlets. Daniela serves in the Editorial Board of several journals including the Journal of Product & Brand Management and Journal of Business Research. She also serves as a reviewer for several highly-ranked international journals.

Md. Ashrafuzzaman is an Assistant Professor in the Department of Education at Bangabandhu Sheikh Mujibur Rahman Digital University, Bangladesh (BDU). He has been working for about eleven years in the field of teaching and educational research with different organizations. In 2014, he received an MPhil degree in English Language Education from the Institute of Education and Research (IER), University of Dhaka (DU). He has also completed his BEd (Hons.) and MEd from IER, DU. He has published research articles in national and international journals. He has researched significant areas such as teachers' training programs, underprivileged children's education (sex workers, transgender, and slum children), English language education, classroom practice, teaching methods and techniques, assessment and feedback practice, and ICT in education.

About the Contributors

Farhan Azim currently works across projects nationally and internationally developing psychometrically sound assessments. His research interests include development of novel assessment instruments, online assessments, measurement theory, teachers' capacity building, and better use of student data for teaching. Farhan has previously worked in areas of assessment including assessment of Mathematical problem solving, teachers' assessment literacy, assessment in STEM, etc. He has also worked in research, monitoring and evaluation of large-scale education projects and taught assessment and research related courses at tertiary institutes in the past. His works have been disseminated through refereed journals, book chapters and international academic conferences.

Smitha Baboo is working as an Assistant Professor in the Department of Psychology, CHRIST University, Bangalore, India. Her expertise area is in School/Educational Psychology, Abuse and Victim Studies, Child, Women and Adolescent Psychology. She has completed her two PhD in the field of Education and Psychology. She has completed 15 scientific manuscripts in the reputed national and international peer-reviewed journals, edited 3 books, 9 book chapters and 3 newspaper articles and has been invited as a guest speaker in the seminars and conferences.

Georgios Bampasidis is a postdoctoral researcher at the Pedagogical Department of Primary Education of the National & Kapodistrian University of Athens (NKUA), working on methodologies that aim to import Astronomy and Remote Sensing in Education. He is also a principal member of the scientific team of the Department's Astronomy and Remote Sensing Club. He taught Astronomy and Remote Sensing at the Master's degree courses of Didactics and Public Understanding of Science and Digital Technology of NKUA, Physics Lab with microsensors at STEM specialization courses of postgraduate students at NKUA and Physics lab and Astrophysics lab to undergraduate students of NKUA. He received his PhD in 2012 in Astrophysics from Paris Observatory in conjunction with the National & Kapodistrian University of Athens working extensively with data from the Cassini-Huygens NASA/ESA joint space mission and he still contributes to Planetary Science.

Meltem Huri Baturay received her Bachelor's and Master's degrees in English Language Teaching from Gazi University. She completed her PhD in the field of Computer Education and Instructional Technology at Middle East Technical University. She published many articles in highly reputable international and SSCI indexed journals and worked as a researcher at an action in COST (European Cooperation in Science and Technology) which was supported by the EU Framework Programme Horizon 2020. She also participated in TUBITAK (The Scientific and Technological Research Council of Turkey) and Erasmus+ KA2 projects as a researcher. She studies technology-assisted language teaching, use of Augmented and Virtual Reality at Education, Distance Education, and Design of Multimedia Enriched Teaching Materials. Currently, she is working as a faculty member and the director of the Center for Teaching and Learning at Atılım University.

Geraldine Bengsch is a postdoctoral researcher at the School of Education, Communication and Society King's College London. Her research interests include interpersonal and intercultural interaction. She works with various research methods and enjoys teaching new methods to students. She has received training as a full stack software engineer and aims to incorporate her knowledge into her research and teaching.

About the Contributors

Annesha Biswas is a Junior Research Fellow and a Ph.D. Candidate at the Department of Economics, Christ (Deemed to be University), Bengaluru, India. Her research area centers around Entrepreneurship, Gender Economics, and Rural Development. Her current research focuses upon the study of Entrepreneurship culture among Tribal women and discusses the issues and barriers of women's venture into entrepreneurship.

Pavlo Brin was born in 1976 in Kharkiv, Ukraine; in 1998 graduated from NTU "KhPI" (Master degree in Management, Magna cum laude); in 2003 presented PhD thesis; from 2005 Associate professor; from 2019 Professor of Management and Taxation Department. Prepared and published more than 150 research and methodical papers, textbooks, manuals for students and monographs in Economics and Management.

Kristina Buttrey has taught in K-12 education for 18 years and post- graduate education for 6. Her areas of expertise include literacy, Dyslexia, assessment, differentiation, classroom management, and Middle School Education. Dr. Buttrey is an assistant professor at Murray State University in Murray, Kentucky.

Anshita Chelawat received her Master Degree in the field of Human Resources in the year 2010 and since then she is consistently serving the educational community by teaching subjects related to general management and human resources. She has nearly 7 years of teaching experience along with 2 years of additional experience as a content writer. To move up in her professional career, she has qualified UGC NET (National Eligibility Test) 2013, NTA NET- 2019 and SET (Maharashtra). Currently, she is pursuing her Ph.D under SNDT women's university. She writes and presents widely in the field of educational technology, e-learning, Learner motivation, etc.

Karthigai Prakasam Chellaswamy has 20 years of teaching experience for UG and PG degree students. He holds a master degree in commerce from PSG College of Arts and Commerce an autonomous college affiliated with Bharathiar University, Coimbatore, M.Phil from Madurai Kamaraj University and PhD from Bharathidasan University Apart from these he has also completed MBA from Periyar University and also an MHRM from Pondicherry University. He has participated and presented in many National and International conferences, attended various workshops, FDP's and MDP's and also chaired sessions in International & National level conferences. He has published in various national and international journals. He has received the faculty excellence award for the academic year 2009 at New Horizon College, Bangalore. As of date, he has completed 2 Major Research Projects. Currently, he is working as an Associate Professor of Commerce & Coordinator for MCOM at the Central Campus, Christ (Deemed to be University), Bangalore.

Cafer Ahmet Çinar got his Bachelor's from the Department of Computer Education and Instructional Technology, Faculty of Education at Canakkale Onsekiz Mart University. At the moment, he is doing his Masters at the same department. He is an expert on Augmented Reality and doing research studies on the use of Augmented and Virtual Reality in Education.

Anacleto Correia (M) is an Associate Professor and lecturer of Management and Information Systems subjects at the Portuguese Navy Academy. He holds a Ph.D. in Computer Science, an M.Sc. in Statistics and Information Management, a B.Sc. degree in Management, and also a B.Sc. at Portuguese Naval Academy. His research interests are focused on requirements engineering, software engineering, process modeling, data mining, machine learning, and business engineering. He has also more than 20 years of experience in industry-leading projects and architecting large software development projects and is the author of dozens of scientific papers in journals and conference proceedings.

Barbara Culatta is Professor Emerita of Communication Disorders at Brigham Young University. She received her PhD from the University of Pittsburgh and completed a postdoctoral fellowship at Johns Hopkins University. She has written books, articles, and chapters on language and literacy interventions. She received federal grants to conduct language and literacy intervention programs and was the creator of the Systematic and Engaging Early Literacy project.

Tinanjali Dam is a PhD Candidate, Department of Economics, CHRIST (Deemed to be University). Studied Integrated Master's in Economics, Hyderabad Central University.

Ankit Dhamija is an accomplished academician and academic administrator with an experience of more than 13 years. Currently working at Amity Business School, Amity University Haryana, he has a demonstrated history of performing and delivering quality content to students in the capacity of Assistant Professor in the higher education industry. He has contributed in the Institution building through teaching, research and publications, accreditation and ranking, coordinating the examination, curriculum design & development and student mentoring. He has also published research papers in leading indexed journals and presented papers at several International/National Conferences. Also, he has published e-books and book chapters with leading publishers. With strong education professional with Doctorate in Information Technology, Double Masters in Computer Applications (MCA)and Information Technology (M.Tech(IT)) and Bachelors in Commerce, Dr Dhamija is skilled in areas like Academic Research Paper Writing, Database Management Systems, Management Information System, Web Design & Development and Microsoft Office, Python Programming, System Analysis and Design, Computer Networks. He is a master in adopting innovative teaching pedagogy for engaging students in classrooms and getting the best out of them.

Deepika Dhamija is an academician with more than10 years of experience as Assistant Professor in Information Technology domain. She has published more than 20 research papers and book chapters in reputed journal and also presented papers in national/International Conferences. Having Scopus indexed book chapters with leading publishers and also published an e-book. Attended various FDP's, workshops and seminars with highly reputed organizations and Researchers. She is comfortable with blended-teaching learning. Won Best paper award, Young Scientist Award, Woman Researcher Award in different conferences and seminars. She is skilled in teaching the Under Graduate and Post graduate students with the subject-Ecommerce, Database Management System, Computers in Management, Computer Applications in business, Management Information System.

About the Contributors

Joaquim Dias Soeiro is currently appointed as Head of School of the School of Hospitality, Tourism and Events at Taylor's University in Malaysia and also a member of the Centre for Research and Innovation in Tourism (CRiT), Taylor's University. He has lived in Malaysia and worked in education for more than a decade and developed his expertise in outcome-based education and experiential learning. He has built his career in Malaysia by benefiting from his education in France and adapting his profile from a multicultural aspect. His current research area focuses on capability development, learning experience and how learning is being constructed while taking into consideration social and cultural involvements.

Hacer Dolanbay is an Assistant Prof. at the Faculty of Education. Her specialization is media and digital literacy, implementation of new approaches in education, and media literacy education at different levels.

Burcu Durmaz is a faculty member at Süleyman Demirel University, Faculty of Education, Department of Mathematics and Science Education. She received her master's and doctorate degrees in mathematics education from Eskişehir Osmangazi University and Uludağ University, respectively. She worked on gifted students' mathematics education in her PhD thesis and post-doctoral research project as a visiting scholar at St. John's University in NY. The author's areas of interest include gifted students' mathematics education, problem solving skills, children's literature and mathematics integration.

Gonca Yangın Ekşi is a Professor in English Language Teaching (ELT) in the Department of Foreign Language Education, Gazi University where she teaches several undergraduate and graduate courses and supervises MA and PhD dissertations. The courses she has offered include Teaching English to Young Learners, Practice Teaching, ICT and CALL, Curriculum development and Materials Evaluation, Language learning theories, and Psychology of the language learner. She received her MA in ELT in Hacettepe University, Department of ELT and she holds her PhD in ELT in Gazi University. She has worked in a number of projects including the national project for the development of the national English curriculum for Primary and Secondary schools. She has managed an Erasmus KA2 Project with distinguished universities in Turkey and abroad. She has published various research articles nationally and internationally focusing on with teaching and learning English as a foreign language. Her research interests include computer-assisted language learning, pre- and inservice teacher education, curriculum and materials development, teaching skills and language components, young learners, use of corpus in language teaching. She has also been working as an editor to ELT Research Journal.

Marta Ferreira Dias has a PhD in Economics from the University of Warwick, UK, a MSc in Economics from the University of Coimbra and a degree in Economics from the University of Coimbra. She is an Assistant Professor in the University of Aveiro, at the Department of Economics, Management, Industrial Engineering and Tourism. She lectures under graduated and graduated courses of Microeconomics, European Economics, Microeconomic Analysis, International Economics and others, Energy Economics and Energy Policy and regulation. Presently, she is a member of the research unit on Competitiveness, Governance and Public Policies (GOVCOPP). She is a member of research teams of the University of Aveiro participating in several European sponsored projects in the fields of Social Economy and Competences for graduates.

About the Contributors

Nagarjuna G. is an Assistant Professor in the Department of Tourism Management, School of Business and Management, Bannerghatta Campus, Christ (Deemed to be University). Before starting his academic career, he worked in Holiday Bliss as an executive in tour operations. Later, he joined Christ University as a Research Assistant for the Major Research Project on "An Evaluation of Eco and Sustainable Tourism Practices of Selected Resorts in Karnataka". He holds a doctoral degree in the sustainable tourism practices of Karnataka. He started his full-Time academic career by joining the Department of Tourism Studies in Indian Academy Degree College, later served as an assistant professor at Mount Carmel College, Bangalore. He has presented research and conceptual papers in seminars and conferences at national and international level. He has published articles in acclaimed journals and also participated in research workshops. He was one of the Organizing committee members for a one-day national seminar on 'Tourism and Community Development'. Apart from his research and academic interest, he is also interested in theatrical performance. He is part of the Thaksh Theatrics play group.

Apostolia (Lia) Galani is an Associate Professor at the Department of Primary Education of the National and Kapodistrian University of Athens, Greece, teaching human and physical geography, as well as the educational use of IT in school geography. Her research interests focus on a) the design of teaching-learning sequences in several areas of science and especially in Remote Sensing and astronomy; b) the use of informal sources in science education; c) the teaching of Socio-Scientific Issues concerning climate change; and d) Cultural Geography in education (i.e. difficult past, the notion of the Other). She has participated in a number of EU and national projects and she has authored or co-authored many articles or chapters in Greek and International Journals or books including the Greek Gymnasium geography textbooks.

María García-Molina holds a Degree in Teaching Primary Education, specialization in Teaching English as a Foreign Language and Bilingual Education, by the University of Córdoba (Spain). She was awarded with a research initiation grant (Beca de colaboración destinada a estudiantes universitarios para realizar tareas de investigación en departamentos universitarios) by the Spanish Ministry of Education. Currently, she works as a language assistant in Dortmund (Germany) thanks to a scholarship (Beca de Auxiliar de Conversación) by the Spanish Ministry of Education.

Leila Goosen is a full professor in the Department of Science and Technology Education of the University of South Africa. Prof. Goosen was an Associate Professor in the School of Computing, and the module leader and head designer of the fully online signature module for the College for Science, Engineering and Technology, rolled out to over 92,000 registered students since the first semester of 2013. She also supervises ten Masters and Doctoral students, and has successfully completed supervision of 43 students at postgraduate level. Previously, she was a Deputy Director at the South African national Department of Education. In this capacity, she was required to develop ICT strategies for implementation. She also promoted, coordinated, managed, monitored and evaluated ICT policies and strategies, and drove the research agenda in this area. Before that, she had been a lecturer of Information Technology (IT) in the Department for Science, Mathematics and Technology Education in the Faculty of Education of the University of Pretoria. Her research interests have included cooperative work in IT, effective teaching and learning of programming and teacher professional development.

About the Contributors

Patrícia Gouveia is Associate Professor at Lisbon University Fine Arts Faculty [Faculdade de Belas-Artes da Universidade de Lisboa]. Integrated member of ITI – Interactive Technologies Institute / LARSyS, Laboratory for Robotics and Engineering Systems, IST. Co-curator of the Playmode exhibition (MAAT 2016-2019). Works in Multimedia Arts and Design since the nineties. Her research focus on playable media, interactive fiction and digital arts as a place of convergence between cinema, music, games, arts and design. Previously she was Associate Professor at the Interactive Media (Games and Animation) degree at Noroff University College (2014-16) in Kristiansand, Norway. Invited Assistant Professor at FCSH/UNL (2007-14) and Assistant Professor at ULHT (2008-13) both in Lisbon. From 2006 to 2014 Patrícia edited the blog Mouseland. In 2010 she published the book Digital Arts and Games, Aesthetic and Design of Ludic Experience [Artes e Jogos Digitais, Estética e Design da Experiência Lúdica] (ed. Universitárias Lusófonas), a synthesis of her doctoral thesis and some articles she published. More information here: https://fbaul.academia.edu/PatriciaGouveia/CurriculumVitae.

Emily Guetzoian works at the University of California, Los Angeles (UCLA) Anderson School of Management supporting MBA students with global field study projects. She enjoys working with students during their academic journey and providing individualized strategies to support each unique learner. Emily is a proud first-generation college graduate. She holds a BA in sociology and a BA in communication from California State University Channel Islands, an MS in counseling and guidance (college student personnel) from California Lutheran University, and an EdD in higher education leadership from Fresno State University. Her dissertation was a mixed-methods, multi-institutional study examining the academic success, feelings of belonging, and commitment to service of first-generation sorority members. Emily has experience in a variety of higher education areas at public and private institutions, including housing and residential life, summer conferencing, academic advising, field studies, international education, writing centers, tutoring services, student employment and development, clubs and organizations, and new student orientation. She enjoys staying actively involved in professional organizations, particularly in the learning center community, to continually discover new ideas and strategies to support students.

Kendra M. Hall-Kenyon is a professor and department chair in the Department of Teacher Education at Brigham Young University. Hall-Kenyon has spent the last twenty years studying or working in early education. She received her B.A. in Family Science from BYU, and her M.S. and Ph.D. from Columbia University, Teacher's College in Cognitive Studies. Dr. Hall-Kenyon's research focuses on early literacy instruction and assessment and early childhood teacher education.

Cristina A. Huertas-Abril is an Associate Professor in the Faculty of Education at the University of Córdoba (Spain). Her research interests include Computer-Assisted Language Learning (CALL), Bilingual Education, Teaching English as a Foreign Language (TEFL) and teacher training. She has participated in several national and international research projects, and published numerous scientific articles in prestigious journals. Dr Huertas-Abril teaches at Master's level at the UCO and UCA (Spain) and at the Ateneum-University in Gdansk (Poland), has taught both in formal and non-formal contents, and has directed and taught several specialization courses on Bilingual Education, Translation Studies, and Second Language Acquisition. She has presented many papers at different (inter)national conferences around the world like Spain, Germany, Poland, France, Turkey and Bahrein, among others. Moreover, she has had international academic stays in Chile and in the US. She is a member of the Research Group 'Research in Bilingual and Intercultural Education' (HUM-1006), and the co-founder of the Ibero-

American Research Network on Bilingual and Intercultural Education (IBIE). ORCID: https://orcid.org/0000-0002-9057-5224.

Nilofer Hussaini is an Assistant Professor in the Department of Professional Studies, Christ University, Bangalore. Her research interests mainly includes Socio-Economic and Political issues of Emerging Economies She obtained her PhD in Commerce & MBA from (Bihar), India in 2014 and 2004, respectively. She qualified National Eligibility Test for Lectureship in Management, India, in 2005. She has 7 years of teaching experience in commerce and management discipline and is an author of several research articles and a book. She has presented research papers at several International and National Conferences.

Fritz Ilongo is a Psychologist and Counsellor, Senior Lecturer in the University of Eswatini. He recently authored; 'Creative Education – DDV: SEE', Outskirts Press, USA; 'AfroSymbiocity as a Psychology of Conflict and Conflict Resolution in Africa', Cambridge Scholars Publishing, UK; 'Psychology of Religion, Violence, and Conflict Resolution.' Nova Science Publishers, USA; 'Workplace Bullying in African Tertiary Institutions.' Nova Science Publishers, USA.

Sheikh Rashid Bin Islam is a Researcher in Bangladesh Consulting Services, Dhaka, Bangladesh. His research interest lies in Education Policy Management, Curriculum Development, Inclusive and Special Education, Educating Children with Disabilities, and Japanese Education. He has worked on various education research projects, including gender equity, social inequality, social justice, and socio-economic research in Bangladesh. He is trained as an education specialist at the University of Dhaka, Bangladesh, and he has conducted his research with multiple international and national NGOs in Japan, Myanmar, and Bangladesh. He proactively participates in civil society activities and plays a courageous role in the unending struggle against human deprivation and social injustice. Further, he also contributes to youth-focused international and national organizations such as the United Nations Youth and Student Association Bangladesh (UNYSAB) to promote and empower youths for decent work and sustainable career development.

Sunitha Abhay Jain, Professor, School of Law, Christ University, Bengaluru, holds a Doctoral Degree in Law from NLSIU, Bengaluru. She is the coordinator for the LLM Program at School of Law, Christ University, Bengaluru. She holds an LL.B. and LL.M degree from Bangalore University and has specialized in Corporate and Commercial Laws and had secured Second Rank in the University for her BA LLB (Hons.) program. She also completed her Master of Human Rights from Pondicherry University and a Post Graduate Diploma in Cyber Laws from NALSAR, Hyderabad. She has been a full time faculty in law and has a teaching experience of over two decades. She has guided many PG., MPhil & Ph.D. research scholars. She has numerous publications to her credit in the form of book chapters and research articles in reputed Scopus indexed and UGC care listed journals. Has been invited as a resource person by various national and international institutions. She has chaired and presented papers at national and international seminars and conferences.

Sunil John is an Associate Professor at the School of Law Christ University. Dr. Sunil John holds a Bachelors and Masters degree in History from the Madras Christian College, M. Phil in Gender Studies from Hyderabad Central University. He was awarded the EKD Germany and Cadburys Foundations Scholarship to study Conflict Resolution and Peace Building from Woodbrooke Quaker College in

About the Contributors

Birmingham, UK. He did his LL.B and LL.M in International Law from the University of Mumbai. He subsequently pursued his P.hD in the Philosophy of Law and Governance from the University of Mumbai. His thesis was on comparative Natural Law theories of Kautilya and Thomas Aquinas. Dr. Sunil John has also pursued Film studies from the Film and Television Institute of India, Pune. He has an experience of working with NGOs and has been teaching for the last 17 years.

Seena Kaithathara is an Assistant Professor, Dept. Statistics, Christ University, Bangalore, India.

Yogesh Kanna Sathyamoorthy is an Assistant Professor of Neurosciences in the Department of Psychology, Christ University. He is teaching biomedical courses to undergraduate and postgraduate students. He has completed his PhD in Neuroscience from University of Madras.

Janna Kellinger is an associate professor in the Curriculum and Instruction department at the University of Massachusetts Boston. She is the author of A Guide to Designing Curricular Games: How to "Game" the System as well as the book chapter, "Coding across the Curriculum." She most recently designed a course-based game for a Coding for Non-Coders class.

Goh Kok Ming is a global Minecraft mentor and Primary Educator in Under-Enrolled School, who loves to integrate Minecraft in teaching and learning. He is also the Winner of International Society for Technology in Education (ISTE) Awards for Games and Stimulations, and Blended and Online Learning Year 2021.

Joseph Varghese Kureethara is heading the Centre for Research at Christ University. He has over sixteen years of experience in teaching and research at CHRIST (Deemed to be University), Bengaluru and has published over 100 articles in the fields of Graph Theory, Number Theory, History, Religious Studies and Sports both in English and Malayalam. Kureethara has co-edited five books including Recent Trends in Signal and Image Processing, Neuro-Systemic Applications in Learning and Data Science and Security, and authored three books. His blog articles, comments, facts and poems have earned about 1.5 lakhs total pageviews. He has delivered invited talks in over thirty conferences and workshops. He is the Mathematics section editor of Mapana Journal of Sciences and member of the Editorial Board and a reviewer of several journals. He has worked as a member of the Board of Studies, Board of Examiners and Management Committee of several institutions. He has supervised 5 PhDs, 12 MPhils and supervising 8 PhDs.

Georgy P. Kurien is the Associate Dean at the School of Business and Management, Christ University, Bengaluru. He teaches MBA students Supply Chain Management and Sustainable Business Management. Before joining academia, Prof Georgy Kurien served in the Indian Army for two decades and retired as a Lieutenant Colonel. He held prestigious military appointments in Command, Instructional and Staff, both during operations and peacetime. Dr Kurien obtained his B.Tech in Mechanical Engineering from Kerala University, M. E. from the University of Pune, Ph D from the M S University of Baroda and PG in Business Management from XLRI Jamshedpur, India. Dr Kurien is also an alumnus and faculty member of the Haggai Institute International. His research interests and publications are in Supply Chain Performance Measurement, Sustainable Business Models and Terramechanics.

Richard Lambert is a Professor in the Department of Educational Leadership at the University of North Carolina at Charlotte, Director of the Center for Educational Measurement and Evaluation, and Editor of NHSA Dialog: A Research-to-Practice Journal for the Early Intervention Field. He earned his Ph.D. in Research, Measurement, and Statistics and Ed.S. in counseling psychology from Georgia State University. He has received over 20 million dollars in funding for research. He serves as the Principal Investigator for an award from the North Carolina Department of Public Instruction entitled "Evaluating the Implementation of a Formative Assessment System in North Carolina Kindergarten Classrooms" and an award from the North Carolina Department of Health and Human Services entitled "Coaching, Mentoring, Performance Evaluation, and Professional Development for BK Licensed Teachers in Non-public School Classrooms". His research interests include formative assessment for young children, applied statistics, and teacher stress and coping. He has served the College Board in the AP Statistics program for 20 years as a Reader, Table Leader, Question Leader, and Rubric Team Member.

Karen Le Rossignol is a Senior Lecturer in creative writing, editing, publishing and freelancing skills in the School of Communication and Creative Arts at Deakin University, Australia. She has extensive experience in developing industry-oriented curriculum and educational digital storyworlds, for which she has received university and national awards. Her work-integrated learning expertise is demonstrated through project-based approaches to editing/publishing and freelancing as applied research across narrative and digital storytelling.

Yixun (Annie) Li is currently an Assistant Professor in the Department of Early Childhood Education at The Education University of Hong Kong. She holds a Ph.D. in Human Development from the University of Maryland, College Park, a Master's degree in Developmental and Educational Psychology from Beijing Normal University, and a Bachelor's degree in Engineering from North China Electric Power University. Her research concentrates on language development and reading acquisition in monolingual and bilingual children and adults, as well as game-based interventions for first and second language learners.

Luciana Lima has a PhD in Psychology from the Faculty of Psychology and Educational Sciences of the University of Porto. Luciana Lima is currently doing post-doctoral studies at the Multimedia Department at the Faculty of Fine Arts of the University of Lisbon with a scholarship from ARDITI, ITI – Interactive Technologies Institute / LARSyS, Laboratory for Robotics and Engineering Systems, IST. She is an effective member of the Portuguese Psychologists Association and her current research interests focus on the intersection between gender, digital games, and gaming culture. Luciana Lima research focus the hegemony of games as interactive and artistic media and their social impacts, with an emphasis on gender equality.

Gaia Lombardi is an Italian Primary School Teacher with over 20 years of experience in teaching Mathematics, Science and English as a Second Language. Expert in CLIL in ages 6-12. Expert in Coding and Computational Thinking; EU Codweek Leading Teacher for Italy. Previous publications: 2006 "L'avventura di crescere insieme. Manuale teorico-pratico per l'asilo nido" (The adventure of growing together. Theorical-practical manual for nursery"), Juiior Edizioni 2020:The Role of Unplugged Coding Activity in Developing Computational Thinking in Ages 6-11" in Kalogiannis, M., & Papadakis, S., Handbook of research on Tools for Teaching Computational Thinking in P-12 Education, Information Science Publishing.

About the Contributors

Hannah Luce is a second-year doctoral student in the Educational Research, Measurement, and Evaluation program at the University of North Carolina at Charlotte (UNCC). She received her Bachelor's Degree in Elementary Education from the University of Vermont (UVM) in 2017 and her Master's in Curriculum and Instruction (Literacy) from UVM in 2020. Since beginning her academic career, Hannah has been awarded the Elementary Education Award from the College of Education at UVM and the Herschel and Cornelia Everett Fellowship from the UNCC Graduate School. Hannah currently works for the Center for Educational Measurement and Evaluation at UNCC where she serves as a co-researcher on an implementation fidelity study. She is primarily interested in the following research areas: formative assessment, interrater reliability, and literacy assessment practices.

Marshall M. is an avid student of visual processing, reading and neuro-modulation. She participates in researching cutting-edge resources to improve the foundational skills needed to advance visual intelligence and plays an integral role in the development of these resources. Her intuition in designing functional models and resources to undergird the approaches proven to support student development with visual skills, vocabulary development, and neuromodulation is well respected. Marinda is passionate to help students reach the next level of skills and personal development.

Mara Madaleno has a Ph.D. in Economics from the University of Aveiro. She currently lectures Finance and Economics at the DEGEIT of UA and is the Director of the Master in Economics. She is also vice-Director of the Master in Data Science for Social Sciences. Highly experiment in publications of peer-reviewed and indexed articles, books, book chapters, and conference proceedings publications. Works in the areas of finance, financial markets, energy and environmental economics and works as a collaborator of research projects in the field of the current publication and in her research interest areas.

Jamie Mahoney is an Associate Professor in the Adolescent, Career, and Special Education Department at Murray State University. She teaches Special Education courses for dual certification Learning Behavior Disorder/ Elementary or Middle School undergraduate students and graduate students in the Alt. Cert, Master LBD, and Moderate Severe Disabilities programs. Dr. Mahoney has recently completed the Level 1 Dyslexia Orton Gillingham Certification through DTI. She currently serves on the KYCEC TED board as Past President. She has taught students with various disabilities in the areas of math, reading, and language arts for over 20 years in the elementary public school setting. She is certified in the areas of special education, general education, reading endorsed, assistive technology certified, and educational leadership certified. Her research interests include preparing preservice and inservice teachers to effectively teach students of all abilities using differentiated instruction methods, dyslexia, response to intervention and progress monitoring, increasing student engagement using technology, collaboration and co-teaching methods, and assessment methodologies.

Anand Manivannan works with the Department of Commerce, Christ University, Bangalore, India. He holds a Ph.D. in Commerce from SRM University (SRM Institute of Science and Technology) Chennai, Tamil Nadu. His area of focus is on mystery shopping and mystery shoppers' profession. His doctoral dissertation was on enhancing job satisfaction through motivation and Emotional Intelligence, a study concerning mystery shoppers. His other research focus is on Work-Life Balance, Gig-Economy, Consumer purchase behavior etc. He has presented his research article at AMA American Marketing Association Conference as an extended feather to his cap.

Rick Marlatt is an associate professor of language, literacy, and culture at New Mexico State University where he received the 2020 Digital Learning Initiatives Leading the Way Award. Rick earned his Ph.D. in Educational Studies from the University of Nebraska-Lincoln and his MFA in Creative Writing from the University of California, Riverside. His work in English language arts bridges the fields of teacher education, digital literacies, literature study, and sociocultural theory. His most recent work appears in English Journal, Journal of Education, Action in Teacher Education, and Journal of Adolescent & Adult Literacy. His co-edited book, Esports Research and its Integration in Education, was published in 2021.

Minda Marshall is an educationalist and researcher focussing on visual processing and cognitive development through the processes of reading. She has successfully developed and implemented such solutions for schools, universities, and various other organizations for more than 20 years. Minda serves on the board of the Destiny Group, oversees Mokopane Destiny Academy and is also a director of Lectorsa, a South African company. In addition, she is a co-founder of M3Line. Minda played an integral role in M3line and Lectorsa launching the Eyebraingym in February 2020. Lectorsa is partnering with various Tertiary Institutions, i.e. Stellenbosch University, University Pretoria, University of the Free State, University of Namibia, and public and private schools to assist students in developing their visual processing reading cognitive skills. The Eyebraingym solution results from more than 100,000 case studies and hours of research compiled into a simplistic user friendly, gauged online visual processing, reading and comprehension development system. Her qualifications include a BA degree, various international leadership training programmes, and Occupational Directed Education and Training Practitioning Skills. In addition, she has authored and co-authored articles, academic articles and books. Minda is passionate about educating and empowering teachers, educators, parents and learners to discover their internal strengths to maximize their abilities. In addition, she trains leaders, educators, parents and students around the world.

Brian McKenzie is a gamer and Associate Professor at Maynooth University in Ireland. He has a PhD in history and research interests in critical literacy, gaming and game design, and innovative pedagogy. He has published historical and pedagogical research and contributed to several Dungeons & Dragons publications as a freelance writer for Goodman Games.

Cora-Lynn Munroe-Lynds is a recent graduate from the School of Information Management, with a Master of Information degree. While attending Dalhousie, she published a prize-winning journal article on the public's perceptions of the government during COVID-19. Her research interests include comprehensive literature searches such as scoping review and systematic reviews, content analyses, business intelligence, information literacy, and information ecosystems. For her master's thesis, she conducted a systematic mapping of information literacy in learning outcomes. Last year she joined a team that conducted a scoping review looking at the impact COVID-19 has had on undergraduate medical education. Cora has been and continues to be a guest speaker for the Information in Society course in the School of Information Management at Dalhousie University. She enjoys sharing her knowledge and speaks on information literacy and information ecosystems.

Shabarisha N. is currently working as Assistant Professor in the School of Business and Management, Christ University, for the last 6 years. He took his Master of Commerce degree in 2012 from Kuvempu University, Shimoga. He also obtained PGDHRM from the same University. He has cleared

About the Contributors

the UGC - National Eligibility Test for Lectureship twice in 2011 and 2012. He has 9 years of teaching experience. He has published a number of articles in the field of finance and accounting. He has also presented a number of research papers at both national and international conferences and seminars etc. He has delivered more than 30 invited talks in the area of Financial Derivatives, International Financial Reporting Standards, and Indian Accounting Standards. His areas of interest are in Empirical finance - asset pricing, volatility modeling, risk management, financial modelling, accounting standards, and cost management.

Larysa Nadolny is an Associate Professor in the School of Education and Human Computer Interaction at Iowa State University. Her research includes examining motivation and engagement in digital learning environments.

Iffat Naomee is a lecturer of Institute and Education and Research (IER), University of Dhaka. She has completed her graduation and post graduation from the same institute and has earned another post graduation degree from University of Worcester, UK. She has been working in the field of education for the past 6 years.

Cathlyn Niranjana Bennett completed her doctoral work in Neuropsychology from the National Institute of Mental Health and Neurosciences, India. Her research interests include Neuropsychological Assessments and Interventions including EEG Neurofeedback. She currently serves as Assistant Professor with the Department of Psychology, Christ University, India.

Ana Nobre, after living and studying in Paris, currently teaches at Universidade Aberta where she has taught since 1998, having previously been a Professor at the Sorbonne University, Paris. She completed a PhD in Didactologie des langues et des Cultures from the University Sorbonne Paris III. She is dedicated to the teaching of foreign languages in eLearning, to digital resources for learning in online environments and recently to the didactic eLearning and gamification in education. She was coordinator of the project "Teaching / learning languages online" and researcher of @ssess project of the Distance Education Laboratory and eLearning (FCT, 2010-2013) where she investigated the problem of digital alternative assessment of orality.

Vasco Nobre, after having worked since 1994 as Commissioner and Executive Director of the OIKOS Space, began his teaching activity at the Open University in October 2009 as a Tutor and in 2012 as a Guest Assistant Professor. He has a PhD in Arts & Media from the Université Sorbonne (Paris) in 2007. He has been a researcher on digital resources for learning in online contexts.

Keiichi Ogawa is a Professor/Department Chair in the Graduate School of International Cooperation Studies at Kobe University in Japan. He is also a Governing Board Member in the UNESCO International Institute for Educational Planning (IIEP). He has served in various graduate schools and international organizations, including Honorary Professor at Kyrgyz National University, Visiting Professor at Columbia University/the University of Dhaka, Affiliate Professor at the University of Hawaii at Manoa/George Washington University, and Education Economist at the World Bank. His research interest lies in the economics of education, education finance, and education policy. He has worked on development assistance activities in over 30 countries and has authored or co-edited eight books and over 90 journal articles/book chapters. Many of them are issues related to educational development and cooperation in national and international settings. He holds his Ph.D. in Comparative International Education and Economics of Education from Columbia University.

Anand Patil is Associate Professor of Business Studies at the School of Business Studies and Social Sciences, CHRIST (Deemed to be University) Bangalore. He has M.Com and M.Phil to his credit in Commerce and Management. He obtained Ph.D. in Commerce from Shivaji University, Kolhapur, Maharashtra. Accounting and Taxation are his areas of expertise. He has 19 years of experience in teaching at the graduate and postgraduate levels. He has also presented papers at various national and international conferences and published articles in reputed journals. Dr. Anand also has a rich administrative and industry experience where he served as Academic Head for MBA at Magnus School of Business (MSB, ICFAI) Bangalore, Program Director for BBA at Alliance University, Bangalore and as an internal auditor for various educational institutions, banks and joint-stock companies.

Sharon Peck is a professor of literacy and play advocate. Sharon believes in authentic and meaningful instruction for all. Sharon studies play, game-based pedagogy, multimodal language arts, and place and community-based literacy instruction.

Giuseppe Pedeliento (PhD) is Associate Professor of Marketing at the Department of Management of the University of Bergamo. Former visiting lecturer at the Aalto School of Business (Helsinki, Finland), at Johannes Kepler University (Linz, Austria) and visiting scholar at the University of Washington Bothell (Seattle, USA), his research focuses mainly on B2B and B2C marketing and branding, and consumer behavior. His articles have appeared in journals such as Organization Studies, Journal of Advertising, Family Business Review, Journal of Business Research, Industrial Marketing Management, Journal of Business Ethics, Journal of Business & Industrial Marketing, Consumption, Markets & Culture, Journal of Service Theory and Practice, Management Decision, Journal of Product & Brand Management, and in other academic outlets. Giuseppe serves in the Editorial Board of the Journal of Business Research, Journal of Product & Brand Management, Management Decision, and of the Italian Journal of Marketing. He is also an Associate Editor for Pearson Management & Marketing Cases, and serves as a reviewer for several highly-ranked international journals. In 2021 he has been appointed member of the board of directors of the Italian Marketing Association (Società Italiana Marketing, SIM).

Reena Raj is currently presently working as an Assistant Professor in the Department of Business Analytics, CHRIST (Deemed to be University), Bengaluru, Karnataka. She has 20 years of experience including industry, academia and management research. Prof Reena has presented papers in various national and international conferences and published research papers and edited books. She has mentored close to 200 projects across various domains in management. Her areas of interest include Analytics and Decision Sciences and Behavioural Sciences. She has been associated with Christ University for 13 years.

Sreedhara Raman is having Bachelor of Engineering from Kuvempu University, Post Graduate Diploma in Business Management from Indian Institute of Rural management, Jaipur, and Doctor of Philosophy from the University of Mysore. He has around 5 years of corporate experience during which he worked for Zenith Rubbers Limited and Falcon Tyres. He has around 18 years of teaching and research experience. Presently, he is working as Associate Professor at School of Business and Management,

About the Contributors

CHRIST (Deemed to be University) in Marketing Specialization, at the Central campus, Bangalore. His core areas of teaching and research are Sales Management, Distribution Management, and Marketing Research and Analytics. He has published research papers in Scopus indexed and UGC approved journals. He has also presented research papers in the International and National conferences.

Jéssica Reuter is Master in Finance and PhD student in Economics and Business Sciences at the University of Aveiro. Researcher at the University of Aveiro. Her research interests include innovation, education, financial market analysis, international finance, behaviour in finance and public policy.

Mohd Ali Samsudin, PhD, is an Associate Professor at School of Educational Studies, Universiti Sains Malaysia (USM). His research interests include Applied Psychometrics and Statistics in Education and Science, Technology, Engineering and Mathematics (STEM) Digital Learning. In the field of Applied Psychometrics, his research focuses on the use of Computerized Adaptive Testing (CAT), as a tool to integrate technology into assessment. As for the Applied Statistic Research. Dr Mohd Ali Samsudin is currently looking into the use of Big Data and Social Network Analysis as well as the emerging trend in data technology for Industrial Revaluation (IR 4.0). In terms of STEM Digital Learning, he is researching the application of Mixed Reality of STEM Learning and the movement of citizen developer among STEM Teachers.

Seema Sant is currently working as an Associate Dean & Professor Human Resources at Vivekanand Education Society Institute of Management Studies and Research (VESIM), Chembur, Mumbai. She is a behavioral certified trainer with extensive academic and industry experience. She has done her MBA (HR) and Ph.D. in Business Administration, Diploma in Training & Development (ISTD). She is also a Certified Trainer for Saville Consulting International Accreditation Programme. She has 24 years of experience working with corporate and academic institutions. Her areas of interest are Organizational Development, Changing Work Culture, Training Effectiveness & Development and HR Analytics.

Elvira Lázaro dos Santos holds a PhD in Education-Mathematic Didactics at the Institute of Education of the University of Lisbon, a Master's in Education and a degree in Mathematics from the Faculty of Sciences of the University of Lisbon. She teaches in both elementary and high schools and has participated in several innovative National and International projects, which include Technologies and Mathematics Education. She has been interested in initial and in-service teacher training, formative assessment and writes Math books for basic education.

Bidisha Sarkar has completed her MBA from ICFAI Business School, India. She has pursued M.Phil and PhD from Christ University, India. Her research area for M.Phil was finance. She explored the area of econometrics-finance in her PhD. She has four years of experience which includes academic and industry. Dr. Sarkar had served several international clients for major and minor research projects. Her area of expertise is the energy sector. She is a social entrepreneur and founder of 'Utthan Foundation' where members serve for youth development. Dr. Sarkar is presently, working with Christ University, India.

Emine Sendurur received her PhD in Computer Education and Instructional Technology from Middle East Technical University, Turkey, in 2012. In 2005, she was hired as a research assistant in the same department. After completing her PhD, she worked as an instructor in Computer Programming department. She recently works as an associate professor doctor in Computer Education and Instructional Technologies department at Ondokuz Mayıs University, Turkey. She teaches courses including instructional design, computer science, learning theories, Internet based programming and human-computer interaction. Her main research interests consist of user experience, informal learning, social networking sites, cognitive load theory, instructional message design, and eye-tracking methodology.

Polat Sendurur received his bachelor degree in Computer Education and Instructional Technology from Middle East Technical University, Turkey, in 2004, and then he was hired as computer science teacher by Turkish Ministry of Education. In 2006, he started to his PhD education and was hired as a research assistant in Computer Education and Instructional Technology from Middle East Technical University. He recently works as an instructor in Computer Education and Instructional Technologies department at Ondokuz Mayıs University, Turkey. He teaches courses including teaching methods, fundamentals of distance education, qualitative research methods in instructional technologies, and introduction to programing. His main research interests consist of technology integration, cognitive tools, computational thinking, and computer science education.

Lee Ann Setzer holds a master's degree in speech-language pathology. She is the project coordinator for Project SEEL (Systematic and Engaging Early Literacy) at Brigham Young University.

M. Mahruf C. Shohel is an academic researcher with special interests in education, childhood studies, international development, technology-enhanced learning and social science research methods. He has written extensively on development issues in the Global South and conducted research on disadvantaged children including socioeconomically deprived children, street children, sex worker's children and displaced refugee children. Currently, he is engaged in the fields of education in emergencies, education for sustainable development and global citizenship, emerging technologies in education, students' learning journeys and their engagement, and teaching and learning in higher education.

Haytham Siala is a Senior Lecturer (Associate Professor) in Digital Marketing at Newcastle University. Haytham received his Ph.D. in Information Systems from Brunel University, UK. His research interests include Social Media & Digital Marketing, Consumer Behavior, Religious Brand Management, Business Ethics and Technology Enhanced Leaning. His research has been published in leading journals such as Business Ethics, Information, Technology and People, Journal of Business Research, and Information System Frontiers.

Constantine-(Kostas) Skordoulis is Professor of Epistemology and Didactical Methodology of Physics at the Department of Primary Education, National and Kapodistrian University of Athens, Greece, where he teaches Physics and Theory of Scientific Knowledge. He is also Coordinator of the Module "History of Science, Epistemology and Didactical Methodology", in the School of Science and Technology of the Hellenic Open University. He has studied Physics at the University of Kent at Canterbury, UK and has a PhD in Quantum Optics from the University of Ioannina. He has worked as a Visiting Researcher at the Universities of Oxford (UK), Jena (Germany) and Groningen (Netherlands) with scholarships from DAAD (Germany) and NWO (Netherlands). He is Effective Member of the International Academy of History of Science and has been Member of the Council of the European Society for History of Science

About the Contributors

(2012-14) and Secretary of the Teaching Commission of the Division of History of Science and Technology of the International Union of History and Philosophy of Science (2007-2017).

Carolyn Stufft is an assistant professor of literacy in the Department of Teacher Education at Berry College. Dr. Stufft is a certified ELAR (English/Language Arts/Reading) teacher, Reading Specialist, and Legacy Master Reading Teacher; she has taught grades 4-8 in charter and Title I public schools. Her research interests include the use of digital literacies to promote K-12 students' literacy practices. Her teaching interests include the preparation of pre-service teachers to effectively incorporate digital literacies within the curriculum.

Binod Sundararajan's research interests lie in organizational, professional and business communication; computer-mediated communication; CSCW, CSCL and social network analysis. He conducts research in adoption and diffusion of mediated technologies, use of CMC in such diverse areas as entrepreneurship, justice, teaching and learning, business ethics education, pedagogical approaches, leadership education, collaborative work and learning and management education, and historical data analysis.

Sanjida Akter Tanni is a lecturer at the Institution of Education and Research, Jagannath University, Dhaka, Bangladesh. Her research interests are online learning, distance education, blended learning, teaching-learning strategies, and technology-based education.

Samantha Taylor is focused on leveraging and integrating technology to increase self-reported efficacy in learners and educators. She supports Open Education Resource (OER) initiatives, sharing original pre-class mini-lectures and active-learning materials via her website. Sam hosts a Guest Speaker podcast available on YouTube and Spotify. She teaches cost management and financial reporting at Dalhousie University, and is an educator and lead policy advisor with CPA Western School of Business.

Rendani Tshifhumulo is the Head of the Department of Arts and Social Sciences. She has presented papers nationally and internationally addressing IKS, Myth, Contemporary social problems including health and domestic violence. Dr. Tshifhumulo teaches Sociology from undergraduate to postgraduate level. She has managed to supervise many students at honours, MA and PhD levels. She has written articles, book chapters and edited a book. Her last article is on the travails of COVID 19 survivors.

Livhuwani Daphney Tshikukuvhe is a lecturer at the university of Venda in the department of Indigenous knowledge systems and heritage. She is an Indigenous Knowledge Holder(IKS) practitioner , She hold her masters of arts degree of African studies department in the School of Human and social sciences. she is currently working towards her PhD. She is a supervisor and supervised students in Indigenous knowledge system and heritage department. She is good in organizing community engagement e.g. celebration of heritage and everything related to cultural days , her researches mostly based on how to preserve culture, it can be on indigenous food/traditional food, morals, values, etc. She is a supervisor and supervised students in Indigenous knowledge system and heritage department.

Anna Rebecca Unterholzner attends the Ph.D. in Fine Arts (Multimedia Art Department) at the Fine Arts Faculty at Lisbon University, Portugal. She completed her Master's degree in Modern and Contemporary European Philosophy in 2019 at the Luxembourg University and received her Bachelor's degree in Economics and Social Sciences in 2016 at the Vienna University of Economics and Business, Austria. She is currently a researcher collaborator at two Lisbon University Research Centres: ITI/LARsyS, Interactive Technologies Institute and CIEBA Center for research and studies in Fine Arts. Anna Unterholzner's research focuses on transdisciplinary art and design territories that merge arts and emotions, neuroaesthetics, gaming, interactive media, and gender equity.

Sharon Varghese is currently working as Assistant Professor in the Department of Statistics, CHRIST University, India and has obtained Ph.D. in Statistics from Pondicherry University, India in 2019. Currently guiding 2 Ph.D. Scholars and 8 M.Sc. students in their research. The research areas are distribution theory, reliability engineering and survival analysis.

Sankar Varma is a Research Scholar in the field of Economics with Christ (Deemed to be University), Bengaluru, Karnataka, India. His area of research interest includes Political Economy, Ecological Economics, Economics of Growth and Development, Cultural Economics and Criticism. He is at present working on contemporary urban development and exclusion. He has his works published in the Economic and Political Weekly (EPW), the Frontline (The Hindu Publishing Group) and various other books and journal platforms both online and physical.

Cláudia Veloso is Professor of Management (Marketing and Finances) at ESTGA - University of Aveiro. She is a researcher at GOVCOPP. She was a Member of the Board of the Centro Hospitalar do Nordeste (ULSNE) and Technical Adviser of the Ministry of Health of Portugal. She participated in 4 R&D projects, published more than 70 publications in peer-reviewed journals, book chapters and proceedings, and won 7 scientific awards.

Sam von Gillern is an Assistant Professor of Literacy Education at the University of Missouri. His primary research interests include digital citizenship and game-based learning in English language arts education.

John R. Woodward hold degrees in theoretical physics, cognitive science, and computer science, all from the University of Birmingham, U.K. Currently, he is with the School of Computer Science and Mathematics at the University of Stirling, He is a member of the Computational Heuristics, Operational Research and Decision Support research group (http://chords.cs.stir.ac.uk/). He was with the European Organization for Nuclear Research (CERN), where he conducted research into particle physics, the Royal Air Force as an Environmental Noise Scientist, and Electronic Data Systems as a Systems Engineer, and has also taught in China, Japan and the UK. He has given tutorials at GECCO, PPSN, and CEC on The Automatic Design of Algorithms, the aim is to generate high-quality algorithms, more cheaply and quickly. He has also organized a workshop at GECCO on this for the past 7 years.

Ahmet Erdost Yastibaş has a Ph.D. degree in English language teaching and has been working as an English language lecturer for more than 11 years. His research interests include technology-enhanced language teaching and foreign language assessment and evaluation.

About the Contributors

Lin Zou is a Chinese language teacher at a primary school affiliated with South China Normal University, P.R. China. She graduated with a Master's degree in Teaching Chinese to Speakers of Other Languages in Jinan University, Guangzhou, P.R. China. She was awarded the China National Teaching Achievement Award in 2018. Her research interests center on game-based interventions for early literacy learning.

Index

21St Century Skills 81, 96, 99, 112, 118, 124, 160-161, 315, 346-347, 377, 430, 472-477, 483, 485-487, 510-511, 515, 528, 580, 582, 597, 715, 748, 750-752, 754, 756-758, 761-765, 767-769, 800, 836, 844-845, 868, 873-876, 881, 889-892, 928, 943

A

Academic Achievement 66, 156, 162, 247, 399, 418, 420, 609, 622, 755, 806, 923, 943
Academics 5, 82, 109, 111, 133, 263, 401, 475-476, 582, 601, 792-793, 796
acquiring 21st century skills through e-learning 580, 582, 597
ACRL framework 220, 222, 240, 243, 245
Activate Background Knowledge 695
active methodology 630, 643
AI teacher 381-392, 395
Algorithms 255, 700, 706, 751, 841, 878, 881, 887-889, 891, 896, 904, 916, 925
Analysing 36, 127, 132, 270, 274, 287, 419, 620, 865
Application (App) 924
Application Programming Interface (API) 924
Applied Computing 180, 801
Artificial Intelligence 9, 12, 30, 70, 72, 75, 83, 136, 381-382, 392-395, 482, 569, 801, 837, 874, 915, 925, 945, 957
Assessment Criteria 31, 39, 42-44, 131, 150, 772-773, 775, 781, 783
assessment rubrics 194, 206
Augmented Reality (AR) 466, 544, 649, 849, 870, 958
automaticity 250, 252-253, 258
Available Designs 269, 281, 287
Avatars 50, 82, 459, 501, 653, 658, 755, 761, 797, 818, 821, 888, 892, 894, 897, 900, 904

B

Behavioral Changes 141, 788

bibliometric analysis 13, 15-18, 26, 28-30
binary method 461-462, 466-467, 471
blood circulatory 750, 760
Blooket 289, 294, 300
Board Games 1, 164, 225, 291, 298, 344, 347, 349, 357-360, 362, 457-458, 513, 541, 553, 833, 890-891, 901, 903
Business Ethics 488-490, 493, 499, 501-508

C

Challenges and Prospects 78, 104
Coding 44, 85, 111, 325, 341, 355, 581, 685, 690, 697, 699, 701-706, 709, 711, 713-715, 755, 758-759, 766, 819, 868-869, 872, 874-879, 881-882, 886-905, 907, 909-910, 913, 918, 920, 922-923
CODING UNPLUGGED 697, 701, 709, 711, 715
Cognitive Development 2, 14, 81, 88, 249, 251, 254, 258, 260, 275-276, 278, 317, 348, 406, 627, 648, 662, 697, 732, 768, 842, 844
Cognitive Load Theory 60, 75, 252, 265, 267, 876, 883
Collaborative Learning 87, 95, 141, 278, 304, 329, 503, 551, 650, 761, 795, 808, 886, 942, 944-945
community engagement 580, 589-590, 594-595, 597, 600
Community Of Practice 222, 269-270, 274, 288, 401, 795
complementary angles 772-773, 777-779, 782
Computational Thinking 24, 26, 85, 697, 699-702, 713-715, 759, 874, 876, 879, 884, 886, 888-891, 893, 901-904
Computer Programming 178, 888, 895, 904
Computer Science 21, 26, 36, 43, 55, 74, 101-102, 161, 225, 361, 392, 470, 600, 602, 700, 714-715, 799, 829, 869, 871-875, 877, 879, 882-887, 889, 901-902, 944, 956
Conceptual Framework 315, 318, 543-545, 547, 552, 597, 601, 773, 807, 921
Content and Language Iintegrated Learning 510-511,

Volume I: 1-471; Volume II: 472-958

Index

526-527, 530-531
Context- or Theme-Based App 695
corporate training 164-167, 176-177
COVID-19 82, 98-99, 104, 106, 110, 115, 123, 133, 139, 165, 167, 169, 176-177, 180-181, 185-186, 189, 191, 193-195, 199-200, 206-210, 212, 215-219, 221, 224, 245, 247, 251, 253, 265, 268, 378, 420, 425, 433, 447, 473-474, 483-485, 562, 582, 647, 665, 721, 729, 742, 757, 802, 811, 874, 937-938
critical theoretical analyses 606, 608
Critical Thinking 5, 57, 82-83, 85-87, 89, 95, 117-118, 133, 138, 144-145, 174, 225, 256, 289-292, 294-295, 322-324, 344-346, 348, 356-357, 359, 364, 366-368, 372-375, 412, 418-423, 425-430, 472-475, 481-483, 507, 510, 514, 519, 525, 558, 581, 607, 665, 750-752, 758, 761, 765, 767, 770, 790, 833-834, 837, 842, 874, 889-891, 901, 928-931, 933, 943, 946-947, 955
Critical Thinking Skills 117, 256, 372, 374, 418-423, 425-429, 475, 481, 665, 751
Cross-Sectional Study 107, 112, 118, 267, 561
Cultural Knowledge 269-270, 273, 276-278, 280-281, 284, 286, 288, 477, 588, 597, 602
Cultural Meaning Systems 269, 288
custom-built solutions 905-906

D

Data Analysis 16-17, 320, 326, 339, 355, 383, 455, 458, 463-464, 518, 541, 561, 584, 665, 756, 777, 915-916, 919, 921-922
decomposition 700, 888, 890, 894-895, 904
Deployment 39, 311, 590, 924, 957
DGBL 99, 468, 554-559, 561-562, 564, 567-569, 571, 574-575, 835
Digital Game-Based Learning (DGBL) 468, 554-556, 561, 574, 835
Digital Games 4-5, 11, 13-15, 17, 26, 61, 69, 77, 79-80, 98, 102-103, 106, 109, 124, 140, 150, 153, 157, 159, 182-183, 186-188, 191, 284-285, 293, 298, 337-338, 341-342, 371-372, 376, 402, 422, 438, 455-456, 505, 510-515, 525-526, 529, 536, 538, 541, 549, 551, 553, 554-556, 558-559, 561-564, 566-570, 572-574, 576-578, 581, 598, 623, 631-632, 644, 660, 662-663, 665, 747-748, 753, 769, 772, 774, 782-783, 800, 846-847, 849-851, 864-865, 869-870, 878, 881-882, 884, 886, 903, 933
digital learning environments 16, 29, 62, 66, 302, 488
digital learning game 731-732, 734, 741, 749
Digital Literacy 84, 99, 140, 160, 233, 284, 301, 307, 320, 333, 335-336, 340, 346, 363, 366, 370-371, 399, 415, 482, 569, 596, 671-672, 790-794, 797-802, 805-808, 884
Digital Media 87, 96, 99, 181, 190, 247, 285, 287, 343, 369, 372, 380, 416, 555, 571, 575, 583, 610, 621, 623, 625, 629-630, 664, 671-674, 676-677, 680, 683-684, 686, 689-690, 692, 695, 767, 797
Digital reading intervention 431
digital scoot 289, 293
Digital Skills 81, 84-85, 98, 100, 105, 181, 473, 475, 486, 816, 828
Digital Storytelling 83, 243, 302-303, 312, 317, 319, 331, 336, 339, 343, 758, 806, 885
digital storyworld 302-312, 314, 319
digital storyworld model 302-306, 308-309, 311-312, 314
digitalization of education 927, 937
dual-teacher classroom 383, 390-391, 394-395
Dungeons n Dragons 220, 225, 230, 242, 247
duvheke 418-429

E

ebook 675, 681, 685, 689, 693, 695-696
Educational digital games 106, 510, 513-514
Educational Games 1-2, 24, 27-28, 31, 49, 59-60, 62, 66, 70, 72, 80, 100-103, 111, 125, 157-158, 161, 217, 346, 349, 360, 387, 417, 430, 488, 513-514, 527, 531, 533-535, 537-539, 541, 543-544, 550, 552-553, 577, 652-653, 666, 758, 765, 768, 830, 836, 842-843, 868-871, 873-874, 879, 882-885, 887, 898
Educational Project 945
Educational Robots 381-382, 386, 393-394, 707
Educational Technologies 25, 83, 334, 371, 511-512, 555-556, 571, 596, 601, 604, 630, 935
Educational Video Games 422, 455-456, 458, 471
Edutainment 1, 4, 59, 80, 323, 551, 869-870
E-Learning 72-73, 83, 88, 96, 99, 101, 104, 140, 157-158, 178, 197, 247, 266, 287, 315, 342-343, 380, 393, 416, 469, 484-485, 506-507, 527, 548, 550, 552, 571, 580, 582, 584, 590, 597, 600-601, 605, 611, 645, 666, 730, 767, 801, 810-818, 822-823, 825-831, 870, 919, 921-922, 927, 938, 945
E-Learning 2.0 83, 927, 945
Emerging Technologies 12, 56-57, 59, 78, 81, 83, 96-97, 118, 484, 581, 644, 668, 792, 799, 804, 886, 957
Emotional Intelligence 358, 548, 606, 608, 615-616, 618-619
Engineering Design Process 650, 660, 668
English Language Arts 320-322, 324, 327, 329, 337, 693
environmental awareness 510-511, 514-515, 517-518,

522-526, 529-531
E-School 370, 584, 590, 597, 605
Esport 750, 757
Experiential Learning 1-2, 9, 53, 60, 71, 89, 93, 125, 135-136, 151, 177, 196-198, 216-217, 269, 274, 280, 302, 305-308, 317, 319, 426, 475-476, 483, 487, 504, 583, 588, 729, 933

F

Fair Game 832
First Language 438, 454
first-year seminar 220-221, 224, 243, 245, 247
Flipped Learning 36, 55, 82, 430, 653-654, 657, 659-661, 668
flow state 194-200, 206, 215-216
Foreign Language 35, 55, 57, 124, 136-137, 390, 392, 429, 437, 454, 457-458, 468-471, 511-512, 526-528, 530, 549, 570, 767, 798
foreign language learners 457-458, 471
Formative Assessment 47, 49, 242, 294, 746, 772-775, 777, 780, 782-784, 810, 812, 814-815, 818, 822-823, 825-828, 830
Fundamental Reading Process 252, 258, 260
funny crazy stories 107

G

game art 180, 186, 188-189
Game Based Pedagogy 144-145, 147-149, 151-152, 344, 837, 842
game coding 868, 875-877, 887
Game Design 11, 29-30, 54, 56, 59, 62, 66, 68-69, 79, 89, 98, 100, 108, 170, 184, 188-190, 243, 246, 280, 286, 317, 344-345, 347-349, 355-356, 358-361, 372, 402, 420-421, 428, 476, 483, 548, 551, 553, 570, 632, 751, 755-756, 768-769, 796, 800-801, 803, 844-845, 857, 866, 868, 875, 878-879, 885-886, 901, 904, 949, 951, 956
Game Designing 887
Game Mechanics 66, 141, 151, 162, 170, 340, 343, 349-350, 361, 632, 673, 676, 796, 814, 822, 863, 903
Game Playing 4, 33, 272-273, 277, 281, 868, 873-874, 880, 892, 894-895, 898
game simulation 194-196, 198-199, 214, 319
Game Theory 24, 176, 182, 366, 751, 832, 835, 838, 840-841, 869, 949
Game-Based 1-2, 4, 8, 10-13, 15-17, 21, 24, 26-29, 31-37, 40, 43, 46-47, 51-76, 78-82, 87-112, 115, 117-127, 130-148, 150, 152-161, 164-165, 178, 188, 194-195, 197-200, 216-218, 249, 254, 269-270, 272, 281, 285, 287, 293-294, 302, 304, 306, 309, 319-321, 323, 336, 340, 342-349, 356-360, 371, 378, 381-382, 385-390, 392, 400-402, 415-418, 420-422, 429-430, 450-451, 468-471, 477, 491-492, 503, 507, 510-514, 526-531, 533-537, 540, 542-553, 554-556, 558, 561, 569-575, 577, 581-583, 587-589, 596, 602, 606-621, 639-640, 645-646, 651, 662-664, 666-667, 673, 676, 686, 697-699, 714-715, 726, 731-732, 747-749, 751, 753-755, 760, 764, 767-769, 772, 774, 788, 800, 804, 808, 810, 812-815, 817-818, 822-823, 826, 828, 830, 834-838, 840-841, 844-845, 868, 871-875, 881-882, 884-888, 893, 899-903, 920, 927, 933-934, 941-945
game-based language learning 511-513, 527-528, 530-531
Game-Based Learning (GBL) 1-5, 8-13, 15-17, 21, 24, 26-29, 31-40, 43, 46-47, 51-76, 78-81, 85, 88-89, 91-112, 115, 117-127, 130-162, 164-165, 178, 194-195, 197-200, 216-218, 249, 270, 285, 287, 294, 302, 304, 306, 319-321, 323, 336, 340, 342-343, 347, 357, 360, 382, 385, 398, 400-403, 407, 415-418, 420-422, 429, 451, 468-471, 477, 491-492, 507, 513-514, 528, 530, 533-537, 540, 542-553, 554-556, 558, 561, 569-575, 582, 587-589, 596, 602, 607, 621, 639, 646, 648, 651, 662-665, 667, 697-699, 714-715, 726, 731-732, 747-749, 751, 753-755, 757, 760, 764-765, 767-769, 772, 788, 800, 808, 810, 812, 815, 817, 828, 830, 834-836, 838, 840-842, 844-845, 868, 871-873, 875, 881-882, 884-888, 893, 899-901, 903, 920, 927-928, 933-934, 941-945
Game-Based Pedagogical Approach 78, 91, 609
Game-Based Pedagogy 13, 17, 26, 89, 91, 93, 95, 130-131, 133, 140, 144-146, 148, 158, 160, 269, 272, 345-346, 348, 356-358, 360, 418, 544, 551, 581-583, 588, 606-621, 836-837, 868, 874
Gamer 182, 187, 190, 193, 324, 342, 492, 868, 888, 891, 893, 897, 901
Gamification 5, 9, 11, 13, 15-17, 21, 24, 26, 28-32, 35-36, 53-56, 59, 62-63, 66, 68-71, 73, 75, 79-80, 82, 85, 88-89, 95, 97, 101-103, 107-110, 112, 114-118, 121, 123-124, 133, 135, 139-142, 158, 162, 164-178, 246, 289, 291, 293, 296, 299, 303-304, 338-339, 342-343, 346, 361-362, 371, 378, 472-474, 476-478, 480-487, 492, 504-505, 533, 537, 539, 544, 546-547, 550, 552-553, 556-557, 570, 573-574, 581, 607, 609-610, 620-621, 630-634, 637-639, 641, 643-645, 665, 710, 716-717, 720-724, 726-730, 788-822, 826-831, 836, 844, 868, 876, 883, 902, 905, 922-923, 943, 946, 949,

955-958
Gaming 4, 8, 10-11, 15, 18, 24-25, 27, 29, 34, 38, 46, 54, 59-60, 62-65, 67, 69, 72-73, 76-77, 98, 101, 104-105, 126, 134, 152, 154, 156-158, 160, 162, 164, 171, 180, 182, 186-192, 196, 220-221, 224-225, 227, 242-243, 269-270, 272-279, 282-284, 286-288, 291, 294, 297, 301, 323-324, 333-336, 339-343, 345-347, 349, 357, 359, 390, 402, 422, 430, 456, 458-459, 463-464, 467, 469-470, 476, 488-492, 495-496, 498-500, 502-505, 517, 550-552, 588, 602, 645, 647-650, 653, 662-663, 665, 668, 726, 728, 731, 733, 735, 740, 746-747, 755, 766-767, 769-770, 772, 784, 788-792, 794, 796, 801, 804, 807, 810-812, 814-819, 821-822, 827-829, 834-836, 841, 843-844, 853, 865-866, 882, 884, 888, 890, 893-894, 897-898, 900-901, 942, 956, 958

Gaming Pedagogy 343
Gender Differences 99, 107, 118, 799
gender equity 180, 186, 188-189
Gimkit 289, 294, 301
Graphical User Interface (GUI) 38, 924
GraphoGame Afrikaans 431-433, 437-443, 445-446

H

Head-Mounted Display (HMD) 958
Higher Education 3, 10-12, 15, 24-26, 29, 31, 36-37, 46-48, 53-61, 65-69, 71, 78-79, 81-84, 88, 93-98, 100-105, 107-110, 112, 116-118, 135, 137-140, 144-145, 147, 154, 158-167, 170, 173-174, 176-178, 180-184, 186-188, 190, 192, 195-196, 199, 215, 221-222, 244, 246, 253, 265, 267-268, 302, 304, 307, 309, 315, 318, 340, 415-416, 421, 429-430, 468-469, 484-485, 533, 540, 546-547, 549-552, 561, 572, 574, 576, 582, 601, 604, 645, 662, 667, 720, 730, 768, 800-801, 803, 805, 814-815, 829, 837, 871-872, 905, 919, 921-923, 927, 929, 942, 944

Higher Order Thinking 39, 81, 95, 399, 419, 512, 526, 606, 608, 615-616, 618-619, 653, 658, 667, 751-752, 764-765, 874, 876, 878, 880
home language 432, 437, 454
honey 757-759
HTML and CSS 924
Human-Centered Design 180, 957
humanoid robot 382, 386-390, 395
Human-Robot Interaction 383-384, 393-395

I

Ignite by Hatch 731, 734-735, 742, 746-747, 749
indigenous games 397-399, 409, 414-419, 423, 426, 428-430
Information and Communications Technologies (ICTs) 605
Information Literacy 34, 55, 84, 104, 153, 164-166, 172-174, 176-178, 221-222, 228, 231, 240, 244-245, 291, 300, 307, 380, 401-402, 415, 417, 510, 528, 606, 646, 648, 660, 662, 664-665, 803-804, 921, 923, 928
Information Literature 646
In-Service Teachers 136, 335-336, 554-555, 561, 566-570, 661
institutional support 91, 533, 539-540, 543, 546-547, 553
Integrated Development Environment (IDE) 925
Interaction Design 143, 180, 394
interactive digital narrative 303, 305, 311, 316, 318-319
interactive instructions 905

J

JavaScript (JS) 925

K

Kahoot! 35, 46-47, 55-57, 166, 168, 175, 177, 300, 643-644, 800
Kinect 34, 50-51, 54-57, 530, 893
Knowledge Retention 131, 164, 166-167, 178-179, 798

L

Language and Communication 731-732, 735-736, 738-739, 742, 744, 746, 749
Language and Communication Domain 735-736, 738, 742, 749
Large Classes 402, 431-432, 435, 447, 592
learner motivation 668, 732, 810, 812, 814-816, 818, 820-822, 828
Learning Management System (LMS) 112, 828, 899, 925
Learning Outcomes 2-4, 8, 14, 31, 34-35, 37, 46, 51, 53, 63, 65, 78-79, 92, 94, 125, 140, 149, 157, 199, 214, 220-221, 228, 235, 237, 241-243, 303, 316, 324, 382, 387-390, 394, 402, 421, 437, 455-457, 460-461, 466-467, 476-477, 481, 492-493, 499, 501, 509, 512, 518, 526, 553, 556, 574, 582, 596, 609, 647, 661, 686, 721, 726, 732, 793-794, 800,

802, 868, 874-876, 879, 881, 887, 927, 933
Learning Skills 5-7, 86, 174, 588, 602, 669, 753, 826, 834, 928, 930, 932, 941
Legal Education 472-473, 483-485, 487
leisure games 648-650, 653, 659, 668, 948
Leveling Up 300, 896, 898-899, 904
Line Game 832-833, 835-838, 840-842
Literacy Domain 153, 736-738, 742, 749
Literacy Learning 285, 287, 293, 315, 320, 322-324, 326, 329-330, 334, 338-339, 344-345, 347-348, 356-357, 381-382, 385-387, 392, 437, 453, 604, 624, 671-672, 677, 686, 689, 692, 944
Literacy Skills 34, 86, 119, 153, 165, 174, 249, 270, 272, 279-280, 284, 289, 291, 293, 295, 299, 333, 335-336, 363-364, 367, 370-372, 377, 379, 397-400, 405-406, 409, 411-412, 415, 422, 434, 535, 581, 589, 596, 606-614, 616-621, 646, 648, 660, 664, 672, 674-676, 680, 682-683, 687, 694, 764, 799, 803, 836, 841, 928-930, 941
logical skills 697-698, 713, 715, 832
Low Code 905, 907, 910, 925

M

Machine Learning 117, 874, 910, 914-916, 921, 923, 925
Mars rover 757, 759-760, 763
Mashing 358, 362
mastering-skills 788
MBA students 122, 124, 126-127, 129, 134
Media Literacy 84-85, 307, 363-364, 366-380, 416, 606, 608, 613-620, 622-623, 625, 628, 692, 928
Meta Plan 31, 40-42
metacognition 609, 713, 749, 837
Misconceptions 68, 474, 582, 646, 648, 651-652, 657, 660, 662, 664, 666
Mobile Learning 24, 26, 54, 164, 434, 469, 630-631, 633-634, 665, 799, 803, 805, 813, 942
mobile-based games 646-650, 652, 655, 658-659, 661
Modding 358-359, 362
mother tongue 433, 438, 454, 460, 471, 511
Mugging Up 111, 118
Multiliteracies 178, 216, 220-223, 241, 244, 269-270, 280-281, 285-288, 308, 315, 317, 322, 337, 340, 345-346, 359, 378, 475, 487, 548, 581-583, 588, 597, 599, 602, 607, 624
multiliteracy framework 194, 198, 200, 205, 216
Multimodal 59, 73, 89, 223, 243, 269-270, 280-281, 288, 290, 294, 308, 321-322, 329-331, 334-336, 340-346, 348, 355, 358-359, 362, 581-583, 607, 612, 619, 621, 691, 770, 805, 905

multimodality 286, 331, 339, 343, 345, 356, 360
Multiple Intelligences 53, 625, 697, 714-715

N

narcissism 607, 613, 615
national language 454
native language learners 457-458, 471
no code 905-907, 917-918, 924-925
Non-Playing Characters 459, 471, 653

O

object-oriented programming 883, 886, 888, 897, 904
official language 438, 454
Online Learning 68, 82, 109, 178, 195, 220-221, 223, 232, 253, 337, 476, 483, 584, 598, 721, 768, 803, 810-813, 815, 817, 821-822, 827-830, 835, 841
On-the-Job Learning 118
Operational Literacy 288
orbital mechanics 649-650, 652, 655, 659, 668

P

parenting style 613-614
pedagogical design 235, 244, 302, 304, 519, 524
Pedagogical Game 832
Pedagogical Soundness 677, 679, 696
Pedagogical Strategies 336, 540, 577-578, 596, 630-631, 638
Pedagogical Tools 139, 163, 304, 668, 837
personality development 606, 619
Personalized Ebook 696
perspective and empathy 302
Phonics 250-251, 258, 400, 434, 453, 671, 676-677, 679, 690, 694
Play-Based Pedagogy 362
Player Experience 304, 316, 846
Player Interpretation 846
Playful Learning 90, 151, 304, 344, 349, 360-361, 732
playful stance 151, 348, 357-358, 362, 538
playfulness 29, 88, 91, 344, 348, 357, 361, 491-492, 495, 499, 503
Political Economy 832
post-millennial 564, 575
Pre-Service Teachers 102, 320-321, 329-330, 449, 562, 567, 575-576, 597, 604, 661
Primary Education 452, 561, 576, 716-724, 726, 728-730
production dice game 122, 128, 136-137
Professional Development 92, 95, 220, 338, 357-358,

Index

384, 429, 500, 533, 535, 540, 550, 553, 571, 576, 598, 603, 661, 694, 768, 920
Project-Based Learning (PBL) 39, 82, 177, 765, 836, 927-933, 941-945
pro-social behaviors 606, 608, 618-619

Q

Qualitative Research 339, 423-424, 462-463, 466, 468, 483, 515, 530, 637, 723, 905-907, 909-911, 914-916, 918, 921-922
qualitative research methods 905, 907, 910, 922
Quality Of Education 372, 448, 452, 716-718, 720, 722-723, 726, 808
Quantitative Research 455, 461-462, 466-467, 554, 561, 661
Quizlet 168, 289, 294, 300
Quizziz 289, 294, 300

R

reading fluency 249-252, 255-256, 258, 260, 265, 434, 452
reading skills 249-252, 254, 256, 266, 268, 330, 348, 389, 431-432, 434-435, 437, 439, 445-447, 515
religiosity 488-492, 495-496, 498, 500-503, 505, 507-508
Religiously Informed Ethics 488
Remote Learning 289, 292, 757, 927
Renewable Energy 512, 757, 759
research literacy 905, 907, 911, 915-916, 918
robot-assisted language learning (RALL) 386, 394-395
Robotics 12, 93, 382, 392, 394-395, 697, 701-702, 711, 715, 872
rocket science 649-652, 655, 657, 659-660, 669
roleplay 35, 45
Role-Play Game 194
Role-Playing Games 98, 220, 227, 469, 504, 513, 794, 829, 836, 852, 862, 865, 894

S

Scaffolded reading support 431
Scaffolding 59, 143, 198, 231, 292, 327, 333, 432, 435, 437, 445, 452, 607, 628, 671, 675, 680, 686-687, 696, 698, 793, 874, 900, 910
Scavenger Hunt 168, 294, 750, 757, 761
school choice 716-717, 723, 726
School Management Team (SMT) 605
Science Learning 136, 159, 400, 416, 623, 646-648, 650, 661, 664, 667

Scuba Diving 948, 958
Second Language 76, 339, 388-389, 393, 433, 438, 454, 457, 469, 471, 511, 527, 529, 711
Second Language Learners 457, 471
SEEL 671-672, 676, 679, 681-682, 685-687, 689, 691, 695, 714
Self-Directed Learning 109, 145, 152, 156, 174, 732-733, 747-749
Sequencing 310, 417, 888, 893-894, 904
Serious Games 2, 5, 9, 11-12, 14-15, 23, 27-29, 66, 68-70, 74, 76, 83, 106, 161, 304, 315, 318-319, 323-324, 337, 339, 343, 347, 359, 362, 417, 470-471, 477, 484, 486, 488-490, 499-502, 504-505, 508, 534, 550-552, 555-556, 570, 573, 647-648, 650, 652-653, 658, 662-663, 667-669, 728, 845, 847, 866, 868, 870, 883, 886, 903, 942, 944, 948, 956-957
simulated reality 946, 948, 958
situated cognition 194, 197, 216, 306
Skill Development 108, 138-139, 156, 198, 538, 648, 879
skinning 344-348, 350-351, 356, 358, 362
Socialization 221-222, 276, 620, 628, 788, 792, 796-797, 843, 847-849, 865, 875-876
Socrative 34, 48-49, 56
Space Station 226, 750, 757, 759-760
storyboard 946, 951, 958
Storytelling 4, 34, 83, 123, 243, 270-271, 279, 281, 302-303, 305-306, 310, 312, 314, 317, 319, 327, 331, 333, 335-336, 339, 343-344, 359, 389, 393, 403, 702, 709, 721, 751, 757-758, 806, 885, 899
Strategic Game 832
student assistant 164, 169, 172, 177, 179
student employee 168, 171, 174, 176, 178
student worker 164-165, 167-170, 172-176, 179
supplementary angles 772-773, 776, 778
supporting-approaches 788
Sustainable Forest 757-758

T

Tabletop Games 344-347, 357-358, 361-362, 664
Tangential Learning 666, 669
Teacher Competencies 160, 360, 533, 544, 551, 553
Teaching And Learning 3, 54, 67, 78-79, 81-83, 87, 91, 93-95, 104, 107, 109-110, 123-124, 139, 150, 171, 220-222, 310, 321-323, 336, 345, 349, 358, 361, 383-385, 399, 401, 409, 414, 422, 429, 431-432, 447, 449, 459, 476, 478, 483, 485, 511, 530, 536-537, 542, 544, 546, 568, 581, 585-586, 589-591, 593-595, 597-598, 600-603, 625, 631,

633, 635-636, 643-644, 668, 699, 714, 748-749, 755, 774, 784, 802, 844, 884, 920, 923, 933, 941
technological tools 117-118, 150, 158, 290, 321, 365, 422
Technology Acceptance Model 334, 341, 343, 491, 505, 508, 816, 830
Technology Adoption 491, 596
Technology Enhanced Learning 70, 484, 488, 499, 550, 574, 665, 804, 829, 920
Tech-savvy kids 107
Theory of Gamification 716-717, 720-721, 723
Tic-Tac-Toe 153, 832, 838
Topic Model 915, 925
TPACK framework 554-555, 561, 566, 586, 598, 601, 693
TPACK model 554-556, 559-562, 564, 567-569, 575, 691
Traditional Methods 118, 591, 941
transformative learning 302, 304, 313, 317
Trent Hergenrader 225, 229
tsetsetse 397, 399-400, 403-407
tutorial games 513

U

Understanding 9, 14, 24-25, 33, 41, 50, 58-59, 61, 65, 67, 78, 86, 92, 94-96, 100, 111, 118, 122, 124-125, 127, 131, 140-141, 143, 148, 152-153, 156, 158, 174, 185, 192, 197, 200, 204-205, 216, 223, 235, 237, 241-243, 249-253, 258-259, 270, 275, 277, 280-282, 286, 292, 296-298, 306-308, 314, 321, 327, 330, 336, 339, 342-343, 346-347, 349, 351, 354-356, 358, 367-369, 372-373, 375-376, 384, 402, 407, 409, 414-415, 417, 423-424, 456, 467-468, 474, 477-478, 482-483, 486, 489, 506-507, 511-512, 515, 536, 547, 552, 561, 567, 577, 583-584, 586, 594-595, 597, 603, 607-610, 619, 621, 623, 626-627, 632, 647, 660, 663, 667, 671, 677, 686, 689-690, 700, 727, 732, 734, 738-739, 749, 751, 758, 765, 774, 776, 778, 782, 792, 805-806, 809, 814, 816, 828, 832-834, 836-838, 841-842, 844, 865-866, 884, 889-890, 911, 915, 920, 927-928, 931-932

V

validity evidence 731-732, 734-735, 738, 740-741, 749
Video Game 62-64, 137, 190, 196, 270-272, 274-284, 286, 319-321, 323-324, 327, 334, 342-343, 345, 350, 361-362, 527, 576, 581, 583, 604, 653-654, 658, 663, 666, 695, 720, 732-734, 751, 753-755, 766, 813, 837, 846, 852, 865, 890, 892-898, 901
Video Game Literacies 343
Video Game-Based Learning (DGBL) 575
Virtual Learning Environments 506, 550, 818, 830
Virtual Reality (VR) 9, 12, 80, 82, 162, 180, 189-190, 279, 319, 338, 466, 504, 512, 528, 551, 569, 665, 806, 849, 885, 946, 948-950, 952-953, 955-958
visual intelligence 249-255, 257, 264-266
visual processing 249, 251-254, 258-261, 264-265
Visualization 34, 71, 83, 118, 596, 883, 887, 921, 924
Vygotskian constructivism 194, 197, 216

W

Web Of Science 13, 16-17, 649
What You See Is What You Get (WYSIWYG) 925
Wikipedia 109, 118, 220, 236-238, 240-241, 244-247, 359
Writing 3, 34-35, 39, 55, 105, 146-147, 220-225, 228, 230, 236-237, 239-244, 247, 266, 278, 288-289, 291-293, 298, 300-301, 303, 309, 311, 317, 324-325, 329, 333-337, 342, 344, 356, 364-365, 374, 399, 427, 448, 456, 474, 478, 480-481, 513, 584, 610, 636, 643, 674-676, 680, 682, 695, 697, 709, 712-713, 738-740, 749, 751-752, 770, 819, 835, 837, 877, 888, 895, 912, 925, 929-930

Z

Zone Of Proximal Development 197, 273, 276-277, 292, 437, 449, 607, 698, 713, 715, 732, 900-901

Recommended Reference Books

IGI Global's reference books are available in three unique pricing formats:
Print Only, E-Book Only, or Print + E-Book.

Shipping fees may apply.

www.igi-global.com

ISBN: 978-1-7998-0420-8
EISBN: 978-1-7998-0421-5
© 2020; 1,757 pp.
List Price: US$ 1,975

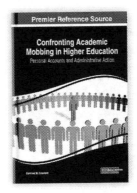

ISBN: 978-1-5225-9485-7
EISBN: 978-1-5225-9487-1
© 2020; 301 pp.
List Price: US$ 195

ISBN: 978-1-5225-9631-8
EISBN: 978-1-5225-9637-0
© 2020; 379 pp.
List Price: US$ 195

ISBN: 978-1-7998-0004-0
EISBN: 978-1-7998-0006-4
© 2020; 337 pp.
List Price: US$ 195

ISBN: 978-1-5225-9833-6
EISBN: 978-1-5225-9835-0
© 2020; 203 pp.
List Price: US$ 155

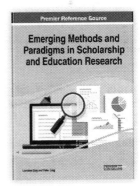

ISBN: 978-1-7998-1001-8
EISBN: 978-1-7998-1003-2
© 2020; 330 pp.
List Price: US$ 195

Do you want to stay current on the latest research trends, product announcements, news, and special offers?
Join IGI Global's mailing list to receive customized recommendations, exclusive discounts, and more.
Sign up at: www.igi-global.com/newsletters.

Publisher of Peer-Reviewed, Timely, and Innovative Academic Research

www.igi-global.com   Sign up at www.igi-global.com/newsletters   facebook.com/igiglobal   twitter.com/igiglobal   linkedin.com/igiglobal

Ensure Quality Research is Introduced to the Academic Community

Become an Evaluator for IGI Global Authored Book Projects

 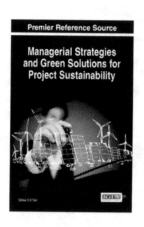  

The overall success of an authored book project is dependent on quality and timely manuscript evaluations.

Applications and Inquiries may be sent to:
development@igi-global.com

Applicants must have a doctorate (or equivalent degree) as well as publishing, research, and reviewing experience. Authored Book Evaluators are appointed for one-year terms and are expected to complete at least three evaluations per term. Upon successful completion of this term, evaluators can be considered for an additional term.

If you have a colleague that may be interested in this opportunity, we encourage you to share this information with them.

IGI Global Author Services

Providing a high-quality, affordable, and expeditious service, IGI Global's Author Services enable authors to streamline their publishing process, increase chance of acceptance, and adhere to IGI Global's publication standards.

Benefits of Author Services:

- **Professional Service:** All our editors, designers, and translators are experts in their field with years of experience and professional certifications.
- **Quality Guarantee & Certificate:** Each order is returned with a quality guarantee and certificate of professional completion.
- **Timeliness:** All editorial orders have a guaranteed return timeframe of 3-5 business days and translation orders are guaranteed in 7-10 business days.
- **Affordable Pricing:** IGI Global Author Services are competitively priced compared to other industry service providers.
- **APC Reimbursement:** IGI Global authors publishing Open Access (OA) will be able to deduct the cost of editing and other IGI Global author services from their OA APC publishing fee.

Author Services Offered:

English Language Copy Editing
Professional, native English language copy editors improve your manuscript's grammar, spelling, punctuation, terminology, semantics, consistency, flow, formatting, and more.

Scientific & Scholarly Editing
A Ph.D. level review for qualities such as originality and significance, interest to researchers, level of methodology and analysis, coverage of literature, organization, quality of writing, and strengths and weaknesses.

Figure, Table, Chart & Equation Conversions
Work with IGI Global's graphic designers before submission to enhance and design all figures and charts to IGI Global's specific standards for clarity.

Translation
Providing 70 language options, including Simplified and Traditional Chinese, Spanish, Arabic, German, French, and more.

Hear What the Experts Are Saying About IGI Global's Author Services

"Publishing with IGI Global has been **an amazing experience** for me for sharing my research. The **strong academic production** support ensures quality and timely completion." – Prof. Margaret Niess, Oregon State University, USA

"The service was **very fast, very thorough, and very helpful** in ensuring our chapter meets the criteria and requirements of the book's editors. I was **quite impressed and happy** with your service." – Prof. Tom Brinthaupt, Middle Tennessee State University, USA

Learn More or Get Started Here:

For Questions, Contact IGI Global's Customer Service Team at cust@igi-global.com or 717-533-8845

Celebrating Over 30 Years of Scholarly Knowledge Creation & Dissemination

www.igi-global.com

InfoSci®-Books

A Database of Nearly 6,000 Reference Books Containing Over 105,000+ Chapters Focusing on Emerging Research

GAIN ACCESS TO **THOUSANDS** OF REFERENCE BOOKS AT **A FRACTION** OF THEIR INDIVIDUAL LIST **PRICE**.

InfoSci®-Books Database

The **InfoSci®-Books** is a database of nearly 6,000 IGI Global single and multi-volume reference books, handbooks of research, and encyclopedias, encompassing groundbreaking research from prominent experts worldwide that spans over 350+ topics in 11 core subject areas including business, computer science, education, science and engineering, social sciences, and more.

Open Access Fee Waiver (Read & Publish) Initiative

For any library that invests in IGI Global's InfoSci-Books and/or InfoSci-Journals (175+ scholarly journals) databases, IGI Global will match the library's investment with a fund of equal value to go toward **subsidizing the OA article processing charges (APCs) for their students, faculty, and staff** at that institution when their work is submitted and accepted under OA into an IGI Global journal.*

INFOSCI® PLATFORM FEATURES

- Unlimited Simultaneous Access
- No DRM
- No Set-Up or Maintenance Fees
- A Guarantee of No More Than a 5% Annual Increase for Subscriptions
- Full-Text HTML and PDF Viewing Options
- Downloadable MARC Records
- COUNTER 5 Compliant Reports
- Formatted Citations With Ability to Export to RefWorks and EasyBib
- No Embargo of Content (Research is Available Months in Advance of the Print Release)

*The fund will be offered on an annual basis and expire at the end of the subscription period. The fund would renew as the subscription is renewed for each year thereafter. The open access fees will be waived after the student, faculty, or staff's paper has been vetted and accepted into an IGI Global journal and the fund can only be used toward publishing OA in an IGI Global journal. Libraries in developing countries will have the match on their investment doubled.

To Recommend or Request a Free Trial:
www.igi-global.com/infosci-books

eresources@igi-global.com • Toll Free: 1-866-342-6657 ext. 100 • Phone: 717-533-8845 x100

www.igi-global.com

Publisher of Peer-Reviewed, Timely, and Innovative Academic Research Since 1988

www.igi-global.com

IGI Global's Transformative Open Access (OA) Model:
How to Turn Your University Library's Database Acquisitions Into a Source of OA Funding

Well in advance of Plan S, IGI Global unveiled their OA Fee Waiver (Read & Publish) Initiative. Under this initiative, librarians who invest in IGI Global's InfoSci-Books and/or InfoSci-Journals databases will be able to subsidize their patrons' OA article processing charges (APCs) when their work is submitted and accepted (after the peer review process) into an IGI Global journal.

How Does it Work?

Step 1: Library Invests in the InfoSci-Databases: A library perpetually purchases or subscribes to the InfoSci-Books, InfoSci-Journals, or discipline/subject databases.

Step 2: IGI Global Matches the Library Investment with OA Subsidies Fund: IGI Global provides a fund to go towards subsidizing the OA APCs for the library's patrons.

Step 3: Patron of the Library is Accepted into IGI Global Journal (After Peer Review): When a patron's paper is accepted into an IGI Global journal, they option to have their paper published under a traditional publishing model or as OA.

Step 4: IGI Global Will Deduct APC Cost from OA Subsidies Fund: If the author decides to publish under OA, the OA APC fee will be deducted from the OA subsidies fund.

Step 5: Author's Work Becomes Freely Available: The patron's work will be freely available under CC BY copyright license, enabling them to share it freely with the academic community.

Note: This fund will be offered on an annual basis and will renew as the subscription is renewed for each year thereafter. IGI Global will manage the fund and award the APC waivers unless the librarian has a preference as to how the funds should be managed.

Hear From the Experts on This Initiative:

"I'm very happy to have been able to make one of my recent research contributions *freely available* along with having access to the *valuable resources* found within IGI Global's InfoSci-Journals database."

– **Prof. Stuart Palmer**, Deakin University, Australia

"Receiving the support from IGI Global's OA Fee Waiver Initiative *encourages me to continue my research work without any hesitation*."

– **Prof. Wenlong Liu**, College of Economics and Management at Nanjing University of Aeronautics & Astronautics, China

For More Information, Scan the QR Code or Contact: IGI Global's Digital Resources Team at eresources@igi-global.com.

Printed in the United States
by Baker & Taylor Publisher Services